Recommended by **Teachers**
Trusted by **Toppers**

Allinone®

CHEMISTRY
Class 12

EVERYTHING YOU NEED TO SCORE

- Simplified NCERT Theory
- In-text & Chapter Exercises
- CBQs; MCQs, A-R, Case Based
- Board Questions Upto 2025
- Sample Question Papers

CBSE Exams 2026

Recommended by **Teachers**
Trusted by **Toppers**

All in One

CHEMISTRY
Class 12

EVERYTHING YOU NEED TO SCORE

- Simplified NCERT Theory
- In-text & Chapter Exercises
- CBQs; MCQs, A-R, Case Based
- Board Questions Upto 2025
- Sample Question Papers

CBSE Exams 2026

Authors
Shikha Soni
Tarnija Midha

arihant
SUCCESS AND NOTHING LESS

ARIHANT PRAKASHAN
(School Division Series)

卐 *ADMINISTRATIVE & PRODUCTION OFFICES*

Regd. Office

'Ramchhaya' 4577/15, Agarwal Road, Darya Ganj, New Delhi -110002
Tele: 011- 47630600, 43518550; Fax: 011- 23280316

卐 *Head Office*

Kalindi, TP Nagar, Meerut (UP) - 250002, Tel: 0121-7156203, 7156204

卐 *SALES & SUPPORT OFFICES*

Agra, Ahmedabad, Bengaluru, Bareilly, Chennai, Delhi, Guwahati, Hyderabad, Jaipur, Jhansi, Kolkata, Lucknow, Nagpur & Pune.

PO No : TXT-XX-XXXXXXX-X-XX

Published By Arihant Publications (India) Ltd.

For further information about the books published by Arihant, log on to www.arihantbooks.com or e-mail at info@arihantbooks.com

Follow us on

卐 *PRICE* ₹475.00

PRODUCTION TEAM

Publishing Managers Mahendra Singh Rawat & Keshav Mohan	*Cover Designer* Salman Shaikh	*Inner Designer* Ankit Tyagi
Project Head Akansha Tomar	*Page Layouting* Sanjay Yadav	*Proof Reader* Nisha Verma

Index *cum* Study Planner

One Book- Endless Features

to Help you Succeed

02

CHAPTER

Electrochemistry is a branch of chemistry that deals with the study of production of electricity from energy released during spontaneous chemical reactions and the use of electrical energy to carry out non-spontaneous chemical transformations.

YOUR STUDY GOALS

- 2.1 Electrochemical Cells
- 2.2 Electrochemical Series
- 2.3 Nernst Equation
- 2.4 Electrochemical Cell and Gibbs Energy of the Reaction
- 2.5 Conductance of Electrolytic Solutions
- 2.6 Electrolytic Cells and Electrolysis
- 2.7 Batteries (Commercial Cells)
- 2.8 Fuel Cells
- 2.9 Corrosion

YOUR PRACTICE GOAL

- Objective Type Questions (41 Qs ; 26 MCQs, 13 A-R & 2 Case Study)
- Subjective Type Questions (41Qs; 18 SA-I, 10 SA-II & 13 LAs)

Electrochemistry

2.1 Electrochemical Cells

Redox Reactions

A chemical reaction in which electrons are lost by one substance and gained by another is called **redox reaction**.

e.g.

$$\overset{-2}{H_2S} + \overset{0}{Cl_2} \longrightarrow \overset{0}{S} + 2H\overset{-1}{Cl}$$

(Oxidation; Reduction; H_2S: Reducing agent; Cl_2: Oxidising agent)

Transfer of electrons from reducing agent to oxidising agent generate electric current. Therefore, the redox reactions setup the basis of electrochemical cells and electrolytic cells which are discussed further.

An electrochemical cell is a device in which chemical energy of the redox reaction is converted into electrical energy, while electrolytic cell do the reverse.

$$\text{Chemical energy} \underset{\text{Electrolytic cell}}{\overset{\text{Electrochemical cell}}{\rightleftharpoons}} \text{Electrical energy}$$

Chapter Intro

A quick information about the coverage of the chapter to explain students about what they are going to study.

2.1 Electrochemical Cells

Redox Reactions

A chemical reaction in which electrons are lost by one substance and gained by another is called **redox reaction**.

e.g.

$$\overset{-2}{H_2S} + \overset{0}{Cl_2} \longrightarrow \overset{0}{S} + 2H\overset{-1}{Cl}$$

(Oxidation; Reduction; H_2S: Reducing agent; Cl_2: Oxidising agent)

Transfer of electrons from reducing agent to oxidising agent generate electric current. Therefore, the redox reactions setup the basis of electrochemical cells and electrolytic cells which are discussed further.

An electrochemical cell is a device in which chemical energy of the redox reaction is converted into electrical energy, while electrolytic cell do the reverse.

$$\text{Chemical energy} \underset{\text{Electrolytic cell}}{\overset{\text{Electrochemical cell}}{\rightleftharpoons}} \text{Electrical energy}$$

The most common electrochemical cell is a galvanic cell or a voltaic cell.

TEACHER'S TIP

The positive (+) sign of the cathode indicates the electrode at which electrons enter the cell, whereas the negative (–) sign of the anode is where the electrons leave the cell.

Teacher Tips

Important Points related to given concept to bring students focus on important points.

Simplified Theory

It contains the necessary study material well supported by Definitions, Facts, Figures, Flowcharts, etc.

Quick Test 1

Conceptual Questions

1. How would you determine the standard electrode potential of the system Mg^{2+}/Mg? *NCERT Intext*
2. Can you store copper sulphate solution in a zinc pot? *NCERT Intext*
3. Given the standard electrode potentials, $K^+/K = -2.93$ V, $Ag^+/Ag = 0.80$ V, $Hg^{2+}/Hg = 0.79$ V, $Mg^{2+}/Mg = -2.37$ V, $Cr^{3+}/Cr = -0.74$ V. Arrange these metals in increasing order of their reducing power. *NCERT*
4. Using E° values of X and Y given below, predict which is better for coating the surface of iron to prevent corrosion and why? *CBSE 2023, 2025*
   Given : $E^\circ_{X^{2+}/X} = -2.36$ V
   $E^\circ_{Y^{2+}/Y} = -0.14$ V
   $E^\circ_{Fe^{2+}/Fe} = -0.44$ V
5. Use the data to answer the following and also justify giving reason. *CBSE 2019*

	Cr	Mn	Fe	Co
$E^\circ_{M^{2+}/M}$	−0.91	−1.18	−0.44	−0.28
$E^\circ_{M^{3+}/M^{2+}}$	−0.41	+1.57	+0.77	+1.97

   (i) Which is a stronger reducing agent in aqueous medium, Cr^{2+} or Fe^{2+} and why?
   (ii) Which is the most stable ion in +2 oxidation state and why?

Numerical Questions

6. Calculate the potential of hydrogen electrode in contact with a solution whose pH is 10. *NCERT Intext*
7. Write the Nernst equation and emf of the following cell at 298 K.
   (i) $Mg(s) \mid Mg^{2+}(0.001\ M) \parallel Cu^{2+}(0.0001\ M) \mid Cu(s)$
   (ii) $Fe(s) \mid Fe^{2+}(0.001\ M) \parallel H^+(1\ M) \mid H_2(g)(1\ bar) \mid Pt(s)$
   Given that, $E^\circ_{Mg^{2+}/Mg} = -2.36$ V, $E^\circ_{Cu^{2+}/Cu} = 0.34$ V, $E^\circ_{Fe^{2+}/Fe} = -0.44$ V *NCERT*
8. Calculate emf of the following cell at 25°C.
   $Sn \mid Sn^{2+}(0.001\ M) \parallel H^+(0.01\ M) \mid H_2(g)(1\ bar) \mid Pt(s)$
   Given: $E^\circ_{(Sn^{2+}/Sn)} = -0.14$ V, $E^\circ_{(H^+/H_2)} = 0.00$ V
   $(\log 10 = 1)$ *CBSE 2024, 2023*
9. The cell in which the following reaction occurs,
   $2Fe^{3+}(aq) + 2I^-(aq) \longrightarrow 2Fe^{2+}(aq) + I_2(s)$
   has $E^\circ_{cell} = 0.236$ V at 298 K, calculate the standard Gibbs energy and the equilibrium constant of the cell reaction. *NCERT Intext*
10. In the button cell, widely used in watches and other devices, the following reaction takes place
   $Zn(s) + Ag_2O(s) + H_2O(l) \longrightarrow Zn^{2+}(aq) + 2Ag(s) + 2OH^-(aq)$
   Determine E° and ΔG° for the reaction.
   (Given, $E^\circ_{Ag^+/Ag} = +0.80$ V, $E^\circ_{Zn^{2+}/Zn} = -0.76$ V)

Answers

6. −0.591 V 7. (i) 2.67 V (ii) 0.53 V
8. 0.11045 V 9. −45.55 kJ mol^{-1}, 9.616×10^7
10. −301.08 kJ mol^{-1}

For Solutions, See QR Code on Pg. 74

Quick Tests

To make students understand the chapter in a smooth part-by-part manner, Quick Tests have been given in each chapter. These Exercises help students to assess the understanding of related concepts at regular interval.

One Book- Endless Features

to Help you Succeed

Illustrative Figures

To make the concepts completely visible, illustrative diagrams have been given at various place.

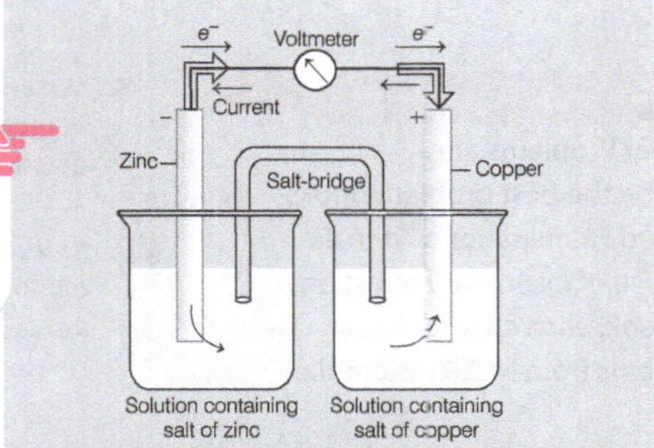

Daniell cell having Zn and Cu electrodes dipped in the solutions of their respective salts

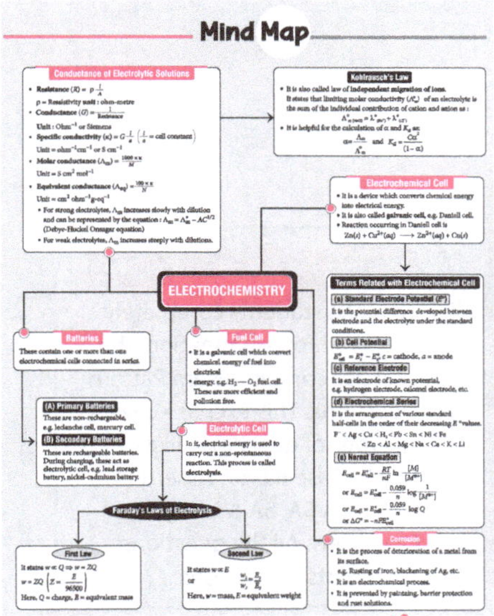

NCERT Questions

To make students completely understand NCERT books, solutions of selected NCERT questions have been given in each chapter.

Example 6 The electrical resistance of a column of 0.05 M NaOH solution of diameter 1 cm and length 50 cm is $5.55 \times 10^3\ \Omega$. Calculate its resistivity, conductivity and molar conductivity. NCERT

Sol. Area, $A = \pi r^2 = 3.14 \times \left(\frac{1}{2}\right)^2 \text{ cm}^2 = 0.785 \text{ cm}^2$

Resistivity, $\rho = \frac{RA}{l}$

$$= \frac{5.55 \times 10^3\,\Omega \times 0.785 \text{ cm}^2}{50 \text{ cm}} = 87.135\ \Omega \text{ cm}$$

Conductivity, $\kappa = \frac{1}{\rho} = \frac{1}{87.135}\ \Omega^{-1} \text{ cm}^{-1}$

$= 0.01148\ \Omega^{-1}\text{cm}^{-1}$

$= 1.148 \times 10^{-2} \text{ S cm}^{-1}$

Mind Map

A quick revision visual tool for the complete chapter.

Board Exams' Questions

Solving Board Exams' Questions while studying the chapters, always prove to be confidence booster. For this purpose, each chapter has selected Questions from last 10 years Board Exams upto 2025.

10. Account for the following:

(i) On the basis of E° values. O_2 gas should be liberated at anode but it is Cl_2 gas which is liberated in the electrolysis of aqueous NaCl.

(ii) Conductivity of CH_3COOH decreases on dilution. **CBSE 2025**

One Book- Endless Features

to Help you Succeed

NCERT Exemplar Problems

NCERT Exemplar Problems are considered to be the best problem books for School/Board Examinations. To make students practice of exemplary questions given in this book, each chapter has selected problems from NCERT Exemplar.

32. Assertion (A) For measuring resistance of an ionic solution an AC source is used.
Reason (R) Concentration of ionic solution will change if DC source is used. **NCERT Exemplar**

29. Assertion (A) E_{cell} should have positive value for the cell to function. **NCERT Exemplar**
Reason (R) $E_{anode} > E_{cathode}$.

SAMPLE QUESTION PAPER 1

A Highly Simulated Sample Question Paper for CBSE Class XII Examination

CHEMISTRY [Fully Solved]

Time : 3 Hours | Max. Marks : 70

General Instructions

Read the following instructions carefully and follow them :

1. This question paper contains **33 questions**. All questions are **compulsory**.
2. Question paper is divided into **FIVE** sections - **Section A, B, C, D and E**.
3. **SECTION-A** question number 1 to 16 are multiple choice type questions. Each question carries 1 mark.
4. **SECTION-B** question number 17 to 21 are very short answer type questions. Each question carries 2 marks.
5. **SECTION-C** question number 22 to 28 are short answer type questions. Each question carries 3 marks.
6. **SECTION-D** question number 29 to 30 are case-based questions. Each question carries 4 marks.
7. **SECTION-E** question number 31 to 33 are long answer type questions. Each question carries 5 marks.
8. There is no overall choice given in the question paper. However, an internal choice has been provided in few questions in all the Sections except section A.
9. Kindely note that there is a separate question paper for Visually Impaired candidates.
10. Use of calculator is NOT allowed.

Section-A

Question No. 1 to 16 are Multiple Choice type Questions, carrying 1 mark each.

1. In an alkaline medium, glycine predominantly exists as an
(a) cation
(b) anion
(c) Zwitter ion
(d) covalent form

2. Examine the following data for a reaction $A + B \longrightarrow P$. Concentrations of reactant A is varied, while the concentration of reactant B is kept constant.

Experiment	$[A]$ (M)	$[B]$ (M)	Rate ($mol\ L^{-1}s^{-1}$)
1	0.1	0.2	0.02
2	0.2	0.2	0.08
3	0.4	0.2	0.32

What will be the order of the reaction with respect to reactant A?
(a) 0 (b) 1
(c) 2 (d) 3

3. Identify the name of the reaction, bromoalkanes are prepared by refluxing the silver salts of acids with bromine in CCl_4.
(a) Borodine-Hunsdiecker reaction
(b) Finkelstein reaction
(c) Swarts reaction
(d) Balz-Schiemann reaction

4. The charge required to liberate 34.5g sodium from fused sodium chloride is
(a) 1 F (b) 1.5 F (c) 0.5 F (d) 2 F

5. The coordination number of Pt in $[Pt(NH_3)_4Cl_2]^{2+}$ ion is
(a) 2 (b) 4 (c) 6 (d) 8

6. Give IUPAC name of the compound given below.
$H_3C—CH(Cl)—CH_2—CH_2—CH(OH)—CH_3$
(a) 5-chlorohexan-2-ol
(b) 2-chlorohexan-5-ol
(c) 2-hydroxy-5-chlorohexane
(d) 2-chloro-5-hydroxyhexane

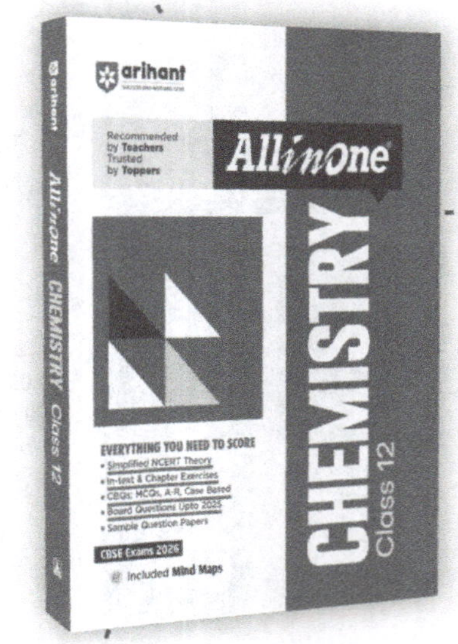

Exam Pattern Exercise

To make students completely prepared for examination, this Exercise contains Exam Pattern Questions. This exercise covers all types of questions, like; MCQs, Case Based, Assertion-Reason, VSA, SA & LA Type Questions. All the questions have Hints & Solutions. .

Sample Question Papers

To make students practice of examination in real sense, there are 5 Sample Question Papers at the end. All these Sample Questions Papers are exactly prepared on the latest syllabus & pattern of examination.

EXAM PATTERN QUESTIONS

Part I Objective Type Questions

Multiple Choice Questions [1 Mark]

1. In an electrochemical process, a salt bridge is used **CBSE 2020**
(a) as a reducing agent
(b) as an oxidising agent
(c) to complete the circuit so that current can flow
(d) None of the above

2. Electrode potential for Mg electrode varies according to the equation $E_{Mg^{2+}/Mg} = E^\circ_{Mg^{2+}/Mg} - \frac{0.059}{2}\log\frac{1}{[Mg^{2+}]}$. The graph of $E_{Mg^{2+}/Mg}$ vs $\log[Mg^{2+}]$ is **NCERT Exemplar**

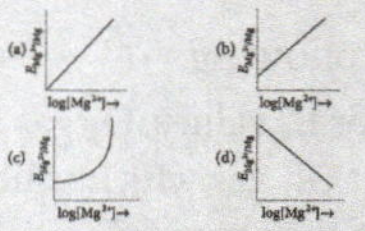

3. Standard electrode potential for Sn^{4+}/Sn^{2+} couple is +0.15 V and that for the Cr^{3+}/Cr couple is −0.74V. The two couples in their standard states are connected to make a cell. The cell potential will be **CBSE 2026**
(a) +1.19 V (b) +0.89 V
(c) + 0.18V (d) +1.83 V

5. The electrochemical cell made up of Zn and Cu half-cell is called Daniell cell. The emf of a Daniell cell is 1.10 V. **Competency Based Que.**

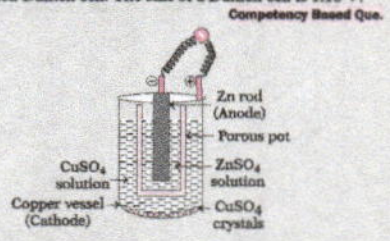

When an external voltage greater than 1.10 V is applied to this cell, which of the following change will be observed in the cell?
(a) Zn electrode will act as an anode.
(b) Current will flow from Cu half cell to Zn half cell.
(c) Electrochemical cell continue to work fast.
(d) Cell will act as electrolytic cell.

6. Calculate the equilibrium constant for the reaction,
$Zn(s) + Cu^{2+}(aq) \longrightarrow Zn^{2+}(aq) + Cu(s)$
[Given, $E^\circ_{cell} = 1.1$ V]
(a) 2×10^{32} (b) 2×10^{34} (c) 2×10^{37} (d) 2×10^{39}

7. In the given reaction,
$2Cu^{+}(aq) \rightleftharpoons Cu^{2+}(aq) + Cu(s)$
$E^\circ_{Cu^{+}/Cu} = 0.62$ V and $E^\circ_{Cu^{2+}/Cu} = 0.26$ V
Find out the equilibrium constant.

Latest Course Structure

Time: 3 Hrs **Total Marks : 70**

Units	Title	Marks
I	Solutions	7
II	Electrochemistry	9
III	Chemical Kinetics	7
IV	*d* -and *f* -Block Elements	7
V	Coordination Compounds	7
VI	Haloalkanes and Haloarenes	6
VII	Alcohols, Phenols and Ethers	6
VIII	Aldehydes, Ketones and Carboxylic Acids	8
IX	Amines	6
X	Biomolecules	7
	Total	**70**

UNIT I

Solutions

Types of solutions, expression of concentration of solutions of solids in liquids, solubility of gases in liquids, solid solutions, Raoult's law, colligative properties - relative lowering of vapour pressure, elevation of boiling point, depression of freezing point, osmotic pressure, determination of molecular masses using colligative properties, abnormal molecular mass, van't Hoff factor.

UNIT II

Electrochemistry

Redox reactions, EMF of a cell, standard electrode potential, Nernst equation and its application to chemical cells, Relation between Gibbs energy change and EMF of a cell, conductance in electrolytic solutions, specific and molar conductivity, variations of conductivity with concentration, Kohlrausch's Law, electrolysis and law of electrolysis (elementary idea), dry cell-electrolytic cells and Galvanic cells, lead accumulator, fuel cells, corrosion.

UNIT III

Chemical Kinetics

Rate of a reaction (Average and instantaneous), factors affecting rate of reaction: concentration, temperature, catalyst; order and molecularity of a reaction, rate law and specific rate constant, integrated rate equations and half-life (only for zero and first order reactions), concept of collision theory (elementary idea, no mathematical treatment), activation energy, Arrhenius equation.

UNIT IV

d and *f* -Block Elements

General introduction, electronic configuration, occurrence and characteristics of transition metals, general trends in properties of the first row transition metals – metallic character, ionisation enthalpy, oxidation states, ionic radii, colour, catalytic property, magnetic properties, interstitial compounds, alloy formation, preparation and properties of $K_2Cr_2O_7$ and $KMnO_4$.

Lanthanoids - Electronic configuration, oxidation states, chemical reactivity and lanthanoid contraction and its consequences.

Actinoids - Electronic configuration, oxidation states and comparison with lanthanoids.

UNIT V

Coordination Compounds

Coordination compounds - Introduction, ligands, coordination number, colour, magnetic properties and shapes, IUPAC nomenclature of mononuclear coordination compounds. Bonding, Werner's theory, VBT, and CFT; structure and stereoisomerism, importance of coordination compounds (in qualitative analysis, extraction of metals and biological system).

UNIT VI

Haloalkanes and Haloarenes

Haloalkanes: Nomenclature, nature of C—*X* bond, physical and chemical properties, optical rotation mechanism of substitution reactions.

Haloarenes: Nature of C—*X* bond, substitution reactions (Directive influence of halogen in monosubstituted compounds only).

Uses and environmental effects of - dichloromethane, trichloromethane, tetrachloromethane, iodoform, freons, DDT.

UNIT VII

Alcohols, Phenols and Ethers

Alcohols: Nomenclature, methods of preparation, physical and chemical properties (of primary alcohols only), identification of primary, secondary and tertiary alcohols, mechanism of dehydration, uses with special reference to methanol and ethanol.

Phenols: Nomenclature, methods of preparation, physical and chemical properties, acidic nature of phenol, electrophillic substitution reactions, uses of phenols.

Ethers: Nomenclature, methods of preparation, physical and chemical properties, uses.

UNIT VIII

Aldehydes, Ketones and Carboxylic Acids

Aldehydes and Ketones: Nomenclature, nature of carbonyl group, methods of preparation, physical and chemical properties, mechanism of nucleophilic addition, reactivity of alpha hydrogen in aldehydes, uses.

Carboxylic Acids: Nomenclature, acidic nature, methods of preparation, physical and chemical properties; uses.

UNIT IX

Amines

Amines: Nomenclature, classification, structure, methods of preparation, physical and chemical properties, uses, identification of primary, secondary and tertiary amines.

Diazonium salts: Preparation, chemical reactions and importance in synthetic organic chemistry.

UNIT X

Biomolecules

Carbohydrates - Classification (aldoses and ketoses), monosaccaharides (glucose and fructose), D-L configuration oligosaccharides (sucrose, lactose, maltose), polysaccharides (starch, cellulose, glycogen); Importance of carbohydrates.

Proteins -Elementary idea of - amino acids, peptide bond, polypeptides, proteins, structure of proteins - primary, secondary, tertiary structure and quaternary structures (qualitative idea only), denaturation of proteins; enzymes. Hormones - Elementary idea excluding structure.

Vitamins - Classification and functions.

Nucleic Acids: DNA and RNA.

Practical

Evaluation Scheme for Examination	Marks
Volumetric Analysis	08
Salt Analysis	08
Content Based Experiment	06
Project Work	04
Class Record and viva	04
Total	**30**

PRACTICAL SYLLABUS

Micro-chemical methods are available for several of the practical experiments. Wherever possible, such techniques should be used.

A. Surface Chemistry

1. Preparation of one lyophilic and one lyophobic sol
   Lyophilic sol - starch, egg albumin and gum
   Lyophobic sol - aluminium hydroxide, ferric hydroxide, arsenous sulphide.
2. Dialysis of sol-prepared in (a) above.
3. Study of the role of emulsifying agents in stabilizing the emulsion of different oils.

B. Chemical Kinetics

1. Effect of concentration and temperature on the rate of reaction between Sodium Thiosulphate and Hydrochloric acid.
2. Study of reaction rates of any one of the following:
   - Reaction of Iodide ion with Hydrogen Peroxide at room temperature using different concentration of Iodide ions.
   - Reaction between Potassium Iodate, (KIO_3) and Sodium Sulphite: (Na_2SO_3) using starch solution as indicator (clock reaction).

C. Thermochemistry

Any one of the following experiments

- Enthalpy of dissolution of Copper Sulphate or Potassium Nitrate.
- Enthalpy of neutralization of strong acid (HCl) and strong base (NaOH).
- Determination of enthaply change during interaction (Hydrogen bond formation) between Acetone and Chloroform.

D. Electrochemistry

Variation of cell potential in $Zn/Zn^{2+}||Cu^{2+}/Cu$ with change in concentration of electrolytes ($CuSO_4$ or $ZnSO_4$) at room temperature.

E. Chromatography

1. Separation of pigments from extracts of leaves and flowers by paper chromatography and determination of R_f values.

2. Separation of constituents present in an inorganic mixture containing two cations only (constituents having large difference in R_f values to be provided).

F. Preparation of Inorganic Compounds

1. Preparation of double salt of Ferrous Ammonium Sulphate or Potash Alum.
2. Preparation of Potassium Ferric Oxalate.

G. Preparation of Organic Compounds

Preparation of any one of the following compounds

1. Acetanilide
2. Di-benzalacetone
3. *p*-nitroacetanilide
4. Aniline yellow or 2-naphthol aniline dye.

H. Tests for the functional groups present in organic compounds:

Unsaturation, alcoholic, phenolic, aldehydic, ketonic, carboxylic and amino (Primary) groups.

I. Characteristic tests of carbohydrates, fats and proteins in pure samples and their detection in given foodstuffs.

J. Determination of concentration/ molarity of $KMnO_4$ solution by titrating it against a standard solution of:

1. Oxalic acid,
2. Ferrous Ammonium Sulphate

   (Students will be required to prepare standard solutions by weighing themselves).

K. Qualitative analysis

Determination of one cation and one anion in a given salt.

Cations : Pb^{2+}, Cu^{2+}, Al^{3+}, Fe^{3+}, Mn^{2+}, Ni^{2+}, Zn^{2+}, Co^{2+}, Ca^{2+}, Sr^{2+}, Ba^{2+}, Mg^{2+}, NH_4^+

Anions : CO_3^{2-}, S^{2-}, SO_3^{2-}, NO_3^-, NO_2^-, Cl^-, Br^-, I^-, SO_4^{2-}, PO_4^{3-}, CH_3COO^-, $C_2O_4^{2-}$

(**Note**: Insoluble salts excluded)

PROJECTS

Scientific investigations involving laboratory testing and collecting information from other sources.

A few suggested Projects.

- Study of the presence of oxalate ions in guava fruit at different stages of ripening.
- Study of quantity of casein present in different samples of milk.
- Preparation of soybean milk and its comparison with the natural milk with respect to curd formation, effect of temperature, etc.
- Study of the effect of Potassium Bisulphate as food preservative under various conditions (temperature, concentration, time, etc.)
- Study of digestion of starch by salivary amylase and effect of pH and temperature on it.
- Comparative study of the rate of fermentation of following materials: wheat flour, gram flour, potato juice, carrot juice, etc.
- Extraction of essential oils present in Saunf (aniseed), Ajwain (carum), Illaichi (cardamom).
- Study of common food adulterants in fat, oil, butter, sugar, turmeric power, chilli powder and pepper.

Note: *Any other investigatory project, which involves about 10 periods of work, can be chosen with the approval of the teacher.*

01 CHAPTER

Solution is one of the most important class of mixtures that contains more than one components. In this chapter, we will not only discuss the different types of solutions but also some possible ways in which concentrations of a solute can be expressed in liquid solutions and terms related to it.

YOUR STUDY GOALS

1.1 Types of Solutions
1.2 Expressing Concentration of Solutions
1.3 Solubility
1.4 Vapour Pressure of Liquid Solutions
1.5 Ideal and Non-ideal Solutions
1.6 Colligative Properties
1.7 Abnormal Molar Mass
1.8 van't Hoff Factor

YOUR PRACTICE GOAL

- Objective Type Questions (38 Qs ; 26 MCQs, 10 A-R, 2 Case Study)
- Subjective Type Questions (29 Qs; 15 SA-I, 7 SA-II, 7 LA)

Solutions

A **solution** is a homogeneous mixture of two or more substances whose composition can be varied within certain limits.

The component that is present in a relatively larger quantity is known as **solvent** and the component which is present in lesser amount is known as **solute.**

The physical state in which solution exists is same as that of the state of solvent.

Characteristics of Solutions

- A solution does not allow a beam of light to scatter.
- A solution is stable and the solute from the solution cannot be separated by filtration process.
- The solute particles in a solution do not settle down.
- 10^{-7} to 10^{-8} cm is the range of the size of solute particles in a solution.

1.1 Types of Solutions

Solutions are classified on different basis which are as follows

On the Basis of Amount of Solute

On the basis of amount of solute present in a solution, the solution may be of following types

(i) **Concentrated solution** It is a solution in which a large amount of solute is dissolved in a given quantity of solvent.

(ii) **Dilute solution** It is a solution in which a small amount of solute is dissolved in large amount of solvent.

On the Basis of Number of Components

On the basis of number of components present, the solution may be of following types

(i) **Binary solution** It is a type of solution which contains two components, e.g. salt solution.

(ii) **Ternary solution** It is a type of solution which contains three components either two solvents and one solute or one solvent and two solutes, e.g. A solution of salt, sugar and water. The naming (binary, ternary, quaternary) goes on as the number of components increases. In this chapter, we will focus on binary solutions only.

On the Basis of Physical State of Components

On the basis of physical state of components, solution can be broadly divided into three types. Their further subdivisions and examples are tabulated below.

Types of solutions	Solute	Solvent	Examples
Solid solutions	Gas	Solid	Solution of hydrogen in palladium.
	Liquid	Solid	Mercury with sodium forming an amalgam.
	Solid	Solid	Alloys like bronze and many others.
Liquid solutions	Gas	Liquid	Oxygen dissolved in water, aerated drinks, carbon dioxide dissolved in water.
	Liquid	Liquid	Alcoholic beverages are basically solutions of ethanol dissolved in water.
	Solid	Liquid	Sucrose (table sugar) or salt in water.
Gaseous solutions	Gas	Gas	Air which is mostly mixture of nitrogen and oxygen gases.
	Liquid	Gas	Chloroform mixed with nitrogen gas, humidity in air.
	Solid	Gas	Camphor in nitrogen gas, dust or smoke in air.

1.2 Expressing Concentration of Solutions

There are several methods by which we can describe the concentration of the solution quantitatively. Some of these are as follows

Concentration Terms	Definition	Formula	Examples
Mass Percentage (w/w %)	The mass percentage of a component in a given solution is the mass of the component per 100 g of the solution.	Mass % of a component $= \frac{\text{Mass of the component in the solution}}{\text{Total mass of the solution}} \times 100$	e.g. A 10% glucose in water by mass means that 10 g of glucose is dissolved in 90 g of water resulting in a 100 g of solution.
Volume Percentage (V/V %)	The volume percentage is the volume of the component per 100 parts by volume of the solution.	Volume % of a component $= \frac{\text{Volume of the component}}{\text{Total volume of solution}} \times 100$	e.g. 100 mL of 35% (V/V) solution of ethylene glycol contains 35 mL of ethylene glycol and 65 mL of water.
Mass by Volume Percentage (w/V %)	It is the mass of solute dissolved in 100 mL of the solution.	Mass by volume % $= \frac{\text{Mass of solute}}{\text{Total volume of solution}} \times 100$	e.g. A 10% solution of sodium chloride (w/V) means that 10 g of sodium chloride is dissolved in 100 mL of solution.
Parts Per Million (ppm)	It is defined as the number of parts of a component per million parts (10^6) of the solution. It is used when a solute is present in trace quantities.	ppm $= \frac{\text{Number of parts of the component}}{\text{Total number of parts of all components of the solution}} \times 10^6$	e.g. (i) The concentration of pollutants in water or atmosphere is often expressed in terms of $\mu g\ mL^{-1}$ or ppm. (ii) Gases like oxygen [weighs 6×10^{-3} g] dissolved in one litre of sea water is expressed in 5.8 g per 10^6 g or 5.8 ppm.

Concentration Terms	Definition	Formula	Examples
Mole Fraction (χ)	It is the ratio of number of moles of one component to the total number of moles of all the components present in the solution.	Mole fraction of a component $= \frac{\text{Number of moles of the component}}{\text{Total number of moles of all the components}}$	e.g. In a binary solution, if the number of moles of A and B are n_A and n_B respectively, then mole fraction of A will be $\chi_A = \frac{n_A}{n_A + n_B}$ Similarly, mole fraction of B, $\chi_B = \frac{n_B}{n_A + n_B} \Rightarrow \chi_A + \chi_B = 1$
Molarity (M)	It is defined as the number of moles of solute dissolved in one litre or one cubic decimetre of the solution. It is expressed in term of mol L^{-1}.	$\text{Molarity} = \frac{\text{Number of moles of solute}}{\text{Volume of solution (in litre)}}$	e.g. 0.25 mol L^{-1} (or 0.25 M) solution of NaOH means that 0.25 moles (or 10 g) of NaOH has been dissolved in one litre (or one cubic decimetre).
Molality (m)	It is defined as the number of moles of solute per kilogram (kg) of the solvent. It is expressed in term of mol kg^{-1}.	$\text{Molality} = \frac{\text{Moles of solute}}{\text{Mass of solvent (in kg)}}$	e.g. 1.00 mol kg^{-1} (or 1.00 m) solution of KCl means that 1 mole (74.5 g) of KCl is dissolved in 1 kg of water.

Note Mass %, ppm, mole fraction and molality are independent of temperature, whereas mass by volume %, volume % and molarity depends on temperature. This is because volume depends on temperature but mass does not.

Example 1 Calculate the mass percentage of benzene (C_6H_6) and carbon tetrachloride (CCl_4), if 22 g of benzene is dissolved in 122 g of CCl_4. NCERT Intext

Sol. Mass of solution = Mass of benzene + Mass of carbon tetrachloride

$$= (22 + 122)\text{ g} = 144\text{ g}$$

$$\text{Mass \% of benzene} = \frac{\text{Mass of benzene}}{\text{Mass of solution}} \times 100$$

$$= \frac{22}{144} \times 100 = 15.28\%$$

$$\text{Mass \% of } CCl_4 = \frac{\text{Mass of } CCl_4}{\text{Mass of solution}} \times 100$$

$$= \frac{122}{144} \times 100 = 84.72\%$$

Example 2 What amount of water is required to make 10% ethanol in water solution using 10 mL of pure ethanol?

Sol. Given, volume of pure ethanol = 10 mL

volume % of ethanol = 10%

Total amount of solution = ?

$$\text{Volume \% of ethanol} = \frac{\text{Volume of ethanol}}{\text{Total volume of solution}} \times 100$$

or $$10 = \frac{10}{\text{Total volume of solution}} \times 100$$

$\Rightarrow$ Total volume of solution = 100 mL

Thus, the amount of water used

$= 100 -$ amount of ethanol $= (100 - 10)$ mL $= 90$ mL

Example 3 If 1L of a solution contains 5 mL of a certain disinfectant then express this concentration in ppm.

Sol. Amount of disinfectant $= 5\text{ mL} = 5 \times 10^{-3}$ L

Amount of solution = 1 L

$$\text{Then, ppm} = \frac{\text{Amount of disinfectant}}{\text{Amount of solution}} \times 10^6$$

$$= \frac{5 \times 10^{-3}}{1} \times 10^6 = 5 \times 10^3 \text{ ppm}$$

Example 4 Calculate the mole fraction of benzene in solution containing 30% by mass in carbon tetrachloride. NCERT Intext

Sol. For 100 g of solution, mass of benzene in the solution = 30 g [Given, benzene in CCl_4 = 30%]

$\therefore$ Mass of carbon tetrachloride (CCl_4) = (100 − 30) g = 70 g

Molar mass of benzene

$(C_6H_6) = 12 \times 6 + 1 \times 6 = 78 \text{ g mol}^{-1}$

Molar mass of $CCl_4 = 12 + 4 \times 35.5 = 154 \text{ g mol}^{-1}$

$$\therefore \text{Number of moles of benzene} = \frac{\text{Mass of benzene}}{\text{Molar mass of benzene}}$$

$$\text{Number of moles of benzene} = \frac{30\text{ g}}{78\text{ g mol}^{-1}} = 0.385\text{ mol}$$

$$\text{Number of moles of } CCl_4 = \frac{\text{Mass of } CCl_4}{\text{Molar mass of } CCl_4}$$

$$= \frac{70 \text{ g}}{154 \text{ g mol}^{-1}} = 0.455 \text{ mol}$$

Mole fraction of benzene (χ_1)

$$= \frac{\text{Moles of benzene}}{\text{Total moles in the solution}}$$

$$= \frac{0.385}{0.385 + 0.455} = \frac{0.385}{0.84} = 0.458$$

And mole fraction of CCl_4 $(\chi_2) = 1 - 0.458 = 0.542$

(as $\chi_1 + \chi_2 = 1$)

Example 5 **Calculate the molarity of each of the following solutions.**

(i) 30 g of $Co(NO_3)_2 \cdot 6H_2O$ in 4.3 L of solution.

(ii) 30 mL of 0.5 M H_2SO_4 diluted to 500 mL.

NCERT Intext

Sol. (i) Molecular mass of $Co(NO_3)_2 \cdot 6H_2O$

$$= 58.7 \text{ g/mol} + 2 \times (14 \text{ g/mol} + 3 \times 16 \text{ g/mol}) + 6 \times (2 \times 1 \text{ g/mol} + 16 \text{ g/mol})$$

$$= (58.7 + 124 + 108) \text{ g mol}^{-1} = 290.7 \text{ g mol}^{-1}$$

Number of moles of $Co(NO_3)_2 \cdot 6H_2O$

$$= \frac{\text{Mass of solute}}{\text{Molecular mass of solute}}$$

$$= \frac{30 \text{ g}}{290.7 \text{ g mol}^{-1}} = 0.103 \text{ mol}$$

$$\text{Molarity of solution} = \frac{\text{Number of moles of solute}}{\text{Volume of solution (L)}}$$

$$= \frac{0.103 \text{ mol}}{4.3 \text{ L}}$$

$$= 0.024 \text{ mol / L} = 0.024 \text{ M}$$

(ii) (a) **First method**

$\because$ 1000 mL of 0.5 M H_2SO_4 will contain

$H_2SO_4 = 0.5$ mol

$\therefore$ 30 mL of 0.5 M H_2SO_4 will contain H_2SO_4

$$= \frac{0.5 \text{ mol}}{1000 \text{ mL}} \times 30 \text{ mL} = 0.015 \text{ mol}$$

$$\text{Molarity of solution} = \frac{\text{Number of moles of solute}}{\text{Volume of solution (L)}}$$

$$= \frac{0.015 \text{ mol}}{0.500 \text{ L}}$$

[$\because$ Given, $V = 500$ mL]

$= 0.03$ M

(b) **Second method**

As we know that, $M_1V_1 = M_2V_2$

$$0.5 \text{ M} \times 30 \text{ mL} = M_2 \times 500 \text{ mL}$$

$$M_2 = 0.03 \text{ M}$$

Example 6 **If the density of some lake water is 1.25 g mL^{-1} and it contains 92 g of Na^+ ions per kg of water. Calculate the molality of Na^+ ions in the lake.** NCERT

Sol. Number of moles in 92 g of Na^+ ions

$$= \frac{\text{Mass}}{\text{Molecular mass}} = \frac{92 \text{ g}}{23 \text{ g/mol}} = 4 \text{ moles}$$

$$\text{Molality of } Na^+ \text{ ions} = \frac{\text{Number of moles of solute}}{\text{Mass of solvent (kg)}}$$

$$= \frac{4 \text{ mol}}{1 \text{ kg}} = 4 \text{ mol kg}^{-1}$$

Quick Test 1

Conceptual Questions

1. Identify the type of solutions that represents the following examples.

(i) Humidity in air (ii) Copper dissolved in gold

(iii) Carbon dioxide dissolved in water

2. Will the molarity of a solution at 50°C be same, less or more than at 25°C?

3. Out of 1 molal and 1 molar aqueous solution which is more concentrated?

Numerical Questions

4. Calculate the mass percentage of aspirin ($C_9H_8O_4$) in acetonitrile (CH_3CN), when 6.5 g of $C_9H_8O_4$ is dissolved in 450 g of CH_3CN. NCERT

5. (i) A solution is obtained by mixing 200 g of 30% and 300 g of 20% solution by weight. Calculate the percentage of solute in the final solution.

(ii) If 1.04 g of $BaCl_2$ is present in 10^5 g of solution, then calculate the concentration of solution in ppm.

6. Calculate the amount of benzoic acid (C_6H_5COOH) required for preparing 250 mL of 0.15 M solution in methanol. NCERT

7. Concentrated nitric acid used in the laboratory work is 68% nitric acid by mass in aqueous solution. What should be the molarity of such a sample of the acid, if the density of the solution is 1.504 g mL^{-1}? NCERT

8. A solution of glucose in water is labelled as 10% w/w. What would be the molality and mole fraction of each component in the solution? If the density of the solution is 1.2 g mL^{-1}, then what shall be the molarity of the solution? NCERT

9. Calculate the mass of urea (NH_2CONH_2) required in making 2.5 kg of 0.25 molal aqueous solution. NCERT Intext

Answers

4. 1.424% 5. (i) 24% (ii) 10.4 ppm 6. 4.575 g
7. 16.23 M 8. 0.67 M 9. 37.5 g

For Solutions, See QR Code on Pg. 34

1.3 Solubility

Solubility of a substance is its maximum amount that can be dissolved in a specified amount of solvent under specified conditions.

The units of solubility are mol dm^{-3} or g dm^{-3} or grams of solute per 100 g of solvent.

It depends on

(i) nature of solute (ii) nature of solvent
(iii) temperature (iv) pressure

Solubility of a Solid in a Liquid

In general, a solute dissolves in a solvent if the intermolecular interactions are similar in the two.

The solubility of a solid in a liquid at any temperature is defined as 'the maximum amount of the solid (solute) in gram which can be dissolved in 100 g of the liquid (solvent) to form the saturated solution at that particular temperature'.

Process of Solubility of a Solid in a Liquid

- **Dissolution** When a solid solute is added to a solvent, the solute dissolves, increasing the concentration of the solution.
- **Crystallisation** Some solute particles in the solution colloide with solid solute particles and get separated out of the solution.

A balance is established when the rate of solute particles dissolving equals the rate of particles crystallising leading to a **state of dynamic equilibrium**.

$$\text{Solute} + \text{Solvent} \underset{\text{Crystallisation}}{\overset{\text{Dissolution}}{\rightleftharpoons}} \text{Solution}$$

At this stage, the concentration of the solute in the solution remains constant under the same temperature and pressure conditions. This process is similar for **gases dissolved in liquids**.

Saturated and Unsaturated Solutions

A solution in which no more solute can be dissolved at the same temperature and pressure is called as **saturated solution**, while **unsaturated solution** is the one in which more solute can be dissolved at the same temperature.

The concentration of solute in saturated solution represents its **solubility**.

Factors Affecting the Solubility of a Solid in a Liquid

Solubility of a solid in a liquid depends upon the following factors

(i) Nature of Solute (solid) **and Solvent** (liquid)

This can be understood by saying "***like dissolves like***". It means that polar or ionic compounds (like NaCl) dissolve in polar solvents (like water) and remains almost insoluble in non-polar solvents (like benzene).

Similarly, non-polar (i.e., covalent or organic) compounds (like naphthalene, anthracene) are soluble in non-polar solvents (like benzene, ether, etc.) and less soluble in polar solvents (like water).

TEACHER'S TIP

If hydration energy (energy released due to intermolecular attraction between solute and solvent molecules) is greater than lattice energy (energy released due to interionic attraction between solute molecules), then solution is easily formed.

(ii) Effect of Temperature

The solubility of a solid in a liquid is significantly affected by temperature changes.

Consider an example of saturated solution which represents equilibrium between undissolved solute and dissolved solute.

$$\text{Solute} + \text{Solvent} \rightleftharpoons \text{Solution}; \Delta_{sol} H = \pm\text{ve}$$

According to Le Chatelier's principle,

- If dissolution process is endothermic i.e. $\Delta H_{sol} > 0$ (+ve) then solubility increases with increase in temperature.
- If dissolution process is exothermic i.e. $\Delta H_{sol} < 0$ (−ve) then solubility decreases with increase in temperature.

  The plots of solubility of a solid *versus* temperature are described as **solubility curves**.

(iii) Effect of Pressure

Pressure does not have any significant effect on solubility of solids in liquids because solids and liquids are highly incompressible and practically remain unaffected by the pressure change.

Solubility of a Gas in a Liquid

Almost all gases are soluble in water but at different extents. **The solubility of any gas in a particular liquid** is the volume of the gas (in cubic centimetre, cc) that can be dissolved in unit volume (1cc) of the liquid to form the saturated solution at certain temperature and under a pressure of one atmosphere.

Factors Affecting the Solubility of a Gas in a Liquid

Solubility of gas in a liquid depends upon the following factors

(i) **Nature of solute** (gas) **and solvent** (liquid) The solubility of different gases in the same solvent varies. The gases which can be easily liquified are more soluble in common solvents.

e.g. Gases like hydrogen, oxygen, nitrogen and helium, etc., dissolve in water to a small extent whereas the gases like NH_3, HCl, SO_2, etc., are highly soluble in water.

Note This dissolved oxygen sustains all aquatic life.

(ii) **Effect of temperature** The solubility of a gas in a liquid decreases with increase in temperature as the dissolution of a gas in a liquid is an exothermic process, i.e. heat is evolved. Thus,

$$\text{Gas} + \text{Solvent} \longrightarrow \text{Solution} + \text{Heat}$$

By applying Le Chatelier's principle, it is clearly evident that increase of temperature would shift the equilibrium in the backward direction, i.e. the solubility would decrease.

Note The solubility of some sparingly soluble gases like hydrogen and inert gases increases slightly with increase in temperature (mainly in the case of non-aqueous solvents such as hydrocarbons, alcohols and acetone).

(iii) **Effect of pressure** The solubility of a gas increases with increase in pressure. In simple words we can say, that the number of gas molecules in the vapour phase decreases whereas, the number of gas molecules dissolved in solution increases on increasing pressure.

Solubility of a gas in liquid varying with change in pressure is governed by the **Henry's law** which is discussed below.

Henry's Law

It states that "at a constant temperature, the solubility of a gas in a liquid is directly proportional to the partial pressure of the gas present above the surface of liquid or solution".

Dalton also independently concluded that the solubility of a gas in a liquid solution is a function of partial pressure of the gas.

If we use the mole fraction of a gas in the solution as a measure of its solubility, then it can be said that *"the mole fraction of the gas (χ) in the solution is proportional to the partial pressure of the gas (p) over the solution".*

The most common form of Henry's law states that *"the partial pressure of the gas in vapour phase (p) is proportional to the mole fraction of the gas (χ) in the solution".* It is expressed as

$$p \propto \chi$$

or $$\boxed{p = K_H \cdot \chi} \quad \text{...(i)}$$

where, K_H is called **Henry's law constant.**

The units of Henry's law constant (K_H) are **torr or kbar.**

It can be concluded that higher the value of K_H at a particular pressure, the lower is the solubility of the gas in the liquid.

Graphical Representation to Validate Henry's Law

If we draw a graph between the partial pressure of the gas against the mole fraction of the gas in solution at a given temperature, then a straight line passing through the origin is obtained as shown in the figure given below.

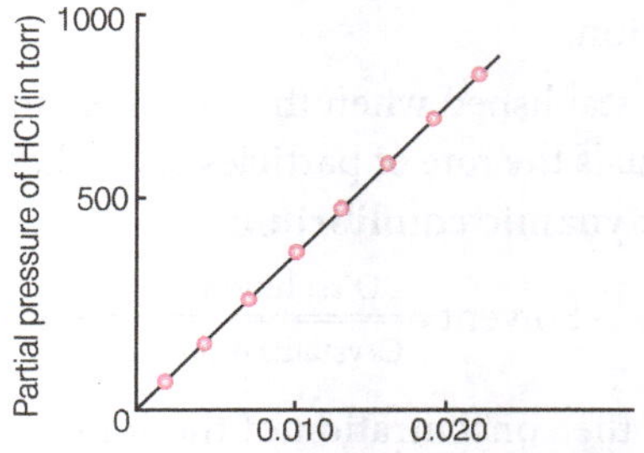

Graph shows solubility of HCl gas in cyclohexane at 293 K.

The value of the slope is equal to value of K_H.

Significance of Henry's Law and Henry's Law Constant

- Henry's law is applied to each gas independent of the presence of other gases.
- Different gases have different K_H values in same solvent and at the same temperature. This suggests that K_H is a function of the nature of the gas.

- The K_H values of a gas is different in different solvents. Moreover, this value increases with the increase in temperature.
- Solubility of gases in liquid decreases with increase of temperature. This is the reason why aquatic species are more comfortable in cold water rather than in warm water.

Example 7 **H_2S, a toxic gas with rotten egg like smell, is used for qualitative analysis. If the solubility of H_2S in water at STP is 0.195 m, calculate Henry's law constant.**
NCERT Intext

Sol. Solubility of H_2S gas $= 0.195$ m, i.e. 0.195 moles in 1 kg of the solvent (water).

$\because$ Number of moles of H_2O in 1 kg of the solvent (water)

$$= \frac{1000 \text{ g}}{18 \text{ g mol}^{-1}} = 55.55 \text{ mol}$$

$\therefore$ Mole fraction of H_2S gas in the solution

$$(\chi) = \frac{0.195 \text{ mol}}{(0.195 + 55.55) \text{ mol}}$$

$$= \frac{0.195 \text{ mol}}{55.745 \text{ mol}} = 0.0035$$

Pressure at STP $= 0.987$ bar

According to Henry's law, $p_{H_2S} = K_H \times \chi_{H_2S}$

or $$K_H = \frac{p_{H_2S}}{\chi_{H_2S}} = \frac{0.987 \text{ bar}}{0.0035} = 282 \text{ bar}$$

Example 8 **At the same temperature, H_2 is more soluble in water than He. Which of them has higher value of K_H and why?**

Sol. He has higher value of K_H because if the gas has more solubility, its K_H value will be low.

Applications of Henry's Law

Henry's law finds several applications in industries. It also explains many biological phenomena.

These are as follows

(i) **In the production of carbonated beverages** To increase the solubility of CO_2 in soft drinks and soda water, the bottle is sealed under high pressure.

(ii) **In deep sea diving** Scuba divers (deep-sea divers) breathe air at high pressure underwater. Increased pressure increases the solubility of atmospheric gases (like nitrogen) in blood.

When divers come towards surface, the pressure gradually decreases resulting in the release of dissolved gases from blood. This leads to the formation of bubbles of nitrogen in the blood, which blocks capillaries and gives rise to an ailment called **bends or decompression sickness.**

To avoid bends as well as the toxic effects of high concentrations of nitrogen in the blood, the tanks used by scuba divers are filled with air diluted with helium (11.7%, helium, 56.2% nitrogen and 32.1% oxygen).

(iii) **For people living at high altitudes or climbers** At high altitudes, the partial pressure of oxygen is less than that at the ground level. This leads to low concentrations of oxygen in the blood and tissues of people living at high altitudes or climbers.

Consequently, they feel weak both physically and mentally. These are the symptoms of a medical condition known as **anoxia.**

Limitations of Henry's Law

It is applicable only when

- the pressure of the gas is not too high.
- temperature is not too low.
- the gas should not undergo any chemical change.
- the gas should not undergo association or dissociation in the solution.

Quick Test 2

Conceptual Questions

1. Based on solute-solvent interactions, arrange the following in the increasing order of solubility in *n*-octane and explain. Cyclohexane, KCl, CH_3OH, CH_3CN
2. K_H value for $Ar(g)$, $CO_2(g)$, $HCHO(g)$ and $CH_4(g)$ are 40.39, 1.67, 1.83×10^{-5} and 0.413 respectively. Arrange these gases in the order of their increasing solubility by giving suitable reason.
3. Give reasons for the following
   (i) Aquatic species are more comfortable in cold water than in warm water.
   (ii) At higher altitudes people suffer from anoxia resulting in inability to think. CBSE 2024

For Solutions, See QR Code on Pg. 34

Numerical Questions

4. At what partial pressure, oxygen will have a solubility of 0.05 g L^{-1} in water at 293 K?
   [Henry's constant (K_H) for O_2 in water at 293 K is 34.86 k bar. Assume the density of the solution to be same as that of the solvent.]
5. The partial pressure of ethane over a solution containing 6.56×10^{-3} g of ethane is 1 bar. If the solution were to contains 5.0×10^{-2} g of ethane, then what will be the partial pressure of the gas? NCERT
6. Henry's law constant for CO_2 in water is 1.67×10^8 Pa at 298 K. Calculate the quantity of CO_2 in 500 mL of soda water when packed under 2.5 atm CO_2 pressure at 298 K. NCERT Intext, CBSE 2025

Answers

4. 0.98 bar 5. 7.62 bar 6. 1.857 g

1.4 Vapour Pressure of Liquid Solutions

Liquid solutions are the solutions in which liquid is the solvent. The solute can be a gas, liquid or a solid. We shall discuss the properties of binary solutions i.e., solution of (i) liquids in liquids and (ii) solids in liquids.

The most important property of liquid-liquid solution is the vapour pressure.

The pressure exerted by the vapours of solvent, when they are in dynamic equilibrium with its liquid at a given temperature is called **vapour pressure.**

Vapour Pressure of Liquid-Liquid Solutions

When a binary solution of two volatile liquids is taken in a closed vessel, both the components would evaporate and finally a state of equilibrium is established between the vapour phase and liquid phase.

The total vapour pressure in this case is equal to the sum of the partial pressures of each of the two components (according to Dalton's law of partial pressure). These partial pressures are related to the mole fractions of the two components.

Relation between partial pressures and mole fraction was further explained by Raoult, which is discussed below.

Raoult's Law

Raoult's law states that "*at a given temperature, for a solution of volatile liquids, the partial vapour pressure of each component of the solution is directly proportional to its mole fraction present in solution*".

Let us consider that two volatile liquids 1 and 2 have mole fractions as χ_1 and χ_2, respectively.

If p_1 and p_2 are the vapour pressures of these components in the solution, respectively, at same temperature then according to Raoult's law,

For component 1, $p_1 \propto \chi_1$ or $p_1 = p_1^\circ \chi_1$

Similarly, **for component 2,** $p_2 = p_2^\circ \chi_2$

where, p_1° and p_2° are the vapour pressures of pure components 1 and 2, respectively, at the same temperature.

Relation between Dalton's Law and Raoult's Law

According to **Dalton's law of partial pressure,** the total pressure (p_{total}) over the solution phase in the container will be sum of the partial pressures of the components of the solution and is given as

$$p_{total} = p_1 + p_2$$

So, $$p_{total} = p_1^\circ \chi_1 + p_2^\circ \chi_2$$

As we know, $\chi_1 + \chi_2 = 1$ or $\chi_1 = 1 - \chi_2$

Then, $$p = p_1^\circ (1 - \chi_2) + p_2^\circ \chi_2$$

$$\boxed{p = p_1^\circ + (p_2^\circ - p_1^\circ)\chi_2}$$

From this equation, following conclusions can be drawn

- The total vapour pressure over the solution can be related to the mole fraction of any one component.
- Total vapour pressure over the solution varies linearly with the mole fraction of component 2.
- The total vapour pressure over the solution increases or decreases with increase in mole fraction of component 1, depending upon the vapour pressures of the pure components 1 and 2.

Graphical Representation of Raoult's Law

A plot of p_1 and p_2 *versus* the mole fractions χ_1 and χ_2 for a solution gives a linear plot as shown in the given figure.

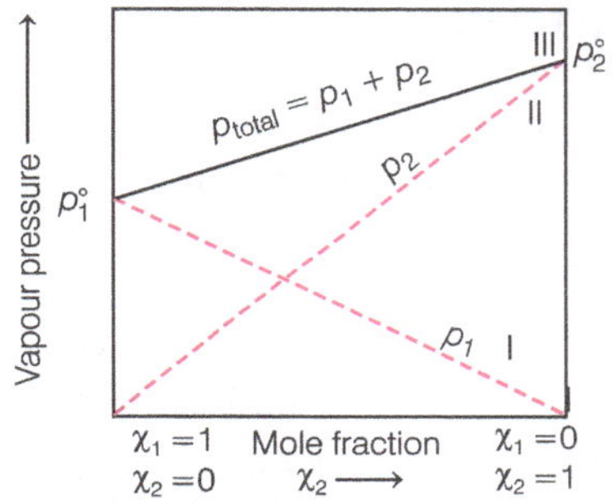

Plot of vapour pressure and mole fraction of an ideal solution at constant temperature

In the above graph,

- The dashed lines I and II represents the partial pressure of the components. (It can be seen from the plot that p_1 and p_2 are directly proportional to χ_1 and χ_2, respectively.) These lines (I and II) pass through the points for which χ_1 and χ_2 are equal to unity.
- The total vapour pressure is given by line marked III in the figure.
- The plot (line III) of p_{total} *versus* χ_2 is a straight line as shown in figure.
- Assuming that $p_1^\circ < p_2^\circ$, i.e. component 1 is less volatile than component 2, then the minimum value of p_{total} is p_1° and the maximum value is p_2°.
- The composition of vapour phase in equilibrium with the solution can be determined by the partial pressures of the components.
- If y_1 and y_2 are the mole fractions of the components 1 and 2 respectively in the vapour phase then, using Dalton's law of partial pressure;

$$p_1 = y_1 p_{\text{total}} \text{ and } p_2 = y_2 p_{\text{total}}$$

- In general, for a solution containing a number of volatile components (liquids), for any component i,

$$p_i = y_i \cdot p_{\text{total}}$$

Raoult's Law as a Special Case of Henry's Law

According to Raoult's law, the vapour pressure of a volatile component in a given solution is given by

$$p_i = \chi_i p_i^\circ$$

If in the solution of a gas in a liquid, the volatile component exists as a gas then, according to Henry's law, $p = K_H \chi$

Thus, partial pressure of the volatile component (gas) is directly proportional to the mole fraction of that component (gas) in the solution.

Therefore, Raoult's and Henry's laws become identical except their proportionality constants (K_H-Henry's constant and p_i° constant for Raoult's law) are different. Therefore, **Raoult's law becomes a special case of Henry's law in which K_H becomes equal to p_i°.**

Example 9 The vapour pressure of ethyl alcohol at 298 K is 20 mm of Hg. Its mole fraction in a solution with methyl alcohol is 0.40. What is its vapour pressure in solution if the mixture obeys Raoult's law?

Sol. According to Raoult's law, $p_A = p_A^\circ \chi_A$

Vapour pressure of pure ethyl alcohol

$(p_A^\circ) = 20$ mm of Hg

Mole fraction of ethyl alcohol $(\chi_A) = 0.40$

Vapour pressure of ethyl alcohol in solution

$(p_A) = 20 \times 0.40 = 8$ mm of Hg

Example 10 The vapour pressures of pure liquids *A* and *B* are 450 and 700 mm of Hg at 350 K, respectively. Find out the composition of the liquid mixture, if total vapour pressure is 600 mm of Hg. Also, find the composition of the vapour phase. NCERT Intext

Sol. Given, $p_A^\circ = 450$ mm of Hg, $p_B^\circ = 700$ mm of Hg

$p_{\text{total}} = 600$ mm of Hg

According to Raoult's law,

$$p_A = \chi_A \times p_A^\circ$$

$$p_B = \chi_B \times p_B^\circ = (1 - \chi_A)\, p_B^\circ$$

$$p_{\text{total}} = p_A + p_B = \chi_A p_A^\circ + (1 - \chi_A)\, p_B^\circ$$

$$= p_B^\circ + (p_A^\circ - p_B^\circ)\, \chi_A$$

On substituting the values, we get

$$600 = 700 + (450 - 700)\, \chi_A$$

or $\quad 250\chi_A = 100$

$$\Rightarrow \quad \chi_A = \frac{100}{250} = 0.40$$

Thus, composition of the liquid mixture will be

Mole fraction of $A(\chi_A) = 0.40$

Mole fraction of $B(\chi_B) = 1 - 0.40 = 0.60$

$$\therefore p_A = \chi_A \times p_A^\circ = 0.40 \times 450 \text{ mm of Hg} = 180 \text{ mm of Hg}$$

$$p_B = \chi_B \times p_B^\circ = 0.60 \times 700 \text{ mm of Hg} = 420 \text{ mm of Hg}$$

Thus, in vapour phase, mole fraction of A

$$= \frac{p_A}{p_A + p_B} = \frac{180}{180 + 420} = 0.30$$

Mole fraction of $B = 1 - 0.30 = 0.70$

Vapour Pressure of Solutions of Solids in Liquids

The vapour pressure of the solution (after an addition of non-volatile solute to a solvent) at the given temperature is found to be lower than the vapour pressure of the pure solvent at the same temperature.

This is because in solid-liquid solution, the surface has both solute and solvent molecules; thereby the fraction of the surface covered by the solvent molecules gets reduced.

Consequently, the number of solvent molecules escaping from the surface is correspondingly reduced, thus, the vapour pressure is also reduced.

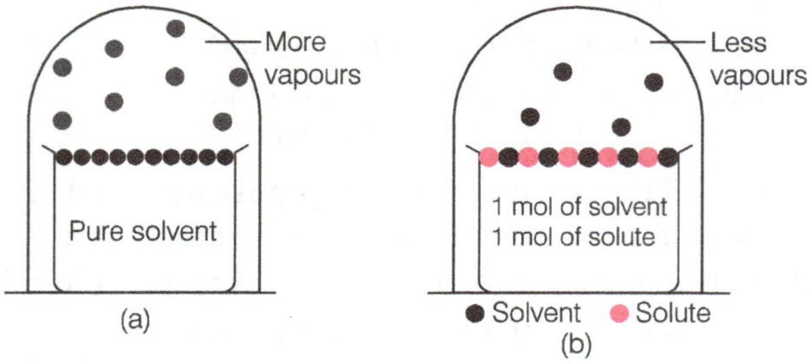

Decrease in the vapour pressure of the solvent due to the presence of solute in the solvent. (a) Evaporation of the molecules of the solvent (denoted by dark dots) from its surface. (b) In a solution, solute particles (denoted by light dots) also occupy part of the surface area.

The decrease in the vapour pressure of solvent depends on the amount of non-volatile solute present in the solution, irrespective of its nature.

Raoult's law in its general form can be stated as, "*for any solution, the partial vapour pressure of each volatile component in the solution is directly proportional to its mole fraction*".

A plot between the vapour pressure and the mole fraction of the solvent is linear as shown below.

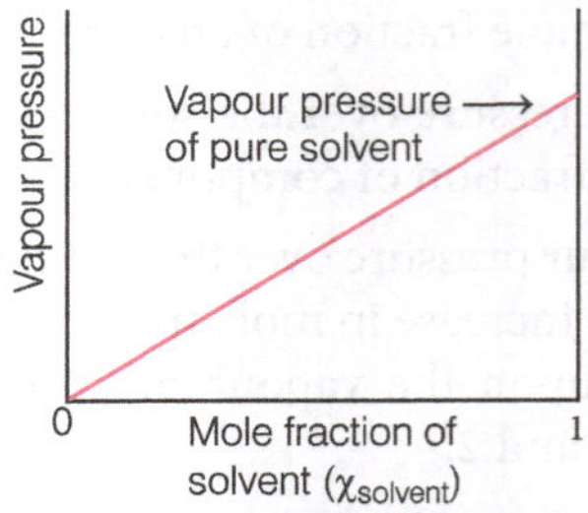

Plot between the vapour pressure and mole fraction of the solvent

1.5 Ideal and Non-ideal Solutions

Liquid-liquid solutions can be divided into ideal and non-ideal solutions on the basis of Raoult's law.

Ideal Solutions

The solutions which obey Raoult's law over the entire range of concentration are called **ideal solutions**.

In ideal solution, no heat is absorbed or evolved when the components are mixed i.e. $\Delta_{mix} H = 0$ and $\Delta_{mix} V = 0$. The volume of the solution is equal to the sum of volumes of two components.

If intermolecular attractive forces between solute-solute molecules (A—A) and solvent-solvent molecules (B—B) are nearly equal to intermolecular forces between solute-solvent (A—B) molecules, then ideal solutions are formed. A perfect ideal solution is rare but nearly ideal solutions can be obtained.

e.g. (i) n-hexane + n-heptane

(ii) Bromoethane + chloroethane

(iii) Benzene + toluene

(iv) Chlorobenzene + bromobenzene

Non-ideal Solutions

The solutions which do not obey Raoult's law over the entire range of concentration are called **non-ideal solutions**. If vapour pressure of solution is higher than that predicted by Raoult's law then such deviation is called **positive deviation**. If vapour pressure of solution is lower than that predicted by Raoult's law then such deviation is called **negative deviation**.

The plots of vapour pressure as a function of mole fractions for such solutions are shown below.

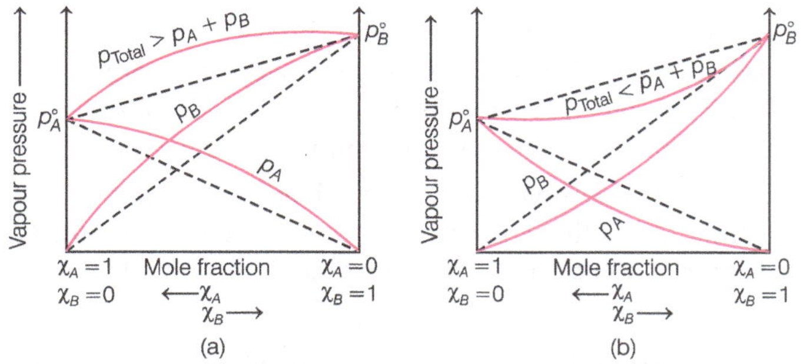

The vapour pressures of two component systems as a function of composition.
(a) A solution that shows positive deviation from Raoult's law and
(b) A solution that shows negative deviation from Raoult's law.

If intermolecular forces between solute-solvent (A—B) are weaker than intermolecular forces between solute-solute molecules (A—A) and solvent-solvent molecules (B—B) then solutions show **positive deviation.**

e.g. (i) Carbon disulphide + acetone
(ii) Ethanol + acetone
(iii) Acetone + benzene

If intermolecular forces between solute-solvent (A—B) are stronger than intermolecular forces between solute-solute molecules (A—A) and solvent-solvent molecules (B—B) then solutions show **negative deviation.**

e.g. (i) Chloroform + acetone
(ii) Phenol + aniline
(iii) Water + nitric acid

Difference between solutions having positive and negative deviation from ideal behaviour are given in the table below.

Solutions having positive deviation from ideal behaviour	Solutions having negative deviation from ideal behaviour
• The intermolecular interactions i.e. A—B interactions are weaker than in pure components i.e. between A—A or B—B.	The intermolecular interactions i.e. A—B interactions are stronger than in pure components i.e. between A—A or B—B
• $p_1 > p_1^0\chi_1$ and $p_2 > p_2^0\chi_2$	$p_1 < p_1^0\chi_1$ and $p_2 < p_2^0\chi_2$
• $\Delta_{mix}H$ = positive (endothermic)	$\Delta_{mix}H$ = negative (exothermic)
• $\Delta_{mix}V$ = positive	$\Delta_{mix}V$ = negative
• Heating increases solubility.	Heating decreases solubility.

Depending upon the extent of deviation from Raoult's law, a new category of binary mixtures, known as azeotropes is formed. It is discussed below.

Azeotropes (Constant Boiling Mixtures)

The binary mixtures (liquid mixtures) having the same composition in liquid and vapour phase and boil at constant temperature are called **azeotropic mixtures** or **azeotropes.**

In such cases, it is not possible to separate the components by fractional distillation. There are two types of azeotropes called **minimum boiling azeotropes** and **maximum boiling azeotropes.**

The azeotropes distil over as if they are pure liquids.

Minimum Boiling Azeotropes

The non-ideal solutions which show a large positive deviation from Raoult's law, form **minimum boiling azeotropes** at a specific composition.

For these type of solutions, there is one intermediate composition for which the total vapour pressure of such a solution will be the highest and boiling point will be the lowest.

e.g. Ethanol-water mixture on fractional distillation gives a solution containing approximately 95% by volume of ethanol.

Maximum Boiling Azeotropes

The non-ideal solutions which show a large negative deviation from Raoult's law form **maximum boiling azeotropes** at specific composition.

For the solution showing these type of deviation, there is one intermediate composition for which the vapour pressure of the solution is lowest and boiling point is highest. e.g. Azeotrope formed from nitric acid and water has the approximate composition of 68% nitric acid and 32% water by mass, with a boiling point of 393.5 K.

TEACHER'S TIP

$\Delta_{mix}S$ and $\Delta_{mix}G$ is always positive and negative respectively for both ideal and non-ideal solutions.

Quick Test 3

Conceptual Questions

1. What role does the molecular interaction play in a solution of alcohol and water? NCERT
2. What type of deviation is shown by a mixture of ethanol and acetone? Give reason. CBSE 2024, 2023
3. On mixing liquids *X* and *Y*, volume of the resulting solution decreases. What type of deviation from Raoult's law is shown by the resulting solution? What change in temperature would you observe after mixing liquids *X* and *Y*? CBSE 2023
4. What type of azeotropic mixture will be formed by a solution of acetone and chloroform? Justify on the basis of strength of intermolecular interactions that develop in the solution. CBSE 2019

Numerical Questions

5. If the vapour pressure of C_2H_5OH at 298 K is 40 mm of Hg. Its mole fraction in a solution with CH_3OH is 0.8. What will be its vapour pressure in solution, if it obeys Raoult's law?
6. The vapour pressure of pure liquid *X* and pure liquid *Y* at 25°C are 120 mm Hg and 160 mm Hg respectively. If equal moles of *X* and *Y* are mixed to form an ideal solution, calculate the vapour pressure of the solution. CBSE 2023
7. A mixture contains 1 mole of volatile liquid A ($p_A^\circ = 100$ mm Hg) and 4 moles of volatile liquid B ($p_B^\circ = 90$ mm Hg). Calculate the total vapour pressure of the distillate assuming solution behave ideally.

Answers

5. 32 mm Hg 6. 140 mm Hg 7. 92 mm Hg

For Solutions, See QR Code on Pg. 34

1.6 Colligative Properties

The properties of solutions which depend only on the number of solute particles irrespective of their nature relative to the total number of particles present in the solution, are called **colligative properties.** (Colligative : From Latin : Co means together, ligare means to bind.)

There are four important colligative properties

- relative lowering of vapour pressure,
- elevation in boiling point,
- depression in freezing point and
- osmotic pressure of solution.

Relative Lowering of Vapour Pressure

We have studied that, on adding non-volatile solute to a solvent, the vapour pressure of the solution decreases. Raoult's established that, relative lowering of vapour pressure depends only on the concentration of the solute particles and it is independent of their identity.

Let χ_1 is the mole fraction of solvent, χ_2 is that of solute, p_1° is the vapour pressure of pure solvent and p_1 is that of solution. Thus, according to Raoult's law.

$$p_1 = p_1^\circ \chi_1$$

The lowering in vapour pressure of solvent,

$$p_1^\circ - p_1 = \Delta p_1$$

Relative lowering in vapour pressure $= \dfrac{p_1^\circ - p_1}{p_1^\circ}$

Relative lowering in vapour pressure is equal to mole fraction of solute.

$$\frac{\Delta p_1}{p_1^\circ} = \frac{p_1^\circ - p_1}{p_1^\circ} = \chi_2 = \frac{n_2}{n_1 + n_2}$$

Here, n_1 and n_2 are number of moles of solvent and solute. In a solution containing several non-volatile solutes, the lowering of the vapour pressure depends on the sum of the mole fraction of different solutes.

Note Relative lowering of vapour pressure is a colligative property while lowering of vapour pressure is not.

Determination of Molar Mass of Solute

For dilute solutions, $n_2 << n_1$

(In dilute solutions, amount of solute is very little as compared to solvent)

$$\therefore \quad \frac{p_1^\circ - p}{p_1^\circ} = \frac{n_2}{n_1} \quad \text{(Neglecting } n_2 \text{ in denominator)}$$

or in terms of molar mass

$$\frac{p_1^\circ - p}{p_1^\circ} = \frac{w_2 \times M_1}{M_2 \times w_1}$$

where, w_1 and w_2 are the masses and M_1 and M_2 are the molar masses of the solvent and solute, respectively.

Example 11 **An aqueous solution of 2% non-volatile solute exerts a pressure of 1.004 bar at the normal boiling point of the solvent. What is the molar mass of the solute?** NCERT

Sol. Vapour pressure of pure water at the boiling point

$(p_1^\circ) = 1 \text{ atm} = 1.013 \text{ bar}$

Vapour pressure of solution (p) = 1.004 bar (Given)

2% non-volatile solute means

Mass of solute (w_2) = 2 g and Mass of solution = 100 g

$\therefore$ Mass of solvent (w_1) = 98 g

Applying Raoult's law for dilute solution, as n_2 (moles of solute) is very small in comparison to n_1 (moles of solvent).

$\therefore$ n_2 can be neglected from denominator.

Lowering in vapour pressure,

$$\frac{p_1^\circ - p}{p_1^\circ} = \frac{n_2}{n_1 + n_2} \approx \frac{n_2}{n_1} = \frac{w_2 / M_2}{w_1 / M_1} = \frac{w_2}{M_2} \times \frac{M_1}{w_1}$$

$$\frac{(1.013 - 1.004)\text{ bar}}{1.013\text{ bar}} = \frac{2\text{ g}}{M_2} \times \frac{18\text{ g mol}^{-1}}{98\text{ g}}$$

or $$M_2 = \frac{2 \times 18}{98} \times \frac{1.013}{0.009}\text{ g mol}^{-1} = 41.35\text{ g mol}^{-1}$$

Elevation in Boiling Point

The **boiling point of a liquid** is that temperature at which its vapour pressure becomes equal to the atmospheric pressure. Generally, the vapour pressure of a liquid increases with increase of temperature.

We can say that when a non-volatile solute is added to a solvent, the boiling point of the solution is always higher than that of pure solvent in which the solution is prepared. This difference in the boiling points of the solution (T_b) and pure solvent (T_b°) is called **elevation in boiling point** (ΔT_b).

It is given by, $\Delta T_b = T_b - T_b^\circ$

Elevation in boiling point depends on the number of solute molecules rather than their nature. The given figure depicts the variation of vapour pressure of the pure solvent and solution as a function of temperature.

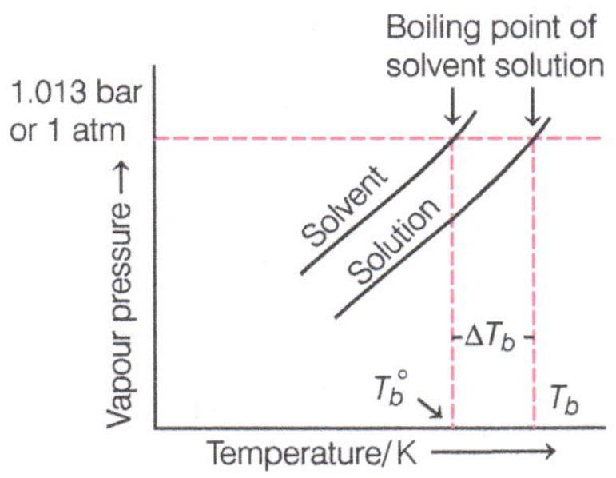

The figure shows that ΔT_b denotes the elevation in boiling point of a solvent in solution.

Experiments have shown that for **dilute solutions**, the elevation in boiling point is directly proportional to the molal concentration of the solute in a solution (m).

Thus, $\Delta T_b \propto m$

or $\Delta T_b = K_b m$

where, m (molality) is the number of moles of solute dissolved in 1 kg of solvent and K_b is the constant of proportionality, called **boiling point elevation constant** or **molal elevation constant** or **ebullioscopic constant.**

The unit of K_b is K kg mol^{-1}.

If $m = 1$ molal

Then, $\Delta T_b = K_b$

Thus, boiling point elevation constant, K_b is defined as "the *elevation in boiling point for 1 molal solution, i.e. a solution containing 1 mole of solute dissolved in 1000 g of the solvent*".

Determination of Molar Mass of Solute

If w_2 gram of solute of molar mass of M_2 is dissolved in w_1 gram of solvent, then

So, $$\Delta T_b = \frac{K_b \times w_2 \times 1000}{M_2 \times w_1}$$

or $$M_2 = \frac{K_b \times w_2 \times 1000}{\Delta T_b \times w_1}$$

Thus, in order to determine M_2, molar mass of the solute, known mass of solute in a known mass of the solvent is taken and ΔT_b is determined experimentally for a known solvent whose K_b value is known.

Example 12 **Boiling point of water at 750 mm of Hg is 99.63°C. How much sucrose is to be added to 500 g of water such that it boils at 100°C? [K_b for water is 0.52 K kg mol^{-1}]** NCERT Intext

Sol. Mass of water (W_A) = 500 g = 0.5 kg

Elevation in boiling point

$(\Delta T_b) = 373\text{ K} - 372.63\text{ K} = 0.37\text{ K}$

Molal elevation constant (K_b) = 0.52 K kg mol^{-1}

Molar mass of sucrose ($C_{12}H_{22}O_{11}$)

$(M_B) = (12 \times 12\text{ g/mol}) + (22 \times 1\text{ g/mol}) + (16 \times 11\text{ g/mol})$

$= 342\text{ g mol}^{-1}$

$$W_B = \frac{M_B \times \Delta T_b \times W_A}{K_b}$$

$$= \frac{(342\text{ g mol}^{-1}) \times (0.37\text{ K}) \times (0.5\text{ kg})}{(0.52\text{ K kg mol}^{-1})}$$

$= 121.7$ g

Depression in Freezing Point

The **freezing point** is that temperature at which the solid and the liquid states of the substance have the same vapour pressure.

When a non-volatile solute is added to a solvent, the freezing point of thus formed solution is always lower than that of pure solvent. This is because the vapour pressure of the solvent decreases in the presence of non-volatile solute. This difference in the freezing point is known as **depression in freezing point**.

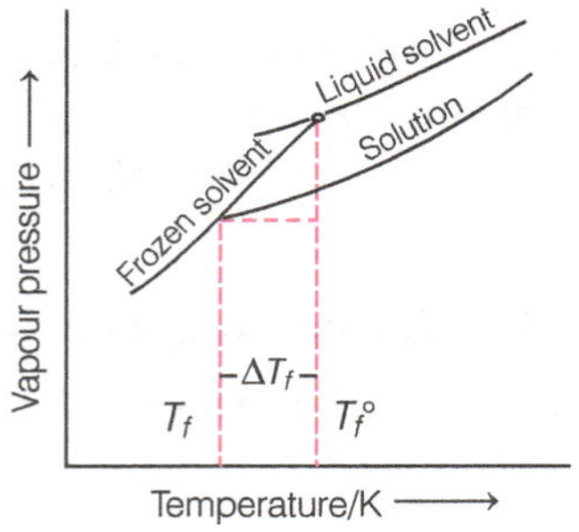

Figure showing ΔT_f, depression in freezing point of a solvent in a solution

If T_f° is the freezing point temperature (in kelvin) of pure solvent and T_f is the freezing point temperature (in kelvin) of the solution when non-volatile solute is dissolved in it then,

Depression in freezing point (ΔT_f),

$$\Delta T_f = T_f^\circ - T_f$$

For dilute solutions, $\Delta T_f \propto m$

or $$\Delta T_f = K_f m$$

where, m is the molal concentration (or molality) of the solution and the proportionality constant K_f, which depends on the nature of the solvent is known as **freezing point depression constant** or **molal depression constant** or **cryoscopic constant**.

The unit of K_f is K kg mol^{-1}. If $m = 1$ molal, then $\Delta T_f = K_f$

Thus, freezing point depression constant is defined as "*the depression in freezing point for 1 molal solution, i.e. a solution containing 1 mole of solute dissolved in 1000 g of solvent*".

Note Elevation in boiling point and depression in freezing point are colligative properties while boiling and freezing points are not.

Determination of Molar Mass of Solute

If w_2 gram of solute of molar mass M_2 is dissolved in w_1 gram of solvent, then

$$\Delta T_f = \frac{K_f \times w_2 \times 1000}{w_1 \times M_2}$$

or $$M_2 = \frac{K_f \times w_2 \times 1000}{\Delta T_f \times w_1}$$

This expression is used to determine the molar mass of solute.

Relation between Enthalpy Changes and Constants (K_f or K_b)

The values of K_f and K_b, which depend upon the nature of solvent, can be shown from the following relations.

$$K_f = \frac{R \times M_1 \times T_f^2}{1000 \times \Delta_{fus} H}$$

$$K_b = \frac{R \times M_1 \times T_b^2}{1000 \times \Delta_{vap} H}$$

where, R and M_1 stand for the gas constant and molar mass of the solvent, respectively and T_f and T_b denotes the freezing point and the boiling point of the pure solvent respectively (in kelvin). $\Delta_{fus} H$ and $\Delta_{vap} H$ represent the enthalpies for the fusion and vaporisation of the solvent, respectively.

Example 13 A 5% solution (by mass) of cane sugar in water has freezing point of 271 K. Calculate the freezing point of a 5% glucose in water, if freezing point of pure water is 273.15 K. NCERT

Sol. **For cane sugar solution**

Molality of sugar solution $= \frac{W_2}{M_2} \times \frac{1000}{W_1}$

Here, $W_2 = 5$ g, $M_2 = 342$ g mol^{-1} (sugar), $W_1 = 95$ g

Molality (m) $= \frac{5}{342} \times \frac{1000}{95} = 0.154$ m

ΔT_f for sugar solution $= 273.15 - 271 = 2.15$ K

$$\Delta T_f = K_f \times m$$

$$\therefore \quad K_f = \frac{2.15}{0.154} \text{ K kg/mol}$$

For glucose solution, $\Delta T_f = K_f \times m$

$$\text{Molality (glucose)} = \frac{W_2'}{M_2'} \times \frac{1000}{W_1'}$$

$$m\text{ (glucose)} = \frac{5}{180} \times \frac{1000}{95}$$

$$= 0.2924 \text{ m}$$

where, $W_2' = 5\text{g}, M_2' = 180 \text{ g mol}^{-1}, W_1' = 95 \text{ g}$

$$\therefore \quad \Delta T_f\text{ (glucose)} = \frac{2.15}{0.154} \times 0.2924 = 4.08 \text{ K}$$

$\therefore$ Freezing point of glucose solution

$$= (273.15 - 4.08) \text{ K} = 269.07 \text{ K}$$

Osmotic Pressure of Solution

Before we will discuss osmotic pressure, let us first understand the term osmosis.

Osmosis

The phenomenon of the flow of solvent molecules through a semipermeable membrane from pure solvent to the solution is known as **osmosis**.

Semipermeable membrane (SPM) is the membrane which allows solvent molecules like water to pass through their holes. However, it hinders the passage for bigger molecules of solute like salt.

If semipermeable membrane is placed between the pure solvent and solution as shown in the figure, the solvent molecules will flow through the membrane from pure solvent to the solution.

These membranes appear to be continuous sheets or films, yet they contain a network of submicroscopic holes or pores.

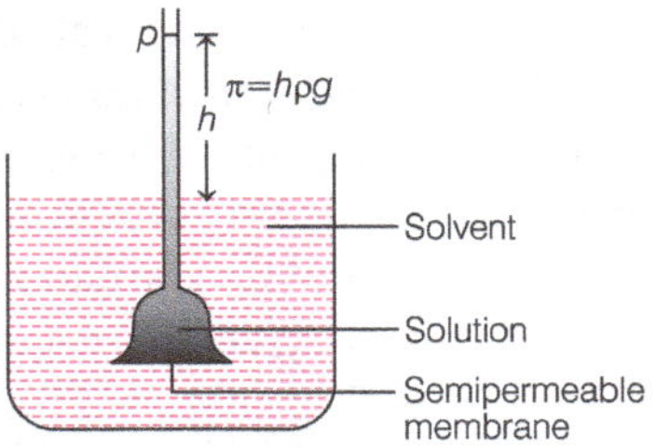

Level of solution rises in the thistle funnel due to osmosis of solvent

If the osmosis takes place between the solutions of different concentrations, then solvent molecules will move from the solution of low solute concentration to that of higher solute concentration. The flow will continue till the equilibrium is attained.

Examples of Osmosis

The examples of osmosis are as follows

- A raw mango placed in concentrated salt solution loses water *via* osmosis and shrivel into pickle.
- Wilted flowers revive when placed in fresh water through osmosis.
- A carrot that has become limp due to water loss into the atmosphere can be placed into the water making it firm once again through osmosis.
- Through osmosis, blood cell collapse due to loss of water when placed in water containing more than 0.9% (mass/volume) salt solution.
- People taking a lot of salt or salty food experience water retention in tissue cells and intercellular spaces because of osmosis. This resulting puffiness or swelling is called **edema**.
- Water movement from soil into plant roots and subsequently into upper portion of the plant is partly due to osmosis.
- The preservation of meat by salting and of fruits by adding sugar protects against bacterial action. Through the process of osmosis, a bacterium on salted meat or fruits loses water, shrivels and dies.

TEACHER'S TIP

In osmosis, solvent molecules can move in both the directions but its net flow is from the region of higher solvent concentration to the lower solvent concentration across a semipermeable membrane.

Osmotic Pressure (π)

The osmotic pressure of a solution is *the excess pressure that must be applied to the solution side of the membrane to prevent osmosis, i.e. to stop the passage of solvent molecules through a semipermeable membrane into the solution.* It is a colligative property as it depends upon the number of solute molecules present in the solution and not on their nature.

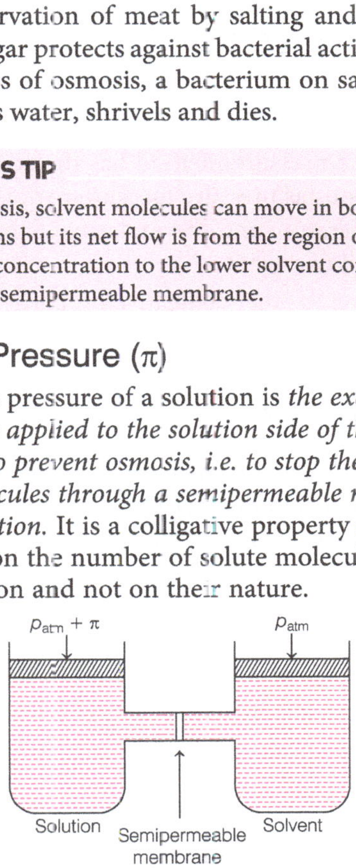

The excess pressure equal to the osmotic pressure must be applied on the solution side to prevent osmosis

The osmotic pressure of a solution depends on its concentration. Larger the concentration, larger will be the osmotic pressure.

Determination of Molar Mass of Solute

Osmotic pressure is proportional to the molarity (C) of the solution at a given temperature (T).

Thus, $\pi \propto C, \pi = CRT$ (For dilute solution)

where, π is the osmotic pressure and R is the gas constant.

But $$C = \frac{n_2}{V}$$

and $$n_2 = \frac{w_2}{M_2}$$

where, n_2 is the number of moles of solute dissolved in V L of solution, w_2 is the weight of solute and M_2 is its molar mass.

Therefore, $$\pi = \frac{w_2 RT}{VM_2}$$

Or, $$M_2 = \frac{w_2 RT}{V\pi}$$

Advantages of Osmotic Pressure Method

- The osmotic pressure method has the advantage over other methods as pressure measurement is around the room temperature and the molarity of the solution is used instead of molality.
- As compared to other colligative properties, its magnitude is large even for very dilute solutions.
- This method is widely used to determine molar masses of proteins, polymers and other macromolecules.

Example 14 **Calculate the osmotic pressure (in pascals) exerted by a solution prepared by dissolving 1.0 g of polymer of molar mass 185000 g mol^{-1} in 450 mL of water at 37°C.** NCERT Intext

Sol. From the relation, $\pi = CRT = \frac{n}{V} RT$, we can find the value of π.

Mass of polymer = 1.0 g

Here, number of moles of solute dissolved (n)

$$= \frac{1.0 \text{ g}}{185000 \text{ g mol}^{-1}} = \frac{1}{185000} \text{ mol}$$

$V = 450 \text{ mL} = 0.450 \text{ L}$

$T = 37°\text{C} = (37 + 273) \text{ K} = 310 \text{ K}$

$R = 8.314 \text{ kPa L K}^{-1} \text{ mol}^{-1}$

$= 8.314 \times 10^3 \text{ Pa L K}^{-1}\text{mol}^{-1}$

Substituting these values, we get

$$\pi = \frac{1}{185000} \text{ mol} \times \frac{1}{0.45 \text{ L}} \times 8.314 \times 10^3 \text{ Pa L K}^{-1}\text{mol}^{-1} \times 310 \text{ K} = 30.96 \text{ Pa}$$

Types of Solution on the Basis of Osmotic Pressure

There are three types of solutions on the basis of concentration and hence the applied osmotic pressure.

(i) **Isotonic solution** Two solutions having same osmotic pressure at a given temperature are called isotonic solutions. There is no osmosis between these two solutions as they have same molar concentration.

e.g. The osmotic pressure associated with the fluid inside the blood cell is equivalent to that of 0.9% (mass/volume) sodium chloride solution, called normal saline solution and it is safe to inject intravenously.

Note Isotonic solutions are often referred to as isoosmotic solutions as they have same osmotic pressure or solute concentration.

(ii) **Hypertonic solution** A solution having more osmotic pressure than the other solution is called hypertonic solution.

e.g. If we place the cells in a solution containing more than 0.9% (mass/volume) sodium chloride, then water will flow out of the cells and they would shrink. This process is called **plasmolysis**.

(iii) **Hypotonic solution** A solution having less osmotic pressure than the other solution is called hypotonic solution. e.g. If the salt concentration is less than 0.9% (mass/volume) sodium chloride, then water will flow into the cells and they would swell, if placed in this solution and they would swell.

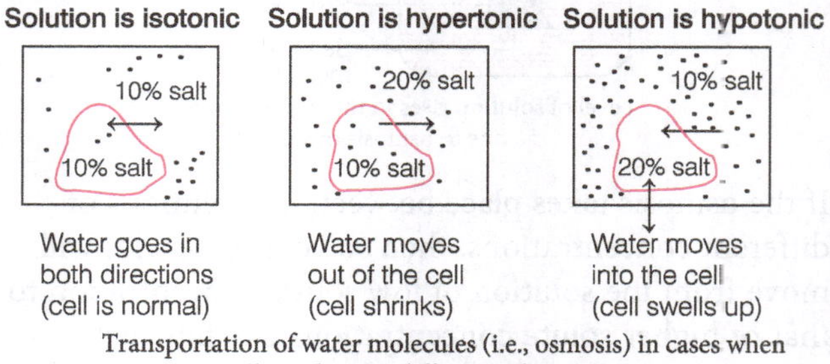

Transportation of water molecules (i.e., osmosis) in cases when cells are kept in different solutions

Reverse Osmosis and Water Purification

The direction of osmosis can be reversed, if a pressure larger than the osmotic pressure is applied to the solution side. Now, the pure solvent flows out of the solution through semipermeable membrane. This phenomenon is called **reverse osmosis.** This method is used in desalination to get salt free-water from sea water as shown in the figure.

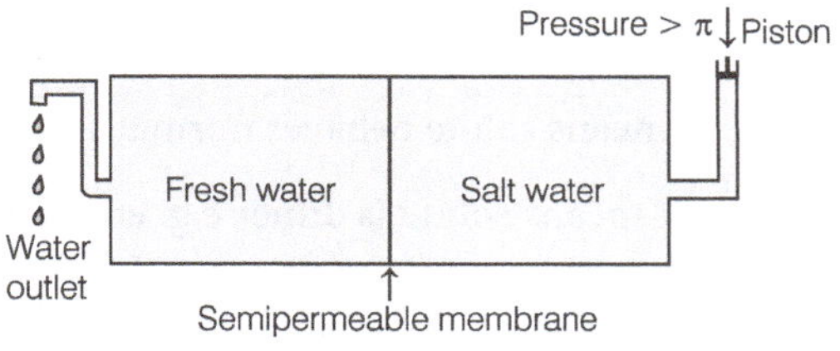

Reverse osmosis occurs when a pressure larger than the osmotic pressure is applied to the solution

When a pressure higher than the osmotic pressure of the sea water is applied, pure water passes through the semipermeable membrane leaving dissolved salt ions and other impurities behind.

The pressure required for the reverse osmosis is quite high. Variety of polymer membranes are available for this purpose.

The most commonly used porous membrane is that of **cellulose acetate** placed over a suitable support as it is permeable to water but not permeable to impurities and ions present in water. This method of purification is boon for the regions where fresh water is scarcely available.

1.7 Abnormal Molar Mass

Ionic compounds when dissolved in water dissociates into cations and anions. We have studied that the colligative properties help us to calculate the molar masses of solutes.

But in case of association or dissociation of compounds, molar masses determined by these methods do not agree with theoretical value. Such molar masses that are either lower or higher than the expected or normal values are called **abnormal molar masses.**

Case of association or dissociation of compounds is described as

(i) **Association** of molecules leads to decrease in the number of particles in solution resulting in a decrease in the value of colligative properties. e.g. ΔT_b or ΔT_f for ethanoic acid will be half of the normal value.

Colligative properties are inversely related to molar mass of a compound. Therefore, higher value is obtained for molar mass than normal values.

e.g. Ethanoic acid in benzene undergoes dimerisation, it shows a molar mass of 120 g/mol (normal molar mass = 60 g/mol)

$$2CH_3COOH \rightleftharpoons (CH_3COOH)_2$$

(ii) **Dissociation** of molecules leads to increase in the number of particles in solution resulting in an increase in the value of colligative properties. Due to this, lower value is obtained for molar mass than normal values.

e.g. Potassium chloride in water dissociates into K^+ and Cl^- ions and it shows a molar mass of 37.25 g/mol (normal molar mass = 74.5 g/mol)

$$KCl \rightleftharpoons K^+ + Cl^-$$

TEACHER'S TIP

Molecules of ethanoic acid tend to form dimers in non-polar solvents or in environments with a low dielectric constant as there is insufficient polarity to break the hydrogen bonds.

1.8 van't Hoff Factor (i)

It is defined as *"the ratio of the experimental value of the colligative property to the calculated value of the colligative property".*

$$i = \frac{\text{Normal (calculated) molar mass}}{\text{Observed (abnormal) molar mass}} = \frac{\text{Observed colligative property}}{\text{Calculated colligative property}}$$

$$\text{Colligative property} \propto \frac{1}{\text{Molar mass}}$$

- In association, observed molar mass is more than the normal, so i has a value less than one ($i < 1$).
- In dissociation, observed molar mass has lesser value than normal, so i is more than one ($i > 1$).
- In case, no association or dissociation takes place, so $i = 1$.

$$i = \frac{\text{Total number of moles of particles after association / dissociation}}{\text{Number of moles of particles before association / dissociation}}$$

Values of van't Hoff factor (*i*) at Various Concentrations of Some Salts

Salt	Values of i 0.1 m	Values of i 0.01 m	van't Hoff factor (i) for complete dissociation of solute
NaCl	1.87	1.94	2.00
KCl	1.85	1.94	2.00
K_2SO_4	2.32	2.7	3.00
$MgSO_4$	1.21	1.53	2.00

Modified forms of Colligative Properties

Due to inclusion of van't Hoff factor, the modified forms of colligative properties are as follows

Relative lowering of vapour pressure,

$$\frac{\Delta p}{p^\circ} = i\chi_2$$

or

$$\frac{p_1^\circ - p_1}{p_1^\circ} = i \cdot \frac{n_2}{n_1}$$

Elevation in boiling point, $\Delta T_b = iK_b m$

Depression in freezing point, $\Delta T_f = iK_f m$

Osmotic pressure of solution, $\pi = iCRT$ or $\frac{in_2RT}{V}$

Example 15 **Determine the amount of $CaCl_2$ ($i = 2.47$) dissolved in 2.5 L of water such that its osmotic pressure is 0.75 atm at 27°C.** NCERT

Sol. From, $\pi = iCRT = i\frac{n}{V}RT$ or $n = \frac{\pi \times V}{i \times R \times T}$

Here, $\pi = 0.75$ atm; $V = 2.5$ L, $i = 2.47$

$T = 300$ K (27 + 273); $R = 0.0821$ L atm $K^{-1} mol^{-1}$

$$\Rightarrow n = \frac{0.75 \text{ atm} \times 2.5 \text{ L}}{2.47 \times 0.0821 \text{ L atm K}^{-1} \text{mol}^{-1} \times 300 \text{ K}}$$

$= 0.0308$ mol

Molar mass of $CaCl_2$ = 40 g / mol + 2× 35.5 g / mol

= 111 g mol^{-1}

∴ Amount of $CaCl_2$ dissolved $= n \times M$

= 0.0308 × 111 g / mol = 3.42 g

Degree of Dissociation and Association

Using van't Hoff factor, the extent of a degree of dissociation or association can be calculated.

(i) **Degree of dissociation** It is defined as the fraction of the total substance that undergoes dissociation.

$$\alpha \text{ (degree of dissociation)} = \frac{(i-1)}{(n-1)}$$

(ii) **Degree of association** It is defined as the fraction of the total substance which exists in the form of associated molecules.

$$\alpha \text{ (degree of association)} = \frac{(1-i)}{\left(1-\frac{1}{n}\right)} \text{ or } \left(\frac{i-1}{\frac{1}{n}-1}\right)$$

- If $i = 1$, it means solute behaves normally.
- If $i = \frac{1}{2}$, it means solute is dimer e.g. ethanoic acid in benzene.
- If $i = \frac{1}{4}$, it means solute is tetra-atomic, e.g. P_4.
- If $i = \frac{1}{8}$, it means solute is octa-atomic, e.g. S_8.
- If $i > 1$, it means solute undergoes dissociation.
- If $i < 1$, it means solute undergoes association.

Example 16 **A 0.5% aqueous solution of KCl was found to be freeze at −0.24°C. Calculate the van't Hoff factor and degree of dissociation of the solute at this concentration. (K_f for water = 1.86 K kg mol^{-1}).**

Sol. Given, $K_f = 1.86$ K kg mol^{-1}, $W_2 = 0.5$ g, $W_1 = 99.5$ g,

$\Delta T_f = T_f^\circ - T_f = (273 - 272.76)$ K = 0.24 K

[∵ $T_f = -0.24$°C = 273K − 0.24 K]

$$\text{Observed molecular mass of KCl} = \frac{1000 \times K_f \times W_2}{\Delta T_f \times W_1}$$

$$= \frac{1000 \times 1.86 \text{ K kg mol}^{-1} \times 0.5 \text{ g}}{0.24 \text{ K} \times 99.5 \text{ g}} = 38.9 \text{ g/mol}$$

Normal molecular mass of KCl = (39. 0 + 35.5) g/mol

= 74.5 g/mol

$$\text{van't Hoff factor} = \frac{\text{Normal molecular mass}}{\text{Observed molecular mass}}$$

$$i = \frac{74.5 \text{ g / mol}}{38.9 \text{ g / mol}} = 1.92$$

$$\underset{(1-\alpha)}{KCl} \rightleftharpoons \underset{\alpha}{K^+} + \underset{\alpha}{Cl^-}$$

Total number of particles $= 1 - \alpha + \alpha + \alpha = 1 + \alpha$

$i = 1 + \alpha$

∴ $1.92 = 1 + \alpha$

So, $\alpha = 1.92 - 1 = 0.92$, i.e. 92% dissociated.

Quick Test 4

Conceptual Questions

1. How does sprinkling of salt help in clearing the snow covered roads in hilly areas? Explain the phenomenon involved in the process. *NCERT Exemplar*
2. Arrange the depression in freezing point of water observed for the same molar concentrations of acetic acid, trichloroacetic acid and trifluoroacetic acid. Explain the order as well. *NCERT*
3. When kept in water, raisin swells in size. Name and explain the phenomenon involved with the help of a diagram. Give three applications of the phenomenon. *NCERT Exemplar*

Numerical Questions

4. Calculate the mass of a non-volatile solute (molar mass 40 g mol^{-1}) which should be dissolved in 114 g of octane to reduce its vapour pressure to 80%. *NCERT*
5. A glucose solution which boils at 101.04°C at 1 atm. What will be relative lowering of vapour pressure of an aqueous solution of urea which is equimolal to given glucose solution? (Given: K_b for water is 0.52 K kg mol^{-1}) *CBSE SQP 2021*
6. 18 g of a non-volatile solute is dissolved in 200 g of H_2O freezes at 272.07 K. Calculate the molecular mass of solute (K_f for water = 1.86 K kg mol^{-1}) *CBSE 2024*
7. Calculate the freezing point of a solution containing 60 g of glucose (molar mass = 180 g mol^{-1}) in 250 g of water. (K_f of water = 1.86 K kg mol^{-1}) *CBSE 2018*
8. At 300 K, 36 g of glucose present in a litre of its solution has an osmotic pressure of 4.98 bar. If the osmotic pressure of the solution is 1.52 bar at the same temperature, what would be its concentration? *CBSE 2019, NCERT*
9. When 19.5 g of F—CH_2—COOH (molar mass =78 g mol^{-1}), is dissolved in 500 g of water, the depression in freezing point is observed to be 1°C. Calculate the degree of dissociation of F—CH_2—COOH.
{Given : K_f for water = 1.86 K kg mol^{-1}} *CBSE 2023*
10. If benzoic acid (M = 122 g mol^{-1}) is associated into a dimer when dissolved in benzene and the osmotic pressure of a solution of 6.1 g of benzoic acid in 100 mL benzene is 6.5 atm at 27°C, then what is the percentage association of benzoic acid ? *CBSE 2023*
{Given : R = 0.0821 L atm K^{-1} mol^{-1}}

Answers

4. 10 g
5. 0.034 atm
6. 180 g mol^{-1}
7. 2.47 K
8. 0.061 mol L^{-1}
9. 3.07×10^{-3}
10. 0.94

For Solutions, See QR Code on Pg. 34

Mind Map

Types of Solutions

Solid Solutions
- Gas – Solid ⟶ Solution of H_2 in Pd
- Liquid – Solid ⟶ Amalgam of Hg with Na
- Solid – Solid ⟶ Alloys like bronze and many other

Liquid Solutions
- Gas – Liquid ⟶ O_2 dissolved in water
- Liquid – Liquid ⟶ Ethanol dissolved in water
- Solid – Liquid ⟶ Salt dissolved in water

Gaseous Solutions
- Gas – Gas ⟶ Mixture of O_2 and N_2
- Liquid – Gas ⟶ Chloroform with N_2 gas
- Solid – Gas ⟶ Camphor in N_2 gas

Methods of Expressing Concentration of Solution

- **Mass percentage** $(w/W) = \dfrac{\text{Mass of solute (g)}}{\text{Total mass of solution (g)}} \times 100$
- **Mass by volume percentage** $(w/V) = \dfrac{\text{Mass of solute (g)}}{\text{Total volume of solution (mL)}} \times 100$
- **Volume percentage** $(v/V) = \dfrac{\text{Volume of solute (mL)}}{\text{Total volume of solution (mL)}} \times 100$
- **ppm** $= \dfrac{\text{No. of parts of components}}{\text{Total no. of parts of all components of solution}} \times 10^6$
- **Mole fraction** $(\chi) = \dfrac{\text{No. of moles of solute}}{\text{Total no. of moles in solution}}$
- **Molarity** $(M) = \dfrac{\text{No. of moles of solute}}{\text{Volume of solution (L)}}$
- **Normality** $(N) = \dfrac{\text{No. of grams equivalent of solute}}{\text{Volume of solution (L)}}$
- **Molality** $(m) = \dfrac{\text{No. of moles of solute}}{\text{Weight of the solvent (in kg)}}$
- Mass%, ppm, mole fraction and molality are independent of temperature, whereas mass by volume %, volume % and molarity depends on temperature.

Solubility

It shows the maximum amount of solute that can be present in a specified amount of solvent at a given temperature.

Solubility of a Solid in a Liquid
- Effect of temperature : Exothermic process-decreases with rise in temperature. Endothermic process-increases with rise in temperature.
- Effect of pressure : Not significant

Solubility of a Gas in a Liquid
- **Effect of temperature** Increases with decrease in temperature.
- **Effect of pressure** Increases with increase in pressure.
- **Henry's law** states that the solubility of a gas in a liquid is directly proportional to partial pressure of the gas present above the solution surface at constant temperature.

$p = K_H \cdot \chi$; K_H = Henry's law constant.

SOLUTIONS

Colligative Properties

These depend only upon the number of solute particles but not on their nature.

Relative Lowering of Vapour Pressure

Relative lowering of vapour pressure ∝ mole fraction of solute.

i.e. $$\frac{p_1^\circ - p_1}{p_1^\circ} = \chi_2 = \frac{w_2/M_2}{\frac{w_1}{M_1} + \frac{w_2}{M_2}}$$

(2 for solute, 1 for solvent)

Elevation in Boiling Point

$\Delta T_b = T_b - T_b^\circ$ or $\Delta T_b = K_b \cdot m$

or $$\Delta T_b = \frac{K_b \times w_2 \times 1000}{M_2 \times w_1}$$

Depression in Freezing Point

$\Delta T_f = T_f^\circ - T_f$ or $\Delta T_f = K_f \cdot m$

or $$\Delta T_f = \frac{K_f \times w_2 \times 1000}{M_2 \times w_1}$$

Osmosis and Osmotic Pressure (π)

Osmosis is the process of movement of solvent particles through a semipermeable membrane from the solution of low concentration to high concentration.

Osmotic pressure is the pressure applied on solution side to stop the process of osmosis.

$$\pi = CRT = \frac{n_2}{V} RT$$

Reverse osmosis, on the other hand, forces water to move from high to low solute concentration, by applying external pressure.

Raoult's Law

It states $p \propto \chi$

Here, p = partial vapour pressure,

χ = mole fraction.

Thus, $p_{total} = p_1\chi_1 + p_2\chi_2 + ...$

Ideal Solutions
- These obey Raoult's law at all conditions of temperature and pressure.
- For such solutions, $\Delta H_{mix} = 0$ and $\Delta V_{mix} = 0$. e.g., *n*-hexane + *n*-heptane.

Non-Ideal Solutions
- These do not obey Raoult's law over the entire range of concentration.
- For such solutions, $\Delta H_{mix} \neq 0$ and $\Delta V_{mix} \neq 0$.

Solutions Showing Positive Deviation
- A–B interactions are weaker than A–A or B–B interactions. For this, ΔH_{mix} = +ve and ΔV_{mix} = +ve. e.g., acetone + benzene.
- Large positive deviation forms minimum boiling azeotropes.

Solutions Showing Negative Deviation
- A–B interactions are greater than A–A or B–B interactions. For this, ΔH_{mix} = –ve and ΔV_{mix} = –ve. e.g., phenol + aniline.
- Large negative deviation forms maximum boiling azeotropes.

Abnormal Molar Mass

Molar masses are either higher or lower than the expected or normal values.

van't Hoff factor (*i*)

It is the ratio of experimental and calculated value of colligative property.
- $i = 1$ for non-electrolyte
- $i > 1$ for dissociation
- $i < 1$ for association

EXAM PATTERN QUESTIONS

Objective Type Questions

Multiple Choice Questions (MCQs)

[1 Mark]

1. **Which of the following is the correct example of solid solution in which the solute is in gas phase?**

(a) Copper dissolved in gold
(b) Camphor in nitrogen gas
(c) Hydrogen in palladium
(d) All of the above

2. **Consider the following table.**

Types of solutions	Solute and solvent	Examples
Gaseous solution	Liquid and Gas	X
Solid solutions	Y	Alloys like bronze

'X' and 'Y' in the above table are Competency Based Que.

(a) X = Dust or smoke in air, Y = Solid and solid
(b) X = Humidity in air, Y = Liquid and solid
(c) X = Camphor in nitrogen gas, Y = Gas and solid
(d) X = Chloroform mixed with nitrogen gas, Y = Solid and solid

3. **184 g ethyl alcohol is mixed with 72 g of water. The ratio of mole fraction of alcohol to water is**

(a) 3 : 4
(b) 1 : 2
(c) 1 : 4
(d) 1 : 1

4. **4 L of 0.02 M aqueous solution of NaCl was diluted by adding 1 L of water. The molarity of the resultant solution is .... .** NCERT Exemplar

(a) 0.004
(b) 0.008
(c) 0.012
(d) 0.016

5. **In a chemistry laboratory, Richa took 5 g of a solute from an unknown box and prepared a 0.25 M basic solution. The volume of the solution was 500 mL.**

Based on the above data, which of the following is likely to be the unknown substance used by Richa?

(Approx. Atomic masses of Ca = 40 u; Na = 23 u; Li = 7 u; Cs = 133 u; O = 16 u; H = 1 u) Competency Based Que.

(a) $Ca(OH)_2$
(b) NaOH
(c) LiOH
(d) CsOH

6. **A glycerine solution, at 293 K, has a molality of 3.89 molal and molarity of 5.33 M.**

Which of these would be correct for molarity and molality of the same glycerine solution at 450 K? Competency Based Que.

(a) Molarity < 5.33 M; Molality = 3.89 molal
(b) Molarity < 5.33 M; Molality < 3.89 molal
(c) Molarity > 5.33 M; Molality = 3.89 molal
(d) Molarity = 5.33 M; Molality = 3.89 molal

7. **A beaker contains a solution of substance 'A'. Precipitation of substance 'A' takes place when small amount of 'A' is added to the solution.**

The solution is ..... . NCERT Exemplar

(a) saturated
(b) supersaturated
(c) unsaturated
(d) concentrated

8. **Pressure does not have any significant effect on solubility of solids in liquids because** CBSE 2021 (Term I)

(a) solids are highly compressible.
(b) liquids are highly compressible.
(c) solubility of solid in liquid is directly proportional to partial pressure.
(d) solids and liquids are highly incompressible.

9. **Solubility of gases in liquids decreases with rise in temperature because dissolution is an** CBSE SQP 2021 (Term I)

(a) endothermic and reversible process
(b) exothermic and reversible process
(c) endothermic and irreversible process
(d) exothermic and irreversible process

10. Value of Henry's constant K_H, CBSE 2023

(a) increases with decrease in temperature.
(b) decreases with increase in temperature.
(c) increases with increase in temperature.
(d) remains constant.

11. **Which of the following statements is not true?** Diksha

(a) A temperature increase will cause an increase in vapour pressure.
(b) The total vapour pressure of a mixture of liquids is equal to the sum of the vapour pressure of each component in the mixture.

(c) At a given temperature, all materials have the same vapour pressure.
(d) The vapour pressure of a liquid in a mixture of liquids is less than the vapour pressure of that pure liquid.

12. Which one of the following pairs will not form an ideal solution? CBSE 2021 (Term I)
(a) Benzene and toluene
(b) *n*-hexane and *n*-heptane
(c) Ethanol and acetone
(d) Bromoethane and chloroethane

13. When 1 mole of benzene is mixed with 1 mole of toluene. The vapours will contain (Given : vapour pressure of benzene = 12.8 kPa and vapour pressure of toluene = 3.85 kPa). CBSE SQP 2021
(a) equal amount of benzene and toluene as it forms an ideal solution.
(b) unequal amount of benzene and toluene as it forms a non-ideal solution.
(c) higher percentage of benzene.
(d) higher percentage of toluene.

14. 1 mole of liquid A and 2 moles of liquid B make a solution having a total vapour pressure 40 torr. The vapour pressure of pure A and pure B are 45 torr and 30 torr respectively. The above solution CBSE 2023
(a) is an ideal solution.
(b) shows positive deviation.
(c) shows negative deviation.
(d) is a maximum boiling azeotrope.

15. An azeotropic mixture of two liquids has a boiling point higher than either of the two liquids when it CBSE 2023
(a) shows large negative deviation from Raoult's law.
(b) shows no deviation from Raoult's law.
(c) shows large positive deviation from Raoult's law.
(d) obeys Raoult's law.

16. Which of the following azeotropic solutions has the boiling point more than the boiling point of its constituents molecules?
(a) $CHCl_3$ and CH_3COCH_3
(b) CS_2 and CH_3COCH_3
(c) CH_3CH_2OH and CH_3COCH_3
(d) C_6H_6 and CH_3COCH_3

17. If molality of a dilute solution is doubled, the value of the molal elevation constant (K_b) will be CBSE 2023
(a) halved (b) doubled
(c) tripled (d) unchanged

18. How much ethyl alcohol must be added to 1 litre of water so that the solution will freeze at – 14°C? (K_f for water = 1.86°C/mol) CBSE SQP 2021 (Term I)
(a) 7.5 mol (b) 8.5 mol
(c) 9.5 mol (d) 10.5 mol

19. An unripe mango placed in a concentrated salt solution to prepare pickle, shrivels because .... CBSE 2025
(a) it gains water due to osmosis
(b) it loses water due to reverse osmosis
(c) it gains water due to reverse osmosis
(d) it loses water due to osmosis

20. At a given temperature, osmotic pressure of a concentrated solution of a substance .... NCERT Exemplar
(a) is higher than that of a dilute solution.
(b) is lower than that of a dilute solution.
(c) is same as that of a dilute solution.
(d) cannot be compared with osmotic pressure of dilute solution.

21. In case of association, abnormal molar mass of solute will CBSE 2025
(a) increase
(b) decrease
(c) remain same
(d) first increase and then decrease

22. We have three aqueous solutions of NaCl labelled as 'A', 'B' and 'C' with concentrations 0.1 M, 0.01 M and 0.001 M, respectively. The value of van't Hoff factor for these solutions will be in the order .... NCERT Exemplar
(a) $i_A < i_B < i_C$ (b) $i_A > i_B > i_C$
(c) $i_A = i_B = i_C$ (d) $i_A < i_B > i_C$

23. Van't Hoff factor for $Na_2SO_4 \cdot 10H_2O$ solution, assuming complete ionisation is CBSE 2024
(a) 1 (b) 3 (c) 13 (d) 2

24. Match the Column I with Column II.

Column I	Column II
A. Urea, glucose	(i) 2 : 3
B. NaCl, $MgCl_2$	(ii) 1 : 1
C. $Al_2(SO_4)_3$, Na_3PO_4	(iii) 1 : 2
D. Glucose, NaCl	(iv) 1 : 0.8

Codes

	A	B	C	D		A	B	C	D
(a)	(ii)	(i)	(iv)	(iii)	(b)	(iv)	(i)	(ii)	(iii)
(c)	(i)	(ii)	(iii)	(iv)	(d)	(iii)	(ii)	(i)	(iv)

25. Which of the following statement is/are true?
I. The freezing point of 0.1 M KCl is higher than that of 0.1 M C_2H_5OH.
II. The freezing point of a 4% aqueous solution of X having molecular weight as m is equal to the freezing point of 12% aqueous solution of Y having molecular weight $3m$ (assume that $i = 1$ for both X and Y).

III. **The boiling point of pure water at sea level is greater than at mount Everest.** **CBSE QB**

(a) I and II
(b) I, II and III
(c) II and III
(d) I and III

26. **If van't Hoff factor of aqueous solutions of *X*, *Y* and *Z* are 1.9, 0.9 and 2.6. Then, which of the following relation is correct?** **Competency Based Que.**

(a) Boiling point : $Z < X < Y$
(b) Freezing point : $Z < X < Y$
(c) Osmotic pressure : $X = Y = Z$
(d) Vapour pressure : $X < Y = Z$

Assertion-Reason [1 Mark]

Directions (Q. Nos. 27-36) In the following questions, an Assertion (A) is followed by a corresponding Reason (R). Use the following keys to choose the appropriate answer.

(a) Both (A) and (R) are true and (R) is the correct explanation of (A).
(b) Both (A) and (R) are true, but (R) is not the correct explanation of (A).
(c) (A) is true, but (R) is false.
(d) (A) is false, but (R) is true.

27. **Assertion** (A) One molar aqueous solution has always higher concentration than one molal.

Reason (R) The molality of a solution depends upon the density of the solution whereas molarity does not.

28. **Assertion** (A) Aquatic species are more comfortable in cold water rather than in warm water. **CBSE SQP 2021**

Reason (R) Different gases have different K_H values at the same temperature.

29. **Assertion** (A) Ethanol and acetone shows positive deviation from Raoult's law.

Reason (R) Pure ethanol molecules exhibit hydrogen bond and on adding acetone hydrogen bond between ethanol molecules breaks.

30. **Assertion** (A) Chloroform and acetone mixture shows negative deviation from Raoult's law.

Reason (R) In chloroform and acetone mixture, *A—A* or *B—B* type intermolecular interactions are weaker than *A—B* type interactions. **CBSE 2024 C**

31. **Assertion** (A) Nitric acid and water form maximum boiling azeotrope. **CBSE SQP 2021**

Reason (R) Azeotropes are binary mixture having the same composition in liquid and vapour phase.

32. **Assertion** (A) The vapour pressure of 0.1M sugar solution is less than that of 0.1M potassium chloride solution.

Reason (R) Lowering of vapour pressure is directly proportional to the number of species present in the solution.

33. **Assertion** (A) When NaCl is added to water, a depression in freezing point is observed. **CBSE 2023**

Reason (R) The lowering of vapour pressure of a solution causes depression in the freezing point.

34. **Assertion** (A) Cryoscopic constant depends on nature of solvent. **CBSE SQP 2021 (Term-I)**

Reason (R) Cryoscopic constant is a universal constant.

35. **Assertion** (A) Osmotic pressure is a colligative property.

Reason (R) Osmotic pressure is proportional to the molality. **CBSE 2023**

36. **Assertion** (A) NaCl in water and organic acids in benzene show abnormal molecular mass.

Reason (R) Abnormal molecular mass is obtained when the substance in the solution undergoes dissociation or association.

Case Study [4 Marks]

37. Read the given case and answer the following questions.

Henry's law and Raoult's law are key principles in understanding solution equilibria, particularly concerning gas-liquid and liquid-liquid interactions. Henry's law is particularly relevant in environmental systems, such as gas exchange between the atmosphere and bodies of water, where factors like temperature, pressure and salinity play crucial roles.

Conversely, Raoult's law applies to ideal solutions, asserting that the vapour pressure of each component is proportional to its mole fraction. However, real solutions often deviate from ideal behaviour. Positive deviations occur when solute-solvent interactions are weaker than in the pure components, leading to higher than expected vapour pressures. Negative deviations, on the other hand, result from stronger solute-solvent interactions, causing lower vapour pressure. Both laws, while idealised provide valuable insights into molecular interactions, with deviations offering further understanding of non-ideal solutions in field like chemical engineering and environmental chemistry.

(i) What role does Henry's law play in explaining gas exchange between the atmosphere and water bodies?

(ii) When the temperature increases, then henry's constant
(a) increases (b) decreases
(c) remains same (d) can't predict

(iii) Real solutions deviate from Raoult's law
(a) due to difference in solute-solute interactions.
(b) due to difference in solvent-solvent interactions.
(c) due to difference in solute-solvent interactions.
(d) None of the above

Or Raoult's law is primarily used for in solution chemistry
(a) to predict the mole fraction.
(b) to predict the vapour pressure.
(c) to predict the molality.
(d) to predict the molarity.

38. Read the given case and answer the following questions.

Boiling point or freezing point of liquid solution would be affected by the dissolved solids in the liquid phase. A soluble solid in solution has the effect of raising its boiling point and depressing its freezing point. The addition of non-volatile substances to a solvent decreases the vapour pressure and the added solute particles affect the formation of pure solvent crystals.

According to many researches the decrease in freezing point is directly correlated to the concentration of solutes dissolved in the solvent. This phenomenon is expressed as freezing point depression and it is useful for several applications such as freeze concentration of liquid food and to find the molar mass of an unknown solute in the solution. Freeze concentration is a high quality liquid food concentration method where water is removed by forming ice crystals. This is done by cooling the liquid food below the freezing point of the solution's identity.

The freezing point depression is referred as a colligative property and it is proportional to the molar concentration of the solution (*m*), along with vapour pressure lowering, boiling point elevation, and osmotic pressure. These are physical characteristics of solutions that depend only on the identity of the solvent and the concentration of the solute. The characters are not depending on the solute's identity.

(i) Why is osmotic pressure preferable to other colligative properties?
(ii) What are the factors on which colligative properties depend?
(iii) Why does water boils above 100°C when non-volatile solid is added to pure water?

Or

Why does osmotic pressure depend on temperature?

Subjective Type Questions

Short Answer Type I Questions [2 Marks]

1. A solution obtained by mixing 300 g of 25% and 400 g of 40% solution by mass. Calculate the mass % of the resulting solution. **NCERT**

2. Calculate the molality of K_2CO_3 solution which is formed by dissolving 2.5 g of it in 1 L of solution. Density of solution is 0.85 g mL^{-1}.

3. (i) Nitrogen gas is soluble in water. At temperature 293 K, the value of K_H is 76.48 kbar. How would the solubility of nitrogen vary (increase, decrease or remain the same) at a temperature above 293 K, if the value of K_H rises to 88.8 kbar?
(ii) Chloroform (boiling point 61.2°C) and acetone (boiling point 56°C) are mixed to form an azeotrope. The mole fraction of acetone in this mixture is 0.339. Predict whether the boiling point of the azeotrope formed will be
(a) 60°C (b) 64.5°C or (c) 54°C
Define your answer with reason.

Or (i) A soda bottle will go flat (loose its fizz) faster in Srinagar than in Delhi. Is this statement correct? Why or why not?
(ii) How does sugar help in increasing the shelf-life of the product? **CBSE SQP 2025**

4. State Henry's law and write its two applications. **CBSE 2024 C**

5. Aquatic animals feel more comfortable in cold water than warm water as the solubility of oxygen in cold water is more than that in warm water. The graph below shows the solubility of oxygen in the water as a function of pressure at different temperatures T_1 and T_2. **Competency Based Que.**

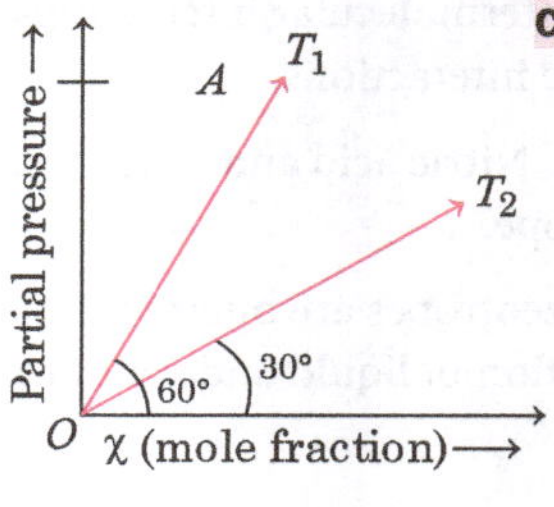

(i) Based on the above graph, what is the ratio of K_H at T_1 and T_2?
(ii) Between T_1 and T_2, which one is greater?

6. (i) Gas (*A*) is more soluble in water than gas (*B*) at the same temperature. Which one of the two gases will have the higher value of K_H (Henry's constant) and why?
(ii) In non-ideal solution, what type of deviation shows the formation of maximum boiling azeotropes? **CBSE 2016**

7. Give reasons:
(i) Cooking is faster in pressure cooker than in an open pan.
(ii) On mixing liquid *X* and liquid *Y*, volume of the resulting solution decreases. What type of deviation from Raoult's law is shown by the resulting solution? What change in temperature would you observe after mixing liquids *X* and *Y*? **CBSE 2025**

8. Define Azeotrope. What type of azeotrope is formed by negative deviation from Raoult's law? Give an example. **CBSE 2025**

9. A solution is prepared by dissolving 10 g of non-volatile solute in 200 g of water. It has a vapour pressure of 31.84 mm Hg at 308 K. Calculate the molar mass of the solute. (Vapour pressure of pure water at 308 K = 32 mm of Hg) **CBSE 2015**

10. Why is the vapour pressure of a solution of glucose in water lower than that of water? **NCERT Exemplar**

Or

If a table spoon of sugar is added to water, then what happens to vapour pressure of water?

11. A solution prepared by dissolving 1.25 g of oil of winter green (methyl salicylate) in 99 g of benzene has a boiling point of 80.31°C and K_b for benzene is 2.53 K kg mol^{-1}. Find molar mass of the solute. Boiling point of benzene = 80.10°C.

12. An aqueous solution of sodium chloride freezes below 273 K. Explain the lowering in freezing point of water with the help of a suitable diagram.

13. (i) Why an increase in temperature observed on mixing chloroform and acetone?
(ii) Why does common salt solution freeze at low temperature than water? **Diksha**

14. Rakesh took 20 g of solute *A* to prepare a 50 mL solution. This solution is isotonic to another solution of the same volume with a weight of 40 g of a different solute *B*.
(i) If both the solution is prepared at the same temperature, then what is the ratio of molecular mass of solute *A* to that of *B*?
(ii) If the two solutions are placed at different temperatures, keeping all other variables constant, and separated by SPM, will the osmosis happen, and why? **Competency Based Que.**

15. (i) When dehydrated fruits and vegetables are placed in water, they slowly swell and return to original shape. Why?
(ii) Prove that relative lowering in vapour pressure of a liquid on addition of non-volatile solute is a colligative property.

Short Answer Type II Questions [3 Marks]

16. One of the key ingredients in some toothpastes is sodium fluoride. However, the concentration of this chemical compound is very low. This concentration can be expressed in ppm (parts per million) that is 1 ppm represents a concentration of 1 mg of sodium fluoride in 1 kg of the toothpaste. **Competency Based Que.**
(i) A 1.00 g sample of toothpaste was found to contain 2.88×10^{-5} mol of sodium fluoride. What is the concentration of sodium fluoride, in ppm, for this sample of toothpaste?
(ii) Sodium fluoride is toxic in high concentrations. Major health problems can occur if concentrations of sodium fluoride are greater than 3.19×10^{-2} g per kilogram of body mass. Deduce the maximum mass of sodium fluoride, (in mg), that a 75 kg person could swallow without reaching the toxic concentration.
(iii) The concentration of sodium fluoride in a prescription toothpaste is 2800 ppm. Use your answer to Question (ii) to deduce the mass of toothpaste, (in kg), that a 75.0 kg person could swallow without reaching the toxic concentration.

17. The air is a mixture of a number of gases. The major components are oxygen and nitrogen with approximate proportion of 20% is to 79% by volume at 298 K, respectively.

The water is in equilibrium with air at a pressure of 10 atm. At 298 K, if the Henry's law constants for oxygen and nitrogen are 3.30×10^7 mm and 6.51×10^7 mm respectively, calculate the composition of these gases in water. **NCERT**

18. Benzene and toluene form ideal solution over the entire range of composition. The vapour pressures of pure benzene and toluene at 300 K are 50.71 mm of Hg and 32.06 mm of Hg, respectively. Calculate the mole fraction of benzene in the vapour phase, if 80 g of benzene is mixed with 100 g of toluene. **NCERT**

19. Water vapour and liquid water are in equilibrium in the image shown below. At room temperature, the vapour pressure of water is 25 mm Hg. The volume of water vapour is V. **Competency Based Que.**

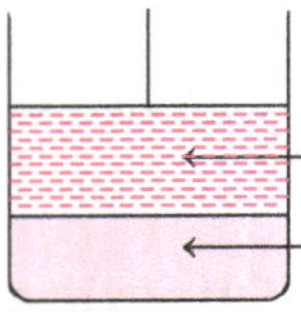

What will be the vapour pressure of the water if the volume of water vapour becomes

(i) $2V$ when the piston is moved upwards

(ii) $\frac{V}{2}$ when the piston is moved downwards

(iii) Explain the reasons for your answers for (i) and (ii).

20. A solution of glucose (molar mass = 180 g mol^{-1}) in water has a boiling point of 100.20°C. Calculate the freezing point of the same solution. Molal constants for water K_f and K_b are 1.86K kg mol^{-1} and 0.512K kg mol^{-1} respectively. **CBSE 2025**

21. A solution containing 15 g urea (molar mass = 60 g mol^{-1}) per litre of solution in water has the same osmotic pressure (isotonic) as a solution of glucose (molar mass = 180 g mol^{-1}) in water. Calculate the mass of glucose present in one litre of its solution. **CBSE 2025**

22. Give reasons for the following.

(i) Measurement of osmotic pressure method is preferred for the determination of molar masses of macromolecules such as proteins and polymers.

(ii) Aquatic animals are more comfortable in cold water than in warm water.

(iii) Elevation of boiling point of 1 M KCl solution is nearly double than that of 1 M sugar solution. **CBSE 2018**

Long Answer Type Questions [5 Marks]

23. Vapour pressures of pure acetone and chloroform at 328 K are 741.8 mm of Hg and 632.8 mm of Hg, respectively. Assuming that they form ideal solution over the entire range of composition, plot p_{total}, $p_{chloroform}$ and $p_{acetone}$ as a function of $\chi_{acetone}$. The experimental data observed for different compositions of mixture is

$100 \times \chi_{acetone}$	0	11.8	23.4	36.0	50.8	58.2	64.5	72.1
$p_{acetone}$/mm Hg	0	54.9	110.1	202.4	322.7	405.9	454.1	521.1
$p_{chloroform}$/mm Hg	632.8	548.1	469.4	359.7	257.7	193.6	161.2	120.7

Plot this data also on the same graph paper. Indicate whether it has positive deviation or negative deviation from the ideal solution. **NCERT**

24. (i) State Raoult's law for a solutions containing volatile components. How does Raoult's law become a special case of Henry's law?

(ii) 2.00 g of a non-electrolyte solute dissolve in 100 g of benzene lowered the freezing point of benzene by 0.80 K. Find the molar mass of the solute (K_f for benzene = 5.12 K kg mol^{-1}). **Diksha**

25. (i) Two liquids X and Y boil at 100°C and 120°C respectively. Which of them has higher vapour pressure at 50°C and why?

(ii) Calculate the boiling point of a solution prepared by adding 15.0 g of NaCl to 250 g water. (K_b for water = 0.512 K kg mol^{-1}; molar mass of NaCl = 58.44 g)

(iii) Determine the osmotic pressure of a solution prepared by dissolving 25 mg of K_2SO_4 in 2 litre of water at 25°C, assuming that it is completely dissociated. **NCERT**

26. (i) Give the differences (any three) between ideal and non-ideal solutions.

(ii) Which of the following solutions will have the highest and lowest osmotic pressure and why?

(a) Sugar in water

(b) Salt in water

27. (i) What is the effect of temperature on the solubility of glucose in water?

(ii) Ibrahim collected a 10 mL each of fresh water and ocean water. He observed that one sample labelled *P* froze at 0°C while the other *Q* at –1.3°C. Ibrahim forgot which of the two, *P* or *Q* was ocean water. Help him identify which container contains ocean water, giving rationalisation for your answer.

(iii) Calculate van't Hoff factor for an aqueous solution of $K_3[Fe(CN)_6]$ if the degree of dissociation (α) is 0.852. What will be boiling point of this solution if its concentration is 1 molal?

(K_b = 0.52 K kg/mol) **CBSE SQP 2024**

28. (i) Why is boiling of 1 M NaCl solution more than that of 1 M glucose solution ?

(ii) A non-volatile solute '*X*' (molar mass = 40 g mol^{-1}) when dissolved in 78 g of benzene reduced its vapour pressure to 90%. Calculate the mass of *X* dissolved in the solution.

(iii) Calculate the boiling point elevation for a solution prepared by adding 10g of $MgCl_2$ to 200 g of water assuming $MgCl_2$ is completely dissociated.
(K_b for water = 0.512 K kg mol^{-1}, molar mass of $MgCl_2$ = 95 g mol^{-1}). **CBSE 2023**

29. (i) An experiment was carried out in the laboratory, to study depression in freezing point. 1 M aqueous solution of $Al(NO_3)_3$ and 1 M aqueous solution of glucose were taken. From the given figure identify solution 1 and solution 2. Give a possible reason for your answer.

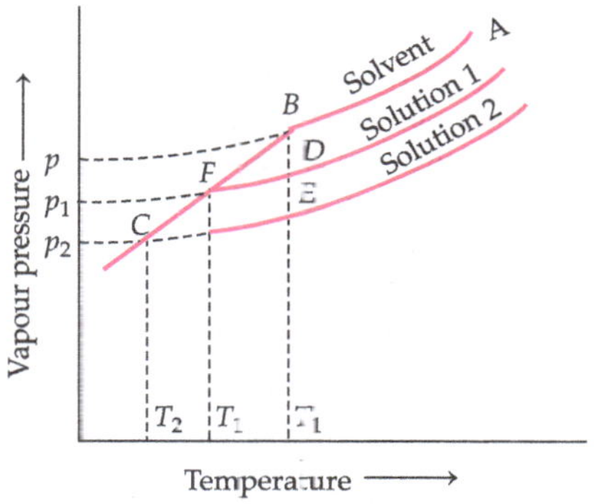

(ii) The osmotic pressure of a solution of cane sugar was found to be 2.46 atm at 300 K. If the solution was diluted five times, calculate the osmotic pressure at the same temperature.
How can the osmotic pressure of the given cane sugar solution be decreased without changing its volume? Give a reason for your answer.

Or

(i) While giving intravenous injections to the patients, the doctors take utmost care of the concentration of the solution used. Why is it necessary to check the concentration of the solution?

(ii) A solution of phenol was obtained by dissolving 2×10^{-2} kg of phenol in 1 kg of benzene. Experimentally it was found to be 73% associated. Calculate the depression in the freezing point recorded. **CBSE SQP 2025**

Hints & Solutions

Objective Type Questions

1. (*c*) Solution of hydrogen in palladium is an example of solid solution in which solute is a gas. It is one of the rare examples in which solute is present in larger volume as compared to the solvent.

2. (*d*) • Chloroform mixed with N_2 gas and humidity in air are examples of gaseous solutions. Thus, X = Chloroform mixed with N_2 gas.
   • Alloys like bronze and many other are examples of solid solutions having solute and solvent both solids.
   Thus, Y = Solid and solid.

3. (*d*) Number of moles of $C_2H_5OH = \frac{184\text{g}}{46\text{g mol}^{-1}} = 4 \text{ mol}$

$$(M_{C_2H_5OH} = 46 \text{ g/mol})$$

Number of moles of $H_2O = \frac{72\text{g}}{18\text{g mol}^{-1}} = 4 \text{ mol}$

$$(M_{H_2O} = 18 \text{ g/mol})$$

Mole fraction, $\chi_{C_2H_5OH} = \frac{4}{4+4} = \frac{4}{8}$

$$\chi_{H_2O} = \frac{4}{4+4} = \frac{4}{8}$$

$$\Rightarrow \quad \frac{\chi_{C_2H_5OH}}{\chi_{H_2O}} = \frac{4/8}{4/8} = \frac{1}{1} = 1:1$$

4. (*d*) Given, $M_1 = 0.02 \text{ M}, \; V_1 = 4 \text{ L}, \; M_2 = ?,$
$V_2 = 4 \text{ L} + 1 \text{ L} = 5 \text{ L}$

As we know, $M_1V_1 = M_2V_2$

$$0.02 \text{M} \times 4 \text{ L} = M_2 \times 5\text{L}$$

$$M_2 = \frac{0.08}{5} = 0.016 \text{ M}$$

5. (*b*) Let, the molar mass of the unknown substance be x.
Molarity of the basic solution is 0.25 M,
i.e. 0.25 moles are present in 1 litre of solution.
So, $\frac{0.25}{2}$ moles are present in 500 mL of solution.

As, moles $= \frac{\text{Mass}}{\text{Molar mass}}$

$$\Rightarrow \quad \frac{5 \text{ g}}{x} = \frac{0.25}{2} \text{ mol} \Rightarrow x = 40 \text{ g mol}^{-1}$$

Among the given compounds, NaOH has molar mass of 40 g mol^{-1}.

6. (*a*) As the temperature increases, molarity decreases due to the increase in volume but it has no effect on molality as molality does not depends on volume.
Hence, the correct relation be
Molarity < 5.33 M; Molality = 3.89 m

7. (*b*) When solute is added to the solution three cases may arise.
   (i) If it dissolves into solution then solution is unsaturated.
   (ii) If it does not dissolve in the solution then solution is known as saturated.
   (iii) When solute get precipitated, solution is known as supersaturated solution.

8. (*d*) Solids and liquids are highly incompressible. Hence, their solubility does not get affected with changes in pressure.
However, solubility of gases in a liquid is directly proportional to the pressure of that gas above the surface of the solution.

9. (*b*) The dissolution of gas in a liquid is an exothermic process, so heat is evolved. According to Le-Chatelier's principle, solubility of gases in liquid decreases with increase in temperature and it is a reversible process.

10. (*c*) Value of Henry's constant K_H, increases with increase in temperature.

11. (*c*) The only incorrect statement is (c). This is because different materials (substances) have different vapour pressures at the same temperature, based on their intermolecular forces.

12. (*c*) Ethanol and acetone solution will not form an ideal solution and shows positive deviation from Raoult's law.

13. (*c*) The vapours will contain a higher percentage of benzene because benzene has a higher vapour pressure than toluene.
So, the vapours above the solution majorly consist of benzene vapours.

14. (*c*) Mole fraction of A, $\chi_A = \frac{1 \text{ mol}}{(1+2) \text{ mol}} = \frac{1}{3}$

Mole fraction of B, $\chi_B = \frac{2 \text{ mol}}{3 \text{ mol}} = \frac{2}{3}$

Also, $p_A^\circ \chi_A + p_B^\circ \chi_B = \left(45 \times \frac{1}{3}\right) + \left(30 \times \frac{2}{3}\right) = 35 \text{ Torr}$

But, observed vapour pressure is 40 Torr. Therefore, it is not an ideal solution. Also, the calculated value is less than the given pressure, i.e 40 torr. Thus, it show negative deviation.

15. (*a*) shows large negative deviation from Raoult's law.

16. (*a*) Among the given solutions, mixture of $CHCl_3$ and CH_3COCH_3 shows negative deviation. Hence, it has higher boiling point or lesser vapour pressure, than its constituents.

17. (*d*) Since, the molal elevation constant (K_b) is a property of the solvent and does not depend on the molality of the solution. Therefore, its value will remain unchanged.

18. (*a*) Given, $V = 1$ L or 1000 mL

$T_f = (273-14)\text{ K} = 259\text{ K}$

$\Delta T_f = (273-259)\text{ K} = 14\text{ K}$

$K_f = 1.86°\text{ C/mol}$

$\because \Delta T_f = K_f \times m$

$\therefore \Delta T_f = \frac{K_f \times n_B \times 1000}{w_A(\text{in mL})}$

where, ΔT_f = depression in freezing point
K_f = molal depression constant
n_B = number of moles of solute
w_A = given mass of solvent

$\therefore \quad 14 = \frac{1.86 \times n_B \times 1000}{1000}$

[$\because$ Density of water = 1 g mL^{-1}
$\therefore$ 1000 mL water = 1000 g]

$n_B = \frac{14 \times 1000}{1.86 \times 1000} = 7.5$ mol

19. (*d*) When an unripe mango is placed in a concentrated solution, it loses water due to osmosis. Water moves from the mango (lower concentration) to the salt solution (higher concentration), which causes the mango to shrivel. This process is used in making pickles.

20. (*a*) According to definition of osmotic pressure, we know, that $\pi = CRT$. For concentrated solution, C has higher value than dilute solution.

Hence, as concentration of solution increases, osmotic pressure will also increase.

21. (*a*) In the case of association, the solute particles combine to form larger units. So, i has a value less than one $(i < 1)$, and the abnormal molar mass increases.

22. (*c*) As the van't Hoff factor is independent of the molarity of solution, hence, $i_A = i_B = i_C$.

23. (*b*) van't Hoff factor for $Na_2SO_4 \cdot 10H_2O$ solution is 3.

$$Na_2SO_4 \cdot 10H_2O \rightleftharpoons \underbrace{2Na^+ + SO_4^{2-}}_{3} + 10H_2O$$

$\therefore$ Total number of ions = 2 + 1 = 3

24. (a) The correct match is A-(ii), B-(i), C-(iv), D-(iii)

Hint : Calculate van't Hoff factor (*i*) for all the compounds and find their ratios.

25. (c)(i) As $\Delta T_f \propto i$, more the number of ions, more will be ΔT_f and lesser is the freezing point.

The minimum freezing point means more is the number of ions.

For KCl, $i = 2$

For C_2H_5OH, $i = 1$

Thus, freezing point of 0.1 M KCl will be less than that of 0.1M C_2H_5OH.

(ii) As, $\Delta T_f(X) = \Delta T_f(Y)$

$K_f \times m_X = K_f \times m_Y$

$m_X = m_Y$

$\Rightarrow \frac{4 \times 1000}{100 \times M_1} = \frac{12 \times 1000}{100 \times M_2}$

where, M_1 = molar mass of X
M_2 = molar mass of Y

$\frac{4}{M_1} = \frac{12}{M_2} \Rightarrow M_2 = 3M_1$

Hence, if m is molar mass of X then, $3m$ will be the molar mass of Y.

(iii) Higher the pressure, higher is the boiling point of water. At low pressure, the boiling of water comes down. The boiling takes place at a lower temperature at the top of a mountain due to low pressure.

Hence, statements (ii) and (iii) are correct.

26. (*b*) Among the given relations, only (b) is the correct match, i.e., freezing point : $Z < X < Y$.

27. (*b*) Both (A) and (R) are true, but (R) is not the correct explanation of (A). The correct explanation is that one molar aqueous solution has 1 mole in less than 1000 g of water. Hence, 1000 g of water will be associated with more than 1 mole while 1 molal has 1 mole in 1000 g of water.

28. (*b*) Aquatic species are more comfortable in cold water rather than in warm water because the solubility of gases decreases with increase of temperature.

Hence both (A) and (R) are true, but (R) is not the correct explanation of (A).

29. (*a*) Ethanol molecules show hydrogen bonding. On adding acetone, its molecules get in between the host molecule and break some of hydrogen bonds between them. Due to weakening of interaction, the mixture of ethanol and acetone shows the positive deviation from Raoult's law. Hence, both (A) and (R) are true and (R) is the correct explanation of (A).

30. (*a*) Both (A) and (R) are correct and (R) is the correct explanation of (A).

31. (*b*) Nitric acid and water form maximum boiling azeotropes. This solution shows large negative deviation from Raoult's law. Thus, both (A) and (R) are true, but (R) is not the correct explanation of (A).

32. (*d*) Lowering of vapour pressure is directly proportional to the number of species present in the solution. Sugar is a non-electrolyte, however KCl is an electrolyte which dissociates in solution to give particles. Hence, there is greater lowering in vapour pressure in case of KCl.

Therefore, the vapour pressure of 0.1 M sugar solution is more than that of 0.1 M potassium chloride solution. Thus, (A) is false, but (R) is true.

33. (*a*) Both (A) and (R) are true and (R) is the correct explanation of (A). Actually lowering of vapour pressure is observed due to intermolecular interaction of solvent-solute particles.

34. (*c*) (A) is true, but (R) is false.

The value of cryoscopic constant depends on the nature of the solvent. Hence, it is not a universal constant.

35. (*c*) (A) is true, but (R) is false. Osmotic pressure is a colligative property as it depends on the number of solute present and not on the nature of the solute. Moreover, it is directly proportional to molarity (C).

$$\pi = CRT$$

36. (*a*) Both (A) and (R) are true and (R) is the correct explanation of (A).

37. (i) Henry's law explains that the solubility of gases, like oxygen and nitrogen in water (or blood) is directly proportional to their partial pressure in the atmosphere. The principle is crucial for understanding gas exchange in aquatic system as well as in human physiology, such as during diving. For example, divers experience decompression sickness when ascending too quickly. The rapid decrease in pressure, causes nitrogen, which had dissolved in the blood at higher pressures to form bubbles which blocks capillaries. **(2)**

(ii) (a) As temperature increases, Henry's constant K_H increases, leading to lower solubility of gases in liquids. **(1)**

(iii) (c) Real solutions deviate from Raoult's law due to differences in solute-solvent interactions compared to the pure components. These deviations can be either positive or negative. **(1)**

Or (iii) (b) Raoult's law is used to predict the vapour pressure of an ideal solution, based on the mole fraction of each component in the mixture. **(1)**

38. (i) The osmotic pressure method has an advantage over other methods because pressure is measured at room temperature and molarity of the solution is used instead of molality. Its magnitude is large in comparison to other colligative properties, even in very dilute solutions. **(2)**

(ii) Colligative properties depends on the identity of the solvent and the concentration of the solute. **(1)**

(iii) Lowering in vapour pressure results in an elevation in boiling point. Therefore, when a non-volatile solid is added to pure water, it will boil at higher temperature. **(1)**

Or (iii) The extra pressure that must be applied to the solution in order to prevent pure solvent osmosis is called osmotic pressure. Osmotic pressure always increases as the temperature increases because of van't Hoff equation $\pi = iCRT$. **(1)**

Subjective Type Questions

1. Mass of solute in 300 g of solution of 25% by mass

$$= \frac{25}{100} \times 300 \text{ g} = 75 \text{ g}$$

$\therefore$Mass of solvent in 300 g of solution $= (300 - 75)$ g $= 225$ g **(½)**

Now, mass of solvent in 400 g of solution of 40% by mass

$$= \frac{40}{100} \times 400 \text{ g} = 160 \text{ g}$$ **(½)**

$\therefore$ Mass of solvent in 400 g of solution $= (400 - 160)$ g $= 240$ g

Total mass of solvent $= (225 + 240)$ g $= 465$ g

Total mass of solute $= (75 + 160)$ g $= 235$ g

Total mass of solution $= (300 + 400)$ g $= 700$ g

$\therefore$ Mass % of solute in solution after mixing

$$= \frac{235 \text{ g}}{700 \text{ g}} \times 100 = 33.57\%$$ **(½)**

and mass % of solvent in solution after mixing

$$= \frac{465 \text{ g}}{700 \text{ g}} \times 100 = 66.43\%$$ **(½)**

2. Density of solution $(d) = 0.85 \text{ g mL}^{-1}$

So, mass of solution $= V \times d = 1000 \text{ mL} \times 0.85 \text{ g mL}^{-1} = 850$ g

Mass of solvent (water) $= 850 \text{ g} - 2.5 \text{ g} = 847.5$ g

Now, number of moles of solute $= \frac{2.5}{138} = 0.018$ mol **(1)**

[$\because$ Molecular mass of $K_2CO_3 = 138$ g/mol]

$\therefore$ Molality of K_2CO_3 solution $= \frac{0.018}{847.5} \times 1000 = 0.021$ m **(1)**

3. (i) Solubility of gas is inversely proportional to the value of Henry's law constant, K_H. On increasing temperature nitrogen gas becomes less soluble because its K_H value increases. **(1)**

(ii) (b) 64.5°C

Chloroform (boiling point 61.2°C) and acetone (boiling point 56°C) mixture shows negative deviation from Raoult's law. Therefore, they form maximum boiling azeotrope at a specific composition. The boiling point of the mixture so obtained will be higher than the individual components. **(1)**

Or

(i) At higher altitudes, i.e., in Srinagar the atmospheric pressure is lower. The solubility of a gas in a liquid is directly proportional to the partial pressure of the gas over the solution. Therefore, the carbon dioxide dissolved in water will be lesser at Srinagar making the soda bottle go flat faster. **(1)**

(ii) Preservation of food is done by adding sugar/salt. It protects the food against bacterial action. Through osmosis, a bacterium on canned food loses water, shrivels and dies. (1)

4. Refer to text on pages 6 and 7. (2)

5. (i) Ratio of $K_H(T_1) : K_H(T_2)$

As per Henry's law, $p = K_H\chi$. So the slope of the p *versus* χ curve will be the Henry's law constant.

$$K_{H_1} : K_{H_2} = \frac{\tan 60}{\tan 30}$$

$$= \frac{\sqrt{3}}{(1/\sqrt{3})} = 3$$ (1)

(ii) As we can see that

$$\chi \propto \frac{1}{K_H}$$

The slope of the graph gives the value of Henry's law constant.

So, K_H for $T_1 > K_H$ for T_2

Thus, $T_1 > T_2$. [$\because K_H \propto T$] (1)

6. (i) Solubility is inversely proportional to K_H, i.e. Henry's constant of the gas. Thus, greater the value of K_H, lower is the solubility of the gas. As gas (A) is more soluble in water than gas (B) at the same temperature, hence the gas (A) has lower value of K_H. In other words, gas (B) has higher value of K_H than gas (A) at the same temperature. (1)

(ii) In non-ideal solutions, the solutions that show large negative deviation from Raoult's law form maximum boiling azeotropes. e.g. Mixture of nitric acid and water. (1)

7. (i) Cooking is faster in a pressure cooker because the pressure inside the cooker higher, which raises the boiling point of water, allowing the food to cook at a higher temperature. (1)

(ii) Refer to ans of Q.3. Quick Test 3. (1)

8. Refer to text on page 11. (2)

9. Molar mass of solute $= 180 \text{ g mol}^{-1}$ (2)

Refer to example 11 on page 12.

10. In the solution, the surface has both solute and solvent molecules, so the fraction of the surface covered by solvent molecules gets reduced. Thus, the number of solvent molecules escaping from the surface is reduced, resulting in lowering the vapour pressure. So, the vapour pressure of the solution of glucose in water is lower than that of pure water. (2)

11. **Ans.** $152.11 \times 10^3 \text{ g mol}^{-1}$ (2)

12. When a non-volatile solute is added to a solvent, the freezing point of the solution is always lower than that of pure solvent as the vapour pressure of the solvent decreases in the presence of non-volatile solute. (1)

Plot for the lowering in freezing point of water when NaCl is added to it is shown below.

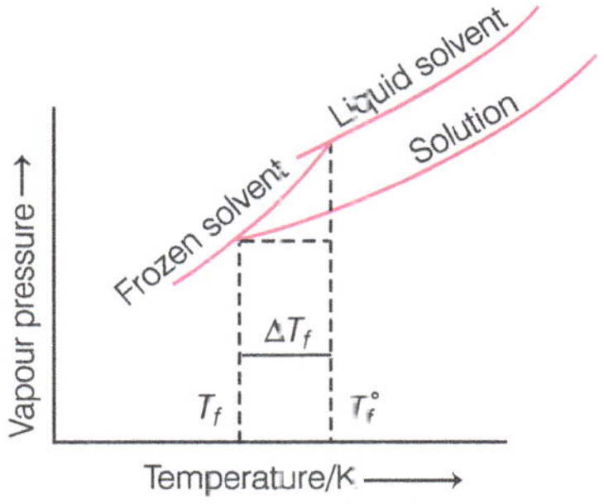

(1)

13. (i) Since, force of attraction between acetone and chloroform is greater than force of attraction between $CHCl_3$—$CHCl_3$ or acetone-acetone. Therefore, $\Delta H = -$ve, i.e., exothermic process and thus, there is increase in temperature. (1)

(ii) When common salt is added, vapour pressure of solution becomes less and at a lower temperature vapour pressure of solid and solution becomes equal, i.e., freezing point is lowered. (1)

14. (i) For any solution, osmotic pressure is given by

$$\pi = (w / MV) \times RT;$$

where,

w = weight of the solute, V = volume of solution, R = gas constant and T is temperature.

For two solutions to be isotonic,

$$\pi_1 = \pi_2$$

$$\Rightarrow \quad \frac{20}{M_1} = \frac{40}{M_2}$$

$$\Rightarrow \quad \frac{M_1}{M_2} = \frac{1}{2}$$ (1)

(ii) Yes, because at different temperature the solutions are no longer isotonic and hence, there will be movement of particles through osmosis. (1)

15. (i) Refer to text on page 15. (1)

(ii) Refer to text on page 12. (1)

16. (i) Moles of NaF $= 2.88 \times 10^{-5}$ mol (Given)

Molar mass of NaF $= 42$ g/mol, so the mass of NaF in 1 g toothpaste $= 42 \times 2.88 \times 10^{-5}$ g

Mass of NaF in 1 kg toothpaste

$$= 42 \times 2.88 \times 10^{-2} \text{ g} = 1.210 \text{ g}$$

Mass in mg = 1210 mg = 1210 ppm (1)

(ii) As concentration should be greater than 3.19×10^{-2} g/ kg of body mass for being toxic.

Thus, for 75 kg of body mass,

Toxic mass $= 75 \times 10^3 \times 3.19 \times 10^{-2} = 2392.5$ g

$= 2.3925$ mg (1)

(iii) Maximum mass of toothpaste that can be swallowed

Mass of toothpaste needed

$$= \frac{\text{Toxic mass}}{\text{Concentration of sodium fluoride}}$$

$$= \frac{2.3925}{2800} \text{ kg} = 0.000854 \text{ kg} = 8.54 \times 10^{-4} \text{ kg} \quad \textbf{(1)}$$

17. Given that, total pressure of air in equilibrium with water = 10 atm

As air contains 20% oxygen and 79% nitrogen by volume.

$\therefore$ Partial pressure of oxygen $(p_{O_2}) = \frac{20}{100} \times 10$ atm

$= 2 \text{ atm} = 2 \times 760 \text{ mm} = 1520 \text{ mm}$ **(1)**

Partial pressure of nitrogen, $(p_{N_2}) = \frac{79}{100} \times 10$ atm

$= 7.9 \text{ atm} = 7.9 \times 760 \text{ mm} = 6004 \text{ mm}$ **(1)**

Given that, $K_H(O_2) = 3.30 \times 10^7$ mm,

$K_H(N_2) = 6.51 \times 10^7$ mm

According to Henry's law, $p_{O_2} = K_H \times \chi_{O_2}$

or $\chi_{O_2} = \frac{p_{O_2}}{K_H} = \frac{1520 \text{ mm}}{3.30 \times 10^7 \text{ mm}} = 4.61 \times 10^{-5}$ **(1/2)**

$p_{N_2} = K_H \times \chi_{N_2}$

or $\chi_{N_2} = \frac{p_{N_2}}{K_H} = \frac{6004 \text{ mm}}{6.51 \times 10^7 \text{ mm}} = 9.22 \times 10^{-5}$ **(1/2)**

18. Molar mass of benzene $(C_6H_6) = 78 \text{ g mol}^{-1}$

Molar mass of toluene $(C_7H_8) = 92 \text{ g mol}^{-1}$

$n_{C_6H_6}$ (number of moles of benzene)

$= \frac{80 \text{ g}}{78 \text{ g mol}^{-1}} = 1.026$ mol

$n_{C_7H_8}$ (number of moles of toluene)

$= \frac{100 \text{ g}}{92 \text{ g mol}^{-1}} = 1.087$ mol **(1)**

Mole fraction of benzene,

$\chi_{C_6H_6} = \frac{1.026 \text{ mol}}{(1.026 + 1.087) \text{ mol}} = 0.486$

Mole fraction of toluene

$\chi_{C_7H_8} = 1 - 0.486 = 0.514$

Applying Raoult's law,

Partial vapour pressure of benzene in solution

$p_{C_6H_6} = p^\circ_{C_6H_6} \times \chi_{C_6H_6}$

$= (50.71 \text{ mm of Hg}) \times (0.486)$

$= 24.65$ mm of Hg

Partial vapour pressure of toluene in solution

$p_{C_7H_8} = p^\circ_{C_7H_8} \times \chi_{C_7H_8} = 32.06 \text{ mm of Hg} \times 0.514$

$= 16.48$ mm of Hg **(1)**

Total vapour pressure of solution

$p = 24.65 \text{ mm of Hg} + 16.48 \text{ mm of Hg}$

$= 41.13$ mm of Hg

Mole fraction of benzene in vapour phase

$$= \frac{\chi_{C_6H_6} \times p^\circ_{C_6H_6}}{p_{\text{total}}} = \frac{0.486 \times 50.71 \text{ mm of Hg}}{41.13 \text{ mm of Hg}} = 0.6 \quad \textbf{(1)}$$

19. (i) When the piston is moved upwards vapour pressure of water will remain same, i.e. 25 mm Hg **(1)**

(ii) When the piston is moved downwards vapour pressure of water will be 25 mmHg. **(1)**

(iii) Explanation of (i) and (ii)

- Vapour pressure is independent of the volume of water.
- When the volume of vapour is changed, for example : decreased, some of the vapour in the container turns into its liquid state. Decreasing volume has no effect on vapour pressure.
- Furthermore, if the volume of vapour is increased, some of the liquid will change into its vapour state. Increasing volume has no effect on vapour pressure. **(1)**

20. $\Delta T_b = T_b - T_b^\circ$

[Given, $T_b = 100.2°C = 373.2K$, $T_b^\circ = 100°C = 373K$]

$\Delta T_b = (373.2 - 373)K$

$\Delta T_b = 0.2K$

$\Delta T_b = K_b m$ $\quad [K_b = 0.512 \text{ K kg mol}^{-1}]$

$m = \frac{\Delta T_b}{K_b} = \frac{0.2K}{0.512K \text{ kg mol}^{-1}} = \frac{0.2}{0.512} \text{mol kg}^{-1}$ **(1)**

Now, $\Delta T_f = K_f m$ $\quad$ [Given, $K_f = 1.86K \text{ kg mol}^{-1}$]

$\Rightarrow \Delta T_f = 1.86 \text{ K kg mol}^{-1} \times \frac{0.2}{0.512} \text{mol kg}^{-1}$

$\Rightarrow \Delta T_f = 0.7266K.$ **(1)**

Also, $\Delta T_f = T_f^\circ - T_f$ $\quad [T_f^\circ = 0°C = 273K]$

$0.7266 = 273 - T_f$

$T_f = (273 - 0.7266)K$

$T_f = 272.2734K = -0.7266°C \approx -0.73°C$ **(1)**

21. (d) $\pi_{\text{urea}} = \pi_{\text{glucose}}$ $\quad$ ($\because$ isotonic solutions)

$C_{\text{urea}}RT = C_{\text{glucose}}RT$ $\quad [V = 1 \text{ L}]$ **(1)**

$\frac{n_{\text{Urea}}}{V} = \frac{n_{\text{Glucose}}}{V}$

$\Rightarrow n_{\text{urea}} = n_{\text{glucose}}$

$\Rightarrow \frac{15 \text{ g}}{60 \text{ g mol}^{-1}} = \frac{W_{\text{glucose}}}{180 \text{ g mol}^{-1}}$ **(1)**

$\Rightarrow W_{\text{glucose}} = \frac{15 \text{ g} \times 180 \text{ g mol}^{-1}}{60 \text{ g mol}^{-1}}$

$\Rightarrow W_{\text{glucose}} = 45$ g **(1)**

22. (i) The osmotic pressure method has the advantage over other methods as pressure measurement is around the room temperature and the molarity of the solution is used instead of molality. **(1)**

(ii) Oxygen is present in dissolved state in water. As per Henry's law when temperature rises, solubility of a gas decreases in solvent, it means solubility of oxygen in warm water is less than cold water. This makes aquatic species breathe comfortably in cold water. (1)

(iii) Elevation in boiling point is directly proportional to 'i'. $\Delta T_b \propto i$. Now as given in the question, elevation of boiling point of 1 M KCl solution is nearly double than that of 1 M sugar solution. It is because KCl being ionic, dissociates into K^+ and Cl^- and therefore, it's van't Hoff factor, i is 2 whereas for sugar, van't Hoff factor is 1 as it does not undergo such a dissociation. (1)

23.

$\chi_{acetone}$	0.0	0.118	0.234	0.360	0.508	0.582	0.645	0.721	
$p_{acetone}$/mm Hg	0	54.9	110.1	202.4	322.7	405.9	454.1	521.1	
$p_{chloroform}$/mm Hg	632.8	548.1	469.4	359.7	257.7	193.6	161.2	120.7	
p_{total}	632.8	603	579.5	562.1	580.4	599.5	615.3	641.8	(3)

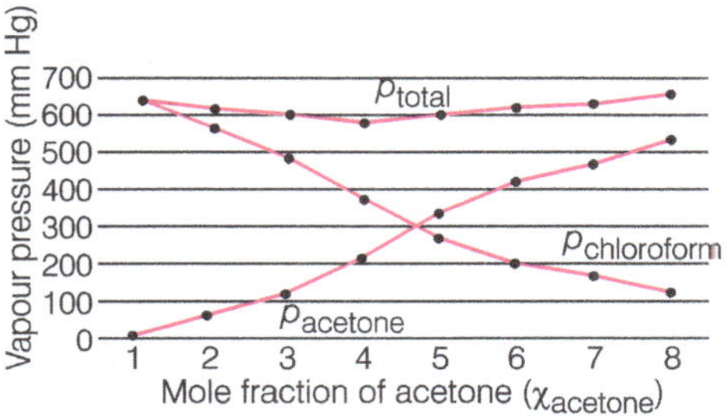

(1)

As the plot for p_{total} dips downwards, hence the solution shows negative deviation from the ideal behaviour. (1)

24. (i) Raoult's law states that the partial vapour pressure of each component is directly propotional to its mole fraction when both solute and solvent are volatile.

$$p_A \propto X_A$$

$$p_A = p_A^\circ \cdot X_A \text{ and } p_B = p_B^\circ X_B \quad (1½)$$

In both the case, partial pressure of volatile component is directly proportional to its mole fraction in solution. Only the proportionality constant K_H differs from p_A. Thus, Raoult's law is a special case of Henry's law. (1½)

(ii) Given, Mass of solute $(w_B) = 2$ g

Mass solvent $(w_A) = 100$ g

$\Delta T_f = 0.80$ K; $K_f = 5.12$ K kg/mol

$$\because \quad \Delta T_f = K_f \times \frac{w_B \times 1000}{M_B \times w_A} \quad (1/2)$$

$$\therefore \quad M_B = \frac{K_f \times w_B \times 1000}{\Delta T_f \times w_A} \quad (1/2)$$

$$M_B = \frac{5.12 \text{ K kg/mol} \times 2 \text{ g} \times 1000}{0.80 \text{ K} \times 100 \text{ kg}}$$

Thus, $M_B = 128$ g/mol (1)

25. (i) Since, X has a lower boiling point than Y, it is more volatile. Further, at 50°C, liquid X, being more volatile, will have a higher vapour pressure as compared to liquid Y. (1)

(ii) **Ans.** 373.53 K, (2)

(iii) **Ans.** 5.27×10^{-3} (2)

26. (i) Refer to text on pages 10 and 11. (3)

(ii) Refer to text on page 17. (2)

27. (i) Addition of glucose to water is an endothermic reaction. So according to Le-Chatelier's principle, the solubility of glucose in water, increases with increase in temperature. (1)

(ii) Q is ocean water as due to the presence of salts in ocean water it freezes at lower temperature as compared to normal water (depression in freezing point). (1)

(iii) Degree of dissociation of $K_3[Fe(CN)_6] = 0.852$

$K_b = 0.52$ K kg/mol

$K_3[Fe(CN)_6]$ gives 4 ions in aqueous solution

$$i = 1 + (n-1)\alpha = 1 + (4-1) \times 0.852 = 3.556 \quad (1)$$

$$\Delta T_b = iK_b m = 3.556 \times 0.52 \text{ K kg / mol} \times 1 \text{ mol/kg}$$

$$= 1.85 \text{ K}$$

$$T_b = 374.85 \text{ K} \approx 101.85° \text{ C}$$

$$[\because \Delta T_b = T_b - T_b^\circ \text{ and } T_b^\circ = 373 \text{ K}] \quad (2)$$

28. (i) In case of 1 M NaCl solution, the concentration of particles is higher as compared to 1 M glucose solution. Also the van't Hoff factor of NaCl is greater than 1, while that of glucose is 1. (1)

(ii) Given,

Molar mass of non volatile solute $X = 40 \text{ g mol}^{-1}$

Amount of benzene = 78 g

Let p be the vapour pressure of pure benzene

The vapour pressure of solution will be

$$= \frac{90}{100} p = 0.9p$$

$$\frac{p - p'}{p} = \frac{W \times 78}{40 \times 78}$$

$$\frac{p - 0.9p}{p} = \frac{W}{40}$$

$$W = 40 \frac{(0.1p)}{p} = 40 \times 0.1 = 4 \text{ g}$$ **(2)**

(iii) Given,

Amount of $MgCl_2 = 10$ g

Amount of water = 200 g

K_b for water = 0.512 K kg mol^{-1}

Molar mass of $MgCl_2 = 95$ g mol^{-1}

$$\Delta T_b = K_b \times m = 0.512 \times m$$

$$= \frac{0.512}{200} \times \frac{100}{95} \times 1000 = 0.269 \text{ K.}$$ **(2)**

29. (i) Depression in the freezing point is a colligative property. In dilute solutions, the depression of freezing point (ΔT_f) is directly proportional to the molality.

From the graph it is interpreted that solution 2 shows more depression in freezing point.

1 M $Al(NO_3)_3$ has higher i value ($i = 3$) than 1 M glucose ($i = 1$).

Thus, 1 M $Al(NO_3)_3$ will have higher depression, hence solution 2 is $Al(NO_3)_3$ solution and solution 1 is glucose solution. **(2)**

(ii) $\pi = \left(\frac{n_2}{V}\right) RT$

Given, $\pi = 2.64$ atm

Let $V_1 = V$, $V_2 = 5V$ (On dilution by 5 times)

$$\frac{\pi_1}{\pi_2} = \frac{\left(\frac{n}{V_1}\right)}{\left(\frac{n}{V_2}\right)} \Rightarrow \frac{2.64}{\pi_2} = \frac{\left(\frac{n}{V}\right)}{\left(\frac{n}{5V}\right)}$$

[n = no. of moles remain same even after dilution]

$\pi_2 = 0.528$ atm

Osmotic pressure is directly proportional to temperature. The osmotic pressure of cane sugar can be decreased by decreasing the temperature. (Without changing its volume). **(3)**

Or

(i) While giving intravenous injections to the patients, utmost care of concentration of the solution is to be taken. The solution must have same concentration as that of blood cells.

If the solution becomes more concentrated than the concentration of the blood it will lead to the shrinking of blood cells and fluid will start flowing out because of osmosis.

If concentration is less concentrated than the concentration of the blood it will lead to swelling of blood cells. Both situations are life-threatening. **(2)**

(ii) Phenol associates in benzene to a certain extent to form dimer.

$$2C_6H_5OH \longrightarrow (C_6H_5OH)_2$$

Initial concentration :	C	0
Final concentration	$C(1-\alpha)$	$\frac{C\alpha}{n}$

where, α is degree of association.

Experimentally, phenol is 73% associated.

Hence, $\alpha = 0.73$

Relation between i (vant Hoff factor) and α is given as

$\alpha = \frac{(i-1)}{\left(\frac{1}{n} - 1\right)}$, where n for phenol = 2 as phenol acts as dimer and association is taking place.

Substituting the values $0.73 = \frac{(i-1)}{\left(\frac{1}{2} - 1\right)}$

$$i = 1 - \frac{0.73}{2} = 0.635$$

Depression in freezing point can be calculated as

$$\Delta T_f = iK_f m = iK_f \left(\frac{w_b}{M_b \times w_a}\right)$$

$K_f = 5.12$ K kg/mol,

$w_b = 2 \times 10^{-2}$ kg = 20 g, $w_a = 1$ kg, $M_b = 94$ g mol^{-1}

$$\Delta T_f = \frac{0.635 \times 5.12 \text{ K kg mol}^{-1} \times 20 \text{ g}}{94 \text{ g mol}^{-1} \times 1 \text{ kg}}$$

$$= 0.692 \text{ K}$$ **(3)**

QR Code for Quick Test 1	QR Code for Quick Test 2	QR Code for Quick Test 3	QR Code for Quick Test 4

SELF ASSESSMENT TEST

Objective Type Questions [1 Mark]

1. Molarity (in mol/L) of distilled or pure water is
(a) 55.56 (b) 18 (c) 49.87 (d) 81

2. The molality of a urea solution in which 0.0100 g of urea, $[(NH_2)_2CO]$ is added to $0.3000\ dm^3$ of water at STP is
(a) 0.555 m (b) 5.55×10^{-4} m
(c) 33.3 m (d) 3.33×10^{-2} m

3. Match the following terms given in Column I with the Column II.

	Column I (Solution mixture)		Column II (van't Hoff factor)
I.	KCl in water	A.	0.5
II.	Ethanoic acid in benzene	B.	2
III.	K_2SO_4 in water	C.	3
IV	$C_{12}H_{22}O_{11}$ in water	D.	1

Codes
(a) I → A; II → C; III → D; IV → B
(b) I → B; II → A; III → C; IV → D
(c) I → D; II → C; III → A; IV → B
(d) I → A; II → B; III → C; IV → D

4.

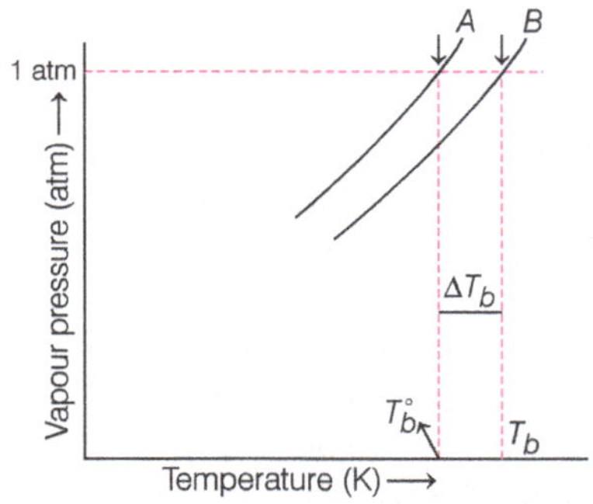

Identify *A* and *B* in the above given diagram.
(a) *A*-Boiling point of solvent; *B*-Boiling point of solution
(b) *A*-Boiling point of solution; *B*-Boiling point of solvent
(c) *A*-Boiling point of solute; *B*-Boiling point of solvent
(d) *A*-Boiling point of solvent; *B*-Boiling point of solute

5. What happens to freezing point of benzene when naphthalene is added?
(a) Increases
(b) Decreases
(c) Remains unchanged
(d) First decreases and then increases

Assertion-Reason [1 Mark]

Directions (Q. Nos. 6-8) In the following questions, an Assertion (A) is followed by a corresponding Reason (R). Use the following keys to choose the appropriate answer.
(a) Both (A) and (R) are true and (R) is the correct explanation of (A).
(b) Both (A) and (R) are true and (R) is not the correct explanation of (A).
(c) (A) is true but (R) is false.
(d) (A) is false but (R) is true.

6. **Assertion** (A) Amalgam of mercury with sodium is an example of solid solutions.
Reason (R) Mercury is solute and sodium is solvent in the solution.

7. **Assertion** (A) Molality of a solution in liquid state changes with temperature.
Reason (R) The volume of a solution changes with temperature.

8. **Assertion** (A) When scuba divers come towards surface, their capillaries get blocked which is painful and dangerous to life.
Reason (R) This occurs due to release of dissolved gases as the pressure decreases and leads to the formation of bubbles of nitrogen in the blood.

Short Answer Type I Questions [2 Marks]

9. (i) What do you mean by the term solution?
(ii) A 400 g toothpaste sample has 0.20 g fluoride concentration. What is its concentration in ppm?

10. (i) Why do smaller particles dissolve faster than larger ones?
(ii) $\Delta_{sol}H$ of NH_4Cl is > 0. What is the effect of temperature on its solubility?

11. (i) It is advised to add ethylene glycol to water in car radiator while driving in hill station. Why?
(ii) Why do doctors advise gargles by saline water in case of sore throat?

Short Answer Type II Questions [3 Marks]

12. The figure below shows a graph of the molarity of two solutions (*A* and *B*) *versus* volume at constant temperature.

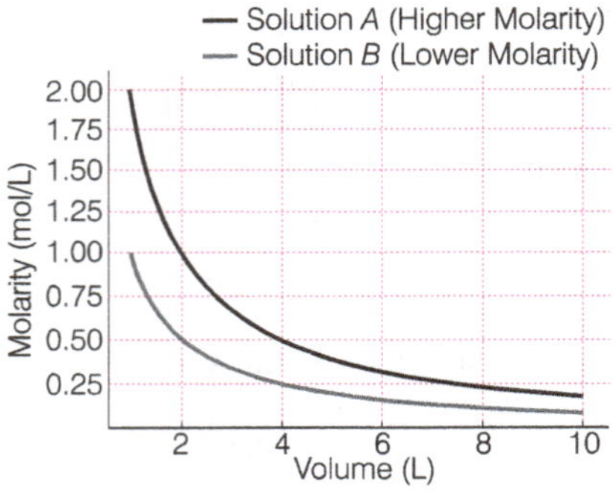

Answer the following questions based on the above given graph.
(i) If the volume of solution *A* is doubled, how does its molarity change? Explain why this happens.
(ii) Compare the molarity of solutions *A* and *B*. What can you infer about the relative amount of solute in each solution if both solutions have the same initial volume?
(iii) If solution *A* becomes more concentrated over time (without a change in volume), what can you say about the behaviour of the solute (e.g., evaporation of solvent, additional solute added)?

13. Water vapours and liquid water are in equilibrium in a container. At room temperature, the vapour pressure of water is 25 mm of Hg. The volume of water is *V* mL.
(i) What will be the vapour pressure of water if the volume of water is reduced to *V*/4 mL without any change in temperature? Give a reason.
(ii) Will there be a change in vapour pressure if more water (at room temperature) is added to the container? Give a reason.

Case Study [4 Marks]

14. The concentration of a solute is very important in studying chemical reactions because it determines how often molecules collide in solution and thus indirectly determine the rate of reactions and the conditions at equilibrium.

There are several ways to express the amount of solute present in a solution. The concentration of a solution is a measure of the amount of solute that has been dissolved in a given amount of solvent or solution. Concentration can be expressed in terms of molarity, molality, parts per million, mass percentage, volume percentage, etc.

Answers the following questions given below.
(i) What would be the concentration of 100 mL solution in which 6.02×10^{20} molecules of urea are present?
(ii) If 0.1M $AgNO_3$ and 0.1 M NaCl solutions are mixed in same volume, then what will be the concentration of nitrate ions?
(iii) Molality of an aqueous solution of urea is 4.44 mol/kg. What will be the mole fraction of urea in a solution?

Or

What do you understand by 20% (*w*/*V*) solution of NaOH?

Long Answer Type Questions [5 Marks]

15. (i) What is van't Hoff factor?
(ii) What possible values can van't Hoff factor have if the solute molecules undergo dissociation?
(iii) An aqueous solution containing 12.48 g of barium chloride in 1.0 kg of water boils at 373.0832 K. Calculate the degree of dissociation of barium chloride.
(Given, K_b for $H_2O = 0.52$ K m^{-1}; molar mass of $BaCl_2 = 208.34$ g mol^{-1}).

Answers

1. (*a*) 2. (*b*) 3. (*b*) 4. (*a*) 5. (*b*) 6. (*a*) 7. (*d*) 8. (*a*) 9. (*ii*) 5×10^2 ppm
14. (i) 0.01 mol/L (ii) 0.05 M (iii) 0.074 15. (iii) $X = 83.55\%$

02 CHAPTER

Electrochemistry is a branch of chemistry that deals with the study of production of electricity from energy released during spontaneous chemical reactions and the use of electrical energy to carry out non-spontaneous chemical transformations.

▼ YOUR STUDY GOALS

2.1 Electrochemical Cells
2.2 Electrochemical Series
2.3 Nernst Equation
2.4 Electrochemical Cell and Gibbs Energy of the Reaction
2.5 Conductance of Electrolytic Solutions
2.6 Electrolytic Cells and Electrolysis
2.7 Batteries (Commercial Cells)
2.8 Fuel Cells
2.9 Corrosion

▼ YOUR PRACTICE GOAL

- Objective Type Questions (41 Qs ; 26 MCQs, 13 A-R & 2 Case Study)
- Subjective Type Questions (41Qs; 18 SA-I, 10 SA-II, 13 LA)

Electrochemistry

2.1 Electrochemical Cells

Redox Reactions

A chemical reaction in which electrons are lost by one substance and gained by another is called **redox reaction**.

e.g.

Oxidation ($S^{-2} \rightarrow S^{0}$)

$$\underset{\text{Reducing agent}}{\overset{-2}{H_2S}} + \underset{\text{Oxidising agent}}{\overset{0}{Cl_2}} \longrightarrow \overset{0}{S} + 2H\overset{-1}{Cl}$$

Reduction ($Cl^{0} \rightarrow Cl^{-1}$)

Transfer of electrons from reducing agent to oxidising agent generate electric current. Therefore, the redox reactions set up the basis of electrochemical cells and electrolytic cells which are discussed further. An electrochemical cell is a device in which chemical energy of the redox reaction is converted into electrical energy, while electrolytic cell do the reverse.

$$\text{Chemical energy} \underset{\text{Electrolytic cell}}{\overset{\text{Electrochemical cell}}{\rightleftharpoons}} \text{Electrical energy}$$

The most common electrochemical cell is a galvanic cell or a voltaic cell.

Galvanic Cells

Electrochemical cells which convert the chemical energy (Gibbs energy) of a spontaneous redox reaction into electrical energy are called **galvanic** or **voltaic cells**. An example of this type of device is **Daniell cell**.

In this cell, an electrode is dipped into the solution of its own salt, this combination is called a **half-cell** or **redox couple**. In a half-cell, either a reduction or an oxidation reaction occurs. Oxidation occurs at **anode** and it has a negative potential with respect to the solution whereas, reduction occurs at the **cathode** and it has a positive potential with respect to the solution.

Oxidation and reduction result in the development of potential difference between the two half-cells and hence, generates electricity.

TEACHER'S TIP

The positive (+) sign of the cathode indicates the electrode at which electrons enter the cell, whereas the negative (–) sign of the anode is where the electrons leave the cell.

Daniell Cell

It consists of two dissimilar metals or electrodes, i.e. zinc and copper. Zinc rod is dipped in zinc sulphate solution and a copper rod in copper sulphate solution. These two solutions are connected by an electric circuit and a salt-bridge as shown in the figure.

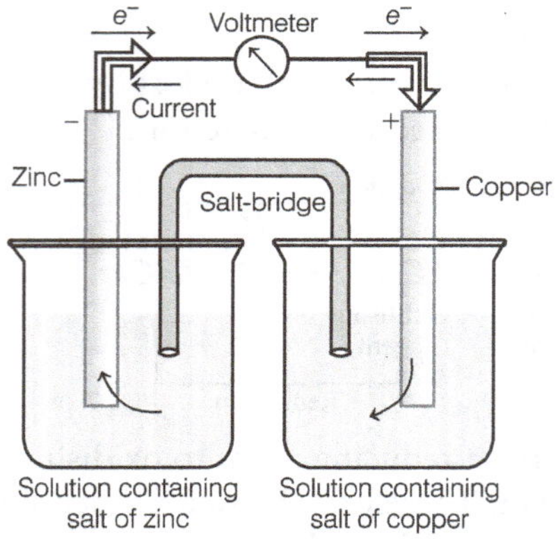

Daniell cell having Zn and Cu electrodes dipped in the solutions of their respective salts

Working

The two half-cell reactions in a Daniell cell are:

- $Zn(s) \longrightarrow Zn^{2+}(aq) + 2e^-$ (oxidation half-reaction)
- $Cu^{2+}(aq) + 2e^- \longrightarrow Cu(s)$ (reduction half-reaction)

The zinc electrode may be called as the **oxidation half-cell** and the copper electrode as the **reduction half-cell.**

The overall redox reaction occurs as

$$Zn(s) + Cu^{2+}(aq) \longrightarrow Zn^{2+}(aq) + Cu(s)$$

- We can construct innumerable number of galvanic cells on the pattern of Daniell cell by taking combinations of different half-cells.
- The two half-cells are connected by a metallic wire through a voltmeter and a switch externally.
- The electrolytes of the two half-cells are connected internally through a salt bridge.
- Sometimes, both the electrodes are dipped in the same electrolyte solution and in such cases, salt bridge is not required.
- An electrical potential energy of 1.1 V is generated from the Daniell cell, when the concentration of Zn^{2+} and Cu^{2+} ions is unity (1 mol dm^{-3}).

Functioning of Daniell Cell in Presence of External Voltage (E_{ext})

Following three cases are possible when E_{ext} is applied.

Case I **When the external potential is lower than 1.1 V.** Under this condition, electrons flow from Zn rod to Cu rod. Hence, current flows from Cu to Zn. Zinc dissolves at anode and copper deposits at cathode.

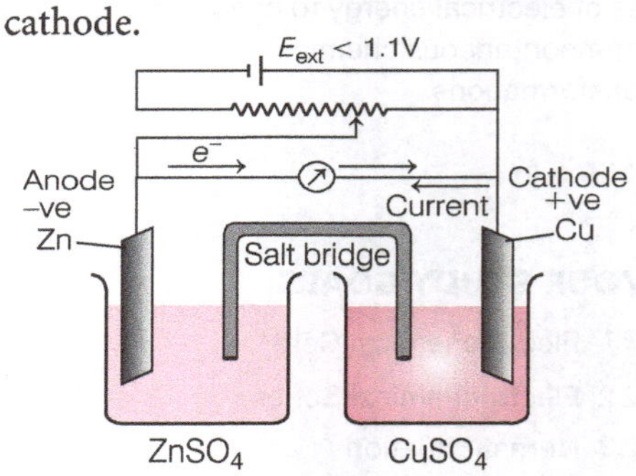

Case II **When the external potential is equal to 1.1V.** If an external opposite potential is applied to the galvanic cell and increased slowly, we find that the reaction continues to take place till the opposing voltage reaches the value of 1.1 V. Once it meets the value, the reaction stops altogether and no current or electrons flows through the cell.

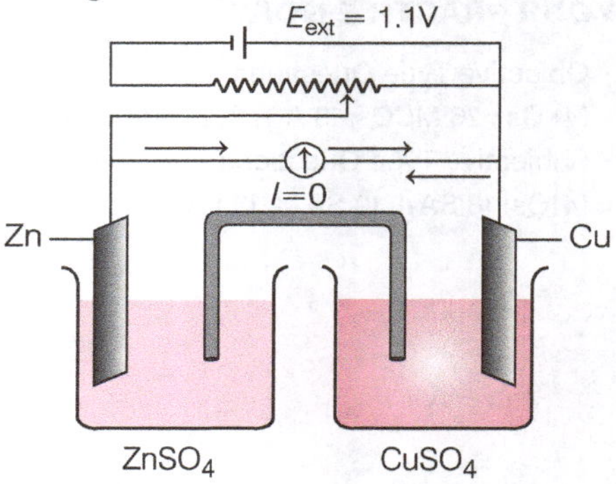

Case III **When the external potential is more than 1.1V.** The reactions get reversed and which also reverses the polarity of the electrodes. This cell is then called an **electrolytic cell**, a device for using electrical energy to carry out non-spontaneous chemical reactions.

Hence, an electrochemical cell can behave like an electrolytic cell, when $E_{ext} > E_{cell}$.

Now, electrons flow from Cu to Zn and current flows from Zn to Cu. Therefore, zinc is deposited at the zinc electrode and copper dissolves at copper electrode.

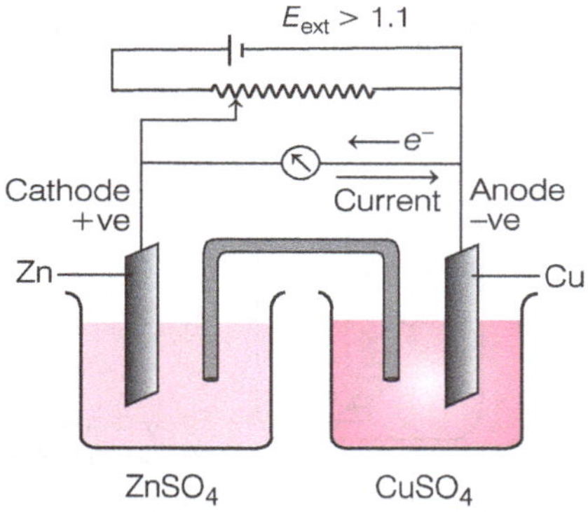

Salt-Bridge

- It is a U-shaped glass tube containing electrolytes (KCl, KNO_3, NH_4Cl, etc.,) mixed in some kind of gel (like gelatine or *agar-agar*).
- It plays an important role in working of an electrochemical cell as it completes the circuit and maintains the electrical neutrality of solutions in each of the respective half-cells.
- Salt-bridge prevents transference or diffusion of the solutions from one half cell to the other. It also prevents liquid-liquid junction-potential, i.e. the potential difference which arises between two solutions when in contact with each other.

Some Important Terms Related to Cell

The various important terms related to cell are as follows

Electrode Potential

It refers to the potential difference developed between electrode and electrolyte in an electrochemical cell. Electrode potential may generate as a result of the following processes:

- Metal atoms of the electrode have a tendency to go into the solution as ions leaving behind the electrons at the electrode making it negatively charged. It means that the metal undergoes oxidation and the potential difference observed will be named as **oxidation potential**.

$$M \longrightarrow M^{n+} + ne^-$$

- On the other hand, metal ions in the solution have a tendency to leave the electrolyte and deposit on the electrode making the electrode positively charged.

Here, the metal undergoes reduction and the resulted potential difference will be named as **reduction potential**.

$$M^{n+} + ne^- \longrightarrow M$$

Cell Potential or EMF of a Cell

The potential difference between the two half-cells is called the **cell potential** and is measured in volts.

In other words, the difference between standard reduction potential of cathode and standard reduction potential of anode is called **cell potential**.

$$E^{\circ}_{cell} = E^{\circ}_{cathode} - E^{\circ}_{anode}$$

It depends upon the following factors

- Nature of metal and its ions
- Concentrations of electrolytes used
- Temperature

Cell potential is also known as **electromotive force** (EMF) when no current flows through the cell.

Cell Representation

While representing the galvanic cell, the **anode** is written on the **left** and the **cathode** on the **right**.

A vertical line (|) separates the metal from the metal ion (electrolyte solution) and a double vertical line (||) indicates a salt-bridge connecting the two half-cells (two electrolytes).

The state of the metal and the solution is written with the concentration of the electrolyte in parenthesis.

$$E_{cell} = E^{\circ}_{right\ (cathode)} - E^{\circ}_{left\ (anode)}$$

Let us consider an example to understand the concept.

Step I Write the cell reaction,

$$Cu(s) + 2Ag^+(aq) \longrightarrow Cu^{2+}(aq) + 2Ag(s)$$

Step II Split the reaction into two half-cell reactions.

At cathode (reduction)

$$2Ag^+(aq) + 2e^- \longrightarrow 2Ag(s)$$

At anode (oxidation)

$$Cu(s) \longrightarrow Cu^{2+}(aq) + 2e^-$$

Step III Represent the complete reaction according to the conversion discussed above.

$$Cu(s)\,|\,Cu^{2+}(aq)\,||\,Ag^{+}(aq)\,|\,Ag(s)$$

$$E^{\circ}_{cell} = E^{\circ}_{Ag^{+}/Ag} - E^{\circ}_{Cu^{2+}/Cu}$$

General representation of an electrochemical cell is given as

$$M_1(s)|M_1^{n+}(aq)||M_2^{n+}(aq)|M_2(s)$$

Anode Oxidation half-cell Reduction half-cell Cathode

Electrons flow this way →

TEACHER'S TIP

In case of electrochemical cell, remember LOAN word to avoid confusion about processes

L → Left, O → Oxidation, A → Anode, N → negative.

Example 1

(i) Formulate the electrochemical cell representing the reaction,

$$2Cr(s) + 3Fe^{2+}(aq) \longrightarrow 2Cr^{3+}(aq) + 3Fe(s)$$

(ii) Calculate E°_{cell}.

[Given, $E^{\circ}_{Cr^{3+}/Cr} = -0.74$ V, $E^{\circ}_{Fe^{2+}/Fe} = -0.44$ V].

Sol. (i) Representation of the given cell,

$$Cr(s)\;|\;Cr^{3+}(aq)||\;Fe^{2+}(aq)|\;Fe(s)$$

(ii) $E^{\circ}_{cell} = E^{\circ}_{right} - E^{\circ}_{left}$

As, $E^{\circ}_{Cr^{3+}/Cr} = -0.74$ V

$E^{\circ}_{Fe^{2+}/Fe} = -0.44$ V

$E^{\circ}_{cell} = -0.44 - (-0.74)$

$E^{\circ}_{cell} = -0.44 + 0.74 = 0.30$ V

Standard Electrode Potential

The electrode potential under the conditions of unit concentration (1M) (i.e. the concentrations of all the species involved in a half-cell is unity) at 1atm pressure and 25°C (298 K) temperature of all the species in the half-cell is called the **standard electrode potential**.

According to the IUPAC convention, standard reduction potential of a cell are now considered as the standard electrode potential.

Measurement of Electrode Potential

The value of electrode potential cannot be determined experimentally because neither the oxidation nor the reduction reaction can occur by itself.

To measure the half-cell potential, one half-cell is assigned a potential value of zero, called as **Standard Hydrogen Electrode** (SHE).

SHE consists of a platinum electrode coated with platinum black. The electrode is dipped in acidic solution of 1M H^{+} ions and pure H_2 gas is bubbled through it at 1 bar pressure. The concentration of both the reduced and oxidised forms of hydrogen is maintained at unity.

The SHE is represented as,

$$Pt(s)\,|\,H_2(g)\,|\,H^{+}(aq)$$

Here, the reaction occurs as,

$$H^{+}(aq) + e^{-} \longrightarrow \frac{1}{2}H_2(g)$$

This electrode has zero potential at all temperatures.

The construction of the SHE is shown in the figure below.

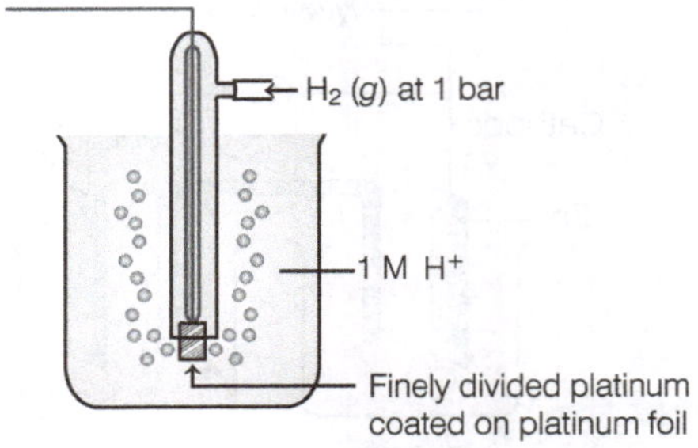

Standard Hydrogen Electrode (SHE)

At 298K, the emf is measured by combining the SHE of the anode (reference half cell) with another half-cell of the cathode, resulting into the standard reduction potential of the other half-cell (cathode).

In this manner, half-cell potentials are measured.

EMF of the cell $= E^{\circ}_{cell} = E^{\circ}_{R} - E^{\circ}_{L}$

As E°_{L} for SHE is zero, $E^{\circ} = E^{\circ}_{R} - 0 = E^{\circ}_{R}$

Note The superscript degree (°) indicates standard conditions.

Calculation of emf of the Cell

In case of Daniell cell,

***Case* I** The measured emf of the cell,

$$Pt(s)|H_2(g, 1bar)|H^{+}(aq, 1M)||Cu^{2+}(aq, 1M)|Cu$$

the value for the standard electrode potential of the half-cell reaction,

$Cu^{2+}(aq, 1M) + 2e^{-} \longrightarrow Cu(s)$ is equal to 0.34 V.

***Case* II** The measured emf of the cell,

$$Pt(s)|H_2(g, 1bar)|H^{+}(aq, 1M)||Zn^{2+}(aq, 1M)|Zn$$

and the value for the standard electrode potential of the half-cell reaction,

$Zn^{2+}(aq, 1M) + 2e^{-} \longrightarrow Zn(s)$ is equal to -0.76V.

- The positive value of the standard electrode potential in the **first case** indicates that Cu^{2+} ions get reduced more easily than H^+ ions.
- In other words, we can say that hydrogen gas can reduce copper ion under the standard conditions.

  Thus, Cu does not dissolve in HCl. In nitric acid, copper is oxidised by nitrate ion and not by hydrogen ion.
- The negative value of the standard electrode potential in the **second case** indicates that H^+ions can oxidise zinc. In other words, we can say that zinc ions can reduce hydrogen ions.
- Taking sign convention, the half-cell reactions for the Daniell cell can be written as:

$$Zn(s) \longrightarrow Zn^{2+}(aq, 1M) + 2e^- \quad \text{(at left electrode)}$$

$$Cu^{2+}(aq, 1M) + 2e^- \longrightarrow Cu(s) \quad \text{(at right electrode)}$$

The overall cell reaction can be written as:

$$Zn(s) + Cu^{2+}(aq) \longrightarrow Zn^{2+}(aq) + Cu(s)$$

$$\text{EMF of the cell} = E^\circ_{cell} = E^\circ_R - E^\circ_L$$
$$= 0.34\ V - (-0.76) V = 1.10 V$$

Inert Electrodes

Some metals like platinum or gold are used as inert electrodes. They do not participate in the reaction but provide their surface for oxidation or reduction reactions and for the conduction of electrons. e.g.,

In hydrogen electrode : $Pt(s) | H_2(g) | H^+(aq)$

Half-cell reaction : $H^+(aq) + e^- \longrightarrow \frac{1}{2}H_2(g)$

Bromine electrode : $Pt(s) | Br_2(aq) | Br^-(aq)$

Half-cell reaction : $\frac{1}{2}Br_2(aq) + e^- \longrightarrow Br^-(aq)$

Note Now a days, **calomel electrode** is also used as a secondary reference electrode. It is a type of a cell in which the electrode is mercury coated with calomel (Hg_2Cl_2) and the electrolyte is a solution of KCl and saturated calomel.

2.2 Electrochemical Series

The arrangement of various standard half-cells in the order of their decreasing values of standard reduction potentials is called **electrochemical series** or **activity series** or **electromotive series.**

Standard Electrode Potentials at 298K

(Electrochemical Series)

Increasing strength of oxidising agent (left) / Increasing strength of reducing agent (right)

Reaction (oxidised form $+ne^-$	$\longrightarrow$ reduced form)	$E^\ominus$/V
$F_2(g) + 2e^-$	$\longrightarrow 2F^-$	2.87
$Co^{3+} + e^-$	$\longrightarrow Co^{2+}$	1.81
$H_2O_2 + 2H^+ + 2e^-$	$\longrightarrow 2H_2O$	1.78
$MnO_4^- + 8H^+ + 5e^-$	$\longrightarrow Mn^{2+} + 4H_2O$	1.51
$Au^{3+} + 3e^-$	$\longrightarrow Au(s)$	1.40
$Cl_2(g) + 2e^-$	$\longrightarrow 2Cl^-$	1.36
$Cr_2O_7^{2-} + 14H^+ + 6e^-$	$\longrightarrow 2Cr^{3+} + 7H_2O$	1.33
$O_2(g) + 4H^+ + 4e^-$	$\longrightarrow 2H_2O$	1.23
$MnO_2(s) + 4H^+ + 2e^-$	$\longrightarrow Mn^{2+} + 2H_2O$	1.23
$Br_2 + 2e^-$	$\longrightarrow 2Br^-$	1.09
$NO_3^- + 4H^+ + 3e^-$	$\longrightarrow NO(g) + 2H_2O$	0.97
$2Hg^{2+} + 2e^-$	$\longrightarrow Hg_2^{2+}$	0.92
$Ag^+ + e^-$	$\longrightarrow Ag(s)$	0.80
$Fe^{3+} + e^-$	$\longrightarrow Fe^{2+}$	0.77
$O_2(g) + 2H^+ + 2e^-$	$\longrightarrow H_2O_2$	0.68
$I_2 + 2e^-$	$\longrightarrow 2I^-$	0.54
$Cu^+ + e^-$	$\longrightarrow Cu(s)$	0.52
$Cu^{2+} + 2e^-$	$\longrightarrow Cu(s)$	0.34
$AgCl(s) + e^-$	$\longrightarrow Ag(s) + Cl^-$	0.22
$AgBr(s) + e^-$	$\longrightarrow Ag(s) + Br^-$	0.10
$\mathbf{2H^+ + 2e^-}$	$\longrightarrow \mathbf{H_2(g)}$	**0.00**
$Pb^{2+} + 2e^-$	$\longrightarrow Pb(s)$	−0.13
$Sn^{2+} + 2e^-$	$\longrightarrow Sn(s)$	−0.14
$Ni^{2+} + 2e^-$	$\longrightarrow Ni(s)$	−0.25
$Fe^{2+} + 2e^-$	$\longrightarrow Fe(s)$	−0.44
$Cr^{3+} + 3e^-$	$\longrightarrow Cr(s)$	−0.74
$Zn^{2+} + 2e^-$	$\longrightarrow Zn(s)$	−0.76
$2H_2O + 2e^-$	$\longrightarrow H_2(g) + 2OH^-(aq)$	−0.83
$Al^{3+} + 3e^-$	$\longrightarrow Al(s)$	−1.66
$Mg^{2+} + 2e^-$	$\longrightarrow Mg(s)$	−2.36
$Na^+ + e^-$	$\longrightarrow Na(s)$	−2.71
$Ca^{2+} + 2e^-$	$\longrightarrow Ca(s)$	−2.87
$K^+ + e^-$	$\longrightarrow K(s)$	−2.93
$Li^+ + e^-$	$\longrightarrow Li(s)$	−3.05

- Negative E° means that the redox couple is stronger reducing agent than H^+/H_2, e.g., Zn (−0.76 V).
- Positive E° means that the redox couple is a weaker reducing agent than H^+/H_2, e.g., Ag (+ 0.80 V).

Applications

Some important applications of electrochemical series are mentioned below.

(i) **Stability of reduced form**

- If the standard electrode potential of an electrode is greater than zero, then its reduced form is more stable as compared to hydrogen gas.
- Similarly, if standard electrode potential is less than zero (negative value), hydrogen gas is more stable than the reduced form of the species.

(ii) **Reducing power of various species**

- Standard reduction potentials of half-cells are arranged from the highest (positive) value to the lowest (negative) value in a table.
- More negative the emf value, stronger is the reducing agent.
- The more positive the emf value, the weaker is the reducing agent as it is compared to H^+/H_2.
- e.g. F_2 has highest reduction potential, hence, it is strongest oxidising agent, while Li^+ has lowest reduction potential, hence, it is a weakest reducing agent.

(iii) **Predicting the feasibility of redox reaction**

- Electrochemical series also helps to predict the feasibility of a redox reaction, thermal stability of metal oxides and spontaneity of an electrochemical cell by choosing the half-cells with appropriate $E°$ values.
- Any cell reaction with negative calculated value of emf will not proceeds.

(iv) **Nature of electrode**

- The electrode with higher electrode potential ($E°$) acts as cathode.
- The electrode with lower electrode potential acts as an anode.

Uses of Electrochemical Cells

These cells are used for determining the pH of solutions, solubility product, equilibrium constant and other thermodynamic properties and for potentiometric titrations.

TEACHER S TIP

More positive the $E°$ value, more easily the species undergo reduction. Whereas, when $E°$ value is more negative, the species undergoes oxidation easily.

2.3 Nernst Equation

The equation which gives the relation between electrode potential, temperature and concentration of metal ions is called **Nernst equation.**

1. Nernst Equation for Electrode Potential

According to Nernst, for the electrode reaction

$$M^{n+}(aq) + ne^- \longrightarrow M(s)$$

The electrode potential at any concentration measured against standard hydrogen electrode, can be written as

$$E_{(M^{n+}/M)} = E^\circ_{(M^{n+}/M)} - \frac{RT}{nF} \ln \frac{[M]}{[M^{n+}]}$$

This is known as the **Nernst equation.**

For pure solids, $[M] = 1$

$$E_{(M^{n+}/M)} = E^\circ_{(M^{n+}/M)} - \frac{RT}{nF} \ln \frac{1}{[M^{n+}]} \quad \ldots(i)$$

Here, $E^\circ_{(M^{n+}/M)}$ is the standard reduction potential of the electrode, R is the universal gas constant having value 8.314 $JK^{-1}mol^{-1}$, n is the number of electrons involved in the reaction, T is the temperature in K, $[M^{n+}]$ is the concentration of the metal ion, M^{n+} and F is the Faraday constant whose value is 96500 C mol^{-1} (approx.).

Using logarithm to the base 10 value, Eq. (i) becomes,

$$E = E^\circ - \frac{2.303RT}{nF} \log \frac{1}{[M^{n+}]}$$

At $T = 298$ K, putting values of all constants, we get,

$$E = E^\circ - \frac{0.059}{n} \log \frac{1}{[M^{n+}]}$$

2. Nernst Equation for EMF of a Cell

For the cathode of Daniell cell, the emf is

$$E_{(Cu^{2+}/Cu)} = E^\circ_{(Cu^{2+}/Cu)} - \frac{RT}{2F} \ln \frac{1}{[Cu^{2+}(aq)]}$$

For the anode of Daniell cell, the emf is

$$E_{(Zn^{2+}/Zn)} = E^\circ_{(Zn^{2+}/Zn)} - \frac{RT}{2F} \ln \frac{1}{[Zn^{2+}(aq)]}$$

The cell potential of the Daniell cell is given by

$$E_{cell} = E_{(Cu^{2+}/Cu)} - E_{(Zn^{2+}/Zn)}$$

$$= E^\circ_{(Cu^{2+}/Cu)} - \frac{RT}{2F} \ln \frac{1}{[Cu^{2+}(aq)]}$$

$$- E^\circ_{(Zn^{2+}/Zn)} + \frac{RT}{2F} \ln \frac{1}{[Zn^{2+}(aq)]}$$

$$E_{cell} = E^\circ_{(Cu^{2+}/Cu)} - E^\circ_{(Zn^{2+}/Zn)} - \frac{RT}{2F}\left[\ln \frac{1}{[Cu^{2+}(aq)]} - \ln \frac{1}{[Zn^{2+}(aq)]}\right]$$

$$E_{cell} = E^\circ_{cell} - \frac{RT}{2F} \ln \frac{[Zn^{2+}]}{[Cu^{2+}]}$$

By converting logarithm to the base 10 and substituting the values of R, F and $T = 298$ K, we get

$$E_{cell} = E^\circ_{cell} - \frac{0.059}{2} \log \frac{[Zn^{2+}]}{[Cu^{2+}]}$$

According to the obtained equation,

- E_{cell} is directly dependent upon concentration of Cu^{2+} and inversely dependent upon the concentration of Zn^{2+} ions.
- E_{cell} decreases as temperature decreases and number of electrons involved in the reaction increases.

TEACHER'S TIP

For a general electrochemical reaction of the type,

$$aA + bB \xrightarrow{ne^-} cC + dD$$

The Nernst equation can be written as

$$E_{cell} = E^\circ_{cell} - \frac{RT}{nF} \ln Q$$

$$\Rightarrow \quad E_{cell} = E^\circ_{cell} - \frac{RT}{nF} \ln \frac{[C]^c [D]^d}{[A]^a [B]^b}$$

At $T = 298$ K,

$$E_{cell} = E^\circ_{cell} - \frac{0.0591}{n} \log \frac{[C]^c [D]^d}{[A]^a [B]^b}$$

Example 2 **Calculate emf of the following cell at 25 °C.**

$Fe|Fe^{2+}(0.001M)||H^+(0.01M)|H_2(g)\ (1bar)|Pt(s)$

$E^\circ_{(Fe^{2+}/Fe)} = -0.44$ V; $E^\circ_{(H^+/H_2)} = 0.00$ V **Delhi 2015**

Sol. For the given cell representation, the cell reaction will be

$$Fe\,(s) + 2H^+(aq) \longrightarrow Fe^{2+}(aq) + H_2(g)$$

The standard emf of the cell will be,

$$E^\circ_{cell} = E^\circ_{H^+/H_2} - E^\circ_{Fe^{2+}/Fe},\quad E^\circ_{cell} = 0 - (-0.44) = 0.44\ V$$

The Nernst equation for the cell reaction at 25°C,

$$E_{cell} = E^\circ_{cell} - \frac{0.0591}{n} \log \frac{[Fe^{2+}]}{[H^+]^2}$$

$$= 0.44 - \frac{0.0591}{2} \log \frac{[0.001]}{[0.01]^2} = 0.44 - 0.02955\ (\log 10)$$

$$= 0.44 - 0.02955\ (1) \qquad [\because \log 10 = 1]$$

$$= 0.41045\ V = 0.41\ V$$

3. Equilibrium Constant from Nernst Equation

In Daniell cell if the ciruit is closed, the following reaction takes place

$$Zn(s) + Cu^{2+}(aq) \longrightarrow Zn^{2+}(aq) + Cu(s)$$

The concentration of Zn^{2+} keeps on increasing while the concentration of Cu^{2+} keeps on decreasing with time. At the same time, voltage of the cell on the voltmeter keeps on decreasing.

After sometime, there is no change in the concentration of Cu^{2+} and Zn^{2+} ions and at that time, voltmeter gives zero reading.

At equilibrium,

$$\text{Therefore, } E_{cell} = 0 = E^\circ_{cell} - \frac{2.303\,RT}{2F} \log \frac{[Zn^{2+}]}{[Cu^{2+}]}$$

At equilibrium,

$$\frac{[Zn^{2+}]}{[Cu^{2+}]} = K_C$$

Therefore, at $T = 298$ K, the above equation can be written as

$$E^\circ_{cell} = \frac{0.0591}{2} \log K_C = 1.1\ V$$

$$\therefore \quad \log K_C = \frac{(1.1\ V \times 2)}{0.059\ V} = 37.288$$

$$K_C = 2 \times 10^{37} \text{ at } 298\ K$$

Such a high value of K_C shows that the reaction has proceeded almost to the completion before attainment of equilibrium condition.

Hence, the value of K_C determines the extent of cell reaction. In general, at equilibrium

$$E^\circ_{cell} = \frac{2.303\,RT}{nF} \log K_C$$

Thus, the above equation gives a relationship between equilibrium constant of the reaction and standard potential of the cell in which that reaction takes place.

Concentration Cells

Two electrodes of the same metal dipped separately into two solutions of the same electrolyte having different concentrations and the solutions are connected through salt bridge, such cells are known as concentration cells, e.g., copper ion concentration cell.

$$Cu|Cu^{2+}(C_1)||Cu^{2+}(C_2)|Cu$$

$$E_{cell} = \frac{0.0591}{n}\log\frac{C_2}{C_1}, \text{ where } C_2 > C_1 \text{ and } E^\circ_{cell} = 0$$

The electrode placed in high concentration electrolyte acts as cathode and that placed in low concentration electrolyte acts as anode.

Example 3 **Calculate the equilibrium constant for the reaction.**

$$Fe(s) + Cd^{2+}(aq) \rightleftharpoons Fe^{2+}(aq) + Cd(s)$$

[Given, $E^\circ_{Cd^{2+}/Cd} = -0.40V$, $E^\circ_{Fe^{2+}/Fe} = -0.44$ V]

Sol.

$$E^\circ_{cell} = E^\circ_{cathode} - E^\circ_{anode}$$
$$= -0.40\text{V} - (-0.44\text{V})$$
$$= -0.40\text{ V} + 0.44\text{ V} = 0.04\text{ V}$$

$$\therefore \quad E^\circ_{cell} = \frac{0.059}{n}\log K_C$$

$$\therefore \quad E^\circ_{cell} = \frac{0.059}{2}\log K_C = 0.04\text{ V}$$

$$\text{or} \quad \log K_C = \frac{2\times 0.04}{0.059} = 1.356$$

$$K_C = \text{antilog}\, 1.356 = 22.70$$

2.4 Electrochemical Cell and Gibbs Energy of the Reaction

Electrical work done (W_{elec}) in one second is equal to the electrical potential multiplied by total charge passed (Q).

$$W_{elec} = \text{emf} \times Q$$

To obtain maximum work from a galvanic cell, charge has to be passed reversibly. The reversible work done by a galvanic cell is equal to the decrease in its Gibbs energy.

Relation between Gibb's energy and emf of cell

Let, nF is the amount of charge passed, E is the emf of the cell and $\Delta_r G$ is the Gibbs energy of the reaction, then

$$W_{elec} = -\Delta G$$
$$\Delta_r G = -nFE_{cell}$$

E_{cell} is an **intensive property** but ΔG is an **extensive thermodynamic property** whose value depends on n.

Thus, if we write the reaction,

$$Zn(s) + Cu^{2+}(aq) \longrightarrow Zn^{2+}(aq) + Cu(s), \Delta_r G = -2FE_{cell}$$

But when we write the reaction,

$$2Zn(s) + 2Cu^{2+}(aq) \longrightarrow 2Zn^{2+}(aq) + 2Cu(s),$$
$$\Delta_r G = -4FE_{cell}$$

Under standard conditions (i.e. when molar concentration of all reacting species is unity at 298 K), the emf of a cell is related to the Gibbs free energy as

$$\Delta_r G^\circ = -nFE^\circ_{cell}$$

where, n is the number of electrons involved in the reaction and F is the Faraday's constant.

Relation between cell potential, free energy and equilibrium constant

The relation between cell potential (E°_{cell}), free energy ($\Delta_r G^\circ$) and equilibrium constant (K_C) is given by

$$\text{or} \quad \Delta_r G^\circ = -2.303\, RT \log K_C$$

as $\Delta_r G^\circ = -nFE^\circ_{cell}$ and $E^\circ_{cell} = \frac{2.303RT}{nF}\log K_C$

Therefore, measurement of E°_{cell} can give us the value of thermodynamic quantity, $\Delta_r G^\circ$ i.e., standard Gibbs energy of the reaction which later help in the calculation of equilibrium constant by the equation given below.

$$\Delta_r G^\circ = -RT\ln K$$

TEACHER'S TIP

At the stage of chemical equilibrium in the cell, $E_{cell} = 0$

$$\Delta_r G = -nFE_{cell} = -nF \times 0 = 0$$

The reaction is feasible only, when

$$E_{cell} = \text{positive} \quad \text{or} \quad \Delta_r G = \text{negative.}$$

Example 4 **The standard electrode potential (E°) for Daniell cell is +1.1 V. Calculate, the $\Delta_r G^\circ$ for the reaction.**

$$Zn(s) + Cu^{2+}(aq) \longrightarrow Zn^{2+}(aq) + Cu(s);$$
$$(1\text{ F} = 96500\text{ C mol}^{-1})$$

All India 2013, Diksha, NCERT

Sol. $Zn(s) + Cu^{2+}(aq) \longrightarrow Zn^{2+}(aq) + Cu(s)$

$$E^\circ_{cell} = +1.1\text{ V}, \Delta_r G^\circ = ?$$
$$1\text{F} = 96500\text{ C mol}^{-1}, n = 2$$
$$\Delta_r G^\circ = -nFE^\circ_{cell} = -2 \times 96500\text{ C mol}^{-1} \times 1.1\text{ V}$$
$$= -212300\text{ J mol}^{-1}$$
$$\Delta_r G^\circ = -212.300\text{ kJ mol}^{-1}$$

Example 5 **Calculate $\Delta_r G^\circ$ and $\log K_C$ for the following reaction**

$$Cd^{2+}(aq) + Zn(s) \longrightarrow Zn^{2+}(aq) + Cd(s)$$

Given : $E^\circ_{Cd^{2+}/Cd} = -0.403$ V

$E^\circ_{Zn^{2+}/Zn} = -0.763$ V **CBSE 2019**

Sol. Given, $E^\circ_{Cd^{2+}/Cd} = -0.403$ V

$E^\circ_{Zn^{2+}/Zn} = -0.763$V

$\therefore \quad E^\circ_{cell} = -0.403 - (-0.763)$

$E^\circ_{cell} = 0.36$ V

$\because \quad \Delta_r G^\circ = -nFE^\circ_{cell}$

where, n = number of moles of electrons used

$n = 2$ (Here), $F = 96500$ C mol^{-1}

$\therefore \quad \Delta_r G^\circ = -2 \times 96500 \times 0.36$

$= 69480$ J / mol

Also, $E^\circ_{cell} = \dfrac{0.0591}{n} \log K_C$

$\therefore \quad \log K_C = \dfrac{n \times E^\circ_{cell}}{0.0591} = \dfrac{2 \times 0.36}{0.0591} = 12.18$

$\log K_C = 12.18$

Quick Test 1

Conceptual Questions

1. How would you determine the standard electrode potential of the system Mg^{2+}/Mg? *NCERT Intext*

2. Can you store copper sulphate solution in a zinc pot? *NCERT Intext*

3. Given the standard electrode potentials,
$K^+/K = -2.93$ V, $Ag^+/Ag = 0.80$ V
$Hg^{2+}/Hg = 0.79$ V, $Mg^{2+}/Mg = -2.37$ V,
$Cr^{3+}/Cr = -0.74$ V
Arrange these metals in increasing order of their reducing power. *NCERT*

4. Using E° values of X and Y given below, predict which is better for coating the surface of iron to prevent corrosion and why? *CBSE 2023, 2025*

Given : $E^\circ_{X^{2+}/X} = -2.36$ V

$E^\circ_{Y^{2+}/Y} = -0.14$ V

$E^\circ_{Fe^{2+}/Fe} = -0.44$ V

5. Use the data to answer the following and also justify giving reason. *CBSE 2019*

	Cr	Mn	Fe	Co
$E^\circ_{M^{2+}/M}$	−0.91	−1.18	−0.44	−0.28
$E^\circ_{M^{3+}/M^{2+}}$	−0.41	+1.57	+0.77	+1.97

(i) Which is a stronger reducing agent in aqueous medium, Cr^{2+} or Fe^{2+} and why?

(ii) Which is the most stable ion in +2 oxidation state and why?

Numerical Questions

6. Calculate the potential of hydrogen electrode in contact with a solution whose pH is 10. *NCERT Intext*

7. Write the Nernst equation and emf of the following cell at 298 K.

(i) $Mg(s) \mid Mg^{2+}(0.001\text{ M}) \| Cu^{2+}(0.0001\text{ M}) \mid Cu(s)$

(ii) $Fe(s) \mid Fe^{2+}(0.001\text{ M}) \| H^+(1\text{ M}) \mid H_2(g)$ (1 bar) $\mid Pt(s)$

Given that, $E^\circ_{Mg^{2+}/Mg} = -2.36$ V,

$E^\circ_{Cu^{2+}/Cu} = 0.34$ V, $E^\circ_{Fe^{2+}/Fe} = -0.44$ V *NCERT*

8. Calculate emf of the following cell at 25°C.

$Sn \mid Sn^{2+}(0.001\text{ M}) \| H^+(0.01\text{ M}) \mid H_2(g)(1\text{ bar})$ Pt (s)

Given: $E^\circ_{(Sn^{2+}/Sn)} = -0.14$ V, $E^\circ_{(H^+/H_2)} = 0.00$ V

($\log 10 = 1$) *CBSE 2024, 2025*

9. The cell in which the following reaction occurs,

$$2Fe^{3+}(aq) + 2I^-(aq) \longrightarrow 2Fe^{2+}(aq) + I_2(s)$$

has $E^\circ_{cell} = 0.236$ V at 298 K, calculate the standard Gibbs energy and the equilibrium constant of the cell reaction. *NCERT Intext*

10. In the button cell, widely used in watches and other devices, the following reaction takes place

$$Zn(s) + Ag_2O(s) + H_2O(l) \longrightarrow Zn^{2+}(aq) + 2Ag(s) + 2OH^-(aq)$$

Determine E° and ΔG° for the reaction.
(Given, $E^\circ_{Ag^+/Ag} = +0.80$ V, $E^\circ_{Zn^{2+}/Zn} = -0.76$ V)

Answers

6. −0.591 V *7.* (i) 2.67 V (ii) 0.53 V
8. 0.11045 V *9.* −45.55 kJ mol^{-1}, 9.616×10^7
10. −301.08 kJ mol^{-1}

For Solutions, See QR Code on Pg. 74

2.5 Conductance of Electrolytic Solutions

Before introducing the concept of conductance of electricity through electrolytic solutions, we must revise few terms related to conductance of electricity given in the tabulated form below:

Term	Definition	Formula/Unit
(i) **Resistance (R)**	It is a property of a substance that restricts or blocks the flow of electric current through it. It can be measured with the help of Wheatstone bridge.	$R = \rho \frac{l}{A}$ where, ρ is resistivity, l is length and A is cross-sectional area. **Unit** : Ohm (Ω)
(ii) **Resistivity (ρ)**	The resistance offered by a substance of 1 m length with area of cross-section equal to 1 m^2.	$\rho = R \frac{l}{A}$ **Units** : Ω cm or Ω m in S.I. unit. [$1\,\Omega\,m = 100\,\Omega\,cm$ or $1\,\Omega\,cm = 0.01\,\Omega\,m$]
(iii) **Conductance (G)**	The ease with which current flows through a conductor. It is the inverse of resistance.	$G = \frac{1}{R} = \frac{A}{\rho l} = \kappa \frac{A}{l}$ **Unit** : SI unit is Siemens (S) which is equal to ohm^{-1} (Ω^{-1}) or mho.
(iv) **Conductivity (κ) or Specific conductivity**	It is the inverse of resistivity. Alternatively it may also be defined as the conductance of 1 cm^3 of the solution of an electrolyte or the conductance of a solution of 1 m length with area of cross-section equal to 1 m^2.	$\kappa = \frac{1}{\rho} = \frac{l}{RA} = G \cdot \frac{l}{A}$ or $\kappa = G \times$ cell constant **Units** : $\Omega^{-1}\,cm^{-1}$ or Scm^{-1}, SI unit is Sm^{-1} [$1\,Scm^{-1} = 100\,Sm^{-1}$]

Note IUPAC recommends the term resistivity over specific resistance and conductivity over specific conductance.

The magnitude of conduction depends upon the nature of the material. It also depends upon the temperature and pressure at which the measurements are made.

Different Types of Materials

Materials are classified into conductors, insulators and semi-conductors depending on the magnitude of their conductivity.

- **Conductors** The substance which have very large conductivity are known as conductors, e.g., metals and their alloys, certain non-metals like carbon-black, graphite and some organic polymers are electronically conducting.
- **Insulators** The substances which have very low conductivity are known as insulators, e.g., glass, ceramics, etc.
- **Semiconductors** The substances which have conductivity between conductors and insulators are known as semiconductors, e.g., silicon, doped silicon and gallium arsenide.
- **Superconductors** The substances which have zero resistivity or infinite conductivity, are known as superconductors, e.g., metals and their alloys at very low temperatures (0 to 15 K). Now a days, a number of ceramic materials and mixed oxides show superconductivity at temperatures as high as 150 K.

Electronic Conductance

Electrical conductance through metals is due to the movement of electrons and termed as **electronic** or **metallic conductance.** It depends upon

- the nature and structure of metal,
- number of valence electrons per atom and
- temperature (it decreases with increase of temperature).

Pure water has very low conductivity but when electrolytes are dissolved in water, they furnish their own ions in the solution, hence its conductivity increases.

The conductance of electricity by ions which are present in the solutions is called **electrolytic** or **ionic conductance.**

Factors affecting the conductivity of electrolytic or ionic solutions are

(i) **Nature of the electrolyte** Strong electrolytes have higher electrical conductivity because they have large tendency to ionise. However, weak electrolytes have low electrical conductivity because of low degree of ionisation.

(ii) **Size of ions and their solvation** Smaller ions and less solvated ions generally exhibits higher electrical conductivity.

(iii) **Nature of the solvent and its viscosity** In polar solvent, the electrolyte will ionise more as compared to non-polar solvent.

However, lower the viscosity of the solvent, higher will be ionic movement and hence, larger will be the electrical conductivity.

(iv) **Concentration of the electrolytic solution** With decrease in concentration of electrolytic solution (dilution), the ionisation of weak electrolyte increases and thus, the electrical conductivity increases.

(v) **Temperature** On increasing the temperature, there is an increase in ionisation as the movement of ions also increases. Consequently, the electrical conductivity of solution increases.

The differences between metallic (electronic) conductors and electrolytic conductors are as follows:

Difference between Electronic Conductors and Electrolytic Conductors

Electronic conductors or Metallic conductors	Electrolytic conductors
Passage of current by movement of electrons in the metallic lattice, e.g., Cu, Ag, etc.	Passage of current by ions in molten state or in aqueous solution of electrolytes, e.g. NaCl (*aq*) or NaCl (fused).
It generally shows no transfer of matter.	It involves transfer of matter in the form of ions.
Due to the vibration of kernels, the electrical conduction decreases with decrease in temperature.	The electrical conduction increases with increase of temperature due to increase in dissociation.
The conducting power of metals is usually high.	The conducting power of electrolytic conductors is relatively low.

Measurement of the Conductivity of Ionic Solutions

In order to measure unknown resistance of an electrolytic solution Wheatstone bridge is used. In this method, we generally encounter two major problems.

- Passing direct current (DC) changes the composition of the solution.
- A solution cannot be connected directly to the bridge.

The first difficulty is resolved by using an alternating current (AC) and the second problem is solved by using a specially designed vessel called **conductivity cell** which consists of two platinum electrodes coated with platinum black, i.e., finely divided metallic Pt is deposited on the electrodes electrochemically.

It is available in several designs and two simple ones are shown below.

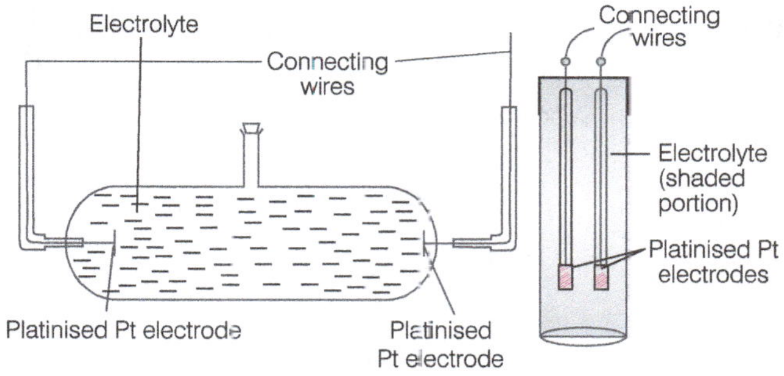

Two different types of conductivity cells

The area of cross-section of these electrodes is A and they are separated by a distance, l.

Thus, the resistance of column containing electrolytic solution between the electrodes is given by equation:

$$R = \rho \frac{l}{A} = \frac{1}{\kappa} \times \frac{l}{A}$$

The quantity $\frac{l}{A}$ is called the **cell constant**. It is denoted by the symbol G^*.

The cell constant will be given by

$$G^* = \frac{l}{A}$$

$$\boxed{G^* = R \times \kappa}$$

Unit of cell constant $(G^*) = \text{m}^{-1}$

Measurement of Cell Constant

For measuring the cell constant, the resistance of the cell is determined using KCl solutions whose conductivity at different temperatures and concentrations is already known. Then, the resistance or conductivity of an electrolyte can be measured by using a cell constant that is based on **Wheatstone bridge principle.**

Measurement of Unknown Resistance

In the figure given below, R_2 is the resistance of the electrolyte to be measured, R_3 and R_4 are known resistances and R_1 is the variable resistance which is adjusted until no current passes through the circuit. O is the source of AC power called oscillator.

Under the no current condition, minimum or no sound can be heard from the earphone, *P* (a detector).

When no current passes, $\frac{R_1}{R_2} = \frac{R_3}{R_4}$. Therefore, $R_2 = \frac{R_1 R_4}{R_3}$

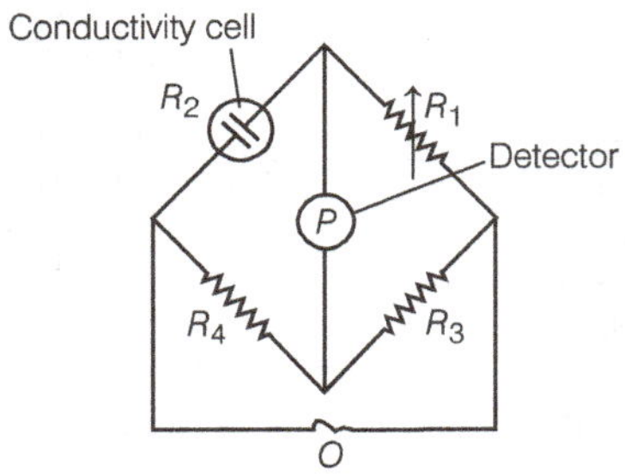

Arrangement for measurement of resistance of an electrolyte

Now a days, inexpensive conductivity meters are available which can directly read the conductance or resistance of the solution in the conductivity cell.

Once the cell constant and the resistance of the electrolyte in the cell are known, the conductivity of the cell is given by,

$$\kappa = \frac{\text{Cell constant}}{R} = \frac{G^*}{R}$$

The conductivity of solutions of different electrolytes in the same solvent and at a given temperature differs due to charge and size of the ions in which they dissociate, the concentration of ions or ease with which the ions move under a potential gradient. It is thus, necessary to define a more meaningful quantity called molar conductivity which is discussed below.

Note The same electrolyte will show different conductivity at different temperatures and different solvents.

Molar Conductivity

Molar conductivity is the conducting power of all the ions produced by dissolving one gram mole of an electrolyte placed between two electrodes with area of cross-section '*A*' and distance of unit length.

It is denoted by Λ_m and given by equation.

$$\Lambda_m = \frac{\kappa}{C}$$

If κ is expressed in $\Omega^{-1}m^{-1}$ or Sm^{-1} unit and the concentration, *C* in mol m^{-3}, then the unit of Λ_m will be $\Omega^{-1}m^2mol^{-1}$ or Sm^2mol^{-1}.

$$\Lambda_m = \frac{\kappa \times 1000}{M}$$

where, *M* is the molarity of the electrolytic solution.

$$1\ Sm^2mol^{-1} = 10^4\ S\ cm^2mol^{-1}$$

or, $$1\ Scm^2mol^{-1} = 10^{-4}\ Sm^2mol^{-1}$$

Note Molar conductivity is the conductance of the electrolytic solution kept between the electrodes of a conductivity cell at unit distance but having area of cross-section large enough to accommodate sufficient volume of solution that contains one mole of the electrolyte.

Example 6 The electrical resistance of a column of 0.05 M NaOH solution of diameter 1 cm and length 50 cm is $5.55 \times 10^3\ \Omega$. Calculate its resistivity, conductivity and molar conductivity. NCERT

Sol. Area, $A = \pi r^2 = 3.14 \times \left(\frac{1}{2}\right)^2 cm^2 = 0.785\ cm^2$

Resistivity, $\rho = \frac{RA}{l}$

$$= \frac{5.55 \times 10^3 \Omega \times 0.785\ cm^2}{50\ cm} = 87.135 \Omega\ cm$$

Conductivity, $\kappa = \frac{1}{\rho} = \frac{1}{87.135} \Omega^{-1}\ cm^{-1}$

$$= 0.01148\ \Omega^{-1}cm^{-1}$$
$$= 1.148 \times 10^{-2}\ S\ cm^{-1}$$

Molar conductivity,

$$\Lambda_m = \frac{\kappa \times 1000}{M} = \frac{1.148\ S\ cm^{-1} \times 10^{-2} \times 1000\ cm^3\ L^{-1}}{0.05\ mol\ L^{-1}}$$
$$= 229.6\ S\ cm^2\ mol^{-1}$$

Variation of Conductivity and Molar Conductivity with Concentration

- Conductivity of a solution always decreases with decrease in concentration (i.e., with dilution) of both the strong and weak electrolytes. This is due to the fact that the number of ions that carry current in a unit volume of solution always decreases with decrease in concentration.
- The molar conductivity can be expressed as

$$\Lambda_m = \kappa V$$

Also, $$\Lambda_m = \frac{\kappa A}{l}$$

[$l = 1$ and $A = V$]

[volume containing 1 mole of electrolyte]

- Molar conductivity increases with decrease in concentration (i.e., with dilution). This is because the total volume V of solution containing one mole of electrolyte increases. It has been found that decrease in κ on dilution is more than compensated by increase in its volume.
- When the concentration approaches zero, the molar conductivity reaches a limiting value, known as **limiting molar conductivity** and is denoted as Λ°_m.

For Strong Electrolytes

Practically, strong electrolytes completely dissociate at all concentrations. For strong electrolytes, Λ_m increases slowly with dilution. This can be represented by equation, **Debye-Huckel-Onsager equation.**

$$\Lambda_m = \Lambda^\circ_m - A\sqrt{C}$$

where, Λ_m = molar conductivity
Λ°_m = limiting molar conductivity
A = constant that depends upon the viscosity and dielectric constant of the solvent
C = concentration of solution

If we plot Λ_m against $\sqrt{C}$, we get a straight line with slope as '$-A$' and intercept as 'Λ°_m'. The value of constant 'A' for a given solvent and temperature depends upon the type of electrolyte, i.e., the charges on the cation and anion produced on the dissociation of electrolyte in the solution.

Thus, NaCl, $CaCl_2$ and $MgSO_4$ are known as 1-1, 2-1 and 2-2 electrolytes, respectively. All electrolytes of a particular type have the same value of 'A'.

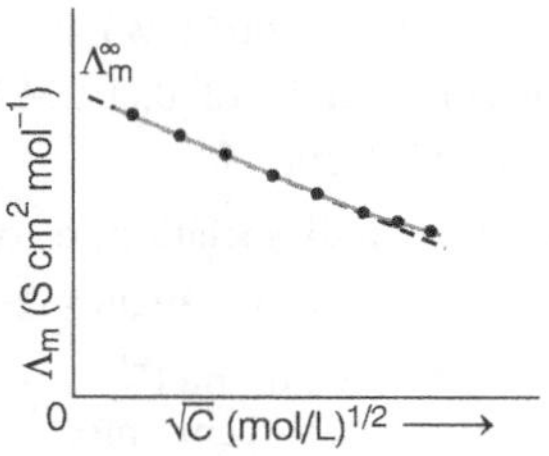

Variation of Λ_m with $\sqrt{C}$ for strong electrolyte (KCl)

For Weak Electrolytes

The electrolytes which do not ionise completely in aqueous as well as in molten state are called **weak electrolytes**, e.g., H_2CO_3, CH_3COOH, etc.

They have lower degree of dissociation at higher concentrations and hence for such electrolytes, the change in Λ_m with dilution is due to increase in the degree of dissociation and consequently the number of ions in total volume of solution that contains 1 mol of electrolyte. The Λ°_m value of weak electrolytes increases steeply with dilution, especially in the low concentration region.

In this region, the graph of weak electrolytes in a plot of Λ_m against $\sqrt{C}$ becomes parallel to the Y-axis. So, the limiting molar conductivity of a weak electrolyte cannot be determined by extrapolation of the plot.

At infinite dilution ($C \rightarrow$ zero) electrolyte dissociates completely ($\alpha = 1$), but at such low concentration the conductivity of the solution is so low that it cannot be measured accurately.

It is rather determined by applying the Kohlrausch law of independent migration of ions. Through Kohlrausch law, we can determined Λ°_m values of weak electrolyte (discussed later in this chapter).

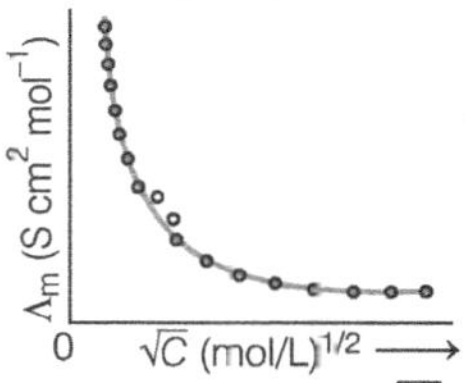

Variation of Λ_m with $\sqrt{C}$ for weak electrolyte (CH_3COOH).

Kohlrausch Law

Kohlrausch law of independent migration of ions states that *"limiting molar conductivity of an electrolyte is the sum of the individual contributions of the cation and the anion of the electrolyte"*.

e.g. $\Lambda^\circ_{m\,(NaCl)} = \lambda^\circ_{Na^+} + \lambda^\circ_{Cl^-}$

where, $\Lambda^\circ_{m\,(NaCl)}$ is the molar conductivity of NaCl and $\lambda^\circ_{Na^+}$ and $\lambda^\circ_{Cl^-}$ are limiting molar conductivity of sodium and chloride ions, respectively.

In general, if an electrolyte on dissociation produces ν_+ cations and ν_- anions, the above equation becomes

$$\boxed{\Lambda^\circ_m = \nu_+\lambda^\circ_+ + \nu_-\lambda^\circ_-}$$

where, λ°_+ and λ°_- are the limiting molar conductivities of the cation and anion, respectively.

Applications of Kohlrausch Law

Some important applications of Kohlrausch law are as follows:

- The molar conductivity of weak electrolytes at infinite dilution can be calculated by using Kohlrausch law.

- The ratio of molar conductivity (Λ_m) at a specific concentration (C) to the molar conductivity at infinite dilution, i.e., limiting molar conductivity, Λ°_m is known as degree of dissociation and can be calculated as :

$$\alpha = \frac{\Lambda^c_m}{\Lambda^\circ_m}$$

- Molar conductivity of weak electrolyte also depends on degree of dissociation. Higher the value of degree of dissociation, higher will be the molar conductivity.
- Knowing the degree of dissociation (α), the dissociation constant (K) of the weak electrolyte at a given concentration of the solution, can be calculated.

$$\text{Dissociation constant, } K = \frac{C\alpha^2}{(1-\alpha)}$$

$$= \frac{C(\Lambda^c_m)^2}{(\Lambda^\circ_m)^2\left(1-\frac{\Lambda^c_m}{\Lambda^\circ_m}\right)} = \frac{C(\Lambda^c_m)^2}{\Lambda^\circ_m(\Lambda^\circ_m - \Lambda^c_m)}$$

- Solubility of sparingly soluble salts like AgCl, $Mg(OH)_2$, $BaSO_4$, etc. can be calculated as

$$\text{Solubility} = \frac{\kappa \times 1000}{\Lambda^\circ_m} \text{ (mol/L)}$$

Example 7 **Calculate Λ°_m for acetic acid,**

Given that, $\Lambda^\circ_{m(HCl)} = 426 \text{ S cm}^2 \text{ mol}^{-1}$

$\Lambda^\circ_{m(NaCl)} = 126 \text{ S cm}^2 \text{ mol}^{-1}$

$\Lambda^\circ_{m(CH_3COONa)} = 91 \text{ S cm}^2 \text{ mol}^{-1}$

Sol. $\Lambda^\circ_{m\,(CH_3COOH)} = \Lambda^\circ_{H^+} + \Lambda^\circ_{CH_3COO^-}$

$= \Lambda^\circ_{H^+} + \Lambda^\circ_{Cl^-} + \Lambda^\circ_{CH_3COO^-} + \Lambda^\circ_{Na^+} - \Lambda^\circ_{Cl^-} - \Lambda^\circ_{Na^+}$

$= \Lambda^\circ_{m\,(HCl)} + \Lambda^\circ_{m\,(CH_3COONa)} - \Lambda^\circ_{m\,(NaCl)}$

$= (426 + 91 - 126) = 391 \text{ S cm}^2 \text{ mol}^{-1}$

Example 8 **Conductivity of 0.00241 M acetic acid solution is 7.896×10^{-5} S cm^{-1}. Calculate its molar conductivity in this solution. If Λ°_m for acetic acid be 390.5 S cm^2 mol^{-1}, what would be its dissociation constant?** **NCERT, Delhi 2008; All India 2008**

Sol. Given, $\kappa = 7.896 \times 10^{-5} \text{ S cm}^{-1}$,

$\Lambda^\circ_{m\,(CH_3COOH)} = 390.5 \text{ S cm}^2 \text{ mol}^{-1}$

and Molarity (M) = 0.00241 M

Molar conductivity,

$$\Lambda^c_m = \frac{\kappa \times 1000}{\text{Molarity}} = \frac{7.896 \times 10^{-5} \text{ S cm}^{-1} \times 1000}{0.00241 \text{ M (mol cm}^{-3})}$$

$\Lambda^c_m = 32.76 \text{ S cm}^2 \text{ mol}^{-1}$

$$\text{Degree of dissociation, } \alpha = \frac{\Lambda^c_m}{\Lambda^\circ_m} = \frac{32.76}{390.5} = 8.4 \times 10^{-2}$$

	CH_3COOH	$\rightleftharpoons$	CH_3COO^-	+	H^+
Initial conc.	C		0		0
Final conc.	$C - C\alpha$		$C\alpha$		$C\alpha$

$$K = \frac{[CH_3COO^-][H^+]}{[CH_3COOH]} = \frac{C\alpha^2}{1-\alpha} = 1.86 \times 10^{-5} \text{ mol L}^{-1}$$

Quick Test 2

Conceptual Questions

1. (i) Why alternating current is used for measuring resistance of an electrolytic solution? *NCERT Exemplar*

(ii) Why does the conductivity of a solution decreases with dilution? *NCERT Intext, Diksha*

2. Explain with a graph, the variation of molar conductivity of a strong electrolyte with dilution. *CBSE 2019*

3. Solutions of two electrolytes 'A' and 'B' are diluted. The Λ_m of 'B' increases 1.5 times while that of A increases 25 times. Which of the two is a strong electrolyte? Justify your answer. Graphically show the behavior of 'A' and 'B'. *CBSE SQP 2022 (Term II)*

4. Why on dilution the Λ_m of CH_3COOH increases drastically, while that of CH_3COONa increases gradually? *NCERT Exemplar*

Numerical Questions

5. The conductivity of sodium chloride at 298 K has been determined at different concentrations and the results are given below.

Concentration/ M	0.001	0.010	0.020	0.050	0.100
$10^{-2} \times \kappa / \text{Sm}^{-1}$	1.237	11.85	23.15	55.53	106.74

Calculate Λ_m for all concentrations and draw a plot between Λ_m and $C^{1/2}$. Find the value of Λ°_m.

6. The resistance of a conductivity cell containing 0.001 M KCl solution at 298 K is 1500 Ω. What is the cell constant, if the conductivity of 0.001 M KCl solution at 298 K is 0.146×10^{-3} S cm^{-1}? *NCERT*

7. Calculate the degree of dissociation (α) of acetic acid, if its molar conductivity (Λ_m) is 39.05 S cm^2 mol^{-1}.

Given : $\lambda^0(H^+) = 349.6 \text{ S cm}^2 \text{ mol}^{-1}$ and $\lambda^0(CH_3COO^-) = 40.9 \text{ S cm}^2 \text{ mol}^{-1}$ *CBSE 2017*

8. Conductivity of 2.5×10^{-4} M methanoic acid is 5.25×10^{-5} S cm^{-1}. Calculate its molar conductivity and degree of dissociation. Given: $\lambda^\circ(H^+) = 349.5 \text{ S cm}^2 \text{ mol}^{-1}$ and $\lambda^\circ(HCOO^-) = 50.5 \text{ S cm}^2 \text{mol}^{-1}$. *CBSE 2015*

Answers

5. 124.05 Scm^{2}mol^{-1} **6.** 0.219 cm^{-1} **7.** 0.1

8. $\Lambda^\circ_m = 400 \text{ S cm}^2 \text{ mol}^{-1}$, $\alpha = 0.525$

For Solutions, See QR Code on Pg. 74

2.6 Electrolytic Cells and Electrolysis

Electrolytic cells are those cells in which electrical energy is used to carry out non-spontaneous chemical reactions and the reactions taking place in an **electrolytic cell** is called **electrolysis**.

In an electrolytic cell, external source of voltage is used to bring about a chemical reaction. One of the simplest electrolytic cell consists of two copper strips (which acts as anode and cathode) dipping in an aqueous solution of copper sulphate.

The diagrammatic representation of the apparatus used in the process of electrolysis is shown in the figure given below.

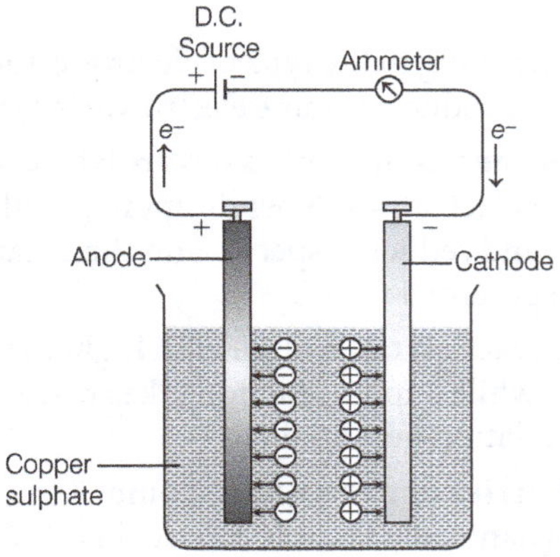

Electrolytic cell

Working of Electrolytic Cells

In an electrolytic cell, when a DC voltage is applied to the two electrodes, then copper is dissolved (oxidised) at anode and deposited (reduced) at cathode and following reactions take place.

At cathode, $Cu^{2+}(aq) + 2e^- \longrightarrow Cu(s)$

At anode, $Cu(s) \longrightarrow Cu^{2+}(s) + 2e^-$

In industrial process, impure copper rod is made as an anode that dissolves on passing current and pure copper rod is made cathode at which Cu^{2+} ions deposits.

Thus, in an electrolytic cell,

- Cations (positive ions) are attracted towards the negative electrode, cathode and discharge by accepting electrons from the cathode. Hence, reduction occurs at cathode. (This is in contrast to galvanic cells, in which a cathode is a positive electrode).
- The anode in an electrolytic cell is positive electrode where oxidation of anions (negative ions) occurs.

Application of Electrolytic Cells

Many metals, e.g., Na, Mg, Al etc., are produced on large scale by electrochemical reduction of their respective cations where no suitable chemical reducing agents are available for this purpose.

Sodium (Na) and magnesium (Mg) metals are produced by the electrolysis of their fused chlorides. Aluminium (Al) is produced by the electrolysis of aluminium oxide in presence of cryolite.

Faraday's Laws of Electrolysis

The **quantitative aspects of electrolysis** was studied extensively by Michael Faraday and his laws of electrolysis are known as **Faraday's laws of electrolysis.** Now, let us discuss these laws as follows

1. Faraday's First Law

It states that "the amount of chemical reaction occurring at any electrode during electrolysis by passing current is directly proportional to the quantity of electricity passed through the electrolyte (in solution or in molten state)".

Thus, w g of the substance gets deposited on passing Q coulomb of electricity.

$$w \propto Q \text{ or } w = ZQ$$
$$w = Z \times it \qquad (\because Q = it)$$

where, Q = quantity of electricity (in C), i = current (in A), t = time (in s), Z = constant of proportionality called **electrochemical equivalent**. It is defined as the amount of the substance deposited when 1A of current is passed for 1s (1C of charge is passed). Its unit is g C^{-1}.

2. Faraday's Second Law

It states that "when the same quantity of electricity is passed through different electrolytes connected in series, the weight of different substances liberated at the electrodes are directly proportional to their equivalent weights.

$$\frac{w_1}{E_1} = \frac{w_2}{E_2} = \frac{w_3}{E_3} = \ldots = \frac{w_n}{E_n}$$

or $$\frac{w_1}{E_1} = \frac{w_2}{E_2}$$

where, w is the mass of substance and E is its equivalent weight.

TEACHER'S TIP

The equivalent mass (weight) of a substance deposited is equal to the atomic mass of an element divided by the number of electrons gained or lost by one atom/ion of the element, i.e.,

$$\text{Equivalent weight } (E) = \frac{\text{Atomic mass}}{\text{No. of electrons gained or lost by one atom / ion}}$$

or, $$E = \frac{\text{Molar mass of element}}{\text{Valency}}$$

Faraday's Constant

The amount of electricity (or charge) required for oxidation or reduction depends on the stoichiometry of the electrode reaction.

e.g. $$Ag^+(aq) + e^- \longrightarrow Ag(s)$$

One mole of the electron is required for the reduction of one mole of silver ions.

The charge on an electron is 1.602×10^{-19} C.

Therefore, the charge on one mole of electrons is

$$N_A \times 1.6021 \times 10^{-19} \text{C} = 6.02 \times 10^{23} \text{ mol}^{-1} \times 1.6021 \times 10^{-19} \text{C}$$
$$= 96487 \text{ C mol}^{-1}$$
$$1\text{F} \approx 96500 \text{ C mol}^{-1}.$$

This quantity of electricity is called **Faraday's constant** and is represented by the symbol *F*.

Note Combining Faraday's laws, we get, $Z = \frac{E}{F} = \frac{W}{Q}$

Example 9 **An aqueous solution of copper sulphate, $CuSO_4$ was electrolysed between platinum electrodes using a current of 0.1287 A for 50 min.**

[Given : Atomic mass of Cu = 63.5 g mol^{-1}]

(i) Write the cathodic reaction.

(ii) Calculate,

(a) electric charge passed during electrolysis.

(b) mass of copper deposited at the cathode.

[Given, 1F = 96500 C mol^{-1}]

Sol. (i) $Cu^{2+} + 2e^- \longrightarrow Cu(s)$

(ii) Given that, $t = 50 \times 60 = 3000$ s, $i = 0.1287$A

(a) $Q = it = 0.1287 \times 3000 = 386.1$ C

(b) $$m = Z \times i \times t = \frac{\text{Eq. wt.}}{96500} \times i \times t$$

$$= \frac{63.5}{2 \times 96500} \times 386.1$$

$$= 0.127 \text{ g}$$

Products of Electrolysis

The products formed during electrolysis depend on the following factors:

(i) **Nature of material being electrolysed** The products of electrolysis depend upon the standard electrode potentials of the material or electrodes. Also, the nature of electrolyte determines the process of electrolysis.

In case of strong electrolyte, the process is fast, whereas the process is slow in case of weak electrolyte.

(ii) **Type of electrodes being used** If the electrode is inert (e.g., Pt or Au electrode), it does not participate in the chemical reaction and acts as source and sink for the electrons. If the electrode is reactive (e.g., Cu or Zn electrode), it participates in the electrode reactions.

Hence, according to the type of electrode, the electrolysis products of same electrolyte may vary.

(iii) **Nature of species present in electrolytic cell** The product of electrolysis depends upon the different oxidising and reducing species and their standard electrode potential values.

Cathodic reaction takes place with higher reduction potential, while anodic reaction takes place with higher oxidation potential.

(iv) **Kinetic barrier or overvoltage** Some of the thermodynamically feasible electrochemical processes are so slow kinetically that these do not seem to take place at lower voltage.

Hence, extra voltage (extra potential) or overvoltage (over potential) is required for them.

The electrolytes which favoured the reaction to take place are present in the molten or in solution form. This is because, in case of solids, the ions are present at specific positions and cannot move at ordinary temperature.

Some Important Examples of Electrolysis

Some important examples of electrolysis are discussed below.

(i) **Electrolysis of molten sodium chloride** It produces sodium metal at the cathode and chlorine gas at the anode. This happens according to the following reactions

At cathode, $Na^+(aq) + e^- \longrightarrow Na(s)$

At anode, $Cl^-(aq) \longrightarrow \frac{1}{2}Cl_2(g) + e^-$

(ii) **Electrolysis of aqueous solution of sodium chloride** (brine) It is more complicated. Since, the solution is in water, so there are two dissociation reactions producing four different ions.

$$NaCl \longrightarrow Na^+ + Cl^-$$
$$H_2O \longrightarrow H^+ + OH^-$$

At cathode, there are two possible reactions

$$Na^+ (aq) + e^- \longrightarrow Na(s); \quad E^\circ_{cell} = -2.71\,V$$
$$H^+ (aq) + e^- \longrightarrow \frac{1}{2} H_2(g); \quad E^\circ_{cell} = 0.00\,V$$

The reaction with the higher value of E° is preferred. Thus, the reaction at the cathode during electrolysis is :

$$H^+ (aq) + e^- \longrightarrow \frac{1}{2} H_2(g) \quad \ldots(i)$$

But $H^+(aq)$ is produced by the dissociation of H_2O,

i.e. $\quad H_2O(l) \longrightarrow H^+(aq) + OH^-(aq) \quad \ldots(ii)$

Therefore, net reaction at the cathode are the sum of Eqs. (i) and (ii)

$$H_2O(l) + e^- \longrightarrow \frac{1}{2} H_2(g) + OH^- \quad \ldots(iii)$$

At anode possible oxidation reactions are

$$Cl^- (aq) \longrightarrow \frac{1}{2} Cl_2(g) + e^-, \; E^\circ_{cell} = 1.36\,V$$
$$OH^- \longrightarrow \frac{1}{2} H_2O + \frac{1}{4} O_2 + e^- \quad \ldots(iv)$$

or, $\quad 2H_2O(l) \longrightarrow O_2(g) + 4H^+(aq) + 4e^-,$

$$E^\circ_{cell} = 1.23\,V \quad \ldots(v)$$

Reaction (v) is the sum of reaction (ii) and reaction (iv). The reaction with the lower value of E° is preferred at the anode.

Thus, we expect oxidation of water to take place at the anode.

However, due to the overpotential of oxygen, liberation of chlorine gas is preferred. Hence,

At cathode, $H_2O(l) + e^- \longrightarrow \frac{1}{2} H_2(g) + OH^-(aq)$

At anode, $\quad Cl^-(aq) \longrightarrow \frac{1}{2} Cl_2(g) + e^-$

Net reaction,

$$NaCl(aq) + H_2O(l) \longrightarrow Na^+(aq) + OH^-(aq) + \frac{1}{2} H_2(g) + \frac{1}{2} Cl_2(g)$$

(iii) **Electrolysis of copper sulphate solution**

- **Very inert electrodes**

$$CuSO_4(aq) \longrightarrow Cu^{2+}(aq) + SO_4^{2-}(aq)$$

At anode, $\quad H_2O(l) \longrightarrow \frac{1}{2} O_2(g) + 2H^+(g) + 2e^-$

At cathode, $\quad Cu^{2+}(aq) + 2e^- \longrightarrow Cu(s)$

Therefore, copper is deposited at the cathode and O_2 gas is liberated of the anode.

- **Using copper electrodes**

$$CuSO_4(aq) \longrightarrow Cu^{2+}(aq) + SO_4^{2-}(aq)$$

At anode, $\quad Cu(s) \longrightarrow Cu^{2+}(aq) + 2e^-$

At cathode, $\quad Cu^{2+}(aq) + 2e^- \longrightarrow Cu(s)$

Therefore, copper dissolves at the anode and is deposited at cathode. The process is used in the purification of copper.

(iv) **Electrolysis of sulphuric acid** During electrolysis of sulphuric acid, following reactions are possible.

At anode,

(a) $2H_2O(l) \longrightarrow O_2(g) + 4H^+(aq) + 4e^-;$

$$E^\circ_{cell} = +1.23\,V$$

(b) $2SO_4^{2-}(aq) \longrightarrow S_2O_8^{2-}(aq) + 2e^-; \; E^\circ_{cell} = 1.96\,V$

For dilute sulphuric acid, reaction (a) is preferred but at higher concentration of H_2SO_4, reaction (b) is preferred.

At cathode,

$$H^+ + e^- \longrightarrow \frac{1}{2} H_2(g); \; E^\circ_{cell} = 0.00V$$

Quick Test 3

Conceptual Questions

1. (a) When acidulated water (dil. H_2SO_4) is electrolysed, will the pH of the solution be affected? Justify your answer. *NCERT Exemplar*

(b) What will happen to pH of brine solution if electrolysed?

2. Write the reaction which is preferred at anode during the electrolysis of H_2SO_4 at higher concentration?

3. What will be the products of electrolysis when an aqueous solution of $CuCl_2$ is electrolysed using platinum electrode?

Numerical Questions

4. (a) Consider the reaction,

$$Cr_2O_7^{2-} + 14H^+ + 6e^- \longrightarrow 2Cr^{3+} + 7H_2O$$

What is the quantity of electricity in coulombs, needed to reduce 1 mole of $Cr_2O_7^{2-}$? *NCERT Intext*

(b) What is the amount of charge required to carry out the conversion of 1 mole of Al^{3+} ions to Al according to the following reaction,

$$Al^{3+} + 3e^- \longrightarrow Al$$

Or How much charge is required for the reduction of 1 mole of Al^{3+} to Al? NCERT

5. How much electricity is required in coulomb for the oxidation of

(a) 1 mole of H_2O to O_2?

(b) 1 mole of FeO to Fe_2O_3? NCERT

6. If a current of 0.5 A flows through a metallic wire for 2 h, then how many electrons would flow through the wire? NCERT Intext

7. Calculate the time required to deposit 1.27 g of copper at cathode when a current of 2 A was passed through the solution of $CuSO_4$.

(Molar mass of Cu = 63.5 g mol^{-1}, F = 96500 C mol^{-1}) CBSE 2015

8. Calculate the mass of Ag deposited at cathode when a current of 2A was passed through a solution of $AgNO_3$ for 15 min.

(Given : Molar mass of Ag = 108 g mol^{-1}
1F = 96500 C mol^{-1}). CBSE 2017

Answers

4. (a) 579000 C (b) 289500 C *5.* (i) 1.93×10^5 C (ii) 96500 C

6. 2.25×10^{22} *7.* 965 sec *8.* 2.014 g

For Solutions, See QR Code on Pg. 74

2.7 Batteries (Commercial Cells)

A battery (which contains one or more than one electrochemical cell connected in series) or a cell used as a source of electrical energy is basically a galvanic cell, which converts the chemical energy of the redox reaction into electrical energy.

For a battery to be of practical use, it should be reasonably light, compact and its voltage should not vary appreciably during its use. There are mainly two types of batteries which are discussed below.

1. Primary Batteries

A primary battery (non-chargeable battery) is a device in which reactions occur only once and after use (over a period of time), battery becomes dead and cannot be reused. It produces electric current for a period of time and with time when no more chemicals remain available to take part in the reaction, the cell dies.

The most familiar examples of this type of batteries are **Leclanche cell** and **mercury cell.**

(i) Leclanche Cell (Dry Cell)

The components of this cells are following:

Anode Zinc metal container.

Cathode Carbon (graphite) rod surrounded by powdered MnO_2 and carbon black.

Electrolyte Moist paste of ammonium chloride (NH_4Cl) and zinc chloride ($ZnCl_2$) is filled in the space between the electrodes.

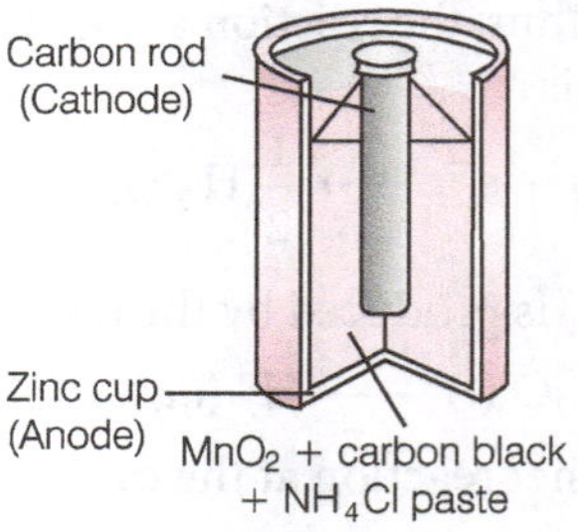

Dry cell

The reactions occurring at the cathode and the anode are:

At cathode, $MnO_2 + NH_4^+ + e^- \longrightarrow MnO(OH) + NH_3$

At anode, $Zn(s) \longrightarrow Zn^{2+} + 2e^-$

In the reaction involved at cathode, manganese is reduced from the +4 oxidation state to the +3 state. NH_3 produced in the reaction forms a complex with Zn^{2+} to give $[Zn(NH_3)_4]^{2+}$ as follows

$$Zn^{2+} + 4NH_3 \longrightarrow [Zn(NH_3)_4]^{2+}$$

The cell has a potential of about 1.5 V.

Uses It is commonly used in transistors and clocks.

(ii) Mercury Cell

The components of this cell are

Anode Zinc-mercury amalgam.

Cathode Paste of mercuric oxide (HgO) and carbon powder.

Electrolyte Paste of KOH and ZnO.

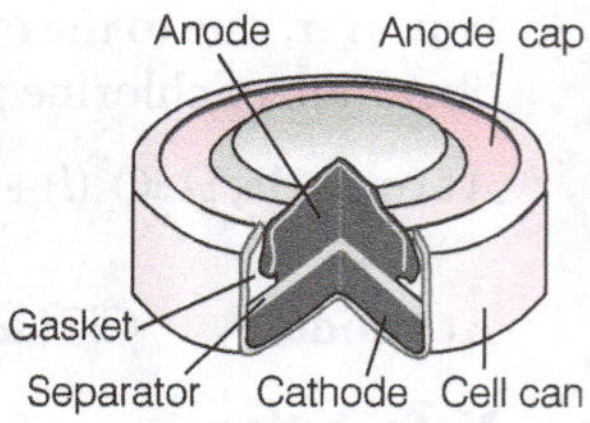

Mercury cell

The reducing agent is zinc and the oxidising agent is mercury (II) oxide.

The electrode reactions of a mercury cell can be written as below:

At cathode, $HgO + H_2O + 2e^- \longrightarrow Hg\,(l) + 2OH^-$

At anode, $\underset{\text{(Amalgam)}}{Zn(Hg)} + 2OH^- \longrightarrow ZnO(s) + H_2O + 2e^-$

The overall reaction of the cell is written as

$$\underset{\text{(Amalgam)}}{Zn(Hg)} + HgO(s) \longrightarrow ZnO\,(s) + Hg\,(l)$$

The potential of a mercury cell is approximately 1.35 V. It remains constant as in the overall cell reaction no ions are involved in solution whose concentration can change during the life span of the cell. Thus, it lasts longer.

Uses It is suitable for low current devices like hearing aids, watches, etc.

2. Secondary Batteries

A secondary cell after use can be recharged by passing current through it in the opposite direction so that it can be used again.

A good secondary cell can undergo a large number of discharging and charging cycles.

Two important secondary batteries are **lead storage battery** and **nickel-cadmium battery**.

(i) Lead Storage Battery (Lead accumulator)

A typical 12V battery consists of six cells connected in series, each cell providing a potential of about 2V.

Anode A series of lead grids packed with spongy lead.

Cathode A grid of lead packed with lead dioxide.

Electrolyte An aqueous solution of H_2SO_4, 38% (H_2) by weight.

When the battery is in use (discharging), the cell reactions are given below:

At cathode,

$$PbO_2(s) + SO_4^{2-}(aq) + 4H^+(aq) + 2e^- \longrightarrow PbSO_4(s) + 2H_2O\,(l)$$

At anode, $Pb\,(s) + SO_4^{2-}(aq) \longrightarrow PbSO_4(s) + 2e^-$

The overall reaction of the cell is written as

$$Pb\,(s) + PbO_2(s) + 2H_2SO_4(aq) \longrightarrow 2PbSO_4(s) + 2H_2O(l)$$

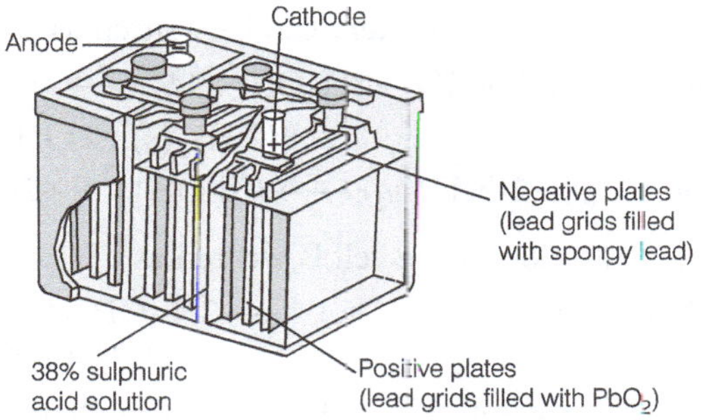

Lead storage battery

During charging, current greater than 12 V is passed from external source.

Due to this, the reactions are forced to reversed and $PbSO_4(s)$ on anode and cathode is converted into Pb and PbO_2, respectively.

At cathode,

$$PbSO_4(s) + 2H_2O\,(l) \longrightarrow PbO_2(s) + SO_4^{2-}(aq) + 4H^+(aq) + 2e^-$$

At anode, $PbSO_4(s) + 2e^- \longrightarrow Pb(s) + SO_4^{2-}(aq)$

Uses It is commonly used in automobiles and power invertors.

TEACHER'S TIP

Sulphuric acid is consumed during discharging and causes the decrease in the density of the electrolytic solution as water is formed during the reactions. When the concentration of H_2SO_4 falls to 1.20 g L^{-1}, it requires recharging.

(ii) Nickel-Cadmium Battery

The components of this battery are

Anode Cadmium metal.

Cathode Metal grid containing NiO_2.

Electrolyte Moist NaOH or KOH solution.

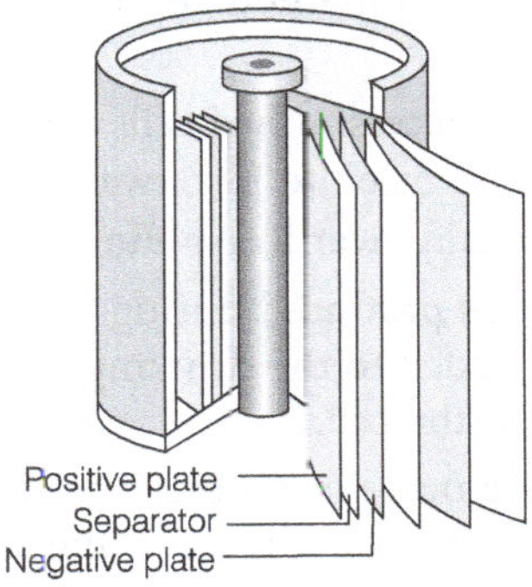

Nickel-cadmium battery

The reactions of Ni-Cd battery can be written as

At cathode, $2NiO(OH)(s) + 2H_2O(l) + 2e^- \longrightarrow 2Ni(OH)_2(s) + 2OH^-(aq)$

At anode, $Cd(s) + 2OH^-(aq) \longrightarrow Cd(OH)_2(s) + 2e^-$

The overall reaction of the cell is written as

$$Cd(s) + 2NiO(OH)(s) + 2H_2O(l) \longrightarrow 2Ni(OH)_2(s) + Cd(OH)_2(s)$$

The overall cell reaction of Ni-Cd cell during discharging is

$$Cd(s) + 2Ni(OH)_3(s) \longrightarrow CdO(s) + 2Ni(OH)_2(s) + H_2O(l)$$

The voltage of this cell = 1.4 V

It has longer life than the lead storage cell but more expensive to manufacture.

Uses It is used in electrical toys, camera, portable power tools, etc.

2.8 Fuel Cells

- A galvanic cells in which chemical energy from combustion of fuels like hydrogen, methane, methanol, etc., is converted into electrical energy are called **fuel cells.**
- In this type of galvanic cells, reactants are continuously fed to the electrodes, which react to produce electricity and products thus formed are continuously removed from the electrolyte compartment.
- In thermal plants, the chemical energy (heat of combustion) of fossil fuels like coal, gas or oil is first used for converting water into high pressure steam.This is then used to run a turbine to produce electricity.
- Thus, production of electricity by thermal plants is not a very efficient method and is a major source of pollution.

One of the most successful fuel cells uses the reaction of hydrogen with oxygen to form water. It was used for providing electrical power in **Apollo space programme.** The water vapours produced during the reaction were condensed and added to the drinking water supply for the astronauts. In the cell,

- **Electrodes** are made of porous carbon impregnated with metallic catalysts (Pt, Ag or metal oxides).
- **Electrolyte** concentrated NaOH or KOH.
- **Catalysts** Finely divided Pt or Pd.

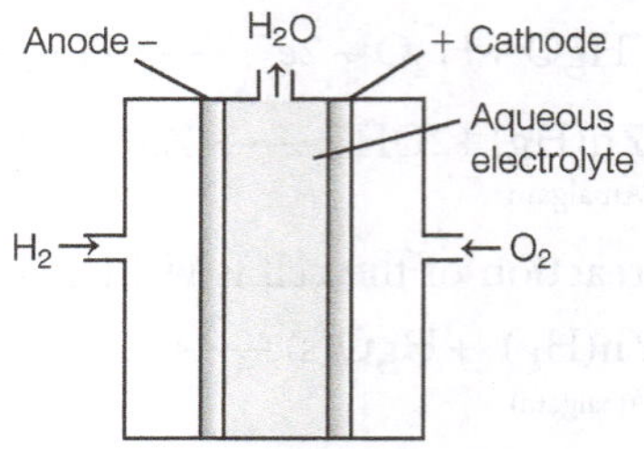

Fuel cell using H_2 and O_2 produces electricity

The electrode reactions for the cell are given below:

At cathode, $O_2(g) + 2H_2O(l) + 4e^- \longrightarrow 4OH^-(aq)$

At anode, $2H_2(g) + 4OH^-(aq) \longrightarrow 4H_2O(l) + 4e^-$

The overall reaction of the cell is written as

$$2H_2(g) + O_2(g) \longrightarrow 2H_2O(l)$$

Advantages of Fuel Cells

Some of the advantages of fuel cells are as follows.

- It is highly efficient (70%) as compared to thermal power plants (40%).
- It does not cause pollution as no harmful products are formed.
- This cell runs as long as the reactants are supplied.
- This cell being light weight have been used in automobiles on an experimental basis.

Disadvantages of Fuel Cells

- Difficulty is faced in handling the gaseous fuels.
- Catalysts used are very costly.
- Electrode preparation is very difficult and time taking.

2.9 Corrosion

An electrochemical process in which a metal is oxidised to metal oxide or other salt of the metal by losing electrons to oxygen or other electronegative element and forms a coating on the metal surface is called **corrosion.**

The rusting of iron, tarnishing of silver surface, surface of copper and bronze turning green are some of the examples of corrosion.

Factors Affecting Corrosion

The following factors are responsible for affecting the rate of corrosion.

(i) **Reactivity of the metal** More the reactive metal, more will be the tendency of corrosion.

(ii) **Presence of impurities** Metal having impurities have more chances to get corrode than pure metal.

(iii) **Air and moisture** The presence of moisture and air can easily cause corrosion. The presence of gases like SO_2, CO_2 and NO_2 in air accelerate the process of corrosion. If metal is placed in vacuum, it does not undergo corrosion.

(iv) **Strains in metal** Corrosion can occur more easily at strains, cuts or scratches present on metal.

(v) **Presence of electrolyte** The presence of electrolyte can make the corrosion process faster.

For example, if iron is placed in sea water, then it will corrode more rapidly than iron placed in pure water.

Mechanism of Corrosion

In corrosion, a metal is oxidised by loss of electrons to oxygen and formation of oxides take place.

- **Rusting** (or corrosion) occurs in the presence of water and air. The place of iron object where rusting takes place, acts as anode. This is the place at which oxidation occurs and iron oxide is formed.
- Electrons released at anodic spot move through the metal and go to another spot on the metal and reduce oxygen in the presence of H^+ which is believed to be available from H_2CO_3 formed due to dissolution of carbon dioxide from air into water. This spot behaves as the cathode.

The reactions at anode and cathode are:

At anode, $2Fe(s) \longrightarrow 2Fe^{2+}(aq) + 4e^-$;

$$E^\ominus_{(Fe^{2+}/Fe)} = -0.44 \text{ V}$$

At cathode, $O_2(g) + 4H^+(aq) + 4e^- \longrightarrow 2H_2O(l)$;

$$E^\ominus_{H^+|O_2|H_2O} = 1.23 \text{ V}$$

The overall reaction of the cell is written as

$$2Fe(s) + O_2(g) + 4H^+(aq) \longrightarrow 2Fe^{2+}(aq) + 2H_2O(l);$$

$$E^\ominus_{(cell)} = 1.67 \text{ V}$$

The ferrous ions obtained are further oxidised by atmospheric oxygen to ferric ions which comes out as rust in the form of hydrated ferric oxide ($Fe_2O_3 . xH_2O$) and with further production of H^+ ions.

e.g. Corrosion of iron in atmosphere.

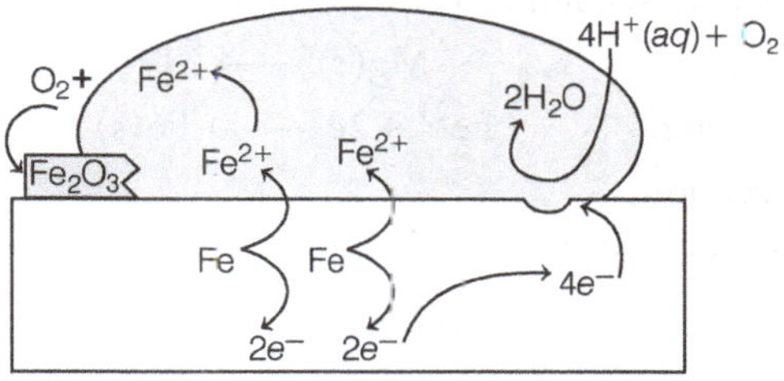

Atmospheric oxidation

$$2Fe^{2+}(aq) + 2H_2O(l) + \frac{1}{2}O_2(g) \longrightarrow Fe_2O_3(s) + 4H^+(aq)$$

Prevention of Corrosion

Prevention of corrosion saves money and helps in preventing accidents such as bridge collapse or failures. It significantly damages buildings, bridges and ships, leading to substantial financial losses each year. Thus, prevention of corrosion is essential.

Methods for Prevention of Corrosion

Some of the common methods used for the prevention of corrosion are as follows:

(i) **Protective layer method** In this method, the coating of the surface of the metal is done to prevent it from coming in contact with moisture and atmospheric oxygen.

This protection can be attained by following methods

(a) Surface coating with paint, some oil, grease some chemicals (e.g. bisphenol), etc., can prevent the corrosion of metal.

(b) Electroplating is the method used for protection of metal in which the corrosion-resistant metal like nickel, chromium, copper etc., is plated on the surface of metal.

(ii) **Sacrificial protection** In this method, the coating of a more reactive metal on a less reactive metal is done. The more reactive metal losses its electrons or oxidises and protect the less reactive metal by sacrificing itself.

e.g. Galvanisation (coating iron with zinc by dipping or electrolysis)

(iii) **Cathodic protection of iron** In this method, the exposed surface of iron is attached to a more reactive metal like magnesium by connecting them with wire. The more reactive metal acts as anode and the iron acts as cathode.

The involved chemical reactions are

At anode, $Mg(s) \longrightarrow Mg^{2+}(aq) + 2e^-$

At cathode, $Fe^{2+} + 2e^- \longrightarrow Fe(s)$

Net reaction,

$$Mg(s) + Fe^{2+}(aq) \longrightarrow Mg^{2+}(aq) + Fe(s)$$

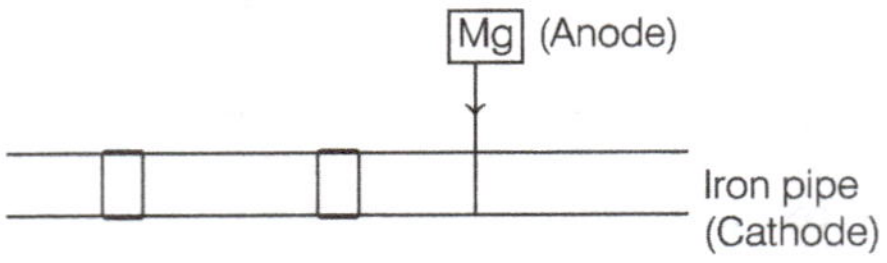

(iv) **Anti-rust solution** The iron articles are dipped into the boiling anti-rust solution containing alkaline solutions of phosphate and chromate salts. This forms a protective insoluble film of **iron phosphate** on the surface thus, preventing rusting.

Hydrogen Economy

- Now-a-days development and economy of a country depends upon consumption of energy. People for the sake of improvement in their lifestyle increases the requirement of energy. At present main source of energy is fossil fuels like coal, oil, gas, etc. With increase in energy consumption the reservoirs of fossil fuels are getting exhausted very rapidly. Also, carbon dioxide produced during the combustion of fossil fuels results in **greenhouse effect**. Therefore, the use of these fuels should be minimized or avoided.
- Hydrogen economy can be an ideal alternative. This vision includes the use of hydrogen as a renewable and non-polluting source of energy. It can be used in both production by electrolysis of water using solar energy as well as in fuel cell. Also, the technologies are truly based on electrochemical principles.

Quick Test 4

1. Write the name of the cell which is generally used in transistors. Write the reactions taking place at the anode and the cathode of the cell. *CBSE 2017*

2. Given reasons :
 (i) Mercury cell delivers a constant potential during its life time.
 (ii) In the experimental determination of electrolytic conductance, direct current (DC) is not used. *CBSE 2023*

3. Write the name of the cell which is generally used in hearing aids. Write the reactions taking place at the anode and the cathode of this cell. *CBSE 2017*

4. Write the cell reaction of a lead storage battery when it is discharged. How does the density of the electrolyte change when the battery is discharged? *NCERT Exemplar*

5. Name the cell which *CBSE 2023*
 (i) was used in Apollo Space programme.
 (ii) is used in automobile and invertors
 (iii) is suitable for hearing aids and watches.
 (iv) does not give a steady potential and is used in transistors.

6. Suggest two materials other than hydrogen that can be used as fuel in fuel cells. *NCERT Intext*

7. Rusting of iron is quicker in saline water than in ordinary water. Give reason.

8. Why rusting of iron pipe can be prevented by joining it with a piece of magnesium?

For Solutions, See QR Code on Pg. 74

Mind Map

Conductance of Electrolytic Solutions

- **Resistance** $(R) = \rho \frac{l}{A}$
  ρ = Ressistivity **unit** : ohm-metre
- **Conductance** $(G) = \frac{1}{\text{Resistance}}$
  Unit : Ohm^{-1} or Siemens
- **Specific conductivity** $(\kappa) = G\frac{l}{a}$ $\left(\frac{l}{a} = \text{cell constant}\right)$
  Unit = $\text{ohm}^{-1}\text{cm}^{-1}$ or S cm^{-1}
- **Molar conductance** $(\Lambda_m) = \frac{1000 \times \kappa}{M}$
  Unit = $\text{S cm}^2 \text{mol}^{-1}$
- **Equivalent conductance** $(\Lambda_{eq}) = \frac{100 \times \kappa}{N}$
  Unit = $\text{cm}^2 \text{ohm}^{-1}\text{g-eq}^{-1}$
  - For strong electrolytes, Λ_m increases slowly with dilution and can be represented by the equation : $\Lambda_m = \Lambda_m^\circ - AC^{1/2}$ (Debye-Huckel Onsagar equation)
  - For weak electrolytes, Λ_m increases steeply with dilutions.

Kohlrausch's Law

- It is also called law of **independent migration of ions**.
  It states that limiting molar conductivity (Λ_m°) of an electrolyte is the sum of the individual contribution of cation and anion as :
  $$\Lambda^\circ_{m\,(NaCl)} = \lambda^\circ_{(Na^+)} + \lambda^\circ_{(Cl^-)}$$
- It is helpful for the calculation of α and K_a as:
  $$\alpha = \frac{\Lambda_m}{\Lambda_m^\circ} \quad \text{and} \quad K_a = \frac{C\alpha^2}{(1-\alpha)}$$

Electrochemical Cell

- It is a device which converts chemical energy into electrical energy.
- It is also called **galvanic cell**, e.g. Daniell cell.
- Reaction occurring in Daniell cell is
  $$Zn(s) + Cu^{2+}(aq) \longrightarrow Zn^{2+}(aq) + Cu(s)$$

ELECTROCHEMISTRY

Terms Related with Electrochemical Cell

(a) Standard Electrode Potential (E°)

It is the potential difference developed between electrode and the electrolyte under the standard conditions.

(b) Cell Potential

$E^\circ_{cell} = E^\circ_c - E^\circ_a$, c = cathode, a = anode

(c) Reference Electrode

It is an electrode of known potential, e.g. hydrogen electrode, calomel electrode, etc.

(d) Electrochemical Series

It is the arrangement of various standard half-cells in the order of their decreasing E°values.

$F^- < Ag < Cu < H_2 < Pb < Sn < Ni < Fe < Zn < Al < Mg < Na < Ca < K < Li$

(e) Nernst Equation

$$E_{cell} = E^\circ_{cell} - \frac{RT}{nF}\ln\frac{[M]}{[M^{n+}]}$$

$$\text{or } E_{cell} = E^\circ_{cell} - \frac{0.059}{n}\log\frac{1}{[M^{n+}]}$$

$$\text{or } E_{cell} = E^\circ_{cell} - \frac{0.059}{n}\log Q$$

$$\text{or } \Delta G^\circ = -nFE^\circ_{cell}$$

Batteries

These contain one or more than one electrochemical cells connected in series.

(A) Primary Batteries

These are non-rechargeable, e.g. leclanche cell, mercury cell.

(B) Secondary Batteries

These are rechargeable batteries. During charging, these act as electrolytic cell, e.g. lead storage battery, nickel-cadmium battery.

Fuel Cell

- It is a galvanic cell which convert chemical energy of fuel into electrical energy.
  e.g. $H_2 - O_2$ fuel cell
- These are more efficient and pollution free.

Electrolytic Cell

In it, electrical energy is used to carry out a non-spontaneous reaction. This process is called **electrolysis**.

Faraday's Laws of Electrolysis

First Law

It states $w \propto Q \Rightarrow w = ZQ$

$w = ZQ \left(Z = \frac{E}{96500}\right)$

Here, Q = charge, E = equivalent mass

Second Law

It states $w \propto E$

or $\frac{w_1}{w_2} = \frac{E_1}{E_2}$

Here, w = mass, E = equivalent weight

Corrosion

- It is the process of deterioration of a metal from its surface.
  e.g. Rusting of iron, blackening of Ag, etc.
- It is an electrochemical process.
- It is prevented by painting, barrier protection and rust solutions.

EXAM PATTERN QUESTIONS

Objective Type Questions

Multiple Choice Questions [1 Mark]

1. In an electrochemical process, a salt bridge is used **CBSE 2020**

(a) as a reducing agent
(b) as an oxidising agent
(c) to complete the circuit so that current can flow
(d) None of the above

2. Electrode potential for Mg electrode varies according to the equation $E_{Mg^{2+}/Mg} = E^{\ominus}_{Mg^{2+}/Mg} - \frac{0.059}{2} \log \frac{1}{[Mg^{2+}]}$.
The graph of $E_{Mg^{2+}/Mg}$ *vs* $\log[Mg^{2+}]$ is **NCERT Exemplar**

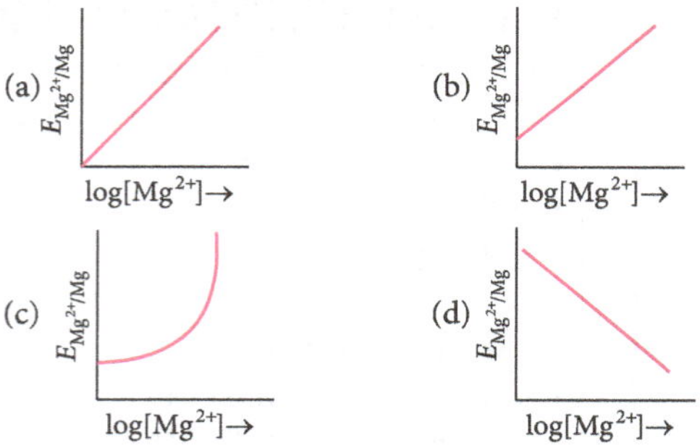

3. Standard electrode potential for Sn^{4+}/Sn^{2+} couple is +0.15 V and that for the Cr^{3+}/Cr couple is −0.74V. The two couples in their standard states are connected to make a cell. The cell potential will be **CBSE 2025**

(a) +1.19 V (b) +0.89 V
(c) + 0.18V (d) +1.83 V

4. At the time of equilibrium inside the Daniell cell, Nernst equation can be expressed as **Diksha**

(a) $0 = E^\circ_{cell} - \frac{2.303\,RT}{nF} \log \frac{[Zn^{2+}]}{[Cu^{2+}]}$

(b) $E_{cell} = 0 - \frac{2.303\,RT}{nF} \log \frac{[Zn^{2+}]}{[Cu^{2+}]}$

(c) $0 = E^\circ - \frac{2.303\,RT}{nF} \log \frac{[Cu^{2+}]}{[Zn^{2+}]}$

(d) $E_{cell} = E^\circ_{cell} - \frac{2.303\,RT}{nF} \log \frac{[Zn^{2+}]}{[Cu^{2+}]}$

5. The electrochemical cell made up of Zn and Cu half-cell is called Daniell cell. The emf of a Daniell cell is 1.10 V. **Competency Based Que.**

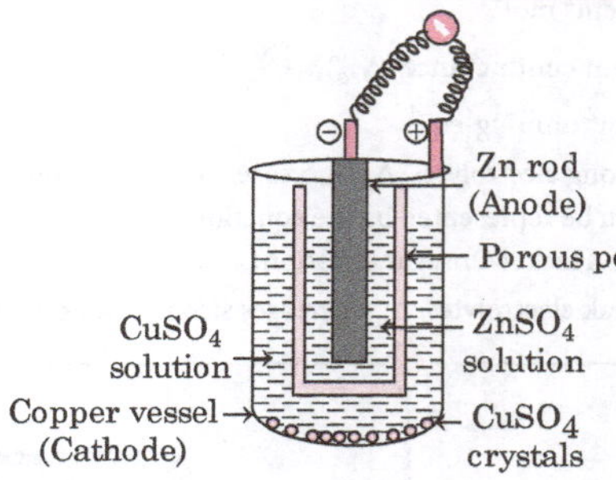

When an external voltage greater than 1.10 V is applied to this cell, which of the following change will be observed in the cell?

(a) Zn electrode will act as an anode.
(b) Current will flow from Cu half cell to Zn half cell.
(c) Electrochemical cell continue to work fast.
(d) Cell will act as electrolytic cell.

6. Calculate the equilibrium constant for the reaction,

$$Zn(s) + Cu^{2+}(aq) \longrightarrow Zn^{2+}(aq) + Cu(s)$$

[Given, $E^\circ_{cell} = 1.1$ V]

(a) 2×10^{32} (b) 2×10^{34} (c) 2×10^{37} (d) 2×10^{39}

7. In the given reaction,

$$2Cu^{+}(aq) \rightleftharpoons Cu^{2+}(aq) + Cu(s)$$

$E^\circ_{Cu^{+}/Cu} = 0.62$ V and $E^\circ_{Cu^{+}/Cu} = 0.26$ V

Find out the equilibrium constant.

(a) 2.76×10^2 (b) 1.2×10^4
(c) 1.2×10^6 (d) 2.76×10^8

8. A voltaic cell is made by connecting two half cells represented by half equations below

$$Sn^{2+}(aq) + 2e^- \longrightarrow Sn(s);\ E^\circ = -0.14 \text{ V}$$
$$Fe^{3+}(aq) + e^- \longrightarrow Fe^{2+}(aq);\ E^\circ = +0.77 \text{ V}$$

Which statement is correct about this voltaic cell?

(a) Fe^{2+} is oxidised and the voltage of the cell is −0.91 V.
(b) Sn is oxidised and the voltage of the cell is 0.91 V.
(c) Fe^{2+} is oxidised and the voltage of the cell is 0.91 V.
(d) Sn is oxidised and the voltage of the cell is 0.63 V.

9. **Which metal cannot replace H_2 from hydrochloric acid?**

(a) Zn (b) Cu (c) Mg (d) Al

10. **Arrange the following species in the increasing order of their reducing power on the basis of standard electrode potential values given below.**

(I) $K^+ / K = -2.93$ V

(II) $Ni^{2+} / Ni = -0.25$ V

(III) $Ag^+ / Ag = 0.80$ V

(a) I < II < III (b) II < III < I
(c) III < II < I (d) III < I < II

11. **Which of the following option will be the limiting molar conductivity of CH_3COOH if the limiting molar conductivity of CH_3COONa is 91 S $cm^2 mol^{-1}$? Limiting molar conductivity for individual ions are given in the following table.** **CBSE SQP 2021**

S.No.	Ions	Limiting molar conductivity (S $cm^2 mol^{-1}$)
1	H^+	349.6
2	Na^+	50.1
3	K^+	73.5
4	OH^-	199.1

(a) 350 S $cm^2 mol^{-1}$ (b) 375.3 S $cm^2 mol^{-1}$
(c) 390.5 S $cm^2 mol^{-1}$ (d) 340.4 S $cm^2 mol^{-1}$

12. **Dilution affects both conductivity as well as molar conductivity. Effect of dilution on both is as follows.** **CBSE 2024**

(a) Both increase with dilution.
(b) Both decreases with dilution.
(c) Conductivity increases whereas molar conductivity decreases on dilution.
(d) Conductivity decreases whereas molar conductivity increases on dilution.

13. **There are two beakers 'A' and 'B' containing KCl and CH_3COOH solutions, respectively. On adding water to beakers A and B, which of the following change in Λ_m of the solutions will be correct?** **Competency Based Que.**

(a) It increases sharply in beaker *A* and slowly in beaker *B*.
(b) It increases slowly in beaker *A* and sharply in beaker *B*.
(c) It decreases in beaker *A* but no change in beaker *B*.
(d) There is no change in beaker *A* but it decreases slowly in beaker *B*.

14. **Kohlrausch give the following relation for strong electrolytes.**

$$\Lambda_m = \Lambda_m^\circ - A\sqrt{C}$$

Which of the following equality holds? **CBSE 2020, 2023**

(a) $\Lambda = \Lambda_m$ as $C \longrightarrow \sqrt{A}$ (b) $\Lambda = \Lambda_m$ as $C \longrightarrow \infty$
(c) $\Lambda = \Lambda_m$ as $C \longrightarrow 0$ (d) $\Lambda = \Lambda_m$ as $C \longrightarrow 1$

15. **Which of the following solutions of KCl will have the highest value of molar conductivity?** **CBSE 2023**

(a) 0.01 M (b) 1 M (c) 0.5 M (d) 0.1 M

16. **The molar ionic conductivities of Al^{3+} and SO_4^{2-} are 189 S cm^2 mol^{-1} and 160 S $cm^2 mol^{-1}$ respectively. The value of limiting molar conductivity of $Al_2(SO_4)_3$ will be** **CBSE 2024**

(a) 198 S cm^2 mol^{-1} (b) 858 S cm^2 mol^{-1}
(c) 588 S cm^2 mol^{-1} (d) 891 S cm^2 mol^{-1}

17. **Match the following Column I with Column II and choose the correct option using the codes given below.**

	Column I		Column II
A.	Faraday's first law	(i)	$\frac{W_1}{E_1} = \frac{W_2}{E_2}$
B.	Faraday's second law	(ii)	$W \times Q$
C.	Faraday's constant	(iii)	$i \times t$
D.	Q	(iv)	96500 C mol^{-1}

Choose the correct option among the given options.

Codes

	A	B	C	D
(a)	(ii)	(i)	(iv)	(iii)
(b)	(i)	(ii)	(iii)	(iv)
(c)	(ii)	(i)	(iii)	(iv)
(d)	(iii)	(i)	(ii)	(iv)

18. **The quantity of charge required to obtain one mole of aluminium from Al_2O_3 is ....** **NCERT Exemplar**

(a) 1 F (b) 3 F (c) 6 F (d) 2 F

Or **The charge required for the reduction of 1 mol of Al^{3+} to Al will** **Diksha**

(a) 1 F (b) 3 F (c) 27 F (d) 13 F

19. **An electrolytic cell contains alumina. If we have to obtain 50 g Al by using 105 A of current, the time required is**

(a) 1.54 h (b) 2.15 h (c) 1.42 h (d) 1.32 h

20. **1.5 A current is flowing through a metallic wire. If it flows for 3 h, how many electrons would flow through the wire?**

(a) 2.05×10^{22} electrons (b) 1.0×10^{23} electrons
(c) 10^{24} electrons (d) 4.5×10^{23} electrons

21. **6 A current with 75% efficiency is passed through a cell for 6 h? ($Z = 4 \times 10^{-4}$). The amount of metal deposited will be**

(a) 22.4 g (b) 36.0 g (c) 32.4 g (d) 38.8 g

22. **Anode in the Leclanche cell is**

(a) zinc container (b) graphite electrode
(c) carbon (d) $MnO_2 + C$

23. **In a lead storage battery** CBSE 2020

(a) PbO_2 is reduced to $PbSO_4$ at the cathode
(b) Pb is oxidised to $PbSO_4$ at the anode
(c) Both electrodes are immersed in the same aqueous solution of H_2SO_4
(d) All the above are true

24. **How many Faradays are required to reduce 1 mole of MnO_4^- to Mn^{2+}?** CBSE 2023

(a) 4 (b) 3 (c) 6 (d) 5

25. **Which of the following cell was used in Apollo space programme?** CBSE 2023, 2024 C

(a) Mercury cell (b) H_2—O_2 fuel cell
(c) Dry cell (d) Ni-Cd cell

26. **Four half reactions I to IV are shown below.** CBSE 2023

I. $2Cl^- \longrightarrow Cl_2 + 2e^-$
II. $4OH^- \longrightarrow O_2 + 2H_2O + 2e^-$
III. $Na^+ + e^- \longrightarrow Na$
IV. $2H^+ + 2e^- \longrightarrow H_2$

Which two of these reactions are most likely to occur when concentrated brine is electrolysed?

(a) I and III (b) I and IV
(c) II and III (d) II and IV

Assertion-Reason [1 Mark]

Directions (Q. Nos. 27-39) In the following questions an Assertion (A) is followed by a corresponding Reason (R). Use the following keys to choose the appropriate answer.

(a) Both (A) and (R) are true and (R) is the correct explanation of (A).
(b) Both (A) and (R) are true, but (R) is not the correct explanation of (A).
(c) (A) is true, but (R) is false.
(d) (A) is false, but (R) is true.

27. **Assertion** (A) 96500 C charge is required for the reduction of one mole of silver ions.

Reason (R) The amount of electricity (or charge) required for oxidation or reduction depends on the stoichiometry of the electrode reaction.

28. **Assertion** (A) $E_{Ag^+/Ag}$ increases with increase in concentration of Ag^+ ions.

Reason (R) $E_{Ag^+/Ag}$ has a positive value.

29. **Assertion** (A) E_{cell} should have positive value for the cell to function. NCERT Exemplar

Reason (R) $E_{anode} > E_{cathode}$.

30. **Assertion** (A) Copper is less reactive than zinc and hydrogen.

Reason (R) The value of $E^\circ_{Cu^{2+}/Cu}$ is negative.

31. **Assertion** (A) For a Daniell cell, $Zn|Zn^{2+}(1\ M) || Cu^{2+}(1\ M)|Cu$ with E° cell = 1.1 V, if the external opposing potential is more than 1.1 V, the electrons flow from Cu to Zn.

Reason (R) Cell acts like a galvanic cell. CBSE 2024

32. **Assertion** (A) For measuring resistance of an ionic solution an AC source is used.

Reason (R) Concentration of ionic solution will change if DC source is used. NCERT Exemplar

33. **Assertion** (A) For strong electrolytes, there is a slow increase in molar conductivity with dilution and can be represented by the equation.

$$\Lambda_m^\circ = \Lambda_m - AC^{1/2}$$

Reason (R) The value of the constant 'A' for NaCl, $CaCl_2$ and $MgSO_4$ in a given solvent at a given temperature is different. CBSE SQP 2025

34. **Assertion** (A) Conductivity decreases with decrease in concentration of electrolyte.

Reason (R) Number of ions per unit volume that carry the current in a solution decreases on dilution. CBSE 2023

35. **Assertion** (A) Λ_m for weak electrolytes shows a sharp decrease when the electrolytic solution is diluted.

Reason (R) For weak electrolytes, degree of dissociation increases with dilution of solution. CBSE 2023

36. **Assertion** (A) Electrolysis of aqueous solution of NaCl gives chlorine gas at anode instead of oxygen gas.

Reason (R) Formation of oxygen gas at anode requires overpotential. CBSE 2023

37. **Assertion** (A) Mercury cells give a constant voltage throughout its life.

Reason (R) Electrolyte KOH is not involved in the reaction.

38. **Assertion** (A) H_2—O_2 fuel cell gives a constant voltage throughout its life.

Reason (R) In this fuel cell, H_2 reacts with OH^- ions yet the overall concentration of OH^- ions does not change.

39. **Assertion** (A) Galvanised iron does not rust.

Reason (R) Zinc has a more negative electrode potential than iron.

Case-Study [4 Marks]

40. **Read the passage given below and answer the following questions.**

Oxidation-reduction reactions are commonly known as redox reactions. They involve transfer of electrons from one species to another. In a spontaneous

reaction, energy is released which can be used to do useful work. The reaction is split into two half reactions. Two different containers are used and a wire is used to drive the electrons from one side to the other and a Voltaic/Galvanic cell is created.

In this cell, chemical energy of a redox reaction is converted into electrical energy. The simplest galvanic cell is in which Zn rod is dipped in a solution of $ZnSO_4$ and Cu rod is placed in a solution of $CuSO_4$. The two rods are connected by a metallic wire through a voltmeter. The two solutions are joined by a salt bridge. The difference between the two electrode potentials of the two electrodes is known as electromotive force.

If E°_{cell} is positive, the reaction is spontaneous and if it is negative, the reaction is non-spontaneous and is referred to as electrolytic cell. The process of electrolysis refers to the decomposition of a substance by an electric current. One mole of electric charge when passed through a cell will discharge half a mole of a divalent metal ion such as Cu^{2+}. This was first formulated by Faraday in the form of laws of electrolysis.

The conductance is the property of materials due to which a material allows the flow of ions through itself and thus conducts electricity. Conductivity is represented by κ and it depends upon nature and concentration of electrolyte, temperature, etc.

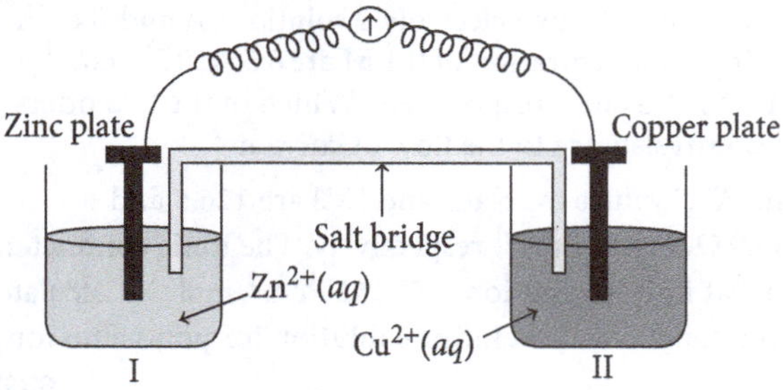

(i) (a) What will happen to the concentration of Zn^{2+} and Cu^{2+}, when $E_{cell} = 0$?

(b) Why does conductivity of a solution decreases with dilution?

(ii) Which plate is going to act as cathode of the cell?

(a) Zn (b) Cu
(c) Both of these (d) None of these

(iii) When does electrochemical cell behaves like an electrolytic cell?

(a) $E_{ext} > E_{cell}$
(b) $E_{ext} < E_{cell}$
(c) $E_{ext} = E_{cell}$
(d) $E_{ext} = 0$

Or

How much charge in terms of Faraday required for the conversion of 1 mol of H_2O to O_2?

(a) 1F (b) 2F
(c) 3F (d) 4F

41. **Read the passage given below and answer the following questions.**

Rahul set-up an experiment to find resistance of aqueous KCl solution for different concentrations at 298 K using a conductivity cell connected to a Wheatstone bridge. He fed the Wheatstone bridge with a.c. power in the audio frequency range 550 to 5000 cycles per second.

Once the resistance was calculated from null point he also calculated the conductivity (κ) and molar conductivity (Λ_m) and recorded his readings in tabular form.

S.No.	Conc. (M)	κ(S cm^{-1})	Λ_m(Scm^{2}mol^{-1})
1.	1.00	111.3×10^{-3}	111.3
2.	0.10	12.9×10^{-3}	129.0
3.	0.01	1.41×10^{-3}	141.0

CBSE 2023

(i) Why does conductivity decrease with dilution ?

(ii) If Λ°_m of KCl is 150.0 S cm^2 mol^{-1}. Calculate the degree of dissociation of 0.01 M KCl.

(iii) If Rahul had used HCl instead of KCl, then would you expect the Λ_m values to be more or less than those per KCl for a given concentration. Justify.

Or Amit, a classmate of Rahul repeated the same experiment with CH_3COOH solution instead of KCl solution.

Give one point that would be similar and one that would be different in his observations as compared to Rahul.

Subjective Type Questions

Short Answer Type I Questions [2 Marks]

1. In a standard hydrogen electrode (SHE), the platinum wire is normally dipped in 1 M conc. HCl solution.

Find out the potential of SHE if the platinum wire is dipped in a solution containing 1×10^{-10} M, H^+ concentration. **Competency Based Que.**

2. Calculate the emf of the following cell

$Ni(s) + 2Ag^+(0.01\text{ M}) \longrightarrow Ni^{2+}(0.1\text{ M}) + 2Ag(s)$

Given that, $E^\circ_{cell} = 1.05$ V, $\log 10 = 1$ **CBSE 2024**

3. The emf of a cell corresponding to the reaction, $Zn(s) + 2H^+(aq) \longrightarrow Zn^{2+}(0.1\text{ M}) + H_2(g, 1\text{ atm})$ is 0.28 V at 25°C.

Write the half-cell reaction and calculate the pH of the solution at the hydrogen electrode.

$$E^\circ_{Zn^{2+}/Zn} = -0.76\text{ V}, E^\circ_{H^+/H_2} = 0$$

4. Observe the following cell and answer the questions that follow : **CBSE SQP 2025**

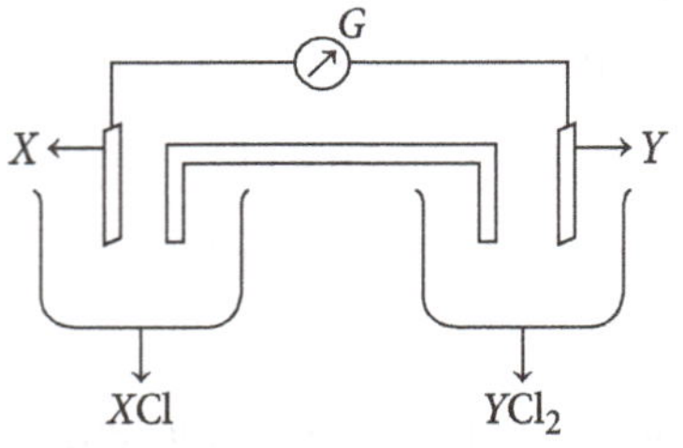

(a) Represent the cell shown in the figure.

(b) Name the carriers of the current in the salt bridge.

(c) Write the reaction taking place at the anode.

5. For an experiment, Aman prepared a 1 litre $FeSO_4$ solution of 1M concentration and stored the solution in a glass jar. Before starting the experiment, Aman wants to stir the solution. Which of the following spoons should he use for this purpose and why?

Aluminium spoon ($Al^{3+}/Al = -1.66$ V)

Copper spoon ($Cu^{2+}/Cu = 0.34$ V)

[Given : E°/V($Fe^{2+}/Fe = -0.44$ V)]

Competency Based Que.

6. The molar conductivity (Λ_m) of KCl solution, at different concentration at 298 K, is plotted as shown in the figure given below.

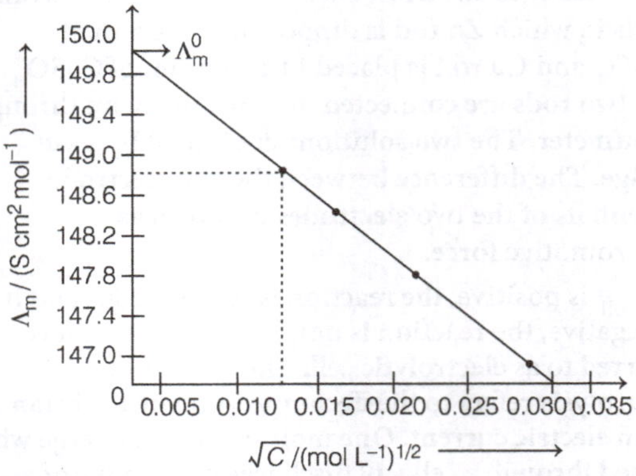

Determine the value of Λ°_m and A for KCl.

7. Which of the following solutions has larger molar conductance?

(i) 0.08 M solution having conductivity equal to $2.0 \times 10^{-2}\ \Omega^{-1}\ cm^{-1}$.

(ii) 0.10 M solution having resistivity equal to 58 Ω cm.

8. Conductivity of two electrolyte solutions *A* and *B* each having a concentration of 0.1 M are 8.5×10^{-2} S cm^{-1} and 4.1×10^{-4} S cm^{-1} respectively. Which of the two offers greater resistance to the flow of current ?

9. The Λ°_m values for NaCl and KCl are 126.5 and 149.9 $\Omega^{-1}\ cm^2\ mol^{-1}$ respectively. The ionic conductance of Na^+ at infinite dilution is 50.1 $\Omega^{-1} cm^2\ mol^{-1}$. Calculate the ionic conductance at infinite dilution for potassium ion (K^+). **CBSE 2024**

10. Account for the following:

(i) On the basis of E° values, O_2 gas should be liberated at anode but it is Cl_2 gas which is liberated in the electrolysis of aqueous NaCl.

(ii) Conductivity of CH_3COOH decreases on dilution. **CBSE 2025**

11. One Faraday of electric charge is passed through the electrolytic cells placed in a series containing solution of Ag^+, Cu^{2+}, Al^{3+}, respectively. Find out the simple mass ratio of the metals deposited at the respective electrodes.

(Given : Atomic mass Ag = 108 g mol^{-1}, Cu = 63.5 g mol^{-1}, Al=27 g mol^{-1}) **Competency Based Que.**

12. One half-cell in a voltaic cell is constructed from a silver wire dipped in silver nitrate solution of unknown concentration. The other half-cell consists of a zinc electrode in a 0.10 M solution of $Zn(NO_3)_2$. A voltage of 1.48 V is measured for this cell. Use this information to calculate the concentration of silver nitrate solution.
[Given, $E^\circ_{Zn^{2+}/Zn} = -0.763$ V, $E^\circ_{Ag^+/Ag} = +0.80$V]

13. Define the following terms. **CBSE 2024**
(i) Limiting molar conductivity (Λ°_m)
(ii) Fuel cell

14. Define the following terms. **CBSE 2024**
(i) Faraday's second law of electrolysis
(ii) Corrosion

15. How is galvanisation different from cathodic protection of iron?

16. Calculate emf of the following cell, **CBSE 2023**
$Zn(s)|Zn^{2+}(0.1\ M)||(0.01\ M)Ag^+|Ag(s)$
Given : $E^\circ_{Zn^{2+}/Zn} = -0.76$ V, $E^\circ_{Ag^+/Ag} = +0.80$ V
[Given : log 10 = 1]

17. Consider the figure and answer the following questions.

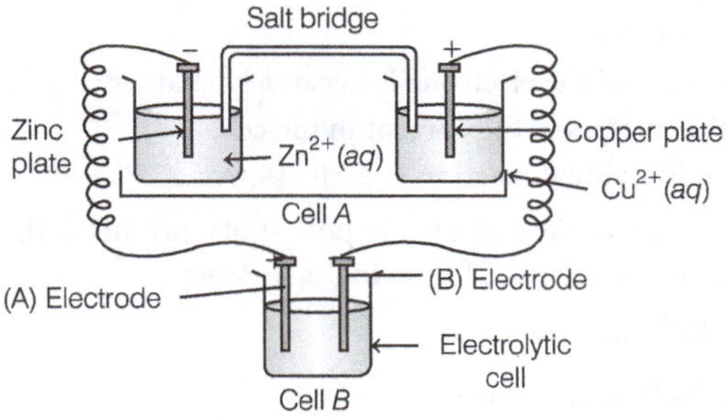

(i) Cell 'A' has $E_{cell} = 2$V and Cell 'B' has $E_{cell} = 1.1$ V. Which of the two cells 'A' or 'B' will act as an electrolytic cell. Which electrode reactions will occur in this cell?
(ii) If cell 'A' has $E_{cell} = 0.5$V and cell 'B' has $E_{cell} = 1.1$V then what will be the reactions at anode and cathode?

18. A strip of nickel metal is placed in a 1 molar solution of $Ni(NO_3)_2$ and a strip of silver metal is placed in a one molar solution of $AgNO_3$. An electrochemical cell is created when the two solutions are connected by a salt bridge and the two strips are connected by wires to a voltmeter.
(i) Write the balanced equations for the overall reaction occurring in the cell.
(ii) Calculate the cell potential E, at 25° C for the cell, if the initial concentration of $Ni(NO_3)_2$ is 0.100 molar and the initial concentration of $AgNO_3$ is 1.00 molar.
[$E^\circ_{Ni^{2+}/Ni} = -0.25$ V, $E^\circ_{Ag^+/Ag} = 0.80$ V, $\log 10^{-1} = -1$]

Short Answer Type II Questions [3 Marks]

19. (i) Calculate the strength of the current required to deposit 1.2 g of magnesium from molten $MgCl_2$ in 1 h. [1 F = 96500 C mol^{-1}, atomic mass of Mg = 24.0]
(ii) An electric current of 0.15 A is passed through 500 mL of 0.15 M copper sulphate solution. How much time is required to deposit all the copper?

20. Calculate $\Delta_r(G^\circ)$ and $\log K_C$ of the reaction:
$$Fe^{2+}(aq) + Ag^+(aq) \longrightarrow Fe^{3+}(aq) + Ag(s)$$
Given : $E^\circ_{Ag^+/Ag} = 0.80$V, $E^\circ_{Fe^{3+}/Fe^{2+}} = 0.77$V
[$R = 8.314 JK^{-1} mol^{-1}$, $F = 96500$ C mol^{-1}] **CBSE 2025**

21. Calculate $\Delta_r G^\circ$ and $\log K_C$ of the reaction.
$$2Cr(s) + 3Cd^{2+}(aq.) \longrightarrow 2Cr^{3+}(aq.) + 3Cd(s)$$
Given, $E^\circ_{Cr^{3+}/Cr} = -0.74$ V
$E^\circ_{Cd^{2+}/Cd} = -0.40$ V
[$R = 8.314 JK^{-1} mol^{-1}$, $F = 96500 C mol^{-1}$] **CBSE 2025**

22. Resistance of a conductivity cell filled with 0.2 mol L^{-1} KCl solution is 200 Ω. If the resistance of the same cell when filled with 0.05 mol L^{-1} KCl solution is 620 Ω, calculate the conductivity and molar conductivity of 0.05 mol L^{-1} KCl solution. The conductivity of 0.2 mol L^{-1} KCl solution is 0.0248 S cm^{-1}. **CBSE 2024**

23. Conductivity of 2×10^{-3} M methanoic acid is 8×10^{-5} S cm^{-1}. Calculate its molar conductivity and degree of dissociation if Λ°_m for methanoic acid is 404 S cm^2 mol^{-1}. **CBSE 2024 C**

24. Chromium metal is electroplated using an acidic solution containing CrO_3 according to the following equation
$$CrO_3(aq) + 6H^+ + 6e^- \longrightarrow Cr(s) + 3H_2O$$
Calculate how many grams of chromium will be electroplated by 24,000 coulombs. How long will it take to electroplate 1.5 g chromium using 12.5 A current?
[Atomic mass of Cr = 52 g mol^{-1}, 1 F = 965000 C mol^{-1}] **CBSE 2019**

25. Calculate the standard free energy change taking place in H_2-O_2 fuel cell in which the following reactions occur.

(i) $O_2 + 4H^+ + 4e^- \longrightarrow 2H_2O$; $E^\circ = 1.229$ V

(ii) $2H_2 \longrightarrow 4H^+ + 4e^-$; $E^\circ = 0.000$ V

26. (i) What should be the signs (positive/negative) for E°_{cell} and ΔG° for a spontaneous redox reaction occurring under standard conditions?

(ii) State Faraday's first law of electrolysis. **CBSE 2023, 2025**

27. A lead-storage cell can act both as galvanic and electrolytic cells. Explain.

28. In the electrolysis of sulphuric acid, there are two possible anodic reactions

$2H_2O(l) \longrightarrow O_2(g) + 4H^+(aq) + 4e^-, E^\circ = 1.23$ V

$2SO_4^{2-}(aq) \longrightarrow S_2O_8^{2-}(aq) + 2e^-, \quad E^\circ = 1.96$ V

Which reaction occurs at anode and why?

Long Answer Type Questions [5 Marks]

29. (i) Calculate the emf of the following cell at 298 K

$Al(s)|Al^{3+}(0.001M)||Ni^{2+}(0.1M)|Ni(s)$ [Given : $E^\circ_{Al^{3+}/Al} = -1.66V, E^\circ_{Ni^{2+}/Ni} = -0.25V$, log 10 = 1]

(ii) With the help of a graph explain why it is not possible to determine Λ°_m for a weak electrolyte by extrapolating the molar conductivity (Λ_m) *versus* $C^{1/2}$ curve as for strong electrolyte. **CBSE 2023**

30. (i) The molar conductivities of NH_4^+ and Cl^- ion are 73.8 S cm^2 mol^{-1} and 76.2 S cm^2 mol^{-1} respectively. The conductivity of 0.1M NH_4Cl is 1.29×10^{-2}S cm^{-1}. Calculate its molar conductivity and degree of dissociation.

(ii) Calculate the half-cell potential at 298 K for the reaction

$$Zn^{2+} + 2e^- \longrightarrow Zn$$

if $[Zn^{2+}] = 0.1$ M and $E^\circ_{Zn^{2+}/Zn} = -0.76$ V. **CBSE 2023**

31. (i) Calculate the emf of the following cell at 25°C.

$Zn(s)|Zn^{2+}(0.1M)||H^+(0.01\ M)|H_2(g)(1\ bar), Pt(s)$

[Given : $E^\circ_{Zn^{2+}/Zn} = -0.76$ V, $E^\circ_{H^+/H_2} = 0.00$ V, log 10 = 1]

(ii) State Kohlrausch law of independent migration of ions. Why does the conductivity of a solute decreases with dilution ? **CBSE 2023**

32. (i) When a bright silver object is placed in the solution of gold chloride, it acquires a golden tinge but nothing happens when it is placed in a solution of copper chloride. Explain this behaviour of silver.

[Given: $E^\circ_{Cu^{2+}/Cu} = +0.34$; $E^\circ_{Ag^+/Ag} = +0.80$ V, $E^\circ_{Au^{3+}/Au} = +1.40$ V]

(ii)

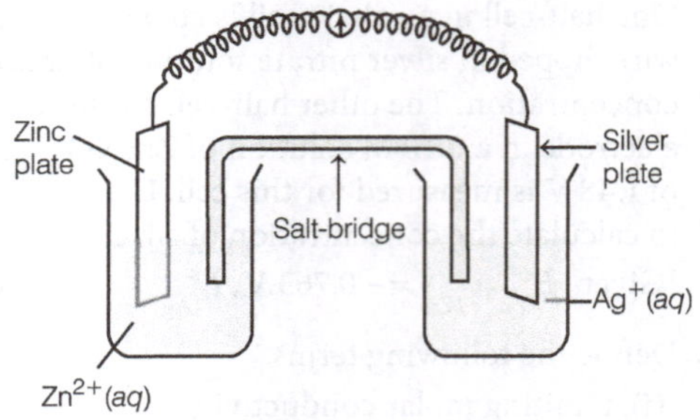

Consider the figure given above and answer the following questions

(a) What is the direction of flow of electrons?

(b) Which one is anode and which one is cathode?

(c) What will happen if the salt-bridge is removed?

(d) How will concentration of Zn^{2+} and Ag^+ ions be affected when the cell functions?

(e) How will concentration of these ions be affected when the cell becomes dead?

33. Depict the galvanic cell in which the reaction

$Zn(s) + 2Ag^+(aq) \longrightarrow Zn^{2+}(aq) + 2Ag(s)$

takes place.

Further show

(i) which of the electrode is negatively charged?

(ii) the carriers of the current in the cell.

(iii) an individual reaction at each electrode. **NCERT**

34. Using the standard electrode potentials, predict if the reaction between the following is feasible.

(i) $Fe^{3+}(aq)$ and $I^-(aq)$

(ii) $Ag^+(aq)$ and $Cu(s)$

(iii) $Fe^{3+}(aq)$ and $Br^-(aq)$

(iv) $Ag(s)$ and $Fe^{3+}(aq)$

(v) $Br_2(aq)$ and $Fe^{2+}(aq)$

Given standard electrode potentials,

$E^\circ_{1/2\,I_2, I^-} = 0.541$ V, $E^\circ_{Cu^{2+},Cu} = 0.34$ V,

$E^\circ_{1/2\,Br_2, Br^-} = 1.09$ V, $E^\circ_{Ag^+, Ag} = 0.80$ V

$E^\circ_{Fe^{3+}, Fe^{2+}} = 0.77$ V **NCERT**

35. (i) Write the anode and cathode reactions and the overall cell reaction occurring in a lead storage battery during its use.

(ii) Calculate the potential for half-cell containing 0.01 M. $K_2Cr_2O_7(aq)$, 0.01M $Cr^{2+}(aq)$ and 10×10^{-4}M$H^+(aq)$ The half-cell reaction is

$Cr_2O_7^{2-}(aq) + 14H^+(aq) + 6e^- \rightarrow 2Cr^{3+}(aq) + 7H_2O(l)$

and the standard electrode potential is given as $E^\circ = 1.38$V [Given: log 10 = 1] **CBSE 2025**

36. (i) State Kohlrausch law. **CBSE 2025**

(ii) Calculate the emf of the following cell at 298 K.

$Al(s)|Al^{3+}$ (0.15M) $||Cu^{2+}$ (0.025 M$|Cu(s)$

(Given: $E^{\circ}_{(Al^{3+}/Al)} = -1.66$ V, $E^{\circ}_{(Cu^{2+}/Cu)} = 0.34$V

$\log 0.15 = -0.8239$, $\log 0.025 = -1.6020$ **CBSE SQP 2021**

37. (i) On the basis of E° values, identify which amongst the following is the strongest oxidising agent?

$$Cl_2(g) + 2e^- \longrightarrow 2Cl^-;\ E^{\circ} = +1.36\text{ V}$$

$$MnO_4^- + 8H^+ + 5e^- \longrightarrow Mn^{2+} + 4H_2O;\ E^{\circ} = 1.51\text{ V}$$

$$Cr_2O_7^{2-} + 14H^+ + 6e^- \longrightarrow 2Cr^{3+} + 7H_2O;\ E^{\circ} = +1.33\text{ V}$$

(ii) The following figure, represents variation of (Λ_m) *vs* $\sqrt{C}$ for an electrolyte. Here Λ_m is the molar conductivity and C is the concentration of the electrolyte.

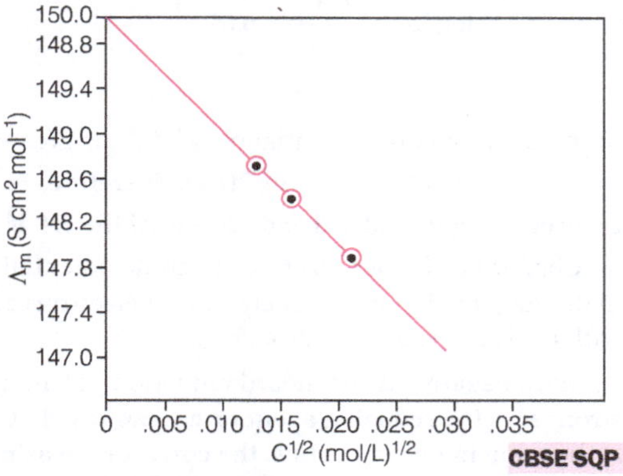

CBSE SQP 2021

(a) Define molar conductivity.

(b) Identify the nature of electrolyte on the basis of the above plot. Justify your answer.

(c) Determine the value of Λ_m for the electrolyte.

(d) Show how to calculate the value of *A* for the electrolyte using the above graph.

38. Look at the diagram and answer the questions that follow. **Competency Based Que.**

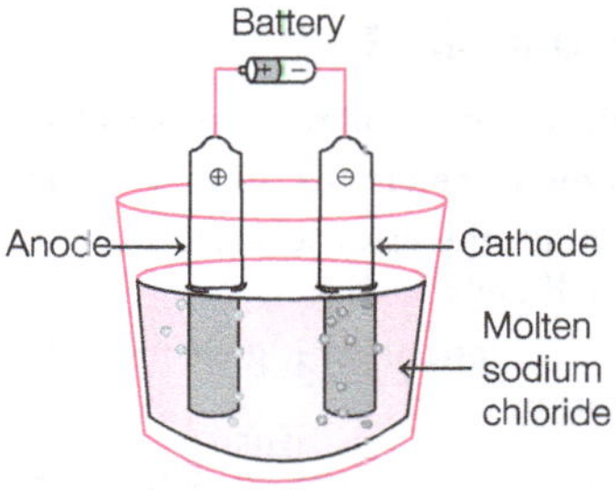

(i) Identify the ion(s) moving towards the cathode. Give a reason for your choice.

(ii) What is the expected product at the anode? Write the reaction (s) occuring at the anode.

(iii) Write the net reaction of the process seen in the above diagram.

(iv) State the laws that govern the above process.

39. Three electrolytic cells *A*, *B* and *C* containing solutions of zinc sulphate, silver nitrate and copper sulphate, respectively are connected in series.

A steady current of 1.5 A was passed through them until 1.45 g of silver deposited at the cathode of cell *B*. How long did the current flow? What mass of copper and zinc were deposited in the concerned cells?

(Atomic mass of Ag = 108, Zn = 65.4, Cu = 63.5) **NCERT**

40. Explain how rusting of iron is envisaged as setting up of an electrochemical cell? **NCERT Intext**

41. Answer the following.

(i) Why hydrogen is considered as a fuel resource for future?

(ii) How can we generate energy from hydrogen fuel?

(iii) Why do we need to reduce our usage of carbonacious fuels?

Hints & Solutions

Objective Type Questions

1. (*c*) In an electrochemical process, a salt-bridge is used.
   (i) To complete the circuit, so that current can flow.
   (ii) To maintain the electrical neutrality of the solution in the half cells.

2. (*b*) Electrode potential for Mg electrode varies according to the equation

$$E_{Mg^{2+}/Mg} = E^{\circ}_{Mg^{2+}/Mg} - \frac{0.059}{2}\log\frac{1}{[Mg^{2+}]}$$

$$E_{Mg^{2+}/Mg} = E^{\circ}_{Mg^{2+}/Mg} + \frac{0.059}{2}\log[Mg^{2+}]$$

$$E_{Mg^{2+}/Mg} = \frac{0.059}{2}\log[Mg^{2+}] + E^{\circ}_{Mg^{2+}/Mg}$$

This equation represents equation of straight line. It can be correlated as

$$\underset{y}{\underset{\uparrow}{E_{Mg^{2+}/Mg}}} = \underset{m}{\underset{\uparrow}{\left(\frac{0.059}{2}\right)}} \underset{x}{\underset{\uparrow}{\log[Mg^{2+}]}} + \underset{C}{\underset{\uparrow}{E^{\circ}_{Mg^{2+}/Mg}}}$$

So, intercept $(C) = E^{\circ}_{Mg^{2+}/Mg}$

Thus, equation can be diagramatically represented as

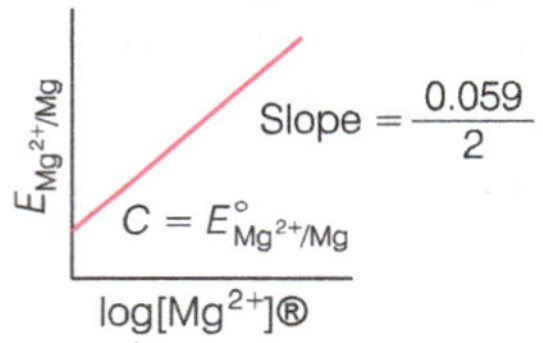

3. (*b*) E° value for $\frac{Sn^{4+}}{Sn^{2+}}$ is higher (more positive), therefore, it will act as cathode, whereas, $\frac{Cr^{3+}}{Cr}$ couple will act as anode.

$$E^{\circ}_{cell} = E^{\circ}_{cathode} - E^{\circ}_{anode}$$

$$E^{\circ}_{cell} = (+0.15) - (-0.74)$$

$$E^{\circ}_{cell} = 0.89\ V$$

4. (*a*) At equilibrium, $E_{cell} = 0$

$\therefore$ Nernst equation can be expressed as

$$0 = E^{\circ}_{cell} - \frac{2.303\ RT}{nF}\log\frac{[Zn^{2+}]}{[Cu^{2+}]}$$

5. (*d*) When an external voltage becomes greater than 1.1 V, electrons flow from Cu to Zn and current flows from Zn to Cu. Reaction starts functioning in opposite direction. Hence, this works as an electrolytic cell.

6. (*c*) $E^{\circ}_{cell} = \frac{0.059}{2}\log K_C$

$\therefore \quad \log K_C = \frac{1.1 \times 2}{0.059} = 37.288$

Thus, $\quad K_C = 2 \times 10^{37}$ at 298 K

7. (*c*) In the given reaction,

$$2Cu^{+}(aq) \rightleftharpoons Cu^{2+}(aq) + Cu(s)$$

$$E^{\circ}_{Cu^{+}/Cu} = 0.62\ V \text{ and } E^{\circ}_{Cu^{2+}/Cu} = 0.26\ V$$

$$E^{\circ}_{cell} = 0.62 - 0.26 = 0.36\ V$$

$$E_{cell} = E^{\circ}_{cell} - \frac{0.0591}{n}\log\frac{[Cu^{2+}]}{[Cu^{+}]^2} = E^{\circ}_{cell} - \frac{0.0591}{n}\log K_C$$

At equilibrium, $E_{cell} = 0V$

$$0 = E^{\circ}_{cell} - \frac{0.0591}{1}\log K_C$$

$$E^{\circ}_{cell} = 0.0591\log K_C$$

$$0.36 = 0.0591\log K_C$$

$$\log K_C = \frac{0.36}{0.0591} = 6.09$$

$$\therefore \quad K_C = 1.2 \times 10^6$$

8. (*b*) As the reduction potential of $Fe^{3+}(aq)$ is greater than the reduction potential of $Sn^{2+}(aq)$. Therefore, Fe^{3+} is reduced or Sn is oxidised and voltage of the cell is 0.91 V.

9. (*b*) Copper has higher positive electrode potential than hydrogen, making it less likely to lose electrons and react with acids to produce hydrogen gas.

10. (*c*) More negative the standard reduction potential value, stronger is the reducing agent or we can say that greater is the reducing power. Thus, the correct increasing order will be

$$\underset{(III)}{Ag^{+}/Ag} < \underset{(II)}{Ni^{2+}/Ni} < \underset{(I)}{K^{+}/K}$$

11. (*c*) Given, $\Lambda^{\circ}_{m(H^{+})} \rightarrow 349.6\ S\ cm^2 mol^{-1}$

$$\Lambda^{\circ}_{m(Na^{+})} \rightarrow 50.1\ S\ cm^2 mol^{-1}$$

$$\Lambda^{\circ}_{m(K^{+})} \rightarrow 73.5\ S\ cm^2 mol^{-1}$$

$$\Lambda^{\circ}_{m(OH^{-})} \rightarrow 199.1\ S\ cm^2 mol^{-1}$$

$$\Lambda^{\circ}_{(CH_3COONa)} \rightarrow 91\ S\ cm^2 mol^{-1}$$

Complete reaction is as follows

$$CH_3COONa + HCl \longrightarrow NaCl + CH_3COOH$$

$$\Lambda^{\circ}_{m(CH_3COOH)} = \Lambda^{\circ}_{m(CH_3COONa)} - \Lambda^{\circ}_{m(Na^{+})} + \Lambda^{\circ}_{m(H^{+})}$$

$$= 91 - 50.1 + 349.6$$

$$= 390.5\ S\ cm^2 mol^{-1}$$

12. (*d*) On dilution, conductivity decreases whereas molar conductivity increases. This can be explained as follows.

On dilution, generally the number of ions per unit volume carrying the current tends to decrease, which results in a decrease in the conductivity of the electrolytic solution.

Whereas, on dilution the total number of ions increases due to increase in the degree of dissociation. Hence, molar conductivity increases.

13. (*b*) Molar conductivity increases sharply for the weak electrolyte with increase in dilution and for strong electrolyte, it increase slightly on dilution.

Hence, for beaker *A*, it increases slowly while for beaker *B*, it increases sharply.

14. (*c*) When the concentration $(\lambda = \lambda_0)$ approaches zero (i.e. $C_0 \longrightarrow 0$), the molar conductivity reaches a limiting value known as limiting molar conductivity (Λ_m°). Thus, among the given option, (c) is correct.

15. (*a*) Molar conductivity, $\Lambda_m = \dfrac{1000 \times \kappa}{M}$

κ is same for both solutions.

$\therefore \quad \Lambda_m \propto \dfrac{1}{M}$

Thus, 0.01 M has the highest value of molar conductivity.

16. (*b*) $Al_2(SO_4)_3 \longrightarrow 2Al^{3+} + 3SO_4^{2-}$

$$\lambda_m^\circ(Al_2(SO_4)_3) = 2\lambda_m^\circ(Al^{3+}) + 3\lambda_m^\circ(SO_4^{2-})$$
$$= 2 \times (189\ S\ cm^2 mol^{-1}) + 3 \times (160\ S\ cm^2\ mol^{-1})$$
$$= 858\ S\ cm^2\ mol^{-1}$$

17. (*a*) The correct match will be

A $\rightarrow$ (ii), B $\rightarrow$ (i), C $\rightarrow$ (iv), D $\rightarrow$ (iii)

18. (*b*) The quantity of charge required to obtain one mole of aluminium from Al_2O_3 is equal to number of electrons required to convert Al_2O_3 to Al.

$$Al^{3+}(aq) + 3e^- \longrightarrow Al(s)$$

Hence, total 3F is required.

19. (*c*) $Al^{3+} + 3e^- \longrightarrow Al$

Equivalent weight of Al $= \dfrac{27}{3} = 9$

From Faraday's first law, $w = Zit = \dfrac{E}{96500} it$

$\therefore \quad t = \dfrac{50 \times 96500}{9 \times 105} = 5105.82 s = 1.42$ h

20. (*b*) Charge on one electron $= 1.6 \times 10^{-19}$ C

As, $Q = it = 1.5 \times 3 \times 3600 = 16200C$

$\therefore$ 16200C charge is on $\dfrac{1 \times 16200}{1.6 \times 10^{-19}} = 1.0 \times 10^{23}$ electrons

21. (*d*) $w = Zit = 4 \times 10^{-4} \times 6 \times \dfrac{75}{100} \times 6 \times 3600 = 38.8$ g

22. (*a*) Leclanche cell consists of zinc container, which acts as the anode.

23. (*d*) All the given statements are correct regarding lead storage battery.

24. (*d*) $MnO_4^- + 8H^+ + 5e^- \longrightarrow Mn^{2+} + 5H_2O$

Thus, 1 mole of MnO_4^- requires 5 moles of electrons = 5 Faradays.

25. (*b*) H_2—O_2 fuel cell was used in Apollo space programme.

26. (*b*) When concentrated brine is electrolysed, then following reactions occur :

At anode $\quad 2Cl^- \longrightarrow Cl_2 + 2e^-$

At cathode $Na^+ + e^- \longrightarrow Na, E^\circ = -2.71$ V

$2H^+ + 2e^- \longrightarrow H_2, E^\circ = 0$ V

The reaction with higher E° value will takes place.

Thus, $2H^+ + 2e^- \longrightarrow H_2$ reaction will occur at cathode.

27. (*a*) Both (A) and (R) are true and (R) is the correct explanation of (A).

28. (*b*) $E = E^\circ - \dfrac{0.0591}{1} \log \dfrac{1}{[Ag^+]} = E^\circ + 0.0591 \log [Ag^+]$

Therefore, $E_{Ag^+/Ag}$ increases with increase in concentration of Ag^+ ions. Hence, both (A) and (R) are true, but (R) is not the correct explanation of (A).

29. (*c*) (A) is true, but (R) is false. For reaction to be spontaneous, E_{cell} should have a positive value. This is true only when $E_{cathode} > E_{anode}$.

30. (*a*) Copper is less reactive than zinc and hydrogen because its standard electrode potential is negative, while the standard electrode potential of zinc is positive and that of hydrogen is zero.

Thus, both (A) and (R) are true and (R) is the correct explanation of (A).

31. (*c*) On applying an external voltage greater than 1.1 V in Daniell cell, the current flows in reverse direction, i.e. from Zn to Cu (cathode to anode) and electron flow from Cu to Zn. Reaction starts functioning in opposite direction. Hence, this cell works as an electrolytic cell. Thus, (A) is true, but (R) is false.

32. (a) Both (A) and (R) are true and (R) is the correct explanation of (A).

Concentration of ionic solution changes on using DC current as a source of energy while on passing AC current concentration does not change. Hence, AC source is used for measuring resistance.

33. (*d*) (A) is false, but (R) is true.

$\Lambda_m^\circ = \Lambda_m - AC^{1/2}$ is an incorrect equation, the correct equation is $\Lambda_m = \Lambda_m^\circ - AC^{1/2}$.

34. (*a*) Both (A) and (R) are true and (R) is the correct explanation of (A).

35. (*a*) Both (A) and (R) are true and (R) is the correct explanation of (A).

36. (*a*) Both (A) and (R) are true and (R) is the correct explanation of (A).

37. (*c*) Mercury cell gives the constant voltage throughout its life because the overall reaction does not involve any ion in the solution. In mercury cell, paste of KOH and ZnO is used as electrolyte. Thus, (A) is true, but (R) is false.

38. (*a*) Both (A) and (R) are true and (R) is the correct explanation of (A).

39. (a) Galvanised iron, i.e., iron coated with zinc does not rust easily so zinc has more negative electrode potential than iron. In other words, zinc is less reactive than iron. Thus, both (A) and (R) are true and (R) is the correct explanation of (A).

40. (i) (a) Increasing concentration of Zn^{2+} and decreasing concentration of Cu^{2+} reaches to an equilibrium.

(b) Conductivity of a solution decreases with dilution due to decrease in number of ions per unit volume. **(2)**

(ii) (*b*) Copper (Cu) plate will acts as a cathode of the cell. **(1)**

(iii) (*a*) An electrochemical cell behave like an electrolytic cell when $E_{ext} > E_{cell}$. If an external opposite potential is applied on the galvanic cell and increased reaction continues to take place till the opposing voltage reaches the value of 1.1 V. **(1)**

Or

(*b*) The chemical equation is

$$H_2O \longrightarrow 2H^+ + \frac{1}{2}O_2 + 2e^-$$

From above chemical equation, we can say that to reduce 1 mol of H_2O, we need two moles of electrons. Hence, we required 2 Faraday charge. **(1)**

41. (i) Refer to text on page 48. **(1)**

(ii) Given, Λ_m° of KCl $= 150.0\,S\,cm^2\,mol^{-1}$

Molarity $(M) = 0.01$ M

$$\text{Molar conductivity} = \frac{\kappa \times 1000}{\text{Molarity}}$$

and κ for 0.1 M KCl solution $= 1.41 \times 10^{-3}$ [Given]

$$\therefore \Lambda_m^c = \frac{1.41 \times 10^{-3} \times 1000}{0.01\,M} = 141\ S\,cm^2 mol^{-1}$$

$$\text{Degree of dissociation, } \alpha = \frac{\Lambda_m^c}{\Lambda_m^\circ} = \frac{141}{150} = 0.94$$ **(1)**

(iii) If Rahul had used HCl instead of KCl, then the molar conductivity will decrease as the molecular mass of KCl is greater than HCl. Also, velocity of K^+ ion is less than that of H^+ ions. **(2)**

Or One similarity between Rahul's and Amit's observations would be that the conductivity of the solution would decrease with dilution.

One difference between Rahul's and Amit's observation would be that the values of conductivity and molar conductivity would be different for the two solutions. This is because the nature of the electrolyte and the solvent used affect the conductivity and molar conductivity.

Since CH_3COOH is a weak acid, it will not dissociate completely in water, resulting in a lower conductivity and molar conductivity compared to KCl. **(2)**

Subjective Type Questions

1. $H^+ + e^- \longrightarrow \frac{1}{2}H_2$

Here, $n = 1$

Concentration $= 1 \times 10^{-10}$ M

Applying Nernst equation,

$$E = E^\circ - \frac{0.0591}{n}\log\frac{1}{[H^+]}$$

$$E = 0 - \frac{0.0591}{1}\log\frac{1}{1\times 10^{-10}}$$

$$= 0.0591 \times 10 \log 10 = 0.591 \quad (\log 10 = 1)$$

Thus, potential of standard hydrogen electrode is 0.591 V. **(2)**

2. Given, $E^\circ_{cell} = 1.05$ V, $\log 10 = 1$

Cell reaction,

$$Ni(s) + 2Ag^+\ (0.01\ M) \longrightarrow Ni^{2+}\ (0.1\ M) + 2Ag(s)$$ **(1)**

We know that,

$$E_{cell} = E^\circ_{cell} - \frac{0.0591}{2}\log\frac{[Ni^{2+}]}{[Ag^+]^2}$$

$$= 1.05 - \frac{0.0591}{2}\log\frac{(0.1)}{(0.01)^2}$$

$$= 1.05 - 0.029\log(1000) = 1.05 - 0.087$$

$$= 0.963\ V \approx 0.97\ V$$ **(1)**

3. **At cathode,** $2H^+ + 2e^- \longrightarrow H_2$

At anode, $Zn(s) \longrightarrow Zn^{2+}(aq) + 2e^-$

$$E^\circ_{cell} = E^\circ_{H^+/H_2} - E^\circ_{Zn^{2+}/Zn} = 0 - (-0.76\,V) = 0.76\ V$$ **(½)**

$$\therefore \quad E_{cell} = E^\circ_{cell} - \frac{0.0591}{2}\log\left(\frac{[Zn^{2+}]}{[H^+]^2}\right)$$

$$\Rightarrow \quad 0.28 = 0.76 - \frac{0.0591}{2}\log\frac{0.1}{[H^+]^2}$$ **(½)**

$$\Rightarrow \quad \frac{0.48 \times 2}{0.0591} = \log\frac{0.1}{[H^+]^2} = \log 0.1 - \log[H^+]^2$$

$$\Rightarrow \quad 16.243 = \log 0.1 - 2\log[H^+] = -1 - 2\log[H^+]$$

$$\Rightarrow \quad \frac{17.243}{2} = -\log[H^+]$$

$$\Rightarrow \quad 8.62 = pH \quad (\because pH = -\log[H^+])$$ **(1)**

4. (a) $X(s)|\,X^+(aq)\,||\,Y^{2+}(aq)\,|Y(s)$

(b) Ions are carrier of current in salt bridge.

(c) $X(s) \longrightarrow X^+(aq) + e^-$ **(2)**

5. Aman should use the copper spoon.

The reduction potential of aluminium is lower than Fe metal hence, aluminium spoon (metal) cannot be used as it undergoes oxidation i.e., would lose e^-.

$$Al(s) \longrightarrow Al^{3+}(aq) + 3e^-$$ **(1)**

Thus, the solution will slowly turn into aluminium sulphate and it will not serve the purpose.

Copper, on the other hand, has a reduction potential higher than Fe (both in ionic state) or we can say it is less reactive than Fe.

$$Cu^{2+} + 2e^- \longrightarrow Cu(s)$$

Moreover, Cu here is in the solid state. Hence Cu spoon can be used to stir the solution as it will not bring any change in the $FeSO_4$ solution. **(1)**

6. A plot of Λ_m(y-axis) and $\sqrt{C}$(x-axis) is shown in figure given in question. It can be seen that it is nearly a straight line. From the intercepts ($\sqrt{C} = 0$), we find that

$\Lambda_m^\circ = 150.0\,\text{S cm}^2\,\text{mol}^{-1}$ and

$A = -\text{Slope} = 87.465\,\text{S cm}^2\text{mol}^{-1}/(\text{mol L}^{-1})^{1/2}$ **(2)**

7. (i) $\Lambda_m = 250\,\Omega^{-1}\text{cm}^2\text{mol}^{-1}$ **(1)**

(ii) $\Lambda_m = 172.4\,\Omega^{-1}\,\text{cm}^2\text{mol}^{-1}$

Thus, solution (i) has larger molar conductance. **(1)**

8. $\kappa \propto \frac{1}{R}$

Hence, B will offer greater resistance. **(2)**

9. $\lambda^\circ_{K^+} = 73.5\,\Omega^{-1}\,\text{cm}^2\,\text{mol}^{-1}$ **(2)**

10. (i) Refer to text on page 53. **(1)**

(ii) Refer to text on page 48. **(1)**

11. 1 Faraday electric charge deposits 1 g equivalent of any substance on the electrodes kept in a series.

Equivalent mass of Ag $= \frac{108}{1} = 108$

Equivalent mass of Cu $= \frac{63.5}{2} = 31.75$

Equivalent mass of Al $= \frac{27}{3} = 9.0$

Hence, simple mass ratio deposited at respective electrodes are

Ag	:	Cu	:	Al
108 g	:	31.75 g	:	9.0 g
12	:	4	:	1

[Cu $= 3.527 \approx 4$] **(2)**

12. **[Ans** $= 1.24 \times 10^{-2}$ M] **(2)**

13. (i) **Limiting molar conductivity** (Λ°_m) When the concentration of the electrolyte approaches zero, then the molar conductivity is known as limiting molar conductivity. **(1)**

(ii) **Fuel cell** It is a galvanic cell in which the chemical energy from combustion of fuels like hydrogen, methane, methanol, etc., is converted into electrical energy. In this type of cells, reactants are continuously feed to the electrode which react to produce electricity. **(1)**

14. (i) **Faraday's second law of electrolysis** It states that, when the same quantity of electricity is passed through different electrolytes, the amount of different substances formed are directly proportional to their equivalent weights.

$$\frac{W_1}{E_1} = \frac{W_2}{E_2} = \frac{W_3}{E_3} = \ldots$$ **(1)**

(ii) **Corrosion** It is an electrochemical process in which a metal is oxidised to metal oxide or other salt of the metal by losing electrons to oxygen or other electronegative element and forms a coating on the metal surface. The rusting of iron, tarnishing of silver surface, development of green coating on copper and bronze are some of the examples of corrosion. **(1)**

15. Refer to text on page 57 and 58. **(2)**

16. Using Nernst equation,

$$E_{cell} = E^\circ_{cell} - \frac{0.059}{n}\log K$$

$$E^\circ_{cell} = E^\circ_{Ag^+/Ag} - E^\circ_{Zn^{2+}/Zn}$$

$$= 0.80 - (-0.76) = 0.80 + 0.76 = 1.56\text{ V}$$

At anode, $Zn \longrightarrow Zn^{2+} + 2e^-$

At cathode, $2Ag^+ + 2e^- \longrightarrow 2Ag$ **(1)**

On combining the overall equation is

$Zn(s) + 2Ag^+(aq) \longrightarrow Zn^{2+}(aq) + 2Ag(s)$

$$E_{cell} = 1.56 - \frac{0.059}{2}\log\frac{[Zn^{2+}]}{[Ag^+]^2}$$

$$= 1.56 - 0.0295\log\frac{10^{-1}}{(10^{-2})^2}$$

$$= 1.56 - 0.0295\log 10^3$$

$$= 1.56 - 0.0295 \times 3\log 10$$

$$= 1.56 - 0.0295 \times 3 = 1.56 - 0.0885$$

$E_{cell} = 1.4715$ V **(1)**

17. (i) Cell 'B' will act as electrolytic cell due to its lesser value of emf.

The electrode reactions will be

At cathode: $Zn^{2+} + 2e^- \longrightarrow Zn$

At anode: $Cu \longrightarrow Cu^{2+} + 2e^-$ **(1)**

(ii) If cell 'B' has higher emf, it acts as galvanic cell. Now it will push electrons into cell 'A'

In this case, the reactions will be

$Zn \longrightarrow Zn^{2+} + 2e^-$ (At anode)

$Cu^{2+} + 2e^- \longrightarrow Cu$ (At cathode) **(1)**

18. (i) $Ni(s) + 2Ag^+(aq) \longrightarrow Ni^{2+}(aq) + 2Ag(s)$ **(½)**

(ii) $Ni(NO_3)_2 \longrightarrow Ni^{2+} + 2NO_3^-$

$Ag(NO_3)_3 \longrightarrow Ag^+ + 3NO_3^-$

$Ni(s) + 2Ag^+(aq.) \longrightarrow Ni^{2+}(aq.) + 2Ag(s)$ **(½)**

$E^\circ_{cell} = E^\circ_{Ag^+/Ag} - E^\circ_{Ni^{2+}/Ni} = 0.80 - (-0.25) = 1.05$ V

$$\therefore E_{cell} = E^\circ_{cell} - \frac{0.0591}{n}\log\frac{[Ni^{2+}]}{[Ag^+]^2} \quad (\because n = 2)$$

$$= 1.05 - \frac{0.0591}{2}\log\frac{0.1}{1^2} = 1.0795 \text{ V}$$ (1)

19. (i) [**Hint** $Q = i \times t$]; [**Ans.** = 2.68 A] (1)

(ii) Given, molarity = 0.15 M, volume = 500 mL

$$\overset{(+2)}{CuSO_4} \longrightarrow \overset{(0)}{Cu(s)},\ n = 2$$

$$M \times V \times n = \text{gram eq.}$$

$$0.15 \times \frac{500}{1000} \times 2 = \text{gram eq.} \quad ...(i)$$

As, $W = Zit$

$$\text{gram eq.} = \frac{it}{96500} = \frac{0.15 \times t}{96500} \quad ...(ii)$$

From (i) and (ii)

$$0.15 \times \frac{500}{1000} \times 2 = \frac{0.15 \times t}{96500}$$

$$\Rightarrow t = 96500 \text{ sec.}$$ (2)

20. $E^\circ_{Ag^+/Ag} = 0.80\text{V} = E^\circ_{cathode}$

$E^\circ_{Fe^{3+}/Fe^{2+}} = 0.77 \text{ V} = E^\circ_{anode}$

$E^\circ_{cell} = E^\circ_{cathode} - E^\circ_{anode} = (0.80 - 0.77)\text{V}$

$E^\circ_{cell} = 0.03\text{V}$

$\Rightarrow \Delta_r G^\circ = -nFE^\circ_{cell}$

Here, $n = 1, F = 96500 \text{ C mol}^{-1}$

$\therefore \Delta_r G^\circ = -1 \times 96500 \times 0.03 = -2895$ J/mol

Also, $E^\circ_{cell} = \frac{0.059}{n}\log K_C$

$$\log K_C = \frac{n \times E^\circ_{cell}}{0.059} = \frac{1 \times 0.03}{0.059} = 0.508$$ (3)

21. $\Delta_r G^\circ = -196860$ J/mol or -1960.860 kJ/mol

$\log K_C = 34.5763.$ (3)

22 Given, for 0.2 mol L^{-1} KCl solution,

Conductivity, $\kappa = 0.0248 \text{ S cm}^{-1}$

Resistance, $R = 200\,\Omega$

Cell constant = Conductivity × Resistance

$= 0.0248 \times 200 = 4.96 \text{ cm}^{-1}$ (1)

For 0.05 mol L^{-1} KCl solution,

Resistance = 620 Ω,

Cell constant = 4.96 cm^{-1}

$$\text{Conductivity} = \frac{\text{Cell constant}}{\text{Resistance}} = \frac{4.96}{620} = 0.008\,\Omega^{-1}\text{cm}^{-1}$$ (1)

$$\text{Molar conductivity} = \frac{\text{Conductivity} \times 1000}{\text{Molarity}}$$

$$= \frac{0.008\,\Omega^{-1}\text{cm}^{-1} \times 1000 \text{ cm}^3\text{L}^{-1}}{0.05 \text{ mol L}^{-1}}$$

$$= 160\,\Omega^{-1} \text{ cm}^2 \text{ mol}^{-1}$$ (1)

23. Molar conductivity,

$$\Lambda_m = \frac{\kappa \times 1000}{C} = \frac{8 \times 10^{-5} \text{ S cm}^{-1} \times 1000}{2 \times 10^{-3} \text{ mol L}^{-1}}$$

$$= \frac{8 \times 10^{-2}}{2 \times 10^{-3}} = 40 \text{ S cm}^2 \text{ mol}^{-1}$$ (1½)

Degree of dissociation,

$$\alpha = \frac{\Lambda_m}{\Lambda^\circ_m} = \frac{40}{404} = 0.099$$ (1½)

24. Given : Charge $(Q) = 24000$ C

Current $(I) = 12.5$ A

Mass of chromium (Cr) deposited = 1.5 g (1)

Molar mass of (Cr) = 52 and 1 F = 96500 C mol^{-1}

$\because$ 6 × 96500 C charge, deposit Cr = 52 g

$$\therefore \text{ 24000 C charge, deposit Cr} = \frac{52 \times 24000}{6 \times 96500} = \frac{1248000}{6 \times 96500}$$

Mass of chromium deposited = 2.16 g (1)

Also,

$\because$ Charge $(Q) = i \times t$ (time)

$$\therefore t = \frac{Q}{i} = \frac{24000}{12.5} = 1920 \text{ s}$$

Thus, duration of current = 32 min. (1)

25. [**Ans** – 474.4 kJ] (3)

26. (i) For spontaneous redox reactions the signs for E°_{cell} and ΔG° is positive and negative, respectively. (1½)

(ii) **Faraday's First Law** It states that "the amount of chemical deposition occuring at any electrode by passing current is directly proportional to the quantity of electricity passed through the electrolyte". (1½)

27. Refer to text on pages 55. (3)

28. Refer to text on page 53. (3)

29. (i) At anode (Oxidation) $2Al \longrightarrow 2Al^{3+} + 6e^-$

At cathode (Reduction) $3Ni^{2+} + 6e^- \longrightarrow 3Ni$ (1)

Total electrons transferred $(n) = 6$

$$E^\circ_{cell} = E^\circ_{cathode} - E^\circ_{anode}$$

$$= -0.25 - (-1.66 \text{ V}) = 1.41 \text{ V}$$

From Nernst equation, we have

$$E_{cell} = E^\circ_{cell} - \frac{0.059}{6}\log\frac{[0.001]^2}{[0.01]^3}$$

$$E_{cell} = 1.41 - 0.00983 = 1.40017 \text{ V}$$ (1)

(ii) Refer to text on page 49. (3)

30. (i) $\Lambda^\circ_{m(NH_4Cl)} = \lambda^\circ_{NH_4^+} + \lambda^\circ_{Cl^-} = (73.8 + 76.2)$

$= 150 \text{ S cm}^2\text{mol}^{-1}$ (1)

Conductivity of 0.1 M $NH_4Cl = 1.29 \times 10^{-2} \text{ S cm}^{-1}$

$$\Lambda_m = \frac{1.29 \times 10^{-2} \times 1000}{0.1} = 129 \text{S cm}^2\text{mol}^{-1}$$ (1)

$$\alpha \text{ (degree of dissociation)} = \frac{\Lambda_m}{\Lambda_m^\circ} = \frac{129}{150} = 0.86$$ **(1)**

(ii) According to Nernst equation

$$E_{Zn^{2+}/Zn^-} = -0.76 - \frac{0.0591}{2}\log\frac{10}{1} = -0.76 - \frac{0.0591}{2}$$

$$= \frac{-1.52 - 0.0591}{2} = -0.789 \text{ V}$$ **(2)**

31. (i) According to question,

Oxidation reaction, $Zn(s) \longrightarrow Zn^{2+}(aq) + 2e^-$

Reduction reaction, $2H^+ + 2e^- \longrightarrow H_2(g)$

$$E^\circ_{cell} = E^\circ_{H^+/H_2} - E^\circ_{Zn^{2+}/Zn}$$

$$= 0 - (-0.76) = 0.76 \text{ V}$$ **(1)**

According to Nernst equation

$$E_{cell} = E^\circ_{cell} - \frac{0.0591}{n}\log\frac{[Zn^{2+}]}{[H^+]^2}$$

$$= 0.76 - \frac{0.0591}{2}\log\frac{0.1}{(0.01)^2}$$

$$= 0.76 - 0.029 \log 1000 = 0.671 \text{ V}$$ **(1)**

(ii) Refer to text on page 48 and 49. **(3)**

32. (i) E° value of silver ($E^\circ_{Ag^+/Ag} = +0.80$ V) is lower than that of gold, hence silver displaces gold ($E^\circ_{Au^{3+}/Au} = +1.40$V), which gets deposited on the silver object.

E° value of copper ($E^\circ_{Cu^{2+}/Cu} = +0.34$) is lower than that of silver, hence silver cannot displace copper from its solution. **(2)**

(ii) (a) Electrons flow from Zn to Ag plate.

(b) Zn acts as anode and Ag acts as cathode.

(c) Cell will stop functioning.

(d) Concentration of Zn^{2+} ions will increase and that of Ag^+ ions will decrease.

(e) No change. **(3)**

33. Refer to diagram on page 38 in Daniell cell. Take, solution containing salt of silver than copper and silver electrode rather than copper. **(1)**

(i) The negatively charged electrode is the zinc electrode. It acts as an anode. **(1)**

(ii) The current will flow from silver to zinc. **(1)**

(iii) Oxidation at anode $Zn(s) \longrightarrow Zn^{2+}(aq) + 2e^-$

Reduction at cathode $Ag^+(aq) + e^- \longrightarrow Ag(s)$ **(2)**

34. The reaction will be feasible, if emf of the cell reaction is positive.

(i) $Fe^{3+}(aq) + I^-(aq) \longrightarrow Fe^{2+}(aq) + \frac{1}{2}I_2$

$$E^\circ_{cell} = E^\circ_{Fe^{3+}/Fe^{2+}} - E^\circ_{1/2\, I_2/I^-} = 0.77 - 0.54 = 0.23 \text{ V}$$

(feasible) **(1)**

(ii) $2Ag^+(aq) + Cu(s) \longrightarrow 2Ag(s) + Cu^{2+}(aq)$

$$E^\circ_{cell} = E^\circ_{Ag^+/Ag} - E^\circ_{Cu^{2+}/Cu}$$

$= 0.80 - 0.34 = 0.46$ V (feasible) **(1)**

(iii) $Fe^{3+}(aq) + Br^-(aq) \longrightarrow Fe^{2+}(aq) + \frac{1}{2}Br_2$

$$E^\circ_{cell} = E^\circ_{Fe^{3+}/Fe^{2+}} - E^\circ_{1/2\, Br_2/Br^-} = 0.77 - 1.09$$

$= -0.32$ V (not feasible) **(1)**

(iv) $Ag(s) + Fe^{3+}(aq) \longrightarrow Ag^+(aq) + Fe^{2+}(aq)$

$$E^\circ_{cell} = E^\circ_{Fe^{3+}/Fe^{2+}} - E^\circ_{Ag^+/Ag}$$

$= 0.77 - 0.80 = -0.03$ V (not feasible) **(1)**

(v) $\frac{1}{2}Br_2(aq) + Fe^{2+}(aq) \longrightarrow Br^- + Fe^{3+}$

$$E^\circ_{cell} = E^\circ_{1/2\, Br_2/Br^-} - E^\circ_{Fe^{3+}/Fe^{2+}}$$

$= 1.09 - 0.77 = 0.32$ V (feasible) **(1)**

35. (i) Refer to text on page 55. **(2)**

(ii) By applying Nernst equation,

$$E_{cell} = E^\circ_{cell} - \frac{0.0591}{n}\log\frac{[Cr^{3+}]^2}{[Cr_2O_7^{2-}][H^+]^{14}}$$

Given, $E^\circ_{cell} = 1.33$V, $n = 6$, $[Cr^{3+}] = 0.01$M, $[Cr_2O_7^{2-}] = 0.01$M, $[H^+] = 1 \times 10^{-4}$M

$$\therefore \quad E_{cell} = 1.33 - \frac{0.0591}{6}\log\frac{(0.01)^2}{(0.01)(1 \times 10^{-4})^{14}}$$

$$E_{cell} = 1.33 - \frac{0.0591}{6}[\log(0.01)(10^{56})]$$

$$E_{cell} = 1.33 - \frac{0.0591}{6}\log 10^{54} = 1.33 - \frac{0.0591}{6} \times 54(\log 10)$$

$$E_{cell} = (1.33 - 0.5319)\text{V} = 0.7981\text{V} \approx 0.798\text{V}$$ **(3)**

36. (i) **Kohlrausch Law** It states that limiting molar conductivity of an electrolyte is the sum of the individual contributions of the cations and the anions of the electrolyte.

Kohlrausch examined Λ°_m values for a number of strong electrolytes and found that for a pair of electrolytes with the same negative ion but differing only in the positive ion, the difference between the Λ°_m values is constant. **(2)**

(ii) $E^\circ_{cell} = E^\circ_{cathode} - E^\circ_{anode} = 0.34 - (-1.66) = 2.00$ V

According to Nernst equation,

$$E_{cell} = E^\circ_{cell} - \frac{0.059}{n}\log\frac{[Al^{3+}]^2}{[Cu^{2+}]^3}$$

Here, $n = 6$

$$E_{cell} = 2 - \frac{0.059}{6}\log\frac{[0.15]^2}{[0.025]^3}$$

$$= 2 - \frac{0.059}{6}(2\log 0.15 - 3\log 0.025)$$

$$= 2 - \frac{0.059}{6}(-1.6478 + 4.806)$$

$$= 2 - 0.0310 = 1.969 \text{ V}$$ **(3)**

37. (i) Oxidising power of metals decrease with an increase in their E° values. Thus, MnO_4^- is the strongest oxidising agent. **(1)**

(ii) (a) Molar conducivity of a solution is the conductance of that volume of solution containing one mole of electrolyte, kept between two electrodes having unit length between them and large cross-sectional areas so as to contain the electrolyte. **(1)**

(b) The nature the electrolyte on the basis of given plot is strong electrolyte. For strong electrolyte, Λ°_m increases slowly with dilution. **(1)**

(c) Using Debye-Huckel Onsager equation,

$$\Lambda_m = \Lambda^\circ_m - A\sqrt{C}$$

Λ° value from graph is 150 S cm^2 mol^{-1}. **(1)**

(d)

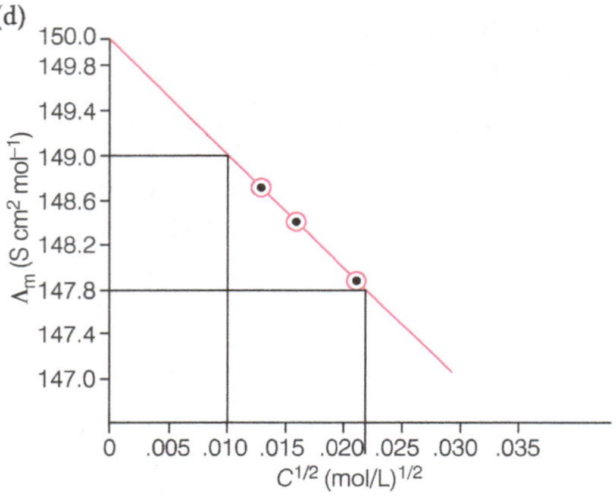

$$A = -\text{ slope} = -\left(\frac{y_2 - y_1}{x_2 - x_1}\right) = -\frac{(149 - 147.8)}{(0.010 - 0.022)}$$

$= 100$ S cm^{2}mol^{-1}/(mol L^{-1})$^{1/2}$ **(1)**

38. (i) The ions moving towards the cathode are Na^+. The electrolyte is molten sodium chloride, so only one cation (Na^+) is present in the reaction medium. **(1)**

(ii) The product expected at the anode is chlorine, as chlorine is negatively charged ion, so it attracts towards positively charged anode.

The reaction at anode is

$$Cl^- \longrightarrow \frac{1}{2}Cl_2(g) + e^-$$ **(1)**

(iii) The molten sodium chloride will decompose into sodium and chlorine gas, when electricity is passed through it.

The net reaction for the process is

$$2NaCl \longrightarrow 2Na + Cl_2(g)$$ **(1)**

(iv) The above process is governed by the Faraday's law of electrolysis. They are as follows:

- The amount of chemical reaction which occurs at any electrode during electrolysis by a current, is proportional to the quantity of electricity passed through the electrolyte.
- The amounts of different substances liberated by the same quantity of electricity passing through the electrolytic solution are proportional to their chemical equivalent weights. **(2)**

39. $\underset{}{Ag^+} + \underset{1F}{e^-} \longrightarrow \underset{1\,mol}{Ag}$

$\because$ 108 g of Ag is deposited by 96500 C

$\therefore$ 1.45 g of Ag will be deposited by $= \dfrac{96500 \times 1.45}{108}$

$= 1295.6$ C

$Q = it$ or $1295.6 \text{ C} = 1.5 \text{ A} \times t$

$\therefore \quad t = \dfrac{1295.6 \text{ C}}{1.5 \text{ A}} \Rightarrow t = 863.7$ s **(2)**

The reaction related to the deposition of copper is

$$Cu^{2+} + 2e^- \longrightarrow \underset{63.5\,g}{Cu}$$

$\because$ 2×96500 C electricity deposits 63.5 g of Cu

$\therefore$ 1295.6 C electricity will deposit

$\dfrac{63.5 \times 1295.6}{2 \times 96500}$ g of Cu, i.e., 0.426 g of Cu. **(1)**

The reaction related to the deposition of zinc is

$$Zn^{2+} + \underset{2 \times 96500\,C}{2e^-} \longrightarrow \underset{65.4\,g}{Zn}$$

$\because$ 2×96500 C electricity deposits 65.4 g of Zn.

$\therefore$ 1295.6 C electricity will deposit $\dfrac{65.4 \times 1295.6}{2 \times 96500}$ g of Zn,

i.e., 0.44 g of Zn. **(2)**

40. In corrosion, a metal is oxidised by the loss of electrons to oxygen with the formation of oxides. So, an electrochemical cell is set-up, e.g., rusting of iron.

Refer to text on pages 57 and 58. **(5)**

41. Refer to text on page 58. **(5)**

QR Code for Quick Test 1

QR Code for Quick Test 2

QR Code for Quick Test 3

QR Code for Quick Test 4

SELF ASSESSMENT TEST

Objective Type Questions [1 Mark]

1. An electrochemical cell can behave like an electrolytic cell when
   (a) $E_{cell} = 0$
   (b) $E_{cell} > E_{ext}$
   (c) $E_{ext} > E_{cell}$
   (d) $E_{cell} = E_{ext}$

2. The electrode potential is known as standard electrode potential
   (a) when it is reduction potential (according to IUPAC).
   (b) when concentrations of all the species involved is unity.
   (c) when it is oxidation potential (according to IUPAC).
   (d) Both (a) and (b)

3. Using the data given below find out the strongest reducing agent.
   $E^\circ_{Cr_2O_7^{2-}/Cr^{3+}} = 1.33$ V; $E^\circ_{Cl_2/Cl^-} = 1.36$ V;
   $E^\circ_{MnO_4^-/Mn^{2+}} = 1.51$ V; $E^\circ_{Cr^{3+}/Cr} = -0.74$ V.
   (a) Cl^-
   (b) Cr
   (c) Cr^{3+}
   (d) Mn^{2+}

4. Which type of electrolyte are used in *A* and *B*?

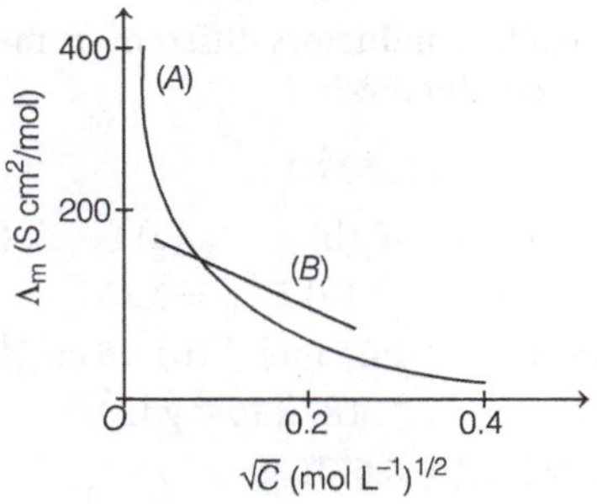

	A	*B*
(a)	Weak electrolyte	Strong electrolyte
(b)	Strong electrolyte	Weak electrolyte
(c)	Weak electrolyte	Weak electrolyte
(d)	Strong electrolyte	Strong electrolyte

Assertion - Reason [1 Mark]

■ **Direction** (Q. Nos. 5-7) In the following questions, an Assertion (A) is followed by a corresponding Reason (R). Use the following keys to choose the appropriate answer.

5. **Assertion** (A) The electrolytic conduction increases with increase in temperature.
   Reason (R) Mobility of ions increases with rise in temperature.

6. **Assertion** (A) Electrolysis of an aqueous solution of KI gives I_2 at the anode but that of KF gives O_2 at the anode not F_2.
   Reason (R) I^- ions have much lower oxidation potential than water while F^- ions have much higher oxidation potential than water.

7. **Assertion** (A) Cu does not dissolve in HCl but dissolved in HNO_3.
   Reason (R) In nitric acid, Cu is oxidised by nitrate ion not by hydrogen ion.

Short Answer Type I Questions [2 Marks]

8. (i) A rusted piece of iron undergoes electrochemical reactions. Write the chemical reaction taking place at
   (a) the electrode that behaves as an anode.
   (b) the electrode that behaves as a cathode.
   (ii) Given that the standard reduction potential for $Al^{3+}/Al = -1.66$ V and $\frac{1}{2}I_2/I^- = 0.54$ V, what will be the standard potential of the cell made by using Al^{3+} and I^-?

9. Following reactions occur at cathode during the electrolysis of aqueous silver chloride solution.
   $$Ag^+(aq) + e^- \longrightarrow Ag(s); E^\circ = +0.80 \text{ V}$$
   $$H^+(aq) + e^- \longrightarrow \frac{1}{2}H_2(g); E^\circ = 0.00 \text{ V}$$
   On the basis of their standard reduction electrode potential (E°) values, which reaction is feasible at the cathode and why?

10. (i) The conductivity of 0.2 M KCl solution is 3×10^{-2} ohm^{-1}cm^{-1}. Calculate its molar conductance.
    (ii) Calculate the cell constant if two Pt electrode fitted in a conductance cell are 1.5 cm apart and the cross-sectional area of each electrode is 0.75 cm^2.

Short Answer Type II Questions [3 Marks]

11. Calculate E°_{cell} for the following reaction at 298 K.

$$2Al(s) + 3Cu^{2+}(0.01M) \longrightarrow 2Al^{3+}(0.01M) + 3Cu(s)$$

Given, $E_{cell} = 1.98$ V

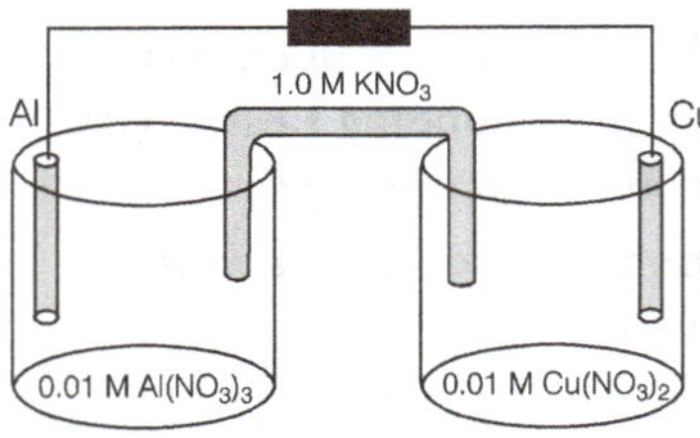

12. At 25°C, the specific conductance of a saturated solution of AgCl is $3.41 \times 10^{-6} \Omega^{-1}$ $cm^{-1}$and that of water is 1.61×10^{-6} $\Omega^{-1}cm^{-1}$. The molar conductance at infinite dilution for Ag^{+} and Cl^{-} ions are $61.92 \Omega^{-1}$ $cm^{2}mol^{-1}$ and 76.34 $\Omega^{-1}cm^{2}$ mol^{-1}, respectively.

Calculate the solubility of AgCl in gram per litre at the given temperature.

$$AgCl \rightleftharpoons Ag^{+} + Cl^{-}$$

Case - Study [4 Marks]

13. Batteries play an essential role in modern society, powering a vast array of devices from small electronics to electric vehicles. Among these, primary batteries, such as dry cells and mercury cells, provide energy through irreversible chemical reactions. Dry cells, commonly used in household items like remote controls and flashlights, utilize a zinc anode and a carbon cathode to generate electricity. They are characterised by their convenience and ease of use, but once depleted, they cannot be recharged. In contrast, mercury cells, though less common today due to environmental concerns, are notable for their stable voltage output and compact design, making them ideal for precision instruments like watches and medical devices.

On the other hand, secondary batteries, including lead storage batteries and nickel-cadmium (Ni/Cd) batteries, offer the advantage of rechargeability. Lead storage batteries are extensively employed in automotive applications due to their robustness and ability to provide high currents, while Ni/Cd batteries have historically been favored for portable electronics and power tools. Additionally, the advent of fuel cells marks a significant advancement in energy technology, as they convert hydrogen and oxygen into electricity with water as the only byproduct. This innovative approach promises a cleaner energy future, reducing reliance on fossil fuels and minimising environmental impact. Understanding the various types of batteries, their operating principles and their applications is crucial for advancing energy storage technologies and meeting the growing demand for sustainable energy solutions.

(i) What factors determine the choice of battery technology for a specific application?

(ii) What is the primary chemical reaction occurring in a dry cell?

(iii) Why are lead storage batteries commonly used in vehicles?

Or

(iii) What is one significant environmental concern associated with mercury cells?

Long Answer Type Questions [5 Marks]

14. Answer the following,

(a) For the reaction,

$$2AgCl(s) + H_2(g)\ (1\ atm) \longrightarrow 2Ag(s) + 2H^{+}(0.1\ M) + 2Cl^{-}(0.1\ M),$$

$\Delta G^{\circ} = -43600$ J at 25° C. [log $10^{-n} = -n$]

Calculate the emf of the cell.

(b) What mass of Ag (At. mass is 108 u) could be plated on a spoon from electrolysis of $AgNO_3$ solution by one ampere current for 10 minutes?

15. (i) Explain the working of a lead storage battery during discharge and recharge.

(ii) How is metallic conductors different from electrolytic conductors?

Answers

1. (c) 2. (d) 3. (b) 4. (a) 5. (a)
6. (c) 7. (a) 8. (ii) $E^{\circ}_{cell} = 2.2$ V
10. (i) $1.5 \times 10^{2} \Omega^{-1}$ cm^{2} mol^{-1} (ii) 2.0 cm^{-1}
11. 2.0 V 12. 1.87×10^{-3} g L^{-1}
14. (a) 0.3382 V (b) 0.6715 g

03
CHAPTER

Chemical kinetics is the branch of chemistry which deals with the study of rates of chemical reactions and the mechanism by which reaction proceeds. Alongwith the rate of reaction, chemical kinetics helps in determining the conditions for altering reaction rates, predicting the yield of products and calculating the time required for a reaction completion.

▼ YOUR STUDY GOALS

▼ YOUR PRACTICE GOAL

- Objective Type Questions (36 Qs ; 23 MCQs, 11 A-R, 2 Case Study)
- Subjective Type Questions (33 Qs; 15 SA-I, 11 SA-II, 7 LA)

Chemical Kinetics

3.1 Rate of a Chemical Reaction

Rate of a chemical reaction means the rate or speed with which the reaction takes place. It can be defined as "*the change in concentration of reactants or products per unit time*".

It can be expressed in terms of

- the rate of decrease in concentration of any one of the reactants, or
- the rate of increase in concentration of any one of the products.

On the basis of their speeds, some reactions (such as ionic reactions) occur **very fast** e.g. precipitation of AgCl from $AgNO_3$ and NaCl. Some reactions are **very slow** e.g. rusting of iron in presence of air and moisture. Also, there are reactions like inversion of cane sugar and hydrolysis of starch, which proceed with a **moderate** speed.

Consider a simple hypothetical reaction, assuming that the volume of the system remains constant such that one mole of the reactant R produces one mole of the product P,

$$R \longrightarrow P$$

If $[R]_1$ and $[P]_1$ are the concentrations of reactant and product respectively at time t_1 and $[R]_2$ and $[P]_2$ are the concentrations at time t_2, then

$$\Delta t = t_2 - t_1$$
$$\Delta R = [R]_2 - [R]_1$$
$$\Delta P = [P]_2 - [P]_1$$

Here, the square brackets are used to express molar concentration.

Rate of disappearance of R

$$=\frac{\text{Decrease in concentration of } R}{\text{Time taken}}=-\frac{\Delta[R]}{\Delta t} \quad \ldots(\text{i})$$

Rate of appearance of P

$$=\frac{\text{Increase in concentration of } P}{\text{Time taken}}=+\frac{\Delta[P]}{\Delta t} \quad \ldots(\text{ii})$$

Thus, rate of reaction = Rate of disappearance of R

= Rate of appearance of P

$$=\frac{-\Delta[R]}{\Delta t}=\frac{+\Delta[P]}{\Delta t}$$

Units of Rate of a Reaction

Unit of rate of a reaction is **concentration time^{-1}**. If concentration is in mol L^{-1} and time is in seconds, then the units of rate of reaction will be **mol L^{-1} s^{-1}**. However, in gaseous reactions, when the concentration of gases is taken in terms of their partial pressures, the unit of rate equation will be **atm s^{-1}**.

TEACHER'S TIP

- In rate expression, the negative sign indicates that the concentration of reactants decreases with time whereas, the positive sign indicates that the concentration of products increases with time.
- The concentration change may be positive or negative but the rate is always positive.

Types of Rate of a Reaction

The rate of a reaction can be classified into following two types.

Average Rate of a Reaction (r_{av})

It is defined as the average value of reactant or product concentration during a specified interval of time.

It is expressed as

For a reaction, $R \longrightarrow P$ (Reactant) (Product)

$$\text{Average rate}=\frac{\text{Change in concentration in given time}}{\text{Time taken}}$$

$$\therefore \quad r_{av}=-\frac{\Delta[R]}{\Delta t}=\frac{+\Delta[P]}{\Delta t}$$

For example, $2N_2O_5(g) \longrightarrow 4NO_2(g)+O_2(g)$

$$r_{av}=\frac{-1}{2}\frac{\Delta[N_2O_5]}{\Delta t}=+\frac{1}{4}\frac{\Delta[NO_2]}{\Delta t}=\frac{+\Delta[O_2]}{\Delta t}$$

Instantaneous Rate of a Reaction (r_{inst})

It is defined as the rate of change of concentration of any one of the species involved in the reaction at a particular instant of time. It is expressed as

$$r_{inst}=-\frac{d[R]}{dt}=+\frac{d[P]}{dt}$$

For example, $2NO(g)+O_2(g) \longrightarrow 2NO_2(g)$

$$r_{inst}=-\frac{1}{2}\frac{d[NO]}{dt}=-\frac{d[O_2]}{dt}=+\frac{1}{2}\frac{d[NO_2]}{dt}$$

As $\Delta t \rightarrow 0$, Instantaneous rate = Average rate

Note If the stoichiometric coefficients of reactant or product are not equal to one, then the rate of disappearance of any of the reactant or the rate of appearance of products is divided by their respective stoichiometric coefficients.

Determination of Rate of a Reaction

Rate of a reaction can be determined from the slope of the graph between the concentration of any of the reactants or products with time. Average and instantaneous rate of a reaction, respectively can be determined as follows.

- **Determination of average rate** is done by measuring concentration of reactant and product after fixed intervals of time.

  In graph (a) and (b), R_1 and R_2 are the concentration of reactants, P_1 and P_2 are the concentration of products in the time interval between t_1 and t_2.

  Then, average rate of reaction

  $$=\frac{-\{[R_2]-[R_1]\}}{t_2-t_1}=\frac{[P_2-P_1]}{t_2-t_1}$$

- **Determination of instantaneous rate** is done by drawing a tangent at time t on either of the curves, concentration of reactant *vs* time t, or concentration of product *vs* time.

  The slope of tangent drawn on any of the curve at time t gives the value of instantaneous rate on that instant.

As shown in graphs (a) and (b), the slope of tangent is $\frac{-d[R]}{dt}$ in graph (a) and $\frac{d[P]}{dt}$ in graph (b), which gives the value of instantaneous rate at time t.

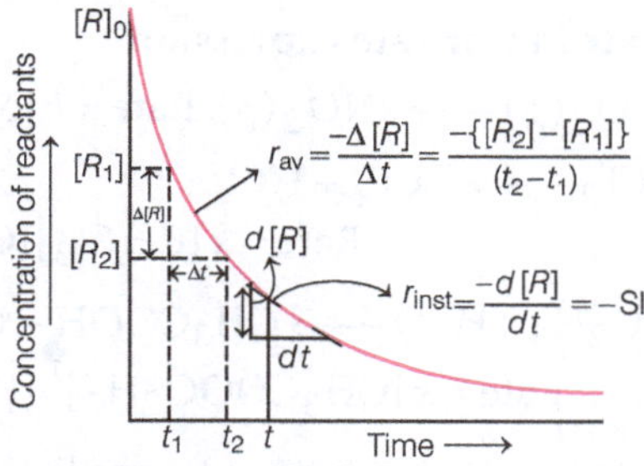

(a) Variation in concentration of reactant with time.

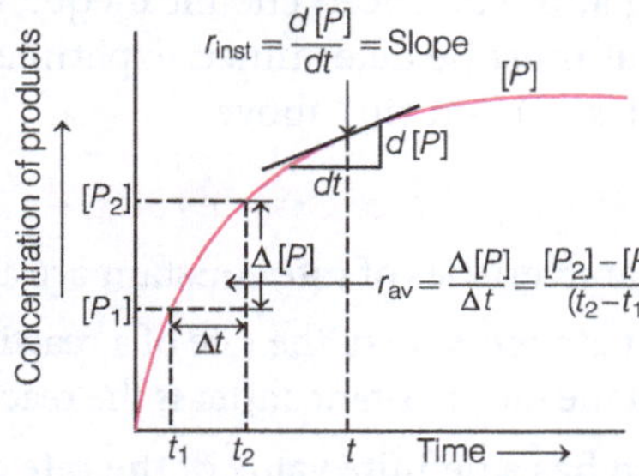

(b) Variation in concentration of product with time

Determination of average and instantaneous rate of a reaction

Note Symbol Δ is used for large change and symbol 'd' is used for small change.

Example 1 **For the reaction, $R \longrightarrow P$, the concentration of a reactant changes from 0.03 M to 0.02 M in 25 min. Calculate the average rate of reaction using units of time both in minutes and seconds.** **NCERT Intext**

Sol. For the reaction, $R \longrightarrow P$

Average rate of reaction

$$= \frac{\text{Change in concentration of reactant / product}}{\text{Time taken}}$$

$$= -\frac{\Delta[R]}{\Delta t} = -\frac{\{[R_2]-[R_1]\}}{t_2 - t_1}$$

$$= -\frac{(0.02 - 0.03)\text{ M}}{25 \text{ min}}$$

$$= \frac{0.01 \text{ M}}{25 \text{ min}} = 4 \times 10^{-4} \text{ mol L}^{-1} \text{ min}^{-1}$$

Converting unit of time in seconds

$$\frac{4 \times 10^{-4}}{60} \text{ mol L}^{-1}\text{s}^{-1} = 6.66 \times 10^{-6} \text{ mol L}^{-1} \text{ s}^{-1}$$

Example 2 **For the reaction, $2A \longrightarrow$ Products, the concentration of A decreases from 0.5 mol L^{-1} to 0.4 mol L^{-1} in 10 min. Calculate the rate during this interval.** **NCERT Intext**

Sol. Rate of reaction = Rate of disappearance of A

$$= -\frac{1}{2}\frac{\Delta[A]}{\Delta t} = -\frac{1}{2}\frac{(0.4 - 0.5)\text{ mol L}^{-1}}{10 \text{ min}}$$

$$= 0.005 \text{ mol L}^{-1} \text{ min}^{-1}$$

Example 3 **The decomposition of N_2O_5 in CCl_4 at 318 K has been studied by monitoring the concentration of N_2O_5 in the solution. Initially the concentration of N_2O_5 is 2.33 mol L^{-1} and after 184 minutes, it is reduced to 2.08 mol L^{-1}. The reaction takes place according to the equation.**

$$2N_2O_5(g) \longrightarrow 4NO_2(g) + O_2(g)$$

Calculate the average rate of this reaction in terms of hours, minutes and seconds. What is the rate of production of NO_2 during this period? **NCERT**

Sol. Average rate $= \frac{1}{2}\left\{-\frac{\Delta[N_2O_5]}{\Delta t}\right\}$

$$= -\frac{1}{2}\left[\frac{(2.08 - 2.33)\text{ mol L}^{-1}}{184 \text{ min}}\right]$$

$$= 6.79 \times 10^{-4} \text{ mol L}^{-1}\text{/min}$$

$$= (6.79 \times 10^{-4} \text{ mol L}^{-1} \text{ min}^{-1}) \times (60 \text{ min/ 1h})$$

$$= 4.07 \times 10^{-2} \text{ mol L}^{-1}\text{/h}$$

$$= 6.79 \times 10^{-4} \text{ mol L}^{-1} \text{ min}^{-1} \times (1 \text{ min/60 s})$$

$$= 1.13 \times 10^{-5} \text{ mol L}^{-1}\text{s}^{-1}$$

According to the given equation,

$$\text{Rate} = \frac{1}{4}\left\{\frac{\Delta[NO_2]}{\Delta t}\right\}$$

$$\frac{\Delta[NO_2]}{\Delta t} = 6.79 \times 10^{-4} \times 4 \text{ mol L}^{-1} \text{ min}^{-1}$$

$$= 2.72 \times 10^{-3} \text{ mol L}^{-1} \text{ min}^{-1}$$

Factors Influencing Rate of a Reaction

Rate of a chemical reaction depends upon the following factors

(i) **Concentration of reactants** The rate of a reaction is directly proportional to the concentration of reactants. It usually increases when concentration of reactant increases due to increase in collision frequency.

(ii) **Temperature** The rate of a reaction is directly proportional to the temperature of the system. Speed of a reaction nearly doubles on 10°C rise in temperature.

(iii) **Catalyst** A catalyst alters the speed of reaction and helps to attain the equilibrium quickly. It participates in the reaction without being consumed.

(iv) **Surface area of the reactants** Smaller the particle size, greater the surface area and faster is the reaction. That's why magnesium powder reacts much more rapidly than magnesium ribbon with dilute sulphuric acid.

(v) **Presence of radiation** The rate of some reactions can be increased when radiation of suitable frequency is available otherwise they are very slow or do not occur. Such reactions are called **photochemical reactions**.

e.g. Chlorine does not react with hydrogen in dark but in presence of sunlight the reaction is explosive.

i.e. $$H_2 + Cl_2 \xrightarrow{h\nu} 2HCl$$

3.2 Rate Law and Rate Constant

The expression in which the reaction rate is given in terms of molar concentration of reactants with each term raised to some power, which may or may not be same as the stoichiometric coefficient of the reacting species in a balanced chemical equation is called **rate law, rate equation** or **rate expression**.

Consider a general reaction,

$$aA + bB \longrightarrow cC + dD$$

where, a, b, c and d are the stoichiometric coefficients of reactants and products, respectively.

The rate expression for the above reaction is

$$\text{Rate} \propto [A]^x [B]^y \quad \ldots(i)$$

where, x and y are exponents which can be determined experimentally. These exponents may or may not be equal to the stoichiometric coefficients (a and b) of the reactants.

Above equation can also be written as

$$\text{Rate} = k[A]^x [B]^y \quad \ldots(ii)$$

This expression is known as rate law where, k is the proportionality constant called **rate constant.**

Rate law can also be written as

$$\frac{-d[R]}{dt} = k[A]^x [B]^y \quad \ldots(iii)$$

This form of equation is known as **differential rate equation.**

Now, if in rate law all concentrations are taken as unity, i.e. $[A] = [B] = 1$ mol/L, then rate $= k$.

Hence, rate constant can be defined as the rate of a reaction when the concentration of each reactant is taken as unity. Rate constant is also called **specific reaction rate or specific rate constant.**

Examples of rate law or rate expression

(i) $2NO(g) + O_2(g) \longrightarrow 2NO_2(g)$, Rate $= k[NO]^2 [O_2]$

(ii) $CHCl_3 + Cl_2 \longrightarrow CCl_4 + HCl$,
Rate $= k[CHCl_3][Cl_2]^{1/2}$

(iii) $CH_3COOC_2H_5 + H_2O \longrightarrow CH_3COOH + C_2H_5OH$,
Rate $= k[CH_3COOC_2H_5]^1 [H_2O]^0$

Thus, rate law for a reaction cannot be predicted by merely looking at the balanced chemical equation, i.e., theoretically but must be determined experimentally as seen in examples (ii) and (iii) above.

Characteristics of Rate Constant

Some of the characteristics of rate constant are as follows.

- Rate constant is a measure of the rate of a reaction. Greater is the value of the rate constant, faster is the reaction.
- Each reaction has a definite value of the rate constant at a particular temperature and its value for the same reaction changes with change in temperature.
- Its value does not depend upon the concentrations of the reactants.
- The unit of rate constant depends upon the order of reaction.

Example 4 The following results have been obtained during the kinetic studies of the reaction,

$$2A + B \longrightarrow C + D.$$

Exp.	$[A]$ / mol L^{-1}	$[B]$ / mol L^{-1}	Initial rate of formation of $[D]$ / mol L^{-1} min^{-1}
1.	0.1	0.1	6.0×10^{-3}
2.	0.3	0.2	7.2×10^{-2}
3.	0.3	0.4	2.88×10^{-1}
4.	0.4	0.1	2.40×10^{-2}

Determine the rate law and the rate constant for the reaction. NCERT

Sol. Rate law may be expressed as

$$\text{Rate} = k[A]^x [B]^y$$

$$(\text{Rate})_1 = 6.0 \times 10^{-3} = k(0.1)^x (0.1)^y \quad \ldots(i)$$
$$(\text{Rate})_2 = 7.2 \times 10^{-2} = k(0.3)^x (0.2)^y \quad \ldots(ii)$$
$$(\text{Rate})_3 = 2.88 \times 10^{-1} = k(0.3)^x (0.4)^y \quad \ldots(iii)$$
$$(\text{Rate})_4 = 2.40 \times 10^{-2} = k(0.4)^x (0.1)^y \quad \ldots(iv)$$

$$\frac{(\text{Rate})_1}{(\text{Rate})_4}=\frac{6.0\times 10^{-3}}{2.40\times 10^{-2}}=\frac{k\,(0.1)^x(0.1)^y}{k\,(0.4)^x(0.1)^y}$$

or $$\frac{1}{4}=\frac{(0.1)^x}{(0.4)^x}=\left(\frac{1}{4}\right)^x$$

$\therefore$ $$x=1$$

$$\frac{(\text{Rate})_2}{(\text{Rate})_3}=\frac{7.2\times 10^{-2}}{2.88\times 10^{-1}}=\frac{k(0.3)^x\,(0.2)^y}{k(0.3)^x(0.4)^y}$$

or $$\frac{1}{4}=\frac{(0.2)^y}{(0.4)^y}=\left(\frac{1}{2}\right)^y$$

$\therefore$ $$y=2$$

Now, rate law expression is given by Rate $=k\,[A]\,[B]^2$

Rate constant, k can be determined by substituting the values of A, B and rate of formation of D. By taking the values from any experiment, say experiment 2.

$$\text{Rate}=k\,[A]\,[B]^2$$

$$k=\frac{\text{Rate}}{[A]\,[B]^2}=\frac{7.2\times 10^{-2}\,\text{mol L}^{-1}\text{min}^{-1}}{(0.3\ \text{mol L}^{-1})(0.2\ \text{mol L}^{-1})^2}$$

or $$k=6.0\ \text{mol}^{-2}\ \text{L}^2\text{min}^{-1}$$

Quick Test 1

Conceptual Questions

1. Why does the rate of any reaction generally decreases during the course of the reaction? NCERT Exemplar

2. Mention the factors that affect the rate of a chemical reaction. NCERT

3. How can you determine the rate law of the following reaction? NCERT Exemplar

$$2\text{NO}(g)+\text{O}_2(g)\longrightarrow 2\text{NO}_2(g)$$

4. For a reaction, $2H_2O_2 \xrightarrow[\text{Alkaline medium}]{I^-} 2H_2O+O_2$

the proposed mechanism is as given below

(1) $H_2O_2+I^-\longrightarrow H_2O+IO^-$(slow)

(2) $H_2O_2+IO^-\longrightarrow H_2O+I^-+O_2$ (fast)

(i) Write the rate law for the reaction.

(ii) Write the overall order of reaction.

(iii) Out of steps (1) and (2), which one is rate determining step?

Numerical Questions

5. For the reaction,

$$2\text{N}_2\text{O}_5(g)\longrightarrow 4\text{NO}_2(g)+\text{O}_2(g),$$

the rate of formation of $NO_2(g)$ is 2.8×10^{-3} Ms^{-1}. Calculate the rate of disappearance of $N_2O_5(g)$. CBSE 2018

6. For the reaction, $2A+B\longrightarrow A_2B$;

The rate $=k\,[A]\,[B]^2$ with $k=2.0\times 10^{-6}\ \text{mol}^{-2}\ \text{L}^2\ \text{s}^{-1}$.

Calculate the initial rate of reaction when $[A]=0.1\ \text{mol L}^{-1}$, $[B]=0.2\ \text{mol L}^{-1}$.

Calculate the rate of reaction after $[A]$ is reduced to $0.06\ \text{mol L}^{-1}$. NCERT

7. In the following reaction

$$K_3PO_4\longrightarrow 3K^+ + PO_4^{3-}$$

The rate of formation of PO_4^{3-} is 50 mol L^{-1}s^{-1}.

(i) What is the rate of formation of potassium ions?

(ii) What is the rate of loss of K_3PO_4? Competency Based Que.

Answers

5. 1.4×10^{-3} mol L^{-1}s^{-1}

6. (i) 8.0×10^{-9} mol L^{-1}s^{-1} (ii) 3.89×10^{-9} mol L^{-1}s^{-1}

7. (i) 150 mol litre^{-1}s^{-1} (ii) -50 mol litre^{-1}s^{-1}

For Solutions, See QR Code on Pg. 107

3.3 Order of a Reaction

The sum of the powers of the concentration of the reactants in the rate law expression is called the **order of the chemical reaction.**

For a general reaction,

$$aA+bB\longrightarrow cC+dD$$

The rate law expression for the reaction is,

$$\text{Rate}=k\,[A]^x\,[B]^y$$

- Here, x and y, calculated experimentally, indicate how sensitive the rate is to the change in concentrations of A and B.
- Sum of these exponents, i.e. $x+y$ gives the overall order of a reaction whereas x and y represent the order with respect to the reactants A and B, respectively.
- Order of a reaction can be 0, 1, 2, 3 and even a fraction. e.g. If rate of any reaction is expressed as

$$\text{Rate}=k[A]^{1/2}[B]^{3/2}$$

Then, order $= x + y = \frac{1}{2} + \frac{3}{2} = 2$

Hence, reaction is said to be of **second order.**

Example 5 **For a reaction, $P \longrightarrow Q$, the rate becomes 8 times when concentration of P is doubled. What is the order of the reaction?**

Sol. Let rate, $r = k[P]^n$ ...(i)

$8r = k[2P]^n$ ...(ii)

On dividing Eq. (ii) by Eq. (i), we get

$$\frac{8r}{r} = \frac{k[2P]^n}{k[P]^n}$$

or $[2]^3 = [2]^n$ or $n = 3$

Therefore, order of the reaction is 3.

Units of Rate Constant for Different Orders of Reaction

The units of rate constants of different orders are different. This can be easily illustrated below

For a general reaction, $aA + bB \longrightarrow cC + dD$

$$\text{Rate} = k[A]^x[B]^y$$

where, $x + y = n =$ order of the reaction

$$k = \frac{\text{Rate}}{[A]^x[B]^y}$$

$$= \frac{\text{concentration}}{\text{time}} \times \frac{1}{(\text{concentration})^n}$$

$$= (\text{concentration})^{1-n}\ \text{time}^{-1}$$

(where, $[A] = [B]$)

Considering SI units of concentration, mol L^{-1} and time s, the unit of $k = (\text{mol L}^{-1})^{1-n}\ s^{-1}$. Thus, the units of k for different orders of reaction are given below.

Reaction with Units of Rate Constant

Reaction	Order	Unit of rate constant (k)
Zero order	$n=0$	$= \frac{\text{mol L}^{-1}}{s} \times \frac{1}{(\text{mol L}^{-1})^0} = \text{mol L}^{-1}\ s^{-1}$
First order	$n=1$	$= \frac{\text{mol L}^{-1}}{s} \times \frac{1}{(\text{mol L}^{-1})^1} = s^{-1}$
Second order	$n=2$	$= \frac{\text{mol L}^{-1}}{s} \times \frac{1}{(\text{mol L}^{-1})^2} = \text{mol}^{-1}\text{L}s^{-1}$
n^{th} order	n	$= \frac{\text{mol L}^{-1}}{s} \times \frac{1}{(\text{mol L}^{-1})^n} = (\text{mol L}^{-1})^{1-n}s^{-1}$

Example 6 **From the rate expression for the following reactions, determine their order of reaction and the dimensions of the rate constant.** **NCERT**

(i) $3NO(g) \longrightarrow N_2O(g)$, Rate $= k[NO]^2$

(ii) $H_2O_2(aq) + 3I^-(aq) + 2H^+ \longrightarrow 2H_2O(l) + I_3^-$, Rate $= k[H_2O_2][I^-]$

(iii) $CH_3CHO(g) \longrightarrow CH_4(g) + CO(g)$, Rate $= k[CH_3CHO]^{3/2}$

(iv) $C_2H_5Cl(g) \longrightarrow C_2H_4(g) + HCl(g)$, Rate $= k[C_2H_5Cl]$

Sol. (i) Rate $= k[NO]^2$,

Order of reaction = 2

Unit (dimension) of rate constant,

$$k = \frac{\text{Rate}}{[NO]^2} = \frac{\text{mol L}^{-1}s^{-1}}{(\text{mol L}^{-1})^2} = \text{mol}^{-1}\text{L s}^{-1}$$

(ii) Rate $= k[H_2O_2][I^-]$

Order of reaction $= 1 + 1 = 2$

$$\text{Dimension of } k = \frac{\text{Rate}}{[H_2O_2][I^-]} = \frac{\text{mol L}^{-1}\ s^{-1}}{(\text{mol L}^{-1})(\text{mol L}^{-1})}$$

$= \text{mol}^{-1}\ \text{L s}^{-1}$

(iii) Rate $= k[CH_3CHO]^{3/2}$

Order of reaction $= \frac{3}{2}$

$$\text{Dimension of } k = \frac{\text{Rate}}{[CH_3CHO]^{3/2}} = \frac{\text{mol L}^{-1}s^{-1}}{(\text{mol L}^{-1})^{3/2}}$$

$= \text{mol}^{-1/2}\ L^{1/2}\ s^{-1}$

(iv) Rate $= k[C_2H_5Cl]$, Order of reaction = 1

$$\text{Dimension of } k = \frac{\text{Rate}}{[C_2H_5Cl]} = \frac{\text{mol L}^{-1}\ s^{-1}}{\text{mol L}^{-1}} = s^{-1}$$

3.4 Molecularity of a Reaction

The number of reacting species (atoms, ions or molecules) taking part in an elementary reaction, which must collide simultaneously in order to bring about a chemical reaction is called **molecularity of the reaction.**

Depending upon the number of participating molecules, the reaction can be unimolecular, bimolecular, trimolecular, etc.

Reaction	No. of participating molecule	Molecularity
$N_2O_4 \longrightarrow 2NO$	One molecule	1 (Unimolecular)
$2HI \longrightarrow H_2 + I_2$	Two molecule	2 (Bimolecular)
$2NO + O_2 \longrightarrow 2NO_2$	Three molecule	3 (Trimolecular)

Reactions with molecularity greater than three (trimolecular) are rare and slow to proceed as probability of more than three molecules colliding simultaneously to form product(s) is very low.

TEACHER'S TIP
Molecularity has no meaning for complex reactions as these reactions are supposed to take place in a sequence of a number of steps. It can be determined only for the elementary reactions.

It is evident that complex reactions involving more than three molecules in the stoichiometric equation must take place in more than one step. This fact can be explained as follows.

Mechanism of Reaction

A series of elementary reactions, proposed to explain the overall reaction is called the **mechanism of the reaction.**

The simple chemical reactions which occur only in one step are called **elementary reactions** whereas the reactions which occur in two or more steps are called **complex reactions.**

A complex reaction proceeds through a series of elementary reactions. Each elementary reaction has its own molecularity and its own rate.

Rate Determining (Slow) Step

The slowest step of the reaction is considered as the rate determining step of the chemical reaction and it decides the **overall rate** of the reaction.

Consider the following reaction,

$$2N_2O_5 \longrightarrow 4NO_2 + O_2$$

The rate law for this equation is found to be,

$$\text{Rate of reaction} = k[N_2O_5]$$

If the reaction occur by the collisions of two N_2O_5 molecules as indicated by the balanced equation, it would be a second order reaction as

$$\text{Rate} = k\,[N_2O_5]^2.$$

But observed rate law suggests that it is a first order reaction which implies that the reaction is a complex reaction. So, it must take place in two steps in such a way that the slowest step should involve only one molecule of N_2O_5.

***Step* I** $N_2O_5 \xrightarrow{\text{Slow}} NO_2 + NO_3$

***Step* II** $N_2O_5 + NO_3 \xrightarrow{\text{Fast}} 3NO_2 + O_2$

From these observations, we can **distinguish between molecularity and order of a reaction** as follows

Molecularity	Order
The number of reacting species which must collide simultaneously in order to carry out a chemical reaction is called molecularity of a reaction.	The sum of powers of the concentrations of the reactants in the rate law expression is called the order of that chemical reaction.
Molecularity is always a whole number value only, i.e. 1, 2, 3 . . .	Order of a reaction may have zero, whole number or fractional values.
Molecularity is a theoretical concept.	Order of a reaction is determined experimentally.
Molecularity is applicable to elementary reactions. For complex reactions, it has no meaning.	Order of a reaction is applicable to elementary as well as complex reactions.
For simple reactions, molecularity can be obtained from the stoichiometry of the equations.	For simple reactions, order of a reaction may not be equal to the number of molecules of the reactants as seen from the balanced equation.
Molecularity of a reaction cannot be zero.	Order of a reaction can be zero.

3.5 Integrated Rate Equations

Instantaneous rate is hard to measure, so the differential rate equations is integrated to relate concentration of reactants or products with time.

These equations are different for reactions of different orders. In this topic, we shall determine these equations only for zero and first order chemical reactions.

Zero Order Reactions

The reaction in which rate of the reaction is proportional to zero power of the concentration of reactants is called **zero order reaction.**

Thus, in these reactions, the rate does not depend on the concentration of any of the reactants.

Consider the reaction, $R \longrightarrow P$

The differential rate equation can be written as

$$\text{Rate} = -\frac{d[R]}{dt} = k[R]^0 = k \times 1$$

$$d[R] = -\,kdt$$

On integrating both sides,

$$[R] = -\,kt + I \qquad \ldots\text{(i)}$$

where, I is the constant of integration.

Initially, at $t=0$, the concentration of the reactant $R=[R]_0$, where R_0 is the initial concentration of the reactant.

From Eq. (i), we have

$$[R]_0 = -k \times 0 + I$$

On substituting, $[R]_0 = I$ in the Eq.(i) we get

$$[R] = -kt + [R]_0 \quad \ldots\text{(ii)}$$

Simplifying Eq. (ii), gives

$$k = \frac{[R]_0 - [R]}{t} \quad \ldots\text{(iii)}$$

The Eq. (iii) **is integrated rate equation of zero order reaction.**

Graphical Representation of Zero Order Reaction

The expression $[R]=[R_0]-kt$ is comparable to straight line equation, i.e. $y=mx+c$ and therefore the value of k can be evaluated by **graphical method.**

If we plot $[R]$ against t, we get a straight line with slope equal to $-k$ and intercept equal to $[R]_0$ as shown in the below figure.

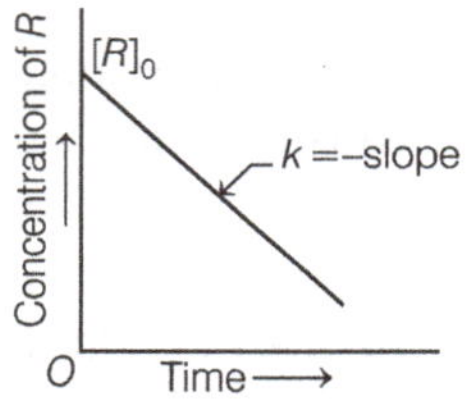

Variation in the concentration *vs* time plot for a zero order reaction

Examples of the Zero Order Reactions

Some enzyme catalysed reactions and reactions which occur on metal surfaces are few examples of zero order reactions. e.g. Decomposition of gaseous ammonia on platinum surface at high temperature and pressure.

$$2NH_3(g) \xrightarrow[\text{Pt catalyst}]{1130\text{ K}} N_2(g) + 3H_2(g)$$

The thermal decomposition of HI on gold surface is another example of zero order reaction.

Note The unit of rate and rate constant for zero order reactions are same.

Example 7 **The rate constant for zero order reaction in A is 0.0030 mol L^{-1} s^{-1}. How long will it take for the initial concentration of A to fall from 0.10 M to 0.075 M ?**

Sol. For zero order reaction,

$$k = \frac{[R]_0 - [R]}{t}$$

Given, $[R]_0 = 0.10$ M

$[R] = 0.075$ M

and $k = 0.0030$ mol L^{-1} s^{-1}

$$t = \frac{[R]_0 - [R]}{k} = \frac{0.10 - 0.075}{0.0030} = 8.33 \text{ s}$$

First Order Reactions

The reaction in which the rate of the reaction is proportional to the first power of the concentration of the reactant, R is called **first order reactions.**

For the reaction, $R \longrightarrow P$

The differential rate equation is given as,

$$\text{Rate} = -\frac{d[R]}{dt} = k[R]$$

On rearranging the above equation

or $$\frac{d[R]}{[R]} = -k\,dt$$

On integrating the equation, we get

$$\ln[R] = -kt + I \quad \ldots\text{(i)}$$

where, I is the constant of integration.

In the beginning when $t=0$, $R=[R]_0$, where $[R]_0$ is the initial concentration of the reactant.

∴ Eq. (i) can be rewritten as

$$\ln[R]_0 = -k \times 0 + I$$

$$\ln[R]_0 = I$$

On substituting $I = \ln[R]_0$ in the Eq. (i) to get

$$\ln[R] = -kt + \ln[R]_0 \quad \ldots\text{(ii)}$$

or $$\ln\frac{[R]}{[R]_0} = -kt \quad \ldots\text{(iii)}$$

or $$\frac{1}{t}\ln\frac{[R]}{[R]_0} = -k \text{ or } k = \frac{1}{t}\ln\frac{[R]_0}{[R]} \quad \ldots\text{(iv)}$$

or $$k = \frac{2.303}{t}\log\frac{[R]_0}{[R]} \quad \ldots\text{(v)}$$

The Eq. (v) is **integrated rate equation of first order reaction**. It is usually written as

$$k = \frac{2.303}{t} \log \frac{a}{(a-x)}$$

where, a is the initial concentration of reactant, R and $(a-x)$ is the concentration of reactant R, left after time t as x moles of it get changed to products after time t.

Expression for Rate Constant at Time t_1 and t_2

Rate constant can be calculated if concentrations of the reactants are measured at time t_1 and t_2.

At time t_1, $\ln [R]_1 = -kt_1 + \ln [R]_0$ ...(vi)

At time t_2, $\ln [R]_2 = -kt_2 + \ln [R]_0$ ...(vii)

Here, $[R]_1$ and $[R]_2$ are concentrations of the reactants at time t_1 and t_2, respectively.

On subtracting Eq. (vi) from Eq. (vii), we have

$$\ln [R]_1 - \ln [R]_2 = -kt_1 - (-kt_2)$$

or, $$\ln \frac{[R]_1}{[R]_2} = k(t_2 - t_1)$$

$$k = \frac{1}{t_2 - t_1} \ln \frac{[R]_1}{[R]_2} \quad \text{...(viii)}$$

$$k = \frac{2.303}{t_2 - t_1} \log \frac{[R]_1}{[R]_2}$$

Exponential form of Eq. (iii) can be written as:

$$[R] = [R]_0 e^{-kt} \quad \text{...(ix)}$$

Graphical Representation of First Order Reaction

If we plot ln $[R]$ against t, we get a straight line with slope $= -k$ and intercept equal to $\ln [R]_0$ as shown in figure (a).

On taking first order rate Eq. (v)

$$k = \frac{2.303}{t} \log \frac{[R]_0}{[R]}$$

or $$\log \frac{[R]_0}{[R]} = \frac{kt}{2.303}$$

If we plot a graph between $\log [R]_0 / [R]$ *vs* t, we get a straight line with the slope $= k/2.303$ as shown in figure (b).

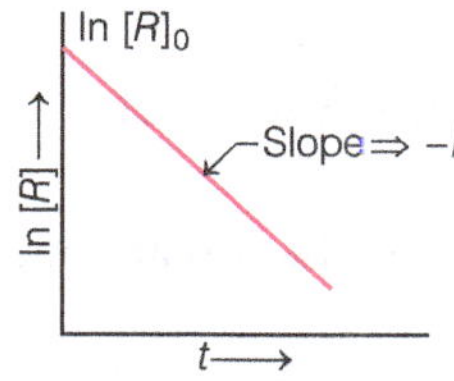

(a) A plot between ln $[R]$ and time $[t]$ for a first order reaction

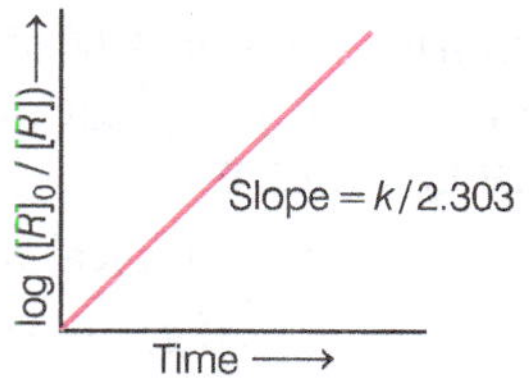

(b) Plot of $\log [R]_0 / [R]$ *vs* time for a first order reaction

Examples of First Order Reactions

(i) All natural and artifical radioactive decay of unstable nuclei takes place by first order kinetics.

$$^{226}_{88}\text{Ra} \longrightarrow {}^{4}_{2}\text{He} + {}^{222}_{86}\text{Rn}; \text{Rate} = k[\text{Ra}]$$

(ii) Hydrogenation of ethene is an example of first order reaction.

$$C_2H_4(g) + H_2(g) \longrightarrow C_2H_6(g); \text{Rate} = k[C_2H_4]$$

(iii) Decomposition of N_2O_5 and N_2O are more examples of first order reactions.

$$N_2O_5(g) \longrightarrow N_2O_4(g) + \frac{1}{2}O_2; \text{Rate} = k[N_2O_5]$$

$$N_2O(g) \longrightarrow N_2(g) + \frac{1}{2}O_2(g); \text{Rate} = k[N_2O]$$

Example 8 **Consider a certain reaction $A \longrightarrow$ Products, with $k = 2.0 \times 10^{-2} \text{s}^{-1}$. Calculate the concentration of A remaining after 100 s if the initial concentration of A is 1.0 mol L^{-1}.** NCERT

Sol. $k = 2.0 \times 10^{-2}\ \text{s}^{-1}$; $[A]_0 = 1.0$ mol L^{-1}; $t = 100$ s

As the unit of rate constant is s^{-1}, so the reaction follows first order kinetics. The rate constant for first order can be given as,

$$k = \frac{2.303}{t} \log \frac{[A]_0}{[A]}$$

Therefore,

$$2.0 \times 10^{-2}\ \text{s}^{-1} = \frac{2.303}{100\ \text{s}} \log \frac{1.0\ \text{mol L}^{-1}}{[A]}$$

$$2.0 \times 10^{-2}\ \text{s}^{-1} = \frac{2.303}{100\ \text{s}} (\log 1 - \log [A])$$

$$2.0 \times 10^{-2}\ \text{s}^{-1} = \frac{2.303}{100\ \text{s}} (0 - \log [A])$$

$$-\log [A] = \frac{2.0 \times 10^{-2}\ \text{s}^{-1} \times 100\ \text{s}}{2.303}$$

or $$[A] = \text{antilog}\left(-\frac{2.0 \times 10^{-2}\ \text{s}^{-1} \times 100\ \text{s}}{2.303}\right)$$

or $$[A] = 0.135\ \text{mol L}^{-1}$$

Pressure Change Method (For Gaseous System) for the Calculation of the Value of Rate Constant

Let us consider a typical first order gas phase reaction,

$$A(g) \longrightarrow B(g)+C(g)$$

Let p_i be the initial pressure of A at time $t=0$ and p_t be the total pressure at time, t. Also, p_A, p_B and p_C are the partial pressures of A, B and C, respectively at time t.

Total pressure, $p_t = p_A + p_B + p_C$ (pressure units)

If x atm be the decrease in pressure of A at time t and one mole each of B and C is being formed, then increase in pressure of B and C will also be x atm each.

	$A(g)$ $\longrightarrow$	$B(g)$ +	$C(g)$
At $t=0$	p_i atm	0 atm	0 atm
At time t	$(p_i - x)$ atm	x atm	x atm

$$p_t = (p_i - x) + x + x = p_i + x$$

$$x = (p_t - p_i)$$

where, $p_A = p_i - x = p_i - (p_t - p_i) = 2p_i - p_t$

Thus, integrated rate equation for gaseous phase can be written as

$$k = \left(\frac{2.303}{t}\right)\left(\log \frac{p_i}{p_A}\right)$$

$$\boxed{k = \frac{2.303}{t} \log \frac{p_i}{(2p_i - p_t)}}$$

Example 9 **The following data were obtained during the first order thermal decomposition of SO_2Cl_2 at a constant volume,**

$$SO_2Cl_2(g) \longrightarrow SO_2(g) + Cl_2(g)$$

Exp. No.	Time/s^{-1}	Total pressure/atm
1.	0	0.5
2.	100	0.6

Calculate the rate of the reaction when total pressure is 0.65 atm. NCERT

Sol.

	$SO_2Cl_2(g)$ $\longrightarrow$	$SO_2(g)$ +	$Cl_2(g)$
Initially at $t=0$	p_i	0	0
After time t	$p_i - p$	p	p

Total pressure after time t, i.e.

$$p_t = p_i - p + p + p = p_i + p$$

$$\therefore \quad p = p_t - p_i$$

So, $p_{SO_2Cl_2} = p_i - p = p_i - (p_t - p_i)$

$$= p_i - p_t + p_i = 2p_i - p_t$$

The rate constant for gaseous phase can be calculated as,

$$k = \frac{2.303}{t} \log \frac{p_i}{(2p_i - p_t)}$$

Given, $p_i = 0.5$ atm; $p_t = 0.6$ atm and $t = 100$ s

$$k = \frac{2.303}{(100\text{ s})} \log \frac{0.5\text{ atm}}{0.4\text{ atm}} = \frac{2.303}{(100\text{ s})} \log 1.25$$

$$= \frac{2.303}{(100\text{ s})} \times 0.0969 = 2.23 \times 10^{-3}\text{s}^{-1}$$

Calculation of reaction rate when total pressure is 0.65 atm

$$p_{SO_2Cl_2} = 2 \times 0.5 - 0.65$$

$$= (1 - 0.65) = 0.35\text{ atm}$$

$$k = 2.23 \times 10^{-3}\text{s}^{-1}$$

$$\text{Rate} = k \times p_{SO_2Cl_2} = (2.23 \times 10^{-3}\text{s}^{-1}) \times (0.35\text{ atm})$$

$$\text{Rate} = 7.8 \times 10^{-4}\text{ atm s}^{-1}$$

Half-Life of a Reaction

The time in which the concentration of a reactant is reduced to one-half of its initial concentration is called the **half-life of a reaction**. It is represented as $t_{1/2}$.

Derivation of Half-life of a Reaction from Zero Order Rate Equation

For a **zero order reaction,** the rate constant is given as

$$k = \frac{[R]_0 - [R]}{t}$$

At $t = t_{1/2}$, $\quad [R] = \frac{1}{2}[R]_0$

The rate constant at $t_{1/2}$ becomes

$$k = \frac{[R]_0 - 1/2[R]_0}{t_{1/2}}$$

$$\Rightarrow \quad \boxed{t_{1/2} = \frac{[R]_0}{2k}}$$

It is clear that $t_{1/2}$ **for a zero order reaction is directly proportional to the initial concentration of the reactants and inversely proportional to the rate constant.**

The graph of $t_{1/2}$ *versus* initial concentration of reactant is shown below.

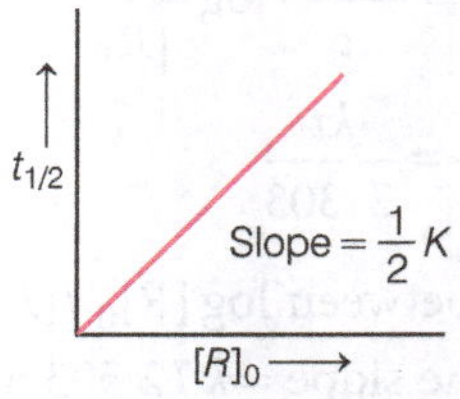

Plot of $t_{1/2}$ *vs* concentration for zero order reaction.

Derivation of Half-life of a Reaction from First Order Rate Equation

For the **first order reaction,** the rate constant is given as

$$k = \frac{2.303}{t} \log \frac{[R]_0}{[R]}$$

At $t_{1/2}$, $\quad [R] = \frac{[R]_0}{2}$

Therefore, $\quad k = \frac{2.303}{t_{1/2}} \log \frac{[R]_0}{[R]_0/2}$

or $\quad k = \frac{2.303}{t_{1/2}} \log 2$ or $k = \frac{2.303}{t_{1/2}} \times 0.301$

or $\quad \boxed{t_{1/2} = \frac{0.693}{k}}$

Thus, for **first order reaction, $t_{1/2}$ is independent of $[R]_0$ and hence, is constant.** The graph of $t_{1/2}$ *versus* initial concentration of reactant is shown below.

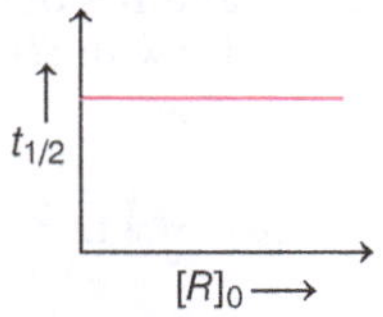

Plot of $t_{1/2}$ *vs* concentration for first order reaction.

The half-life of a reaction with *n*th order is given as

$$\boxed{t_{1/2} \propto \frac{1}{[R]_0^{n-1}}}$$

Expressions for the Reactions of Zero and First Order

Order	0	1
Reaction type	$R \rightarrow P$	$R \rightarrow P$
Differential rate law	$d[R]/dt = -k$	$d[R]/dt = -k[R]$
Integrated rate law	$kt = [R]_0 - [R]$	$[R] = [R]_0 e^{-kt}$ or or $kt = \ln \{[R]_0/[R]\}$
Straight line plot	$[R]$ *vs* t	$\ln [R]$ *vs* t
Half-life	$[R]_0 / 2k$	$\ln 2/k$
Units of k	conc. time^{-1} or mol L^{-1}s^{-1}	time^{-1} or s^{-1}

TEACHER'S TIP

Zero order reaction for 100% completion takes two half-life. On the other hand, first order reaction for 100% completion takes infinite half-life.

Example 10 **A reaction is 50% complete in 10 minutes. It is allowed to proceed another 5 minutes. How much the reaction would complete at the end of 15 minutes if it follows zero order kinetics?**

Sol. Let initial concentration, $[R]_0 = 100$ mol L^{-1}

At $t_{1/2}$, half of the reactant is consumed

$$k = \frac{[R]_0}{2t_{1/2}} = \frac{100}{2 \times 10} = 5 \text{ mol L}^{-1} \text{ min}^{-1}$$

Using integrated zero order kinetics,

At time $t = 15$ min.

$$k = \frac{[R]_0 - [R]}{t} \Rightarrow 5 = \frac{100 - [R]}{15}$$

$75 = 100 - [R]$

$[R] = 25$ mol L^{-1} and $[R]_0 = 100$ mol L^{-1} (Given)

$\therefore$ 75% of the reaction would be completed after 15 min.

Example 11 **The half-life for radioactive decay of ^{14}C is 5730 yrs. An archaeological artifact containing wood had only 80% of the ^{14}C found in a living tree. Estimate the age of the sample.** NCERT

Sol. For first order reaction, $t_{1/2} = \frac{0.693}{k}$

$$\therefore \quad k = \frac{0.693}{t_{1/2}} = \frac{0.693}{5730} \text{yr}^{-1}$$

We know that, $t = \frac{2.303}{k} \log \frac{[R]_0}{[R]}$

$$= \frac{2.303}{\frac{0.693}{5730}} \log \frac{100}{80} \quad \left(\text{As, } k = \frac{0.693}{t_{1/2}}\right)$$

$$= \frac{2.303 \times 5730}{0.693} \log \frac{100}{80} = \frac{2.303 \times 5730}{0.693} \log 1.25$$

$$= \frac{2.303 \times 5730}{0.693} \times 0.0969 = 1845 \text{ yrs (approx.)}$$

Therefore, the age of the given archaeological artifact containing wood is 1845 yrs.

Pseudo First Order Reaction

The reactions which are not actually of first order but behave so due to altered conditions are called **pseudo first order reactions** or **pseudo unimolecular reactions.** In such a chemical reaction between two substances, one reactant is present in large or excess amounts.

e.g.

- **Acid hydrolysis of ethyl acetate**

$$CH_3COOC_2H_5 + H_2O \xrightarrow{H^+} CH_3COOH + C_2H_5OH$$

	$CH_3COOC_2H_5$	H_2O	CH_3COOH	C_2H_5OH
$t = 0$	0.01mol	10 mol	0 mol	0 mol
t	0 mol	9.99 mol	0.01mol	0.01mol

$$\text{Rate} = k\,[CH_3COOC_2H_5]$$

Here, H_2O is taken in large excess.

- **Inversion of cane sugar** is another pseudo first order reaction.

$$\underset{\text{Cane sugar}}{C_{12}H_{22}O_{11}} + H_2O \xrightarrow{H^+} \underset{\text{Glucose}}{C_6H_{12}O_6} + \underset{\text{Fructose}}{C_6H_{12}O_6}$$

Rate $= k[C_{12}H_{22}O_{11}]$

Example 12 **In a pseudo first order hydrolysis of an ester in water, the following results were obtained :**

t/s	0	30	60	90
[Ester]/mol L^{-1}	0.55	0.31	0.17	0.085

Calculate the average rate of reaction between the time interval 30 to 60 s. NCERT

Sol. Average rate during the interval 30-60 s.

$$-\frac{[C_2 - C_1]}{t_2 - t_1} = \frac{-(0.17 - 0.31)}{60 - 30} = \frac{0.14}{30} \text{ mol L}^{-1}\text{s}^{-1}$$
$$= 4.67 \times 10^{-3} \text{ mol L}^{-1}\text{s}^{-1}$$

Quick Test 2

Conceptual Questions

1. For a certain reaction, the rate law is,
Rate $= k[A][B]^{3/2}$.
Can this belong to an elementary reaction? NCERT Exemplar

2. (i) Write the rate equation for the reaction, $2A + B \longrightarrow C$, if the order of the reaction is zero. NCERT Exemplar

(ii) Molecularity of any reaction can not be equal to zero. Give reason. NCERT Exemplar

3. A reaction is of second order with respect to a reactant. How is its rate affected if the concentration of the reactant is (a) tripled (b) reduced to half? Diksha

4. A reaction, reactant $\longrightarrow$ product is represented by (the graph)

(i) Predict the order of the reaction in this case.

(ii) What does the slope of the graph represent? Write the unit of the represented quantity.

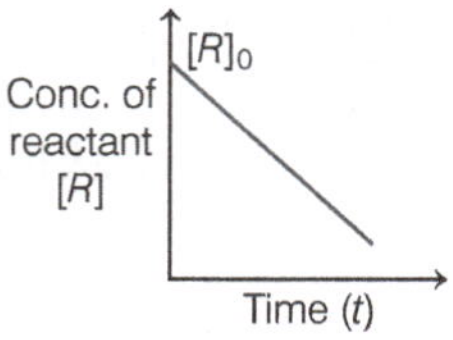

NCERT Exemplar, CBSE 2019

5. Show that in case of a first order reaction, the time taken for completion of 99% reaction is twice the time required for 90% completion of the reaction. (log 10 = 1) NCERT, CBSE 2024

Numerical Questions

6. The decomposition of NH_3 on platinum surface, $2NH_3(g) \xrightarrow{Pt} N_2(g) + 3H_2(g)$ is a zero order with $k = 2.5 \times 10^{-4}$ mol $L^{-1}s^{-1}$. What are the rates of production of N_2 and H_2? NCERT

7. The decomposition of NH_3 on platinum surface is zero order reaction. If rate constant (k) is 4×10^{-3} Ms^{-1}, how long will it take to reduce the initial concentration of NH_3 from 0.1 M to 0.064 M. CBSE 2019

8. A first order reaction has a rate constant 1.15×10^{-3} s^{-1}. How long will 5 g of this reactant take to reduce to 3 g? NCERT Intext

9. The reaction between A and B is of first order with respect to A and zero order with respect to B. Fill in the blanks in the following table.

Exp. No.	$[A]$ /mol L^{-1}	$[B]$ /mol L^{-1}	Initial rate/ mol L^{-1} min^{-1}
1.	0.1	0.1	2.0×10^{-2}
2.	–	0.2	4.0×10^{-2}
3.	0.4	0.4	–
4.	–	0.2	2.0×10^{-2}

NCERT

10. The following data were obtained during the first order thermal decomposition of C_2H_5Cl at a constant volume.

$$C_2H_5Cl\,(g) \longrightarrow C_2H_4\,(g) + HCl(g)$$

Experiment	Time (s^{-1})	Total pressure (atm)
1	0	0.4
2	100	0.6

Calculate the rate constant
(Given : log 2 = 0.3010, log 3 = 0.4771, log 4 = 0.6021) CBSE 2023

Answers

6. $\frac{d[N_2]}{dt} = 2.5 \times 10^{-4}$ mol $L^{-1}s^{-1}$, $\frac{d[H_2]}{dt} = 7.5 \times 10^{-4}$ mol $L^{-1}s^{-1}$

7. 9s **8.** 443.8s or 444s

9. 0.2 mol L^{-1}, 8×10^{-2} mol L^{-1} min^{-1}, 0.1mol L^{-1}

10. 6.9×10^{-3} sec^{-1}

For Solutions, See QR Code on Pg. 107

3.6 Temperature Dependence of the Rate of a Reaction

Most of the chemical reactions are accelerated by increase in temperature. It has been found that "*for a chemical reaction with rise in temperature by 10°, the rate constant is nearly doubled*".

The effect of temperature is usually expressed in terms of **temperature coefficient.** It is the ratio of rate constant of the reaction at two temperatures differing by 10°.

$$\text{Temperature coefficient} = \frac{\text{Rate constant at } (T + 10\,°\text{C})}{\text{Rate constant at } T\,°\text{C}}$$

Arrhenius Equation

The temperature dependence of the rate of a chemical reaction was first proposed by J.H. van't Hoff but Arrhenius provided its physical justification and interpretation and thus, is expressed by Arrhenius equation,

$$k = Ae^{-E_a/RT}$$

where, A is the **Arrhenius factor** or the **frequency factor,** also called **pre-exponential factor**. It is a constant specific to a particular reaction. R is gas constant and E_a is the activation energy measured in joules/mole (J mol^{-1}).

Explanation of Arrhenius Equation

- According to Arrhenius, a reaction takes place only when reactant molecules collide with each other.
- Collision of reactant molecules forms an unstable intermediate, which exists for a very short time and then breaks up to form the product molecules.

e.g. $H_2(g) + I_2(g) \longrightarrow 2HI(g)$

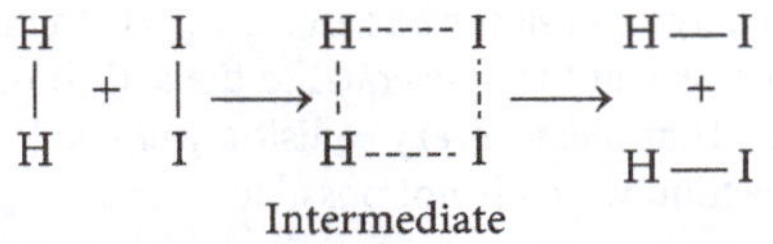

Formation of HI through the intermediate

- The energy required to form intermediate, called **activated complex** is known as activation energy. In other words, **activation energy** is the extra amount of energy which has to be supplied to the reacting species in their normal energy state to make their energy equal to threshold energy.

  i.e. **Activation energy** = Threshold energy − Average kinetic energy of the reacting molecules.

  Here, threshold energy is the minimum amount of energy required by any reacting molecules to collide with each other to form product.
- Some energy is released when activated complex breaks into product, this energy is the **final enthalpy** (ΔH) of the reaction and depends upon the nature of reactants and products.

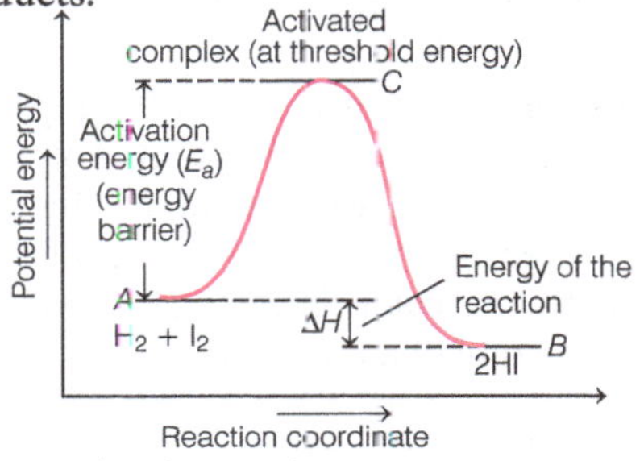

Showing plot of potential energy *versus* reaction coordinate

All the molecules in the reacting species do not have the same kinetic energy. Since, it is difficult to predict the behaviour of any one molecule with precision, Boltzmann and Maxwell used statistics to predict the behaviour of large number of molecules. This is discussed below after example.

Example 13 The decomposition of hydrocarbon follows the equation, $k = (4.5\times 10^{11}\ \text{s}^{-1})e^{-28000\ \text{K}/T}$. Calculate E_a. **NCERT**

Sol. According to Arrhenius equation,

$$k = Ae^{-E_a/RT} \quad \ldots(\text{i})$$

According to the available data

$$k = (4.5\times 10^{11}\ \text{s}^{-1})e^{-28000\ \text{K}/T} \quad \ldots(\text{ii})$$

On comparing both equations, we have

$$-\frac{E_a}{RT} = \frac{-28000\ \text{K}}{T} \Rightarrow E_a = (28000\ \text{K})\times R$$

$$= (28000\ \text{K})\times(8.314\text{K}^{-1}\ \text{J mol}^{-1}) = 232792\ \text{J mol}^{-1}$$

$$E_a = 232.792\ \text{kJ mol}^{-1}$$

Maxwell Boltzmann Distribution Curve

- According to Maxwell and Boltzmann, distribution of kinetic energy may be described by plotting the fraction of molecules (N_E/N_T) *versus* kinetic energy (E).

  Here, N_E is the number of molecules with energy E and N_T is the total number of molecules.

- The peak of the curve represents the kinetic energy possessed by the maximum fraction of molecules, that is known as **most probable kinetic energy**.

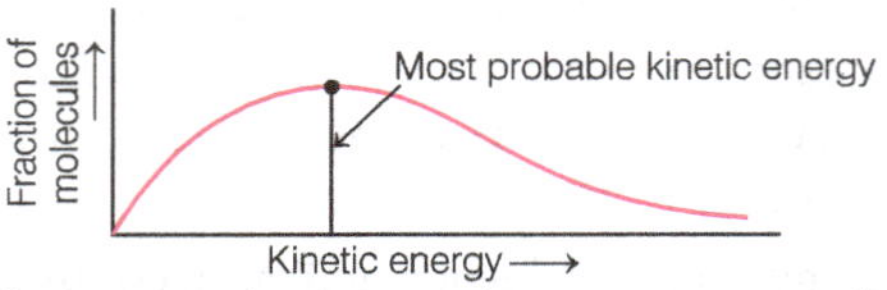

Distribution curve showing energies among gaseous molecules

- On raising the temperature, the maximum of the curve moves to the higher energy value and the curve broadens out.
- The proportion of molecules with higher energy increases, i.e., the fraction of reactant molecules which collide with energies greater than E_a increases with increasing the temperature. Thus, the molecules having energy equal to or greater than E_a gets doubled leading to doubling the rate of a reaction.

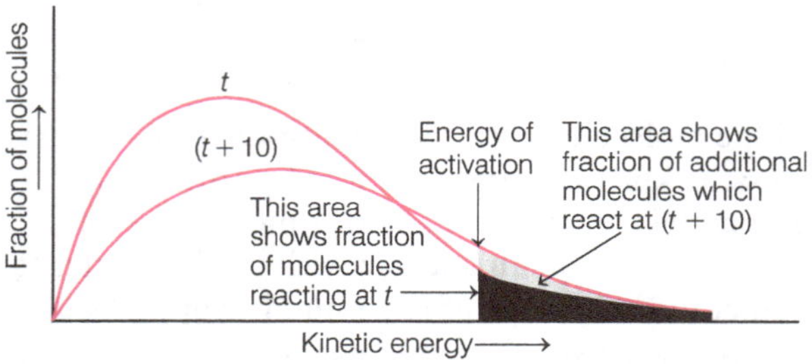

Distribution curve showing temperature dependence of rate of a reaction

Calculation of Activation Energy from Arrhenius Equation

In Arrhenius equation, $k = Ae^{-E_a/RT}$, the factor $e^{-E_a/RT}$ represents the fraction of molecules that have kinetic energy more than the activation energy (E_a) and is called **Boltzmann factor**.

Thus, it is clear from *Arrhenius equation that increasing the temperature or decreasing the activation energy will result in an increase in the rate of the reaction and an exponential increase in the rate constant.*

The calculation of activation energy can be carried out by two methods which are as follows.

(i) **Graphical Method** Taking natural logarithm on both sides, the Arrhenius equation becomes,

$$\ln k = -\frac{E_a}{RT} + \ln A$$

The plot of $\ln k$ *versus* $1/T$ gives a straight line.

Slope of this plot gives the value of $-\frac{E_a}{R}$ and the intercept gives the value of $\ln A$.

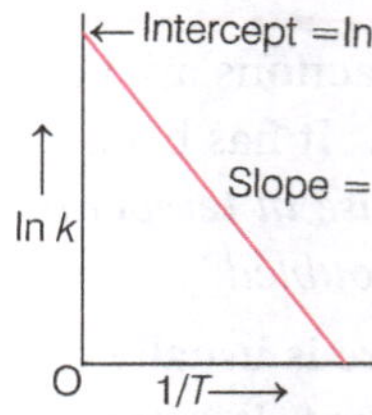

A plot between $\ln k$ and $1/T$

(ii) **Experimental method** E_a and A can also be determined from the rate constants at two different temperatures.

$$\ln k = -\frac{E_a}{RT} + \ln A$$

or

$$\log k = -\frac{E_a}{2.303\,RT} + \log A$$

Let k_1 and k_2 be the rate constants at temperatures T_1 and T_2, respectively. Then,

$$\log k_1 = -\frac{E_a}{2.303\,RT_1} + \log A \quad \ldots\text{(i)}$$

$$\log k_2 = -\frac{E_a}{2.303\,RT_2} + \log A \quad \ldots\text{(ii)}$$

A = constant for the given reactions.

Subtracting Eq. (i) from Eq. (ii), we have

$$\log k_2 - \log k_1 = \frac{E_a}{2.303\,RT_1} - \frac{E_a}{2.303\,RT_2}$$

$$\log \frac{k_2}{k_1} = \frac{E_a}{2.303\,R}\left[\frac{1}{T_1} - \frac{1}{T_2}\right]$$

$$\log \frac{k_2}{k_1} = \frac{E_a}{2.303\,R}\left[\frac{T_2 - T_1}{T_1 T_2}\right]$$

TEACHER'S TIP

Activation energy can never be zero. If $E_a = 0$, then the initial energy of the reactant will be equal to the activation energy of the reaction. That means every collision will result into chemical reaction which is not possible.

Example 14 **In general it is observed that the rate of chemical reaction becomes doubled with every 10° rise in temperature. If this generalisation holds for a reaction in the temperature range 298 to 308 K what would be the value of E_a for this reaction?**

Or

The rate of the chemical reaction doubles for an increase of 10 K in temperature from 298 K. Calculate E_a.

NCERT Intext

Sol. According to integrated Arrhenius equation

$$\log\frac{k_2}{k_1} = \frac{E_a}{2.303\,R}\left[\frac{1}{T_1} - \frac{1}{T_2}\right]$$

Given, $T_1 = 298\text{K}, T_2 = 308\text{ K}, \frac{k_2}{k_1} = 2$

Now, $\log 2 = \frac{E_a}{2.303 \times 8.314}\left[\frac{1}{298} - \frac{1}{308}\right]$

$$0.3010 = \frac{E_a}{2.303 \times 8.314} \times \frac{10}{298 \times 308}$$

$$E_a = \frac{0.3010 \times 2.303 \times 8.314 \times 298 \times 308}{10}$$

$$= 52898\text{ J mol}^{-1} = 52.898\text{ kJ mol}^{-1}$$

Effect of Catalyst

A catalyst is a substance which alters the rate of reaction without itself undergoing any permanent chemical change. e.g.

MnO_2 catalyses the following reaction in the order to raise its rate considerably.

$$2KClO_3 \xrightarrow{MnO_2} 2KCl + 3O_2$$

If the catalyst reduces rate of reaction, then it is called **inhibitor.**

The action of the catalyst can be explained by intermediate complex theory which is discussed below.

Intermediate Complex Theory

According to this theory, a catalyst participates in a chemical reaction by forming temporary bonds with the reactants resulting in an intermediate complex and decomposes to form products and the catalyst.

Catalysed reaction proceed as,

$$\underset{\text{Reactants}}{A+B} + \underset{\text{Catalyst}}{C} \longrightarrow \underset{\text{Intermediate complex}}{ABC} \rightarrow \underset{\text{Product}}{A-B} + \underset{\text{Catalyst regenerated}}{C}$$

Since, the catalyst is regenerated after the decomposition of the intermediate so, a small amount of catalyst is enough for a large amount of reactants. It is believed that '*the catalyst provides an alternate pathway or reaction mechanism by reducing the activation energy between reactants and products, hence lowering the potential energy barrier*' as shown in the figure.

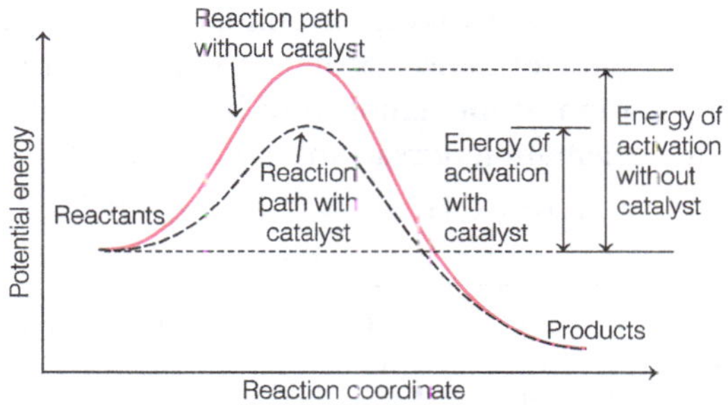

Effect of catalyst on activation energy

It is also clear from the Arrhenius equation ($k = Ae^{-E_a/RT}$) that lower the value of E_a faster will be the rate of reaction.

Characteristics of a Catalyst

Some of the characteristics of a catalyst are as follows

- A small amount of the catalyst can catalyse a large amount of reactions.
- A catalyst does not alter **Gibbs energy**, ΔG of a reaction.
- It does not change the equilibrium constant rather, it helps in attaining the equilibrium faster.
- A catalyst catalyses the **spontaneous reactions** but does not catalyse **non-spontaneous reactions.**
- A catalyst is highly specific. They have an ability to direct the reaction to yield a particular product.

3.7 Collision Theory of Chemical Reactions

- Collision theory developed by Trautz and William is based on kinetic theory of gases. According to this theory, the reactant molecules are assumed to be hard spheres and reaction is postulated to occur when molecules collide with each other.
- **Collision Frequency** (Z) is the number of collisions per second per unit volume of the reaction mixture.

  For a bimolecular elementary reaction,

  $$A + B \longrightarrow \text{Products}$$

  Rate of reaction can be expressed as

  $$\boxed{\text{Rate} = Z_{AB}\, e^{-E_a/RT}} \quad \ldots\text{(i)}$$

  where, Z_{AB} is the collision frequency of the reactants, A and B.
- **Effective Collisions** are the collisions in which reactant molecules collide with sufficient kinetic energy (which is also called threshold energy) and with proper orientation

so as to facilitate breaking of bonds between the reacting molecules and formation of new bonds to form products. e.g. Formation of methanol from bromomethane depends upon the orientation of reactant molecules.

$$CH_3Br + OH^- \longrightarrow CH_3OH + Br^-$$

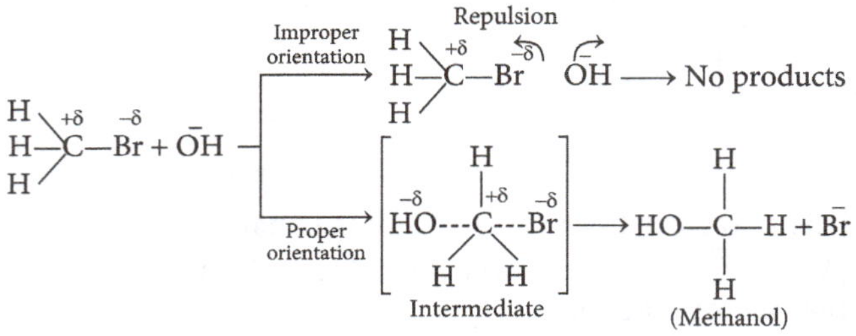

Proper and improper orientations of colliding molecules

In collision theory, activation energy and proper orientation of the molecules together determine the criteria for an effective collision and thus, the rate of a chemical reaction.

$$\text{Reaction rate} = PZ_{AB}\, e^{-E_a/RT} \quad \ldots\text{(ii)}$$

where, P is **orientation factor** or **steric factor** or **probability factor.**

Limitations of Collision Theory

This theory explains the results of a number of reactions but it does not give satisfactory explanation in some cases as it considers atoms/molecules to be hard spheres and ignores their structural aspect.

Quick Test 3

Conceptual Questions

1. Oxygen is available in plenty in air yet fuels do not burn by themselves at room temperature. Explain. *NCERT Exemplar*

2. Why in redox titration of $KMnO_4$ *versus* oxalic acid, we heat oxalic acid solution before starting the titration? *NCERT Exemplar*

3. In some case, it is found that a large number of colliding molecules have energy more than threshold energy, yet the reaction is slow. Why? *CBSE 2013; NCERT Exemplar*

4. The reaction between $H_2(g)$ and $O_2(g)$ is highly feasible yet allowing the gases to stand at room temperature in the same vessel does not lead to the formation of water. Explain. *NCERT Exemplar*

Numerical Questions

5. The rate constant of a reaction quadruples when the temperature changes from 700 K to 720 K. Calculate the activation energy for this reaction.
[log 2 = 0.30, log 4 = 0.60, 2.303 R = 19.15 J K^{-1} mol^{-1}] *CBSE 2024*

6. The rate constant for the decomposition of hydrocarbons is $2.418 \times 10^{-5} s^{-1}$ at 546 K. If the energy of activation is 179.9 kJ mol^{-1}, what will be the value of pre-exponential factor? *NCERT*

7. The decomposition of A into product has value of k as $4.5 \times 10^3\ s^{-1}$ at 10°C and energy of activation 60 kJ mol^{-1}. At what temperature would k be $1.5 \times 10^4 s^{-1}$? *NCERT; CBSE 2013*

8. The activation energy for the reaction, $2HI(g) \longrightarrow H_2(g) + I_2(g)$ is 209.5 kJ mol^{-1} at 581 K. Calculate the fraction of molecules of reactants having energy equal to or greater than activation energy. *NCERT Intext*

9. The rate constant for the first order decomposition of N_2O_5 is given by the following equation

$$\log k = 23.6 - \frac{2 \times 10^4}{T} K$$

Calculate E_a for this reaction (Given, $R = 8.314\ JK^{-1}\ mol^{-1}$) *CBSE 2023*

10. The time required for 10% completion of a first order reaction at 298 K is equal to that required for its 25% completion at 308 K. If the value of A is $4 \times 10^{10} s^{-1}$. Calculate k at 318 K and E_a. *NCERT*

For Solutions, See QR Code on Pg. 107

Answers

5. 289.548 kJ mol^{-1}	6. $3.9 \times 10^{12} s^{-1}$
7. 24.02°C	8. 1.471×10^{-19}
9. 382.8 kJ mol^{-1}	10. $1.035 \times 10^{-2} s^{-1}$, 76.640 kJ mol^{-1}

Mind Map

CHEMICAL KINETICS

Order of Reaction

It is the sum of powers of concentration terms in the rate law expression.
e.g. Rate = $k[A][B]^2$
$\therefore$ Order = 1 + 2 = 3
It is determined experimentally.

Molecularity of Reaction

It shows number of species taking part in an elementary (one step) reaction.
- It can never be equal to zero. It is always a whole number.
- It has no meaning in complex reactions (reactions involving more than one steps).

Temperature Dependence of Rate of Reaction

For a chemical reaction with rise in temperature by 10°C, the rate constant is nearly doubled.

(A) Arrhenius Equation

$$k = Ae^{-E_a/RT}$$

Here, A = pre-exponential factor,
R = gas constant,
E_a = activation energy.

$$\log k = \log A - E_a/2.303\,RT$$

$$\log\frac{k_2}{k_1} = \frac{E_a}{2.303R}\left(\frac{T_2 - T_1}{T_1T_2}\right)$$

(B) Activation Energy (E_a)

- It is energy required by the reactant molecules to form an intermediate called **activated complex**.
- The slope of ln k vs $1/T$ has the value $-\frac{E_a}{R}$ and is used to calculate value of E_a.

Collision Theory

According to it, rate = $PZ_{AB}e^{-E_a/RT}$
P is steric or orientation factor
Z_{AB} = Collision frequency of the reactants.

Requirements for Proper Collision

- Proper orientation.
- Suitable activation energy.

Average Rate

- It is rate of change of concentration of reactant / product over a long time interval.

$$r_{av} = -\frac{\Delta[R]}{\Delta t} = \frac{\Delta[P]}{\Delta t}$$

- For a reaction, $aA \longrightarrow bB + cC$

$$\text{rate} = -\frac{\Delta[A]}{a\Delta t} = +\frac{\Delta[B]}{b\Delta t} = +\frac{\Delta[C]}{c\Delta t}$$

a, b, c = integers of balanced equation.

Instantaneous Rate

It is the rate of change of concentration of reactant / product at a particular instant.
For $R \rightarrow P$

$$r_{ins} = -\frac{d[R]}{dt} = \frac{d[P]}{dt}$$

(–ve because concentration of R decreases with time.)

Rate of Reaction

It is defined as change in concentration per unit time. (Unit : mol L^{-1} s^{-1})

Factors Influencing Rate of Reaction

- **Concentration** Higher the concentration of reactants, faster is the rate of reaction.
- **Temperature** Increases with increase in temperature. Becomes almost double with 10°C rise.
- **Presence of Catalyst** Increases with a catalyst.
- **Activation Energy** Lower the activation energy, faster is the reaction.

Rate Law

- It is the expression of rate in terms of molar concentration of reactants with each term raised to power which may or may not be same as stoichiometric coefficients of reactants in a balanced chemical equation.
- For a reaction,

$$xA + yB \longrightarrow zC$$

- Rate = $k[A]^p[B]^q$, p and q may or may not be equal to x and y.

Rate Constant (k)

- It is the rate of chemical reaction when concentration of each reactant is taken as unity.
- It is also called specific reaction rate.
- It depends only upon temperature.
- Unit of $k = \left(\frac{\text{mol}}{\text{L}}\right)^{1-n} s^{-1}$

where, n = order of reaction.

Integrated Rate Equations

Zero Order Reaction

- Rate, $-\frac{d[R]}{dt} = k$ or $kt = [R]_0 - [R]$
- $t_{1/2}$ (half-life) = $\frac{[R]_0}{2k}$
- Plot of $[R]$ vs t is a straight line with slope $-k$ and intercept $[R_0]$.

First Order Reaction

Rate, $-\frac{d[R]}{dt} = k[R]$ or $kt = \ln\frac{[R]_0}{[R]}$

$$k = \frac{2.303}{t}\log\frac{a}{(a-x)},$$

a = initial concentration

$$t_{1/2} = \frac{\ln 2}{k} = \frac{0.693}{k}$$

- Plot of ln $[R]$ vs t is a straight line with slope $-k$ and intercept ln $[R]_0$.
- In terms of pressure (For gas phase reaction), $A(g) \longrightarrow B(g) + C(g)$

$$k = \frac{2.303}{t}\log\frac{p_i}{2p_i - p_t},$$

Pseudo First Order Reaction

These reactions are not actually of first order but behave so due to altered conditions, e.g. hydrolysis of ester.

EXAM PATTERN QUESTIONS

Objective Type Questions

Multiple Choice Questions [1 Mark]

1. Which of the following expressions is correct for the rate of reaction given below?

$5\,Br^-(aq) + BrO_3^-(aq) + 6\,H^+(aq) \longrightarrow 3\,Br_2(aq) + 3H_2O(l)$

NCERT Exemplar

(a) $\frac{\Delta[Br^-]}{\Delta t} = 5\frac{\Delta[H^+]}{\Delta t}$ (b) $\frac{\Delta[Br^-]}{\Delta t} = \frac{6}{5}\frac{\Delta[H^+]}{\Delta t}$

(c) $\frac{\Delta[Br^-]}{\Delta t} = \frac{5}{6}\frac{\Delta[H^+]}{\Delta t}$ (d) $\frac{\Delta[Br^-]}{\Delta t} = 6\frac{\Delta[H^+]}{\Delta t}$

2. For the reaction $3A \rightarrow 2B$, rate of reaction $\frac{d[B]}{dt}$ is equal to **CBSE 2023**

(a) $\frac{-3}{2}\frac{d[A]}{dt}$ (b) $\frac{-2}{3}\frac{d[A]}{dt}$

(c) $\frac{-1}{3}\frac{d[A]}{dt}$ (d) $\frac{+2d[A]}{dt}$

3. A graph of volume of hydrogen released *vs* time for the reaction between zinc and dil. HCl is given in figure. On the basis of this, mark the correct option. **NCERT Exemplar**

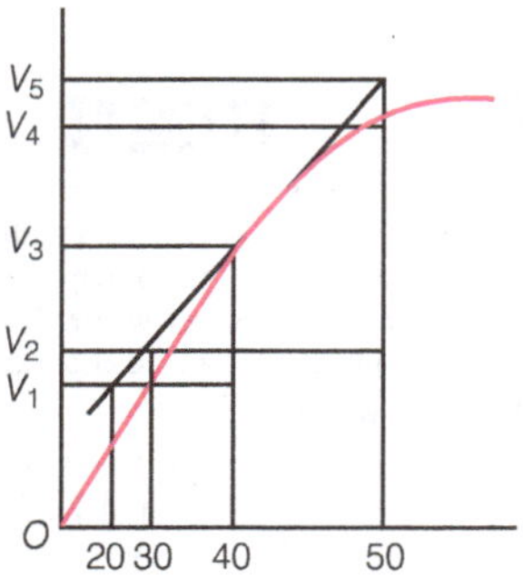

(a) Average rate upto 40s is $\frac{V_3 - V_2}{40}$

(b) Average rate upto 40s is $\frac{V_3 - V_2}{40 - 30}$

(c) Average rate upto 40s is $\frac{V_3}{40}$

(d) Average rate upto 40s is $\frac{V_3 - V_1}{40 - 20}$

4. Which of the following can increase the rate of a chemical reaction ? **Competency Based Que.**

P. Increasing the temperature

Q. Increasing the concentration of products

R. Adding a catalyst

S. Increasing the concentration of reactants

(a) Q and S (b) P and Q

(c) P, R and S (d) P, Q, R and S

5. Which of the pairs represents the same order of reaction ? **Competency Based Que.**

(a)

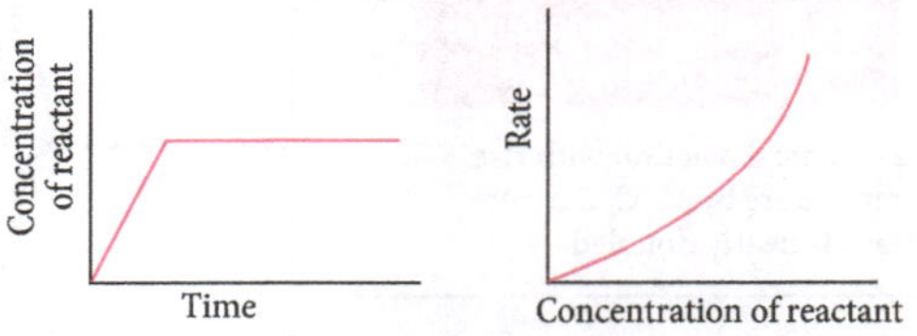

(b)

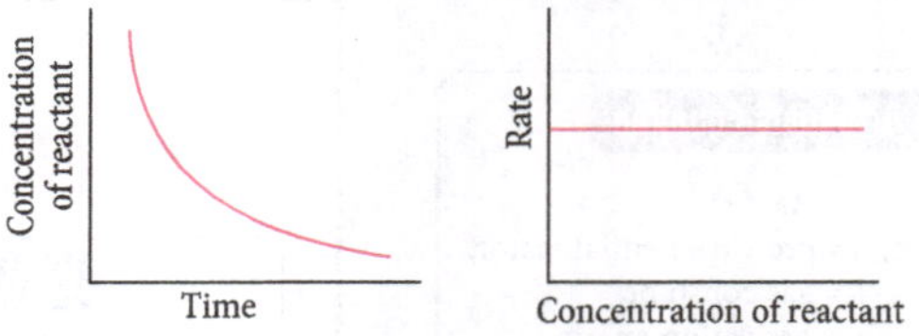

(c)

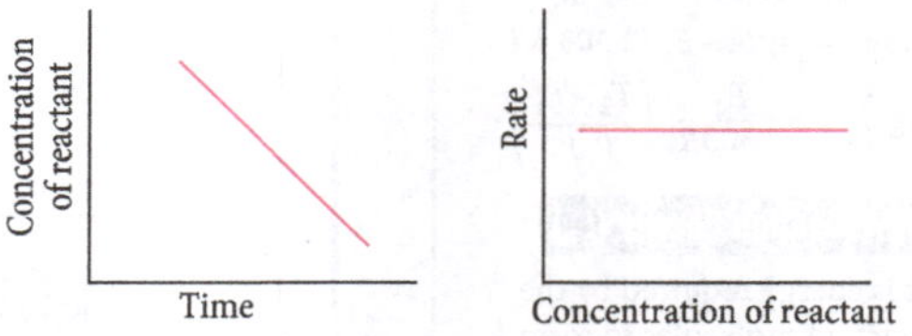

(d)

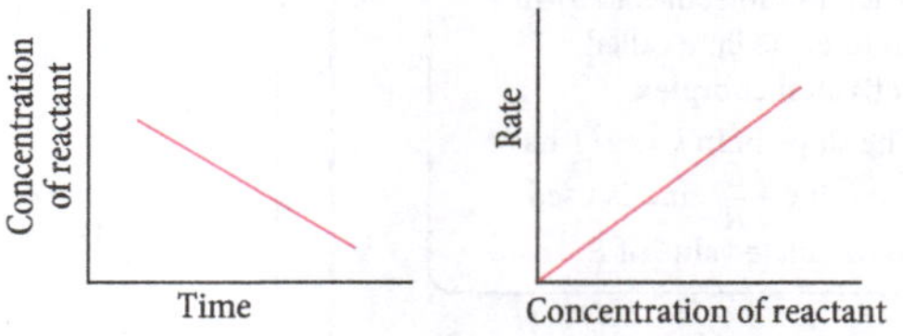

6. For the reaction , $A + 2B \longrightarrow C + D$, the order of reaction is **CBSE 2024**

(a) 1 with respect to A

(b) 2 with respect to B

(c) can't be predicted as order is determined experimentally.

(d) 3

7. Which of the following statement is true ?

(a) Molecularity of a reaction can be zero or a fraction.
(b) Molecularity has no meaning for complex reactions.
(c) Molecularity of a reaction is an experimental quantity.
(d) Reactions with molecularity three are very rare but are fast.

8. The rate of a reaction increases sixteen times when the concentration of the reactant increases four times. The order of the reaction is CBSE 2024

(a) 2.5 (b) 2.0
(c) 1.5 (d) 0.5

9. In a given graph of zero order reaction, the slope and intercept are CBSE 2024

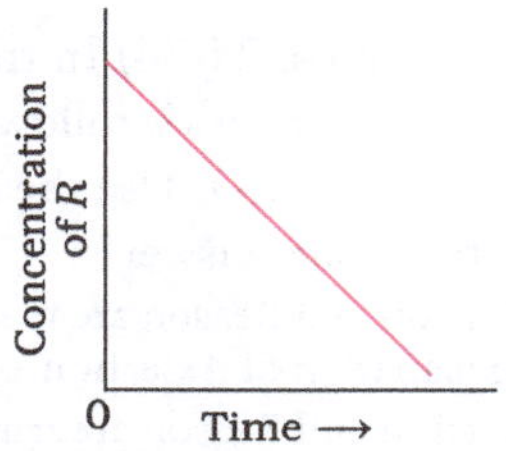

(a) Slope $= k$, Intercept $= [R]_0$
(b) Slope $= -k$, Intercept $= [R]_0$
(c) Slope $= k/2.303$, Intercept $= \ln[R]_0$
(d) Slope $= -k/2.303$, Intercept $= \ln A$

10. Match the Column I with Column II and choose the correct option.

Column I (Reaction)	Column II (Order of reaction)
A. Inversion of cane sugar	(i) Zero order reaction
B. Decomposition of N_2O	(ii) First order reaction
C. Thermal decomposition of HI on gold surface	(iii) Pseudo order reaction

Codes

	A	B	C		A	B	C
(a)	(i)	(ii)	(ii)	(b)	(ii)	(iii)	(i)
(c)	(iii)	(ii)	(i)	(d)	(ii)	(i)	(iii)

11. The following experimental rate data were obtained for a reaction carried out at 25°C

$$A(g) + B(g) \longrightarrow C(g) + D(g)$$

Initial $[A(g)]$ / mol dm^{-3}	Initial $[B(g)]$ / mol dm^{-3}	Initial rate/ mol $dm^{-3}s^{-1}$
3.0×10^{-2}	2.0×10^{-2}	1.89×10^{-4}
3.0×10^{-2}	4.0×10^{-2}	1.89×10^{-4}
6.0×10^{-2}	4.0×10^{-2}	7.56×10^{-4}

What are the orders with respect to $A(g)$ and $B(g)$? CBSE 2023

	Order with respect to $A(g)$	Order with respect to $B(g)$
(a)	Zero	Second
(b)	First	Zero
(c)	Second	Zero
(d)	Second	First

12. The slope in the plot of $\ln[R]$ *vs* time for a first order reaction is CBSE 2022

(a) $\frac{+k}{2.303}$ (b) $-k$ (c) $\frac{-k}{2.303}$ (d) $+k$

13. The half-life for a zero order reaction equals CBSE 2023

(a) $\frac{2k}{[R]_0}$ (b) $\frac{1}{2}\frac{k}{[R_0]^2}$
(c) $\frac{[R_0]^2}{2k}$ (d) $\frac{[R]_0}{2k}$

14. Rate law for the reaction $A + 2B \longrightarrow C$ is found to be

$$\text{Rate} = k[A][B]$$

Concentration of reactant 'B' is doubled, keeping the concentration of 'A' constant, the value of rate constant will be.... . NCERT Exemplar

(a) the same (b) doubled
(c) quadrupled (d) halved

15. A first order reaction is 50% completed in 1.26×10^{14} s. How much time would it take for 100% completion?

(a) 1.26×10^{15} s (b) 2.52×10^{14} s
(c) 2.52×10^{28} s (d) Infinite

16. The rate of reaction $A + B \rightarrow$ Products, is given by the equation $r = k[A][B]$. If B is taken in large excess, the order of reaction would be CBSE 2023

(a) 2 (b) 0
(c) 1 (d) Cannot be predicted

17. In effective collisions the colliding molecules must have: CBSE 2024

(a) proper orientation only.
(b) a certain minimum amount of activation energy.
(c) threshold energy only.
(d) threshold energy and proper orientation both.

18. Activation energy of a chemical reaction can be determined by .... NCERT Exemplar

(a) determining the rate constant at standard temperature
(b) determining the rate constant at two different temperatures
(c) determining probability of collision
(d) using catalyst

19. What is the activation energy for a reaction, if its rate doubles when the temperature is raised from 20°C to 35°C? ($R = 8.314$ J mol^{-1}K^{-1})

(a) 342 kJ mol^{-1} (b) 269 kJ mol^{-1}
(c) 34.7 kJ mol^{-1} (d) 15.1 kJ mol^{-1}

20. The graph below shows the volume of carbon dioxide formed with time during a chemical reaction.

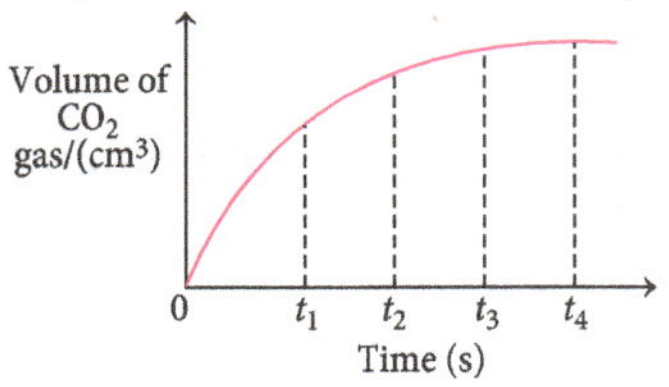

Based on the graph, at what time is the rate of reaction the highest ? **Competency Based Que.**

(a) t_1 (b) t_2 (c) t_3 (d) t_4

21. According to Arrhenius equation, rate constant k is equal to $A\,e^{-E_a/RT}$. Which of the following options represents the graph of ln k vs $\frac{1}{T}$? **NCERT Exemplar**

(a)
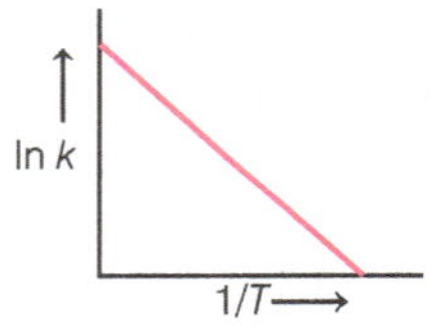

(b)
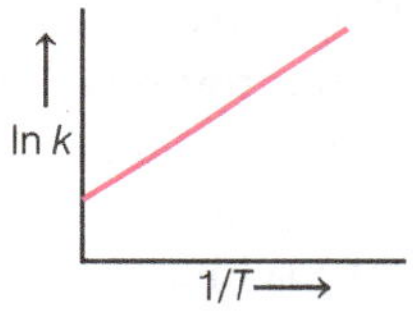

(c)
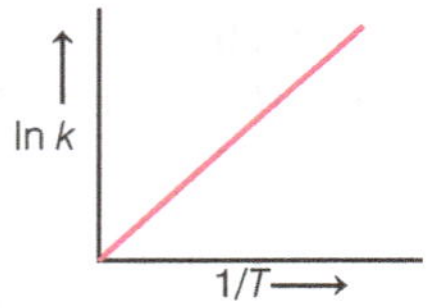

(d)
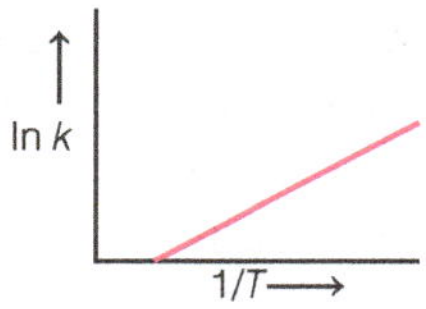

22. The diagram below shows the potential energy variation for a reaction using a catalyst and for the same reaction without a catalyst. **Competency Based Que.**

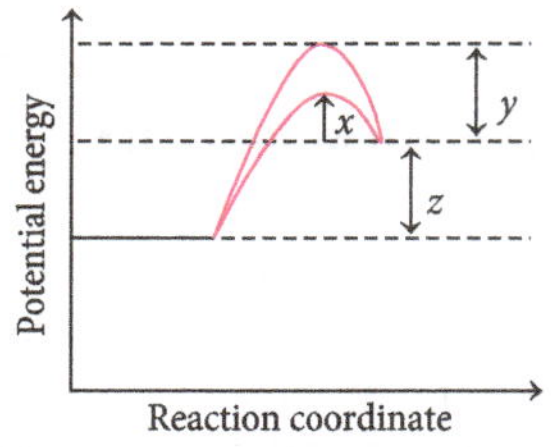

Which of the following represents the enthalpy change (ΔH) and activation energy (E_a) for the reaction with a catalyst?

Option	ΔH	E_a with catalyst
P	z	$x + z$
Q	z	$y + z$
R	$z + x$	x
S	z	y

(a) P (b) Q (c) R (d) S

23. Which of the following statements is/are correct?

I. A catalyst lowers the activation energy of a reaction.

II. A catalyst allows the same rate of reaction to be achieved at a lower temperature.

III. A catalyst mixes with reactants and increases the overall concentration of reactants in the rate equation. **Competency Based Que.**

(a) Only I (b) I and II
(c) II and III (d) I, II and III

Assertion-Reason [1 Mark]

Directions (Q. Nos. 24-34) In the following questions, an Assertion (A) is followed by a corresponding Reason (R). Use the following keys to choose the appropriate answer.

(a) Both Assertion and Reason are true and Reason is the correct explanation of Assertion.
(b) Both Assertion and Reason are true, but Reason is not the correct explanation of Assertion.
(c) Assertion is true, but Reason is false.
(d) Assertion is false, but Reason is true.

24. Assertion (A) Rate of reaction is a measure of change in concentration of reactant with respect to time.

Reason (R) Rate of reaction is a measure of change in concentration of product with respect to time.

25. Assertion (A) For a zero order reaction, the unit of rate constant and rate of reaction are same.

Reason (R) Rate of reaction for zero order reaction is independent of concentration of reactant. **CBSE 2023, 24 C**

Or **Assertion** (A) The units of rate constant of a zero order reaction and the rate of reaction are the same.

Reason (R) In zero order reaction, the rate of reaction is independent of the concentration of reactants. **CBSE 2024**

26. Assertion (A) For complex reactions, molecularity and order are not same.

Reason (R) Order of reaction may be zero. **CBSE 2020**

27. Assertion (A) Rate constant determined from Arrhenius equation are fairly accurate for simple as well as complex molecules.

Reason (R) Reactant molecules undergo chemical change irrespective of their orientation during collision.

28. Assertion (A) Order and molecularity of a reaction are always same.

Reason (R) Complex reactions involve a sequence of elementary reactions and the slowest step is rate determining. **CBSE 2023**

29. Assertion (A) A catalyst increases the rate of reaction.

Reason (R) Catalyst also changes the equilibrium constant.

30. Assertion (A) Hydrolysis of an ester follows first order kinetics. **CBSE 2020**

Reason (R) Concentration of water remains nearly constant during the course of the reaction.

31. Assertion (A) The unit of k is independent of order of reaction.

Reason (R) The unit of k for zero order reaction is mol $L^{-1}s^{-1}$.

32. Assertion (A) Reactions of higher order are rare.

Reason (R) The chances of simultaneous multimolecular collision are extremely small.

33. Assertion (A) Rate of reaction increase with increase in temperature.

Reason (R) Number of collisions increases with increase in temperature.

34. Assertion (A) All collisions of reactant molecules lead to product formation.

Reason (R) Only those collisions in which molecules have correct orientation and sufficient kinetic energy lead to compound formation.

Case-Study [4 Marks]

35. Read the given case and answer the following questions.

Arrhenius equation for first order reactions are useful for modeling the timing and temperature of petroleum generation from organic rich shales and kerogens at laboratory scales (e.g. per minute), based on pyrolysis 52 peak data is measured at multiple heating rates, and for burial histories occurring over geological time scales (e.g. per millions of years).

First order reactions are accompanied by second order reactions and physical changes impacting the kerogens as they thermally mature, so simple Arrhenius equation, first order reaction modeling can only provide an approximation of the complete petroleum generation process. Thermally immature shale and/or kerogen samples yield less complex pyrolysis S2-peaks than thermally mature sample and provide more credible kinetic distributions when modeled at multiple heating rates with the Arrhenius equation.

More credible kinetic fits to the S2-peak pyrolysis data are derived by allowing the activation energy (*E*) and the frequency factor (*A*) to vary for each reaction to derive good-fit kinetic distributions than by applying the commonly used assumption that the *A* value remain constant for the set of parallel reactions included in the distribution.

(i) The plot of ln k *versus* $\frac{1}{T}$ gives a straight line.

What is the value of slope and intercept in this graph?

(ii) If the activation energy for a reaction is zero and rate constant is $1.72 \times 10^5 \text{ s}^{-1}$ at 300 K. Calculate the rate constant at 310 K.

(iii) What will be the SI unit for Arrhenius factor in Arrhenius equation of a second order reaction ?

Or Give the relation between rate constant and activation energy.

36. Read the given case and answer the following questions.

The rate of a chemical reaction is expressed either in terms of decrease in the concentration of reactants or increase in the concentration of a product per unit time. Rate of the reaction depends upon the nature of reactants, concentration of reactants, temperature, presence of catalyst, surface area of the reactants and presence of light. Rate of reaction is directly related to the concentration of reactant. Rate law states that, the rate of reaction depends upon the concentration terms on which the rate of reaction actually depends, as observed experimentally. The sum of powers of the concentration of the reactants in the rate law expression is called order of reaction while the number of reacting species taking part in an elementary reaction which must collide simultaneously in order to bring about a chemical reaction is called molecularity of the reaction.

Answer the following questions

(i) (a) What is a rate determining step?

(b) Define complex reaction.

(ii) What is the effect of temperature on the rate constant of a reaction?

Or

Why is molecularity applicable only for elementary reactions whereas order is applicable for elementary as well as complex reactions?

(iii) The conversion of molecule X to Y follows second order kinetics. If concentration of X is increased 3 times, how will it affect the rate of formation of Y? **CBSE 2025**

Subjective Type Questions

Short Answer Type I Questions [2 Marks]

1. We do not determine the order of a reaction by taking into consideration the balanced chemical equation? Give reason.

2. One-fourth of reaction is completed in 32 min. What is the half-life period of this reaction?

3. (i) Give an example of first order reaction.
(ii) Plot the graph between $\log[R]_0/[R]$ *vs* time (t) for a first order reaction.

4. The C-14 content of an ancient piece of wood was found to have three tenths of that in living trees. How old is that piece of wood ?
($\log 3 = 0.4771$, $\log 7 = 0.8540$, half-life of C-14 $= 5730$ years) **CBSE SQP 2021**

5. (i) A first order reaction takes 40 minutes for 30% decomposition. Calculate the rate constant.
(ii) Give the unit of rate constant for first order reaction.

6. The concentration of R in the reaction; $R \longrightarrow P$; was measured as a function of time and the following data is obtained

$[R]$ mol L^{-1}	1.0	0.75	0.40	0.10
t (min)	0.0	0.05	0.12	0.18

Determine the order of reaction.

7. The rate constant of a reaction of zero order in A is 3.0×10^{-3} mol L^{-1} s^{-1}. How long will it take for the initial concentration of A to fall from 0.10 M to 0.075 M?

8. For an elementary reaction, $X(g) \longrightarrow Y(g) + Z(g)$ the half-life period is 10 min. In what period of time would the concentration of X be reduced to 10% of original concentration?

9. If time taken for half of the first order reaction to complete is t_1, whereas that for $3/4^{th}$ of the reaction to complete is t_2. How are t_1 and t_2 related to each other?

10. Nitrogen dioxide reacts differently with carbon monoxide at different temperatures. The equation below shows the original reaction and reaction mechanism at two different temperatures. **Competency Based Que.**

Original reaction

$$NO_2 + CO \longrightarrow NO + CO_2$$

Reaction mechanism at $T > 770$ K

$$NO_2 + CO \longrightarrow NO + CO_2 \text{ (slow)}$$

Reaction mechanism at $T < 770$ K

$$2NO_2 \longrightarrow NO + NO_3 \text{ (slow)}$$
$$NO_3 + CO \longrightarrow NO_2 + CO_2 \text{ (fast)}$$

Write down the equation for the rate of the reaction for
(i) $T > 770$ K (ii) $T < 770$ K

11. (i) Why a reaction does not have a zero activation energy?
(ii) Why equilibrium constant remain unchanged in the presence of a catalyst?

12. (i) Illustrate graphically the effect of catalyst on activation energy.
(ii) Catalysts have no effect on the equilibrium constant, why?

13. What happens to the rate constant (k) and activation energy (E_a) as the temperature of a chemical reaction is increased? Justify. **CBSE 2023**

14. (i) Explain why H_2 and O_2 do not react at room temperature.
(ii) Write the rate equation for the reaction, $A_2 + 3B_2 \longrightarrow 2C$, if the overall order of the reaction is zero. **CBSE 2017 C**

15. For the following reaction,

$$2H_2O_2 \longrightarrow O_2 + 2H_2O$$

The curve below shows how the volume of oxygen formed varies with time.

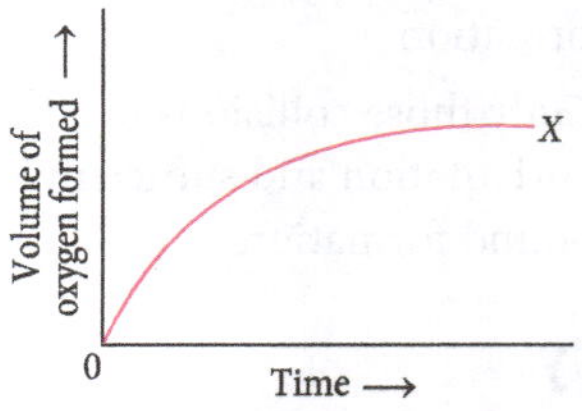

Explain the shape of the graph in terms of the rate of formation of oxygen.

Short Answer Type II Questions [3 Marks]

16. The following results have been obtained during the kinetic studies of the reaction,

$$P + 2Q \longrightarrow R + 2S$$

Exp.	Initial P (mol/L)	Initial Q (mol/L)	Initial rate of formation of R (M min^{-1})
1.	0.10	0.10	3.0×10^{-4}
2.	0.30	0.30	9.0×10^{-4}
3.	0.10	0.30	3.0×10^{-4}
4.	0.20	0.40	6.0×10^{-4}

Determine the rate law expression for the reaction. **CBSE SQP 2021**

17. The decomposition of phosphine, PH_3 proceeds according to the following equation,

$$4PH_3(g) \longrightarrow P_4(g) + 6H_2(g)$$

It is found that the reaction follows the following rate equation, Rate $= k[PH_3]$

The half-life of PH_3 is 37.9 s at 120°C.

(i) How much time is required for $3/4^{th}$ of PH_3 to decompose?

(ii) What fraction of the original sample of PH_3 remains behind after 1 min ?

18. The rate constant for the first order decomposition of N_2O_5 is given by the following equation:

$$k = (2.5 \times 10^{14} s^{-1}) e^{(-25000 \text{ K})/T}$$

Calculate E_a for this reaction and rate constant, if its half-life period be 300 minutes.

19. Rate constant 'k' of a reaction varies with temperature 'T' according to the equation.

$$\log k = \log A - \frac{E_a}{2.303R}\left(\frac{1}{T}\right)$$

where, E_a is the activation energy. When a graph is plotted for $\log k$ vs $\frac{1}{T}$, a straight line with a slope of -4250 K is obtained. Calculate E_a for the reaction [$R = 8.314 \text{ K}^{-1}\text{mol}^{-1}$].

20. What will be the initial rate of a reaction if its rate constant is 10^{-3} min^{-1} and the concentration of reactant is 0.2 mol dm^{-3}? How much of the reactant will be converted into products in 200 min?

21. The rate constant for a first order reaction is 60 s^{-1}. How much time will it take to reduce the concentration of the reactant of 1/10 th of its initial value?

22. A certain reaction is 50% complete in 20 min at 300 K and the same reaction is 50% complete in 5 min at 350 K. Calculate the activation energy if it is a first order reaction.

[$R = 8.314 \text{ J K}^{-1}\text{mol}^{-1}$; $\log 4 = 0.602$] **CBSE 2025**

23. When the temperature changes from 27°C to 37°C, the rate of the chemical reaction is double. Calculate the energy of activation for the reaction.

(Given, $R = 8.314 \text{ J mol}^{-1}\text{K}^{-1}$, $\log 2 = 0.3010$, $\log 3 = 0.4771$, $\log 4 = 0.6021$) **CBSE 2023**

24. The decomposition of N_2O_5 according to the equation.

$$2N_2O_5(g) \longrightarrow 4NO_2(g) + O_2(g)$$

is a first order reaction. After 30 min, in a closed vessel, the total pressure is found to be 284.5 mm of Hg and on complete decomposition, the total pressure is 584.5 mm of Hg. Then, find the rate constant of the reaction.

25. The rate constant of a certain reaction is given by

$$\log k = 5.4 - \frac{212}{T}$$

Calculate E_a at 127°C.

26. The activation energy of a first order reaction is 187.06 kJ mol^{-1} at 750 K and the value of pre-exponential factor, A is $1.97 \times 10^{12} s^{-1}$.

Calculate the rate constant and half-life.

(Given : $e^{-30} = 9.35 \times 10^{-14}$)

Long Answer Type Questions [5 Marks]

27. (i) For a reaction, $2NH_3 \longrightarrow N_2 + 3H_2$ (in the presence of Pt catalyst at 1130 K), Rate $= k$. Write the order of the reaction and unit of the rate constant of the reaction.

(ii) Write three differences between order of reaction and molecularity of the reaction.

28. During nuclear explosion one of the products is ^{90}Sr with half-life of 28.1 yr. If 1 μg of ^{90}Sr was absorbed in the bones of a newly born baby instead of calcium, how much of it will remain after 10 yr and 60 yr if it is not lost metabolically? **NCERT**

29. (i) Consider the reaction $R \rightarrow P$ for which the change in concentration of R with time is shown by the following graph :

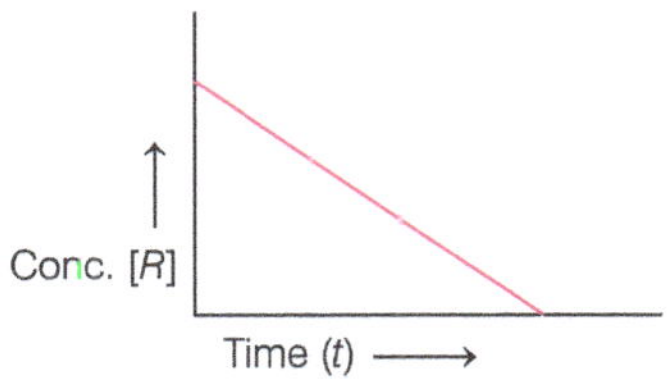

(a) Predict the order of reaction.

(b) What does the slope of the curve indicate?

(ii) The rate of reaction quadruples when temperature changes from 293 K to 313 K. Calculate E_a assuming that it does not change with time.

[$R = 8.314 \text{ JK}^{-1}\text{mol}^{-1}$] **NCERT, CBSE 2019, 2025**

30. (i) A first order reaction is 50% complete in 30 minutes at 300 K and in 10 minutes at 320 K. Calculate activation energy (E_a) for the reaction.
($R = 8.314\ JK^{-1}\ mol^{-1}$) **CBSE 2020, 2022**

(ii) Write the two conditions for collisions to be effective collisions.

(iii) How order of reaction and molecularity differ towards a complex reaction?

31. The rate constant for the decomposition of N_2O_5 at various temperatures is given below

$T/°C$	0	20	40	60	80
$10^5 \times k/s^{-1}$	0.0787	1.70	25.7	178	2140

Draw a graph between $\ln k$ and $1/T$ and calculate the values of A and E_a. Predict the rate constant at 30°C and 50°C. **NCERT**

32. A drug becomes ineffective after 30% decomposition. The original concentration was 10 mg mL^{-1} which becomes 8.4 mg mL^{-1} during first 40 months. Assuming the decomposition of first order, calculate the expiry time of the drug in months. What is the half-life of the drug?

33. The experimental data for the reaction;

$$2A + B_2 \longrightarrow 2AB; \text{ is}$$

Experiment	$[A]$ M	$[B_2]$ M	Initial rate ($mol\ L^{-1}\ s^{-1}$)
1.	0.50	0.5	1.6×10^{-4}
2.	0.50	1.0	3.2×10^{-4}
3.	1.00	1.0	3.2×10^{-4}

Write the most probable rate equation for the reaction.

Hints & Solutions

Objective Type Questions

1. (c) Given, chemical reaction is

$$5Br^-(aq) + BrO_3^-(aq) + 6H^+(aq) \longrightarrow 3Br_2(aq) + 3H_2O(l)$$

Rate law expression for the above equation can be written as

$$-\frac{1}{5}\frac{\Delta[Br^-]}{\Delta t} = -\frac{\Delta[BrO_3^-]}{\Delta t} = \frac{-1}{6}\frac{\Delta[H^+]}{\Delta t} = \frac{+1}{3}\frac{\Delta[Br_2]}{\Delta t}$$

$$\Rightarrow \quad \frac{\Delta[Br^-]}{\Delta t} = \frac{5}{6}\frac{\Delta[H^+]}{\Delta t}$$

2. (b) For $3A \longrightarrow 2B$

$$\text{Rate of reaction} = -\frac{1}{3}\frac{d[A]}{dt} = +\frac{1}{2}\frac{d[B]}{dt}$$

$$\therefore \quad \frac{d[B]}{dt} = -\frac{2}{3}\frac{d[A]}{dt}$$

3. (c) $Zn + \text{Dil. } HCl \longrightarrow ZnCl_2 + H_2\uparrow$

Average rate of reaction

$$= \frac{\text{Change in concentration of } H_2}{\text{Change in time}} = \frac{V_3 - 0}{40 - 0} = \frac{V_3}{40}$$

4. (c) The rate of reaction increases with increase in the concentration of reactant, surface area, temperature and catalyst.

Thus, statements I, III and IV can increase the rate of a chemical reaction.

5. (c) The graph given in option (c) is for zero order reaction.

6. (c) The order of a reaction can't be predicted just by looking at the reaction equation. It is actually determined experimently.

7. (b) Statement (b) is true and the correct form of other given statements are

Statement (a): Molecularity of a reaction is always a whole number.

Statement (c): Molecularity is a theoretical concept.

Statement (d): Reactions with molecularity three are very rare as probability of formation of product is low.

8. (b) As, rate $(r) = k\,[a]^n$ ...(i)

According to question,

$$16r = k\,[4a]^n \quad \text{...(ii)}$$

From Eqs. (i) and (ii),

$$\Rightarrow \quad \frac{1}{16} = \left[\frac{1}{4}\right]^n$$

$$\Rightarrow \quad 16 = 4^n$$

$$\Rightarrow \quad n = 2$$

9. (b) For a zero order reaction, rate equation is as follows

$$x = -kt + [R]_0 \quad \text{...(i)}$$

where x is concentration of product in time t

k is rate constant and $[R]_0$ is initial concentration of reactant.

$\therefore$ From Eq. (i), slope $= -k$ and intercept $= [R]_0$

10. (c) The correct match is A $\rightarrow$ (iii), B $\rightarrow$ (ii), C $\rightarrow$ (i).

11. (c) Let, rate of reaction be $k[A]^x[B]^y$

$$1.89 \times 10^{-4} = k[3.0 \times 10^{-2}]^x[2.0 \times 10^{-2}]^y \quad \text{...(i)}$$

$$1.89 \times 10^{-4} = k[3 \times 10^{-2}]^x[4 \times 10^{-2}]^y \quad \text{...(ii)}$$

$$7.56 \times 10^{-4} = k[6 \times 10^{-2}]^x[4 \times 10^{-2}]^y \quad \text{...(iii)}$$

From Eqs. (ii) $\div$ (i), we get

$$1 = 2^y$$

$$2^0 = 2^y$$

$$y = 0$$

From Eqs. (iii) $\div$ (ii), we get

$$4 = 2^x$$

$$2^2 = 2^x$$

$$x = 2$$

Therefore, the order of reaction with respect to $A = 2$ and w.r.t $B = 0$.

12. (a) The plot between $\ln[R]$ *vs* time (t) for first order reaction is shown below

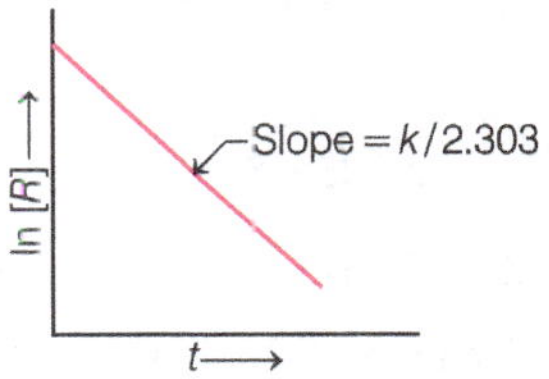

$$\text{Slope of this graph} = \frac{k}{2.303}$$

13. (d) For zero order reaction, rate constant is

$$k = \frac{[R]_0 - [R]}{t}$$

$$\text{At } t = t_{1/2},\ [R] = \frac{1}{2}[R]_0$$

$$k = \frac{[R]_0 - \frac{1}{2}[R]_0}{t_{1/2}}$$

$$t_{1/2} = \frac{[R]_0}{2k}$$

14. (b) Rate law can be written as

$$\text{Rate, } R_1 = k[A][B]$$

$$R_2 = k\,[A]\,[2B] = 2R_1$$

$\therefore$ As concentration of B is doubled, keeping the concentration of A constant, rate of reaction gets doubled.

15. (*d*) It is impossible to confirm that the whole of the substance will react completely because in its half-life, 50% of the substance reacts. Hence, time taken for 100% completion of reaction is infinite.

16. (*c*) For, $A + B \longrightarrow$ Products

$$r = k[A][B]$$

If $[B]$ is taken in large excess, the reaction will become pseudo first order reaction.

17. (*d*) In effective collision, colliding molecule must have energy equal to or greater than threshold energy with proper orientation to give rise to product.

18. (*b*) Activation energy of a chemical reaction is related to rate constant of a reaction at two different temperatures, i.e. k_1 and k_2 respectively

$$\ln\left(\frac{k_2}{k_1}\right) = \frac{E_a}{R}\left[\frac{1}{T_1} - \frac{1}{T_2}\right]$$

This equation is known as Arrhenius equation.

19. (*c*) Given,

Initial temperature

$$T_1 = 20 + 273 = 293 \text{ K}$$

Final temperature, $T_2 = 35 + 273 = 308$ K

$$R = 8.314 \text{ J mol}^{-1} \text{ K}^{-1}$$

As rate constant, $k \propto r \Rightarrow \frac{k_2}{k_1} = 2$

From Arrhenius equation, we know that

$$\log\frac{k_2}{k_1} = \frac{E_a}{2.303\,R}\left(\frac{T_2 - T_1}{T_1 T_2}\right)$$

$$\log 2 = \frac{E_a}{2.303 \times 8.314}\left[\frac{308 - 293}{293 \times 308}\right]$$

$$E_a = 34673.48 \text{ J mol}^{-1} = 34.7 \text{ kJ mol}^{-1}$$

20. (*a*) The rate of reaction is highest at t_1.

21. (*a*) According to Arrhenius equation, $k = A\,e^{-E_a/RT}$

Taking ln on both sides, $\ln k = \ln\left(Ae^{-\frac{E_a}{RT}}\right) = -\frac{E_a}{RT} + \ln A$

On comparing with equation of straight line, graph 'a' represents the graph of $\ln k$ *vs* $\frac{1}{T}$.

22. (*a*)

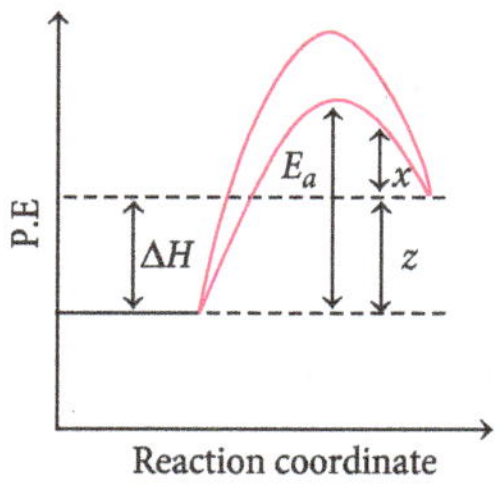

As the catalyst provides an alternate pathway or reaction mechanism by reducing the activation energy between reactant and products hence, lowering the potential energy barrier.

Thus, according to given value in the graph, E_a with catalyst and ΔH are $x + z$ and z, respectively.

23. (*b*) The addition of a catalyst will not affect the concentration of either the reactants. Hence, only statements I and II are correct.

24. (*b*) Rate of reaction is a measure of change in concentration of reactant and product with respect to time. As, concentration of product increases with increase in time, concentration of reactant decreases.

For reaction, $R \rightarrow P$

$$\text{Rate} = \frac{-\Delta[R]}{\Delta t} = +\frac{\Delta[P]}{\Delta t}$$

Hence, both statements (A) and (R) are true, but (R) is not the correct explanation of (A).

25. (*a*) For zero order reaction

$$\text{Rate} = k[A]^0$$

$$\boxed{\text{Rate} = k}$$

$\therefore$ Both (A) and (R) are true and (R) is the correct explanation of (A).

26. (*b*) Order of overall reaction is equal to molecularity of slowest step. They are equal for elementary reaction, but for complex reactions, they may be different.

However, order can be zero and fractional but molecularity cannot be zero. Thus, both (A) and (R) are true but (R) is not the correct explanation of (A).

27. (*c*) Rate constant determined from Arrhenius equation are fairly accurate for both simple and complex molecules because only those molecules undergo chemical change which have proper orientation during collision, i.e. effective collision. Thus, (A) is true but (R) is false.

28. (*d*) Order and molecularity differs in case of complex reactions.

$\therefore$ (A) is false, but (R) is true.

29. (*c*) A small amount of the catalyst can catalyse a large amount of reactants. A catalyst does not alter Gibbs energy, ΔG of a reaction. It does not change the equilibrium constant rather, it helps in attaining the equilibrium faster, i.e., it catalyses the forward and backward directions both to the same extent so that the equilibrium state remains same and is achieved earlier.

Thus, (A) is true, but (R) is false.

30. (*a*) Consider the hydrolysis of an ester

$$CH_3COOC_2H_5 + H_2O \longrightarrow CH_3COOH + C_2H_5OH$$

$$\text{Rate} = k[CH_3COOC_2H_5][H_2O]$$

Hydrolysis of an ester follows first order because the concentration of water, $[H_2O]$ remains nearly constant and the change in the concentration of acid will result in very negligible change in the concentration of H^+/OH^- ion during the course of the reaction.

Thus, both (A) and (R) are true and (R) is the correct explanation of (A).

31. (*d*) The unit of k depends on order of reaction and it is mol L^{-1} s^{-1} for a zero order reaction.
Hence, (A) is false, but (R) is true.

32. (*a*) The reactions of higher order are rare because the chances of multimolecular collisions at the same time to give product are very low.
Hence, (A) and (R) are true and (R) is the correct explanation of (A).

33. (*a*) With increase in temperature, the kinetic energy of molecules is increased as the number of collisions increases and hence, the rate of reaction gets increased.
Hence, (A) and (R) are true and (R) is the correct explanation of (A).

34. (*d*) Not all collisions of reactant molecules lead to product formation, only effective collisions, means molecules which have proper and correct orientation and sufficient kinetic energy during collisions can form product.
Hence, (A) is false, but (R) is true.

35. (i)

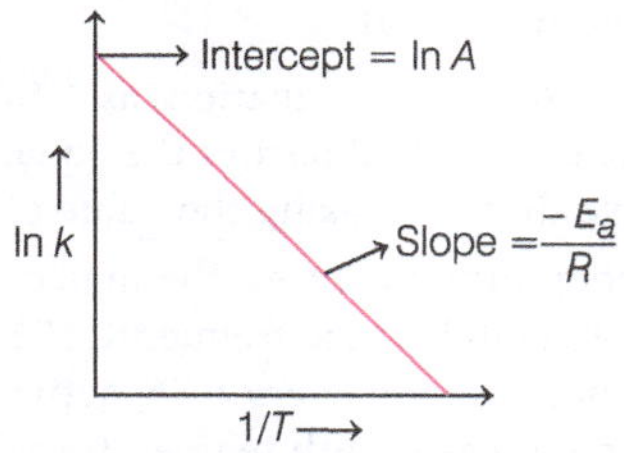

(1)

(ii) $E_a = 0 \Rightarrow \log\frac{k_2}{k_1} = 0 \Rightarrow \frac{k_2}{k_1} = 1$

Therefore, $k_2 = k_1 = 1.72 \times 10^5\ s^{-1}$ (1)

(iii) The factor A has the same unit as that of k.
$\therefore$ SI unit of $A = L\ mol^{-1}\ s^{-1}$. (2)

Or The relationship between rate constant and activation energy is

$$\log k = \log A - \frac{E_a}{2.303RT}$$ (2)

36. (i) (a) The rate determining step is the slowest step of a chemical reaction that determines the speed (rate) at which the overall reaction proceeds. (1)

(b) Complex reaction is the reaction in which the mechanism consists of more than one elementary step. (1)

(ii) The rate constant of a reaction is nearly doubled with the rise in temperature by 10°C. The temperature dependence of the rate constant on temperature is given by Arrhenius equation,
$k = Ae^{-E_a/RT}$, where A is called the frequency factor and E_a is the activation energy of the reaction. (1)

Or

A complex reaction takes place through a number of elementary reactions. Each elementary reaction may have different molecularity. Therefore, it is meaningless to talk of molecularity of the overall complex reaction. However, order of a complex reaction is determined by the slowest step in its mechanisms, therefore order can be calculated for both elementary and complex reactions. (1)

(iii) For the reaction $X \rightarrow Y$
Reaction rate $(r) = k[X]^2$ (For second order) ...(i)
If the concentration of X is increased three times, then reaction rate, $(r') = k[3X]^2 = k[9X^2]$ ...(ii)
On dividing Eq. (i) by Eq. (ii), we get

$$\frac{r'}{r} = \frac{k[9X^2]}{k[X^2]} = 9$$

It means that the rate of formation of Y will increase by 9 times. (1)

Subjective Type Questions

1. The rate of reaction may not depend upon all the molecules of a reactant present in the balanced chemical equation. Thus, balanced chemical equation often leads to incorrect order or rate law.

$$5Br^-(aq) + BrO_3^-(aq) + 6H^+(aq) \longrightarrow 3Br_2(aq) + 3H_2O(l)$$

This is actually a fourth order reaction but it seems to be a twelfth order reaction. Actually, the reaction is complex and occurs in several steps.
The order of such reaction is determined by the slowest step in the reaction mechanism. (2)

2. One fourth of the reaction is completed means 75% reactant is left. For the first order reaction,

$$k = \frac{2.303}{32}\log\frac{a}{0.75a} = \frac{2.303}{32}\log(1.33)$$

$$k = (0.072) \times (0.124) = 0.0089\ min^{-1}$$

$$t_{1/2} = \frac{0.693}{k} = \frac{0.693}{0.0089\ min^{-1}} = 77.86\ min$$ (2)

3. (i) All natural and artificial radioactive decay of unstable nuclei takes place by first order kinetics.

$$^{226}_{88}Ra \longrightarrow {}^4_2He + {}^{222}_{86}Rn$$

Hydrogenation of ethene and decomposition of N_2O_5 and N_2O are also the examples of first order reactions. (1)

(ii) For the first order reaction,

$$k = \frac{2.303}{t}\log\frac{[R]_0}{[R]}$$

If we plot a graph between $\log[R]_0/[R]$ *vs* t we get a straight line with the slope $= \frac{k}{2.303}$ as shown below.

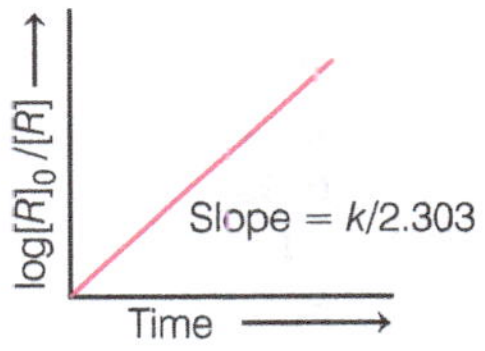

(1)

4. The given reaction is a first order . So,

$$k = \frac{0.693}{t_{1/2}} = \frac{0.693}{5730}$$

Using the equation for first order,

$$t = \frac{2.303}{k} \log \frac{C_0}{C_t} \quad ...(i) \quad \textbf{(1)}$$

Let $C_0 = 1$ and $C_t = \frac{3}{10}$

So, $\frac{C_0}{C_t} = \frac{1}{\frac{3}{10}} = \frac{10}{3}$

Putting values in Eq. (i),

$$t = \frac{2.303}{0.693} \times 5730 \log \frac{10}{3}$$

$$t = 19042 \times (1 - 0.4771) = 9957 \text{ years} \quad \textbf{(1)}$$

5. (i) $[R]_0 = 100$, $[R] = 100 - 30 = 70$, $t = 40$ min

$$k = \frac{2.303}{t} \log \frac{[R]_0}{[R]} = \frac{2.303}{40} \log \frac{100}{70} = \frac{2.303}{40} \times 0.1548$$

$k = 8.91 \times 10^{-3}$ min^{-1}. **(1)**

(ii) The unit of k for first order reaction is s^{-1}. **(1)**

6.

$a - x$	0.75	0.4	0.1
Δx	−0.25	− 0.6	−0.9
Rate $= \frac{-\Delta x}{\Delta t}$	$\frac{0.25}{0.05} = 5$	$\frac{0.6}{0.12} = 5$	$\frac{0.9}{0.18} = 5$

As rate $= \frac{-\Delta x}{\Delta t}$ = constant for different concentration values so the reaction is of zero order. **(2)**

7. $t = \frac{[A]_0 - [A]}{k}$

$$t = \frac{(0.1 - 0.075) \text{ mol L}^{-1}}{3.0 \times 10^{-3} \text{ mol L}^{-1} \text{s}^{-1}}$$

$t = 8.33$ s **(2)**

8. $t_{1/2} = 10$ min (Given)

$$k = \frac{0.693}{t_{1/2}} = \frac{0.693}{10 \text{ min}} = 0.0693 \text{ min}^{-1}$$

$$t = \frac{2.303}{k} \log \frac{a}{0.1a}$$

$$t = \frac{2.303}{0.0693 \text{ min}^{-1}} \log 10 = 33.23 \text{ min}$$

$t \approx 33$ min **(2)**

9. For 3/4 decay, $t_{3/4} = t_2 = \frac{2.303}{k} \log \frac{100}{25} = \frac{2.303}{k} \log 4$

$$t_2 = \frac{1.386}{k} \quad ...(i)$$

For $\frac{1}{2}$ decay, $t_{1/2} = t_1 = \frac{0.693}{k}$ ...(ii)

(i) ÷ (ii)

$$\frac{t_2}{t_1} = \frac{\frac{1.386}{k}}{\frac{0.693}{k}} = 2 \Rightarrow t_2 = 2t_1$$

(2)

10. The slowest step is the rate determining step.

(i) Rate of reaction for $T > 770$ K

Rate $= k [NO_2] [CO]$ **(1)**

(ii) Rate of reaction for $T < 770$ K

Rate $= k [NO_2]^2$ **(1)**

11. (i) According to Arrhenius equation,

$$k = Ae^{-E_a/RT}$$

If $E_a = 0$, $k = A$, i.e. rate constant equals to collision frequency which suggests that every collision results into a chemical reaction that cannot be true. Hence, $E_a \neq 0$. **(1)**

(ii) It catalyses the forward and backward reactions to the same extent so that the equilibrium state remains same. **(1)**

12. Refer to text on page 91. **(2)**

13. According to Arrhenius equation, as T increases, the value of the exponential part of the equation becomes less negative thus increasing the value of k.

As the temperature increases, the molecules move faster and therefore collide more frequently. The molecules also carry more kinetic energy. So, activation energy for the reaction increases with temperature. **(2)**

14. (i) The activation energy for the reaction of H_2 with O_2 is very high at room temperature. **(1)**

(ii) In zero order reaction, the rate does not depend on the concentration of any of the reactants.

Thus, overall order is zero.

∴ Rate $= k[A]^0[B]^0$. **(1)**

15. The slope of the curve defines the rate of formation of oxygen. Initially, the slope is high which means the rate of formation is high.

After sometime, slope is constant which means the reactants are exhausted and the reaction is completed so the volume is constant. **(2)**

16. For reaction, $P + 2Q \longrightarrow R + 2S$,

Let the rate law expression be rate $= k[P]^x[Q]^y$

For experiment 1,

$$\text{Rate (1)} = 3.0 \times 10^{-4} = k(0.10)^x(0.10)^y \quad ...(i)$$

For experiment 2,

$$\text{Rate (2)} = 9.0 \times 10^{-4} = k(0.30)^x(0.30)^y \quad ...(ii)$$

For experiment 3,

$$\text{Rate (3)} = 3.0 \times 10^{-4} = k(0.10)^x(0.30)^y \quad ...(iii) \quad \textbf{(1)}$$

Dividing (i) and (iii), $\frac{\text{Rate(1)}}{\text{Rate(3)}} = \left(\frac{1}{3}\right)^y \Rightarrow 1 = \left(\frac{1}{3}\right)^y$

So, $y = 0$, and similarly, $\frac{\text{Rate (2)}}{\text{Rate (3)}} = (3)^x \Rightarrow 3 = (3)^x$

So, $x = 1$

$\therefore$ Rate law $= k[P]$ **(2)**

17. **Given**, $t_{1/2} = 37.9$ s

Initial concentration $= [R]_0$

Concentration after time $(t) = \frac{[R]_0}{4}$

(i) $k = \frac{0.693}{37.9} = 0.0183\ s^{-1} = 1.83 \times 10^{-2} s^{-1}$

$$t = \frac{2.303}{k} \log \frac{[R]_0}{[R]}$$

$$t_{3/4} = \frac{2.303}{1.83 \times 10^{-2} s^{-1}} \log \frac{[R]_0}{[R]_0/4}$$

$$t_{3/4} = \frac{2.303 \times 100 \times 2 \times 0.30105}{1.83} = \frac{138.66}{1.83} s = 75.77 \text{ s}$$ **(1½)**

(ii) $t = 1$ min $= 60$ s and $k = 0.0183\ s^{-1}$

$$\text{and } 60 = \frac{2.303}{0.0183} \log \frac{[R]_0}{[R]}$$

$$\log \frac{[R]_0}{[R]} = \frac{60 \times 0.0183}{2.303} = 0.4768$$

$$\frac{[R]_0}{[R]} = 2.998$$

$$\Rightarrow \frac{100}{2.998} = [R]$$

$$[R] = 33.35\%$$ **(1½)**

18. According to Arrhenius equation,

$$k = A \cdot e^{-E_a/RT} \quad \text{...(i)}$$

Given data

$$k = 2.5 \times 10^{14}\ s^{-1} e^{-25000\ K/T} \quad \text{...(ii)}$$ **(1)**

On comparing both equations, we have

$$-\frac{E_a}{RT} = \frac{-25000\ K}{T}$$

$$E_a = 25000\ K \times 8.314\ JK^{-1} mol^{-1}$$

$$= 207850\ J/mol = 207.8\ kJ/mol$$ **(1)**

Given, half-life $= 300$ min

For first order reaction, we have

$$t_{1/2} = \frac{0.693}{k}$$

$$k = \frac{0.693}{300} = 0.00231\ min^{-1}$$

$$k = 2.31 \times 10^{-3}\ min^{-1}$$ **(1)**

19. Given : Slope $= -4250$ K

$R = 8.314\ JK^{-1} mol^{-1}$

From equation, $\log k = \log A - \frac{E_a}{2.303\,RT}$

$$\Rightarrow \frac{-E_a}{2.303\,R} = -4250$$

$$\Rightarrow E_a = 81.37\ kJ\ mol^{-1}$$ **(3)**

20. Initial rate $= k[A] = 10^{-3} \times 0.2 = 2 \times 10^{-4}$ mol dm^{-3} min^{-1} **(1)**

$$k = \frac{2.303}{t} \log \frac{a}{a-x}$$

$$10^{-3} = \frac{2.303}{200} \log \frac{0.2}{(a-x)}$$

$$\frac{0.2}{2.303} = \log(0.2) - \log(a-x)$$

$$\Rightarrow 0.0868 = -0.6990 - \log(a-x)$$

$$\Rightarrow \log(a-x) = -0.6990 - 0.0868$$

$$(a-x) = \text{Antilog}(-0.7858)$$

$$(a-x) = 0.164\ mol\ dm^{-3}$$ **(2)**

21. $k = 60\ s^{-1}$

$$t = \frac{2.303}{k} \log \frac{a}{a-x}$$

$$t = \frac{2.303}{60} \log \frac{a}{a/10} = \frac{2.303}{60} \log 10$$

$$t = 3.8 \times 10^{-2}\ s^{-1}$$ **(3)**

22. By using half-life equation, we get

$$k = \frac{0.693}{t_{1/2}}$$

At 300 K, $k_1 = \frac{0.693}{20\,\text{min}}$

At 350 K, $k_2 = \frac{0.693}{5\,\text{min}}$

$$\Rightarrow \frac{k_2}{k_1} = \frac{\left(\frac{0.693}{5}\right)}{\left(\frac{0.693}{20}\right)} = \frac{20}{5} = 4$$

From the Arrhenius equation,

$$\log \frac{k_2}{k_1} = \frac{E_a}{2.303R}\left[\frac{1}{T_1} - \frac{1}{T_2}\right]$$

$$E_a = \frac{2.303 \times R \times T_1 \times T_2}{(T_2 - T_1)} \log\left(\frac{k_2}{k_1}\right)$$

$$E_a = \frac{2.303 \times 8.314 \times 300 \times 350}{(350 - 300)} \log(4)$$

$$E_a = 24205.82\ J\ mol^{-1} \approx 24.206\ kJ\ mol^{-1}$$ **(3)**

23. $$\log \frac{k_2}{k_1} = \frac{E_a}{2.303R}\left[\frac{1}{T_1} - \frac{1}{T_2}\right]$$

$$\log \frac{2k}{k} = \frac{E_a}{2.303 \times 8.314} \times \left[\frac{1}{300} - \frac{1}{310}\right]$$

$$\Rightarrow E_a = \frac{0.3010 \times 2.303 \times 8.314 \times 300 \times 310}{10} = 53.60\ kJ/mol$$ **(3)**

24. Use, $k = \frac{2.303}{t} \log \frac{p_i}{2p_i - p_t}$

Refer to example given on page 86.

[**Ans.** $k = 0.0052\ min^{-1}$] **(3)**

25. Compare the given equation by

$\log k = \log A - \frac{E_a}{2.303RT}$ and then calculate E_a.

[**Ans.** $E_a = 4.059$ kJ/mol] **(3)**

26. $$\log k = \log A - \frac{E_a}{2.303RT}$$

$$\log k = \log(1.97 \times 10^{12}) - \frac{187060}{2.303 \times 8.314 \times 750}$$

$$\log k = 12.3 - 13.026 \Rightarrow \log k = -0.726$$

$$\Rightarrow \quad k = 0.188$$

$$t_{1/2} = \frac{0.693}{k} = \frac{0.693}{0.188} = 3.686 \text{ s}$$ **(3)**

27. (i) Zero order reaction,

Unit of rate constant = mol L^{-1} s^{-1} **(2)**

(ii)

Order of reaction	Molecularity
1. The sum of powers of the concentration of the reactants in the rate law expression is called the order of reaction.	The number of reacting species taking part in an elementary reaction is called molecularity of the reaction.
2. It can be fractional or zero.	It is always a whole number and cannot be zero.
3. It is determined experimentally.	It can be calculated by simply adding the molecules of the slowest step.

(3)

28. $t_{1/2} = 28.1$ yr ; $k = \frac{0.693}{t_{1/2}} = \frac{0.693}{28.1}$ yr^{-1} **(1)**

For Ist order reaction

$$t = \frac{2.303}{k} \log \frac{a}{(a-x)}$$

***Case* I** $a = 1\,\mu g$; $t = 10$ yr; $k = \frac{0.693}{28.1}$ yr^{-1}

$$10 \text{ yr} = \frac{2.303}{0.693} \times 28.1 \text{ yr} \log \frac{a}{(a-x)}$$

$$\log \frac{a}{(a-x)} = \frac{10 \text{ yr} \times 0.693}{2.303 \times 28.1 \text{ yr}} = 0.107$$

$$\frac{a}{(a-x)} = \text{Antilog}(0.107) = 1.279$$

$$(a-x) = \frac{a}{1.279} = \frac{(1\,\mu g)}{1.279}$$

$$= 0.7819\,\mu g$$

Amount left after 10 yr = 0.7819 μg **(2)**

***Case* II** $a = 1$ μg, $t = 60$ yr ; $k = \frac{0.693}{28.1}$ yr^{-1}

$$60 \text{ yr} = \frac{2.303}{0.693} \times 28.1 \text{ yr} \times \log \frac{a}{(a-x)}$$

$$\log \frac{a}{(a-x)} = \frac{60 \text{ yr} \times 0.693}{28.1 \text{ yr} \times 2.303} = 0.642$$

$$\frac{a}{(a-x)} = \text{Antilog } 0.642 = 4.385$$

$$(a-x) = \frac{a}{4.385} = \frac{(1\,\mu g)}{4.385}$$

$$= 0.2280\,\mu g$$

Amount left after 60 yr = 0.2280 μg **(2)**

29. (i) (a) The reaction is of zero order. Since, the integrated rate equation for zero order reaction is $k = \frac{[R]_0 - [R]}{t}$.

If we plot $[R]$ against t, we get a straight line with slope equal to $-k$ and intercept equals to $[R]_0$ as shown.

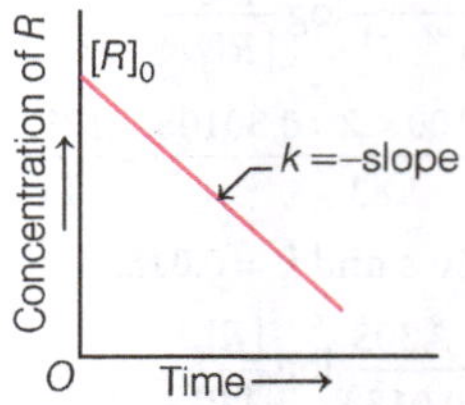

(1)

(b) Slope of curve indicates that concentration of reactant decreases with the time (t) and is numerically equal to the value of k.

i.e. Slope of the graph $= -k = -\frac{d[R]}{dt}$ **(1)**

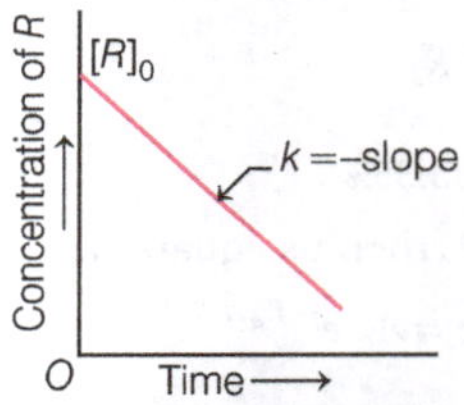

Variation in the concentration *vs* time plot for a zero order reaction **(1)**

(ii) Given, $T_1 = 293$ K, $T_2 = 313$ K, $k_2/k_1 = 4$,

$R = 8.314$ J K^{-1} mol^{-1}, log 4 = 0.6021

$$\because \quad \log \frac{k_2}{k_1} = \frac{E_a}{2.303R}\left[\frac{T_2 - T_1}{T_1 T_2}\right]$$

$$\therefore \quad \log 4 = \frac{E_a}{2.303 \times 8.314}\left[\frac{313 - 293}{313 \times 293}\right]$$

$$0.6021 = \frac{E_a}{19.147}\left[\frac{20}{91709}\right]$$

$$E_a = \frac{0.6021 \times 19.147 \times 91709}{20} = 52862.94 \text{ J mol}^{-1}$$

Hence, $E_a = 52.86294$ kJ mol^{-1} **(2)**

30. (i) By using half life equation, we get $k = \frac{0.693}{t_{1/2}}$

At 300 K, $k_1 = \frac{0.693}{30 \text{ min}} = 0.0231 \text{ min}^{-1}$

At 320 K, $k_2 = \frac{0.693}{10 \text{ min}} = 0.0693 \text{ min}^{-1}$

From the Arrhenius equation

$$\log\frac{k_2}{k_1}=\frac{E_a}{2.303R}\left[\frac{1}{T_1}-\frac{1}{T_2}\right]$$

$$E_a=\frac{2.303\times R\times T_1\times T_2}{T_2-T_1}\log\left(\frac{k_2}{k_1}\right)$$

$$\Rightarrow \quad E_a=\frac{2.303\times 8.314\times 300\times 320}{(320-300)}\times\log\left(\frac{0.0693}{0.0231}\right)$$

$$E_a=43.85 \text{ kJ mol}^{-1}$$ **(3)**

(ii) Refer to pages 91 and 92 (Collision theory of chemical reactions). **(1)**

(iii) Refer to pages 82 and 83 (Molecularity of a reaction). **(1)**

31. To draw the graph between $\ln k$ *versus* $1/T$, we rewrite the data as follows

T (K)	$1/T$	$\ln k$
273(0°C)	$0.003663 = 3.66\times10^{-3}$	8.971
293(20°C)	$0.003413 = 3.41\times10^{-3}$	12.044
313(40°C)	$0.003195 = 3.19\times10^{-3}$	14.759
333(60°C)	$0.003003 = 3.00\times10^{-3}$	16.695
353(80°C)	$0.002833 = 2.83\times10^{-3}$	19.181

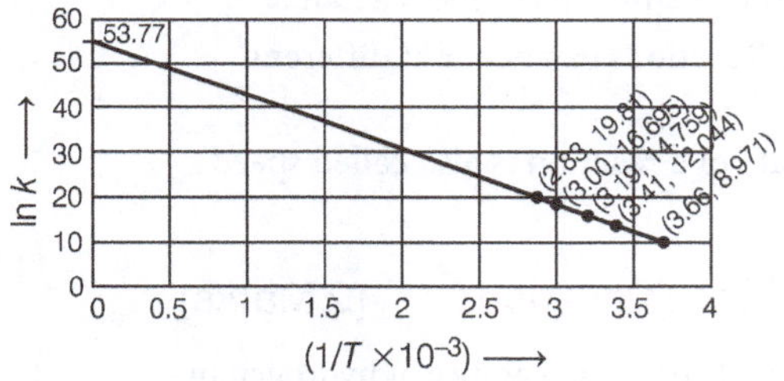

(2)

From the graph, we find the slope

$$\text{Slope}=\frac{-E_a}{R}=\frac{(8.971-19.181)}{(3.66-2.83)\times10^{-3}}$$

$$\frac{-E_a}{R}=\frac{-10.21}{0.83\times10^{-3}}$$

∴ Activation energy,

$$E_a=\frac{10.21\times 8.314 \text{ J mol}^{-1}}{0.00083}$$

$$=102272 \text{ J mol}^{-1}$$

$$=102.272 \text{ kJ mol}^{-1}$$

$$\Rightarrow \quad E_a=102.272 \text{ kJ mol}^{-1}$$ **(1)**

According to Arrhenius equation,

$$\ln k=\ln A+\left(\frac{-E_a}{RT}\right)$$

On comparing it with $y = mx + c$. The equation of line in intercept form,

$$\ln k=\left(-\frac{E_c}{R}\right)\frac{1}{T}+\ln A.$$

$\log A$ = value of intercept on Y-axis, i.e. on the $\ln k$-axis = 53.77

Frequency factor, $A = e^{53.77}$

or, $\quad A = 2.249\times10^{23}$ collisions s^{-1}

Value of rate constant k can be find by the study of graph.

T(K)	$1/T$	Values of $\ln k$ from graph	Values of k
303	0.003300	13.402	$6.63\times10^5 \text{ s}^{-1}$
323	0.003096	15.727	$6.763\times10^6 \text{ s}^{-1}$

(2)

32. $k=\dfrac{2.303}{t}\log\dfrac{a}{a-x}$

$$k=\frac{2.303}{40}\log\left(\frac{10}{8.4}\right)=\frac{2.303}{40}\times0.0757$$

$$k=0.00436 \text{ month}^{-1}$$ **(2)**

Calculation of expiry time of the drug,

$$t=\frac{2.303}{0.00436}\log\frac{a}{0.7a}$$

$$=\frac{2.303}{0.00436}\times0.155$$

$$t=81.87 \text{ months}$$ **(2)**

or $\quad t\approx 82$ months.

$$t_{1/2}=\frac{0.693}{k}=\frac{0.693}{0.00436}$$

$$t_{1/2}=158.94 \text{ months.}$$ **(1)**

33. Refer to example 4 on pages 80 and 81. **(5)**

QR Code for Quick Test 1

QR Code for Quick Test 2

QR Code for Quick Test 3

SELF ASSESSMENT TEST

Objective Type Questions [1 Mark]

1. For a hypothetical reaction, $R \longrightarrow$ Products; rate $= -k[R]$. The negative sign used in the rate expression indicates

(a) decrease in the concentration of reactants with time.

(b) decrease in the rate with time.

(c) reaction is reversible.

(d) None of the above

2. For an elementary reaction $M \longrightarrow N$, the rate of disappearance of M increases by a factor of 8 upon doubling the concentration of M. The order of the reaction with respect to M is

(a) 4 (b) 3

(c) 2 (d) 1

3. For the given rate expression $= k[A]^{3/2}[B]^{-1}$, the overall order of a reaction is

(a) zero (b) half

(c) one (d) two

4. Which of the following statements is not correct for the catalyst?

(a) It catalyses the forward and backward reactions to the same extent.

(b) It alters ΔG of the reaction.

(c) It is a substance that does not change the equilibrium constant of a reaction.

(d) It provides an alternate mechanism by reducing activation energy between reactants and products.

5. For the decomposition of azoisopropane into hexane and nitrogen at 543 K, the following data is obtained.

$$(CH_3)_2CHN{=}NCH(CH_3)_2 \longrightarrow N_2 + C_6H_{14}$$

Experiment	**Time** (s)	**Total pressure** (mm Hg)
I	0	35.0
II	360	54.0

The value of rate constant at 360s is

(a) $2.17 \times 10^{-3} s^{-1}$ (b) $3.25 \times 10^{-3} s^{-1}$

(c) $3.25 \times 10^{-3} min^{-1}$ (d) $1.98 \times 10^{-3} s^{-1}$

Assertion-Reason [1 Mark]

Direction (Q. Nos. 6-8) In the following questions, an Assertion (A) is followed by a corresponding Reason (R). Use the following keys to choose the appropriate answer.

(a) Both (A) and (R) are true and (R) is the correct explanation of (A).

(b) Both (A) and (R) are true, but (R) is not the correct explanation of (A).

(c) (A) is true, but (R) is false.

(d) (A) is false, but (R) is true.

6. Assertion (A) Some zero order reactions may have order in fractions.

Reason (R) Order cannot be determined from the balanced chemical equation.

7. Assertion (A) For a reaction: $P + 2Q \longrightarrow$ products, Rate $= k[P]^{1/2}[Q]^1$ so the order of reaction is 1.5

Reason (R) Order of reaction is the sum of stoichiometric coefficients of the reactants.

8. Assertion (A) Reactions can occur at different speeds.

Reason (R) Rate of a reaction is also called speed of reaction.

Short Answer Type I Questions [2 Marks]

9. (i) What is the rate of disappearance of hydrogen in the following reaction?

$$3H_2 + N_2 \longrightarrow 2NH_3$$

(ii) How is the rate law different from law of mass action?

10. How can average and instantaneous rates of a reaction can be determined from the plot of concentration *versus* time?

11. A first order reaction is 25% complete in 40 minutes.

(i) Calculate the value of rate constant.

(ii) In what time will the reaction be 80% completed?

Short Answer Type II Questions [3 Marks]

12. A first order reaction is 50% completed in 40 minutes at 300 K and in 20 minutes at 320 K. Calculate the activation energy of the reaction. (Given : $\log 2 = 0.3010$, $\log 4 = 0.6021$, $R = 8.314\ JK^{-1}\ mol^{-1}$)

13. The activation energy of a reaction is 94.14 kJ mol^{-1} and the value of rate constant at 298 K is $18 \times 10^{-5} s^{-1}$. Calculate the frequency factor or pre-exponential factor, A.

14. Consider the following reaction,

$$2NO(g) + Cl_2(g) \longrightarrow 2NOCl(g)$$

The following data were collected at 263 K.

Exp. No.	Initial [NO] (M)	Initial $[Cl_2]$ (M)	Initial rate of disappearance of Cl_2 (M/min)
1.	0.15	0.15	0.60
2.	0.15	0.30	1.20
3.	0.30	0.15	2.40
4.	0.25	0.25	?

Answer the following questions.

(i) What is the order of reaction with respect to NO and Cl_2.

(ii) Determine the rate constant of reaction.

(iii) Determine the initial rate of disappearance of Cl_2 in exp. 4.

Case-Study [4 Marks]

15. Brownian motion provides a window to microscopic dynamics. Observing the erratic motion of a colloid in a fluid delivers information on the strong interconnection of fluctuation and dissipation summarised.

Breaking this equilibrium by introducing, for example, a single laser-heated particle to the solution also breaks the fundamental assumption of equipartition and new physical descriptions are required.

However, hot Brownian motion can be still mapped onto the well known fluctuation-dissipation relation when introducing effective quantities for temperature and viscosity. Recent theoretical studies have shown that the effective temperatures are not unique for all degrees of freedom due to their coupling to the generated hydrodynamic flow fields.

The effective configurational temperature of hot Brownian motion governing the diffusion coefficient at long times shall, therefore, also differ from the effective kinetic temperature that would enter a Maxwell-Boltzmann like description.

Answers the following questions given below

(i) The rate constant of a reaction is $1.5 \times 10^7 s^{-1}$ at 50°C and $4.5 \times 10^7 s^{-1}$ at 100°C. Calculate the value of activation energy, E_a for the reaction. ($R = 8.314$ J K^{-1} mol^{-1})

Or

With the help of Arrhenius equation, how can you say that increasing the temperature result in an increase in the rate of reaction?

(ii) Give the Maxwell Boltzmann distribution curve showing temperature dependence of rate of reaction.

(iii) What does the peak of the distribution curve represents?

Long Answer Type Questions [5 Marks]

16. (i) Consider the reaction, $2A + B \longrightarrow C + D$

Following results were obtained from experiments designed to study the rate of reactions.

Exp. No.	Initial concentration (mol L^{-1}) [A]	[B]	Initial rate of formation [D] (M/min)
1.	0.10	0.10	1.5×10^{-3}
2.	0.20	0.20	3.0×10^{-3}
3.	0.20	0.40	6.0×10^{-3}

(a) Write the rate law for the reaction.

(b) Calculate the value of rate constant for the reaction.

(c) Which of the following possible reaction mechanisms is consistent with the rate law?

I. $A + B \longrightarrow C + E$ (slow)

$A + E \longrightarrow D$ (fast)

II. $B \longrightarrow C + E$ (slow)

$A + E \longrightarrow F$ (fast)

$A + F \longrightarrow D$ (fast)

(ii) Discuss any four factors which affect the rate of a chemical reaction.

Answers

1. (a) 2. (b) 3. (b) 4. (b) 5. (a) 6. (d)
7. (c) 8. (b) 11. (a) 0.0072 min^{-1} (b) 223.6 mins
12. 27.664 $kJmol^{-1}$ 13. $5.7 \times 10^{12} s^{-1}$
14. (i) 2 and 1 (ii) 177.78 $mol^{-2} L^2 min^{-1}$ (iii) 2.78 M/min
15. (i) 22.01 kJ mol^{-1}
16. (i) Rate $= k[B]$ (ii) $1.5 \times 10^{-2} min^{-1}$ (iii) II

04

CHAPTER

The *d*-block of the periodic table includes the elements of the groups 3 to 12. They are often called as **transition metals.**

The elements constituting the *f*-block are those in which the 4*f*- and 5*f*-orbitals are progressively filled. They are often called as **inner-transition metals.**

The two series of the inner-transition metals (4*f* and 5*f*) are called **lanthanoids** and **actinoids**, respectively.

d-and *f*-Block Elements

YOUR STUDY GOALS

YOUR PRACTICE GOAL

- Objective Type Questions (37 Qs ; 23 MCQs, 12 A-R, 2 Case Study)
- Subjective Type Questions (60 Qs; 24 SA-I, 16 SA-II, 20 LA)

4.1 *d*-Block Elements (Transition Elements)

The elements which have incompletely filled *d*-orbitals in its ground state or in any of its oxidation state are called ***d*-block elements** (transition elements).

The presence of partly filled *d*-or *f*-orbitals in their atoms sets the study of the transition elements and their compounds apart from that of the main group elements.

Various precious metals like silver, gold, platinum and industrially important metals like iron, copper, titanium are part of the **transition metals.**

Position of *d*-Block Elements in the Periodic Table

The *d*-block occupies the large middle section flanked between *s*-and *p*-blocks in the periodic table.

The *d*-orbitals of the penultimate energy level in their atoms receive electrons giving rise to the three rows of the transition metals, i.e. 3*d*, 4*d* and 5*d*. The fourth row of 6*d* is still incomplete.

- **First transition series** or **3*d*- series** Scandium ($_{21}Sc$) to Zinc ($_{30}Zn$).
- **Second transition series** or **4*d*-series** Yttrium ($_{39}Y$) to Cadmium ($_{48}Cd$).
- **Third transition series** or **5*d*-series** Lanthanum ($_{57}La$) to Mercury ($_{80}Hg$), excluding $_{58}Ce$ to $_{71}Lu$.
- **Fourth transition series** or **6*d*-series** Actinium ($_{89}Ac$) to Copernicium ($_{112}Cn$), excluding $_{90}Th$ to $_{103}Lr$.

Occurrence

d-block elements are present as oxides, hydroxides and carbonates in low oxidation state, these are basic in nature. Halides and other salts of *d*-block elements are generally stable in water.

Electronic Configuration

General electronic configuration of transition metals is $(n-1)d^{1\text{-}10}ns^{1\text{-}2}$, where *n* is the outermost shell which may have one or two electrons, whereas $(n-1)$ stands for the inner *d*-orbitals which may have one to ten electrons.

Exceptions

- All the *d*-block elements however, are not transition elements. Last members of different series such as Zn, Cd and Hg has completely filled *d*-orbital $(n-1)d^{10}ns^2$.
- The orbitals in these elements are completely filled in the ground state as well as in their common oxidation states. They do not show any characteristic properties of transition elements except complex formation. Hence, these are not considered as **transition elements**.
- Some of the exceptions are observed in electronic configuration due to very little energy difference between $(n-1)d$ and ns orbitals such as

$$Cr: 3d^5 4s^1 \text{ instead of } 3d^4 4s^2$$
$$Cu: 3d^{10} 4s^1 \text{ instead of } 3d^9 4s^2$$

This can be explained on the basis of electronic repulsion and energy exchange which proves that half-filled and completely filled *d*-orbitals have more stable configuration.

- In the transition elements, the *d*-orbitals project to the periphery of an atom more than the other orbitals (i.e., *s* and *p*). Thus, they are more influenced by the surroundings as well as affecting the atoms or molecules surrounding them.
- In some respect, ions of a given d^n configuration $(n = 1\text{-}9)$ have similar electronic and magnetic properties.

Outer Electronic Configuration of Transition Elements (Ground State)

1st series	**Sc**	**Ti**	**V**	**Cr**	**Mn**	**Fe**	**Co**	**Ni**	**Cu**	**Zn**
Atomic number (*Z*)	21	22	23	24	25	26	27	28	29	30
Electronic configuration	$3d^1 4s^2$	$3d^2 4s^2$	$3d^3 4s^2$	$3d^5 4s^1$	$3d^5 4s^2$	$3d^6 4s^2$	$3d^7 4s^2$	$3d^8 4s^2$	$3d^{10} 4s^1$	$3d^{10} 4s^2$
2nd series	**Y**	**Zr**	**Nb**	**Mo**	**Tc**	**Ru**	**Rh**	**Pd**	**Ag**	**Cd**
Atomic number (*Z*)	39	40	41	42	43	44	45	46	47	48
Electronic configuration	$4d^1 5s^2$	$4d^2 5s^2$	$4d^4 5s^1$	$4d^5 5s^1$	$4d^6 5s^1$	$4d^7 5s^1$	$4d^8 5s^1$	$4d^{10} 5s^0$	$4d^{10} 5s^1$	$4d^{10} 5s^2$
3rd series	**La**	**Hf**	**Ta**	**W**	**Re**	**Os**	**Ir**	**Pt**	**Au**	**Hg**
Atomic number (*Z*)	57	72	73	74	75	76	77	78	79	80
Electronic configuration	$5d^1 6s^2$	$5d^2 6s^2$	$5d^3 6s^2$	$5d^4 6s^2$	$5d^5 6s^2$	$5d^6 6s^2$	$5d^7 6s^2$	$5d^9 6s^1$	$5d^{10} 6s^1$	$5d^{10} 6s^2$
4th series	**Ac**	**Rf**	**Db**	**Sg**	**Bh**	**Hs**	**Mt**	**Ds**	**Rg**	**Cn**
Atomic number (*Z*)	89	104	105	106	107	108	109	110	111	112
Electronic configuration	$6d^1 7s^2$	$6d^2 7s^2$	$6d^3 7s^2$	$6d^4 7s^2$	$6d^5 7s^2$	$6d^6 7s^2$	$6d^7 7s^2$	$6d^8 7s^2$	$6d^{10} 7s^1$	$6d^{10} 7s^2$

General Properties of the Transition Elements

General properties of transition elements are as follows

Physical Properties

- They are very much hard and have very low volatility except Zn, Cd and Hg.
- Their reactivity decreases with the increase in their atomic number. Some other physical properties are discussed below.

1. Metallic Character

- All transition elements are metals having hcp, ccp or bcc lattices. With the exceptions of Zn, Cd, Hg and Mn, they have one or more typical metallic structures at normal temperatures.
- Transition elements display typical metallic properties such as high tensile strength, ductility, malleability, high thermal and electrical conductivity and metallic lustre.

2. Melting and Boiling Points

- They have high melting and boiling points. The high melting point of these metals is due to the involvement of greater number of electrons from $(n-1)d$ in addition to the *ns*-electrons in the **interatomic metallic bonding**.
- In any row, the melting points of these metals rise to a maximum at d^5 and fall regularly with the increase in atomic number except Mn and Tc.

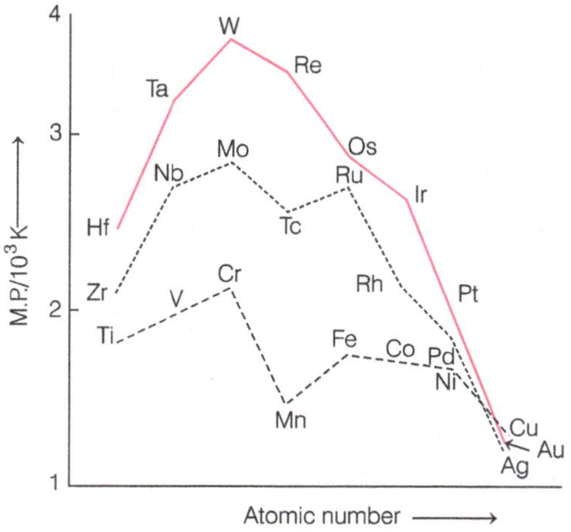

Trends in melting points of transition elements

3. Enthalpy of Atomisation

- Energy required to convert metallic crystal into individual atom is known as **enthalpy of atomisation.**
- The transition metals have high enthalpy of atomisation because of strong interatomic interaction due to unpaired electrons. It first increases, reaches to the maximum in the middle of each series and then decreases.
- Metals of second (4*d*) and third (5*d*) series have high enthalpy of atomisation than the corresponding elements of first (3*d*) series because of stronger metal-metal bond.
- Order of enthalpy of atomisation ($\Delta_a H°$) of 3*d* series is Zn < Mn < Sc < Cu < Cr < Fe < Co < Ni < Ti < V.

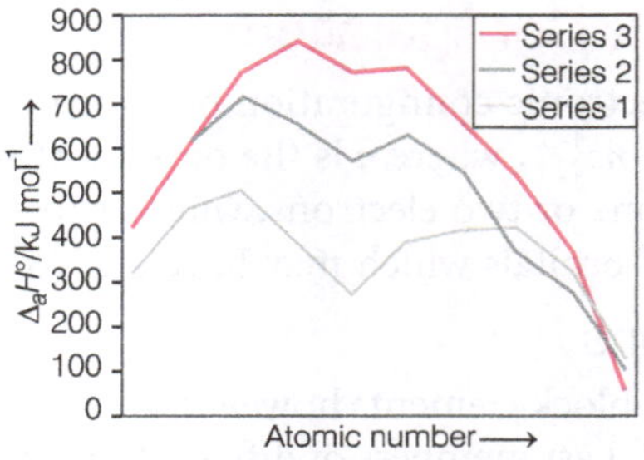

Trends in $\Delta_a H°$ (kJ/mol) of transition elements

Atomic and Ionic Radii

Variation in atomic and ionic radii of transition metals are as follows

Atomic radii

The atomic radii of the transition elements are intermediate between those of *s* and *p*-block elements. The following trend in atomic radii of transition elements are observed.

Along the Period

- On moving from left to right, generally atomic radii first decreases till the middle, becomes almost constant and then increases towards the end of periods.
  (i) In the beginning, the curve of the graph decreases as the atomic radius decreases. This is because the new electron enters a *d*-orbital each time, the nuclear charge increases by unity. Due to poor shielding of *d*-electrons, attractive forces increase between the nucleus and valence electrons and hence size decreases.

(ii) Further, in the midway, the atomic radii becomes almost constant. This is because, the increased in **nuclear charge** and increased **screening effect** balance each other. [See middle section of the curve of the graph.]

(iii) However, at the end of the series, size of elements increases due to the increase in the magnitude of repulsive forces between electrons.

- On comparing the atomic sizes, we obtained the following graph.

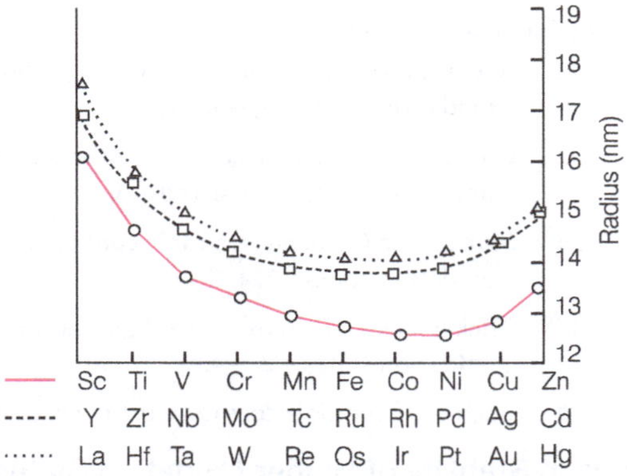

Trends in atomic radii of transition elements

Note Also, density of transition metals increases from left to right in a period because atomic radius decreases and atomic mass increases.

Along the Group

- The atomic radii of transition metals increases down the group upto second series. As, the transition elements of third series have nearly the same radii as metals of second transition series.
- The reason is the intervention of the $4f$-orbitals which must be filled before the $5d$ series of elements.
- The filling of $4f$-orbital before $5d$-orbital results in a regular decrease in atomic radii called **lanthanoid contraction** (discussed later in this chapter).

Note Due to this contraction, the second and third d-series exhibit similar radii, e.g. Zr (160 pm) and Hf (159 pm) have similar physical and chemical properties.

Ionic Radii

It has the same trend as that of atomic radii for transition elements. Moreover, the ionic radii of the transition metals are smaller than those of s-and p-block elements belonging to same period. s-and d-block elements form positive ions, whereas p-block elements mostly form negative ions.

Ionisation Enthalpies (IE)

- The first ionisation enthalpy of d-block elements usually lie between those of s-block elements and p-block elements.
- Ionisation energy increases in a period with atomic number. This is due to increase in the nuclear charge with atomic number which accompanies the filling of inner d-orbitals.
- The irregularities in the trend of first I.E. of $3d$ metals series is because of the fact that the removal of the electrons alters the relative energies of $4s$ and $3d$-orbitals. This alteration release the exchange energy.

  e.g. Cr ($3d^5 4s^1$), has very low first I.E. as loss of one electron gives stable configuration (i.e. $3d^5$), Zn shows quite high value of IE_1 due to extra stability of completely filled orbitals (i.e. $3d^{10} 4s^2$).
- First ionisation energy $(IE)_1$ of $5d$-elements are higher than those of the $3d$ and $4d$-elements. This is due to greater effective nuclear charge acting on outer valence electrons because of the weak shielding of the nucleus by $4f$-electrons. The ionisation energies of the $3d$ and $4d$-elements are irregular.
- In $3d$-series, first four members show little difference in values of IE_1 and these values for last four elements are also fairly close.
- Although **second** and **third** I.E. also increases from left to right. However, the magnitude of increase for the successive elements is much higher.

  Some of the exceptions are as follows

  (i) 3rd IE of Mn is very high because loss of 3rd electron gives the stable half-filled configuration.

  (ii) IE_3 change from Fe^{2+} to Fe^{3+} is small because loss of electrons gives the stable configuration of $3d^5$.
- There is a fall in IE_2 from Cr to Mn and from Cu to Zn because after the removal of first electron, Cr and Cu acquire a stable configuration, i.e. d^5 and d^{10}. The high values of IE_3 for Cu, Ni and Zn explain why they show a maximum oxidation state of +2.

Oxidation States

- Transition metals show a great variety of oxidation states (or variable valency) in its compounds except the first and the last element. This is because of the fact that the difference in the energy of $(n-1)$ d-electrons and ns-electrons is low which implies that electrons from both energy levels can take part in bonding.

- Oxidation states first increases from Sc to Mn due to increase in number of unpaired electrons and then decreases because pairing takes place. e.g. In 3*d*-series, Mn exhibits all the oxidation states from +2 to +7.
- The elements which give the greatest number of oxidation states occur in near the middle of the series.

Oxidation states of the first row transition metals
(The most common ones are typed in bold)

Sc	Ti	V	Cr	Mn	Fe	Co	Ni	Cu	Zn
	+2	+2	+2	**+2**	+2	+2	**+2**	+1	**+2**
+3	+3	+3	**+3**	+3	**+3**	**+3**	+3	**+2**	
	+4	+4	+4	+4	+4	+4	+4		
		+5	+5	+5					
			+6	+6	+6				
				+7					

- **Stability of higher oxidation states** increases in a group from top to bottom due to increase in the distance from the outermost shell.

  e.g. In group 6, Mo (VI) and W (VI) are found to be more stable than Cr (VI). That's why, Cr (VI) in the form of dichromate in acidic medium is a strong oxidising agent, whereas MoO_3 and WO_3 are not.
- **Variability of oxidation states** of transition elements arises due to incomplete filling of *d*-orbitals in such a way that their oxidation states differ from each other by unity.

  e.g. V^{II}, V^{III}, V^{IV}, V^{V}. This in contrast with the variability of oxidation states of non-transition elements, where oxidation states normally differ by a unit of two.
- Mostly **ionic bonds** are formed in lower oxidation states. However, in compounds of higher oxidation state, mostly **covalent bonds** are formed.
- An interesting feature in the variability of oxidation states of *d*-block elements is noticed among the groups 4 to 10.
- Although, the lower oxidation states of *p*-block are favoured by the heavier members due to **inert pair effect**, the opposite is true in case of *d*-block elements.
- Low oxidation states are found if a complex compound has ligands capable of π-acceptor character and σ-bonding.

  e.g. $Ni(CO)_4$ and $Fe(CO)_5$, the oxidation state of nickel and iron is zero.

Example 1 **What may be the stable oxidation state of the transition element with the following *d*-electron configurations in the ground state of their atoms $3d^3$, $3d^5$, $3d^8$ and $3d^4$?** NCERT

Hint
(i) In case of *d*-block elements upto 7 group, the maximum oxidation state = *ns* electrons + (*n* − 1) *d* unpaired electrons.
(ii) Minimum oxidation state is generally +2, but in scandium, it is +3.
(iii) Write the outer shell configuration of the atoms having the given configuration to find the stable oxidation states.

Sol. Stable oxidation states :

$3d^3$: Vanadium (General electronic configuration $3d^3 4s^2$)
: oxidation states +2, +3, +4 and +5.

$3d^5$: Chromium (General electronic configuration $3d^5 4s^1$)
: oxidation states +3, +4 and +6.

$3d^5$: Manganese (General electronic configuration $3d^5 4s^2$)
: oxidation states +2, +4, +6, +7.

$3d^8$: Nickel (General electronic configuration $3d^8 4s^2$)
: oxidation states +2, +4.

$3d^4$: Such configuration does not exist in ground state.

Trends in Stability of Higher Oxidation States

- Transition metals show their highest oxidation states with **fluorine and oxygen** because F and O are small in size and the most electronegative elements.
- The ability of fluorine to stabilise the highest oxidation state is due to either higher lattice enthalpy as in the case of CoF_3 or higher bond enthalpy, e.g. VF_5 and CrF_6.
- 3*d* transition metals form **stable halides**. The highest oxidation states are shown in $\mathbf{TiX_4}$**,** $\mathbf{VF_5}$ **and** $\mathbf{CrF_6}$.

  While, +7 oxidation state by Mn is shown in the compound $\mathbf{MnO_3F}$.
- In low oxidation states, fluorine is unstable, e.g. VX_2 (X = Cl, Br or I). However, **Cu (II) halides** are known including $\mathbf{CuF_2}$ **except iodide.**

$$2Cu^{2+} + 4I^- \longrightarrow Cu_2I_2 + I_2$$

- However, most of the Cu(I) compounds are unstable in aqueous solution and undergo disproportionation.

$$2Cu^+(aq) \longrightarrow Cu^{2+} + Cu(s)$$

The stability of $Cu^{2+}(aq)$ than $Cu^+(aq)$ is due to much more negative $\Delta_{hyd}H^\circ$ of $Cu^{2+}(aq)$ than Cu^+, which more than compensates for the IE_2 of Cu.

Note **Disproportionation** is a special type of redox reaction in which a species is simultaneously reduced and oxidised to form two different products.

In disproportionation, same substance behaves as oxidising agent for one molecule and at the same time as reducing agent for another molecule.

e.g. $2\overset{III}{Mn^{3+}}(aq) + 2H_2O \longrightarrow \overset{IV}{Mn}O_2(s) + Mn^{2+}(aq) + 4H^+(aq)$

Formulae of Halides of 3*d*-Transition Metals

Oxidation no./ Group no.	4	5	6	7	8	9	10	11	12
+6			CrF_6						
+5		VF_5	CrF_5						
+4	TiX_4	VX_4^I	CrX_4	MnF_4					
+3	TiX_3	VX_3	CrX_3	MnF_3	FeX_3^I	CoF_3			
+2	TiX_2^{III}	VX_2	CrX_2	MnX_2	FeX_2	CoX_2	NiX_2	CuX_2^{II}	ZnX_2
+1								CuX^{III}	

Key : $X = F \rightarrow I$, $X^I = F \rightarrow Br$, $X^{II} = F \rightarrow Cl$, $X^{III} = Cl \rightarrow I$

Trends in the Stability of Higher Oxidation States of Transition Metal Oxides

- Oxygen stabilises the highest oxidation state in the oxides more than fluorine (highest fluoride of Mn is MnF_4, whereas its highest oxide is Mn_2O_7) due to the ability of oxygen to form multiple bonds with the metal atoms,

  e.g. In the covalent oxide Mn_2O_7, each Mn is tetrahedrally surrounded by oxygen including a Mn—O—Mn bridge.

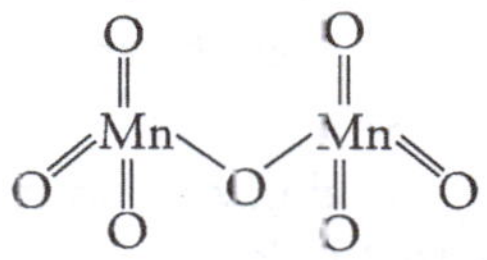

- The tetrahedral $[MO_4]^{n-}$ ions are known for V^V, Cr^{VI}, Mn^V, Mn^{VI} and Mn^{VII}.
- The highest oxidation state in the oxide is same as that of group number upto group 7. Beyond group 7, no higher oxides of Fe above Fe_2O_3 are known, although ferrates (VI) $(FeO_4)^{2-}$ are formed in alkaline medium but they readily decompose to Fe_2O_3 and O_2. Besides the oxides, oxocations stabilise V^V as VO_2^+, V^{IV} as VO^{2+} and Ti^{IV} as TiO^{2+}.

Note Highest oxidation state of manganese is +7, exhibited in stable compounds. Although osmium (76) is the element having highest oxidation state in periodic table, i.e. +8.

Groups Containing Oxides of 3*d*-Transition Metals

Oxidation no./ Group no.	3	4	5	6	7	8	9	10	11	12
+7					Mn_2O_7					
+6				CrO_3						
+5			V_2O_5							
+4		TiO_2	V_2O_4	CrO_2	MnO_2					
+3	Sc_2O_3	Ti_2O_3	V_2O_3	Cr_2O_3	Mn_2O_3	Fe_2O_3				
					$Mn_3O_4^*$	$Fe_3O_4^*$	$Co_3O_4^*$			
+2		TiO	VO	(CrO)	MnO	FeO	CoO	NiO	CuO	ZnO
+1									Cu_2O	

*Mixed oxides

Electrode Potential

- In aqueous solution, the thermodynamic stability of transition metal compounds depends on **electrode potential** ($E°$).
- A lower $E°$ value indicates greater stability in a particular oxidation state of the transition metal ion.
- If hydration enthalpy is lower, $E°$ is **positive** and if it is higher, $E°$ is **negative**. The observed values of $E°$ and those calculated using the data are compared in the given figure.

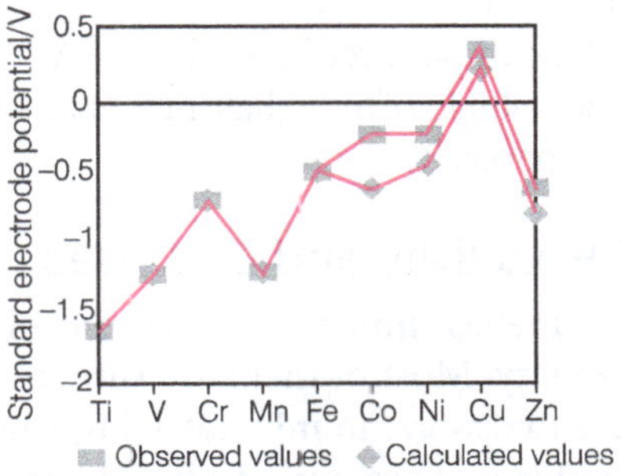

Observed and calculated values for the standard electrode potentials ($M^{2+} \rightarrow M^0$) of the elements from Ti to Zn

Trends in the M^{2+}/M Standard Electrode Potentials

The above result given in the graph of electrode potential value for 3*d*-series can be explained as :

- The values of E° across the series are less negative because of general increase in the sum of the first and second ionisation enthalpies.
- The E° value for Mn, Zn and Ni are more negative than expected from the trend.
- Copper is the only metal having positive value for E°. This is the reason that it does not liberate H_2 gas from acids. It reacts only with the oxidising acids (HNO_3 and H_2SO_4) which are reduced.

Example 2 The $E^\circ_{(M^{2+}/M)}$ value for copper is positive (+0.34 V). What is the possible reason for this?

NCERT Intext, CBSE 2025

Sol. $E^\circ_{(M^{2+}/M)}$ value for any metal depends on three factors

(i) $\Delta_a H$ (Enthalpy of atomisation);

$$M(s) + \Delta_a H \longrightarrow M(g)$$

(ii) $\Delta_i H$ (Enthalpy of ionisation);

$$M(g) + \Delta_i H \longrightarrow M^{2+}(g)$$

(iii) $\Delta_{hyd} H$ (Hydration enthalpy);

$$M^{2+}(g) + \Delta_{hyd} H\,(aq) \longrightarrow M^{2+}(aq)$$

Copper has high value of enthalpy of atomisation and low value of enthalpy of hydration. It means that $\Delta_i H$ required is not compensated by the energy released. Therefore, $E^\circ_{(Cu^{2+}/Cu)}$ is positive.

Trends in M^{3+}/M^{2+} Standard Electrode Potentials

- The low value of E° for Sc^{3+}/Sc^{2+} reflects the stability of Sc^{3+} which has a **noble gas configuration**.
- The highest value of E° for Zn^{3+}/Zn^{2+} is due to the removal of an electron from the stable d^{10} configuration of Zn^{2+}.
- The comparatively high value of E° value for Mn^{3+}/Mn^{2+} indicates the stability of $Mn^{2+}(d^5)$, whereas comparatively low value for Fe indicates the extra stability of Fe^{3+} (d^5).
- Similarly, the comparative low value for V^{3+}/V^{2+} indicates the stability of V^{2+} (half-filled t_{2g} level, discussed in chapter 5).

Chemical Reactivity and E° Values

The transition metals show wide variations in their chemical reactivity. Most of them are sufficiently electropositive to dissolve in **mineral acids**, whereas some of them are noble and are not affected by **single acids**.

The metals of first transition series (with the exception of copper) are relatively more reactive.

However, the actual rate of reaction of these metals with oxidising agents like hydrogen ion (H^+) is sometimes slow.

- **The E° values for M^{2+}/M** indicate a decreasing tendency to form divalent cations across the series. The general trend towards less negative E° values is related to the increase in the sum of the first and second ionisation enthalpies.
- **The E° values for Mn, Ni and Zn** are more negative than expected from the general trend. It is due to the stabilities of half-filled *d*-subshell (d^5) in Mn^{2+} and completely filled *d*-subshell (d^{10}) in zinc.

  It explains their tendencies to form stable divalent ions. For Ni^{2+}, the more negative E° value than expected is due to its highest negative enthalpy of hydration.
- **The E° values for M^{3+}/M^{2+}** shows that Mn^{3+} and Co^{3+} ions are strong oxidising agents in aqueous solutions due to high positive E° values.
- V^{2+} and Cr^{2+} ions are strong reducing agents and will therefore liberate H_2 from a dilute acid.

  e.g. $2Cr^{2+}(aq) + 2H^+(aq) \longrightarrow 2Cr^{3+}(aq) + H_2(g)$

Magnetic Properties

- On applying a magnetic field to substances, two types of magnetic behaviour are observed : **diamagnetism** and **paramagnetism**.
- Many of the transition metal ions have one or more unpaired electron. So, they are paramagnetic in nature.
- Greater is the number of unpaired electrons in an ion, greater is its paramagnetic nature and paramagnetism.
- Those transition elements which have paired electrons are called **diamagnetic**.
- A paramagnetic substance is characterised by its magnetic moment which is calculated by 'spin only' formula, i.e.

$$\mu = \sqrt{n(n+2)}\ \text{BM}$$

where, *n* is the number of unpaired electrons and BM is Bohr Magneton, the unit of magnetic moment.

- Magnetic moment increases with the increasing number of unpaired electrons.

Magnetic Moments of Some Ionic Species

Ion	Outer electronic configuration	Number of unpaired electrons	Magnetic moment (BM)
			Calculated
Sc^{3+}	$3d^0$	0	0
Ti^{3+}	$3d^1$	1	1.73
V^{3+}	$3d^2$	2	2.83
Cr^{3+}	$3d^3$	3	3.87
Mn^{2+}	$3d^5$	5	5.92
Fe^{2+}	$3d^6$	4	4.90
Co^{2+}	$3d^7$	3	3.87
Ni^{2+}	$3d^8$	2	2.83
Cu^{2+}	$3d^9$	1	1.73
Zn^{2+}	$3d^{10}$	0	0.0

Note Substances which are attracted very strongly by a magnetic field and their domains are aligned in one direction are called **ferromagnetic substances**, e.g. Fe, Co, Ni. In fact, ferromagnetism is an extreme form of paramagnetism.

Example 3 Calculate the magnetic moment of a divalent ion in aqueous solution, $[Fe(H_2O)_6]^{2+}$, if atomic number of Fe is 26.

Sol. Magnetic moment $(\mu) = \sqrt{n(n+2)}$ BM

Atomic number of $Fe = 26 = [Ar]3d^6 4s^2$

$$Fe^{2+} = [Ar]3d^6 4s^0 = \boxed{\uparrow\downarrow}\boxed{\uparrow}\boxed{\uparrow}\boxed{\uparrow}\boxed{\uparrow}$$

Thus, unpaired electrons, $n = 4$

So,
$$\mu = \sqrt{n(n+2)}$$
$$= \sqrt{4(4+2)} = \sqrt{24} = 4.89 \text{ BM}$$

Formation of Coloured Ions

- When an electron from a lower energy *d*-orbital is excited to a higher energy *d*-orbital, the energy of excitation corresponds to the frequency of light absorbed. This frequency generally lies in the visible region.
- The colour observed corresponds to the complementary colour of the light absorbed. The frequency of light absorbed is determined by the nature of the ligand.
- Thus, most of the compounds of transition metals are coloured due to ***d-d* transition**. Transition metal ions having **d^0 configuration are colourless.**

TEACHER'S TIP

Few compounds in which transition metal has d^0 configuration, may also exhibit colour due to charge transfer, e.g. CrO_3 has d^0 configuration of Cr and shows orange colour due to charge transfer.

Formation of Complex Compounds

The transition metals form a large number of complex compounds due to *the comparatively smaller size of the metal ions, their high charge density and vacant d-orbitals for bond formation.*

Catalytic Properties

- Many transition metals and their compounds are used as catalyst. Their catalytic activity is due to their ability to adopt multiple oxidation states and to form complexes.

  e.g. V_2O_5 (contact process), finely divided iron (in Haber's process) and nickel (in catalytic hydrogenation).
- Catalysts at a solid surface involve the bond formation between reactant molecules and atoms of the surface of catalyst.
- In some cases, transition metals provide a suitable surface for the reaction to take place. The reactants are adsorbed on the surface of the catalyst. This weakens the bonds between atoms in the reactant molecules.
- Transition metals because of their variable valencies sometimes form unstable intermediate compounds and provide a new path with lower activation energy for the reaction.
- For e.g., iron (III) catalyses the reaction between iodide and persulphate ions.

$$2I^- + S_2O_8^{2-} \xrightarrow{\text{Fe (III)}} I_2 + 2SO_4^{2-}$$

Thus, catalytic action of iron (III) in this reaction is explained as follows

$$2Fe^{3+} + 2I^- \longrightarrow 2Fe^{2+} + I_2$$
$$2Fe^{2+} + S_2O_8^{2-} \longrightarrow 2Fe^{3+} + 2SO_4^{2-}$$

Thus, Fe^{3+} oxidises I^- ions to iodine.

Formation of Interstitial Compounds

- Interstitial compounds are those which are formed when small atoms such as H, C, N, etc. are trapped inside the crystal lattices of metals.
- They are generally **non-stoichiometric** and are neither typically ionic nor covalent, e.g. Mn_4N, TiC, Fe_3H, $TiH_{1.7}$, $VH_{0.56}$, etc.
- The formulas quoted do not correspond to any normal oxidation state of the metal. These compounds are hard (some borides are as hard as diamond), chemically inert, metallic conductors and have high melting points than those of pure metals.

Alloy Formation

- An alloy is a blend of metals prepared by mixing the components. An alloy is a homogeneous solid solution.
- Atoms of transition metal due to similar sizes, can mutually substitute the position in the crystal lattice in the molten state and are miscible with each other forming alloys. Alloys are generally hard, resistant to corrosion and have high melting points.
- Ferrous alloys (with Cr, V, W, Mo and Mn), form varieties of steels and stainless steel, which are best of the class. Brass (Cu-Zn) and bronze (Cu-Sn) are the alloys of transition metals and have considerable industrial importance.

Note Alloys of mercury with metals are known as **amalgams**.

Quick Test 1

1. Silver atom has completely filled d-orbitals ($4d^{10}$) in its ground state. How can you say that it is a transition element? *NCERT Intext*
2. The second and third rows of transition elements resemble each other much more than they resemble the first row. Why? *NCERT Exemplar*
3. Write down the electronic configuration of
   (i) Cr^{3+} (ii) Cu^{+} (iii) Co^{2+} (iv) Mn^{2+} *NCERT*
4. In the series Sc($Z = 21$) to Zn ($Z = 30$), the enthalpy of atomisation of zinc is lowest, i.e., 126 kJ mol^{-1}. Why? *NCERT Intext*
5. (i) Why are Mn^{2+} compounds more stable than Fe^{2+} towards oxidation to their +3 state? *NCERT*
   (ii) Why is the highest oxidation state of a metal exhibited in its oxide or fluoride only? *NCERT Intext*
6. Name the oxometal anions of the first series of the transition metals in which the metal exhibits the oxidation state equal to its group number. *NCERT*
7. Which metal in the first series of transition metals exhibit +1 oxidation state most frequently and why? *NCERT*
8. (i) Which transition metal of the 3d-series has positive $E^{\circ}_{M^{2+}/M}$ value and why?
   (ii) Calculate the 'spin only' magnetic moment of $M^{2+}(aq)$ ion. ($Z = 27$) *NCERT Intext*
9. Predict which of the following will be coloured in aqueous solution? Ti^{3+}, V^{3+}, Cu^{+}, Sc^{3+}, Mn^{2+}, Fe^{3+} and Co^{2+}. Give reasons for each. *NCERT*
10. The standard electrode potential $E^{\circ}_{(M^{2+}/M)}$ for three metals X, Y and Z are as follows

X	Y	Z
−1.18 V	−0.91 V	−0.44 V

Which metal out of X, Y and Z will be the most stable in the M^{2+} state? Give reason. *Competency Based Ques.*

For Solutions, See QR Code on Pg. 143

4.2 Oxides and Oxoanions of Metals

- Transition metals combine with oxygen at high temperature to give metallic oxides.
- Except scandium (Sc), all the transition metals form monoxides (MO) which are ionic in nature.
- As oxidation number increases, covalent nature and acidic character increases, while ionic nature and basic character decreases.
- In general, the oxides in lower oxidation states of metals are basic and in their higher oxidation states, are acidic, whereas in the intermediate oxidation state, the oxides are **amphoteric**.

Behaviour of oxides of manganese are as follows

$$\underset{\text{Basic}}{\overset{+2}{MnO}},\ \underbrace{\overset{+8/3}{Mn_3O_4}, \overset{+3}{Mn_2O_3}, \overset{+4}{MnO_2}}_{\text{Amphoteric}},\ \underset{\substack{\text{Acidic}\\ \text{(Covalent green oil)}}}{\overset{+7}{Mn_2O_7}}$$

Basic oxides Sc_2O_3, TiO, Ti_2O_3, VO, V_2O_3, MnO, FeO, CuO, CoO, NiO, Cu_2O, CrO, etc.

Acidic oxides Mn_2O_7, CrO_3, OsO_4, etc.

Amphoteric oxides TiO_2, ZnO, Cr_2O_3, Mn_2O_3, MnO_2, V_2O_5, Mn_3O_4, Fe_3O_4

Note Highest oxidation number of metal in its oxides is equal to its group number in the periodic table.

1. Potassium Dichromate, $K_2Cr_2O_7$

The preparation and properties of $K_2Cr_2O_7$ are as follows.

Preparation

Potassium dichromate is prepared by chromite ore ($FeCr_2O_4$). The various steps involved in this preparation are as follows

(i) **Conversion of chromite ore into sodium chromate**

Chromite ore is fused with sodium or potassium carbonate in free access of air.

$$4FeCr_2O_4 + 8Na_2CO_3 + \underset{\text{(Excess air)}}{7O_2} \longrightarrow 2Fe_2O_3 + \underset{\substack{\text{Sodium chromate}\\ \text{(Yellow)}}}{8Na_2CrO_4} + 8CO_2\uparrow$$

(ii) **Conversion of sodium chromate into sodium dichromate** Yellow solution of sodium chromate is filtered and acidified with sulphuric acid to give orange sodium dichromate solution.

$$2Na_2CrO_4 + 2H^+ \longrightarrow \underset{\substack{\text{Sodium dichromate}\\\text{(Orange)}}}{Na_2Cr_2O_7} + 2Na^+ + H_2O$$

(iii) **Conversion of sodium dichromate into potassium dichromate** $K_2Cr_2O_7$ is prepared by treating the solution of $Na_2Cr_2O_7$ with KCl because sodium dichromate is more soluble than potassium dichromate.

$$Na_2Cr_2O_7 + 2KCl \longrightarrow \underset{\substack{\text{Potassium}\\\text{dichromate}}}{K_2Cr_2O_7} + 2NaCl$$

Orange coloured crystals of $K_2Cr_2O_7$ separates out.

Structure

The structure of chromate ion (CrO_4^{2-}) is tetrahedral and dichromate ion ($Cr_2O_7^{2-}$) consists of two tetrahedra sharing one corner with Cr—O—Cr bond angle of 126°.

Dichromate ion ($Cr_2O_7^{2-}$)

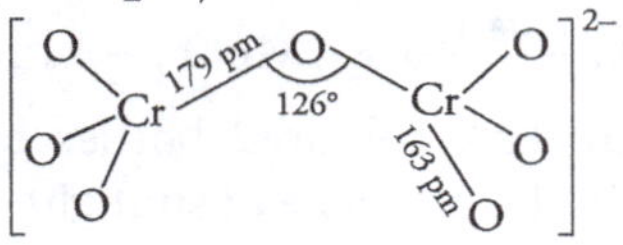

Chromate ion (CrO_4^{2-})

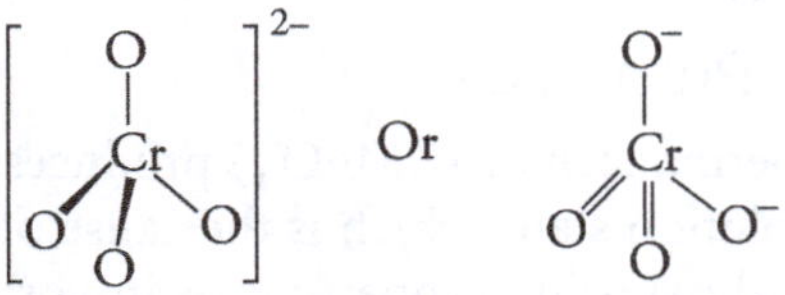

Physical Properties

- It is a crystalline ionic solid having bright, reddish-orange colour.
- It is odourless, with density around 2.67 g cm^{-3}.
- It is soluble in water and insoluble in alcohol, acetone, etc.

Chemical Properties

- Depending upon the pH of the solution, the chromates and dichromates are interconvertible in aqueous solution.

$$\underset{\text{(Orange)}}{Cr_2O_7^{2-}} + H_2O \rightleftharpoons \underset{\text{(Yellow)}}{2CrO_4^{2-}} + 2H^+$$

- In **acidic medium** backward reaction is favoured.

$$2CrO_4^{2-} + 2H^+ \longrightarrow \underset{\text{(Orange)}}{Cr_2O_7^{2-}} + H_2O$$

- In **alkaline medium** forward reaction is favoured,

$$Cr_2O_7^{2-} + 2OH^- \longrightarrow 2CrO_4^{2-} + H_2O$$

- The oxidation state of chromium in chromate and dichromate ion is same.
- One molecule of potassium dichromate, in the presence of dilute sulphuric acid furnishes three atoms of available oxygen or we can say that $Cr_2O_7^{2-}$ ion takes up 6 electrons and act as oxidising agent.

$$K_2Cr_2O_7 + 4H_2SO_4 \longrightarrow K_2SO_4 + Cr(SO_4)_3 + 4H_2O + 3[O]$$

or $$Cr_2O_7^{2-} + 14H^+ + 6e^- \longrightarrow 2Cr^{3+} + 7H_2O \quad [E° = 1.33\ V]$$

Some of the oxidising reactions of K_2CrO_7 are as follows

(i) It oxidises iodides to iodine.

$$Cr_2O_7^{2-} + 14H^+ + 6e^- \longrightarrow 2Cr^{3+} + 7H_2O$$
$$[2I^- \longrightarrow I_2 + 2e^-] \times 3$$
$$Cr_2O_7^{2-} + 6I^- + 14H^+ \longrightarrow 2Cr^{3+} + 3I_2 + 7H_2O$$

(ii) It oxidises acidified ferrous sulphate to ferric sulphate.

$$Cr_2O_7^{2-} + 14H^+ + 6e^- \longrightarrow 2Cr^{3+} + 7H_2O$$
$$[Fe^{2+} \longrightarrow Fe^{3+} + e^-] \times 6$$
$$Cr_2O_7^{2-} + 14H^+ + 6Fe^{2+} \longrightarrow 2Cr^{3+} + 6Fe^{3+} + 7H_2O$$

(iii) It oxidises hydrogen sulphide (H_2S) to sulphur.

$$Cr_2O_7^{2-} + 14H^+ + 6e^- \longrightarrow 2Cr^{3+} + 7H_2O$$
$$[H_2S \longrightarrow S + 2H^+ + 2e^-] \times 3$$
$$Cr_2O_7^{2-} + 3H_2S + 8H^+ \longrightarrow 2Cr^{3+} + 3S + 7H_2O$$

(iv) Similarly, it oxidises stannous salts (Sn^{2+}) to stannic salts (Sn^{4+}).

$$\underset{\substack{\text{Stannous}\\\text{salts}}}{3Sn^{2+}} + Cr_2O_7^{2-} + 14H^+ \longrightarrow \underset{\substack{\text{Stannic}\\\text{salts}}}{3Sn^{4+}} + 2Cr^{3+} + 7H_2O$$

(v) Similarly, it oxidises nitrites to nitrates.

$$\underset{\text{Nitrite}}{3NO_2^-} + Cr_2O_7^{2-} + 8H^+ \longrightarrow \underset{\text{Nitrate}}{3NO_3^-} + 2Cr^{3+} + 4H_2O$$

TEACHER'S TIP

- Orange crystals of dichromate ion are moderately soluble in cold water but readily soluble in hot water.
- In basic medium, $K_2Cr_2O_7$ does not undergo redox reactions and it forms **chromate** ions.

Uses

Potassium dichromate is used

- as an oxidising agent in many reactions.
- in preparation of azo compounds.

- as a disinfectant.
- for tanning of leather, in photography and for hardening of gelatin.
- as a primary standard solution in volumetric analysis in acidic medium.

2. Potassium Permanganate, $KMnO_4$

The preparation and properties of $KMnO_4$ are as follows

Preparation

(i) Potassium permanganate is prepared by pyrolusite (MnO_2) ore. When pyrolusite ore is fused with alkali metal hydroxide in the presence of air or an oxidising agent like KNO_3, potassium manganate is formed.

$$2MnO_2 + 4KOH + O_2 \longrightarrow \underset{\text{Potassium manganate}}{2K_2MnO_4} + 2H_2O$$

Potassium manganate (K_2MnO_4) is of **green colour** which disproportionates in a neutral or acidic solution to produce potassium permanganate.

$$3MnO_4^{2-} + 4H^+ \longrightarrow 2MnO_4^- + MnO_2 + 2H_2O$$

$$\text{Or } 3K_2MnO_4 + 4H^+ \longrightarrow \underset{\text{Potassium permanganate}}{2KMnO_4} + MnO_2 + 2H_2O + 4K^+$$

(ii) Commercially, it is prepared by alkaline oxidative fusion of MnO_2 followed by electrolytic oxidation of manganate (VI).

$$MnO_2 \xrightarrow[\text{Oxidised with air or } KNO_3]{\text{Fused with KOH}} \underset{\text{Manganate ion}}{MnO_4^{2-}}$$

$$MnO_4^{2-} \xrightarrow[\text{in alkaline solution}]{\text{Electrolytic oxidation}} \underset{\text{Permanganate ion}}{MnO_4^-}$$

(iii) In the laboratory, a manganese (II) ion salt is oxidised by peroxodisulphate to permanganate.

$$2Mn^{2+} + 5S_2O_8^{2-} + 8H_2O \longrightarrow 2MnO_4^- + 10SO_4^{2-} + 16H^+$$

(iv) Dark purple crystals are formed which are isostructural with $KClO_4$.

Structure

The manganate, MnO_4^{2-} and permanganate, MnO_4^- are tetrahedral, the green MnO_4^{2-} is paramagnetic with one unpaired electron but the purple MnO_4^- is diamagnetic.

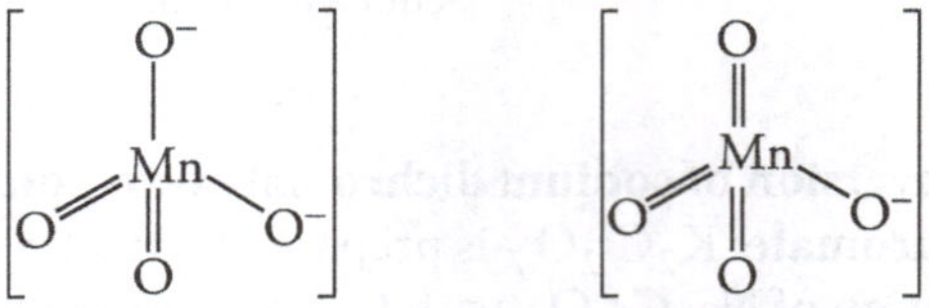

Tetrahedral manganate ion (green, paramagnetic)   Tetrahedral permanganate ion (purple, diamagnetic)

The π-bonding takes place by overlapping of *p*-orbitals of oxygen with *d*-orbitals of manganese.

Physical Properties

- It is dark purple coloured (the deep purple colour of $KMnO_4$ is due to charge transfer from O to Mn) crystalline solid. It is moderately soluble in water at room temperature (6.4 g/100 g of H_2O at 293 K) and more soluble in hot water. On heating, it decomposes at 513 K and O_2 is evolved.

$$2KMnO_4 \xrightarrow{513\text{ K}} K_2MnO_4 + MnO_2 + O_2$$

- It is stored in dark coloured bottles because it gets decomposed in the presence of sunlight.
- It shows weak paramagnetism which depends upon temperature.

Chemical Properties

Potassium permanganate ($KMnO_4$) produces nascent oxygen in solution state, which is the cause of its bleaching and oxidising properties. Its important reactions are as follows

Bleaching Action of $KMnO_4$ in Different Solutions

(i) **Neutral solution**

$$2KMnO_4 + H_2O \longrightarrow 2KOH + 2MnO_2 + 3[O]$$

$$MnO_4^- + 2H_2O + 3e^- \longrightarrow MnO_2 + 4OH^-$$

(ii) **Alkaline solution**

$$2KMnO_4 + 2KOH \longrightarrow 2K_2MnO_4 + H_2O + [O]$$

$$MnO_4^- + e^- \longrightarrow MnO_4^{2-}$$

(iii) **Acidic solution**

$$2KMnO_4 + 3H_2SO_4 \longrightarrow K_2SO_4 + 2MnSO_4 + 3H_2O + 5[O]$$

$$MnO_4^- + 8H^+ + 5e^- \longrightarrow Mn^{2+} + 4H_2O$$

- **Oxidation reactions of acidified $KMnO_4$**

(i) **Iodide to iodine**

$$[MnO_4^- + 8H^+ + 5e^- \longrightarrow Mn^{2+} + 4H_2O] \times 2$$
$$[2I^- \longrightarrow I_2 + 2e^-] \times 5$$
$$\overline{2MnO_4^- + 10I^- + 16H^+ \longrightarrow 2Mn^{2+} + 5I_2 + 8H_2O}$$

(ii) **Ferrous salt to ferric salt**

$$MnO_4^- + 8H^+ + 5e^- \longrightarrow Mn^{2+} + 4H_2O$$
$$[\underset{\text{(Green)}}{Fe^{2+}} \longrightarrow \underset{\text{(Yellow)}}{Fe^{3+}} + e^-] \times 5$$
$$\overline{MnO_4^- + 5Fe^{2+} + 8H^+ \longrightarrow Mn^{2+} + 5Fe^{3+} + 4H_2O}$$

(iii) **Oxalate to carbon dioxide** (at 333 K)

$$[MnO_4^- + 8H^+ + 5e^- \longrightarrow Mn^{2+} + 4H_2O] \times 2$$
$$[C_2O_4^{2-} \longrightarrow 2CO_2 + 2e^-] \times 5$$
$$\overline{2MnO_4^- + 5C_2O_4^{2-} + 16H^+ \longrightarrow 2Mn^{2+} + 10CO_2 + 8H_2O}$$

(iv) **Hydrogen sulphide to sulphur**

$$H_2S \longrightarrow 2H^+ + S^{2-}$$
$$[MnO_4^- + 8H^+ + 5e^- \longrightarrow Mn^{2+} + 4H_2O] \times 2$$
$$[S^{2-} \longrightarrow S + 2e^-] \times 5$$
$$\overline{2MnO_4^- + 5S^{2-} + 16H^+ \longrightarrow 2Mn^{2+} + 5S + 8H_2O}$$

(v) **Sulphurous acid or sulphite to sulphate or sulphuric acid**

$$[MnO_4^- + 8H^+ + 5e^- \longrightarrow Mn^{2+} + 4H_2O] \times 2$$
$$[SO_3^{2-} + H_2O \longrightarrow SO_4^{2-} + 2H^+ + 2e^-] \times 5$$
$$\overline{5SO_3^{2-} + 2MnO_4^- + 6H^+ \longrightarrow 2Mn^{2+} + 5SO_4^{2-} + 3H_2O}$$

(vi) **Nitrite to nitrate**

$$MnO_4^- + 8H^+ + 5e^- \longrightarrow Mn^{2+} + 4H_2O] \times 2$$
$$[NO_2^- + H_2O \longrightarrow NO_3^- + 2H^+ + 2e^-] \times 5$$
$$\overline{2MnO_4^- + 5NO_2^- + 6H^+ \longrightarrow 2Mn^{2+} + 5NO_3^- + 3H_2O}$$

Oxidation reaction of neutral or mildly alkaline $KMnO_4$

(i) **Iodide to iodate**

$$[MnO_4^- + 2H_2O + 3e^- \longrightarrow MnO_2 + 4OH^-] \times 2$$
$$I^- + 6OH^- \longrightarrow IO_3^- + 3H_2O + 6e^-$$
$$\overline{2MnO_4^- + I^- + H_2O \longrightarrow IO_3^- + 2MnO_2 + 2OH^-}$$

(ii) **Thiosulphate to sulphate**

$$8MnO_4^- + 3S_2O_3^{2-} + H_2O \longrightarrow 8MnO_2 + 6SO_4^{2-} + 2OH^-$$

(iii) **Manganous salt to MnO_2**

$$2MnO_4^- + 3Mn^{2+} + 2H_2O \xrightarrow{ZnO \text{ or } ZnSO_4} 5MnO_2 + 4H^+$$

Uses

Uses of potassium permanganate are as follows

- In analytical chemistry, it is used as an oxidant in the preparation of organic compounds.
- It is used in bleaching of wool, cotton and silk, in decolourisation of oils and cleaning surgical instruments in hospitals.
- Volumetric titrations involving $KMnO_4$ are carried out only in the presence of dil. H_2SO_4. In case HCl is used, it is oxidised to Cl_2.

4.3 Applications of Transition Metals

Important applications of transition metals are as follows.

- Iron and steel are the most important construction materials.
- TiO is used in pigment industry.
- MnO_2, Zn, Ni and Cd are used in battery industries.
- Cu, Ag and Au are used for making coins and ornaments.
- V_2O_5 is used as a catalyst in the manufacture of sulphuric acid.
- $TiCl_4$ with $Al(CH_3)_3$ is used in the manufacture of polythene.
- Iron catalyst is used in Haber's process for the manufacture of ammonia.
- Ni catalyst is used for hydrogenation of fats.
- $PdCl_2$ is used as a catalyst in the Wacker process (oxidation of ethyne to ethanal).
- Nickel complexes are used in the polymerisation of alkynes, benzene, etc.
- Light sensitive properties of AgBr are used in photographic industries.

Quick Test 2

1. Give reasons for the following. CBSE SQP 2021
   (i) Transition elements act as catalysts.
   (ii) It is difficult to obtain oxidation state greater than two for copper.
   (iii) CrO is basic but Cr_2O_3 is amphoteric.
2. When orange solution containing $Cr_2O_7^{2-}$ ion is treated with an alkali, a yellow solution is formed and when H^+ ions are added to yellow solution, an orange solution is obtained. Explain, why does this happen? NCERT Exemplar
3. Explain why does colour of $KMnO_4$ disappear when oxalic acid is added to its solution in acidic medium? NCERT Exemplar
4. Complete and balance the following chemical equations: CBSE 2018
   (i) $Fe^{2+} + MnO_4^- + H^+ \longrightarrow$
   (ii) $MnO_4^- + H_2O + I^- \longrightarrow$
5. Describe the preparation of potassium dichromate from chromite ore. What is the effect of the increasing pH on a solution of potassium dichromate? CBSE 2019, 2020, NCERT
6. What happens when acidified $KMnO_4$ reacts with the following in acidic medium ? Diksha
   (i) H_2S (ii) Oxalic acid (iii) KNO_2
7. A solution of $KMnO_4$ on reduction yields either a colourless solution or a brown precipitate or a green solution depending on pH of the solution. What different stages of the reduction do these represent and how are they carried out? NCERT Exemplar
8. Substance *D* is used for the bleaching of wool, cotton, silk and other textile fibres and for the decolourisation of oils. It is dark purple in colour and is almost insoluble in water. The shape of the molecule is tetrahedral. Competency Based Que.
   (i) Calculate the magnetic moment of this substance.
   (ii) What is the magnetic nature of the compound *D*?
   (iii) What is the bond angle of the central atom with the other atoms?

For Solutions, See QR Code on Pg. 143

4.4 *f*-Block Elements (Inner-Transition Elements)

- Elements in which the **last electron** or **differentiating electrons** fill up in *f*-orbital are called ***f*-block elements.**
- These elements are also known as **inner-transition elements** as $(n-2)f$-orbitals lie deep with respect to the penultimate shell.

These elements are divided into two series

(i) $4f$-series or lanthanoids (ii) $5f$-series or actinoids

4.5 Lanthanoids

The 14 elements, from cerium(Ce) to lutetium (Lu) in which $4f$-orbitals are being filled up are called **lanthanoids.** These elements are also called rare earth elements, as they occur very rarely.

Properties of Lanthanoids

Some properties of lanthanoids are discussed below

Electronic Configuration

General electronic configuration of lanthanoids are $6s^2 5d^{0\text{-}1} 4f^{1\text{-}14}$. In these elements, last electron enters into the $4f$-orbital till Yb($4f^{14}$).

Only cerium, gadolinium and lutetium have electron in 5*d*-orbital as well.

The general trend in electronic configurations of lanthanoids are tabulated below.

Electronic Configurations of Lanthanum and Lanthanoids

Atomic number	Name	Symbol	Outer electronic configurations Ln
57	Lanthanum	La	[Xe] $5d^1 6s^2$
58	**Cerium**	**Ce**	**[Xe] $4f^1 5d^1 6s^2$**
59	Praseodymium	Pr	[Xe] $4f^3 5d^0 6s^2$
60	Neodymium	Nd	[Xe] $4f^4 5d^0 6s^2$
61	Promethium	Pm	[Xe] $4f^5 5d^0 6s^2$
62	Samarium	Sm	[Xe] $4f^6 5d^0 6s^2$
63	Europium	Eu	[Xe] $4f^7 5d^0 6s^2$
64	**Gadolinium**	**Gd**	**[Xe] $4f^7 5d^1 6s^2$**
65	Terbium	Tb	[Xe] $4f^9 5d^0 6s^2$
66	Dysprosium	Dy	[Xe] $4f^{10} 5d^0 6s^2$
67	Holmium	Ho	[Xe] $4f^{11} 5d^0 6s^2$
68	Erbium	Er	[Xe] $4f^{12} 5d^0 6s^2$
69	Thulium	Tm	[Xe] $4f^{13} 5d^0 6s^2$
70	Ytterbium	Yb	[Xe] $4f^{14} 5d^0 6s^2$
71	**Lutetium**	**Lu**	**[Xe] $4f^{14} 5d^1 6s^2$**

Atomic and Ionic Radii

The atomic and ionic radii decreases from lanthanum to lutetium. This is due to the unique property of lanthanoids which is known as **lanthanoid contraction.**

Lanthanoid Contraction

The filling of 4*f*-orbital before 5*d*-orbital results in a regular decrease in atomic radii called **lanthanoid contraction.**

Causes of Lanthanoid Contraction

- The factor responsible for the lanthanoid contraction is similar to that of ordinary transition series, i.e., the imperfect shielding of one electron by another in the same set of orbitals.

  However, the shielding of one 4*f*-electron by another is less than that of one *d*-electron by another.
- As the atomic number increases in lanthanoid series, for every proton in the nucleus the extra electron enters into $4f$-orbitals. Therefore, there is a gradual increase in the effective nuclear charge experienced by the outer electrons.

  Accordingly, the attraction of the nucleus for the electrons in the outermost shell increases as the atomic number of lanthanoids increases.
- The decrease in atomic radii is not regular but the decrease in ionic radii of their M^{3+} ions is quite regular as represented by the following graph.

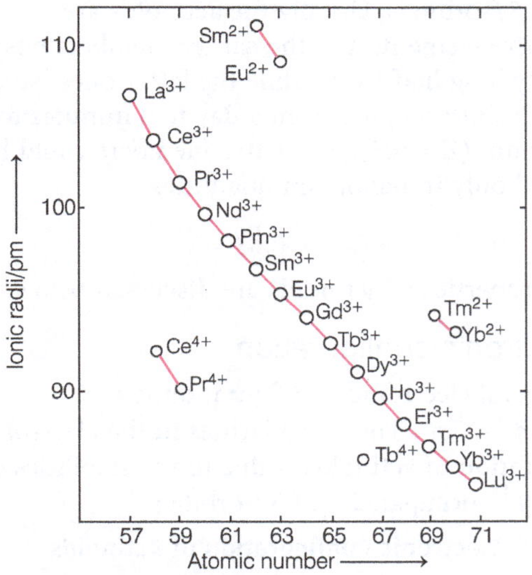

Trends in ionic radii of lanthanoids

Consequences of Lanthanoid Contraction

(i) **Basic character of oxides and hydroxides** Due to the lanthanoid contraction, the covalent nature of Ln—OH bond increases as the basic character of oxides and hydroxides decreases from $La(OH)_3$ to $Lu(OH)_3$.

(ii) **Similarity in the size or radii of elements of second and third transition series** Because of lanthanoid contraction, elements which follow the third transition series are considerably smaller than that would otherwise be expected. The normal size increases from Sc → Y → La and disappears after lanthanoids. Thus, pairs of elements such as Zr/Hf, Nb/Ta and Mo/W are almost identical in size.

Due to almost similar size, such pairs have very similar properties which make their separation difficult and hence, are also called as **chemical twin.**

(iii) **Separation of lanthanoids** Due to lanthanoid contraction, there is a small difference in the size of lanthanoids.

So, there is difference in some properties of lanthanoids like solubility, degree of hydration and complex formation. These differences enable the separation of lanthanoids by **ion exchange method.**

Oxidation States

- The most common and **stable oxidation state of lanthanoid is +3.** This oxidation state are especially stable in lanthanum, gadolinium and lutetium.
- +2 and +4 oxidation states also exist but they changes to +3 in some cases, e.g. Sm^{2+}, Eu^{2+} lose one electron to attain +3 state and hence are **good reducing agents.**
- The +4 oxidation state in cerium and terbium is stable as +4 ions of these elements have empty and half-filled $4f$ subshell respectively. Also, $Sm^{2+}(4f^6)$, Eu^{2+} $(4f^7)$ and Yb^{2+} $(4f^{14})$ ions are also exist in aqueous solutions.
- Similarly, Yb^{2+} with $4f^{14}$ configuration act as a **reductant** and Tb^{4+} with half-filled f-orbitals acts as an **oxidant.** While Ce^{4+}, Pr^{4+} in aqueous solution gain one electron to attain +3 state and hence are **oxidising agents.**

General Characteristics

(i) **Appearance** Lanthanoids are silvery white soft metals and tarnish rapidly in air. The hardness increases with increasing atomic number (samarium is steel hard).

(ii) **Density and melting point** Lanthanoids are highly dense metals and have high melting points (1000 to 1200 K). Sm has exceptionally high melting point of 1623 K.

(iii) **Metallic property** They have typical metallic structure and are good conductors of heat and electricity.

(iv) **Alloy formation** With other metals especially Fe they easily form alloys, e.g., alloy **mischmetal** of rare earth element i.e., lanthanoid (94%-95%), iron (upto 5%) and traces of S, C, Ca and Al.

(v) **Magnetic properties**

(a) Generally, paramagnetism is shown by lanthanoid ions. The paramagnetism arises due to the presence of unpaired electrons in f-orbital.

(b) Magnetic moment depends upon orbital and spin magnetic moment together. Neodymium shows maximum paramagnetism.

(vi) **Colour** Most of the trivalent ions are coloured in solid as well as in aqueous solution due to partly filled f-orbital. Generally, lanthanoid ions with xf-electrons have a similar colour to those with $(14-x)$ f-electrons. e.g. La^{3+} and Lu^{3+} are colourless. The absorption bands are narrow, probably because of the excitation within f-level.

(vii) **Complex formation** Lanthanoids have large size and low charge to radius ratio. As a result, they have poor tendency to form complex.

(viii) **Ionisation enthalpy**

(a) The first ionisation enthalpies of lanthanoids are around 600 kJ mol^{-1}, the second about 1200 kJ mol^{-1} comparable with those of calcium.

(b) The variation of the third ionisation enthalpies indicates that the exchange enthalpy consideration (as in $3d$-orbital of first transition series) appears to impart a certain degree of stability to empty, half-filled and completely filled f-orbitals as indicated by the abnormally low third ionisation enthalpies of La, Gd and Lu.

Chemical Behaviour

- The first few members of the series are quite reactive, almost like calcium. However, with increasing atomic number, their behaviour becomes similar to that of aluminium. These combine with hydrogen, carbon, nitrogen, sulphides and halides. They also form oxides (M_2O_3 type) and hydroxides [$M(OH)_3$ type], which are basic like alkaline earth metal oxides and hydroxides.

Some of the chemical reactions are shown below in the form of flow chart

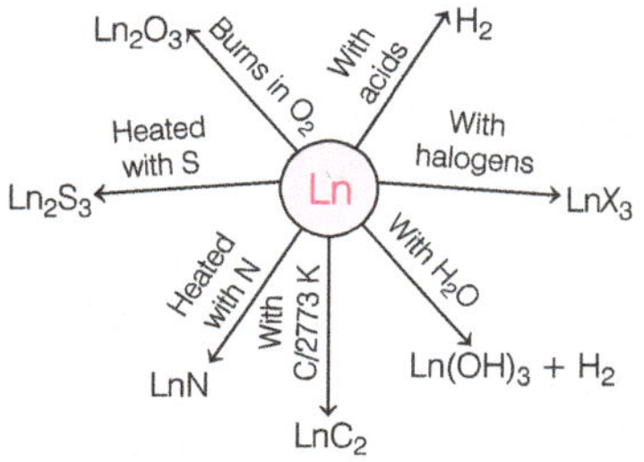

Chemical reactions of the lanthanoids

Uses

- Lanthanoids are used for the production of alloy steels for plates and pipes.
- Mischmetal alloy of lanthanoid is used in Mg-based alloy to produce bullets, shell and lighter flint.
- Mixed oxides of lanthanoids are used as catalysts in **cracking** of petroleum.
- Some lanthanum oxides are used as phosphors in television screens.
- Compounds of some of these elements are used as oxidising agent in volumetric analysis, e.g. cerium sulphate (i.e. $Ce(SO_4)_2$).
- Oxides of lanthanoids are used to produce red colour on television screen.

4.6 Actinoids

These are the elements in which the last electron is filled in $5f$-orbitals. Usually the actinoids are radioactive elements and the earlier members possess relatively long half-lives, while the latter ones have half-life values ranging from a day to 3 minutes for lawrencium ($Z = 103$). The latter members could be prepared only in nanogram quantities.

Properties of Actinoids

Some properties of actinoids are discussed below.

(i) Electronic configuration

The general electronic configuration is $5f^{0-14}6d^{0-1}7s^2$. The irregularities in the electronic configuration of actinoids is due to the stabilities of f^0, f^7 and f^{14} occupancies of $5f$-orbitals.

Electronic Configuration of Actinoids

Atomic number	Name	Symbol	Outer electronic structure
89	Actinium	Ac	$[Rn]6d^1 7s^2$
90	Thorium	Th	$[Rn]5f^0 6d^2 7s^2$
91	Protactinium	Pa	$[Rn]5f^2 6d^1 7s^2$
92	Uranium	U	$[Rn]5f^3 6d^1 7s^2$
93	Neptunium	Np	$[Rn]5f^4 6d^1 7s^2$
94	Plutonium	Pu	$[Rn]5f^6 6d^0 7s^2$
95	Americium	Am	$[Rn]5f^7 6d^0 7s^2$
96	**Curium**	**Cm**	**$[Rn]5f^7 6d^1 7s^2$**

Atomic number	Name	Symbol	Outer electronic structure
97	Berkelium	Bk	$[Rn]5f^9 6d^0 7s^2$
98	Californium	Cf	$[Rn]5f^{10} 6d^0 7s^2$
99	Einsteinium	Es	$[Rn]5f^{11} 6d^0 7s^2$
100	Fermium	Fm	$[Rn]5f^{12} 6d^0 7s^2$
101	Mendelevium	Md	$[Rn]5f^{13} 6d^0 7s^2$
102	Nobelium	No	$[Rn]5f^{14} 6d^0 7s^2$
103	**Lawrencium**	**Lr**	$\mathbf{[Rn]5f^{14} 6d^1 7s^2}$

(ii) Ionic size

The radii of trivalent and quadrivalent ions of actinoids contract slightly with increasing atomic number due to **actinoid contraction**. This contraction results from poor shielding experienced by $5f$-electrons.

(iii) Oxidation States

- Actinoids show a variety of oxidation states due to comparable energies of $5f$, $6d$ and $7s$ energy levels.
- The dominant oxidation state of actinoids is $+3$, which shows increasing stability for the heavier elements.

(iv) Magnetic Properties

Actinoids are generally paramagnetic due to the presence of unpaired electrons in their $5f$-orbitals. Actinoids tend to have more complex magnetic properties with lower values of magnetic moments compared to that of lanthanoids due to the poorer shielding of $5f$-electrons.

(v) Colour of the ions

Actinoid ions are generally coloured due to f-f transition. It depends upon the number of unpaired electrons in $5f$-orbitals.

(vi) Complex formation

Actinoids have greater tendency to form complexes due to higher nuclear charge and smaller size of their atoms.

(vii) Density

All the actinoids have high density except thorium and americium.

(viii) Ionisation Enthalpies

The ionisation enthalpies of actinoids are very low.

(ix) Radioactive Nature

Generally all the actinoids are radioactive in nature.

Similarities between Lanthanoids and Actinoids

There are some similarities between lanthanoids and actinoids, which are as follows

- Both exhibit $+3$ oxidation state predominantly.
- Both are electropositive and have high reactivity.
- Like lanthanoid contraction, there is actinoid contraction also.
- They show ion exchange behaviour.
- In both series, f-orbitals are being progressively filled.

Difference between Lanthanoids and Actinoids

Property	Lanthanoids	Actinoids
Oxidation states	They show mainly $+3$ oxidation state. $+2$ and $+4$ oxidation states also exist.	In addition to $+3$ oxidation state, actinoids also show higher oxidation states like $+4$, $+5$, $+6$ and $+7$.
Binding energies	Binding energies of $4f$ are higher.	Binding energies of $5f$ are lower.
Shielding effect	They have poor shielding effect.	They have even poor shielding effect than lanthanoids.
Magnetic properties	They are paramagnetic and their magnetic properties can be easily explained.	They are also paramagnetic, but their magnetic properties cannot be easily explained.
Chemical reactivity		
(i) Tendency to form complexes	Less	More
(ii) Radioactivity	Except promethium, these are non-radioactive substances.	These are radioactive substances.
(iii) Basic character	These are less basic.	These are more basic.
(iv) Tendency to form oxoions	They do not form oxoions.	They form oxoions such as UO_2^+, NpO_2^+, PuO_2^+, etc.

Uses

Some important uses of actinoids are as follows

- Uranium is used as nuclear fuel in nuclear reactors, while its salts are used in glass industry and also in medicines.
- For atomic reactors as well as in atomic bombs, plutonium is used as fuel.
- Thorium is used in treatment of cancer.
- Thorium is also used as fuel rods in atomic reactors.
- Some actinoids are used for the synthesis of transuranic elements.

Quick Test 3

1. (i) What are the different oxidation states exhibited by lanthanoids? *NCERT*

(ii) Name a member of the lanthanoid series which is well known to exhibit +4 oxidation state. *CBSE 2014*

2. What are inner-transition elements? Decide which of the following atomic numbers are of the inner-transition elements 29, 59, 74, 95, 102, 104? *NCERT*

3. Use Hund's rule to derive the electronic configuration of Ce^{3+} ion and calculate its magnetic moment on the basis of 'spin only' formula. *NCERT*

4. What are alloys? Name an important alloy which contains some of the lanthanoid metals. Mention its uses. *NCERT*

5. The chemistry of the actinoid elements is not so smooth as that of the lanthanoids. Justify this statement by giving some examples from the oxidation state of these elements. *NCERT*

6. Actinoid contraction is greater from element to element than lanthanoid contraction. Why? *NCERT Intext*

For Solutions, See QR Code on Pg. 143

Mind Map

Lanthanoids

- Electronic configuration = $[Xe]4f^{1-14}\,5d^{0-1}6s^2$
- Atomic and ionic radii decrease from La to Lu and this decrease is called **lanthanoid contraction**. It is due to poor sheilding of $4f$-orbitals.
- Common oxidation state = +3
- They are paramagnetic, coloured, have second I.E. comparable to Ca.

Consequences of Lanthanoid Contraction

- Decrease in basic character of oxide and hydroxide from La to Lu.
- Same size of Zr and Hf, Nb and Ta etc.

Potassium Dichromate ($K_2Cr_2O_7$)

- Prepared as

$$\text{Chromite ore} \xrightarrow[\text{Air}]{Na_2CO_3} \text{Chromate} \xrightarrow{H^+} \text{Dichromate of Na} \xrightarrow{KCl} K_2Cr_2O_7$$

- **Structure**

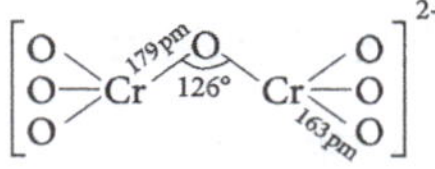

$Cr_2O_7^{2-} + 14H^+ + 6e^- \longrightarrow 2Cr^{3+} + 7H_2O$

- It oxidises I^- to I_2, H_2S to S, Fe^{2+} to Fe^{3+} and itself gets reduced to Cr^{3+}.

Potassium Permaganate ($KMnO_4$)

- Prepared as

$$\text{Pyrolusite } (MnO_2) \xrightarrow[O_2]{KOH} MnO_4^{2-} \xrightarrow{H^+} MnO_4^-$$

Structure

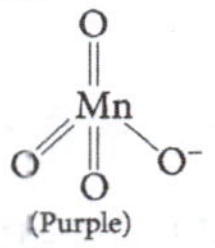

(Purple)
(Tetrahedral permanganate ion)

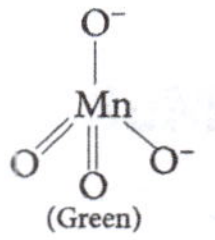

(Green)
(Tetrahedral manganate ion)

- **Properties** In acidic medium, it oxidises I^- to I_2, Fe^{2+} to Fe^{3+}, $C_2O_4^{2-}$ to CO_2, H_2S to S and itself converts into Mn^{2+}.
- In neutral or faintly alkaline medium, it oxidises I^- to IO_3^-, $S_2O_3^{2-}$ to SO_4^{2-} and itself gets reduced to MnO_2.

Actinoids

- Electronic configuration = $[Rn]5f^{0-14}\,6d^{0-1}7s^2$
- Shows **actinoid contraction**.
- Shows the large number of O.S. due to less difference in energy of $6d$, $7s$ and $5f$ orbitals.
- Mostly radioactive.
- They are also coloured and paramagnetic.

Compounds of *d*-Block Elements

THE *d*-AND *f*- BLOCK ELEMENTS

f-Block Elements

These are also called inner-transition elements.

d-Block Elements

These are also called transition elements.
Electronic configuration = $(n-1)d^{1-10}ns^{1-2}$

USES

- TiO in pigment industry.
- MnO_2 in dry battery cells.
- Mischmetal, an alloy of lanthanoid used in Mg-based alloy to produce bullets, shell etc.
- Uranium is used as a nuclear fuel in nuclear reactors.

Properties of *d*-Block Elements

Physical Properties

- They have high m.p., b.p. conductivity, ductility, etc.
- They are hard and less volatile except Zn, Cd and Hg [due to the absence of $(n-1)d\ e^-$ in them].

Atomic and Ionic Radii

- It usually decreases with increase in atomic number across a series due to increase in effective nuclear charge.
- At the end of the series, it increases due to increased repulsive forces.

Enthalpy of Atomisation

- It is the energy required to convert the metallic crystal into atom.
- It first increases upto middle and then decreases.

Interstitial Compounds

They trap small atoms like C, H, N, etc. in their crystals to modify properties.

Complex Formation

They all from complex due to their small size, high charge density and availability of vacant d-orbitals.

Oxidation States (OS)

Show oxidation states from + 2 to + 7 but – 3 is most common.
Maximum O.S. = $(n-1)d$ unpaired $e^- + ns\ e^-$

Alloy Formation

They form alloy with other metals. Alloy of Hg is called amalgam.

Catalytic Property

They act as good catalyst due to their variable valency and availability of vacant d-orbitals.

Magnetic Property and Colour

These are generally paramagnetic and coloured due to the presence of unpaired d-electrons.

$E°$ Values

$E°$ values become less negative across the series due to general increase in the sum of the first and second ionisation enthalpies. The values of $E°$ for Mn, Ni and Zn are more negative than expected from the trend.

Ionisation Enthalpy

It increases with decrease in size. However, there are some irregularities due to electronic configuration and stability factors.

EXAM PATTERN QUESTIONS

Objective Type Questions

Multiple Choice Questions (MCQs) [1 Mark]

1. The ions of metals of Group 12 [Zn, Cd and Hg] have completely filled *d*-orbitals and so they **CBSE 2023**

(a) behave like semiconductors.
(b) have very high melting points.
(c) do not behave like transition metals.
(d) behave like superconductors.

2. Metallic radii of some transition elements are given below. Which of these elements will have highest density?

Element	Fe	Co	Ni	Cu
Metallic radii/pm	126	125	125	128

NCERT Exemplar

(a) Fe (b) Ni (c) Co (d) Cu

3. Which of the following statement is not correct?

(a) Copper liberates hydrogen from acids. **NCERT Exemplar**
(b) In its higher oxidation states, manganese forms stable compounds with oxygen and fluorine.
(c) Mn^{3+} and Co^{3+} are oxidising agents in aqueous solution.
(d) Ti^{2+} and Cr^{2+} are reducing agents in aqueous solution.

4. Which of the following transition metals does not show variable oxidation state ? **CBSE 2023**

(a) Ti (b) Cr (c) Cu (d) Sc

5. Which of the following characteristics of transition metals is associated with their catalytic activity?

(a) Paramagnetic nature **CBSE 2023**
(b) Colour of hydrated ions
(c) High enthalpy of atomisation
(d) Variable oxidation states

6. The magnetic moment is associated with its spin angular momentum and orbital angular momentum. Spin only magnetic moment value of Cr^{3+} ion (Atomic no : Cr = 24) is .... **CBSE 2025**

(a) 2.87 B.M (b) 3.87 B.M (c) 3.47 B.M (d) 3.57 B.M.

7. Which of the following characteristics make transition elements good catalysts? **Competency Based Que.**

P. Their tendency to form reaction intermediates with the reactants thereby reducing the activation energy.
Q. Their ability to have multiple oxidation states.
R. Their ability to form complex compounds.

(a) Only P (b) Only Q
(c) Only Q and R (d) P, Q and R

8. Two important compounds of transition element chromium are $K_2Cr_2O_7$ and K_2CrO_4. Compound $K_2Cr_2O_7$ is orange in colour and K_2CrO_4 is yellow in colour. The colour observed is because chromium ion in their compounds **Competency Based Que.**

(a) contain completely filled *d*-orbitals.
(b) contain empty *d*-orbitals.
(c) undergo *d*-*d* transition of electrons.
(d) undergo charge transfer between oxide ion and itself.

9. Which of the following statement is not correct?

(a) $La(OH)_3$ is less basic than $Lu(OH)_3$. **Diksha**
(b) La is actually an element of transition series rather than lanthanoids.
(c) Atomic radius of Zr and Hf is same.
(d) In lanthanoid series, the ionic radius of Lu^{3+} is smallest.

10. The silver UK coins are an alloy of **Diksha**

(a) Cu and Zn (b) Cu and Fe
(c) Cu and Ni (d) Cu and Al

11. From the elements of 3*d*-series given below, which element shows the maximum number of oxidation states? **CBSE 2024**

(a) Scandium (b) Manganese
(c) Chromium (d) Titanium

12. Transition metals are known to make interstitial compounds. Formation of interstitial compounds makes the transition metal **CBSE 2024**

(a) more hard (b) more soft
(c) more ductile (d) more metallic

13. The magnetic nature of elements depends on the presence of unpaired electrons. Identify the configuration of transition element, which shows highest magnetic moment? **NCERT Exemplar**

(a) $3d^7$ (b) $3d^5$ (c) $3d^8$ (d) $3d^2$

14. Interstitial compounds are formed when small atoms are trapped inside the crystal lattice of metals. Which of the following is not the characteristic property of interstitial compounds? **CBSE 2020, NCERT Exemplar**

(a) They have high melting points in comparison to pure metals.
(b) They are very hard.
(c) They retain metallic conductivity.
(d) They are chemically very reactive.

15. **Which of the following reactions are disproportionation reactions?** **NCERT Exemplar**

(i) $Cu^+ \longrightarrow Cu^{2+} + Cu$

(ii) $3MnO_4^- + 4H^+ \longrightarrow 2MnO_4^- + MnO_2 + 2H_2O$

(iii) $2KMnO_4 \longrightarrow K_2MnO_4 + MnO_2 + O_2$

(iv) $2MnO_4^- + 3Mn^{2+} + 2H_2O \longrightarrow 5MnO_2 + 4H^+$

(a) (i) (b) (i), (ii) and (iii)
(c) (ii), (iii) and (iv) (d) (i) and (iv)

16. **In which of the following oxo metal anions does the metal not exhibit an oxidation state equal to its group number?** **Competency Based Que.**

(a) CrO_4^{2-} (b) MnO_4^- (c) $Cr_2O_7^{2-}$ (d) MnO_4^{2-}

17. **Out of the following transition elements, the maximum number of oxidation states is shown by** **CBSE 2024 C**

(a) Sc (b) Cr (c) Mn (d) Fe

18. **Acidified $KMnO_4$ oxidises sulphite to** **CBSE 2025**

(a) $S_2O_3^{2-}$ (b) $S_2O_8^{2-}$
(c) $SO_2(g)$ (d) SO_4^{2-}

19. **$KMnO_4$ acts as an oxidising agent in acidic medium. The number of moles of $KMnO_4$ that will be needed to react with one mole of sulphide ions in acidic solution is** **NCERT Exemplar**

(a) $\frac{2}{5}$ (b) $\frac{3}{5}$ (c) $\frac{4}{5}$ (d) $\frac{1}{5}$

20. **$KMnO_4$ acts as an oxidising agent in alkaline medium. When alkaline $KMnO_4$ is treated with KI, iodide ion is oxidised to ....** **NCERT Exemplar**

(a) I_2 (b) IO^- (c) IO_3^- (d) IO_4^-

21. **On addition of small amount of $KMnO_4$ to concentrated H_2SO_4, a green oily compound is obtained which is highly explosive in nature. Identify the compound from the following** **NCERT Exemplar**

(a) Mn_2O_7 (b) MnO_2 (c) $MnSO_4$ (d) Mn_2O_3

22. **Which of the following has abnormally low value of third ionisation enthalpy?** **NCERT Exemplar**

(a) Lanthanum (b) Gadolinium
(c) Lutetium (d) All of these

23. **Match the properties given in Column I with the metals in Column II.** **CBSE SQP 2025**

	Column I		Column II
(i)	Actinoid having configuration $[Rn]5f^7 6d^1 7s^2$	(A)	Ce
(ii)	Lanthanoid which has $4f^{14}$ electronic configuration in +3 oxidation state.	(B)	Lu
(iii)	Lanthanoid which show +4 oxidation state	(C)	Cm

Choose the correct option among them

(a) (i)-(C), (ii)-(B), (iii)-(A)
(b) (i)-(C), (ii)-(A), (iii)-(B)
(c) (i)-(A), (ii)-(B), (iii)-(C)
(d) (i)-(B), (ii)-(A), (iii)-(C)

Assertion - Reason [1 Mark]

Directions (Q. Nos. 24-35) In the following questions an Assertion (A) is followed by a corresponding Reason (R). Use the following keys to choose the appropriate answer.

(a) Both (A) and (R) are true, and (R) is the correct explanation of (A).
(b) Both (A) and (R) are true, but (R) is not the correct explanation of (A).
(c) (A) is true, but (R) is false.
(d) (A) is false, but (R) is true.

24. **Assertion** (A) The electronic configuration of Cu(II) is $3d^9$, whereas that of Cu(I) is $3d^{10}$.

Reason (R) Cu(II) has greater effective nuclear charge.

25. **Assertion** (A) Zinc is not regarded as a transition element.

Reason (R) In zinc, 3*d* orbitals are completely filled in its ground state as well as in its oxidised state. **CBSE 2023**

26. **Assertion** (A) Copper is a non-transition element.

Reason (R) Copper has completely filled *d*-orbitals in its ground state. **CBSE 2023**

27. **Assertion** (A) Zn do not show any characteristic properties of transition elements except complex formation.

Reason (R) Zinc has completely filled 3*d*-subshell.

28. **Assertion** (A) Zr and Hf have almost identical radii.

Reason (R) Both Zr and Hf exhibit similar properties. **CBSE 2023**

29. **Assertion** (A) Highest oxidation state of manganese in fluoride is +4 (MnF_4) but highest oxidation state in oxides is +7 (Mn_2O_7).

Reason (R) Fluorine stabilises lower oxidation state.

30. **Assertion** (A) When $KMnO_4$ solution is added to oxalic acid solution, the decolourisation is slow in the beginning but becomes instantaneous after some time.

Reason (R) When $KMnO_4$ solution is added to oxalic acid solution CO_2 is formed as product.

31. **Assertion** (A) As the atomic number of lanthanoids increases, their atomic radius decreases.

Reason (R) From Eu to Yb, as the atomic number increases atomic radius decreases.

32. **Assertion** (A) Cr^{2+} is reducing, while Mn^{3+} is oxidising even when both have d^4-configuration.

Reason (R) Configuration of Cr changes from d^3 to d^4.

33. **Assertion** (A) $KMnO_4$ oxidises oxalic acid to CO_2 and itself changes to Mn^{2+} ion.

Reason (R) $KMnO_4$ acts as an oxidising agent.

34. **Assertion** (A) The highest oxidation state of osmium is +8.

Reason (R) Osmium is a 5d-block element. **NCERT Exemplar**

35. **Assertion** (A) Ce^{4+} ion is good analytical reagent.

Reason (R) Ce^{4+} has a stable electronic configuration.

Competency Based Que.

Case Study [4 Marks]

36. **The elements which show the greatest number of oxidation states occur in or near the middle of the series. Manganese, for example exhibits all the oxidation states from (+ 2) to (+ 7). The lesser number of oxidation states at the extreme ends is due to either too few electrons to lose or share (Sc, Ti) or too many d electrons (hence fewer orbitals available in which to share electrons with others) for higher valence (Cu, Zn). Thus early in the series scandium (II) is virtually unknown and titanium (IV) is more stable than Ti (III) or Ti (II). On the other end, the only oxidation state of zinc is + 2 (no d electrons are involved). The maximum oxidation states of reasonable stability correspond in value to the sum of the s and d electrons upto manganese ($T^{IV}O_2$, $V^{V}O_2^+$, $Cr^{VI}O_4^{2-}$, $Mn^{VII}O_4^-$) followed by a rather abrupt decrease in stability of higher oxidation states, so that the typical species to follow are $Fe^{II, III}$, $Co^{II, III}$, Ni^{II}, $Cu^{I, II}$, Zn^{II}.**

The variability of oxidation states, a characteristic of transition elements, arises out of incomplete filling of d-orbitals in such a way that their oxidation states differ from each other by unity, e.g., V(II), V(III), V(IV), V(V). This is in contrast with the variability of oxidation states of non-transition elements where, oxidation states normally differ by a unit of two. An interesting feature in the variability of oxidation states of the d-block elements is noticed among the groups. Although in the p-block, the lower oxidation states are favoured by the heavier members (due to inert pair effect), the opposite is true in the group of d-block.

For example in group 6, Mo (VI) and W (VI) are found to be more stable than Cr (VI). Thus Cr (VI), in the form of dichromate in acidic medium is a strong oxidising agent, whereas MoO_3 and WO_3 are not. Low oxidation states are found when a complex compound has ligands capable of π-acceptor character in addition to the σ-bonding.

For example, in $Ni(CO)_4$ and $Fe(CO)_5$, the oxidation state of nickel and iron is zero.

(i) Why Fe^{2+} compounds are less stable than Mn^{2+} compounds towards +3 oxidation states?

(ii) Calculate the magnetic moment of
(a) Ti^{3+} (b) Ni^{2+}

(iii) Why Cu^+ ion is not stable in aqueous solution?

Or Why transition metal exhibit highest oxidation states with oxide or fluoride only?

37. **The first ionisation enthalpies of the lanthanoids are around 600 kJ mol^{-1}, the second about 1200 kJ mol^{-1} comparable with those of calcium. A detailed discussion of the variation of the third ionisation enthalpies indicates that the exchange enthalpy considerations appear to impart a certain degree of stability of empty, half-filled and completely filled orbitals f level. This is indicated from the abnormally low value of the third ionisation enthalpy of lanthanum, gadolinium and lutetium. In their chemical behaviour, in general, the earlier members of the series are quite reactive similar to calcium but, with increasing atomic number, they behave more like aluminium. Values for $E°$ for the half-reaction.**

$$Ln^{3+}(aq) + 3e^- \longrightarrow Ln(s)$$

are in the range of – 2.2 to – 2.4 V except for Eu for which the value is – 2.0 V. This is, of course, a small variation. The metals combine with hydrogen when gently heated in the gas. The carbides, Ln_3C, Ln_2C_3 and LnC_2 are formed when the metals are heated with carbon. They liberate hydrogen from dilute acids and burn in halogens to form halides. They form oxides M_2O_3 and hydroxides $M(OH)_3$. The hydroxides are definite compounds, not just hydrated oxides. They are basic like alkaline earth metal oxides and hydroxides. The best single use of the lanthanoids is for the production of alloy steels for plates and pipes. A well known alloy is mischmetal which consists of a lanthanoid metal (~ 95%) and iron (~ 5%) and traces of S, C, Ca and Al. A good deal of mischmetall is used in Mg-based alloy to produce bullets, shell and lighter flint.

(i) (a) What is the nature of bonding in La_2O_3 and Lu_2O_3.

(b) What is the trend in the stability of oxo salts of lanthanoid from La to Lu?

(ii) Among lanthanoids, Ln (III) compounds predominate over Ln (II) and Ln (IV).

(iii) Ionisation enthalpies of Ce, Pr and Nd are higher than Th, Pa and U. Why?

Or Why irregularities in electronic configuration of actinoids are more than lanthanoids?

Subjective Type Questions

Short Answer Type I Questions [2 Marks]

1. Explain briefly how + 2 state becomes more and more stable in the first half of the first row transition elements with increasing atomic number? **NCERT**

Or

Compare the stability of + 2 oxidation state for the elements of the first transition series. **NCERT**

2. Explain why Cu^+ ion is not stable in aqueous solution? **NCERT Intext**

Or Explain why Cu (I) ion is not known in aqueous solution? **CBSE 2020**

3. Calculate the number of unpaired electrons in the following gaseous ions Mn^{3+}, Cr^{3+}, V^{3+} and Ti^{3+}. Which one of these is the most stable in aqueous solution? **NCERT**

4. The halides of transition elements become more covalent with increasing oxidation state of the metal. Why? **NCERT Exemplar**

5. Separation of a mixture of lanthanoid elements is difficult. Give reason. **CBSE 2020**

6. How would you account for the following? Lanthanoids form primarily +3 ions, while the actinoids usually have higher oxidation states in their compounds, +4 or even +6 being typical.

7. The melting points of three elements *J*, *K* and *L* were recorded. These three elements are from 1st, 2nd and 3rd transition series (not necessarily in the order). All of them have half-filled *d*-orbital. The melting point of *J* is more than *K* and melting point of *K* is more than *L*. Which element is expected to have valence electrons in $5f$-orbitals and why? **Competency Based Que.**

8. How would you account for the following? Among lanthanoids, Ln (III) compounds are predominant. However, ocassionaly in solutions or in solid compounds, +2 and +4 ions are also obtained.

9. The elements of 3*d* transition series are given as

Sc, Ti, V, Cr, Mn, Fe, Co, Ni, Cu, Zn

Answer the following.

(i) Which element is a strong reducing agent in +2 oxidation state and why?

(ii) Zn^{2+} salts are colourless. Why? **CBSE 2025**

10. Explain the following observation.

The members of the actinoid series exhibit a larger number of oxidation states than the corresponding numbers of the lanthanoid series. **CBSE 2012**

11. How would you account for the following?

The oxidising power of the following three oxoions in the series follows the order.

$$VO_2^+ < Cr_2O_7^{2-} < MnO_4^-$$

12. Why do transition elements show variable oxidation states?

(i) Name the element showing maximum number of oxidation states among the first series of transition metals from Sc ($Z = 21$) to Zn ($Z = 30$).

(ii) Name the element which shows only +3 oxidation state. **CBSE 2013**

13. The ionic radii of certain elements of the 3rd transition series are tabulated below. **Competency Based Que.**

Element	Ionic Radii
X^{3+}	87 pm
Y^{3+}	106 pm
Z^{3+}	95 pm

(i) Arrange the elements in the decreasing order of atomic number.

(ii) Define the phenomenon seen in this table.

14. (i) What happens when

(a) $KMnO_4$ is heated? (b) $K_2Cr_2O_7$ is heated?

(ii) Why fluorine stabilises the highest oxidation states of transition metals?

15. (i) Write the oxidation reaction of iodide to iodate ion by potassium permanganate.

(ii) Explain why $Cr_2O_7^{2-}$ ion is a powerful oxidant in acidic medium but weak oxidant in basic medium?

16. Complete the following chemical equations.

(i) $Cr_2O_7^{2-} + 6Fe^{2+} + 14H^+ \longrightarrow$ **CBSE 2025**

(ii) $2CrO_4^{2-} + 2H^+ \longrightarrow$

(iii) $2MnO_4^- + 5C_2O_4^{2-} + 16H^+ \longrightarrow$ **CBSE 2013, 2019, 2020**

(iv) $2MnO_4^- + 5S^{2-} + 16H^+ \longrightarrow$

17. (i) Account for the following.

The lowest oxide of a transition metal is basic, the highest is amphoteric or acidic.

(ii) Complete the following ionic equation.

$$3MnO_4^{2-} + 4H^+ \longrightarrow$$

Or (i) How $KMnO_4$ can be obtained from MnO_2, KOH and KNO_3?

(ii) K_2PtCl_6 is a well known compound, whereas corresponding Ni compound is not known. State the reason for it.

18. Which oxoanion (among VO_4^{3-}, CrO_4^{2-}, MnO_4^{2-} or FeO_4^{2-}) is the strongest oxidant and which is a weak oxidant?

19. Although Cu^+ does not exist in solution state, but $CuCl(s)$ is formed in the presence of Cl^- ions in aqueous solution of $Cu(s)$ and Cu^{2+}. Explain.

20. Chromium is used extensively in steel alloys. It is extracted from its chromite ore ($FeCr_2O_4$), which contains chromium in +3 oxidation state.

(i) Give the electronic configuration of the elements iron and chromium.

(ii) What is the oxidation state of iron in chromite?

21. Name the members of the lanthanoid series which exhibit +4 oxidation states and those which exhibit + 2 oxidation states. Try to correlate this type of behaviour with the electronic configuration of these elements. **NCERT**

22. Although, Zr belongs to 4*d* and Hf belongs to 5*d* transition series but it is quite difficult to separate them, why? **NCERT Exemplar**

23. Compare the chemistry of actinoids with that of the lanthanoids with reference to

(i) electronic configuration (ii) oxidation state

(iii) chemical reactivity **NCERT**

24. Which is the last element in the series of the actinoids? Write the electronic configuration of this element. Comment on the possible oxidation state of this element. **NCERT**

Short Answer Type II Questions [3 Marks]

25. (i) Why are fluorides of transition metals more stable in their higher oxidation state as compared to the lower oxidation state? **CBSE SQP 2025**

(ii) Which one of the following would feel attraction when placed in magnetic field Co^{2+}, Ag^+, Ti^{4+} and Zn^{2+}?

(iii) It has been observed that first ionisation energy of 5*d*-series of transition elements are higher than that of 3*d* and 4*d* series, explain why?

26. When MnO_2 is fused with KOH in the presence of KNO_3 as an oxidising agent, it gives a dark green compound (*A*). Compound (*A*) disproportionates in acidic solution to give purple compound (*B*). An alkaline solution of compound (*B*) oxidises KI to compound (*C*) whereas an acidified solution of compound (*B*) oxidised KI to (*D*). Identify (*A*), (*B*), (*C*) and (*D*). **CBSE 2019**

27. Give reasons for the following.

(i) Mn^{3+} is a good oxidising agent. **CBSE 2020**

(ii) $E^\circ_{M^{2+}/M}$ values are not regular for first row of transition metals (3*d*-series).

(iii) Although F is more electronegative than O, the highest fluoride of Mn is MnF_4, whereas the highest oxide is Mn_2O_7.

28. Account for the following.

(i) The lowest oxide of transition metal is basic and highest is acidic.

(ii) Chromium is a hard metal while mercury is a liquid metal.

(iii) The ionisation energy of elements of the 3*d*-series does not vary much with increasing atomic number. **CBSE SQP 2025**

29. How would you account for the following?

(i) Of the d^4 species, Cr^{2+} is strongly reducing agent, while manganese (III) is strongly oxidising agent.

(ii) Cobalt (II) is stable in aqueous solution but in the presence of complexing reagents, it is easily oxidised.

(iii) The d^1 configuration is very unstable in ions. **NCERT**

30. Observed and calculated values for the standard electrode potentials of elements from Ti to Zn in the first reactivity series are depicted in figure (Refer to page 115): **CBSE SQP 2021**

Explain the following observations.

(i) The general trend towards less negative E° values across the series.

(ii) The unique behaviour of copper.

(iii) More negative E° values of Mn and Zn.

31. Give reasons.

(i) E° value for Mn^{3+}/Mn^{2+} couple is much more positive than that for Fe^{3+}/Fe^{2+}.

(ii) Iron has higher enthalpy of atomisation than that of copper.

(iii) Sc^{3+} is colourless in aqueous solution, whereas Ti^{3+} is coloured. **CBSE 2018**

32. Account for the following.

(i) Ti(IV) is more stable than the Ti (II) or Ti(III).

(ii) In case of transition elements, ions of the same charge in a given series show progressive decrease in radius with increasing atomic number.

(iii) Zinc is comparatively a soft metal, iron and chromium are typically hard. **CBSE SQP (Term II)**

33. Give examples and suggest reasons for the following features of the transition metal chemistry.

(i) The lowest oxide of transition metal is basic; the highest is amphoteric/acidic.

(ii) A transition metal exhibits highest oxidation state in oxides and fluorides.

(iii) The highest oxidation state is exhibited in oxoanions of a metal

34. The E° value in respect of electrodes of chromium ($Z = 24$), manganese ($Z = 25$) and iron ($Z = 26$) are

$Cr^{3+}/Cr^{2+} = -0.4$ V; $Mn^{3+}/Mn^{2+} = 1.5$ V

$Fe^{3+}/Fe^{2+} = +0.8$ V

On the basis of the above information, compare the feasibilities of further oxidation of their +2 oxidation state.

35. Write the chemical equations for the following reactions

(i) Oxidation of nitrite ion by MnO_4^- in acidic medium.

(ii) Acidification of sodium chromate solution.

(iii) Disproportionation of Mn(VI) in acidic solution.

36. Describe the factors on which the stability of an oxidation state of lanthanoid elements depends.

37. The first few members of the series are quite reactive. They usually form oxides and hydroxides. Complete the following reactions of lanthanoids.

(i) $Ln \xrightarrow{\text{Heated with N}}$ (ii) $Ln \xrightarrow{\text{With halogens}}$

(iii) $Ln \xrightarrow{\text{Burns in } O_2}$

38. Write the chemical equations for the following reactions:

(i) Oxidation of SO_3^{2-} in acidic medium by $KMnO_4$.

(ii) Oxidation of Mn^{2+} by $KMnO_4$ in alkaline medium.

(iii) Oxidation of ferrous salt to ferric salt by $KMnO_4$ in acidic medium.

39. Complete the following reactions: **CBSE 2025**

(i) $MnO_4^-(aq) + S_2O_3^{2-}(aq) + H_2O(l) \longrightarrow$

(ii) $Cr_2O_7^{2-}(aq) + H_2S(g) + H^+(aq) \longrightarrow$

(iii) $MnO_4^-(aq) + Fe^{2+}(aq) + H^+(aq) \longrightarrow$

40. The graph below shows the first, second and third ionisation energies of a set of elements.

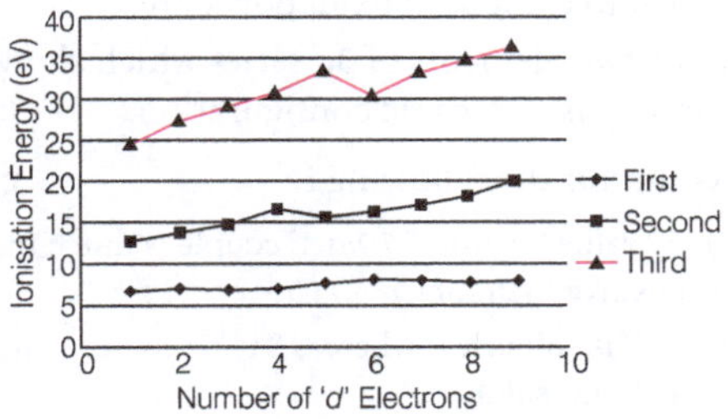

In the graph, we can see a deviation in the fifth element in the trend for second ionisation energy and a deviation in the sixth element in the trend for third ionisation energy. Identify the elements and explain why the deviation occurs. **Competency Based Que.**

Long Answer Type Questions [5 Marks]

41. What are the characteristics of the transition elements and why are they called transition elements? Which of the d-block elements may not be regarded as the transition elements? **NCERT**

42. Explain giving reasons

(i) The enthalpies of atomisation of the transition metals are high.

(ii) Transition metals and many of their compounds show paramagnetic behaviour.

(iii) The transition metals generally form coloured compounds.

(iv) Transition metals and their many compounds act as good catalyst.

(v) Transition metals have high melting points. **NCERT**

43. Compare the general characteristics of the first series of the transition metals with those of the second and third series metals in the respective vertical columns. Give special emphasis on the following points.

(i) Electronic configurations (ii) Oxidation states

(iii) Ionisation enthalpies (iv) Atomic sizes **NCERT**

44. Comment on the statement that elements of the first transition series possess many properties different from those of heavier transition elements. **NCERT**

45. What can be inferred from the magnetic moment values of the following complex species?

Examples	Magnetic moment (BM)
$K_4[Mn(CN)_6]$	2.2
$[Fe(H_2O)_6]^{2+}$	5.3

NCERT

46. Write down the number of 3d-electrons in each of the following ions; Ti^{2+}, V^{2+}, Cr^{3+}, Mn^{2+}, Fe^{2+}, Fe^{3+}, Co^{2+}, Ni^{2+} and Cu^{2+}.

Indicate how would you expect the five 3d-orbitals to be occupied for these hydrated ions (octahedral)? **NCERT**

47. Describe the preparation of potassium permanganate. How does the acidified permanganate solution react with (i) iron (II) ions, (ii) SO_2 and (iii) oxalic acid?

Write the ionic equations for the reactions. **CBSE 2020, NCERT**

48. (i) When $FeCr_2O_4$ is fused with Na_2CO_3 in the presence of air it gives a yellow solution of compound (A). Compound (A) on acidification gives compound (B). Compound (B) on reaction with KCl forms an orange coloured (C). An acidified solution of compound (C) oxidises iodide to (D). Identify (A), (B), (C) and (D). **CBSE 2025**

(ii) Complete and balance the following chemical equations:

(a) $2MnO_4^-(aq) + 10I^-(aq) + 16H^+(aq) \longrightarrow$

(b) $Cr_2O_7^{2-} + 3Sn^{2+} + 14H^+ \longrightarrow$

(c) $3NO_2^- + Cr_2O_7^{2-} + 8H^+ \longrightarrow$ **CBSE 2025**

49. Attempt **any five** of the following. **CBSE 2024**

(i) Why zinc is not regarded as a transition element?

(ii) What is lanthanoid contraction?

(iii) Why is first ionisation enthalpy of chromium lower than that of Zn?

(iv) Why are transition elements good catalysts?

(v) Compounds of transition metals are generally coloured. Give reason.

(vi) Out of $KMnO_4$ and K_2MnO_4, which one is paramagnetic and why?

(vii) Complete the following ionic equation:

$$Cr_2O_7^{2-} + 14H^+ + 6e^- \longrightarrow$$

50. Attempt **any five** of the following.

(i) Out of Cr^{3+} and Mn^{3+}, which one is a strong oxidising agent and why?

(ii) Which ion amongst the following is colourless and why?

$$Ti^{4+}, Cr^{3+}, V^{3+}$$

(Atomic number : Ti = 22, Cr = 24, V = 23)

(iii) Why is Ce^{4+} a strong oxidising agent?

(iv) Why is highest oxidation state of a metal shown in oxide or fluoride only?

(v) Write one similarity between lanthanoids and actinoids.

(vi) Explain why Cu^+ ion is not stable in aqueous solution.

(vii) Why do transition elements have high enthalpies of atomisation? **CBSE 2024 C**

51. Attempt **any five** of the following.

(i) Ce(III) is easily oxidised to Ce(IV). Comment.

(ii) $E^\circ_{(Mn^{2+}/Mn)}$ is – 1.18 V. Why is this value highly negative in comparison to neighbouring *d*-block elements?

(iii) Which element of 3*d*-series has lowest enthalpy of atomisation and why?

(iv) What happens when sodium chromate is acidified?

(v) Zn, Cd and Hg are soft metals. Why?

(vi) Why is permanganate titration not carried out in the presence of HCl?

(vii) The lower oxides of transition metals are basic whereas the highest are amphoteric/acidic. Given reason. **CBSE 2024**

52. Answer the following questions.

(i) Out of Ag_2SO_4, CuF_2 and MgF_2 and CuCl, which compound will be coloured and why?

(ii) Explain

(a) CrO_4^{2-} is a strong oxidising agent while MnO_4^{2-} is not.

(b) Zr and Hf have identical sizes.

(c) The lowest oxidation state of manganese is observed in basic medium while, the highest in acidic medium.

(d) Mn (II) shows maximum paramagnetic character amongst the divalent ions of the first transition series.

53. Shown below is a step-wise process for the fomation of an orange-coloured crystalline compound *C*. Identify the compound *C* and write the chemical reactions to show the formation of compounds *A*, *B* and *C*.

Chromate ore fused with NaOH in presence of air forms a yellow coloured compound *A*. ⟶ Yellow coloured compound *A* on acidification with dil. sulphuric acid gives compound *B*. ⟶ Compound *B* on reaction with KCl forms an orange coloured crystalline compound *C*.

54. (i) Account for the following :

(a) Zn^{2+} salts are colourless while Ni^{2+} salts are coloured.

(b) Cr^{2+} is a strong reducing agent.

(c) Transition metals and their compounds show catalytic activities.

(ii) Write the ionic equations for the oxidising action of MnO_4^- in acidic medium with

(1) I^- ion and (2) Fe^{2+} ion **CBSE 2023**

55. (i) Name two oxometal anions of the 3*d* series of the transition metals in which the metal exhibits the oxidation state equal to its group number.

(ii) What is the effect of increasing pH on a solution of $K_2Cr_2O_7$?

(iii) Why is Cu^+ not stable in aqueous solution ?

(iv) Name a member of lanthanoid series which is well-known to exhibit +4 oxidation state.

(v) Name two elements of 3*d* series which show anomalous electronic configuration. **CBSE 2023**

56. (i) Account for the following : **CBSE 2023**

(a) E° value for Mn^{3+}/Mn^{2+} couple is much more positive than for Cr^{3+}/Cr^{2+}.

(b) Sc^{3+} is colourless whereas Ti^{3+} is coloured in an aqueous solution.

(c) Actinoids show wide range of oxidation states.

(ii) Write the chemical equations for the preparation of $KMnO_4$ from MnO_2.

57. (i) Account for the following :

(a) Transition metals form alloys.

(b) Ce^{4+} is a strong oxidising agent.

(ii) Write one similarity and one difference between chemistry of lanthanoids and actinoids.

(iii) Complete the following ionic equation.

$$Cr_2O_7^{2-} + 2OH^- \longrightarrow$$ **CBSE 2023**

58. (i) Why is chemistry of actinoids complicated as compared to lanthanoids ?

(ii) Complete the following reaction and justify that it is a disproportionation reaction :

$$3\,MnO_4^{2-} + 4H^+ \longrightarrow \_\_ + \_\_ + 2H_2O$$

(iii) The given graph shows the trends in melting points of transition metals.

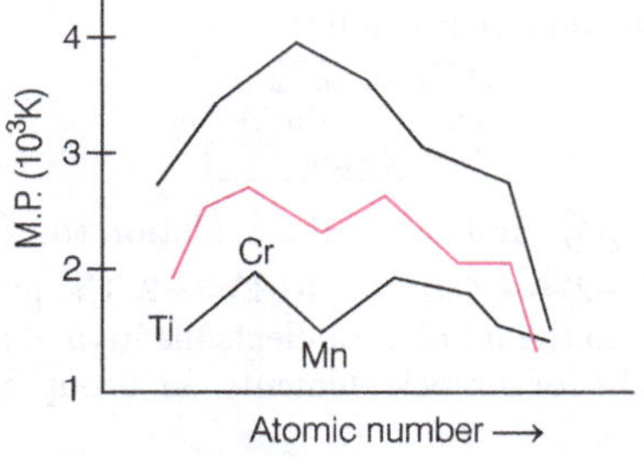

Explain the reason why Cr has highest melting point and manganese (Mn) a lower melting point. **CBSE 2023**

59. (i) Account for the following :

(a) Transition metals form complex compounds

(b) The $E^\circ_{Mn^{2+}/Mn}$ value for manganese is highly negative, whereas $E^\circ_{Mn^{3+}/Mn^{2+}}$ is highly positive.

(c) Cu^+ ion is unstable in aqueous solution.

(ii) Write the equations involved in the preparation of $KMnO_4$ from pyrolusite ore (MnO_2). **CBSE 2023**

60. (i) Identify the following:

(a) Transition metal of 3*d* series that exhibits only one oxidation state.

(b) Transition metal of 3*d* series that acts as a strong reducing agent in +2 oxidation state in aqueous solution.

(ii) Complete and balance the following equations :

(a) $Cr_2O_7^{2-} + 14H^+ + 6Fe^{2+} \longrightarrow$

(b) $KMnO_4 \xrightarrow{\text{Heat}}$

(iii) What is Mischmetall ? Write its one use. **CBSE 2023**

Hints & Solutions

Objective Type Questions

1. (*c*) Zn, Cd and Hg have completely filled *d*-orbitals, so they do not behave like transition metals

2. (*d*) On moving left to right along period, metallic radius decreases, while atomic mass increases. Decrease in metallic radius coupled with increase in atomic mass results in increase in density of metals.

   Hence, among the given four choices Cu belongs to right side of periodic table in transition metal, and it has highest density (89 g/cm^3).

3. (*a*) Copper lies below hydrogen in the electrochemical series and hence does not liberate H_2 from acids. Therefore, option (a) is not correct.

   Other three options (b, c, d) are correct.

4. (*d*) Scandium does not show variable oxidation state.

5. (*d*) Catalytic properties of transition element is due to its variable oxidation state.

6. (*b*) $Cr = [Ar]3d^4 4s^1$

   $Cr^{3+} = [Ar]3d^3 4s^0$

   So, $n = 3$

   $\therefore \mu_{\text{spin only}} = \sqrt{n(n+2)}\,\text{B.M.} = \sqrt{3(3+2)}\,\text{B.M.}$

   $= \sqrt{3(5)}\,\text{B.M.}$

   $\mu = \sqrt{15}\,\text{B.M.} = 3.87\,\text{B.M.}$

7. (*d*) All the given statements are correct.

8. (*d*) The orange colour of dichromate is due to charge (electron) transfer from O^{2-} ligands to the empty *d*-orbitals of the central metal Cr^{6+}, i.e., ligand to metal charge transfer.

9. (*a*) Only statement (a) is incorrect. The correct form of statement (a) is : $La(OH)_3$ is more basic than $Lu(OH)_3$.

10. (*c*) The silver UK coins are an alloy of Copper (Cu) and Nickel (Ni).

11. (*b*) Manganese (Mn) exhibits maximum number of oxidation states. It shows +2, +3, +4, +5, +6 and +7 oxidation states.

12. (*a*) Formation of interstitial compound makes the transition metal more hard.

13. (*b*) Greater the number of unpaired electron, higher will be its value of magnetic moment.

    Since, $3d^5$ has 5 unpaired electrons hence highest magnetic moment.

    $$\mu = \sqrt{5(5+2)} = \sqrt{35} = 5.95\ \text{BM}$$

14. (*d*) Interstitial compounds are formed when small atoms are trapped inside the crystal lattice of metals.

    Some of their important characteristics are as follows

    (i) They are very hard and rigid.

    (ii) They have high melting points which are higher than those of the pure metals.

    (iii) They show conductivity like that of the pure metal.

    (iv) They acquire chemical inertness.

15. (*a*) The reaction in which oxidation as well as reduction, occur upon same atom simultaneously is known as disproportionation reaction.

    Oxidation

    $$Cu^+ \longrightarrow Cu^{2+} + Cu$$

    Reduction

16. (*d*) In $Cr_2O_7^{2-}$ and CrO_4^{2-} the oxidation state of Cr is +6. $(2x)+7(-2)=-2$ and $x+4(-2)=-2$. The group number is equal to the number of electrons in $(n-1)d$ and ns sub-shells for *d*-block elements. So, group number $=5+1=6$.

    In MnO_4^- the oxidation state of Mn is +7. $(2x)+7(-2)=-1$ The group number is equal to the number of electron in $(n-1)d$ and ns subshell for *d*-block elements. So, group no. is $5+2=7$.

17. (*c*) Manganese, which is in the middle of the period, has the highest number of oxidation states, and indeed the highest oxidation state in the whole period since it has five unpaired electrons.

18. (*d*) Acidified $KMnO_4$ oxidises sulphite to sulphate in acidic medium.

    $$\underset{\text{(Sulphite)}}{5SO_3^{2-}} + 2MnO_4^- + 6H^+ \longrightarrow 2Mn^{2+} + \underset{\text{(Sulphate)}}{5SO_4^{2-}} + 3H_2O$$

19. (*a*) The reaction of $KMnO_4$ in which it acts as an oxidising agent in acidic medium is

    $$2KMnO_4 + 3H_2SO_4 \longrightarrow K_2SO_4 + 2MnSO_4 + 3H_2O + 5[O]$$

    $$[H_2S + [O] \longrightarrow H_2O + S] \times 5$$

    $$2KMnO_4 + 3H_2SO_4 + 5H_2S \longrightarrow K_2SO_4 + 2MnSO_4 + 8H_2O + 5S$$

    5 moles of S^{2-} ions react with 2 moles of $KMnO_4$. So, 1 mole of S^{2-} ion will react with $\frac{2}{5}$ moles of $KMnO_4$.

20. (*c*) $KMnO_4$ acts as an oxidising agent in alkaline medium. When alkaline $KMnO_4$ is treated with KI, iodide ion is oxidised to IO_3^-.

    Reaction $2KMnO_4 + H_2O + KI \longrightarrow 2MnO_4 + 2KOH + KIO_3$

21. (*a*) On addition of $KMnO_4$ to concentrated H_2SO_4, a green oily compound Mn_2O_7 is obtained which is highly explosive in nature.

    $$2KMnO_4 + 2H_2SO_4(\text{Conc.}) \longrightarrow Mn_2O_7 + 2KHSO_4 + H_2O$$

22. (*d*) La, Gd and Lu, all have abnormally low value of third ionisation enthalpy.

23. (*a*) The correct match is (i)-(C), (ii)-(B), (iii)-(A).

24. (*a*) Cu(II) is more stable than Cu(I).

As it is known that, Cu(I) has $3d^{10}$ stable configuration, while Cu(II) has $3d^9$ configuration.

But Cu(II) is more stable due to greater effective nuclear charge of Cu(II), i.e., it holds 17 electrons instead of 18 in Cu(I). Thus, both (A) and (R) are true and (R) is the correct explanation of (A).

25. (*a*) Both A and R are true and R is the correct explanation of A.

26. (*d*) (A) is false, but (R) is true.

Cu is a transition metal as Cu^{2+}ion has an incomplete *d*-level.

27. (*a*) The 3*d*-subshell of zinc is completely filled in ground state as well as in their oxidised state. Thus, it does not show any characteristic properties of transition elements except complex formation. Thus, both (A) and (R) are true and (R) is correct explanation of (A).

28. (*b*) Both Zr and Hf have almost same atomic radii due to lanthanoid contraction.

29. (*c*) Highest oxidation state of manganese in fluoride is +4 (MnF_4) but highest oxidation state in oxides is +7(Mn_2O_7).

The reason is that in covalent compounds fluorine can form single bond while oxygen forms double bond.

Thus, (A) is true, but, (R) is false.

30. (*b*) When $KMnO_4$ solution is added to oxalic acid solution, the decolourisation is slow in the beginning but becomes instantaneous after some time because Mn^{2+} acts as autocatalyst.

Reduction half

$$MnO_4^- + 8H^+ + 5e^- \longrightarrow Mn^{2+} + 4H_2O] \times 2$$

Oxidation half

$$C_2O_4^{2-} \longrightarrow 2CO_2 + 2e^-] \times 5$$

Overall equation

$$2MnO_4^- + 16H^+ + 5C_2O_4^{2-} \longrightarrow 2Mn^{2+} + 10CO_2 + 8H_2O$$

Thus, both (A) and (R) is true, but (R) is not the correct explanation of (A).

31. (*b*) Both (A) and (R) are true, but (R) is not the correct explanation of (A).

32. (*c*) Cr^{2+} is reducing, while Mn^{3+} is oxidising even when both have d^4 configuration. Cr^{2+} is reducing as its configuration changes from d^4 to d^3, the later having a half-filled t_{2g} level. On the contrary, the change from $Mn^{3+}$to Mn^{2+} results in the half-filled (d^5) configuration which has extra stability. Thus, (A) is true but (R) is false.

33. (*a*) $KMnO_4$ oxidises oxalic acid to CO_2 and itself changes to Mn^{2+} ion, which is colourless, because $KMnO_4$ acts as an oxidising agent.

Both (A) and (R) are true and (R) is the correct explanation of (A).

34. (*b*) Both (A) and (R) are true, but (R) is not the correct explanation of (A). The highest oxidation state of osmium is +8 due to its ability to expand their octet by using its all 8 electrons (2 from 6*s* and 6 from 5*d*).

35. (*b*) Both (A) and (R) are true, but R is not the correct explanation of (A).

36. (i) Fe^{2+} ion has d^6 configuration while Mn^{2+} ion has d^5 electronic configuration which is half-filled and more stable. So Mn^{2+} compounds are more stable than Fe^{2+} compounds towards oxidation state. **(1)**

(ii) (a) $Ti^{3+} = 3d^1$; $n = 1$

$$\mu = \sqrt{n(n+2)} \text{ B.M.} = \sqrt{1(1+2)} \text{ B.M.}$$

$$\mu = 1.73 \text{ B.M}$$ **(1)**

(b) $Ni^{2+} = 3d^8$; $n = 2$

$$\mu = \sqrt{n(n+2)} \text{ B.M.} = 2\sqrt{2(2+2)} \text{ B.M.}$$

$$\mu = 2.83 \text{ B.M.}$$ **(1)**

(iii) In aqueous solution Cu^+ ions is not stable because of its less negative enthalpy of hydration than that of Cu^{2+} ion in aqueous solution. **(1)**

Or A transition metal exhibits higher oxidation states in oxides and fluorides because oxygen and fluorine are highly electronegative elements and have small size. **(1)**

37. (i) (a) As the size decreases covalent character increases. Therefore, La_2O_3 is ionic in nature and Lu_2O_3 is covalent in nature. **(1)**

(b) As the atomic radius decreases due to lanthanoid contraction. Hence, from La to Lu the stability of oxo salts also decreases. **(1)**

(ii) All lanthanoids possess (+3) oxidation state but some lanthanoids such as Ce (IV), Nd (II), Nd (IV). Sm (II), Eu (II), Tm (II),Yb (II), Tb (IV), Dy (IV) also exhibit (+ 2) and (+4) oxidation states to attain extra stable f^0 and f^7 configuration. **(1)**

(iii) It is because in the starting when 5*f* orbitals begin to be occupied, it will penetrate less into the inner core of electrons. The 5*f* electrons therefore, be more effectively shielded from the nuclear charge than, 4*f* electrons of the corresponding lanthanoids. Therefore, outer electrons experience less force of attraction and they are available for bonding in the actinoides. **(1)**

Or Actinoids exhibit irregularities in the electronic configuration due to stabilities of the f^0, f^7 and f^{14} occupancies of the 5*f*-orbital. **(1)**

Subjective Type Questions

1. Elements (+2 state) $_{21}Sc^{2+}$, $_{22}Ti^{2+}$, $_{23}V^{2+}$, $_{24}Cr^{2+}$ and $_{25}Mn^{2+}$ have more stable +2 oxidation state and the outer electronic configuration are $3d^1, 3d^2, 3d^3, 3d^4$ and $3d^5$, respectively. In all the elements listed, the removal of two 4*s* electrons (in Cr^{2+}, $1e^-$ from 4*s* and $1e^-$ from 3*d*), the 3*d*-orbitals get gradually occupied. Since, the

number of empty d-orbitals decreases or the number of unpaired electrons in $3d$-orbitals increases with increase in atomic number of cations, so the stability of the cations (M^{2+}) increases from Sc^{2+} to Mn^{2+}. **(2)**

2. In aqueous solution, copper (I) undergoes disproportionation reaction as follows

$$2Cu^+ (aq) \longrightarrow Cu^{2+} + Cu(s)$$

The highest stability of Cu^{2+} ion in aqueous solution is due to negative enthalpy of hydration.
Hence, Cu^+ is not known (or unstable) in aqueous solution. **(2)**

3. $Mn^{3+} (Z = 25) = [Ar]\, 3d^4$ | ↿ | ↿ | ↿ | ↿ | | **(½)**

$Cr^{3+} (Z = 24) = [Ar]\, 3d^3$ | ↿ | ↿ | ↿ | | | **(½)**

$V^{3+} (Z = 23) = [Ar]\, 3d^2$ | ↿ | ↿ | | | | **(½)**

$Ti^{3+} (Z = 22) = [Ar]\, 3d^1$ | ↿ | | | | | **(½)**

Cr^{3+} is the most stable among these in aqueous solution because it has half-filled t_{2g} level $(= t_{2g}^3)$.

4. This problem is based on the concept of Fajans' rule. As the oxidation state increases, size of the ion of transition element decreases. As per Fajans' rule, when the size of metal ion decreases, covalent character of the bond formed increases.

Therefore, the halide of transition elements become more covalent with increasing oxidation state of the metal. **(2)**

5. Refer to text on page 123. **(2)**

6. The wide range of oxidation states of actinoids is attributed to the fact that the $5f$, $6d$ and $7s$ energy levels are of comparable energies. Therefore, all these three subshells can participate in bonding. But the most common oxidation state of actinoids is also +3. **(2)**

7. Element J is expected to have valence electrons in the $5f$-orbitals. The melting point of the element J is the highest among the three. So, it is expected to belong to the 3rd transition series with the valence electrons in $5f$-orbitals. **(2)**

8. +2 and +4 oxidation states are also obtained due to high stabilities of f^0, f^7 and f^{14} configuration. **(2)**

9. (i) Cr is a strong reducing agent in +2 oxidation state because Cr^{2+} has $3d^4$ configuration, which after losing one electron forms Cr^{3+}, which has a stable half-filled $t_{2g}(t_{2g}^3)$ configuration. **(1)**

(ii) Refer to Q.54 (i) (a). **(1)**

10. Actinoids have lower ionisation energy and less effective nuclear charge, hence more number of valence electrons can take part in bond formation. It is due to the fact that $5f, 6d$ and $7s$ levels are of comparable energies. Therefore, actinoids exhibit $+3, +4, +5, +6$ and $+7$ oxidation states due to the participation of $5f, 6d$ and $7s$ electrons in bond formation. Hence, actinoids exhibit greater range of oxidation states than lanthanoids. **(2)**

11. It is because V in the lower oxidation state is less stable than Cr which in turn is less stable than Mn. Thus, MnO_4^- has a great tendency to get reduced and hence, behave as a good oxidising agent. Similarly, VO_2^+ has the least oxidising power. **(2)**

12. Transition elements show variable oxidation state due to their ability of utilising single or multiple $4s$ and $3d$ electrons.

(i) Mn (manganese) shows the maximum number of oxidation states. **(1)**

(ii) Scandium shows only +3 oxidation state. **(1)**

13. (i) The elements in decreasing order of atomic number is given as $X > Z > Y$. **(1)**

(ii) The overall decrease in atomic and ionic radii from lanthanum to lutetium (the lanthanoid contraction) is a unique feature in the chemistry of the lanthanoids. This is called "lanthanoid contraction". **(1)**

14. (i) (a) Refer to text on page 120. **(½)**

(b) $2K_2Cr_2O_7 \xrightarrow{\Delta} 2K_2CrO_4 + Cr_2O_3 + \frac{3}{2}O_2$ **(½)**

(ii) **Hint** Fluorine is electronegative element and can form only single bonds (Refer to text on page 114). **(1)**

15. (i) Refer to text on page 121. **(1)**

(ii) Refer to text on page 119. **(1)**

16. (i) Refer to text on page 119.

(ii) Refer to text on page 119.

(iii) Refer to text on page 121.

(iv) Refer to text on page 121. **(2)**

17. (i) In lower oxidation states, transition metals behave like metals and their metal oxides are basic in nature. Thus, in lower oxidation states, transition metal oxides are basic.

As the oxidation state increases, its metallic character decreases due to decrease in size, thus, it becomes less metallic or more non-metallic. Oxides of a non-metal may be acidic or neutral.

Thus, in higher oxidation states, transition metal oxides are amphoteric or acidic. **(1)**

(ii) $3MnO_4^{2-} + 4H^+ \longrightarrow 2MnO_4^- + MnO_2 + 2H_2O$ **(1)**

Or

(i) Refer to text on page 120. **(1)**

(ii) This is because Pt^{4+} is more stable then Ni^{4+} as the sum of four ionisation enthalpies of Pt is less than of Ni. **(1)**

18. Strongest oxidant = MnO_4^{2-} **(1)**

Weakest oxidant = VO_4^{3-} **(1)**

19. Refer to text on page 114. **(2)**

20. (i) Refer to text on page 111. **(1)**

(ii) **Hint** Oxidation state of Fe = +2 **(1)**

21. Refer to text on page 123. **(2)**

22. Refer to text on page 123. **(2)**

23. Refer to text on pages 124 and 125. (2)

24. Refer to text on page 125. (2)

25. (i) Since, fluorine has smaller atomic size and higher electronegativity, therefore, it oxidises the metal to their higher oxidation state (due to higher lattice energy). (1)

(ii) Electronic configuration of Co^{2+} : $[Ar]3d^7$

= | ↑↓ | ↑↓ | ↑ | ↑ | ↑ |

$3d^7$

It has **three unpaired electrons.**

Electronic configuration of Ag^+ : $[Kr]4d^{10}5s^0$

| ↑↓ | ↑↓ | ↑↓ | ↑↓ | ↑↓ |

It does **not have any unpaired electron.**

Electronic configuration of Ti^{4+} : [Ar]
Unpaired electron is absent.

Electronic configuration of Zn^{2+} : $[Ar]3d^{10}$

Unpaired electron is absent.

Thus, since unpaired electron is present only in Co^{2+}, it is paramagnetic in nature, hence Co^{2+} ion would be attracted to magnetic field. (1)

(iii) First ionisation energy of $5d$-series of transition elements are higher than that of $3d$ and $4d$-series because $5d$-series have intervening $4f$-orbitals.

There is greater effective nuclear charge acting on outer valence electrons due to the weak shielding by $4f$-electrons.

Therefore, large amount of energy is required to remove the outer electron in this case as compared to $3d$ and $4d$-series. (1)

26. When MnO_2 is fused with KOH in presence of KNO_3, green coloured compound K_2MnO_4 (*A*) is formed. Since, (*A*) disproportionates in acidic medium to give purple compound (*B*), thus (*B*) is $KMnO_4$. In alkaline medium, $KMnO_4$ (*B*) oxidises KI to **(*C*)**, thus compound (*C*) is KIO_3; whereas in acidic medium, KI is oxidised to compound (*D*) which is I_2. (1)

The reactions involved are

(i) $MnO_2 + 2KOH + KNO_3 \longrightarrow \underset{\substack{\text{(Green)} \\ (A)}}{K_2MnO_4} + KNO_2 + H_2O$

(ii) $3K_2MnO_4 + 2H_2SO_4 \longrightarrow \underset{\substack{\text{(Purple)} \\ (B)}}{2KMnO_4} + MnO_2 + 2H_2O + 2K_2SO_4$ (1)

(iii) $2KMnO_4 + KI + H_2O \longrightarrow \underset{(C)}{KIO_3} + 2MnO_2 + 2KOH$

(iv) $2KMnO_4 + 10KI + 3H_2SO_4 \longrightarrow 2MnSO_4 + K_2SO_4 + \underset{(D)}{5I_2} + 8H_2O$ (1)

27. (i) Mn^{3+}/Mn^{2+} has large positive $E°$ value. Hence, Mn^{3+} can be easily reduced to Mn^{2+} because Mn^{2+} has half-filled electronic configuration, so it is stable and Mn^{3+} is least stable. Therefore, it is a good oxidising agent. (1)

(ii) There is decreasing negative electrode potential of M^{2+}/M in the first transition series due to increase in the sum of IE_1 and IE_2. It shows that in general, the stability of +2 oxidation state decreases from left to right. Exceptions are Mn and Zn in which the greater stability of +2 state for Mn is due to half-filled *d*-subshell (d^5) in Mn^{2+} and that of Zn is due to completely filled *d*-subshell (d^{10}) in Zn^{2+}. (1)

(iii) It is because oxygen can form multiple bonds, whereas fluorine can only form single bonds with metals. (1)

28. (i) In the case of a lower oxide of a transition metal, the metal atom has some electrons present in the valence shell of the metal atom that are not involved in bonding.

As a result, it can donate electrons and behave as a base. Whereas in higher oxide of a transition metal, the metal atom does not have an electron in the valence shell for donation as they are involved in bonding. As a result, it can accept electrons and behave as an acid. (1)

(ii) Chromium has unpaired electrons which result in strong metallic bonding and hence it is a hard solid and the absence of unpaired electrons in Hg results in it being a liquid. (1)

(iii) The increase in effective nuclear charge responsible for steady increase in ionisation energy is counter balanced by shielding effect of $(n-1)d$ electrons. Thus, the ionisation energy of elements of the 3*d*-series does not very much with increasing atomic number. (1)

29. (i) $E°$ value of Cr^{3+}/Cr^{2+} is negative (– 0.41 V) while that of Mn^{3+}/Mn^{2+} is positive (+ 1.57 V). This means that Cr^{2+} ions can lose electrons to form Cr^{3+} ions and acts as a reducing agent, while Mn^{3+} ions can accept electrons and can act as an oxidising agent. (1)

(ii) Cobalt (III) ion has greater tendency to form complexes than cobalt (II) ion. Therefore, Co (II) ion being stable in aqueous solution, changes to Co (III) ion in the presence of complexing reagents and gets oxidised. (1)

(iii) Ions of transition metals with d^1 configuration tend to lose one electron to acquire d^0 configuration that is quite stable. Therefore, such ions (with d^1) undergo either oxidation or disproportionation, hence are unstable. (1)

30. (i) The general trend towards less negative $E°$ values across the series is related to the general increase in the sum of the first and second ionisation enthalpies. (1)

(ii) The high energy to transform Cu(*s*) to $Cu^{2+}(aq)$ is not balanced by its hydration enthalpy.

Most of Cu (I) compounds are unstable in aqueous solution and undergo disproportionation.

$2Cu^+ \longrightarrow Cu^{2+} + Cu$ (1)

(iii) The stability of the half-filled d-subshell in Mn^{2+} and the completely filled d^{10} configuration in Zn^{2+} are related to their more negative $E°$ values. **(1)**

31. (i) Mn^{2+} compounds are more stable due to half-filled d-orbitals. Fe^{2+}compounds are comparatively less stable as they have six electrons in their orbitals. So, they tend to lose one electron from Fe^{2+} and get stable $3d^5$-configuration in Fe^{3+}.

Therefore, comparatively high positive value of $E°$ for Mn^{3+}/Mn^{2+}indicates the stability of $Mn^{2+}(d^5)$, whereas comparatively low value for Fe^{3+}/Fe^{2+} indicates the extra stability of $Fe^{3+}(d^5)$. **(1)**

(ii) Energy required to convert metallic crystal into individual atom is **enthalpy of atomisation**. In transition row elements, it first increases and reaches to maximum upto middle element and then decreases. This is because of strong inter atomic interaction due to unpaired electron.

Greater the number of unpaired electron, stronger will be bonding and thus enthalpy of atomisation will also be more. Since, iron has more unpaired electrons than copper therefore, its enthalpy of atomisation is more. **(1)**

(iii) The metal ions with partially or incomplete filled d-orbitals will be coloured in aqueous solution. While the metal ions having either empty or completely filled d-orbitals are colourless.
The colour will be due to d-d transition of electrons.
Thus, the outer electronic configuration of metal ions are Sc^{3+} : $3d^0$, Ti^{3+} : $3d^1$
Hence, among the given ions, Ti^{3+} will exhibit colour in aqueous solution, while Sc^{3+} will be colourless. **(1)**

32. (i) Electronic configuration of Ti : $[Ar]3d^2 4s^2$

Electronic configuration of Ti^{4+} is [Ar]. It has stable noble gas configuration.

Electronic configuration of Ti^{2+} : $[Ar]3d^2$

Electronic configuration of Ti^{3+} : $[Ar]3d^1$

As Ti^{4+} acquires nearest noble gas configuration on loss of 4 electrons, thus it is more stable than the Ti^{3+} and Ti^{2+}. **(1)**

(ii) In case of transition elements, ions of the same charge in a given series show progressive decrease in radius with increasing atomic number.

As with increase in atomic number, the new electron enters in d-orbitals and the element is expected to show increase in atomic size, but due to poor shielding effect of d-orbitals, the electrostatic attraction between nucleus and outermost orbital increases and hence, the ionic radii decreases. **(1)**

(iii) Zinc is a soft metal as compared to iron and chromium because it has low enthalpy of atomisation (due to the absence of unpaired electron), whereas, iron and chromium have high enthalpy of atomisation (due to the presence of unpaired electrons), which account for their hardness. **(1)**

33. (i) Refer to solution 17. **(1)**

(ii) Refer to text on pages 114 and 115. **(1)**

(iii) Oxometal anions have the highest oxidation state e.g. Cr in $Cr_2O_7^{2-}$ has an oxidation state of +6.

This is due to the combination of metal with oxygen which is highly electronegative and strong oxidising agent. **(1)**

34. Negative value of $E°$ for Cr^{3+}/Cr^{2+} shows that Cr^{2+} is least stable. Greater positive value for Mn^{3+}/Mn^{2+} than that for Fe^{3+}/Fe^{2+} shows that Mn^{2+} is more stable than Fe^{2+}.
Hence, stability of +2 oxidation state is in the order : $Cr^{2+} < Fe^{2+} < Mn^{2+}$ or the oxidation of their +2 state to +3 state is in the order : $Cr^{2+} > Fe^{2+} > Mn^{2+}$. **(3)**

35. (i) Refer to text on page 121. **(1)**

(ii) Refer to text on page 119. **(1)**

(iii) Refer to text on page 120. **(1)**

36. Refer to text on page 123. **(3)**

37. Refer to text on page 124. **(3)**

38. Refer to text on pages 121. **(3)**

39. (i) Refer to text on page 121. **(1)**

(ii) Refer to text on page 119. **(1)**

(iii) Refer to text on page 121. **(1)**

40. The element that shows deviation in the trend for the second ionisation energy is manganese, whereas the element that shows deviation in the trend for the third ionisation energy is iron.

The deviation occurs because Mn^{2+} ion and Fe^{3+} have $3d^5$ configuration which is more stable than the configuration of Cr^{2+} and Mn^{3+} ions. **(3)**

41. Refer to text on pages 110 and 111. **(5)**

42. (i) Refer to text on page 112. **(1)**

(ii) Refer to text on pages 116 and 117. **(1)**

(iii) Refer to text on page 117. **(1)**

(iv) Refer to text on page 117. **(1)**

(v) Refer to text on page 112. **(1)**

43. (i) **Electronic configuration** The elements in the same vertical column generally have similar electronic configuration. Although, the first series has only two exceptions,

$$Cr = 3d^5\,4s^1 \text{ and } Cu = 3d^{10}4s^1$$

Second transition series have six exceptions,

$$Mo = 4d^5 5s^1,\ Nb = 4d^4 5s^1,\ Ru = 4d^7 5s^1$$
$$Rh = 4d^8 5s^1,\ Pd = 4d^{10} 5s^0,\ Ag = 4d^{10} 5s^1$$

Third transition series has three exceptions,

$$W = 4f^{14}5d^4 6s^2,\quad Pt = 4f^{14}5d^9 6s^1$$
$$Au = 4f^{14}5d^{10}6s^1$$

(2)

(ii) **Oxidation states** Refer to text on pages 113 to 114. **(1)**

(iii) **Ionisation enthalpies** The first ionisation enthalpy in each series generally increase gradually as we move from left to right. Though some exceptions are observed in each series.

The first ionisation enthalpies of some elements in the second (4*d*) series are higher, while some of them have lower value than the elements of 3*d*-series in the same vertical column. **(1)**

(iv) **Atomic size** Generally, ions of the same charge or atoms in a given series show progressive decrease in radius with increasing atomic number though the decrease is quite small.

But the size of the atoms of the 4*d*-series is larger than the corresponding elements of the 3*d*-series whereas those of corresponding elements of the 5*d*-series are nearly the same as those of 4*d*-series due to lanthanoid contraction. **(1)**

44. The heavier transition elements belong to fourth (4*d*), fifth (5*d*) and sixth (6*d*) transition series. Their properties are expected to be different from the elements belonging to the first (3*d*) transition series due to the following reasons.

(i) Atomic radii of heavier transition elements (4*d* and 5*d* series) are larger than those of the corresponding elements of the first transition series though those of 4*d* and 5*d*-series are very close to each other. **(1)**

(ii) Ionisation enthalpies of 5*d*-series are higher than the corresponding elements of 3*d* and 4*d*-series. **(1)**

(iii) Enthalpies of atomisation of 4*d*-and 5*d*-series are higher than the corresponding elements of the first series. **(1)**

(iv) Melting and boiling points of heavier transition elements are greater than those of the first transition series due to stronger intermetallic bonding. **(1)**

(v) The elements of the first transition series generally form low spin or high spin complexes, depending upon the strength of ligand field.

However, the heavier transition elements form low spin complexes irrespective of the strength of the ligand field. **(1)**

45. Magnetic moment $(\mu) = \sqrt{n(n+2)}$ BM

For $n = 1$, $\mu = \sqrt{1(1+2)} = \sqrt{3} = 1.73$ BM ≈ 2

For $n = 2$, $\mu = \sqrt{2(2+2)} = \sqrt{8} = 2.83$ BM ≈ 3

For $n = 3$, $\mu = \sqrt{3(3+2)} = \sqrt{15} = 3.87$ BM ≈ 4

For $n = 4$, $\mu = \sqrt{4(4+2)} = \sqrt{24} = 4.90$ BM ≈ 5

For $n = 5$, $\mu = \sqrt{5(5+2)} = \sqrt{35} = 5.92$ BM ≈ 6

In $K_4[Mn(CN)_6]$, Mn is in +2 oxidation state, i.e. given value of μ (2.2 BM $\approx$ 2) indicates the presence of one unpaired electron. Since, CN^- is a strong field ligand.

Hence, when CN^- ligands approach Mn^{2+} ion, the electrons in 3*d* pair up. Hybridisation involved is d^2sp^3 forming inner orbital octahedral complex.

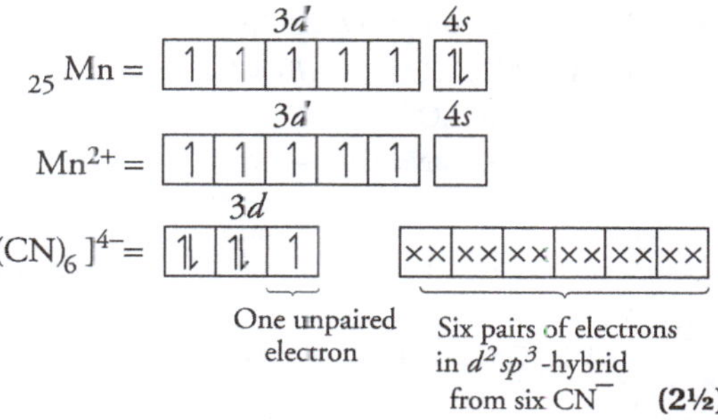

(2½)

In $[Fe(H_2O)_6]^{2+}$, Fe is in +2 oxidation state. Given, $\mu = 5.3$ BM (≈ 5), shows that there are four unpaired electrons. Since, H_2O is a weak ligand. Hence, the electrons in 3*d* do not pair up when the ligands, i.e. H_2O molecules, approach. To accommodate the electrons donated by H_2O molecules, the hybridisation is sp^3d^2. Therefore, it will be an outer orbital octahedral complex.

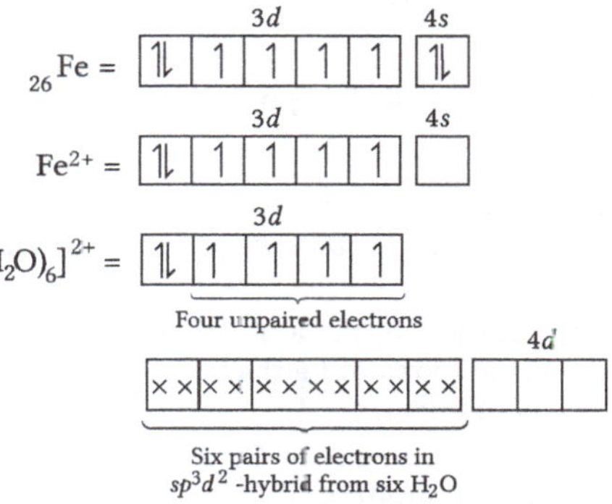

(2½)

46. All the ions form complex of the type $[M(H_2O)_6]^{n+}$. As water is a weak field ligand, therefore, in case of octahedral complex, pairing takes place, when each t_{2g} and e_g orbital is singly occupied [t_{2g} (d_{xy}, d_{yz}, d_{zx}) set is of lower energy and e_g $(d_{z^2}, d_{x^2-y^2})$ is of higher energy].

Ions	Configuration	Number of 3*d* electrons	Number of unpaired electrons	Occupancy of 3*d*-orbitals
Ti^{2+}	$3d^2$	2	2	t_{2g}^2
V^{2+}	$3d^3$	3	3	t_{2g}^3
Cr^{3+}	$3d^3$	3	3	t_{2g}^3
Mn^{2+}	$3d^5$	5	5	$t_{2g}^3e_g^2$
Fe^{2+}	$3d^6$	6	4	$t_{2g}^4e_g^2$
Fe^{3+}	$3d^5$	5	5	$t_{2g}^3e_g^2$
Co^{2+}	$3d^7$	7	3	$t_{2g}^5e_g^2$
Ni^{2+}	$3d^8$	8	2	$t_{2g}^6e_g^2$
Cu^{2+}	$3d^9$	9	1	$t_{2g}^6e_g^3$

47. Refer to text on pages 120 to 121. (5)

48. (i) (A) = Na_2CrO_4 (B) = $Na_2Cr_2O_7$
(C) = $K_2Cr_2O_7$ (D) I_2

$$4FeCr_2O_4 + 8Na_2CO_3 + \underset{\text{(Excess air)}}{7O_2} \longrightarrow 2Fe_2O_3 + \underset{\substack{\text{Sodium chromate}\\ \text{(yellow)}\\ (A)}}{8Na_2CrO_4} + 8CO_2\uparrow$$

$$2Na_2CrO_4 + 2H^+ \longrightarrow \underset{\substack{(B)\\ \text{Sodium dichromate}\\ \text{(Orange)}}}{Na_2Cr_2O_7} + 2Na^+ + H_2O$$

$$Na_2Cr_2O_7 + 2KCl \longrightarrow \underset{\substack{\text{Potassium dichromate}\\ \text{(Orange)}\\ (C)}}{K_2Cr_2O_7} + 2NaCl$$

$$Cr_2O_7^{2-} + 6I^- + 14H^+ \longrightarrow 2Cr^{3+} + \underset{\substack{(D)\\ \text{(Iodine)}}}{3I_2} + 7H_2O$$

(ii) (a) $$2MnO_4^-(aq) + 10I^-(aq) + 16H^+(aq) \longrightarrow 2Mn^{2+}(aq) + 5I_2(s) + 8H_2O(l)$$

(b) $$Cr_2O_7^{2-} + 3Sn^{2+} + 14H^+ \longrightarrow 3Sn^{4+} + 2Cr^{3+} + 7H_2O$$ (2)

49. (i) Zinc is not a transition metal because Zn has 10 electrons in 3*d*-orbital in its ground state as well as oxidised state. (1)

(ii) Lanthanoid contraction is gradual decrease in size of atoms and ions of lanthanoids with an increase in atomic number. (1)

(iii) Ionisation enthalpy of Cr is less than Zn because Cr has a configuration of $[Ar]3d^5 4s^1$ therefore electron will easily come out from 4*s*-orbital (to attain stable half-filled ($3d^5$) configuration) and will require very less energy. But in case of Zn, electron comes out from a completely filled $4s^2$ orbital and require more energy as compared to the chromium. (1)

(iv) Transition metals have partially filled *d*-orbitals so they can easily withdraw the electrons from the reagent or give electrons to them depending on nature of reaction. They also have a tendency to show large number of oxidation states and ability to form complexes which makes them a good catalyst. (1)

(v) Coloured compounds of transition elements is associated with partially filled $(n-1)\,d$ orbitals, the transition metal ions containing unpaired *d*-electrons undergoes electronic transition from one *d*-orbital to another. During this *d-d* transition process, the element absorbs certain energy from radiation and emits the remaining of energy as coloured light. The colour of ion is complementary of colour absorbed by it. Hence, coloured ions is formed due to *d-d* transition. (1)

(vi) K_2MnO_4 is paramagnetic due to presence of unpaired electrons, while $KMnO_4$ is diamagnetic due absence of any unpaired electron. (1)

(vii) $Cr_2O_7^{2-} + 14H^+ + 6e^- \longrightarrow 2Cr^{3+} + 7H_2O$ (1)

50. (i) Mn^{3+} is a stronger oxidising agent as the change from Mn^{3+} to Mn^{2+} results in half-filled, d^5-configuration which has extra stability. (1)

(ii) Ti^{4+} will be colourless due to its empty 3*d*-orbital. (1)

(iii) Cerium (IV) ion (Ce^{4+}) is a good oxidising agent because of its high oxidation state, small size and high positive charge. (1)

(iv) The highest oxidation state of a metal is usually exhibited in its oxide or fluoride because oxygen and fluorine are small in size and highly electronegative. (1)

(v) Refer to text on Page 125. (1)

(vi) In aqueous solution, copper (I) undergoes disproportionation reaction as follows

$$2Cu^+(aq) \longrightarrow Cu^{2+} + Cu(s)$$

The highest stability of Cu^{2+} ion in aqueous solution is due to negative enthalpy of hydration. Hence, Cu^+ is not known in aqueous solution. (1)

(vii) Transition elements have high enthalpies of atomisation because of large number of unpaired electrons in their atoms, so they have stronger interatomic interaction and hence stronger bonding between atoms resulting in higher enthalpies of atomisation. (1)

51. (i) Ce(III) ion have the outer electronic configuration $4f^1 5d^0 6s^0$ which can easily lose the electron from 4*f* orbital to acquire the stable configuration, i.e. $4f^0 5d^0 6s^0$ and form Ce(IV) ion. (1)

(ii) The $E^\circ_{(Mn^{2+}/Mn)}$ value is −1.18 V, which is highly negative as compared to other neighbouring *d*-block elements due to extra stability of half-filled orbital of Mn^{2+} (i.e. $3d^5$). (1)

(iii) Greater is the number of unpaired electrons stronger is the resultant bonding, hence greater is the enthalpy of atomisation.

In 3*d* series elements, Zn has the lowest enthalpy of atomisation, it is due to the absence of unpaired electrons in *ns* and $(n-1)d$ shells. (1)

(iv) When sodium chromate is acidified then orange colour solution of sodium dichromate is formed.

$$\underset{\substack{\text{Sodium}\\ \text{chromate}}}{2Na_2CrO_4} + 2H^+ \longrightarrow \underset{\substack{\text{Sodium}\\ \text{dichromate}\\ \text{(Orange)}}}{Na_2Cr_2O_7} + 2Na^+ + H_2O$$ (1)

(v) Zn, Hg and Cd have completely filled *d*-orbitals in the ground state as well as in their common oxidation states. Thus, formation of strong metallic bond is not possible and they are soft. (1)

(vi) Permanganate titration is not carried out in the presence of HCl because if HCl is used, the oxygen produced from the reaction of $KMnO_4$ and HCl is partly utilised in oxidising HCl to Cl_2, which itself acts as an oxidising agent and partially oxidises the reducing agent. (1)

(vii) In lower oxidation states, transition metals behave like metals and their metal oxides are basic in nature. Thus, in lower oxidation states, transition metal oxides are basic.

As the oxidation state increases, its metallic character decreases due to decrease in size, thus, it becomes less metallic or more non-metallic. Oxides of a non-metal may be acidic or neutral.

Thus, in higher oxidation states, transition metal oxides are amphoteric or acidic. **(1)**

52. (a) CuF_2 is coloured because it has unpaired electron present in it. **(1)**

(b) (i) Cr in CrO_4^{2-} is in the highest oxidation state, i.e., +6 while Mn in MnO_4^{2-} is not. **(1)**

(ii) Zr and Hf have identical size due to lanthanoid contraction. **(1)**

(iii) The lowest oxidation state of Mn in basic medium is +2 while in acidic medium the highest oxidation state is +7. **(1)**

(iv) Mn^{2+} have five unpaired electrons present in it and that is why it shows maximum paramagnetic character. **(1)**

53. The above given process is depicting the preparation of potassium dichromate. **(1)**

The unknown compound '*C*' is potassium dichromate ($K_2Cr_2O_7$) **(1)**

Stepwise chemical equations involved are as follows

$$4FeCr_2O_4 + 16NaOH + 7O_2 \longrightarrow \underset{(A)}{8Na_2CrO_4} + 2Fe_2O_3 + 8H_2O \quad \textbf{(1)}$$

$$2Na_2CrO_4 + H_2SO_4 \longrightarrow \underset{(B)}{Na_2Cr_2O_7} + Na_2SO_4 + H_2O \quad \textbf{(1)}$$

$$Na_2Cr_2O_7 + 2KCl \longrightarrow \underset{(C)}{K_2Cr_2O_7} + 2NaCl \quad \textbf{(1)}$$

54. (i) (a) Zn^{2+} with configuration $[Ar]3d^{10}$ has completely filled orbitals. Therefore, its salts are colourless. Ni^{2+} with configuration $[Ar]3d^8$ has two unpaired electrons in 3*d*-orbitals. So, it forms coloured salts. **(1)**

(b) As after the loss of one electron Cr^{2+} becomes Cr^{3+} which has more stable half-filled (t_{2g}^3) configuration. **(1)**

(c) Due to variable oxidation state. **(1)**

(ii) (a) $2MnO_4^- + 10I^- + 16H^+ \longrightarrow 2Mn^{2+} + 5I_2 + 8H_2O$ **(1)**

(b) $MnO_4^- + 5Fe^{2+} + 8H^+ \longrightarrow Mn^{2+} + 5Fe^{3+} + 4H_2O$ **(1)**

55. (i) MnO_4^-: Mn has +7 oxidation state and group number is 7.

CrO_4^{2-}: Cr has +6 oxidation state and group number is 6. **(1)**

(ii) Refer to text on page 119 **(1)**

(iii) Refer to text on page 114. **(1)**

(iv) Cerium exhibits +4 oxidation state. **(1)**

(v) Cr and Cu

Cr : $[Ar]3d^5 4s^1$ Cu : $[Ar]3d^{10} 4s^1$ **(1)**

56. (i) (a) Refer to text on page 116. **(1)**

(b) Refer to text on page 117. **(1)**

(c) Refer to text on page 125. **(1)**

(ii) Refer to text on page 120. **(2)**

57. (i) (a) Refer to text on page 118. **(1)**

(b) Refer to text on page 123. **(1)**

(ii) Refer to text on page 125. **(2)**

(iii) $Cr_2O_7^{2-} + 2OH^- \longrightarrow 2CrO_4^{2-} + H_2O$ **(1)**

58. (i) Refer to text on page 125. **(1)**

(ii) $3MnO_4^{2-} + 4H^+ \longrightarrow 2MnO_4^- + MnO_2 + 2H_2O$

Here, MnO_4^{2-} is reduced to MnO_2 as well as oxidised to MnO_4^-. Hence, it is a disproportionation reaction. **(2)**

(iii) Refer to text on page 112. **(2)**

59. (i) (a) Refer to text on page 117. **(1)**

(b) Refer to text on page 116. **(1)**

(c) Refer to text on page 114. **(1)**

(ii) Refer to text on page 120. **(2)**

60. (i) (a) Scandium exhibit only +3 oxidation state. **(1)**

(b) Cr is strongest reducing agent in +2 oxidation state which on losing electron gains a stable configuration. **(1)**

(ii) (a) $Cr_2O_7^{2-} + 14H^+ + 6Fe^{2+} \longrightarrow 2Cr^{3+} + 6Fe^{3+} + 7H_2O$ **(1)**

(b) $2KMnO_4 \xrightarrow{\text{Heat}} K_2MnO_4 + MnO_2 + O_2$ **(1)**

(iii) Refer to text on page 123.

- Mischmetal alloy of lanthanoid is used in Mg-based alloy to produce bullets, shell and lighter flint. **(1)**

QR Code for Quick Test 1

QR Code for Quick Test 2

QR Code for Quick Test 3

SELF ASSESSMENT TEST

Objective Type Questions [1 Mark]

1. Which of the following compounds is used as the starting material for the preparation of potassium dichromate?
   (a) $K_2SO_4 \cdot Cr_2(SO_4)_3 \cdot 24H_2O$ (Chrome alum)
   (b) $PbCrO_4$ (Chromite yellow)
   (c) $FeCr_2O_4$ (Chromite)
   (d) $PbCrO_4 \cdot PbO$ (Chrome red)
2. Which of the following element show catalytic property?
   (a) Ca (b) Fe (c) Pb (d) None of these
3. Transition elements have unique property that
   (a) they show variable oxidation state.
   (b) these elements acts as catalyst.
   (c) they form coloured compounds.
   (d) All of the above
4. Choose the appropriate option about the mischmetal.
   (a) It is an alloy which consists of a lanthanoid metal (~95%) and iron (~5%) and traces of S, C, Ca and Al.
   (b) It is used in Mg based alloy to produce bullets, shell and lighter flint.
   (c) It finds application in making aeroplane body.
   (d) Both (a) and (b).
5. A solution of $KMnO_4$ is reduced to form various products. At pH > 7, it gives a green solution (*A*) and at pH < 7, it is reduced to a colourless solution (*B*). Identify (*A*) and (*B*) from the options given below.

	(*A*)	(*B*)
(a)	MnO_4^{2-}	Mn^{2+}
(b)	MnO_2	MnO_4^{2-}
(c)	Mn^{2+}	MnO_2
(d)	Mn^{2+}	MnO_4^{2-}

Assertion - Reason [1 Mark]

Directions (Q. Nos. 6-8) In the following questions an Assertion (A) is followed by a corresponding Reason (R). Use the following keys to choose the appropriate answer.

6. **Assertion** (A) Many trivalent lanthanoid ions are coloured both in solid state and in aqueous solution.
   Reason (R) Colour of these ions is due to the presence of *f*-electrons.
7. **Assertion** (A) Highest oxidation state is exhibited by transition metal lying in the middle of the series.
   Reason (R) The highest oxidation state exhibited corresponds to number of $(n-1)d$ electrons.
8. **Assertion** (A) The highest oxidation states of the 3*d*-metals depends only on electronic configuration of the metal.
   Reason (R) The number of electrons in the $(n-1)d$ and *ns*-subshells determine the oxidation states exhibited by the metal.

Short Answer Type I Questions [2 Marks]

9. (i) Which of the following are amphoteric oxides?
   Mn_2O_7, CrO_3, Cr_2O_3, CrO, V_2O_5, V_2O_4
   (ii) What happens when dichromate ion is dissolved in alkali?
10. (i) Write the formula of compound in which transition metal is in +7 oxidation state.
    (ii) What happens when $KMnO_4$ is treated with KI in alkaline medium?
11. (i) In the titration of Fe^{2+} ions with $KMnO_4$ in acidic medium, dil. H_2SO_4 is used but not the dil. HCl. Why?
    (ii) Arrange the following oxides of Mn in the order of their decreasing acidic nature.
    MnO, Mn_2O_3, Mn_3O_4, MnO_2, Mn_2O_7.

Short Answer Type II Questions [3 Marks]

12. On the basis of the figure given below, answer the following questions:

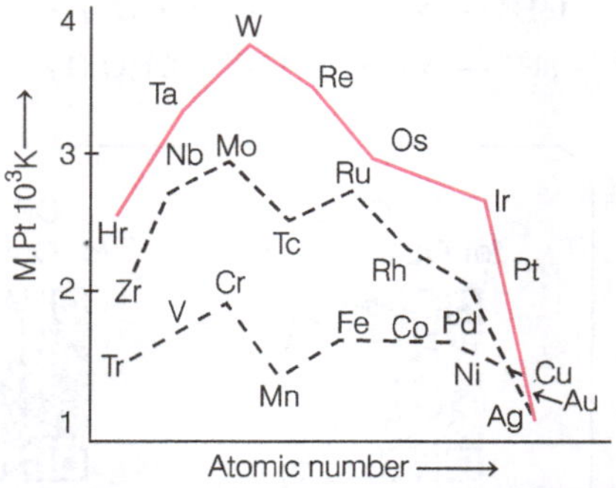

(i) Why manganese has lower melting point than chromium?

(ii) Why do transition metals of 3*d*-series have lower melting point as compared to 4*d*-series?

(iii) In the third transition series, identify and name the metal with the highest melting point.

13. (i) Name the elements which are used for the synthesis of transuranic elements.

(ii) What are the uses of mischmetal?

(iii) Write two similarities between chemistry of lanthanoids and actinoids.

14. Name a compound of

(i) transition metal which is used in the manufacture of sulphuric acid.

(ii) transition metal that is used in Haber's process for the manufacture of ammonia.

(iii) transition metal that have light sensitive properties and act as valuable source in photographic industry.

Case-Study [4 Marks]

15. Except for the first and last individuals in the series, all of the transition elements exhibit different oxidation states. They use variable valence electrons to signify varied valency in their compound.

The *s*-block, *d*-block and *f*-block elements have positive oxidation states, (except for H, which has a −1 oxidation state as well), but the majority of the *p*-block elements have both positive and negative oxidation states. The number of electrons used by an electropositive element for bonding is equal to its positive oxidation state. The capacity of *d*-block elements to display a range of oxidation states in their compounds is a distinguishing feature.

As a result, multiple oxidation states emerge depending on the number of *d*-electrons participating in bonding. The amount of *s*-electrons, present is generally equal to the lowest oxidation state (except Sc). Compounds containing fluorine and oxygen, the two most electronegative elements, have the greatest oxidation states. Compounds with oxidation states +2 and +3 of these elements contain ionic bonds, but those in higher oxidation states are mainly covalent.

In the case of the permanganate ion, MnO_4^-, the bonds produced between manganese and oxygen are covalent. Given the acid-base nature of the oxides, it can be deduced that a rise in oxidation state leads to a decrease in basic character and *vice-versa*. Because transition metals have several oxidation states, their compounds in the higher oxidation levels are potent oxidising agents because they take electrons and transition to stable lower oxidation states.

(i) Why do transition elements exhibit a wide range of oxidation states? Discuss the role of *d*-electrons in this behaviour.

(ii) Why are lower oxidation states of transition elements generally more stable in ionic compounds?

(iii) In the case of MnO_4^- (permanganate ion), is the bond between manganese and oxygen ionic or covalent? Justify your answer.

Or

What is the relation between oxidation state and the acidic or basic nature of transition metal oxides?

Long Answer Type Questions [5 Marks]

16. (i) Distinguish the structure of chromate ion from that of dichromate ion.

(ii) Give two equations that explains the nature of $K_2Cr_2O_7$ as an oxidising agent.

(iii) What is meant by the term lanthanoid contraction? Write any one consequence of it.

17. (a) What happens when $KMnO_4$ reacts with nitrite ion?

(b) What happens when a lanthanoid reacts with water?

(c) Why are alloys mostly prepared from transition metals?

(d) Write the ionic equation for reaction of KI with acidified $KMnO_4$.

(e) Write the outer shell electronic configuration of an element with atomic number 24. Why is this element different from the elements that are adjacent to it in the periodic table?

Answers

1. (c)	2. (b)	3. (d)	4. (d)
5. (a)	6. (a)	7. (c)	8. (d)

05

CHAPTER

Certain elements, that include mostly transition metals, forms a large number of **complex compounds** in which the metal atoms are bound to a number of anions or neutral molecules by sharing of electrons. Today, such compounds are named as **coordination compounds.**
The branch of inorganic chemistry which deals with its study is called **coordination chemistry.**

YOUR STUDY GOALS

YOUR PRACTICE GOAL

- Objective Type Questions (44 Qs ; 28 MCQs, 13 A-R, 3 Case Study)
- Subjective Type Questions (56 Qs ; 24 SA-I, 25 SA-II, 7 LA)

Coordination Compounds

5.1 Addition Compounds

When two or more stable compounds combine together in stoichiometric ratio, then the compound formed is called **addition compound.**

e.g. $KCl + MgCl_2 + 6H_2O \longrightarrow \underset{\text{Carnallite}}{KCl \cdot MgCl_2 \cdot 6H_2O}$

$(NH_4)_2SO_4 + FeSO_4 + 6H_2O \longrightarrow \underset{\text{Mohr's salt}}{FeSO_4 \cdot (NH_4)_2SO_4 \cdot 6H_2O}$

On the basis of how the addition compounds dissociate, these are classified into two main types, namely, coordination compounds and double salts.

Coordination Compounds

- Addition compounds which exhibit properties completely different from their constituents and retain their identity in the solid as well as in the dissolved state are called **coordination compounds.**

  e.g. Potassium hexacyanoferrate(II), ($K_4[Fe(CN)_6]$), when dissolved in water gives K^+ and $[Fe(CN)_6]^{4-}$ ions in the solution. This solution does not show any properties of Fe^{2+} or CN^- ions. The ion $[Fe(CN)_6]^{4-}$ is a **complex ion.**

- Complex ions are the ions in which the central metal ion is bonded to one or more molecules or ions. They are also known as **coordination complexes** because they are Lewis acid-base complexes.
- The salts of the complex ions are called complex compounds or coordination compounds. This is because in all such compounds, the central metal ion forms dative or co-ordinate bonds with surrounding species.

Double Salts

- These are the addition compounds which are stable in the solid state but break up into its constituents in dissolved state.
- These compounds show some properties of their constituent ions too. It contains two salts in equimolar ratio which are crystallised together to form their saturated solution.
- For example, Mohr's salt, $FeSO_4 \cdot (NH_4)_2SO_4 \cdot 6H_2O$, when dissolved in water gives Fe^{2+}, NH_4^+ and SO_4^{2-} ions and shows the properties of these ions during their respective tests. Similarly, carnallite, $KCl \cdot MgCl_2 \cdot 6H_2O$ and potash alum, $KAl(SO_4)_2 \cdot 12H_2O$, etc., dissociate into simple ions completely when dissolved in water.

Difference between Coordination Compounds and Double Salts

Coordination compounds	Double salts
They don't completely lose their identity in solution.	They lose their identity in solution.
They exist in solid state as well as in the form of complex ions when dissolved in water or any other solvent. They don't dissociate into simple ions completely.	They exist only in solid state and dissociate into ions in aqueous solution or in other solvent.
Their properties are different from their constituents.	Their properties are essentially same as those of its constituent compounds.
In a complex compound or coordination compound, metal ion satisfies two types of valencies called primary and secondary valencies.	In a double salt, metal ions exhibit their normal valency.
e.g. $[Ni(NH_3)_6]Cl_2$, $K_4[Fe(CN)_6]$, etc.	e.g. Mohr's salt $[FeSO_4 \cdot (NH_4)_2SO_4 \cdot 6H_2O]$, potash alum $[K_2SO_4 \cdot Al_2(SO_4)_3 \cdot 24H_2O]$, etc.

5.2 Werner's Theory of Coordination Compounds

- **Alfred Werner** (1866-1919), a Swiss chemist was the first to formulate his ideas about the structures of coordination compounds. He proposed the concept of a **primary valence** and a **secondary valence** for a metal ion.

  Binary compounds such as $CrCl_3$, $CoCl_2$ and $PdCl_2$ have primary valence of 3, 2 and 2 respectively.
- In a series of compounds of cobalt(III) chloride with ammonia, it was found that some of the chloride ions could be precipitated as AgCl on adding excess of $AgNO_3$ solution in cold but some remained in the solution.

  The above observations, together with the results of conductivity measurements in solution is shown below in the table.

Formulation of Cobalt(III) Chloride-Ammonia Complexes

Complex Compounds	Colour	No. of Cl^- ion precipitated per mole of the complex by Ag^+	Formula	Solution conductivity corresponds to
$CoCl_3 \cdot 6NH_3$	Yellow	3	$[Co(NH_3)_6]^{3+} 3Cl^-$	1 : 3 electrolyte
$CoCl_3 \cdot 5NH_3$	Purple	2	$[CoCl(NH_3)_5]^{2+} 2Cl^-$	1 : 2 electrolyte
$CoCl_3 \cdot 4NH_3$	Green	1	$[CoCl_2(NH_3)_4]^+ Cl^-$	1 : 1 electrolyte
$CoCl_3 \cdot 4NH_3$	Violet	1	$[CoCl_2(NH_3)_4]^+ Cl^-$	1 : 1 electrolyte

TEACHER'S TIP

The two compounds in the above table have identical empirical formula, $CoCl_3 \cdot 4NH_3$ but they have distinct properties. Such compounds are termed as **isomers**.

Postulates of Werner's Theory

The **Werner** in **1898**, propounded his theory of coordination compounds and the main postulates are as follows

- In coordination compounds, metal has two types of linkages (valencies)-primary and secondary.
- **Primary valency** is equal to the oxidation number of central ion. It is non-directional and ionisable. It is satisfied by negative ions.
- **Secondary valency** is equal to the coordination number of central atom/ion. It is directional and non-ionisable. It is commonly satisfied by neutral molecules or negative ions and is always fixed for a metal. Each metal ion has a fixed number of secondary valency.
- The ions or groups bounded by the secondary valencies to the metal have characteristic spatial arrangements called **coordination polyhedra** corresponding to different coordination number.

  e.g. Structure of $[CoCl_2(NH_3)_4]^+ Cl^-$ is as follows

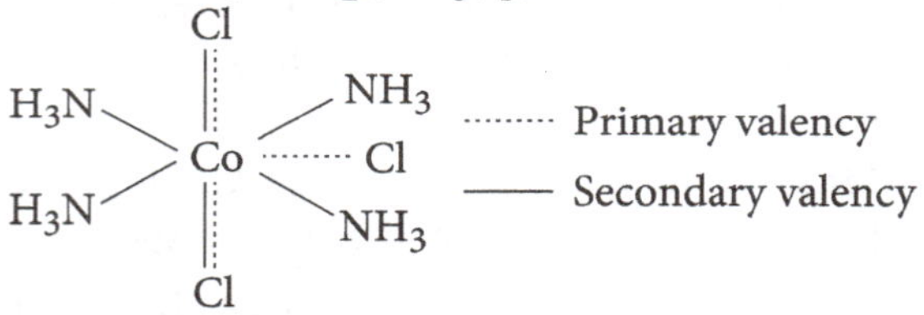

  The solid and dotted lines together indicate Cl-atom satisfying both primary and secondary valency.
- Werner further postulated that octahedral, tetrahedral and square planar geometrical shapes are more common in coordination compounds of transition metals.

  Thus, $[Co(NH_3)_6]^{3+}$, $[CoCl(NH_3)_5]^{2+}$ and $[CoCl_2(NH_3)_4]^+$ are octahedral entities, while $[Ni(CO)_4]$ and $[PtCl_4]^{2-}$ are tetrahedral and square planar, respectively.

5.3 Definitions of Some Important Terms Used in Coordination Compounds

Coordination Entity

Coordination entity complex constitutes a central metal atom or ion attached to a fixed number of ions or molecules. It may be positive, negative or neutral, e.g. $[CoCl_3(NH_3)_3]$ is a coordination entity in which cobalt ion is surrounded by three NH_3 molecules and three Cl^- ions.

Other examples are $[Fe(CN)_6]^{4-}$, $[Co(NH_3)_6]^{3+}$, $[Ni(CO)_4]$ and $[PtCl_2(NH_3)_2]$.

The complex ion carrying a positive charge is called **cationic complex,** the one with a negative charge is called **anionic complex** and the one with no charge is called a **neutral complex**.

Central Metal Atom or Ion

In a coordination entity, the metal atom or ion to which a fixed number of ions/groups are bounded in a definite geometrical arrangements around it is called **central metal atom** or **ion.**

e.g. In $[NiCl_2(H_2O)_4]$, $[CoCl(NH_3)_5]^{2+}$ and $[Fe(CN)_6]^{3-}$, Ni^{2+}, Co^{3+} and Fe^{3+} respectively are central metal atoms or ions which are also called **Lewis acids.**

Ligands

Ligands are the ions or molecules bound to the central atom/ion through a coordinate bond in the coordination entity. It is a **Lewis base.** These may be simple ions such as Cl^-, small molecules such as H_2O or NH_3, larger molecules such as $H_2NCH_2CH_2NH_2$ or even macromolecules, such as proteins.

Ligands are classified into three categories on the basis of charge.

(i) **Neutral ligands** $H_2\ddot{O}$, CO, $\ddot{N}H_3$, NO, etc.

(ii) **Negative ligands** F^-, Cl^-, Br^-, I^-, OH^-, CN^-, SO_4^{2-}, etc.

(iii) **Positive ligands** NO^+, NO_2^+, $NH_2—NH_3^+$, etc.

On the basis of denticity (donor sites/number of ligating groups), ligands are classified as follows

(i) **Unidentate or Monodentate** When a ligand is bonded through one donor site to a central metal atom/ion, it is said to be unidentate ligand, e.g. Cl^-, CO, NH_3, H_2O, etc.

(ii) **Didentate or Bidentate** When a ligand is bonded through two donor sites to a central metal atom/ion, it is said to be a didentate ligand, e.g.

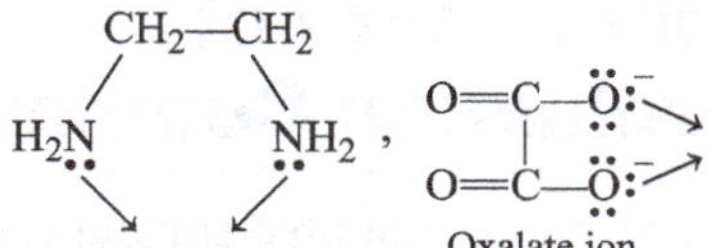

Ethylenediamine, Oxalate ion

(iii) **Polydentate** The ligands which contains three or more donor atoms, are called polydentate ligands, e.g.

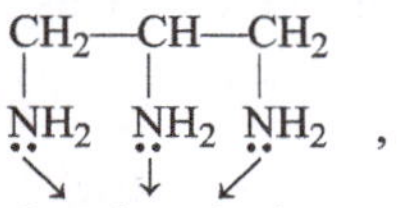

Propylenetriamine

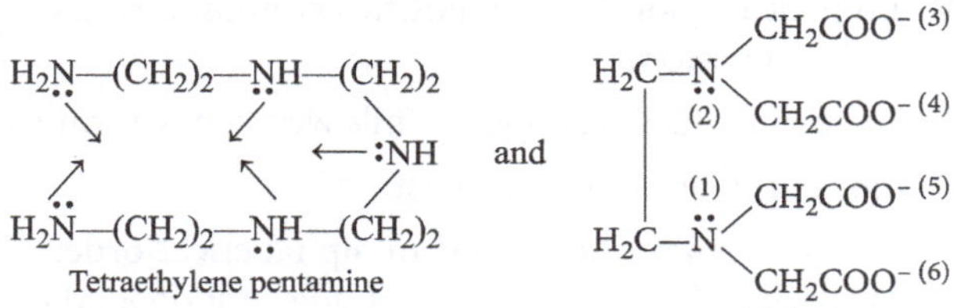

Tetraethylene pentamine and EDTA^{4-}

(iv) **Ambidentate ligands** Ligand which has two different donor atoms and either of the two gets attached to the central metal atom/ion is called an ambidentate ligand. e.g.

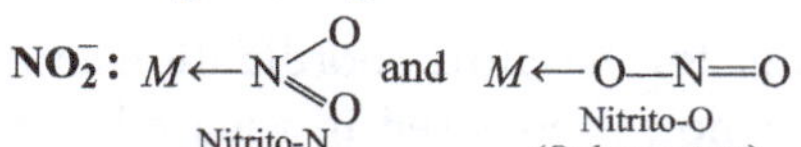

Nitrito-N (N-donor atom) and Nitrito-O (O-donor atom)

SCN$^-$: $M \leftarrow SCN$ and $M \leftarrow NCS$ etc.

Thiocyanato (S-donor atom), Isothiocyanato (N-donor atom)

(v) **Chelating ligands** When a di- or polydentate ligand uses its two or more donor sites simultaneously to bind a single metal ion, it is called a chelating ligand.

The number of such ligating groups is called the **denticity** of the ligand. Complexes formed have a ring like structure and are called **chelate complexes**.

The chelating ligands form more stable complexes than the unidentate analogs. This is called **chelate effect**.

e.g.

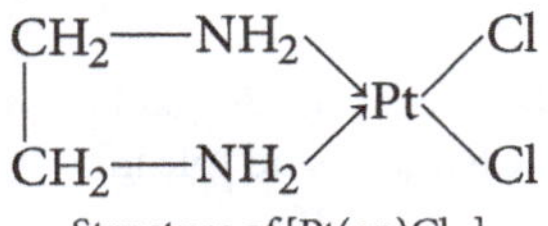

Structure of $[Pt(en)Cl_2]$

Coordination Number (CN)

The total number of ligand donor atoms directly attached to the metal ion in a complex is called the **coordination number of that metal ion.**

e.g.

$[Co(NH_3)_6]^{3+}$, CN of Co = 6 ; $[Ni(CO)_4]$, CN of Ni = 4

$[Co(en)_3]^{3+}$, CN of Co = 3 × 2 = 6 (en = didentate)

$[Fe(C_2O_4)_3]^{3-}$, CN of Fe = 3 × 2 = 6 ($C_2O_4^{2-}$ = didentate)

$[PtCl_6]^{2-}$, CN of Pt = 6 ; $[Ni(NH_3)_4]^{2+}$, CN of Ni = 4

> **TEACHER'S TIP**
> π(pi) bonds, if formed between the ligand and the central atom/ion, are not counted for the coordination number.
> The coordination number is determined only by the number of sigma (σ) bonds formed by the ligand with the central atom/ion.

Coordination Sphere and Counter Ions

The central atom/ion and the ligands attached to it are enclosed in the square bracket and are collectively known as **coordination sphere**. These are non-ionisable.

The ionisable groups are written outside the bracket and are known as **counter ions or ionisation sphere**.

e.g. In $K_4[Fe(CN)_6]$, the coordination sphere is $[Fe(CN)_6]^{4-}$ and the counter ion is K^+.

Coordination Polyhedron

It is the spatial arrangement of the ligand atoms which are directly attached to the central atom/ion.

The most common coordination polyhedra are octahedral, square planar and tetrahedral as shown in the figures given below.

e.g. $[Co(NH_3)_6]^{3+}$ is octahedral, $[Ni(CO)_4]$ is tetrahedral and $[PtCl_4]^{2-}$ is square planar.

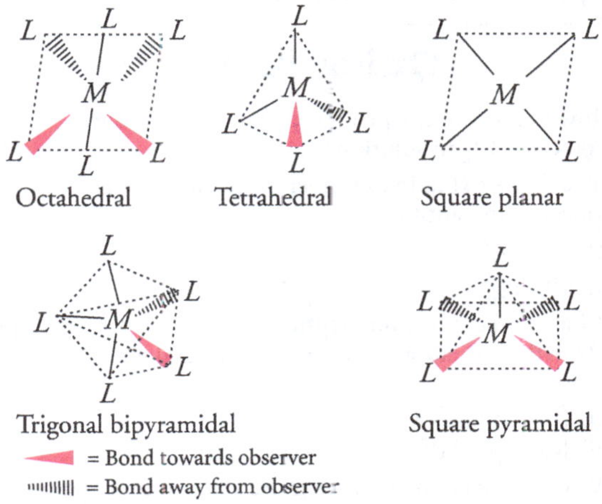

Shapes of different coordination polyhedra, where, M is central atom/ ion and L is a unidentate ligand

Oxidation Number of Central Atom

Oxidation number of the central atom in a complex is defined as the charge it would carry when all the ligands are removed along with electron pairs which are shared with the central atom.

The oxidation number is represented by a Roman numeral in parenthesis following the name of the coordination entity.

e.g. In $[Cu(CN)_4]^{3-}$, oxidation number of Cu is +1 and it is written as Cu(I).

In the complex $[CoBr_2(en)_2]^+$, the charge on the complex is +1, charge on central metal ion may be calculated as : $[Co \quad Br_2 \quad (en)_2]^+$

$$\begin{array}{ccc} \downarrow & \downarrow & \downarrow \\ x & +2(-1) & +2(0) = +1 \end{array}$$

$$x = +3$$

Depicting various terms used in a complex

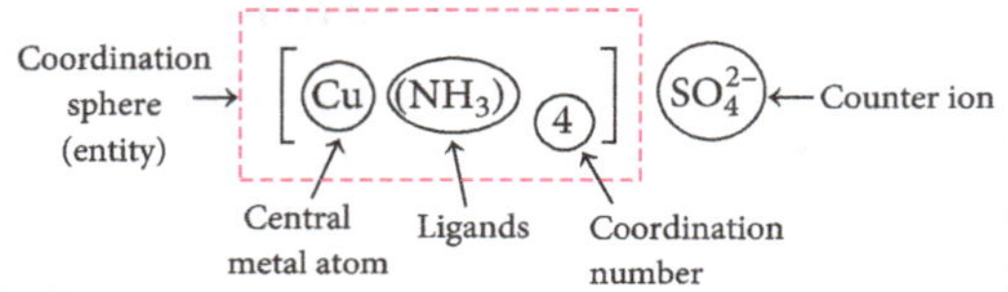

Homoleptic and Heteroleptic Complexes

- Complexes in which a metal is bound to only one kind of donor groups, are known as **homoleptic complexes,** e.g. $[Co(NH_3)_6]^{3+}$.
- Complexes in which a metal is bound to more than one kind of donor groups, are known as **heteroleptic complexes,** e.g. $[Co(NH_3)_4Cl_2]^+$.

Quick Test 1

1. How many ions are produced from the complex $Co(NH_3)_6Cl_2$ in solution? NCERT
2. Specify the oxidation number of metal in the following coordination entities. NCERT
   (i) $[Co(H_2O)(CN)(en)_2]^{2+}$ (ii) $[CoBr_2(en)_2]^+$
   (iii) $[PtCl_4]^{2-}$ (iv) $K[Co(CO)_4]$
3. What is meant by homoleptic complex? Give an example.
4. Write the oxidation number of metal in the following complexes.
   (i) $[Fe(CN)_6]^{4-}$ (ii) $[FeF_6]^{3-}$
   (iii) $[Co(C_2O_4)_3]^{3-}$ (iv) $[CoF_6]^{3-}$
5. Why chelate complexes are more stable than complexes with unidentate ligands?

For Solutions, See QR Code on Pg. 182

5.4 Nomenclature of Coordination Compounds

The formulae and names adopted for the coordination entities are based on the recommendations of the International Union of Pure and Applied Chemistry (IUPAC). The rules for the nomenclature of coordination compounds are as follows.

1. Formulae of Mononuclear Coordination Entities

Mononuclear coordination entities contain a single central metal atom.

The following rules are applied while writing the formulae.

- The central atom is listed first.
- The ligands are then listed in alphabetical order. The placement of a ligand in the list does not depend on its charge.
- **Polydentate ligands** are also listed alphabetically. In case of abbreviated ligand, the first letter of the abbreviation is used to determine the position of the ligand in the alphabetical order.
- The formula for the entire coordination entity, whether charged or not, is enclosed in square brackets. When ligands are polyatomic, their formulae are enclosed in parentheses. Ligand abbreviations are also enclosed in parentheses.
- There should be no space between the ligands and the metal within a **coordination sphere.**
- When the formula of a charged coordination entity is to be written without that of the counter ion, the charge is indicated outside the square brackets as a right superscript with the number before the sign.
  e.g. $[Co(CN)_6]^{3-}$, $[Cr(H_2O)_6]^{3+}$, etc.
- The charge of the cation(s) is balanced by the charge of the anion(s).

Note IUPAC, in 2004, recommends that ligands will be sorted alphabetically. Charge has no role in it.

2. Naming of Mononuclear Coordination Compounds

The names of coordination compounds are derived by following the principles of additive nomenclature, i.e., the groups that surround the central atom must be identified in the name.

The following rules are used while naming coordination compounds.

- The cation is named first in both positively and negatively charged coordination entities.
- The ligands are named in an alphabetical order before the name of the central atom/ion. (This procedure is reversed from writing formula).
- Names of the anionic ligands end in -'o', those of neutral and cationic ligands are the same except *aqua* for H_2O, ammine for NH_3, carbonyl for CO and nitrosyl for NO. These are placed within enclosing brackets ( ).

Examples of Unidentate Ligands

Name	Formula	Charges	Name of ligands
Neutral ligands			
Ammonia	NH_3	zero	ammine
Water	H_2O	zero	*aquo* or *aqua*
Phosphine	$\ddot{P}H_3$	zero	phosphine
Nitrogen oxide	NO	zero	nitrosyl
Carbon monoxide	CO	zero	carbonyl
Triphenyl phosphine	$(C_6H_5)_3\ddot{P}$	zero	triphenyl phosphine
Pyridine	$C_5H_5\ddot{N}$	zero	pyridine (py)
Negative ligands			
Halide ion	X^- (X = Cl, Br, I)	−1	halo or halido
Hydroxide ion	$:OH^-$	−1	hydroxo
Cyanide ion	$:CN^-$	−1	cyano
Oxide ion	O^{2-}	−2	oxo
Peroxide ion	O_2^{2-}	−2	peroxo
Carbonate ion	CO_3^{2-}	−2	carbonato
Sulphate ion	SO_4^{2-}	−2	sulphato
Nitrite ion	NO_2^-	−1	nitro or nitrito
Thiocyanate ion	SCN^-	−1	thiocyanato or isothiocyanato
Acetate ion	CH_3COO^-	−1	acetato
Sulphide ion	S^{2-}	−2	sulphido
Sulphite ion	SO_3^{2-}	−2	sulphito
Nitrate ion	NO_3^-	−1	nitrato
Amide ion	NH_2^-	−1	amido
Positive ligands			
Nitrosonium	NO^+	+1	nitrosonium
Nitronium	NO_2^+	+1	nitronium

- Prefixes mono, di, tri, etc., are used to indicate the number of the individual ligands in the coordination entity.
- When the names of the ligands include a numerical prefix, then the terms, *bis, tris, tetrakis* are used, the ligand to which they refer is placed in parentheses. e.g., $[NiCl_2(PPh_3)_2]$ is named as dichlorido*bis*(triphenylphosphine)nickel(II).
- Oxidation state of the metal in cation, anion or neutral coordination entity is indicated by Roman numeral in parenthesis.
- If the complex ion is a cation, the metal is named same as the element, e.g. Co in a complex cation is called **cobalt** and Pt is called **platinum**. If the complex ion is an anion, the name of the metal ends with the suffix—'ate', e.g. Co in a complex anion, $[Co(SCN)_4]^{2-}$ is called **cobaltate**. For some metals, the Latin names are used in the complex anions, e.g. ferrate for Fe.
- The neutral complex molecule is named similar to that of the complex cation.
- For naming ambidentate ligands, when a ligand can coordinate through more than one atom, then the point of attachment is indicated by putting the symbol of atom through which it coordinates, e.g.

(i) $[Pt(NH_3)_2Cl(NO_2)]$ is named as Diamminechloridonitrito-N-platinum(II)

(ii) $K_3[Cr(C_2O_4)_3]$ is named as Potassium trioxalatochromate(III)

(iii) $[CoCl_2(en)_2]Cl$ is named as Dichlorido*bis* (ethane-1,2-diamine)cobalt (III) chloride

(iv) $[Cr(NH_3)_3(H_2O)_3]Cl_3$ is named as Triamminetriaquachromium(III) chloride

(v) $[Co(H_2NCH_2CH_2NH_2)_3]_2(SO_4)_3$ is named as *tris*(ethane-1,2-diamine)cobalt(III) sulphate.

Example 1 **Write the formulae for the following coordination compounds.**

(i) Tetraamminediaquacobalt(III) chloride

(ii) Potassium tetracyanonickelate(II) **NCERT Intext**

Sol. (i) $\underbrace{\text{Tetraamminediaqua}}_{\text{Ligand}}\ \underbrace{\text{cobalt (III)}}_{\text{Metal}}\ \underbrace{\text{chloride}}_{\text{Counter ion}}$

$\overset{\text{III}}{[Co(NH_3)_4(H_2O)_2]}Cl_x$

To find the value of x, we have to find the charge on the complex.

$$\overset{III}{[Co(NH_3)_4(H_2O)_2]^{x+}}$$

$$\Rightarrow \quad +3 + 4 \times 0 + 2 \times 0 = x$$

$$x = +3$$

So, the formula of the complex is $[Co(NH_3)_4(H_2O)_2]Cl_3$

(ii) $\dfrac{\text{Potassium}}{\text{Counter ion}}\ \dfrac{\text{tetracyano}}{\text{Ligand}}\ \dfrac{\text{nickelate (II)}}{\text{Metal}}$

$K_x[\overset{II}{Ni}(CN)_4]$

To find the value of x, find the charge on the complex.

$[Ni(CN)_4]^{x-}$ (as K^+ is positive)

$$+2 + (-1) \times 4 = -x$$

$$-x = -2 \quad \text{or} \quad x = +2$$

So, the formula of the complex is $K_2[Ni(CN)_4]$

Example 2 **Write down the IUPAC names of the following coordination compounds.**

(i) $[Co(NH_3)_5Cl]Cl_2$ (ii) $K_2[PdCl_4]$ NCERT Intext

Sol. (i) $[Co(NH_3)_5Cl]Cl_2$

Let, the oxidation state of Co is x.

$$x + (0) \times 5 + (-1) \times 1 + (-1) \times 2 = 0$$

$$x + 0 - 3 = 0$$

$$x = +3$$

So, the name of the complex is pentaamminechloridocobalt(III) chloride.

(ii) $K_2[PdCl_4]$

Let the oxidation state of Pd is x.

$$(+1)\,2 + x + (-1)\,4 = 0$$

$$2 + x - 4 = 0$$

$$\Rightarrow \quad x = +2$$

So, the name of the complex is potassium tetrachloridopalladate(II).

5.5 Isomerism in Coordination Compounds

Two or more compounds having the same molecular formula but different arrangement of atoms are said to exhibit **isomerism**. They differ in one or more physical or chemical properties.

Isomerism in coordination compounds are of two types. These are as follows

Isomerism

Structural isomerism
- Linkage isomerism
- Coordination isomerism
- Ionisation isomerism
- Solvate isomerism

Stereoisomerism
- Geometrical isomerism
- Optical isomerism

1. Structural Isomerism

The coordination compounds having same chemical formula but different structural arrangement are known as **structural isomers**. It is further subdivided into following types.

Linkage Isomerism

It is shown by the coordination compounds containing ambidentate ligand such as NO_2, SCN^-, etc. SCN^- can bind to a metal through N and S as *M*—NCS and *M*—SCN, respectively. Similarly, NO_2 can bind either by N or by O. e.g.

$$\underset{\text{Yellow}}{[Co(NH_3)_3(NO_2)]Cl_2} \text{ and } \underset{\text{Red}}{[Co(NH_3)_3ONO]Cl_2}.$$

Coordination Isomerism

It arises from the interchange of ligands between cationic and anionic entities of different metal ions present in a complex. e.g. $[Co(NH_3)_6]^{3+}[Cr(CN)_6]^{3-}$ in which the NH_3 ligands are bound to Co^{3+} and the CN^- ligand to Cr^{3+} and in its coordination isomer $[Cr(NH_3)_6]^{3+}[Co(CN)_6]^{3-}$, the NH_3 ligands are bound to Cr^{3+} and CN^- ligands to Co^{3+}. Similarly, $[Pt(NH_3)_4]^{2+}[PtCl_4]^{2-}$ shows coordination isomerism.

Ionisation Isomerism

It arises when compounds give different ions in the solution although they have same composition. It arises when the counter ion in a complex salt is itself a potential ligand and can displace a ligand which can then become the counter ion. e.g.

$$\underset{\text{(Red)}}{[Co(NH_3)_5SO_4]Br} \text{ and } \underset{\text{(Violet)}}{[Co(NH_3)_5Br]SO_4}$$

Hydrate Isomerism or Solvate Isomerism

This type of isomerism arises in case where water is involved as a solvent. Solvate isomers differ by whether or not a solvent molecule is directly bonded to the metal ion or merely present as free solvent molecules in the crystal lattice. e.g., *aqua* complex $[Cr(H_2O)_6]Cl_3$ (violet) and its solvate isomer $[Cr(H_2O)_5Cl]Cl_2 \cdot H_2O$ (grey-green).

2. Stereoisomerism

Coordination compounds having same molecular as well as structural formulae but different arrangement in space in the polyhedra are called **stereoisomers**. This phenomenon is called **stereoisomerism**. It is further subdivided into two types.

Geometrical Isomerism

Heteroleptic complexes with coordination numbers 4 and 6 show this type of isomerism. It arises due to the difference in the geometrical arrangement of the ligands around the central metal ion.

When same ligands occupy the adjacent position in the polyhedra, it is known as ***cis*-isomer**, whereas when same ligands occupy the opposite position in the polyhedra, it is known as ***trans*-isomer**.

(i) Isomerism in Complexes with Coordination Number 4.

- **Square planar complexes** of $[MX_4]$, $[MX_3L]$, $[MXL_3]$ type (where X and L are unidentate ligands) do not show geometrical isomerism, since all the possible spatial arrangement of four ligands around the central metal atom is the same.
- **Type $[MX_2L_2]$** A square planar complex of the type $[MX_2L_2]$ (X and L are unidentate) shows these two geometrical isomers, e.g.

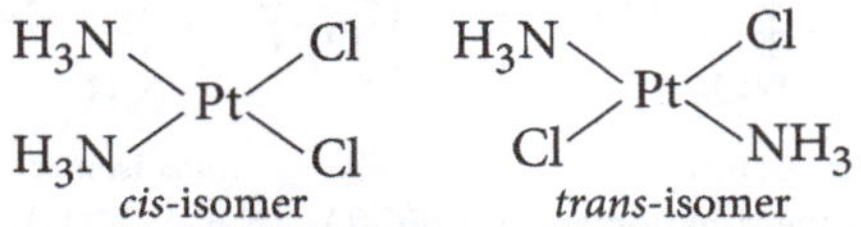

cis-isomer *trans*-isomer
Geometrical isomers of $[Pt(NH_3)_2Cl_2]$

Note *cis*-isomer of $[Pt(NH_3)_2Cl_2]$ is also known as ***cis*-platin**, which is used as an anticancer drug in the chemotherapy process of cancer treatment.

- **Type $[MABXL]$** Square planar complex of this type (A, B, X and L are unidentate) shows three isomers.

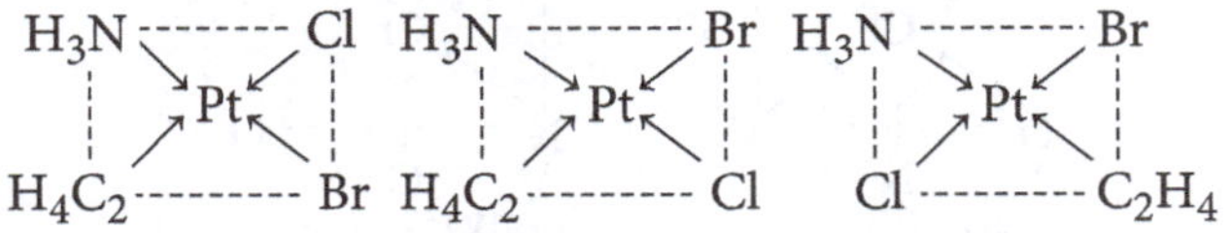

Geometrical isomers of $[Pt(NH_3)(C_2H_4)BrCl]$

- **Type $[MA_2XL]$**

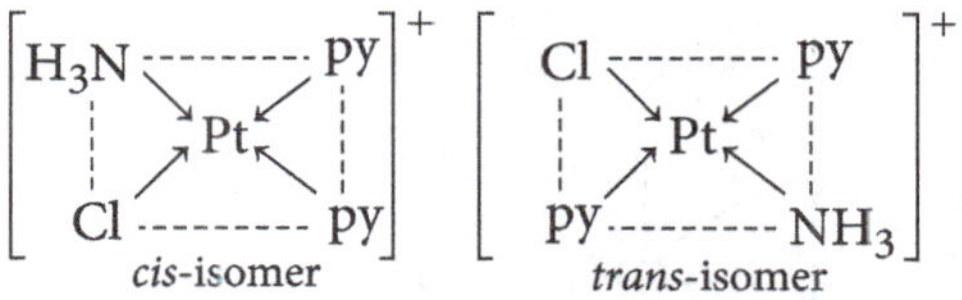

cis-isomer *trans*-isomer
Geometrical isomers of $[Pt(py)_2(NH_3)Cl]^+$

- **Type $[M(ab)_2]$** where, (ab) is an asymmetrical bidentate ligand having two different donor atoms. e.g. Glycine, $NH_2—CH_2—COO^-$ which has N and O atoms as donor atoms.

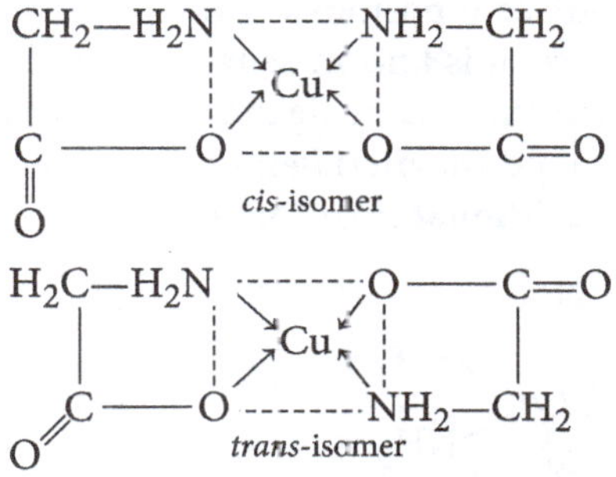

cis-isomer
trans-isomer
cis-and *trans*-isomers of $[Cu(gly)_2]$

> **TEACHER'S TIP**
> **Tetrahedral complex** does not show geometrical isomerism because the relative positions of unidentate ligands attached to the central metal atom are the same with respect to each other.

(ii) Isomerism in Complexes with Coordination Number 6

- **Octahedral complexes** of $[MX_6]$, $[MX_5L]$ and $[M(aa)_3]$ type do not exhibit geometrical isomerism.
- **Type $[MX_2L_4]$** *cis-trans* isomerism is possible in octahedral complexes of the type $[MX_2L_4]$ in which two ligands X may be oriented *cis* or *trans* to each other.

e.g.

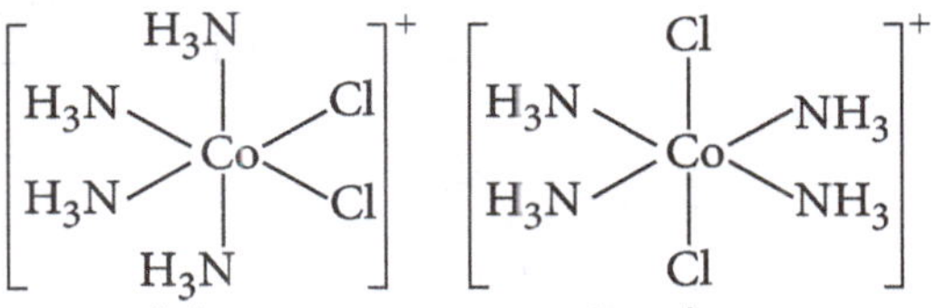

cis-isomer *trans*-isomer
Geometrical isomers of $[Co(NH_3)_4Cl_2]^+$

• **Type [$MAXL_4$]**

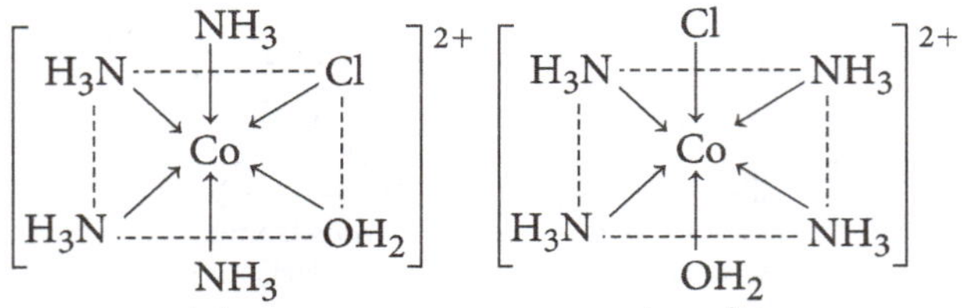

cis-isomer *trans*-isomer

Geometrical isomers of $[Co(NH_3)_4(H_2O)Cl]^{2+}$

• **Type [MX_3L_3]** Octahedral coordination entities of the type [MX_3L_3] shows geometrical isomerism. When three donor atoms of same ligands are occupying adjacent positions at the corners of an octahedral face, it is known as **facial (*fac*) isomer**, whereas when three same ligands are occupying positions around the meridian of the octahedron, it is known as **meridional (*mer*) isomer**.

e.g.

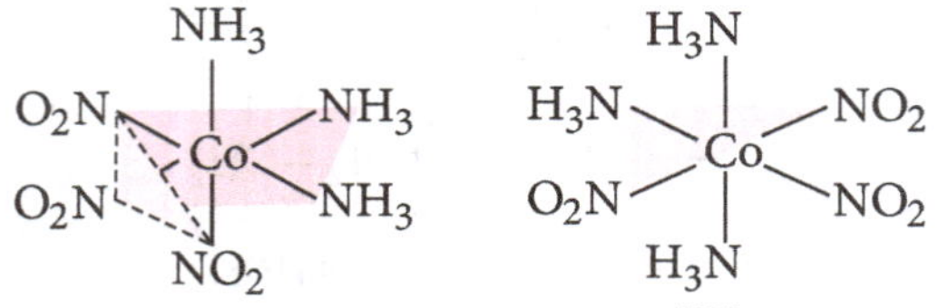

fac- *mer-*

Facial *(fac)* and meridional *(mer)* isomers of $[Co(NH_3)_3(NO_2)_3]$

Hence, these isomers differ in one or more physical or chemical properties.

• **Type [$MA_2X_2L_2$]**

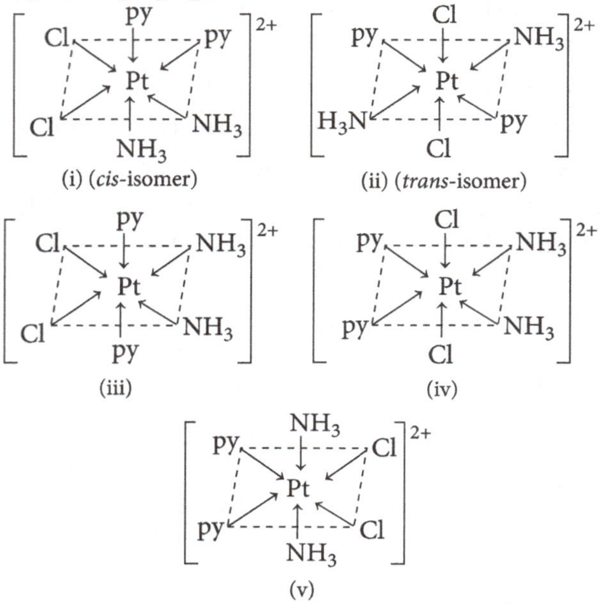

Five geometrical isomers of $[Pt(NH_3)_2(py)_2Cl_2]^{2+}$

• **Type [*MABCDXL*]** There is only one example of this type of complex where all the six monodentate ligands are different.
e.g. $[Pt(py)NH_3(NO_2)Cl(Br)(I)]^+$.

• The geometrical isomer of this type of complex may be written by fixing a ligand at one position and then placing the other ligands *trans* to it. Theoretically, 15 geometrical isomers are possible for this complex compound. But only three of them have been isolated.

• **Type [$M(aa)_2X_2$]**

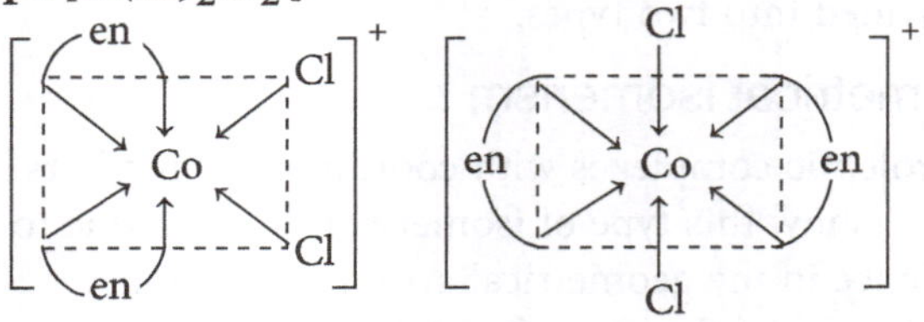

cis-isomer *trans*-isomer

cis-and *trans*-isomers of $[Co(en)_2Cl_2]^+$ ion

• **Type [$M(aa)_2XL$]**

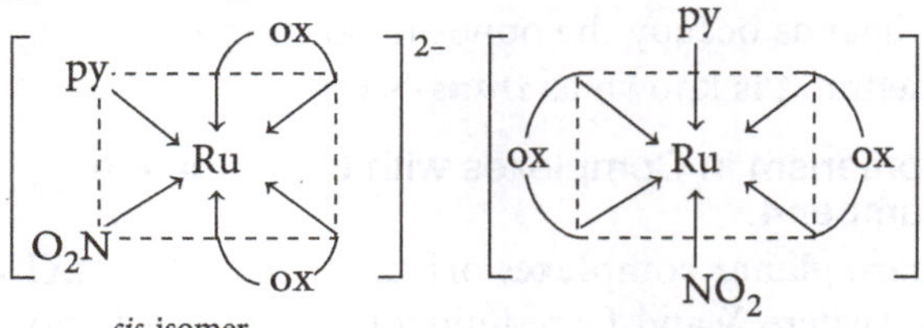

cis-isomer *trans*-isomer

Geometrical isomers of $[Ru(C_2O_4)_2py(NO_2)]^{2-}$

• **Type [$M(aa)X_2L_2$]**

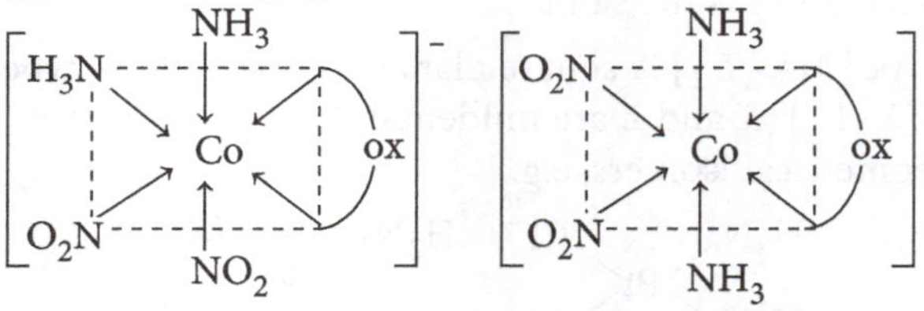

cis-isomer *trans*-isomer

Geometrical isomers of $[Co(C_2O_4)(NH_3)_2(NO_2)_2]^-$

• **Type [$M(ab)_3$]** where, (*ab*) is an unsymmetrical bidentate ligand in which (*a*) and (*b*) are two different donor atoms, e.g. $[Cr(gly)_3]$.

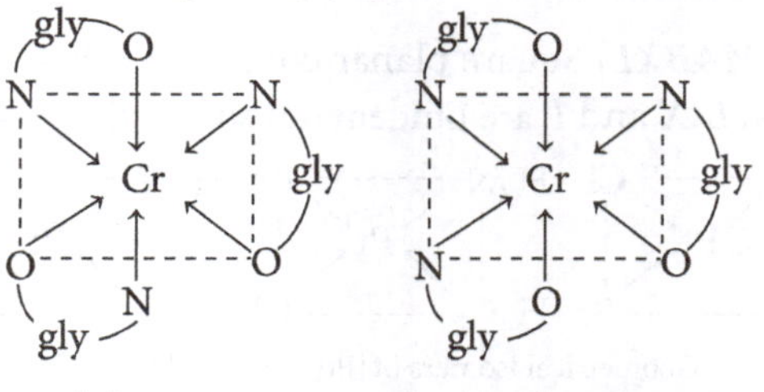

cis-isomer *trans*-isomer

cis- and *trans*- isomers of $[Cr(gly)_3]$

Optical Isomerism

- The compounds which do not have a plane of symmetry show optical isomerism. The **optically active** isomers have non-superimposable mirror images or they cannot be superimposed on one another.
- The molecules or ions which cannot be superimposed are called **chiral.**
- The two forms called *dextro* (*d*) or *laevo* (*l*), depending upon the direction they rotate the plane of polarised light in a polarimeter and are called **enantiomers.**
- The isomer which rotates the plane of polarised light to the right is called *dextro* (*d*) rotatory, whereas the isomer which rotates the plane of polarised light to the left is called *laevo* (*l*) rotatory.

  An equimolar mixture of *dextro* (*d*) and *laevo* (*l*) rotatory isomers is called **racemic mixture.**

(i) Optical Isomerism in Complexes with Coordination Number 4

- **Tetrahedral complexes** of $[MX_4]$ and $[MX_3L]$ type do not show optical isomerism because all possible arrangements of ligands around the central metal atom are exactly equivalent.
- **In [*MABXL*]** type of tetrahedral complexes where the central metal atom *M* is surrounded by four different ligands are expected to produce a pair of enantiomers. For example, $[As(CH_3)(C_2H_5)(S)(C_6H_5COO)]^{2-}$ ion exists in two optical isomers as it has a chiral centre and has no plane of symmetry.

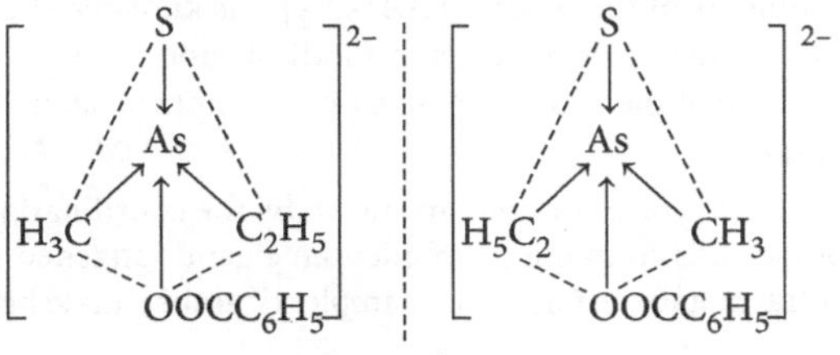

Mirror plane

Optical isomers of $[As(CH_3)(C_2H_5)S(C_6H_5COO)]^{2-}$

- **Square planar complexes** Square planar complexes do not show optical isomerism as they have all the four ligands and the central metal atom in the same plane and hence have a plane or axis of symmetry. Thus, these coordination compounds are optically inactive.

(ii) Optical Isomerism in Coordination Number 6

- Octahedral complexes of $[MX_4L_2]$ and $[MX_3L_3]$ type exist in *cis*-and *trans* and *fac*- and *mer*- isomers. These isomers are optically inactive due to presence of symmetry and hence do not show optical isomerism.
- **Type $[MA_2X_2L_2]$**

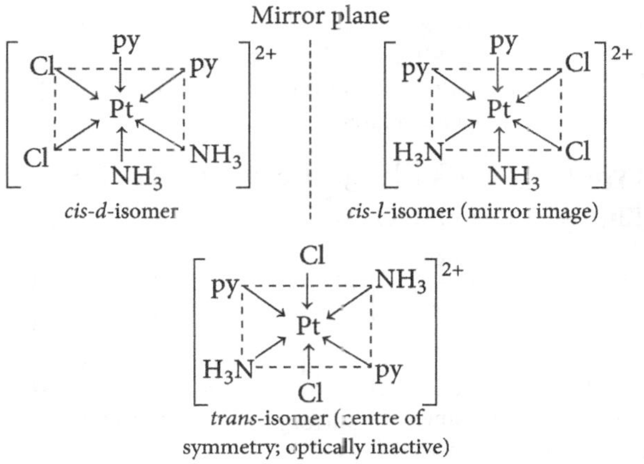

Optical isomers of $[Pt(NH_3)_2Cl_2(py)_2]^{2+}$

- **Type [*MABCDXL*]** Each of the 15 geometrical isomers of $[Pt(py)(NH_3)(NO_2)ClBrI]^+$ complex exists in optically active *d*-and *l*-forms, giving a total of 30 optically active isomers.

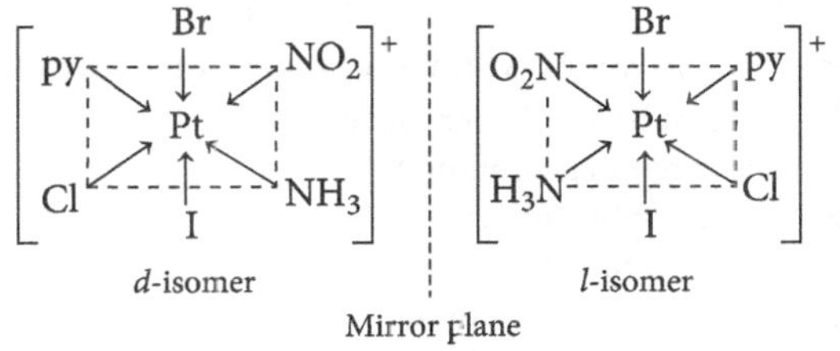

Optical isomers of $[Pt(NO_2)(NH_3)ClBrIpy]^+$

- **Type $[M(aa)_3]$**, e.g. $[Co(en)_3]^{3+}$, $[Cr(ox)_3]^{3-}$.

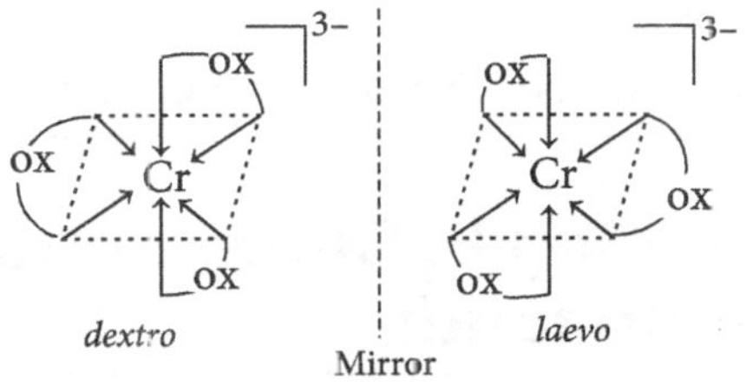

Optical isomers of $[Cr(ox)_3]^{3-}$

- **Type** $[M(aa)_2X_2]$, e.g. *cis*-$[Co(en)_2Cl_2]^+$, *cis*-$[Pt(en)_2Cl_2]^+$, *cis*-$[Cr(ox)_2Cl_2]^{3-}$.

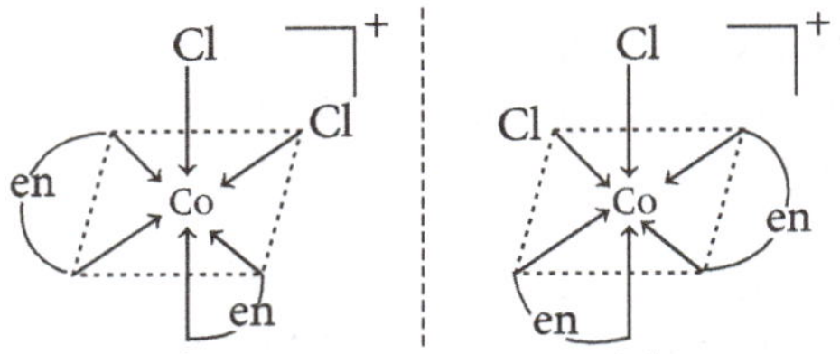

cis-dextro Mirror *cis-laevo*

Optical isomers of $[Co(en)_2Cl_2]^+$

- **Type** $[M(aa)_2XY]$, e.g. $[Co(en)_2(NH_3)(Cl)]^{2+}$, $[Rh(C_2O_4)_2(py)(NO_2)]^{2-}$

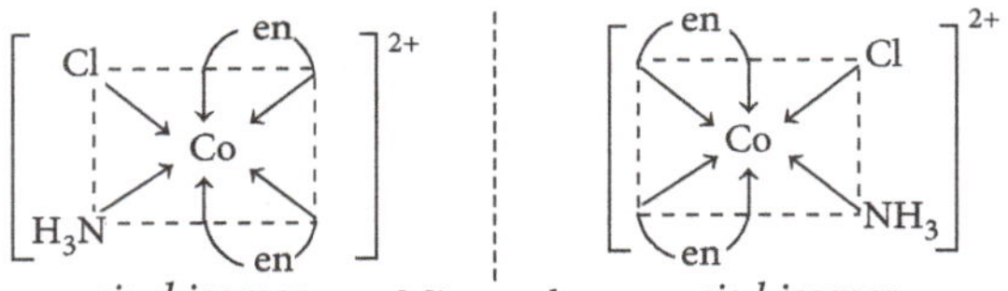

cis-d-isomer (optically active) Mirror plane *cis-l*-isomer

Optical isomers of $[Co(en)_2(NH_3)(Cl)]^{2+}$

- **Type** $[M(aa)X_2Y_2]$, e.g. $[Co(en)(NH_3)_2Cl_2]^+$

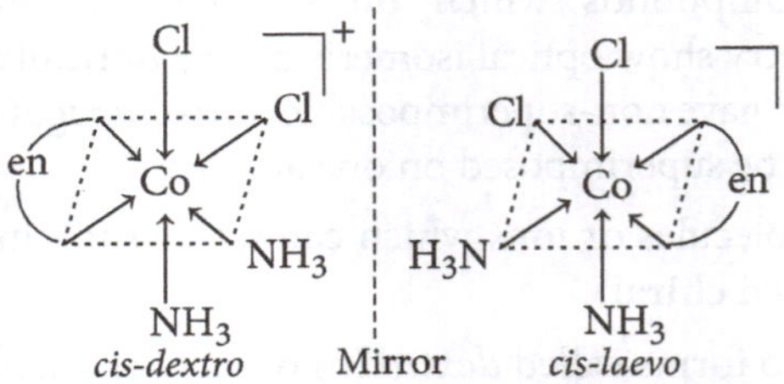

cis-dextro Mirror *cis-laevo*

Optical isomers of $[Co(NH_3)_2(en)Cl_2]^+$

- **Type** $[M(aa)_3]$ Each of *cis*- and *trans*-isomers of $[Cr(gly)_3]$ is optically active and hence each gives a pair of optical isomers (*d*- and *l*- forms)

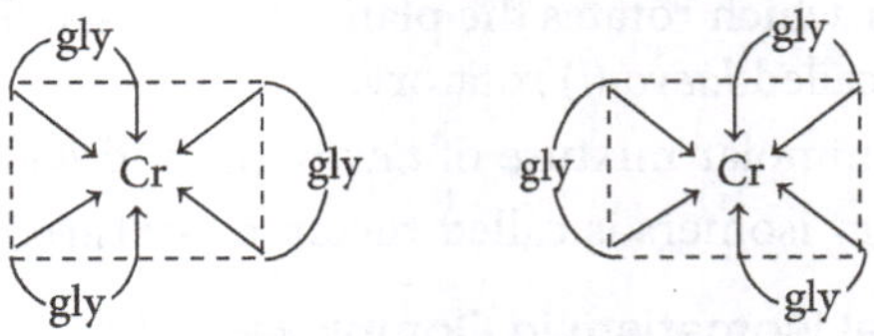

cis-or *trans d*-isomer *cis*-or *trans l*-isomer

d- and *l*-optical isomers of *cis*- and *trans*- forms of $[Cr(gly)_3]$

Quick Test 2

1. Write the IUPAC names of the following coordination entities.
   (i) $[Co(H_2O)(CN)(en)_2]^{2+}$ (ii) $[CoBr_2(en)_2]^+$
   (iii) $[PtCl_4]^{2-}$ (iv) $K[Co(CO)_4]$
2. Using IUPAC norms, write the formulae for the following.
   (i) Potassium trioxalatochromate(III)
   (ii) Hexaammineplatinum(IV)
   (iii) Tetrabromidocuprate(II)
   (iv) Pentaamminenitrito-N-cobalt(III) NCERT
3. Write the IUPAC name of the following
   (i) $[Co(NH_3)_5(ONO)]^{2+}$
   (ii) $K_2[NiCl_3]$ CBSE 2023
4. Using IUPAC norms, write the systematic names of the following.
   (i) $[Co(NH_3)_6]Cl_3$ (ii) $[Pt(NH_3)_2Cl(NH_2CH_3)]Cl$
   (iii) $[Ti(H_2O)_6]^{3+}$ NCERT
5. Write the IUPAC name of the complex $[Cr(NH_3)_4Cl_2]^+$. What type of isomerism does it exhibit?
6. Draw all the isomers (geometrical and optical) of
   (i) $[CoCl_2(en)_2]^+$ (ii) $[Co(NH_3)Cl(en)_2]^{2+}$
   (iii) $[Co(NH_3)_2Cl_2(en)]^+$ NCERT
7. A complex of the type $[M(AA)_2X_2]^{n+}$ is known to be optically active. What does this indicate about the structure of the complex? Give one example of such complex. NCERT Exemplar
8. Write the type of isomerism shown by the coordination compounds containing ambidentate ligands attached to a central metal ion. Give two examples of ambidentate ligands.

For Solutions, See QR Code on Pg. 182

5.6 Bonding in Coordination Compounds

Werner was the first to explain the nature of bonding in coordination compounds but his theory was not able to answer the basic questions like :

- Why only some elements can form coordination compounds?
- Why the directional properties are exhibited by the bonds in coordination compounds?
- Why magnetic and optical properties are characteristic for coordination compounds?

Many approaches have been put forth to explain the nature of bonding in coordination compounds. These are Valence Bond Theory (VBT), Crystal Field Theory (CFT), Ligand Field Theory (LFT) and Molecular Orbital Theory (MOT).

Valence Bond Theory

This theory was put forward by **L. Pauling** in 1930 to explain the shapes of the complexes.

The main points of this theory are as follows

- Central atom/ion makes a required number of empty orbitals available for the formation of coordinate bonds with suitable orbitals of the ligand.
- These orbitals undergo hybridisation by using $(n-1)d$, ns, np or ns, np, nd orbitals of central atom/ion under the influence of ligands to give same number of hybrid orbitals of equal energy and definite geometry.

Hybridisation and Geometry of Complexes

Coordination number	Type of hybridisation	Distribution of hybrid orbitals in space
4	sp^3	Tetrahedral
4	dsp^2	Square planar
5	sp^3d	Trigonal bipyramidal
6	sp^3d^2	Octahedral
6	d^2sp^3	Octahedral

- The empty hybrid orbitals of the central metal atom or ion overlap with the filled orbitals of the ligands containing the lone pair of electrons. In this way, a metal-ligand coordinate bond is formed.
- The inner orbital (low spin) or the outer orbital (high spin) complexes are formed depending upon whether the *d*-orbitals of inner shell or *d*-orbitals of outer shell are used in hybridisation.
- The complex will be **diamagnetic** if the electrons are paired whereas, if unpaired electrons are present then the complex will be **paramagnetic**.
- Ligands must have one sigma orbital containing lone pair of electrons.

Applications of Valence Bond Theory

It is usually possible to predict the geometry of a complex from the knowledge of its magnetic behaviour on the basis of the valence bond theory.

Octahedral Complexes

Octahedral complexes involve one *s*, three *p* and two *d*-orbitals. Let us take some examples to explain octahedral complexes.

(i) **$[Co(NH_3)_6]^{3+}$** In this complex, oxidation state of cobalt is +3 and electronic configuration of Co^{3+} ion is $[Ar]3d^6$.

Its hybridisation scheme can be shown as

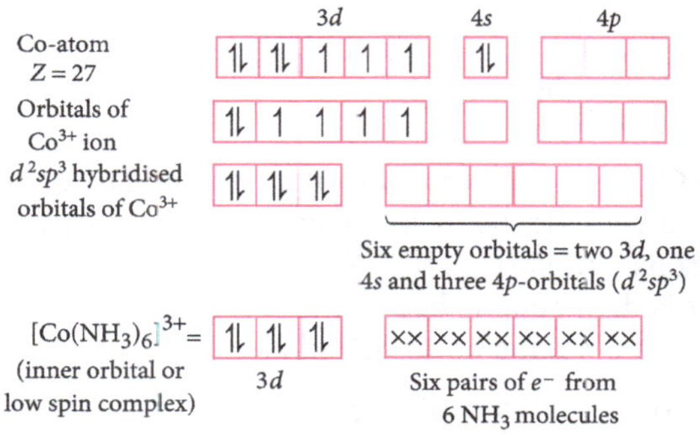

Six pairs of electrons, one from each NH_3 molecule, occupy the six hybrid orbitals. Thus, complex has octahedral (d^2sp^3) geometry and is diamagnetic because of the absence of unpaired electrons.

In this complex, inner *d*-orbital (3*d*) is used in hybridisation, thus, it is called an **inner orbital** or **low spin** or **spin paired** complex.

(ii) **$[CoF_6]^{3-}$** In this complex outer orbital 4*d* is used in hybridisation. Thus, it is called **outer orbital** or **high spin** or **spin free complex**.

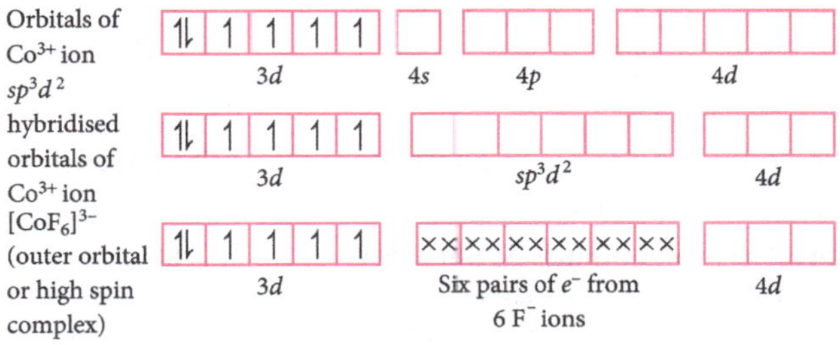

Six pairs of electrons, one from each F^- ion occupy the six hybrid orbitals. Thus, the complex has octahedral geometry (sp^3d^2) and is paramagnetic because of the presence of four unpaired electrons.

Tetrahedral Complexes

In tetrahedral complexes, one *s* and three *p*-orbitals are hybridised to form four equivalent orbitals oriented tetrahedrally. Let us take an example to explain tetrahedral complexes.

$[NiCl_4]^{2-}$ In this complex ion, oxidation state of Ni is +2 and its valence shell configuration is $[Ar]3d^8$.

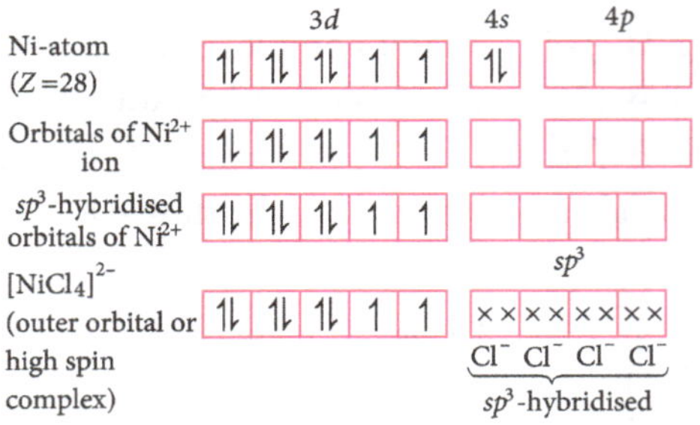

Each Cl^- ion donates a pair of electrons. The compound is paramagnetic, because it contains two unpaired electrons. Similarly, $[Ni(CO)_4]$ has tetrahedral geometry but it is diamagnetic because nickel is in zero oxidation state and contains no unpaired electrons.

Square Planar Complexes

Square planar complexes involve one *d*, one *s* and two *p*-orbitals for bonding. The hybridisation involved is dsp^2. Let us take an example to understand it clearly, e.g. $[Ni(CN)_4]^{2-}$ has square planar shape.

Ni-atom (ground state) = $[Ar]3d^8 4s^2 4p^0$

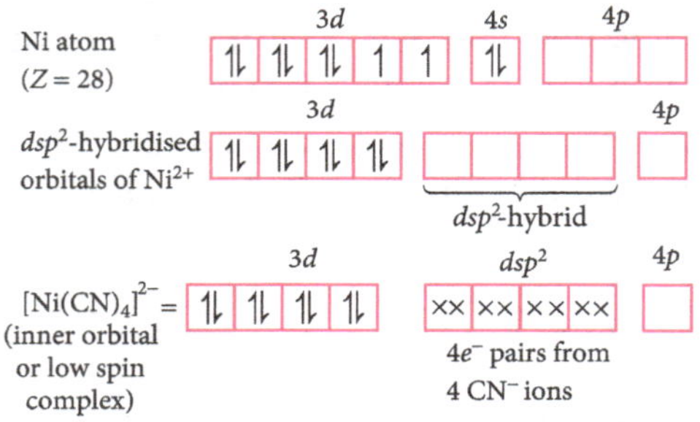

The compound is diamagnetic because of the absence of unpaired electrons.

Note The hybrid orbitals do not actually exist. Infact, hybridisation is a mathematical manipulation of wave equation for the atomic orbitals involved.

Inner Orbital and Outer Orbital Complexes

Inner orbital octahedral complexes	Outer orbital octahedral complexes
• These are formed by d^2sp^3 hybridisation involving two $(n-1)d$ orbitals (i.e., $(n-1)d_{z^2}$ and $(n-1)d_{x^2-y^2}$ orbitals), one *ns* and three *np* orbitals.	• These are formed by sp^3d^2 hybridisation involving one *ns*, three *np* and two *nd* orbitals (i.e. nd_{z^2} and $nd_{x^2-y^2}$ orbitals).
• These complexes have comparatively lesser number of unpaired electrons and hence are called low spin or spin paired octahedral complexes.	• These complexes have comparatively greater number of unpaired electrons and hence are called high spin or spin free octahedral complexes.
• These are given by strong field ligands.	• These are given by weak field ligands.

Magnetic Properties of Coordination Compounds

The magnetic moment of coordination compounds can be measured by the magnetic susceptibility experiments. The results can be used to obtain information about the number of unpaired electrons and hence structures of metal complexes.

Some complications revealed on critical study of magnetic data of coordination compounds of metals of the first transition series which are as follows.

- For metal ions upto three electrons in *d*-orbital [Ti^{3+} (d^1), V^{3+} (d^2), Cr^{3+} (d^3)], two vacant *d*-orbitals are available for octahedral hybridisation using 4*s* and 4*p*-orbitals. The magnetic behaviour of these free ions and their coordination entities are similar.
- When more than three 3*d* electrons are present, the required pair of 3*d* orbitals for octahedral hybridisation are not directly available because of Hund's rule. e.g. For d^4 (Cr^{2+}, Mn^{3+}), d^5(Mn^{2+}, Fe^{3+}), d^6(Fe^{2+}, Co^{3+}) cases, a vacant pair of *d*-orbitals result only by pairing of 3*d* electrons which leaves two, one and zero unpaired electrons, respectively.
- The magnetic data agree with maximum spin pairing in many cases especially with coordination compound containing d^6 ions. However, with species containing d^4 and d^5 ions there are complications. Some examples are given below.
  - $[Mn(CN)_6]^{3-}$ has magnetic moment of two unpaired electrons, while $[MnCl_6]^{3-}$ has a paramagnetic moment of four unpaired electrons.
  - $[Fe(CN)_6]^{3-}$ has paramagnetic moment of one unpaired electron, while $[FeF_6]^{3-}$ has a paramagnetic moment of five unpaired electrons.
  - $[CoF_6]^{3-}$ is paramagnetic due to the presence of four unpaired electrons, while $[Co(C_2O_4)_3]^{3-}$ is diamagnetic.

This is explained by VBT in terms of formation of inner orbital (d^2sp^3-hybridisation) and outer orbital (sp^3d^2-hybridisation) coordination entities. $[Mn(CN)_6]^{3-}$, $[Fe(CN)_6]^{3-}$ and $[Co(C_2O_4)_3]^{3-}$ are inner orbital complexes involving d^2sp^3 hybridisation, the former two complexes are paramagnetic and the latter diamagnetic, while $[MnCl_6]^{3-}$, $[FeF_6]^{3-}$ and $[CoF_6]^{3-}$ are outer orbital complex involving sp^3d^2-hybridisation and are paramagnetic.

Magnetic moment (μ) of a substance containing '*n*' unpaired electrons is approximately given by the following expression $\mu = \sqrt{n(n+2)}$ **BM.**

BM (Bohr Magneton) is the unit of magnetic moment.

Limitations of VBT

Although valence bond theory is advantageous to explain the formation, structures and magnetic properties of coordination compounds but it comes with few limitations, listed as follows.

- It is based on a number of assumptions and provides only qualitative explanations for complexes.
- It does not distinguish between weak and strong ligands.
- It does not give quantitative interpretations of magnetic data.
- It does not give a quantitative interpretation of the thermodynamic or kinetic stabilities of coordination compounds.
- It fails to explain relative energies of different shapes.
- It does not explain the colour and spectral properties of coordination compounds.
- It fails to predict the exact tetrahedral and square planar structures of 4-coordinate complexes.
- It does not take into account the splitting of d-energy levels.

Description of Some Important Metal Complexes using VBT

Ion/Complex	Central metal ion	Configuration of metal ion	Hybridisation of metal ion involved	Geometry of the complex	Number of unpaired electrons	Magnetic behaviour
$[Ti(H_2O)_6)]^{3+}$	Ti^{3+}	d^1	d^2sp^3	Octahedral	1	Paramagnetic
$[V(H_2O)_6]^{3+}$	V^{3+}	d^2	d^2sp^3	Octahedral	2	Paramagnetic
$[Cr(H_2O)_6]^{3+}$	Cr^{3+}	d^3	d^2sp^3	Octahedral	3	Paramagnetic
$[Cr(NH_3)_6]^{3+}$	Cr^{3+}	d^3	d^2sp^3	Octahedral	3	Paramagnetic
$[MnF_6]^{3-}$	Mn^{3+}	d^4	sp^3d^2	Octahedral	4	Paramagnetic
$[Mn(CN)_6]^{3-}$	Mn^{3+}	d^4	d^2sp^3	Octahedral	2	Paramagnetic
$[MnCl_4]^{2-}$	Mn^{2+}	d^5	sp^3	Tetrahedral	5	Paramagnetic
$[FeF_6]^{3-}$	Fe^{3+}	d^5	sp^3d^2	Octahedral	5	Paramagnetic
$[Fe(H_2O)_6]^{3+}$	Fe^{3+}	d^5	sp^3d^2	Octahedral	5	Paramagnetic
$[Fe(CN)_6]^{3-}$	Fe^{3+}	d^5	d^2sp^3	Octahedral	1	Paramagnetic
$[Fe(CN)_6]^{4-}$	Fe^{2+}	d^6	d^2sp^3	Octahedral	0	Diamagnetic
$[FeCl_4]^{2-}$	Fe^{2+}	d^6	sp^3	Tetrahedral	4	Paramagnetic
$[Co(NH_3)_6]^{3+}$	Co^{3+}	d^6	d^2sp^3	Octahedral	0	Diamagnetic
$[CoF_6]^{3-}$	Co^{3+}	d^6	sp^3d^2	Octahedral	4	Paramagnetic
$[Ni(CO)_4]$	Ni	$3d^84s^2$	sp^3	Tetrahedral	0	Diamagnetic
$[Ni(CN)_4]^{2-}$	Ni^{2+}	d^8	dsp^2	Square planar	0	Diamagnetic
$[NiCl_4]^{2-}$	Ni^{2+}	d^8	sp^3	Tetrahedral	2	Paramagnetic
$[Ni(H_2O)_6]^{2+}$	Ni^{2+}	d^8	sp^3d^2	Octahedral	2	Paramagnetic
$[CuCl_4]^{2+}$	Cu^{2+}	d^9	sp^3	Tetrahedral	1	Paramagnetic
$[Zn(NH_3)_4]^{2+}$	Zn^{2+}	d^{10}	sp^3	Tetrahedral	0	Diamagnetic
$[Pt(NH_3)Cl_2]$	Pt^{2+}	d^8	dsp^2	Square planar	0	Diamagnetic

Crystal Field Theory (CFT)

CFT is an electrostatic model which considers the metal-ligand bond to be ionic arising purely from electrostatic interactions between the metal ion and the ligand.

The main points of this theory are as follows

- The transition metal ion is surrounded by the ligands with lone pairs of electrons and the complex is a combination of central metal ion surrounded by other ions or molecules or dipoles, e.g. ligands.
- All types of ligands are regarded as point charges in case of anions and as point dipoles in case of neutral molecules.
- The interactions between the metal ion and the negative ends of anion (or ion dipoles) is purely electrostatic, i.e., the bond between the metal and ligand is considered to be 100% ionic.
- The ligands surrounding the metal ion produce electrical field and this electrical field influences the energies of the orbitals of central metal ion, particularly *d*-orbitals.
- In the case of free metal ion, all five *d*-orbitals have the same energy. Orbitals having the same energies are called **degenerate orbitals**.
- The five degenerate *d*-orbitals of the metal ion split into different sets of orbital having different energies in the presence of electrical field of ligands. This is called **crystal field splitting**.
- The number of ligands and their arrangement (geometry) around the central metal ion will have different effect on the relative energies of the five *d*-orbitals. In simple words, the crystals field splitting will be different in different structures having different coordination numbers.
- The magnetic properties, spectra and preference for particular geometry can be explained in terms of splitting of *d*-orbitals in different crystal fields.

Crystal Field Splitting in Octahedral Coordination Entities

In an octahedral coordination entity with six ligands surrounding the metal atom/ion, there will be repulsion between the electrons in metal *d*-orbitals and the electrons (or negative charges) of the ligands.

Such a repulsion is more when the metal *d*-orbital is directed towards the ligand than when it is away from the ligand. Thus,

- the $d_{x^2-y^2}$ and d_{z^2} orbitals which point towards the axes along the direction of the ligand will experience more repulsion and will be raised in energy; and
- the d_{xy}, d_{xz} and d_{yz} orbitals which are directed between the axes will be lowered in energy relative to the average energy in the spherical crystal field.

Thus, the degeneracy of the *d*-orbitals has been removed due to ligand electron-metal electron repulsions in the octahedral complex to yield three orbitals of lower energy, t_{2g} set and two orbitals of higher energy, e_g set. This splitting of the degenerate levels due to the presence of ligands in a definite geometry is termed as crystal field splitting.

The difference of energy between the two sets of degenerate orbitals as a result of crystal field splitting is known as **Crystal Field Stabilisation Energy (CFSE)**, it is denoted by Δ_o (the subscript *o* is for octahedral).

Thus, the energy of the two e_g orbitals will increase by (3/5) Δ_o and that of the three t_{2g} will decrease by (2/5) Δ_o. The splitting of *d*-orbitals in an octahedral crystal field can be seen in following diagram.

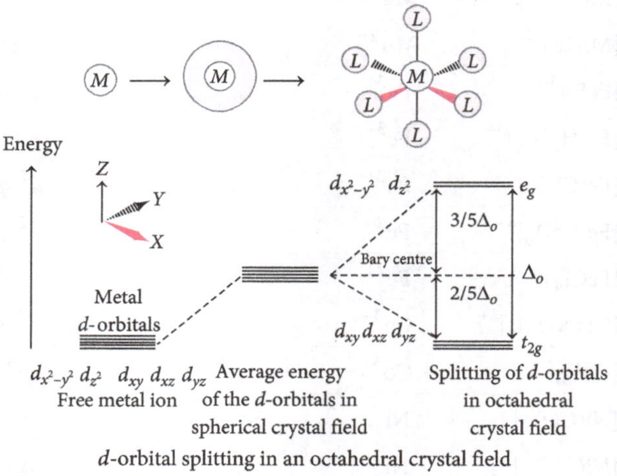

d-orbital splitting in an octahedral crystal field

Here, CFSE can be calculated as

$$\text{CFSE} = [-0.4x + 0.6y]\Delta_o$$

where, Δ_o = CFSE in octahedral complex

x = number of electrons in t_{2g} orbitals

y = number of electrons in e_g orbitals.

Spectrochemical Series

- The crystal field splitting, Δ_o, depends upon the field produced by the ligand and charge on the metal ion.
- Some ligands are able to produce strong fields in which case, the splitting will be large, whereas others produce weak fields and consequently result in small splitting of *d*-orbitals.
- So, ligands can be arranged in a series in the order of increasing field strength. This series is known as **spectrochemical series**.

  e.g. $I^- < Br^- < SCN^- < Cl^- < S^{2-} < F^- < OH^- < C_2O_4^{2-} < H_2O < NCS^- < EDTA^{4-} < NH_3 < en < CN^- < CO$
- It is an experimentally determined series, based on the absorption of light by complexes with different ligands.

Let us assign electrons in the *d*-orbitals of metal ion in octahedral coordination entities.

- The single *d*-electron of metal ion occupies one of the lower energy t_{2g}-orbitals.
- In d^2 and d^3 coordination entities, the *d*-electrons occupy the single t_{2g}-orbitals in accordance with the Hund's rule.
- For d^4 ions, two possible patterns of electron distribution arise:
  - the fourth electron could either enter the t_{2g} level and pair with an existing electron, or
  - it could avoid paying the price of the pairing energy by occupying the e_g level.

These possibilities depends on the relative magnitude of the crystal field splitting, Δ_o and the pairing energy, *P* (*P* represents the energy required for electron pairing in a single orbital).

The two options are given below

- If $\Delta_o < P$, the fourth electron enters one of the e_g orbitals giving the configuration $t_{2g}^3 e_g^1$. Ligands for which $\Delta_o < P$ are known as **weak field ligands** and form **high spin complexes**.
- If $\Delta_o > P$, it becomes more energetically favourable for the fourth electron to occupy t_{2g} orbital with configuration $t_{2g}^4 e_g^0$. Ligands which produce this effect are known as **strong field ligands** and form **low spin complexes**.

  Calculations show that d^4 to d^7 coordination entities are more stable for strong field as compared to weak field cases.

Crystal Field Splitting in Tetrahedral Coordination Entities

In tetrahedral coordination entity formation, the *d*-orbital splitting is inverted and is smaller as compared to the octahedral field splitting. It can be easily illustrated from the given figure.

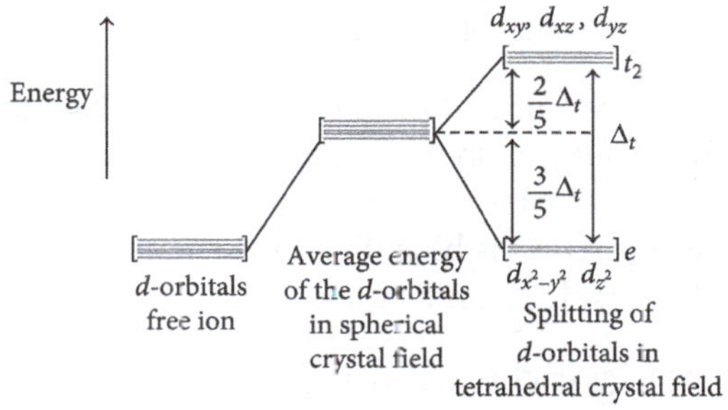

d-orbital splitting in a tetrahedral crystal field

Here, CFSE can be calculated as

$$\text{CFSE} = [-0.6x + 0.4y]\Delta_t$$

where, Δ_t = CFSE in tetrahedral complex

x = number of electrons in *e*-orbitals

y = number of electrons in t_2-orbitals.

For the same metal, the same ligands and metal-ligand distances, it can be shown that $\Delta_t = (4/9)\Delta_o$.

Consequently, the orbital splitting energies are not sufficiently large for forcing pairing and, therefore, low spin configurations are rarely observed.

Note The '*g*' **subscript** is used for the octahedral and square planar complexes which have centre of symmetry. Since, tetrahedral complexes lack symmetry, '*g*' subscript is not used with energy levels (i.e. t_2 and *e*).

Colour in Coordination Compounds

The most distinctive properties of transition metal complexes is their wide range of colours.

When light of certain frequency falls on the complex, it absorbs light from visible range for transition of electron from lower to higher level.

Colour of the compound is complementary (the colour generated from the wavelength left over) to the colour of absorbed light. This is known as ***d-d* transition**. e.g. The complex $[Ti(H_2O)_6]^{3+}$ appears violet in colour due to the transition of electron from t_{2g} level to the e_g level $(t_{2g}^1 e_g^0 \rightarrow t_{2g}^0 e_g^1)$. The crystal field theory attributes the colour of the coordination compounds due to *d-d* transition of the electron.

It can be easily understood by following energy diagram.

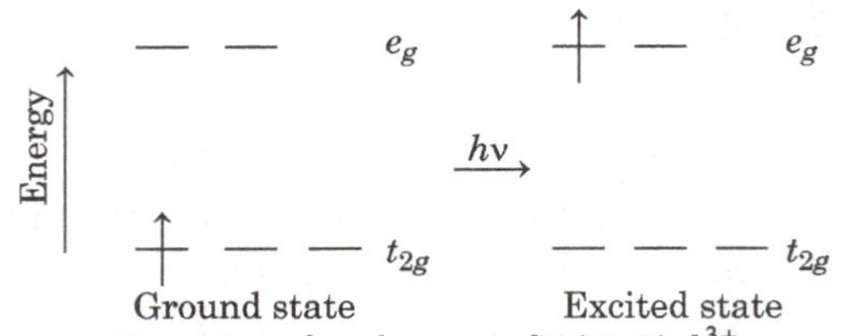

Transition of an electron in $[Ti(H_2O)_6]^{3+}$

It is important to note that in the absence of ligand, crystal field splitting does not occur and hence the substance is colourless. e.g. Anhydrous $CuSO_4$ is white, while $CuSO_4 \cdot 5H_2O$ is blue. Similarly, removal of water from $[Ti(H_2O)_6]Cl_3$ on heating renders it colourless.

Effect of Ligand on the Colour of a Complex

Ligand plays an important role in exhibiting the colour to the complex. This can be easily illustrated by considering the example of $[Ni(H_2O)_6]^{2+}$ complex which forms when nickel(II) chloride is dissolved in water.

If the didendate ligand, ethane-1, 2-diamine (en) is progressively added in the molar ratio en : Ni, 1 : 1, 3 : 1; complexes with different colours are formed as shown below

$$\underset{\text{Green}}{[Ni(H_2O)_6]^{2+}(aq)} + en(aq) \longrightarrow \underset{\text{Pale blue}}{[Ni(H_2O)_4(en)]^{2+}} + 2H_2O$$

$$\underset{\text{Green}}{[Ni(H_2O)_4(en)]^{2+}(aq)} + en(aq) \longrightarrow \underset{\text{Blue/Purple}}{[Ni(H_2O)_2(en)_2]^{2+}(aq)} + 2H_2O$$

$$[Ni(H_2O)_2(en)_2]^{2+}(aq) + en(aq) \longrightarrow \underset{\text{Violet}}{[Ni(en)_3]^{2+}(aq)} + 2H_2O$$

Colour of Some Gemstones

- Ruby is aluminium oxide (Al_2O_3) containing about 0.5-1% Cr^{3+} ions (d^3), which are randomly distributed in positions normally occupied by Al^{3+}. We may view these chromium(III) species as octahedral chromium(III) complexes incorporated into the alumina lattice, *d-d* transitions at these centres give rise to the colour.
- In Emerald, Cr^{3+} ions occupy octahedral sites in the mineral beryl ($Be_3Al_2Si_6O_{18}$). The absorption bands seen in the ruby shift to longer wavelength, namely yellow-red and blue, causing emerald to transmit light in the green region.

Limitations of CFT

CFT is successful in explaining the formation, structures, colour, magnetic properties, the effects of weak and strong field ligands in **coordination compounds**. However, it has the following limitations

- As the ligands are point charges, the anionic ligands should exert the greatest splitting effect. However, the anionic ligands actually are found at the left (or lower) end of the spectrochemical series.
- CFT treats the metal-ligand bond as purely ionic and it does not take into account the covalent character of bonding between the ligand and the central atom.

Note Valence bond theory considers the ***M*—*L* bond** as covalent, while crystal field theory considers the ***M*—*L* bond** to be ionic.

Example 3 On the basis of crystal field theory, explain why Co(III) forms paramagnetic octahedral complex with weak field ligands whereas it forms diamagnetic octahedral complex with strong field ligands? **NCERT Exemplar**

Sol. With weak field ligands, $\Delta_o < P$, (pairing energy) so, the electronic configuration of Co(III) will be $t_{2g}^4 e_g^2$, i.e. it has 4 unpaired electrons and is paramagnetic.

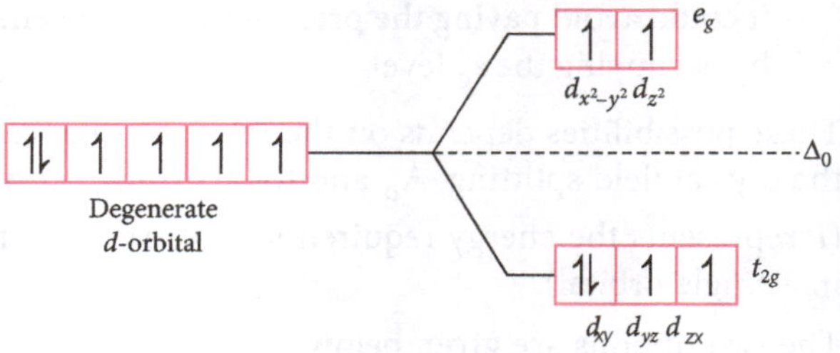

With strong field ligands, $\Delta_o > P$ (pairing energy), so pairing occurs thus, the electronic configuration will be $t_{2g}^6 e_g^0$. It has no unpaired electrons and is diamagnetic.

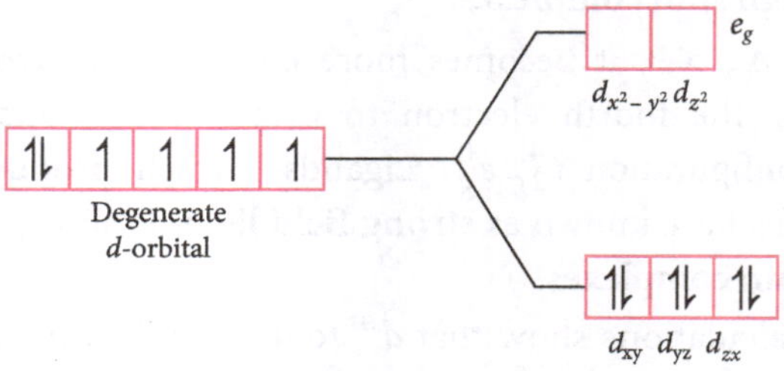

5.7 Bonding In Metal Carbonyls

The homoleptic carbonyls, i.e., the compounds containing carbonyl ligands only, are formed by most of the transition metals. These carbonyls have simple and well defined structures.

In these compounds, CO acts as a donor ligand and donates lone pairs of electrons of carbonyl carbon into vacant orbital of metal forming σ-bond.

It also behaves as an acceptor ligand and forms π-bond by back donation of electrons from filled *d*-orbital of metal to vacant antibonding (π^*)-orbital of CO.

This back-bonding stabilises the metal-ligand interaction. It is also called **synergic bonding**.

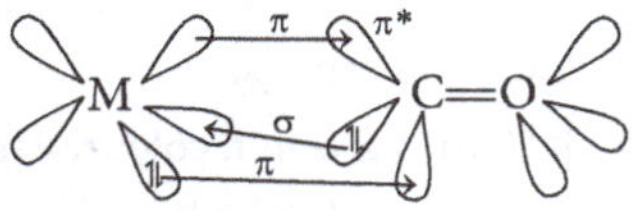

Synergic bonding

Structures of some representative homoleptic metal carbonyls are given below.

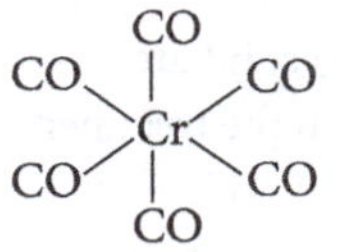

$Cr(CO)_6$, Octahedral

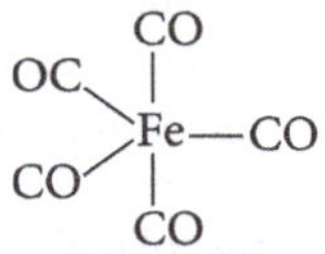

$Fe(CO)_5$, Trigonal bipyramidal

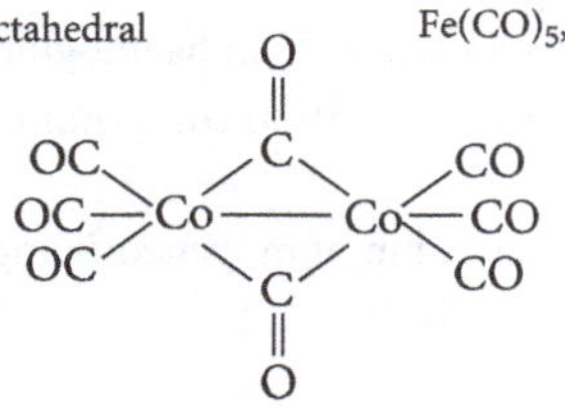

$Co_2(CO)_8$, Octacarbonyldicobalt(0)

Structures of some representative homoleptic metal carbonyls

5.8 Significance of Coordination Compounds

Due to their complex structures, coordination compounds hold very important significance in the natural as well as man-made realms. Important applications of these compounds are discussed below.

In Biological Systems

- Haemoglobin, the red pigment of blood, which acts as the oxygen carrier is a coordination compound of Fe^{2+} with porphyrin ring.
- The pigment chlorophyll in plants, responsible for photosynthesis, is a coordination compound of Mg^{2+} with porphyrin.
- Vitamin B_{12} also called cyanocobalamin, the anti-pernicious anaemia factor, is a coordination compound of cobalt.
- Enzymes like carboxypeptidase *A* and carbonic anhydrase (catalysts of biological systems) are also coordinated to metal ions.

In Medicinal Chemistry

- The platinum complex *cis*-$[Pt(NH_3)_2Cl_2]$, commonly known as *cis*-platin, is used in the treatment of cancer.
- EDTA complex of calcium is used in the treatment of lead poisoning.
- Chelate therapy is widely used in medicinal chemistry. For example, the excess of copper and iron present in plant/animal system are removed by the chelating ligands D-penicillamine and desferrioxime B *via* the formation of complexes.

In Analytical Chemistry

Coordination compounds are used in qualitative and quantitative chemical analysis. The familiar colour reactions given by metal ions with a number of ligands, as a result of formation of coordination entities, form the basis for their detection and estimation by classical and instrumental methods of analysis. For example, EDTA, DMG, α-nitroso-β-naphthol, cupron, etc.

- Detection of Cu^{2+}.
- The hardness of water is estimated by titration with Na_2EDTA. EDTA forms stable complexes with the metal ions (Ca^{2+} and Mg^{2+}) present in the hard water. Since, stability constants of calcium and magnesium complexes of EDTA are different, the selective estimation of these ions can be done.
- Ni^{2+} is detected by the formation of a red complex with dimethylglyoxime (DMG).
- The separation of Ag^+ and Hg^{2+} in group I is based on the fact that AgCl dissolves in NH_3, while Hg_2Cl_2 makes an insoluble black substance with it.

In the Extraction/Metallurgy of Metals

- Extraction of various metals from their ore involves complex formation. e.g. Silver and gold are extracted from their ore by dissolving it in NaCN in the presence of oxygen and water to form $[Ag(CN)_2]^-$ and $[Au(CN)_2]^-$ respectively.

$$M^+ + 2NaCN(aq) \longrightarrow \underset{\text{Soluble complex}}{Na[M(CN)_2]} + 2Na^+$$

$(M = Ag \text{ or } Au)$

- This soluble complex is treated with Zn dust and Au/Ag gets precipitated.

$$2Na[M(CN)_2] + Zn \longrightarrow Na_2[Zn(CN)_4] + 2M\downarrow$$

- Also used for the purification of metals, e.g. Mond's process for the purification of nickel, in which impure Ni is converted to $[Ni(CO)_4]$, which is decomposed to yield pure nickel.

In other Areas

- **Electroplating** of metals with the complex salts as electrolyte like $[Ag(CN)_2]^-$ and $[Au(CN)_2]^-$, is done much more smoothly and evenly than that from a solution of simple metal ions.
- It is used for many industrial processes in homogeneous and heterogeneous catalysis. e.g. Wilkinson catalyst $[(Ph_3P)_3RhCl]$ which is a rhodium complex is used for the hydrogenation of alkenes.
- It is used as an **antiknock**, agent in gasoline and jet fuels. e.g. $[(C_2H_5)_4Pb]$.
- In **black and white photography**, the developed film is fixed by washing with hypo solution which dissolves the undecomposed AgBr to form a complex ion, $[Ag(S_2O_3)_2]^{3-}$.

Quick Test 3

1. Amongst the following ions which one has the highest magnetic moment value?
(i) $[Cr(H_2O)_6]^{3+}$ (ii) $[Fe(H_2O)_6]^{2+}$
(iii) $[Zn(H_2O)_6]^{2+}$ *NCERT*

2. $[NiCl_4]^{2-}$ is paramagnetic while $[Ni(CO)_4]$ is diamagnetic though both are tetrahedral. Why? *NCERT Intext*

3. For the complex ion $[CoF_6]^{3-}$, write the hybridisation type, magnetic character and spin nature.
[Atomic number : Co = 27] *CBSE 2017*

4. Predict the number of unpaired electrons in the square planar $[Pt(CN)_4]^{2-}$ ion. *NCERT Intext*

5. Why are different colours observed in octahedral and tetrahedral complex for the same metal and same ligands? *NCERT Exemplar*

6. Answer the following questions. *CBSE SQP 2022*
(i) $[Ni(H_2O)_6]^{2+}(aq)$ is green in colour, whereas $[Ni(H_2O)_4(en)]^{2+}(aq)$ is blue in colour, give reason in support of your answer.
(ii) Write the formula and hybridisation of the following compound.
tris (ethane-1,2-diamine)cobalt(III) sulphate

7. A coordination compound (X) is used in the treatment of cancer, what is 'X' here?

8. Name the following.
(i) Ring that is attached to Fe^{2+} in haemoglobin.
(ii) Vitamin B_{12} is a coordination compound of this element.
(iii) Complex that is used in homogeneous and heterogeneous catalysis.

For Solutions, See QR Code on Pg. 182

Mind Map

COORDINATION COMPOUNDS/ COMPLEX COMPOUNDS

Do not dissociate into simple ions when dissolved in water.

TERMINOLOGY

Coordination Entity

It contains central metal atom/ion surrounded by the fixed number of ions or molecules.

Central Metal Atom/Ion

Atom/ion to which a fixed number of ions/groups are bonded in a definite geometrical arrangement around it.

Ligands

- These are the ions/molecules which donate their lone pair to central metal atom/ion.
- These may be positive (e.g. NO^+, NO_2^+), negative (e.g. CN^-, Cl^-), neutral (e.g. H_2O, CO, NO, etc.)
- Further, on the basis of donor sites or denticity, these are called unidentate (e.g. Cl^-, CO), bidentate (e.g. en, oxalate), polydentate (e.g. EDTA) and ambidentate (e.g. nitrito, thiocyanate) or chelating.

Coordination Number (CN)

It shows the number of ligands bonded to central metal.

CN = number of unidentate ligands

or

CN = number of ligands × denticity

Oxidation Number (ON or OS)

It shows the charge carried by the central metal atom/ion if all the ligands are removed along with electron pairs which are shared with central atom.

Homoleptic and Heteroleptic Complexes

Homoleptic Metal is bound to one kind of donor groups.

Heteroleptic Metal is bound to more than one kind of donor groups.

NOMENCLATURE

For Cationic Complexes

Counter ion name + ligand name with quantity in alphabetical order + metal name + ate + (OS of metal). e.g.

$K_2[Ni(CN)_4]$ - Potassium tetracyanonickelate(II)

For Anionic/Neutral Complexes

Ligand no. + ligand name (alphabetically) + metal name + (OS of metal) + counter ion name (if present).

e.g. $[Co(NH_3)_4(H_2O)_2]Cl_3$.
Tetraaminediaquacobalt(III) chloride

H_2O-aqua, NO-nitrosyl, Cl^-- chlorido, CN^-- cyano, etc.

Double Salt

Dissociate completely into simple ions when dissolved in water (Mohr's salt $FeSO_4 (NH_4)_2SO_4{\cdot}6H_2O$)

Isomerism

It is shown by such compounds which has same molecular formula but different arrangement of atoms.

Structural Isomerism

It is due to difference in structural arrangement.

It may be

- **Linkage isomerism** (due to the presence of ambidentate ligand like NO_2, NCS^-, etc. e.g. [*M*—NCS] and [*M*—SCN].
- **Ionisation isomerism** (due to difference in counter ion.) e.g. $[Co(NH_3)_5SO_4]Br$ and $[Co(NH_3)_5Br]SO_4$
- **Hydrate or solvate isomerism** (due to difference in H_2O molecule inside the sphere). e.g. $[Cr(H_2O)_6]Cl_3$ and $[Cr(H_2O)_5Cl]Cl_2 \cdot H_2O$
- **Coordination isomerism** (when both the ions are complexes), e.g. $[Co(NH_3)_6]\ [Cr(CN)_6]$ and $[Co(CN)_6]\ [Cr(NH_3)_6]$

Stereoisomerism

Complexes shows different arrangement in space.

It may be

- **Geometrical isomerism** (shown by complexes of the type MX_2L_2, $MABXL$, MX_2L_4, etc., but not by tetrahedral complexes.
- **Optical isomerism** (shown by complexes having at least one bidentate ligand, e.g. $[PtCl_2(en)_2]^{2+}$.

BONDING

Crystal Field Theory

Here, *d*-orbital of metal splits into $d_{x^2-y^2}$ and d_{z^2} (i.e. e_g set) and d_{xy}, d_{yz}, d_{zx} (i.e. t_{2g} set).
For tetrahedral, $e < t_2$.
For octahedral, $e_g > t_{2g}$.

- A series in which ligand are arranged in order of increasing magnitude of crystal field splitting, is called **spectrochemical series**.
$I^- < Br^- < SCN^- < Cl^- < S^{2-} < F^- < OH^- < C_2O_4^{2-} < H_2O < NCS^- < EDTA^{4-} < NH_3 < en < CN^- <$ CO.
- If $\Delta_o < P$, then complex is high spin or weak field.
- If $\Delta_o > P$, then complex is low spin or strong field.

Valence Bond Theory

Using this theory, property of a complex can be calculated as:

- Predict the OS of central metal atom/ion.
- Write E.C. of central metal atom/ion.
Pair up the *d*-electron, if ligand is strong like CN^-, CO, NH_3, etc.
- Fill ligands in empty *d*-orbitals and predict hybridisation and structure as:

Orbital Used	Hybridisation	Structure
one *s* + three *p*	sp^3	Tetrahedral
one *d*+one *s*+two *p*	dsp^2	Square planar
two *d*+one *s*+three *p*	sp^3d^2 or d^2sp^3	Octahedral

- If unpaired electron(s) present, then paramagnetic otherwise diamagnetic.
- $(n-1)$ *d*-orbital used by ligand = inner orbital, *nd*-orbital used by ligand = outer orbital.

Werner's Theory

According to it, primary valency (oxidation state) is ionisable but secondary valency (also called coordination number) are non-ionisable and is represented inside the coordination sphere.

EXAM PATTERN QUESTIONS

Objective Type Questions

Multiple Choice Questions [1 Mark]

1. **How many ions will be produced by the complex compound $[Cr(en)_3]Cl_3$, when it is dissolved in water?** **Competency Based Que.**

(a) 2 (b) 4
(c) 7 (d) 10

2. **On adding $AgNO_3$ solution to 1 mole of $PdCl_2.4NH_3$, two moles of AgCl are formed. The secondary valency of Pd in the complex will be** **Diksha**

(a) 0 (b) 2
(c) 4 (d) 1

3. **In the complex compound $Fe_4[Fe(CN)_6]_3$, oxidation states of counter ion Fe and central metal ion Fe respectively are** **Competency Based Que.**

(a) II, III (b) III,II
(c) IV, III (d) II, II

4. **In which of the following does the central atom exhibit an oxidation state of +3 ?** **CBSE 2023**

(a) $K_2[Ni(CN)_4]$ (b) $K_4[Fe(CN)_6]$
(c) $[Fe(C_2O_4)_3]^{3-}$ (d) $[Cu(NH_3)_4]^{2+}$

5. **A chelating agent has two or more than two donor atoms to bind to a single metal ion. Which of the following is not a chelating agent?** **NCERT Exemplar**

(a) Thiosulphato
(b) Oxalato
(c) Glycinato
(d) Ethane-1, 2-diamine

6. **Which of the following complexes is a 'Chelate' complex ?** **CBSE 2023**

(a) $[Co(NH_3)_6]^{3+}$ (b) $[Co(en)_3]^{3+}$
(c) $[Co(NH_3)_4Cl_2]^+$ (d) $[CoF_6]^{3-}$

7. **Amongst the following, the most stable complex is** **NCERT**

(a) $[Fe(H_2O)_6]^{3+}$ (b) $[Fe(NH_3)_6]^{3+}$
(c) $[Fe(C_2O_4)_3]^{3-}$ (d) $[FeCl_6]^{3-}$

8. **The formula of the complex dichloridobis(ethane-1, 2-diamine)platinum(IV) nitrate is** **CBSE 2023**

(a) $[PtCl_2(en)_2(NO_3)_2]$
(b) $[PtCl_2(en)_2]\ (NO_3)_2$
(c) $[PtCl_2(en)_2(NO_3)]NO_3$
(d) $[Pt(en)_2(NO_3)_2]Cl_2$

9. **The correct IUPAC name of $[Pt(NH_3)_2Cl_2]^{2+}$ is** **CBSE 2025**

(a) Diamminedichloridoplatinum (II)
(b) Diamminedichloridoplatinum (IV)
(c) Diamminedichloridoplatinum (0)
(d) Diamminedichloridoplatinate (IV)

10. **Due to the presence of ambidentate ligands coordination compounds show isomerism. Palladium complexes of the type $[Pd(C_6H_5)_2(SCN)_2]$ and $[Pd(C_6H_5)_2(NCS)_2]$ are** **NCERT Exemplar**

(a) linkage isomers
(b) coordination isomers
(c) ionisation isomers
(d) geometrical isomers

11. **$[Co(NH_3)_5NO_3]SO_4$ and $[Co(NH_3)_5SO_4]NO_3$ exhibit** **CBSE 2023**

(a) linkage isomerism
(b) ionisation isomerism
(c) optical isomerism
(d) coordination isomerism

12. **A co-ordination compound pentaamminechlorido-cobalt(III) sulphate is dissolved in water. When a few drops of chemical '*A*' is added to the solution, it gives white precipitate.**

Identify chemical '*A*'. **Competency Based Que.**

(a) AgCl (b) $AgNO_3$
(c) $BaSO_4$ (d) $BaCl_2$

13. **The complexes $[Co(NH_3)_6][Cr(CN)_6]$ and $[Cr(NH_3)_6][Co(CN)_6]$ are the examples of which type of isomerism?** **Diksha**

(a) Linkage isomerism
(b) Ionisation isomerism
(c) Coordination isomerism
(d) Geometrical isomerism

14. **Indicate the complex ion which shows geometrical isomerism.** **NCERT Exemplar**

(a) $[Cr(H_2O)_4Cl_2]^+$
(b) $[Pt(NH_3)_3Cl]$
(c) $[Co(NH_3)_6]^{3+}$
(d) $[Co(CN)_5(NC)]^{3-}$

15. $[M(AA)X_2Y_2]$ is a type of a co-ordinate compound in which M = metal ion, AA = didentate ligand, X = monodentate ligand, and Y = monodentate ligand.

Which of the following isomerisms does this compound exhibit? **Competency Based Que.**

(a) Co-ordination isomerism
(b) Linkage isomerism
(c) Geometrical isomerism
(d) Optical isomerism

16. Optical isomerism is not shown by the complex **CBSE 2023**

(a) $[Co(en)_2Cl_2]^+$ *trans*-form
(b) $[Co(en)_2Cl_2]^+$ *cis*-form
(c) $[Cr(ox)_2]^{3-}$
(d) $[Cr(en)_3]^{3+}$

17. The magnetic moment of $[NiCl_4]^{2-}$ **CBSE 2023**

(a) 1.82 BM
(b) 2.82 BM
(c) 4.42 BM
(d) 5.46 BM

18. Which one of the following is an outer orbital complex and exhibits paramagnetic behaviour?

(a) $[Ni(NH_3)_6]^{2+}$
(b) $[Zn(NH_3)_6]^{2+}$
(c) $[Cr(NH_3)_6]^{3+}$
(d) $[Co(NH_3)_6]^{3+}$

19. Which one of these statements about $[Co(CN)_6]^{3-}$ is true?

(a) $[Co(CN)_6]^{3-}$ has no unpaired electrons and will be in a low-spin configuration.
(b) $[Co(CN)_6]^{3-}$ has four unpaired electrons and will be in a low-spin configuration.
(c) $[Co(CN)_6]^{3-}$ has four unpaired electrons and will be in a high-spin configuration.
(d) $[Co(CN)_6]^{3-}$ has no unpaired electrons and will be in a high-spin configuration.

20. Which of the following facts about the complex $[Cr(NH_3)_6]Cl_3$ is incorrect? **Diksha**

(a) The complex involves d^2sp^3 hybridisation and is octahedral in shape.
(b) The complex is paramagnetic.
(c) The complex is in outer orbital complex.
(d) The complex gives white precipitate with $AgNO_3$ solution.

21. Atomic number of Mn, Fe and Co are 25, 26 and 27 respectively. Which of the following inner orbital octahedral complex ions are diamagnetic?

I. $[Co(NH_3)_6]^{3+}$
II. $[Mn(CN)_6]^{3-}$
III. $[Fe(CN)_6]^{4-}$
IV. $[Fe(CN)_6]^{3-}$

Choose the correct option.

(a) II and III
(b) I and IV
(c) I and III
(d) II and IV

22. The CFSE for octahedral $[CoCl_6]^{4-}$ is 18,000 cm^{-1}. The CFSE for tetrahedral $[CoCl_4]^{2-}$ will be **NCERT Exemplar**

(a) 18,000 cm^{-1}
(b) 16,000 cm^{-1}
(c) 8,000 cm^{-1}
(d) 20,000 cm^{-1}

23. The colour of the coordination compounds depends on the crystal field splitting. What will be the correct order of absorption of wavelength of light in the visible region, for the complexes, $[Co(NH_3)_6]^{3+}$, $[Co(CN)_6]^{3-}$, $[Co(H_2O)_6]^{3+}$? **NCERT Exemplar**

(a) $[Co(CN)_6]^{3-} > [Co(NH_3)_6]^{3+} > [Co(H_2O)_6]^{3+}$
(b) $[Co(NH_3)_6]^{3+} > [Co(H_2O)_6]^{3+} > [Co(CN)_6]^{3-}$
(c) $[Co(H_2O)_6]^{3+} > [Co(NH_3)_6]^{3+} > [Co(CN)_6]^{3-}$
(d) $[Co(CN)_6]^{3-} > [Co(NH_3)_6]^{3+} > [Co(H_2O)_6]^{3+}$

24. EDTA is used for the estimation of **Diksha**

(a) Na^+ and K^+ ions
(b) Cu^{2+} and Cs^+ ions
(c) Cl^- and Br^- ions
(d) Ca^{2+} and Mg^{2+} ions

25. For lead-poisoning, the antidote used is

(a) white of an egg
(b) *cis*-platin
(c) nickel
(d) EDTA

26. In photography, the use of $Na_2S_2O_3 \cdot 5H_2O$ is

(a) for converting AgBr into Ag_2SO_4.
(b) for converting AgBr into soluble thiosulphate complex.
(c) for converting AgBr into silver thiosulphate.
(d) in reduction of Ag metal from AgBr.

27. **Formulation of Cobalt (III) Chloride-Ammonia Complexes**

Colour	Formula	Solution conductivity corresponds to
Yellow	$[Co(NH_3)_6]^{3+}3Cl^-$	Y
Purple	$[CoCl(NH_3)_5]^{2+}2Cl^-$	1 : 2 electrolyte
Green	X	1 : 1 electrolyte

'X' and 'Y' in the above table are **CBSE SQP 2025**

(a) $X = [Co(NH_3)_6]^{2+}3Cl^-, Y = 1:3$
(b) $X = [Co(NH_3)_4Cl_2]^{+}Cl^-, Y = 1:3$
(c) $X = [Co(NH_3)_4Cl_2]^{+}Cl^-, Y = 1:1$
(d) $X = [Co(NH_3)_4Cl_2]^{3+}3Cl^-, Y = 1:1$

28. Which of the following is the most stable complex species? **CBSE 2024 C**

(a) $[Fe(CN)_6]^{3-}$
(b) $[Fe(CO)_5]^{3+}$
(c) $[Fe(C_2O_4)_3]^{3-}$
(d) $[Fe(H_2O)_6]^{3+}$

Assertion-Reason [1 Mark]

Directions (Q. Nos. 29-41) In the following questions an Assertion (A) is followed by a corresponding Reason (R). Use the following keys to choose the appropriate answer.

(a) Both (A) and (R) are true and (R) is the correct explanation of (A).
(b) Both (A) and (R) are true, but (R) is not the correct explanation of (A).
(c) (A) is true, but (R) is false.
(d) (A) is false, but (R) is true.

29. **Assertion** (A) In the coordination compound $[Co(H_2NCH_2CH_2NH_2)_3]_2(SO_4)_3$, ethane-1,2-diamine is a neutral ligand.

Reason (R) Oxidation number of Co in the complex ion is +3.

30. **Assertion** (A) The stability of $[Ni(en)_3]Cl_2$ is more than that of $[Ni(NH_3)_6]Cl_2$.

Reason (R) The geometry of Ni is trigonal bipyramidal in $[Ni(en)_3]Cl_2$.

31. **Assertion** (A) $[Cr(H_2O)_6]Cl_2$ and $[Fe(H_2O)_6]Cl_2$ are examples of homoleptic complexes. **CBSE 2025**

Reason (R) All the ligands attached to the metal are the same.

32. **Assertion** (A) The ligands of nitro and nitrito are called ambidentate ligands.

Reason (R) These ligands give linkage isomers.

33. **Assertion** (A) *trans*-$[CrCl_2(ox)_2]^{3-}$ shows optical isomerism.

Reason (R) Optical isomerism is common in octahedral complexes involving didentate ligands. **CBSE 2023**

34. **Assertion** (A) Complexes of MX_6 and MX_5L type (X and L are unidentate) do not show geometrical isomerism. **NCERT Exemplar**

Reason (R) Geometrical isomerism is not shown by complexes of coordination number 6.

35. **Assertion** (A) The total number of isomers shown by $[Co(en)_2Cl_2]^+$ complex ion is three.

Reason (R) $[Co(en)_2Cl_2]^+$ complex ion has an octahedral geometry.

36. **Assertion** (A) Tetrahedral complexes do not show geometrical isomerism.

Reason (R) The relative positions of the unidentate ligands attached to the central metal atom are the same with respect to each other.

37. **Assertion** (A) $[Mn(CN)_6]^{3-}$ has a magnetic moment of two unpaired electrons while $[MnCl_6]^{3-}$ has a magnetic moment of four unpaired electrons.

Reason (R) $[Mn(CN)_6]^{3-}$ is inner orbital complex involving d^2sp^3-hybridisation, on the other hand, $[MnCl_6]^{3-}$ is outer orbital complex involving sp^3d^2-hybridisation. **CBSE SQP 2025**

38. **Assertion** (A) $[Fe(CN)_6]^{3-}$ ion shows magnetic moment corresponding to two unpaired electrons.

Reason (R) Because it has d^2sp^3 type hybridisation. **NCERT Exemplar**

39. **Assertion** (A) $[Ni(CN)_4]^{2-}$ is square planar and diamagnetic. **NCERT Exemplar**

Reason (R) It has no unpaired electrons due to presence of strong field ligand.

40. **Assertion** (A) Low spin tetrahedral complexes are rarely observed. **NCERT Exemplar**

Reason (R) Crystal field splitting energy is less than pairing energy for tetrahedral complexes. **CBSE 2020**

41. **Assertion** (A) Toxic metal ions are removed by the chelating ligands. **NCERT Exemplar**

Reason (R) Chelate complexes tend to be more stable.

Case-Study [4 Marks]

42. Read the given case and answer the following questions.

In 1893, Werner was the first to propose correct structures for coordination compounds containing complex ions, in which a central transition metal atom is surrounded by neutral or anionic ligands. For example, it was known that cobalt forms a "complex" hexamminecobalt(III) chloride, with formula $CoCl_3 \cdot 6NH_3$, but the nature of the association indicated by the dot was mysterious. Werner proposed the structure $[Co(NH_3)_6]Cl_3$, with the Co^{3+} ion surrounded by six NH_3, at the vertices of an octahedron.

The three Cl^- are dissociated as free ions, which Werner confirmed by measuring the conductivity of the compound in aqueous solution, and also by chloride anion analysis using precipitation with silver nitrate. Later, magnetic susceptibility analysis was also used to confirm Werner's proposal for the chemical nature of $CoCl_3 \cdot 6NH_3$.

For complexes with more than one type of ligand, Werner succeeded in explaining the number of isomers observed. For example, he explained the existence of two tetraammine isomers, for $(Co(NH_3)_4Cl_3$, one green and one purple. Werner proposed that these are two geometrical isomers of formula $[Co(NH_3)_4Cl_2]Cl$, with one Cl^- ion dissociated as confirmed by conductivity measurements.

The Co atom is surrounded by four NH_3 and two Cl ligands at the vertices of an octahedron. The green isomer is "*trans*" with the two Cl ligands at opposite vertices and the purple is "*cis*" with the two Cl at adjacent vertices.

Werner also prepared complexes with optical isomers, and in 1914 he reported the first synthetic chiral compound lacking carbon, known as hexol with formula $[Co(Co(NH_3)_4(OH)_2)_3]Br_6$.

Based on the above information. Answer the following questions.

(i) Why is CO a stronger ligand than NH_3 in complexes?

(ii) Write the IUPAC name of the following complex $[CoBr_2(en)_2]^+$

Or What type of isomerism is shown by the complex $[Co(NH_3)_5SO_4]Br$?

(iii) For the complex ion $[Ni(NH_3)_6]^{2+}$, state the geometry of the ion.

43. **Read the given case and answer the following questions.**

Complex compounds play an important role in our daily life. These compounds contain central metal and ligands. Ligands can be negatively charged or neutral molecules. Ligands can be differentiated on the basis of the number of donor sites which is simply called as denticity. It can be monodentate, didentate, polydentate, ambidentate ligands.

Polydentate ligands are more stable than monodentate ligands.

Complex compounds are named according the IUPAC system. Many approaches have been put forth to explain the nature of bonding in complex compounds. These are valence bond theory (VBT), crystal field theory (CFT), ligand field theory (LFT) and Molecular orbital theory (MOT).

Based on the above information, answer the following questions.

(i) (a) What is the oxidation state of Cu in $[Cu(NH_3)_4Cl_2]$?

(b) What is the IUPAC name of the complex $[Ni(NH_3)_6]Cl_2$?

(ii) Which one of the following forms a low spin complex?

(a) $[Co(CN)_6]^{3-}$ (b) $[NiCl_4]^{2-}$

(c) $[Ni(H_2O)_6]^{2+}$ (d) $[MnF_6]^{3-}$

(iii) The magnetic property and the number of unpaired electrons in the complex $[Co(NH_3)_6]^{3+}$ will be

(a) Paramagnetic, 2 (b) Paramagnetic, 1

(c) Diamagnetic, 0 (d) Diamagnetic, 2

Or The hybridisation and geometry for the complex $[Co(NH_3)_6]^{3+}$ is

(a) d^2sp^3, octahedral (b) sp^3d, trigonal bipyramidal

(c) sp^3, tetrahedral (d) dsp^2, tetrahedral

44. **Read the given case and answer the following questions.**

Crystal field theory was proposed by H. Bethe and John van Vleck in 1930. L. Orgel in 1952, gave a much more satisfactory explanation for the bonding and the properties of complexes. The Crystal Field Theory (CFT) is an electrostatic model which considers the metal-ligand bond to be ionic arising purely from electrostatic interactions between the metal ion and the ligand. In an octahedral coordination entity with six ligands surrounding the metal atom/ion, there will be repulsion between the electrons in metal *d*-orbitals and the electrons (or negative charges) of the ligands. Such a repulsion is more when the metal *d*-orbital is directed towards the ligand than when it is away from the ligand.

The degeneracy of the *d*-orbitals has been removed due to ligand-metal electron repulsions in the octahedral complex to yield three orbitals of lower energy, t_{2g} set and two orbitals of higher energy, e_g set.

(i) What will be the correct order for the wavelengths of absorption in the visible region for the following $[Ni(NO_2)_6]^{4-}$, $[Ni(NH_3)_6]^{2+}$, $[Ni(H_2O)_6]^{2+}$? **NCERT**

(ii) Explain the violet colour of the complex $[Ti(H_2O)_6]^{3+}$ on the basis of crystal field theory. **NCERT**

Or How does the colour of the coordination complex $[Ti(H_2O)_6]^{3+}$ ion change on heating?

(iii) What is meant by spectrochemical series ?

Subjective Type Questions

Short Answer Type I Questions [2 Marks]

1. $FeSO_4$ solution mixed with $(NH_4)_2SO_4$ solution in 1 : 1 molar ratio gives the test of Fe^{2+} ion but $CuSO_4$ solution mixed with aqueous ammonia in 1 : 4 molar ratio does not give the test of Cu^{2+} ion. Why? **NCERT**

2. What is meant by the unidentate, bidentate and ambidentate ligands? Give two examples of each. **NCERT, Diksha**

3. (i) What is a chelate complex? Give one example.

(ii) What are heteroleptic complexes? Give one example. **CBSE 2023**

4. Give the formula of each of the following coordination compound entities.

(i) Co^{3+} ion is bound to one Cl^-, one NH_3 molecule and two bidentate ethylene diamine (en) molecules.

(ii) Ni^{2+} ion is bound to two water molecules and two oxalate ions.

5. Using IUPAC norms, write the formulae for the following

(i) Sodium dicyanidoaurate(I).

(ii) Tetraamminechloridonitrito-N-platinum(IV) sulphate. **CBSE 2017**

6. Write IUPAC name of the following coordination entities

(i) $[Co(NH_3)_4Cl(NO_2)]Cl$ **CBSE 2023**

(ii) $[PtCl_2(en)_2]^{2+}$

7. How many geometrical isomers are possible in the following coordination entities?

(i) $[Cr(C_2O_4)_3]^{3-}$

(ii) $[Co(NH_3)_3Cl_3]$ **NCERT**

8. Write the types of isomerism exhibited by the following complexes.

(i) $[Co(NH_3)_5Cl]SO_4$

(ii) $[Co(en)_3]^{3+}$

(iii) $[Co(NH_3)_6][Cr(CN)_6]$

9. What type of isomerism is exhibited by $[Co(NH_3)_4Cl_2]^+ Br^-$? Write the structures of the possible isomers and the state of hybridisation of the central metal atom.

10. Write all the geometrical isomers of $[Pt(NH_3)(Br)(Cl)(py)]$ and how many of these will exhibit optical isomers? **NCERT**

11. (i) Which of the following species cannot act as a ligand ? Give reason.

OH^-, NH_4^+, CH_3NH_2, H_2O

(ii) The complex $[Co(NH_3)_5(NO_2)]Cl_2$ is red in colour. Give IUPAC name of its linkage isomer. **CBSE 2023**

12. Explain why

(i) geometrical isomerism is not possible for tetrahedral complexes?

(ii) optical isomerism is not shown by square planar complexes? **CBSE 2023**

13. Why do compounds having similar geometry have different magnetic moment? **NCERT Exemplar**

14. Give reasons

(i) Low spin tetrahedral complexes are not formed.

(ii) $[Co(NH_3)_6]^{3+}$ is an inner orbital complex, whereas $[Ni(NH_3)_6]^{2+}$ is an outer orbital complex. **NCERT Intext, CBSE 2023**

15. What is the coordination entity formed when excess of aqueous KCN is added to an aqueous solution of copper sulphate? Why is it that no precipitate of copper sulphide is obtained when $H_2S(g)$ is passed through this solution? **NCERT**

16. Explain why $[Fe(H_2O)_6]^{3+}$ has magnetic moment value of 5.92 BM whereas $[Fe(CN)_6]^{3-}$ has a value of only 1.74 BM? **Diksha**

17. (i) Predict the geometry of $[Ni(CN)_4]^{2-}$.

(ii) Calculate the spin only magnetic moment of $[Cu(NH_3)_4]^{2+}$ ion. **CBSE SQP 2021**

18. Draw the diagram showing splitting of *d*-orbital in tetrahedral complex.

19. (i) Define the following terms

(a) Crystal field splitting energy

(b) Ambidentate ligand **CBSE 2025**

(ii) What is meant by the chelate effect? Give an example. **CBSE 2024 C, 2025**

20. (i) On the basis of crystal field theory, write the electronic configuration for d^5 ion with a strong field ligand for which $\Delta_o > P$.

(ii) $[NiCO)_4]$ has tetrahedral geometry, while $[Ni(CN)_4]^{2-}$ has square planar yet both exhibit diamagnetism. Explain.
[Atomic number Ni = 28] **CBSE 2023**

21. $[Fe(CN)_6]^{4-}$ and $[Fe(H_2O)_6]^{2+}$ are of different colours in dilute solutions. Why? **NCERT**

22. $[Ti(H_2O)_6]^{3+}$ absorbs light of wavelength 500 nm. Name one ligand which would form Ti(III) complex absorbing light of lower wavelength than 500 nm and one ligand which would form a complex absorbing light of wavelength higher than 500 nm. **Competency Based Que.**

23. Discuss the nature of bonding in metal carbonyls. **NCERT**

24. What is the relationship between observed colour of the complex and the wavelength of light absorbed by the complex?

Short Answer Type II Questions [3 Marks]

25. (i) Give the IUPAC name and electronic configuration of central metal atom in terms of t_{2g} and e_g of $K_4[Mn(CN)_6]$.

(ii) How many ions are produced from the complex $[Cr(NH_3)_6]Cl_2$ in solution? **CBSE 2024 C**

26. Explain the bonding in coordination compounds in terms of Werner's postulates. **NCERT**

27. Using IUPAC norms, write the formulae for the following
(i) Tetrahydroxidozincate(II)
(ii) Potassium tetrachloridopalladate(II)
(iii) Diamminedichloridoplatinum(II)
(iv) Potassium tetracyanidonickelate(II)
(v) Hexaamminecobalt(III) sulphate **NCERT**

28. Using IUPAC norms, write the systematic names of the following
(i) $[Ni(NH_3)_6]Cl_2$ (ii) $[Co(en)_3]^{3+}$
(iii) $[Ni(CO)_4]$ **NCERT**

29. Write the IUPAC name of the following coordination compounds.
(i) $[Cr(NH_3)_3Cl_3]$ (ii) $K_3[Fe(CN)_6]$ **CBSE 2025**
(iii) $[CoBr_2(en)_2]^+$ (en = ethylene diamine)

30. Write the IUPAC names of the following coordination compounds. (Any three) **CBSE 2024, 2025**
(i) $[Co(NH_3)_4Cl(NO_2)]Cl$ (ii) $[Ni(NH_3)_6]Cl_2$
(iii) $K_3[Cr(C_2O_4)_3]$ (iv) $[Co(en)_2Br_2]^+$

31. Give the evidence that $[Co(NH_3)_5Cl]SO_4$ and $[Co(NH_3)_5SO_4]Cl$ are ionisation isomers. **NCERT Intext**

32. (i) Write the IUPAC name and hybridisation of the complex $[Fe(CN)_6]^{3-}$. **CBSE 2020**
(Given : Atomic number of Fe = 26)
(ii) What is the difference between an ambidentate ligand and a chelating ligand?

33. (i) Write the electronic configuration of iron in the following complex ion and predict its magnetic behaviour : $[Fe(H_2O)_6]^{2+}$
(ii) Write the IUPAC name of the coordination complex: $[CoCl_2(en)_2]NO_3$ **CBSE SQP 2021**

34. Write the hybridisation and magnetic character of the following complexes :
(i) $[Fe(H_2O)_6]^{2+}$ (ii) $[Ni(CN)_4]^{2-}$ **CBSE 2019**
[Atomic number : Fe = 26, Ni = 28]

35. (i) Write the formula of the following coordination compound:
Iron (III) hexacyanoferrate(II)
(ii) What type of isomerism is exhibited by the complex $[Co(NH_3)_5Cl]SO_4$?
(iii) Write the hybridisation and number of unpaired electrons in the complex $[CoF_6]^{3-}$.
(Atomic number of Co = 27) **CBSE 2018**

36. (i) Why Co^{2+} is easily oxidised to Co^{3+} in the presence of a strong ligand? [At. no. of Co = 27]
(ii) Using IUPAC norms, write the name of $[Cr(C_2O_4)_3]^{3-}$.
(iii) If $PtCl_2 \cdot 2NH_3$ does not react with $AgNO_3$, what will be its formula? **CBSE 2025**

37. Explain the hybridisation, geometry, magnetic properties and IUPAC nomenclature of $[Fe(CN)_6]^{4-}$ and $[Fe(CN)_6]^{3-}$.

38. (i) What type of isomerism is shown by the complex $[Co(NH_3)_5(SCN)]^{2+}$?
(ii) Why $[NiCl_4]^{2-}$ is paramagnetic, while $[Ni(CN)_4]^{2-}$ is diamagnetic?
(Atomic number of Ni = 28)
(iii) Why are low spin tetrahedral complexes rarely observed? **CBSE 2017**

Or Why are low spin tetrahedral complexes not formed? **CBSE 2017, 2025**

39. (i) Draw the geometrical isomers of the given complex $[Co(en)_2Cl_2]^+$.
(ii) Write the electronic configuration of d^4 ion if $\Delta_o > P$.
(iii) What is a didentate ligand? Give one example. **CBSE 2024**

40. One mole of an isomer of complex $[Cr(H_2O)_6]Cl_3$ when treated with $AgNO_3$ produces 2 moles of a white precipitate of AgCl. Write the formula of this isomer of the complex and show how the metal-ligand bonding differs in the two isomers though both are octahedral. **Competency Based Que.**

41. What is the crystal field stabilisation energy? How does the magnitude of Δ_o decide the actual configuration of *d*-orbital in a coordination entity? **NCERT**

Or What is meant by crystal field splitting energy? On the basis of crystal field theory, write the electronic configuration of d^4 in terms of t_{2g} and e_g in an octahedral field when
(i) $\Delta_o > P$ (ii) $\Delta_o < P$

42. (i) What type of isomerism is shown by the complex $[Co(NH_3)_6][Cr(CN)_6]$?
(ii) Why a solution of $[Ni(H_2O)_6]^{2+}$ is green while a solution of $[Ni(CN)_4]^{2-}$ is colourless?
(iii) Write the IUPAC name of the following complex : $[Co(NH_3)_5(CO_3)]Cl$ **CBSE 2017, 2025**

43. Answer any three of the following questions. **CBSE 2023**
(i) Explain the type of hybridisation in $[Fe(CN)_6]^{3-}$ on the basis of valence bond theory. (Given : Atomic number of Fe = 26)
(ii) Draw the geometrical isomers of $[PtCl_2(en)_2]^{2+}$ ion.
(iii) $[NiCl_4]^{2-}$ is paramagnetic, while $[Ni(CO)_4]$ is diamagnetic though both are tetrahedral. Why ?
(iv) Name the type of isomerism when ambidentate ligands are attached to central metal ion. Give one example of ambidentate ligand.

44. (i) What is the basis of formation of the spectrochemical series?

(ii) Draw the structures of geometrical isomers of the following coordination complexes.

$[Co(NH_3)_3Cl_3]$ and $[CoCl_2(en)_2]^+$

(en = ethylene diamine and atomic number of Co is 27).

45. In a coordination entity, the electronic configuration of the central metal ion is $t_{2g}^3 e_g^1$.

(i) Is the coordination compound a high spin or low spin complex?

(ii) Draw the crystal field splitting diagram for the above complex.

46. The hexaaquamanganese(II) ion contains five unpaired electrons, while the hexacyano ion contains only one paired electron. Explain using crystal field theory. **NCERT Intext**

47. Name the compound $[Fe(H_2O)_5 NO]^{2+}$ and explain the magnetic properties of $[Fe(H_2O)_5 NO]^{2+}$ and oxidation state of iron in this complex.

48. Give detailed description of CFT for different types of ligand and explain how CFT explain colour of coordination compounds? Use suitable example to explain.

49. A metal ion M^{n+} having d^4 valence electronic configuration combines with three bidentate ligands to form a complex compound. Assuming $\Delta_o > P$.

(i) Draw the diagram showing d-orbital splitting during this complex formation.

(ii) Write the electronic configuration of the valence electrons of the metal M^{n+} ion in terms of t_{2g} and e_g.

(iii) What type of hybridisation will M^{n+} ion have?

Long Answer Type Questions [5 Marks]

50. $PtCl_4$ and NH_3 may form five complexes, A $(PtCl_4 \cdot 6NH_3)$, $B(PtCl_4 \cdot 5NH_3)$, C $(PtCl_4 \cdot 4NH_3)$, $D(PtCl_4 \cdot 3NH_3)$ and $E(PtCl_4 \cdot 2NH_3)$. One mole of each A, B, C, D and E reacts with excess of $AgNO_3$ to yield 4, 3, 2 and 1 mole(s) of AgCl respectively, while E gives no AgCl. The conductance of their solutions are in the order $A > B > C > D > E$. On the basis of Werner's theory, write their structures and give the total number of ions given by one complex.

51. (i) Write IUPAC names of the following **CBSE 2025**

(a) $[Co(H_2O)(CN)en)_2]^{2+}$ (b) $[PtCl_4]^{2-}$

(c) $Cr(NH_3)_4Cl(ONO)]^+$

(ii) What is spectrochemical series? Write the difference between a strong field ligand and a weak field ligand.

52. Indicate the types of isomerism exhibited by the following complexes and draw the structures for these isomers.

(i) $K[Cr(H_2O)_2(C_2O_4)_2]$ (ii) $[Co(en)_3]Cl_3$

(iii) $[Co(NH_3)_5(NO_2)](NO_3)_2$

(iv) $[Pt(NH_3)(H_2O)Cl_2]$ **NCERT Intext**

53. Discuss the nature of bonding in the following coordination entities on the basis of valence bond theory. **NCERT**

(i) $[Fe(CN)_6]^{4-}$ (ii) $[FeF_6]^{3-}$

(iii) $[Co(C_2O_4)_3]^{3-}$ (iv) $[CoF_6]^{3-}$

54. For the complex $[Fe(en)_2Cl_2]Cl$, identify

(i) the oxidation number of iron.

(ii) the hybridisation and the shape of the complex.

(iii) the magnetic behaviour of the complex.

(iv) whether there is an optical isomer of the complex? If so draw its structure.

(v) IUPAC name of the complex.

(At. no. of Fe= 26) **CBSE 2025**

55. In the following complex ions, explain the type of hybridisation, shape and magnetic property: **CBSE 2025**

(i) $[Fe(H_2O)_6]^{2+}$ (ii) $[NiCl_4]^{2-}$

(At. Nos.: Fe =26 and Ni= 28)

56. (i) A purple colour compound A, which is a strong oxidising agent and used for bleaching of wool, cotton, silk and other textile fibres was added to each of the three test tubes along with H_2SO_4. It was followed by strong heating.

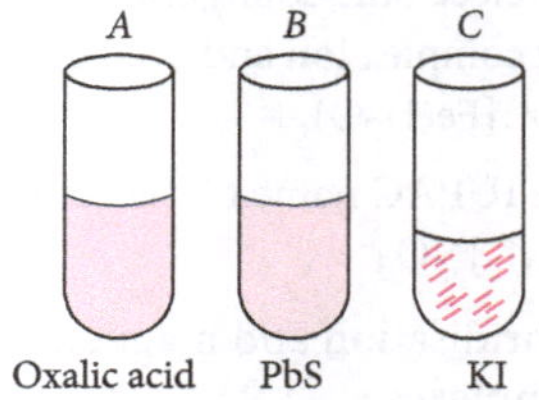

In which of the above test tubes A, B or C.

(a) Violet vapours will be formed

(b) The bubbles of gas evolved will extinguish a burning matchstick.

Write an equation for each of the above observations.

(ii) A metal ion Mn^{n+} of the first transition series having d^5 configuration combines with three didentate ligands. Assuming $\Delta_o < P$.

(a) Draw the crystal field energy level diagram for the 3d orbital of this complex.

(b) What is the hybridisation of Mn^{n+} in this complex and why?

(c) Name the type of isomerism exhibited by this complex. **Competency Based Que.**

Hints & Solutions

Objective Type Questions

1. (*b*) When $[Cr(en)_3]Cl_3$ dissolves in water, it gives $3Cl^-$ ions and one $[Cr(en)_3]^{3+}$ cationic complex.
So, total number of ions produced is 4.

2. (*c*) $PdCl_2 \cdot 4NH_3 + 2AgNO_3 \longrightarrow [Pd(NH_3)_4]^{2+} + 2AgCl + 2NO_3^-$

Since, 4 NH_3 ligands are attached to Pd, thus its coordination number or secondary valency is 4.

3. (*b*) $Fe_4[Fe(CN)_6]_3$ dissociates as

$$Fe_4[Fe(CN)_6]_3 \longrightarrow 4Fe^{3+} + 3[Fe(CN)_6]^{4-}$$

Thus, the oxidation state of counter ion is +3. Now, for $[Fe(CN)_6]^{4-}$ complex, let the oxidation state of Fe be x.

$\therefore \quad x + 6(-1) = -4$

$\Rightarrow \quad x = +2$

Thus, the oxidation state of central metal ion Fe is +2.

4. (*c*) $[Fe(C_2O_4)_3]^{3-}$ exhibit an oxidation state of +3.

5. (*a*) A chelating ligand has two or more binding donor atoms to a single metal ion.

e.g.

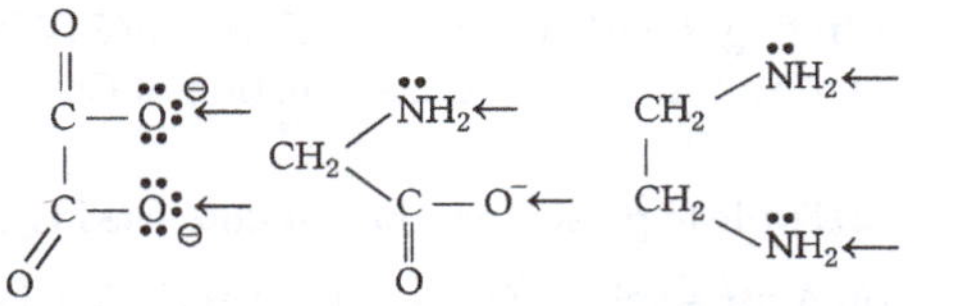

Oxalato Glycinato Ethane-1, 2 diamine

Here, (←) denotes binding site.

Thiosulphato ($S_2O_3^{2-}$) is not a chelating ligand because geometrically it is not favourable for $S_2O_3^{2-}$ to chelate a metal ion.

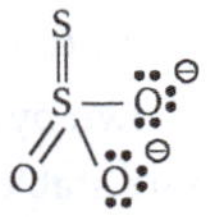

6. (*b*) $[Co(en)_3]^{3+}$ is a chelate complex. Here, 'en' is a chelating ligand that form a stable complex by forming a ring.

7. (*c*) In all these complexes, Fe is in +3 oxidation state. However, the complex (c) is a chelate because three $C_2O_4^{2-}$ ions act as the chelating ligands. Thus, the most stable complex is $[Fe(C_2O_4)_3]^{3-}$.
Hence, correct answer is (c).

8. (*b*) The formula of the complex dichlorido *bis* (ethane-1, 2-diamine)platinum(IV) nitrate is $[PtCl_2(en)_2](NO_3)_2$.

9. (*b*) The correct IUPAC name of $[Pt(NH_3)_2Cl_2]^{2+}$ is diamminedichloridoplatinum (IV).

10. (*a*) The ligand(s) which has two different binding sites are known as ambident ligands, e.g. SCN, NO_2, etc.

Here, SCN has two binding sites at S and N. Hence, SCN (thiocyanate) can bind to the metal ion in two ways.

$$M \leftarrow NCS \text{ or } M \leftarrow SCN$$

Thus, coordination compounds containing SCN as a ligand can show linkage iscmerism, i.e. $[Pd(C_6H_5)_2(SCN)_2]$ and $[Pd(C_6H_5)_2(NCS)_2]$ are linkage isomers.

Hence, correct choice is (a).

11. (*b*) Refer to text on page 152.

12. (*d*) Pentaamminechloridocobalt(III) sulphate dissolves in water and reacts with barium chloride (*A*) ($BaCl_2$) to form a white precipitate of barium sulphate.

13. (*c*) The complexes $[Co(NH_3)_6][Cr(CN)_6]$ and $[Cr(NH_3)_6][Co(CN)_6]$ are the examples of coordination isomerism. This isomerism occurs only in those complexes in which both cations and anions are complex. It occurs due to exchange of ligands between cation and anions.

14. (*a*) $[Cr(H_2O)_4Cl_2]^+$ shows geometrical isomerism because it is a MA_4B_2 type coordination compound which contains two set of equivalent ligands, 4 H_2O and 2 Cl.

Hence, the possible geometrical isomers are

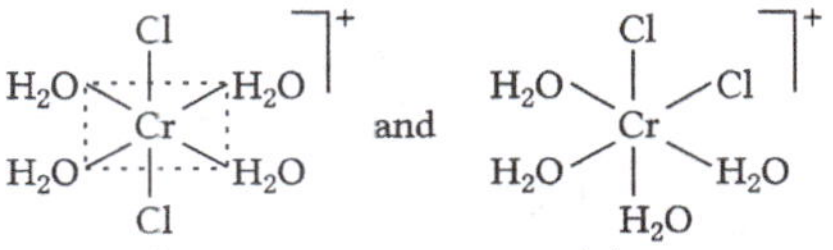

trans-isomer *cis*-isomer

Hence, correct choice is (a).

15. (*d*) The compound $[M(AA)X_2Y_2]$ has the same formula but a different arrangement of ligands around the central metal ion. It exhibits optical isomerism as it does not have a plane of symmetry.

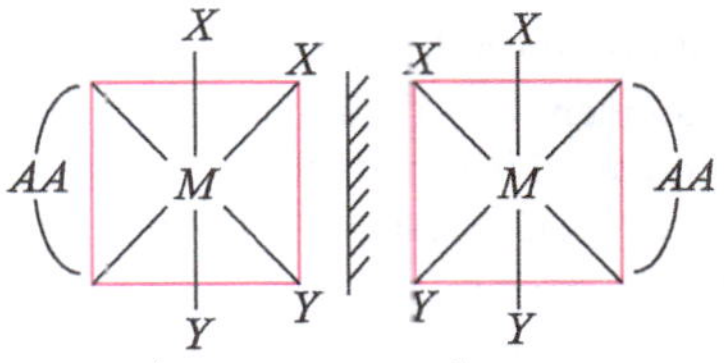

dextro *laevo*

16. (*a*) *trans* form of $[Co(en)_2Cl_2]^+$ does not show optical isomerism due to the superimposable mirror images (on page no. 154).

17. (*b*) For the complex, $[NiCl_4]^{2-}$

Let the oxidation state of Ni = x

$\therefore \quad x + 4(-1) = -2$

$x = -2 + 4$

$x = +2$

Now, electronic configuration of $Ni^{2+} = 3d^8 4s^0$

$\therefore \quad Ni^{2+} =$ | ⇅ | ⇅ | ⇅ | ↑ | ↑ |

Two unpaired electrons are present in $[NiCl_4]^{2-}$.

Thus, magnetic moment

$$= \sqrt{n(n+2)} = \sqrt{2(2+2)} = \sqrt{8}$$

$\Rightarrow \quad \mu = 2.82$ BM

18. (*a*) Outer orbital complex utilises 4*d*-orbitals for bonding and exhibit paramagnetic behaviour, only if unpaired electrons are present.

In $[Ni(NH_3)_6]^{2+}$, $Ni^{2+} = [Ar]\ 3d^8 4s^0$

$[Ni(NH_3)_6]^{2+} =$

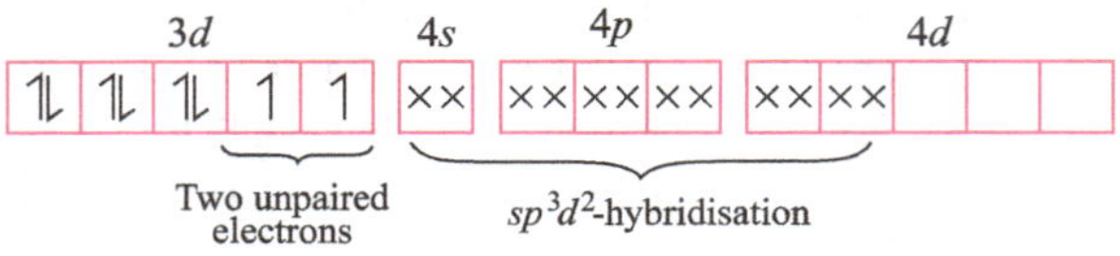

So, this is an outer orbital complex having paramagnetic character.

19. (*a*) $[Co(CN)_6]^{3-}$

$Co^{3+} = 1s^2\ 2s^2\ 2p^6\ 3s^2\ 3p^6\ 3d^6$

CN^- is a strong field ligand and as it approaches the metal ion, the electrons get paired up. The splitting of the *d*-orbitals into two sets of orbitals in an octahedral complex $[Co(CN)_6]^{3-}$ may be represented as

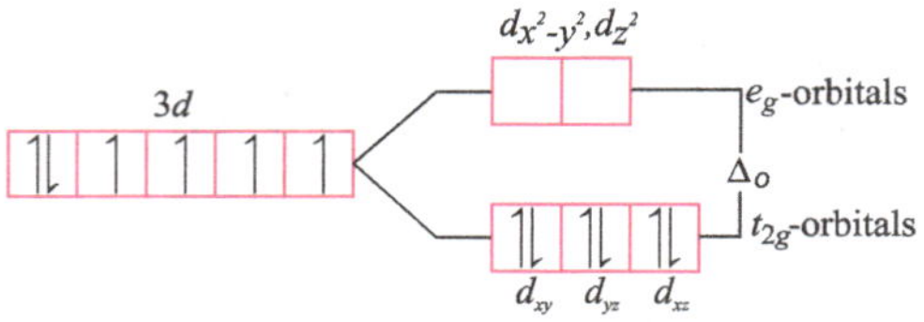

Here, for d^6 ions, three electrons first enter orbitals with parallel spin and the remaining may pair up in t_{2g}-orbital giving rise to a low spin complex.

$\therefore$ $[Co(CN)_6]^{3-}$ has no unpaired electrons and will be in low spin configuration.

20. (*c*) The statements (a), (b) and (d) are correct while any statement (c) is incorrect. Its correct form can be explained as, Cr exists as Cr^{3+} ion in the given complex.

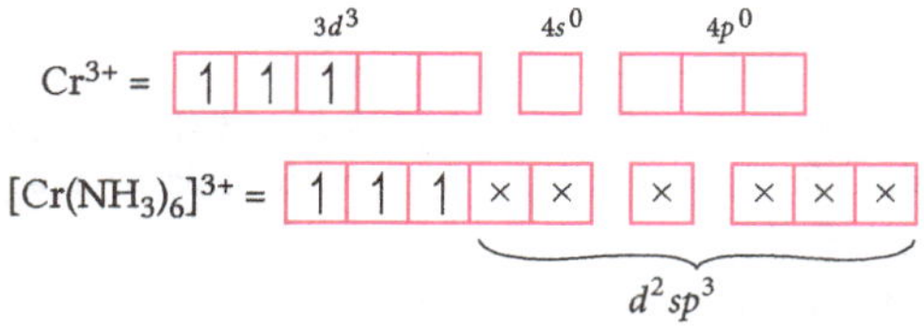

Thus, it forms inner orbital complex.

21. (*c*) $[Co(NH_3)_6]^{3+}$ and $[Fe(CN)_6]^{4-}$, inner orbital complex ions are diamagnetic. [For explanation refer to text on pages 157, 158 and 159].

22. (*c*) CFSE for octahedral and tetrahedral complexes are closely related to each other by the formula $\Delta_t = \frac{4}{9}\Delta_o$.

where, Δ_o = CFSE for octahedral complex,

Δ_t = CFSE for tetrahedral complex

According to question, $\Delta_o = 18{,}000\ cm^{-1}$

$$\therefore \quad \Delta_t = \frac{4}{9}\Delta_o = \frac{4}{9} \times 18{,}000\ cm^{-1}$$

$$= 4 \times 2{,}000 = 8{,}000\ cm^{-1}$$

Hence, correct choice is (c).

23. (*c*) As we know that, strong field ligand split the five degenerate energy levels with more energy separation than weak field ligand, i.e., with increase in strength of ligand, crystal field splitting energy increases.

Hence, $\quad \Delta E = \frac{hc}{\lambda}$

$$\Rightarrow \quad \Delta E \propto \frac{1}{\lambda} \Rightarrow \lambda \propto \frac{1}{\Delta E}$$

As energy separation increases, the wavelength decreases. Thus, the correct order is

$$[Co(H_2O)_6]^{3+} > [Co(NH_3)_6]^{3+} > [Co(CN)_6]^{3-}$$

Here, strength of ligand increases, ΔE increases, CFSE increases and λ absorption decreases.

Hence, correct choice is (c).

24. (*d*) The hardness of a water sample is estimated by titrating it with a standard solution of EDTA. In other words, it is used for the estimation of Ca^{2+} and Mg^{2+} ions.

25. (*d*) For lead poisoning, the antidote used is EDTA.

26. (*b*) $AgBr + 2Na_2S_2O_3 \longrightarrow \underset{\text{Soluble complex}}{Na_3[Ag(S_2O_3)_2]} + NaBr$

27. (*b*) $X = [Co(NH_3)_4Cl_2]^+Cl^-$, $Y = 1:3$

$X = [Co(NH_3)_4Cl_2]^+ Cl^-$ solution conductivity corresponds to 1 : 1. $[Co(NH_3)_6]^{3+}3Cl^-$ solution conductivity corresponds to $Y = 1:3$ electrolyte.

28. (*c*) More stability is shown by $[Fe(C_2O_4)_3]^{3-}$ because metal chelates are more stable than non-chelates. Oxalate is a bidentate ligand and forms metal chelates. Hence, $[Fe(C_2O_4)_3]^{3-}$ is more stable.

29. (*b*) Ethane-1, 2-diamine is a neutral ligand as it carries no charge. Moreover, oxidation number of Co in the complex ion is +3. Thus, both (A) and (R) are true but (R) is not the correct explanation of (A).

30. (*c*) $[Ni(en)_3]Cl_2$ is more stable than $[Ni(NH_3)_6]Cl_2$, because $[Ni(en)_3]Cl_2$ is a chelating compound which are more stable than complexes with unidentate ligands as the dissociation of this complex involves breaking of two bonds instead of one.

Further, $[Ni(en)_3Cl_2]$ shows octahedral geometry with d^8 configuration. Thus, (A) is true, but (R) is false.

31. (*a*) Both (A) and (R) are true and (R) is the correct explanation of (A).

$[Cr(H_2O)_6]Cl_2$ and $[Fe(H_2O)_6]Cl_2$ are examples of homoleptic complexes as all the ligands attached to the metal are the same.

32. (*b*) When a ligand has two possible donor atoms and can be attached in two ways to the central metal atom then that ligand is called ambidentate ligand, e.g. Nitro (NO_2) and nitrito (ONO). Moreover, these ligands show linkage isomerism. Thus, both (A) and (R) are true, but (R) is not the correct explanation of (A).

33. (*d*) Assertion is false, but Reason is true.
The correct (A) is; *trans* -$[CrCl_2(ox)_2]^{3-}$ does not show optical isomerism.

34. (*c*) (A) is true, but (R) is false.
Complexes of MX_6 and MX_5L type (X and L are unidentate) do not show geometrical isomerism due to presence of same type of ligands.

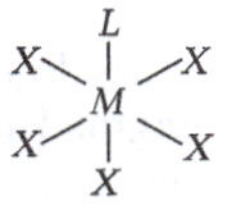

Plane of symmetry

35. (*b*) $[Co(en)_2Cl_2]^+$ exist in *cis* and *trans*-isomers out of which *cis* isomer will be optically active (*cis-d*-isomer) and (*cis-l*-isomer). Thus, both (A) and (R) are true, but (R) is not the correct explanation of (A).

36. (*a*) Tetrahedral complexes do not show geometrical isomerism because the relative positions of the unidentate ligands attached to the central metal atom are same with respect to each other. Thus, both (A) and (R) are true and R is correct explanation of (A).

37. (*a*) Both A and R are true and R is the correct explanation of A.
In both complexes, manganese is present in +3 oxidation state. The electronic configuration of Mn^{3+} is [Ar] $3d^4$.
Cyanide (CN^-) is a strong field ligand which causes pairing of electrons. This leads to the formation of low spin and inner orbital complex with d^2sp^3 hybridisation. This complex shows a magnetic moment of two unpaired electrons.
Chloride (Cl^-) is a weak field ligand which do not cause pairing of electrons. This leads to the formation of high spin and outer orbital complex with sp^3d^2 hybridisation. This complex shows a magnetic moment of four unpaired electrons.

38. (*d*) (A) is false, but (R) is true.
According to VBT, For the complex $[Fe(CN)_6]^{3-}$,

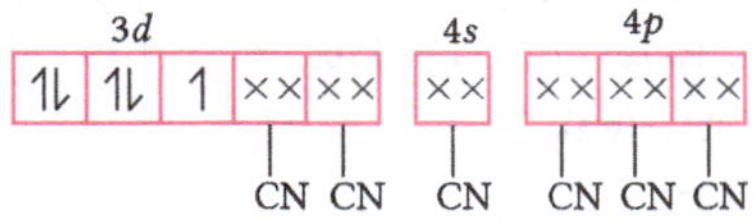

Hybridisation $= d^2sp^3$
Number of unpaired electrons is 1.
Thus, $[Fe(CN)_6]^{3-}$ ion shows magnetic moment corresponding to one unpaired electron.

i.e.
$$\mu = \sqrt{n(n+2)}$$
$$= \sqrt{1(1+2)}$$
$$= \sqrt{3} = 1.73 \text{ BM}$$

39. (*a*) $[Ni(CN)_4]^{2-}$ is square planar and diamagnetic.

$Ni \rightarrow 3d^8\,4s^2$; $Ni^{2+} \rightarrow 3d^8\,4s^0$

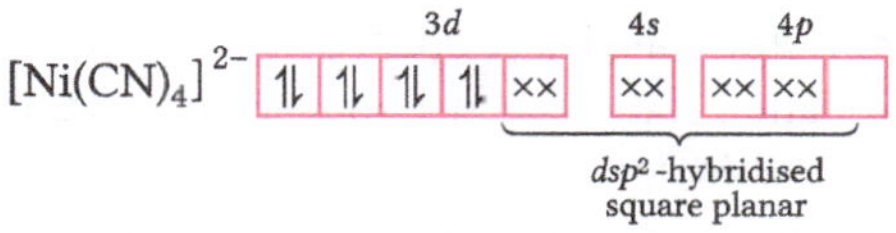

∴ This complex has no unpaired electron.
Thus, both (A) and (R) are true and (R) is the correct explanation of (A).

40. (*a*) Both (A) and (R) are true and (R) is the correct explanation of (A).

41. (*a*) Both (A) and (R) are true and (R) is the correct explanation of (A).
Toxic metal ions are removed by chelating ligands. When a solution of chelating ligand is added to solution containing toxic metals, ligands chelate the metal ions by the formation of a stable complex.

42. (i) Ligand such as CO have empty π orbitals which overlap with the filled *d* orbitals (t_{2g}) of transition metals forming π bonds (back bonding).
These π interactions increases the value of Δ_0. This account for the position of these ligands as strong ligand.
On the other hand, NH_3 do not form π bonds by back bonding. **(1)**

(ii) The IUPAC name of the complex $[CoBr_2(en)_2]^+$ is dibromido*bis*(ethane-1,2-diamine)cobalt(III) ion. **(1)**

Or

$[Co(NH_3)_5SO_4]Br$ shows ionisation isomerism as $[Co(Br)(NH_3)_5]SO_4$ and $[Co(SO_4)(NH_3)_5]Br$. **(1)**

(iii) Oxidation number of Ni in the complex $[Ni(NH_3)_6]^{2+}$ is
$$x + 6 \times (0) = +2$$
$$\Rightarrow \quad x = +2$$
Electronic configuration of Ni is $[Ar]3d^8 4s^2$.

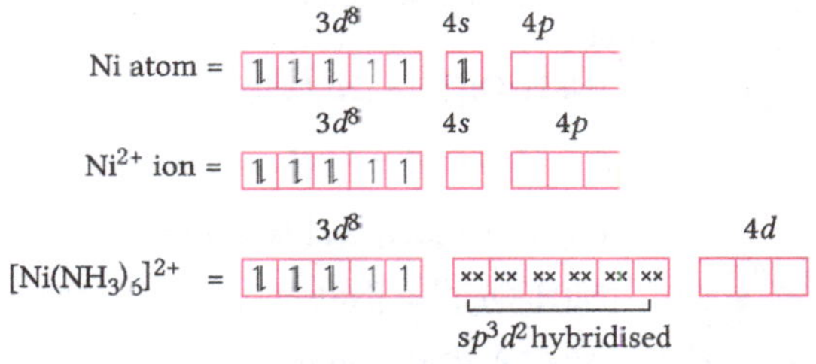

Thus, geometry of complex ion is octahedral. **(2)**

43. (i) (a) Let the oxidation state of Cu in $[Cu(NH_3)_4Cl_2]$ be x.

$\Rightarrow \quad x + 0 \times 4 + (-1 \times 2) = 0$

$\Rightarrow \quad x = +2$

Thus, oxidation state of Cu is +2. **(1)**

(b) IUPAC name of the complex $[Ni(NH_3)_6]Cl_2$ is hexaamminenickel(II) chloride. **(1)**

(ii) (a) In the complex $[Co(CN)_6]^{3-}$, Co is in +3 oxidation state. The electronic configuration of Co^{3+} is $[Ar]3d^6$.

The splitting of d-orbitals into two sets of orbitals in the given complex is represented as

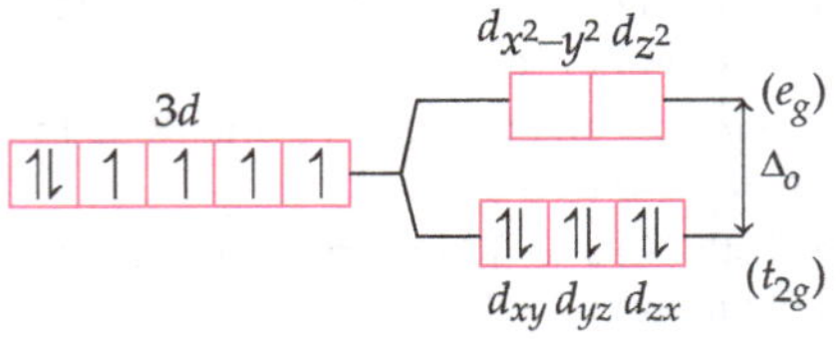

Since, CN^- is a strong field ligand therefore, pairing of electrons takes places giving rise to low spin complex. **(1)**

(iii) (c) In the complex $[Co(NH_3)_6]^{3+}$, the oxidation state of Co is +3. It has the electronic configuration as $[Ar]3d^6$. NH_3 ligand in this case behave as a strong field ligand. Thus, it causes pairing of electrons in 3d-orbital. As a result, there are no unpaired electrons present in the complex. Thus, the complex is diamagnetic in nature. **(1)**

Or

(a) In, $[Co(NH_3)_6]^{3+}$, Co is in +3 oxidation state. Its electronic configuration is $[Ar]3d^6$. NH_3 is a strong field ligand, which causes pairing of electrons in 3d orbitals.

So, this complex involves d^2sp^3 hybridisation and the complex has octahedral geometry. **(1)**

44. (i) In all the given complexes, the metal ion is Ni^{2+}. The increasing field strengths of the ligands present as per electrochemical series are in the order :

$$H_2O < NH_3 < NO_2^-$$

The energies absorbed for excitation will be in the order :

$$[Ni(H_2O)_6]^{2+} < [Ni(NH_3)_6]^{2+} < [Ni(NO_2)_6]^{4-}$$

As $E = \frac{hc}{\lambda}$, *i.e.*, $E \propto \frac{1}{\lambda}$; the wavelengths will be in the opposite order, that is as follows

$$[Ni(H_2O)_6]^{2+} > [Ni(NH_3)_6]^{2+} > [Ni(NO_2)_6]^{4-}$$ **(2)**

(ii) In $[Ti(H_2O)_6]^{3+}$ titanium is present in +3 oxidation state.

E.C. of $Ti^{3+} = 3d^1$

E.C. of

$[Ti(H_2O)_6]^{3+}$ =

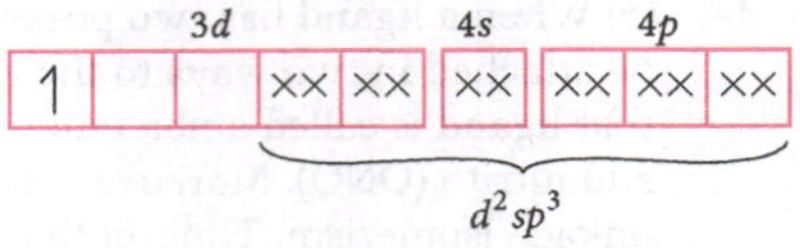

$[Ti(H_2O)_6]^{3+}$ has one unpaired electron. This unpaired electron when excited from t_{2g} level to e_g level absorb yellow light and hence, appears violet coloured. **(1)**

Or

On heating $[Ti(H_2O)_6]^{3+}$ ion, it loses H_2O molecules. As in the absence of ligand, crystal filled splitting does not occur and hence the complex becomes colourless. **(1)**

(iii) Ligands can be arranged in a series in the order of increasing field strength. This series is known as spectrochemical series. **(1)**

Subjective Type Questions

1. When $FeSO_4$ and $(NH_4)_2SO_4$ solutions are mixed in 1:1 molar ratio, Mohr's salt (a double salt) is formed.

$$FeSO_4(aq) + (NH_4)_2SO_4(aq) \longrightarrow \underset{\text{Mohr's salt}}{FeSO_4 \cdot (NH_4)_2SO_4 \cdot 6H_2O}$$

$$FeSO_4 \cdot (NH_4)_2SO_4 \cdot 6H_2O \rightleftharpoons Fe^{2+}(aq) + 2NH_4^+(aq) + 2SO_4^{2-}(aq) + 6H_2O$$

Because Fe^{2+} ions are formed on dissolution of Mohr's salt, its aqueous solution gives the test of Fe^{2+} ions. **(1)**

But when $CuSO_4$ is mixed with ammonia, following reaction occurs

$$CuSO_4(aq) + 4NH_3(aq) \longrightarrow [Cu(NH_3)_4]SO_4$$

This complex does not produce Cu^{2+} ion, so the solution of $CuSO_4$ and NH_3 does not give the test of Cu^{2+} ion. **(1)**

2. **Unidentate** Which has only one donor atom to form a coordinate bond with central metal atom/ion. e.g. H_2O, NH_3, etc.

Bidentate Which has two donor atoms that can form two coordinate bonds with central metal atom/ion. e.g. ethylene diamine, $C_2O_4^{2-}$, etc.

Ambidentate Which has two donor atoms but can only form one coordinate bond at a particular time with central metal atom/ion.
e.g. ^-SCN or ^-NCS and NO_2^- or $O{-}N{-}O^-$. **(2)**

3. (i) Refer to text on page 149. **(1)**

(ii) Refer to text on page 150. **(1)**

4. (i) $[Co(NH_3)(en)_2Cl]^{2+}$ **(1)**

(ii) $[Ni(H_2O)_2(C_2O_4)_2]^{2-}$ **(1)**

5. (i) $Na[Au(CN)_2]$ **(1)**

(ii) $[Pt(NH_3)_4Cl(NO_2)]SO_4$ **(1)**

6. (i) Tetraamminechloridonitrito-N-cobalt(III) chloride **(1)**

(ii) Dichlorido*bis*(ethane-1,2-diamine)platinum(IV) ion **(1)**

7. (i) No geometrical isomer is possible. **(1)**

(ii) Two geometrical isomers are possible for $[Co(NH_3)_3Cl_3]$.

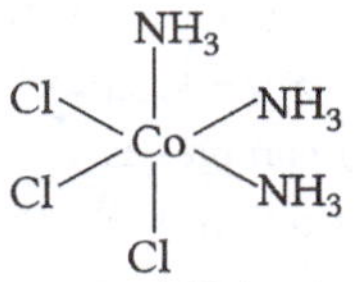
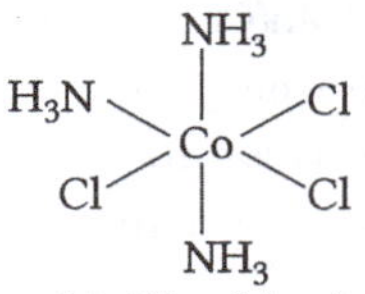

Facial (*fac*) Meridional (*mer*) **(1)**

8. (i) $[Co(NH_3)_5Cl]SO_4$ shows ionisation isomerism.
$[Co(NH_3)_5Cl]SO_4$ and $[Co(NH_3)_5SO_4]Cl$ are ionisation isomers.

(ii) $[Co(en)_3]^{3+}$ shows optical isomerism.
Refer to text on page 155.

(iii) $[Co(NH_3)_6][Cr(CN)_6]$ exhibit coordination isomerism.
Refer to text on page 152. **(2)**

9. Ionisation isomerism and geometrical isomerism are exhibited by $[Co(NH_3)_4Cl_2]Br$. **(1)**

- The ionisation isomers are $[Co(NH_3)_4Cl_2]Br$ and $[Co(NH_3)_4(Cl)(Br)]Cl$.
- The geometrical isomers are;

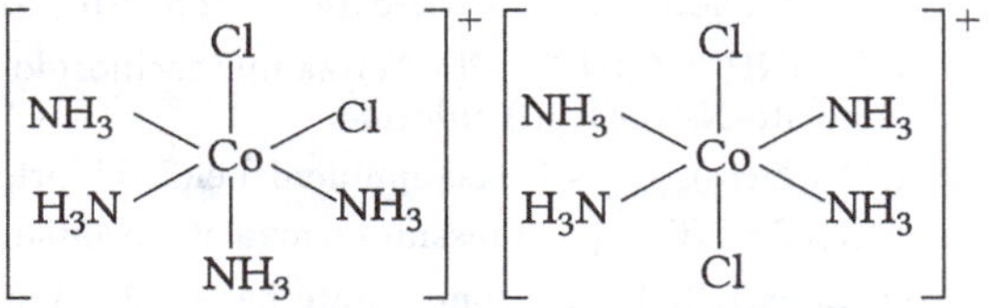

cis *trans*

The central atom has d^2sp^3 hybridisation. **(1)**

10. There are three geometrical isomers of $[Pt(NH_3)Br(Cl)(py)]$ (These structures are obtained by fixing the position of one ligand, i.e. NH_3 and placing at the *trans*-position any one of the remaining three ligands one by one. Two of these are *cis* and one is *trans*).

(i) 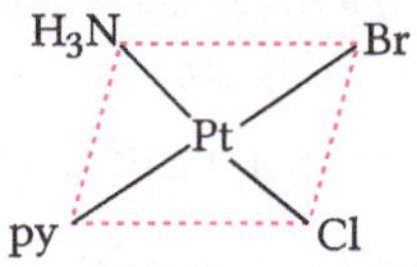

(ii) 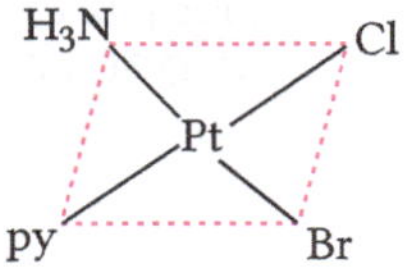

(iii) 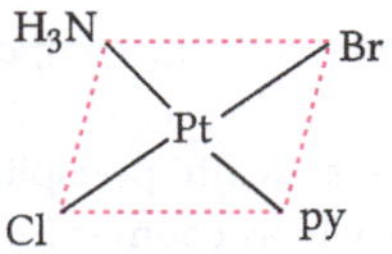 **(1)**

Optical isomerism is not exhibited by the compound with square planar geometry because of the presence of horizontal plane of symmetry. **(1)**

11. (i) NH_4^+ ion does not posses any lone pair of electrons which it can donate to the central metal ion. **(1)**

(ii) **Linkage isomer** : $[Co(NH_3)_5(ONO)]Cl_2$
IUPAC name : Pentaamminenitrito-O-cobalt (III) chloride **(1)**

12. (i) Because relative positions of ligands attached to central metal atom are same with respect to each other. **(1)**

(ii) Because square planar complexes contain a plane of symmetry. **(1)**

13. It is due to the presence of weak or strong field ligands in complexes. **(1)**

If CFSE is high, the complex will show low value of magnetic moment and *vice-versa*, e.g. $[CoF_6]^{3-}$ and $[Co(NH_3)_6]^{3+}$, the former is paramagnetic, and the latter is diamagnetic because F^- is a weak field ligand and NH_3 is a strong field ligand, while both have similar geometry.

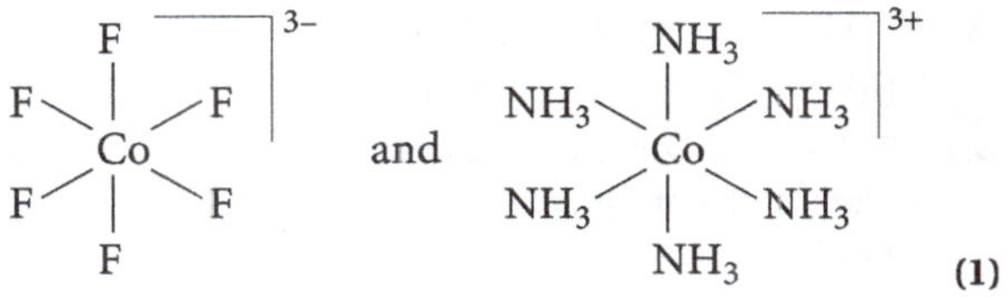 **(1)**

14. (i) For tetrahedral complexes, the crystal field stabilisation energy is lower than pairing energy. So, they are rarely found in low spin state. **(1)**

(ii) $[Co(NH_3)_6]^{3+}$: Refer to text on page 157.

$[Ni(NH_3)_6]^{2+} = [Ar]\,3d^8$

$\Rightarrow$ 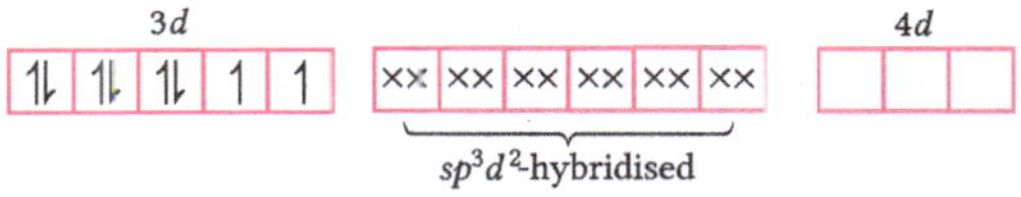

Since, $(n-1)$ *d*-orbitals are not available. So, the *nd*-orbitals are used in bond formation, i.e., in hybridisation and the complex is called outer orbital complex. **(1)**

15. Cu^{2+} forms complex with excess KCN. Cu^{2+} ions are absent in the solution of the complex.

When excess of KCN(*aq.*) is mixed with $CuSO_4$(*aq.*), a complex named potassium tetracyanocuprate(II) is formed. Since, CN^- ions are strong ligands, the complex is quite stable and when H_2S gas is passed, free Cu^{2+} ions are not available to form CuS precipitate. **(1)**

$$\underset{\text{(Excess)}}{4KCN(aq)} + CuSO_4(aq) \longrightarrow \underset{\text{(Soluble)}}{K_2[Cu(CN)_4](aq)} + K_2SO_4(aq)$$

$\downarrow +H_2S$

No cleavage and no production of Cu^{2+} ions **(1)**

16. • H_2O is a weak ligand, electrons do not pair up. Hybridisation is sp^3d^2, $n = 5$, therefore magnetic moment = 5.92 B.M.

• CN^- is a strong ligand. Electrons pair up, hybridisation is d^2sp^3, $n = 1$, therefore magnetic moment = 1.74 BM. **(2)**

17. (i) $[\mathbf{Ni(CN)_4}]^{2-}$ Refer to text on page 158. **(1)**

(ii) In $[Cu(NH_3)_4]^{2+}$ ion, copper is in +2 state.

The electronic configuration is $3d^9 4s^0$.

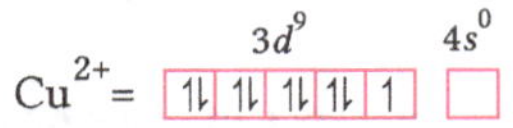

Number of unpaired electron =1

$\mu = \sqrt{n(n+2)} = \sqrt{1(1+2)} = \sqrt{3} = 1.73$ BM **(1)**

18. Refer to text on page 161. **(2)**

19. (i) (a) Refer to text on page 160. **(1/2)**

(b) Refer to text on page 149. **(1/2)**

(ii) Refer to text on page 149. **(1)**

20. (i) Refer to text on page 161. **(1)**

(ii) Refer to text on page 158 and 159. **(1)**

21. In both the complex compounds, Fe is in +2 oxidation state with configuration $3d^6$, i.e., it has four unpaired electrons.

In the presence of weak H_2O ligands, electrons do not pair up hence, due to *d-d* transition $[Fe(H_2O)_6]^{2+}$ possess colour, but in the presence of strong ligand CN^-, electrons get paired up and $[Fe(CN)_6]^{4-}$ remains colourless.

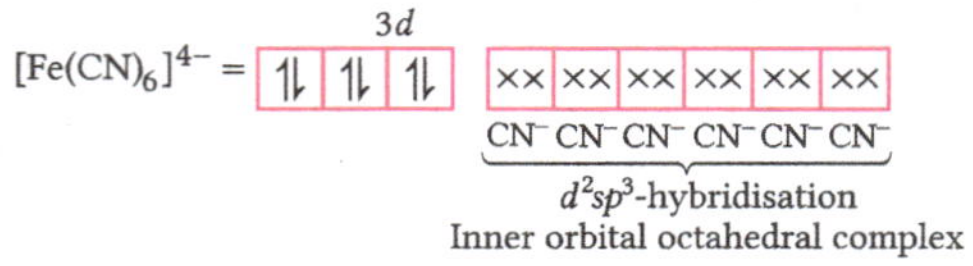

(2)

22. $\because \quad E = \frac{hc}{\lambda}$ or $E \propto \frac{1}{\lambda}$

$\therefore$ Wavelength > 500 nm requires minimum energy and wavelength < 500 nm requires maximum energy.

Now, $F^- < H_2O < NH_3 < CN^-$

$\therefore F^-$ is a weak field ligand, thus due to splitting it requires minimum energy (small energy gap) and hence absorb wavelength > 500 nm. **(1)**

Similarly, CN^- is a strong field ligand, thus due to splitting it requires more energy (more energy gap) and hence absorb wavelength < 500 nm. **(1)**

23. Refer to text on page 163. **(2)**

24. When white light falls on the complex, some part of it is absorbed. Higher the crystal field splitting energy, lower will be the wavelength absorbed by the complex. The observed colour of complex is the colour generated from the wavelength left over,

e.g. If green light is absorbed, the complex appears red.

In terms of crystal field theory, suppose there is an octahedral complex with empty e_g level and an unpaired electrons in the t_{2g} level in ground state. If the unpaired electron absorbs light corresponding to blue-green region, it will excite to e_g level and the complex will appear violet in colour.

In the absence of ligand, crystal field splitting does not occur and the substance is colourless, e.g. anhydrous $CuSO_4$ is white, but $CuSO_4 \cdot 5H_2O$ is blue in colour. **(2)**

25. (i) $K_4[Mn(CN)_6]$: Potassium hexacyanomanganate(II) **(1)**

Electronic configuration of Mn is $3d^5 4s^2$

Oxidation state of Mn in complex is +2

Hence, electronic configuration is $d^5 : t_{2g}^5 e_g^0$ **(1)**

(ii) The chemical compound $[Cr(NH_3)_6]Cl_2$ produces three ions in solution.

$$[Cr(NH_3)_6]Cl_2 \longrightarrow [Cr(NH_3)_6]^{2+} + 2Cl^-$$ **(1)**

26. Refer to text on page 147 and 148. **(3)**

27. (i) $[Zn(OH)_4]^{2-}$ (ii) $K_2[PdCl_4]$ **(3)**

(iii) $[Pt(NH_3)_2Cl_2]$ (iv) $K_2[Ni(CN)_4]$

(v) $[Co(NH_3)_6]_2(SO_4)_3$

28. (i) Hexaamminenickel(II) chloride. **(1)**

(ii) *Tris*(ethane-1,2-diamine)cobalt(III) ion. **(1)**

(iii) Tetracarbonylnickel(0). **(1)**

29. (i) Triamminetrichloridochromium(III). **(1)**

(ii) Potassium hexacyanoferrate(III). **(1)**

(iii) Dibromido*bis*(ethane-1,2-diamine)cobalt(III) ion. **(1)**

30. (i) $[Co(NH_3)_4Cl(NO_2)]Cl$ = Tetraamminechlorido-nitrito-N-cobalt(III) chloride. **(1)**

(ii) $[Ni(NH_3)_6]Cl_2$ = Hexaamminenickel(II) chloride. **(1)**

(iii) $K_3[Cr(C_2O_4)_3]$ = Potassium trioxalatochromate(III). **(1)**

(iv) $[Co(en)_2Br_2]^+$ = Dibromido*bis*(ethane-1,2-diamine) cobalt(III) ion. **(1)**

31. We dissolve both the compounds in water using different test tubes. To both the test tubes:

Case I Add $BaCl_2$ solution, one compound gives white ppt. indicating the presence of SO_4^{2-} ions.

The other compound does not give white precipitate, indicating the absence of SO_4^{2-} ions.

$$[Co(NH_3)_5Cl]SO_4 + BaCl_2\,(aq) \longrightarrow [Co(NH_3)_5Cl]Cl_2 + \underset{\text{White ppt.}}{BaSO_4(s)}$$

$$[Co(NH_3)_5SO_4]Cl + BaCl_2(aq) \longrightarrow \text{No reaction}$$ **(1½)**

Case II Add $AgNO_3$ solution to both the compounds in separate test tubes.

Only II compound gives white precipitate, not I, due to the absence of Cl^- as counter ion.

$$[Co(NH_3)_5SO_4]Cl + AgNO_3\,(aq) \longrightarrow [Co(NH_3)_5SO_4]NO_3 + \underset{\text{White ppt.}}{AgCl(s)}$$

$$[Co(NH_3)_5Cl]SO_4 + AgNO_3(aq) \longrightarrow \text{No reaction}$$

These two tests prove that the given two compounds are a pair of ionisation isomers. **(1½)**

32. (i) IUPAC name of the complex $[Fe(CN)_6]^{3-}$ is Hexacyanoferrate(III) ion.

Hybridisation of $[Fe(CN)_6]^{3-}$ In this complex, Fe is present as Fe^{3+}.

$Fe = [Ar]3d^6 4s^2$ and $Fe^{3+} = 3d^5 4s^0$

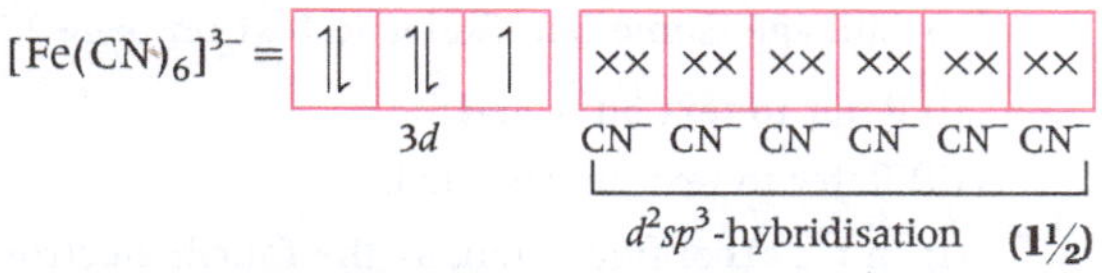

(1½)

(ii) Refer to text on page 149. (1½)

33. (i) In the complex, $[Fe(H_2O)_6]^{2+}$, Fe is in +2 oxidation state.

$Fe = [Ar]3d^6 4s^2$

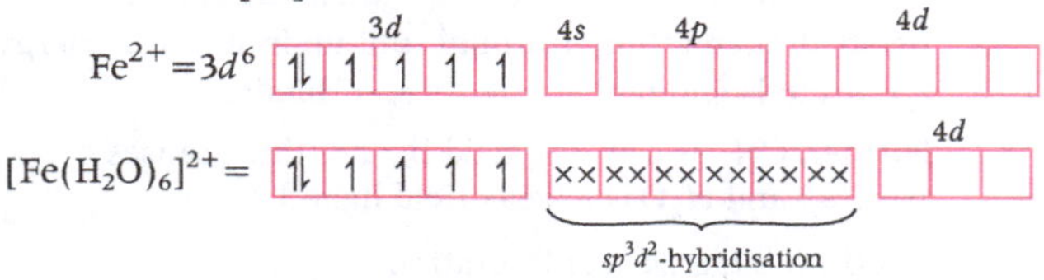

Since, four unpaired electrons are present. Thus, it is paramagnetic. (2)

(ii) The IUPAC name of the coordination complex $[CoCl_2(en)_2]NO_3$ is dichlorido*bis*(ethane-1, 2-diamine)cobalt(III) nitrate. (1)

34. (i) Refer to Q. 33 (i). (1½)

(ii) Refer to text on page 158. (1½)

35. (i) Iron (III) hexacyanoferrate(II) has formula—$Fe_4[Fe(CN)_6]_3$ (1)

(ii) $[Co(NH_3)_5Cl]SO_4$ exhibit ionisation isomerism. Its ionisation isomer is $[Co(NH_3)_5SO_4]Cl$ (1)

(iii) $[CoF_6]^{3-}$: Oxidation state of cobalt is +3.

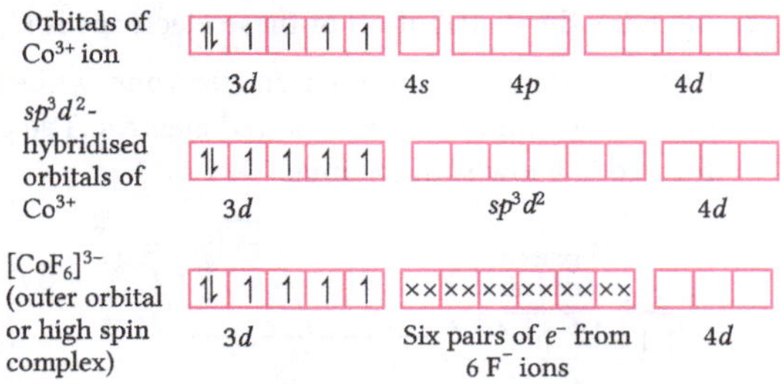

Six pairs of electrons one from each F^- ion occupy the six hybrid orbitals. Thus, the complex has octahedral geometry (sp^3d^2) and is paramagnetic due to four unpaired electrons. (1)

36. (i) Co^{2+} has an electronic configuration of $3d^7 4s^0$. In the presence of a strong ligand, it has a configuration of $t_{2g}^6 e_g^1$, as the electrons get paired up. So, one electron shifts to the higher energy level, which can be lost easily to form Co^{3+} especially to attain a stable electronic configuration (fully-filled t_{2g}). Therefore, Co^{2+} is oxidised easily to Co^{3+} in the presence of strong ligand. (1)

(ii) IUPAC name of $[Cr(C_2O_4)_3]^{3-}$ is trioxalatochromate (III) ion. (1)

(iii) If $PtCl_2 \cdot 2NH_3$ does not react with $AgNO_3$, then it means that chloride ions are not free to react and they are coordinated with the metal ion in the coordination sphere. Thus, the formula of compound can be: $[PtCl_2(NH_3)_2]$. (1)

37. In $Fe(CN)_6]^{4-}$, $Fe^{2+} = [Ar]3d^6 4s^0$

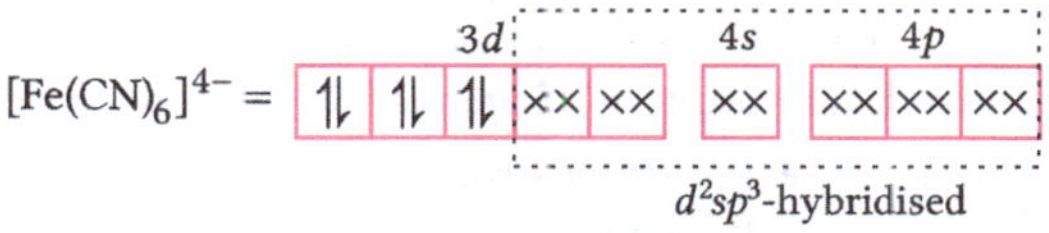

Hybridisation = d^2sp^3, Geometry = Octahedral

Diamagnetic due to no unpaired electron.

IUPAC name = Hexacyanoferrate(II) ion (1½)

$[Fe(CN)_6]^{3-}$, $Fe^{3+} = [Ar]3d^5$

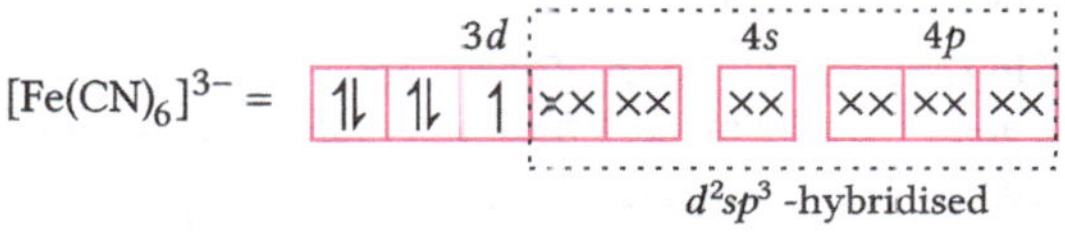

Hybridisation = d^2sp^3, Geometry = Octahedral

Paramagnetic due to the presence of one unpaired electron.

IUPAC name = Hexacyanoferrate(III) ion (1½)

38. (i) Linkage isomerism arises in a coordination compound containing ambidentate ligand. (1)

Hence, $[Co(NH_3)_5(SCN)]^{2+}$ exhibit linkage isomerism due to presence of SCN^- which is an ambidentate ligand. Thus, it can be linked with metal either through N or S.

$[Co(NH_3)_5SCN]^{2+}$ and $[Co(NH_3)_5NCS]^{2+}$

(ii) The complex in which one or more unpaired electrons are present is paramagnetic, while those which does not contain any unpaired electron is diamagnetic. (1)

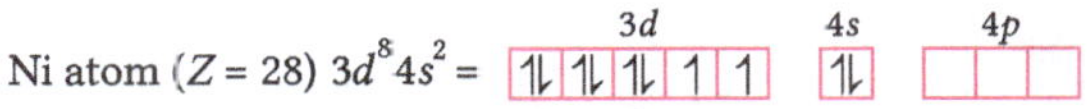

Oxidation state of Ni is +2 in both the complexes, i.e. $[NiCl_4]^{2-}$ and $[Ni(CN)_4]^{2-}$.

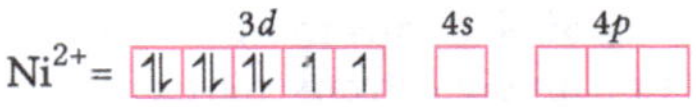

In case of $[NiCl_4]^{2-}$, Cl^- is a weak field ligand so pairing of electrons in 3d-orbital does not occur, hence compound is paramagnetic with two unpaired electrons.

In $[Ni(CN)_4]^{2-}$, CN^- is a strong field ligand, hence pairing occurs and $[Ni(CN)_4]^{2-}$ is diamagnetic.

(iii) For tetrahedral complexes, the crystal field stabilisation energy is lower than pairing energy, so they are rarely formed in low spin state. (1)

39. (i) Geometrical isomers of $[Co(en)_2Cl_2]^+$

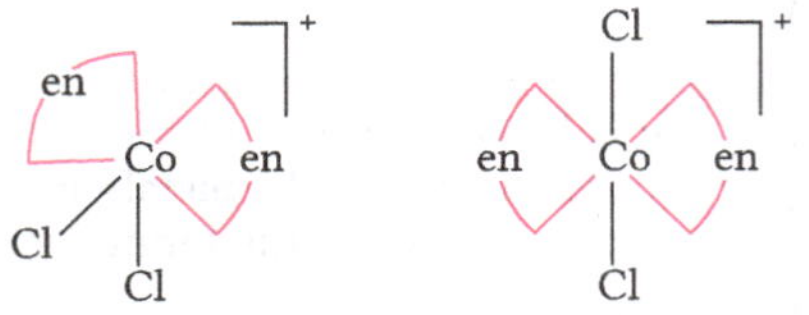

cis-isomer *trans*-isomer **(1)**

(ii) If $\Delta_o > P$, it becomes more energetically favourable for the fourth electron to occupy t_{2g} orbital with configuration $t_{2g}^4 e_g^0$. Ligands which produce this effect are known as strong field ligands. **(1)**

(iii) Didentate ligand have two donor atoms which allow them to bind to a central metal atom or ion at two sites. e.g. Ethylenediamine (en). **(1)**

40. The formula of the isomer is $[Cr(H_2O)_5Cl]Cl_2$. **(1)**

Since two mole AgCl is produced, hence 2 chloro groups are present as primary valencies.

In complex $[Cr(H_2O)_6]Cl_3$ six aqua ligands make direct bond with Cr metal ion thus complex is octahedral. **(1)**

Whereas in complex $[Cr(H_2O)_5Cl]Cl_2 \cdot H_2O$, only 5 aqua and one Cl ligands make direct bond with metal. This complex is also octahedral. The remaining one aqua is present as water of crystallisation. **(1)**

41. Refer to text on pages 160 and 161. **(3)**

42. (i) The type of isomerism exhibited by the complex $[Co(NH_3)_6][Cr(CN)_6]$ is coordination isomerism. Here, both the positive and negative ions are complex ions. Isomerism may be caused by the interchange of ligands between the anion and cation.

The two isomers are $[Co(NH_3)_6][Cr(CN)_6]$ and $[Cr(NH_3)_6][Co(CN)_6]$. **(1)**

(ii) Electronic configuration of Ni = $[Ar]3d^8 4s^2$ (Z = 28)

Ni atom (Z = 28) $3d^8 4s^2$ = 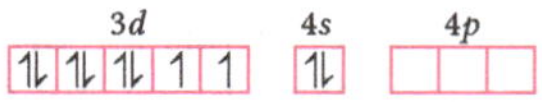

Oxidation state of Ni is +2 in both $[Ni(H_2O)_6]^{2+}$ and $[Ni(CN)_4]^{2-}$.

Ni^{2+} = 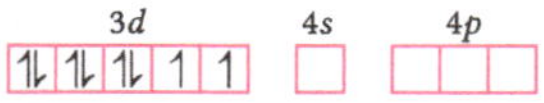

In case of $[Ni(H_2O)_6]^{2+}$, H_2O is a weak field ligand so pairing of electrons in 3*d*-orbital does not occur. These unpaired electrons get excited from a lower energy *d*-orbital to a higher energy *d*-orbital.

Due to *d*-*d* transition, $[Ni(H_2O)_6]^{2+}$ possess green colour, whereas CN^- is a strong field ligand so pairing occurs and a solution of $[Ni(CN)_4]^{2-}$ is colourless (as no unpaired electrons). **(1)**

(iii) The IUPAC name of the complex $[Co(NH_3)_5(CO_3)]Cl$ is pentaamminecarbonatocobalt (III) chloride. **(1)**

43. (i) Refer to ans. of Q.31 (i).

(ii) Refer to text on page 154.

(iii) Refer to ans. of Q.38 (ii).

(iv) Linkage isomerism (Refer to text on page 152). **(3)**

44. (i) Refer to text on page 161. **(1)**

(ii) Refer to text on page 154. **(2)**

45. (i) In $t_{2g}^3 e_g^1$ configuration, as the fourth electron enters in one of the e_g orbitals, thus it is a high spin complex. **(1½)**

(ii) Refer to text on page 160. **(1½)**

46. Because of the presence of six ligands the complex is octahedral and thus, *d*-orbital split up into lower energy t_{2g}-orbitals and higher energy e_g-orbitals.

Further, CN^- is a strong field ligand (thus, causes pairing) and H_2O is a weak field ligand.

Mn (II) ion has $3d^5$ configuration.

In the presence of H_2O molecules (acting as weak field ligand), the distribution of these five electrons is $t_{2g}^3 e_g^2$, i.e., all the electrons remain unpaired to form a high spin complex.

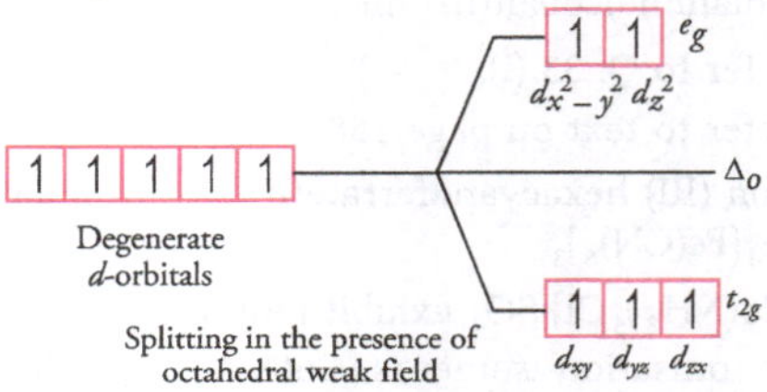

(1½)

However, in the presence of CN^- (acting as strong field ligands), the distribution of these electrons is $t_{2g}^5 e_g^0$, i.e., two t_{2g}-orbitals contain paired electrons, while the third t_{2g}-orbital contains one unpaired electron.The complex formed is a low spin complex.

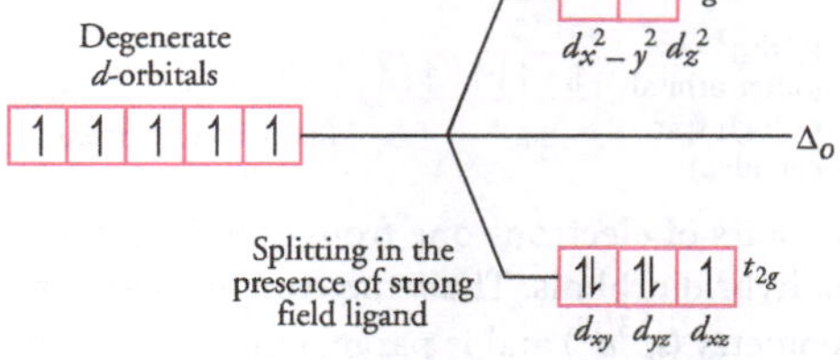

(1½)

47. **IUPAC name** Pentaaquanitrosyliron(I) **(1)**

Oxidation state of Fe =+1 **(1)**

$[Fe(H_2O)_5(NO)]^{2+}$ =

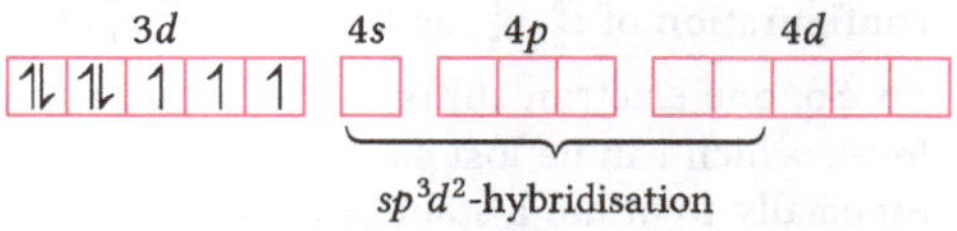

Paramagnetic due to presence of 3 unpaired electrons. **(1)**

48. Refer to text on pages 160, 161 and 162. **(3)**

49. Refer to text on pages 160 and 161. **(3)**

50. Similar to text given on page 147. **(5)**

51. (i) (a) Aquacyano*bis*-(ethane-1,2-diamine)cobalt(III) ion **(1)**

(b) Tetrachloridoplatinate (II) ion **(1)**

(c) Tetraamminechloridonitrito-o-chromium(III) ion **(1)**

(ii) Refer to text on page 161. **(2)**

52. (i) It exists as both geometrical (*cis* and *trans*) and optical isomers.

(a) **Geometrical isomers**

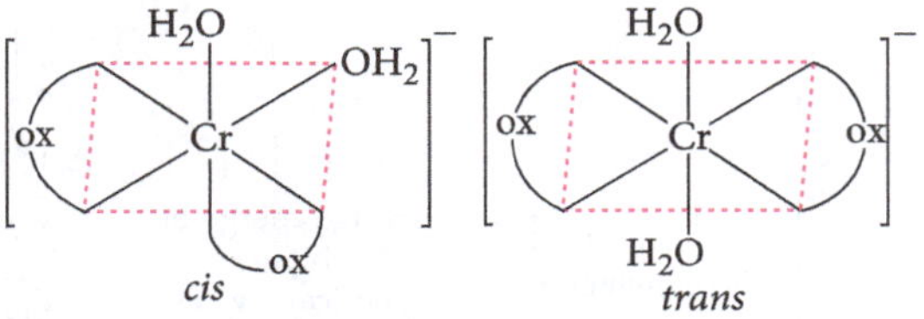

(b) **Optical isomers**

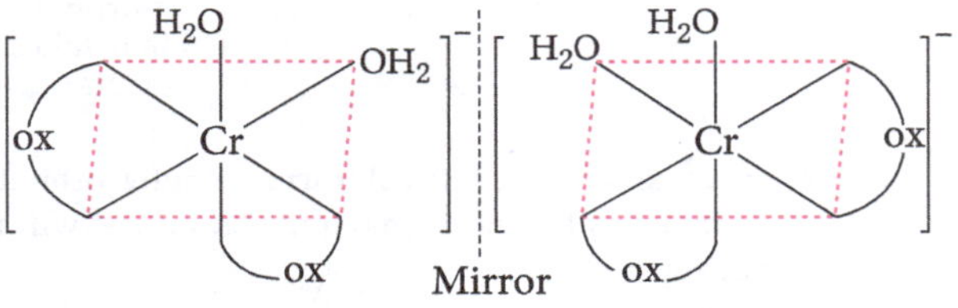

(ii) It shows two optical isomers.

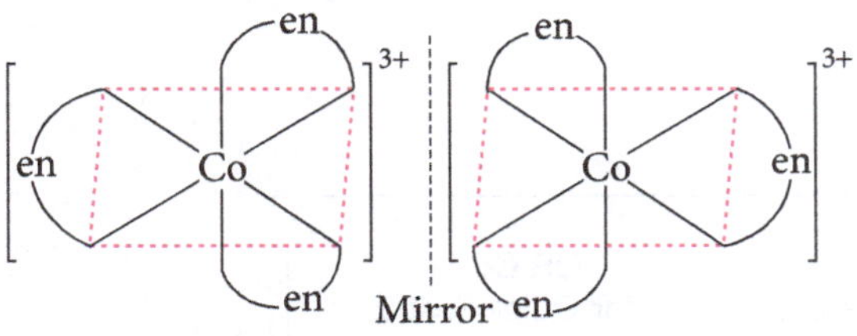

(iii) **Ionisation isomers**

$[Co(NH_3)_5(NO_2)](NO_3)_2$,

$[Co(NH_3)_5(NO_3)](NO_2)(NO_3)$

Linkage isomers

$[Co(NH_3)_5(NO_2)](NO_3)_2$,

$[Co(NH_3)_5(ONO)](NO_3)_2$

(iv) **Geometrical isomers** (*cis* and *trans*)

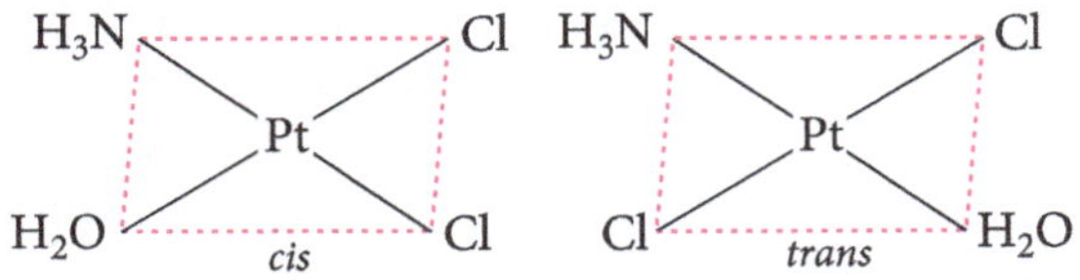

(5)

53. (i) $[\mathbf{Fe(CN)_6}]^{4-}$ In this complex, Fe is present as Fe^{2+}.

$$Fe = [Ar]\, 3d^6\, 4s^2$$

Outer configuration of $Fe^{2+} = 3d^6\, 4s^0$

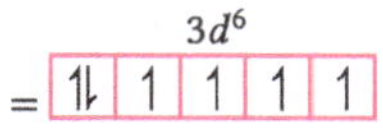

CN^- being strong field ligand, pairs up the unpaired d-electrons. Thus, two $3d$-orbitals are now available for CN^- ions.

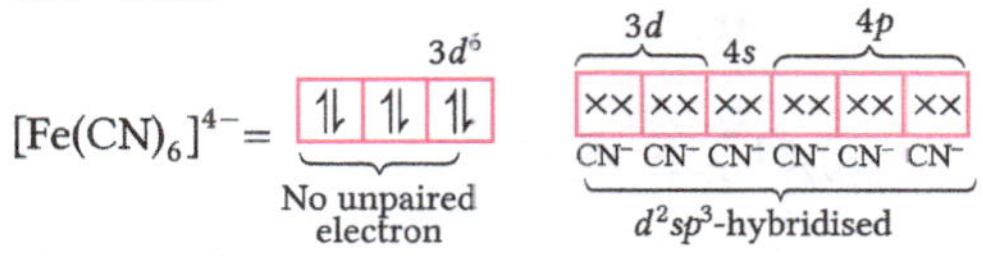

Since, all the electrons are paired, the complex is diamagnetic. Moreover, $(n-1)\,d$-orbitals are involved in bonding. So, it is an inner orbital or low spin complex.

(ii) $[\mathbf{FeF_6}]^{3-}$ In this complex, the oxidation state of Fe is +3.

$Fe^{3+} = 3d^5\, 4s^0$

F^- is a weak field ligand, so no pairing occurs. Thus, $3d$-orbitals are not available to take part in bonding.

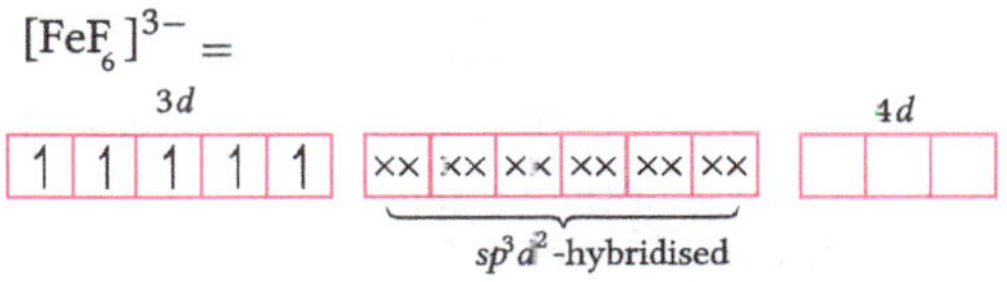

Because of the presence of five unpaired electrons, the complex is paramagnetic. Moreover, nd-orbitals are involved in bonding, so it is an outer orbital or high spin complex.

(iii) $[\mathbf{Co(C_2O_4)_3}]^{3-}$ In this complex, the oxidation state of Co is +3.

Outer configuration of $Co = 3d^7 4s^2$

$$Co^{3+} = 3d^6 4s^0$$

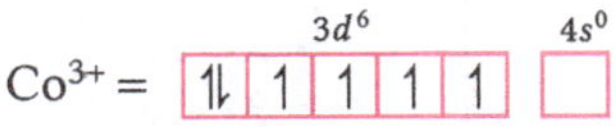

Oxalate ion being a strong field ligand pairs up the $3d$-electrons, thus two out of the five $3d$-orbitals are available for oxalate ions.

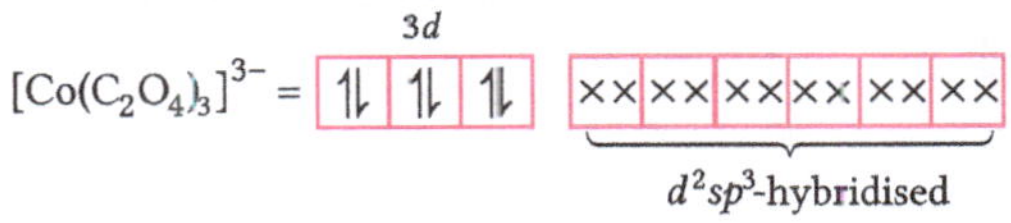

Since, all the electrons are paired, hence this complex is diamagnetic. It is an inner orbital complex because of the involvement of $(n-1)\,d$-orbital for bonding.

(iv) Refer to text on page 157. **(5)**

54. (i) In $[Fe(en)_2Cl_2]Cl$, let the oxidation number of iron be x.
Oxidation number of (en) is 0 and Cl is -1.

$$\therefore \quad x + 2(0) + 2(-1) = +1$$
$$x + 0 - 2 = +1$$
$$x = +3$$

Hence, the oxidation number of iron is +3. **(1)**

(ii) $Fe = [Ar]\,3d^6 4s^2$.

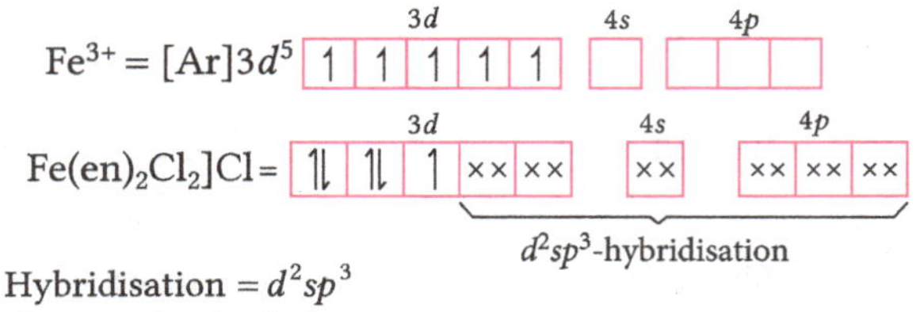

Hybridisation = d^2sp^3
Shape = Octahedral **(1)**

(iii) Since, there is one unpaired electron therefore the complex is paramagnetic.

(iv) Yes, the complex exhibits optical isomerism.

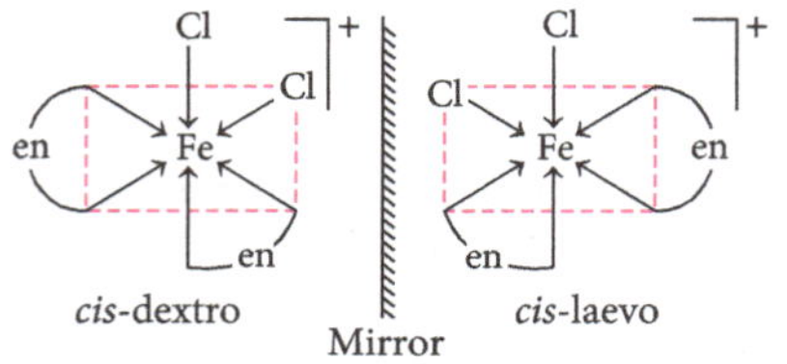

Optical isomers of $[Fe(en)_2Cl_2]^+$ or $[Fe(en)_2Cl_2]Cl$. **(1)**

(v) IUPAC name of the complex is
Dichlorido*bis*-(ethane-1, 2-diamine) iron (III) chloride. **(1)**

55. (i) Refer to Q-33 (i). [Shape = Octahedral] **(2½)**

(ii) Refer to text on pages 157 and 158. **(2½)**

56. (i) (a) **Test tube *C***

$$10I^- + 2MnO_4^- + 16H^+ \longrightarrow \underset{\text{(Violet vapours)}}{5I_2\uparrow} + 2Mn^{2+} + 8H_2O$$ **(1)**

(b) **Test tube *A***

$$5C_2O_4^{2-} + 2MnO_4^- + 16H^+ \longrightarrow \underset{\substack{\text{(Bubbles of gas}\\ \text{that extinguishes}\\ \text{a burning matchstick)}}}{10CO_2\uparrow} + 2Mn^{2+} + 8H_2O$$ **(1)**

(ii) (a)

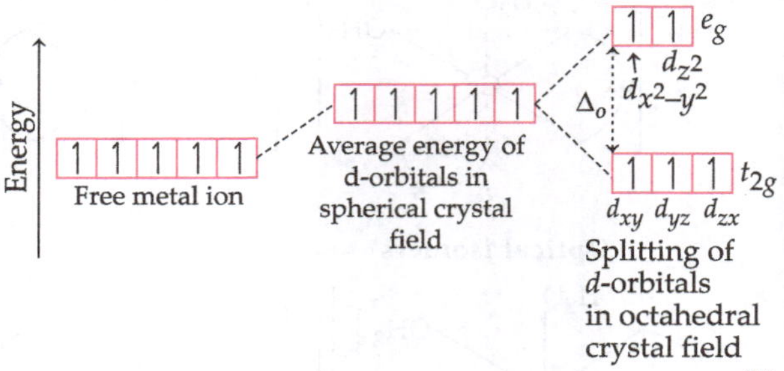

(1)

(b) sp^3d^2, since $\Delta_o < P$ it will form an outer orbital complex as the electrons in the 3*d*-orbital will not pair up. **(1)**

(c) Optical isomerism. **(1)**

QR Code for Quick Test 1

QR Code for Quick Test 2

QR Code for Quick Test 3

SELF ASSESSMENT TEST

Objective Type Questions [1 Mark]

1. A complex compound in which the oxidation number of a metal is zero, is

(a) $[Ni(CO)_4]$ (b) $[Pt(NH_3)_4]Cl_2$
(c) $K_3[Fe(CN)_6]$ (d) $K_4[Fe(CN)_6]$

2. Which of the following complex species is not expected to exhibit optical isomerism?

(a) $[Co(en)_3]^{3+}$
(b) $[Co(en)_2Cl_2]^+$
(c) $[Co(NH_3)_3Cl_3]$
(d) $[Co(en)(NH_3)_2Cl_2]^+$

3. Match the complex ions given in Column I with the hybridisation and number of unpaired electrons given in Column II and assign the correct code.

Column I (Complex ion)	Column II (Hybridisation, number of unpaired electrons)
A. $[Cr(H_2O)_6]^{3+}$	1. $dsp^2, 1$
B. $[Co(CN)_4]^{2-}$	2. $sp^3d^2, 5$
C. $[Ni(NH_3)_6]^{2+}$	3. $d^2sp^3, 3$
D. $[MnF_6]^{4-}$	4. $sp^3, 4$
	5. $sp^3d^2, 2$

(a) A-3, B-1, C-5, D-2 (b) A-4, B-3, C-2, D-1
(b) A-3, B-2, C-4, D-1 (d) A-4, B-1, C-2, D-3

4. Which of the following statements are correct?

I. In octahedral complexes, d_{z^2}, $d_{x^2-y^2}$ orbitals have higher energy than d_{xy}, d_{yz} and d_{zx} orbitals.

II. In tetrahedral complexes, d_{xy}, d_{yz}, d_{zx} orbitals have higher energy than d_{z^2} and $d_{x^2-y^2}$ orbitals.

III. The colours of complexes are due to electronic transitions from one set of *p*-orbitals to another set of orbitals.

IV $\Delta_{(tetrahedral)} = \frac{9}{4}\Delta_{(octahedral)}$

(a) I and II only (b) III and IV only
(c) II and III only (d) II and IV only

5. The correct order of the increasing magnitude of Δ_o for the octahedral complexes of Co (Atomic number = 27) is

(a) $[Co(CN)_6]^{3-} < [Co(C_2O_4)_3]^{3-} < [Co(H_2O)_6]^{3+} < [Co(NH_3)_6]^{3+}$
(b) $[Co(C_2O_4)_3]^{3-} < [Co(H_2O)_6]^{3+} < [Co(NH_3)_6]^{3+} < [Co(CN)_6]^{3-}$
(c) $[Co(H_2O)_6]^{3+} < [Co(NH_3)_6]^{3+} < [Co(CN)_6]^{3-} < [Co(C_2O_4)_3]^{3-}$
(d) $[Co(NH_3)_6]^{3+} < [Co(H_2O)_6]^{3+} < [Co(C_2O_4)_3]^{3-} < [Co(CN)_6]^{3-}$

Assertion-Reason [1 Mark]

Directions (Q. Nos. 6-8) In the following questions an Assertion (A) is followed by a corresponding Reason (R). Use the following keys to choose the appropriate answer.

(a) Both (A) and (R) are true and (R) is the correct explanation of (A).
(b) Both (A) and (R) are true but (R) is not the correct explanation of (A).
(c) (A) is true, but (R) is false.
(d) (A) is false, but (R) is true.

6. **Assertion** (A) $[Co(NH_3)_3(NO_2)_3]$ form facial and meridional isomers.

Reason (R) *fac* and *mer* are geometrical isomers.

7. **Assertion** (A) Central atom in $[NiCl_2(H_2O)_4]$ and $[CoCl(NH_3)_5]^{2+}$ behave as Lewis acid.

Reason (R) Ni^{2+} and Co^{3+} have empty *d*-subshell. So, they can accept a pair of electron.

8. **Assertion** (A) Potassium ferrocyanide is diamagnetic whereas potassium ferricyanide is paramagnetic.

Reason (R) Crystal field splitting in ferrocyanide ion is greater than that of ferricyanide ion.

Short Answer Type I Questions [2 Marks]

9. Differentiate between coordination compounds and double salts.

10. When a coordination compound $CoCl_3 \cdot 6NH_3$ is mixed with $AgNO_3$, 3 moles of AgCl are precipitated per mole of the compound. Write

(i) structural formula of the complex.
(ii) IUPAC name of the complex.

11. (i) Magnetic moment of $[MnCl_4]^{2-}$ is 5.92 BM. Give reason.
(ii) $[Co(NH_3)_6]^{3+}$ has d^2sp^3-hybridisation and octahedral geometry. Justify.

Short Answer Type II Questions [3 Marks]

12. Explain linkage isomerism. Give an example of complexes which exhibit this type of isomerism. Also, find out the type of isomerism in the given pair of coordination compounds $[Cr(H_2O)_5Cl]Cl_2 \cdot H_2O$ and $[Cr(H_2O)_6]Cl_3$.

13. The magnetic moments of few transition metal ions are given below.

Metal ion	Magnetic moment (BM)
Sc^{3+}	0.00
Cr^{2+}	4.90
Ni^{2+}	2.84
Ti^{3+}	1.73

(Atomic no. of Sc = 21, Ti =22, Cr = 24, Ni = 28)
(i) Which of the given metal ions has the maximum number of unpaired electrons and forms colourless aqueous solution respectively?
(ii) On the basis of crystal field theory, write the electronic configuration of d^5 ion if
(a) $\Delta_o > P$ (b) $\Delta_o < P$

14. Using crystal field theory, draw energy level diagram, write electronic configuration of central atom/ion and determine the magnetic moment of the given coordination complexes.
(a) $[FeF_6]^{3-}$ (b) $[Fe(H_2O)_6]^{2+}$
(c) $[Fe(CN)_6]^{4-}$

Case-Study [4 Marks]

15. Coordination compounds exhibit an array of colours, which can be explained through the principles of crystal field theory. This theory provides a framework for understanding how the interaction between the metal ion and surrounding ligands affects the metal, leading to the absorption of specific wavelengths of light. The colour observed for a complex is actually the complementary colour of the light that is absorbed.

Coordination complex	Colour
$[Fe(CN)_6]^{3-}$	Yellow
$[Ti(H_2O)_6]^{3+}$	Violet
$[Ni(CO)_4]$	Colourless
$[Cu(NH_3)_4]^{2+}$	Deep blue

Read the given case and answer the following questions.
(i) According to crystal field theory, why does the colour of a coordination complex depend on the nature of its ligands?
(ii) What is the magnetic behaviour shown by $[Ti(H_2O)_6]^{3+}$?
(iii) How many unpaired electrons are present in $[Ni(CO)_4]$?
Or (iii) $[Cu(NH_3)_4]^{2+}$ has how many unpaired electrons in the 3*d*-orbital?

Long Answer Type Questions [5 Marks]

16. (i) Name the type of isomerism shown by the following pairs of coordination compounds.
(a) $[Cu(NH_3)_4][PtCl_4]$ and $[Pt(NH_3)_4][CuCl_4]$
(b) $[Cr(SCN)(H_2O)_5]^{2+}$ and $[Cr(NCS)(H_2O)_5]^{2+}$
(c) $[Cr(H_2O)_6]Cl_3$ and $[CrCl(H_2O)_5]Cl_2 \cdot H_2O$
(ii) Explain the following cases giving appropriate reasons.
(a) Nickel does not form low spin octahedral complexes.
(b) Co^{2+} is easily oxidised to Co^{3+} in the presence of a strong ligand.

17. To explain bonding in coordination compounds various theories were proposed. One of the important theory was valence bond theory. According to that, the central metal ion in the complex makes available a number of empty orbitals for the formation of coordination bonds with suitable ligands. The appropriate atomic orbitals of the metal hybridise to give a set of equivalent orbitals of definite geometry.
The various complex ion are $[Fe(H_2O)_6]^{2+}$ and $[Mn(CN)_6]^{3-}$.
Answer the following questions.
(i) Write the type of hybridisation in $[Fe(H_2O)_6]^{2+}$ and $[Mn(CN)_6]^{3-}$ respectively.
(ii) Write the magnetic nature of $[Fe(H_2O)_6]^{2+}$.
(iii) Calculate the magnetic moment value of $[Mn(CN)_6]^{3-}$.
(iv) What type of complex is $[Mn(CN)_6]^{3-}$ (inner, outer orbital complex)?
(v) Write the limitations of VBT.

Answers

1. (a) 2. (c) 3. (a) 4. (a) 5. (b) 6. (b)
7. (a) 8. (c)

06

CHAPTER

The compounds formed by the replacement of hydrogen atom(s) from a hydrocarbon, aliphatic or aromatic, by halogen atom(s) (i.e., F, Cl, Br, I) are called **alkyl halide** (haloalkane) and **aryl halide** (haloarene) respectively.

YOUR STUDY GOALS

- 6.1 Classification
- 6.2 Nomenclature
- 6.3 Nature of C—*X* Bond
- 6.4 Preparation of Haloalkanes
- 6.5 Preparation of Haloarenes
- 6.6 Physical Properties of Haloalkanes and Haloarenes
- 6.7 Chemical Reactions of Haloalkanes
- 6.8 Chemical Reactions of Haloarenes
- 6.9 Polyhalogen Compounds

YOUR PRACTICE GOAL

- Objective Type Questions (40 Qs ; 26 MCQs, 12 A-R, 2 Case-study)
- Subjective Type Questions (38 Qs; 18 SA-I, 16 SA-II, 4 LA)

Haloalkanes and Haloarenes

Haloalkanes contain halogen atom(s) attached to the sp^3-hybridised carbon atom(s) of an alkyl group whereas haloarenes contain halogen atom(s) attached to sp^2-hybridised carbon atom(s) of an aryl group.

6.1 Classification

Haloalkanes and haloarenes may be classified as follows

On the Basis of Number of Halogen Atoms

For Monosubstituted Haloalkane

Depending on the number of halogen atoms in their structures, haloalkanes and haloarenes may be classified as mono, di, tri or polyhalogen (tetra, penta, etc.) compounds.

Monohaloalkane	Dihaloalkane	Trihaloalkane
CH_3X or C_2H_5X	CH_2X—CH_2X	CH_2X—CHX—CH_2X

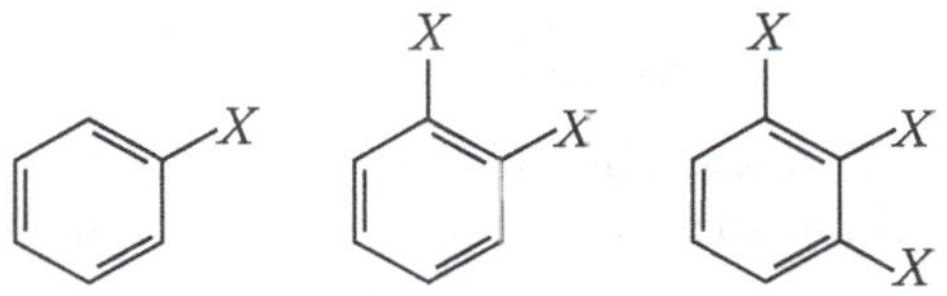

Monohaloarene Dihaloarene Trihaloarene

(where, X = F, Cl, Br, I)

For Disubstituted Haloalkane

The dihalo-compounds having same type of halogen atoms are further classified as

(i) ***Geminal* or *gem*-halides** Here, both the halogen atoms are present on the same carbon atom.

e.g.

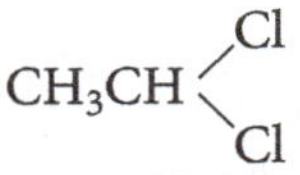

gem-dihalide

1,1-dichloroethane

(ii) ***Vicinal* or *vic*-halides** Here, both the halogen atoms are present on the adjacent carbon atoms.

e.g.

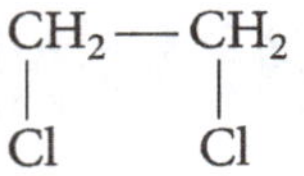

vic-dihalide

1,2-dichloroethane

On the Basis of Nature of Carbon in C—*X* Bond

Monohalocompounds may further be classified according to the hybridisation of the carbon atom to which halogen is bonded, as discussed below.

1. Compounds Containing sp^3C—*X* Bond

These are classified into three categories as follows

(i) **Alkyl halides** or **Haloalkanes** (R—X) In these halides, the halogen atom (X) is bonded to an alkyl group (R).

They form a homologous series of compounds represented by the formula, $C_nH_{2n+1}X$.

They are further classified as primary (1°), secondary (2°) or tertiary (3°) depending upon the nature of carbon atom to which the halogen is attached.

e.g.

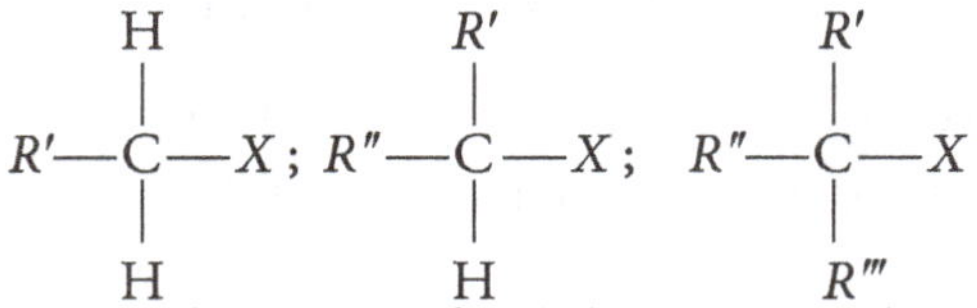

Primary (1°) Secondary (2°) Tertiary (3°)

If in R—X, R is an alicyclic, i.e., cyclic aliphatic hydrocarbons such as cyclopropane, cyclobutane etc.

They are known as halocycloalkane or cycloalkyl halide.

e.g.

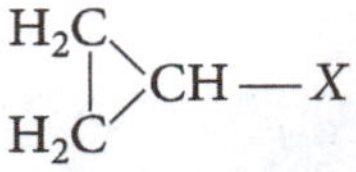

Halocyclopropane

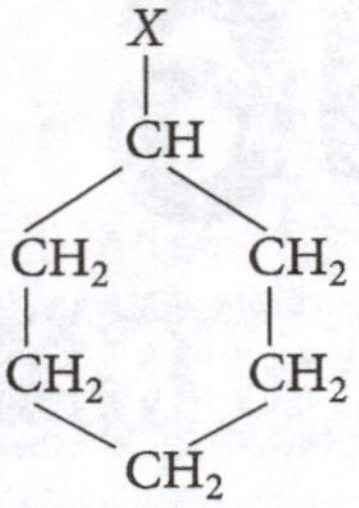

Halocyclohexane

(ii) **Allylic halides** In these halides, the halogen is bonded to the sp^3-hybridised carbon atom next to carbon-carbon double bond which is also called allylic carbon. Hence, these halides are called allylic halides.

e.g.

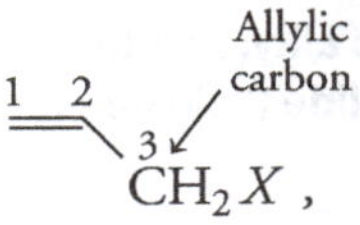

3-haloprop-1-ene (Allyl halide)

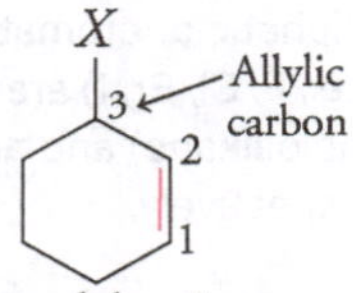

3-halocyclohex-1-ene

$CH_2{=}CH—CH_2—Cl$,

3-chloroprop-1-ene

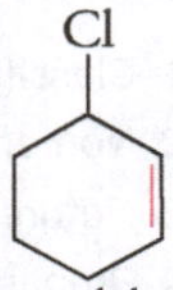

3-chlorocyclohex-1-ene

(iii) **Benzylic halides** In these halides, the halogen atom is bonded to the sp^3-hybridised carbon atom next to an aromatic ring, i.e., to a benzylic carbon.

e.g.

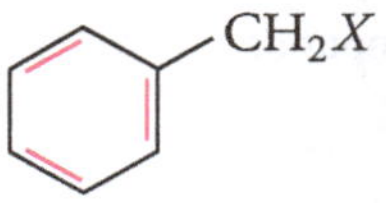

(1°)

;

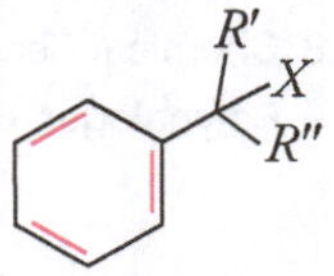

[If $R' = CH_3$, $R'' = H$ (2°)
If $R' = R'' = CH_3$ (3°)]

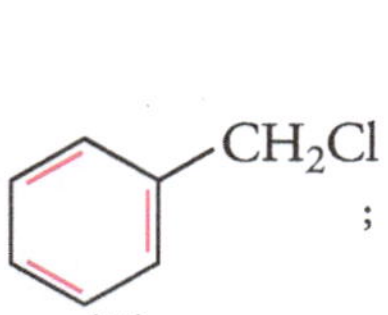

(1°)

;

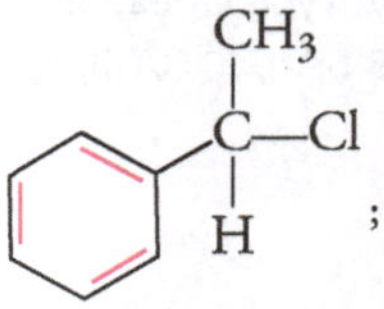

(2°)

;

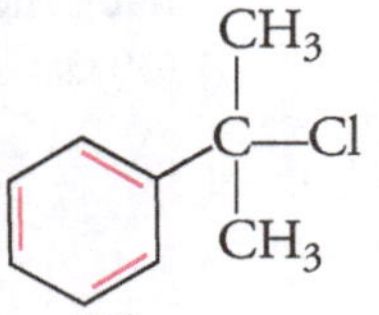

(3°)

2. Compounds Containing sp^2 C—*X* Bond

In these compounds, halogen is directly attached to one of the double bonded carbon atom.

$(-\overset{|}{C}=\overset{|}{C}-X)$.

These are classified into the following two types

(i) **Vinylic halides** In these halides, the halogen atom is bonded to the sp^2-hybridised carbon atom of a carbon-carbon double bond, i.e., vinylic carbon.

e.g.

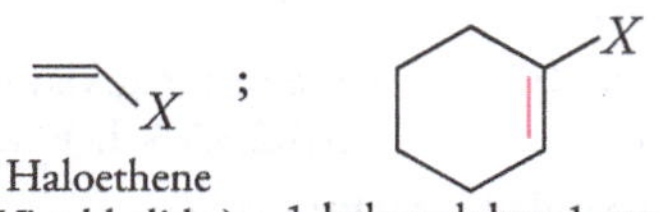

Haloethene (Vinyl halide) ; 1-halocyclohex-1-ene

(ii) **Aryl halides** In these halides, the halogen atom is directly bonded to the sp^2-hybridised carbon atom of an aromatic ring.

e.g.

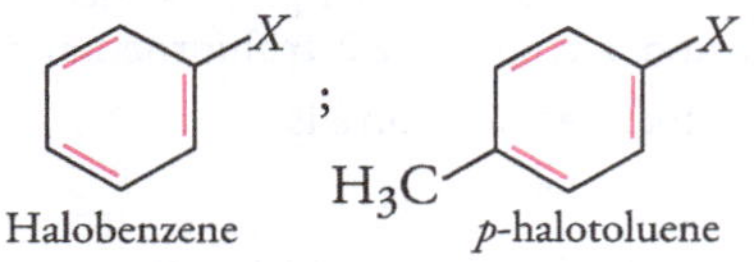

Halobenzene ; *p*-halotoluene

6.2 Nomenclature

The nomenclature of haloalkanes and haloarenes are discussed below.

For Monosubstituted Haloalkane

The **common names** of alkyl halides are derived by naming the alkyl group followed by the name of halide (chloride, bromide, etc). Here, the prefixes *n*-, *iso*-, *sec*-, *tert*-, etc., are used.

In **IUPAC system**, alkyl halides are named as halosubstituted hydrocarbons, i.e., haloalkanes.

The names are written by prefixing the word 'halo' to the name of alkane corresponding to the longest continuous carbon chain having the halogen atom.

e.g. $CH_3CH_2CH_2I$;

Common name *n*-propyl iodide
IUPAC name (1-iodopropane)

$$CH_3-\underset{\underset{CH_3}{|}}{CH}-CH_2-Br;$$

Common name *iso*-butyl bromide
IUPAC name (1-bromo-2-methylpropane)

$$CH_3-\overset{\overset{CH_3}{|}}{\underset{\underset{CH_3}{|}}{C}}-CH_2Cl$$

Common name *neo*-pentyl chloride
IUPAC name (1-chloro-2, 2-dimethylpropane)

For Disubstituted Haloalkane

The dihaloalkanes having the same type of halogen atoms are named as alkylidene or alkylene dihalides. In common name system, *gem*-dihalides are named as **alkylidene halides**, whereas *vic*-dihalides are named as **alkylene dihalides**. In IUPAC system, they are named as **dihaloalkanes**.

e.g.

$$CH_3CH\genfrac{}{}{0pt}{}{Cl}{Cl} \qquad \underset{Cl}{\underset{|}{CH_2}}-\underset{Cl}{\underset{|}{CH_2}}$$

	gem-dihalide	*vic*-dihalide
Common name	Ethylidene chloride	Ethylene dichloride
IUPAC name	1,1-dichloroethane	1,2-dichloroethane

For Haloarenes

They are named by prefixing 'halo' before the name of the aromatic hydrocarbon.

For monohalogen substituted derivatives of benzene, common and IUPAC names are the same.

For dihalogen derivatives, the prefixes *o*-, *m*-, *p*- are used in common system but in IUPAC system, the numerals 1,2 ; 1,3 and 1,4 are used respectively.

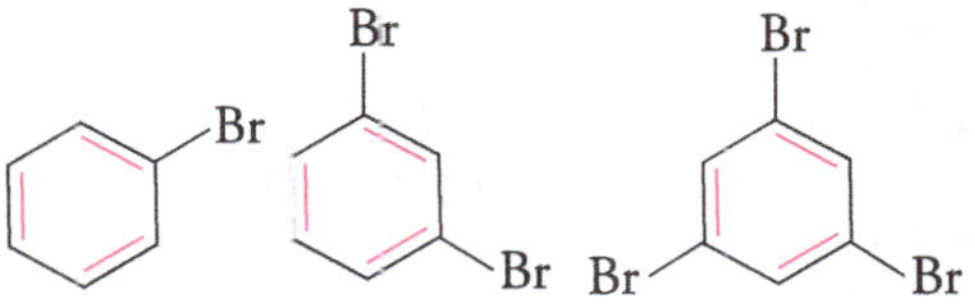

	(a)	(b)	(c)
Common name	Bromobenzene	*m*-dibromobenzene	*sym*-tribromobenzene
IUPAC name	Bromobenzene	1, 3-dibromobenzene	1,3,5-tribromobenzene

In case, if a halogen (functional group) is attached to a benzene ring which in turn, is attached to an alkane or alkene then the position of that halogen will be written in bracket.

e.g.

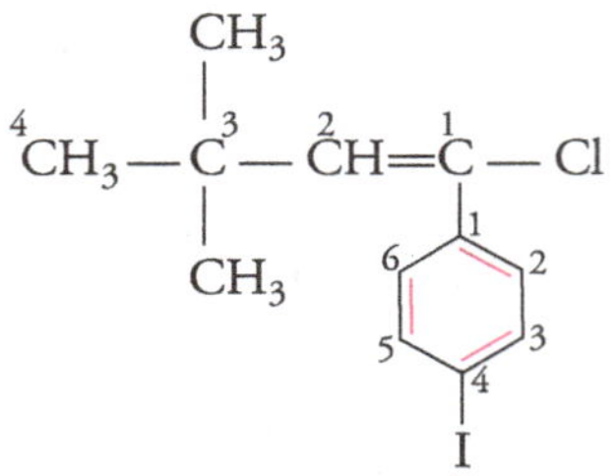

IUPAC name 1-chloro-(4-iodophenyl)-3,3-dimethylbut-1-ene.

Common and IUPAC Names of some Halides

Structure	Common name	IUPAC name
$CH_3CH_2CH_2F$	*n*-propyl fluoride	1-fluoropropane
$(CH_3)_3CCH_2—Br$	*neo*-pentyl bromide	1-bromo-2,2-dimethyl propane
$CH_3CH_2CH(Cl)CH_3$	*sec*-butyl chloride	2-chlorobutane
$(CH_3)_3C—Br$	*tert*-butyl bromide	2-bromo-2-methyl propane
$CH_2=CH—CH_2Br$	Allyl bromide	3-bromopropene
$CH_2=CHCl$	Vinyl chloride	Chloroethene
CH_2Cl_2	Methylene chloride	Dichloromethane
$CHCl_3$	Chloroform	Trichloromethane
$CHBr_3$	Bromoform	Tribromomethane
CCl_4	Carbon tetrachloride	Tetrachloromethane
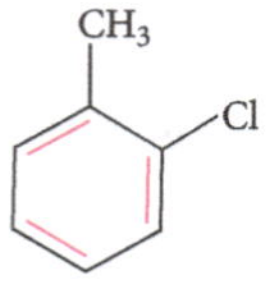	*o*-chlorotoluene	1-chloro-2-methyl benzene or 2-chlorotoluene
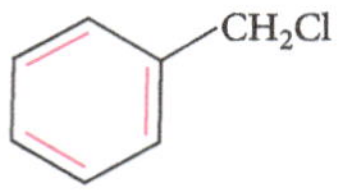	Benzyl chloride	Chlorophenylmethane

Example 1 Write the IUPAC names of the following compounds

(i) $(CCl_3)_3CCl$

(ii) $CHF_2CBrClF$

(iii) $ClCH_2C\equiv CCH_2Br$ **NCERT**

Sol. (i) The expanded structure is

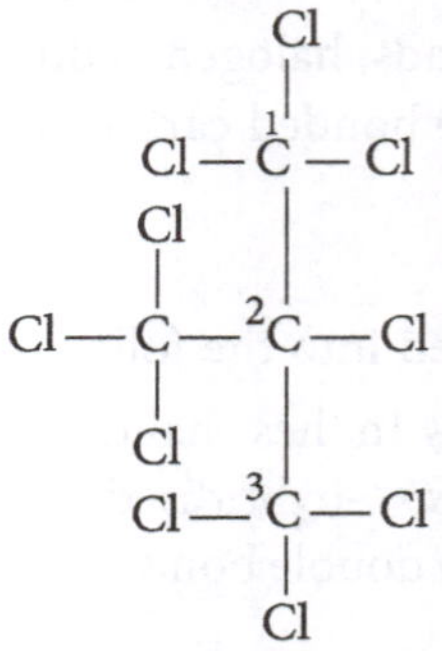

Thus, the IUPAC name of the given structure is 2-(trichloromethyl)-1,1,1,2,3,3,3,-heptachloropropane.

(ii) The expanded structure is

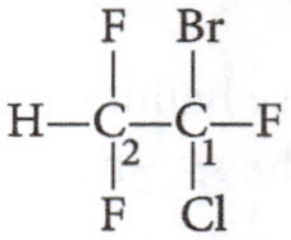

The IUPAC name of the given structure is 1-bromo-1-chloro-1,2,2-trifluoroethane

(iii) The expanded structure is

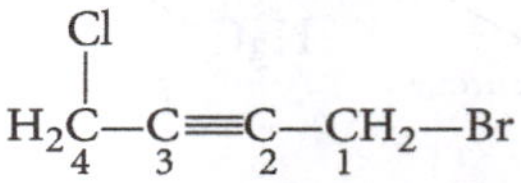

The IUPAC name of the given structure is 1-bromo-4-chloro-but-2-yne

Example 2 **Draw the structure of**

(i) 2-chloro-3-methylpentane

(ii) *p*-bromochlorobenzene **NCERT**

Sol.

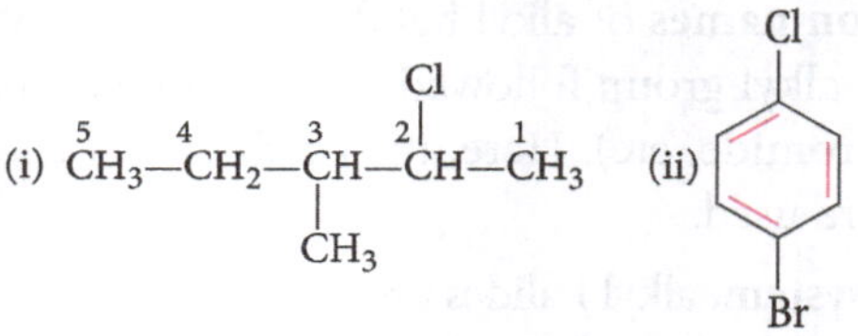

6.3 Nature of C—*X* Bond

Electronegativity of halogen atom is greater than that of carbon atom due to which the shared pair of electron in C—*X* bond lies closer to the halogen atom.

As a result, the halogen atom bears a partial negative charge whereas, the carbon atom bears a partial positive charge, i.e., carbon-halogen bond of alkyl halide is polarised.

$$>\overset{\delta+}{C}-\overset{\delta-}{X}$$

As we go down the group in the modern periodic table, the size of halogen atom increases, fluorine atom is the smallest and iodine atom is the largest.

Consequently, the carbon-halogen bond length also increases from C—F to C—I.

Also, on moving from F to I, the electronegativity of the halogen decreases, therefore the polarity of the C—X bond decreases accordingly.

Carbon-Halogen (C—X) Bond Lengths, Bond Enthalpies and Dipole Moments

Bond between carbon and halogen	Bond length/pm	C—X Bond enthalpies / kJ mol^{-1}	Dipole moment/Debye
CH_3-F	139	452	1.847
CH_3-Cl	178	351	1.860
CH_3-Br	193	293	1.830
CH_3-I	214	234	1.636

Quick Test 1

1. Out of 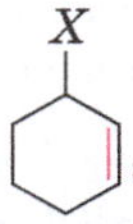 and 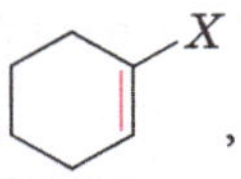, which is an example of allylic halide? *CBSE 2017*

2. Name the following halides according to IUPAC system and classify them as alkyl, allyl, benzyl (primary, secondary, tertiary), vinyl or aryl halides.

(i) $(CH_3)_2CHCH(Cl)CH_3$

(ii) $CH_3CH_2CH(CH_3)CH(C_2H_5)Cl$

(iii) $CH_3CH_2C(CH_3)_2CH_2I$

(iv) $(CH_3)_3CCH_2CH(Br)C_6H_5$

(v) $CH_3CH(CH_3)CH(Br)CH_3$

(vi) $CH_3C(C_2H_5)_2CH_2Br$ *NCERT*

3. Write the IUPAC name of the following compounds.

(i) 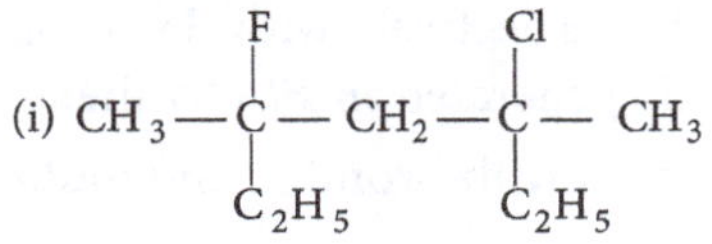

(ii) 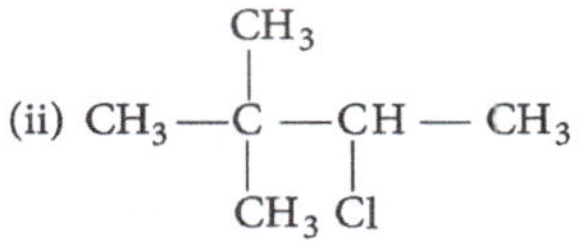

4. Give the IUPAC names of the following compounds.

(i) $CH_3CH(Cl)CH(Br)CH_3$

(ii) $CHF_2CBrClF$

(iii) $ClCH_2C{\equiv}CCH_2Br$

(iv) $CH_3C(p\text{-}ClC_6H_4)_2CH(Br)CH_3$ *NCERT*

5. Write the structures of the following organic halogen compounds

(i) 1-bromo-4-*sec*-butyl-2-methylbenzene

(ii) 1, 4-dibromobut-2-ene

(iii) 4-*tert*-butyl-3-iodoheptane *NCERT Intext*

6. Write the structures of different dihalogen derivatives of propane. *NCERT Intext*

7. The dipole moment of CH_3Br is less as compared to the dipole moment of CH_3F. Give reason.

For Solutions, See QR Code on Pg. 227

6.4 Preparation of Haloalkanes

Haloalkanes can be prepared from wide range of organic compounds through various methods. Some important methods of preparation are discussed below.

Preparation from Alcohols

In this method, the hydroxyl group of an alcohol is replaced by halogen on reaction with concentrated halogen acids, phosphorus halides or thionyl chloride.

(i) By the Action of Halogen Acids

Haloalkanes are prepared by the treatment of alcohols with halogen acids as follows

$$\underset{\text{Alcohol}}{ROH} + \underset{\text{Halogen acid}}{HX} \longrightarrow \underset{\text{Haloalkane}}{RX} + \underset{\text{Water}}{H_2O}$$

The rate of reaction depends on the nature of alcohol as well as the halogen acid.

- The reaction of primary (1°) and secondary (2°) alcohols with halogen acids require the presence of a catalyst, $ZnCl_2$, which acts as a Lewis acid and helps in the cleavage of C—O bond.

- Chloroalkanes are prepared by the action of hydrochloric acid on the primary and secondary alcohols in the presence of anhydrous zinc chloride (**Groove's process**).

$$\underset{\text{Ethyl alcohol }(1^\circ)}{CH_3CH_2OH} + HCl(g) \xrightarrow{\text{Anhydrous }ZnCl_2} \underset{\text{Ethyl chloride}}{CH_3CH_2Cl} + H_2O$$

$$\underset{iso\text{-propyl alcohol }(2^\circ)}{CH_3-\overset{\overset{CH_3}{|}}{\underset{\underset{H}{|}}{C}}-OH} + HCl(g) \xrightarrow{\text{Anhydrous }ZnCl_2} \underset{iso\text{-propyl chloride}}{CH_3-\overset{\overset{CH_3}{|}}{\underset{\underset{H}{|}}{C}}-Cl} + H_2O$$

- Tertiary alcohols are very reactive and therefore, their reactions are conducted by simply shaking with concentrated HCl at room temperature even in the absence of zinc chloride.

$$\underset{tert\text{-butyl alcohol}}{CH_3-\overset{\overset{CH_3}{|}}{\underset{\underset{CH_3}{|}}{C}}-OH} + HCl\,(\text{conc.}) \xrightarrow{\text{Room temperature}} \underset{\substack{tert\text{-butyl chloride}\\(2\text{-chloro-}2\text{-methylpropane})}}{CH_3-\overset{\overset{CH_3}{|}}{\underset{\underset{CH_3}{|}}{C}}-Cl} + H_2O$$

- Bromoalkanes are prepared by heating an alcohol with constant boiling of HBr (48%) in the presence of conc. H_2SO_4, which acts as a catalyst.

$$\underset{\text{Ethyl alcohol}}{CH_3CH_2OH} + HBr \xrightarrow[\Delta]{\text{Conc. }H_2SO_4} \underset{\text{Ethyl bromide}}{CH_3CH_2Br} + H_2O$$

HBr can also be generated *in situ* by the action of conc. H_2SO_4 on KBr or NaBr.

$$\underset{\text{Ethyl alcohol}}{CH_3CH_2OH} + KBr + H_2SO_4(\text{conc.}) \xrightarrow{\Delta} \underset{\text{Ethyl bromide}}{CH_3CH_2Br} + KHSO_4 + H_2O$$

- Iodoalkanes are prepared by heating an alcohol with constant boiling HI (57%).

$$\underset{\text{Ethyl alcohol}}{CH_3CH_2OH} + HI \xrightarrow{\text{Reflux}} \underset{\text{Iodoethane}}{CH_3CH_2I} + H_2O$$

HI can also be generated *in situ* by the action of 95% orthophosphoric acid on KI or NaI

$$\underset{\text{Ethyl alcohol}}{CH_3CH_2OH} + KI + \underset{\text{Phosphoric acid}}{H_3PO_4} \xrightarrow{\Delta} \underset{\text{Iodoethane}}{CH_3CH_2I} + KH_2PO_4 + H_2O$$

This reaction gives good yield of alkyl iodides.

Note
- Secondary and tertiary bromides and iodides cannot be prepared from their respective alcohols in the presence of conc. H_2SO_4 as they undergo dehydration to form alkenes.
- The order of reactivity of alcohols with a given haloacid is $3^\circ > 2^\circ > 1^\circ$.
- The order of reactivity of halogen acids with alcohols is HI > HBr > HCl (as order of bond dissociation energy is HI < HBr < HCl).

(ii) By the Action of Phosphorus Halides

Chloroalkanes are obtained by the action of PCl_5 or PCl_3 on alcohols.

$$R-OH + PCl_5 \longrightarrow R-Cl + POCl_3 + HCl$$

$$\underset{\text{Ethyl alcohol}}{CH_3CH_2OH} + PCl_5 \longrightarrow \underset{\text{Chloroethane}}{CH_3CH_2Cl} + \underset{\text{Phosphoryl chloride}}{POCl_3} + HCl$$

$$\underset{\text{Ethyl alcohol}}{3CH_3CH_2OH} + PCl_3 \longrightarrow \underset{\text{Chloroethane}}{3CH_3CH_2Cl} + \underset{\text{Phosphorus acid}}{H_3PO_3}$$

Bromoalkanes and iodoalkanes are prepared by the reaction of PBr_3 and PI_3 respectively with the alcohols. PBr_3 and PI_3 are usually generated *in situ* by the reaction of red phosphorus with bromine and iodine respectively.

$$R-OH \xrightarrow{\text{red P}/X_2} R-X \;(\text{where}, X = Br, I)$$

$$CH_3-OH \xrightarrow{\text{red P}/Br_2} CH_3-Br$$

(iii) By the Action of Thionyl Chloride

Chloroalkanes are prepared by refluxing the alcohols with $SOCl_2$ in the presence of pyridine.

$$\underset{\text{Ethyl alcohol}}{CH_3CH_2OH} + \underset{\text{Thionyl chloride}}{SOCl_2} \xrightarrow{\text{Pyridine}} \underset{\text{Chloroethane}}{CH_3CH_2Cl} + SO_2\uparrow + HCl\uparrow$$

This method is usually preferred since both the products of this reaction (SO_2 and HCl) are escapable gases. Hence, the reaction gives pure alkyl halide.

TEACHER'S TIP

The above three methods are not applicable for the preparation of aryl halides because the C—O bond in phenol has a partial double bond character and is difficult to break being stronger than a single bond.

Preparation from Hydrocarbons

Alkyl halides can be prepared from alkanes through substitution and from alkenes through addition of halogen acids or through allylic substitution.

By Free Radical Halogenation of Alkanes

Alkanes react with halogens (Cl_2 and Br_2) in the presence of UV light to form haloalkanes.

The reaction proceeds through free radical mechanism and gives a complex mixture of isomeric mono- and polyhaloalkanes, which are difficult to separate as pure compounds. As a result, yield of any single compound is low.

e.g. $$\underset{n\text{-butane}}{CH_3CH_2CH_2CH_3} \xrightarrow[\text{or Heat}]{Cl_2/\text{UV light}} \underset{n\text{-butylchloride}}{CH_3CH_2CH_2CH_2Cl} + \underset{sec\text{-butylchloride}}{CH_3\underset{\underset{Cl}{|}}{C}H\,CH_2CH_3}$$

Note The relative amounts of these isomeric haloalkanes depend upon the nature of the halogen and the number and type of hydrogen atoms (1°, 2° and 3°) which are being substituted. For the ease of substitution, various hydrogens follows the sequence as

benzylic, allylic > 3° > 2° > 1° > vinylic, aryl

From Alkenes

(i) Addition of Hydrogen Halides

An alkene on reaction with hydrogen halide, is converted to the corresponding alkyl halide.

e.g. $$\underset{\text{Alkene}}{>C=C<} + HX \longrightarrow \underset{\text{Haloalkane}}{-\underset{\underset{H}{|}}{\overset{|}{C}}-\underset{\underset{X}{|}}{\overset{|}{C}}-}$$

The decreasing order of reactivity of the halogen acids is

$$HI > HBr > HCl > HF$$

In case of addition to symmetrical alkenes, only one addition product is formed.

But in case of addition to unsymmetrical alkenes, **Markovnikov's** rule is followed.

e.g. propene yields two products but only one predominates according to Markovnikov's rule.

$$\underset{\text{Propene}}{CH_3CH=CH_2} + HI \longrightarrow \underset{\substack{\text{1-iodopropane}\\ \text{(Minor)}}}{CH_3CH_2CH_2I} + \underset{\substack{\text{2-iodopropane}\\ \text{(Major)}}}{CH_3-\underset{\underset{I}{|}}{C}H-CH_3}$$

However, in the presence of a peroxide, the addition of HBr to an unsymmetrical alkene, proceeds in contrary to the Markovnikov's rule. This effect is known as **Kharasch effect or peroxide effect.**

$$\underset{\text{Propene}}{CH_3CH=CH_2} + HBr \xrightarrow{\text{Peroxide}} \underset{\text{1-bromopropane}}{CH_3CH_2CH_2Br}$$

It is informally called as **anti-Markovnikov's addition.**

(ii) Addition of Halogens

In the laboratory, addition of bromine (Br_2) in CCl_4 to an alkene results in discharge of reddish-brown colour of bromine. This constitutes an important method for the detection of double bond in a molecule.

The addition results in the synthesis of *vic*-dibromides which are colourless. On adding Br_2 or Cl_2 to alkenes, the addition occurs at the double bond forming *vic*-dihalides,

e.g. $$\underset{\text{Alkene}}{H_2C=CH_2} + Br_2 \xrightarrow{CCl_4} \underset{vic\text{-dibromide}}{BrCH_2CH_2Br}$$

Preparation by Halogen Exchange

Alkyl iodides are often prepared by the reaction of alkyl chlorides/bromides with NaI in dry acetone. This reaction is known as **Finkelstein reaction.**

$$R—X + NaI \longrightarrow R—I + NaX \quad [X = Cl, Br]$$

e.g. $$CH_3CH_2Br + NaI \xrightarrow[\Delta]{\text{Acetone}} CH_3CH_2I + NaBr$$

NaBr or NaCl, thus formed gets precipitated in dry acetone which facilitates the forward reaction according to Le-Chatelier's principle.

Fluoroalkanes are best prepared by heating an alkyl chloride/bromide in the presence of a metallic fluoride such as AgF, Hg_2F_2, CoF_2 or SbF_3. This reaction is known as **Swarts reaction.**

$$\underset{\text{Methyl bromide}}{CH_3Br} + \underset{\text{Silver fluoride}}{AgF} \longrightarrow \underset{\text{Fluoromethane}}{CH_3F} + \underset{\text{Silver bromide}}{AgBr}$$

Note Generally, bromoalkanes are prepared by refluxing the silver salts of acids with bromine in CCl_4. This reaction is known as **Borodine-Hunsdiecker reaction**. The reaction can be depicted as

$$CH_3CO\overset{-}{O}\overset{+}{Ag} + Br_2 \xrightarrow{CCl_4} \underset{\text{Methyl bromide}}{CH_3Br} + CO_2\uparrow + AgBr$$

Preparation of Haloalkanes (At a Glance)

R—OH (Alcohols)

- $\xrightarrow[\text{Lucas reagent}]{HCl + \text{Anhyd. } ZnCl_2} R\text{—}Cl + H_2O$ (Groove's process)
- $\xrightarrow{NaBr + H_2SO_4} R\text{—}Br + H_2O + NaHSO_4$
- $\xrightarrow{PX_3} 3R\text{—}X + H_3PO_3$ (X = Cl, Br)
- $\xrightarrow{PCl_5} R\text{—}Cl + POCl_3 + HCl$
- $\xrightarrow[X_2 = Br_2, I_2]{\text{red P}/X_2} R\text{—}X$
- $\xrightarrow[SOCl_2]{\text{Pyridine}} R\text{—}Cl + SO_2\uparrow + HCl\uparrow$

- $CH_3CH_2CH_3 \xrightarrow[\text{or Heat}]{Cl_2/\text{UV light}} \underset{n\text{-butyl chloride}}{CH_3CH_2CH_2Cl} + \underset{sec\text{-butyl chloride}}{CH_3CH_2CHClCH_3}$
- $>C{=}C< \; H\text{—}X \longrightarrow >\underset{H}{C}\text{—}\underset{X}{C}<$ (X = Cl, Br, I)
- $R\text{—}X \xrightarrow{NaI} R\text{—}I + NaX$; $R\text{—}X \xrightarrow{AgF} R\text{—}F + AgX$ [X = Cl and Br]

6.5 Preparation of Haloarenes

Haloarenes can be prepared by the following methods

By Electrophilic Substitution of Aromatic Hydrocarbons

Aryl chlorides and bromides can be easily prepared by electrophilic substitution of arenes with chlorine and bromine, respectively in dark, at ordinary temperature in the presence of a Lewis acid catalysts such as iron or ferric halides or aluminium halides ($FeCl_3$, $FeBr_3$, $AlCl_3$).

Lewis acid is used to generate the electrophile, i.e., Cl^+ and Br^+ which reacts with aryl halide.

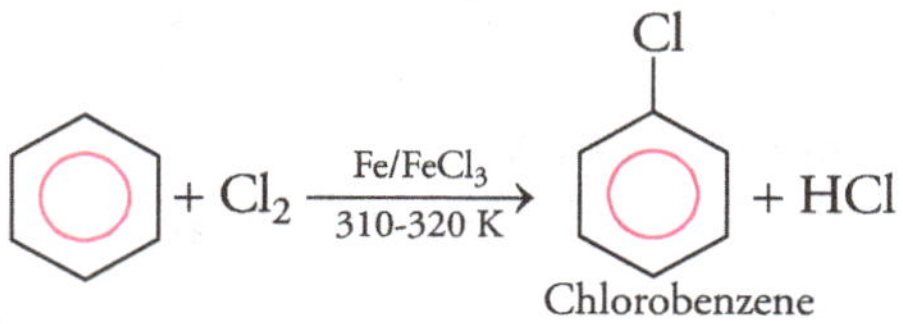

Chlorobenzene

- In case of toluene, a mixture of *o*-chlorotoluene and *p*-chlorotoluene is obtained as —CH_3 group is an *ortho* and *para* directing group.

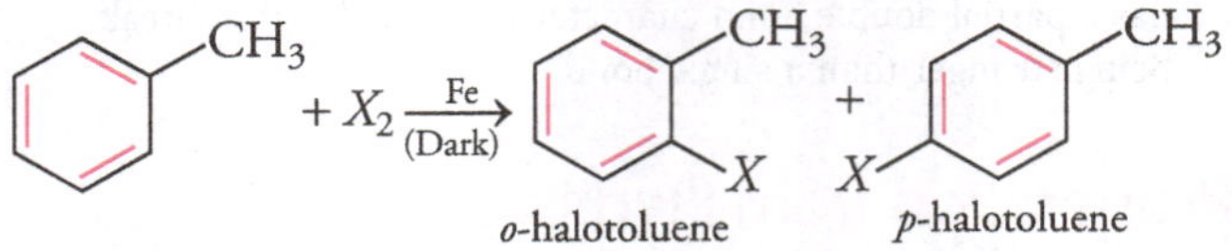

o-halotoluene *p*-halotoluene

- *o*- and *p* -isomers can be easily separated due to large difference in their melting points.
- Reaction with iodine is reversible in nature and require the presence of an oxidising agent (HNO_3, HIO_4, $AgClO_4$) to oxidise the HI formed during iodination.

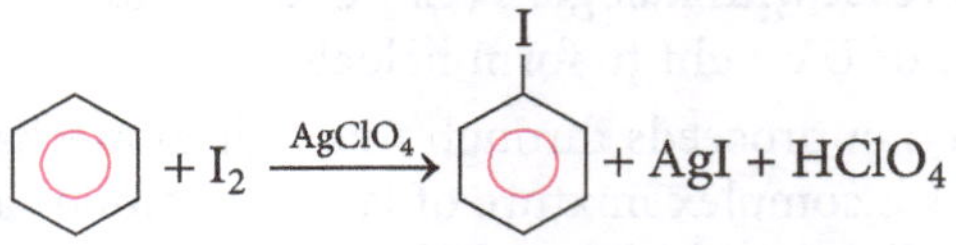

- The reaction with fluorine is violent and cannot be controlled. Therefore, fluoroarene cannot be prepared by direct fluorination of aromatic hydrocarbon.

From Diazonium Salts (Sandmeyer's Reaction)

The diazonium salt is prepared by treating aniline dissolved or suspended in cold aqueous mineral acid with an aqueous solution of sodium nitrite at low temperature (0-5°C).

Bromo- and chloroarenes can be prepared by treating a freshly prepared diazonium salt solution with cuprous bromide or cuprous chloride.

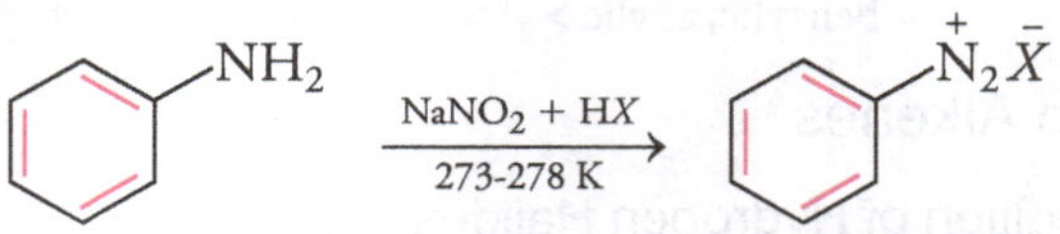

Benzene diazonium halide

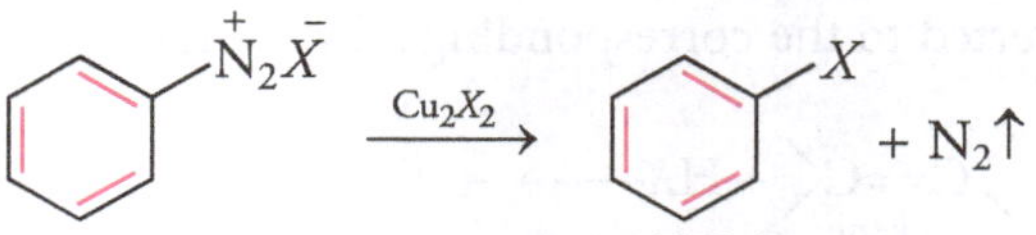

Aryl halide

(X = Cl, Br)

Replacement of the diazonium group by iodine is done simply by shaking the diazonium salt with potassium iodide.

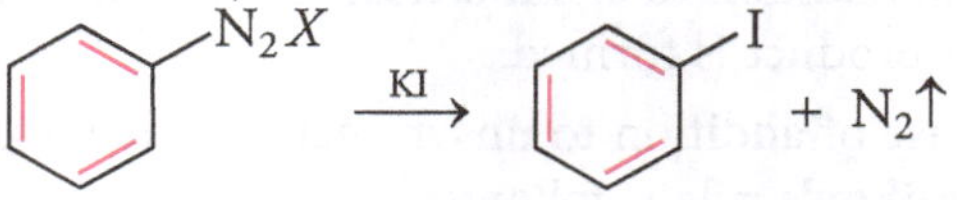

The Sandmeyer's reaction has been modified by using copper powder in place of cuprous halide. This reaction is called **Gattermann reaction.**

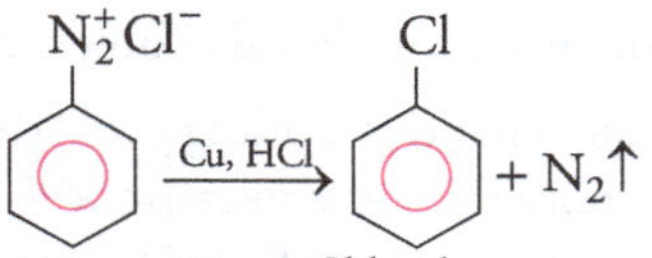

Chlorobenzene

Note If the diazonium group is replaced using fluoroboric acid, the reaction is called **Balz-Schiemann reaction.**

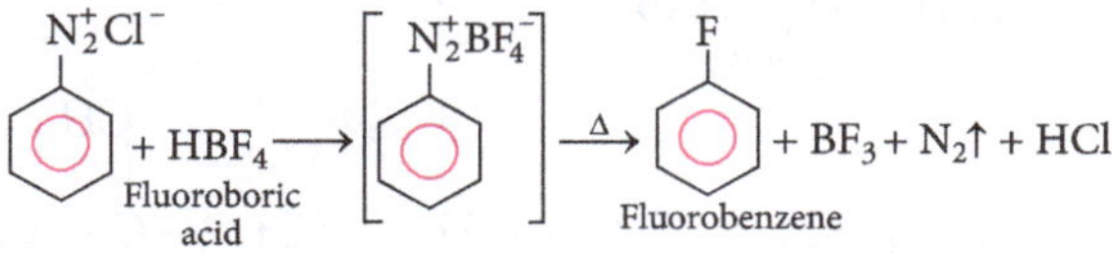

Preparation of Haloarenes (At a glance)

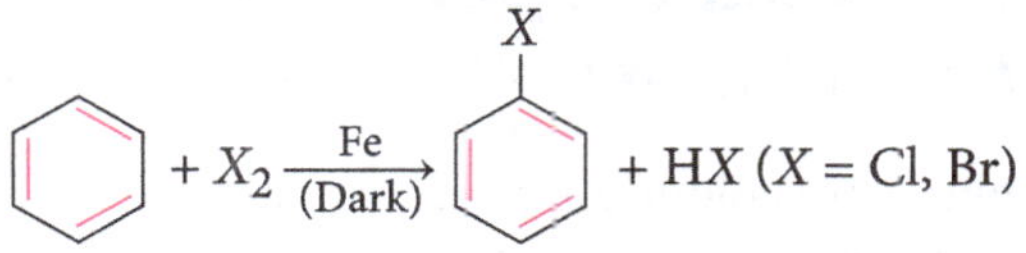

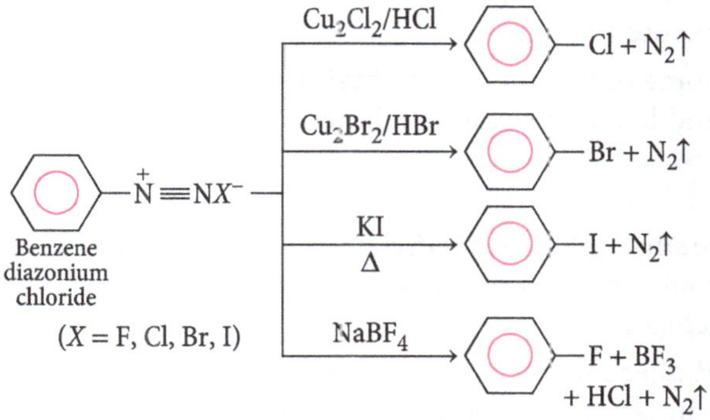

Quick Test 2

1. Among the following alcohols, which will yield the corresponding alkyl chloride on reaction with concentrated HCl at room temperature?

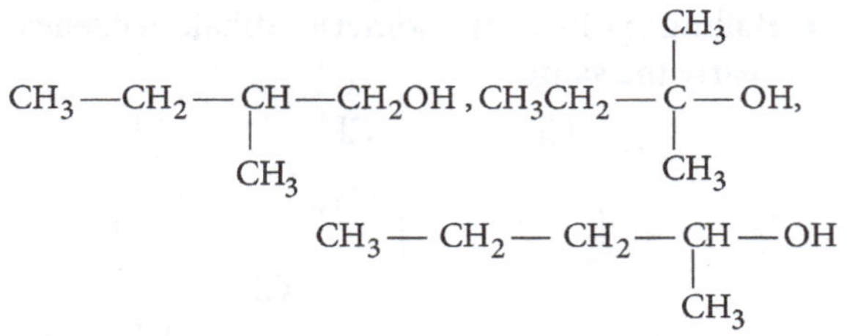

2. Identify the products A and B formed in the following reaction.

$CH_3-CH_2-CH=CH-CH_3 + HCl \longrightarrow A + B$ *NCERT Exemplar*

3. Name the alkene which will yield 1-chloro-1-methylcyclohexane by its reaction with HCl. Write the reactions involved.

4. Write the structure of the major organic products in each of the following reactions.

(i) $CH_3CH_2CH_2Cl + NaI \xrightarrow[\text{Heat}]{\text{Acetone}}$

(ii) $CH_3CH_2CH_2OH + SOCl_2 \xrightarrow{\text{Pyridine}}$

(iii) $CH_3CH_2CH=CH_2 + HBr \xrightarrow{\text{Peroxide}}$

(iv) $CH_3CH=\underset{\displaystyle CH_3}{\underset{|}{C}}(CH_3) + HBr \longrightarrow$ *NCERT*

5. Why aryl halides cannot be prepared by the reaction of phenol with HCl in the presence of $ZnCl_2$? *NCERT Exemplar*

6. Write the structures and names of the compounds formed, when compound A with molecular formula C_7H_8, is treated with Cl_2 in the presence of $FeCl_3$. *NCERT Exemplar*

7. How will you carry out the following conversions?

(i) 2-bromopropane to 1-bromopropane

(ii) Benzene to p-chloronitrobenzene *CBSE 2017*

8. Draw the structures of the major monohalo product for each of the following reactions.

(i) 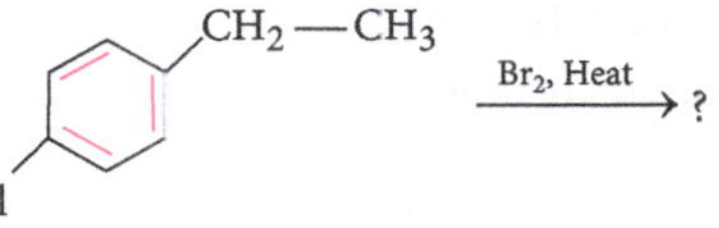

(ii) 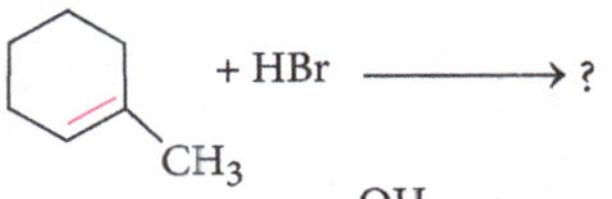

(iii) 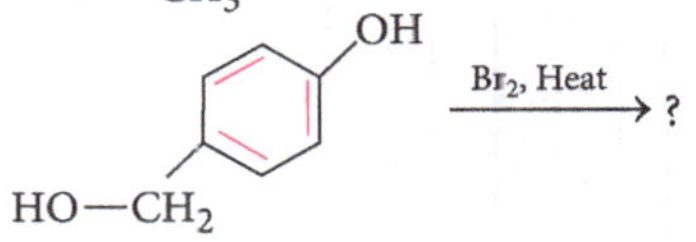

CBSE 2017

For Solutions, See QR Code on Pg. 227

6.6 Physical Properties of Haloalkanes and Haloarenes

Alkyl halides are colourless when they are pure. However, bromides and iodides develop colour when exposed to light.

Some of the important physical properties of haloalkanes and haloarenes are as follows

(i) Physical state

Methyl chloride, methyl bromide, ethyl chloride and some chlorofluoromethanes are gases at room temperature.

Higher members are liquids or solids. Many volatile halogen compounds have sweet smell. Haloarenes are generally colourless liquids or crystalline solids.

(ii) Melting and Boiling points

- The boiling points of chlorides, bromides and iodides are higher than those of the hydrocarbons of comparable molecular mass. This is because molecules of organic halogen compounds are generally polar.

  Due to greater polarity and higher molecular mass as compared to the parent hydrocarbon, the intermolecular forces of attraction (dipole-dipole and van der Waals') between molecules are stronger in the halogen derivatives.
- As the molecular mass increases, the melting and boiling points increases. This is because the attraction get stronger as the molecules get bigger in size and have more electrons.

  The pattern of variation of boiling points of different halides is depicted in table given below

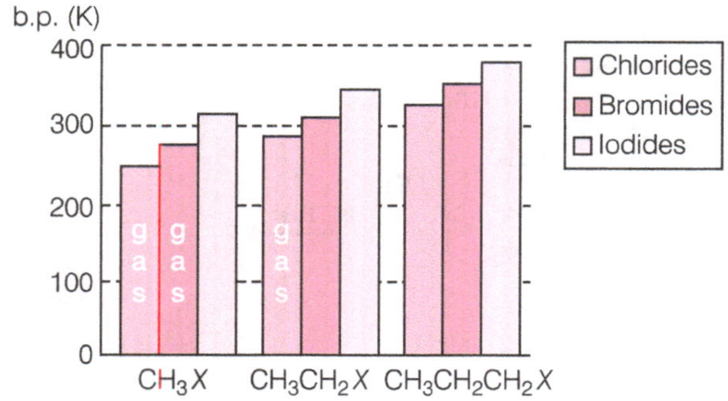

Comparison of boiling points of some alkyl halides

- For the same alkyl group, the boiling point of alkyl halides decreases in the order $RI > RBr > RCl > RF$, because with increase in size and mass of halogen atom, the magnitude of van der Waals' forces increases.
- For isomeric alkyl halides, boiling point decreases as the branching increases. This is because with increase in branching, the surface area of alkyl halide decreases and hence, the magnitude of the van der Waals' forces of attraction decreases.

$$\underset{\text{(b.p.} = 375\text{ K)}}{CH_3CH_2CH_2CH_2Br} > \underset{\text{(b.p.} = 364\text{ K)}}{CH_3CH_2-\underset{\underset{Br}{|}}{CH}-CH_3} > \underset{\text{(b.p.} = 346\text{ K)}}{CH_3-\overset{\overset{CH_3}{|}}{\underset{\underset{Br}{|}}{C}}-CH_3}$$

- Generally, the boiling points of chloro, bromo and iodo compounds increases as the number of halogen atom increases.

  e.g. $\underset{249\text{ K}}{CH_3Cl} < \underset{313\text{ K}}{CH_2Cl_2} < \underset{334\text{ K}}{CHCl_3} < \underset{350\text{ K}}{CCl_4}$
- Boiling points of isomeric dihalobenzenes are nearly the same.

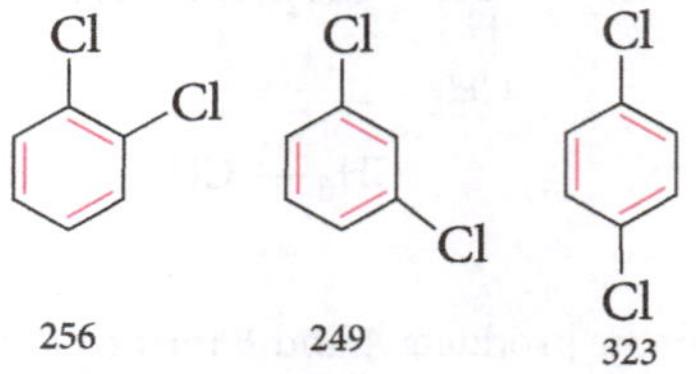

m.p./K	256	249	323
b.p./K	453	446	448

However, the *p*-isomers have high melting point as compared to their *o*-and *m*-isomers. This is due to the symmetry of *p*-isomers that fits in the crystal lattice better as compared to *o*- and *m*-isomers.

(iii) Density

- Fluoro and chloroalkanes are lighter than water, while bromo, iodo and polychloro derivatives are heavier than water.
- With the increase in the number of C-atoms, halogen atoms and atomic mass of halogen atom, density increases.

(iv) Solubility

- The solubility of haloalkanes in water is low. This is because the amount of energy released during the setup of new attractions between haloalkane and water molecules are not-sufficient to break the hydrogen bond between the water molecules.
- They are soluble in organic solvents because the new intermolecular attractions between haloalkanes and solvent molecules are of same strength as the ones being broken in the separate alkyl halide molecules and solvent molecules.

6.7 Chemical Reactions of Haloalkanes

Due to the presence of a polar C—X bond, haloalkanes are highly reactive compounds. The reactions may be divided into following three categories

(i) Nucleophilic substitution reactions

(ii) Elimination reactions

(iii) Reaction with metals

Nucleophilic Substitution Reactions

- When a nucleophile (i.e. electron rich species) stronger than the halide ion, reacts with haloalkane having a partial positive charge on the carbon atom bonded to halogen, a substitution reaction takes place and the halogen atom called **leaving group** departs as halide ion.

  Since, the substitution reaction is initiated by a nucleophile, it is called **nucleophilic substitution reaction**.

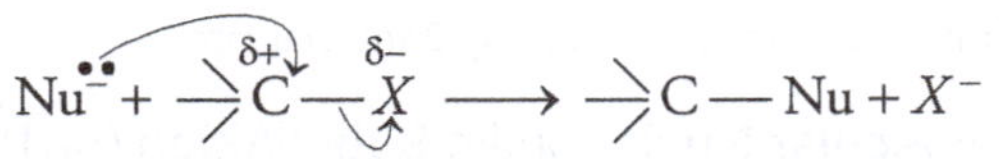

- It is one of the most useful classes of organic reactions of haloalkanes in which halogen is bonded to sp^3-hybridised carbon.
- The products formed by the reaction of haloalkanes with some common nucleophiles are shown in the table given below.

Nucleophilic Substitution of Alkyl Halides (R—X)

$$R—X + Nu^- \longrightarrow R—Nu + X^-$$

Reagent	Nucleophile (Nu^-)	Substitution product (R—Nu)	Class of main product
NaOH(KOH)	HO^-	ROH	Alcohol
H_2O	H_2O	ROH	Alcohol
NaOR'	$R'O^-$	ROR'	Ether
NaI	I^-	R—I	Alkyl iodide
NH_3	NH_3	RNH_2	Primary amine
$R'NH_2$	$R'NH_2$	$RNHR'$	*sec*-amine
$R'R''NH$	$R'R''NH$	$RNR'R''$	*tert*-amine
KCN	$\bar{C}{\equiv}N:$	RCN	Nitrile (cyanide)
AgCN	Ag— CN:	RNC (isocyanide)	Isonitrile
KNO_2	O=N—O	R—O—N=O	Alkyl nitrite
$AgNO_2$	Ag—$\ddot{O}$—N=O	$R—NO_2$	Nitroalkane
R'COOAg	$R'COO^-$	$R'COOR$	Ester
$LiAlH_4$	H^-	RH	Hydrocarbon
R'^-M^+	R'^-	RR'	Alkane

- **Formation of cyanides and isocyanides** Groups like cyanides and nitrites possess two nucleophilic centres and are called **ambident nucleophiles**.

  Cyanide group is a hybrid of two contributing structures and therefore, can act as nucleophile in two different ways [$^{\ominus}C{\equiv}N \longleftrightarrow :C{=}N^{\ominus}$].

  When it links through carbon atom, it results in formation of **alkyl cyanides** and when it links through nitrogen atom, it results in formation of **isocyanides**.
- **Formation of nitroalkanes and alkyl nitrites** : In nitrite ion, there are two different points of linkage ($^-O—\ddot{N}{=}O$). The linkage through oxygen results in **alkyl nitrites**, while that through nitrogen atom, results in **nitroalkanes**.

Note Among alkyl halides, iodide ion is the best leaving group. Hence, iodoalkanes undergo **nucleophilic substitution reactions** at the fastest rate in comparison to fluoroalkane, as fluoride ion is the poorest leaving group.

Better the leaving group, more facile is the nucleophilic substitution reaction.

Mechanism

The nucleophilic substitution reactions can proceed by following two different mechanisms.

I. Bimolecular Nucleophilic Substitution (S_N2)

When two molecules takes part in determining the rate of the reaction, it is called **bimolecular nucleophilic substitution (S_N 2).**

e.g., The reaction between CH_3Cl and hydroxide ion to yield methanol and chloride ion follows a second order kinetics. i.e., the rate depends upon the concentration of both the reactants.

This can be represented diagrammatically as shown below

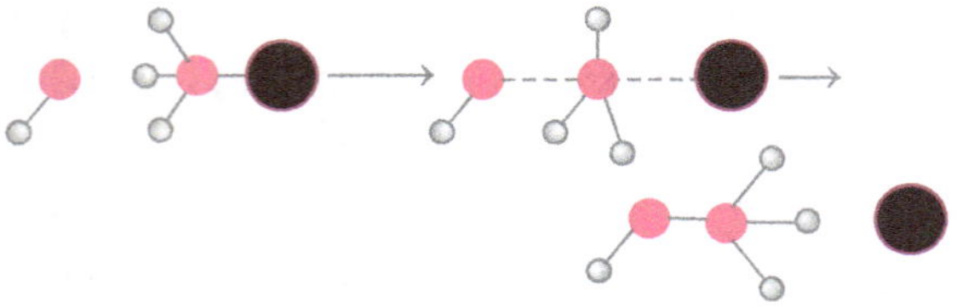

Grey dot represents the incoming hydroxide ion and black dot represents the outgoing halide ion

- In S_N 2 mechanism, the incoming nucleophile approaches the alkyl halide (CH_3X) molecule and starts interacting with it due to which the carbon-halide (C—X) bond starts breaking and a new carbon-nucleophile (C—OH) bond starts forming.

  These two processes take place simultaneously in a single step and no intermediate is formed.

  Such reaction occurs through the formation of a **transition state**. In transition state, the C-atom is simultaneously bonded to incoming nucleophile and also to the outgoing leaving group, i.e. carbon is bonded to five atoms.

  Thus, this state is unstable and results in the formation of the product.

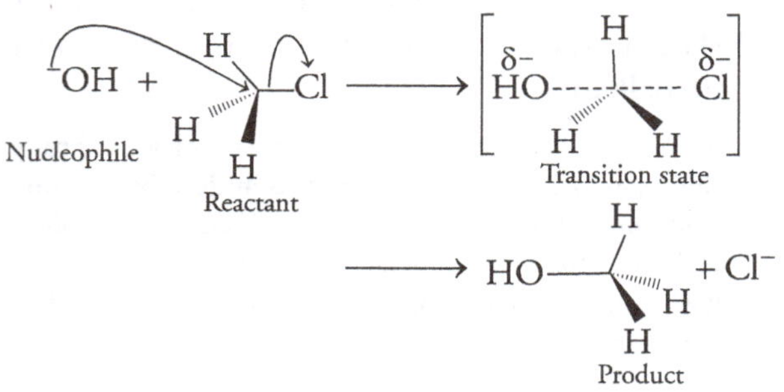

- As the attacking nucleophile approaches closer to the carbon, C—H bonds still keep on moving in the same direction till the attacking nucleophile attaches to carbon and leaving group leaves the carbon.

  As a result configuration is inverted. This process is called as **inversion of configuration.**
- Since, S_N 2 reaction requires the backside approach of nucleophile to the carbon bearing the leaving group, i.e. X-atom, the presence of bulky alkyl groups blocks the approach of the nucleophile to carbon due to steric hindrance.

  That's why the simple alkyl halides, methyl halides and primary alkyl halides always react predominantly by S_N 2 mechanism.
- Tertiary halides are least reactive because of the presence of bulky groups which hinders the approaching nucleophiles.

  Thus, the order of reactivity of alkyl halides towards S_N 2 reactions is as follows:

  Methyl halide > Primary halide > Secondary halide > Tertiary halide

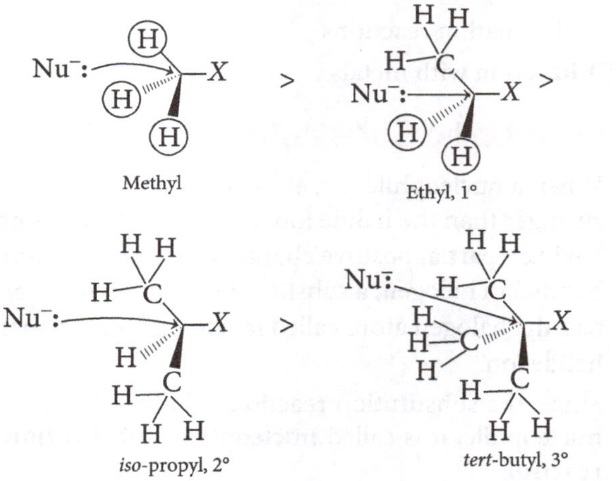

Note Non-polar solvents favour S_N 2 mechanism.

II. Unimolecular Nucleophilic Substitution (S_N1)

- When only one molecule is involved in determining the rate of the reaction, it is called **unimolecular nucleophilic substitution (S_N 1).**
- Such type of reactions are generally carried out in polar protic solvents such as water, alcohol, acetic acid, etc., because they stabilise the carbocation by solvation.

  e.g., The reaction between *tert*-butyl bromide and hydroxide ion yield *tert*-butyl alcohol.

  $(CH_3)_3C—Br + OH^- \longrightarrow (CH_3)_3COH + Br^-$

S_N1 reaction occurs *via* two steps.

Step I **Formation of carbocation intermediate**

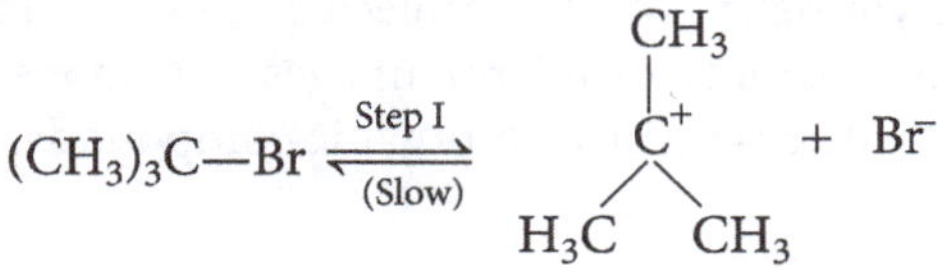

In this step, formation of carbocation takes place due to the heterolytic cleavage of $\gtrdot C—X$ ($\gtrdot C—Br$) bond. This step is slow and reversible **(rate determining step)**. It involves only one reactant, i.e., alkyl halide, therefore, rate of reaction depends only on the concentration of alkyl halide and not on the concentration of nucleophile.

Thus, it follows **first order kinetics**. Energy for $C—X$ bond breaking is obtained through solvation of halide ion with the proton of protic solvent.

Step II **Attack of nucleophile on carbocation formed.**

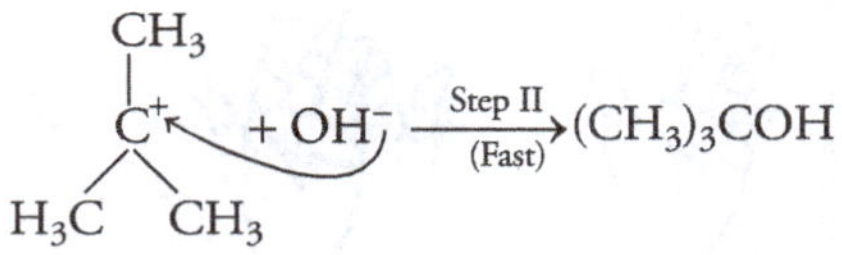

In this step, nucleophile attack the carbocation formed in step I and the substitution reaction completes.

- Greater the stability of carbocation, greater will be its ease of formation from alkyl halide and faster will be the rate of reaction. That's why, 3° alkyl halides undergo S_N1 reaction very fast because of high stability of 3° carbocations.

  Therefore, the order of reactivity of alkyl halides towards S_N1 reactions is as

  Methyl halide < Primary halide < Secondary halide < Tertiary halide

- We can sum up the order of reactivity of alkyl halides towards S_N1 and S_N2 reactions as

S_N1 reactivity order ←

Tertiary halide, Secondary halide, Primary halide, CH_3X

→ S_N2 reactivity order

- Allylic and benzylic halides show high reactivity towards the S_N1 reaction because carbocation thus formed gets stabilised through resonance.

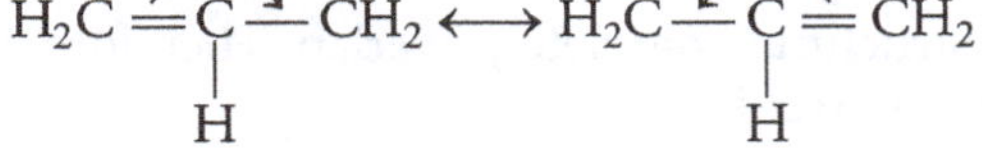

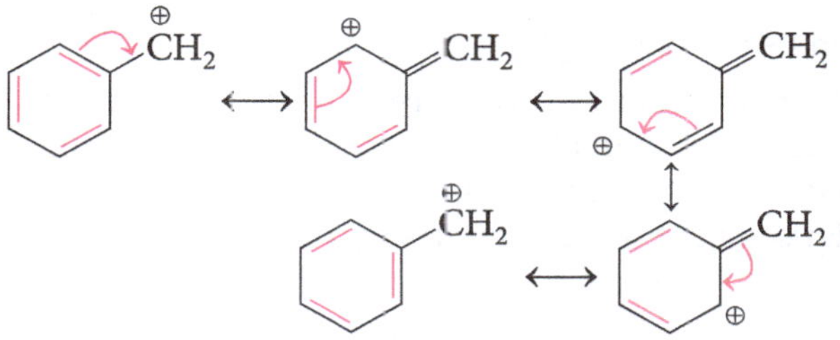

- For a given alkyl group, the reactivity of the halide, $R—X$ follows the same order in both the mechanisms, S_N1 and S_N2.

$$R—I > R—Br > R—Cl > R—F$$

Differences between S_N1 and S_N2 reactions

	S_N1	S_N2
1.	It follows first order reaction.	It follows second order reaction.
2.	It involves the formation of carbocation as intermediate.	It involves the formation of transition state.
3.	Rate depends only on concentration of alkyl halide.	Rate depends on concentration of alkyl halide and nucleophile.
4.	Rate of reaction follows the order : 3° > 2° > 1° > CH_3X	Rate of reaction follows the order : CH_3X > 1° > 2° > 3°
5.	Reaction is favoured by polar solvents.	Reaction is favoured by non-polar solvents.

Example 3 **Which one compound from the following pairs would undergo S_N2 faster?**

(i) 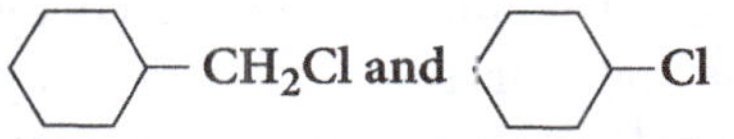

(ii) $CH_3CH_2CH_2I$ and $CH_3CH_2CH_2Cl$ **NCERT Intext**

Sol. (i) Since, 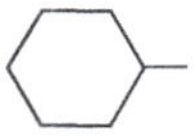 is a primary halide. Thus, it undergoes S_N2 faster than 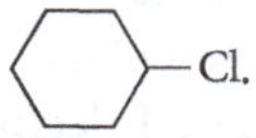.

(ii) Since, iodine is a better leaving group than chlorine, 1-iodo propane undergoes S_N2 reaction faster than 1-chloropropane.

Stereochemical Aspects of Nucleophilic Substitution Reactions

Stereochemistry refers to the study of structure as well as their reactivity. S_N2 reaction proceeds with the complete **stereochemical inversion** while S_N1 reaction proceeds with **racemisation**.

To understand these concepts, some basic stereochemical principles and notations are need to be learnt, which are given as follows

Plane Polarised Light

A beam of ordinary light consists of electromagnetic waves vibrating in all planes in space. When this light is passed through a nicol prism, it becomes plane polarised light, which vibrates only in one plane.

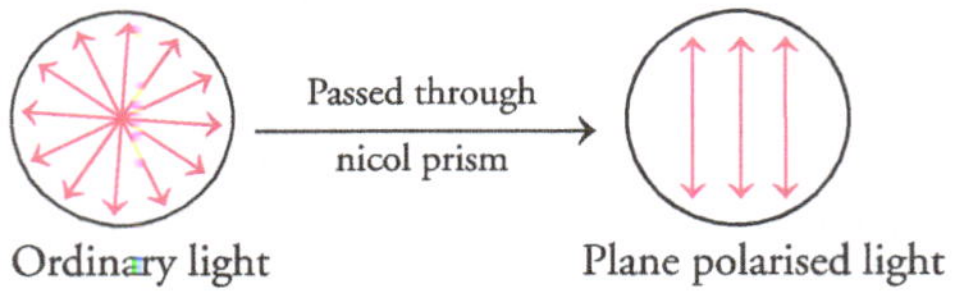

Polarisation of ordinary light

Optical Activity

- When the solutions of certain organic compounds are placed in the path of plane polarised light, they rotate the path of the light either to left or right. Such substances are called **optically active substances.**
- The property of rotating the plane of polarisation either towards left or towards right is called **optical rotation.**
- A substance which rotates the plane polarised light to the right (clockwise direction) is called **dextrorotatory** or ***d*-form** and is indicated by placing a positive (+) sign before the degree of rotation.
- The substance which rotates the plane polarised light towards the left (anticlockwise direction) is called **laevorotatory** or ***l*-form** and is indicated by placing a negative (–) sign before the degree of rotation.
- Such *d*-and *l*-forms of compound are called **optical isomers** and the phenomenon is called **optical isomerism**. The angle by which the plane polarised light is rotated can be measured by an instrument called **polarimeter**.
- **Specific rotation** It is defined as degree of rotation observed when plane of polarised light is passed through a tube 1 decimeter (10 cm) long having a solution with concentration 1 g mL^{-1} at a specific temperature and wavelength.

  Specific rotation $[\alpha]$

$$= \frac{\text{Observed rotation } (d_{obs})}{\text{Length of tube (dm)} \times \text{Concentration of solution } (g\ mL^{-1})}$$

Molecular Asymmetry

- The spatial arrangement of four groups such that all the substituents attached to carbon are different, the mirror image of the molecule is not superimposed on the molecule. Such a rotation is called **asymmetric** carbon or **stereocentre**.
- The asymmetry of the molecule along with non-superimposability of mirror images is responsible for the optical activity in such organic compounds.

Chirality

- All molecules or objects have mirror images. An object or molecule which is non-superimposable on its mirror image is called **chiral** and this property is called **chirality**, e.g., human hand.
- If we hold our left hand in front of a mirror, the image looks like the right hand. If we try to superimpose left and right hands, by putting the one on the other one, we observe that the hands cannot be superimposed, hence the hands are chiral. Chiral molecules are **optically active**.

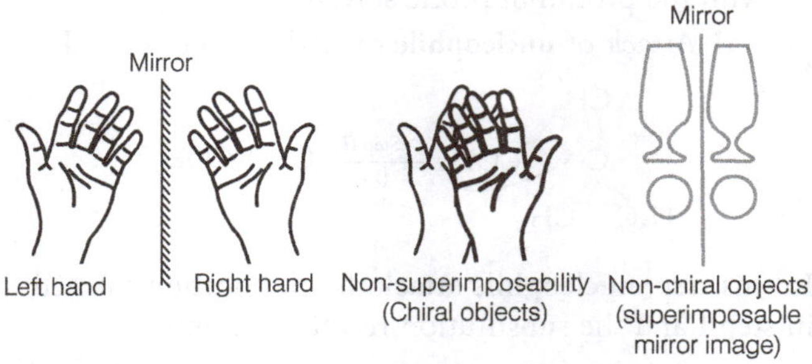

Some common examples of chiral and achiral objects

- The objects which are superimposable on their mirror images are called **achiral** as the glass and the sphere in the above figure. Chiral molecules are **optically inactive**.
- Let us take two simple molecules, propan-2-ol and butan-2-ol and their mirror images.

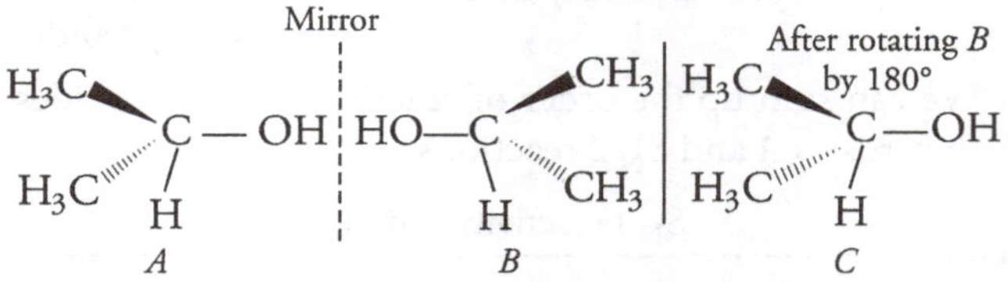

B is mirror image of *A*; *B* is rotated by 180°
and *C* is obtained, *C* is superimposable on *A*.

Propan-2-ol does not contain asymmetric carbon atom as all the four groups attached to the tetrahedral carbon are not different. We rotate the mirror image (*B*) of the molecule by 180° (structure *C*) and try to overlap the structure (*C*) with the structure (*A*), these structures completely overlap. Therefore, it is an **achiral molecule**.

- **Butan-2-ol** molecule contains asymmetric carbon atom and as expected is **chiral**. It has non-superimposable mirror images as shown in the figure given below.

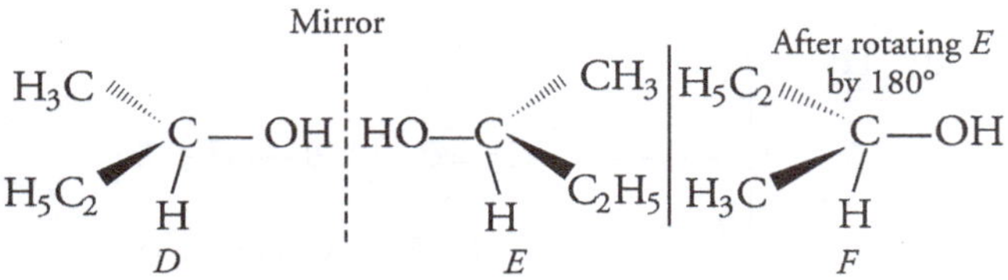

E is mirror image of *D*; *E* is rotated by 180° and *F* is obtained, *F* is non-superimposable on *D*.

Some common examples of chiral molecules are

(i) 2-Chlorobutane, $(CH_3CH(Cl)CH_2CH_3)$,
(ii) 2,3-Dihydroxypropanal (OHC—CHOH—CH_2OH),
(iii) Bromochloroiodomethane (BrClCHI),
(iv) 2-Bromopropanoic acid (H_3C—CHBr—COOH).

Enantiomers

- The stereoisomers related to each other as non-superimposable mirror images are called **enantiomers.** In the above fig. of propan-2-ol and butan-2-ol, *A* and *B* and *D* and *E* are enantiomers and the phenomenon is called **enantiomerism.**
- The enantiomers have identical physical and chemical properties but differ with respect to the rotation of plane polarised light. If one of the enantiomer is dextrorotatory then other will be laevorotatory.

TEACHER S TIP
The sign of optical rotation is not necessarily related to the absolute (actual) configuration of the molecule.

Racemic Mixtures and Racemisation

A mixture containing two enantiomers in equal proportions will have zero optical rotation, as the rotation due to one isomer will be cancelled by the rotation due to the other isomer. Such a mixture is called **racemic mixture.**

It is represented as *dl* or ± forms (before the name) and will be **optically inactive.** The process of converting *d*- or *l*-form of an optically active compound into racemic form (*dl*) is called **racemisation.**

Retention

- When the relative spatial arrangement of bonds at an asymmetric centre in a chiral molecule remains the same before and after the reaction, the reaction is said to occur with **retention of configuration.**

e.g.

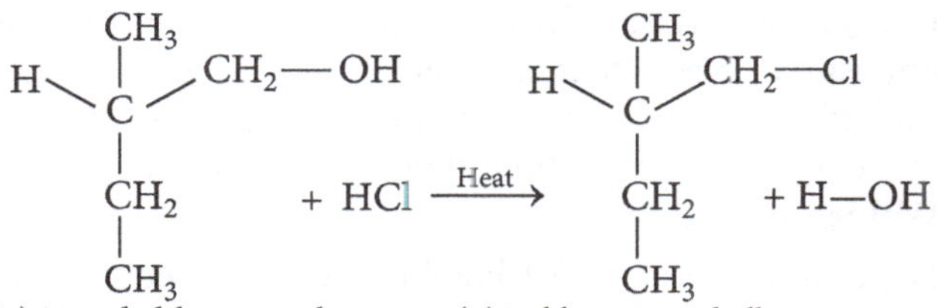

- In the above example, no bond at the asymmetric carbon is broken, and the product will have the same general configuration of groups around the stereocentre as that of reactants.

  Therefore, the reaction proceeds with retention of configuration inspite of change of optical rotation from (–) to (+). This is because two different compounds with same configuration at asymmetric centre may have different optical rotation.

Inversion

- If the relative spatial arrangement of bonds at an asymmetric carbon atom becomes opposite as compared to reactant after the reaction, then the reaction is called **inversion.**
- During the substitution of a group *X* by *Y* in the reactions given below, three possible products may be formed.

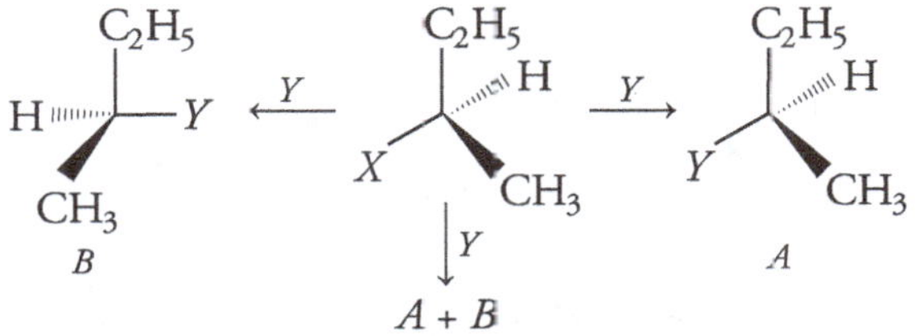

- If *A* is the only product, the process is called **retention of configuration** because *A* has same configuration as that of reactant.

  If *B* is the only product, the process is called **inversion of configuration** because *B* has the configuration opposite to that of reactant.
- If an equimolar mixture, i.e. 50 : 50 mixture of *A* and *B* is formed, the process is called **racemisation** and the product is **optically inactive.**

  Now, stereochemical aspects of nucleophilic substitution reactions can easily be understood as follows

Stereochemical Aspects of S_N2 Reaction

In S_N2 mechanism, the nucleophile attacks on the side opposite to one, where halogen atom is present. Therefore, S_N2 reaction is always accompanied by inversion of configuration, that is referred to as **Walden inversion**.

For example, when (–) 2-halobutane is allowed to react with potassium hydroxide, (+) butan-2-ol is formed with the —OH group occupying the position opposite to halogen had occupied.

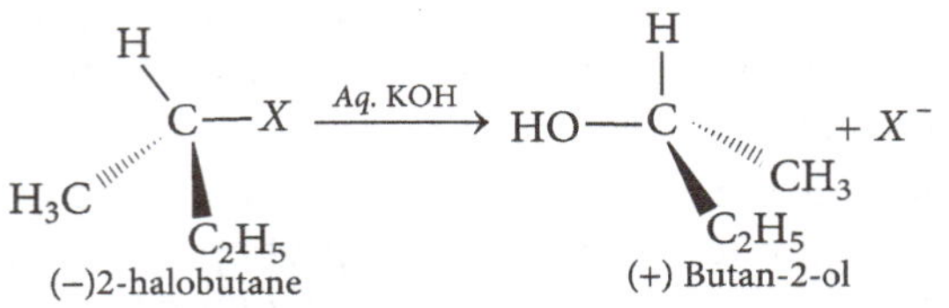

Stereochemical Aspects of S_N1 Reaction

In S_N1 reactions, if the alkyl halide is optically active, the product obtained is a **racemic mixture**. The intermediate carbocation formed in slowest step being sp^2 hybridised is planar (achiral) species.

Therefore, the attack of the nucleophile (OH^-) can occur from either side of the plane of carbocation with equal ease of forming a mixture of two enantiomers.

Thus, S_N1 reaction of optically active alkyl halides are accompanied by racemisation.

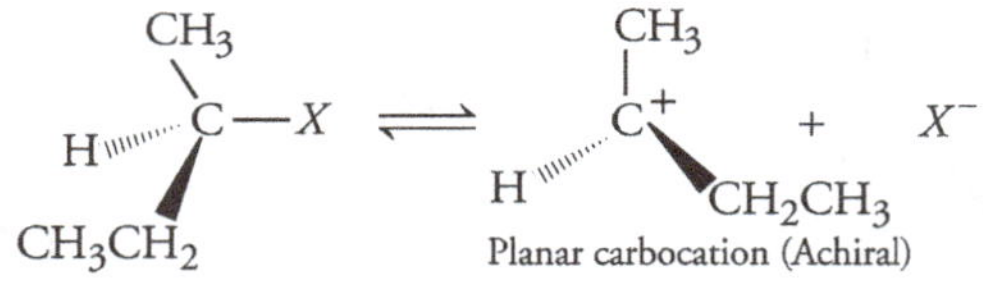

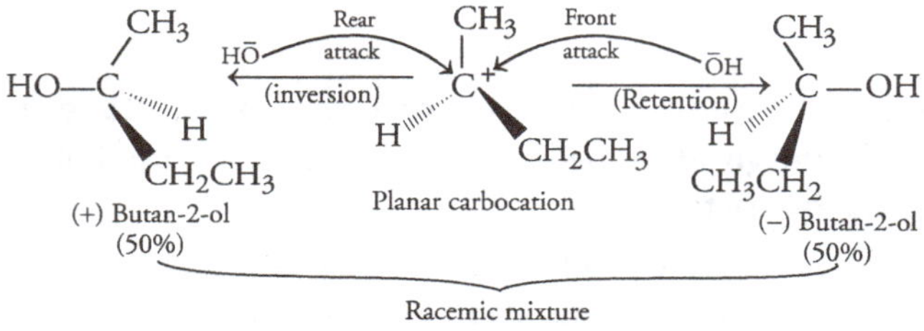

Elimination Reactions: Dehydrohalogenation (Formation of Alkenes)

- When a haloalkane with β-hydrogen atom is heated with alc. KOH solution, hydrogen is eliminated from β-carbon and the halogen is lost from α-carbon atom.
- As a result, an alkene is formed as a product. Due to the involvement of elimination of β-hydrogen atom, the process is often called as β-**elimination**.

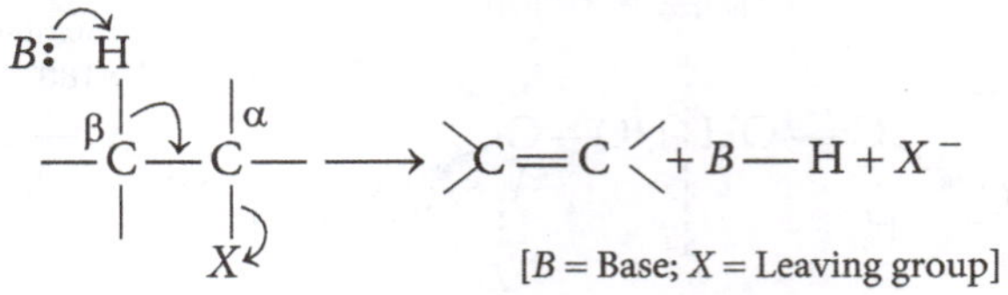

e.g. $H—CH_2—CH_2Br + KOH\ (alc.) \xrightarrow{Heat} CH_2=CH_2 + KBr + H_2O$

- If more than one β-hydrogens are present, then β-elimination takes place according to **Saytzeff rule**, which can be summarised as *"in dehydrohalogenation reactions, the preferred product is that alkene which has the greater number of alkyl groups attached to the doubly bonded carbon atoms"*.

  e.g. 2-bromopentane gives pent-2-ene as the major product.

$$\underset{\text{2-bromopentane}}{H_3C—CH_2—CH_2—\overset{Br}{\overset{|}{C}}H—\underset{\underset{H}{|}}{CH_2}} \xrightarrow[\text{(alc.)}]{\bar{O}H} \underset{\text{Pent-1-ene (19\%)}}{H_3C—CH_2—CH_2—CH=CH_2} + \underset{\substack{\text{Pent-2-ene (81\%)}\\ \text{(Major product)}}}{H_3C—CH_2—CH=CH—CH_3}$$

Elimination *vs* Substitution

- When alkyl halide reacts with nucleophile or base it may undergo either substitution *via* S_N1 and S_N2 or elimination reaction.
- Primary alkyl halide will prefer S_N2 reaction, i.e., nucleophilic substitution reaction *via* S_N2 mechanism.
- Secondary alkyl halide can undergo substitution (S_N2) or elimination depending upon the strength of the **nucleophile** or **base**.
- Tertiary alkyl halide will undergo substitution (S_N1) or elimination depending upon the stability of carbocation or the more substituted alkene.
- A bulkier nucleophile will carry out the elimination more easily than substitution as it prefers to act as a base and abstracts a proton rather than approaching a tetravalent carbon atom (due to steric reasons) and *vice-versa*.

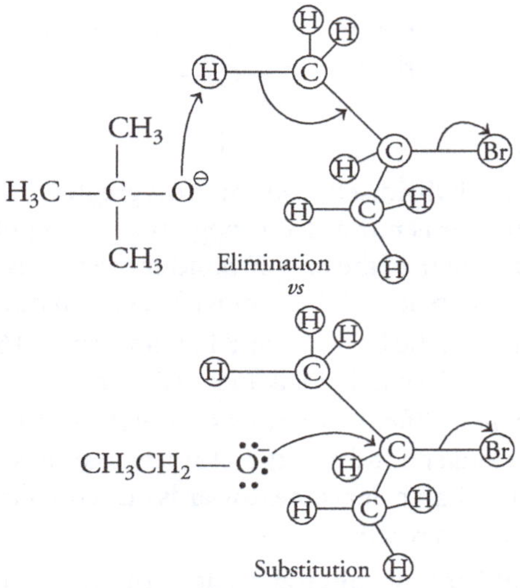

Reaction with Metals

Most organic chlorides, bromides and iodides react with certain metals to give compounds containing carbon-metal bonds. Such compounds are known as **organometallic compounds**.

(i) Action with Magnesium (Formation of Grignard Reagents)

The Grignard reagents are obtained by the reaction of haloalkanes with magnesium metal in the presence of dry ether.

$$CH_3CH_2Br + Mg \xrightarrow{\text{Dry ether}} \underset{\text{Grignard reagent}}{CH_3CH_2MgBr}$$

In the Grignard reagent, the carbon-magnesium bond is covalent but highly polar while, magnesium halogen bond is ionic.

$$\overset{\delta^-}{R} — \overset{\delta^+}{Mg}\,\overset{\delta^-}{X}$$

These are highly reactive and react with any source of proton to give hydrocarbons. Even alcohols, amines, water are sufficiently acidic to convert them to corresponding hydrocarbons.

$$RMgX + H_2O \longrightarrow RH + Mg(OH)X$$

Due to its high reactivity, it is necessary to avoid even traces of moisture from a Grignard reagent and that is why reaction is carried out in dry ether.

(ii) Action with Sodium (Wurtz Reaction)

The reaction in which alkyl halides react with sodium in the presence of dry ether to form hydrocarbons containing double the number of carbon atoms present in the halide, is known as **Wurtz reaction**.

$$2RX + 2Na \xrightarrow{\text{Dry ether}} RR + 2NaX$$

This reaction is useful in the preparation of symmetrical alkanes with higher number of carbon atoms. Tertiary halides do not undergo this reaction.

Chemical Reactions of Haloalkanes (At a glance)

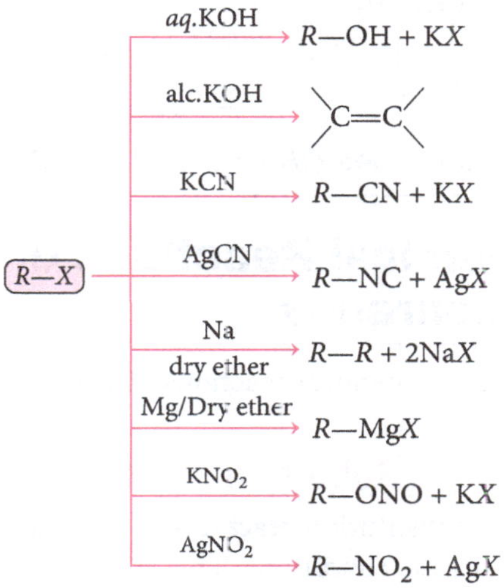

Quick Test 3

1. Out of *o*- and *p*-dibromobenzene, which one has higher melting point and why? NCERT Exemplar

Or Why *p*-dichlorobenzene has higher melting point than those of *ortho*- and *meta*- isomers? CBSE 2023

2. Arrange each set of compounds in the order of increasing boiling points.
   (i) Bromomethane, bromoform, chloromethane, dibromomethane
   (ii) 1-chloropropane, *iso*-propyl chloride, 1-chlorobutane NCERT Intext

3. Which of the following compounds will have the highest melting point and why? NCERT Exemplar

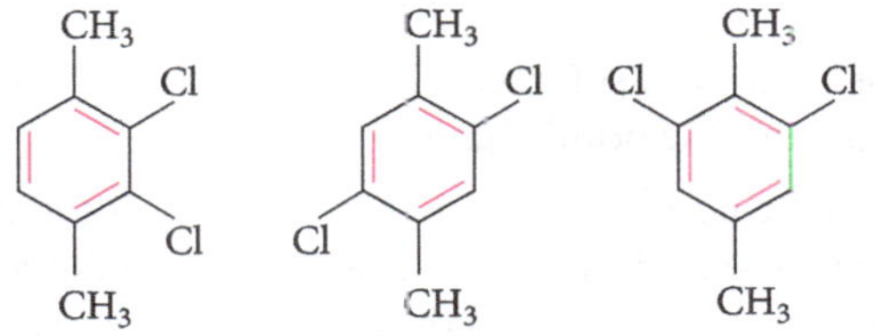

(I) (II) (III)

4. *Tert*-butylbromide reacts with *aq* NaOH by S_N1 mechanism, while *n*-butylbromide reacts by S_N2 mechanism. Why? NCERT Exemplar

5. Which compound in each of the following pairs will react faster in S_N2 reaction with OH^- and why?
   (i) CH_3Br or CH_3I (ii) $(CH_3)_3CCl$ or CH_3Cl NCERT

6. Identify A, B, C, P, Q, R and R' in the following

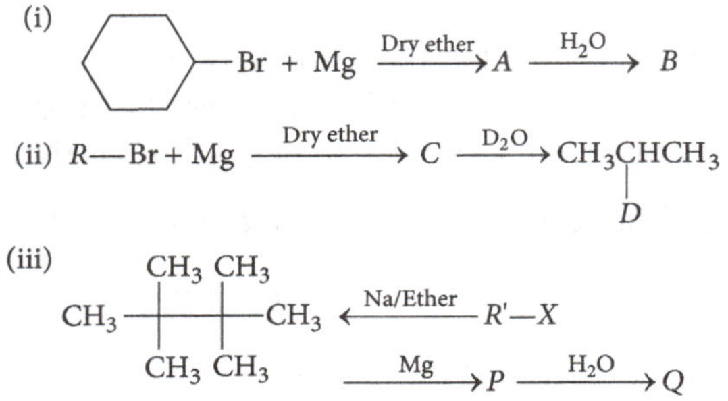

For Solutions, See QR Code on Pg. 227

6.8 Chemical Reactions of Haloarenes

Some important chemical reactions of haloarenes are as follows

Nucleophilic Substitution Reactions

Nucleophilic substitution reactions in aryl halides occur only under drastic conditions. This is because haloarenes are chemically less reactive towards nucleophilic substitution reactions (than haloalkanes) due to the following reasons :

(i) **Resonance effect** In haloarenes like chlorobenzene, the lone pair of electrons on halogen atom are in conjugation with π-electrons of the ring and hence, these are delocalised on the benzene ring as shown below

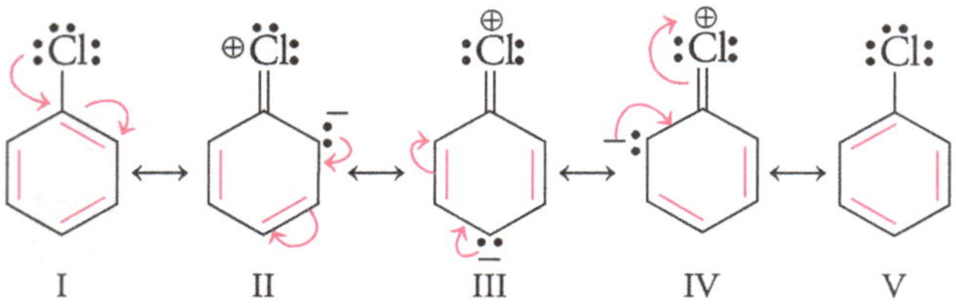

As a result of resonance, C—Cl bond acquires a partial double bond character.

Thus, the bond cleavage in haloarene is difficult than haloalkane (where carbon is attached to halogen by a pure single bond) and thus, they are less reactive towards nucleophilic substitution reaction.

(ii) **Difference in hybridisation of carbon atom in C—*X* bond** In haloalkanes, the carbon atom attached to halogen is sp^3-hybridised, while in haloarenes, it is sp^2-hybridised.

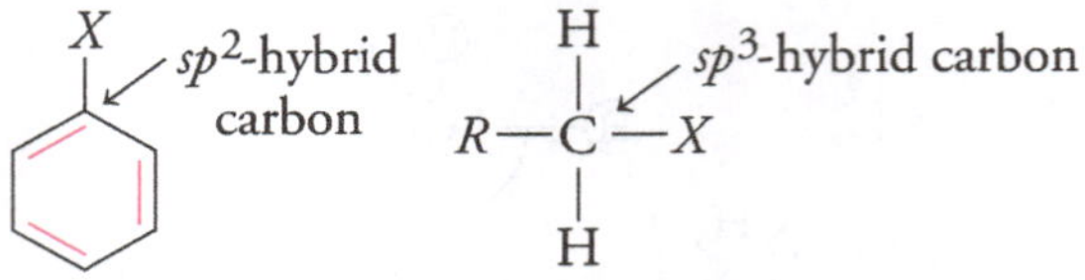

The sp^2-hybridised C-atom with greater *s*-character is more electronegative. It can hold the electron pair of the C—*X* bond more tightly than the sp^3-hybridised C-atom with less *s*-character.

As a result, the C—Cl bond in haloarenes (169 pm) is shorter than in haloalkanes (177 pm).

Since, it is difficult to break a shorter (C—*X*) bond than a longer bond and therefore, haloarenes are less reactive than haloalkanes towards nucleophilic substitution reaction.

(iii) **Unstability of phenyl cation** In haloarenes, the phenyl cation formed as a result of self-ionisation will not be stabilised by resonance, hence S_N1 mechanism cannot occur.

(iv) **Repulsive interaction** It is less likely for the electron rich nucleophile to approach electron rich arenes due to repulsion.

Replacement by Hydroxyl Group

Chlorobenzene when heated in *aq*. NaOH solution at a temperature of 623 K and a pressure of 300 atm, phenol is formed.

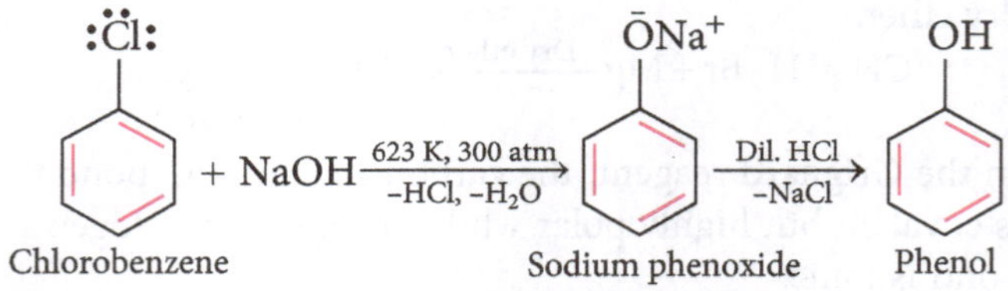

The presence of electron withdrawing groups such as $—NO_2$, —CN at *o*- and *p*-positions of haloarenes with respect to halogen, greatly activates the benzene ring towards nucleophilic substitution.

Further, greater the number of such groups at *o*-and *p*-positions with respect to halogen, more reactive is the haloarene.

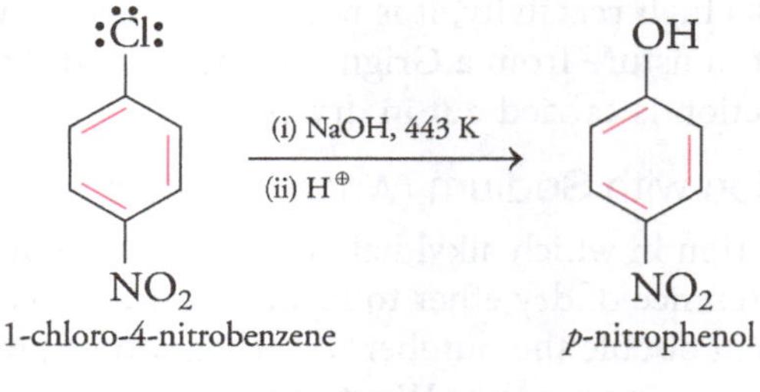

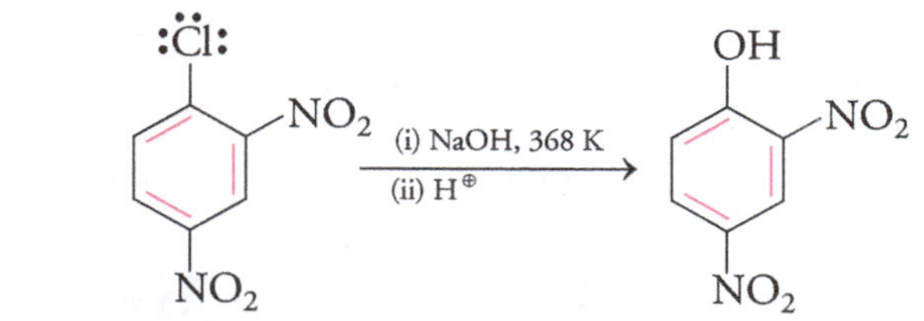

2, 4-dinitrochlorobenzene → 2, 4-dinitrophenol

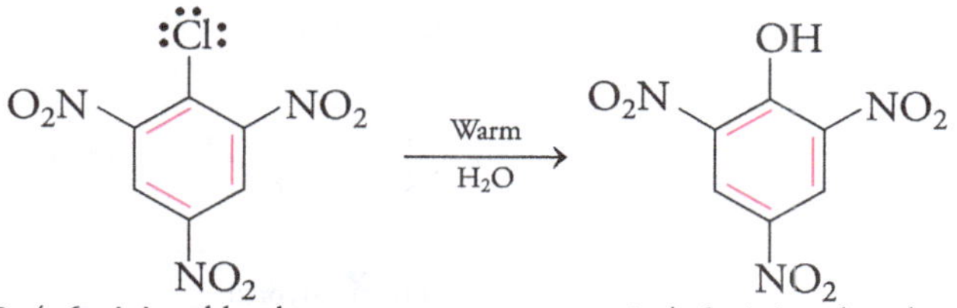

2, 4, 6-trinitrochlorobenzene → 2, 4, 6-trinitrophenol (Picric acid)

The —NO_2 group at *m*-position to the chlorine has no effect on reactivity.

Mechanism

The presence of —NO_2 groups at *o*- and *p*-positions withdraws electrons density from benzene ring and facilitates the attack of nucleophile on haloarenes. The carbanion thus formed is stabilised through resonance as depicted below.

(i) **—NO_2 at *para*-position** The negative charge appeared at *para*-position (structure II) with respect to halogen substitutent is stabilised by —NO_2 group.

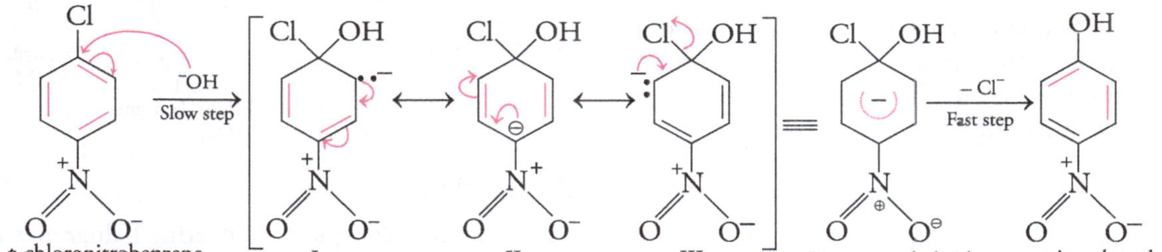

p-chloronitrobenzene; I; II; III; Resonance hybrid; *p*-nitrophenol

(ii) **—NO_2 at *ortho*-position** The negative charge appeared at *ortho*-position (structure IV) with respect to halogen substituent is stabilised by —NO_2 group.

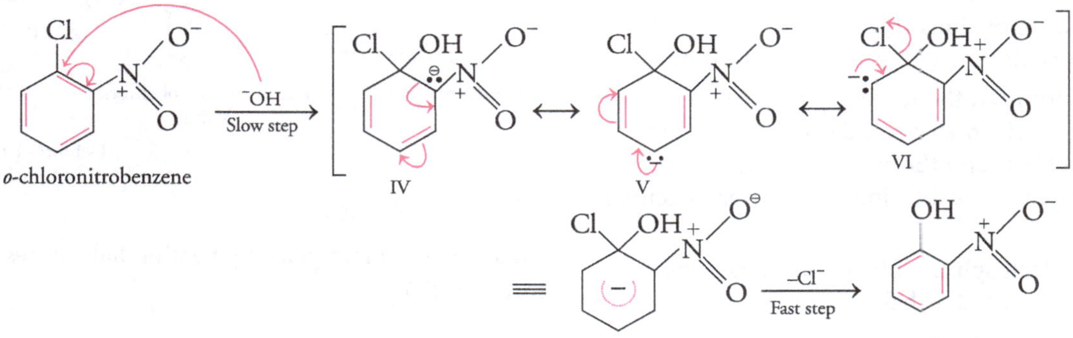

o-chloronitrobenzene; IV; V; VI; Resonance hybrid; *o*-nitrophenol

(iii) **—NO_2 at *meta*-position** In the below structures showing —NO_2 at *meta*-position, there is no such structure in which the negative charge is present on carbon atom bearing the —NO_2 group. Therefore, the presence of nitro group at *meta*-position does not stabilise the negative charge. Hence, no effect on reactivity is observed by the presence of — NO_2 group at *meta*-position.

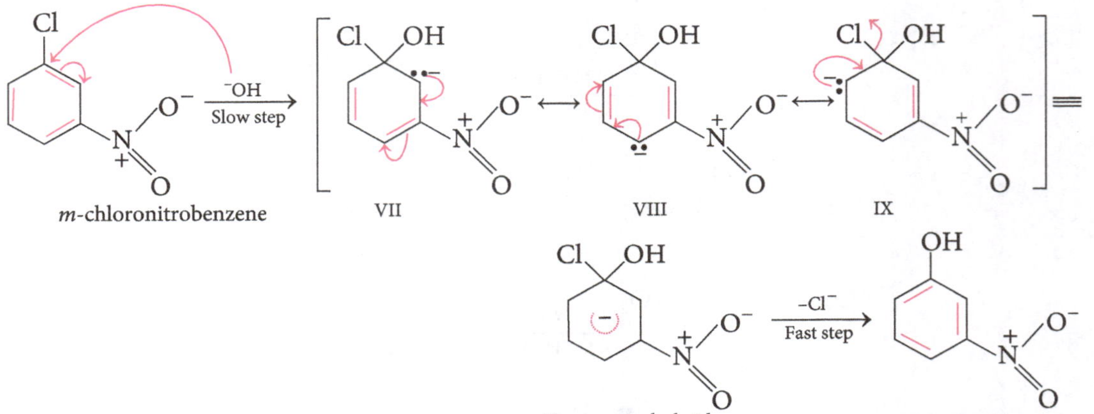

m-chloronitrobenzene

Electrophilic Substitution Reactions

Haloarenes undergo the usual electrophilic reactions of the benzene ring such as halogenation, nitration, sulphonation and Friedel-Crafts reactions. In these reactions, stronger electrophile replaces weaker electrophile.The electrophilic substitution reactions in haloarenes occur slowly and require more drastic conditions. This is due to the *ortho* and *para*-directing influence of halogen atom attached to a benzene ring which can be understood by the following resonating structures of halobenzene.

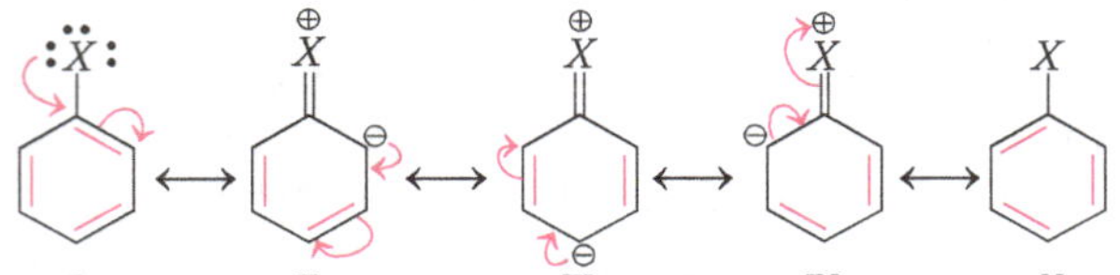

I II III IV V

Thus, due to resonance, the electron density increases more at *o*- and *p*-positions than at *m*-positions. Hence, electrophilic reactions occur at *o*- and *p*-position.

The halogen atom has the tendency to withdraw electrons due to which electron density on benzene ring decreases (–*I*-effect) and the ring gets deactivated. Hence, electrophilic substitution in haloarene occurs at a slower rate.

The common electrophilic substitution reactions of haloarenes are depicted as below.

(i) Halogenation

This reaction takes place by treating haloarenes with halogens in the presence of ferric salt.

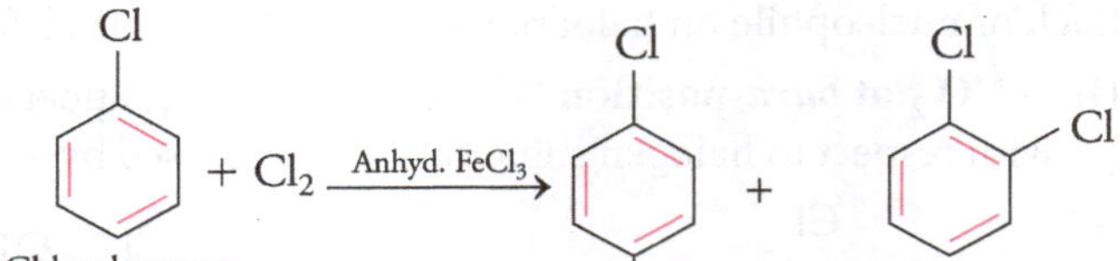

Chlorobenzene; 1, 4-dichlorobenzene (Major); 1, 2- dichlorobenzene (Minor)

(ii) Nitration

This reaction takes place by heating haloarenes with conc. HNO_3 in the presence of conc. H_2SO_4.

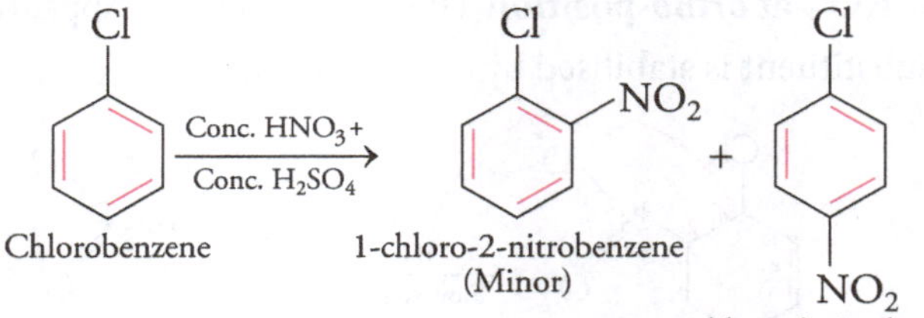

Chlorobenzene; 1-chloro-2-nitrobenzene (Minor); 1-chloro-4-nitrobenzene (Major)

(iii) Sulphonation

This reaction takes place by heating haloarenes with conc. H_2SO_4.

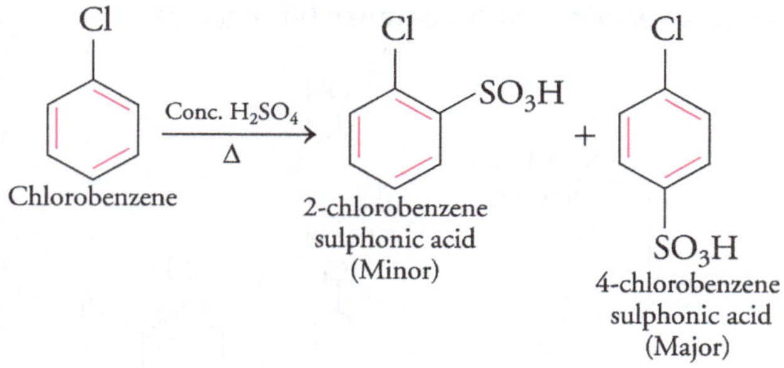

(iv) Friedel-Crafts Reactions

This reaction is carried out by treating haloarenes with alkyl chloride or acyl chloride in the presence of anhydrous $AlCl_3$ acting as a catalyst.

There are two main types of Friedel-Crafts reactions.

(a) Alkylation

In alkylation, haloarenes are treated with alkyl chloride.

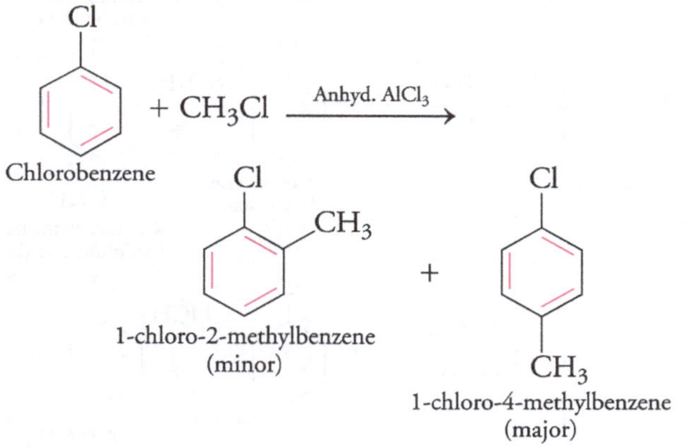

(b) Acylation

In acylation, haloarenes are treated with acyl chloride.

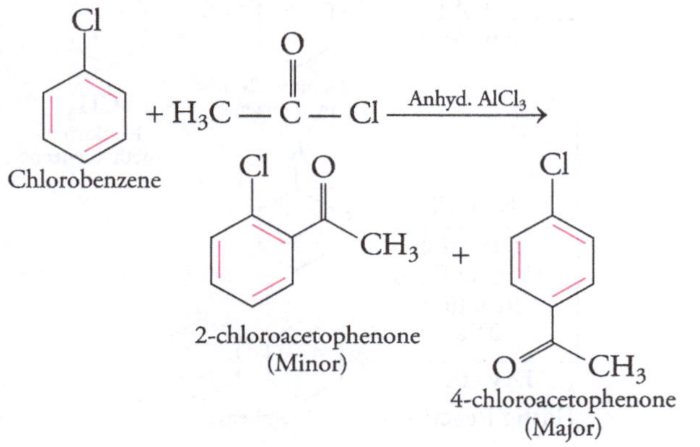

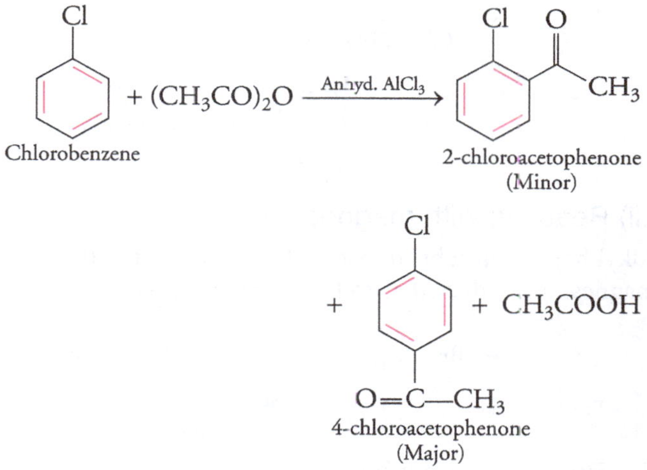

Reaction with Metals

(i) Fittig reaction

When haloarenes react with sodium in the presence of dry ether, two aryl groups are joined together and diphenyl is formed. This reaction is called **Fittig reaction**.

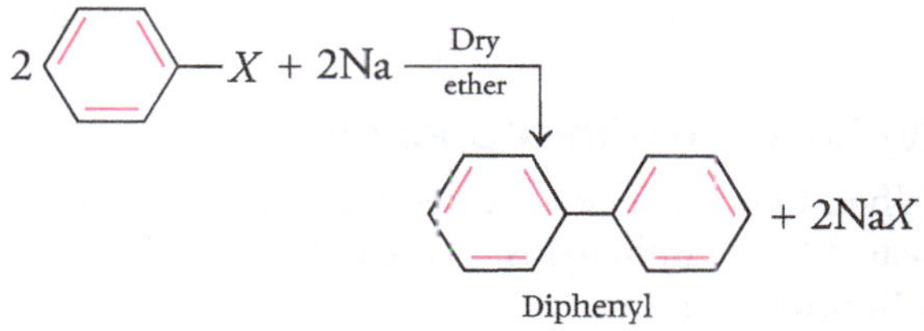

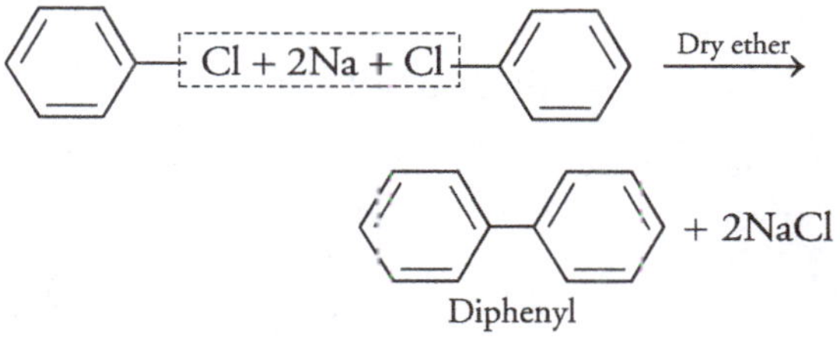

(ii) Wurtz-Fittig reaction

When aryl halide is heated with alkyl halide in the presence of sodium in dry ether, halogen atom is replaced by alkyl group and alkylarene is formed. This reaction is called **Wurtz-Fittig reaction**.

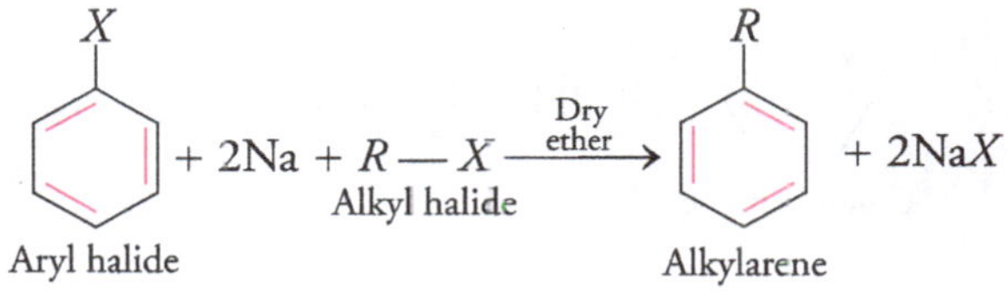

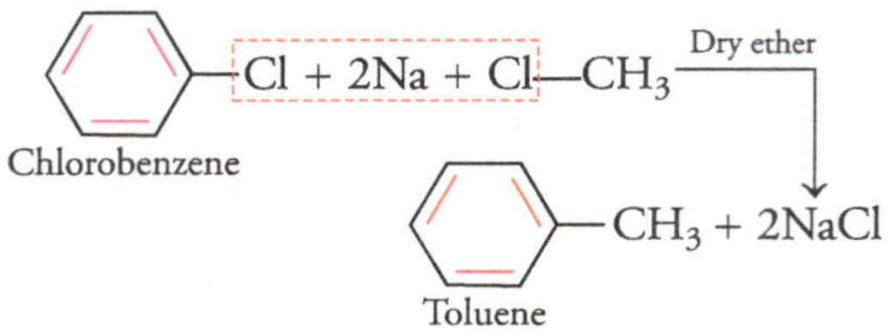

(iii) Reaction with magnesium

Alkyl halides, aryl bromides and iodides react with magnesium in dry ether to form Grignard reagent.

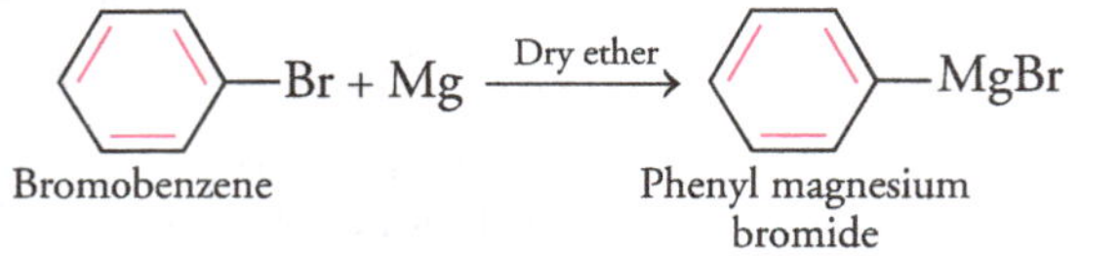

(iv) Reaction with lithium

Bromo- and iodoarenes react with lithium metal in the presence of dry ether to form their corresponding organometallic compounds.

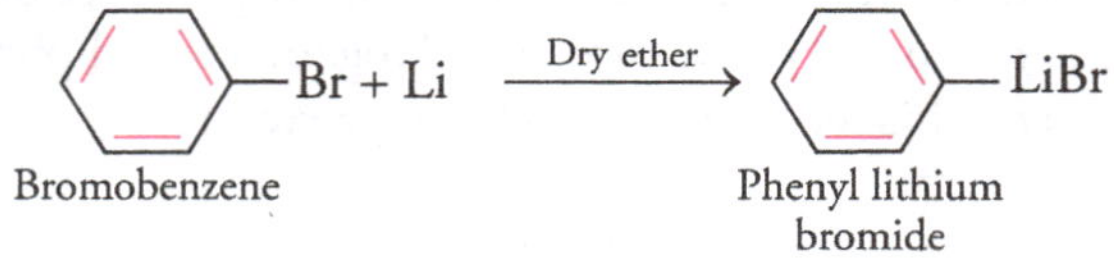

(v) Reaction with copper powder

When iodobenzene is heated with copper powder in a sealed tube, diphenyl is formed. This reaction is called **Ullmann reaction.**

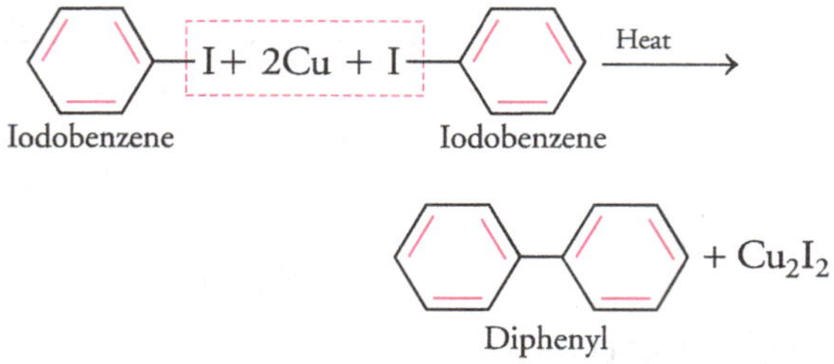

Reduction

On reduction of haloarenes, its parent hydrocarbon is formed.

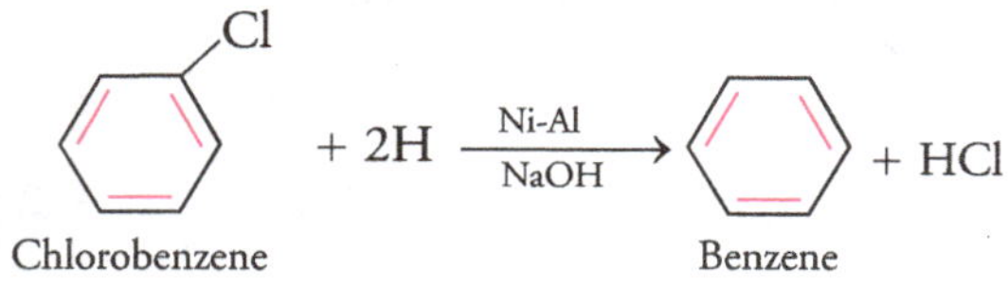

Chemical Reactions of Haloarenes (At a glance)

(i)

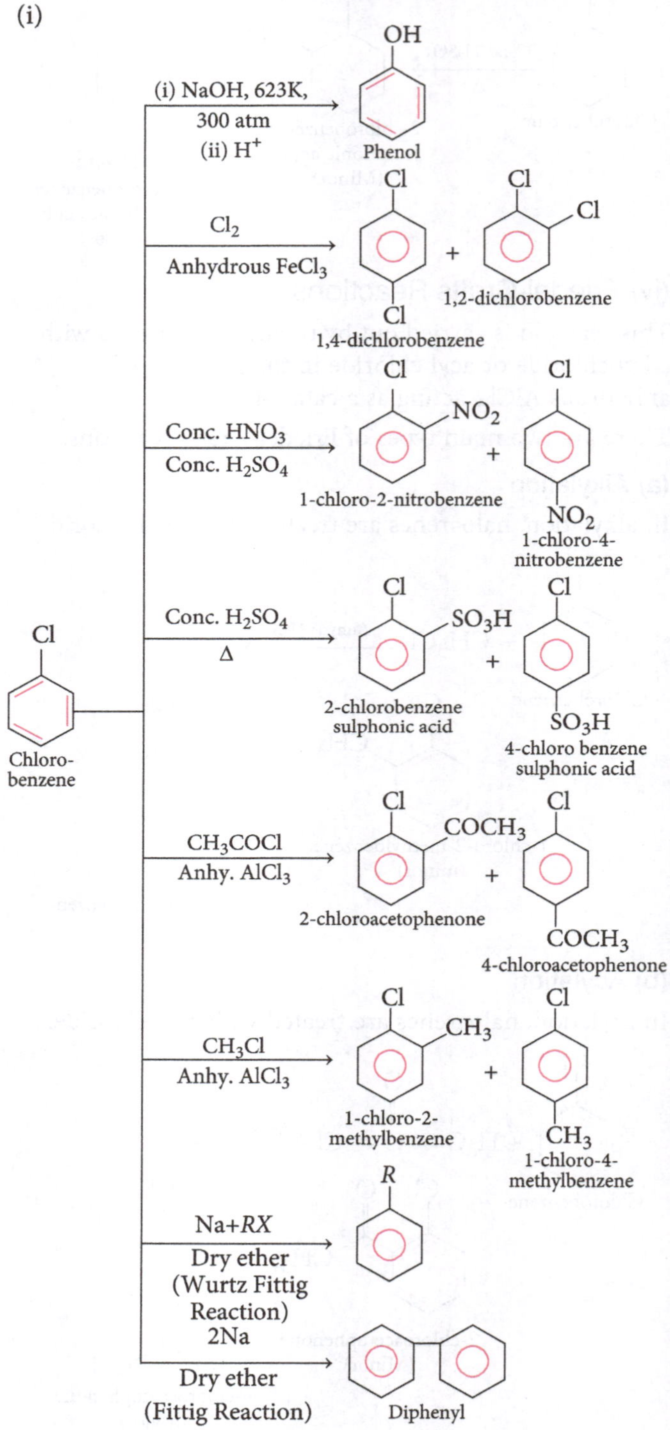

(ii)

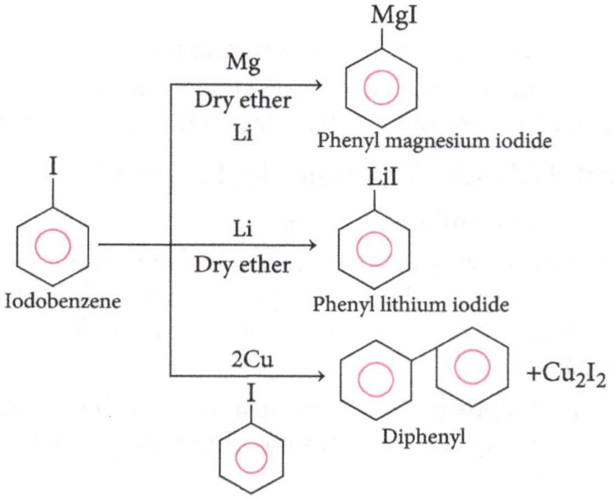

Example 4 **How can the following conversions be carried out?**

(i) 2-bromopropane to 1-bromopropane
(ii) But-1-ene to *n*-butyl iodide
(iii) 2-chloropropane to 1-propanol
(iv) *iso*-propyl alcohol to iodoform
(v) Chlorobenzene to *p*-nitrophenol

All India 2017, NCERT

Sol. (i) $CH_3-\underset{\underset{Br}{|}}{CH}-CH_3 \xrightarrow{\text{Alc. KOH}} CH_3CH=CH_2 \xrightarrow[H_2O_2]{HBr} CH_3-CH_2-\underset{\underset{Br}{|}}{CH_2}$

2-bromopropane ... 1-bromopropane

(ii) $\underset{\text{But-1-ene}}{CH_3CH_2CH=CH_2} \xrightarrow[\text{Peroxide}]{HBr} \underset{n\text{-butyl bromide}}{CH_3CH_2CH_2CH_2Br}$

$\xrightarrow[\text{Acetone (Finkelstein reaction)}]{NaI} \underset{n\text{-butyl iodide}}{CH_3CH_2CH_2CH_2I}$

(iii) $CH_3-\underset{\underset{Cl}{|}}{CH}-CH_3 \xrightarrow[\Delta]{\text{KOH(alc.)}} \underset{\text{Propene}}{CH_3-CH=CH_2}$

2-chloropropane

$\xrightarrow[\text{Anti-Markovnikov's addition}]{\text{HBr, Peroxide}} \underset{\text{1-bromopropane}}{CH_3CH_2CH_2Br} \xrightarrow[\text{Nucleophilic substitution}]{KOH(aq),\ \Delta} \underset{\text{Propanol}}{CH_3CH_2CH_2OH}$

(iv) $CH_3-\underset{\underset{OH}{|}}{CH}-CH_3 + 4I_2 + 6NaOH \xrightarrow[\text{(Iodoform reaction)}]{\text{Heat}} \underset{\text{Iodoform}}{CHI_3\downarrow}$

iso-propyl alcohol

$+ \underset{\text{Sodium ethanoate}}{CH_3COONa} + 5NaI + 5H_2O$

(v)

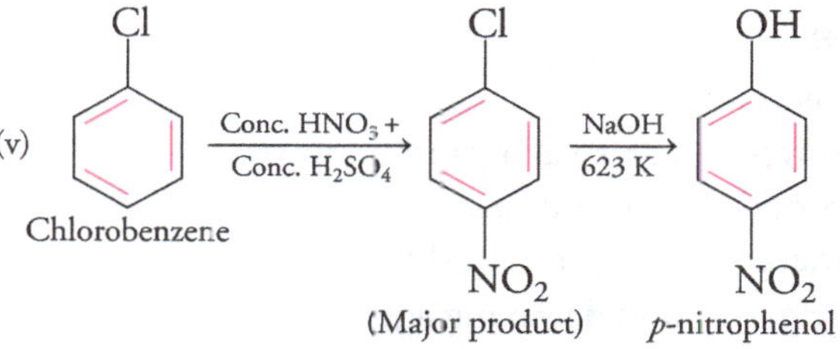

Quick Test 4

1. What happens when
(i) Chlorobenzene is treated with ethanoyl chloride in presence of anhydrous $AlCl_3$.
(ii) Iodobenzene is heated with copper powder.

2. With the help of resonating structures explain the effect of presence of nitro group at *ortho* position in chlorobenzene. **CBSE SQP 2021**

3. Complete the following reactions.

(i)

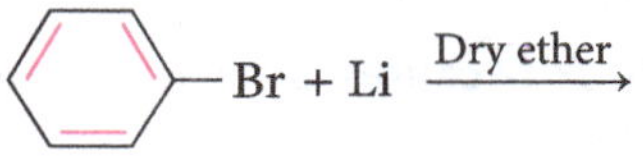

(ii)

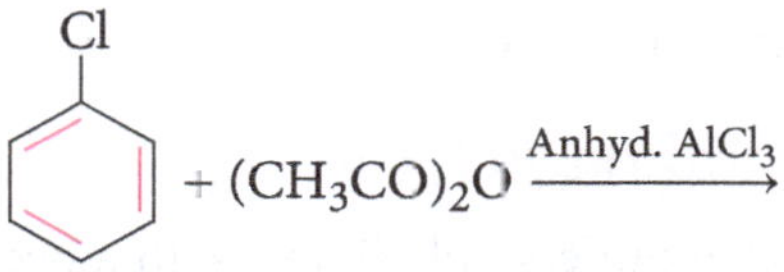

4. Write a short note on Wurtz-fittig reaction.

For Solutions, See QR Code on Pg. 227

6.10 Polyhalogen Compounds

Carbon compounds having more than one halogen atom are usually referred to as **polyhalogen compounds**. Many of these compounds are useful in industry and agriculture.

Some important polyhalogen compounds are described as follows.

Dichloromethane (Methylene Chloride, CH_2Cl_2)

It is colourless, sweet smelling volatile liquid, having low boiling point of 313 K and specific gravity of 1.37. It is prepared industrially by the direct chlorination of methane in the presence of diffused sunlight.

$$CH_4 + 2Cl_2 \xrightarrow{h\nu} CH_2Cl_2 + 2HCl$$

Uses

It is used as

- a solvent and also as a paint remover.
- a propellant in aerosols.
- a metal cleaning and finishing solvent.
- refrigerant and dewaxing agent.
- a process solvent in the manufacture of drugs.

Harmful Effects (Physiological Effects)

Some of the harmful effects of methylene chloride are as follows

- It harms the human central nervous system.
- Exposure to lower levels of methylene chloride in air can lead to slightly impaired hearing and vision.
- Exposure to higher levels of methylene chloride can cause dizziness, nausea, tingling and numbness in the fingers and toes.
- Direct contact with skin causes intense burning and mild redness of the skin.
- Direct contact with eyes can burn the cornea.

Trichloromethane (Chloroform, $CHCl_3$)

Chloroform is a colourless, oily liquid with a peculiar sickly smell and a burning taste. It is slowly oxidised by air in the presence of light to an extremely poisonous gas, carbonyl chloride also called **phosgene**.

$$2CHCl_3 + O_2 \xrightarrow{\text{Sunlight}} \underset{\text{Phosgene}}{2COCl_2} + 2HCl$$

Preservation of Chloroform

To prevent the oxidation of chloroform, it is preserved in the following ways :

- Chloroform is stored in dark coloured bottles to protect it from sunlight to avoid its oxidation.
- These bottles are completely filled with chloroform upto the brim and are properly stoppered to keep air out.
- 1% ethanol is added so, as to convert phosgene gas to diethyl carbonate which is non-volatile and non-toxic.

$$\underset{\text{Phosgene}}{COCl_2} + 2C_2H_5OH \longrightarrow \underset{\text{Diethyl carbonate}}{(C_2H_5)_2CO_3} + 2HCl$$

Uses

It is used

- as a solvent for fats, alkaloids, iodine and other substances.
- as a laboratory reagent.
- in the preparation of chloropicrin, chloretone, etc.
- in medicines.
- in the production of freon refrigerant, *R*-22.
- as an anaesthetic in surgery but now it has been replaced by less toxic, safer anaesthetics, such as ether.

Harmful Effects (Physiological Effects)

Some of its harmful effects are

- Chloroform vapours depresses the central nervous system. Inhaling about 900 ppm (in air) of chloroform for a short time, causes dizziness, fatigue and headache.
- Chronic exposure to chloroform damages liver and kidney due to the formation of phosgene gas inside the body.
- Skin develop sore if immersed directly into the chloroform.

Triiodomethane (Iodoform, CHI_3)

It is a yellow coloured crystalline solid with characteristic unpleasant odour. It is insoluble in water but soluble in organic solvents.

Uses

It is used

- as an antiseptic due to the liberation of free iodine.

$$4CHI_3 + 5O_2 \xrightarrow{\text{Heat}} 6I_2 + 4CO_2 + 2H_2O$$

But due to its unpleasant smell, it has been replaced by other formulations containing iodine.

- in the manufacture of pharmaceuticals.

Tetrachloromethane (Carbon Tetrachloride, CCl_4)

It is a colourless oily liquid with sickly smell. Its boiling point is 350 K. It is formed from chloroform as follows

$$CHCl_3 + Cl_2 \xrightarrow{h\nu} CCl_4 + HCl$$

Uses

It is used

- in large quantities, in the manufacture of refrigerants and propellants for aerosol cans.
- as a feedstock in the synthesis of chlorofluoro-carbons (freons) and other chemicals, pharmaceutical manufacturing.
- as a cleaning fluid, degreasing agent (in industry) and spot remover (in home).
- as fire extinguisher.

Harmful Effects (Physiological Effects)

- Exposure to CCl_4 causes liver cancer in humans.
- The most common effects are dizziness, light headedness, nausea and vomiting, which can cause permanent damage to nerve cells. In severe cases, these effects can lead to coma, unconsciousness or even death.
- Exposure of CCl_4 vapours can make heartbeat irregular or even can stop it. When brought in contact with eyes, it may cause irritation in eyes.
- It is also harmful to environment. When it is released into the air, it rises to the atmosphere and depletes the ozone layer. Depletion of ozone layer increases the human exposure to UV rays which lead skin cancer, eye diseases and disorders and possible disruption of the immune system.

Freons

Chlorofluorocarbon compounds (CFC) of methane and ethane are collectively known as freons. They are extremely stable, unreactive, non-toxic, non-corrosive and easily liquefiable gases. Freon-12 (dichlorodifluoromethane, CCl_2F_2) is one of the most common freons in industrial use. It is manufactured from tetrachloro methane by **Swarts reaction.**

$$3CCl_4 + 2SbF_3 \xrightarrow{SbCl_5} 2SbCl_3 + \underset{\text{Freon-12}}{3CCl_2F_2}$$

Uses

It is used

- as refrigerants in refrigerators and air conditioners.
- as propellants for aerosols and foams to spray out deoderants, cleansers, shaving creams, hair sprays and insecticides.

Harmful Effects (Environmental Effects)

Most freons make its way into the atmosphere, where it undergoes photochemical decomposition and initiates radical chain reactions for depletion of the ozone layer. Therefore, the use of freons as propellants and refrigerants has been drastically discouraged.

p, p' Dichlorodiphenyltrichloroethane (DDT)

DDT, the first chlorinated organic insecticide, was originally prepared in 1873. **Paul Muller** of Geigy Pharmaceuticals in Switzerland discovered the effectiveness of DDT as an insecticide and was awarded the Nobel prize in medicine and physiology in 1948.

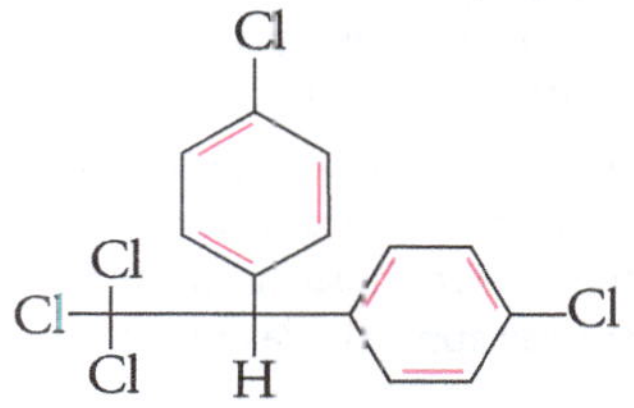

(DDT)

It is a white powder, insoluble in water but soluble in oil.

Uses

- DDT is a cheap but powerful insecticide.
- It is popularly very effective against anopheles mosquitoes (causes malaria) and lice which carry typhus.

Harmful Effects
(Environmental and Physiological Effects)

- DDT is non-biodegradable and extremely stable compound which acts as water pollutant and kills aquatic animals thus imbalancing the water ecosystem.
- When higher animals (including humans) feed on dead fishes killed by DDT, it enters in their food chains.
- DDT gets deposited and stored in fat tissues of animal and increases in amount over the time if ingestion continues at a steady rate.
- Researches have shown that such deposition in long run may cause cancer and other harmful diseases.

  Hence, DDT has been banned in many countries but it is still in use, due to its magical effects of controlling disease, in most of the developing countries.

Quick Test 5

1. Chloroform is stored in closed dark coloured bottles completely filled, so that air is kept out. Explain.

Or Chloroform is stored in closed dark coloured bottles. CBSE 2023

2. (i) Give the reaction for the formation of phosgene gas.
   (ii) What happens when phosgene gas reacts with ethanol? (Give chemical reaction only).

3. Name the non-volatile, non-toxic compound, which is formed when 1% ethanol is added to the bottles of chloroform to convert phosgene gas to that compound.

4. Why iodoform has appreciable antiseptic property? NCERT Exemplar

5. Which polyhalogen compound is used in the production of freon refrigerant *R*-22?

6. What is Freon-12 ? Why freons are not environment friendly ? CBSE 2019

7. Write one use for each of the following.
   (i) DDT (ii) Iodoform CBSE 2019

8. What is the IUPAC name of DDT? Why is its use banned in many countries?

9. Name the following polyhalogen compounds.
   (i) Compound that act as a propellant in aerosols.
   (ii) Compound that is used in the preparation of chloropicrin.

10. Mention polyhalogen compounds that
   (i) act as fire extinguisher. (ii) is a cheap insecticide.
   (iii) is used in hair sprays.

For Solutions, See QR Code on Pg. 227

Mind Map

HALOALKANES AND HALOARENES

Methods of Preparation

1. From Hydrocarbon

- **By free radical halogenation**

$$CH_3CH_2CH_2CH_3 \xrightarrow{Cl_2/UV} CH_3CH_2CH_2CH_2Cl + CH_3CH_2CHClCH_3$$

- **By electrophilic substitution**

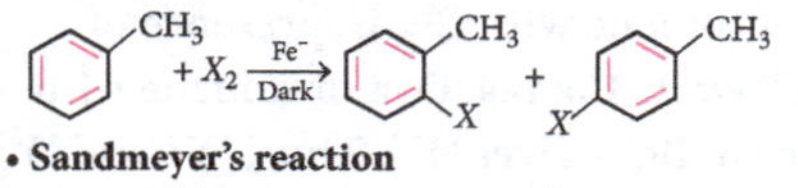

- **Sandmeyer's reaction**

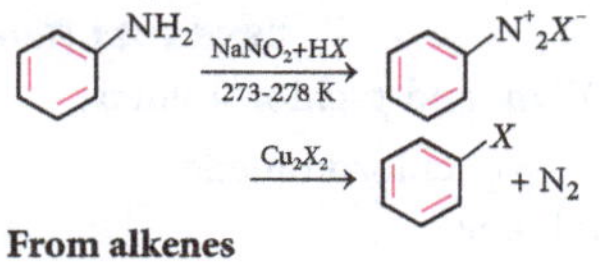

- **From alkenes**

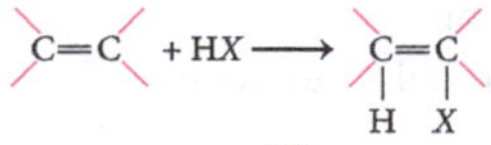

$$H_2C{=}CH_2 + Br_2 \xrightarrow{CCl_4} BrCH_2{-}CH_2Br$$

2. From Alcohol

$$R{-}OH + HCl \xrightarrow{ZnCl_2} R{-}Cl + H_2O$$

$$3R{-}OH + PX_3 \longrightarrow 3R{-}X + H_3PO_3$$

$$R{-}OH + PCl_5 \longrightarrow R{-}Cl + POCl_3 + HCl$$

3. Halogen Exchange

$$RX + NaI \xrightarrow{Acetone/\Delta} RI + NaX$$

(Finkelstein reaction)

$$RBr + AgF \longrightarrow RF + AgBr$$

(Swarts reaction)

Polyhalogen Compounds

1. Dichloromethane (CH_2Cl_2)

- Used as propellant and refrigerant.
- Used as a metal cleaning and finishing solvent.
- Harms CNS and leads to impaired hearing and vision.

2. Trichloromethane ($CHCl_3$)

- Also called as chloroform.
- In air, oxidises to give poisonous gas, phosgene ($COCl_2$).
- Oxidation is prevented by using dark coloured bottles and by adding 1% ethanol.
- Used as a reagent, solvent and anaesthetic.

3. Iodoform (CHI_3)

- Used as an antiseptic and in the manufacture of pharmaceuticals.

4. Carbon Tetrachloride (CCl_4)

- Used as fire extinguisher (under the name pyrene) and cleaning fluid.
- Leads to liver cancer, ozone depletion, etc.

5. Freons

- These are chlorofluorocarbon compounds of methane and ethane.
- These are non-toxic, unreactive, stable and non-corrosive.
- Used as refrigerant and coolant.
- Leads to ozone layer depletion.

6. DDT

- It is *p*, *p*′-dichlorodiphenyltrichloroethane.
- Used as an insecticide.
- Non-biodegradable so causes air pollution, water pollution and soil pollution.

Physical Properties

- **Physical** Colourless, volatile, sweet smell.
- Lower members are gases at room temperature while, higher are solids or liquids.
- **Boiling point** $RI > RBr > RCl > RF$.
- **Melting Point** *para*-isomers have high m.p. than *ortho* and *meta*-isomers.
- **Density** Increases with increase in number of C/X atoms and atomic masses of the X atoms.
- **Solubility** Very slightly soluble in water.

Nomenclature

- **Common name** For haloalkanes, alkyl group followed by the name of halides.
  For haloarenes, prefixing halo before the name of the aromatic ring.
- **IUPAC name** Alkyl halides are named haloalkanes.
- Dihalogen derivatives of haloarenes are named by using numerals.

Chemical Properties

(a) Nucleophilic substitution reaction

$$Nu^- + \overset{\delta+}{>C}{-}\overset{\delta-}{X} \rightarrow >C{-}Nu^- + X^-$$

- S_N1 reaction involves the formation of carbocation intermediate. It gives racemic mixture.
- S_N2 reaction involves the formation of transition state. It results in inversion of configuration.

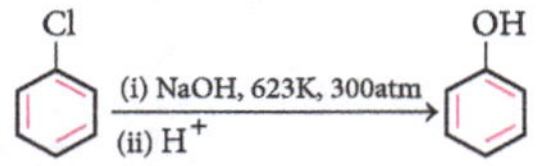

(b) Elimination reaction

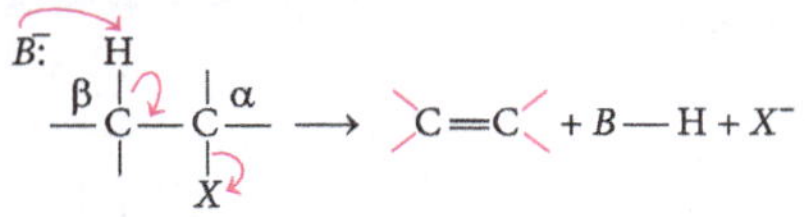

B = Base; X = Leaving group

(c) Reaction with metals

$$CH_3CH_2Br + Mg \xrightarrow{Dry\ ether} CH_3CH_2MgBr$$

Grignard reagent

Wurtz reaction

$$2RX + 2Na \xrightarrow{Dry\ ether} R{-}R + 2NaX$$

Wurtz-Fittig reaction

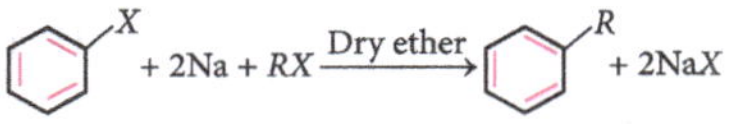

Fittig reaction

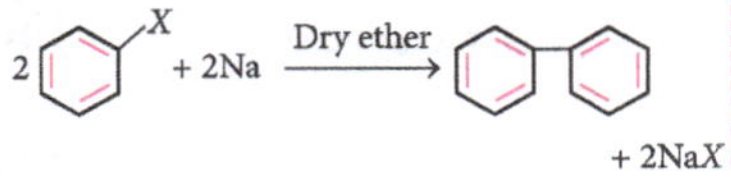

(d) Electrophilic substitution reaction

Haloarenes are *o*, *p*-directing.

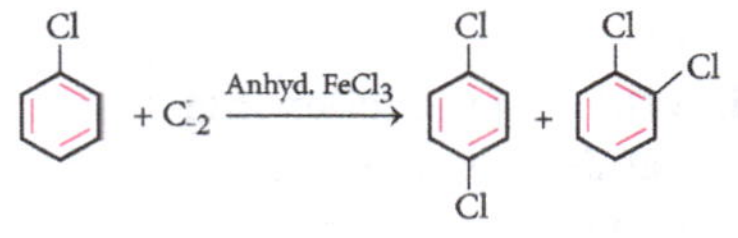

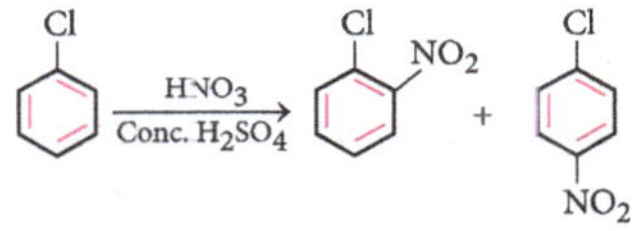

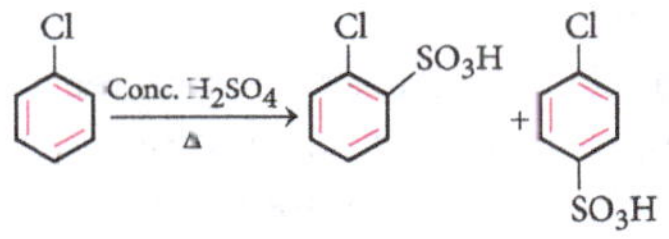

EXAM PATTERN QUESTIONS

Objective Type Questions

Multiple Choice Questions [1 Mark]

1. **Which one of the following has the highest dipole moment?** **CBSE SQP 2025**

(a) CH_3F (b) CH_3Cl

(c) CH_3I (d) CH_3Br

2. **What should be the correct IUPAC name for diethylbromomethane?** **NCERT Exemplar**

(a) 1-bromo-1, 1-diethylmethane

(b) 3-bromopentane

(c) 1-bromo-1-ethylpropane

(d) 1-bromopentane

3. The IUPAC name of benzene hexachloride is **Diksha**

(a) 1, 2, 3, 4, 5, 6-hexachlorocyclohexane

(b) 1, 1, 1, 6, 6, 6-hexachlorocyclohexane

(c) 1, 6-phenyl-1, 6-chlorohexane

(d) 1, 1-phenyl-6, 6-chlorohexane

4. **Match the Column I with Column II and choose the correct option using the codes given below.**

	Column I (Common Name)		Column II (IUPAC Name)
A.	Methylene chloride	(i)	3-bromopropene
B.	Vinyl chloride	(ii)	Dichloromethane
C.	Allyl bromide	(iii)	Chloroethene

Codes

	A	B	C
(a)	(i)	(ii)	(iii)
(b)	(ii)	(i)	(iii)
(c)	(ii)	(iii)	(i)
(d)	(i)	(iii)	(ii)

5. **Which of the following reagent produces pure alkyl halides when heated with alcohols?** **Diksha**

(a) PCl_5 (b) PCl_3

(c) $SOCl_2$ (d) Dry HCl

6. **Toluene reacts with a halogen in the presence of iron (III) chloride giving *ortho* and *para* halo compounds. The reaction is** **NCERT Exemplar**

(a) electrophilic elimination reaction

(b) electrophilic substitution reaction

(c) free radical addition reaction

(d) nucleophilic substitution reaction

7. **The reaction of toluene with Cl_2 in presence of $FeCl_3$ gives '*X*', while the reaction of toluene with Cl_2 in presence of light gives '*Y*'. Thus, '*X*' and '*Y*' are** **CBSE 2021 (Term I)**

(a) X = benzyl chloride Y = *o*- and *p*-chlorotoluene

(b) X = *m*-chlorotoluene Y = *p*-chlorotoluene

(c) X = *o*- and *p*-chlorotoluene
Y = trichloromethylbenzene

(d) X = benzyl chloride, Y = *m*-chlorotoluene

8. **Which of the following is a free radical substitution reaction?**

(a) 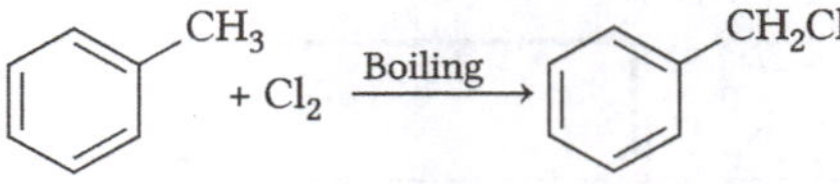

(b) 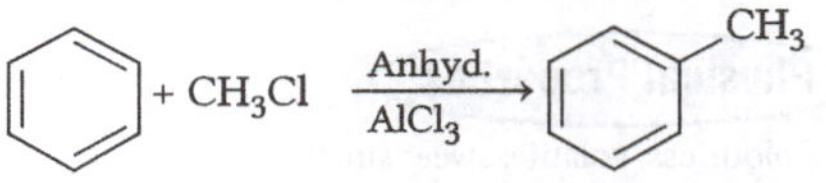

(c) 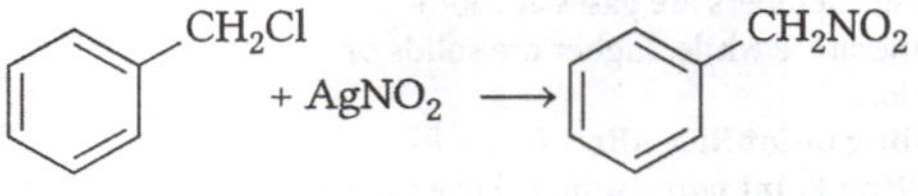

(d) $CH_3CHO + HCN \longrightarrow CH_3CH(OH)CN$

9. **Which reagent is required for one step conversion of benzene diazonium chloride to bromobenzene?** **CBSE 2021 (Term I)**

(a) PBr_3 (b) HBr (c) Cu_2Br_2 (d) Br_2

10. **Arrange the following compounds in increasing order of their boiling points:** **CBSE 2025**

(i) $(CH_3)_2CH-CH_2Br$

(ii) $CH_3CH_2CH_2CH_2Br$

(iii) $H_3C-\underset{Br}{\overset{CH_3}{C}}-CH_3$

The correct order is

(a) (ii) < (i) < (iii)

(b) (i) < (ii) < (iii)

(c) (iii) < (i) < (ii)

(d) (iii) < (ii) < (i)

11. **Study the graph showing the boiling points of bromoalkanes and identify the compounds.**

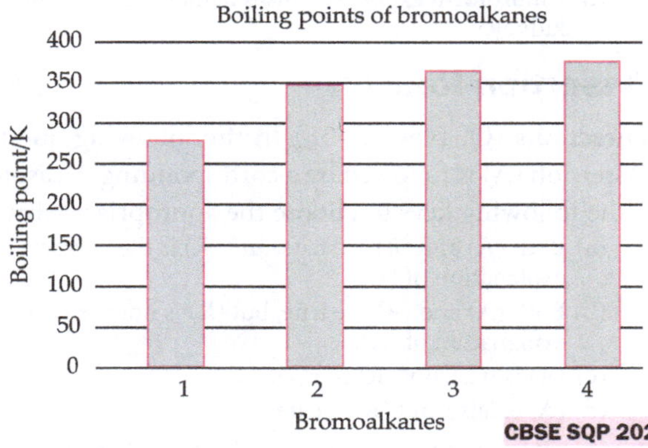

CBSE SQP 2025

(a) 1 = Bromomethane, 2 = 2-bromobutane, 3 = 1-bromobutane, 4 = 2-bromo-2-methylpropane
(b) 1 = 1-bromobutane, 2 = 2-bromo-2-methylpropane, 3= 2-bromobutane, 4 = Bromomethane
(c) 1 = Bromomethane, 2 = 1-bromobutane, 3 = 2-bromo-2-methylpropane, 4 = 2-bromobutane
(d) 1 = Bromomethane, 2 = 2-bromo-2-methylpropane, 3 = 2- bromobutane, 4 = 1-bromobutane

12. **Which one of the following undergoes nucleophilic substitution exclusively by S_N1 mechanism?** **Diksha**

(a) Ethyl chloride (b) Isopropyl chloride
(c) Chlorobenzene (d) Benzyl chloride

13. **Which alkyl halide from the given options will undergo S_N1 reaction faster?** **CBSE 2024**

(a) $(CH_3)_3C—Br$ (b) $(CH_3)_2CH—Br$
(c) $CH_3—CH_2—Br$ (d) $(CH_3)_3C—CH_2—Br$

14. **The order of reactivity of following alcohols with halogen acids is ....** **NCERT Exemplar**

(A) $CH_3CH_2—CH_2—OH$

(B) 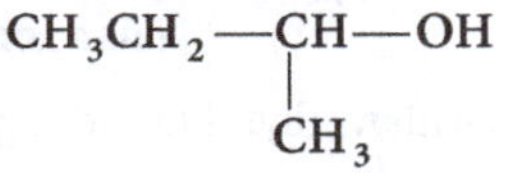

(C) 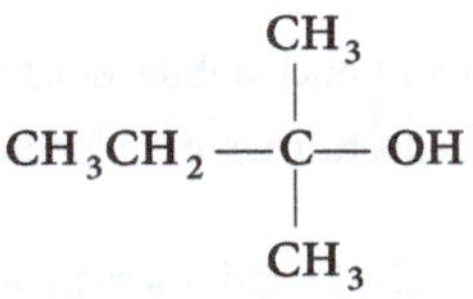

(a) (A) > (B) > (C) (b) (C) > (B) > (A)
(c) (B) > (A) > (C) (d) (A) > (C) > (B)

15. **Alkyl halides undergoing nucleophilic bimolecular substitution reaction involve** **CBSE 2025**

(a) retention of configuration
(b) formation of racemic mixture
(c) inversion of configuration
(d) formation of carbocation

16. **The table given below shown some of the features of S_N1 and S_N2 reaction mechanism.**

	S_N1	S_N2
(i)	First order kinetics	2nd order kinetics
(ii)	Reaction favoured by any type of nucleophile	Reaction favoured by a non-bulky nucleophile
(iii)	Reaction favoured by a good leaving group	Reaction not favoured by a good leaving group
(iv)	Stereochemistry : racemisation	Stereochemistry : Inversion

Which of the rows shows an incorrect feature for at least one of the mechanisms? **Competency Based Que.**

(a) (i) (b) (ii)
(c) (iii) (d) (iv)

17. **Which of the following molecules has a chiral centre correctly labelled with an asterisk (*)?** **CBSE 2023**

(a) $CH_3C^*HBrCH_3$
(b) $CH_3C^*HClCH_2Br$
(c) $HOCH_2C^*H(OH)CH_2OH$
(d) $CH_3C^*Br_2CH_3$

18. **Which of the following compounds will undergo racemisation when solution of KOH hydrolyses ?**

(i) 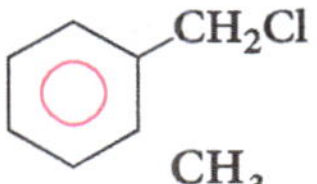 (ii) $CH_3CH_2CH_2Cl$

(ii) 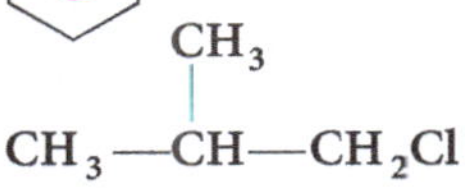 (iv) 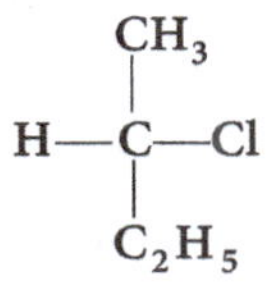

Choose the correct option.

(a) (i) and (ii) (b) (ii) and (iv)
(c) (iii) and (iv) (d) Only (iv)

19. **Which of the following compounds is expected to be optically active?**

(a) $CH_3CH_2CHBrCHO$ (b) $CH_3CH_2CBr_2CHO$
(c) $CH_3CH_2CH_2CHO$ (d) $(CH_3)_2CHCHO$

20. **Identify *A*, *B*, *C* and *D*** **CBSE SQP 2021**

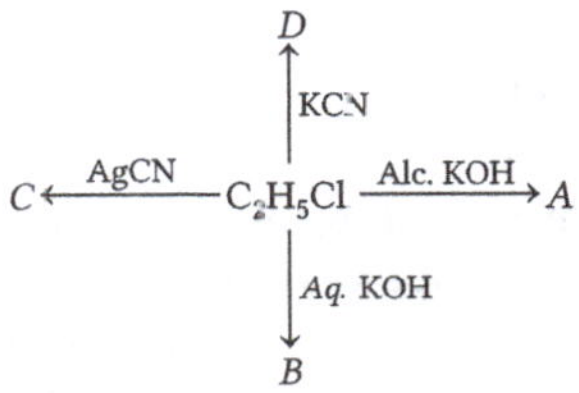

(a) $A = C_2H_4$, $B = C_2H_5OH$, $C = C_2H_5NC$, $D = C_2H_5CN$
(b) $A = C_2H_5OH$, $B = C_2H_4$, $C = C_2H_5CN$, $D = C_2H_5CN$
(c) $A = C_2H_4$, $B = C_2H_5OH$, $C = C_2H_5CN$, $D = C_2H_5NC$
(d) $A = C_2H_5OH$, $B = C_2H_4$, $C = C_2H_5NC$, $D = C_2H_5CN$

21. **Consider the following table.**

Reactant	Reagent	Product formed
Chlorobenzene	(i) NaOH, 623 K, 300 atm (ii) H^+	*X*
Y	2Cu	Diphenyl
Methyl bromide	*Z*	Fluoromethane

'*X*', '*Y*' and '*Z*' in the above table are

(a) $X=$ phenol, $Y=$ Iodobenzene, $Z=$ Silver fluoride
(b) $X=$ Benzene, $Y=$ Phenyl magnesium iodide, $Z=$ Sodium fluoride
(c) $X=$ Phenol, $Y=$ Chlorobenzene, $Z=$ Silver fluoride
(d) $X=$ Benzene, $Y=$ Iodobenzene, $Z=$ Sodium fluoride

22. **Chlorination of toluene in presence of light and heat followed by treatment with aqueous NaOH gives**

(a) benzoic acid
(b) 2,4-dihydroxytoluene
(c) *p*-cresol
(d) *o*-cresol

23. **Which of the following is the correct increasing order for the rate of reaction of the given compounds towards nucleophilic substitution?**

(i) 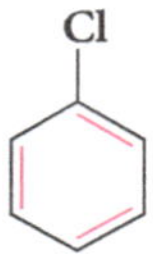

(ii) 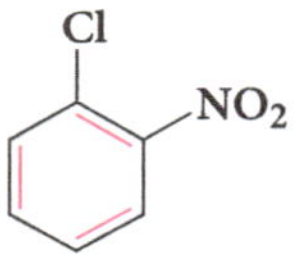

(iii) 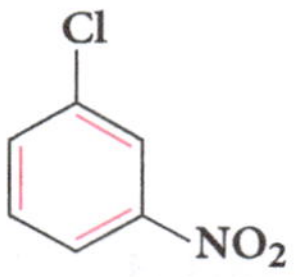

NCERT Exemplar

(a) (i) < (ii) < (iii) (b) (iii) < (ii) < (i)
(c) (i) < (iii) < (ii) (d) (iii) < (i) < (ii)

24. **Which of the following is the correct increasing order for the rate of reaction of the given compounds towards nucleophilic substitution?**

(i) 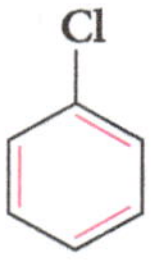

(ii) 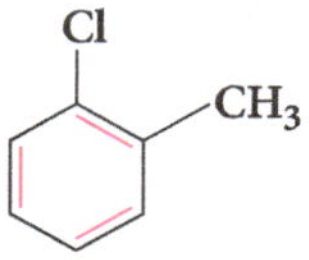

(iii) 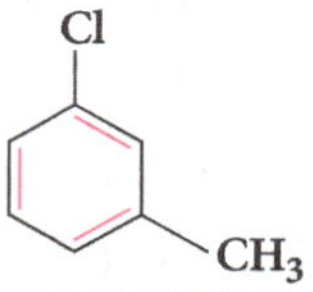

NCERT Exemplar

(a) (i) < (ii) < (iii) (b) (i) < (iii) < (ii)
(c) (iii) < (ii) < (i) (d) (ii) < (iii) < (i)

25. **Auto-oxidation of chloroform in air and light produces a poisonous gas known as** **CBSE 2024**

(a) phosphine (b) mustard gas
(c) phosgene (d) tear gas

26. **Which of the following statement is incorrect for chloroform?**

(a) Breathing about 900 ppm of chloroform can cause diziness.
(b) Chloroform has no effect on central nervous system.
(c) People develop sores when skin is immersed in chloroform.
(d) Chloroform exposure causes damage to liver and kidney.

Assertion-Reason [1 Mark]

Directions (Q. Nos. 27-38) In the following questions, an Assertion (A) is followed by a corresponding. Reason (R). Use the following keys to choose the appropriate answer.

(a) Both (A) and (R) are true, and (R) is the correct explanation of (A).
(b) Both (A) and (R) are true, but (R) is not the correct explanation of (A).
(c) (A) is true, but (R) is false.
(d) (A) is false, but (R) is true.

27. **Assertion** (A) Phosphorus chlorides (tri and penta) are preferred over thionyl chloride for the preparation of alkyl chlorides from alcohols.

Reason (R) Thionyl chloride give pure alkyl halides.

28. **Assertion** (A) *neo*-pentyl chloride is formed when *neo*-pentyl alcohol reacts with HCl.

Reason (R) *neo*-pentyl alcohol is a primary alcohol.

29. **Assertion** (A) Aryl iodides can be prepared by reaction of arenes with iodine in the presence of an oxidising agent.

Reason (R) Oxidising agent oxidises I_2 into HI.

30. **Assertion** (A) The boiling points of alkyl halides decreases in the order $RI > RBr > RCl > RF$.

Reason (R) The boiling points of alkyl chlorides, bromides and iodides are considerably higher than that of the hydrocarbon of comparable molecular mass.

NCERT Exemplar, CBSE 2025

31. **Assertion** (A) Alkyl halides are insoluble in water.

Reason (R) Alkyl halides have halogen attached to sp^3-hybridised carbon. **CBSE 2021 (Term I)**

32. **Assertion** (A) KCN reacts with methyl chloride to give methyl isocyanide.

Reason (R) CN^- is an ambident nucleophile. **NCERT Exemplar**

33. **Assertion** (A) Nucleophilic substitution of iodoethane is easier than chloroethane.

Reason (R) Bond enthalpy of C—I bond is less than that of C—Cl bond. **CBSE 2023**

34. **Assertion** (A) Hydrolysis of (–)-2-bromooctane proceeds with inversion of configuration.

Reason (R) This reaction proceeds through the formation of a carbocation. **NCERT Exemplar**

35. **Assertion** (A) Inversion of configuration is observed in S_N2 reaction.

Reason (R) The reaction proceeds with the formation of carbocation. **CBSE 2024**

36. **Assertion** (A) Inversion of configuration is observed when 1-bromobutane is hydrolysed.

Reason (R) The reaction is S_N2 and proceeds with the formation of transition state. **CBSE 2024**

37. **Assertion** (A) Nitration of chlorobenzene leads to the formation of *m*-nitrochlorobenzene.

Reason (R) —NO_2 group is a *m*-directing group.

38. **Assertion** (A) Presence of a nitro group at *ortho* or *para* position increases the reactivity of haloarenes towards nucleophilic substitution.

Reason (R) Nitro group, being an electron withdrawing group decreases the electron density over the benzene ring. **NCERT Exemplar**

Case-Study [4 Marks]

39. Read the given passage and answer the questions that follow.

Observe the table in which physical data of halomethanes, polyhalogen derivatives and haloarenes is given. Answer the questions based on them.

Some physical data of halomethanes, polyhalogen derivatives and haloarenes.

		Bond C—*X* length	Bond enthalpy	Dipole moment	
1.	CH_3F	139	452	1.847 D	
2.	CH_3Cl	178	351	1.860 D	
3.	CH_3Br	193	293	1.83 D	
4.	CH_3I	214	234	1.636 D	
5.	CH_2Cl_3			1.62 D	
6.	$CHCl_3$			1.03 D	
7.	CCl_4			Zero	
				Dipole moment	**Melting point**
8.	*p*-dichloro benzene			Zero	325 K
9.	*o*-dichloro benzene			2.54 D	216 K
10.	*m*-dichloro benzene			1.72 D	249 K
					Boiling point
11.	C_6H_5F			1.60 D	358 K
12.	C_6H_5Cl			1.69 D	405 K
13.	C_6H_5Br			1.70 D	429 K
14.	C_6H_5I			1.70 D	462 K

Study the above data and answer the following questions.

(i) Why is melting point of *p*-dichlorobenzene higher than *o*-dichlorobenzene but boiling point of *o*-isomer is higher than *p*-isomer?

(ii) Why is dipole moment of CH_3F less than CH_3Cl ?

Or Why is CH_3I more reactive than CH_3Cl?

(iii) Why does C_6H_5I has higher dipole moment than C_6H_5F?

40. Read the given case and answer the questions that follow.

Haloalkanes are colourless (when pure), sweet smelling liquids. CH_3Cl, CH_3Br and C_2H_5Cl and freons are gases. The boiling point of haloalkanes increases with an increase in molecular weight and the length of the carbon chain, but it decreases with branching. They are insoluble in water due to their inability to form H-bonds with water. The dipole moment of haloalkanes increases with polarity and their density increases with increase in molar mass. *p*-dichloro benzene has zero dipole moment and a higher melting point than *o*-dichloro benzene due to its symmetrical structure, which allows it to fit into the crystal lattice readily.

Haloalkanes undergo nucleophilic substitution reaction by S_N2 mechanism, where the order of reactivity is 1° > 2° > 3°, provided the carbocation formed is stable. They also undergo nucleophilic elimination reactions in the presence of alcoholic KOH. Haloarenes are less reactive than haloalkanes towards nucleophilic substitution due to resonance. Haloarenes undergo electrophilic substitution reaction like nitration, sulphonation, Friedel Crafts alkylation, acylation.

Chloroform is used as solvent, Freon is used as refrigerant, dichloromethane is used as paint remover. Iodoform is used as antiseptic. DDT is insecticide but non- biodegradable.

(i) Complete the following

(a) 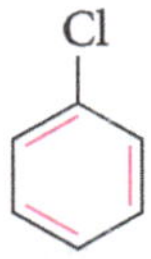 + Conc. $H_2SO_4 \xrightarrow{\Delta}$

(b) $(CH_3)_3CBr + OH^- \longrightarrow$

(ii) The compound which undergoes S_N1 reaction with fastest rate is

(a) 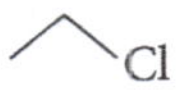

(b) 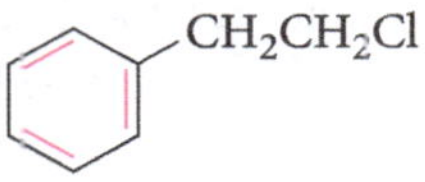

(c) 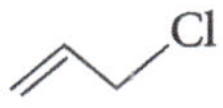

(d) 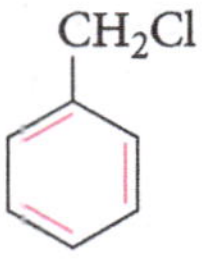

(1)

Or Identify '*A*' in the following reaction.

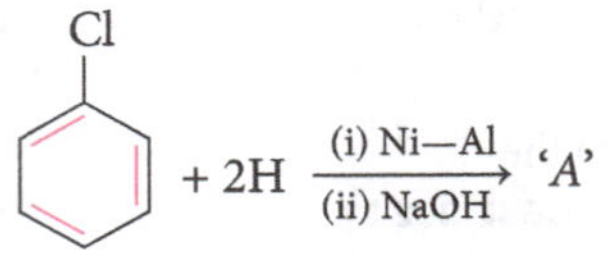

(a) 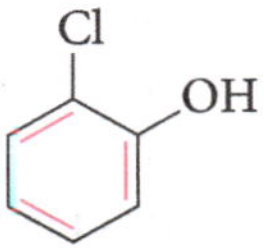 (b)  (c)  (d) 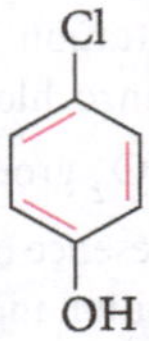

(iii) The antiseptic property of triodomethane is due to
(a) liberation of free iodine. (b) liberation of iodoform. (c) formation of chloroform. (d) formation of phosgene. **(1)**

Subjective Type Questions

Short Answer Type I Questions [2 Marks]

1. Write the IUPAC name, structure and one isomer for each of the following compounds.
(i) *tert*-butyl bromide (ii) Allyl chloride

2. Give the IUPAC names of the following compounds

(i) $H_3C-C(CH_3)_2-CH_2Cl$ (ii) $CH_3CH{=}C(CH_3)-CH(Br)-CH_3$

(iii) $(CH_3)_3CCH_2-CH_2Cl$

(iv) $CH_3-C(C_2H_5)(Cl)-CH_2-C(C_2H_5)(Cl)-CH_3$

3. Complete the following reactions by writing the major and minor product in each case. (Any 2) **CBSE SQP 2025**
(i) $CH_3CH_2Br + KCN \longrightarrow$
(ii) $CH_3CH_2CH{=}CH_2 + HBr \longrightarrow$
(iii) $(CH_3)_2CHCHClCH_3 + \text{alc. } KOH \longrightarrow$

4. Why is sulphuric acid not used during the reaction of alcohols with KI? **NCERT Intext**

5. How will you obtain monobromobenzene from aniline? **NCERT Exemplar**

6. *Para*-dichlorobenzene has higher melting point than those of *ortho* and *meta* isomers. Why? **Diksha**

7. Haloalkanes react with KCN to form alkyl cyanides, while AgCN forms isocyanides as the chief product. Why? **NCERT Intext**

8. Haloalkanes react with KNO_2 to form alkyl nitrites, while $AgNO_2$ forms nitroalkanes as the chief product. Why? **NCERT Intext**

9. What do you mean by a chiral compound? Give an example? **Diksha**

10. (i) Which one of the following pair undergo S_N1 reaction faster and why?
$H_2C{=}CHCHClCH_3$ or $CH_3-CH_2CHClCH_3$
(ii) Benzyl chloride is highly reactive towards S_N1 reaction. **CBSE 2023**

11. Allyl chloride is hydrolysed more readily than *n*-propyl chloride. Why? **NCERT Exemplar**

12. *P*, *Q*, *R* and *S* undergoes S_N2 reaction with KI in acetone. What is the order of the rate of reaction?

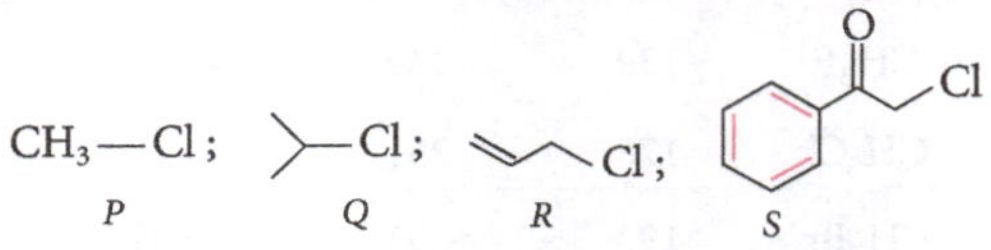

13. Which of the following compounds will react more rapidly by S_N2 reaction and why?
(i) $CH_3-C(CH_3)_2-Br$ or $CH_3-CH_2-CH(Br)-CH_3$
(ii) Arrange the following compounds in the increasing order of their boiling points:
$CH_3CH_2CH_2CH_2Br$, $(CH_3)_2CH-CH_2Br$
$CH_3-C(CH_3)(Br)-CH_3$ **CBSE 2024**

14. To prepare a Grignard reagent, Udita mixes magnesium metal in dry ether with the compound shown below.
$CH_3-CHOH-CH_2-CH_2Br$
Will she obtain the Grignard reagent? Justify your answer. **Competency Based Que.**

15. Aryl halides are extremely less reactive towards nucleophilic substitution. Predict and explain the order of reactivity of the following compounds towards nucleophilic substitution.

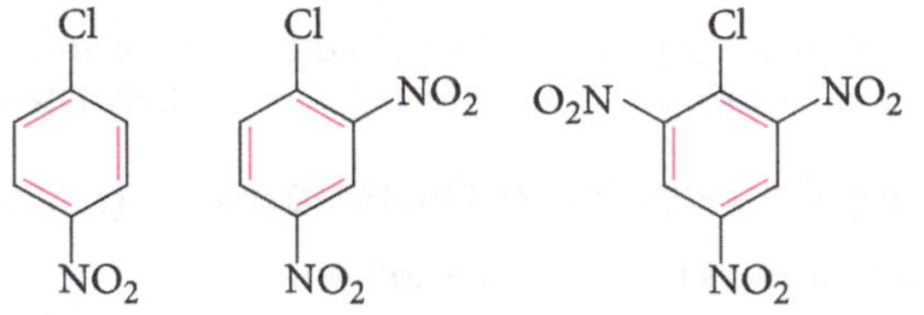

(I) (II) (III)

NCERT Exemplar

16. Carry out the following conversions in not more than 2 steps **CBSE SQP 2021**

(i) Aniline to chlorobenzene

(ii) 2-bromopropane to 1-bromopropane

17. An alkyl halide (*A*) of molecular formula, $C_6H_{13}Cl$ on treatment with alcoholic KOH gives two isomeric alkenes (*B*) and (*C*) of molecular formula, C_6H_{12}. Both alkenes on hydrogenation gives 2, 3-dimethylbutane. Write the structures of (*A*), (*B*) and (*C*). **CBSE 2023**

18. Write one physiological and environmental effect for each of the following

(i) Tetrachloromethane

(ii) DDT **CBSE 2019**

Short Answer Type II Questions [3 Marks]

19. Write the structures of the following organic halogen compounds.

(i) *p*-bromochlorobenzene

(ii) 2-(2-chlorophenyl)-1-iodooctane

(iii) 2-bromobutane **NCERT**

20. A hydrocarbon, C_5H_{10} does not react with chlorine in dark but gives a single monochloro compound, C_5H_9Cl in bright sunlight. Identify the hydrocarbon. **NCERT**

Or Which isomer of C_5H_{10} gives a single monochloro compound, C_5H_9Cl in bright sunlight ? **CBSE 2023**

21. Among the isomeric alkanes of molecular formula C_5H_{12}, identify the one that on photochemical chlorination yields

(i) a single monochloride.

(ii) three isomeric monochlorides.

(iii) four isomeric monochlorides. **NCERT Intext**

22. Draw the structure of the major monohalo product for each of the following reaction :

(i) 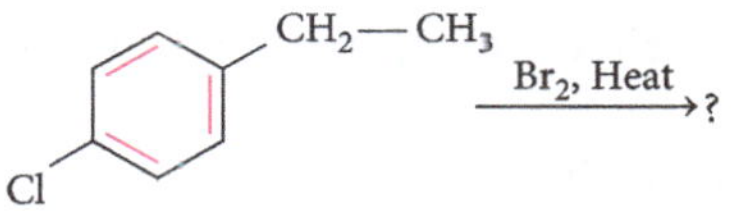

(ii) 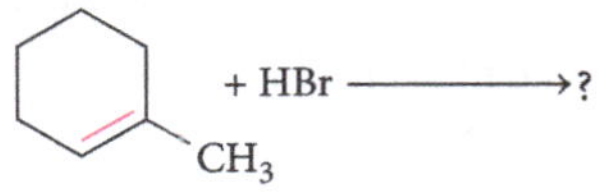

(iii) 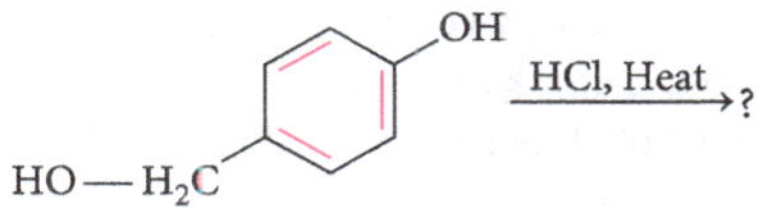

CBSE 2025

23. How do you convert

(i) chlorobenzene to biphenyl?

(ii) propene to 1-iodopropane?

(iii) 2-bromobutane to but-2-ene? **CBSE 2025**

24. How will you bring about the following conversions? [Any three]

(i) 1-bromobutane to 2-bromobutane

(ii) Aniline to chlorobenzene

(iii) Ethanol to ethyl bromide

(iv) Ethyl alcohol to Iodoethane

25. Which of the following compounds will react more rapidly by S_N1 reaction and why?

(i) $CH_3-C(CH_3)_2-Br$ or CH_3CH_2Br

(ii) Arrange the following compounds in the increasing order of their boiling points:
Bromoform, Dibromomethane, Chloromethane, Bromomethane **CBSE 2024**

26. Out of $C_6H_5CHClC_6H_5$ and $C_6H_5CH_2Cl$, which is more easily hydrolysed by aqueous KOH? **NCERT**

27. Define the following terms

(i) Racemic mixture (ii) Chiral carbon

(iii) Enantiomers **CBSE 2024 C**

28. Give reasons for the following.

(i) Ethyl iodide undergoes S_N2 reaction faster than ethyl bromide.

(ii) (±) 2-butanol is optically inactive, though it contains a chiral carbon atom. **CBSE 2023**

(iii) C—*X* bond length in halobenzene is smaller than C—*X* bond length in CH_3—*X*.

Or The C—Cl bond length in chlorobenzene is shorter than that in CH_3Cl.

29. Explain

(i) Why the dipole moment of chlorobenzene is lower than that of cyclohexyl chloride?

(ii) Why alkyl halides, though polar, are immiscible with water?

Or Why is the solubility of haloalkanes in water is very low? **NCERT Exemplar, CBSE 2017**

(iii) Why Grignard reagents should be prepared under anhydrous conditions? **NCERT**

30. The image below shows two competing routes or reactions when a haloalkane reacts with water in the presence of alcohol. The major products under each of the routes are shown.

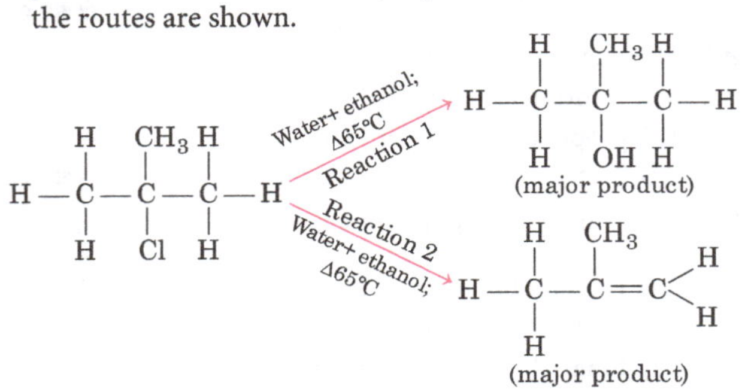

(i) Explain the mechanism for both these reactions.

(ii) Which out of two reactions will predominate? Give reasons. **Competency Based Que.**

31. (i) Comment on the strength and size of the nucleophile or base.

(ii) Chlorobenzene is extremely less reactive towards a nucleophilic substitution reaction. Give two reasons for the same.

Or Why aryl halides are less reactive towards nucleophilic substitution reactions than alkyl halides?

(iii) Which of the following two substances undergo S_N1 reaction faster and why? **NCERT Exemplar**

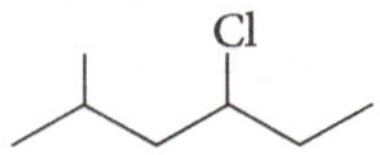

Or

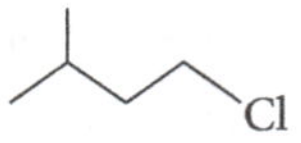

32. Give reasons

(i) *n*-butyl bromide has higher boiling point than *t*-butyl bromide.

(ii) Racemic mixture is optically inactive.

(iii) The presence of nitro group (—NO_2) at *o*/*p* positions, increases the reactivity of haloarenes towards nucleophilic substitution reactions. **CBSE 2015, 2019**

33. **(i) Write the IUPAC name of the given compound:**

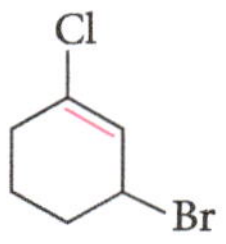

(ii) The presence of —NO_2 group at *ortho* - or *para*-position increases the reactivity of haloarenes towards nucleophilic substitution reactions. Give reason to explain the above statement.

(iii) What happens when ethyl chloride is treated with alcoholic potassium hydroxide? **CBSE 2024**

34. Diphenyls are potential threat to the environment. How are these produced from aryl halides? **NCERT Exemplar**

Long Answer Type Questions [5 Marks]

35. Give reasons for each of the following.

(i)(a) S_N1 reactions are generally carried out in the presence of polar solvents.

(b) Allyl chloride is hydrolysed more readily than *n*-propyl chloride.

(ii) Compound *A* with molecular formula C_4H_9Br is treated with *aq.* KOH solution. The rate of this reaction depends upon the concentration of '*A*' only. When another optically active isomer '*B*' of this compound was treated with *aq.* KOH solution the rate of reaction was found to depend on concentration of both compound and KOH.

(a) Write down the structural formula of both the compounds '*A*' and '*B*'.

(b) Which one of the two will be converted to the product with inverted configuration? **Diksha**

36. (i) Write the chemical equations for the conversion of :

(a) Propene to Propyne **Diksha**

(b) But-1-ene to But-2-ene

(c) Benzene to Biphenyl

(ii) How will you distinguish between Ethyl chloride and ethyl bromide?

(iii) What is the role of lewis acid in the preparation of aryl halide in dark?

37. How can the following conversions be carried out?

(i) Ethyl chloride to propanoic acid

(ii) Ethanol to propane nitrile

(iii) 1-bromopropane to 2-bromopropane

(iv) 2-chlorobutane to 3,4-dimethylhexane

(v) 2-methyl-1-propene to 2-chloro-2-methylpropane **NCERT**

38. What happens when

(i) *n*-butyl chloride is treated with alcoholic KOH?

(ii) Bromobenzene is treated with Mg in the presence of dry ether?

(iii) Chlorobenzene is subjected to hydrolysis?

(iv) Methyl bromide is treated with sodium in the presence of dry ether?

(v) Methyl chloride is treated with KCN? **NCERT**

Hints & Solutions

Objective Type Questions

1 (*b*) CH_3Cl

The increasing order of dipole moment of the given compound is as follows :

$$CH_3I < CH_3Br < CH_3F < CH_3Cl.$$

Though F is most electronegative, the bond length is small as compared to C—Cl. Since, dipole moment is the product of the charge and the bond length.

2 (*b*) Structure of the diethylbromomethane is given below:

$$\overset{5}{H_3C}-\overset{4}{H_2C}-\overset{3}{\underset{}{HC}}(Br)-\overset{2}{CH_2}-\overset{1}{CH_3}$$

Thus, the IUPAC name is 3-bromopentane.

3 (*a*) The structure of the given structure is

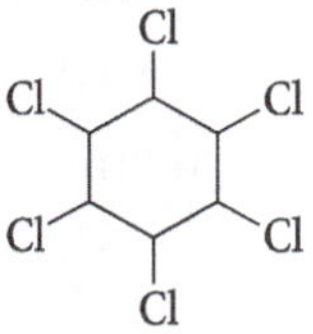

The IUPAC name of the given compound is 1, 2, 3, 4, 5, 6- hexachlorocyclohexane.

4 (*c*) The correct match is A → (ii), B → (iii), C → (i).

5 (*c*) Thionyl chloride is preferred because the other two products formed in the reaction are escapable gases. Hence, the reaction gives pure alkyl halides.

$$ROH + SOCl_2 \longrightarrow R\text{—}Cl + SO_2\uparrow + HCl\uparrow$$

6 (*b*) Toluene reacts with a halogen in the presence of iron (III) chloride giving *ortho* and *para* halo compounds.The reaction is electrophilic substitution reaction.

It has the following mechanism

$$Cl\text{—}Cl \xrightarrow{FeCl_3} FeCl_4^- + Cl^+$$

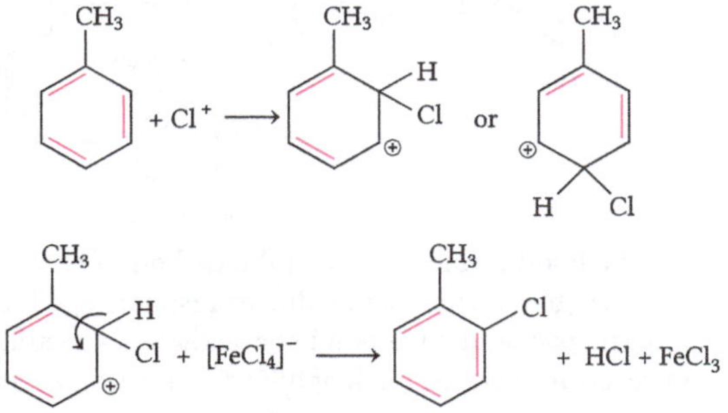

In this mechanism, electrophile Cl^+ attacks to electron rich benzene ring and replaces hydrogen. So, the reaction is electrophilic substitution reaction.

7. (*c*)

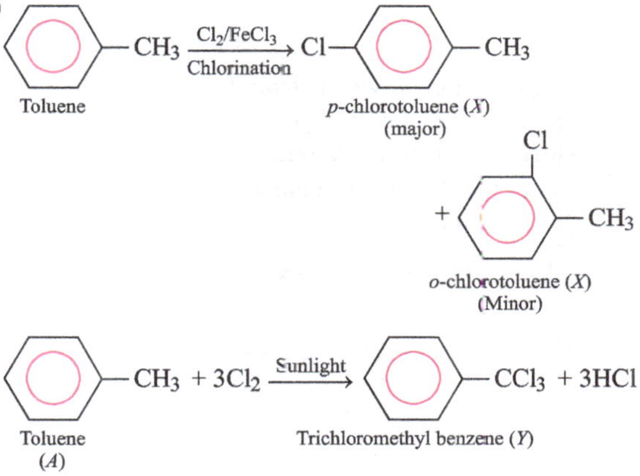

8. (*a*)

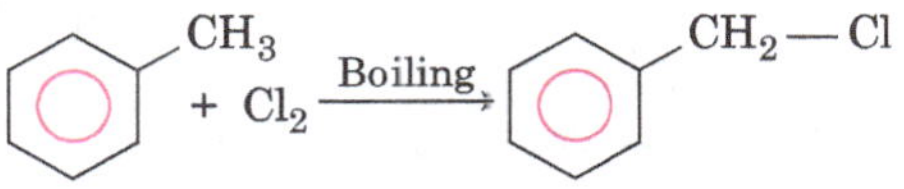

The mechanism is as follows.

$$Cl_2 \xrightarrow{hv} \dot{C}l + \dot{C}l \text{ (chlorine free radical) form.}$$

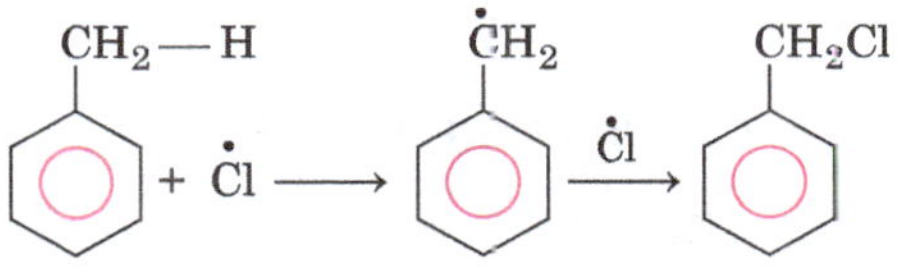

9. (*c*)

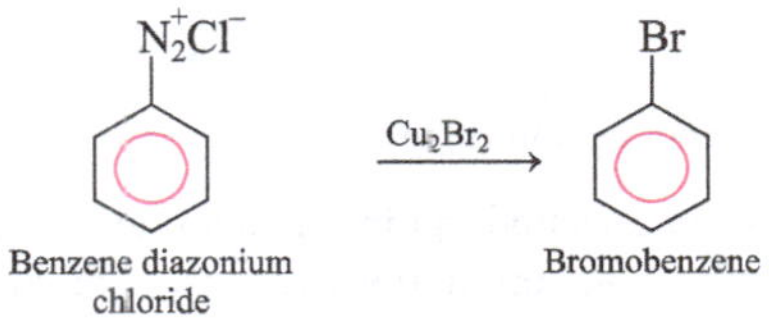

10. (*c*) Smaller the surface area of the compound, higher will be the boiling point, i.e., as the branching increases, boiling point decreases. This is because surface area decreases with increase in branching. Therefore, the correct order of boiling points is (iii) < (i) < (ii).

11. (*d*) 1 = bromomethane,

2 = 2-bromo-2-methylpropane,

3 = 2- bromobutane, 4 = 1-bromobutane

Boiling point increases with increase in molecular weight, as van der Waal's forces increases. But, boiling point decreases with increase in branching, as less surface area is available for van der waal's interactions.

12. (*d*) Benzyl chloride undergoes exclusively S_N1 mechanism because it forms resonance stabilised benzyl carbocation.

13. (*a*) $(CH_3)_3C$—Br (2-bromo-2-methylpropane) undergoes S_N1 reaction faster as it will form 3° carbocation in first step of mechanism of S_N1 reaction.

$$CH_3-\overset{CH_3}{\underset{CH_3}{C}}-Br \xrightarrow{-Br^{\ominus}} CH_3-\overset{CH_3}{\underset{CH_3}{C^{\oplus}}}$$

3° stable carbocation

14 (*b*) Reaction between alcohols and halogen acid follows S_N1 mechanism. In S_N1 mechanism, carbocations are formed as intermediates.

Let us consider the formation of carbocations with the given three alcohols.

$$CH_3-CH_2-CH_2-OH \longrightarrow CH_3-CH_2-\overset{+}{C}H_2 + OH^-$$

1° carbocation (Least stable)

$$CH_3-CH_2-\underset{CH_3}{CH}-OH \longrightarrow CH_3-CH_2-\underset{CH_3}{\overset{+}{CH}} + OH^-$$

2° carbocation (more stable than 1° carbocation)

$$CH_3-CH_2-\overset{CH_3}{\underset{CH_3}{C}}-OH \longrightarrow H_3C-CH_2-\overset{CH_3}{\underset{CH_3}{C^+}} + OH^-$$

3° carbocation (most stable)

Thus the correct order is

$$\underset{(C)}{CH_3CH_2-\overset{CH_3}{\underset{CH_3}{C}}-OH} > \underset{(B)}{CH_3CH_2-\underset{CH_3}{CH}-OH} > \underset{(A)}{CH_3CH_2-CH_2-OH}$$

So, the correct option is (b).

15. (*c*) Alkyl halides undergoing nucleophilic bimolecular substitution reaction involves inversion of configuration.

16. (*c*) If the carbocation is stabilised in the intermediate, then S_N1 reaction is favoured while, if the steric hindrance is low, then it helps the S_N2 transition state. Morever, a good leaving group favours both reaction.

17. (*b*) Asymmetric carbon is a sp^3-hybridised carbon which is attached to four different substituents. This is also called as chiral centre.

Thus, $CH_3-\overset{H}{\underset{Cl}{C^*}}-CH_2Br$ has a chiral centre.

18. (*d*) Only compound (iv), i.e., $H-\overset{CH_3}{\underset{C_2H_5}{C}}-Cl$ will undergo racemisation as it is the only compound which contains a chiral carbon atom.

19. (*a*) The compounds which are chiral are said to be optically active. Among the given compounds only $CH_3-CH_2-\overset{H}{\underset{CHO}{C^*}}-Br$ is optically active.

20. (*a*) Reactions given in flow chart (*D*, *C*, *B*) are nucleophilic substitution reactions. When a nucleophile stronger than the halide ion reacts with haloalkane having a partial positive charge on the carbon atom bonded to halogen, then substitution reaction takes place.

Reaction (*A*) leads to elimination reaction. Complete reactions are as follows

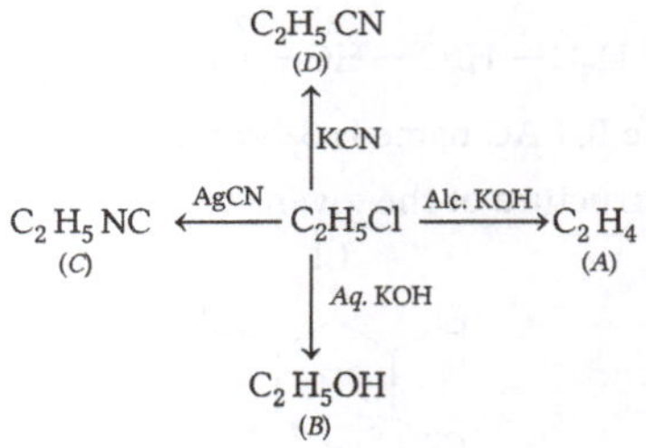

21. (*a*)

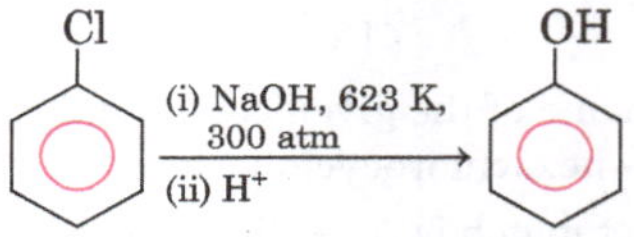

Phenol (*X*)

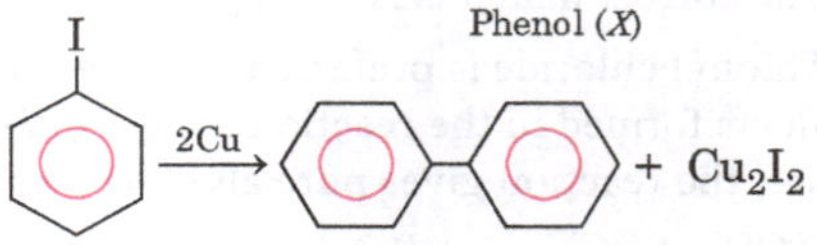

Iodobenzene (*Y*) Diphenyl

$$\underset{\text{Methyl bromide}}{CH_3Br} + \underset{\substack{\text{Silver fluoride}\\(Z)}}{AgF} \longrightarrow \underset{\text{Fluoro methane}}{CH_3F} + \underset{\text{Silver bromide}}{AgBr}$$

22 (*a*)

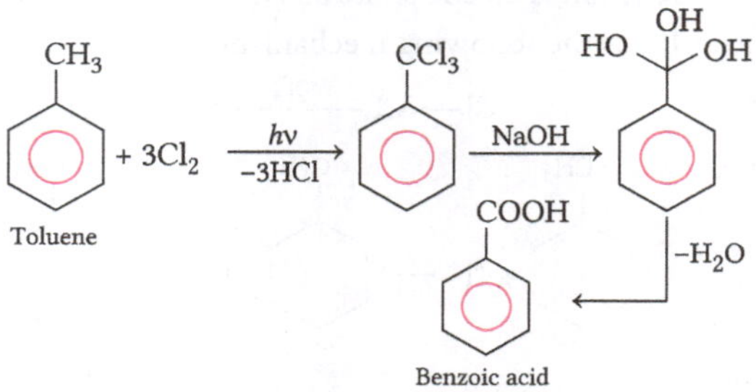

23. (*c*) The bond formed between the carbon of benzene ring and halogen is more stable due to resonance, which imparts partial double bond character. As a result, rate of reaction towards nucleophilic substitution is slow.

However, the presence of an electron withdrawing group at the *ortho* and *para*-positions facilitates nucleophilic substitution because it decreases the electron density at these positions, making the reaction more favourable.

Compound (ii) and (iii) both have one electron withdrawing group, but in compound (ii), electron withdrawing (— NO_2) group is present at the *ortho* position. So, rate of reaction in compound (ii) is more than that of compound (iii). On the other hand, compound (i) has no electron withdrawing group.

Hence, the correct option is (c).

24. (*d*) Presence of electron releasing group at *ortho* or *para* position decreases the rate of nucleophilic substitution reaction.

In compound (iii), electron releasing group is present at *meta* position w.r.t. chlorine, so the impact is less but in compound (ii) it is present at *ortho* position.

Thus, the rate of reaction towards nucleophilic substitution is least in compound (ii) and highest in compound (i) as there is no electron releasing group in this compound.

25 (*c*) Auto-oxidation of chloroform in air and light produces a poisonous gas known as phosgene. The reaction involved is given as

$$\underset{\text{Chloroform}}{2CHCl_3} + \underset{\text{Oxygen}}{O_2} \xrightarrow[\text{Air}]{\text{Light,}} \underset{\text{Phosgene}}{2COCl_2} + \underset{\text{Hydrochloric acid}}{2HCl}$$

26 (*b*) Only statement (b) is incorrect. Its correct form is; inhaling chloroform vapours depress the central nervous system.

27 (*d*) (A) is false but (R) is true. The correct (A) is; the use of thionyl chloride is preferred over phosphorus chlorides for preparing haloalkanes from alcohols because the other products of the reaction, $HCl(g)$ and $SO_2(g)$ being gases escape out leaving behind pure haloalkane.

28 (*d*) 2- chloro -2 methylbutane (not *neo* pentyl chloride) is formed when *neo*-pentyl alcohol reacts with HCl. The initially formed primary carbocation undergoes rearrangement to form more stable tertiary carbocation. The reaction is given as

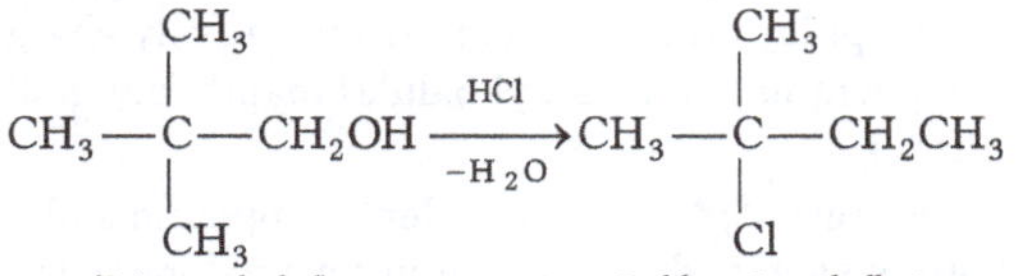

(Primary alcohol) 2-chloro-2-methylbutane

Thus (A) is false, but (R) is true.

29 (*d*) (A) is false, but (R) is true. The correct (A) is; Aryl halides are less reactive towards nucleophilic substitution reactions due to the partial double bond character of the C—*X* bond in aryl halides.

30 (*b*) For the same alkyl group, the boiling point of alkyl halides decreases in the order $RI > RBr > RCl > RF$, because with increase in size and mass of halogen atom, the magnitude of van der Waals' forces increases.

Thus, both (A) and (R) are true, but (R) is not the correct explanation of (A).

31 (*b*) Here, both (A) and (R) are true, but (R) is not the correct explanation of (A).

Alkyl halides are insoluble in water because they are unable to form hydrogen bonds with water or break pre-existing hydrogen bonds.

32 (*d*) Assertion is false but reason is true.

Correct Assertion KCN reacts with methyl chloride to give the mixture of methyl cyanide and methyl isocyanide in which methyl cyanide predominates because of stable C—C bond in methyl cyanide.

33 (*a*) Nucleophilic substitution of iodoethane is easier than chloroethane because bond energy or enthalpy of C—I bond is less than that of C—Cl bond. Thus, both (A) and (R) are true and (R) is the correct explanation of (A).

34 (*c*) Assertion is true, but reason is false.

Correct Reason This reaction proceeds through S_N2 mechanism, in which $\bar{O}H$ ion, attacks at 180° to the halogen atom of 2-bromooctane which leads to the inversion of configuration.

35 (c) S_N1 reaction proceeds with the formation of carbocation, while S_N2 reaction proceeds through the transition state formation. Hence, Assertion (A) is true, but Reason (R) is false.

36 (*a*) Both (A) and (R) are true and (R) is the correct explanation of (A).

37 (*d*) (A) is false but (R) is true. Presence of —Cl in chlorobenzene activates the ring at *ortho* and *para*-positions and therefore, nitration of chlorobenzene leads to the formation of o- and *p*-chloronitrochlorobenzene.

38 (*a*) Nitro group being an electron withdrawing group, decreases the electron density of benzene ring, thus increasing the reactivity of haloarenes towards nucleophilic substitution.

Hence, both (A) and (R) are true and (R) is the correct explanation of (A).

39 (i) *p*-dichlorobenzene fits into crystal lattice more readily than *o*-isomer, therefore, has higher melting point. On the other hand, *o*-isomer has higher boiling point due to higher dipole moment and more polarity than *p*-isomer. **(2)**

(ii) It is because $\mu = e \times d$, C—F bond distance is less than C—Cl, therefore, product of charge and distance is slightly lower in CH_3F than CH_3Cl. **(1)**

Or (ii) It is due to lower bond dissociation enthalpy of C—I bond than C—Cl bond. **(1)**

(iii) It is becuase C—I bond is longer than C—F bond and $\mu = e \times d$. **(1)**

40 (i)

(a) 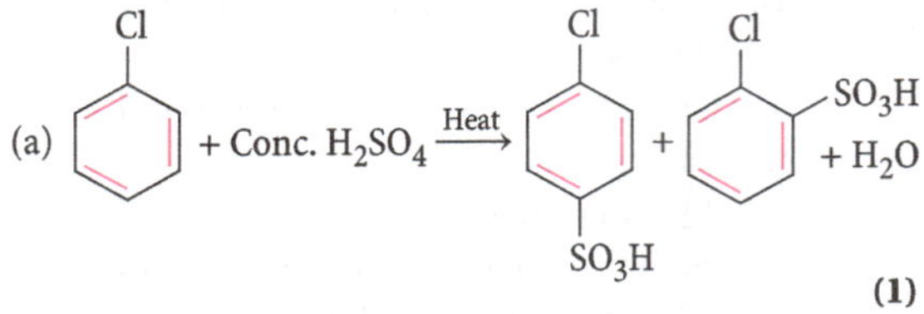

(1)

(b) $(CH_3)_3CBr + OH^- \longrightarrow (CH_3)_3COH + Br^-$ (1)

(ii) (*d*) The compound, 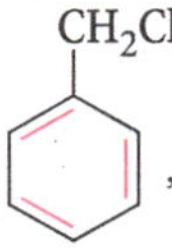 , will react faster due to resonance stabilisation of carbocation.

Whereas in, CH_3CH_2Cl, $C_6H_5CH_2CH_2Cl$ and $CH_2{=}CH{-}CH_2{-}Cl$ carbocation is stabilised only through hyperconjugation. (1)

Or

(*c*) 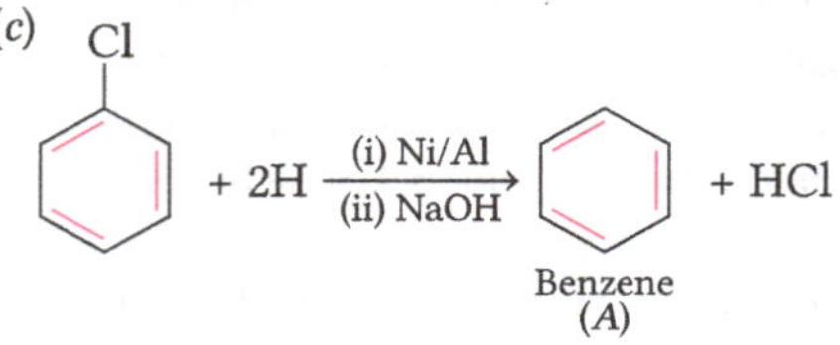

(1)

(iii) (*a*) The antiseptic property of triiodomethane is due to liberation of free iodine. (1)

Subjective Type Questions

1. (i)

$$H_3C-\underset{\underset{CH_3}{|}}{\overset{\overset{CH_3}{|}}{C}}-Br$$

tert-butyl bromide

IUPAC name 2-bromo-2-methylpropane

Its isomer is : $H_3C-\overset{\overset{CH_3}{|}}{CH}-CH_2-Br$

1-bromo-2-methylpropane (1)

(ii) Allyl chloride ($CH_2{=}CH{-}CH_2Cl$)

Isomer of $CH_2{=}CH{-}CH_2Cl$ (allyl chloride) is

$CH_3{-}CH{=}CH{-}Cl$ (1-chloroprop-1-ene). (1)

2. (i) 1-chloro-2, 2-dimethylpropane (1/2)

(ii) 4-bromo-3-methylpent-2-ene (1/2)

(iii) 1-chloro-3,3-dimethylbutane (1/2)

(iv) 3, 5-dichloro-3, 5-dimethylheptane (1/2)

3. (i) $\underset{\text{Ethyl bromide}}{CH_3CH_2Br} + \underset{\text{Potassium cyanide}}{KCN} \longrightarrow \underset{\text{Ethyl cyanide (Major)}}{CH_3CH_2CN} + \underset{\text{Potassium bromide}}{KBr}$

(ii) $\underset{\text{But-1-ene}}{CH_3CH_2CH{=}CH_2} + \underset{\text{Hydrogen bromide}}{HBr} \longrightarrow$

$\underset{\text{2-bromobutane (Major)}}{CH_3CH_2CHBrCH_3} + \underset{\text{1-bromobutane (Minor)}}{CH_3CH_2CH_2CH_2Br}$

(iii) $\underset{\text{2-chloro-3-methylbutane}}{(CH_3)_2CHCHClCH_3} + \underset{\text{Potassium hydroxide}}{\text{Alc. KOH}} \longrightarrow$

$\underset{\substack{\text{2-methylbut-2-ene}\\ \text{(Major)}}}{(CH_3)_2C{=}CHCH_3} + \underset{\substack{\text{3-methylbut-1-ene}\\ \text{(Minor)}}}{(CH_3)_2CHCH{=}CH_2}$ (2)

4. Refer to text on page 190. (2)

5. When aniline, dissolved or suspended in cold aqueous mineral acid, is treated with sodium nitrite, a diazonium salt is formed. This diazonium salt on treatment with cuprous bromide gives monobromobenzene. (1)

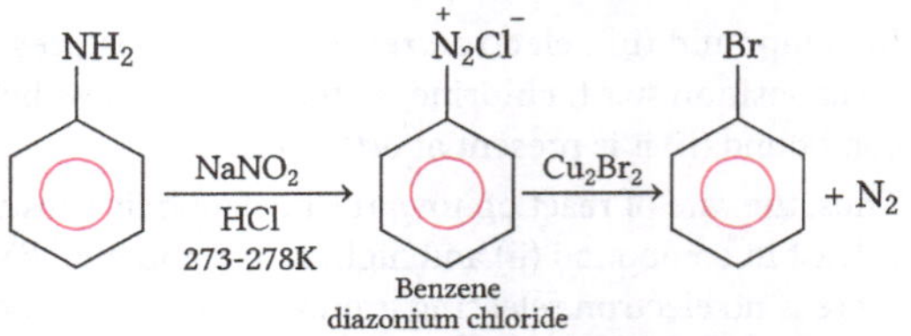

This reaction is named as Sandmeyer's reaction. If benzene diazonium chloride is treated with copper in HBr then the product formed is bromobenzene. This reaction is known as Gattermann reaction. (1)

6. The *p*-isomer is more symmetrical and thus, fit closely in the lattice. Due to which it has stronger intermolecular forces of attractions than those of *ortho* and *meta* isomers. Hence, a large amount of energy is needed to melt *p*-isomer. (2)

7. K^+CN^- is predominantly ionic and provides cyanide ions in solution. Although, both carbon and nitrogen atoms are in position to donate electron pairs, the attack takes place mainly through carbon atom and not through nitrogen atom as, C—C bond is more stable than C—N bond.

However, Ag—CN is mainly covalent in nature and only electron pair of nitrogen is available for bond formation. As a result, alkyl isocyanides are the chief products. (2)

8. KNO_2 (or $O{=}N{-}O^-K^+$) is predominantly ionic and one of the oxygen atom have a negative charge. Nucleophilic attack through this negatively charged oxygen atom on the alkyl halides mainly gives alkyl nitrites.

In contrast, $AgNO_2$ is a covalent compound and both oxygen and nitrogen atoms carry lone pair of electrons. Since, nitrogen is less electronegative than oxygen, therefore, lone pair of electrons of nitrogen is more easily available for bond formation. As a result, nitroalkanes are the chief products. (2)

9. Any compound that is non superimposable on its mirror image is called as a chiral compound.

For example, butan-2-ol is a chiral compound as it has a chiral carbon with four different substituents attached to it. (2)

10. (i) $CH_2{=}CHCHClCH_3$, Allylic halides show high reactivity towards S_N1 reaction because carbocation formed gets stabilised through resonance. (1)

(ii) Benzyl chloride is highly reactive towards the S_N1 reaction because the intermediate benzyl carbocation formed in the slowest step is stabilised through resonance.

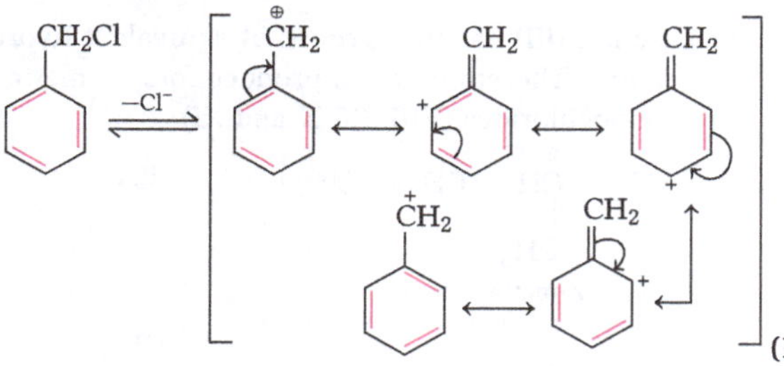

(1)

11. $CH_2{=}CH{-}CH_2Cl \xrightarrow{-Cl^-} CH_2{=}CH{-}\overset{+}{C}H_2 + \overset{-}{Cl}$

Allyl chloride

$CH_2{=}CH{-}\overset{+}{C}H_2 \longleftrightarrow \overset{+}{C}H_2{-}CH{=}CH_2$

(Resonance stabilised carbocation) **(1)**

$CH_3{-}CH_2{-}Cl \xrightarrow{-Cl^-} CH_3{-}CH_2{-}\overset{+}{C}H_2 + Cl^-$

n-propyl chloride (Not stabilised by resonance) **(1)**

Hence, allyl chloride undergoes hydrolysis much faster than *n*-propyl chloride.

12. The order of the rate of reaction is $S > P > R > Q$

Refer to text on page 196. **(2)**

13. (i) 2-bromobutane is a secondary alkyl halide. So, it can undergo S_N2 reaction faster as compared to 2-bromo-2-methylpropane.

In S_N2 reactions, nucleophile attack on less hindered carbon from the back side in the transition state. The minimum hindrance is provided by the primary carbon and maximum hindrance is provided by the tertiary carbocation. **(1)**

(ii) Smaller the surface area of the compounds, higher will be the boiling point, i.e., as the branching increases, boiling point decreases because surface area decreases which result in decrease in attraction.

Thus, the correct boiling point order is,

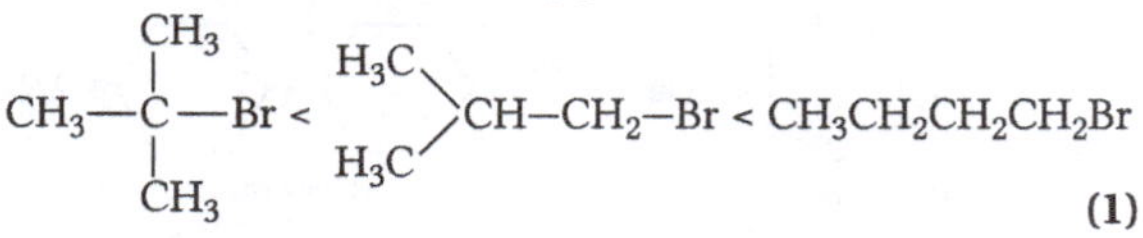

(1)

14. She will not obtain the Grignard reagent.

As the Grignard reagent formed will immediately be protonated by the alcoholic group in the given compound. **(2)**

15. Aryl halides are less reactive towards nucleophilic substitution reaction. Presence of electron withdrawing group at *ortho* and *para* position increases the stability of intermediates and hence increases the reactivity of aryl halides towards nucleophilic substitution reaction.

Now, more the number of EWG at *ortho* and *para* position, higher will be the reactivity of aryl halide. Compound (III) has three EWG so, it is most reactive and compound (I) has only one EWG so, it is least reactive. So, the order of reactivity is (I)<(II)<(III). **(2)**

16. (i)

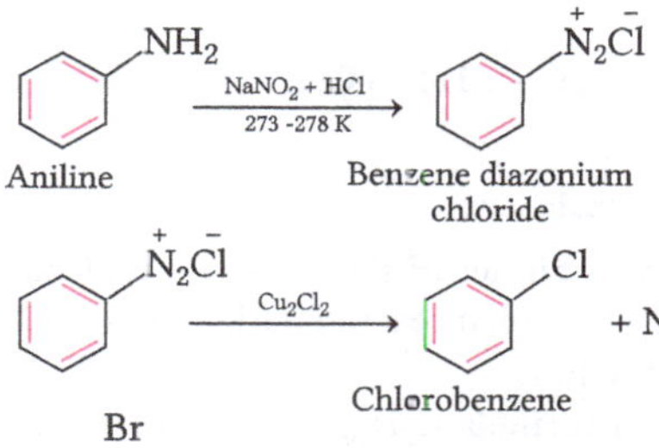

(1)

(ii)

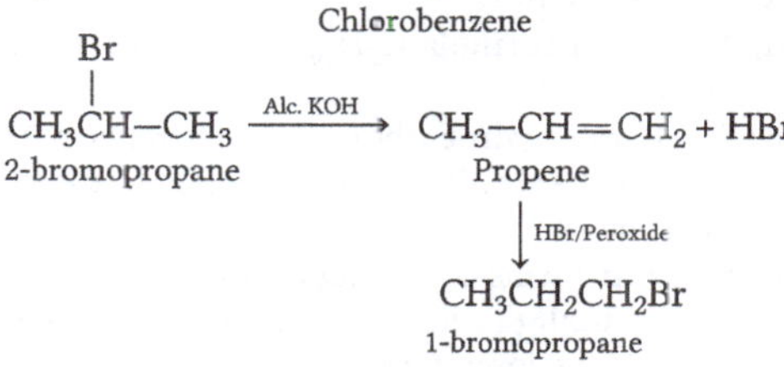

(1)

17. The reaction takes place as follows

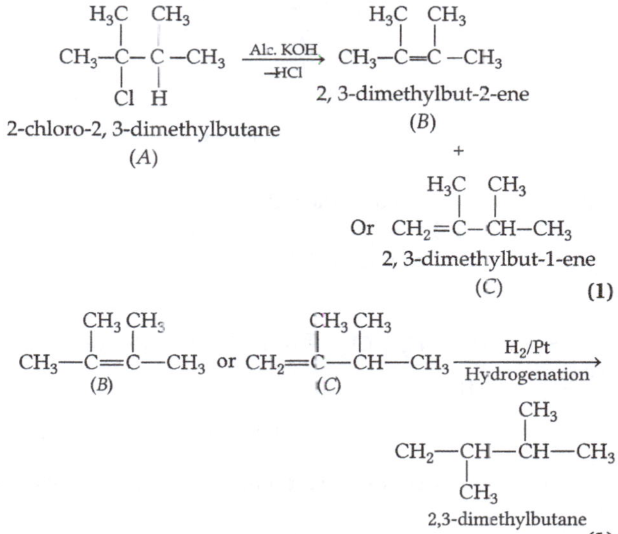

(1) **(1)**

18. (i) Refer to text on page 208. **(1)**

(ii) Refer to text on page 209. **(1)**

19. (i)

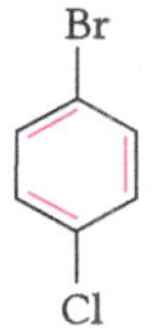

p-bromochlorobenzene **(1)**

(ii) 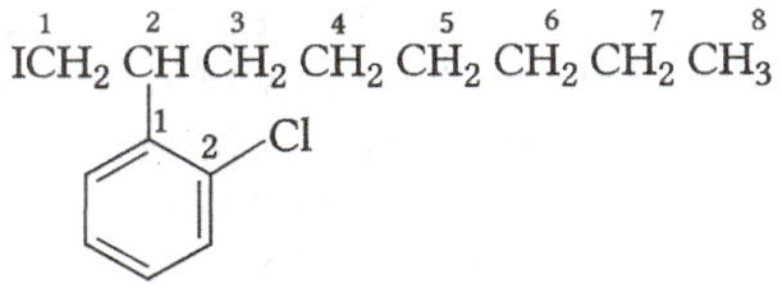

2-(2-chlorophenyl)-1-iodooctane **(1)**

(iii) $\overset{1}{C}H_3-\overset{2}{C}H(Br)-\overset{3}{C}H_2-\overset{4}{C}H_3$

2-bromobutane **(1)**

20. Enlist the possibilities of structures for molecular formula, C_5H_{10} which react in dark and in sunlight. In the given reaction,

(i) Molecular formula C_5H_{10} can be either alkene or cycloalkane.

(ii) Since, the hydrocarbon does not react with chlorine in dark, hence, it is not an alkene but is a cycloalkane.

(iii) Since, it forms only single monochloro derivative in bright sunlight, all the H-atoms should be identical. So, it is cyclopentane. **(2)**

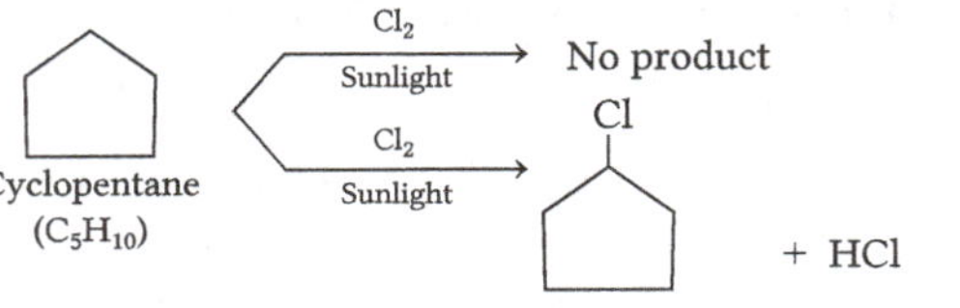

Cyclopentane (C_5H_{10}) — Chlorocyclopentane (C_5H_9Cl) **(1)**

21 (i) A single monochloride (IV) can be produced only when all the hydrogen atoms are equivalent. This isomer must be symmetrical. Its structure is given by (I).

$$H_3C-C(CH_3)_2-CH_3 + Cl_2 \xrightarrow{h\nu} H_3C-C(CH_3)_2-CH_2Cl + HCl$$

(I) (IV)

1-chloro -2, 2-dimethylpropane **(1)**

(ii) Isomer (II) has three groups of equivalent hydrogen atoms.

Therefore, three isomeric monochlorides (V, VI and VII) are produced.

$$\overset{5}{C}H_3-\overset{4}{C}H_2-\overset{3}{C}H_2-\overset{2}{C}H_2-\overset{1}{C}H_3 + Cl_2 \xrightarrow{h\nu}$$

Pentane (II)

$$\overset{5}{C}H_3-\overset{4}{C}H_2-\overset{3}{C}H_2-\overset{2}{C}H_2-\overset{1}{C}H_2-Cl$$

1-chloropentane (V)

$$+\ \overset{5}{C}H_3-\overset{4}{C}H_2-\overset{3}{C}H_2-\overset{2}{C}H(Cl)-\overset{1}{C}H_3$$

2-chloropentane (VI)

$$+\ \overset{5}{C}H_3-\overset{4}{C}H_2-\overset{3}{C}H(Cl)-\overset{2}{C}H_2-\overset{1}{C}H_3$$

3-chloropentane (VII) **(1)**

(iii) Isomer (III) has four groups of equivalent hydrogen atoms. Therefore, it can produce four isomeric monochlorides (VIII, IX, X and XI).

$$\overset{1}{C}H_3-\overset{2}{C}H(CH_3)-\overset{3}{C}H_2-\overset{4}{C}H_3 + Cl_2 \xrightarrow{h\nu}$$

2-methylbutane (III)

$$Cl-H_2\overset{1}{C}-\overset{2}{C}H(CH_3)-\overset{3}{C}H_2-\overset{4}{C}H_3 + \overset{1}{C}H_3-\overset{2}{C}Cl(CH_3)-\overset{3}{C}H_2-\overset{4}{C}H_3$$

1-chloro-2-methylbutane (VIII) — 2-chloro-2-methyl butane (IX)

$$+\ \overset{4}{C}H_3-\overset{3}{C}H(CH_3)-\overset{2}{C}H(Cl)-\overset{1}{C}H_3 + \overset{4}{C}H_3-\overset{3}{C}H(CH_3)-\overset{2}{C}H_2-\overset{1}{C}H_2-Cl$$

2-chloro -3-methylbutane (X) — 1-chloro-3-methylbutane (XI) **(1)**

22 (i) 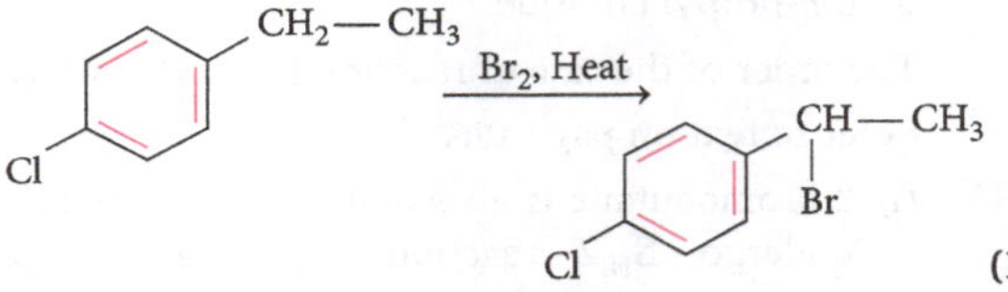

(1)

(ii) 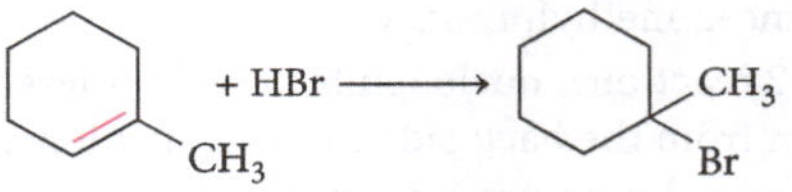

(1)

(iii) 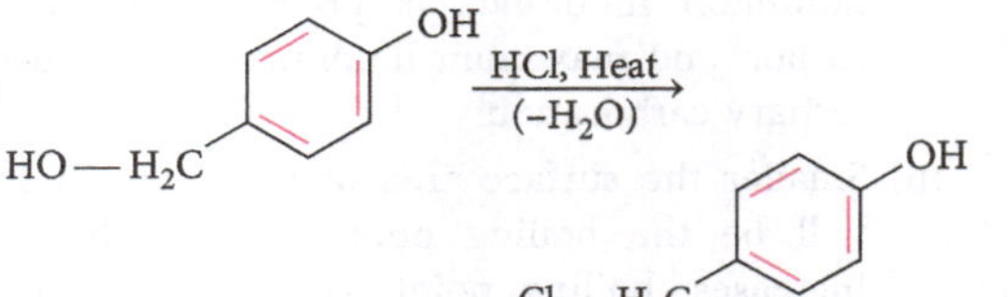

(1)

23. (i) 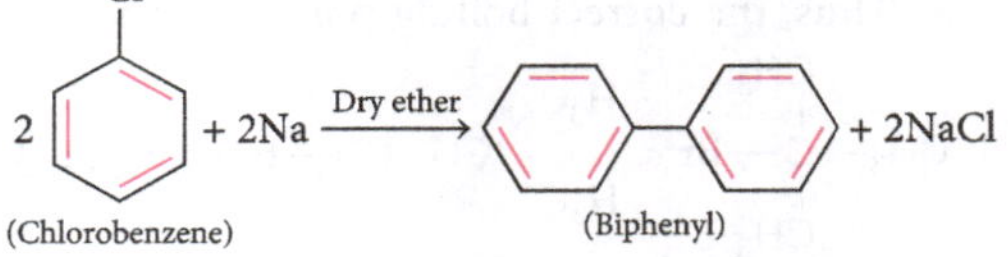

(1)

(ii) $CH_3-CH=CH_2 + HBr \xrightarrow{\text{Peroxide}} \underset{\text{(1-bromopropane)}}{CH_3-CH_2-CH_2-Br} \xrightarrow[\text{Dry acetone}]{\text{NaI}} \underset{\text{(1-iodopropane)}}{CH_3-CH_2-CH_2-I}$ **(1)**

(Propene)

(iii) $\underset{\text{(2-bromobutane)}}{CH_3-CH(Br)-CH_2-CH_3} \xrightarrow{\text{Alc. KOH}} \underset{\text{(But-2-ene)}}{CH_3-CH=CH-CH_3}$ **(1)**

24. (i) $\underset{\text{1-bromobutane}}{CH_3—CH_2—CH_2—CH_2—Br} \xrightarrow[-HBr]{\text{Alc. KOH}}$

$$\underset{\text{But-1-ene}}{CH_3—CH_2—CH=CH_2} \xrightarrow[\text{Markovnikov's addition}]{HBr} \underset{\text{2-bromobutane}}{CH_3CH_2—\underset{\underset{Br}{|}}{CH}—CH_3}$$ **(1)**

(ii) Refer to text on pages 192 and 193. **(1)**

(iii) Refer to text on page 190. **(1)**

(iv) Refer to text on page 190. **(1)**

25 (i) $$H_3C—\underset{CH_3}{\overset{CH_3}{C}}—Br \xrightarrow{-Br^{\ominus}} H_3C—\underset{CH_3}{\overset{CH_3}{C^{\oplus}}} \quad (3° \text{ carbocation})$$

$$CH_3CH_2Br \xrightarrow{-Br^{\ominus}} CH_3\overset{+}{C}H_2 \quad (1° \text{ carbocation})$$ **(1)**

3° carbocation is more stable than 1° carbocation.

Hence, $CH_3—\underset{CH_3}{\overset{CH_3}{C}}—Br$ will react more rapidly by S_N1 mechanism. **(1)**

(ii) Boiling point increases with increase in molecular mass due to greater magnitude of van der Waals' force of attraction. Therefore, the boiling point of compounds increases in the order:

Chloromethane (CH_3Cl) < Bromomethane (CH_3Br) < Dibromoethane (CH_2Br_2) < Bromoform ($HCBr_3$) **(1)**

26 In S_N1 reaction, $C_6H_5CHClC_6H_5$ gets hydrolysed more easily than $C_6H_5CH_2Cl$.

However, under S_N2 reaction, $C_6H_5CH_2Cl$ (with lesser steric hindrance) gets hydrolysed more easily than $C_6H_5CHClC_6H_5$.

Refer to text on pages 196 and 197. **(3)**

27 (i) Refer to text on page 199. **(1)**

(ii) Refer to text on page 198. **(1)**

(iii) Refer to text on page 199. **(1)**

28. (i) Iodide is a better leaving group because of its larger size than bromide, therefore, ethyl iodide undergoes S_N2 reaction faster than ethyl bromide. **(1)**

(ii) (±) 2-butanol is a racemic mixture. It is a mixture which contains two enantiomers in equal proportion and thus, have zero optical rotation due to internal compensation. Therefore, it is optically inactive through it contains a chiral carbon atom. **(1)**

(iii) In halobenzenes (like chlorobenzene), the lone pair of electrons on halogen atom is delocalised on the benzene ring. As a result, $C — X$ bond ($C — Cl$ bond in case of chlorobenzene) acquires some double bond character while in $CH_3—X$, $C—X$ bond is a pure single bond. Therefore, $C—X$ bond in halobenzene is shorter than in $CH_3—X$. **(1)**

29. **Hint:**
- Find the hybridisation of C-atoms in chlorobenzene and cyclohexyl chloride and electronegativity to find the bond polarity and thus, dipole moment.
- Strong intermolecular H-bonding exist among water molecules.
- Consider the reactive nature of Grignard reagents with water.

(i) 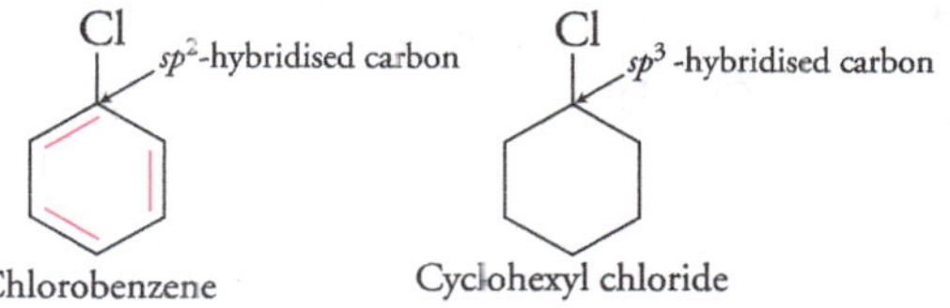

Chlorobenzene Cyclohexyl chloride

Due to sp^2-hybridisation of C-atom in chlorobenzene, C-atom is more electronegative (greater *s*-character), whereas in cyclohexyl chloride, C-atom is sp^3-hybridised, i.e., less electronegative (lesser *s*-character). So, polarity of C—Cl bond in chlorobenzene is less than the C—Cl bond in cyclohexyl chloride.

Further, due to delocalisation of lone pair of electrons of Cl-atom over the benzene ring, C—Cl bond in chlorobenzene acquires some double bond character, while C—Cl bond in cyclohexyl chloride is a pure single bond.

Thus, C—Cl bond in chlorobenzene is shorter than in cyclohexyl chloride. As dipole moment is a product of charge and distance, therefore, the dipole moment of chlorobenzene is lower than that of cyclohexyl chloride. **(1)**

(ii) Water molecules have enough strong intermolecular H-bonding which is difficult to be broken by alkyl halides, though they are polar in nature as well. Therefore, alkyl halides do not dissolve in water and form separate layers. **(1)**

(iii) Grignard reagents ($R—Mg—X$) are readily decomposed by water to produce alkanes. That is why, they should be prepared under anhydrous conditions. Instead, ether is used as a solvent during the preparation of Grignard reagent.

$$R—Mg—X + H_2O \xrightarrow{\text{Ether}} \underset{\text{Alkane}}{R—H} + Mg\begin{matrix} X \\ OH \end{matrix}$$ **(1)**

30. (i) **Reaction 1** (Substitution reaction)

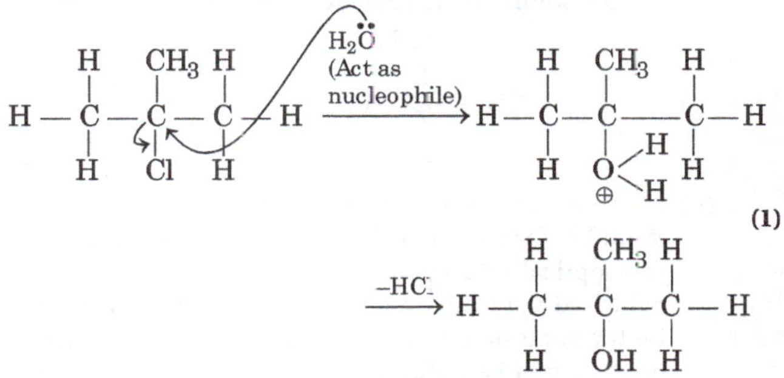

In this reaction, water can behave as a nucleophile and donate a lone pair (from oxygen) and attack (positive) carbon (originally attached to Cl) carbocation.

Reaction 2 (Elimination reaction)

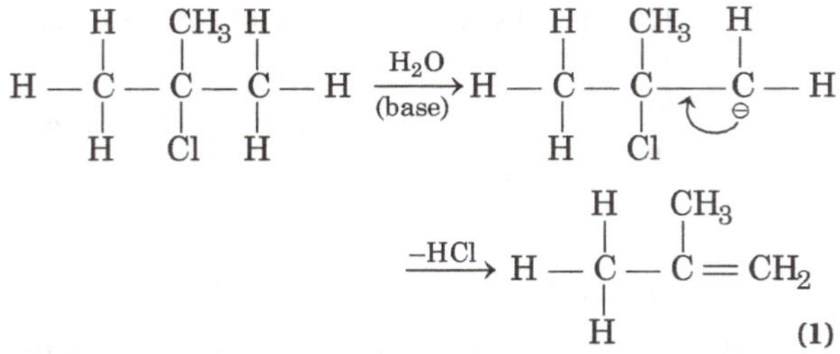

(1)

In this reaction water behaves as a base and accepts a hydrogen ion/proton. This leads to elimination of HCl from the reactant.

(ii) **Reaction 2 Reasons** Tertiary carbocation formed during intermediate stage is stabilised by the electron density from three alkyl groups. (1)

To avoid bulky group effect, elimination reaction dominates over substitution reaction.

31. (i) Refer to text on page 200. (1)

(ii) Refer to text on pages 202 and 203. (1)

(iii) In S_N1 reaction, reactivity depends upon the stability of intermediate carbocation.

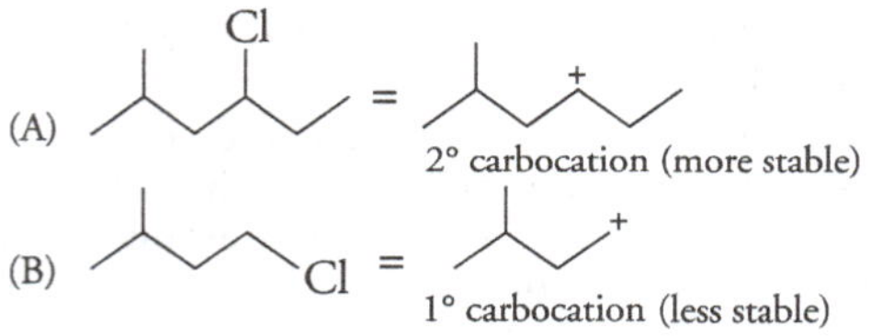

Former carbocation being secondary, is more stable than the latter being primary. Hence, first (A) alkyl halide undergoes S_N1 reaction faster. (1)

32. (i) For isomeric alkyl halides, the boiling points decreases with branching because with branching, the surface area of the molecule decreases and hence, the magnitude of van der Waals' forces of attraction decreases.

Therefore, *n*-butyl bromide ($CH_3CH_2CH_2CH_2Br$) has higher boiling than *tert*-butyl bromide,

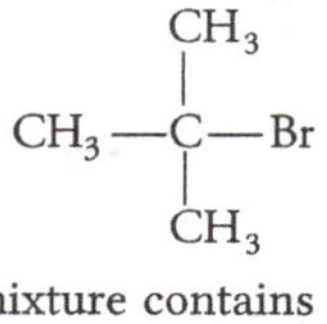

(1)

(ii) Racemic mixture contains two enantiomers, i.e., *d*- and *l*- forms in equal proportions and possesses zero optical rotation as the rotation of plane polarised light due to one isomer will be cancelled by the rotation due to the other isomer. Thus, the mixture will be optically inactive. (1)

(iii) Refer to text on page 203. (1)

33. (i)

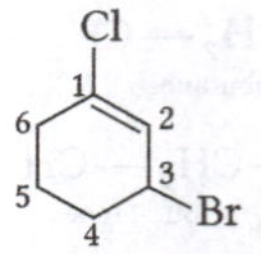

3-bromo-1-chlorocyclohexene (1)

(ii) The presence of nitro-group at *ortho* or *para*-position increases the reactivity of haloarenes towards nucleophilic substitution because —NO_2 is electron withdrawing group which will decrease density of electron over the benzene ring. (1)

(iii) Ethyl chloride when treated with alc. KOH, it will give ethene as a product. This reaction is known as an elimination reaction. (1)

$$\underset{\text{Ethyl chloride}}{CH_3CH_2Cl} \xrightarrow{\text{Alc. KOH}} \underset{\text{Ethene}}{CH_2=CH_2} + \underset{\text{Hydrochloric acid}}{HCl}$$

34. In environment, diphenyl is formed during the incomplete combustion of mineral oil and coal. It is present in the exhaust gases of vehicles and in exhaust air from residential and industrial heating devices.

Acute exposure to high levels of diphenyl has been observed to cause eye and skin irritation and toxic effect on the liver, kidneys and central/peripheral nervous system. Kidneys of animals are also affected due to the ingestion of biphenyls.

Fittig reaction (Preparation of diphenyls from aryl halides). Refer to text on page 205. (3)

35. (i) (a) Polar solvents stabilise the carbocations formed by solvation and hence favours S_N1 reaction. (1)

(b) Allyl halide forms allyl carbocation which is stabilised by resonance. Allyl carbocation is more stable than the carbocation formed by *n*-propylchloride and hence allyl chloride is hydrolysed more easily. (1)

(ii) (a) The rate of reaction of compound '*A*' with *aq*. KOH depends only on the concentration of A. This shows that the reaction follows S_N1 pathway and the compound is tertiary alkyl halide. Thus, *A* is

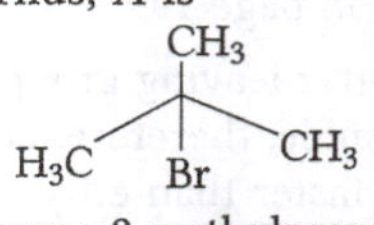

2-bromo-2-methylpropane

Since, compound *B* is optically active and the rate of its reaction with aq. KOH depends on the concentration of both *B* and *aq*. KOH. Thus, the reaction occurs by S_N2 mechanism and the compound is 2-bromobutane.

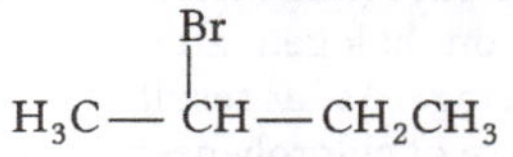

(2)

(b) Since, the reaction of compound *B* with *aq*. KOH follows S_N2 pathway. Hence, it will be converted to the product with inverted configuration. (1)

36. (i) (a) $CH_3—CH{=}CH_2 \xrightarrow{Br_2/CCl_4} CH_3—CH(Br)—CH_2(Br)$

Propene → 1,2-dibromopropane

$\xrightarrow[NaNH_2]{Liq.\ NH_3} CH_3—C{\equiv}CH$ (Propyne) **(1)**

(b) $CH_3CH_2CH{=}CH_2 \xrightarrow{HBr} CH_3CH_2CH(Br)CH_3$

But-1-ene

$\xrightarrow[\Delta]{alc.\ KOH} CH_3CH{=}CHCH_3$ (But-2-ene) **(1)**

(c) 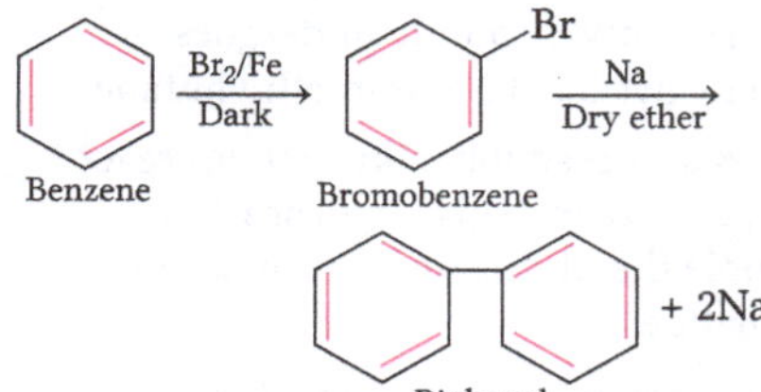

Benzene → (Br₂/Fe, Dark) Bromobenzene → (Na, Dry ether) Biphenyl + 2NaBr **(1)**

(ii) When ethyl chloride is treated with *aq.* KOH followed by reaction with $AgNO_3$, a white ppt is obtained which is soluble in NH_4OH whereas ethyl bromide reacts to give pale yellow ppt which is insoluble in NH_4OH. **(1)**

(iii) Lewis acid helps in the generation of electrophile from the dihalogens and thus facilitate electrophilic substitution reaction. **(1)**

37. (i) $CH_3—CH_2—Cl \xrightarrow{KCN} CH_3—CH_2—C{\equiv}N$

Ethyl chloride (Chloroethane) → Ethyl nitrile (Cyanopropane)

$\xrightarrow{2H_2O/H^+} CH_3—CH_2—COOH$ (Propanoic acid) **(1)**

(ii) $CH_3—CH_2—OH \xrightarrow{Red\ P/I_2}$ (Ethanol)

$CH_3—CH_2—I \xrightarrow{KCN} CH_3—CH_2—CN$

Iodoethane → Propane nitrile **(1)**

(iii) $CH_3CH_2CH_2Br \xrightarrow[\Delta]{KOH\ (alc.)} CH_3CH{=}CH_2 \xrightarrow{HBr} CH_3CH(Br)—CH_3$

1-bromopropane → Prop-1-ene → 2-bromopropane **(1)**

(iv) $2CH_3—CH_2—CH(CH_3)—Cl + 2Na \xrightarrow[Wurtz\ reaction]{Dry\ ether}$

2-chlorobutane

$CH_3—CH_2—CH(CH_3)—CH(CH_3)—CH_2—CH_3 + 2NaCl$

3, 4-dimethylhexane **(1)**

(v) $CH_3—C(CH_3){=}CH_2 \xrightarrow{HCl} CH_3—C(Cl)(CH_3)—CH_3$

2-methylprop-1-ene → 2-chloro-2-methylpropane **(1)**

38. (i) But-1-ene is formed as a result of dehydrohalogenation.

$CH_3—CH_2—CH_2—CH_2—Cl + KOH\ (Alc.) \longrightarrow$

n-butyl chloride

$CH_3—CH_2—CH{=}CH_2 + KCl + H_2O$

But-1-ene **(1)**

(ii) Phenyl magnesium bromide is formed.

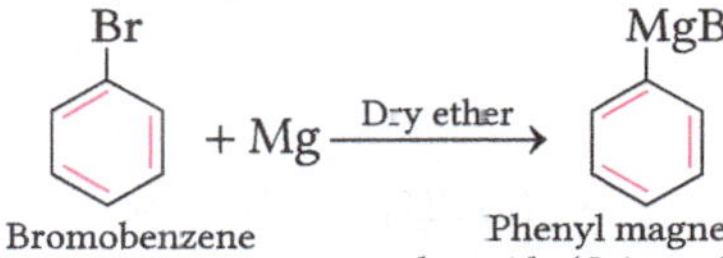

Bromobenzene + Mg → (Dry ether) Phenyl magnesium bromide (Grignard reagent) **(1)**

(iii) At room temperature and pressure, no reaction occurs but when chlorobenzene is heated with 6-8 % NaOH solution at 623K under 320 atmospheric pressure, phenol is obtained.

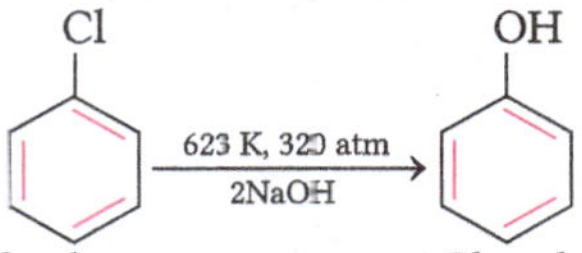

Chlorobenzene → (623 K, 320 atm, 2NaOH) Phenol **(1)**

(iv) Ethane is formed as a result of Wurtz reaction.

$CH_3—Br + 2Na + Br—CH_3 \xrightarrow{Dry\ ether} CH_3—CH_3 + 2NaBr$

Methyl bromide → Ethane **(1)**

(v) Cyanomethane is formed.

$CH_3—Cl + KCN \longrightarrow CH_3—C{\equiv}N + KCl$

Chloromethane (Methyl chloride) → Acetonitrile (Cyanomethane) **(1)**

QR Code for Quick Test 1

QR Code for Quick Test 2

QR Code for Quick Test 3

QR Code for Quick Test 4

QR Code for Quick Test 5

SELF ASSESSMENT TEST

Objective Type Questions [1 Mark]

1. The IUPAC name of *iso*-butyl bromide is
   (a) 1-bromo-3-methylbutane
   (b) 3-bromo-2-methylpropane
   (c) 2-bromo-2-methylpropane
   (d) 1-bromo-2-methylpropane
2. Reaction of 1-phenyl-2-chloropropane with alcoholic KOH gives mainly
   (a) 1-phenylpropene (b) 3-phenylpropene
   (c) 1-phenylpropan-3-ol (d) 1-phenylpropan-2-ol
3. Which of the following compounds undergoes racemisation on hydrolysis with aqueous KOH?
   (a) $CH_3—CH_2—Br$ (b) $CH_3—CH(CH_3)—CH_2—Br$
   (c) $CH_3—Br$ (d) $CH_3—CH(C_2H_5)—Br$
4. Which reagents are required for one step conversion of chlorobenzene to toluene?
   (a) CH_3Cl / $AlCl_3$ (b) CH_3Cl, Na, Dry ether
   (c) CH_3Cl /Fe, Dark (d) $NaNO_2$/HCl/0-5°C
5. Match the reactions given in Column I with the names given in Column II.

Column I	Column II
A. 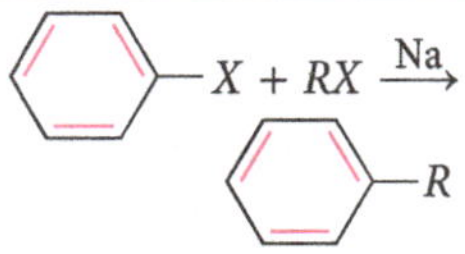	1. Fittig reaction
B. 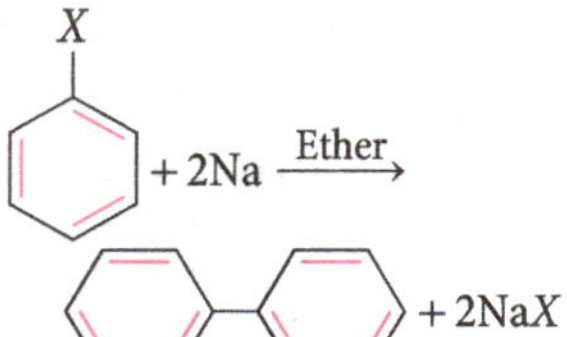	2. Wurtz-Fittig reaction
C. 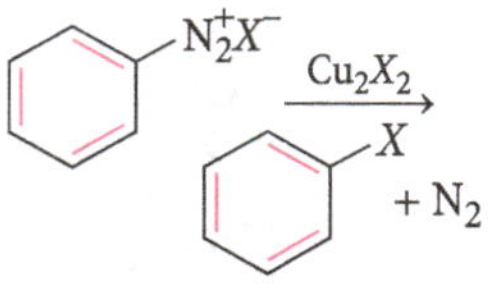	3. Sandmeyer's reaction

(a) A-1, B-2, C-3 (b) A-2, B-1, C-3
(c) A-3, B-2, C-1 (d) A-2, B-3, C-1

Assertion - Reason [1 Mark]

Directions (Q. Nos. 6-8) In the following questions, an Assertion (A) is followed by a corresponding. Reason (R). Use the following keys to choose the appropriate answer.

6. **Assertion** (A) *tert*-butyl bromide undergoes Wurtz reaction to give 2,2,3,3-tetramethylbutane.
   Reason (R) In Wurtz reaction, alkyl halides react with sodium in dry ether to give hydrocarbon containing double the number of carbon atoms present in the halide.
7. **Assertion** (A) *iso*-propyl bromide on Wurtz reaction gives 2, 3-dimethylbutane.
   Reason (R) When same alkyl halides react with sodium in dry ether to give hydrocarbon which contains double the number of carbon atoms present in the alkyl halide, it is called Wurtz reaction.
8. **Assertion** (A) S_N1 mechanism is ruled out in case of haloarene.
   Reason (R) Phenyl cation is formed as a result of self ionisation which is not stabilised by resonance.

Short Answer Type I Questions [2 Marks]

9. Write the major product(s) in the following. (Any 2)
   (i) 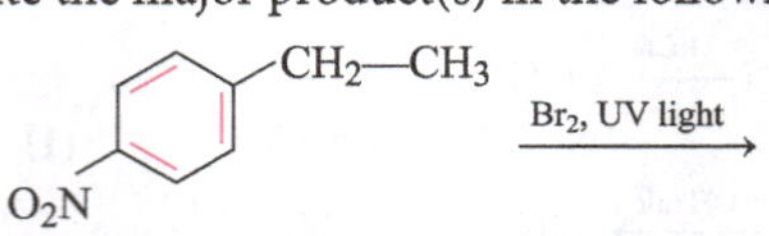
   (ii) $2CH_3—CH(Cl)—CH_3 \xrightarrow[\text{Dry ether}]{\text{Na}}$
   (iii) $CH_3—CH_2—Br \xrightarrow{\text{AgCN}}$
10. (i) Identify the chiral molecule in the following pair
    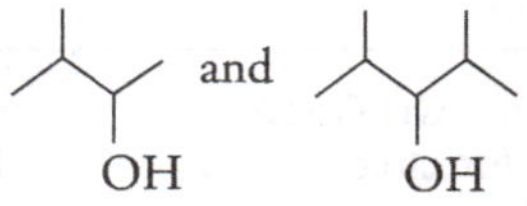
    (a) (b)
    (ii) Write the structure of the product when chlorobenzene is treated with methyl chloride in the presence of sodium metal and dry ether.

11. How are polyhalogens different from other organic halogens? Explain with example.

Short Answer Type II Questions [3 Marks]

12. (i) Write equation for preparation of 1-iodoethane from ethylalcohol.

(ii) Out of 2-bromopentane, 2-bromo-2-methylbutane and 1-bromopentane, which compound is most reactive towards elimination reaction and why?

(iii) Give IUPAC name of

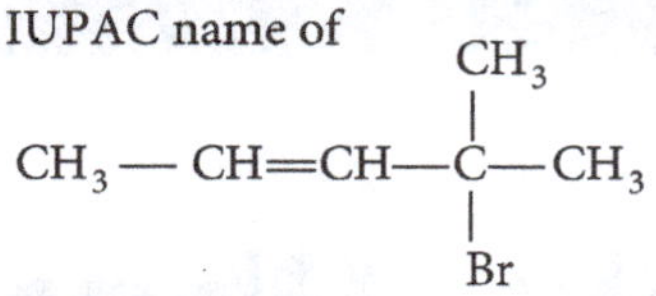

13. (i) For the following reaction.

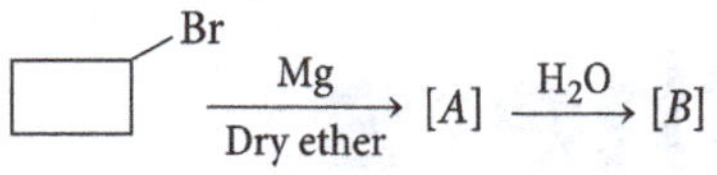

Identify *A* and *B*.

(ii) Haloalkanes easily dissolve in organic solvents. Why?

14. How would you differentiate between S_N1 and S_N2 mechanism of substitution reactions? Give one example of each.

Case-Study [4 Marks]

15. The following questions are case-based questions. Each question has an internal choice and carries 4 (2 + 1 + 1) marks each. Read the passage carefully and answer the questions that follow.

Nucleophilic substitution reaction of haloalkane can be conducted according to both S_N1 and S_N2 mechanisms. S_N1 is a two step reaction while S_N2 is a single step reaction. For any haloalkane which mechanism is followed depends on factors such as structure of haloalkane, properties of leaving group, nucleophilic reagent and solvent.

Influences of solvent polarity In S_N1 reaction, the polarity of the system increases from the reactant to the transition state, because a polar solvent has a greater effect on the transition state than the reactant, thereby reducing activation energy and accelerating the reaction In S_N2 reaction, the polarity of the system generally does not change from the reactant to the transition state and only charge dispersion occurs.

At this time, polar solvent has a great stabilising effect on Nu than the transition state, thereby increasing activation energy and slow down the reaction rate. For example, the decomposition rate (S_N1) of tertiary chlorobutane at 25°C in water (dielectric constant 79) is 300000 times faster than in ethanol (dielectric).

The reaction rate (S_N2) of 2-bromopropane and NaOH in ethanol containing 40% water is twice slower than in absolute ethanol. Hence, the level of solvent polarity has influence on both S_N1 and S_N2 reaction, but with different results. Generally, weak polar solvent is favourable for S_N1 reaction.

The substitution reaction of tertiary haloalkane is based on S_N1 mechanism in solvents with a strong polarity (for example ethanol containing water).

(i) Which one of the following in each pair is more reactive towards S_N2 reaction?

(a) $CH_3—CH_2—I$ or $CH_3—CH_2—Cl$

(b) 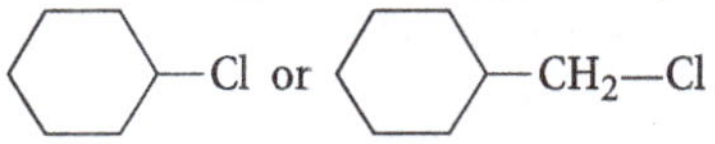

(ii) Why racemisation occurs in S_N1 reactions?

Or

Why is ethanol less polar than water?

(iii) Ethyl iodide undergoes S_N2 reaction faster than ethyl bromide.

Long Answer Type Questions [5 Marks]

16. (i) Primary alkyl halide C_4H_9Br (*A*) reacts with alcoholic KOH to give compound *B*. Compound *B* is reacted with HBr to give *C*, which is an isomer of *A*. When *A* is reacted with sodium metal, it gives compound *D*, C_8H_{18} which is different from the compound formed when *n*-butyl bromide is reacted with sodium. Give the structural formula of *A* and write the equations for all the reactions.

(ii) Write the product(s) of the following reactions.

(a) $CH_3—Cl + KCN \longrightarrow ?$

(b) 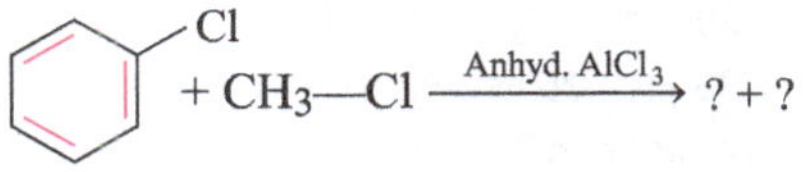

Answers

1. (d)	2. (a)	3. (d)	4. (b)
5. (b)	6. (a)	7. (a)	8. (a)

07 CHAPTER

An alcohol contains one or more hydroxyl group(s) (—OH), directly attached to carbon atom(s) of an aliphatic system (like CH_3OH), while a phenol contains (—OH) group(s), directly attached to carbon atom(s) of an aromatic system (like C_6H_5OH).

YOUR STUDY GOALS

YOUR PRACTICE GOAL

- Objective Type Questions (38 Qs ; 25 MCQs, 11 A-R, 2 Case Study)
- Subjective Type Questions (41 Qs; 13 SA-I, 22 SA-II, 6 LA)

Alcohols, Phenols and Ethers

Alcohols and phenols are formed by replacing one hydrogen atom from a **hydrocarbon** (aliphatic or aromatic) by —OH group. Ethers are formed by the substitution of a hydrogen atom in a hydrocarbon by an alkoxy or aryloxy group (—O*R* / —OAr).

7.1 Classification of Alcohols and Phenols

These may be classified as mono-, di-, tri- or polyhydric compounds depending on whether they contain one, two, three or many hydroxyl groups respectively, in their structures.

Classification of Alcohols and Phenols

Monohydric (alcohols/phenols)	Dihydric (alcohols/phenols)	Trihydric (alcohols/phenols)
• Having one —OH group attached to the carbon atom of a compound.	• Having two —OH groups attached to the two carbon atoms of a compound.	• Having three —OH groups attached to the three carbon atoms of a compound.
• e.g. CH_3OH, 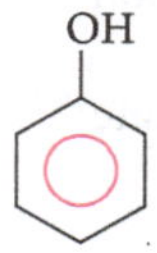	• e.g. CH_2OH–CH_2–CH_2OH, 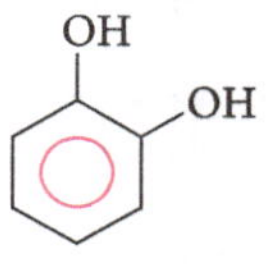	• e.g. CH_2OH–$CHOH$–CH_2OH, 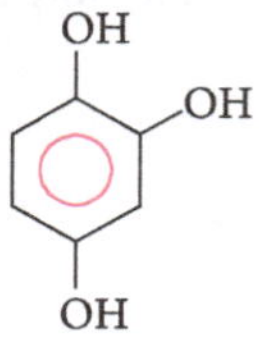

Classification of Monohydric Alcohols

Monohydric alcohols may be further classified according to the hybridisation of the carbon atom to which the hydroxyl group is attached.

Compounds Containing C_{sp^3} — OH Bond

In this class of alcohols, the —OH group is attached to a sp^3-hybridised carbon atom of an alkyl group.

These are further classified as follows

(i) **Primary, Secondary and Tertiary Alcohols**
In these alcohols, the —OH group is attached to primary, secondary and tertiary carbon atom respectively.

e.g. $—\overset{1°}{C}H_2OH$, $>\overset{2°}{C}HOH$, $\geq\overset{3°}{C}OH$,
Primary (1°) Secondary (2°) Tertiary (3°)

(ii) **Allylic Alcohols** In these alcohols, the —OH group is attached to a sp^3-hybridised allylic carbon (i.e. carbon atom next to the carbon-carbon double bond).

e.g. $CH_2{=}CH—CH_2—OH$

(iii) **Benzylic Alcohols** In these alcohols, the —OH group is attached to a sp^3-hybridised benzylic carbon atom (i.e. carbon atom next to an aromatic ring).

e.g.

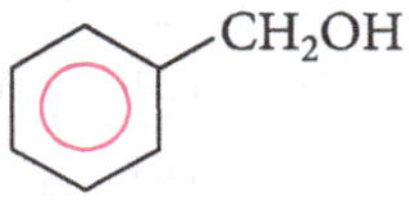

Compounds Containing C_{sp^2}— OH Bond

In these alcohols, the —OH group is attached to a carbon-carbon double bond, i.e. to a vinylic carbon ($CH_2 = CH—$) or to an aryl carbon. These alcohols are also known as **vinylic alcohols**.

e.g. $CH_2{=}CH—OH$
Vinylic alcohol

Phenols These contain —OH groups attached to the carbon atoms of benzene ring.

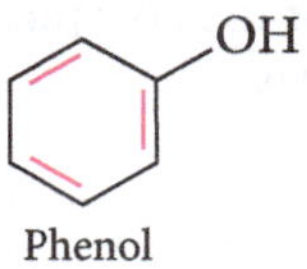

Phenol

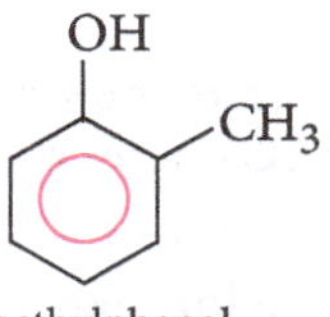

2-methylphenol

7.2 Nomenclature of Alcohols and Phenols

For Alcohols

The **common name** of an alcohol is derived from common name of alkyl group and adding the word alcohol to it.

e.g. $CH_3OH \longrightarrow \underbrace{CH_3 \text{ (methyl group)} + \text{alcohol}}_{\downarrow}$
Methyl alcohol

In **IUPAC system,** the name of an alcohol is derived from the name of the alkane from which the alcohol is derived, by replacing 'e' of alkane with the suffix 'ol'. Here, the position of substituents are indicated by numerals.

Steps for writing the **IUPAC name** of the alcohols are as follows

Step I Select the longest carbon chain (parent chain) containing —OH group.

Step II The selected longest chain is numbered from the end nearest to the hydroxyl group.

Step III Replace the 'e' of alkane by adding suffix 'ol'.

Step IV The positions of the —OH group and other substituents are indicated by using the numbers of carbon atoms to which these are attached.

- **For naming polyhydric alcohols,** the 'e' of alkane is retained and the ending or suffix 'ol' is added.
- Indicate the number of (—OH) groups by adding prefix like di, tri, etc., before 'ol'.
- **Cyclic alcohols** are named by using the prefix cyclo to the common or IUPAC name and considering the —OH group attached to C-1.
- The position of the substituents are indicated by 1, 2, 3 etc., for IUPAC system. However, α, β, γ etc., are used to indicate the substituent position for common name system.

Common and IUPAC Name of Some Alcohols

Compound	Common name	IUPAC name
CH_3OH	Methyl alcohol	Methanol
CH_3CH_2OH	Ethyl alcohol	Ethanol
$CH_3CH_2CH_2OH$	*n*-propyl alcohol	Propan-1-ol

Compound	Common name	IUPAC name
$CH_3-CH(OH)-CH_3$	*iso*-propyl alcohol	Propan-2-ol
$CH_3-CH(OH)-CH_2-CH_3$	*sec*-butyl alcohol	Butan-2-ol
$CH_3-CH(CH_3)-CH_2OH$	*iso*-butyl alcohol	2-methyl-propan-1-ol
$CH_3-C(CH_3)_2-OH$	*tert*-butyl alcohol	2-methyl propan-2-ol
$HOCH_2-CH(OH)-CH_2OH$	Glycerol	Propane-1, 2, 3-triol
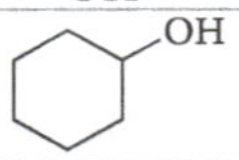	—	Cyclohexanol
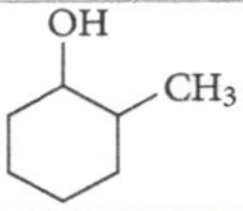	—	2-methylcyclo-hexanol

For Phenols

- The name phenol is given to simplest hydroxy derivative of benzene. It is accepted as common name as well as **IUPAC name.**
- As the structure of phenol involves a benzene ring in its substituted compounds, the terms *ortho* (1, 2-disubstituted), *meta* (1,3-disubstituted) and *para* (1,4-disubstituted) are often used in the common names.
- In **IUPAC system,** Arabic numericals are used to indicate the position of the substituent w.r.t —OH group. The carbon carrying the —OH group gets the number 1.
- The phenols having substituted methyl group, get their names as hydroxyl derivatives of the parent aromatic compound.

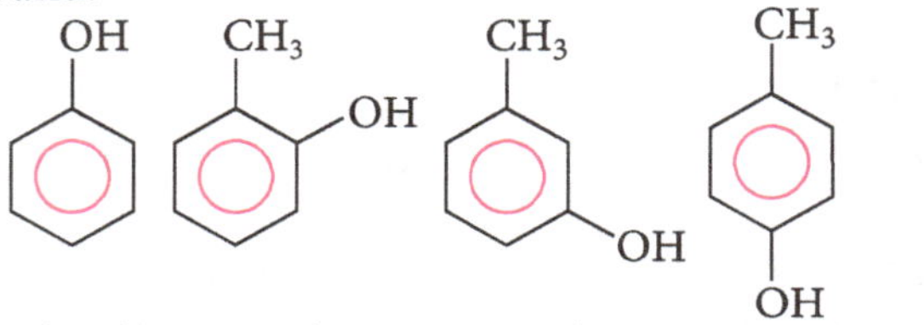

Common name	Phenol	*o*-cresol	*m*-cresol	*p*-cresol
IUPAC name	Phenol	2-methylphenol	3-methylphenol	4-methylphenol

- Dihydroxy derivatives of benzene are known as 1,2-, 1,3- and 1,4-benzene diol.

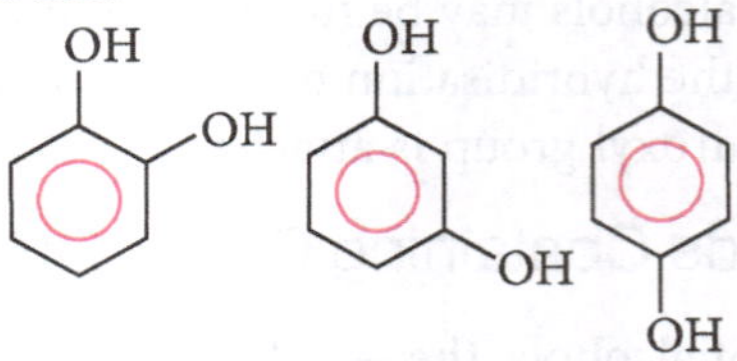

Common name	Catechol	Resorcinol	Quinol or Hydroquinone
IUPAC name	Benzene-1, 2-diol	Benzene-1, 3-diol	Benzene-1,4-diol

Example 1 **Name the following compounds according to IUPAC system.**

(i) 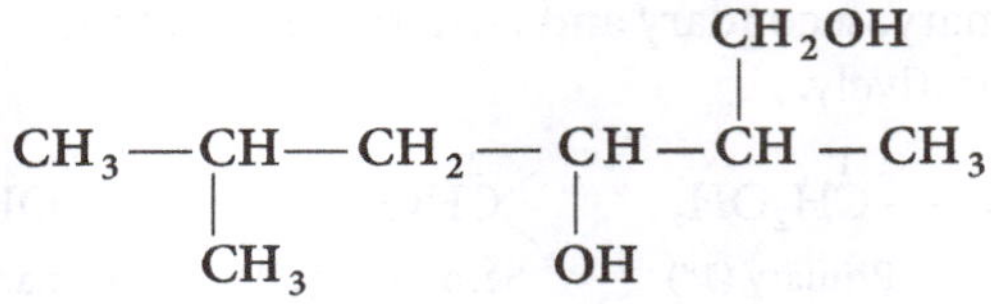

(ii) 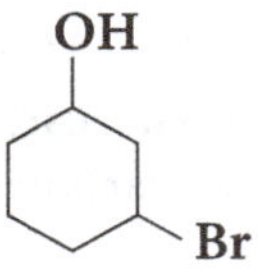

(iii) 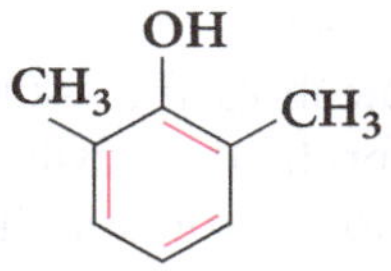

NCERT Intext

Sol. (i) 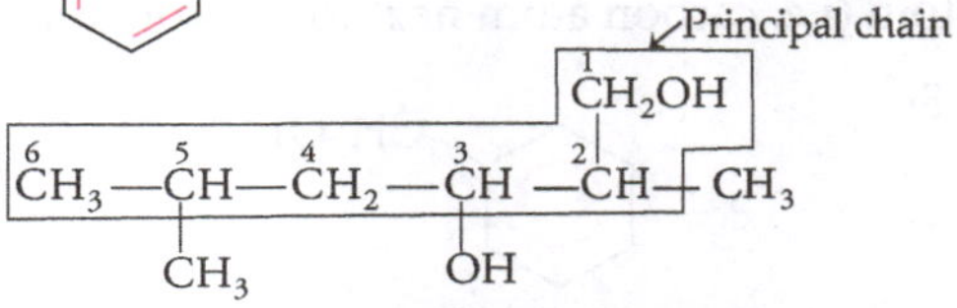

IUPAC name 2, 5-dimethylhexane-1, 3-diol

(ii) 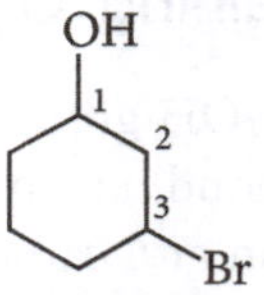

IUPAC name 3-bromocyclohexanol

(iii) 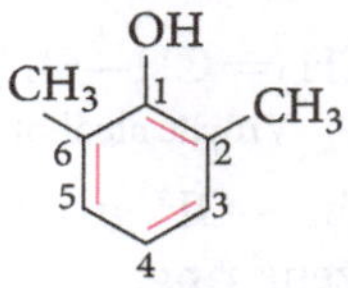

IUPAC name 2, 6-dimethylphenol

Example 2 **Write the structures of the compounds whose IUPAC names are as follows**

(i) Hex-1-en-3-ol

(ii) 2-methylpropan-2-ol

(iii) 2, 6-dimethylphenol

Sol. (i)

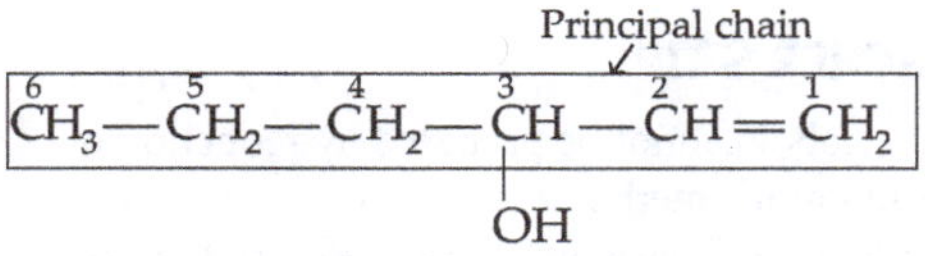

Hex-1-en-3-ol

(ii)

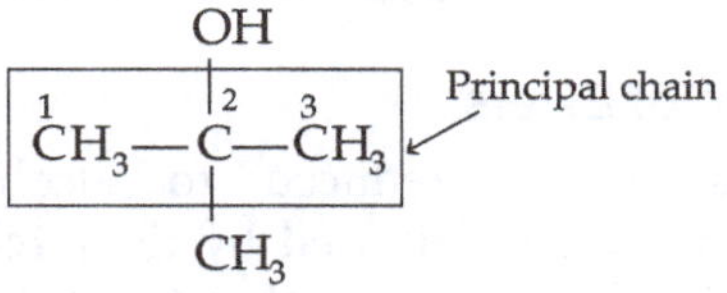

2-methylpropan-2-ol

(iii)

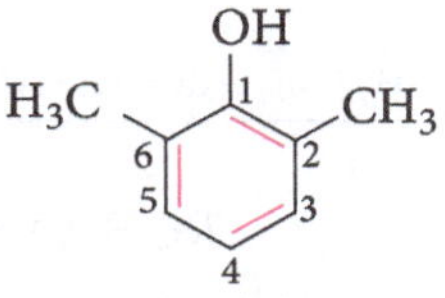

2, 6-dimethylphenol

7.3 Structures of Functional Groups (Alcohols and Phenols)

The structures of alcohols and phenols are tabulated as

Compounds	Nature of hybridisation, bond angle and bond length
Alcohols e.g. Methanol 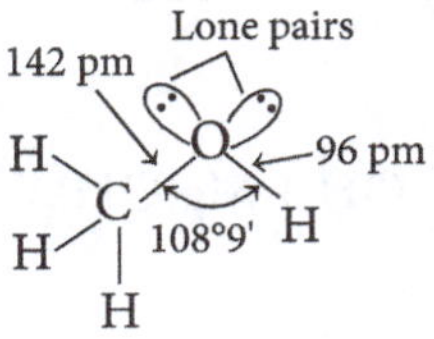	• The oxygen atom of —OH group is attached to carbon atom by a σ (sigma) bond which is formed by overlapping of a sp^3-hybridised orbital of carbon with sp^3-hybridised orbital of oxygen. • The OH bond is polar in nature as electronegativity of oxygen is more than that of hydrogen. • The 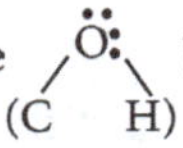 bond angle is slightly less (108°9′) than the tetrahedral angle (109°28′). This is due to the repulsion between the unshared electron pairs of oxygen. • The C—OH bond length is 142 pm.
Phenols 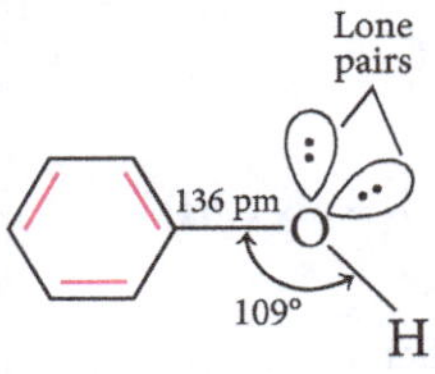	• The C—O bond is formed by overlapping of sp^2-hybridised carbon atom of aromatic ring. • The C—O bond length is slightly less (136 pm) than that in methanol. This is due to partial double bond character on account of the conjugation of unpaired electron pairs of oxygen with aromatic ring. It is also due to sp^2-hybridised state of carbon to which oxygen is attached.

7.4 Methods of Preparation (Alcohols and Phenols)

Preparation of Alcohols

These are prepared by the following methods

From Alkenes

(i) By Acid Catalysed Hydration

Alkenes react with water in the presence of acid (as catalyst) to form alcohols. In case of unsymmetrical alkenes, the addition of water takes place in accordance with **Markovnikov's rule.**

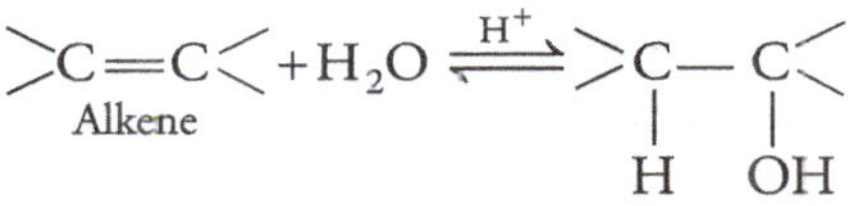

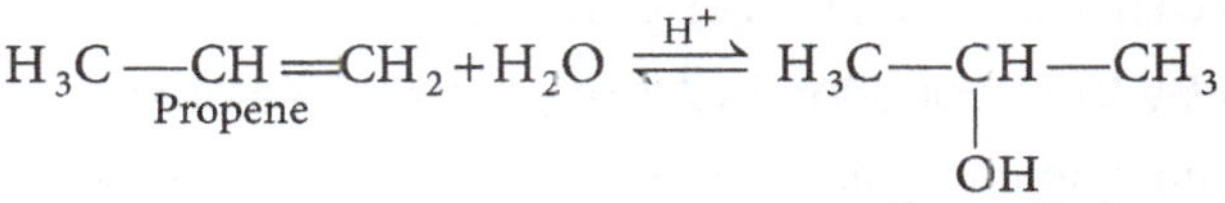

The mechanism of the hydration of alkene involves following three steps.

Step I Protonation of alkene to form a stable carbocation by electrophilic attack of H_3O^+.

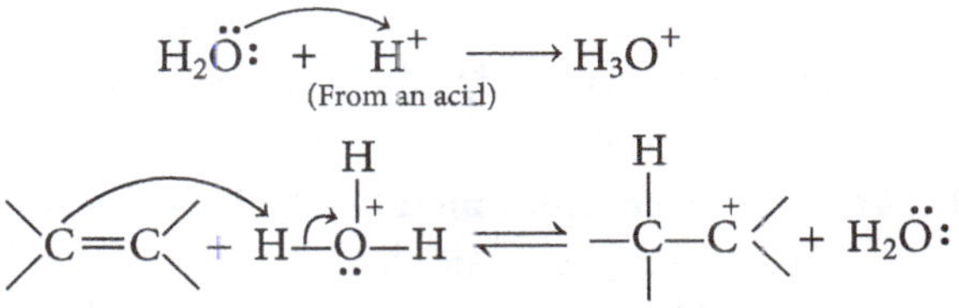

Step II Nucleophilic attack of water on carbocation.

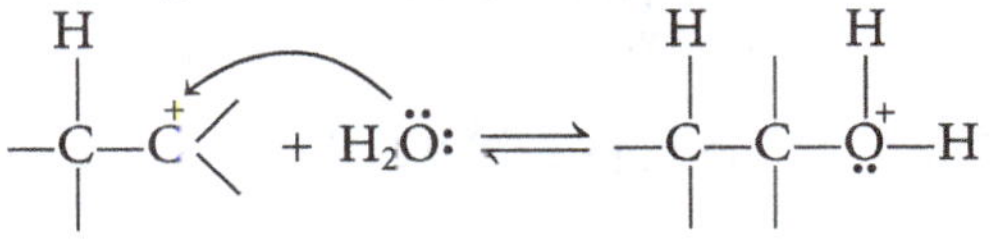

Step III Deprotonation to form an alcohol.

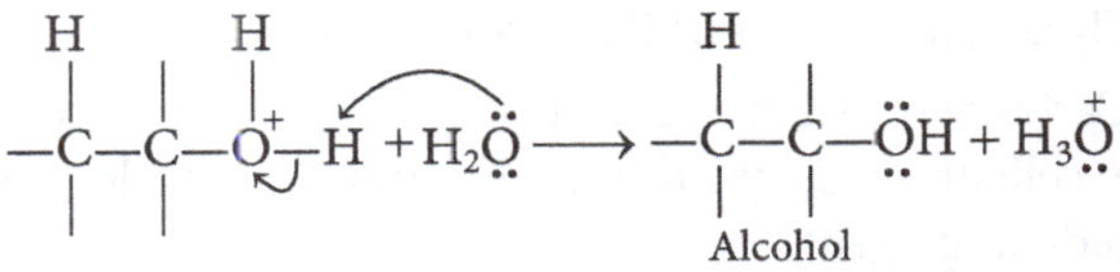

(ii) By Hydroboration-Oxidation

Diborane $(BH_3)_2$ reacts with alkenes to give trialkyl boranes as addition product which upon subsequent oxidation by H_2O_2 (hydrogen peroxide) in the presence of aqueous sodium hydroxide give alcohols.

$$\underset{\text{Propene}}{CH_3-CH=CH_2} + \underset{\text{Diborane}}{(H-BH_2)_2} \longrightarrow$$

$$\underset{\text{Propylborane}}{CH_3-\underset{|}{\overset{}{C}}H(H)-CH_2(BH_2)} \xrightarrow{CH_3-CH=CH_2}$$

$$(CH_3-CH_2CH_2)_2BH \xrightarrow{CH_3-CH=CH_2}$$

$$\underset{\text{Tripropylborane}}{(CH_3-CH_2-CH_2)_3B} \xrightarrow[3H_2O_2, OH^-]{H_2O}$$

$$B(OH)_3 + 3\underset{\text{Propan-1-ol}}{CH_3-CH_2-CH_2-OH}$$

Note Here, the addition of borane to the alkene follows **anti-Markovnikov's** rule, resulting in the formation of alcohol on oxidation.

In this reaction, alcohol is obtained in excellent yield.

From Carbonyl Compounds

(i) By the Reduction of Aldehydes and Ketones

Following methods are used to reduce aldehydes and ketones to the corresponding alcohols.

I. **Addition of H_2** in the presence of a finely divided catalyst like Pt, Pd, or Ni metals (catalytic hydrogenation).

$$\underset{\text{Aldehyde}}{R-CHO} + H_2 \xrightarrow{Ni/Pd} \underset{\text{Alcohol}}{R-CH_2OH}$$

$$\text{e.g. } \underset{\text{Acetaldehyde}}{CH_3CHO} + H_2 \xrightarrow{Ni/Pd} \underset{\text{Ethanol } (1^\circ)}{CH_3CH_2OH}$$

II. **Addition of complex metal hydrides** such as $LiAlH_4$, $NaBH_4$, etc. Aldehydes yield primary alcohols whereas, ketones give secondary alcohols.

$$\underset{\text{Aldehyde}}{R-CHO} \xrightarrow{LiAlH_4} \underset{1^\circ \text{ alcohol}}{R-CH_2OH}$$

$$\underset{\text{Ketone}}{\begin{matrix}R\\R'\end{matrix}\!\!>C=O} \xrightarrow{NaBH_4} \underset{2^\circ \text{ alcohol}}{\begin{matrix}R\\R'\end{matrix}\!\!>CH-OH}$$

(ii) By Reduction of Carboxylic Acids

Carboxylic acids are reduced to primary alcohols in excellent yield by lithium aluminium hydride (a strong reducing agent).

$$\underset{\text{Carboxylic acid}}{R-COOH} \xrightarrow[\text{(ii) } H_2O^+]{\text{(i) } LiAlH_4} \underset{2^\circ \text{ alcohol}}{RCH_2OH}$$

$$\underset{\text{Benzoic acid}}{C_6H_5-COOH} \xrightarrow[\text{(ii) } H_2O^+]{\text{(i) } LiAlH_4} \underset{\text{Benzyl alcohol}}{C_6H_5-CH_2OH}$$

TEACHER'S TIP

- 3° alcohol cannot be prepared by reduction of carbonyl compounds method.
- Reduction of carbonyl compounds and esters to alcohols by using alcoholic sodium is called **Bouveault-Blanc reduction**.

(iii) By Reduction of Esters

Commercially, acids are reduced to alcohols by converting them to esters, followed by their reduction using hydrogen in the presence of catalyst (catalytic hydrogenation).

$$\underset{\text{Carboxylic acid}}{RCOOH} \xrightarrow[H^+]{R'OH} \underset{\text{Ester}}{RCOOR'} \xrightarrow{H_2/\text{Copper chromite catalyst}} RCH_2OH + R'OH$$

From Grignard Reagents

Aldehydes and ketones react with Grignard reagent to form alcohol in two steps. These are as follows

Step I This step involves the nucleophilic addition of Grignard reagent to the carbonyl group to form an adduct.

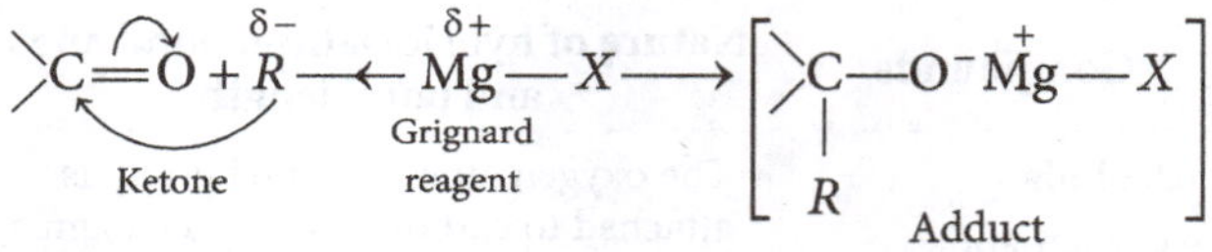

Step II This step involves the hydrolysis of an adduct to yield an alcohol.

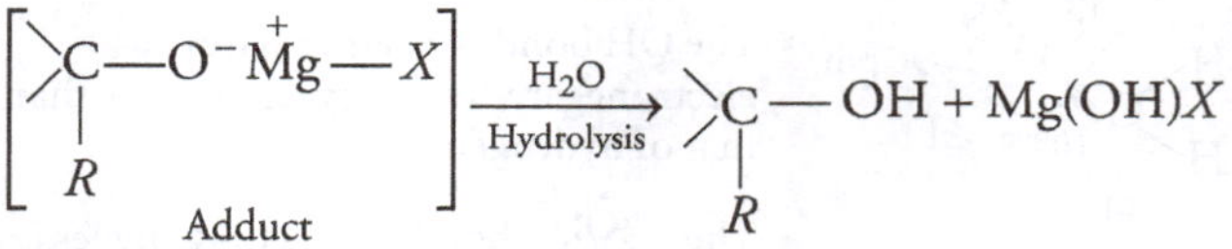

The overall reactions using different aldehydes and ketones are as follows

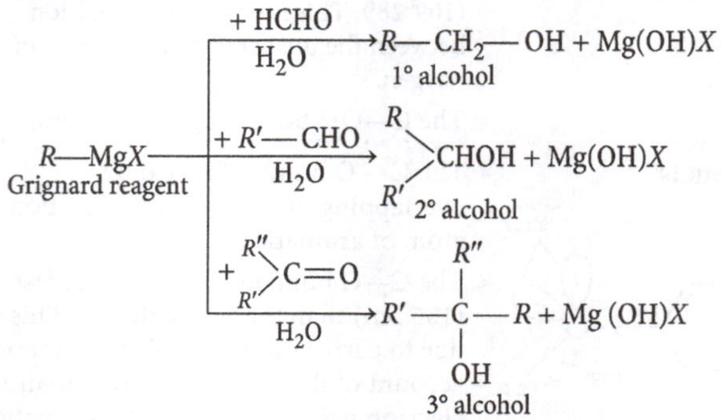

Note Only **formaldehyde yields**, primary alcohol on reaction with Grignard reagents whereas, all other aldehydes and ketones give secondary and tertiary alcohols, respectively.

By Hydrolysis of Haloalkanes

Haloalkanes are hydrolysed to the corresponding alcohols by treatment with an aqueous alkali.

$$CH_3—Cl + KOH(aq) \longrightarrow CH_3OH + HCl$$

Preparation of Alcohol

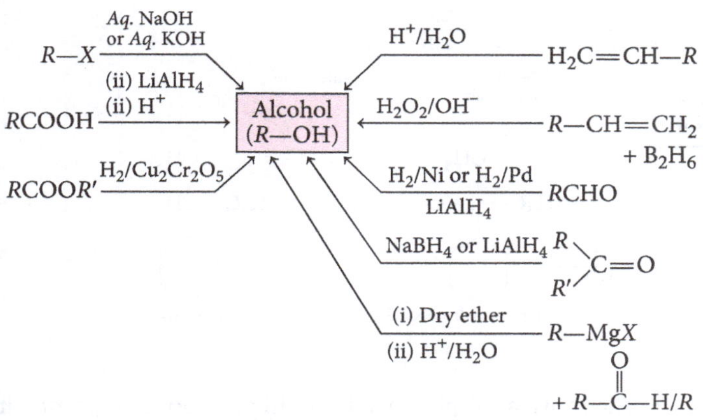

Example 3 **Write a chemical equation when**

(i) ethyl chloride is treated with *aq*.KOH.

(ii) butene is treated with H_2O in presence of dil. H_2SO_4.

(iii) propene is treated with B_2H_6 followed by H_2O_2/OH^-.

Sol. (i) $\underset{\text{Ethyl chloride}}{C_2H_5Cl} + KOH(aq) \longrightarrow \underset{\text{Ethanol}}{C_2H_5OH} + KCl$

(ii) $\underset{\text{Butene}}{CH_3—CH_2—CH=CH_2} + H_2O \xrightarrow{\text{Dil. } H_2SO_4} \underset{\text{Butan-2-ol}}{CH_3—CH_2—\underset{\underset{OH}{|}}{CH}—CH_3}$

(iii) $\underset{\text{Propene}}{CH_3—CH=CH_2} \xrightarrow[\text{(b) } H_2O_2/OH^-]{\text{(a) } B_2H_6} \underset{\text{Propan-1-ol}}{CH_3CH_2CH_2OH}$

Preparation of Phenols

In the laboratory, phenols can be prepared from benzene derivatives by the following methods.

From Benzene Sulphonic Acid

When benzene is sulphonated with oleum ($H_2S_2O_7$= conc. $H_2SO_4 + SO_3$), then benzene sulphonic acid is formed which gets further converted to sodium phenoxide.

On heating with molten sodium hydroxide, acidification of sodium phenoxide gives phenol.

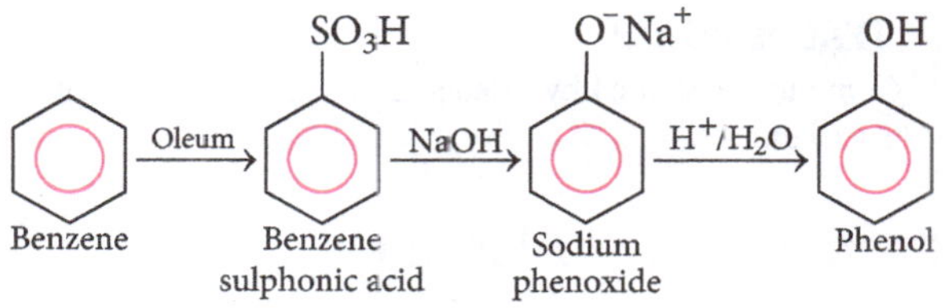

From Haloarenes (Dow's Process)

Chlorobenzene on fusion with NaOH at 623 K and 320 atm pressure gives sodium phenoxide which on acidification yields phenol.

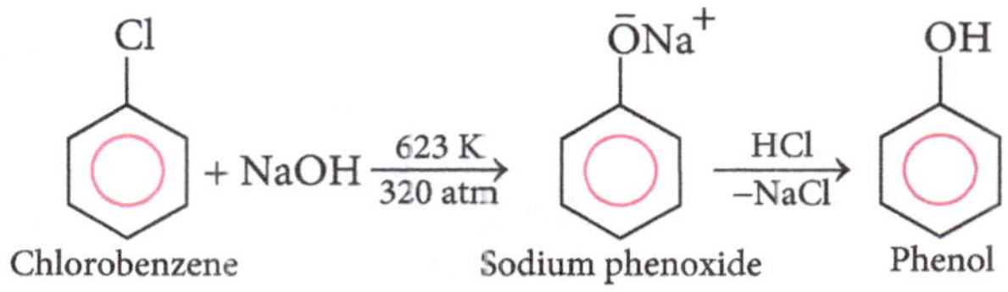

From Diazonium Salts

A diazonium salt of aromatic amine (i.e. aniline) is formed by treating amine with nitrous acid ($NaNO_2$ + HCl) at 273 K-278 K.

Diazonium salts on hydrolysis with warm water or dilute acids give phenols.

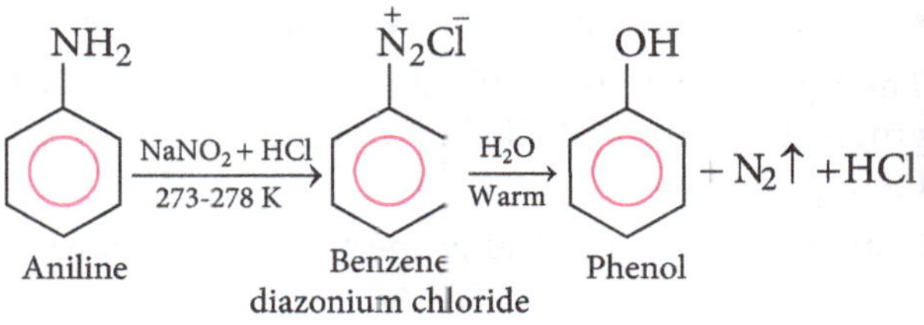

From Cumene

Cumene (*iso*-propyl benzene) on **aerial oxidation** forms cumene hydroperoxide which upon subsequent hydrolysis with dilute acid gives phenol and propanone (acetone). Acetone (a by-product) is obtained in large quantities.

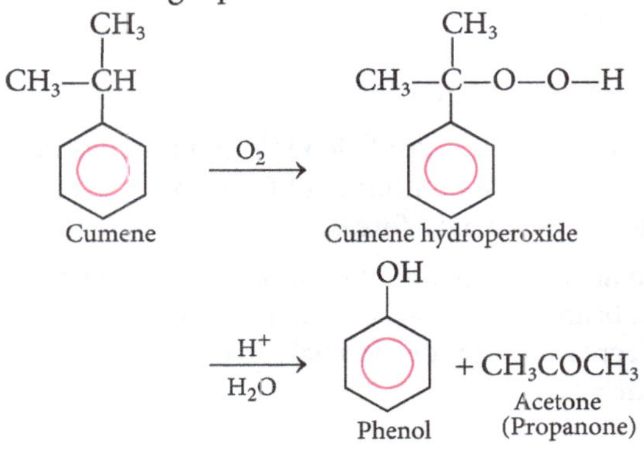

TEACHER'S TIP

Cumene is obtained by Friedel-Crafts alkylation of benzene with propylene. Most of the worldwide production of phenol is done from cumene.

Preparation of Alcohol

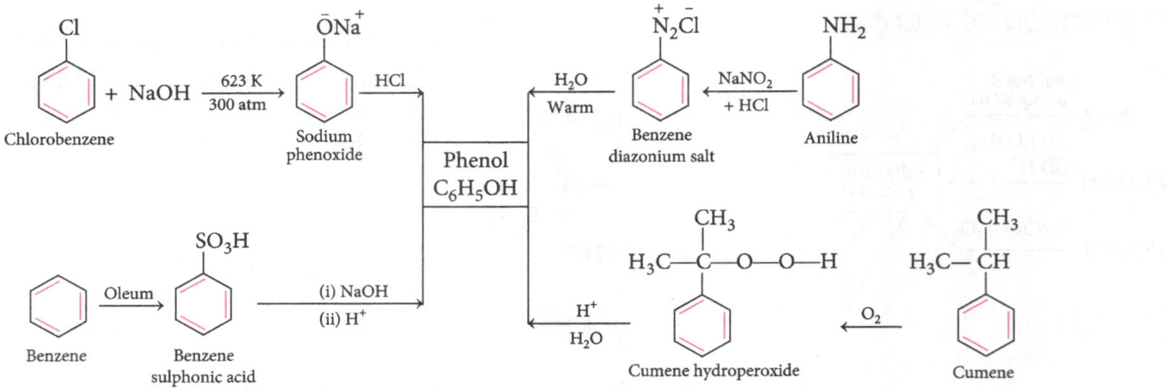

7.5 Physical Properties of Alcohols and Phenols

The alcohols and phenols consist of two parts,

- Alkyl or aryl group
- Hydroxyl group

Their properties are chiefly due to hydroxyl (—OH) group. The nature of alkyl or aryl groups simply modify these properties.

Some important physical properties are as follows

1. Physical State

- At room temperature, lower alcohols are colourless liquids with distinct smell and burning taste. The higher members are colourless, odourless, waxy solids.
- Pure phenols are either colourless liquids or solids and usually turn reddish-brown due to atmospheric oxidation.

2. Boiling Points

- The boiling points of alcohols and phenols increase with increase in number of C-atoms (due to increase in van der Waals' forces).
- In alcohols, the boiling point decreases with increase of branching in carbon chain. This is because of decrease in van der Waals' forces with decrease in surface area.
- Alcohols and phenols have higher boiling points in comparison to hydrocarbons, ethers, haloalkanes and haloarenes of comparable molecular masses.

This is because the —OH group in alcohols and phenols is involved in intermolecular hydrogen bonding due to which they exist as associated molecules, whereas H-bonding is absent in ethers and hydrocarbons.

Hydrogen bonding between alcohol and water; phenol and water are shown below.

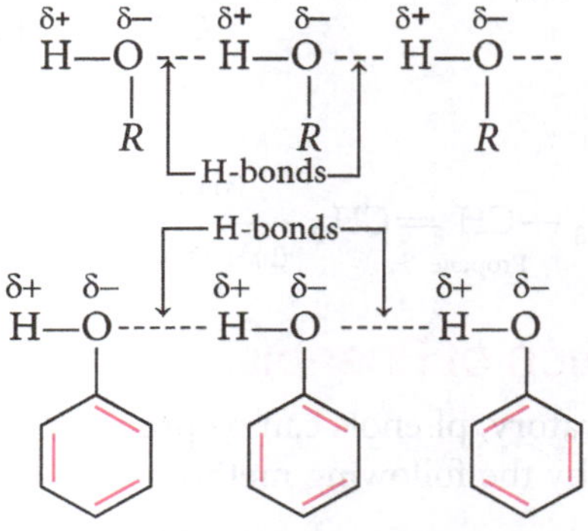

- Boiling point of ethanol, methoxy methane and propane decreases as follows

$$C_2H_5OH \quad > \quad CH_3OCH_3 \quad > CH_3CH_2CH_3$$

Ethanol	**Methoxymethane**	**Propane**
Molecular mass = 46	Molecular mass = 46	Molecular mass = 44
Boiling point = 351 K	Boiling point = 248 K	Boiling point = 231 K

3. Solubility

- The solubility of alcohols and phenols in water is due to their ability to form H-bonds with water molecules. Many lower molecular mass alcohols are miscible with water in all proportions.

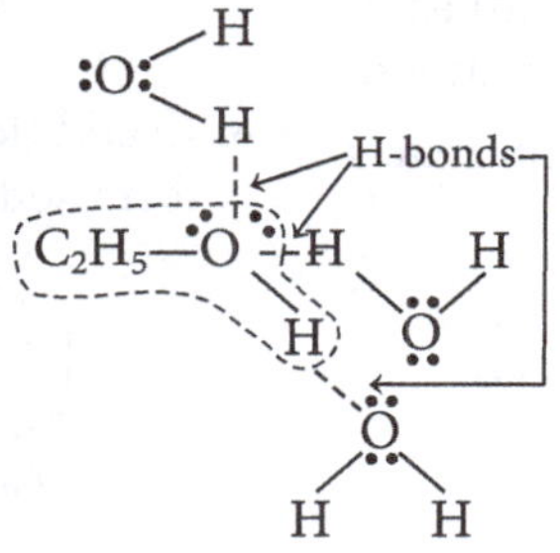

H-bonding between alcohol and water molecules

- Solubility decreases with increase in size of alkyl/aryl (i.e. hydrophobic) groups.
- Solubility of isomeric alcohols increases with branching due to decrease in surface area of hydrophobic part.

Quick Test 1

1. Classify the following as primary, secondary and tertiary alcohols.

(i) $CH_3—C(CH_3)_2—CH_2OH$

(ii) $H_2C{=}CH—CH_2OH$

(iii) $CH_3—CH_2—CH_2—OH$

(iv) 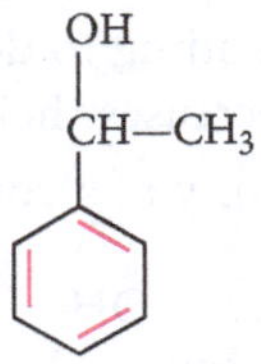

(v) 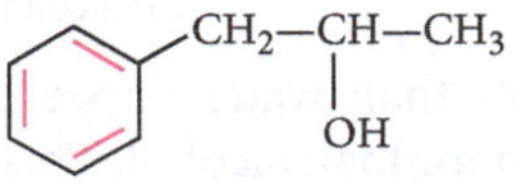

(vi) 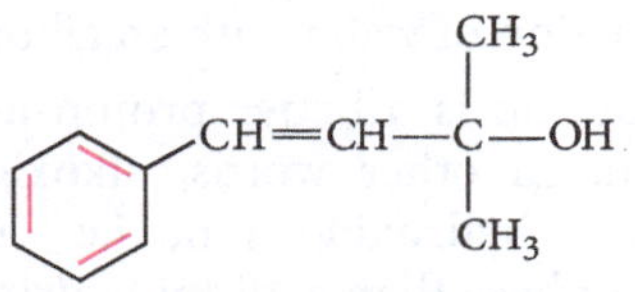

NCERT

2. Write the IUPAC name of the following compounds.

(i) $H_3C—C(CH_3){=}C(Br)—CH_2OH$

(ii) $HO—CH_2—CH(OH)—CH_2OH$

3. Write the mechanism of the following reaction.

$$CH_2{=}CH_2 + H_2O \xrightarrow{H^+} CH_3CH_2OH$$ CBSE 2023

Or

Write the mechanism of hydration of ethene to form ethanol. NCERT

4. Show how will you synthesise?

(i) 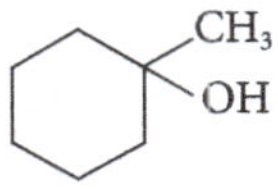 from a suitable alkene. CBSE 2023

(ii) 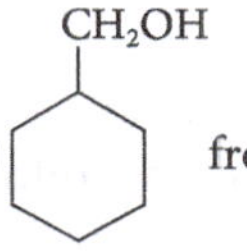 from methanal using a suitable Grignard reagent.

5. How will you convert

(i) Benzene to phenol?

(ii) Cumene hydroperoxide to phenol?

6. (i) Explain with reason :
Solubility of alcohols in water decreases with increase in molecular mass.

(ii) Complete the following reaction.

$$CH_3COOH \xrightarrow[H^+]{CH_3CH_2OH} 'A' \xrightarrow[\text{Catalyst}]{H_2/\text{Copper chromite}} 'B' + CH_3CH_2OH$$

For Solutions, See QR Code on Pg. 272

7.6 Chemical Reactions of Alcohols and Phenols

Alcohols are versatile compounds. They react both as nucleophiles and electrophiles in the following manner.

- **When bond between O—H is broken, alcohol reacts as nucleophiles.**

$$R-\ddot{O}-H + >C^+ \longrightarrow R-\overset{+}{O}(H)-\overset{|}{\underset{|}{C}}- \longrightarrow R-O-\overset{|}{\underset{|}{C}}- + H^+$$

Alcohol as nucleophile

- **When bond between C—O is broken, alcohols react as electrophiles.**

$$R-CH_2-OH + H^+ \longrightarrow RCH_2-\overset{+}{O}H_2$$

$$Br^- + \underset{R}{\underset{|}{CH_2}}-\overset{+}{O}H_2 \longrightarrow Br-\underset{R}{\underset{|}{CH_2}} + H_2O$$

Alcohol as electrophile

- **Based on the cleavage of O—H and C—O bonds,** the reactions of alcohols and phenols may be divided into following two groups.

I. Reactions Involving Cleavage of O—H Bond

Some typical reactions of alcohols and phenols involving the cleavage of O—H bond are as follows

Acidity of Alcohols and Phenols

(i) Reaction with Metals

- Alcohols and phenols react with active metals like Na, K, Al to produce corresponding alkoxides or phenoxides with the evolution of hydrogen gas.

$$\underset{\text{Alcohol}}{2R-O-H} + 2Na \longrightarrow \underset{\text{Sodium alkoxide}}{2R-\overset{-}{O}\overset{+}{Na}} + H_2\uparrow$$

$$\underset{\text{Ethyl alcohol}}{2CH_3-CH_2-OH} + 2Na \longrightarrow \underset{\text{Sodium ethoxide}}{2CH_3-CH_2-\overset{-}{O}\overset{+}{Na}} + H_2\uparrow$$

$$\underset{\textit{tert}\text{-butyl alcohol}}{6(CH_3)_3C-OH} + 2Al \longrightarrow \underset{\text{Aluminium } \textit{tert}\text{-butoxide}}{2[(CH_3)_3C-O)]_3Al} + 3H_2\uparrow$$

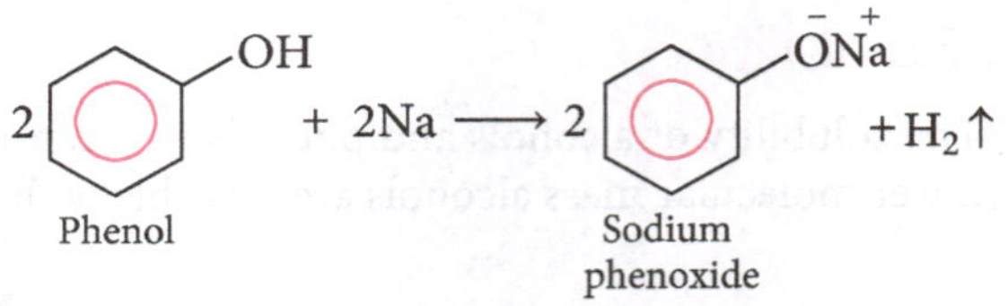

- In addition to this, phenol react with aqueous NaOH to form sodium phenoxide.

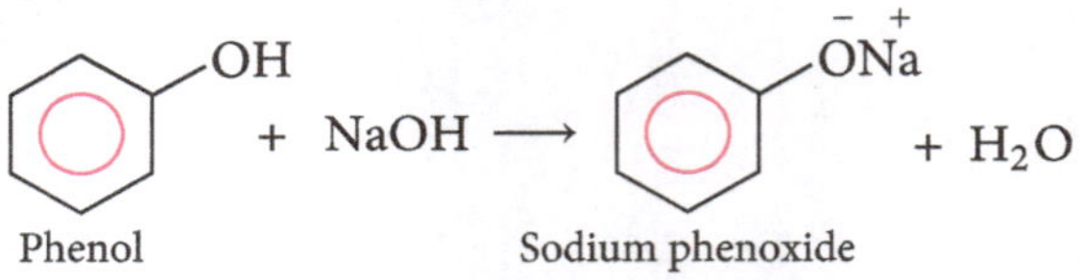

- All the above reactions show that alcohols and phenols are acidic in nature. Actually, alcohols and phenols are **Bronsted acids**, i.e. they can donate a proton to a stronger base (B:).

$$\underset{\text{Base}}{B:} + \underset{\text{Acid}}{H-\ddot{O}-R} \longrightarrow \underset{\text{Conjugate acid}}{B-H} + \underset{\text{Conjugate base}}{:\ddot{\overset{-}{O}}-R}$$

(ii) Acidity of Alcohols

Polar nature of O—H bond is responsible for the acidic character of alcohols. An electron releasing group (alkyl group, CH_3, C_2H_5) increases electron density on oxygen tending to decrease the polarity of O—H bond, which decreases their acidic strength.

Thus, acidity of alcohols decreases in the following order

$$\underset{(1°\text{alcohol})}{R\rightarrow CH_2-OH} > \underset{(2°\text{ alcohol})}{R_2CH-OH} >> \underset{(3°\text{ alcohol})}{RR'R''C-OH}$$

- Alcohols are weaker acids than water or we can say water is a better proton donor than alcohol. This can be illustrated by the reaction of water with an alkoxide.

  Conversely, alkoxide ion is a better proton acceptor than hydroxide ion. In other words, alkoxides are stronger bases than hydroxide ion, i.e., sodium ethoxide is a stronger base than sodium hydroxide.

$$\underset{\text{Base}}{R-\ddot{\overset{-}{O}}:} + \underset{\text{Acid}}{H-\ddot{O}-H} \longrightarrow \underset{\text{Conjugate acid}}{R-O-H} + \underset{\text{Conjugate base}}{:\ddot{\overset{-}{O}}H}$$

- In the presence of strong acids, alcohols act as **Bronsted bases** as well due to the presence of unshared electron pairs on oxygen, which makes them proton acceptors.

$$\underset{\text{Base}}{R-\ddot{O}-H} + \underset{\text{Acid}}{H_2SO_4} \longrightarrow \underset{\text{Protonated alcohol}}{R-\overset{+}{O}H_2} + HSO_4^-$$

(iii) Acidity of Phenols

- **Resonance effect** The reactions of phenol with metals such as Na, Al and sodium hydroxide indicate its acidic nature. In phenol, —OH group is directly attached to sp^2-hybridised carbon of benzene ring which acts as electron withdrawing group.

  Due to this, the lone pairs of electrons of —OH are involved in resonance with C-atom of benzene ring. This delocalisation of electrons (or resonance) can be represented as

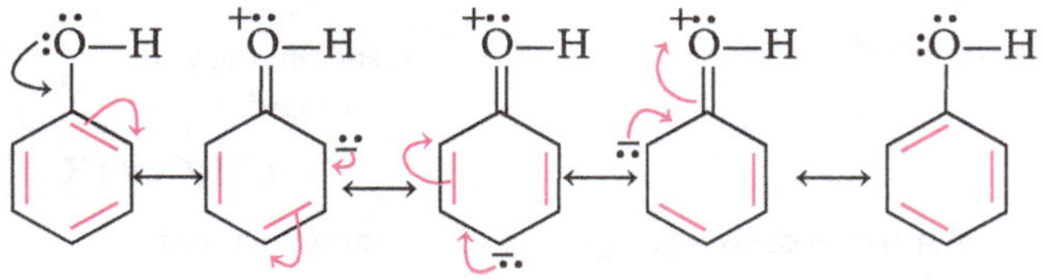

  This resonance imparts a partial positive charge on oxygen, weakening the O—H bond and facilitating proton release, thereby making phenols behave as Bronsted acids.

- **Comparison with alcohols** The reaction of phenol with aqueous NaOH indicates that phenols are strong acids than alcohols. A compound in which hydroxyl group. This is because the higher electronegativity of sp^2-hybridised carbon in phenol decreases electron density on oxygen, increasing the polarity of O—H bond and enhancing the ionisation of phenols compared to alcohols.
- **Phenoxide *vs* Alkoxide stability** In an alkoxide ion, the negative charge is localised on oxygen while in phenoxide ion, the charge is delocalised around aromatic ring. This delocalisation of negative charge makes phenoxide ion more stable and favours the ionisation of phenol.

$$R—\ddot{\underset{\cdot\cdot}{O}}—H \rightleftharpoons R—\ddot{\underset{\cdot\cdot}{O}}:^- + H^+$$

Alcohol   Alkoxide ion (not stabilised by resonance)

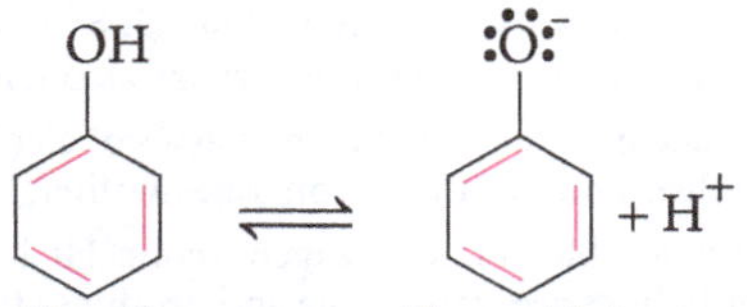

Phenol   Phenoxide ion

Phenol is less stable than phenoxide ion. It is because the resonating structures of phenol involves the separation of charges. Whereas phenoxide ion exists as a resonance hybrid of stable structures.

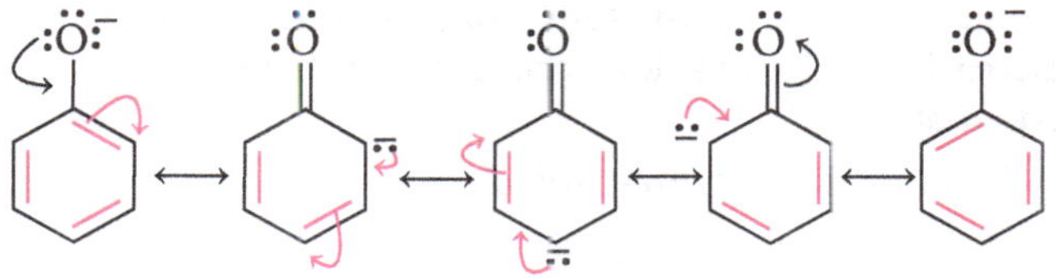

Effect of electron withdrawing group

- In substituted phenols, presence of electron withdrawing groups such as $—NO_2$, —CHO, COOH, —CN etc. stabilise the phenoxide ion by dispersing the negative charge and increase the acidic strength of phenols. The acidity of phenols further increases if these groups are attached at *ortho* and *para*-positions.
- *Ortho* and *para*-nitrophenols are more acidic than *meta*-nitrophenol. It is due to the effective delocalisation of negative charge in phenoxide ion. Further, *o*-nitrophenol is slightly less acidic than *p*-nitrophenol due to intramolecular H-bonding which makes loss of a proton more difficult.

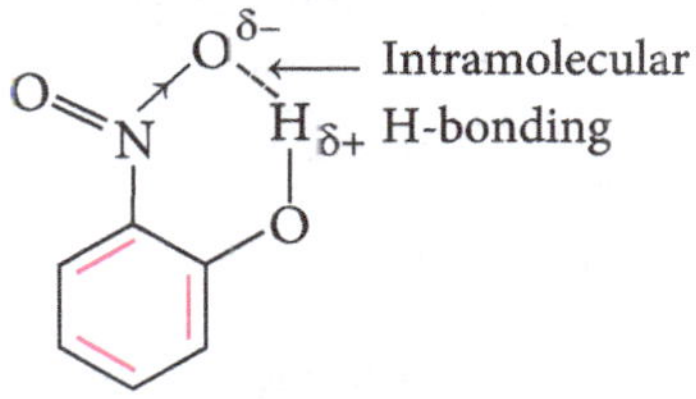

Effect of Electron Releasing Group

Presence of electron releasing groups such as —OR, $—NH_2$, $—NR_2$, alkyl groups in substituted phenols do not favour the formation of phenoxide ion. This result in decrease the acidic strength of phenol. That's why, cresols are less acidic than phenol.

pK_a Values of Some Phenols and Ethanol

Compound	Formula	pK_a
o-nitrophenol	*o*-$O_2N—C_6H_4—OH$	7.2
m-nitrophenol	*m*-$O_2N—C_6H_4—OH$	8.3
p-nitrophenol	*p*-$O_2N—C_6H_4—OH$	7.1
Phenol	$C_6H_5—OH$	10.0
o-cresol	*o*-$CH_3—C_6H_4—OH$	10.2
m-cresol	*m*-$CH_3—C_6H_4—OH$	10.1
p-cresol	*p*-$CH_3—C_6H_4—OH$	10.2
Ethanol	C_2H_5OH	15.9

Note Greater the pK_a value, weaker is the acid.

Example 4 **Arrange the following compounds in increasing order of acidity and give a suitable explanation.**

(i) Phenol, *o*-nitrophenol, *o*-cresol

(ii) H_2O, *ROH*, $HC{\equiv}CH$

Sol. (i) Due to $-I$ and $-R$ effect of $—NO_2$ group, *o*-nitrophenol is a stronger acid than phenol. On the other hand, $—CH_3$ group produces $+I$ effect. $-I$ and $-R$ effect increases the acidic strength by increasing the polarity of —OH bond, while $+I$ effect decreases the polarity due to increase in electron density on —OH bond. So, *o*-cresol is a weaker acid than phenol.

Thus, the correct acidity order is

o-cresol < phenol < *o*-nitrophenol.

(ii) A stronger acid displaces a weaker acid from its salt. When $RO^- \ Na^+$ is treated with H_2O, it forms *ROH*. So, water is a stronger acid than *ROH*.

$$\underset{\text{Stronger acid}}{HOH} + R\overset{-}{O}\overset{+}{Na} \longrightarrow NaOH + \underset{\text{Weaker acid}}{ROH}$$

Similarly, when sodium ethynide is treated with water and alcohol, then acetylene is obtained.

$$\underset{\text{Stronger acid}}{HOH} + CH\equiv \overset{-}{C}\overset{+}{N}a \longrightarrow \underset{\text{Weaker acid}}{HC\equiv CH} + NaOH$$

$$\underset{\text{Stronger acid}}{ROH} + HC\equiv \overset{-}{C}\overset{+}{Na} \longrightarrow HC\equiv CH + \underset{\text{Weaker acid}}{R\overset{-}{O}\overset{+}{Na}}$$

Thus, water and alcohol are stronger acid than ethyne. Therefore, the decreasing order of acidity of given compounds are

$$HOH > ROH > HC\equiv CH$$

Esterification

- Alcohols and phenols react with carboxylic acids, acid chlorides and acid anhydrides to form esters. (R' = alkyl or aryl group)

$$\underset{\text{Carboxylic acid}}{R'—COOH} + \underset{\text{Alcohol}}{R/Ar—OH} \underset{}{\overset{H^+}{\rightleftharpoons}} \underset{\text{Ester}}{R/Ar—COOR'} + H_2O$$

$$\underset{\text{Acid anhydride}}{(R'—CO)_2O} + R/Ar—OH \overset{H^+}{\rightleftharpoons} \underset{\text{Ester}}{R/Ar—COOR'} + R'—COOH$$

Both the above reactions are carried out in the presence of small amount of conc. H_2SO_4. Also, these reactions are reversible and hence water is removed as soon as it is formed.

- Reaction with acid chloride is carried out in the presence of pyridine (base) so as to neutralise HCl which is formed during the reaction. It shifts the equilibrium towards right hand side.

$$\underset{\text{Acyl chloride}}{R'—COCl} + \underset{\text{Alcohol}}{R/Ar—OH} \xrightarrow{\text{Pyridine}} \underset{\text{Ester}}{R/Ar—COOR'} + HCl$$

The introduction of acetyl ($CH_3CO—$) group in alcohols or phenols is known as **acetylation.**

- Acetylation of salicylic acid produces aspirin.

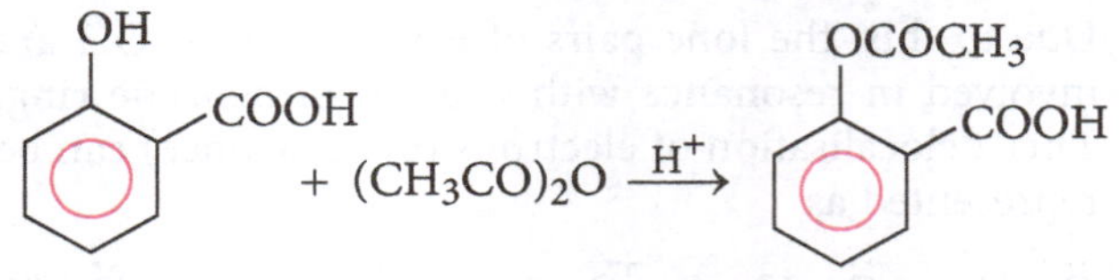

Salicylic acid

Acetylsalicylic acid (Aspirin)

$+ CH_3COOH$

Note **Aspirin** possesses analgesic, anti-inflammatory and antipyretic properties.

II. Reactions Involving Cleavage of (C—O) Bond

The reactions involving cleavage of C—O bond takes place only in alcohols. Phenols show this type of reaction only with Zn.

(i) Reaction with Hydrogen Halides

Alcohols react with hydrogen halides to form alkyl halides.

$$\underset{\text{Alcohol}}{R—OH} + H—X \longrightarrow \underset{\text{Alkyl halide}}{R—X} + H_2O$$

e.g. $$\underset{\text{Ethanol}}{C_2H_5OH} + HCl \xrightarrow[\text{ZnCl}_2]{\text{Anhydrous}} \underset{\text{Ethyl chloride}}{C_2H_5Cl} + H_2O$$

- The order of reactivity of various alcohols towards this reaction is tertiary > secondary > primary.
- Order of reactivity of hydrogen halides is

HI > HBr > HCl

Lucas Test

- This reaction is used as a test to distinguish between the three classes (primary, secondary, tertiary alcohols).
- The difference in reactivity of three classes of alcohols with conc. HCl distinguishes them from one another.
- Alcohols are soluble in Lucas reagent (conc. HCl + $ZnCl_2$) while their halides are immiscible and produces turbidity in solution.
- Tertiary alcohols produce turbidity immediately as they form halides easily. Secondary alcohols produce turbidity after 5 minutes, while primary alcohols do not produce turbidity at room temperature.

(ii) Reaction with Phosphorus Halides

Alcohols are converted to alkyl halides by reaction with phosphorus halides.

$$R—OH + PCl_5 \longrightarrow R—Cl + POCl_3 + HCl$$

$$3R—OH + PX_3 \longrightarrow 3R—X + H_3PO_3 \ (X = \text{Cl, Br or I})$$

(iii) Reaction with Thionyl Chloride ($SOCl_2$)

Alcohols on reacting with $SOCl_2$ in presence of pyridine form chloroalkanes.

$$R—OH + SOCl_2 \xrightarrow{\text{Pyridine}} RCl + SO_2\uparrow + HCl\uparrow$$

(iv) Dehydration

Alcohols undergo dehydration (i.e. removal of a molecule of water) to form alkenes on treatment with a protic acid such as H_2SO_4 or H_3PO_4 or catalysts such as anhydrous $ZnCl_2$ or Al_2O_3.

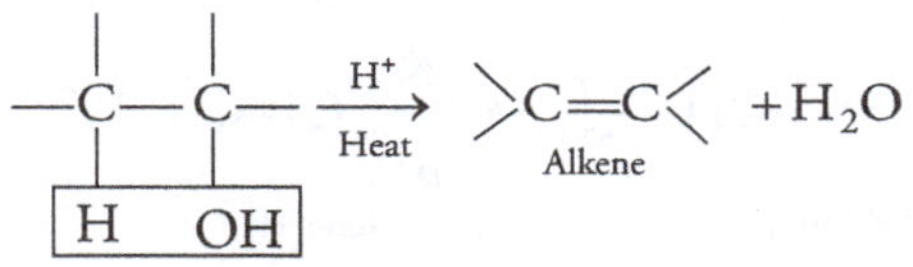

Ethanol undergoes dehydration by heating with conc. H_2SO_4 at 443 K.

$$\underset{\substack{\text{Ethyl alcohol} \\ (1^\circ \text{ alcohol})}}{CH_3—CH_2OH} \xrightarrow[\text{443 K}]{\text{Conc.} H_2SO_4} \underset{\text{Ethylene}}{CH_2=CH_2} + H_2O$$

Secondary and tertiary alcohols are dehydrated under milder conditions,

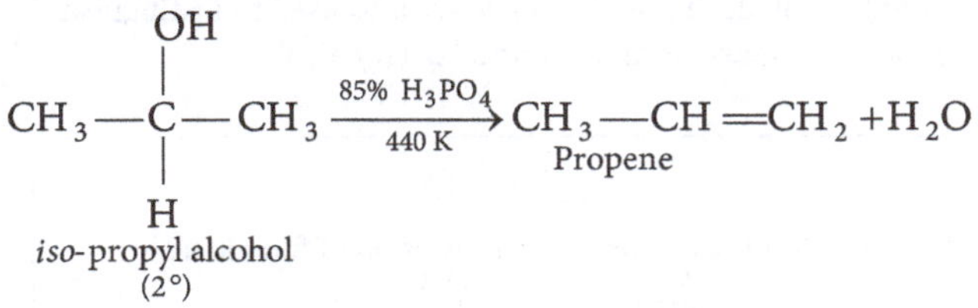

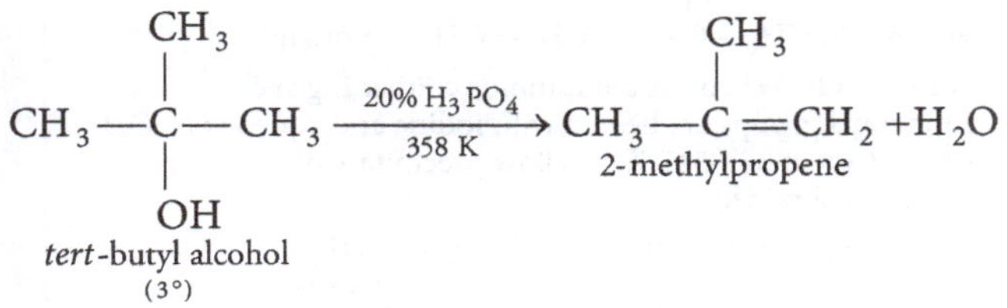

Note Order for ease of dehydration is 3° alcohol > 2° alcohol > 1° alcohol.

Tertiary carbocations are more stable and therefore, are easier to form than secondary and primary carbocations. Thus, tertiary alcohols are the easiest to dehydrate.

Mechanism

The mechanism of dehydration of ethanol involves the following steps

Step I Formation of protonated alcohol

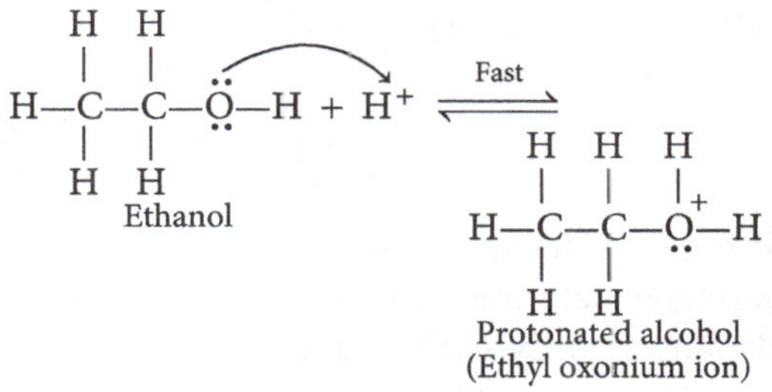

Step II Formation of carbocation

It is the slowest step and hence, it is the rate determining step of the reaction.

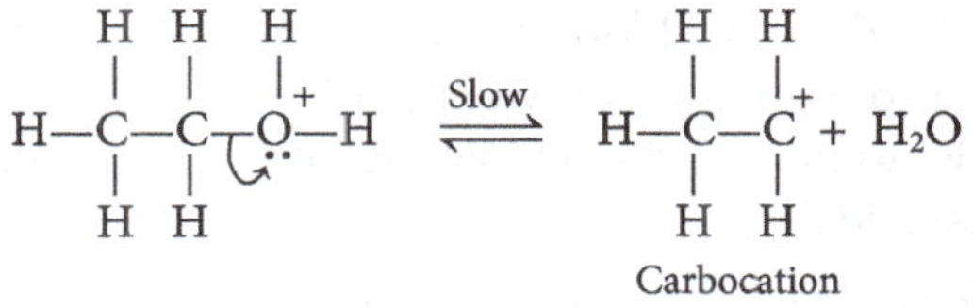

Step III Formation of ethene by the elimination of a proton

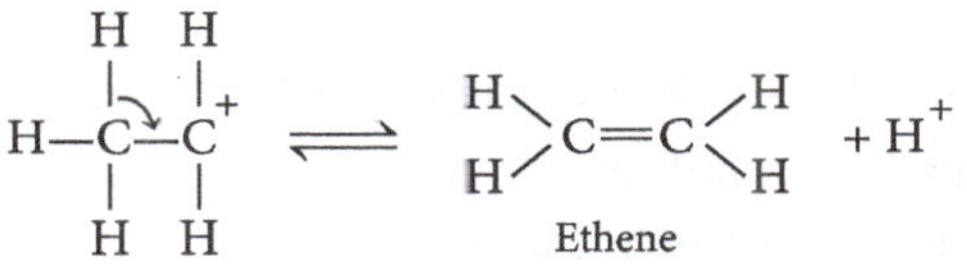

The acid used in step I is released in step III. To drive the equilibrium to the right, ethene is removed as it is formed.

(v) Oxidation

Oxidation of alcohols involves the formation of C=O bond with the cleavage of an O—H and C—H bonds.

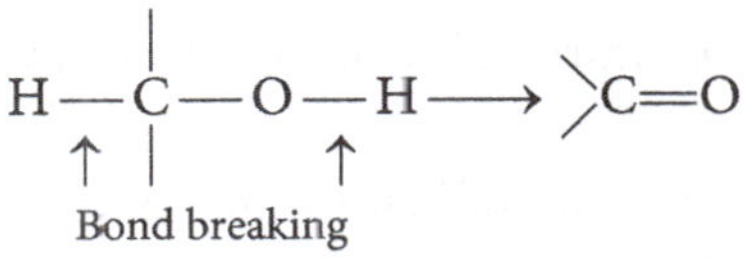

This reaction involves the loss of H_2 molecule from an alcohol molecule, therefore these reactions are known as **dehydrogenation reactions**.

Some reagents used to oxidise primary, secondary and tertiary alcohols are as follows

(a) Oxidation of Primary (1°) Alcohols

- Depending upon the oxidising agent used, a primary alcohol is oxidised to an aldehyde which in turn is oxidised to a carboxylic acid.

$$\underset{\text{Ethanol}}{CH_3—CH_2—OH} \xrightarrow[K_2Cr_2O_7/H_2SO_4]{[O]} \underset{\text{Acetaldehyde}}{CH_3CH{=}O} \xrightarrow{[O]} \underset{\text{Acetic acid}}{CH_3COOH}$$

- Strong oxidising agents like acidified potassium permanganate are used to get carboxylic acids from alcohols directly. CrO_3 in anhydrous medium is used as an oxidising agent for the isolation of aldehydes.

$$\underset{1°\text{ alcohol}}{RCH_2OH} \xrightarrow{CrO_3} \underset{\text{Aldehyde}}{RCHO}$$

- Pyridinium chlorochromate (PCC) is a complex of chromium trioxide with pyridine and HCl. This reagent is used for the oxidation of primary alcohols to aldehydes.

$$\underset{1°\text{ alcohol}}{CH_3—CH{=}CH—CH_2OH} \xrightarrow{PCC} \underset{\text{Crotonaldehyde}}{CH_3—CH{=}CH—CHO}$$

(b) Oxidation of Secondary (2°) Alcohols

Secondary alcohols are oxidised to ketones by using chromic anhydride (CrO_3).

$$\underset{2°\text{ alcohol}}{\begin{matrix}R' \\ R\end{matrix}\!\!>CH—OH} \xrightarrow{CrO_3} \underset{\text{Ketone}}{\begin{matrix}R' \\ R\end{matrix}\!\!>C{=}O}$$

(c) Oxidation of Tertiary (3°) Alcohols

Tertiary alcohols do not undergo oxidation reaction. But in the presence of strong oxidising agents such as acidified $K_2Cr_2O_7$ and acidified $KMnO_4$ and at elevated temperatures, cleavage of various C—C bonds takes place.

As a result, a mixture of ketone and an acid, each containing lesser number of carbon atoms than the original alcohol is obtained.

$$\underset{\substack{3°\text{ alcohol} \\ \textit{tert}\text{-butyl alcohol}}}{(CH_3)_3C—OH} \xrightarrow[-H_2O]{H^+} \underset{\textit{Iso}\text{-butylene}}{CH_3—\overset{\overset{CH_3}{|}}{C}{=}CH_2}$$

$$\xrightarrow{[O]} \underset{\text{Propanone}}{CH_3COCH_3} + \underset{\text{Methanoic acid}}{HCOOH}$$

$$HCOOH \xrightarrow{[O]} H_2O + CO_2\uparrow$$

(vi) Action of Heated Copper

When the vapours of a primary or secondary alcohols are passed over heated copper at 573 K, dehydrogenation takes place and an aldehyde or a ketone is formed, while tertiary alcohols undergo dehydration to form alkenes.

$$\underset{1°\text{ alcohol}}{R—CH_2—OH} \xrightarrow[573\text{ K}]{Cu} \underset{\text{Aldehyde}}{R—CHO} + H_2\uparrow$$

$$\underset{2°\text{ alcohol}}{\begin{matrix}R \\ R'\end{matrix}\!\!>CH—OH} \xrightarrow[573\text{ K}]{Cu} \underset{\text{Ketone}}{\begin{matrix}R \\ R'\end{matrix}\!\!>C{=}O} + H_2\uparrow$$

$$\underset{\substack{\text{(2-methyl propan-2-ol)} \\ 3°\text{ alcohol}}}{CH_3—\overset{\overset{CH_3}{|}}{\underset{\underset{OH}{|}}{C}}—CH_3} \xrightarrow[573\text{ K}]{Cu} \underset{\text{2-methylpropene}}{CH_3—\overset{\overset{CH_3}{|}}{C}{=}CH_2} + H_2O$$

TEACHER'S TIP

Reactions of alcohol with copper are also used to distinguish between primary, secondary and tertiary alcohols.

Iodoform Test

Iodoform test is used for the identification of functional groups like $CH_3—\overset{\overset{O}{\|}}{C}—$ and $CH_3—\overset{\overset{OH}{|}}{C}H—$ in organic compounds. When the compounds containing such functional groups are heated with iodine and aqueous NaOH or Na_2CO_3 at 333-343 K, a yellow precipitate of iodoform (CHI_3) is obtained.

e.g. $CH_3CH_2OH + 4I_2 + 6NaOH \xrightarrow{\Delta} \underset{\text{Iodoform}}{CHI_3\downarrow} + HCO\overset{-}{O}\overset{+}{N}a + 5NaI + 5H_2O$

$$CH_3OH + I_2 + NaOH \xrightarrow{\Delta} \text{No reaction}$$

Chemical Reactions of Alcohols (At a Glance)

$R\text{—}OH$ reacts with:

- Na → $R\text{—}O^-Na^+ + H_2\uparrow$
- $(CH_3)_3C\text{—}OH + Al$ → $2\,[(CH_3)_3C\text{—}O]_3\,Al + H_2\uparrow$
- HX/Anhyd. $ZnCl_2$, Δ → $R\text{—}X + H_2O$
- PX_3 → $R\text{—}X + H_3PO_3$
- PCl_5 → $R\text{—}Cl + POCl_3 + HCl$
- $SOCl_2$, Pyridine → $RCl + SO_2\uparrow + HCl\uparrow$
- $R'\text{—}COOH/(R'CO)_2O$, Conc. H_2SO_4/Δ → $RCOOR' + H_2O$
- $R'COCl$, Pyridine → $RCOOR' + HCl$
- 443K or Conc. H_2SO_4, Conc. H_2SO_4 → $>C=C< + H_2O$
- $KMnO_4/H^+$ or H^- or $K_2Cr_2O_7/H^+$ → $RCOOH$
- Cu/573K → $RCHO$ [From 1° alcohol], $RCOR$ [From 2° alcohol], Alkene [From 3° alcohol]

III. Reactions of Phenols

Following reactions are shown by phenols only.

(i) Electrophilic Aromatic Substitution

Phenols undergo electrophilic aromatic substitution reaction readily. This is because the lone pair present on oxygen is being shared with the benzene ring of phenol through **resonance**. As a result of which, the electron density at the benzene ring increases.

Hence, it becomes more reactive towards electrophilic substitution. Further, it directs the incoming group to *ortho* and *para*-positions in the ring as these positions become electron rich due to the **resonance effect**.

TEACHER'S TIP

The *ortho* and *para*-isomers can be separated by **steam distillation.** *o*-nitrophenol is steam volatile due to intramolecular H-bonding, while p-nitrophenol is less volatile due to association of molecules by intermolecular H-bonding.

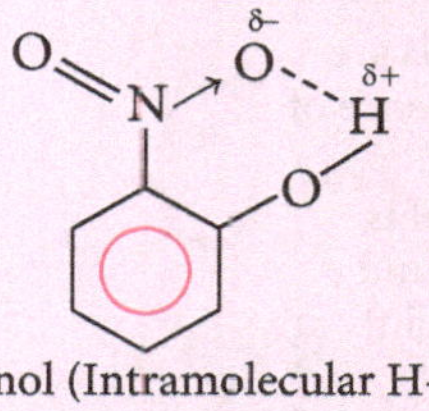

o-nitrophenol (Intramolecular H-bonding)

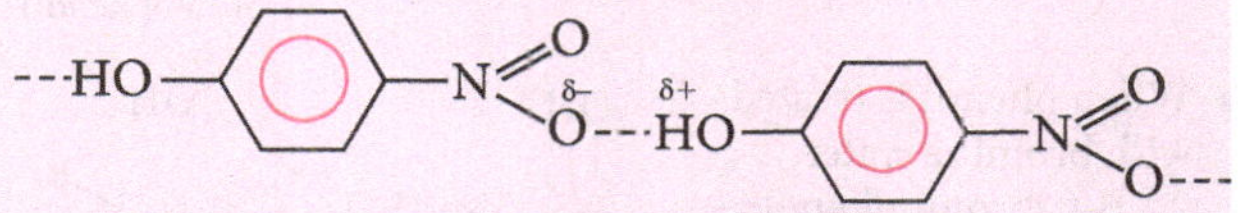

p-nitrophenol (Intermolecular H-bonding)

Common Electrophilic Aromatic Substitution Reactions

Types of Reactions	Reactions involved
A. Nitration • With dilute HNO_3 at low temperature, i.e. 298 K, phenol yields a mixture of *ortho* and *para*-nitrophenols. • With conc. HNO_3, phenol gives 2,4,6-trinitrophenol which is commonly known as **picric acid.**	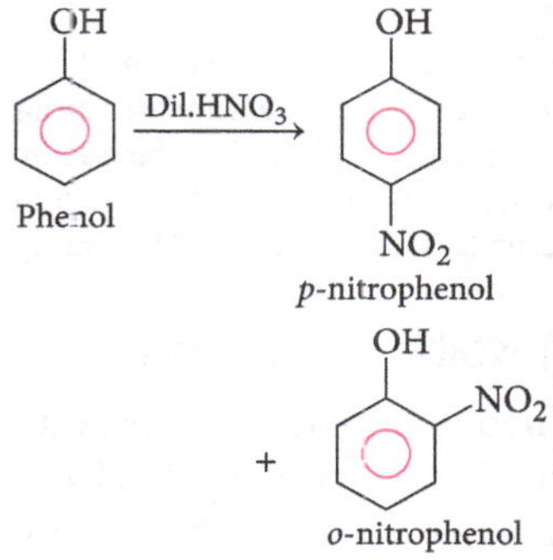
It is prepared by first treating phenol with conc. H_2SO_4 at 373 K to form phenol-2, 4-disulphonic acid and then with conc. HNO_3 to get picric acid.	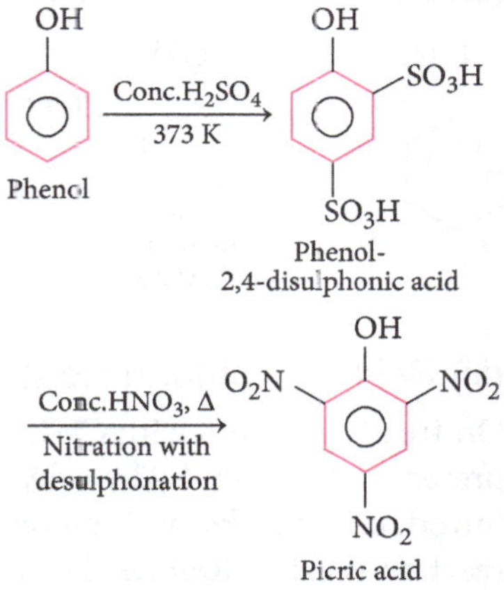

B. **Halogenation**

- When bromination is carried out in solvents of low polarity such as $CHCl_3$ or CS_2 at low temperature, monobromophenols are formed. In the presence of non-polar solvents, ionisation of phenol is greatly suppressed and ring is activated slightly at 1,4-positions.

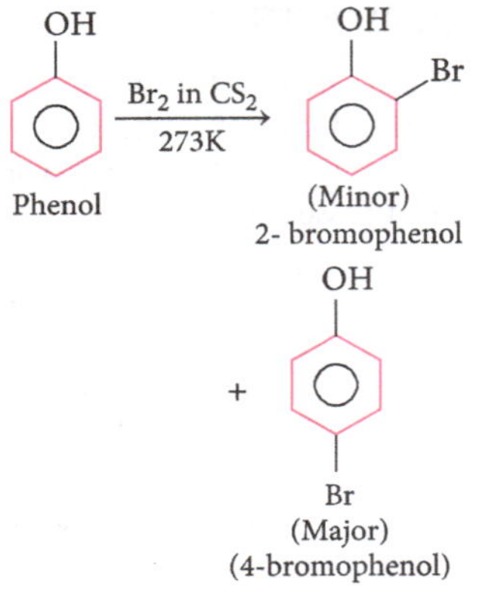

- When phenol is treated with bromine water, 2,4,6-tribromophenol is formed as white precipitate.

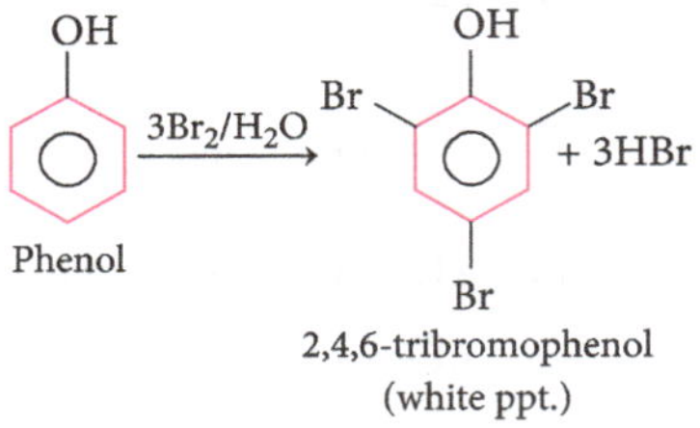

Note Usually, halogenation of benzene is carried out in the presence of Lewis acid which polarises the halogen molecule. But in case of phenol, polarisation of Br_2 molecule takes place even in the absence of Lewis acid because of the highly activating effect of —OH group.

(ii) Kolbe's Reaction

When phenoxide ion (produced by treating phenol with NaOH) undergoes electrophilic substitution with CO_2 (weak electrophile), *o*-hydroxybenzoic acid (salicylic acid) is formed as the main product.

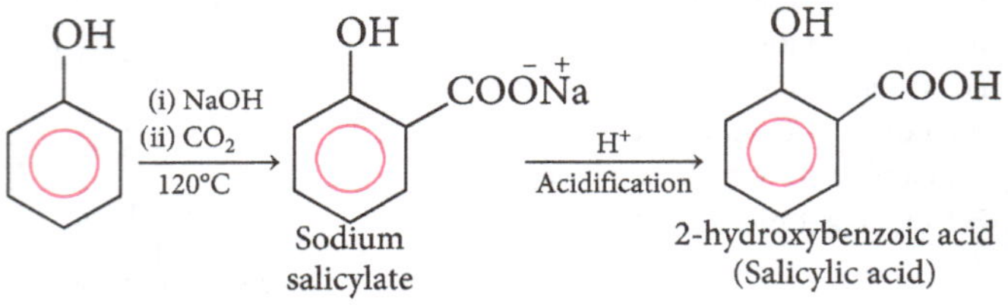

(iii) Reimer-Tiemann Reaction

On treating phenol with $CHCl_3$ (chloroform) in the presence of sodium hydroxide, a —CHO group is introduced at *ortho*-position of benzene ring. This reaction is called **Reimer-Tiemann reaction**.

In this reaction, electrophilic attack occurs by dichlorocarbene ($:CCl_2$), generated from chloroform. The intermediate formed is substituted benzal chloride which is further hydrolysed in the presence of alkali to produce salicylaldehyde.

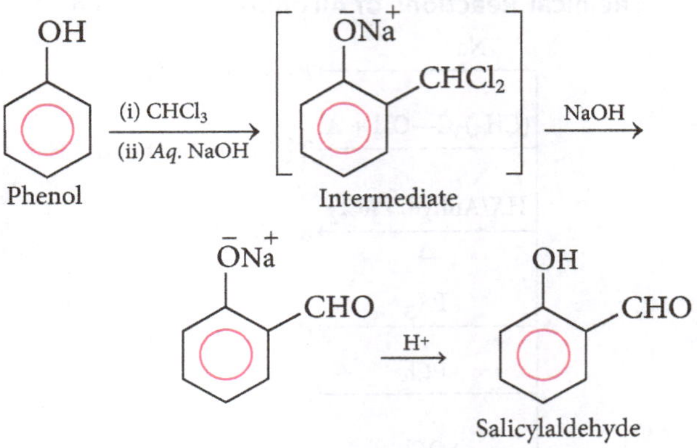

(iv) Reaction of Phenol with Zinc Dust

Phenol is converted to benzene on heating with zinc dust.

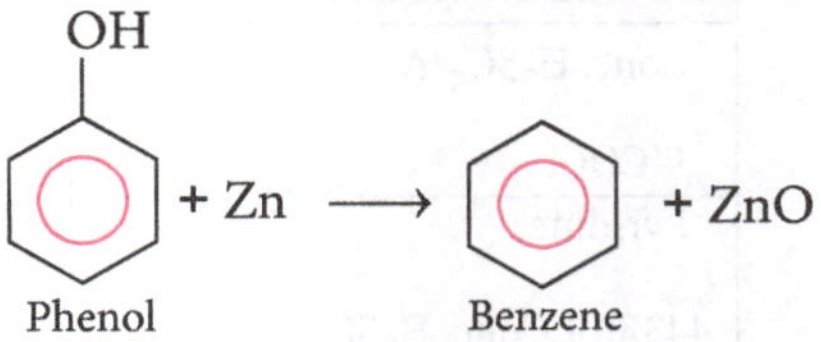

(v) Oxidation

Oxidation of phenol with chromic acid produces a conjugated diketone known as benzoquinone.

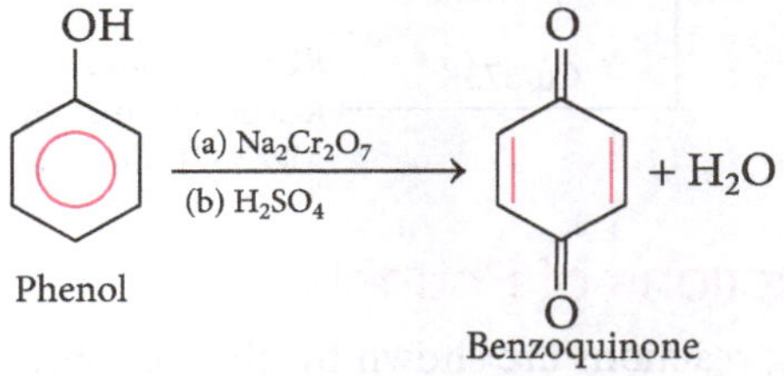

Note In the presence of air, phenol undergoes oxidation and gives dark-coloured mixtures containing quinones.

(vi) Ferric Chloride Test

Phenol gives a violet-coloured water soluble complex with ferric chloride.

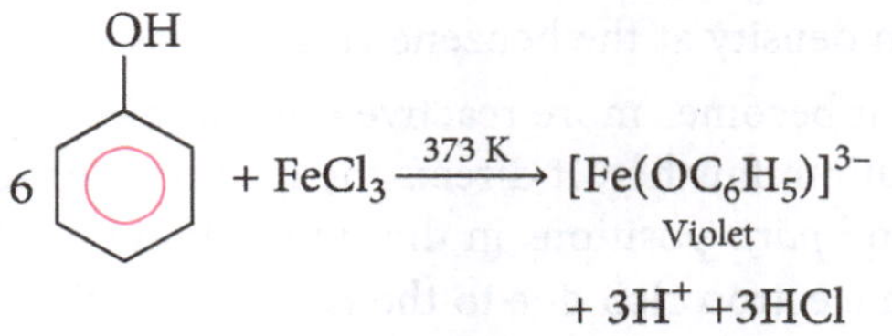

Note Generally, all compounds containing enolic group (=C—OH) respond to this test. However, the colours of complexes are different (such as green, blue, violet etc) and depend upon the structure of phenols.

Chemical Reactions of Phenols (At a Glance)

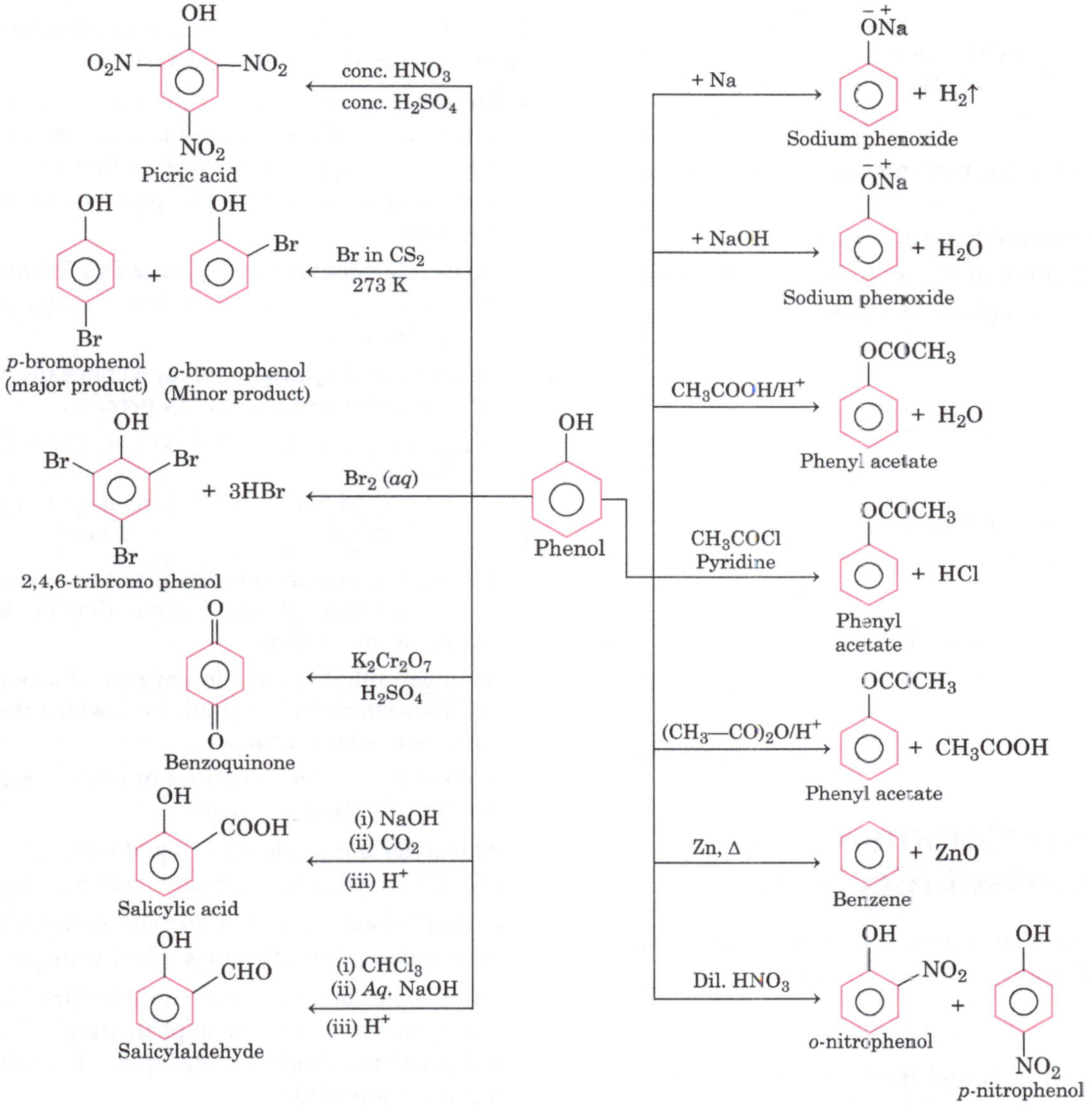

Example 5 **Complete the following reactions.**

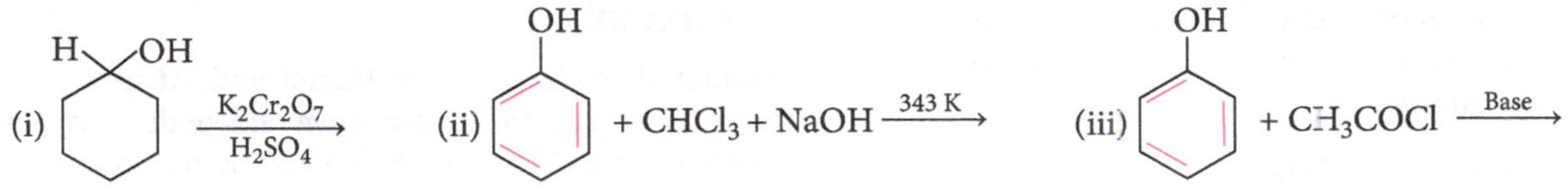

Sol.

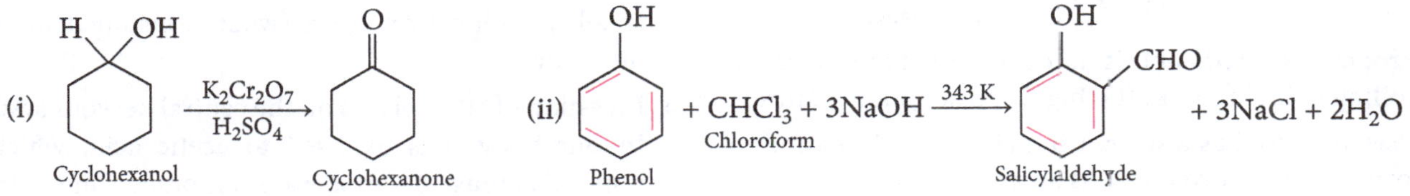

(iii)

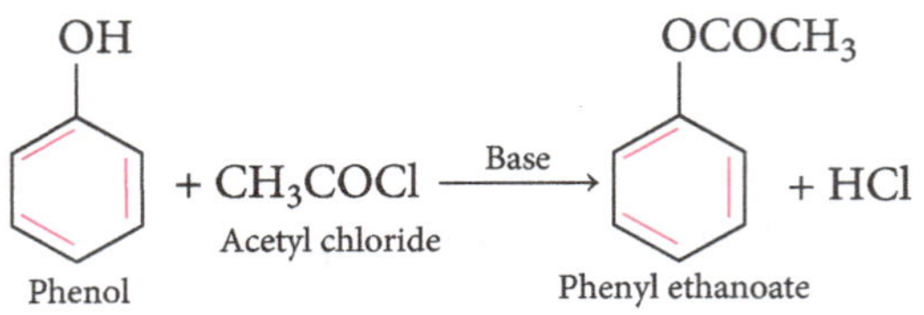

Example 6 **Name the reagents used in the following reactions.**

(i) Cyclohexanol to cyclohexene

(ii) Bromination of phenol to 2, 4, 6-tribromophenol

Sol. (i) Conc. phosphoric acid (H_3PO_4)

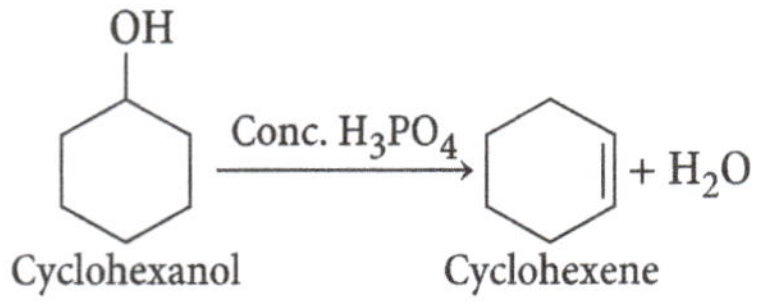

(ii) Bromine water [$Br_2(aq)$]

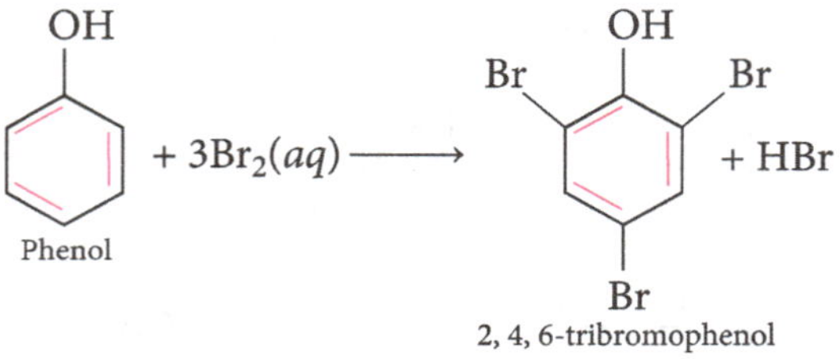

7.7 Some Commercially Important Alcohols

Methanol and ethanol are some of the commercially important alcohols. These are discussed below.

1. Methanol (CH_3OH)

It is also known as **'wood spirit'**, as earlier it was produced by the destructive distillation of wood.

- **Preparation** Now-a-days, methanol is produced by the catalytic hydrogenation of carbon monoxide at high pressure and temperature in the presence of $ZnO-Cr_2O_3$ catalyst.

$$\underset{}{CO + 2H_2} \xrightarrow[\substack{200-300\text{ atm} \\ 575-673\text{ K}}]{ZnO-Cr_2O_3} \underset{\substack{\text{Methyl alcohol} \\ \text{or Methanol}}}{CH_3-OH}$$

- **Properties** Methanol is a colourless liquid with a boiling point of 337 K. It is highly poisonous in nature.
- **Uses** It is used as a solvent in paints, varnishes and in formaldehyde formation, as an antioxidant.

2. Ethanol (C_2H_5OH)

Ethanol is a volatile, flammable, colourless liquid having chemical formula C_2H_5OH.

- **Preparation** It is obtained commercially by the fermentation of sugar present in molasses, sugarcane or fruits like grapes. This sugar is first converted into glucose and fructose in the presence of an enzyme invertase.

  Further, **fermentation** of glucose and fructose occurs in the presence of another enzyme, i.e. zymase which is found in yeast.

  The action of zymase is inhibited once the percentage of alcohol formed exceeds 14 percent.

$$\underset{\text{Sucrose}}{C_{12}H_{22}O_{11}} + H_2O \xrightarrow{\text{Invertase}} \underset{\text{Glucose}}{C_6H_{12}O_6} + \underset{\text{Fructose}}{C_6H_{12}O_6}$$

$$\underset{\substack{\text{Glucose} \\ \text{or Fructose}}}{C_6H_{12}O_6} \xrightarrow{\text{Zymase}} \underset{\text{Ethanol}}{2C_2H_5OH} + 2CO_2\uparrow$$

  Fermentation takes place in anaerobic conditions, i.e. in the absence of air. Carbon dioxide is released during fermentation.

  If air gets into fermentation mixture, the oxygen of air oxidises ethanol to ethanoic acid which destroys the taste of alcoholic drinks.

  Now-a-days, large quantities of ethanol are obtained by the hydration of ethene.

- **Properties** It is a colourless liquid with boiling point of 351 K. It has a pleasant odour and burning taste.
- **Uses** It is used as a solvent in paint industry and in wine making. 99% ethanol is called **absolute alcohol**.

  Commercial alcohol is made unfit for drinking by mixing in it some copper sulphate (to give it colour) and pyridine (a foul smelling liquid). It is known as **denaturation** of **alcohol**.

Physiological Effects of Methanol and Ethanol

- Biological oxidation of methanol and ethanol in the body produces their respective aldehyde and acid. Methanol oxidises to methanal and then to methanoic acid which can lead to blindness (when consumed in small quantities) or death (when consumed in large quantities).
- Ingestion of ethanol acts on the central nervous system. In our body it is oxidised to acetic acid, which is non-poisonous in moderate amounts and affects

judgement and lowers inhibition. However, higher concentration causes nausea and loss of consciousness. Even at higher concentrations it, interferes with spontaneous respiration and can be fatal.

Note Methanol poisoning is treated by administering diluted ethanol, which competes for the enzyme that oxidise methanol, giving the kidneys time to excrete it.

Quick Test 2

1. Suggest a reagent for the following conversion.

NCERT Exemplar

2. Predict the major product of acid catalysed dehydration of
(i) 1-methyl cyclohexanol (ii) butan-1-ol NCERT Intext

3. Name the reagent in the following reactions.
(i) Oxidation of primary alcohol to a carboxylic acid.
(ii) Oxidation of primary alcohol to an aldehyde.
(iii) Bromination of phenol to 2,4,6-tribromophenol.
(iv) Benzyl alcohol to benzoic acid.
(v) Dehydration of propan-2-ol to propene.
(vi) Butan-2-one to butan-2-ol. NCERT

4. Describe the chemical test to distinguish between ethanol and phenol.

5. Why do phenols not give the protonation reaction readily?

6. Predict the major product formed when phenol reacts with following reagents.
(i) Br_2 in CS_2 at 273 K (ii) $Na_2Cr_2O_7$ and H_2SO_4

For Solutions, See QR Code on Pg. 272

7.8 Ethers

Ethers are the organic compounds with general formula of $C_nH_{2n+2}O$ and characterised by an oxygen atom bonded to two alkyl or aryl groups. These are represented by general structure **R—O—R′** where R and R' may be alkyl or aryl group.

Ethers are obtained by the substitution of a hydrogen atom in a hydrocarbon (aliphatic/aromatic) by an alkoxy (O*R*)/aryloxy (OAr) group.

e.g. $\underset{\text{Alkane}}{R\text{—}H} \xrightarrow[-H]{+OR} \underset{\text{Ether}}{R\text{—}OR}$;

$Ar\text{—}H \xrightarrow[-H]{+OR} \underset{\text{Ether}}{Ar\text{—}O\text{—}R}$

Ethers can be classified as

(i) **Simple or symmetrical ethers** The ethers containing same alkyl or aryl groups attached to the oxygen atom are called simple or symmetrical ethers.

e.g. $\underset{\text{Dimethyl ether}}{CH_3OCH_3}$; $\underset{\text{Diethyl ether}}{C_2H_5OC_2H_5}$; $\underset{\text{Diphenyl ether}}{C_6H_5OC_6H_5}$

(ii) **Unsymmetrical ethers** The ethers containing different alkyl or aryl groups attached to the oxygen atom are called unsymmetrical ethers.

e.g. $\underset{\text{Methyl phenyl ether}}{C_6H_5\text{—}O\text{—}CH_3}$; $\underset{\text{Ethyl methyl ether}}{C_2H_5\text{—}O\text{—}CH_3}$;

$\underset{\text{Benzyl phenyl ether}}{C_6H_5\text{—}O\text{—}CH_2C_6H_5}$

Nomenclature

Common names of ethers are derived from the names of alkyl or aryl groups written as a separate word in an alphabetical order and adding the word 'ether' at the end. In case of symmetric ethers, the prefix '*di*' is attached before the name of the alkyl group.

In IUPAC system, ethers are named as alkoxy alkane. Larger alkyl group is considered as a part of alkane. While lower alkyl group is taken as ethereal oxygen and taken as alkoxy group. For example, $CH_3OC_2H_5$ is ethyl methyl ether.

Common and IUPAC Names of Some Ethers

Compound	Common name	IUPAC name
CH_3OCH_3	Dimethyl ether	Methoxymethane
$C_2H_5OC_2H_5$	Diethyl ether	Ethoxyethane
$CH_3O\overset{1}{C}H_2\overset{2}{C}H_2\overset{3}{C}H_3$	Methyl *n*-propyl ether	1-methoxypropane
$C_6H_5OCH_3$	Methyl phenyl ether (anisole)	Methoxybenzene
$C_6H_5O\overset{1}{C}H_2\overset{2}{C}H_3$	Ethyl phenyl ether (phenetole)	Ethoxybenzene
$C_6H_5O(CH_2)_6—CH_3$	Heptyl phenyl ether	1-phenoxyheptane
$CH_3O—\overset{2}{C}H(\,^{3}CH_3)—\overset{1}{C}H_3$	Methyl *iso*-propyl ether	2-methoxypropane
$C_6H_5—O—\overset{1}{C}H_2—\overset{2}{C}H_2—\overset{3}{C}H(CH_3)—\overset{4}{C}H_3$	Phenyl *iso*-pentyl ether	3-methylbutoxybenzene
$CH_3—O—\overset{1}{C}H_2—\overset{2}{C}H_2—OCH_3$	--	1, 2-dimethoxyethane
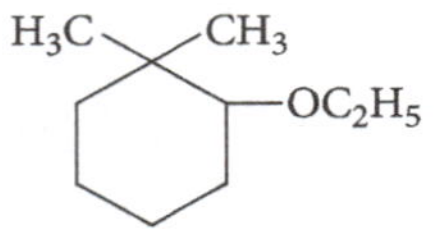	--	2-ethoxy-1,1-dimethylcyclohexane

Example 7 Write the IUPAC names of the following compounds

(i) $CH_3—O—CH_2—\underset{\displaystyle CH_3}{\underset{|}{CH}}—CH_3$

(ii) $C_6H_5—O—C_2H_5$

(iii) $C_6H_5—O—C_7H_{15}$

(iv) $CH_3—CH_2—O—\underset{\displaystyle CH_3}{\underset{|}{CH}}—CH_2CH_3$ **NCERT**

Sol. (i) 1-methoxy-2-methylpropane (ii) Ethoxybenzene
(iii) 1-phenoxyheptane (iv) 2-ethoxybutane

Example 8 Draw the structures of the compounds whose IUPAC names are as follows

(i) 1-ethoxypropane

(ii) 2-ethoxy-3-methylpentane **NCERT**

Sol. (i) $CH_3CH_2—O—CH_2CH_2—CH_3$

(ii) $CH_3—\underset{\displaystyle CH_3—CH_2O}{\underset{|}{CH}}—\underset{\displaystyle CH_3}{\underset{|}{CH}}—CH_2—CH_3$

Structure

- In ethers, the four electron pairs, i.e. the two bond pairs and two lone pairs of electrons on oxygen are arranged in approximate tetrahedral arrangement.
- The (C—O—C or $R—O—R'$) bond angle is slightly greater i.e. 111.7° than the tetrahedral angle because of the repulsive interaction between the two attached alkyl or aryl groups.
- Bulkier the alkyl groups, greater will be the repulsive interactions. Consequently, larger will be deviation in angle. The C—O bond length (141 pm) is almost the same as in alcohols.

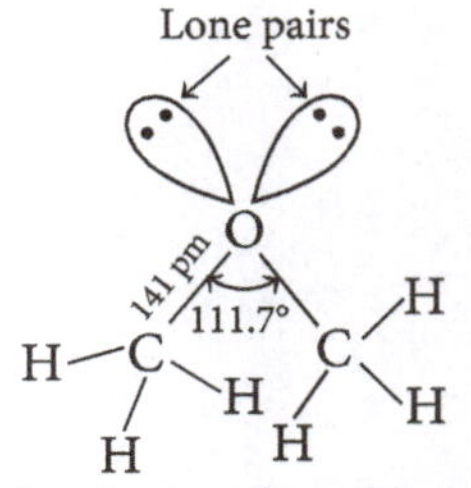

Structure of methoxymethane (Dimethyl ether)

Preparation

Ethers can be prepared by the following methods.

By Dehydration of Alcohols

- In this method excess of primary alcohol is heated with protic acid (conc. sulphuric acid) at 413 K to get symmetrical ethers.

$$\underset{\text{Ethanol (excess)}}{2CH_3CH_2OH} \xrightarrow[\text{413 K}]{\text{Conc. } H_2SO_4} \underset{\text{Ethoxyethane}}{C_2H_5OC_2H_5} + H_2O$$

- If in this reaction alcohol is not present in excess and the temperature is higher, then alcohol will preferably give alkene after dehydration.

  At 443 K, ethene is the main product.

$$\underset{\text{Ethanol}}{CH_3CH_2OH} \xrightarrow[\text{443 K}]{\text{Conc. } H_2SO_4} \underset{\text{Ethene}}{CH_2{=}CH_2} + H_2O$$

Mechanism

The formation of ether is a **nucleophilic bimolecular reaction**, (S_N2). It involves the attack of alcohol molecule on a protonated alcohol as shown below

Step I **Formation of proton** Dissociation of sulphuric acid into proton and bisulphate.

$$H_2SO_4 \rightleftharpoons H^+ + HSO_4^-$$

Step II **Protonation of alcohol** In this step, the alcohol(s) oxygen atom is protonated *via* an acid-base reaction. It leads to the formation of an **oxonium ion.**

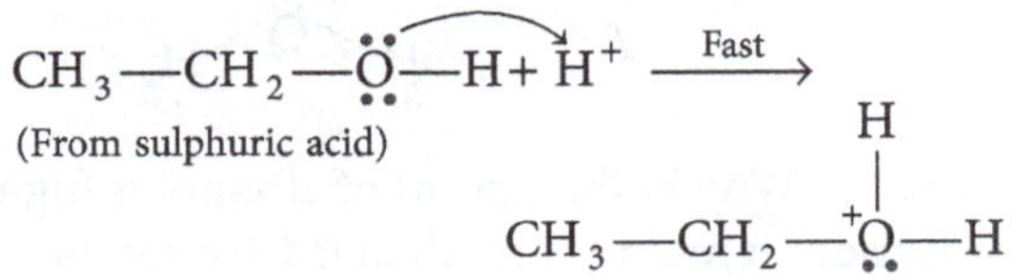
(An oxonium ion)

Step III **Nucleophilic attack by unprotonated alcohol molecule on protonated alcohol molecule.** In this step, the reaction between the carbocation and a second molecule of alcohol takes place. It also leads to the formation of another oxonium ion.

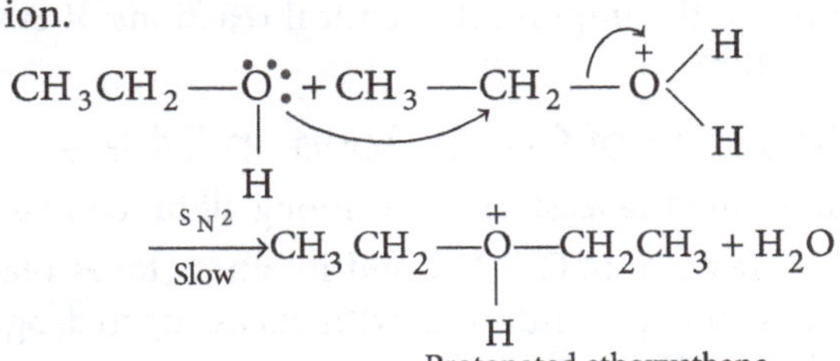
Protonated ethoxyethane (Oxonium ion)

Step IV **Loss of proton to form ethoxy ethane** The oxonium ion liberates a proton to yield the ether.

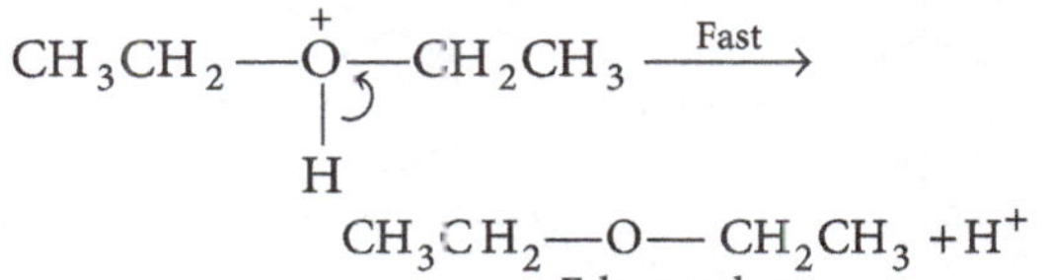
Ethoxy ethane

Limitations

- This method is suitable for the preparation of ethers having primary alkyl groups only.
- The alkyl group should be unhindered and the temperature should be kept low otherwise alkene is formed.
- The order of dehydration of alcohols leading to the formation of ethers follows the order 1° > 2° > 3° alcohols.

> **TEACHER'S TIP**
> The above reaction follows S_N1 pathway when the alcohol is secondary or tertiary.

Williamson's Synthesis

- This is one of the best and important laboratory methods for the preparation of symmetrical and unsymmetrical ethers.

  In this method, an alkyl halide is allowed to react with sodium alkoxide.

$$\underset{\text{Alkyl halide}}{R{-}X} + \underset{\text{Sodium alkoxide}}{R'{-}\ddot{\underset{..}{O}}\overset{+}{Na}} \longrightarrow \underset{\text{Ether}}{R{-}\ddot{\underset{..}{O}}{-}R'} + \underset{\text{Sodium halide}}{NaX}$$

- Ethers containing substituted alkyl groups (secondary or tertiary) may be prepared by this method. This reaction involves S_N2 attack of an alkoxide ion on primary alkyl halide. Better results are obtained, if the alkyl halide is primary and alkoxide is tertiary.

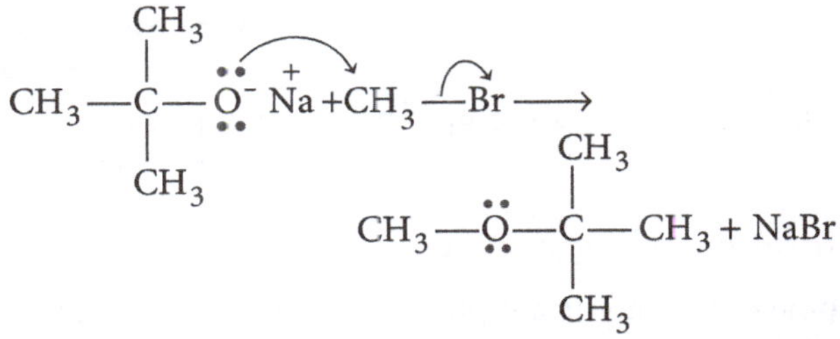
2-methoxy-2-methylpropane

- Phenols are also converted to ethers by this method. In this case, phenol is used as the phenoxide moiety.

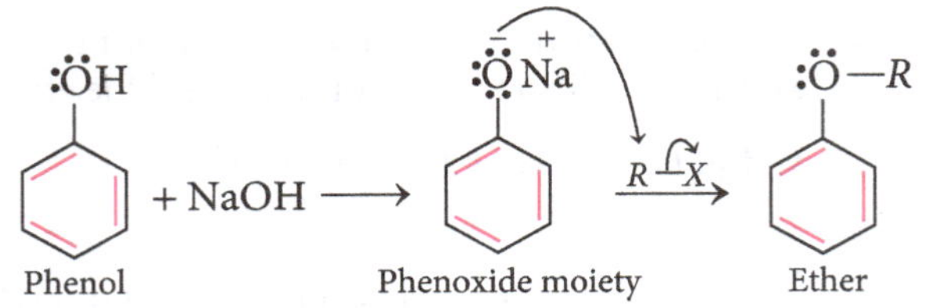

Limitations

- In case of 2° and 3° alkyl halides, due to steric hindrance, elimination competes over substitution and alkenes are formed. It is because alkoxides are not only nucleophiles but strong bases as well. These react with alkyl halides leading to the elimination reaction.

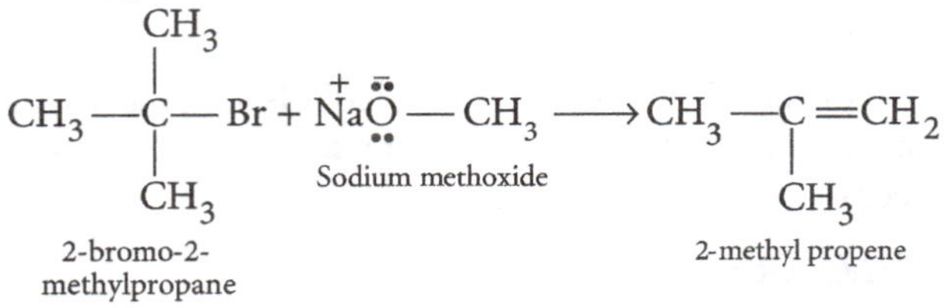

$+ CH_3OH + NaBr$

- Aryl halides have less reactivity towards nucleophilic substitution.

  Thus, aryl halide and sodium alkoxide cannot be used for preparing phenolic ethers.

  e.g. 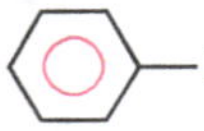 $—Br + CH_3\overset{-}{O}\overset{+}{Na} \longrightarrow$ No reaction

Example 9 **Write the names of reagents and equations for the preparation of the following ethers by Williamson's synthesis.**

(i) 2-methoxy-2-methylpropane

(ii) 1-methoxy ethane

Sol. (i)

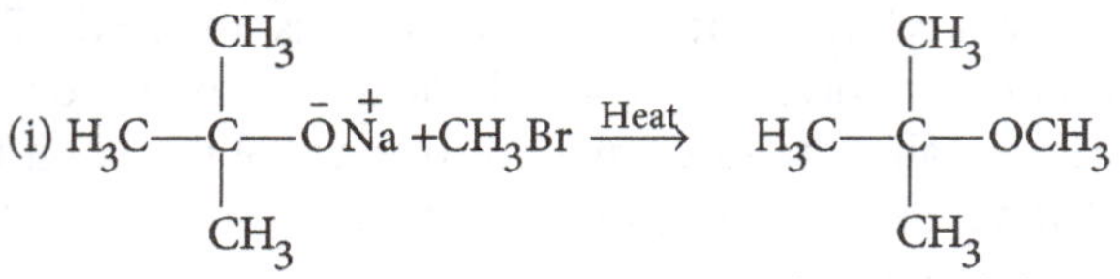

2-methoxy-2-methylpropane

+ NaBr

(ii) $CH_3CH_2\overset{-}{O}\overset{+}{Na} + CH_3Br \xrightarrow{\text{Heat}} CH_3CH_2OCH_3 + NaBr$
1-methoxy ethane

Physical Properties

Some of the important physical properties of ethers are as follows

(i) **Physical state** Dimethyl ether and ethyl methyl ethers are gases at ordinary temperature, whereas higher ones are liquids with characteristic smell.

(ii) **Dipole moment** The C—O bonds in ether molecules are polar in nature thus, its dipole moment is greater than zero.

(iii) **Boiling point** Boiling points of ether are much lower than the boiling points of isomeric alcohols due to the presence of H-bonding in alcohols. Further, the boiling points of ethers are comparable to alkanes of comparable molecular masses due to their low polarity.

Formula	Nomenclature	b.p./K
$CH_3(CH_2)_3CH_3$	*n*-pentane	309.1
$C_2H_5—O—C_2H_5$	Ethoxy ethane	307.6
$CH_3(CH_2)_3—OH$	Butan -1-ol	390

(iv) **Solubility** Lower ethers (upto three carbon atoms) are soluble in water and their miscibility with water resembles to those of alcohols of the same molecular mass.

Both ethoxyethane and butan-1-ol are miscible to almost the same extent, i.e. 7.5 and 9 g per 100 mL H_2O, respectively while pentane is essentially immiscible with H_2O. This is due to the fact that just like alcohols, oxygen of ether can also form H-bonds with the water molecule.

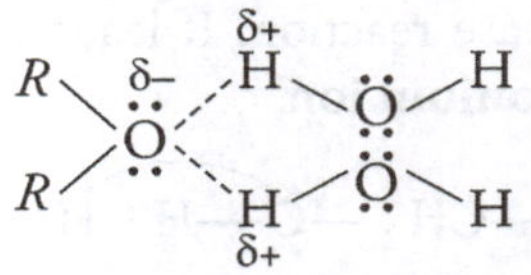

Example 10 **Why boiling point of ethanol is higher in comparison to methoxy methane? Give reason.**

Sol. It is because ethanol is associated with intermolecular H-bonding, therefore, ethanol has higher boiling point than that of methoxy methane which is not associated with intermolecular H-bonding.

Chemical Reactions

Some of the important chemical reactions of ethers are as follows

Cleavage of C— O Bond in Ethers

Ethers are the least reactive among all functional groups.

The cleavage of C—O bond in ethers takes place under drastic conditions with excess of hydrogen halides, HX.

(i) For Symmetrical Ethers

The C—O bond in the ethers can be cleaved by the use of halogen acid (like hydroiodic acid and hydrobromic acid) to give alkyl halide and alcohol.

$$\underset{\text{Ether}}{R\text{—O—}R} + HX \xrightarrow{373\,K} \underset{\text{Alcohol}}{ROH} + \underset{\text{Alkyl halide}}{RX}$$

If excess of halogen acid is used, then alcohol formed reacts further with halogen acid to produce alkyl halide.

$$\underset{\text{Alcohol}}{R\text{—OH}} + \underset{\text{(Excess)}}{HX} \xrightarrow{373\,K} \underset{\text{Alkyl halide}}{R\text{—}X} + H_2O$$

The order of reactivity of hydrogen halides is HI > HBr > HCl. The cleavage of ethers takes place with conc. HI or HBr at high temperature.

Note Diaryl ethers are not cleaved by HI.

(ii) For Unsymmetrical Ethers

Ethers with two different alkyl groups are also cleaved in the same manner. If primary and secondary alkyl groups are present, the alkyl halide is always formed from the smaller alkyl group.

e.g. $$CH_3\text{—}\underset{\substack{|\\CH_3}}{CH}\text{—O—}CH_3 + HI \longrightarrow CH_3I + CH_3\text{—}\underset{\substack{|\\CH_3}}{CHOH}$$

Mechanism

Reaction of an ether with conc. HI starts with protonation of ether molecule.

Step I Protonation of ether to form oxonium ion

$$CH_3\text{—}\ddot{\underset{..}{O}}\text{—}CH_2CH_3 + H\text{—}I \rightleftharpoons \underset{\text{Oxonium ion}}{CH_3\text{—}\overset{H}{\overset{|}{\underset{..}{O^+}}}\text{—}CH_2CH_3} + I^-$$

The reaction takes place with HI or HBr as these reagents are sufficiently acidic and Br^-/I^- are good nucleophiles.

Step II Iodide being a good nucleophile attacks the least substituted carbon of the oxonium ion formed in step I and it displaces an alcohol molecule by S_N2 mechanism.

Therefore, in the cleavage of mixed ethers with two different alkyl groups, the alcohol and alkyl iodide formed, depend on the nature of alkyl groups. When 1° and 2° alkyl groups are present, it is the lower alkyl group that forms alkyl iodide (S_N2 reaction).

$$I^- + CH_3\text{—}\overset{H}{\overset{|}{\underset{..}{O^+}}}\text{—}CH_2CH_3 \xrightarrow[\text{Slow}]{S_N2} \left[I\ldots CH_3\text{—}\overset{H}{\overset{|}{\underset{..}{O^+}}}\text{—}CH_2CH_3 \right]^- \longrightarrow CH_3\text{—}I + CH_3CH_2\text{—}OH$$

Step III If HI is in excess and the reaction is carried out at high temperature, ethanol reacts with another molecule of HI and is converted to ethyl iodide.

$$CH_3CH_2\text{—}\ddot{\underset{..}{O}}\text{—}H + H\text{—}I \rightleftharpoons CH_3CH_2\text{—}\overset{H}{\overset{|}{\underset{..}{O^+}}}H + I^-$$

$$I^- + \overset{CH_3}{\overset{|}{C}}H_2\text{—}\overset{+}{O}H_2 \longrightarrow CH_3CH_2I + H_2O$$

(iii) For Tertiary Ethers

When, one of the alkyl group is a tertiary group, then halide formed is tertiary halide and primary alkyl group converts into alcohol.

$$\underset{\textit{tert}\text{-butyl methyl ether}}{CH_3\text{—}\underset{\substack{|\\CH_3}}{\overset{\substack{CH_3\\|}}{C}}\text{—}OCH_3} + HI \xrightarrow{373\,K} \underset{\textit{tert}\text{-butyl iodide}}{CH_3\text{—}\underset{\substack{|\\CH_3}}{\overset{\substack{CH_3\\|}}{C}}\text{—}I} + \underset{\text{Methyl alcohol}}{CH_3OH}$$

This reaction follows S_N1 mechanism. This is due to the formation of a more stable carbocation, $(CH_3)_3C^+$ with the departure of leaving group, CH_3—OH.

Mechanism

Step I

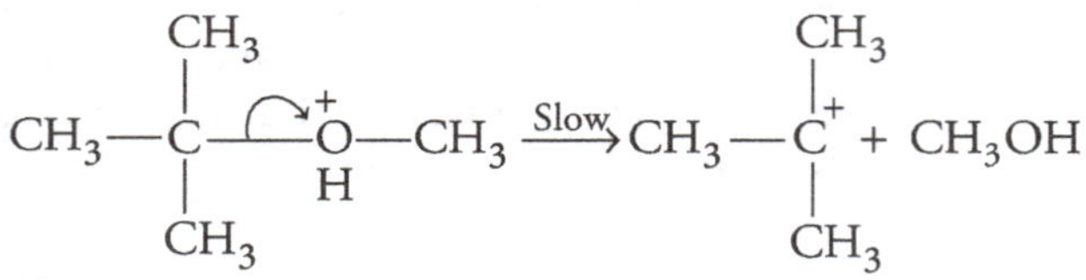

Step II

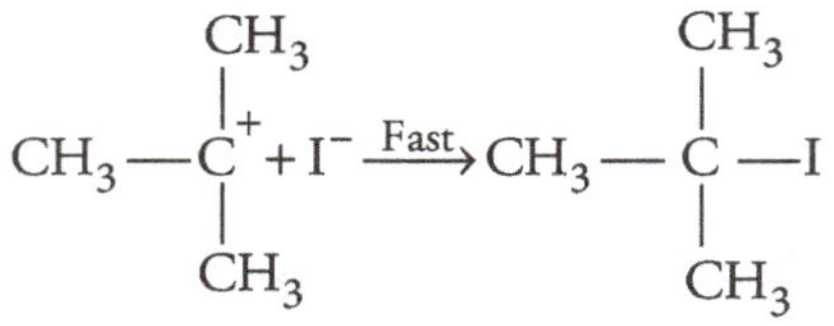

(iv) For Alkyl Aryl Ethers

In case of alkyl aryl ethers such as in anisole, methyl phenyl oxonium ion is formed by the protonation of ether.

The bond between O—CH_3 is weaker than the bond between O—C_6H_5 because the carbon of phenyl group is sp^2-hybridised and there is a partial double bond character. Thus, the reaction yields phenol and alkyl halide.

Phenol does not react further to give halides because sp^2-hybridised carbon of phenol cannot undergo nucleophilic substitution reaction required for conversion to halide.

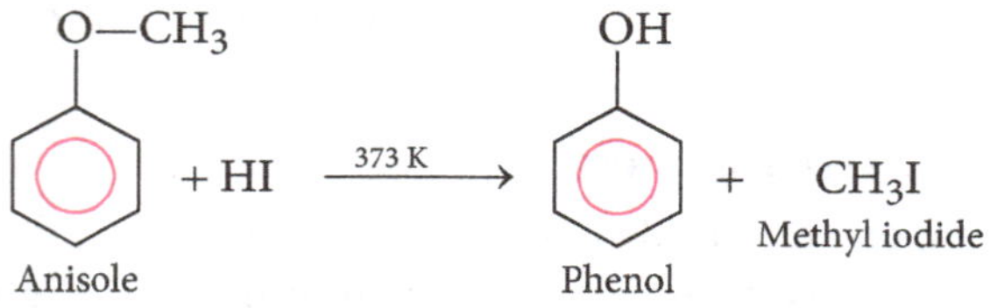

(v) For Benzyl Alkyl Ethers

In case of benzyl alkyl ethers, cleavage of C—O bond gives alkyl alcohol and benzyl halide through S_N1 mechanism because benzyl carbocation is more stable towards S_N1 mechanism.

Electrophilic Substitution Reaction of Aromatic Ethers

Alkoxy group (—O*R*) is *ortho, para*-directing and activates the aromatic ring towards electrophilic substitution. It directs the incoming electrophile at *o*-and *p*-positions.

This is because of the presence of the negative charges at *o*-and *p*-positions indicate the more electron density at these positions.

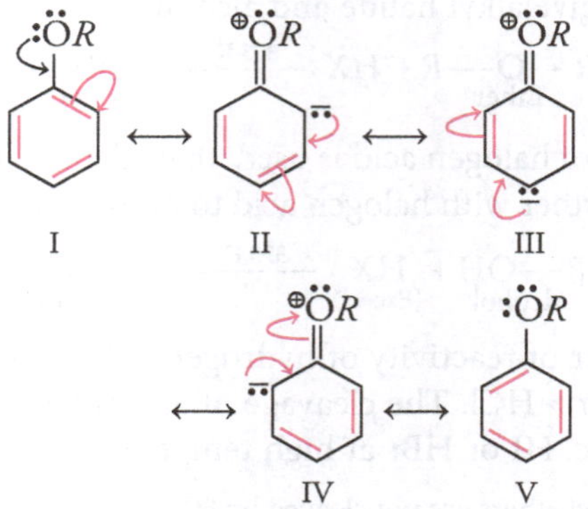

Important electrophilic substitution reactions are as follows

(i) Halogenation

Phenylalkyl ethers undergo usual halogenation in the benzene ring, e.g. anisole (methyl phenyl ether) undergoes bromination with bromine in the presence of ethanoic acid even in the absence of iron (III) bromide catalyst. It is due to the activation of benzene ring by the methoxy group.

Halide group is introduced at *o*-and *p*-positions of the ring. *p*-isomer is obtained in 90% yield.

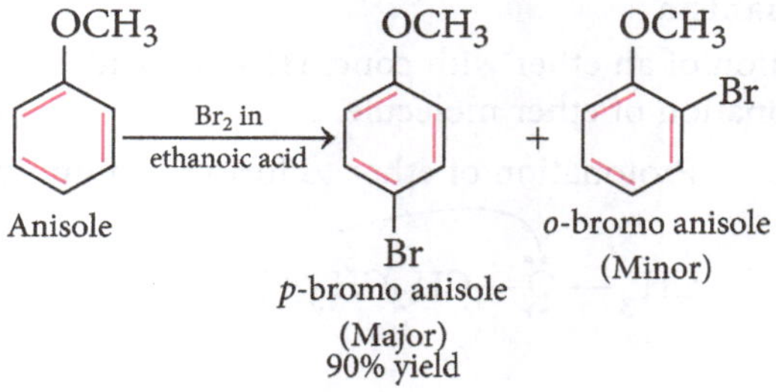

(ii) Friedel-Crafts Reaction

Anisole undergoes Friedel-Crafts reaction, i.e. the alkyl and acyl groups are introduced at *o*- and *p*-positions by reaction with alkyl and acyl halides in the presence of anhydrous aluminium chloride (a Lewis acid) as catalyst.

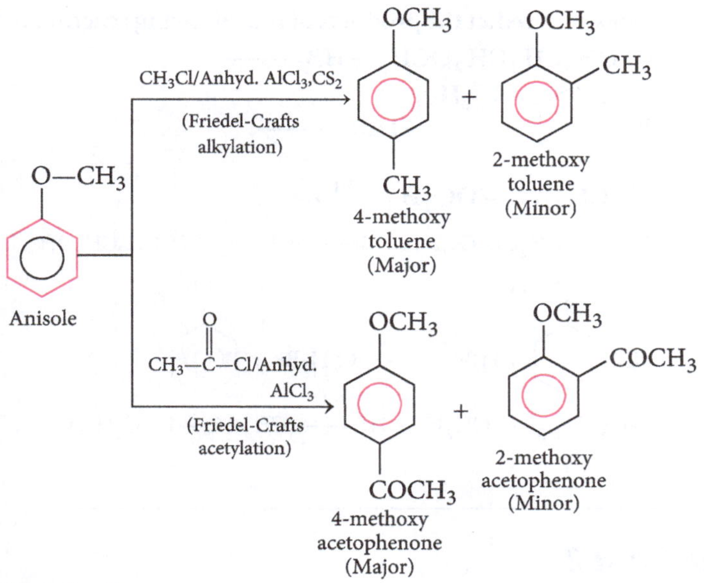

(iii) Nitration

Anisole reacts with a mixture of concentrated sulphuric acid and nitric acids to yield a mixture of *ortho* and *para* nitroanisole.

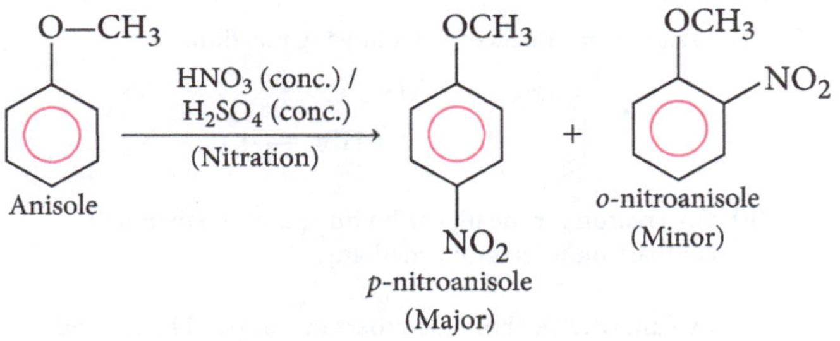

Chemical Reactions of Ethers (At a Glance)

(i) **Aliphatic Ethers**

$$R-O-R \xrightarrow[373\ K]{HX} \underset{\text{Alcohol}}{ROH} + \underset{\text{Alkyl halide}}{RX}$$

(ii) **Aromatic Ethers**

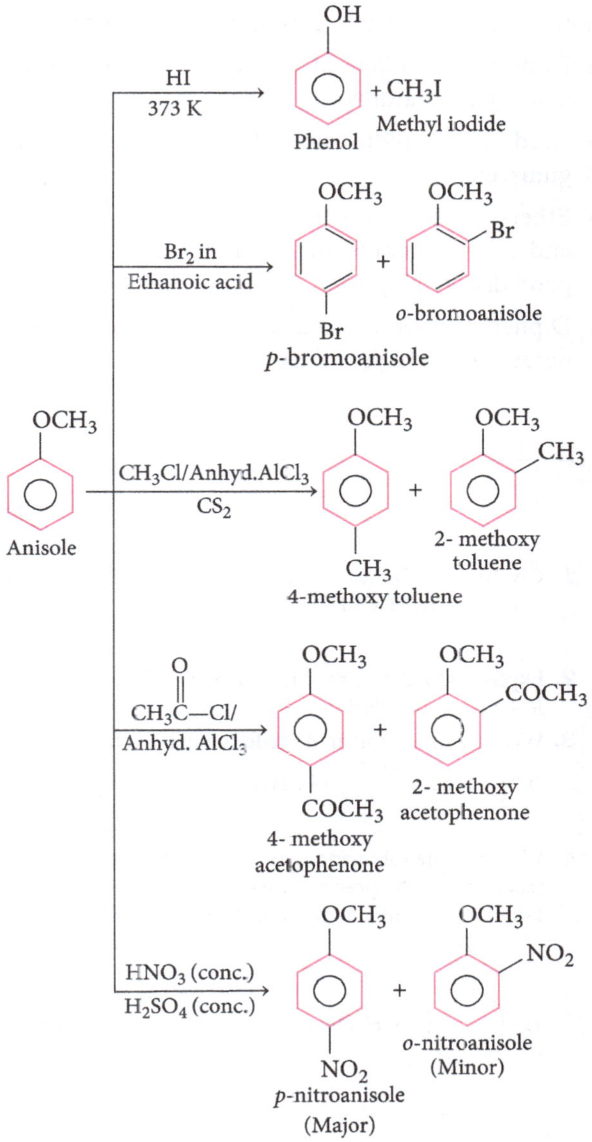

Uses of Ethers

Some of the important uses of ethers are as follows

- Dimethyl ether is used as refrigerant and as solvent at low temperatures.
- Used as an industrial solutions for oils, resins, gums, etc.
- Ethers are used as extracting solvents in laboratory and industry because of their almost inert nature and good dissolving power.
- Diphenyl ether is used as heat transfer medium because of its high boiling point.

Example 11 **Predict the products of the following reactions**

(i) $CH_3CH_2CH_2OCH_3 + HBr \longrightarrow$

(ii) 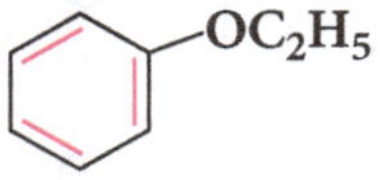

+ HBr $\longrightarrow$

(iii) $(CH_3)_3C—OC_2H_5 \xrightarrow{HI}$

Sol. (i) $CH_3CH_2CH_2OCH_3 + HBr \longrightarrow CH_3Br + CH_3CH_2CH_2OH$

(ii) 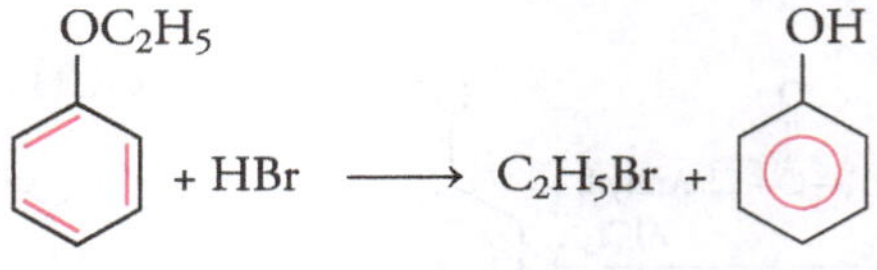

(iii) $(CH_3)_3C—OC_2H_5 + HI \longrightarrow (CH_3)_3C—I + C_2H_5OH$

Quick Test 3

1. Give IUPAC names of the following ethers : NCERT
   (i) $CH_3CH_2CH_2OCH_3$ (ii) $C_2H_5OCH_2—\underset{\underset{CH_3}{|}}{CH}—CH_3$
2. Explain why $O=C=O$ is non-polar, while $R—O—R$ is polar? NCERT Exemplar
3. Write the mechanism of the following reaction.
   $$2CH_3CH_2OH \xrightarrow[413\ K]{Conc.\ H_2SO_4} CH_3CH_2—O—CH_2—CH_3$$
   CBSE 2016, 2017C, 2023
4. Which of the following is an appropriate set of reactants for the preparation of 1-methoxy-4-nitrobenzene and why? NCERT Intext

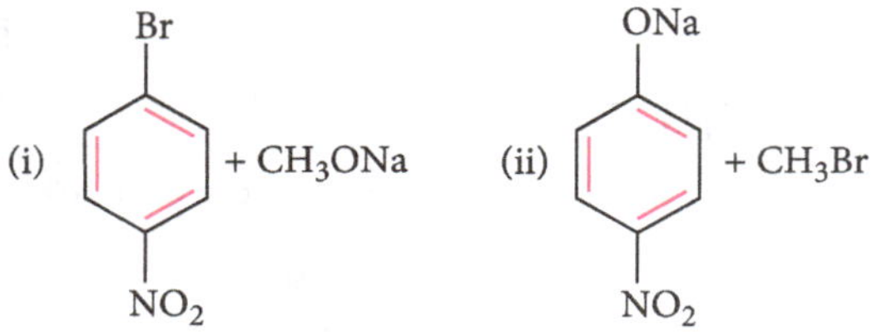

5. Illustrate with examples, the limitations of the Williamson's synthesis for the preparation of certain types of ethers. NCERT
6. Write the mechanism of the reaction of HI with methoxy methane. NCERT, CBSE 2017 C
7. (i) Write the products of the following reaction.

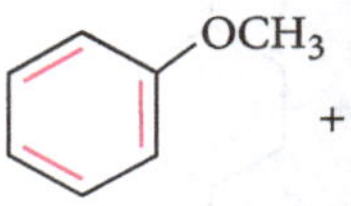

$+ HBr \longrightarrow$

CBSE 2023

(ii) Give reason for the higher boiling point of ethanol in comparison to methoxy methane. NCERT

Or

Explain why alcohols and ethers of comparable molecular mass, have different boiling points? NCERT Exemplar

For Solutions, See QR Code on Pg. 272

Mind Map

ALCOHOLS, PHENOLS AND ETHERS

Methods of Preparation

1. Alcohols

(i) **Alkene** — H_2O/H^+ or $B_2H_6/H_2O_2,OH^-$ (Hydroboration-oxidation) → $R—OH$

(ii) **Aldehyde, ketone** — Ni/Pd or $NaBH_4$ → $R—OH$

(iii) **Carboxylic acid** — (a) $LiAlH_4$, (b) H_2O → $R—OH$

(iv) ***RMgX*** — $>C=O$ → $R—OH$

HCHO → 1° alcohol

Other aldehyde → 2° alcohol

Ketone → 3° alcohol

2. Phenols

(i) **Benzene** — (i) Oleum (ii) (a) NaOH, (b) H^+ → C_6H_5OH

(ii) **Chlorobenzene + NaOH** — 623 K, 300atm → C_6H_5OH

(iii) **Diazonium salt** — HCl; H_2O warm → C_6H_5OH

(iv) **Cumene** $[C_6H_5CH(CH_3)_2]$ — (i) O_2 (ii) H^+, H_2O → C_6H_5OH

3. Ethers

ROH — Dehydration → *ROR*

RX(1°) — RONa (Williamson's synthesis) → *ROR*

Physical Properties

Alcohols and Phenols

- Boiling point increases with molecular mass but decreases with branching.
- Solubility decreases with increase in molar mass or in size of alkyl/aryl groups.

Ethers

- C—O bonds are polar and dipole moment is greater than zero.
- Boiling points are comparable to alkanes of comparable molecular mass.
- Lower ethers (upto 3C-atoms) are soluble in water.

Nomenclature

Alcohols (*R* — OH)

- **Common name** Alkyl group + alcohol
- **IUPAC name** Replacing '*e*' of alkane with suffix 'ol'.

Phenols (C_6H_5OH)

- **Common name** *o*-, *p*- and *m*- terms are used.
- **IUPAC name** Dihydroxy derivatives as 1,2-,1,3-,1,4-benzendiols

Ethers (*R* — O — *R'*)

- **Common name** Alkyl/Aryl groups in alphabetical order followed by ether.
- **IUPAC name** Ethers are named as alkoxyl alkanes (larger part alkane and smaller part alkoxy group).

Chemical Properties

1. Alcohols

ROH:

- Na → *R*ONa (Acidity –1°>2°>3° alcohols)
- *R'*COOH, H^+ (Esterification) → *R'*COO*R* (Ester)
- HX; PCl_5 or $SOCl_2$ → *RX* or *R*Cl
- Conc. H_2SO_4 (Dehydration) → Alkene (more substituted)
- [O] → Aldehyde → Acid or ketone

2. Phenols

- Shows all the properties of aliphatic alcohols.
- Also exhibit following reactions:

C_6H_5OH:

- Dil. HNO_3 (Nitration) → *o*/*p*-Nitrophenol
- Conc. HNO_3 (Nitration) → Picric acid(2,4,6 trinitrophenol)
- Br_2 in CS_2 (Halogenation) → *o*/*p*-product
- Br_2 water → 2,4,6-Tribromophenol
- (i) NaOH (ii) CO_2,H^+ Kolbe's reaction → 2-Hydroxybenzoic acid (Salicylic acid)
- (i) $CHCl_3$+NaOH (ii) H^+ Reimer-Tiemann reaction → Salicylaldehyde
- Zn dust → C_6H_6
- (i) $Na_2Cr_2O_7$ (ii) H_2SO_4 → Benzoquinone

3. Ethers

R—O—R:

- HX → *RX* + *R'*OH
- (If $R = C_6H_5$) HX → C_6H_5OH + *R'X*
- Halogenation X_2 → *o*/*p*-haloanisole
- Friedel-Crafts reaction RCl or RCOCl → *o*/*p*-Methoxytoluene or *o*/*p*-Methoxy Acetophenone
- Nitration → *o*/*p*-nitroanisole

Commercially Important Alcohols

Methanol (CH_3OH)

- It is also known as wood spirit.
- It is used as solvent in paint, varnishes and making formaldehyde.

Ethanol

- It is used as a solvent in paint industry and preparation of number of carbon compounds.

EXAM PATTERN EXERCISE

Objective Type Questions

Multiple Choice Questions [MCQs]

[1 Mark]

1. Out of the following alkene, the one which will produce tertiary butyl alcohol on acid catalysed hydration is CBSE 2024

(a) $CH_3CH_2CH{=}CH_2$

(b) $CH_3CH{=}CH_2$

(c) $CH_3{-}CH{=}CH{-}CH_3$

(d) $(CH_3)_2C{=}CH_2$

2. What would be the reactant and reagent used to obtain 2, 4-dimethyl pentan-3-ol? CBSE SQP 2025

(a) Propanal and propyl magnesium bromide

(b) 3-methylbutanal and 2-methyl magnesium iodide

(c) 2-dimethylpropanone and methyl magnesium iodide

(d) 2-methylpropanal and *iso*-propyl magnesium iodide

3. A tertiary alcohol is obtained by the reaction of Grignard reagent with Diksha

(a) butanone (b) propanone

(c) acetone (d) All of these

4. Nucleophilic addition of Grignard reagent to ketones followed by hydrolysis with dilute acids forms CBSE 2024

(a) alkene

(b) primary alcohol

(c) tertiary alcohol

(d) secondary alcohol

5. Select the incorrect statement about hydroboration oxidation reaction.

(a) Addition is against Markovnikov's rule.

(b) Intermediate is a carbocation.

(c) It does not involve rearrangement.

(d) Alcohol is obtained in excellent yield.

6. For conversion of propene into 1- propanol, which of the following reagents and conditions should be used ?

(a) Conc. H_2SO_4; H_2O and heat

(b) B_2H_6; H_2O_2 / OH^-

(c) Dil. H_2SO_4

(d) H_2O / H^+

7. Monochlorination of toluene in sunlight followed by hydrolysis with *aq.* NaOH yields .... NCERT Exemplar

(a) *o*-cresol (b) *m*-cresol

(c) *p*-cresol (d) benzyl alcohol

8. Arnav when reacted aniline with sodium nitrite and hydrochloric acid at certain temperature, a compound formed. This compound further gives phenol on reaction with Competency Based Que.

(a) C_2H_5OH (b) H_2O

(c) KOH (d) $Ca(OH)_2$

9. The boiling points of four compounds, an ether, an aldehyde, an alcohol and a haloalkane of comparable molecular weights, are given (not necessarily in the same order) in the table below. Competency Based Que.

Compound	Boiling point
P	35°C
Q	76°C
R	47°C
S	118°C

Identify, which of the following compound is the alcohol?

(a) *P* (b) *Q*

(c) *R* (d) *S*

10. Which is the correct order of acid strength from the following? CBSE 2025

(a) $C_6H_5OH > H_2O > ROH$

(b) $C_6H_5OH > ROH > H_2O$

(c) $ROH > C_6H_5OH > H_2O$

(d) $H_2O > C_6H_5OH > ROH$

11. Which of the following species can act as the strongest base? CBSE 2024

(a) OH^- (b) $C_6H_5O^-$

(c) RO^- (d)

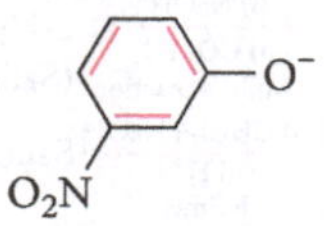

12. Mark the correct order of decreasing acid strength of the following compounds.

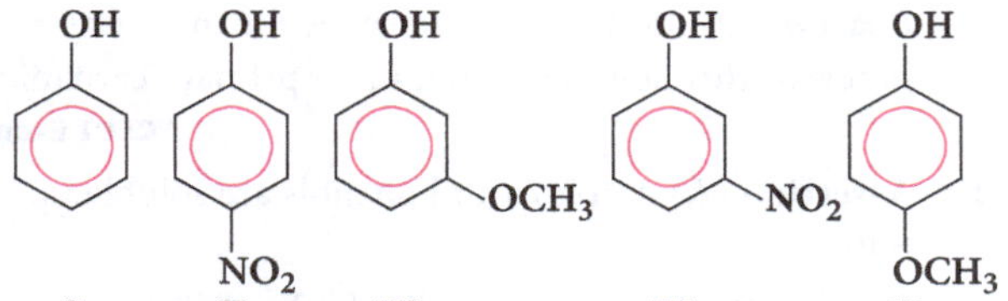

I II III IV V

NCERT Exemplar

(a) V > IV > II > I > III
(b) II > IV > I > III > V
(c) IV > V > III > II > I
(d) V > IV > III > II > I

13. On oxidation, an alcohol gave a product *X* which reduces Tollen's reagent. Which of the following could the alcohols be? **Competency Based Que.**

I. $CH_3—CH_2—CH_2OH$
II. $CH_3—CH_2—CHOH—CH_3$
III. $CH_3—CH_2—C(CH_3)_2—OH$

(a) Only I (b) Only I and II
(c) Only II and III (d) Any of I, II and III

14. A compond (*X*) with the molecular formula C_3H_8O can be oxidised to another compound (*Y*) whose molecular formula is $C_3H_6O_2$. The compound (*X*) may be **CBSE 2021 (Term I)**

(a) $CH_3CH_2—O—CH_3$
(b) $CH_3—\underset{\displaystyle OH}{\underset{|}{C}}H—CH_3$
(c) $CH_3—CH_2—CH_2—OH$
(d) $CH_3—CH_2—CHO$

15. Which of the following alcohols will not undergo oxidation? **CBSE 2023**

(a) Butanol
(b) Butan-2-ol
(c) 2-methylbutan-2-ol
(d) 3-methylbutan-2-ol

16. Match the Column I with Column II and choose the correct option.

Column I	Column II
A. $CH_3—CH_2—OH \xrightarrow[573\text{ K}]{Cu}$	(i) $CH_2=CH_2 + H_2O$
B. $CH_3—CH=CH—CH_2—OH \xrightarrow{PCC}$	(ii) CH_3CHO
C. $CH_3—CH_2—OH \xrightarrow[443\text{ K}]{H_2SO_4,\ \Delta}$	(iii) $CH_3—CH=CH—CHO$

Codes

	A	B	C		A	B	C
(a)	(ii)	(iii)	(i)	(b)	(i)	(ii)	(iii)
(c)	(iii)	(ii)	(i)	(d)	(i)	(iii)	(ii)

17. Phenol does not undergo nucleophilic substitution reaction easily due to **CBSE SQP (Term I)**

(a) acidic nature of phenol.
(b) partial double bond character of C—OH bond.
(c) partial double bond character of C—C bond.
(d) instability of phenoxide ion.

18. The major product(s) formed by the mononitration of 3-methylphenol is

(a)
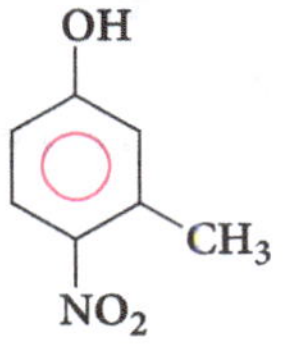

(b)
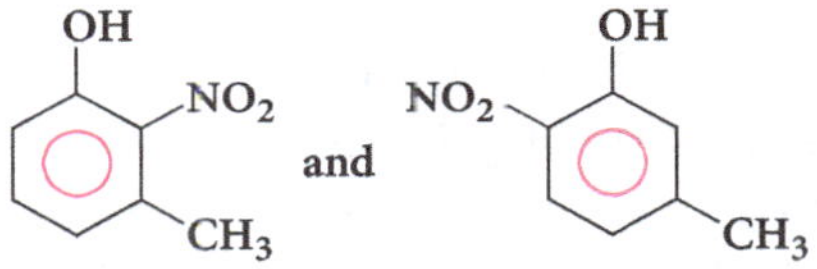

(c)
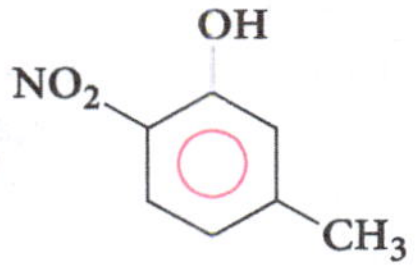

(d)
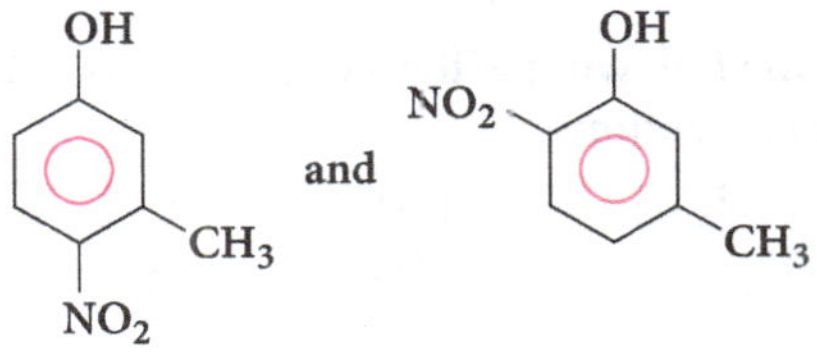

19. Phenol on being heated with concentrated H_2SO_4 and then with concentrated HNO_3 gives **CBSE 2021 (Term I)**

(a) *o* -nitrophenol (b) 2, 4, 6-trinitrophenol
(c) *p*-nitrophenol (d) *m*-nitrophenol

20. Consider the table given below.

Formula	Common name	IUPAC name
X	Heptylphenyl ether	1-phenoxyheptane
$C_6H_5—O—CH_2—CH_2—CH(CH_3)—CH_2—$	*Y*	3-methylbutoxy-benzene
$C_6H_5OCH_3$	Anisole	*Z*

Identify 'X', 'Y' and 'Z' in the above table.

(a) $X = C_6H_5O(CH_2)_5—CH_3$, Y = Phenyl *iso*-pentylether
Z = Methoxybenzene

(b) $X = C_6H_5O(CH_2)_6—CH_3$, Y = Methyl *iso*-pentylether,
Z = Ethoxybenzene

(c) $X = C_6H_5O(CH_2)_6—CH_3$, Y = Phenyl *iso*-pentyl ether,
Z = Methoxybenzene

(d) $X = C_6H_5O(CH_2)_5—CH_3$, Y = Phenyl *iso*-pentyl ether,
Z = Ethoxybenzene

21. **The major product formed when ethanol is dehydrated with Conc. H_2SO_4 at 413 K is**

(a) ethoxyethane (b) methoxyethane
(c) ethene (d) methoxymethane

22. **Williamson's synthesis of preparing dimethyl ether is a/an** **CBSE SQP 2025**

(a) S_N1 reaction
(b) elimination reaction
(c) S_N2 reaction
(d) nucleophilic addition reaction

23. **The reaction of $CH_3OC_2H_5$ with HI gives** **Diksha**

(a) Only CH_3I (b) Only C_2H_5OH
(c) $CH_3I + C_2H_5OH$ (d) $C_2H_5I + CH_3OH$

24. **When diethyl ether is heated with excess of HI, it produces** **CBSE 2023**

(a) ethanol (b) iodoform
(c) methyl iodide (d) ethyl iodide

25. **Which of the following will undergo electrophilic substitution reaction?** **Diksha**

(a) $C_2H_5OC_2H_5$ (b) $CH_3OC_2H_5$
(c) CH_3OCH_3 (d) $C_6H_5OCH_3$

Assertion-Reason [1 Mark]

Directions (Q. 26 to 36) In the following questions an Assertion (A) is followed by a corresponding Reason (R). Use the following keys to choose the appropriate answer.

(a) Both (A) and (R) are true and (R) is the correct explanation of (A).
(b) Both (A) and (R) are true, but (R) is not the correct explanation of (A).
(c) (A) is true, but (R) is false.
(d) (A) is false, but (R) is true.

26. **Assertion** (A) Carbon oxygen bond length of phenol is slightly less than that of methanol.

Reason (R) There exist a partial double bond character and sp^2-hybridisation of carbon to which oxygen is attached in phenol.

27. **Assertion** (A) Addition reaction of water to but-1-ene in acidic medium yields butan-2-ol.

Reason (R) Addition of water in acidic medium proceeds through the formation of primary carbanion. **NCERT Exemplar**

28. **Assertion** (A) Alcohols and phenols are soluble in water.

Reason (R) There occurs a dipole-dipole interaction of OH group of alcohol and phenol with water molecules which is responsible for their solubility in water.

29. **Assertion** (A) Boiling point of *p*-nitrophenol is more than *o*-nitrophenol.

Reason (R) *p*-nitrophenol is steam volatile, due to intermolecular H-bonding. **Compentency Based Que.**

30. **Assertion** (A) The boiling point of ethanol is higher than that of methoxymethane.

Reason (R) There is intramolecular hydrogen bonding in ethanol. **CBSE 2025**

31. **Assertion** (A) C_2H_5OH is a weaker base than phenol but is a stronger nucleophile than phenol.

Reason (R) In phenol, the lone pair of electrons on oxygen is withdrawn towards the ring due to resonance. **CBSE SQP 2020**

32. **Assertion** (A) *p*-methoxyphenol is a stronger acid than *m*-methoxyphenol.

Reason (R) Methoxy group exerts + *R* effect at both *ortho* and *para* position. **CBSE 2024**

33. **Assertion** (A) Bromination of phenol can be carried out even in the absence of Lewis acid.

Reason (R) —OH group of phenol has the high activation effect. **CBSE 2024**

34. **Assertion** (A) Like bromination of benzene, bromination of phenol is also carried out in the presence of Lewis acid. **NCERT Exemplar**

Reason (R) Lewis acid polarises the bromine molecule.

35. **Assertion** (A) IUPAC name of the compound

$$CH_3—\underset{\underset{CH_3}{|}}{CH}—O—CH_2—CH_2—CH_3$$ is

2-ethoxy-2-methylethane

Reason (R) In IUPAC nomenclature, ether is regarded as hydrocarbon derivative in which a hydrogen atom is replaced by —*OR* or —OAr group [where, *R* = alkyl group and Ar = aryl group]. **NCERT Exemplar**

36. **Assertion** (A) Bond angle in ethers is slightly less than the tetrahedral angle.

Reason (R) There is a repulsion between the two bulky (— *R*) groups. **NCERT Exemplar**

Case-Study [4 Marks]

37. Read the case given below and answer the questions that follow

Alcohols are soluble in water due to their ability to form hydrogen bonds. The boiling point of alcohol generally increases with increase in molar mass and decreases with increased branching in the carbon chain. Alcohols on dehydration gives alkenes at 443 K. This reaction is commonly observed in compounds such as anisole and chlorobenzene. Phenol, on the other hand is used to prepare salicylaldehyde, salicylic acid, aspirin, methyl salicylate and *p*-benzoquinone. In addition, phenol undergoes electrophilic substitution reaction at *o* and *p*-position.

Observe the following table showing boiling points of alcohol, their respective molar mass. Study the table and answer the questions based on table and related studied concept.

	Alcohol	Boiling points	Molar mass
1.	CH_3OH	64°C	32 g mol^{-1}
2.	C_2H_5OH	78°C	46 g mol^{-1}
3.	C_3H_7OH (*n*-propyl alcohol)	97°C	60 g mol^{-1}
4.	*Iso*-propyl alcohol	82.5°C	60 g mol^{-1}
5.	*n*-butanol	118°C	74 g mol^{-1}
6.	*Iso*-butyl alcohol	108°C	74 g mol^{-1}
7.	Butan-2-ol	100°C	74 g mol^{-1}
8.	*Tert*-butyl alcohol	83°C	74 g mol^{-1}

(i) Why does tertiary butyl alcohol have lower boiling point than *n*-butyl alcohol?

(ii) Considering intermolecular forces, which alcohol would be expected to exhibit the strongest hydrogen bonding interactions?

(a) *iso*-propyl alcohol (b) Methanol
(c) Ethanol (d) *n*-butanol

Or

Which of the following alcohols would have the highest vapour pressure at room temperature?

(a) *n*-butanol (b) *n*-propanol
(c) Ethanol (d) Methanol

(iii) If Rahul have to mix an alcohol with water, which structural feature of the alcohol would likely make it less soluble?

(a) Low molecular weight with no branching.
(b) Presence of a hydroxyl group.
(c) Low molecular weight with branching.
(d) High molecular weight with no branching.

38. Read the case given below and answer the questions that follow

Phenols undergo electrophilic substitution reactions readily due to the to strong activating effect of OH group attached the benzene ring. Since, the OH group increases the electron density more to *o*- and *p*-positions therefore OH group is *ortho*, *para*-directing. Reimer-Tiemann reaction is one of the examples of aldehyde group being introduced on the aromatic ring of phenol, *ortho* to the hydroxyl group. This is a general method used for the *ortho*-formylation of phenols. **CBSE 2025**

(i) What happens when phenol reacts with
(i) Br_2 / CS_2 (ii) Conc. HNO_3

(ii) Why phenol does not undergo protonation readily?

(iii) Which is a stronger acid phenol or cresol? Give reason.

Or

(iii) Write the IUPAC name of the product formed in the Reimer-Tiemann reaction.

Subjective Type Questions

Short Answer Type I Questions [2 Marks]

1. Give the structures and IUPAC names of monohydric phenols of molecular formula C_7H_8O. **NCERT**

2. Write the steps to show how will you convert nitrobenzene to phenol.

3. (i) Arrange the following in increasing order of their boiling point. **Diksha**

$CH_3CH_2OH, CH_3CHO, CH_3—O—CH_3$

(ii) Reena is comparing the solubility of 1-butanol and 1-pentanol in water. Which is likely to be less soluble in water and why?

4. Arrange the following compounds in the increasing order of the property indicated.

(i) *p*-nitrophenol, ethanol, phenol (acidic character)

(ii) Propanol, propane, propanal (boiling point) **CBSE 2017**

5. (i) Write hydroboration-oxidation reaction with an example.

(ii) Why is *p*-nitrophenol more acidic than phenol? **CBSE 2023**

6. Out of 2-chloroethanol and ethanol, which one is more acidic and why? **NCERT Exemplar**

7. For the pair phenol and cyclohexanol, answer the following.

(i) Why is phenol more acidic than cyclohexanol?

(ii) Give one chemical test to distinguish between the two. **CBSE 2023**

8. (i) How will you distinguish between the following compounds?

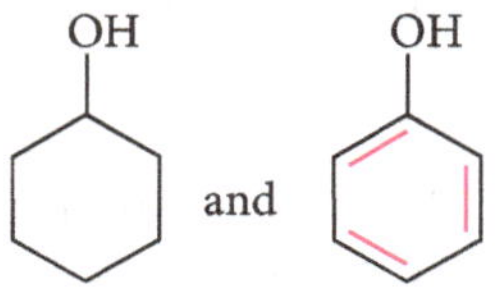

(ii) C—O bond in phenol is much shorter than ethanol. Why? **Diksha**

9. Name the reagents used in the following reactions

(i) Bromination of phenol to 2,4,6-tribromophenol

(ii) Conversion of butan-2-one to butan-2-ol. **CBSE 2024 C**

10. What happens when

(i) salicylic acid is treated with $(CH_3CO)_2O / H^+$?

(ii) anisole is treated with CH_3Cl / anhyd. $AlCl_3$? **CBSE 2017**

Write chemical equation in support of your answer. **CBSE 2019**

11. Give the industrial uses of methanol and ethanol.

12. (i) Methyl tertiary butyl ether is an important additive of gasoline.

How it can be prepared using Williamson's synthesis?

(ii) What happens when anisole is heated with HI?

13. Explain the fact that in aryl alkyl ether,

(i) the alkoxy group activates the benzene ring towards electrophilic substitution and

(ii) it directs the incoming substituents to *ortho* and *para*-positions in benzene ring. **NCERT**

Short Answer Type II Questions [3 Marks]

14. Write structures of the products of the following reactions.

(i) $CH_3—CH{=}CH_2 \xrightarrow{H_2O/H^+}$

(ii)

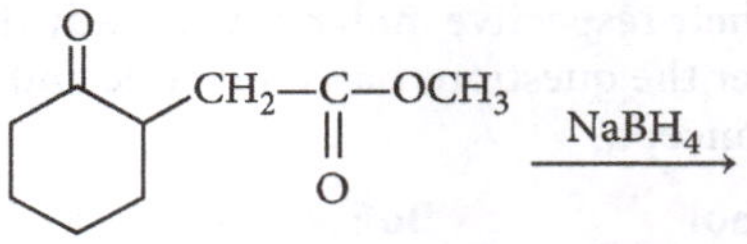

(iii) $CH_3—CH_2—\underset{\displaystyle CH_3}{\underset{|}{CH}}—CHO \xrightarrow{NaBH_4}$ **NCERT Intext**

15. Show how will you synthesise

(i) 1-phenyl ethanol from a suitable alkene?

(ii) cyclohexyl methanol using an alkyl halide by an S_N2 mechanism?

(iii) pentan-1-ol using an alkyl halide? **NCERT**

16. Give two reactions that show the acidic nature of phenol. Compare acidity of phenol with that of ethanol. **NCERT**

17. Neeta was experimenting in the lab to study the chemical reactivity of alcohols. She carried out a dehydration reaction of propanol at 140°C to 180° C.

Different products were obtained at these two temperatures.

(a) Identify the major product formed at 140°C and the substitution mechanism followed in this case.

(b) Identify the major product formed at 180°C and the substitution mechanism followed in this case. **CBSE SQP 2025**

18. (i) Predict the main product of the following reaction.

$$CH_3—\underset{\displaystyle CH_3}{\underset{|}{CH}}—\underset{\displaystyle OH}{\underset{|}{CH}}—CH_2—CH_3 \xrightarrow{HBr} ?$$

(ii) Write the reaction mechanism to explain why this isomer (the main product in the above reaction) predominates. **Competency Based Que.**

19. How does Lucas reagent help in the distinction of primary, secondary and tertiary alcohols? Discuss the reactions involved. **Competency Based Que.**

20. Why is the reactivity of all the three classes of alcohols with conc. HCl and $ZnCl_2$ (Lucas reagent) different? **NCERT Exemplar**

21. Draw the structure and name the product formed, if the following alcohols are oxidised. Assuming that an excess of oxidising agent is used.

(i) $CH_3CH_2CH_2CH_2OH$

(ii) 2-butanol

(iii) 2-methyl-1-propanol

22. (i) How will you distinguish between the following pair by suitable chemical tests?

Butan-1-ol and butan-2-ol

(ii) Complete the following reaction.

$HOCH_2—CHOH—CH_2OH \xrightarrow{HI}$ **CBSE 2019**

23. Give the structure of the major product expected from the following reactions.

(i) Reaction of ethanal with methyl-magnesium bromide followed by hydrolysis.

(ii) Hydration of but-1-ene in the presence of dilute sulphuric acid.

(iii) Reaction of phenol with bromine water. **CBSE 2024**

24. Complete the following equations and name the products formed.

(i) $C_6H_5OH + Br_2 \xrightarrow{H_2O}$

(ii) $(CH_3)_2C{=}O \xrightarrow{LiAlH_4}$

(iii) $C_6H_5OH + CHCl_3 \xrightarrow[340\ K]{Aq.\ NaOH}$

25. Explain the following. **CBSE 2024C**

(i) Reimer-Tiemann reaction

(ii) Kolbe's reaction

(iii) Williamson synthesis

26. Write the reaction of Williamson's synthesis of 2-ethoxy-3-methylpentane, starting from ethanol and 3-methylpentan-2-ol. **NCERT Intext**

27. Aartha's teacher gave her three test tubes. Out of three test tubes one on reduction with H_2/Ni forms alkane. How will she identify that test tube.

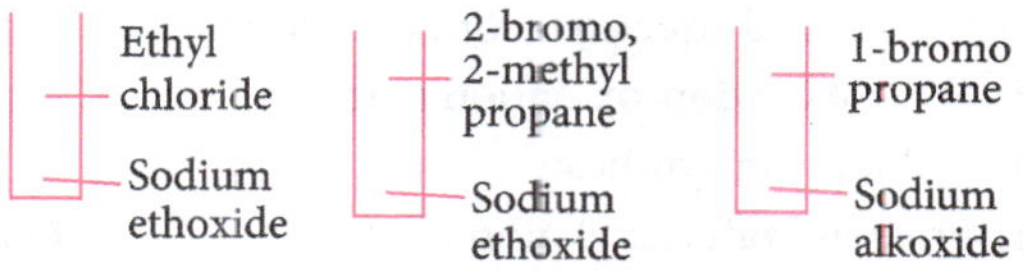

A B C

28. How is 1-propoxy propane synthesised from propan-1-ol? Write the mechanism of this reaction. **NCERT**

29. Write the main product(s) in each of the following reactions.

(i) $CH_3—C(CH_3)_2—O—CH_3 + HI \longrightarrow$

(ii) $CH_3—CH{=}CH_2 \xrightarrow[(b)\ 3H_2O_2/OH^-]{(a)\ B_2H_6}$

(iii) $C_6H_5OH \xrightarrow[(b)\ CO_2,\ H^+]{(a)\ Aq.\ NaOH}$ **CBSE 2016**

30. Write the equation for the reaction of hydrogen iodide with **NCERT**

(i) 1-propoxy propane (ii) methoxy benzene and

(iii) benzyl ethyl ether

31. (i) How will you convert.

(a) Phenol to 4-bromophenol?

(b) Phenol to 2-hydroxy benzoic acid?

(ii) Arrange the following compounds in the decreasing order of their boiling points.

$C_2H_5—O—C_2H_5$ (I), $CH_3—O—C_2H_5$ (II),

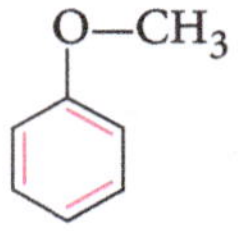

(III)

32. (i) What happens when phenol reacts with

(a) conc. HNO_3 and

(b) $CHCl_3$ in presence of aqueous NaOH followed by acidification?

(ii) Why does the reaction of CH_3ONa with $(CH_3)_3C—Br$ gives 2-methylpropene and not $(CH_3)_3C—O—OCH_3$? **CBSE 2023**

33. (i) Why is the C—O bond length in phenols less than that in methanol?

(ii) Arrange the following in order of increasing boiling point :

Ethoxyethane, Butanal, Butanol, *n*-butane

(iii) How can phenol be prepared from anisole? Give reason. **CBSE 2023**

34. Write chemical equations for the following reactions:
(i) Hydroboration-oxidation reaction
(ii) Williamson synthesis
(iii) Friedel-Crafts alkylation of anisole **CBSE 2024**

35. What happens when
(i) Anisole is treated with CH_3Cl/anhydrous $AlCl_3$?
(ii) Phenol is oxidised with $Na_2Cr_2O_7/H^+$?
(iii) $(CH_3)_3C$—OH is heated with Cu/573 K?
Write chemical equation in support of your answer. **CBSE 2023**

Long Answer Type Questions [5 Marks]

36. (i) Draw the structures of all isomeric alcohols of molecular formula $C_5H_{12}O$ and give their IUPAC names.
(ii) Classify the isomers of alcohols in question 36. (i) as primary, secondary and tertiary alcohols. **NCERT**

37. (i) How are the following conversions carried out?
(a) Propene → Propan-2-ol
(b) Benzyl chloride → Benzyl alcohol
(c) Ethyl magnesium chloride → Propan-1-ol
(d) Methyl magnesium bromide → 2-methyl propan-2-ol. **NCERT**
(ii) Explain why propanol has higher boiling point than that of butane? **NCERT**

38. (i) Give equations of the following reactions. (Any three)
(a) Oxidation of propan-1-ol with alkaline $KMnO_4$ solution.
(b) Bromine in CS_2 with phenol.
(c) Dilute HNO_3 with phenol.
(d) Treating phenol with chloroform in presence of aqueous NaOH. **NCERT**
(ii) Explain how does the —OH group attached to a carbon of benzene ring activate it towards electrophilic substitution? **NCERT**

39. (i) How is phenol obtained from (a) aniline (b) benzene sulphonic acid?
(ii) How it can be converted into (a) salicylaldehyde (b) benzoquinone (c) toluene? **CBSE 2015**

40. Preparation of ethers by acid-catalysed dehydration of secondary and tertiary alcohols is not a suitable method. Give reason. **NCERT**

41. (i) Give one chemical test to distinguish between
(a) phenol and benzoic acid
(b) propan-1-ol and propan-2-ol
(c) methanol and ethanol
(ii) Why is bimolecular dehydration not appropriate for preparation of ethyl methyl ether? Write a suitable method for its preparation. **Diksha**

Hints & Solutions

Objective Type Questions

1. (*d*) 2-methyl propene an acid catalysed hydration produce tertiary butyl alcohol.

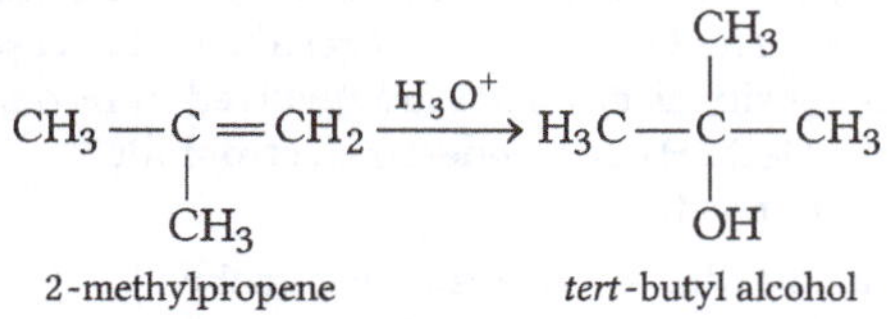

2. (*d*)

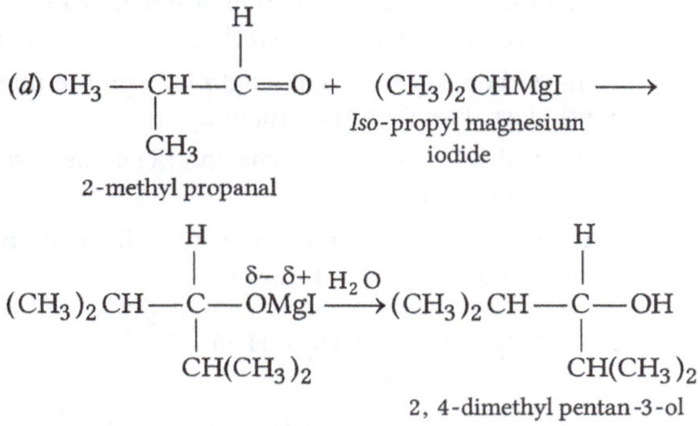

3. (*d*) Since, all the given three compounds are ketones and therefore they will react with a Grignard reagent to yield tertiary alcohols.

4. (*c*) Nucleophilic addition of Grignard's reagent to ketone followed by hydrolysis will give tertiary (3°) alcohol as a product.

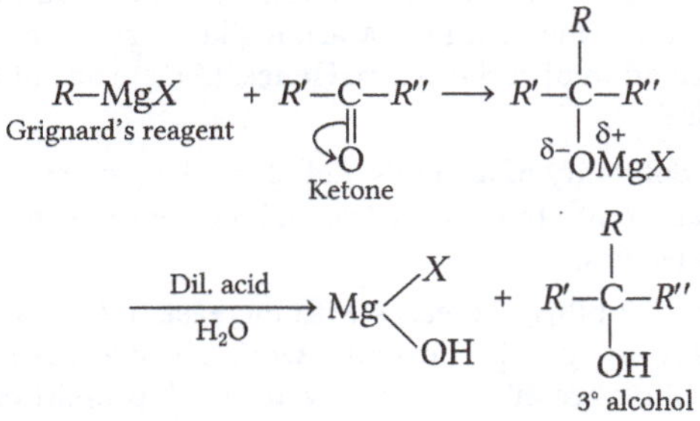

5. (*b*) Only statement (b) is incorrect. Its corrected form is; No intermediate is formed in hydroboration oxidation reaction.

6. (*b*) $CH_3CH{=}CH_2 \xrightarrow[H_2O_2/\bar{O}H]{B_2H_6} CH_3CH_2CH_2OH$

Propene — Propan-1-ol

7. (*d*)

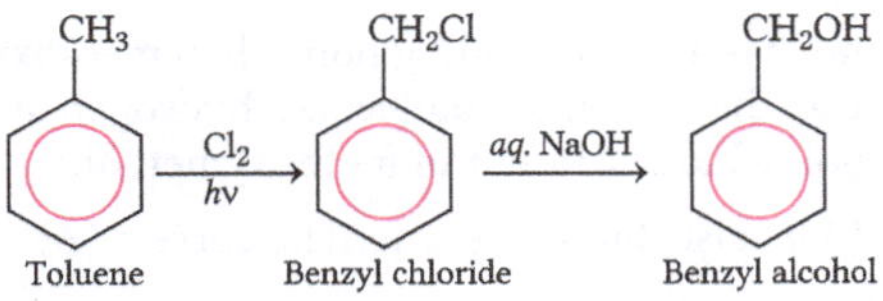

8. (*b*)

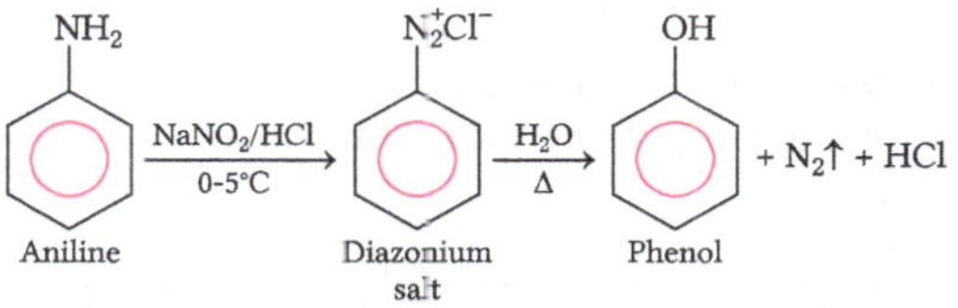

9. (*d*) Compound (*S*) will be an alcohol molecule. This is because alcohol have higher boiling point as compared to ether, aldehyde and haloalkane due to presence of intermolecular hydrogen bonding.

10. (*a*) Phenol is the most acidic among the given options as phenoxide ion formed after losing proton is resonance stabilised. Also, water is more acidic than alcohol because the electron releasing alkyl group, increase the electron density on oxygen, which decreases the polarity of O—H bond, thereby decreasing their acidity.

Thus, the correct order of acid strength is

$$C_6H_5OH > H_2O > ROH$$

11. (*c*) Among the given options, RO^- is the strongest base as its conjugate acid, i.e. *R*OH is the weakest acid as compared to the other conjugate acids, i.e. C_6H_5OH, HOH and

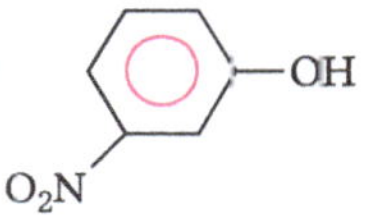

12. (*b*)

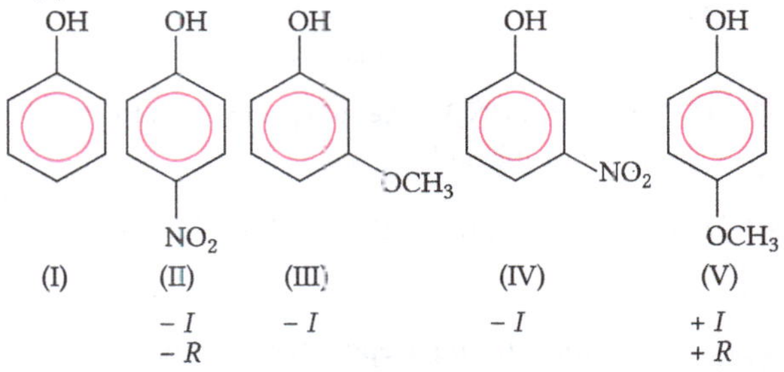

Order of acidic strength : (II) > (IV) > (I) > (III) > (V).

Electron withdrawing group like $—NO_2$ group increases the acidic strength due to $-I$ effect, while electron releasing group i.e. $—OCH_3$ group decreases the acidic strength due to $+I$ effect.

Moreover, *p*-nitrophenol is more acidic than *m*-nitrophenol whereas, *p*-methoxyphenol is less acidic than *m*-methoxyphenol.

13. (*a*) Primary alcohols on oxidation gives aldehyde (*X*) which reduce Tollen's reagent. However, secondary and tertiary alcohols gives ketone and alkene respectively. Thus, among the given alcohols, $CH_3—CH_2—CH_2—OH$ (1°) is the alcohol that will give aldehyde.

14. (c) $\underset{\text{Propanol}}{\underset{(X)}{CH_3CH_2CH_2—OH}} \xrightarrow{\text{On oxidation}} \underset{\text{Propanoic acid}}{\underset{(Y)}{CH_3CH_2COOH}}$

15. (c) Among the given alcohols, 2-methylbutan-2-ol will not undergo oxidation as it is a tertiary alcohol.

16. (a)

A. $\underset{\text{Ethanol}}{CH_3—CH_2—OH} \xrightarrow[573\text{ K}]{Cu} \underset{\text{Ethanal}}{CH_3CHO} + H_2\uparrow$

B. $\underset{\text{But-2-en-1-ol}}{CH_3—CH=CH—CH_2—OH} \xrightarrow{PCC} \underset{\text{(Crotonaldehyde)}}{\underset{\text{But-2-en-1-al}}{CH_3—CH=CH—CHO}}$

C. $CH_3—CH_2—OH \xrightarrow[443\text{ K}]{H_2SO_4,\ \Delta} CH_2=CH_2 + H_2O$

Thus, the correct match is (A)→(ii), (B)→(iii), (C)→(i)

17. (b) Phenol does not undergo nucleophilic substitution reaction easily due to partial double bond character of C—OH bond.

18. (d) Since, —OH and —CH_3 groups are *ortho* and *para*-directing in nature.

Thus, the major products formed in the given reaction is as follows :

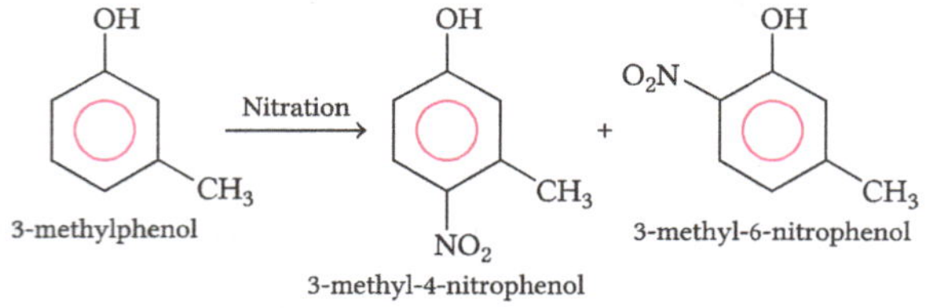

19. (b) With conc. HNO_3, phenol is converted to 2, 4, 6-trinitrophenol.

20. (c) • X is $C_6H_5—O—\overset{1}{C}H_2—\overset{2}{C}H_2—\overset{3}{C}H_2—\overset{4}{C}H_2—\overset{5}{C}H_2—\overset{6}{C}H_2—\overset{7}{C}H_3$

Common name Heptylphenyl ether

IUPAC name 1-phenoxyheptane

- Y is phenyl *iso*-pentyl ether
- Z is methoxybenzene, i.e. $C_6H_5OCH_3$

21. (a) $\underset{\text{Ethanol}}{2CH_3CH_2OH} \xrightarrow[413\text{ K}]{\text{Conc. }H_2SO_4} \underset{\text{Ethoxyethane}}{C_2H_5OC_2H_5} + H_2O$

22. (c) In Williamson's synthesis, alkoxide ion reacts with primary alkyl halide in a single step to form ether. Hence, it is an S_N2 reaction.

23. (c) In the case of mixed ethers such as methyl ethyl ether, the halogen attaches to simpler alkyl group. Thus, the reaction takes place as

$$CH_3OC_2H_5 + HI \longrightarrow CH_3I + C_2H_5OH$$

24. (d) $\underset{\text{Diethyl ether}}{CH_3—CH_2—O—CH_2—CH_3} + \underset{\text{(Excess)}}{2HI} \longrightarrow \underset{\text{Ethyl iodide}}{2CH_3CH_2I} + H_2O$

25. (d) As alkyl groups are usually electron donating so there would be less chance of electrophilic substitution. C_6H_5 group and O attached to it results in decrease of electron density as electrons are involved in resonance. Hence, $C_6H_5OCH_3$ can undergo electrophilic substitution reaction.

26. (a) In phenols, the —OH group is attached to sp^2-hybridised carbon atom of an aromatic ring. As a result, a partial double bond exist between C—O bond.

So, the carbon oxygen bond length (136 pm) in phenol is slightly less than that in methanol.

Hence, both (A) and (R) are true and (R) is the correct explanation of (A).

27. (c) Addition of water to but-1-ene in acidic medium yields butan-2-ol. It is as follows

$$\underset{\text{But-1-ene}}{CH_3—CH_2—CH=CH_2} + H_2O \xrightarrow{H_2SO_4} CH_3—CH_2—\underset{OSO_3H}{\underset{|}{CH}}—CH_3 \xrightarrow{H_2SO_4} \underset{\text{Butan-2-ol}}{CH_3—CH_2—\underset{OH}{\underset{|}{CH}}—CH_3}$$

Addition of H_2O to unsymmetrical alkenes takes place in accordance with the Markovnikov's rule *via* the formation of carbocation. Hence, (A) is true but (R) is false.

28. (c) Solubility of alcohols and phenols in water is due to their ability to form hydrogen bonds with water molecules.

The solubility decreases with increase in size of the alkyl/aryl groups. Several lower molecular mass alcohols are miscible with water in all proportions. Hence, (A) is true, but (R) is false.

29. (c) (A) is true, but (R) is false.

The correct (R) is : *o*-nitrophenol is steam volatile due to intramolecular H-bonding while *p*-nitrophenol is less volatile due to association of molecules by intermolecular hydrogen bonding.

30. (c) (A) is true, but (R) is false.

Ethanol has a higher boiling point than methoxymethane because there is inter-molecular hydrogen bonding in ethanol, which is absent in methoxymethane.

31. (d) (A) is false, but (R) is true. The correct (A) is;

C_2H_5OH is a weaker acid than phenol as in phenol, the lone pair of electrons on oxygen is withdrawn towards the ring due to resonance, leaving oxygen with a positive charge and thus increasing the acidity.

32. (*d*) Methoxy group exerts $-I$ effect at *m*-position and $+R$ effect at *p*-position thereby making *m*-methoxyphenol a stronger acid than *p*-methoxyphenol.

Hence, (A) is false, but (R) is true.

33. (*a*) In case of phenol, the —OH group (electron releasing group) attached to benzene ring is highly activated which polarises the bromine molecule even in the absence of Lewis acid.

Hence, both (A) and (R) are true and (R) is correct explanation of (A).

34. (*d*) (A) is false, but (R) is true.

Correct (A) Bromination of benzene but not of phenol is carried out in presence of a Lewis acid.

In case of phenol, the polarisation of bromine molecule takes place even in the absence of Lewis acid. It is due to the highly activating effect of —OH group attached to the benzene ring.

35. (*d*) (A) is false, but (R) is true.

Correct (A) The IUPAC name of the given compound is 2-propoxypropane.

36. (*d*) (A) is false, but (R) is true.

Correct (A) Bond angle in ether is slightly more than the tetrahedral angle.

37. (i) Tertiary butyl alcohol has a lower boiling point than *n*-butyl alcohol because it has a more branched structure, which decreases its surface area and the attractive forces between its molecules. **(2)**

(ii) (*d*) Hydrogen bonding strength increases with more extended alkyl chains that support the hydroxyl groups hydrogen bonding.

Among the given options, *n*-butanol has the longest chain, and does exhibit the strongest hydrogen bonding interactions. **(1)**

Or

(*d*) Vapour pressure is inversely related to boiling point. Thus, methanol with the lowest boiling point, will have the highest vapour pressure at room temperature. **(1)**

(iii) (*d*) Higher molecular weight alcohol with no branching are less soluble in water because the larger hydrocarbon part makes the molecule more hydrophobic reducing its ability to mix with water. **(1)**

38. (i)

(a) 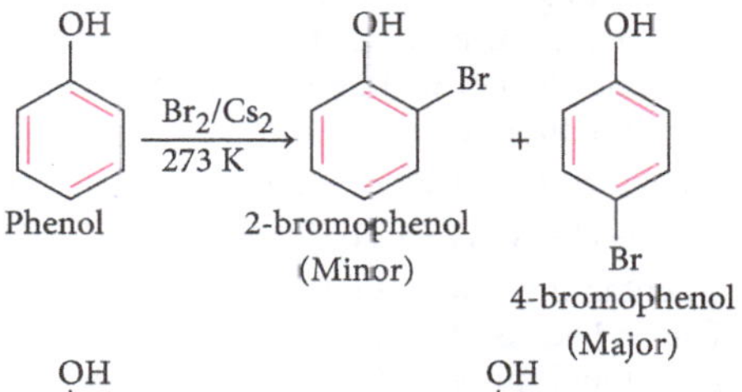

(b) 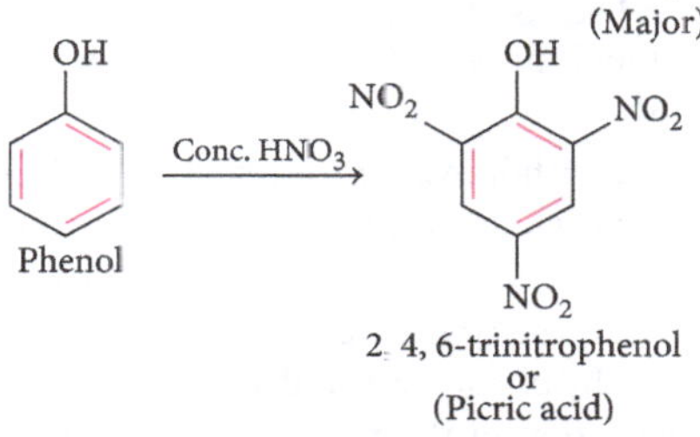

(1 + 1)

(ii) The lone pair on oxygen of —OH in phenol is involved in resonance with the benzene ring. Thus, the lone pair is not available for accepting protons, and hence, phenols do not undergo protonation readily. (1)

(iii) Phenol is a stronger acid than cresol as $—CH_3$ group in cresol produces $+I$ effect, which increases the electron density on —OH bond. This decreases the polarity of —OH bond, and hence, makes it a weaker acid than phenol. (1)

Or (iii) **Reimer-Tiemann Reaction**

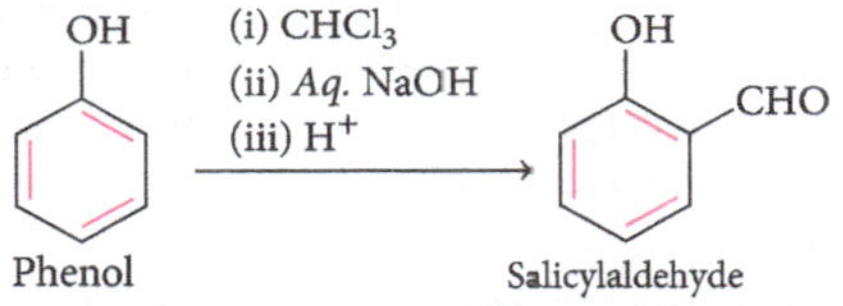

IUPAC name of salicylaldehyde is 2-hydroxybenzaldehyde.

Subjective Type Questions

1. The phenolic compound with molecular formula C_7H_8O, has three isomers that are as follows

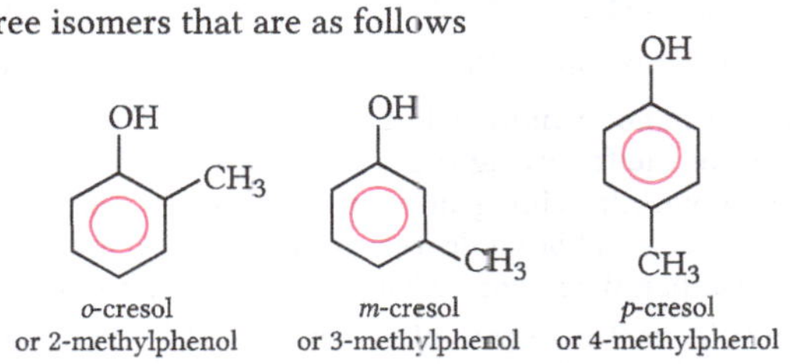

(2)

2. Conversion of nitrobenzene to phenol takes place as

(i) Reduction of nitrobenzene to aniline with Sn/HCl or Fe/HCl.

(ii) Diazotisation of aniline to benzene diazonium chloride with sodium nitrite and hydrochloric acid at 0 to 5°C.

(iii) Hydrolysis of benzene diazonium chloride to phenol with water.

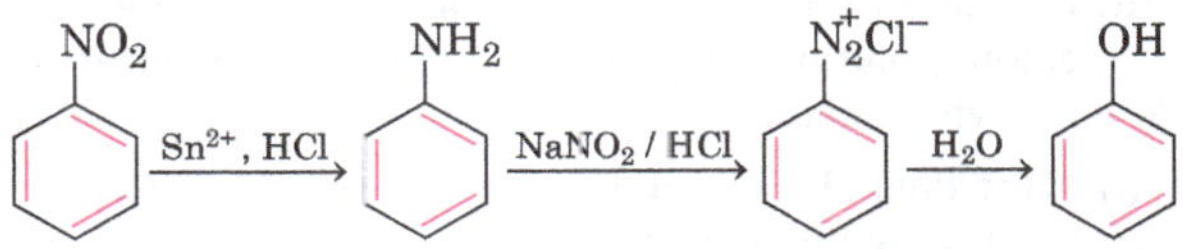

(2)

3. (i) The boiling point of a compound depends on intermolecular hydrogen bonding. Further, boiling point of ethanol will be highest followed by ethanol and dimethyl ether.

Thus the correct increasing order of boiling point is

$CH_3—O—CH_3 < CH_3CHO < CH_3CH_2OH$ **(1)**

(ii) 1-pentanol is less soluble in water than 1-butanol. This is because the larger alkyl group makes 1-pentanol more hydrophobic in nature than 1-butanol. **(1)**

4. (i) Electron withdrawing group such as $—NO_2$ increases the acidic character, while electron releasing group such as $— CH_3$ decreases the acidic character.

Moreover, the phenoxide ion, produced by the loss of a proton by phenol, is stabilised by resonance due to delocalisation of the negative charge on the benzene ring. Therefore, the increasing order of acidic character is

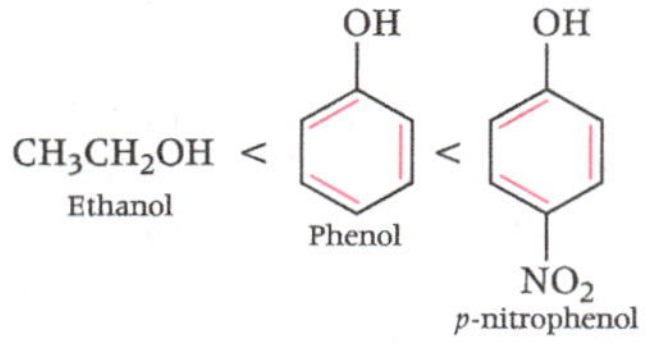

(1)

(ii) Alcohols (CH_3CH_2OH) undergoes strong hydrogen bonding, while hydrocarbon such as propane does not exhibit hydrogen bonding. Moreover, aldehydes show hydrogen bonding but not stronger than alcohols.

Thus, the correct increasing order of boiling point is

$CH_3CH_2CH_3 < CH_3CH_2CHO < CH_3CH_2OH$
(Propane) (Propanal) (Propanol)

(Increasing order of boiling point)

5. (i) Refer to text on pages 233 and 234. **(1)**

(ii) Refer to text on pages 239. **(1)**

6. 2-chloroethanol is more acidic than ethanol. This is because of the following reasons; Due to $-I$-effect (electron withdrawing group) of the Cl-atom, electron density on O—H bond decreases. So, O—H bond of 2-chloroethanol becomes weaker than O—H bond of ethanol. Thus, the release of H^+ ion from O—H bond of 2-chloroethane becomes easier. **(2)**

7. (i) Phenol is more acidic than cyclohexanol as phenoxide ion is more stable than alkoxide ion. (In this case alkoxide is derived from cyclohexanol). This is because, the negative charge is localised at the oxygen atom in case of phenoxide ion. **(1)**

(ii) Phenol on reacting with neutral $FeCl_3$ gives violet colour solution whereas, cyclohexane does not give any violet colour. **(1)**

8. (i) **Hint** Phenol gives violet colouration with $FeCl_3$ solution, while cyclohexanol does not react. **(1)**

(ii) The C—O bond has partial double bond character due to resonance. Also, the carbon attached to oxygen is sp^2-hybridised in phenol and more electronegative compared to that in ethanol which is sp^2-hybridised. **(1)**

9. (i)

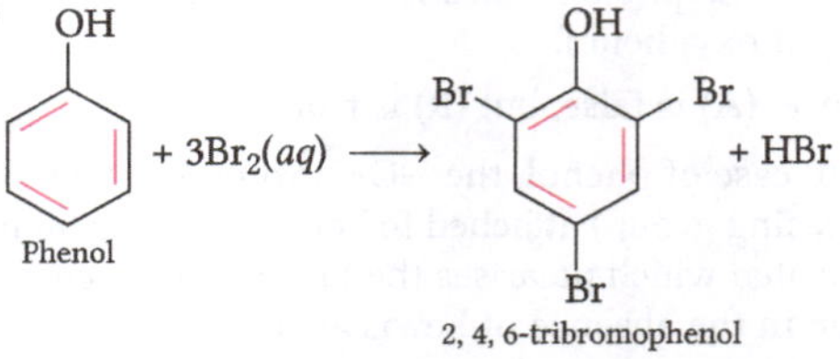

Here, reagent used is $Br_2(aq)$ **(1)**

(ii)

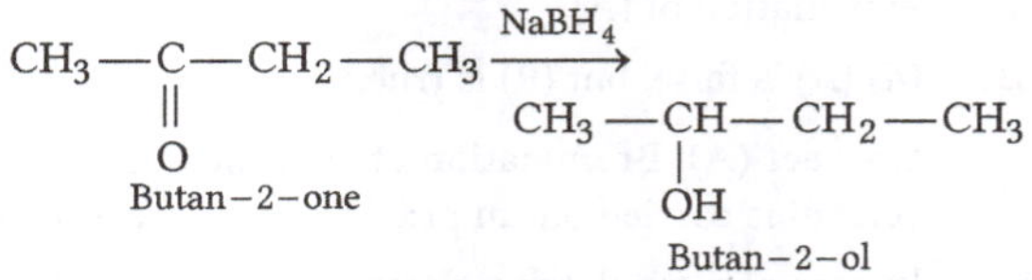

Here, reagent used is $NaBH_4$. **(1)**

10. (i)

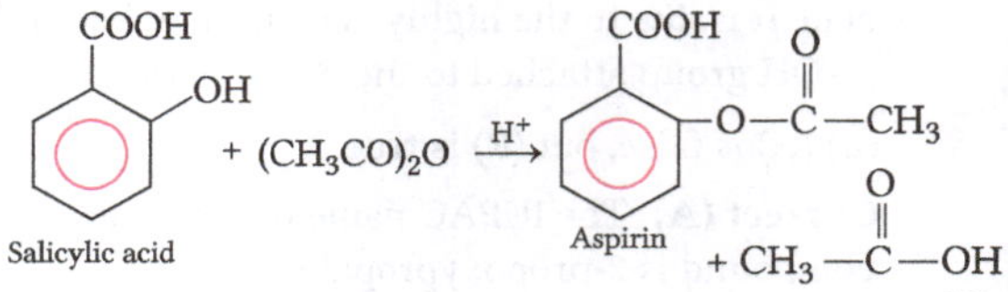

(1)

(ii)

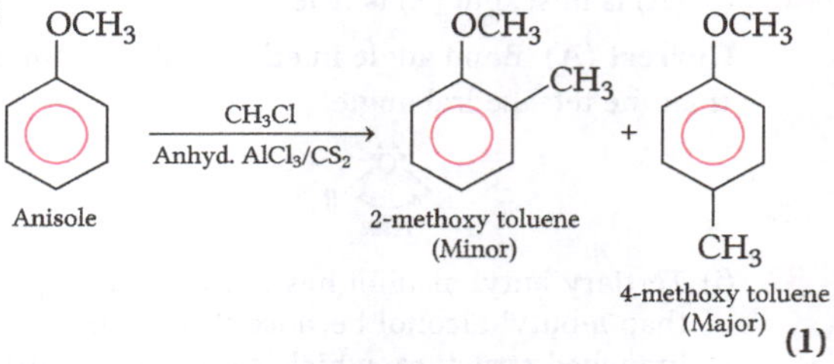

(1)

11. Refer to text on pages 246 and 247. **(2)**

12. (i) Refer to text on page 249. **(1)**

(ii) Refer to text on page 253. **(1)**

13. (i) In aryl alkyl ethers, $+R$-effect of the alkoxy group ($—OR$) increases the electron density on the benzene ring thereby, activating the benzene ring towards electrophilic substitution reactions.

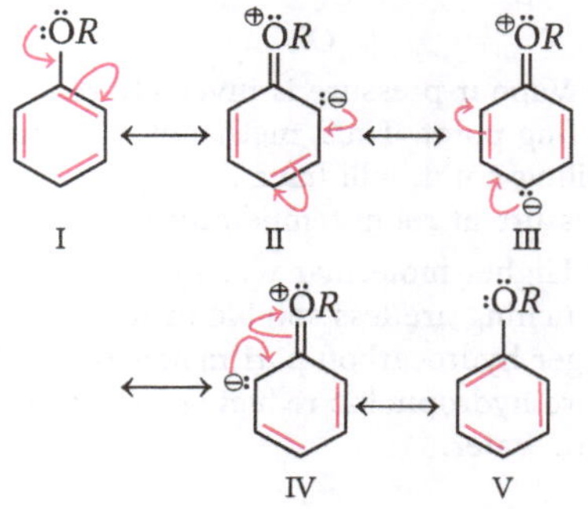

(1)

(ii) Alkoxy group (—O*R*) is ortho, para directing and activates the aromatic ring towards electrophilic substitution.

It directs the incoming electrophile at *o*- and *p*-positions. This is because of the presence of the negative charges at *o*- and *p*-positions which increases the more electron density at these positions. **(1)**

14. (i)
$$\underset{\text{Propene}}{CH_3—CH{=}CH_2} \xrightarrow[\text{Markovnikov's rule}]{H_2O/H^+} \underset{\text{Propan-2-ol}}{\overset{1}{C}H_3—\overset{2}{C}H(OH)—\overset{3}{C}H_3}$$ **(1)**

(ii)

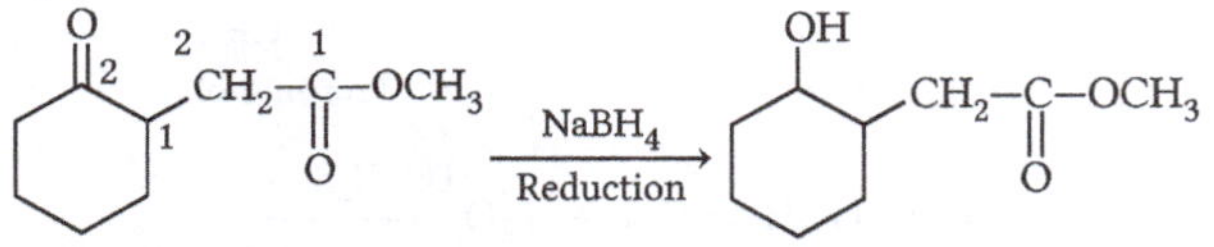

Methyl-2-oxocyclohexyl ethanoate → Methyl (2-hydroxycyclohexyl) ethanoate **(1)**

(iii)
$$\overset{4}{C}H_3—\overset{3}{C}H_2—\overset{2}{C}H(CH_3)—\overset{1}{C}HO \xrightarrow[\text{Reduction}]{NaBH_4}$$
2-methylbutanal

$$\overset{4}{C}H_3—\overset{3}{C}H_2—\overset{2}{C}H(CH_3)—\overset{1}{C}H_2—OH$$
2-methylbutan-1-ol **(1)**

15. (i) On adding H_2O to ethenyl benzene in the presence of dil. H_2SO_4, we get 1-phenyl ethanol.

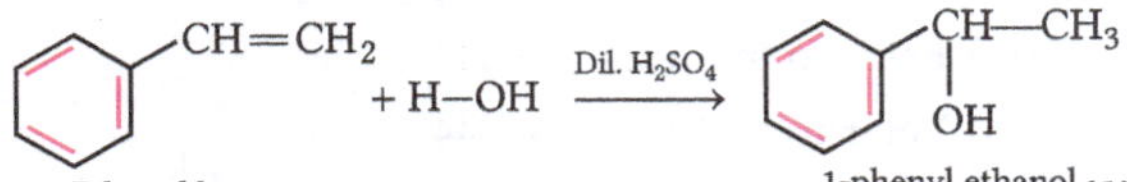

Ethenyl benzene → 1-phenyl ethanol **(1)**

(ii) Hydrolysis of cyclohexylmethylbromide by aqueous NaOH gives cyclohexyl methanol.

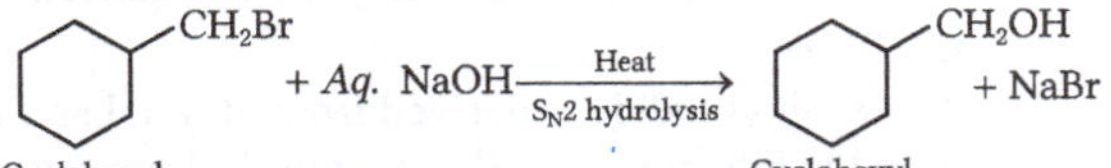

Cyclohexyl methyl bromide → Cyclohexyl methanol **(1)**

(iii) Hydrolysis of 1-bromopentane by aqueous NaOH, gives pentan-1-ol.

$$\underset{\text{1-bromopentane}}{CH_3CH_2CH_2CH_2CH_2—Br} + NaOH \xrightarrow[S_N2\ \text{hydrolysis}]{\text{Heat}}$$
$$\underset{\text{Pentan-1-ol}}{CH_3CH_2CH_2CH_2CH_2—OH} + NaBr$$ **(1)**

16. Following reactions show the acidic nature of phenol :

(i) **Reaction with sodium** H_2 gas is produced.

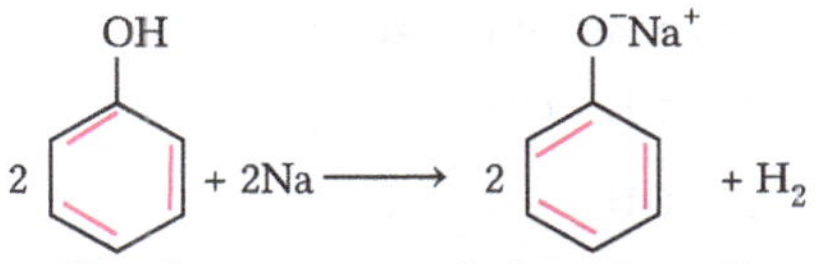

Phenol → Sodium phenoxide **(1)**

(ii) **Reaction with sodium hydroxide** Forms sodium salt and water.

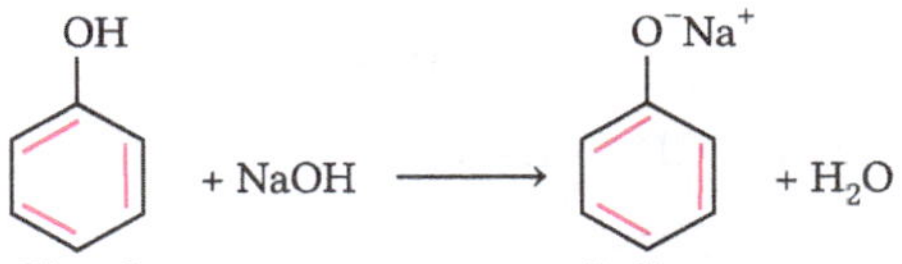

Phenol → Sodium phenoxide **(1)**

Comparison of acidic character of phenol and ethanol

Phenol is more acidic than ethanol because after losing a proton (H^+), phenol forms phenoxide ion which is stabilised by resonance whereas ethoxide ion is not.

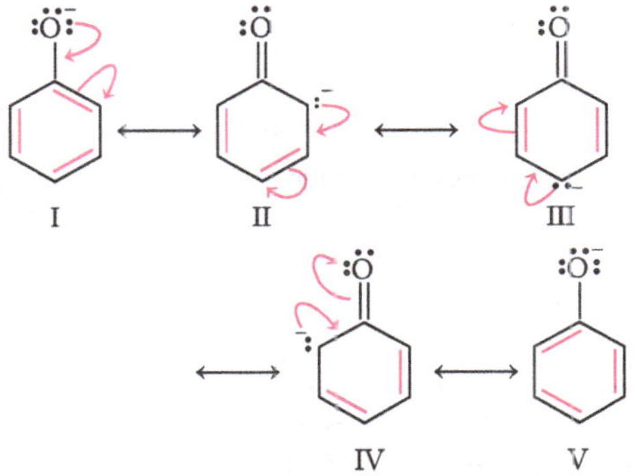

I II III IV V **(1)**

17. (a) At 140°C, dipropyl ether is formed. The formation of ether is a bimolecular nucleophilic substitution (S_N2) reaction.

$$\underset{\text{(Propanol)}}{CH_3CH_2CH_2OH} \xrightarrow[413\ K]{H_2SO_4}$$
$$\underset{\text{(Dipropyl ether)}}{CH_3CH_2CH_2—O—CH_2—CH_2—CH_3}$$ **(2)**

(b) At 180°C, propene is the major product formed by unimolecular nucleophilic substitution reaction (S_N1).

$$\underset{\text{(Propanol)}}{CH_3CH_2CH_2OH} \xrightarrow[443\ K]{H_2SO_4} \underset{\text{(Prop-1-ene)}}{CH_3—CH{=}CH_2}$$ **(1)**

18. (i)
$$CH_3—CH(CH_3)—CH(OH)—CH_2—CH_3 \xrightarrow{HBr}$$
$$CH_3—C(Br)(CH_3)—CH_2—CH_2—CH_3$$
2-bromo-2-methylpentane (Major) **(1)**

(ii) The mechanism of the given reaction is as follows :

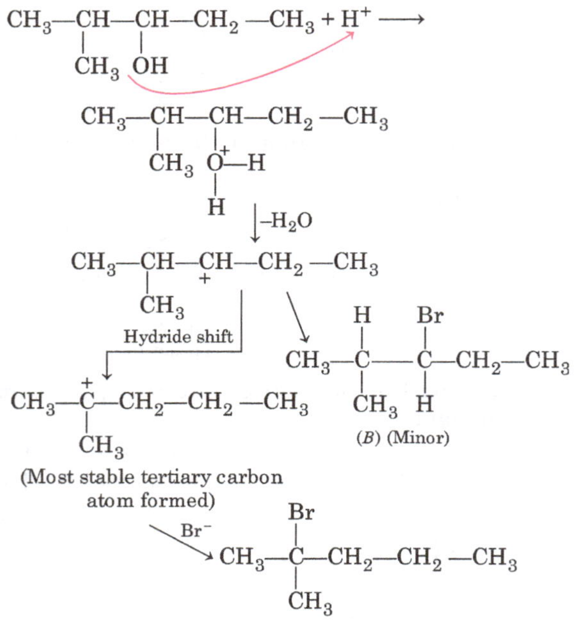

(*A*) 2-bromo-2-methylpentane (Major)

The product (*A*) is major because the carbocation formed is 3° carbocation which is more stable than the carbocation formed in product (*B*). **(2)**

19. Refer to text on page 240. **(3)**

20. The reaction of alcohols with Lucas reagent (conc. HCl and $ZnCl_2$) follows S_N1 mechanism which depends upon the stability of carbocations (intermediate). More stable the intermediate carbocation, more reactive is the alcohol. Tertiary carbocations are most stable among the three classes of carbocations and the order of the stability of carbocation is 3° > 2° > 1°. This order, in turn, reflects the order of reactivity of three classes of alcohols, i.e. 3° > 2° > 1°.

Thus, as the stability of carbocations are different so the reactivity of all the three classes of alcohols with Lucas reagent is different. **(3)**

21. (i) $\underset{\text{Butanol}}{CH_3CH_2CH_2CH_2OH} \xrightarrow[\text{Oxidation}]{[O]} \underset{\text{Butanoic acid}}{CH_3CH_2CH_2COOH}$ **(1)**

(ii) $\underset{\text{Butan-2-ol}}{CH_3CH(OH)CH_2CH_3} \xrightarrow[\text{Oxidation}]{[O]} \underset{\text{Butan-2-one}}{CH_3-C(=O)-CH_2CH_3}$ **(1)**

(iii) $\underset{\text{2-methylpropanol}}{CH_3-CH(CH_3)-CH_2OH} \xrightarrow[\text{Oxidation}]{[O]} \underset{\text{2-methyl propanoic acid}}{CH_3-CH(CH_3)-COOH}$ **(1)**

22. (i) Refer to text on page 242. **(2)**

(ii) **Hint** $CH_3-CH(I)-CH_3$ **(1)**

23. (i)

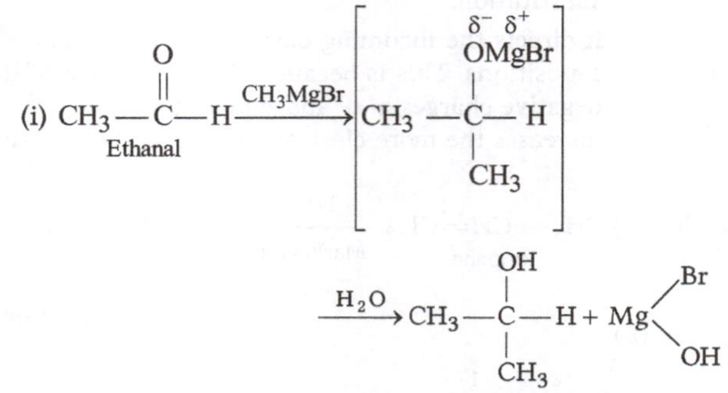

Propan-2-ol **(1)**

(ii) $\underset{\text{But-1-ene}}{CH_3CH_2CH=CH_2} + H_2O \xrightarrow{\text{Dil. } H_2SO_4} \underset{\text{Butan-2-ol}}{CH_3-CH_2-CH(OH)-CH_3}$ **(1)**

(iii)

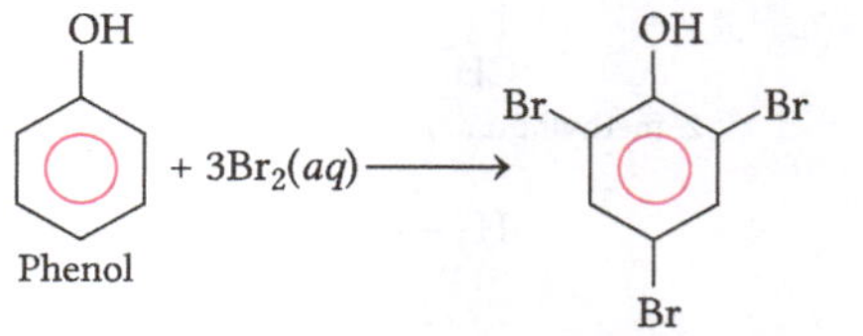

2,4,6-tribromophenol (Main product) **(1)**

24. (i) Refer to text on page 244. **(1)**

(ii) Refer to text on page 234. **(1)**

(iii) Refer to text on page 244. **(1)**

25. (i) Refer to text on page 244. **(1)**

(ii) Refer to text on page 244. **(1)**

(iii) Refer to text on page 249 and 250. **(1)**

26. Alkyl halide should be primary for Williamson's synthesis.

Hence, alkyl halide is derived from ethanol and the alkoxide ion from 3-methylpentan-2-ol.

$$\underset{\text{Ethanol}}{CH_3CH_2OH} + HBr \xrightarrow{\Delta} \underset{\text{Ethyl bromide}}{CH_3CH_2Br} + H_2O$$ **(1)**

$$2\overset{5}{C}H_3\overset{4}{C}H_2-\overset{3}{C}H(CH_3)-\overset{2}{C}H(\overset{1}{C}H_3)-OH + 2Na \longrightarrow$$

3-methylpentan-2-ol

$$2CH_3CH_2-CH(CH_3)-CH(CH_3)-O^-Na^+ + H_2\uparrow$$

Sodium-3-methyl-pent-2-oxide **(1)**

$CH_3CH_2-CH(CH_3)-CH(CH_3)-O^-Na^+ + CH_3CH_2-Br$

$\xrightarrow{S_N2} \overset{5}{C}H_3\overset{4}{C}H_2-\overset{3}{C}H(CH_3)-\overset{2}{C}H(\overset{1}{C}H_3)-O-C_2H_5 + NaBr$

2-ethoxy-3-methylpentane **(1)**

27. As Aartha knows reagent and substrate of each test tube, so she can get idea of product if she have knowledge of Williamson ether synthesis reaction.

- In test tube *A*, alkyl halide is 1° so ether will form. **(1)**

$C_2H_5-Cl + C_2H_5\overset{\ominus}{O}\overset{\oplus}{Na} \longrightarrow C_2H_5-O-C_2H_5 + NaCl$

- In test tube *B*, alkyl halide is 3° (highly branched) so elimination occurs and alkene will form which gives alkane on reduction with H_2/Ni. **(1)**

$CH_3-C(CH_3)_2-Br + C_2H_5ONa \longrightarrow CH_3-C(CH_3)=CH_2$

$\xrightarrow[Ni]{H_2} CH_3-CH(CH_3)-CH_3$

Thus, reaction in test *B* will form alkane. **(1)**

- Test tube *C* will give ether as *R–X* is primary.

$CH_3CH_2CH_2Br + C_2H_5O^-Na^+ \longrightarrow CH_3CH_2CH_2OC_2H_5 + NaBr$

28. Two methods can be employed for this preparation

(i) *Via* Williamson's synthesis

(a) $3CH_3CH_2CH_2OH + PBr_3 \longrightarrow 3CH_3CH_2CH_2Br + H_3PO_3$
Propan-1-ol → 1-bromopropane

(b) $2CH_3CH_2CH_2OH + 2Na \longrightarrow 2CH_3CH_2CH_2O^-Na^+ + H_2$
Propan-1-ol → Sodium propoxide

$CH_3CH_2CH_2O^-Na^+ + CH_3CH_2CH_2-Br \xrightarrow[\text{Heat}]{\text{Dry ether}} CH_3CH_2CH_2-O-CH_2CH_2CH_3 + NaBr$
Sodium propoxide, 1-bromopropane → 1-propoxypropane **(1½)**

(ii) By the dehydration of propan-1-ol with conc. H_2SO_4 at 413 K

$CH_3CH_2CH_2OH + H^+ \xrightarrow{413\,K} CH_3CH_2CH_2-\overset{+}{\ddot{O}}H_2$
Propan-1-ol → Protonated propan-1-ol

$CH_3CH_2CH_2-\ddot{O}H + CH_3CH_2CH_2-\overset{+}{\ddot{O}}H_2 \xrightarrow[-H_2O,\,-H^+]{413\,K} CH_3CH_2CH_2-O-CH_2CH_2CH_3$
1-propoxypropane **(1½)**

29. (i) Refer to text on page 251. **(1)**
(ii) Refer to text on page 234. **(1)**
(iii) Refer to text on page 244. **(1)**

30. (i) $CH_3CH_2CH_2-O-CH_2CH_2CH_3 \xrightarrow[373K]{HI} CH_3CH_2CH_2-OH + CH_3CH_2CH_2-I$
1-propoxypropane → Fropan-1-ol + 1-iodopropane

$CH_3CH_2CH_2-OH + \underset{(Excess)}{HI} \longrightarrow CH_3CH_2CH_2-I$ **(1)**

(ii)

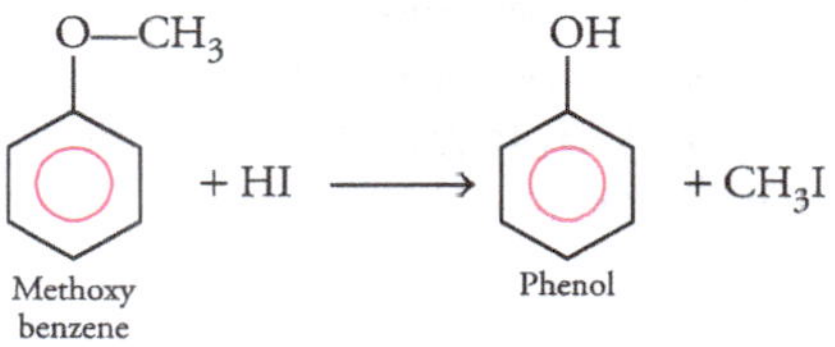

(1)

(iii)

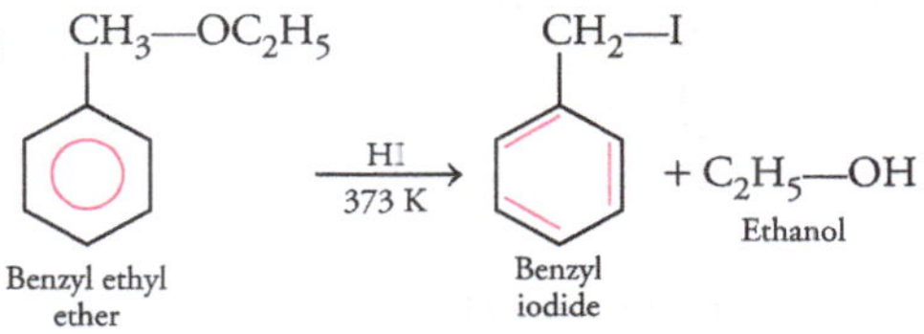

(1)

31. (i) (a) Refer to text on page 244. **(1)**
(b) Refer to text on page 244. **(1)**
(ii) The correct decreasing order of boiling points of the given ethers is as follows :
Anisole (III) > Diethyl ether (I) > Ethyl methyl ether (II)
This is because anisole being an aromatic ether have larger molecular size and as a result, higher van der waal's forces of interactions followed by diethyl ether and ethylmethyl ether. **(1)**

32. (i) Refer to text on pages 243 and 244. **(2)**
(ii) Refer to text on page 250. **(1)**

33. (i) The C—O bond length in phenol is shorter than that in methanol. This is due to the partial double bond character of the unshared electron pair of oxygen conjugated with the aromatic ring and the sp^2-hybridised state of carbon to which oxygen is attached. **(1)**
(ii) The correct increasing order of boiling point of given compounds are **(1)**
n-butane < ethoxyethane < butanal < butanol

(iii)

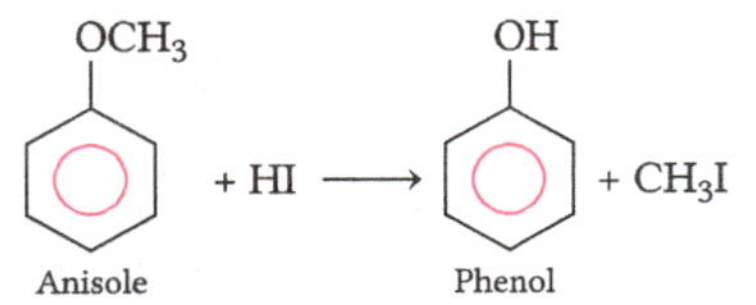

(1)

34. (i) Hydroboration-oxidation reaction is the addition of borane followed by oxidation.

$$3CH_3{-}CH = CH_2 + (BH_3)_2 \text{ or } B_2H_6 \longrightarrow (CH_3CH_2CH_2)_3B$$

Propene

$$\xrightarrow{H_2O_2/OH} H_3BO_3 + 3CH_3CH_2CH_2OH$$ (1)

(ii) The reaction of alkyl halides with solution alkoxide to form ether is called Williamson's synthesis.

$$\underset{\text{Alkyl halide}}{R{-}X} + \underset{\text{Sodium alkoxide}}{R'{-}\overset{-}{O}{-}\overset{+}{Na}} \longrightarrow \underset{\text{Ether}}{R{-}O{-}R'} + NaX$$ (1)

(iii) Anisole reacts with alkyl halide in presence of anhydrous $AlCl_3$ to give the desired products as shown below.

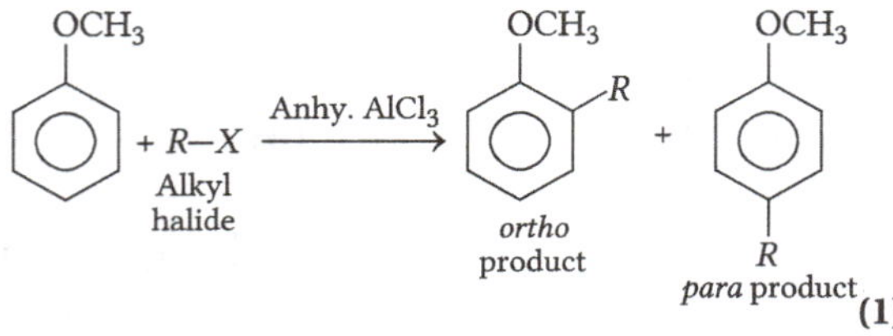

(1)

35. (i) Refer to solution 10 (ii) (SA I Type Ques). (1)

(ii) Refer to text on page 244 (1)

(iii)

$$\underset{t\text{-butyl alcohol}}{CH_3{-}\overset{CH_3}{\underset{CH_3}{C}}{-}OH} \xrightarrow{Cu,\ 573\ K} \underset{\text{2-methyl propene}}{CH_3{-}\overset{CH_3}{C}{=}CH_2}$$ (1)

36. (i) Molecular formula $C_5H_{12}O$ represents eight isomeric alkanols. These are :

(a) $\overset{5}{C}H_3{-}\overset{4}{C}H_2{-}\overset{3}{C}H_2{-}\overset{2}{C}H_2{-}\overset{1}{C}H_2{-}OH$

Pentan-1-ol (½)

(b) $\overset{4}{C}H_3{-}\underset{CH_3}{\overset{3}{C}H}{-}\overset{2}{C}H_2{-}\overset{1}{C}H_2{-}OH$

3-methyl butan-1-ol (½)

(c) $\overset{4}{C}H_3{-}\overset{3}{C}H_2{-}\underset{CH_3}{\overset{2}{C}H}{-}\overset{1}{C}H_2{-}OH$

2-methyl butan-1-ol (½)

(d) $\overset{3}{C}H_3{-}\underset{CH_3}{\overset{CH_3}{\overset{2}{C}}}{-}\overset{1}{C}H_2{-}OH$

2, 2-dimethyl propan-1-ol (½)

(e) $\overset{5}{C}H_3{-}\overset{4}{C}H_2{-}\overset{3}{C}H_2{-}\underset{OH}{\overset{2}{C}H}{-}\overset{1}{C}H_3$

Pentan-2-ol (½)

(f) $\overset{4}{C}H_3{-}\underset{CH_3}{\overset{3}{C}H}{-}\underset{OH}{\overset{2}{C}H}{-}\overset{1}{C}H_3$

3-methyl butan-2-ol (½)

(g) $\overset{1}{C}H_3{-}\underset{OH}{\overset{CH_3}{\overset{2}{C}}}{-}\overset{3}{C}H_2{-}\overset{4}{C}H_3$

2-methyl butan-2-ol (½)

(h) $\overset{5}{C}H_3{-}\overset{4}{C}H_2{-}\underset{OH}{\overset{3}{C}H}{-}\overset{2}{C}H_2{-}\overset{1}{C}H_3$

Pentan-3-ol (½)

(ii) Primary : (a), (b), (c) and (d); Secondary : (e), (f), (h) and Tertiary : (g). (1)

37. (i) (a) Propene ⟶ Propan-2-ol

$$\underset{\text{Propene}}{CH_3{-}CH{=}CH_2} \xrightarrow{H^+/H_2O} \underset{\text{Propan-2-ol}}{CH_3{-}\underset{OH}{CH}{-}CH_3}$$ (1)

(b) Benzyl chloride ⟶ Benzyl alcohol

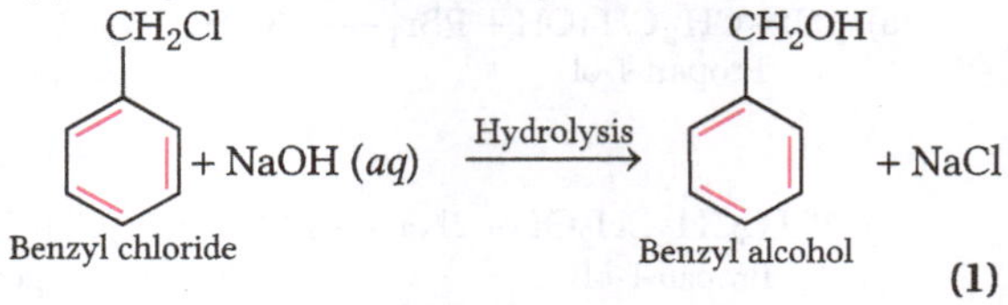

(1)

(c) Ethyl magnesium chloride ⟶ Propan-1-ol

$$\underset{\text{Formaldehyde}}{\overset{H}{\underset{H}{>}}\overset{\delta+}{C}{=}\overset{\delta-}{O}} + \overset{\delta-}{CH_3CH_2}{-}\overset{\delta+}{MgCl} \xrightarrow{\text{Dry ether}}$$

$$\underset{\text{Adduct}}{\left[CH_3CH_2CH_2\overset{\delta-}{O}\overset{\delta+}{MgCl}\right]} \xrightarrow[\text{Hydrolysis}]{H^+/H_2O} \underset{\text{Propan-1-ol}}{CH_3CH_2CH_2OH} + Mg(OH)Cl$$ (1)

(d) Methyl magnesium bromide ⟶ 2-methylpropan-2-ol

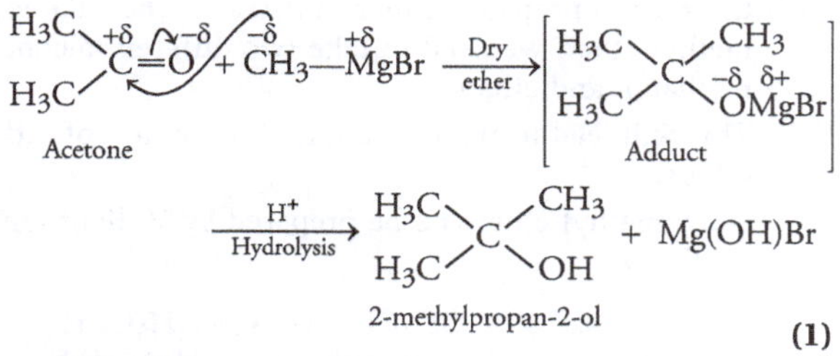

(1)

(ii) Refer to text on page 236. (1)

38. (i) (a) $CH_3CH_2CH_2OH \xrightarrow[\text{(Oxidation)}]{KMnO_4/OH^-} CH_3\,CH_2\,CHO$
Propan-1-ol → Propanal

$\xrightarrow[\text{(Oxidation)}]{KMnO_4/OH^-} CH_3CH_2COOH$
Propanoic acid (1)

(b)

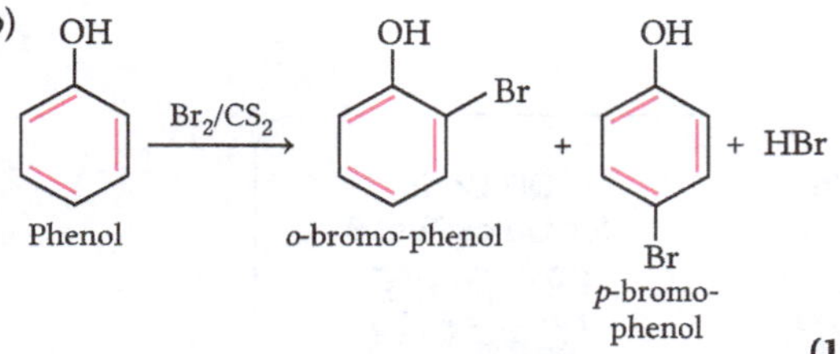

(1)

(c)

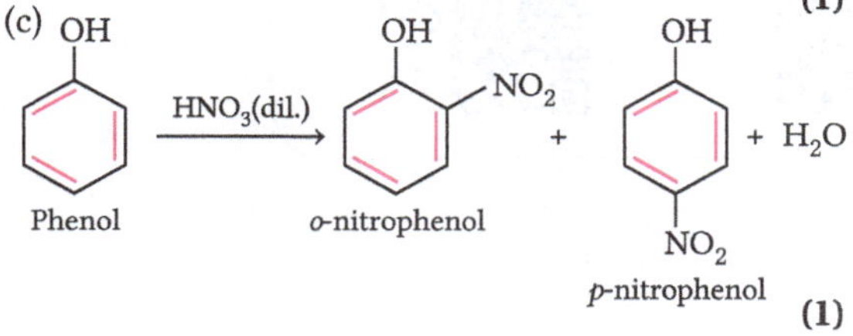

(1)

(d)

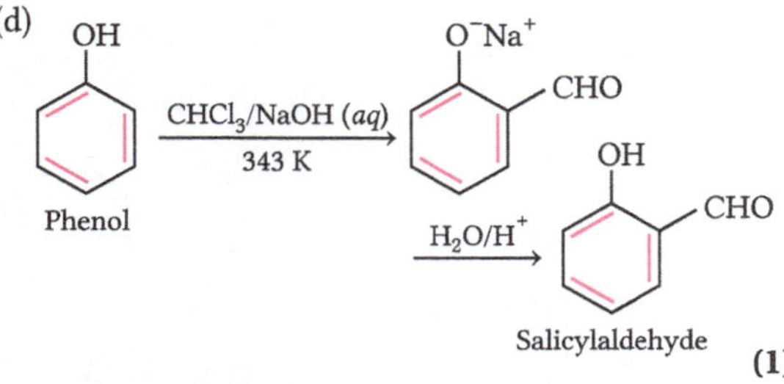

(1)

(ii) In the presence of attacking electrophile, –OH group exerts +*R* effect on the benzene ring. So, electron density in the ring increases particularly at the *ortho* and *para* positions.

When an electrophile attacks, substitution takes place readily at these (*o* and *p* –) positions.

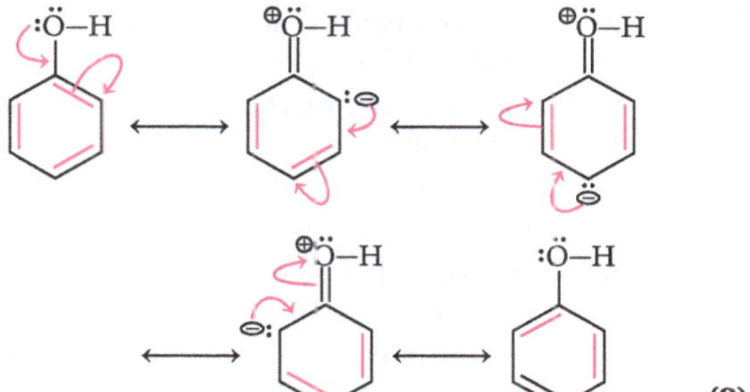

(2)

39. (i) Refer to text on page 235. (2)

(ii) (a), (b) Refer to text on page 244. (2)

(c)

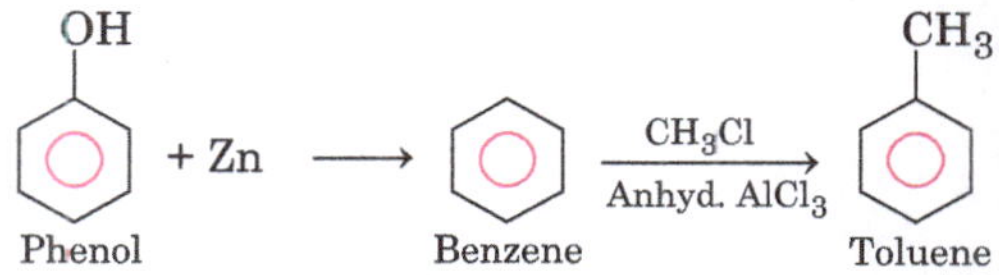

(1)

40. Under acid catalysed dehydration, 2° and 3° alcohols give alkenes rather than ethers.

Thus is due to steric hindrance caused by bulky groups, nucleophilic attack by the alcohol molecule on the protonated alcohol molecule does not occur.

Instead protonated 2° and 3° alcohols lose a water molecule to form stable 2° and 3° carbocations. These carbocations prefer to lose a proton to form alkenes rather than undergoing nucleophilic attack by alcohol molecule to form ethers. (2)

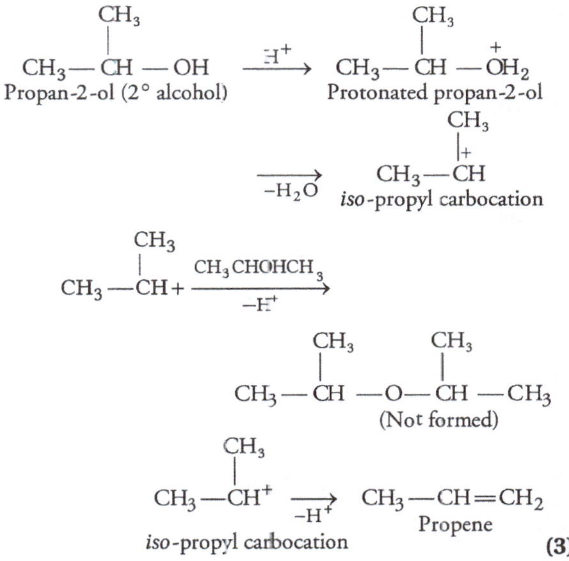

(3)

41. (i) (a) Phenol and benzoic acid can be distinguished by adding $NaHCO_3$ to each.

Phenol does not react while benzoic acid gives effervescence. **(1)**

(b) Propan-2-ol gives iodoform test whereas, propan-1-ol does not. **(1)**

(c) Methanol and ethanol are distinguished by a type of test known as iodoform test.

When ethanol is warmed with iodine in the presence of NaOH, it forms a yellow coloured precipitate but methanol do not react positively to the iodoform test. **(1)**

(ii) In order to prepare an unsymmetrical ether like ethyl methyl ether, we need to take two different alcohols, i.e. methanol and ethanol.

This will lead to the formation of a mixture of different ethers.

Ethyl methyl ether can be prepared by Williamson's synthesis.

$$\underset{\text{Sodium ethoxide}}{C_2H_5\ddot{O}^-Na^+} + \underset{\text{Methyl chloride}}{CH_3Cl} \longrightarrow \underset{\text{Ethylmethyl ether (Methoxy ethane)}}{C_2H_5OCH_3} + NaCl$$

(2)

QR Code for Quick Test 1

QR Code for Quick Test 2

QR Code for Quick Test 3

SELF ASSESSMENT TEST

Objective Type Questions [1 Mark]

1. 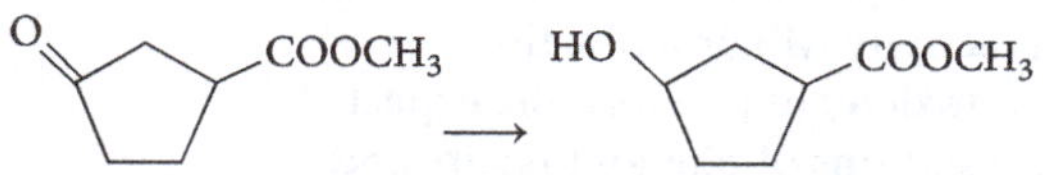

Which of the following reagents should be used to carry out the above conversion?

(a) $LiAlH_4$ (b) $NaBH_4$
(c) Zn-Hg/HCl (d) $KMnO_4$

2. Select the strongest acid among the following compounds.

(a) $FCH_2CH_2CH_2OH$
(b) $H_3CCH_2CH(F)—CH_2OH$
(c) $CH_3CH_2CF_2CH_2OH$
(d) $CH_3CH(F)CH_2CH_2OH$

3. Lucas reagent produces cloudiness immediately with

(a) $CH_3—C(CH_3)(OH)—CH_3$
(b) $CH_3—CH(OH)—CH_2—CH_3$
(c) $CH_3—CH_2—CH_2—OH$
(d) $CH_3—CH(CH_3)—CH_2—OH$

4. Match the Column I with Column II.

Column I		Column II	
(i)	Methanol	(a)	Wood spirit (produced by destructive distillation of wood)
(ii)	Kolbe's reaction	(b)	Reaction of alkyl halide with sodium alkoxide
(iii)	Williamson's synthesis	(c)	Conversion of phenol to *o*-hydroxy salicylic acid

(a) (i)-(b), (ii)-(a), (iii)-(c)
(b) (i)-(a), (ii)-(b), (iii)-(c)
(c) (i)-(a), (ii)-(c), (iii)-(b)
(d) (i)-(c), (ii)-(a), (iii)-(b)

5. In ethers, the two bond pairs and two lone pairs of electrons on oxygen are arranged in a

(a) planar arrangement
(b) tetrahedral arrangement
(c) trigonal bipyramidal arrangement
(d) linear arrangement

Assertion-Reason [1 Mark]

■ **Directions** (Q. Nos. 6-8) In the following questions, an Assertion (A) is followed by a corresponding Reason (R). Use the following keys to choose the appropriate answer.

(a) Both (A) and (R) are correct and (R) is the correct explanation of (A).
(b) Both (A) and (R) are correct but (R) is not the correct explanation of (A).
(c) (A) is correct but (R) is incorrect.
(d) (A) is incorrect but (R) is correct.

6. Assertion (A) Alcohols react both as nucleophiles and electrophiles.

Reason (R) The bond between C—O is broken when alcohols react as nucleophiles.

7. Assertion (A) Reimer-Tiemann reaction of phenol with CCl_4 in NaOH at 340 K gives salicylic acid as the major product.

Reason (R) The reaction occurs through intermediate formation of dichlorocarbene.

8. Assertion (A) Ether behaves as bases in the presence of mineral acids.

Reason (R) Due to the presence of lone pair of electrons on oxygen.

Short Answer Type I Questions [2 Marks]

9. Write the chemical test to distinguish between the following pairs of compounds.

(i) Propan-1-ol and propan-2-ol
(ii) Phenol and ethanol

10. Give reason for the following.
   (i) Phenol is more acidic than methanol.
   (ii) The C—O—H bond angle in alcohols is slightly less than the tetrahedral angle (109°28′).

11. Account for the following :
   (i) Diethyl ether does not react with sodium.
   (ii) Phenol is more easily nitrated than benzene.

Short Answer Type II Questions [3 Marks]

12. Write the equations for the following reaction.
   (i) Phenol is treated with zinc dust and then with conc. HNO_3 and H_2SO_4.
   (ii) Ethanol is treated with PCC.
   (iii) Chloroethane is treated with *aq.* NaOH and then followed by $KMnO_4$.

13. An organic compound '*X*' with molecular mass C_3H_6 on treatment with aqueous H_2SO_4 gives '*Y*' which on further treatment with $HCl/ZnCl_2$ yields '*Z*'. The compound '*Z*' on treatment with ethanolic KOH gives back the compound. Deduce the structures of *X*, *Y* and *Z*.

Case-Study [4 Marks]

14. **The following questions are case-based questions. Each quation has an internal choice and carries 4 (2+1+1) marks each. Read the given case carefully and answer the questions that follows.**

Alcohols and phenols consist of two parts, an alkyl/aryl group and a hydroxyl group. The properties of alcohols and phenols are chiefly due to the hydroxyl group.

Alcohol consumption, particularly heavier drinking is an important risk factor for many health problems and thus, is a major contributor to the global burden of disease. Alcohol or alcoholic bevarages contain ethanol, a psychoactive and toxic substance that can cause dependence. Worldwide, around 2.6 million deaths were caused by alcohol consumption in 2019. Infact, alcohol is a necessary underlying cause for more than 30 conditions and a contributing factor to many more.

The most common disease categories that are entirely or partly caused by alcohol consumption includes infectious diseases cancer, diabetes, neuropsychiatric diseases, cardiovascular disease, liver and pancreatic disease. Phenol is a historical disinfectant with continued use in industrial laboratories, and some health care settings.

Phenol is mildly acidic and requires careful handling due to its propensity to cause chemical burns. It is a protoplasmic poison that can result in multisystem organ failure in severe toxicity. This activity will describe the mechanism of toxicity of phenols, the expected clinical manifestations of phenol toxicity and the management of phenol poisoned patients.

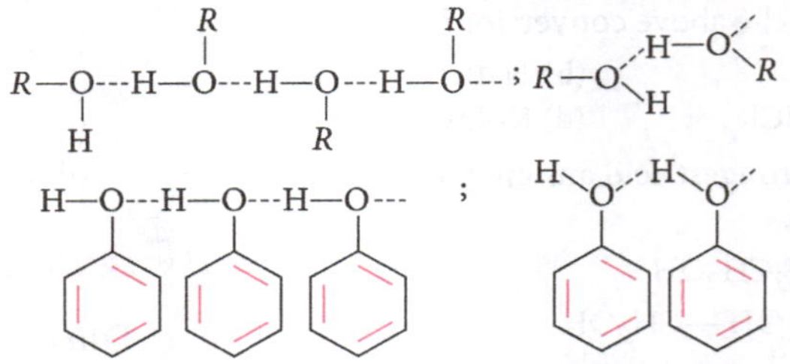

   (i) Write the increasing order of the basicity of the following compounds.
   $H_2O, OH^-, CH_3OH, CH_3O^-$
   (ii) Which among the following, methanol, butan-2-ol, butan-1-ol, 2-methyl-propan-2-ol, will have the highest boiling point?
   Or Write the decreasing order of the boiling point of the following alcohols.
   (i) Pentan-1-ol (ii) 2-methylbutan-2-ol
   (iii) 3-methylbutan-2-ol
   (iii) Why is *o*-nitrophenol more steam volatile than *p*-nitrophenol?

15. (i) An alcohol *A* $(C_4H_{10}O)$ on oxidation with acidified potassium dichromate gives acid *B* $(C_4H_8O_2)$. Compound *A* when dehydrated with conc. H_2SO_4 at 443 K gives compound *C*. Treatment of *C* with aqueous H_2SO_4 gives compound *D* $(C_4H_{10}O)$ which is an isomer of *A*.
   Compound *D* is resistant to oxidation but compound *A* can be easily oxidised.
   Identify *A*, *B*, *C* and *D*. Name the type of isomerism exhibited by *A* and *D*.
   (ii) Sulphuric acid is not used during the reaction of alcohols in the conversion of an alcohol to the alkyl iodide. Explain.

Answers

1. (b)	2. (c)	3. (a)	4. (c)
5. (b)	6. (c)	7. (d)	8. (a)

08

CHAPTER

Aldehydes, Ketones and Carboxylic Acids

The organic compounds containing carbon-oxygen double bond (represented as $>C=O$) are known as **carbonyl compounds** and the group present is known as carbonyl group.
The carbonyl group plays an important role in many biochemical processes of life including the role of β-carotene in promoting healthy vision. It is responsible for many flavours and fragrances such as vanillin (from vanilla beans), cinnamaldehyde (from cinnamon) etc.

YOUR STUDY GOALS

- 8.1 Nomenclature of Aldehydes and Ketones
- 8.2 Structure of the Carbonyl Group
- 8.3 Preparation of Aldehydes and Ketones
- 8.4 Physical Properties of Aldehydes and Ketones
- 8.5 Chemical Reactions of Aldehydes and Ketones
- 8.6 Uses of Aldehydes and Ketones
- 8.7 Carboxylic Acids

YOUR PRACTICE GOAL

- Objective Type Questions (38 Qs ; 24 MCQs, 12 A-R, 2 Case Study)
- Subjective Type Questions (51Qs; 18 SA-I, 17 SA-II, 16 LA)

Depending upon the atoms or group of atoms attached on either sides of the carbonyl group, carbonyl compounds are divided into three major classes, i.e., aldehydes, ketones and carboxylic acids.

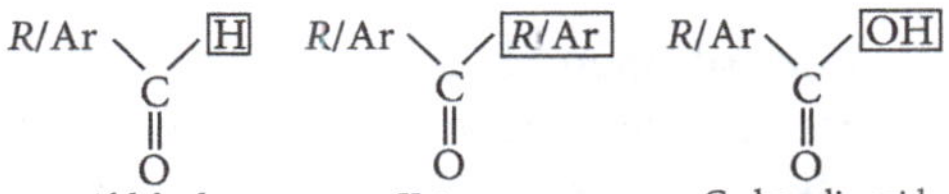

Aldehyde Ketone Carboxylic acid

Aldehydes and ketones are the simplest and most important carbonyl compounds with general formula; $C_nH_{2n}O$.

8.1 Nomenclature of Aldehydes and Ketones

There are two systems of nomenclature of aldehydes and ketones. These are as follows

Common Names

- Common names of aldehydes are derived from common names of corresponding carboxylic acids (—COOH) just by replacing the ending '-ic' of carboxylic acid with aldehyde.

- The location of the substituent in the carbon chain is indicated by Greek letters α, β, γ, δ, etc. The α-carbon being the one directly linked to the $>C=O$ group, β-carbon the next and so on. e.g.

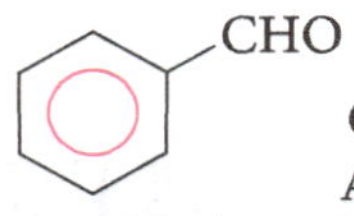

Benzaldehyde

CH_3CHO
Acetaldehyde

$$\underset{\gamma}{H_3C}-\underset{\beta}{\overset{Br}{\overset{|}{CH}}}-\underset{\alpha}{CH_2}-\overset{O}{\overset{\|}{C}}-H$$

β-bromobutyraldehyde

- The common names of ketones are derived by naming the two alkyl or aryl groups bonded to the carbonyl group in alphabetical order.
- Alkyl phenyl ketones are usually named by adding the acyl group as prefix to phenone.
- The locations of substituents are indicated by Greek letters α α′, ββ′, etc., beginning with the carbon atoms next to the carbonyl group, indicated as αα′.

e.g. $$Cl-\overset{\alpha'}{CH_2}-\overset{O}{\overset{\|}{C}}-\overset{\alpha}{CH_2}-Cl,$$

α, α′-dichloroacetone

$$Cl-\overset{\alpha}{CH_2}-\overset{O}{\overset{\|}{C}}-\overset{\alpha'}{CH_2}\overset{\beta'}{CH_2}Br,$$

β′-bromoethyl-α-chloromethylketone

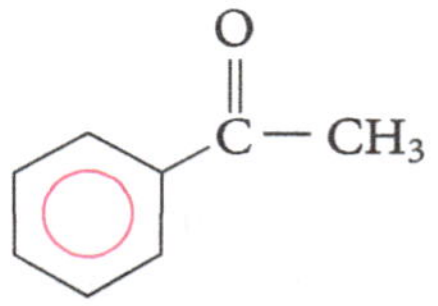

Acetophenone

IUPAC Names

- The IUPAC names of open chain aliphatic aldehydes and ketones are derived from the names of the corresponding alkanes by replacing the ending-'e' with '-al' and-'one' respectively.
- In case of aldehydes, the longest carbon chain is numbered from the carbon of the aldehyde group whereas in case of ketones, the numbering begins from the end nearer to the carbonyl group.
- The substituents are prefixed in alphabetical order along with numerals indicating their positions in the carbon chain. The same applies to cyclic ketones, where the carbonyl carbon is numbered one.
- When the aldehydic group is attached to a ring, the suffix '**carbaldehyde**' is added after the full name of cycloalkane.
- The numbering of the ring carbon atom starts from the carbon atom attached to the aldehyde group.

$$CH_3-CH_2-CH_2-\overset{Br}{\overset{|}{CH}}-\overset{CH_3}{\overset{|}{CH}}-\overset{O}{\overset{\|}{C}}-H,$$

3-bromo-2-methylhexan-1-al

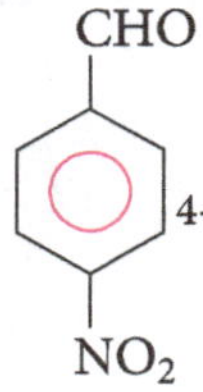

4-nitrobenzaldehyde, or 4-nitrobenzene-carbaldehyde

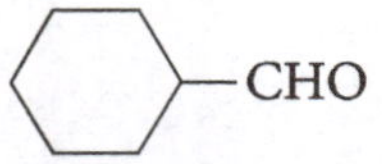

Cyclohexanecarbaldehyde ,

$$OHC-CH_2-\underset{\underset{CHO}{|}}{CH}-CH_2-CHO$$

Propane-1,2,3-tricarbaldehyde

$$CH_3-\overset{CH_3}{\overset{|}{CH}}-\overset{O}{\overset{\|}{C}}-\overset{CH_3}{\overset{|}{CH}}-CH_3,$$

2, 4-dimethylpentan-3-one

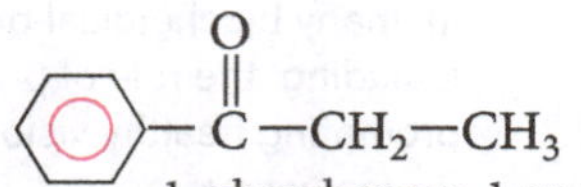

1-phenylpropan-1-one ,

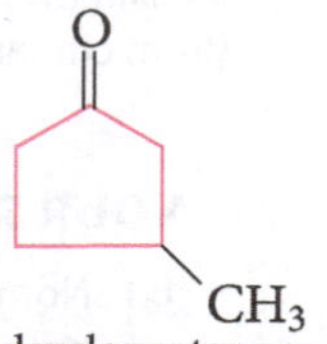

3-methylcyclopentanone ,

$$H_3C-CH_2-\overset{O}{\overset{\|}{C}}-CH_2-\overset{O}{\overset{\|}{C}}-H,$$

3-oxopentanal

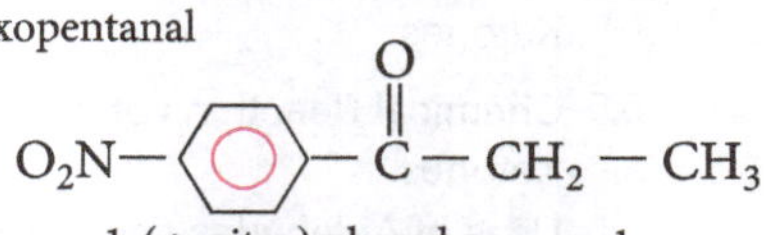

1-(*p*-nitro) phenyl propan-1-one or *p*-nitropropiophenone

Note The name of the simplest aromatic aldehyde carrying the aldehyde group on a benzene ring is **benzenecarbaldehyde** or **benzaldehyde.**

Common and IUPAC Names of Some Aldehydes and Ketones

Structural formula	Common name	IUPAC name
Aldehydes		
HCHO	Formaldehyde	Methanal
CH_3-CHO	Acetaldehyde	Ethanal
$CH_3-CH_2-\overset{\alpha}{C}H(CH_3)-CHO$	α-methylbutyraldehyde	2-methylbutanal
$(CH_3)_2CHCHO$	*iso*-butyraldehyde	2-methylpropanal
$CH_3-CH_2-CH_2-CH_2-CHO$	Valeraldehyde	Pentanal
$CH_2=CH-CHO$	Acrolein	Prop-2-en-1-al
$CH_3-\overset{\alpha}{C}H(OCH_3)-CHO$	α-methoxypropionaldehyde	2-methoxypropanal
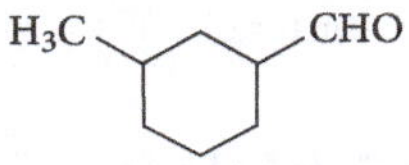	γ-methylcyclohexanecarbaldehyde	3-methylcyclohexanecarbaldehyde
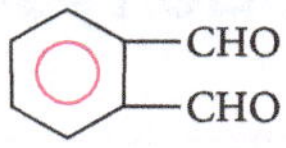	Phthaldehyde	Benzene-1,2-dicarbaldehyde
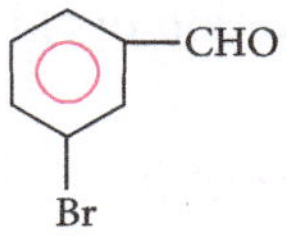	*m*-bromobenzaldehyde	3-bromobenzenecarbaldehyde or 3-bromobenzaldehyde
$CH_3-CH=CH-CHO$	Crotonaldehyde	But-2-enal
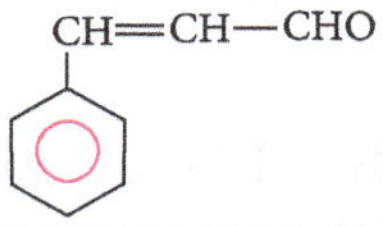	Cinnamaldehyde	3-phenylprop-2-enal
Ketones		
CH_3COCH_3	Acetone	Propanone
$CH_3-CH(CH_3)-C(=O)-CH(CH_3)-CH_3$	Di*iso*propyl ketone	2, 4-dimethylpentan-3-one
$CH_3-C(CH_3)=CH-COCH_3$	Mesityl oxide	4-methylpent-3-en-2-one
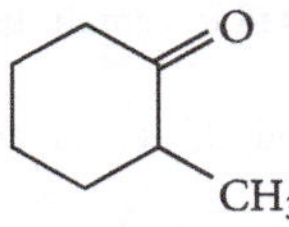	α-methylcyclohexanone	2-methylcyclohexanone

Example 1 **Draw the structures of the following compounds**

(i) **α-methoxypropionaldehyde**
(ii) **3-hydroxybutanal**
(iii) **2-hydroxycyclopentanecarbaldehyde**
(iv) **4-oxopentanal**
(v) **Di-*sec*-butylketone**
(vi) **4- fluoroacetophenone** **NCERT Intext**

Sol. (i) 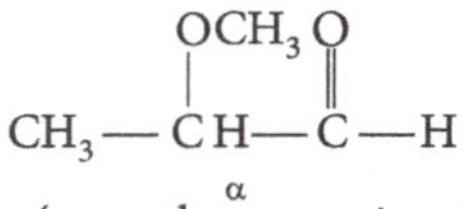

(α-methoxypropionaldehyde)

(ii) 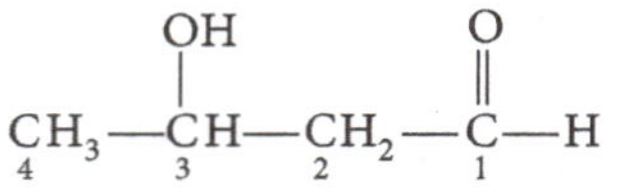 (3-hydroxybutanal)

(iii) 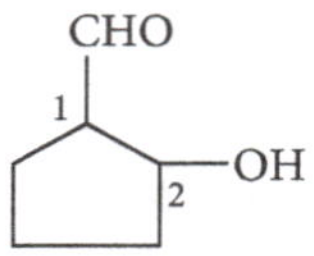 (2-hydroxycyclopentane carbaldehyde)

(iv) 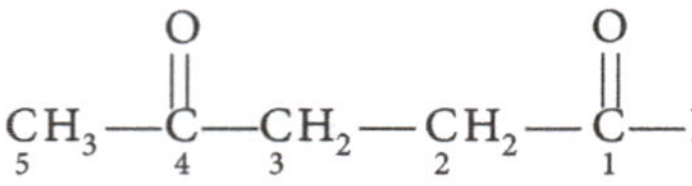 (4 - oxopentanal)

(v) 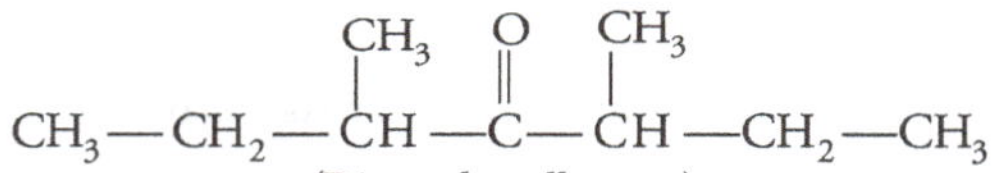

(Di-*sec*-butylketone)

(vi) 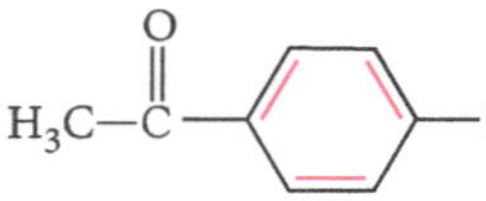 (4- fluoroacetophenone)

8.2 Structure of the Carbonyl Group

The carbonyl carbon atom is sp^2-hybridised and forms 3 sigma (σ) bonds. The fourth valence electron of carbon remains in its *p*-orbital where it forms a π-bond by overlapping with *p*-orbital of an oxygen.

The oxygen atom also have two non-bonding electron pairs. Thus, the carbonyl carbon and the three atoms attached to it lie in the same plane and π-electron cloud is present above and below this plane.
It possesses a trigonal coplanar structure with bond angles are approximately 120°.

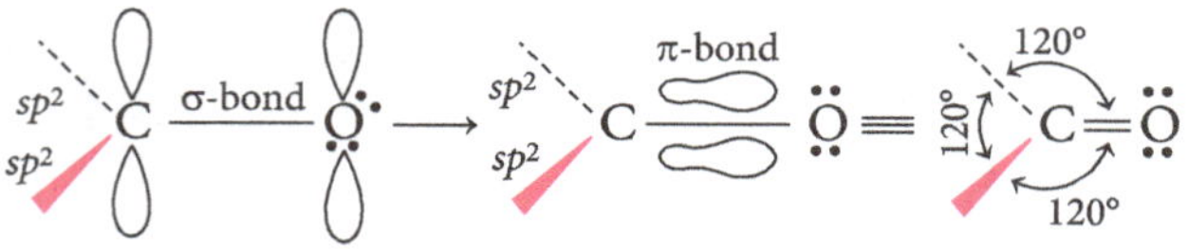

Orbital diagram for the formation of carbonyl group

Resonance of Carbonyl Group

The carbon-oxygen double bond is polarised due to higher electronegativity of oxygen relative to carbon. As a result, carbonyl-carbon acquires partial positive charge and oxygen carries a partial negative charge. Hence, the carbonyl-carbon becomes electrophilic (Lewis acid) and carbonyl-oxygen a nucleophilic (Lewis base) centre. Carbonyl compounds have substantial dipole moments and are polar than ethers.

The high polarity of the carbonyl group can be explained on the basis of resonance involving a neutral (*A*) and dipolar (*B*) structures as shown below.

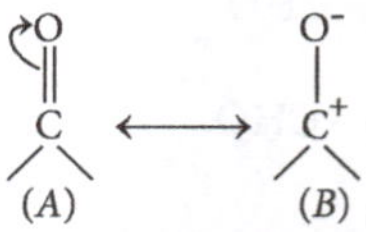

Resonance involving neutral (*A*) and dipolar (*B*) structures

8.3 Preparation of Aldehydes and Ketones

Some important methods of preparation of aldehydes and ketones are discussed below

Preparation of both Aldehydes and Ketones

These are prepared by the following methods.

1. From Alcohols

(i) **By the oxidation of alcohols** Aldehydes and ketones can be prepared by the oxidation of alcohols with $K_2Cr_2O_7/H_2SO_4$ or $KMnO_4/KOH$.

$$\underset{1^\circ \text{ alcohol}}{RCH_2OH} + [O] \xrightarrow{K_2Cr_2O_7/H_2SO_4} \underset{\text{Aldehyde}}{R-CHO} + H_2O$$

$$\underset{2^\circ \text{ alcohol}}{\begin{matrix} R \\ R' \end{matrix}\!\!>CHOH} + [O] \xrightarrow{K_2Cr_2O_7/H_2SO_4} \underset{\text{Ketone}}{\begin{matrix} R \\ R' \end{matrix}\!\!>C{=}O} + H_2O$$

Note The aldehydes formed in the above reaction are readily oxidised to carboxylic acids if allowed to remain in the reaction mixture.

Therefore, the aldehydes are distilled off as soon as they are formed.

(ii) **By the catalytic dehydrogenation of alcohols** This method is suitable for volatile alcohols and has industrial application.

In this method, alcohol vapours are passed over heavy metal catalysts (Ag or Cu) at 573 K.

$$\underset{1^\circ \text{ alcohol}}{R—CH_2OH} \xrightarrow{Cu/573\ K} \underset{\text{Aldehyde}}{R—CHO} + H_2$$

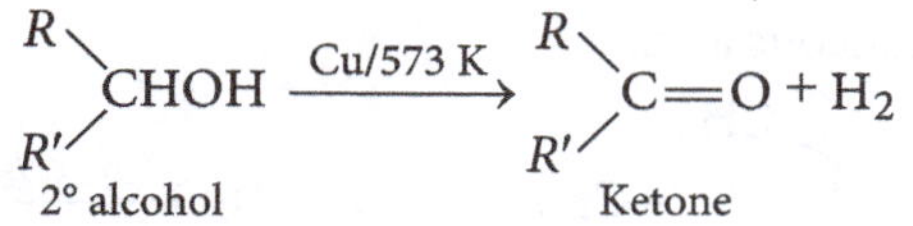

2. From Hydrocarbons

(i) **By the reductive ozonolysis of alkenes** Ozonolysis of alkenes followed by the reaction with zinc dust and water gives aldehydes, ketones or both depending on the substitution pattern of the alkene.

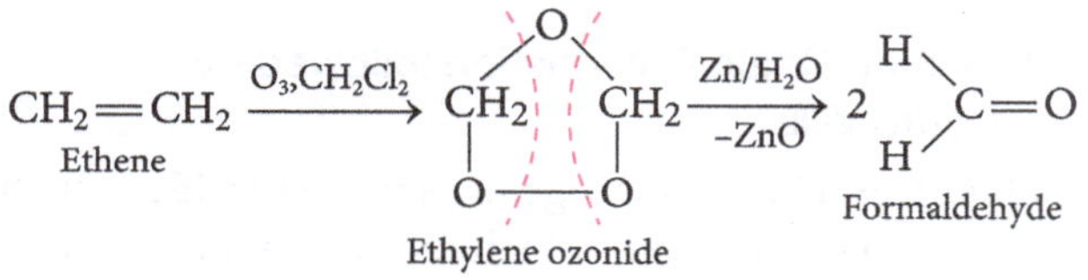

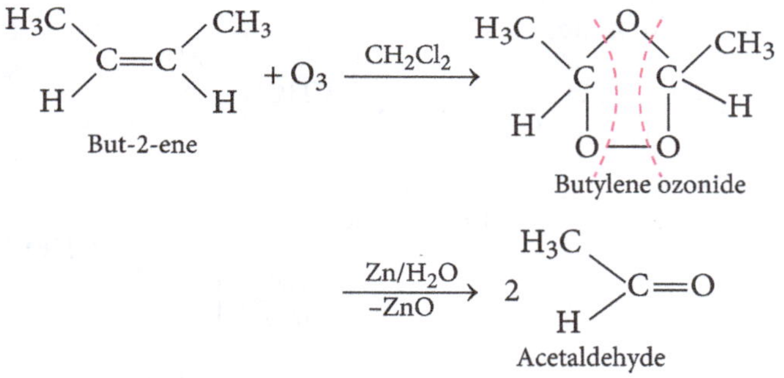

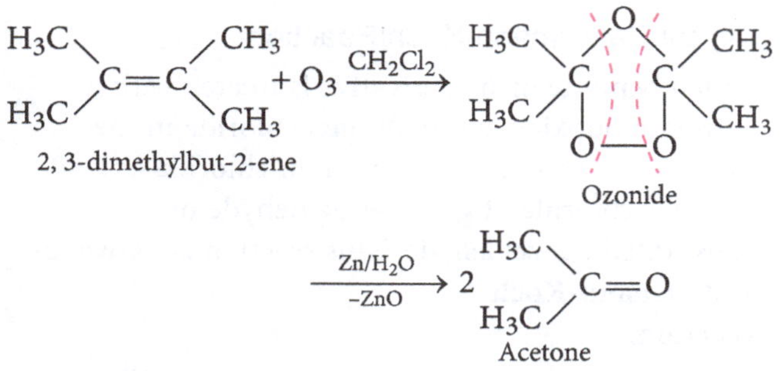

(ii) **By the hydration of alkynes** Addition of water to ethyne in the presence of dil. H_2SO_4 and $HgSO_4$ gives acetaldehyde. All other alkynes give ketones in this reaction.

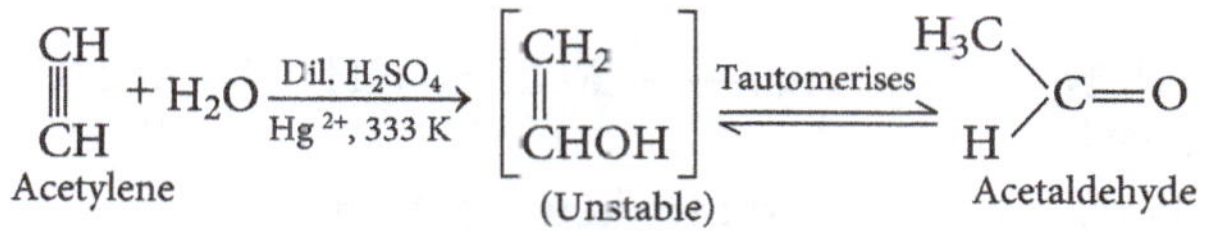

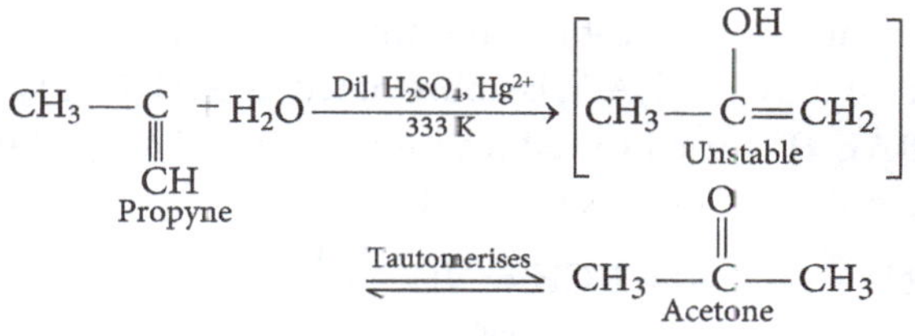

Preparation of both Aldehydes and Ketones

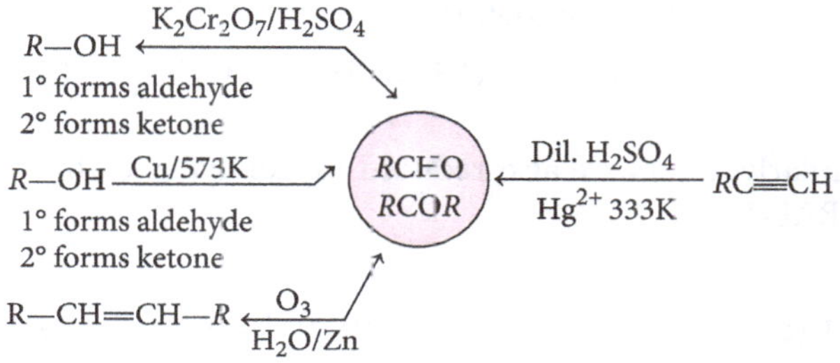

Preparation of Aldehydes

Some important methods for the preparation of only aldehydes are given below.

1. From Acyl Chloride

Acyl chloride or acid chloride is hydrogenated in the presence of palladium catalyst supported over and partially poisoned by the addition of sulphur or barium sulphate. This reaction is called **Rosenmund reduction.**

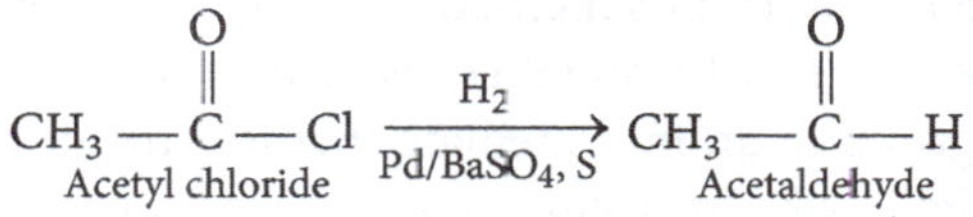

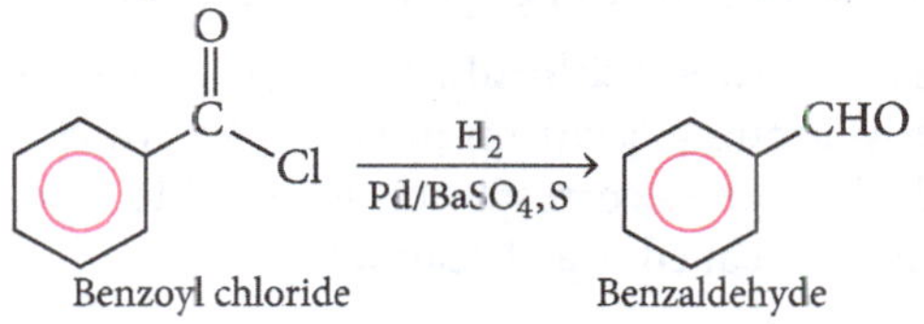

TEACHER'S TIP

Formaldehyde cannot be prepared by the above method as formyl chloride is unstable at room temperature.

2. From Nitriles and Esters

Nitriles are reduced to corresponding imine with stannous chloride in the presence of hydrochloric acid, which on hydrolysis give corresponding aldehyde.

$$\underset{\text{Nitrile}}{RCN} + SnCl_2 + HCl \longrightarrow \underset{\text{Imine}}{RCH = NH} \xrightarrow{H_3O^+} \underset{\text{Aldehyde}}{RCHO}$$

This reaction is called **Stephen reaction.**

Alternatively, di-*iso*-butylaluminium hydride, $[(CH_3)_2CHCH_2]_2AlH$ is abbreviated as $AlH(i\text{-}Bu)_2$ or **DIBAL-H** is used to reduce nitriles (selectively) to imines which upon hydrolysis give aldehydes.

$$RCN \xrightarrow{\text{(a) } AlH(i\text{-}Bu)_2} \underset{\text{Imine}}{RCH{=}NH} \xrightarrow[\text{Hydrolysis}]{\text{(b) } H_2O} \underset{\text{Aldehyde}}{RCHO} + NH_3$$

$$\underset{\text{Hex-4-en-1-nitrile}}{CH_3{-}CH{=}CH{-}CH_2CH_2CN} \xrightarrow[\text{(ii) } H_2O]{\text{(i) } AlH(i\text{-}Bu)_2} \underset{\text{Hex-4-en-1-al}}{CH_3{-}CH{=}CH{-}CH_2CH_2{-}CHO}$$

Similarly, esters are also reduced to aldehydes with DIBAL-H.

$$\underset{\text{Ethyl undecanoate}}{\underset{\text{(Ester)}}{CH_3(CH_2)_9{-}\overset{\overset{\displaystyle O}{\|}}{C}{-}OC_2H_5}} \xrightarrow[\text{(ii) } H_2O]{\text{(i) DIBAL-H}} \underset{\text{Undecanal}}{CH_3(CH_2)_9{-}\overset{\overset{\displaystyle O}{\|}}{C}{-}H}$$

3. From Aromatic Hydrocarbons

Aromatic aldehydes (benzaldehyde and its derivatives) are prepared from aromatic hydrocarbons by the following methods.

(i) By the Oxidation of Methylbenzene

Strong oxidising agents oxidise toluene and its derivatives to benzoic acid. In this method, oxidation is stopped at the aldehyde stage with suitable reagents that converts the methyl group to an intermediate that is difficult to oxidise further. Following oxidising agents are used for this purpose.

(a) **Use of Chromyl chloride** (CrO_2Cl_2) It oxidises methyl group to a chromium complex which on hydrolysis gives corresponding benzaldehyde. This reaction is called **Etard reaction.**

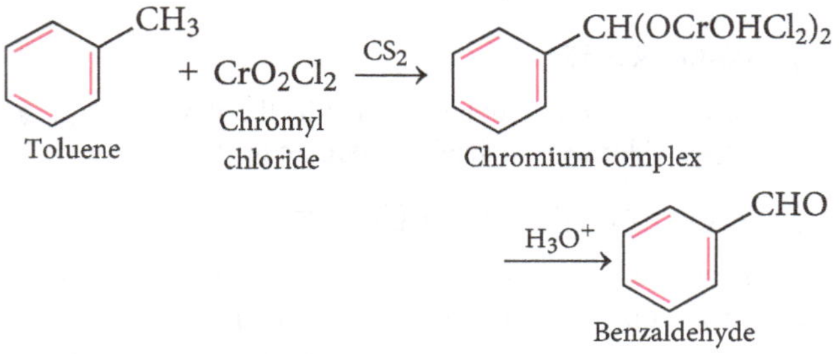

(b) **Use of Chromic oxide** (CrO_3) Toluene or substituted toluene on treatment with CrO_3 in acetic anhydride, gets converted to benzylidene diacetate. This benzylidene diacetate is hydrolysed to corresponding benzaldehyde with aqueous acid.

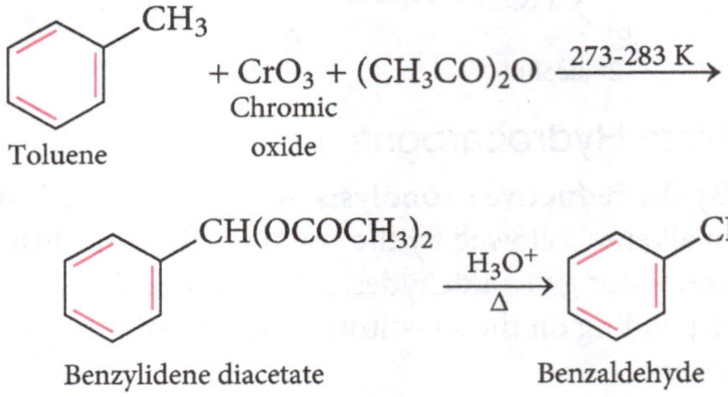

(ii) By Side Chain Chlorination followed by Hydrolysis

Toluene on chlorination gives benzal chloride, which on hydrolysis gives benzaldehyde. This reaction is a **commercial method for the manufacture of benzaldehyde.**

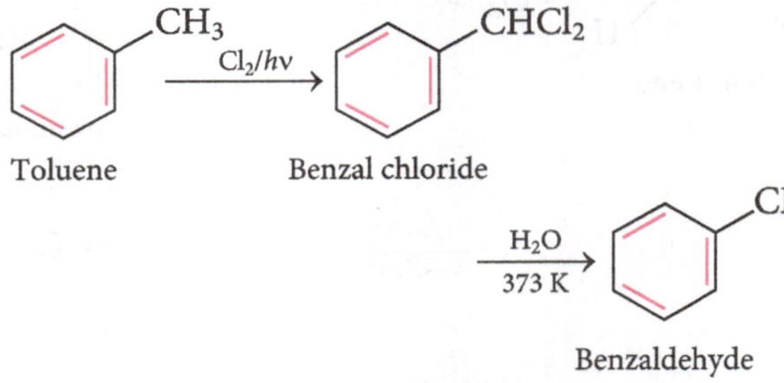

(iii) By Gattermann-Koch Reaction

When benzene or its derivative is treated with carbon monoxide and hydrogen chloride in the presence of anhydrous aluminium chloride or cuprous chloride, it gives benzaldehyde or substituted benzaldehyde. This reaction is known as **Gattermann-Koch reaction.**

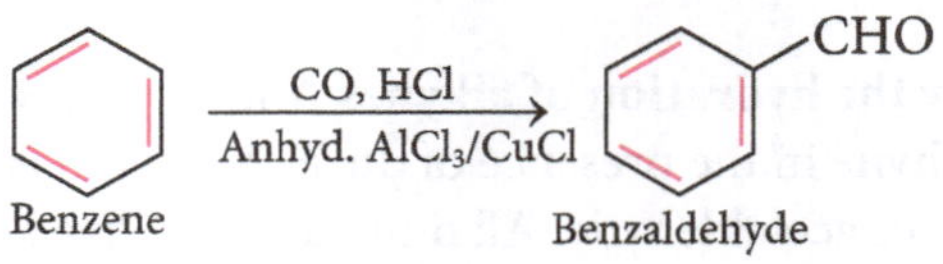

Preparation of Aldehydes

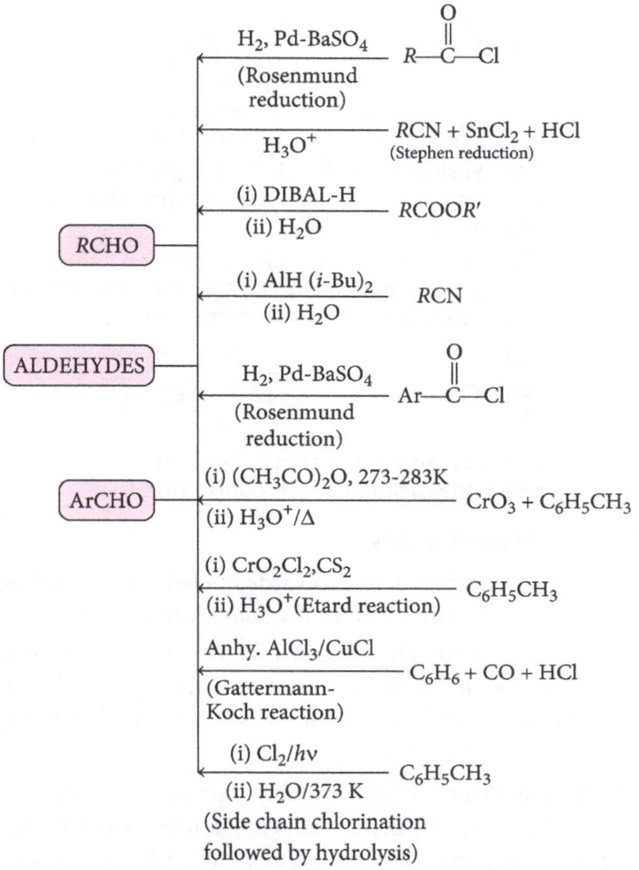

Preparation of Ketones

Some important methods for the preparation of ketones are given below.

1. From Acyl Chlorides

Acyl chlorides, on treatment with dialkylcadmium gives ketones.

$$\underset{\text{Grignard reagent}}{2R\text{—Mg—}X} + CdCl_2 \xrightarrow{\text{Dry ether}} \underset{\text{Dialkyl cadmium}}{R_2Cd} + 2Mg(X)Cl$$

$$2R'\text{—}\underset{\underset{O}{\|}}{C}\text{—Cl} + \underset{\text{Dialkyl cadmium}}{R_2Cd} \xrightarrow{\text{Dry ether}} 2R'\text{—}\underset{\underset{O}{\|}}{C}\text{—}R + CdCl_2$$

2. From Nitriles

When a nitrile is treated with Grignard reagent followed by hydrolysis yields a ketone.

$$C_6H_5MgBr + CH_3\text{—}CH_2\text{—}C\equiv N \xrightarrow{\text{Ether}}$$

$$CH_3CH_2\text{—}C(=NMgBr)(C_6H_5) \xrightarrow{H_3O^+} \underset{\text{Propiophenone (1-phenylpropanone)}}{CH_3CH_2\text{—}C(=O)(C_6H_5)}$$

3. From Benzene or Substituted Benzene

When benzene or substituted benzene is treated with acid chloride in the presence of anhydrous aluminium chloride, a corresponding ketone is obtained. This reaction is known as **Friedel-Crafts acylation reaction.**

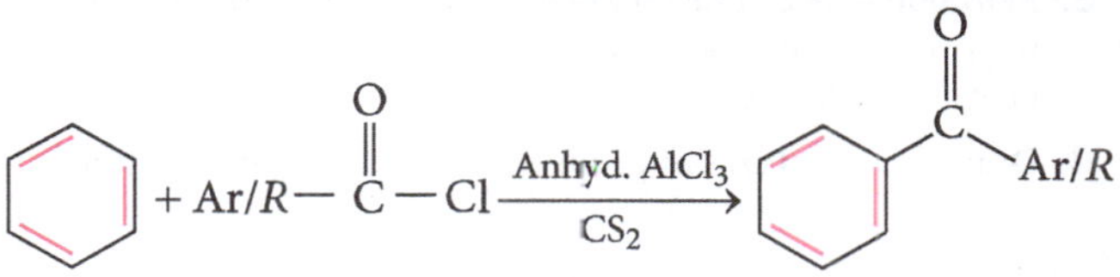

8.4 Physical Properties of Aldehydes and ketones

The physical properties of aldehydes and ketones are described in the given table.

Physical Properties of Aldehydes and Ketones

	Aldehydes	Ketones
Physical State	Aldehydes upto eleven carbon atoms are colourless liquids at room temperature. While higher members are solid. **Exception** Methanal is a pungent smelling at room temperature and ethanal is a volatile liquid.	Higher member of aliphatic and aromatic ketones are solids. While lower members are colourless liquids.
Boiling points	Both have higher boiling point than hydrocarbons and ethers of comparable molecular masses due to weak molecular association in aldehydes and ketones arising out of dipole-dipole interaction. However, their boiling points are lower than that of alcohols due to absence of intermolecular H-bonding.	
Solubility	Lower aldehydes are soluble in water due to H-bonding. It decreases as chain length increases.	Lower ketones are also soluble in water. It decreases with increase in molecular mass.
Odour	Lower members have sharp while higher members have sweet pungent odours.	Typically pleasant and sweet odour.

Quick Test 1

1. Write the IUPAC names of the following ketones and aldehydes. Wherever possible, give their common names.

(i) $CH_3CO(CH_2)_4CH_3$ (ii) $CH_3CH_2CHBrCH_2CH(CH_3)CHO$

(iii) $CH_3(CH_2)_5CHO$ NCERT

2. (i) Draw the molecular structure of the compound 4-methylpent-3-en-2-one.

(ii) Write the reagent required in the following reaction: CBSE 2015

$$CH_2=CH-CH_2OH \xrightarrow{?} CH_2=CH-CHO$$

3. Benzaldehyde can be obtained from benzal chloride. Write the reactions for obtaining benzal chloride and then benzaldehyde from it. NCERT Exemplar

4. Draw the structures of products of the following reactions

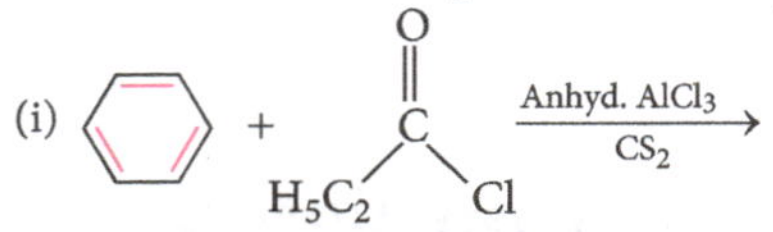

(ii) $(C_6H_5CH_2)_2Cd + 2CH_3COCl \longrightarrow$

5. Arrange the following compounds in the increasing order of their boiling points.

CH_3CHO, CH_3CH_2OH, CH_3OCH_3, $CH_3CH_2CH_3$ NCERT Intext

For Solutions, See QR Code on Pg. 321

8.5 Chemical Reactions of Aldehydes and Ketones

Aldehydes and ketones are highly reactive compounds. Since, both of these possess the same functional group, i.e. polarised carbonyl group, they undergo a number of common reactions.

Some important reactions of aldehydes and ketones are as follows

Nucleophilic Addition Reactions

Unlike alkenes which undergo electrophilic addition reactions, aldehydes and ketones undergo nucleophilic addition reactions.

Mechanism

Step I The nucleophile readily attacks the electrophilic carbon atom of carbonyl group in the direction perpendicular to the plane of sp^2-hybridised orbitals of carbonyl carbon.

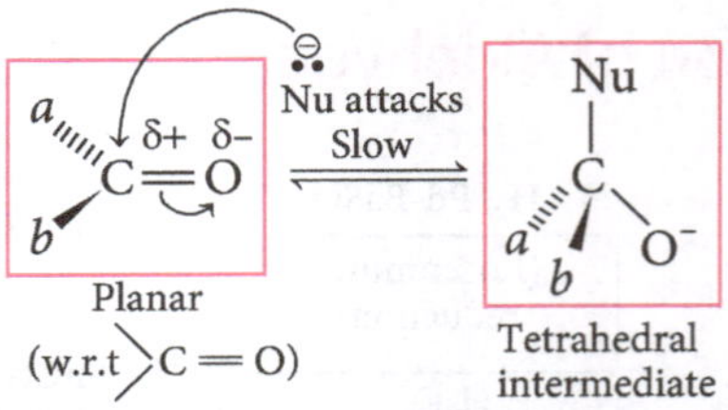

The hybridisation of carbon changes from sp^2 to sp^3 in this process and a tetrahedral alkoxide intermediate is formed.

Step II The intermediate then picks up a proton either from the solvent (usually H_2O) or from the reagent to give electrically neutral addition product.

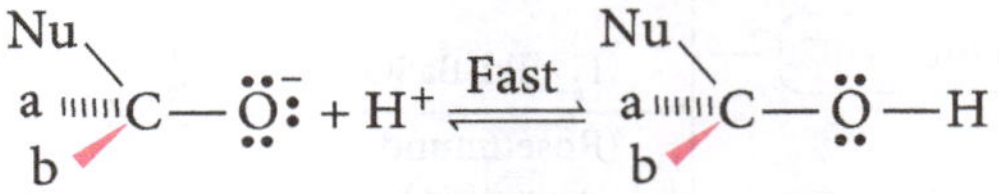

The net result is addition of Nu^- and H^+ across the carbon oxygen double bond.

Relative Reactivities

Aldehydes are more reactive towards nucleophilic addition reactions than ketones due to the following reasons.

- **Steric hindrance** The presence of two relatively large substituents in ketones hinders the approach of nucleophile to carbonyl carbon than in aldehyde having only one such substituent.
- **Inductive effect** Since, an alkyl group has electron donating $(+I)$ inductive effect. Hence, greater the number of alkyl groups attached to carbonyl group, greater the electron denstiy on carbonyl carbon. As ketones has more alkyl groups attached to carbonyl carbon, it has greater electron density and thus, it lowers the attack of nucleophile that results in a decrease in reactivity.

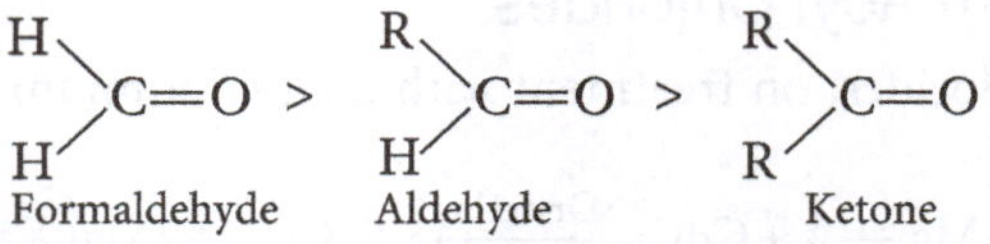

- **In case of aromatic aldehyde or ketones**, the carbon atom of the carbonyl group is less electrophilic due to $+R$ effect. Thus, aromatic aldehydes and ketones are less reactive than aliphatic aldehydes and ketones. However, amongst aromatic aldehydes and ketones, aromatic aldehydes are more reactive than alkyl aryl ketones which in turn are more reactive than diaryl ketones.

$$C_6H_5CHO > C_6H_5COCH_3 > C_6H_5COC_6H_5$$

Some Important Examples of Nucleophilic Addition Reactions

(i) Addition of Hydrogen Cyanide (HCN)

Aldehydes and ketones on reaction with HCN give **cyanohydrins**. This reaction occurs very slow with pure HCN. So, it is catalysed by a base and the generated CN^- being a stronger nucleophile readily attacks on carbonyl-carbon to yield corresponding cyanohydrin.

$$HO^{\ominus} + H-CN \rightleftharpoons :\bar{C}N + H_2O$$

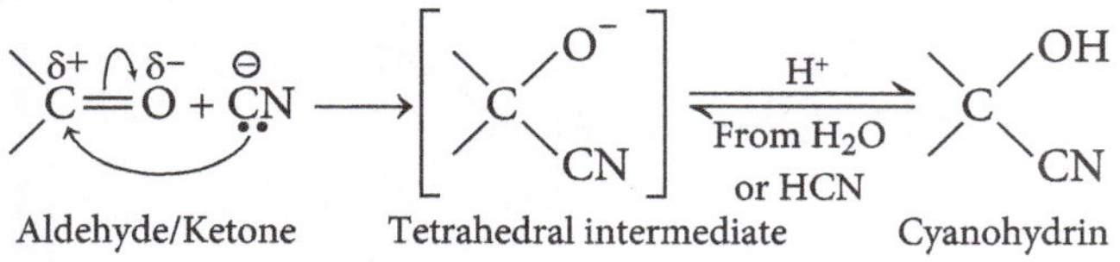

e.g.

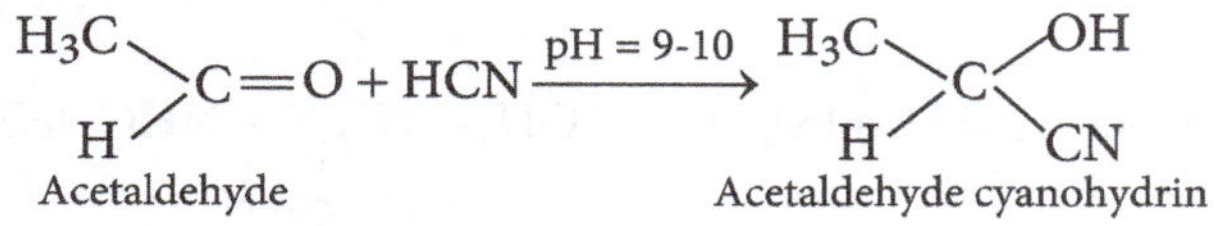

(ii) Addition of Sodium Hydrogensulphite ($NaHSO_3$)

Carbonyl on reaction with $NaHSO_3$ gives bisulphite addition product.

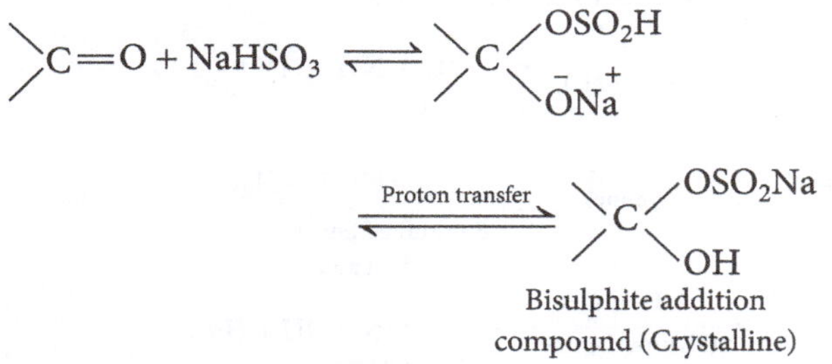

e.g.

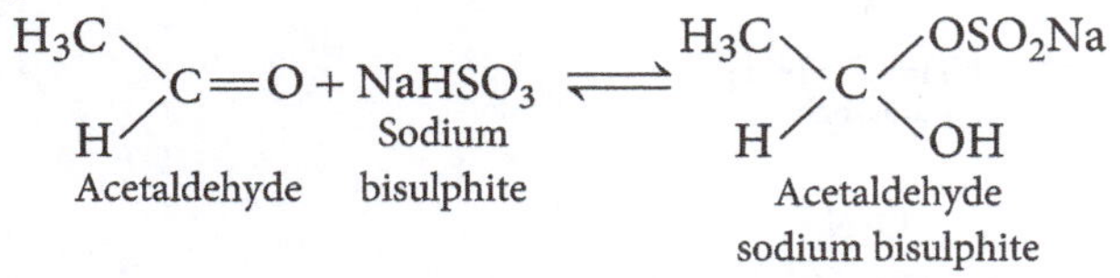

The position of the equilibrium lies largely to the right hand side for most aldehydes and to the left for most ketones due to steric reasons.

The bisulphite addition compound is water soluble and can be converted back to the original carbonyl compound by treating it with dilute mineral acid or alkali.

Therefore, these are useful for separation and purification of aldehydes.

(iii) Addition of Grignard Reagents

Aldehydes and ketones on reaction with Grignard reagent give addition products which upon hydrolysis with water or dilute mineral acids give alcohols.

The type of alcohol formed depends upon the aldehyde or ketone used (formaldehyde $\rightarrow 1^\circ$ alcohols, other aldehydes $\rightarrow 2^\circ$ alcohols and ketones $\rightarrow 3^\circ$ alcohols as discussed in chapter 7).

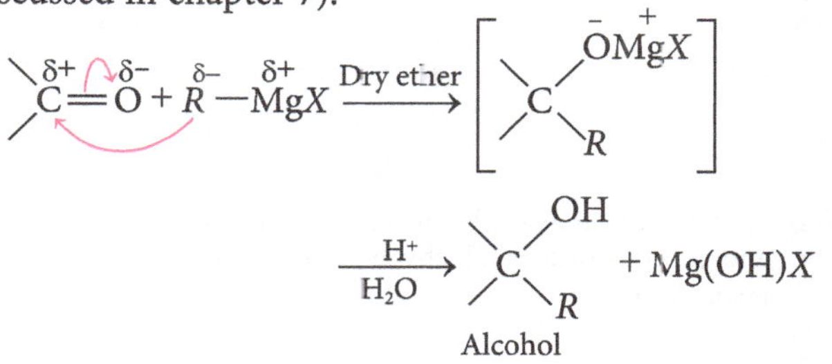

(iv) Addition of Alcohols

Aldehydes react with one equivalent of a monohydric alcohol in the presence of dry HCl gas to yield alkoxy alcohol intermediate known as **hemiacetals.** Hemiacetals on further reaction with one more molecule of alcohol give **acetals.** (Hemiacetals are alkoxy alcohols while acetals are *gem*-dialkoxy compounds). e.g.

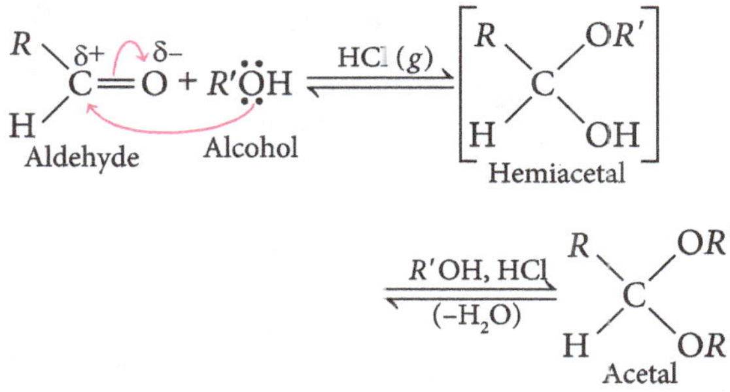

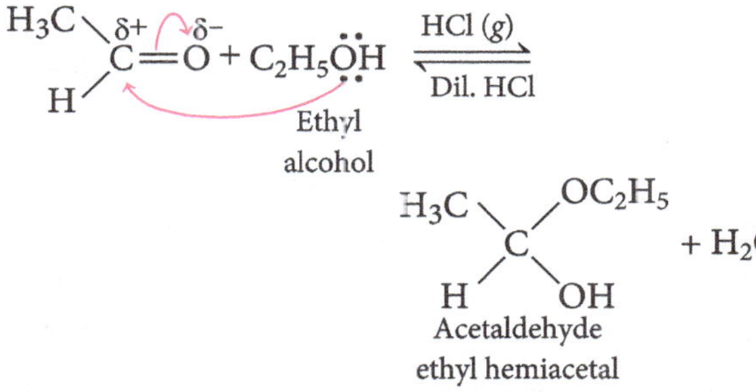

In this reaction, dry HCl gas protonates the oxygen atom of the carbonyl compound, thereby increasing the electrophilicity of the carbonyl carbon and hence facilitating the nucleophilic attack by the alcohol molecule. Ketones, however, do not react with monohydric alcohols but they react with dihydric alcohol such as ethylene glycol to give cyclic **ketals**.

e.g.

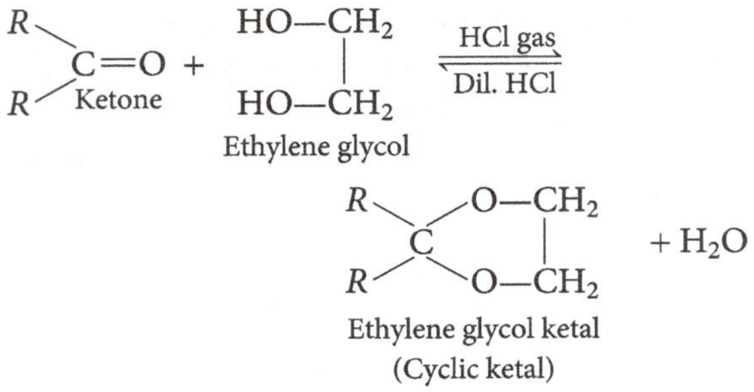

Note Acetals and ketals are hydrolysed by dilute acids and generate original aldehydes and ketones respectively.

Nucleophilic Addition Elimination Reactions

These are two step reactions involving addition followed by elimination of some small molecules. Their first step is similar to nucleophilic addition reactions.

Examples of nucleophilic addition elimination reaction are as follows

Addition of Ammonia and its Derivatives

Aldehydes and ketones react with ammonia and a number of its derivatives, $H_2N—Z$ in weakly acidic medium to form compounds containing $>C=N$ group with the elimination of water molecule.

The reaction is reversible and catalysed by acid. The equilibrium favours the product formation due to rapid dehydration of intermediate to form $>C=N—Z$

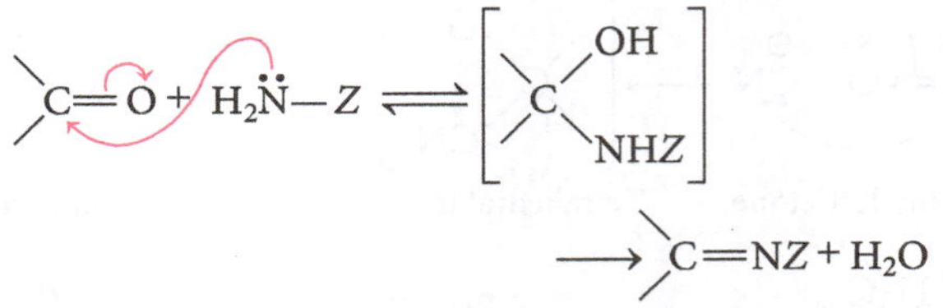

where, Z = H, alkyl, aryl, —OH, $—NH_2$, $—NHCONH_2$

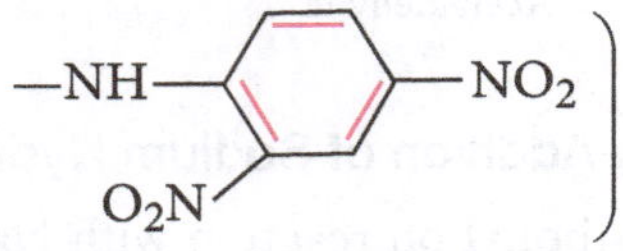

Reactions of Carbonyl Group with Substituted N-derivatives

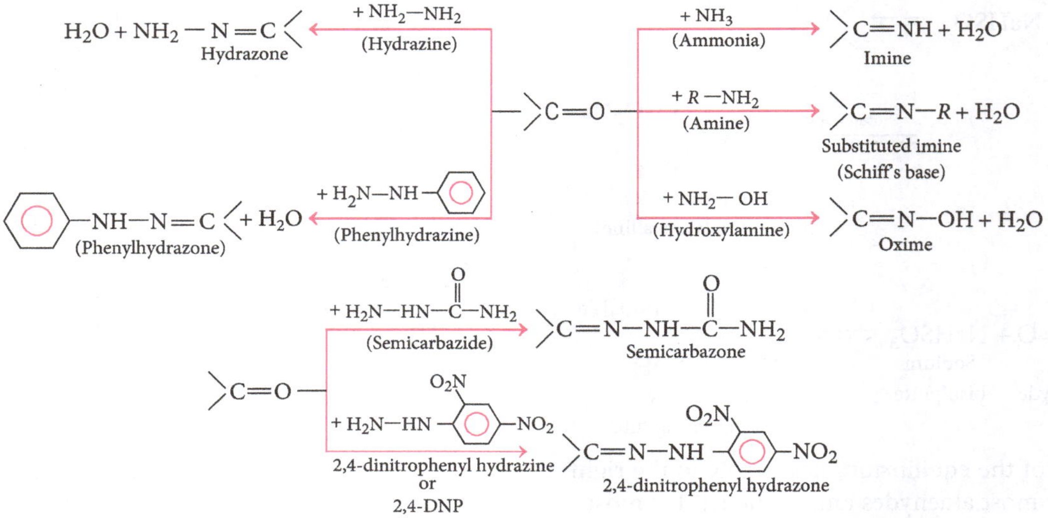

Note 2,4-dinitrophenyl hydrazine is **Brady's reagent**. Aldehydes and ketones react with it to form yellow, orange or red ppt. of 2,4-dinitrophenyl hydrazone. These are useful for the characterisation of aldehydes and ketones.

Example 2 **Predict the products of the following reactions.**

(i) $R—CH=CHCHO + NH_2—\overset{\overset{O}{||}}{C}—NH—NH_2 \xrightarrow{H^+}$

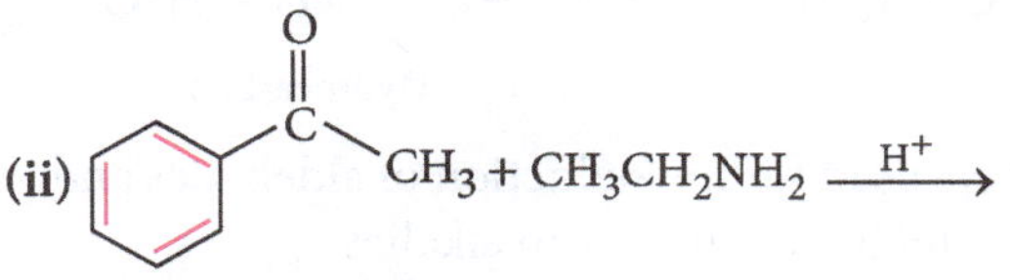

Note Elimination of H_2O from carbonyl and amine group and formation of $C=N$ bond.

Sol. (i) $R—CH=CH—CHO + H_2N—NH—\overset{\overset{O}{||}}{C}—NH_2$
Unsaturated aldehyde Semicarbazide

$\xrightarrow[-H_2O]{H^+} R—CH=CH—CH=N—NH—\overset{\overset{O}{||}}{C}—NH_2$
Semicarbazone

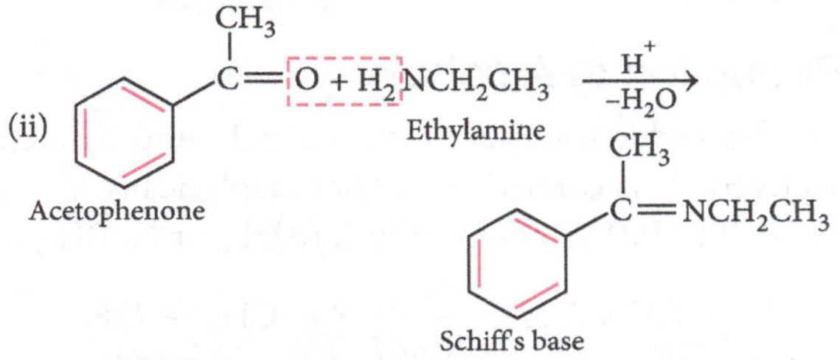

Note Reaction (ii) is used to test the presence of carbonyl group.

Oxidation

Oxidation of Aldehydes

Aldehydes differ from ketones in their oxidation reactions. Aldehydes are easily oxidised to carboxylic acids because of having H-atom attached to carbonyl group.

Aldehydes are easily oxidised not only by strong oxidising agents like HNO_3, $KMnO_4$ and $K_2Cr_2O_7$ but also by weak oxidising agents like Tollen's reagent, Fehling solution and Benedict's reagent.

$$R—CHO \xrightarrow{[O]} R—COOH$$

Oxidation of Ketones

Unlike aldehydes, ketones do not contain H-atom attached to $\rangle C=O$ group and hence, they cannot be oxidised by weak oxidising agent.

These are generally oxidised by strong oxidising agents like HNO_3, acidified $KMnO_4$, acidified $K_2Cr_2O_7$ at high temperature. Their oxidation involves carbon-carbon bond cleavage with the formation of a mixture of carboxylic acids each containing lesser number of carbon atoms than the original ketone.

$$R—\overset{1}{C}H_2—\underset{\underset{O}{||}}{\overset{2}{C}}—\overset{3}{C}H_2—R' \xrightarrow{[O]} R—COOH +$$

$$\underset{\text{(By cleavage of } C_1—C_2 \text{ bond)}}{R'—CH_2COOH + R—CH_2COOH} + \underset{\text{(By cleavage of } C_2—C_3 \text{ bond)}}{R'—COOH}$$

The mild oxidising agents given below are used to distinguish aldehydes from ketones.

Tollen's Test

Tollen's reagent is an ammoniacal solution of silver nitrate.

When an aldehyde is heated with freshly prepared Tollen's reagent, a bright silver mirror is produced due to the formation of silver metal. Aldehydes are oxidised to the corresponding carboxylate anion.

The reaction occurs in alkaline medium.

$$\underset{\text{Aldehyde}}{RCHO} + \underset{\text{Tollen's reagent}}{2[Ag(NH_3)_2]^+} + 3OH^- \xrightarrow{\Delta}$$
$$RCOO^- + \underset{\text{Silver mirror}}{2Ag\downarrow} + 2H_2O + 4NH_3\uparrow$$

The silver thus formed shines like mirror. Hence, this test is called **silver mirror test**.

Note Both aliphatic and aromatic aldehydes reduce Tollen's reagent.

Fehling's Test

Fehling's reagent is a mixture of two solutions, i.e., Fehling's solution *A* and *B*. Fehling's solution *A* is an aqueous copper sulphate and Fehling's solution *B* is an alkaline sodium potassium tartarate **(Rochelle salt)**. These two solutions are mixed in equal amounts before test. When an aldehyde is heated with Fehling's reagent, a reddish-brown precipitate is obtained. Aldehydes are oxidised to corresponding carboxylate anion.

$$\underset{\text{Aldehyde}}{RCHO} + \underset{\text{Fehling's solution}}{2Cu^{2+} + 5OH^-} \xrightarrow{\Delta} RCOO^- + \underset{\text{Red-brown ppt.}}{Cu_2O\downarrow} + 3H_2O$$

Note Aromatic aldehydes do not reduce Fehling's solution.

Benedict's Test

Benedict's solution is an alkaline solution of Cu^{2+} ions complexed with citrate ions. (whereas, Fehling's solution is an alkaline solution of Cu^{2+} ions complexed with tartarate ions.)

Benedict's solution reacts in the same way as Fehling's solution. Being weak oxidising agent, it oxidises only aliphatic aldehyde but are not capable of oxidising aromatic aldehydes.

Note There reagents are used to distinguish aldehydes and ketones.

Oxidation of Methyl Ketones by Haloform Reaction

Aldehydes and ketones having atleast one methyl group linked to the carbonyl carbon atom (methyl ketones) are oxidised by sodium hypohalite to sodium salts of corresponding carboxylic acids having one carbon atom less than that of carbonyl compound.

The methyl group is converted into haloform. This oxidation does not affect a carbon-carbon double bond, if present in the molecule.

$$R—\overset{O}{\overset{\|}{C}}—CH_3 \xrightarrow{NaOX} R—\overset{O}{\overset{\|}{C}}—\overset{-}{O}\overset{+}{Na} + CHX_3$$

$(X = Cl, Br, I)$

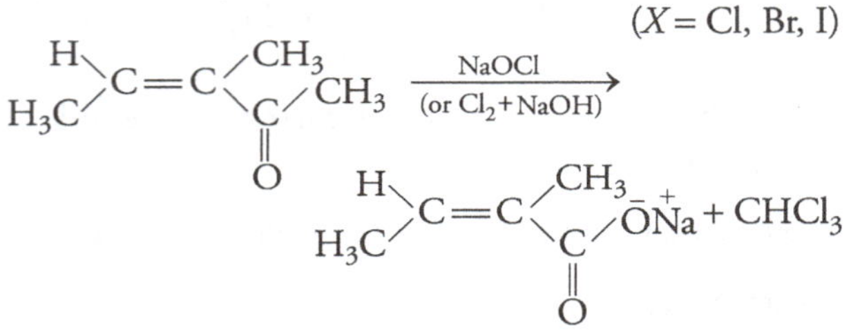

> **TEACHER'S TIP**
> Iodoform reaction with sodium hypoiodite is also used for the detection of CH_3CO — group or $CH_3CH(OH)$ — group which produces CH_3CO — group on oxidation.

Reduction

Aldehydes and ketones can be reduced to a variety of compounds under different conditions.

1. Reduction to Hydrocarbons

The carbonyl group of an aldehyde or ketone is reduced to methylene group to form a hydrocarbon. This can be achieved by either one of the following two reactions.

(i) **Clemmensen reduction** It involves the reduction of carbonyl group ($>C=O$) to $>CH_2$ group and it is carried out in the presence of Zn amalgam and conc. HCl.

$$>C=O + 4[H] \xrightarrow{Zn\text{-}Hg/Conc.\ HCl} \underset{\text{Hydrocarbon}}{>CH_2} + H_2O$$

It is widely used for the reduction of aldehydes and ketones which are sensitive to alkalies.

(ii) **Wolff-Kishner reduction** In this method, the aldehyde or ketone is heated with hydrazine and KOH or NaOH in high boiling solvent such as ethylene glycol. It is used when carbonyl compounds are sensitive to acids.

$$\underset{\text{Aldehyde or Ketone}}{>C=O} \xrightarrow[-H_2O]{+NH_2—NH_2} >C=N—NH_2 \xrightarrow[\text{Ethylene glycol}]{KOH/\Delta} >CH_2 + N_2\uparrow$$

2. Reduction to Alcohols

Aldehydes and ketones are reduced to 1° and 2° alcohols respectively. It is carried out either catalytically (H_2 + Ni / Pt / Pd) or chemically ($LiAlH_4$ or $NaBH_4$).

$$\underset{\text{Aldehyde}}{R—CHO} + 2[H] \xrightarrow[\text{or } NaBH_4]{LiAlH_4} \underset{1^\circ\text{alcohol}}{R—CH_2—OH}$$

$$\underset{\text{Ketone}}{\overset{R}{\underset{R'}{>}}C=O} + H_2 \xrightarrow{\text{Ni or Pt}} \underset{2^\circ\text{alcohol}}{\overset{R}{\underset{R'}{>}}CH—OH}$$

Reactions due to α-Hydrogen

The aldehydes and ketones undergo a number of reactions due to the acidic nature of α-H which in turn is due to the strong electron withdrawing effect of $>C=O$ group.

Acidity of α-Hydrogens of Aldehydes and Ketones

The carbon atom next to carbonyl group is called **α-carbon atom** and hydrogens attached to α-carbon atom are called **α-hydrogens**.

The α-hydrogen of aldehydes and ketones are acidic in nature. The acidity is due to the fact that the anion, which results from the removal of an α-hydrogen by a base $B:^-$ is stabilised by resonance.

The resonance stabilised anion is called **enolate ion.**

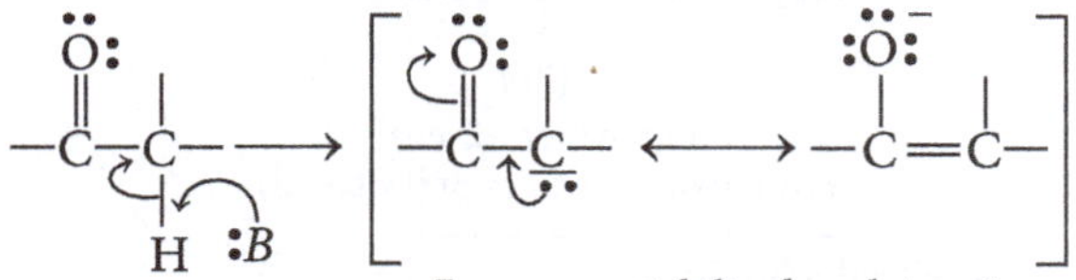

Resonance stabilised enolate anion

The α-carbon of the enolate ion is negatively charged and can acts as a nucleophile.

The reactions due to α-hydrogens are as follows

1. Aldol Condensation

Aldehydes and ketones containing atleast one α-H atom undergo a reaction in the presence of dilute alkali as catalyst to form **β-hydroxy aldehydes (aldol) or β-hydroxy ketones (ketol)** respectively.

Mechanism

Step I Formation of enolate ion by the removal of α-hydrogen.

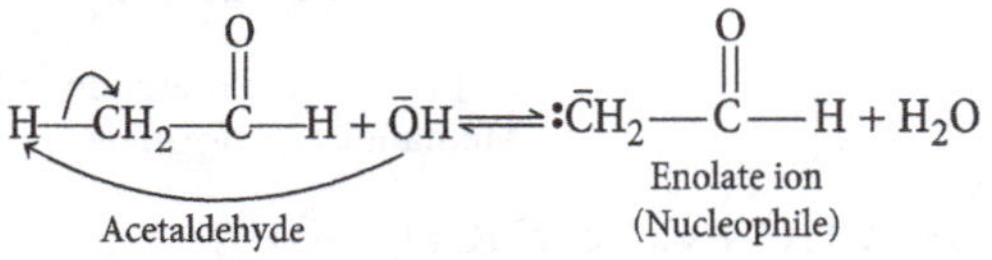

Step II The attack of enolate ion on carbonyl carbon of another un-ionised aldehyde molecule.

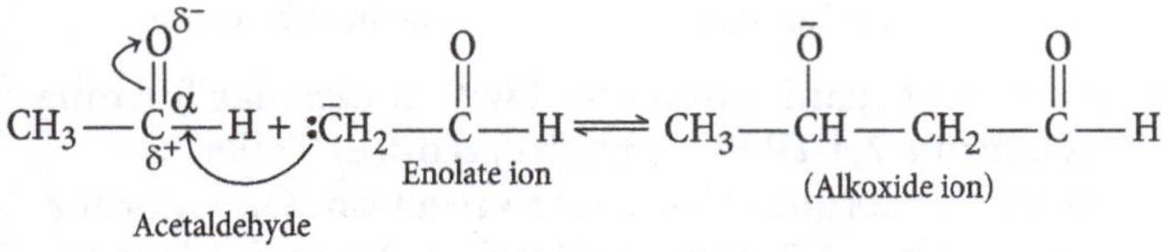

Step III The oxygen (carrying negative charge) in the product accept a proton from water to yield alcohol.

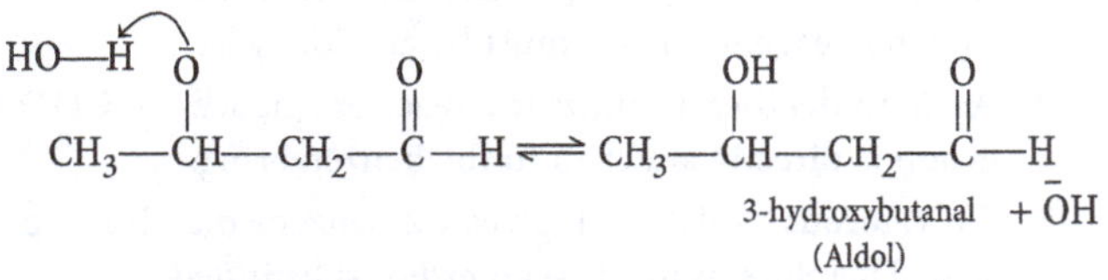

Step IV Heating of aldol gives α,β-unsaturated compound.

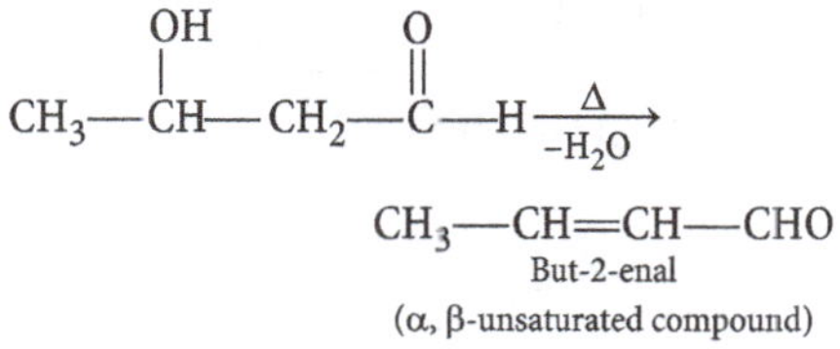

Similarly,

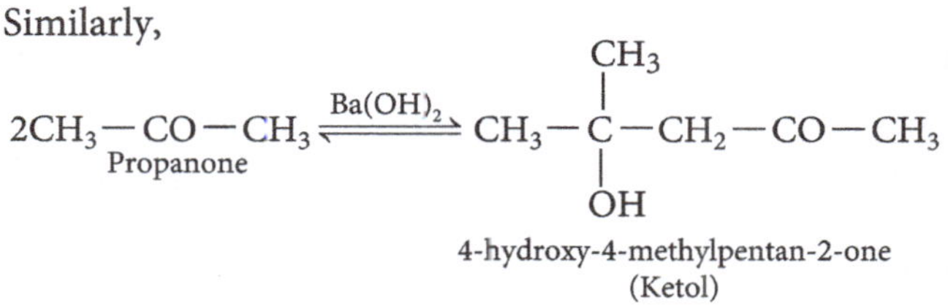

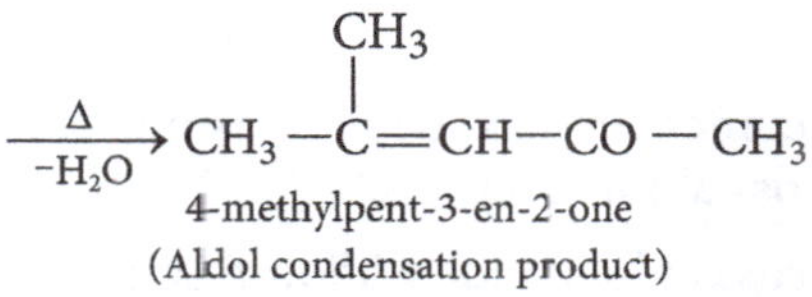

> **Difference between Aldol and Ketol**
>
> - The name aldol (or ketol) is derived from the names of the two functional groups, aldehyde (or ketone) and alcohol present in the product.
> - Aldols readily lose water to give α,β-unsaturated carbonyl compounds which are aldol condensation products.
> - Though, ketones give ketol compounds containing a keto group and alcoholic group, yet the name aldol is used for the condensation products of two molecules of ketones due to their similarity with aldehydes.

> **TEACHER'S TIP**
>
> Formaldehyde (HCHO), benzaldehyde (C_6H_5CHO) and benzophenone ($C_6H_5COC_6H_5$) do not undergo aldol condensation as they do not contain α-H atoms.

2. Cross Aldol Condensation

When aldol condensation is carried out between the two different aldehydes or ketones then reaction is said to be **cross aldol condensation.**

If both the reactants contain α-hydrogen atoms, the reaction gives a mixture of four products due to self condensation and cross-condensation.

$$\begin{matrix} CH_3CHO \\ + \\ CH_3CH_2CHO \end{matrix} \xrightarrow[\text{(ii)}\,\Delta]{\text{(i) NaOH}} \underset{\substack{\text{But-2-enal} \\ \text{(From two molecules of ethanal)}}}{CH_3-CH=CH-CHO} + \underset{\substack{\text{2-methylpent-2-enal} \\ \text{(From two molecules of propanal)}}}{CH_3CH_2-CH=\underset{\displaystyle CH_3}{\underset{|}{C}}-CHO}$$

Simple or self aldol products

$$+$$

$$\underset{\text{2-methylbut-2-enal}}{CH_3-CH=\overset{\displaystyle CH_3}{\overset{|}{C}}-CHO} + \underset{\text{Pent-2-enal}}{CH_3CH_2-CH=CHCHO}$$

(From one molecule of ethanal and one molecule of propanal)

Cross aldol products

Ketones can also be used as one component in the cross aldol reactions.

Cross aldol condensation reactions are of great synthetic use even if one of the carbonyl compounds does not possess α -H atoms.

e.g.

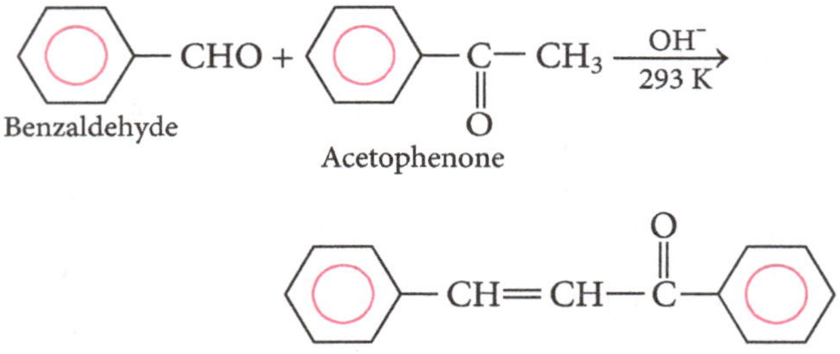

1, 3-diphenylprop-2-en-1-one
(Benzal acetophenone)
(Major product)

Other Reactions

1. Cannizzaro Reaction

Aldehydes which do not have α -H atom undergo self oxidation and reduction (disproportionation) reactions on heating with conc. alkali.

In this reaction, one molecule of aldehyde is reduced to alcohol, while another molecule is oxidised to salt of carboxylic acid.

The sequence of reactions are as follow.

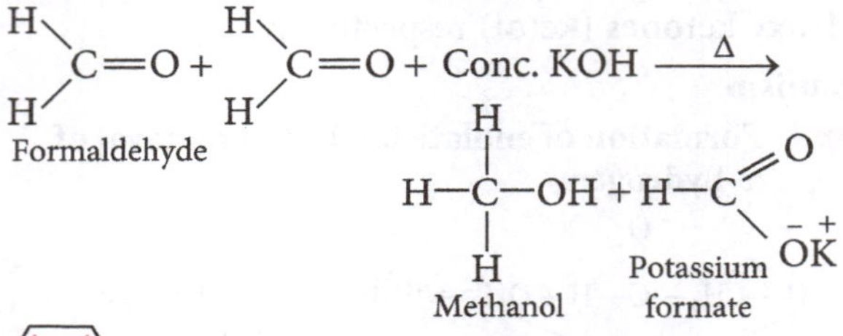

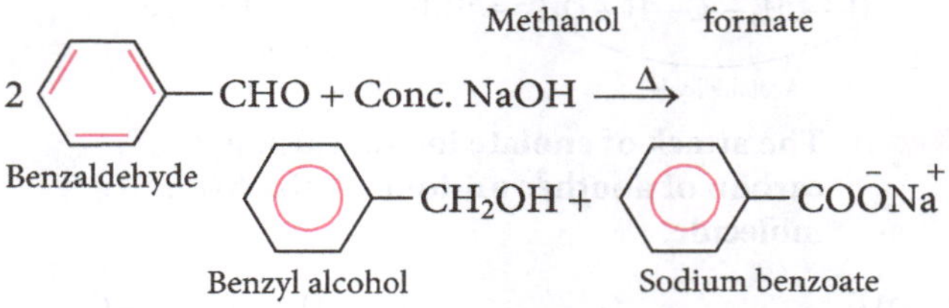

Example 3 **An organic compound with molecular formula $C_9H_{10}O$, forms 2,4-DNP derivative, reduces Tollen's reagent and undergoes Cannizzaro reaction. On vigorous oxidation, it gives 1,2-benzenedicarboxylic acid. Identify the compound.** NCERT

Sol. (i) As the given compound with molecular formula $C_9H_{10}O$, forms a 2,4-DNP derivative and reduces Tollen's reagent, thus it must be an aldehyde.

(ii) As it undergoes Cannizzaro reaction, hence — CHO group is directly attached to the benzene ring.

(iii) On vigorous oxidation, it gives 1,2-benzene dicarboxylic acid. Therefore, it must be an *ortho*- substituted benzaldehyde and the only o-substituted aromatic aldehyde which have $C_9H_{10}O$ molecular formula is o-ethyl benzaldehyde or 2-ethylbenzaldehyde.

The sequence of reactions are as follows :

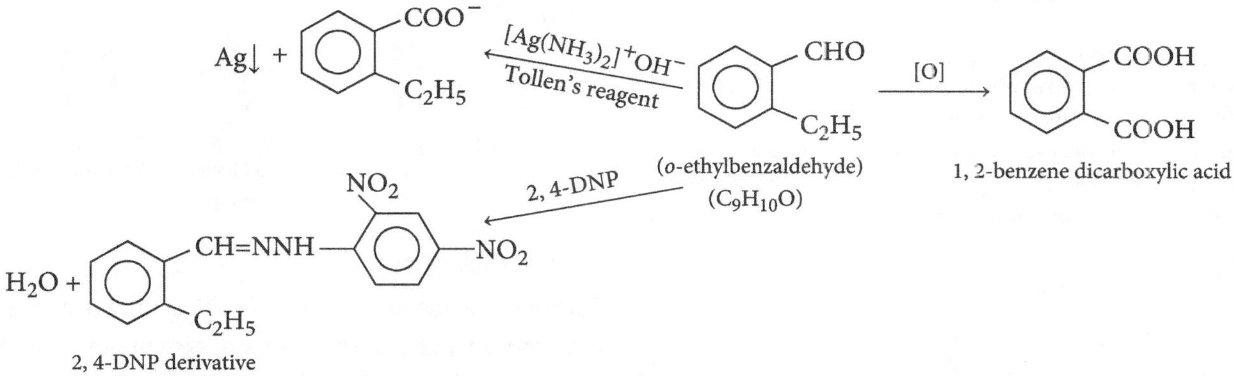

2. Electrophilic Substitution Reactions

Aromatic aldehydes and ketones undergo usual electrophilic substitution reactions of the benzene nucleus such as halogenation, nitration and sulphonation. Since, the both aldehydic group and ketonic group are electron withdrawing groups, so they act as deactivating and *meta*-directing groups.

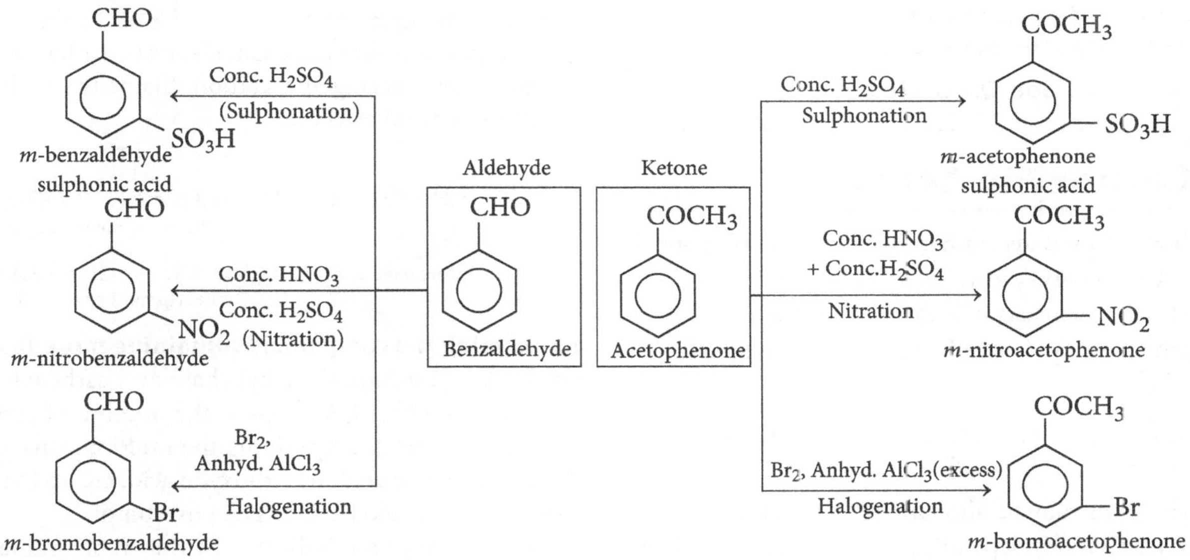

8.6 Uses of Aldehydes and Ketones

Some of the important uses of aldehydes and ketones are as follows

- They are used as solvents, starting materials and reagents for the synthesis of other products in chemical industry.
- Formalin (40% solution of formaldehyde) solution is used to preserve biological specimens and in making bakelite, urea-formaldehyde glues and other polymeric products.
- Acetaldehyde is used primarily as a starting material in the manufacture of acetic acid, ethyl acetate, vinyl acetate, polymers and drugs.
- Benzaldehyde is used in perfumery and dye industries. Some other are also known for their odours and flavours like butyraldehyde, camphor, vanillin, acetophenone, salicylaldehyde, cinnamaldehyde, etc.
- Some of the aldehydes and ketones are used for preparing materials like adhesives, paints, resins, perfumes, plastics, fabrics, etc.

Quick Test 2

1. Arrange the following compounds in the increasing order of their reactivity towards nucleophilic addition reactions.
   (i) Ethanal, propanal, propanone, butanone
   (ii) Benzaldehyde, *p*-tolualdehyde, *p*-nitrobenzaldehyde, acetophenone *NCERT Intext*
2. Complete the following reactions,
   (i)
   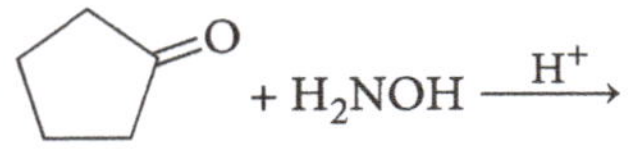
   (ii)
   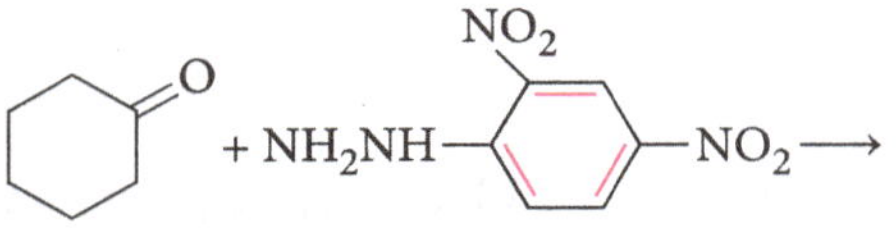
3. What is Tollen's reagent? Write one application/usefulness of this reagent.
4. Illustrate the following name reaction giving suitable example: Wolff-Kishner reduction.
5. Write two important uses of formalin.

For Solutions, See QR Code on Pg. 321

8.7 Carboxylic Acids

The carbon compounds containing a carboxyl functional group, —**COOH** are known as carboxylic acids. Carboxyl group consists of a carbonyl group attached to a hydroxyl group, hence it is named as **carboxyl**.

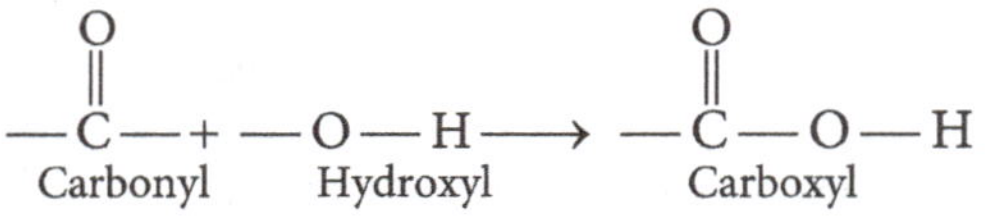

Carboxylic acids may be aliphatic (*R*COOH) or aromatic (ArCOOH) depending on the groups alkyl or aryl attached to carboxylic carbon respectively.

e.g. $CH_3CH_2CH_2COOH$ (Butanoic acid), CH_3COOH (Ethanoic acid),

Benzoic acid

Some higher members of aliphatic carboxylic acids (C_{12} -C_{18}) known as **fatty acids**, occur in natural fats as esters of glycerol.

When carbonyl group gets attached with groups like —O*R*, —NH_2, —*X* and —OCO*R*, the compounds are called **derivatives of carboxylic acids** and known by the name, **ester, amide, acyl halide** and **acid anhydride** respectively.

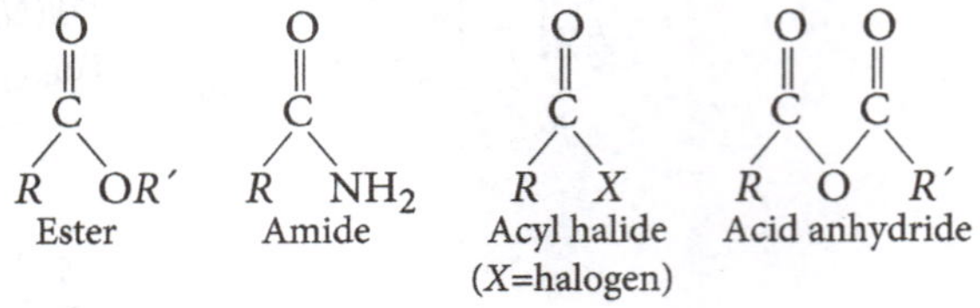

Nomenclature

Carboxylic acids are named according to two systems

- **Common system** In common system, the common names end with the suffix -'ic acid' e.g. Formic acid (HCOOH), acetic acid (CH_3COOH), butyric acid ($CH_3CH_2CH_2COOH$).
- **IUPAC system** IUPAC name of carboxylic acid is alkanoic acid. Thus in IUPAC system, their names are derived by replacing the terminal 'e' from the name of corresponding straight chain alkane by suffix 'oic acid'. During numbering the carbon chain, the carboxylic carbon is numbered one.

e.g. $CH_3—CH(CH_3)—CH_2—COOH$; 3-methylbutanoic acid

$CH_3—CH(Br)—COOH$; 2-bromopropanoic acid

$C_6H_5—CH=CH—COOH$ 3-phenylprop-2-enoic acid

For naming the compounds containing more than one carboxyl group, the alkyl chain and carboxylic carbon is numbered. Moreover, the number of carboxyl groups are indicated by adding the multiplicative prefix like dicarboxylic acid, tricarboxylic acid, etc. to the name of parent alkyl chain. The position of —COOH groups are indicated by the arabic numeral before the multiplicative prefix.

IUPAC Names and Structures of Some Carboxylic Acids

Structure	Common name	IUPAC name
HCOOH	Formic acid	Methanoic acid
CH_3COOH	Acetic acid	Ethanoic acid
CH_3CH_2COOH	Propionic acid	Propanoic acid
$CH_3CH_2CH_2COOH$	Butyric acid	Butanoic acid
$(CH_3)_2CHCOOH$	*iso*-butyric acid	2-methylpropanoic acid
HOOC—COOH	Oxalic acid	Ethanedioic acid

Structure	Common name	IUPAC name
$HOOC—CH_2—COOH$	Malonic acid	Propanedioic acid
$HOOC—(CH_2)_2—COOH$	Succinic acid	Butanedioic acid
$HOOC—(CH_2)_3—COOH$	Glutaric acid	Pentanedioic acid
$HOOC—(CH_2)_4—COOH$	Adipic acid	Hexanedioic acid
$HOOC—CH_2—CH(COOH)—CH_2—COOH$	Tricarballylic acid or Carballylic acid	Propane-1,2,3-tricarboxylic acid
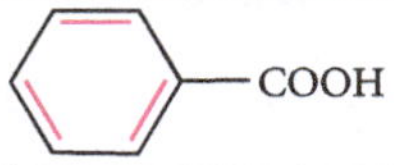	Benzoic acid	Benzene carboxylic acid (Benzoic acid)
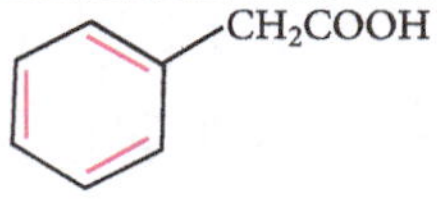	Phenyl acetic acid	2-phenyl ethanoic acid
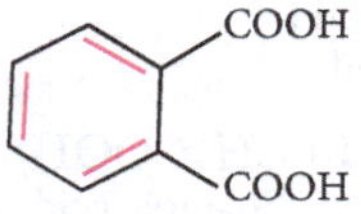	Phthalic acid	Benzene-1, 2-dicarboxylic acid

Example 4 **Give the IUPAC names of the following compounds.**

(i) $PhCH_2CH_2COOH$ (ii) $(CH_3)_2C{=}CHCOOH$

(iii) 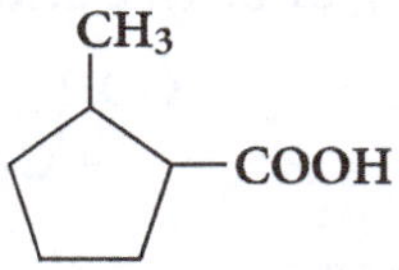 **(iv)** 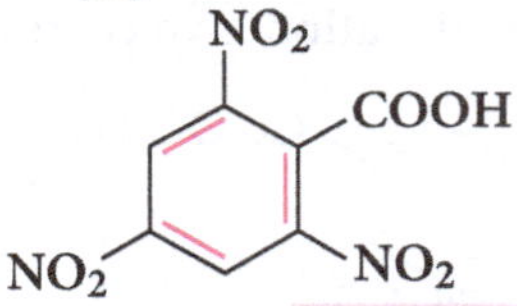

NCERT Intext

Sol. (i) $\overset{3}{Ph—CH_2}—\overset{2}{CH_2}—\overset{1}{COOH}$
3-phenylpropanoic acid

(ii) $\overset{4}{CH_3}\overset{3}{C}(CH_3){=}\overset{2}{C}H—\overset{1}{C}OOH$
3-methylbut-2-en-1-oic acid

(iii) 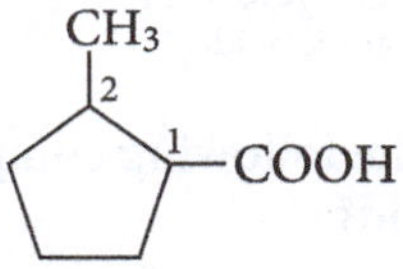
2-methylcyclopentane carboxylic acid

(iv) 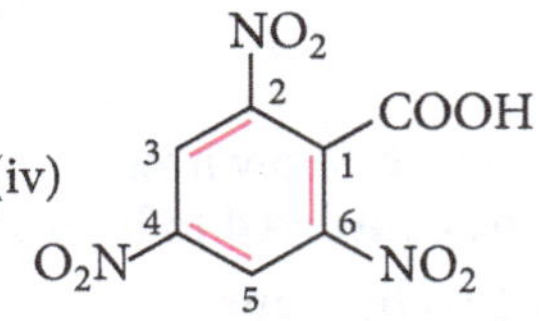
2,4,6-trinitrobenzoic acid

Structure

In carboxylic acids, the bonds attached to the carboxyl carbon are in one plane and are separated by about 120°.

The carboxylic carbon is less electrophilic than carbonyl carbon because of the following possible resonance structures.

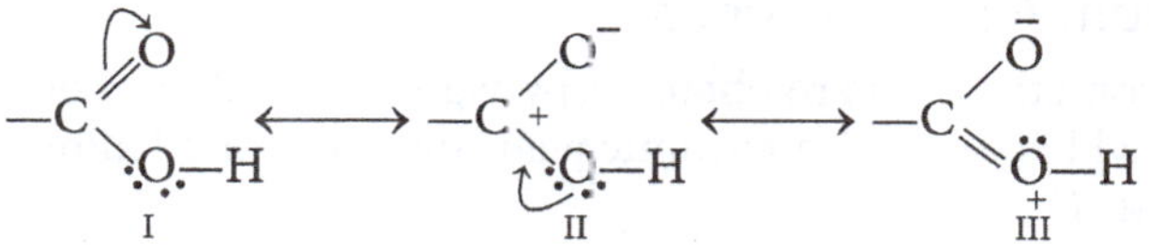

Methods of Preparation

Carboxylic acids are prepared by the following methods.

From Primary Alcohols

Primary alcohols are readily oxidised to corresponding carboxylic acids with common oxidising agents such as potassium permanganate ($KMnO_4$) in neutral, acidic or alkaline medium or by potassium dichromate ($K_2Cr_2O_7$) and chromium trioxide (CrO_3) in acidic medium (Jones reagent).

$$\underset{\text{Alcohol}}{RCH_2OH} \xrightarrow[\text{(ii) } H_3O^+]{\text{(i) Alkaline } KMnO_4} \underset{\text{Acid}}{RCOOH}$$

$$\underset{\text{Decan-1 -ol}}{CH_3(CH_2)_8CH_2OH} \xrightarrow[\text{(Jones reagent)}]{CrO_3,\ aq\ H_2SO_4} \underset{\text{Decanoic acid}}{CH_3(CH_2)_8COOH}$$

From Aldehydes

Carboxylic acids are also prepared from aldehydes by the use of mild oxidising agents like Tollen's reagent or other usual oxidising agents.

$$\underset{\text{Acetaldehyde}}{CH_3CHO} \xrightarrow[\text{Tollen's reagent}]{[O]} \underset{\text{Acetic acid}}{CH_3COOH}$$

From Nitriles and Amides

Nitriles are first hydrolysed to amides and then to acids in the presence of H^+ or $\bar{O}H$ as catalyst. Mild reaction conditions are used to stop the reaction at the amide stage.

$$R—CN \xrightarrow[H_2O]{\overset{+}{H} \text{ or } \bar{O}H} R—\overset{O}{\overset{\|}{C}}—NH_2 \xrightarrow[\Delta]{\overset{+}{H} \text{ or } \bar{O}H} RCOOH + NH_3\uparrow$$

$$\underset{\text{Ethanamide}}{CH_3CONH_2} \xrightarrow[H_3O^+]{\Delta} \underset{\text{Ethanoic acid}}{CH_3COOH} + NH_3\uparrow$$

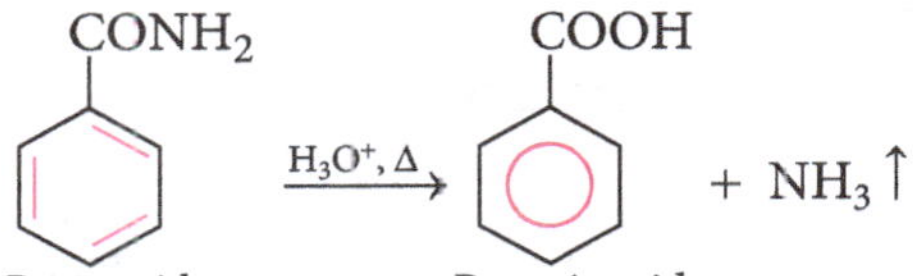

From Alkyl Benzenes

Aromatic acids are obtained by vigorous oxidation of alkyl benzene with chromic acids or acidic or alkaline $KMnO_4$.

During oxidation, the aromatic nucleus remains intact but the entire chain is oxidised to —COOH group irrespective of the length of carbon chain.

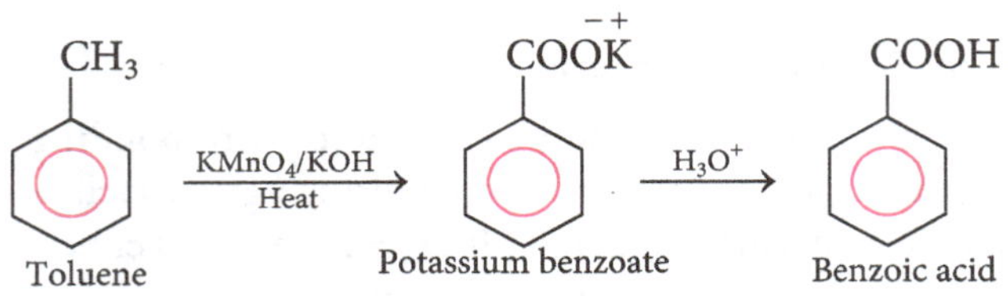

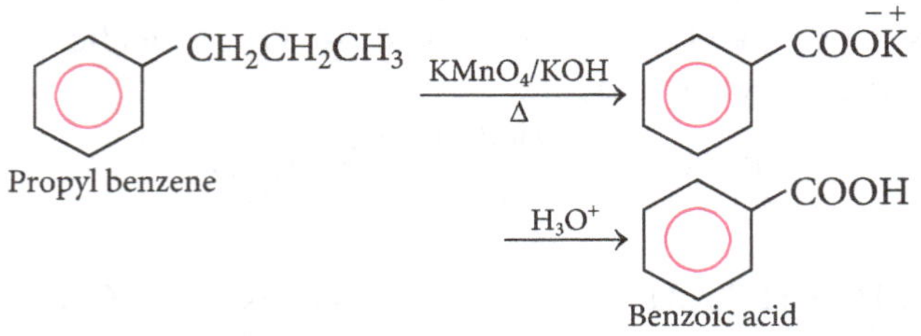

TEACHER'S TIP

1° and 2° alkyl chains contain benzylic hydrogen so, these are oxidised to carboxyl groups, while 3° alkyl chains contain no benzylic hydrogen so, these are not oxidised.

e.g.

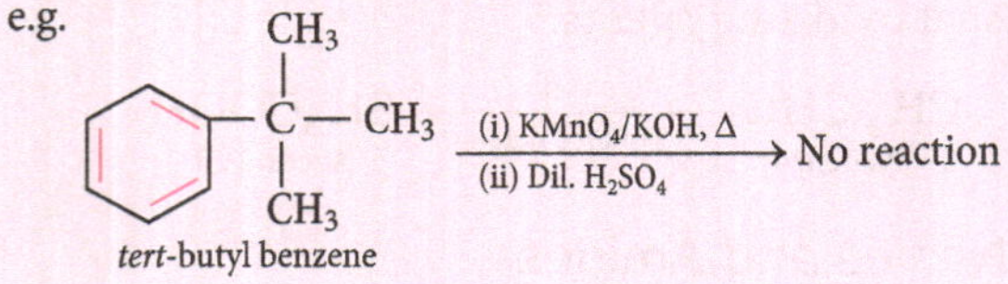

From Alkenes

Same oxidising agents can be used to oxidise alkenes to carboxylic acids.

e.g. $\underset{\text{But-2-ene}}{CH_3CH{=}CHCH_3} \xrightarrow[\text{Dil. } H_2SO_4]{KMnO_4/KOH,\ \Delta} \underset{\text{Ethanoic acid}}{2CH_3COOH}$

From Grignard Reagents

Grignard reagents react with dry ice (CO_2) in ethereal solution to produce salts of carboxylic acids, which on acidification with mineral acids give corresponding carboxylic acids.

$$R^{\delta-}—\overset{\delta+}{Mg}X + O{=}C{=}O \xrightarrow{\text{Dry ether}} \underset{\text{Adduct}}{R—\underset{\underset{O}{\|}}{C}—\overset{-}{O}\overset{+}{Mg}X}$$

$$\xrightarrow[-Mg(OH)X]{H^+ / H_2O} R—COOH$$

Note The acid formed by this method contains one more carbon than the original Grignard reagent.

From Acyl Halides and Anhydrides

Acid chlorides when hydrolysed with water give carboxylic acids or more readily hydrolysed with aqueous base to give carboxylate ions which on acidification provide corresponding carboxylic acids.

Anhydrides on the other hand are hydrolysed to corresponding acids with water.

$$RCOCl \xrightarrow{H_2O} RCOOH + Cl^-$$

$$RCOCl \xrightarrow{\overset{-}{O}H/H_2O} RCOO^- + \overset{-}{Cl} \xrightarrow{H_3O^+} RCOOH$$

$$\underset{\text{Benzoic anhydride}}{(C_6H_5CO)_2O} \xrightarrow{H_2O} \underset{\text{Benzoic acid}}{2C_6H_5COOH}$$

$$\underset{\text{Benzoic ethanoic anhydride}}{C_6H_5COOCOCH_3} \xrightarrow{H_2O} \underset{\text{Benzoic acid}}{C_6H_5COOH} + \underset{\text{Ethanoic acid}}{CH_3COOH}$$

From Esters

Acidic hydrolysis of esters gives directly carboxylic acids while basic hydrolysis gives carboxylates, which on acidification give corresponding carboxylic acids.

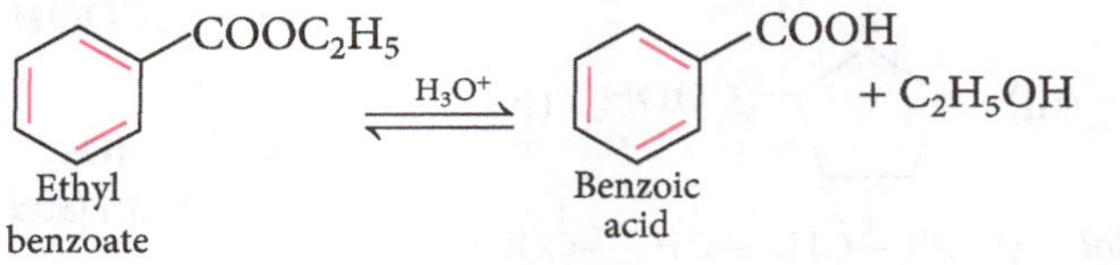

$$\underset{\text{Ethyl butanoate}}{CH_3CH_2CH_2COOC_2H_5} \xrightleftharpoons{NaOH} CH_3CH_2CH_2CO\overset{-}{O}\overset{+}{Na} + C_2H_5OH$$

$$\xrightarrow{H_3O^+} \underset{\text{Butanoic acid}}{CH_3CH_2CH_2COOH}$$

Example 5 **Show how each of the following compounds can be converted to benzoic acid?**

(i) Ethyl benzene **(ii) Acetophenone**

(iii) Bromobenzene **(iv) Phenylethene (styrene)**

NCERT Intext

Sol.

(i)

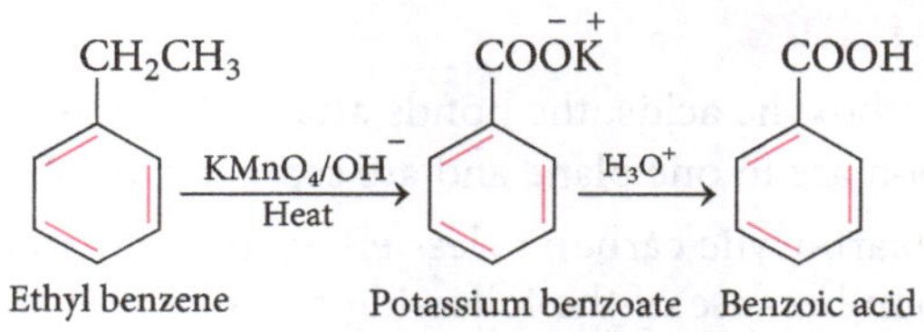

(ii) 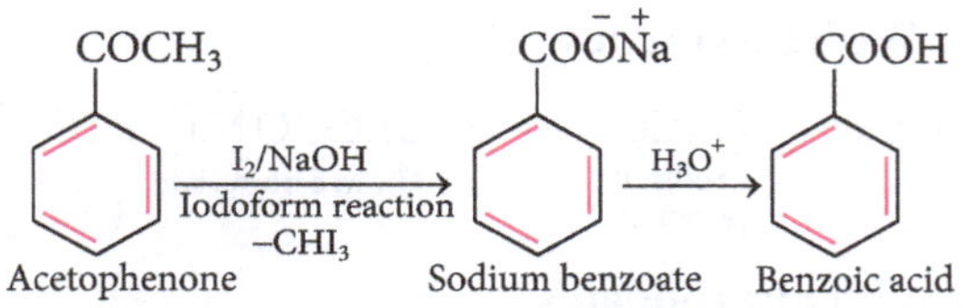

(iii) 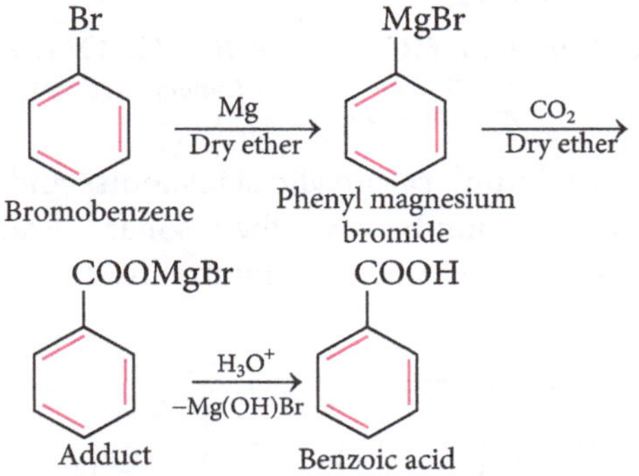

(iv) 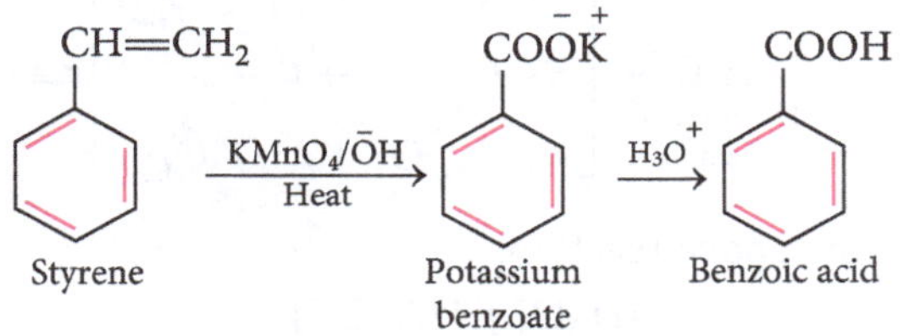

Preparation of Carboxylic acids

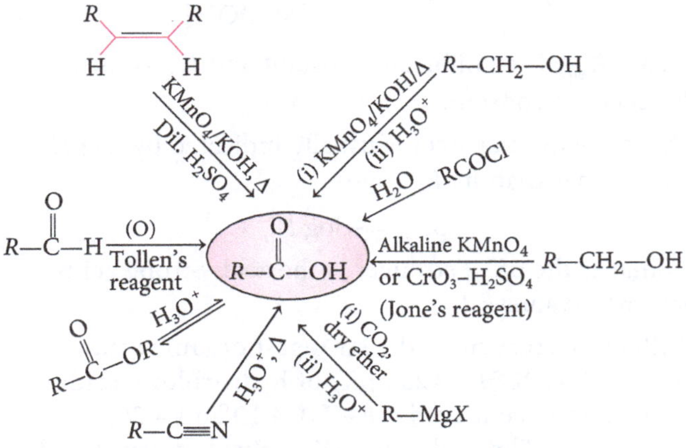

Physical Properties

The physical properties of carboxylic acids are described below in the table.

Physical Properties of Carboxylic Acid

Physical state	Lower carboxylic acids (i.e. upto C_9 atoms) are liquids at room temperature while higher ones are wax like solids.
Odour	Lower members are of sharp and pungent odour, e.g. vinegar while higher acids are odourless.
Solubility	Simple aliphatic carboxylic acids having upto C_4 atoms are miscible in water due to hydrogen bonding. Solubility decreases with increasing chain length. Carboxylic acids are also soluble in less polar organic solvents like benzene, ether, alcohol, chloroform, etc. Exceptionally high due to dimerisation *via* hydrogen bonding.
Boiling point	Boiling point increase with increase in molecular weight. 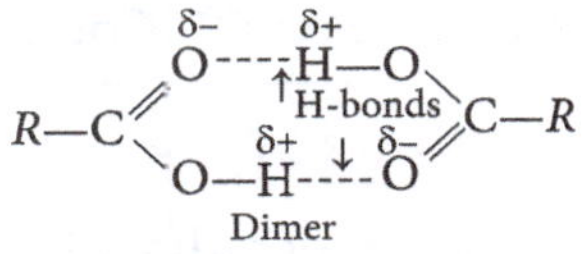 In vapour state or in aprotic solvent. 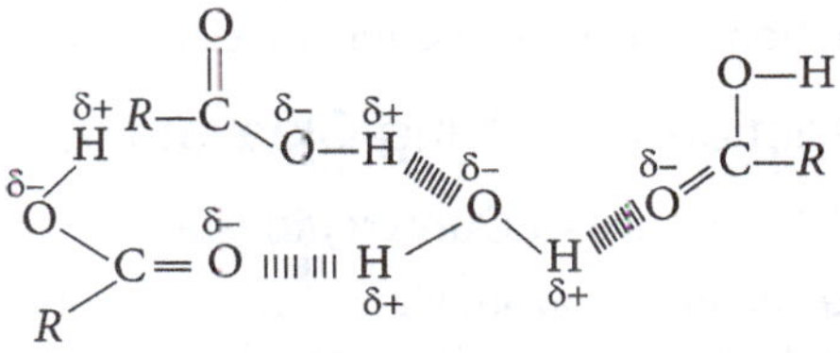 Hydrogen bonding of RCOOH with H_2O
Melting point	Higher than comparable hydrocarbons or alcohols due to strong intermolecular hydrogen bonding.

Quick Test 3

1. (i) Write the IUPAC name of the following compound:

$$CH_3-\underset{\substack{|\\OH}}{CH}-CH_2-COOH$$

(ii) Draw the structural formula of hex-2-en-4-ynoic acid. *NCERT*

2. (i) Give the IUPAC name of the compound $(CH_3)CCH_2COOH$

(ii) Draw the structural formula of 3-bromo-4-phenylpentanoic acid. *NCERT*

3. How will you convert the following?

(i) Ethanal to 2-hydroxy propanoic acid

(ii) Toluene to benzoic acid

4. Complete the following reactions :

(i) $CH_3CH{=}CHCH_3 \xrightarrow[\text{Dil. } H_2SO_4]{KMnO_4, KOH, \Delta}$

(ii) $C_6H_5COOCOCH_5 \xrightarrow{H_2O}$

5. Melting point of carboxylic acids are higher than hydrocarbons and alcohols of comparable molecular mass. Explain.

For Solutions, See QR Code on Pg. 321

Chemical Properties

Chemical properties of carboxylic acids are characteristic of carboxyl group and the alkyl or the aryl group. The reactions of carboxylic acids are classified as follows

Reactions Involving Cleavage of O—H Bond

Acidic Nature of Carboxylic Acids

Like alcohols, carboxylic acids also evolve hydrogen with metals and form salts with alkalies similar to phenols. However, unlike phenols, they react with weaker bases like sodium carbonate and hydrogen carbonates to evolve carbon dioxide.

Reactions Showing Acidic Character of —COOH Group

(a) **With active metal** (Na)

$$2R\text{—}COOH + 2Na \longrightarrow \underset{\text{Sodium carboxylate}}{2R\text{—}CO\overset{-}{O}\overset{+}{Na}} + H_2\uparrow$$

(b) **With alkali**

$$R\text{—}COOH + \underset{\substack{\text{Sodium}\\\text{hydroxide}}}{NaOH} \longrightarrow \underset{\substack{\text{Sodium}\\\text{carboxylate}}}{R\text{—}CO\overset{-}{O}\overset{+}{Na}} + H_2O$$

(c) **With carbonates**

$$RCOOH + \underset{\substack{\text{Sodium}\\\text{carbonate}}}{Na_2CO_3} \longrightarrow \underset{\text{Sodium carboxylate}}{2RCO\overset{-}{O}\overset{+}{Na}} + CO_2\uparrow + H_2O$$

(d) **With bicarbonates**

$$R\text{—}COOH + \underset{\substack{\text{Sodium}\\\text{bicarbonate}}}{NaHCO_3} \longrightarrow \underset{\text{Sodium carboxylate}}{R\text{—}CO\overset{-}{O}\overset{+}{Na}} + H_2O + CO_2\uparrow$$

In aqueous solution, carboxylic acids ionise and exist in dynamic equilibrium between the resonance stabilised carboxylate ions and the hydronium ions.

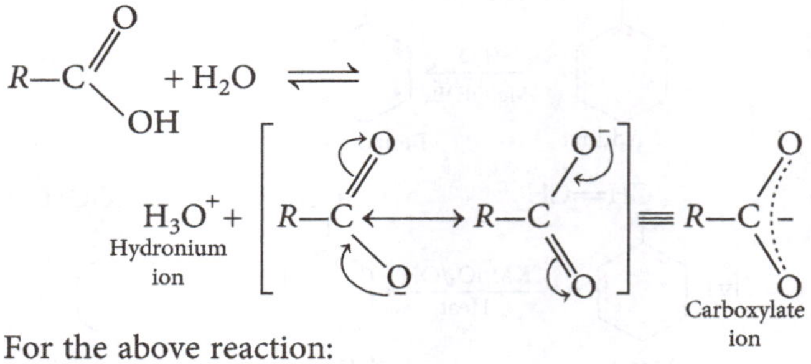

For the above reaction:

$$K_{eq} = \frac{[H_3O^+][RCOO^-]}{[H_2O][RCOOH]};$$

$$K_a = K_{eq}[H_2O] = \frac{[H_3O^+][RCOO^-]}{[RCOOH]}$$

where, K_{eq}, is equilibrium constant and K_a is the acid dissociation constant.

The strength of an acid is usually indicated by its pK_a value rather than its K_a value.

$$pK_a = -\log K_a$$

∴ Smaller the pK_a, stronger is the acid. Strong acids have pK_a values < 1.

Trifluoroacetic acid is the strongest organic acid (pK_a of $CF_3COOH = 0.23$). pK_a of hydrochloric acid, benzoic and acetic acid are –7.0, 4.19 and 4.76, respectively. The acids with pK_a value between 1 and 5 are considered to be moderately strong acids, weak acids have pK_a values between 5 and 15 and extremely weak acids have pK_a values >15.

Cause of Acidic Nature of Carboxylic Acids

Carboxylic acids may be regarded as a resonance hybrid of the structures I and II.

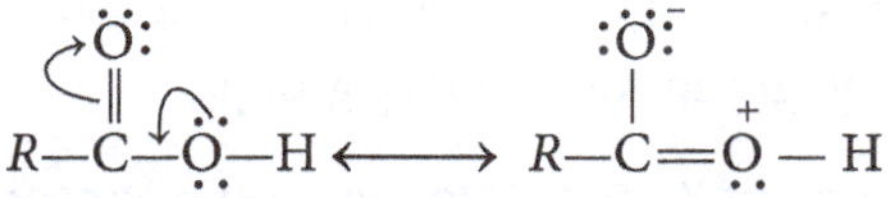

(I) (II)

Being more electronegative, oxygen having positive charge weakens the O—H bond. This results in the acidic nature of carboxyl group.

Carboxylate anion formed by the removal of a proton is also stabilised by resonance as follows

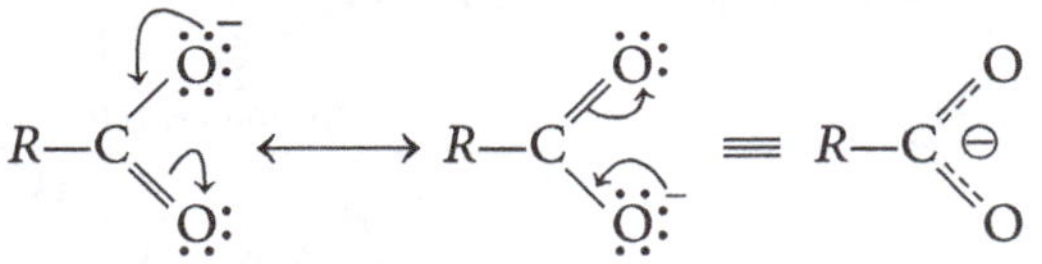

(III) (IV) (V)

Resonance stabilisation of carboxylate anion is more than that of undissociated carboxylic acid. Therefore, greater stability of carboxylate ion is responsible for the acidic character of carboxylic acids.

Note Carboxylic acids are weaker than mineral acids but they are stronger acids than alcohols (pK_a is ~16 for ethanol) and phenols (pK_a is ~ 10).

(i) **Carboxylic acid *vs* Alcohol** Carboxylic acids are more acidic than alcohols because carboxylate anions are more stable than alkoxide ions, so carboxylic acids have strong tendency to release a proton.

(ii) **Carboxylic acid *vs* Phenol** Similarly, carboxylic acids are stronger acids than phenols because carboxylate ion is much more inductive and/or resonance stabilised than phenoxide ion.

Effect of Substituents on the Acidity of Carboxylic Acids

Substituents may affect the stability of the conjugate base and thus, also affect the acidity of the carboxylic acids.

(i) **Electron withdrawing groups (EWGs)** increase the stability of the carboxylate ion by delocalising the negative charge through inductive and/or resonance effect on the conjugate base.

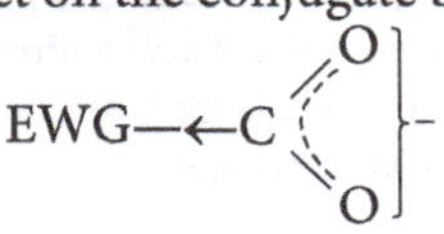

Acidity of carboxylic acids increases due to the presence of Electron Withdrawing Groups (EWGs)

The effect of the following substituent groups in the increasing acidity order is

$$\text{Ph} < \text{I} < \text{Br} < \text{Cl} < \text{F} < \text{CN} < \text{NO}_2 < \text{CF}_3.$$

(ii) **Electron donating groups (EDGs)** decreases the stability of the carboxylate ion by intensifying the negative charge.

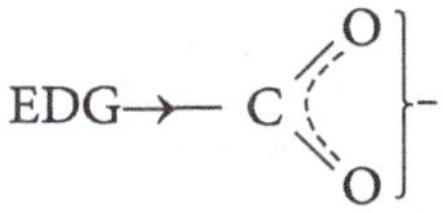

Acidity of carboxylic acids decreases due to the presence of Electron Donating Groups (EDGs)

As the $+I$ effect of electron donating group increases, the relative acidic strength decreases as

$$-CH_3 < -C_2H_5 < -CH(CH_3)_2 < -C(CH_3)_3$$

($+I$-effect increases)

$$\underset{\text{Acetic acid}}{CH_3COOH} > \underset{\text{Propionic acid}}{CH_3CH_2COOH} > \underset{\text{Isobutyric acid}}{(CH_3)_2CHCOOH} > \underset{\text{2,2-dimethylpropanoic acid}}{(CH_3)_3CCOOH}$$

(Relative acidic strength decreases)

Order of Decreasing Acidity of Different Carboxylic Acids Based on pK_a Value

$CF_3COOH > CCl_3COOH > Cl_2CHCOOH > NO_2CH_2COOH > NCCH_2COOH > FCH_2COOH > ClCH_2COOH > BrCH_2COOH > HCOOH > ClCH_2CH_2COOH > C_6H_5COOH > C_6H_5CH_2COOH > CH_3COOH > CH_3CH_2COOH$

(iii) **Effect of hybridisation on acidity** direct attachment of groups such as phenyl or vinyl to the carboxylic acid, increases the acidity of corresponding carboxylic acid, contrary to the decrease expected due to resonance effect shown below.

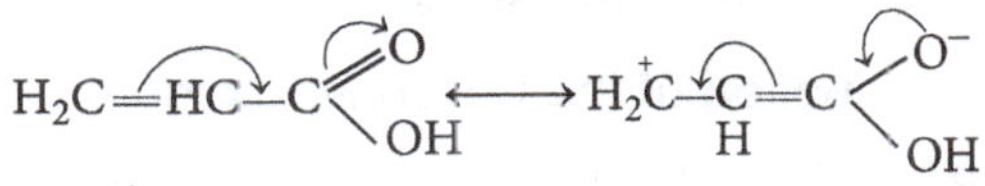

As sp^2-hybridised carbon is more electronegative than that of sp^3-hybridised carbon.

Therefore, as the hybridisation of carbon atom directly attached to —COOH changes from $sp^3 \longrightarrow sp^2 \longrightarrow sp$, the acidic strength increases in the order as

$$\underset{sp^3}{CH_3COOH} < \underset{sp^2}{CH_2{=}CHCOOH} < \underset{sp}{HC{\equiv}C{-}COOH}$$

(iv) Electron withdrawing group attached to phenyl ring of aromatic carboxylic acid increases the acidity while electron donating group decreases their acidity.

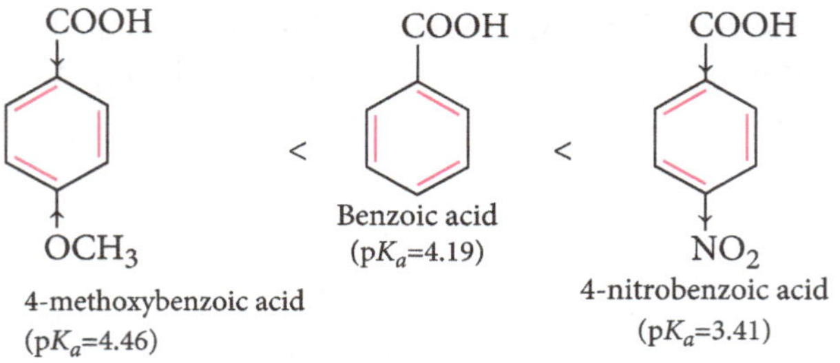

TEACHER'S TIP

The acidity of unsubstituted aliphatic carboxylic acids are less than the unsubstituted aromatic carboxylic acids. Further, since formic acid does not contain any alkyl group, therefore, it is a stronger acid than benzoic acid. Thus, the order of acidic character is formic acid > Benzoic acid > Acetic acid.

Reactions Involving Cleavage of C—OH Bond

1. Esterification

Carboxylic acids react with alcohols or phenols in the presence of a mineral acid such as conc. H_2SO_4 or HCl gas (as a catalyst) to form an ester. This reaction is called **esterification**.

$$R\text{—COOH} + R'\text{—OH} \overset{H^+}{\rightleftharpoons} R\text{—COO}R' + H_2O$$

$$\underset{\text{Acetic acid}}{CH_3\text{—COOH}} + \underset{\text{Methanol}}{CH_3\text{—OH}} \rightleftharpoons \underset{\text{Methyl acetate}}{CH_3\text{—COOCH}_3} + H_2O$$

Mechanism

It is a type of nucleophilic acyl substitution reaction that involves majorly three steps:

Step I Protonation of the Carbonyl Oxygen

This step activates the carbonyl group towards nucleophilic addition of the alcohol.

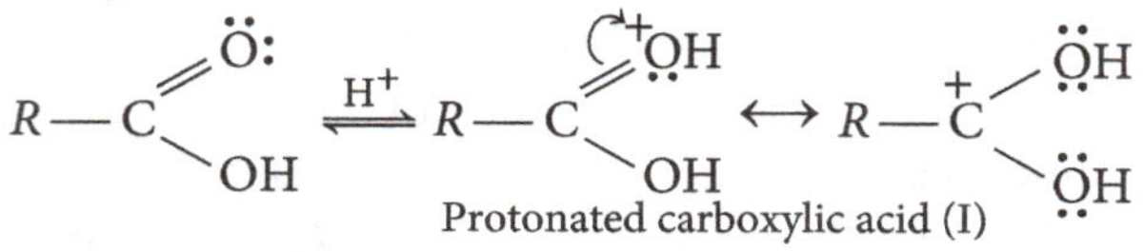

Protonated carboxylic acid (I)

Step II Nucleophilic Addition of the Alcohol

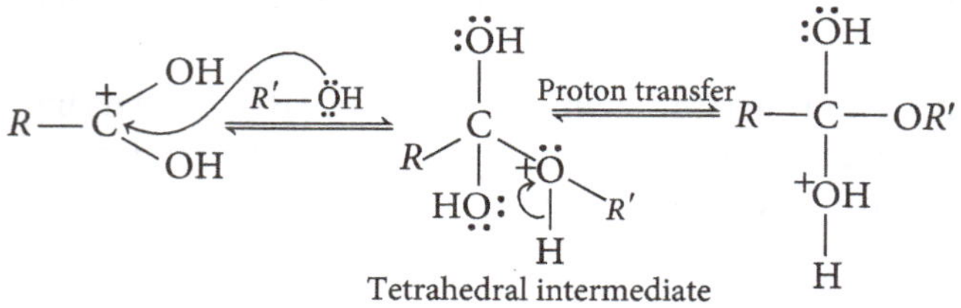

Tetrahedral intermediate

Proton transfer in the tetrahedral intermediate converts the hydroxyl group into $—\overset{+}{O}H_2$ group.

Step III Loss of Water Molecule and a Proton

The $—\overset{+}{O}H_2$ group being better leaving group is eliminated as neutral water molecule. The protonated ester so formed finally loses a proton to give the ester.

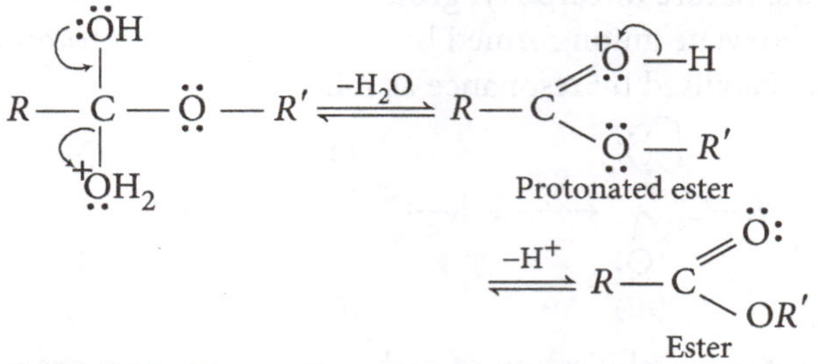

2. Anhydride Formation

Carboxylic acids on heating with mineral acids such as H_2SO_4 or with P_2O_5 give corresponding anhydride. Acid anhydrides are obtained by the elimination of water molecule.

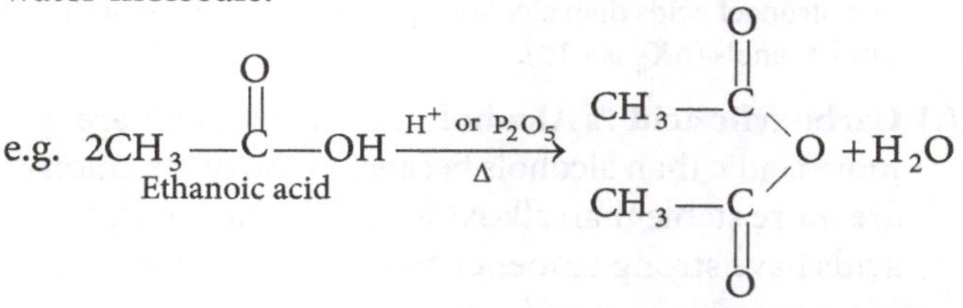

3. Reactions with Phosphorus Trihalides, Phosphorus Pentahalides and Thionyl Chloride

The hydroxyl group of carboxylic acids behaves like that of alcohols and is easily replaced by chlorine atom on treating with PCl_5, PCl_3 or $SOCl_2$.

$$R\text{—COOH} + PCl_5 \longrightarrow \underset{\text{Acyl chloride}}{RCOCl} + POCl_3 + HCl$$

$$3R\text{COOH} + PCl_3 \longrightarrow 3R\text{—COCl} + H_3PO_3$$

$$R\text{—COOH} + SOCl_2 \longrightarrow R\text{—COCl} + SO_2\uparrow + HCl\uparrow$$

Note Thionyl chloride ($SOCl_2$) reagent is preferred to carry out reaction because the other two products obtained are gaseous and escape the reaction mixture making the purification of products easier.

4. Reaction with Ammonia

Carboxylic acids react with ammonia to give ammonium salt which on further heating at high temperature give amides.

$$\underset{\text{Acetic acid}}{CH_3COOH} + NH_3 \rightleftharpoons \underset{\text{Ammonium acetate}}{CH_3CO\overset{-}{O}\overset{+}{N}H_4} \xrightarrow[-H_2O]{\Delta} \underset{\text{Acetamide}}{CH_3CONH_2}$$

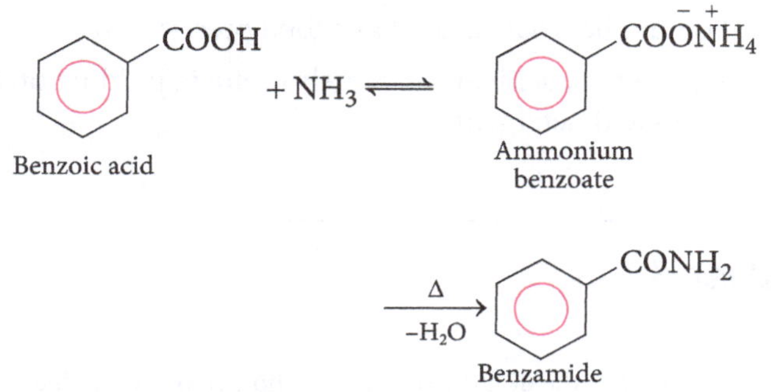

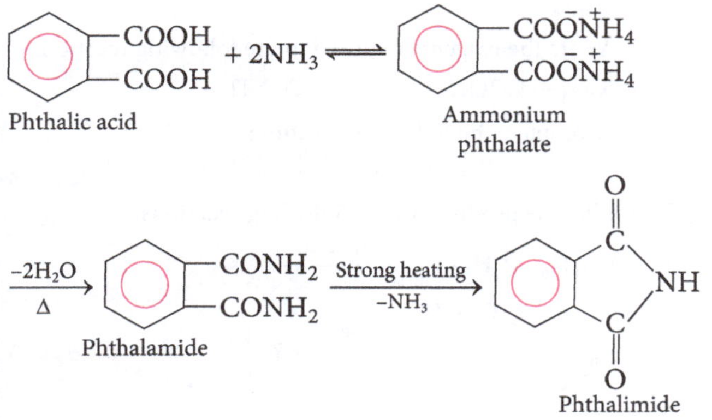

Reactions Involving —COOH Group

1. Reduction

Carboxylic acids are reduced to primary alcohols by $LiAlH_4$ and more easily with diborane.

$$\underset{\text{Acid}}{R—COOH} \xrightarrow[\text{(ii) } H_3O^+]{\text{(i) } LiAlH_4/\text{Ether or } B_2H_6} \underset{\text{Alcohol}}{R—CH_2OH}$$

Note Diborane does not easily reduce functional groups such as ester, nitro, halo, etc. Further, $NaBH_4$ does not reduce the carboxyl group.

2. Decarboxylation

The loss of CO_2 molecule from a carboxylic acid to form hydrocarbons is called **decarboxylation.**

(i) **Using soda lime** Carboxylic acids lose carbon dioxide to form hydrocarbons when their sodium salts are heated with sodalime (NaOH and CaO in the ratio of 3 : 1).

$$R—CO\overset{-}{O}\overset{+}{Na} \xrightarrow[\text{Heat}]{\text{NaOH and CaO}} \underset{\text{Alkane}}{R—H} + Na_2CO_3$$

(ii) **Electrolytic decarboxylation** (Kolbe electrolysis)

Alkali metal salts of carboxylic acids also undergo decarboxylation on electrolysis of their aqueous solutions and form hydrocarbons having twice the number of carbon atoms present in the alkyl group of acid. This reaction is known as **Kolbe electrolysis.**

e.g. $2CH_3CO\overset{-}{O}\overset{+}{Na} + 2H_2O \xrightarrow{\text{Electrolysis}} CH_3—CH_3 + 2CO_2 + H_2 + 2NaOH$

Substitution Reactions in the Hydrocarbon Part

1. Halogenation

Carboxylic acids having an α-hydrogen are halogenated at the α-position on treatment with chlorine or bromine in the presence of small amount of red phosphorus to give α-halocarboxylic acids.

This reaction is known as **Hell-Volhard-Zelinsky reaction.**

$$R—CH_2—COOH \xrightarrow[\text{(ii) } H_2O]{\text{(i) } X_2/\text{Red phosphorus}} \underset{\alpha\text{-halocarboxylic acid}}{R—\underset{X}{\underset{|}{C}H}—COOH}$$

(where, X=Cl, Br)

2. Ring Substitution Reaction

Aromatic carboxylic acids undergo electrophilic substitution reactions in which the carboxyl group acts as a deactivating and *meta*-directing group.

However, they do not undergo **Friedel-Crafts reaction** because the carboxyl group is deactivating and the catalyst aluminium chloride (Lewis acid) gets bonded to the carboxyl group.

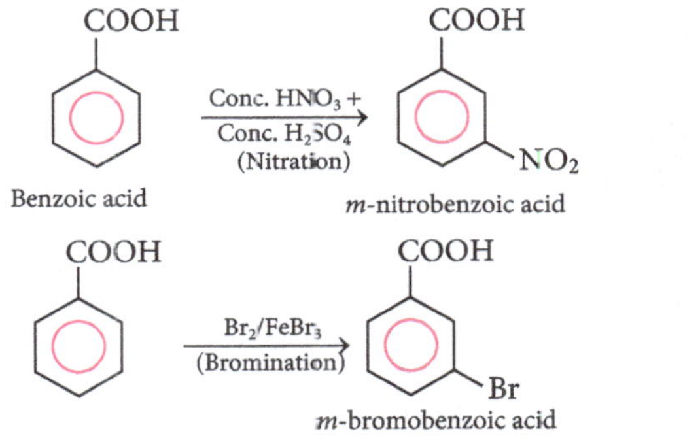

Uses of Carboxylic Acid

Some important uses of carboxylic acids are as follows

- Methanoic acid is used in rubber, textile, dyeing, leather and electroplating industries.
- Ethanoic acid is widely used as a solvent and it is also used as vinegar in food industry.
- In the manufacture of nylon-6,6, hexanedioic acid (adipic acid) is used.
- In perfume industry, esters of benzoic acid are used.
- Sodium benzoate is used as a food preservative.
- Higher fatty acids are extremely useful in production of soaps and detergents.

Quick Test 4

1. Arrange the given compounds in the increasing order of their acidic strength.

$CH_3CH_2CH(Br)COOH$, $CH_3CH(Br)CH_2COOH$, $(CH_3)_2CHCOOH$, $CH_3CH_2CH_2COOH$.

2. Identify the compounds *A*, *B* and *C* in the following reaction.

$$CH_3—Br \xrightarrow{Mg/Ether} [A] \xrightarrow[\text{(ii) Water}]{\text{(i) } CO_2} [B] \xrightarrow{CH_3OH/H^+} [C]$$

NCERT Exemplar

3. Predict the product of the following reaction

$$CH_3COONa \xrightarrow[\Delta]{NaOH/CaO} ?$$

CBSE 2015

Or

Illustrate the decarboxylation reaction giving a suitable example.

4. (i) Write the reagents required in the following reaction:

$$CH_3—COOH \xrightarrow{?} CH_3—CONH_2$$

(ii) Complete the following reaction:

$$CH_3COOH \xrightarrow{Br_2/P}$$

CBSE 2015

5. Predict the products of the following reactions:

(i) $C_6H_5—CH_3 \xrightarrow[\text{(b) } H^+]{\text{(a) } KMnO_4/KOH} ?$

(ii) 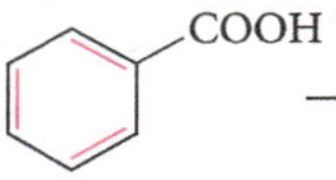 $\xrightarrow{Br_2/FeBr_3}$?

CBSE 2015

For Solutions, See QR Code on Pg. 321

Mind Map

Methods of Preparation

Carboxylic Acids

$RCH_2OH \xrightarrow[\text{(ii) } H_3O^+]{\text{(i) Alk. } KMnO_4} RCOOH$

$R—CN \xrightarrow[H_2O,\ \Delta]{H^+ \text{ or } OH^-} RCOOH$

$R—CONH_2 \xrightarrow{H_3O^+,\ \Delta} RCOOH$

$C_6H_5CH_3 \xrightarrow[\text{(ii) } H_3O^+]{\text{(i) } KMnO_4,\ KOH,\ \Delta} RCOOH$

$RMgX + CO_2 \xrightarrow[H^+/H_2O]{\text{Dry ether}} RCOOH$

$(RCO)_2O \xrightarrow{H_2O} RCOOH$

For both Aldehydes and Ketones

RCH_2OH or $R_2CHOH \xrightarrow[\text{Oxidation}]{K_2Cr_2O_7/H_2SO_4}$ RCHO or RCOR

RCH_2OH or $R_2CHOH \xrightarrow[573\text{ K}]{Cu}$ RCHO or RCOR

$RCH{=}CH \xrightarrow[Hg^{2+},\ 333\text{K}]{\text{Dil. } H_2SO_4}$ RCHO or RCOR

$RCH{=}CHR$ or $R_2C{=}CR_2 \xrightarrow[Zn/H_2O]{O_3}$ RCHO or RCOR

For Aldehydes

$RCOCl \xrightarrow[\text{Rosenmund reduction}]{H_2,Pd/BaSO_4} RCHO$

$RCN \xrightarrow[\text{(ii) } H_3O^+]{\text{(i) } SnCl_2,HCl} RCHO$ (Stephen reaction)

$C_6H_5CH_3$ (Toluene) $\rightarrow RCHO$: (i) $Cl_2/h\nu$ (ii) H_2O/Δ Or (i) CrO_2Cl_2,CS_2 (ii) H_3O^+ (Etard reaction) or (i) $CrO_3,(CH_3CO)_2O$ (ii) H_3O^+/Δ

$C_6H_6 \xrightarrow[\text{Anhyd.} AlCl_3/CuCl]{CO,\ HCl} RCHO$ (Gattermann-Koch reaction)

For Ketones

$R'COCl \xrightarrow{R_2Cd} RCOR$

$RCN \xrightarrow[\text{Ether, } H_3O^+]{RMgBr} RCOR$

ALDEHYDES, KETONES AND CARBOXYLIC ACIDS

Nomenclature

Aldehydes and Ketones (RCHO/RCOR)

Common names

- Replacing corresponding 'ic' of carboxylic acids with aldehyde.
- Naming the two alkyl or aryl groups bonded to the carbonyl groups.

IUPAC names

- Replace –e with –al and –one as required.

Carboxylic Acids (RCOOH)

Common names

- End with suffix -'ic acid'

IUPAC names

- Replacing –e in the corresponding alkane with –oic acid.

Physical Properties

Aldehydes and Ketones

Boiling points are higher than hydrocarbons and ethers of comparable molecular masses.

Carboxylic Acids

Boiling points is exceptionally high due to dimerisation.

Chemical Properties

Aldehydes and Ketones

(a) Nucleophilic Addition Reactions

Order of reactivity

$HCHO > CH_3CHO > CH_3COCH_3 > C_2H_5COCH_3$

$>C{=}O \xrightarrow{HCN}$ Cyanohydrin

$\xrightarrow{NaHSO_3}$ Bisulphite addition product

$\xrightarrow[\text{(a) HCl (g) (b) dil. HCl}]{2\ ROH}$ Acetal or ketal

$\xrightarrow{NH_2—Z}$ (Ammonia derivative) $>C(OH)(NHZ) \longrightarrow >C{=}NZ + H_2O$

(b) Aldol Condensation

It is given by aldehydes having α-H atom.

e.g. $2RCH_2CHO \underset{}{\overset{\text{Dil. NaOH}}{\rightleftharpoons}} RCH_2CH(OH)CH(R)CHO \xrightarrow[-H_2O]{\Delta} RCH_2CH{=}C(R)—CHO$

(c) Oxidation

$R—CHO \xrightarrow{\text{Tollen's reagent}}$ Silver mirror

$R—CHO \xrightarrow{\text{Fehling's solution}}$ Red–brown ppt. of Cu_2O

$R—CO—CH_3$ (Methyl ketone) $\xrightarrow[NaOH]{I_2} R—CO—\overset{-}{O}\overset{+}{Na} + CHI_3$

$RCHO \xrightarrow[HNO_3]{[O]} RCOOH$

(d) Reduction

$>C{=}O \xrightarrow[\text{(Clemmensen reduction)}]{\text{Zn/Hg, Conc. HCl}} >CH_2$

Or

$\xrightarrow[\text{(Wolff-Kishner reduction)}]{NH_2—NH_2,\ KOH} >CH_2$

$>C{=}O \xrightarrow{LiAlH_4} >CHOH$

Aldehydes are reduced to 1° alcohols

Ketones are reduced to 2° alcohols

(e) Cannizzaro Reaction

It is given by aldehydes not having α-H.

$2HCHO \xrightarrow[\text{or NaOH}]{\text{Conc. KOH},\Delta} HCH_2OH$ (Methanol) $+ HCO\overset{-}{O}\overset{+}{K}$

Carboxylic Acids

$RCOOH \xrightarrow[H^+]{R'OH} RCOOR'$ (Ester)

$\xrightarrow{P_2O_5} (RCO)_2O$ (Anhydride)

$\xrightarrow[\text{or } PCl_3]{PCl_5} RCOCl$ (Acyl halide)

$\xrightarrow[\Delta]{NH_3} RCONH_2$ (Amide)

$\xrightarrow[\text{(ii) } H_3O^+]{\text{(i) } LiAlH_4/\text{Ether}} RCH_2OH$

$R—CH_2—COOH \xrightarrow[\text{(HVZ reaction)}]{X_2/\text{Red P}} R—\overset{\alpha}{C}H(X)—COOH$

$RCO\overset{-}{O}\overset{+}{Na} \xrightarrow[\Delta]{\text{NaOH or CaO}} RH$

$RCO\overset{-}{O}\overset{+}{Na} \xrightarrow[\text{Kolbe's electrolysis}]{2H_2O} R–R$

EXAM PATTERN QUESTIONS

Objective Type Questions

Multiple Choice Questions (MCQs) [1 Mark]

1. Which among the following compounds, contain —CHO group, benzene ring, —OCH_3 group, —OH group?

(a) Salicylic acid (b) Salicylaldehyde
(c) Vanillin (d) Cinnamaldehyde

2. Addition of water to butyne occurs in acidic medium and in the presence of Hg^{2+} ions as a catalyst. The product formed is **NCERT Exemplar**

(a) $CH_3-CH_2-CH_2-\overset{O}{\overset{\|}{C}}-H$

(b) $CH_3-CH_2-\overset{O}{\overset{\|}{C}}-CH_3$

(c) $CH_3-CH_2-\overset{O}{\overset{\|}{C}}-OH + CO_2$

(d) $CH_3-\overset{O}{\overset{\|}{C}}-OH + H-\overset{O}{\overset{\|}{C}}-H$

3. The reaction,

$$RCN + SnCl_2 + HCl \longrightarrow RCH{=}NH \xrightarrow{H_3O^+} RCHO$$

is known as

(a) Etard reaction
(b) Haloform reaction
(c) Gattermann-Koch reaction
(d) Stephen reaction

4. In the equation,

$$CH_3COCl \xrightarrow[BaSO_4]{H_2/Pd} X$$

X is **Diksha**

(a) acetaldehyde (b) propionaldehyde
(c) acetone (d) acetic acid

5. Rosenmund reduction is used for the preparation of aldehydes. The catalyst used in this reaction is **CBSE 2024**

(a) Pd—$BaSO_4$ (b) anhydrous $AlCl_3$
(c) iron (III) oxide (d) $HgSO_4$

6. The compound formed as a result of oxidation of ethyl benzene by $KMnO_4$ is **Diksha**

(a) benzyl alcohol (b) acetophenone
(c) benzophenone (d) benzoic acid

7. Which of the following is most reactive in nucleophilic addition reactions? **CBSE 2023**

(a) HCHO (b) CH_3CHO
(c) CH_3COCH_3 (d) $CH_3COC_2H_5$

8. Which of the following compounds will give butanone on oxidation with alkaline $KMnO_4$ solution? **NCERT Exemplar**

(a) Butan-1-ol (b) Butan-2-ol
(c) Both (a) and (b) (d) None of these

9. The reagent which does not react with both, acetone and benzaldehyde? **NCERT Exemplar**

(a) Sodium hydrogen sulphite
(b) Phenyl hydrazine
(c) Fehling's solution
(d) Grignard reagent

10. A compound (A) with molecular formula $C_5H_{10}O$, forms a phenyl hydrazone and gives negative Tollen's and iodoform tests. The compound on reduction gives *n*-pentane. The compound (A) is **CBSE 2023**

(a) pentan-3-one (b) pentanal
(c) pentanol (d) pentan-2-one

11. When $C_6H_5COOCOCH_3$ is treated with H_2O, the product obtained is **CBSE SQP 2025**

(a) benzoic acid and ethanol
(b) benzoic acid and ethanoic acid
(c) acetic acid and phenol
(d) benzoic anhydride and methanol

12. Consider the following reaction. **CBSE 2024**

$$\begin{matrix}H\\ \ \ \ \ \ \ C{=}O\\ H\end{matrix} + \begin{matrix}H\\ \ \ \ \ \ \ C{=}O\\ H\end{matrix} + Conc\cdot KOH \xrightarrow{\Delta} A + B$$

Identify A and B from the given options.

(a) A-Methanol, B-Potassium formate
(b) A-Ethanol, B-Potassium formate
(c) A-Methanal, B-Ethanol
(d) A-Methanol, B-Potassium acetate

13. Which of the following does not give aldol condensation reaction? **CBSE 2023**

(a) $CH_3—CHO$ (b) 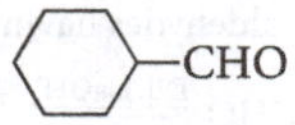

(c) 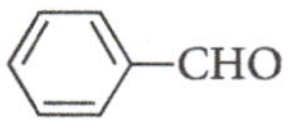 (d) CH_3COCH_3

14. **A carbonyl compound X undergoes the reactions given in the table below.**

Reaction	Result
Tollens' test	+ve
Iodoform test	+ve
Aldol condensation	Forms aldol product

Which of the following could compound X be? **Competency Based Ques**

(a) $CH_3—CH_2—CHO$ (b) $CH_3—CO—CH_3$
(c) $CH_3—CHO$ (d) H—CHO

15. **Which of the following compound gives an oxime with hydroxylamine?** **CBSE SQP 2025**

(a) CH_3COCH_3 (b) CH_3COOH
(c) $(CH_3CO)_2O$ (d) CH_3COCl

16. **What is the correct IUPAC name of the given compound?** **CBSE 2020**

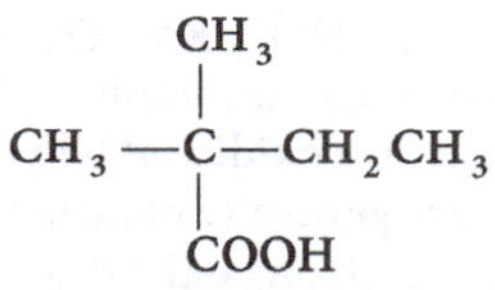

(a) 2, 2-dimethylbutanoic acid
(b) 2-carboxyl-2-methylbutane
(c) 2-ethyl-2-methylpropanoic acid
(d) 3-methylbutane carboxylic acid

17. **The acid formed when propyl magnesium bromide is treated with CO_2 followed by acid hydrolysis.** **CBSE 2025**

(a) C_3H_7COOH (b) C_2H_5COOH
(c) CH_3COOH (d) C_3H_7OH

18. **Which of the following acid is the strongest ?** **Diksha**

(a) CH_3COOH (b) $CH_2ClCOOH$
(c) $CHCl_2COOH$ (d) CCl_3COOH

19. **The carboxylic acid group does not give the usual addition and elimination reactions of aldehydes and ketones because** **Diksha**

(a) O—H bond is more polar than C═O group.
(b) COOH group gets ionised.
(c) carboxylate ion gets stabilised by resonance.
(d) COOH group does not contain carbonyl group.

20. **Arrange the following acids in the decreasing order of acidic strength.**

$HC \equiv C—COOH$ (I) C_6H_5COOH (II)

$CH_2═CH—COOH$ III CH_3COOH (IV)

(a) I > II > III > IV (b) I < II < III < IV
(c) I > III > II > IV (d) I > IV > III > II

21. **Match Column I with Column II.**

Column-I		Column-II
A.	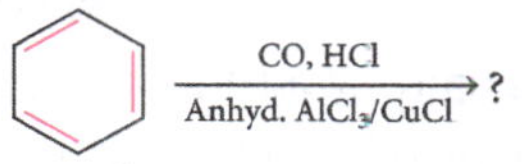	(i) Haloform reaction
B.	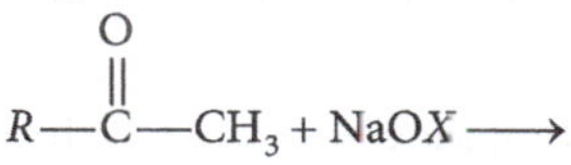	(ii) Gattermann-Koch reaction
C.	$R—CH_2—OH + R'COOH \xrightarrow{\text{Conc. } H_2SO_4}$	(iii) Esterification

Codes

	A	B	C
(a)	(ii)	(i)	(iii)
(b)	(i)	(ii)	(iii)
(c)	(i)	(iii)	(ii)
(d)	(iii)	(ii)	(i)

22. **The product formed during Hell-Volhard-Zelinsky reaction is**

(a) 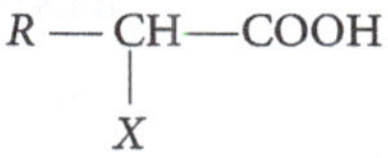 (b) $R—CH_2—COX$

(c) 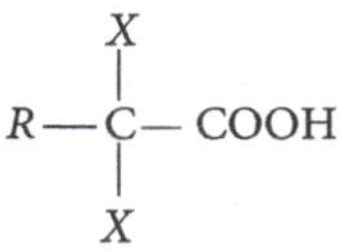 (d) 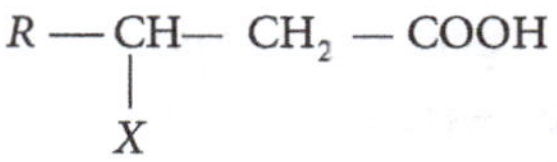

23. **Carboxylic acids do not undergo Friedel Crafts reaction because** **Diksha**

(a) COOH group is *meta* directing.
(b) COOH group is resonance stabilised.
(c) Carboxyl group is deactivating and gets bonded to Friedel-Craft's catalyst.
(d) All of the above

24. **Electrophilic substitution in benzoic acid takes place at the *meta*-position.**

Which of the following is the reason for the reaction above? **Competency Based Ques**

(a) The carboxyl group activates only the *meta*-position.
(b) The carboxyl group deactivates only the *ortho* and *para*-positions.
(c) The carboxyl group activates the *meta*-position more than the ortho and *para*-positions.
(d) The carboxyl group deactivates the *meta*-position less than the *ortho* and *para*-positions.

Assertion-Reason [1 Mark]

Directions (Q. Nos. 25-36) In the following questions, an Assertion (A) is followed by a corresponding Reason (R). Use the following keys to choose the appropriate answer.

(a) Both (A) and (R) are true, and (R) is the correct explanation of (A).
(b) Both (A) and (R) are true, but (R) is not the correct explanation of (A).
(c) (A) is true, but (R) is false.
(d) (A) is false, but (R) is true.

25. **Assertion** (A) Formaldehyde is a planar molecule.

Reason (R) It contains sp^2-hybridised carbon atom. **NCERT Exemplar**

26. **Assertion** (A) The solubility of aldehydes and ketones in water decreases with increase in the size of alkyl group.

Reason (R) Alkyl groups are electron-repelling groups.

27. **Assertion** (A) Compounds containing —CHO group are easily oxidised to corresponding carboxylic acids.

Reason (R) Carboxylic acids can be reduced to alcohols by treatment with $LiAlH_4$. **NCERT Exemplar**

28. **Assertion** (A) Aldehydes and ketones, both react with Tollen's reagent to form silver mirror.

Reason (R) Both aldehydes and ketones contain a carbonyl group. **NCERT Exemplar**

29. **Assertion** (A) Pentan-2-one can be distinguished from pentan-3-one by iodoform test.

Reason (R) Pentan-2-one is a methyl ketone, while the pentan-3-one is not.

30. **Assertion** (A) α-hydrogen atoms of carbonyl compounds are acidic.

Reason (R) The strong electron releasing effect of the carbonyl group make the stabilisation of the conjugate base by the resonance.

31. **Assertion** (A) Aromatic aldehydes and formaldehyde undergo Cannizzaro reaction.

Reason (R) Aromatic aldehydes are almost as reactive as formaldehyde. **NCERT Exemplar**

32. **Assertion** (A) A carboxylate ion ($RCOO^-$) is stabilised by resonance to a greater extent as compared to the acid ($RCOOH$).

Reason (R) The contributing structures of $RCOO^-$ are equivalent, while those of $RCOOH$ are not.

33. **Assertion** (A) Acetic acid but not formic acid can be halogenated in the presence of red P and Cl_2. **CBSE 2023**

Reason (R) Acetic acid is a weaker acid than formic acid.

34. **Assertion** (A) Benzoic acid does not undergo Friedel-Crafts reaction.

Reason (R) Carboxyl group is deactivating and the catalyst aluminium chloride gets bonded to the carboxyl group. **CBSE 2024**

35. **Assertion** (A) Aromatic carboxylic groups do not undergo Friedel- Crafts reaction.

Reason (R) Carboxyl group is deactivating and the catalyst aluminium chloride gets bonded to the carboxyl group. **NCERT Exemplar**

36. **Assertion** (A) Bromination of benzoic acid gives *m*-bromobenzoic acid.

Reason (R) Carboxyl group increases the electron density at the *meta*-position. **CBSE 2023**

Case-Study [4 Marks]

37. Read the case given below and answer the following questions.

Aldehydes and ketones are reduced to primary and secondary alcohols respectively by $NaBH_4$ or $LiAlH_4$ as well as catalytic hydrogenation. The carbonyl group of aldehydes and ketones is reduced to $>CH_2$ group on treatment with Zn-Hg and conc, HCl (Clemmensen reduction) or with hydrazine followed by NaOH or KOH in highly boiling solvent such, as ethylene glycol (Wolff-Kishner reduction).

Aldehydes differ from ketones in their oxidation reactions. Aldehydes are easily oxidised to carboxylic acids on treatment with HNO_3, $KMnO_4$, $K_2Cr_2O_7$, etc. Even mild oxidising agents mainly Tollen's reagent and Fehling's solution also oxidise aldehydes. On the other hand, ketones are generally oxidised under vigorous conditions, i.e. strong oxidising agents and at elevated temperature, to give mixture of carboxylic acids having lesser number of C-atoms than the parent ketone.

(i) A substance $C_4H_{10}O(X)$ yields on oxidation a compound C_4H_8O which gives an oxime and a positive iodoform test. The substance X on treatment with conc. H_2SO_4 gives C_4H_8. Deduce structure of the compund (X) is

(a) $CH_3CH_2CH_2CH_2OH$ (b) $CH_3CH(OH)CH_2CH_3$
(c) $(CH_3)_3COH$ (d) $CH_3CH_2—O—CH_2CH_3$

(ii) Which of the following compound cannot be obtained by reduction of ketone or aldehyde with $NaBH_4$?

(a) Butan-1-ol (b) Butan-2-ol
(c) 2-methyl-1-propan-1-ol (d) 2-methyl-propan-2-ol

Or

The carbonyl compound producing an optically active product by reaction with $LiAlH_4$ is

(a) propanone (b) butanone
(c) pentan-3-one (d) benzophenone

(iii) Which of the following test/reactions is given by aldehydes as well as ketones?

(a) Fehling's test
(b) Tollen's test
(c) 2, 4-DNP test
(d) Cannizzaro's reaction

38. **Read the case given below and answer the following questions.**

A student conducted the following experiments on three organic compounds labelled *A*, *B* and *C*.

Compound *A* When treated with Tollen's reagent, a silver mirror was observed. On reaction with Fehling's solution, a brick-red precipitate was formed. The compound also reacted with sodium bisulphite to produce a crystalline solid.

Compound *B* On treatment with Brady's reagent (2,4-dinitrophenylhydrazine), an orange precipitate was formed. However, it did not give a positive test with Tollen's reagent or Fehling's solution. When heated with iodine in the presence of alkali, a yellow precipitate with an antiseptic odour was observed.

Compound *C* On adding to a solution of sodium bicarbonate, vigorous effervescence was observed. When treated with neutral $FeCl_3$, a violet coloration appeared.

(i) Explain the following observations:

(a) Formation of a silver mirror with Tollen's reagent for compound *A*.

(b) Yellow precipitate with iodine and alkali for compound *B*.

(ii) Write the structures of the compound '*A*' and '*B*' based on the tests performed.

Or Identify the functional groups present in compounds *A* and *B*.

(iii) What is the reason behind effervescence with sodium bicarbonate for compound *C*.

Subjective Type Questions

Short Answer Type I Questions [2 Marks]

1. Acetone on reaction with HCN gives one compound, whereas acetaldehyde gives two compounds that are difficult to separate. Explain why?

2. Why is it necessary to control the pH during the reaction of aldehydes and ketones with ammonia derivatives?

3. (i) Out of *p*-tolualdehyde and *p*-nitrobenzaldehyde, which one is more reactive towards nucleophilic addition reactions, why? **CBSE SQP 2024**

(ii) Write the structure of the product formed when acetone reacts with 2,4-DNP reagent.

4. Predict the products formed when propanone reacts with following reagents : **CBSE 2024**

(i) CH_3MgBr and then H_3O^+

(ii) Zinc amalgam and concentration HCl

5. Would you expect benzaldehyde to be more reactive or less reactive in nucleophilic addition reactions than propanal? Justify your answer. **CBSE 2025**

6. What is α-hydrogen in a carbonyl compounds? Write the similarities and differences on the reactivity of the compounds CH_3CHO and C_6H_5CHO with the reagents

(i) NaOH (ii) Fehling's reagent

7. Write the products of the following reactions

(i) 

CBSE 2023

(ii) 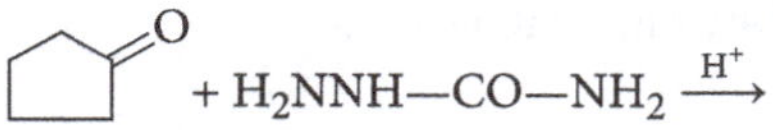

8. Give reasons to support the answer. **CBSE SQP (Term-II)**

(i) Presence of alpha hydrogen in aldehydes and ketones is essential for aldol condensation.

(ii) 3-hydroxypentan-2-one shows positive Tollen's test.

9. Write the reactions involved in the following reactions:

(i) Clemmensen reduction

(ii) Cannizzaro reaction **Delhi 2017**

10. (i) Is benzaldehyde less or more reactive to electrophilic substitution reactions than benzene (C_6H_6) ? Give an explanation for your answer.

(ii) State the position on the ring at which electrophilic substitution is likely to predominate in benzaldehyde. Explain why? **Competency Based Ques.**

11. Show how each of the following compounds can be converted to benzoic acid?

(i) Benzamide

(ii) Propyl benzene

12. How will you bring about the following conversions?

(i) 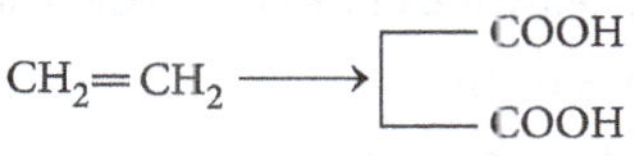

(Succinic acid)

(ii) 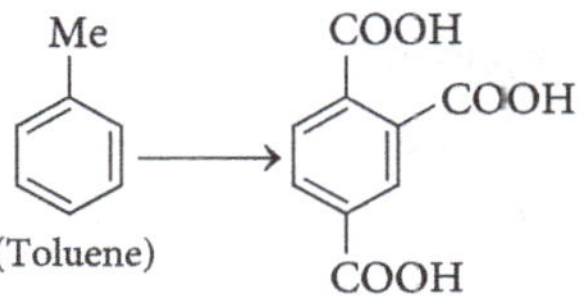

(Toluene)

(Benzene-1,2,4-tricarboxylic acid)

13. Do the following conversions is not more than two steps.
(i) Toluene to Benzoic acid
(ii) Benzaldehyde to 1-phenyl ethanol **CBSE 2023**

14. Account for the following.
(i) $Cl—CH_2COOH$ is a stronger acid than CH_3COOH.
(ii) Carboxylic acids do not give reactions of carbonyl group.

15. Do the following conversions is not more than two steps:
(i) CH_3CN to $CH_3—\underset{\underset{O}{\|}}{C}—CH_3$
(ii) 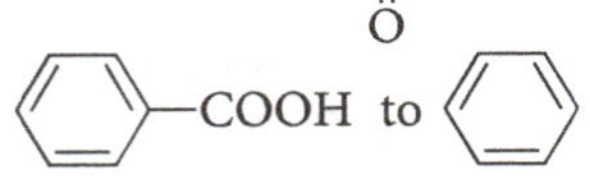

CBSE 2023

16. Give reasons for the following. **CBSE 2023**
(i) Carboxylic carbon is less electrophilic than carbonyl carbon of aldehydes and ketones.
(ii) Propanal is more reactive than propanone towards addition of HCN.

17. Carry out the following conversions
(i) Ethanal to but-2-enal
(ii) Propanoic acid to ethane **CBSE 2025**

18. Account for the following.
(i) Aromatic carboxylic acids do not undergo Friedel-Crafts reaction.
(ii) pK_a value of 4-nitrobenzoic acid is lower than that of benzoic acid. **CBSE 2018**

Short Answer Type II Questions [3 Marks]

19. Write down the IUPAC and common name for the following.
(i) 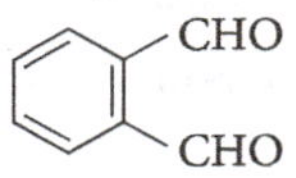

(ii) 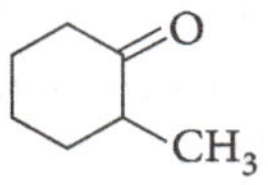

(iii) $CH_2═CHCHO$

20. Draw the structures of the following derivatives.
(i) 2,4-dinitrophenylhydrazone of benzaldehyde
(ii) Cyclopropanone oxime
(iii) Acetaldehyde dimethylacetal
(iv) Semicarbazone of cyclobutanone
(v) Ethylene ketal of hexan-3-one
(vi) Methyl hemiacetal of formaldehyde **NCERT**

21. Write structures of compounds *A*, *B* and *C* in each of the following reactions:

(i) $C_6H_5Br \xrightarrow{\text{Mg/dry ether}} A \xrightarrow[\text{(b) } H_3O^+]{\text{(a) } CO_2(g)} B \xrightarrow{PCl_5} C$

(ii) $CH_3CN \xrightarrow[\text{(b) } H_3O^+]{\text{(a) } CuCl_2/HCl} A \xrightarrow{\text{Dil. NaOH}} B \xrightarrow{\Delta} C$ **CBSE 2017**

22. (i) Give the chemical reaction involved when *p*-nitrotoluene undergoes Etard reaction.
(ii) Why does benzoic acid exist as a dimer in an aprotic solvent?
(iii) Benzene on reaction with methyl chloride in the presence of anhydrous $AlCl_3$ forms toluene. What is the expected outcome if benzene is replaced by benzoic acid? Give a reason for your answer.

Or

An organic compound '*X*', does not undergo aldol condensation. However, '*X*' with compound '*Y*' in the presence of a strong base react to give the compound 1,3-diphenylprop-2-en-1-one.
(i) Identify '*X*' and '*Y*'.
(ii) Write the chemical reaction involved.
(iii) Give one chemical test to distinguish between *X* and *Y*. **NCERT Exemplar**

23. Write the reaction and IUPAC name of the product formed when 2-methylpropanal (*iso*-butyraldehyde) is treated with ethyl magnesium bromide followed by hydrolysis. **CBSE SQP 2023**

24. Complete the following reaction sequence.

$$CH_3—\overset{\overset{O}{\|}}{C}—CH_3 \xrightarrow[\text{(ii) } H_2O/H^+]{\text{(i) } CH_3MgBr} A \xrightarrow[\text{Ether}]{\text{Na metal}} B \xrightarrow{CH_3—Br} C$$

NCERT Exemplar

25. (i) Ethyl benzene is generally prepared by acetylation of benzene followed by the reduction and not by direct alkylation. Think of a possible reason. **NCERT Exemplar**
(ii) Can Gattermann-Koch reaction be considered similar to Friedel-Crafts acylation? Discuss. **NCERT Exemplar**

26. Complete the following reaction.
(i) 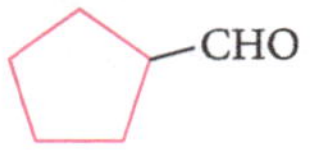

$+ HCN \longrightarrow$

(ii) $HCHO + \text{Methyl alcohol} \xrightleftharpoons{HCl}$

(iii) $HCHO + \text{Conc. NaOH} \longrightarrow$

27. An aldehyde $A(C_{11}H_8O)$, which does not undergo self aldol condensation, gives benzaldehyde and 2 moles of B on ozonolysis. Compound B on oxidation with silver ion gives oxalic acid. Identify the compounds A and B.

28. A, B and C are three non-cyclic functional isomers of a carbonyl compound with molecular formula C_4H_8O. Isomers A and C give positive Tollen's test, whereas isomer B does not give Tollen's test, but gives positive iodoform test.
Isomers A and B on reduction with Zn(Hg)/conc. HCl give the same product D.
(i) Write the structures of A, B, C and D.
(ii) Out of A, B and C isomers, which one is least reactive towards addition of HCN? **CBSE 2018**

29. An alkene 'A' (molecular formula C_5H_{10}) on ozonolysis gives a mixture of two compounds 'B' and 'C'. Compound 'B' gives positive Fehling's test and also forms iodoform on treatment with I_2 and NaOH. Compound 'C' does not give Fehling's test but forms iodoform. Identify the compounds A, B and C. Write the reaction for ozonolysis and formation of iodoform from B and C. **CBSE SQP (Term II), 2025**

30. Give the structures of the following.
(i) Phthaldehyde
(ii) 3-methyl cyclohexane carbaldehyde
(iii) 3-methylbut-2-enoic acid

31. Account for the following differences in the acidic character of the following.
(i) $Me_3C—CH_2—COOH > Me_3SiCH_2COOH$
(ii) $H_2C{=}CHCH_2COOH > CH_3CH_2COOH$
(iii) $N{\equiv}C—CH_2COOH > CH_3COCH_2—COOH$

32 Which acid of each pair shown here would you expect to be stronger? (Any three)
(i) CH_3COOH or CH_2FCOOH
(ii) CH_2FCOOH or $CH_2ClCOOH$
(iii) $CH_2FCH_2CH_2COOH$ or CH_3CHFCH_2COOH
(iv)
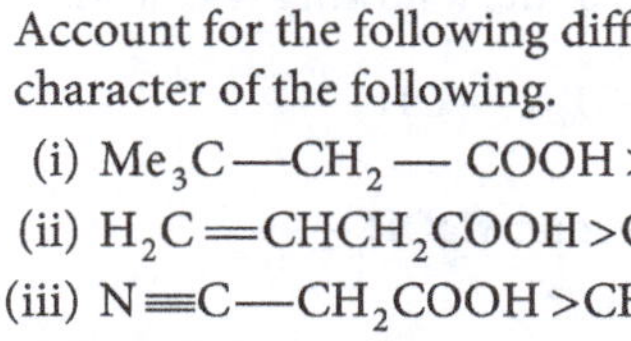

33. Although phenoxide ion has more number of resonating structures than carboxylate ion, carboxylic acid is a stronger acid than phenol. Give two reasons. **CBSE SQP 2016; NCERT**

34. Predict the products formed when cyclohexane-carbaldehyde reacts with following reagents:
(i) PhMgBr and then H_3O^+
(ii) Tollen's reagent
(iii) Semicarbazide and weak acid
(iv) Excess ethanol and acid
(v) Zinc amalgam and dilute hydrochloric acid **NCERT**

35. (i) (a) Write the chemical equation for the haloform reaction of acetone with sodium hypochlorite solution.
(b) Will pentan-3-one undergo the haloform reaction with sodium hypochlorite? Justify your answer.
(c) Name the one aldehyde that also undergoes the haloform reaction.
(ii) Both aldehydes and ketones produce carboxylic acids on oxidation.
(a) With respect to the number of carbon atoms, state the difference in the carboxylic acids formed when
(I) an aldehyde is used as a reactant
(II) a ketone is used as a reactant.
(b) Give one reason for this difference in each case.
Competency Based Que.

Long Answer Type Questions [5 Marks]

36. An organic compound 'A' C_8H_6 on treatment with dilute H_2SO_4 containing mercuric sulphate gives compound 'B'. This compound 'B' can also be obtained from a reaction of benzene with acetyl chloride in presence of anhy. $AlCl_3$. 'B' on treatment with I_2 in *aq*. KOH gives 'C' and a yellow compound 'D'.
Identify A, B, C and D. Give the chemical reactions involved. **CBSE SQP 2021**

37. A hydrocarbon (A) with molecular formula C_5H_{10} on ozonolysis gives two products (B) and (C). Both (B) and (C) gives a yellow precipitate when heated with iodine in presence of NaOH while only (B) gives a silver mirror on reaction with Tollen's reagent.
(i) Identify (A), (B) and (C). **CBSE SQP 2023**
(ii) Write the reaction of B with Tollen's reagent.
(iii) Write the equation for iodoform test for C.
(iv) Write down the equation for aldol condensation reaction of B and C.

38. (i) Write the reaction involved in Cannizzaro reaction.
(ii) Why are the boiling points of aldehydes and ketones lower than that of corresponding carboxylic acids?
(iii) An organic compound 'A' with molecular formula $C_5H_8O_2$ is reduced to n-pentane with hydrazine followed by heating with NaOH and glycol. 'A'

forms a dioxime with hydroxylamine and gives a positive iodoform and Tollen's test. Identify '*A*' and give its reaction for iodoform and Tollen's test. **CBSE 2023**

39. Which of the following compounds would undergo aldol condensation and/or Cannizzaro reaction or neither of these two reactions. Write the structures of the expected products of aldol condensation or Cannizzaro reaction.

(i) Methanal (ii) 2-methyl pentanal
(iii) Benzaldehyde (iv) Benzophenone
(v) Cyclohexanone (vi) 1-phenyl propanone
(vii) Phenyl acetaldehyde (viii) Butan-1-ol
(ix) 2,2-dimethyl butanal **NCERT**

40. (i) Write structures of *A*, *B*, *C* and D in the following reaction sequence:

$$CH_3COCl \xrightarrow{H_2/Pd\text{-}BaSO_4} A \xrightarrow{\text{Dil. NaOH}} B \xrightarrow{\Delta} C$$
$$A \xrightarrow{CH_3MgBr/H_3O^+} D$$

(ii) Arrange the following compounds in the increasing order of their boiling points:

$CH_3CHO, CH_3CH_2OH, CH_3OCH_3, CH_3COOH$ **CBSE 2017 C**

41. (i) How will you bring about the following conversion in not more than two steps?

(a) Propanone to propene
(b) Ethanol to 3-hydroxybutanal
(c) Benzene to *m*-nitroacetophenone
(d) Bromobenzene to 1-phenylethanol
(e) Benzaldehyde to benzophenone
(f) Benzaldehyde to α-hydroxy phenylacetic acid

(ii) Arrange the following compounds in the increasing order of their property as indicated:

Acetaldehyde, acetone, di-*tert*-butyl ketone, *tert*-butyl methyl ketone (reactivity towards HCN) **NCERT**

42. (i) Draw structure of the 2-4-dinitrophenyl hydrazone of benzaldehyde.

(ii) Which acid of the following pair is a stronger acid?

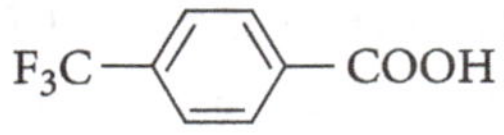

or 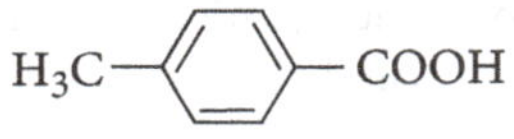

(iii) Write the chemical equation involved in Rosenmund's reduction.

(iv) Why are α-hydrogen atoms of aldehydes and ketones acidic in nature?

(v) Write a chemical test to distinguish between benzaldehye and benzoic acid. **CBSE 2023**

43. (i) What happens when

(a) CH_3COCl is treated with $(CH_3)_2Cd$,
(b) CH_3CHO is treated with HCN, and
(c) Benzaldehyde is treated with conc. $(HNO_3 + H_2SO_4)$?

(ii) Which acid of each pair shown below would you expect to be stronger?

(a) Acetic acid or fluoroacetic acid
(b) *p*-nitrobenzoic acid or *p*-methyl benzoic acid **CBSE 2024 C**

44. (i) Write the reaction for cross aldol condensation of acetone and ethanal. **CBSE SQP 2021**

(ii) How will you carry out the following conversions?

(a) Benzyl alcohol to phenyl ethanoic acid
(b) Propanone to propene
(c) Benzene to *m*-nitroacetophenone

45. (i) Account for the following.

(a) The alpha (α)-hydrogens of aldehydes and ketones are acidic in nature.
(b) Oxidation of aldehydes is easier than ketones.

(ii) Arrange the following in

(a) decreasing reactivity towards nucleophilic addition reaction propanal, acetone, benzaldehyde.
(b) increasing order of boiling point :
Propane, ethanol, dimethylether, propanal

(iii) Give simple chemical test to distinguish between benzoic acid and benzaldehyde. **CBSE 2024**

46. (i) Write the products of the following reactions:

(a) 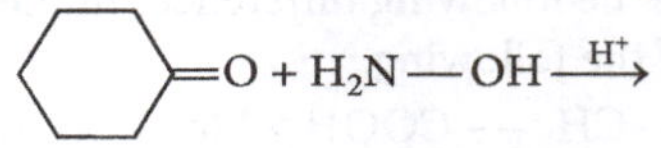

(b) $2C_6H_5CHO + \text{conc. NaOH} \longrightarrow$

(c) $CH_3COOH \xrightarrow{Cl_2/P}$

(ii) Give simple chemical tests to distinguish between the following pairs of compounds.

(a) Benzaldehyde and benzoic acid.
(b) Propanal and propanone **CBSE 2020**

47. Give the simple chemical tests to distinguish between the following pairs of compounds.

(i) Acetophenone and benzophenone
(ii) Phenol and benzoic acid
(iii) Benzoic acid and ethyl benzoate
(iv) Pentan-2-one and pentan-3-one
(v) Ethanal and propanal **NCERT**

48. (i) How can you convert each of the following compounds to benzoic acid? **CBSE 2023**

1. Acetophenone 2. Ethylbenzene
3. Bromobenzene

(ii) Arrange the following compounds in increasing order of their property as indicated.

1. O_2NCH_2—COOH, F—CH_2COOH, CN—CH_2COOH (Acidic character)
2. Ethanal, Propanal, Butanone, Propanone (Reactivity in nucleophilic addition reaction).

49. (i) Differentiate between the following:

(a) Propanoic acid and acrylic acid (CH_2 =CH—COOH)

(b) 2-bromopropanoic acid ($CH_3CHBrCOOH$) and pyruvic acid ($CH_3COCOOH$).

(c) Malonic acid (COOH—CH_2—COOH, drawn vertically) and succinic acid (CH_2COOH—CH_2COOH, drawn vertically).

(ii) (a) Write the chemical equations when acetic acid reacts with

(I) Br_2 in the presence of phosphorus.

(II) Cl_2 in the presence of phosphorus

(b) Give two reactions in which aliphatic aldehydes differ from aromatic aldehydes.

50. An organic compound (*A*) (molecular formula $C_8H_{16}O_2$) was hydrolysed with dilute sulphuric acid to get a carboxylic acid (*B*) and an alcohol (*C*). Oxidation of (*C*) with chromic acid produced (*B*). (*C*) on dehydration gives but-1-ene. Identify (*A*), (*B*) and (*C*) and write chemical equations for the reactions involved. **CBSE 2025**

51. Write short notes on the following :

(i) Wolff-Kishner reduction

(ii) Aldol condensation

(iii) Rosenmund reduction

(iv) Cannizzaro reaction

(v) Hell-Volhard-Zelinsky reaction **CBSE 2024 C**

Hints & Solutions

Objective Type Questions

1. (*c*) The structures of the given compounds in options are as follow

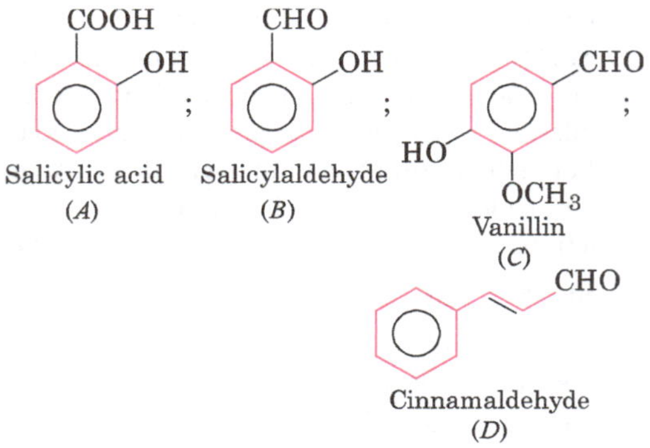

Thus, compound (*C*) contains —CHO group, benzene ring, —OCH_3 group and —OH group.

2. (*b*) But-1-yne on reaction with water in presence of Hg^{2+} ions as a catalyst produces butan-2-one.

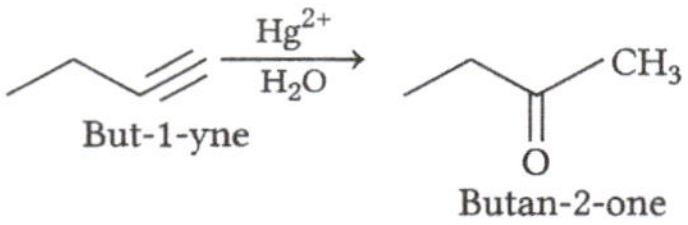

3. (*d*) Preparation of aldehydes from nitriles using $SnCl_2$, HCl and quenching the resulting iminium salt with water is called Stephen reaction.

4. (*a*) $\underset{\text{Acetyl chloride}}{CH_3—COCl} + H_2 \xrightarrow{\text{Pd, BaSO}_4} \underset{\substack{\text{Acetaldehyde}\\(X)}}{CH_3CHO} + HCl$

5. (*a*) Pd-$BaSO_4$ is the catalyst used in rosenmund reduction reaction. In this reaction, aldehydes are prepared.

6. (*d*) Any aliphatic carbon with hydrogen attached to it, in combination with benzene ring, will be oxidised to benzoic acid by $KMnO_4/H^+$.

7. (*a*) In case of aliphatic aldehydes and ketones, greater the number of alkyl groups attached to the carbonyl greater is the electron density on the carbonyl carbon and hence, lower is its reactivity towards nucleophilic addition reactions.

8. (*b*) Butan-2-ol on oxidation with alkaline $KMnO_4$ solution produces butanone as

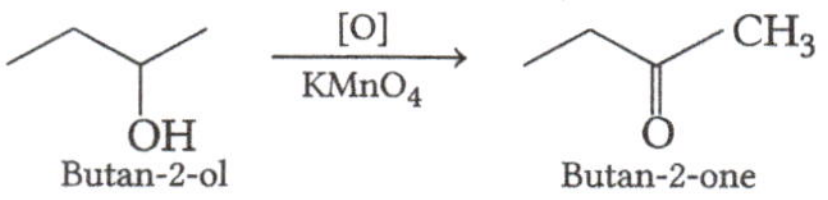

9. (*c*) Acetone and benzaldehyde both do not react with Fehling's solution. Fehling's solution do not react with acetone as it is a ketone, while benzaldehyde is an aromatic aldehyde having no α-hydrogen.

10. (*a*) Compound (*A*) is pentan-3-one.
This is because of the following reasons :
It has a ketone functional group so, gives negative Tollen's test. Moreover, it does not have $—\underset{\underset{O}{\|}}{C}—CH_3$ group thus, it gives negative iodoform test. (*A*) on reduction gives *n*-pentane, it shows that it contains 5 carbon chains.

11. (*b*) When $C_6H_5COOCOCH_3$ is treated with H_2O, the product obtained is benzoic acid and ethanoic acid.

$$C_6H_5COOCOCH_3 \xrightarrow{H_2O} \underset{\text{Benzoic acid}}{C_6H_5COOH} + \underset{\text{Ethanoic acid}}{CH_3COOH}$$

12. (*a*) Formaldehyde undergoes Cannizaro reaction in presence of concentrated base KOH forming methanol and potassium formate salt.

$$\begin{matrix}H_3C\\H_3C\end{matrix}\!\!>C=O + \underset{\text{Formaldehyde}}{\begin{matrix}H\\H\end{matrix}\!\!>C=O} + \text{Conc. KOH} \xrightarrow{\Delta} \underset{\substack{\text{Methanol}\\(A)}}{CH_3OH} + \underset{\substack{\text{Potassium formate}\\(B)}}{HCOO^-K^+}$$

13. (*c*) 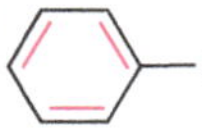—CHO, Due to the lack of α-hydrogen, benzaldehyde does not undergo aldol condensation.

14. (*c*) As Tollen's test is given by aldehyde only. Iodoform test is given by carbonyl compound which have either

CH_3 — CH(OH) group or $CH_3 —\overset{\overset{O}{\|}}{C}—$ group.

Aldol condensation is given by aldehyde and ketones with α-hydrogen atom.

Hence, among the given compound, *X* is CH_3 — CHO which can give all the test.

15. (*a*) CH_3COCH_3

Aldehydes and ketones undergoes nucleophilic addition reactions to give an oxime with hydroxylamine.

Other carbonyl compounds do not give nucleophilic addition reactions.

$$\underset{\text{Acetone}}{\begin{matrix}H_3C\\H_3C\end{matrix}\!\!>C=O} + \underset{\text{Hydroxylamine}}{H_2NOH} \xrightarrow{H^+} \underset{\text{Acetoxime}}{\begin{matrix}H_3C\\H_3C\end{matrix}\!\!>C=NOH} + H_2O$$

16. (*a*) Correct IUPAC name is 2, 2-dimethylbutanoic acid.

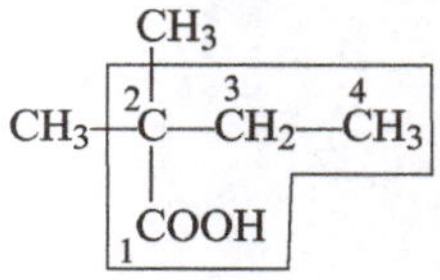

17. (*a*) When propyl magnesium bromide is treated with CO_2, followed by acid hydrolysis, butanoic acid is formed.

$$\underset{\text{(Propyl magnesium bromide)}}{CH_3CH_2CH_2MgBr} \xrightarrow[\text{(ii) } H^+/H_3O^+]{\text{(i) } CO_2 \text{ in dry ether}} \underset{\substack{\text{(Butanoic acid)} \\ \text{M.F. : } C_3H_7COOH}}{CH_3CH_2CH_2—COOH}$$

18. (*d*) Acidity of carboxylic acid increases due to the presence of electron withdrawing groups.

Thus, CCl_3COOH is the strongest acid among the given options due to presence of three chlorine atoms.

19. (*c*) Due to resonance in carboxylate ion, the double bond character of $C=O$ bond in carboxylic acids is greatly reduced as compared to that in aldehydes and ketones.

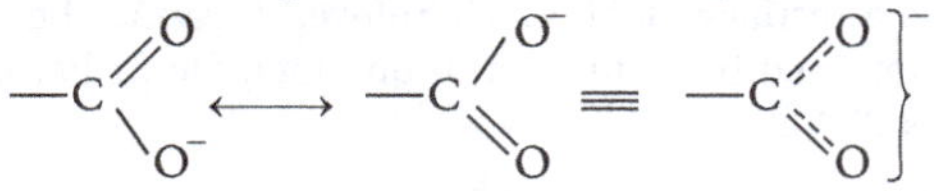

20. (*a*) Acidity increases as the electronegativity of the C-atom directly attached to —COOH group or the hybridisation of the C-atom directly attached to COOH changes from $sp^3 \rightarrow sp^2 \rightarrow sp$.

Thus, the correct decreasing order of acidic strength is

$$\underset{\text{I}}{HC\equiv C—COOH} > \underset{\text{II}}{C_6H_5COOH} > \underset{\text{III}}{CH_2=CH—COOH} > \underset{\text{IV}}{CH_3COOH}$$

21. (*a*) The correct match is (A)-(ii), B-(i), C-(iii).

A. **Gattermann-Koch reaction**

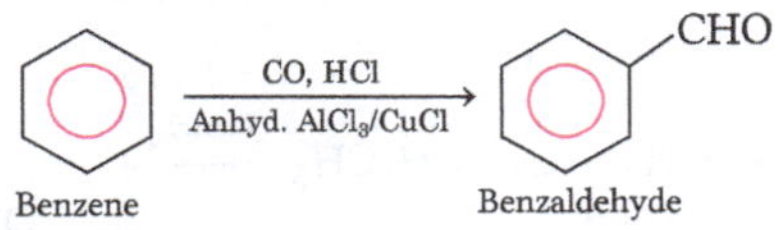

B. **Haloform reaction**

$$R—\underset{\underset{O}{\|}}{C}—CH_3 + NaOX \longrightarrow RCOO^-Na^+ + \underset{(X=Cl,\ Br,\ I)}{CHX_3\downarrow}$$

C. **Esterification**

$$R—CH_2—OH + R'COOH \xrightleftharpoons{\text{Conc. } H_2SO_4} R'—COO—CH_2—R + H_2O$$

22. (*a*) Carboxylic acids having an α-hydrogen are halogenated at the α-position on treatment with chlorine or bromine in the presence of small amount of red phosphorus to give α-halocarboxylic acids. The reaction is known as Hell-Volhard-Zelinsky reaction.

23. (*c*) Carboxylic acids do not undergo Friedal Crafts reaction because the —COOH group is deactivating and the catalyst aluminium chloride gets bonded to the carboxyl group.

24. (*d*) Electrophilic substitution in benzoic acid takes place at *meta*-position because carboxylic group is a deactivating group. Its presence decreases electron density at *ortho* and *para*- positions. Due to this, the electron density at *meta*-position will be more as compared to that of *ortho* and *para*. Hence, positively charged electrophile will attack at the *meta*-position rather than attacking the *ortho* and *para*-positions.

25. (*a*) Since, the carbon atom is formaldehyde is bonded to three regions of electron density (two single bonds with hydrogen and one double bond with oxygen). This corresponds to sp^2-hybridisation. Thus, the molecular geometry is trigonal coplanar with bond angle of 120°. Thus, both (A) and (R) both are true and (R) is the correct explanation of (A).

26. (*c*) The solubility of aldehydes and ketones decreases when the length of alkyl chain increases because of the increase in the magnitude of non-polar (hydrophobic) part in the molecule. Thus, (A) is true, but (R) is false.

27. (*b*) (A) and (R) both are true, but (R) is not the correct explanation of (A).

Easy oxidation of aldehydes is due to the presence of a hydrogen atom on the carbonyl group.

$$R—\overset{\overset{H}{|}}{C}=O \xrightarrow{[O]} R—C\begin{matrix}\nearrow O \\ \searrow OH\end{matrix}$$

Further, carboxylic acids can be reduced to alcohol by using reducing agents such as $LiAlH_4$ or better by diborane.

$$RCOOH \xrightarrow{LiAlH_4} RCH_2OH + H_2O$$

28. (*d*) Ketones do not react with Tollen's reagent to give silver mirror test, because ketone cannot reduce silver ions of Tollen's reagent to give silver metal.

Aldehydes react with Tollen's reagent to form silver mirror. Hence, (A) is false, but (R) is true.

29. (*a*) Both (A) and (R) are true and (R) is the correct explanation of (A). Pentan-2-one having $—CH_3CO$ group undergoes iodoform reaction whereas, pentan-3-one cannot

$$\underset{\text{Pentan-2-one}}{CH_3CH_2—CH_2—\overset{\overset{O}{\|}}{C}—CH_3} + 3NaOI \longrightarrow CH_3CH_2CH_2COO^-Na^+ + \underset{\substack{\text{Iodoform} \\ \text{(Yellow ppt.)}}}{CHI_3\downarrow} + 2NaOH$$

30. (*c*) The acidity of α-hydrogen atoms of carbonyl compounds is due to the strong electron withdrawing effect of the carbonyl group and resonance stabilisation of the conjugate base.

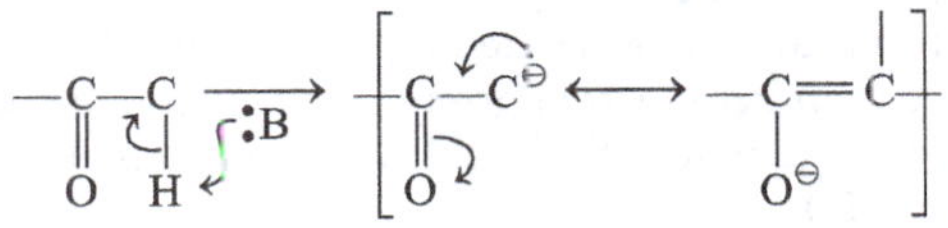

Hence, (A) is true, but (R) is false.

31. (*c*) Aromatic aldehydes are less reactive than aliphatic aldehyde like formaldehyde. Cannizzaro's reaction is shown by aldehydes which do not contain any α-H atom. Such aldehydes in the presence of concentrated solution of an alkali undergo self oxidation-reduction to give a mixture of alcohol and a salt of the carboxylic acid. For example, formaldehyde (HCHO) gives methanol and sodium methanoate.

$$\underset{\text{(2 molecules of formaldehyde or methanal)}}{H{-}\overset{\overset{H}{|}}{C}{=}O} + H{-}\overset{\overset{H}{|}}{C}{=}O \xrightarrow{\text{NaOH (conc.)}} \underset{\text{Methanol}}{CH_3OH} + \underset{\text{Sodium methanonate}}{H{-}\overset{\overset{O}{\|}}{C}{-}\overset{-}{O}\overset{+}{Na}}$$

Hence, (A) is true, but (R) is false.

32. (*a*) Both (A) and (R) are true and (R) is the correct explanation of (A).

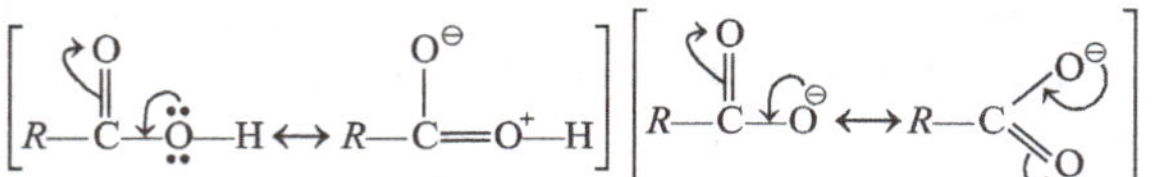

Resonating structures of *R*COOH (non-equivalent)   Resonating structures of *R*COO⁻ (equivalent)

33. (*b*) Acetic acid is halogenated in the presence of red P and Cl_2, but formic acid is not because it lacks an α-hydrogen atom. Further, acetic acid is a weaker acid than formic acid. Thus, both Assertion and Reason are true but Reason is not the correct explanation of Assertion.

34. (*a*) Benzoic acid doesn't undergo Friedel-craft reaction because carbonyl group is *meta*-directing and deactivating in electrophilic aromatic substitution reactions. It directs electrophile to *meta*-position making reaction difficult.

Also, aluminium chloride used as an catalyst for Friedel-Crafts can form complex with carboxyl group which decreases the reactivity of reaction.

Hence, both (A) and (R) are true and (R) is correct explanation of (A).

35. (*a*) Aromatic carboxylic groups do not undergo Friedel-Crafts reaction because carboxyl group is deactivating and the catalyst aluminium chloride gets bonded to the carboxyl group.

36. (c) (A) is true, but (R) is false. The correct reason is, carboxyl group decreases the electron density at the *meta*-position.

37. (i) (b) Since, compound (X) on oxidation yields a product which gives positive iodoform test and also forms an oxime. Therefore, product must contain keto methyl group. Further, compound (X) on treatment with conc. H_2SO_4 forms an alkene (C_4H_8).

Thus, compound (X) is $CH_3\underset{\underset{OH}{|}}{CH}{-}CH_2{-}CH_3$, i.e. butan-2-ol. **(1)**

$$\underset{(X)}{CH_3{-}\overset{\overset{OH}{|}}{CH}{-}CH_2{-}CH_3} \xrightarrow{[O]} \underset{\text{Butanone (M.F. } C_4H_8O)}{CH_3{-}\overset{\overset{O}{\|}}{C}{-}CH_2{-}CH_3}$$

$$\downarrow \text{Conc. } H_2SO_4$$

$$\underset{\text{Butene (M.F. } C_4H_8)}{CH_3{-}CH{=}CH{-}CH_3}$$ **(1)**

(ii) (*d*) Since, 2-methyl-propan-2-ol, i.e. $CH_3{-}\overset{\overset{OH}{|}}{\underset{\underset{CH_3}{|}}{C}}{-}CH_3$ is a tertiary alcohol. Therefore, it, cannot be obtained by reduction of an aldehyde or ketone with $NaBH_4$.

Or

(*b*) The reactions of the given compounds with $LiAlH_4$ are as follows.

$$\underset{\text{Propanone}}{CH_3\overset{\overset{O}{\|}}{C}{-}CH_3} \xrightarrow{LiAlH_4} \underset{\text{Propan-2-ol}}{CH_3\overset{\overset{OH}{|}}{CH}CH_3}$$

$$\underset{\text{Butanone}}{CH_3\overset{\overset{O}{\|}}{C}{-}CH_2CH_3} \xrightarrow{LiAlH_4} \underset{\text{Butan-2-ol (Optically active)}}{CH_3{-}\overset{\overset{OH}{|}}{\underset{\underset{H}{|}}{C^*}}{-}CH_2CH_3}$$

$$\underset{\text{Pentan-3-one}}{H_3C{-}CH_2{-}\overset{\overset{O}{\|}}{C}{-}CH_2CH_3} \xrightarrow{LiAlH_4} \underset{\text{Pentan-3-ol}}{H_3C{-}CH_2{-}\overset{\overset{OH}{|}}{\underset{\underset{H}{|}}{C}}{-}CH_2CH_3}$$

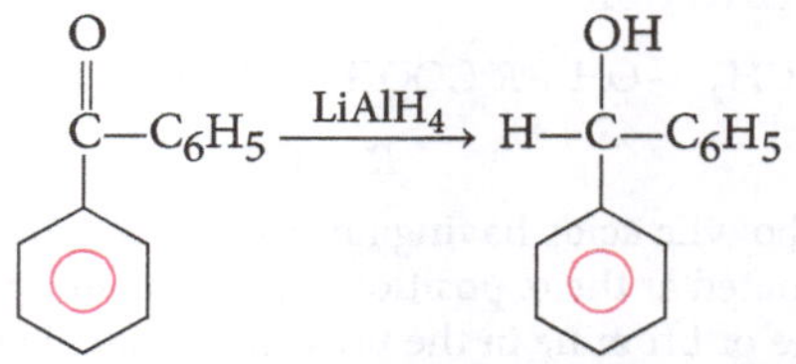

Benzophenone   Diphenyl methanol

Thus, option (b) is correct. **(1)**

(iii) (*c*) 2, 4-DNP test is shown by carbonyl groups in aldehyde and ketones, whereas, Fehling's, Tollen's and Cannizzaro reactions are shown by aldehydes. **(1)**

38. (i) (a) **Compound *A*** Aldehydes reduces Tollen's reagent (Ag^+ ions) to metallic silver, forming a silver mirror. **(1)**

(b) **Compound *B*** Ketones react with 2,4-DNP to form hydrazones (orange precipitate). The iodoform test confirms the presence of a methyl ketone group (i.e. —CH_3CO group), forming iodoform (CHI_3) as a yellow solid. **(1)**

(ii) **Compound *A*** is likely acetaldehyde (CH_3CHO) **(1/2)**

Compound *B* likely to be acetone (CH_3COCH_3)**(1/2)**

Or

In compound *A*, positive Tollen's test and Fehling's test indicate the presence of an **aldehydic group**.

In compound *B*, positive test with 2,4-DNP and the yellow precipitate with iodine in alkali indicate a **methyl ketone group** (i.e. CH_3CO group). **(1)**

(iii) **Compound *C***, i.e. Carboxylic acids react with sodium bicarbonate, releasing CO_2 gas (effervescence). The phenolic OH reacts with $FeCl_3$, forming a **violet-coloured complex**. **(1)**

Subjective Type Questions

1. Acetone on reaction with HCN gives one compound whereas acetaldehyde gives enantiomers (optical isomers) due to the chiral centre. They are difficult to separate since the chemical and physical properties of enantiomers are same. **(1)**

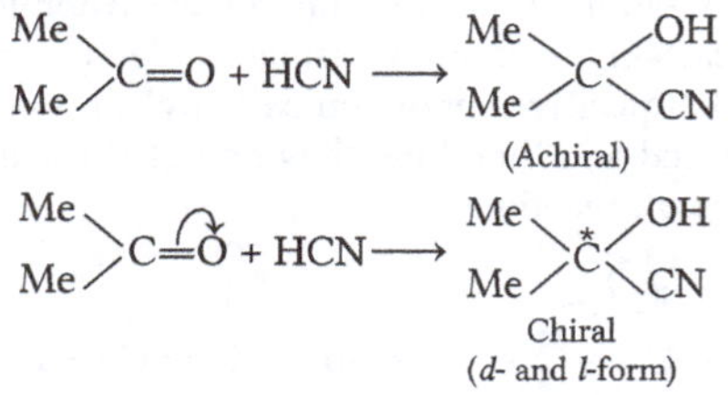

(1)

2. The addition of ammonia derivatives to aldehydes and ketones is done in weakly acidic medium. In case the medium is strongly acidic, then the ammonia derivative will the also gets protonated and will not be able to act as a nucleophile. **(2)**

3. (i) *p*-nitrobenzaldehyde is more reactive towards the nucleophilic addition reaction than *p*-tolualdehyde as —NO_2 group is electron withdrawing in nature. Presence of nitro group decreases electron density.

Hence, facilitates the attack of nucleophile whereas presence of —CH_3 leads to +*I*-effect as CH_3 is electron donating group.

(ii)

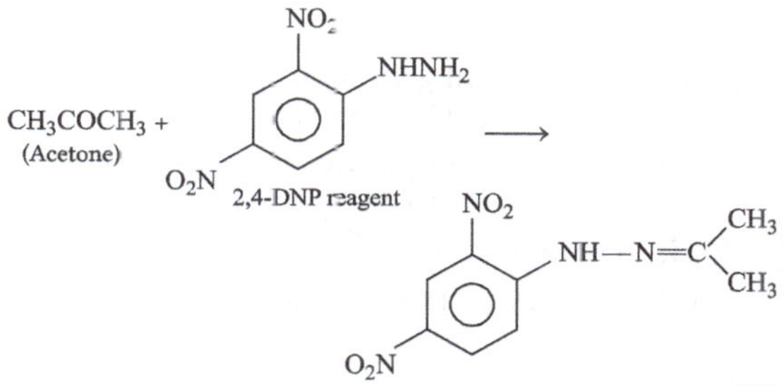

(1)

4. (i) 1, 1,-dimethyl ethanol is formed.

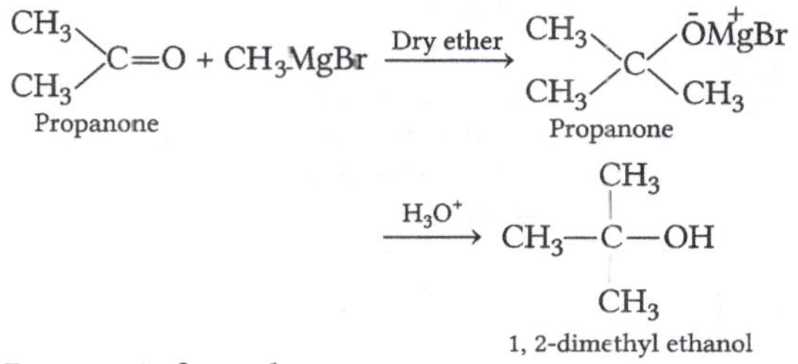

(ii) Propane is formed.

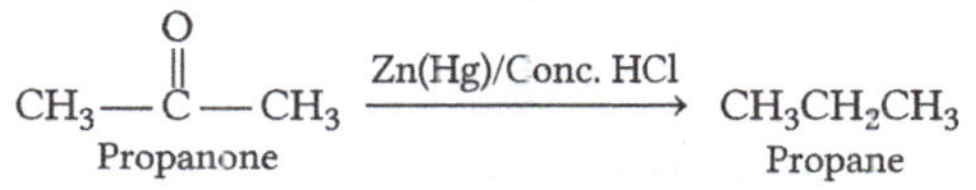

(1)

5. (*d*) Benzaldehyde is less reactive than propanal in nucleophilic addition reactions. This is because the aromatic ring in benzaldehyde decreases the electrophilicity of the carbonyl carbon due to +*R* effect. **(1)**

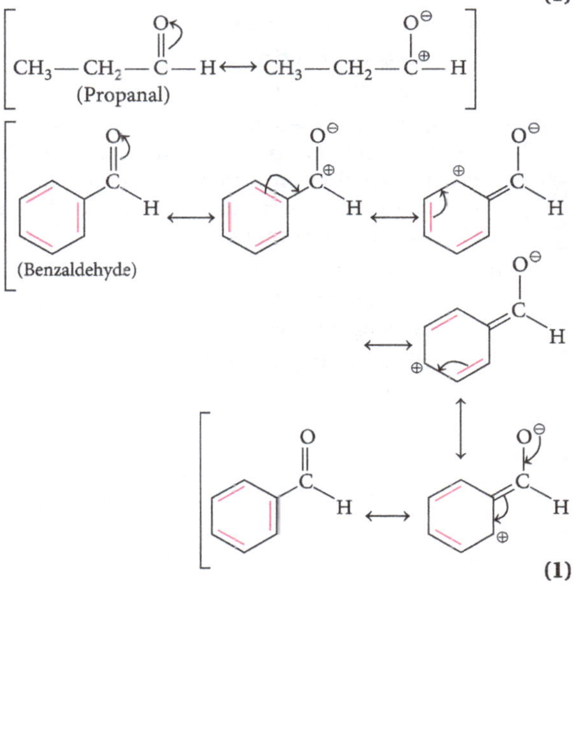

(1)

6. 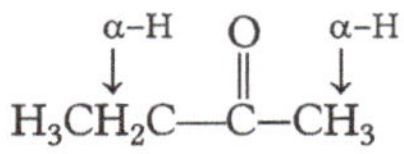 (1)

(i) CH_3CHO will give aldol condensation with NaOH, while C_6H_5CHO does not. (1)

(ii) CH_3CHO gives positive test with Fehling's reagent whereas C_6H_5CHO does not. (1)

7. (i) Refer to text on page 288 (Cannizzaro reaction) (1)

(ii) 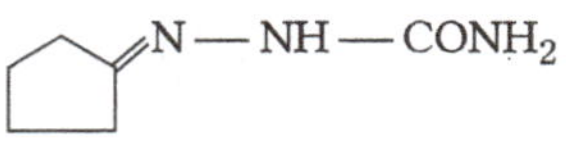

(1)

8. (i) The presence of alpha hydrogen in aldehydes and ketones is essential for aldol condensation because they are acidic in nature (due to the presence of electron withdrawing carbonyl group).

As a result, the electron density at αC—H bond decreases and hence, H-atom becomes weakly held which can be easily abstracted by strong bases forming enolate ion, which are stabilised by resonance. (1)

(ii) The structure of 3-hydroxypentan-2-one is

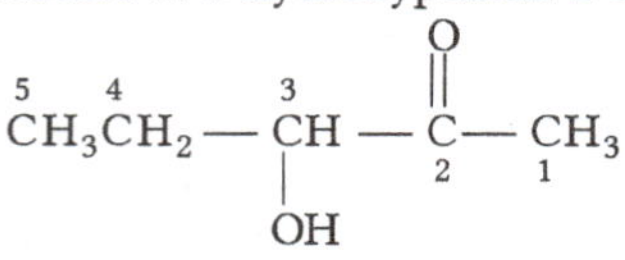

All alpha hydroxy ketones gives Tollen's test. Since, α-hydroxy ketones have the ability to tautomerises to aldehydes and aldehydes gives positive Tollen's test. The given compound is also a α-hydroxy ketone. Thus, it gives this test. (1)

9. (i) **Clemmensen reduction**

Refer to text on page 286. (1)

(ii) **Cannizzaro reaction**

Refer to text on page 288. (1)

10. (i) Benzaldehyde is less reactive to electrophilic substitution than benzene because the aldehyde group is an electron withdrawing group and it destabilises the intermediate carbocation formed in electrophilic substitution reactions. (1)

(ii) In benzaldehyde, the ring becomes deactivated at *ortho* and *para*-positions due to an electron withdrawing aldehydic group.

Therefore, electrophilic substitution occurs only at *m*-position. (1)

11. (i)

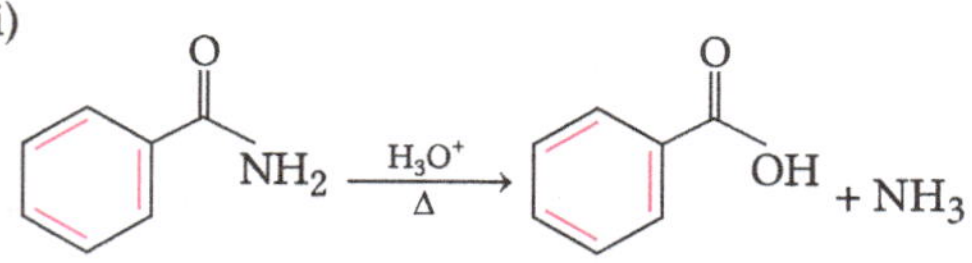

Benzamide Benzoic acid (1)

(ii)

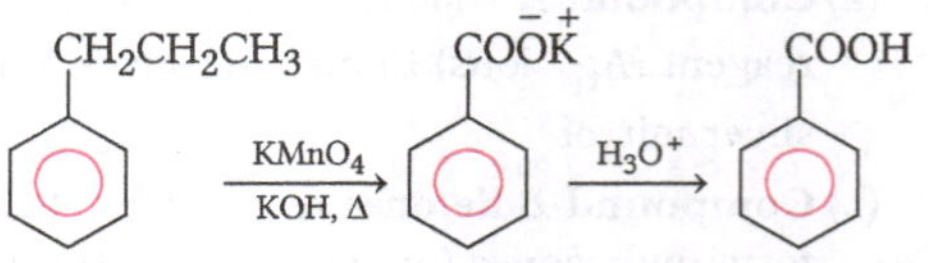

Propyl benzene Benzoic acid (1)

12. (i) $CH_2 = CH_2 \xrightarrow{Br_2} Br\,CH_2\,CH_2\,Br \xrightarrow{CN^-}$

$NCCH_2CH_2CN \xrightarrow{H_3O^+} \begin{array}{l} CH_2—COOH \\ | \\ CH_2—COOH \end{array}$ (1)

(ii) **Hint** Alkylation followed by oxidation. (1)

13. (i) Refer to text on page 292. (From alkyl benzene) (1)

(ii) Refer to text on page 283. (Addition of Grignard reagent) (1)

14. (i) Cl— CH_2COOH is a stronger acid than CH_3COOH. It is because —Cl group exhibits –*I*-effect which makes the carboxylate ion more stable.

Higher the stability of carboxylate ion, easier is the removal of proton from the carboxylic acid and stronger is the acid. In CH_3COOH, —CH_3 group has +*I*-effect which destabilised it. Hence, CH_3COOH is a weaker acid. (1)

(ii) Carboxylic acids contain carbonyl group but do not show the reactions of carbonyl group such as nucleophilic addition reaction like aldehydes and ketones.

Because of the presence of lone pair of electrons on the O-atom of –OH group, the electrophilic character of carbonyl carbon by resonance decreases, hence the partial positive charge on carbonyl carbon atom is reduced and therefore, they do not show nucleophilic addition reactions.

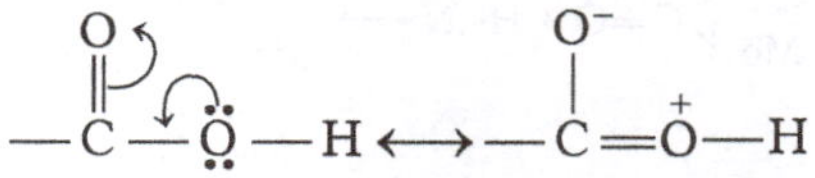 (1)

15. (i) Refer to text on page 281. (Preparation from nitriles) (1)

(ii)

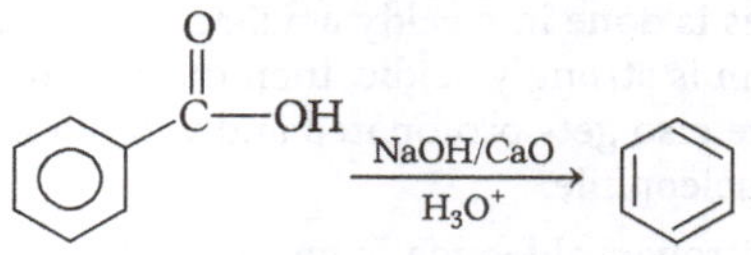

Benzoic acid Benzene (1)

16. (i) This is due to the presence of lone pairs on oxygen atom attached to hydrogen atom in the —COOH group which are involved in resonance and hence makes the carbon atom less electrophilic. (1)

(ii) This is due to the presence of alkyl groups on both sides of the carbonyl carbon, propanone is sterically

17. (d) (i) Refer to text on page - 287.

(ii) $CH_3CH_2—COOH + NaOH \longrightarrow$ (Propanoic acid)

$$\underset{\text{(Sodium propanoate)}}{CH_3CH_2CO\overset{\ominus}{O}\,Na^{\oplus}} + H_2O \xrightarrow[\text{Heat}]{\text{NaOH and CaO}} \underset{\text{(Ethane)}}{CH_3CH_3} + Na_2CO_3$$

18. (i) The —COOH group attached to benzene ring is electron withdrawing in nature and thus deactivates the ring. Secondly, the catalyst used in the reaction, i.e. $AlCl_3$ is a Lewis acid, which has the tendency to bonded to carboxyl group. That's why aromatic carboxylic acid does not undergo Friedel-Crafts reaction. **(1)**

(ii) Lower pK_a value means stronger acid. pK_a value of 4-nitrobenzoic acid is lower than benzoic acid due to following reasons:

(a) Due to $-I$ and $-R$ effect of $—NO_2$ group, electron density in O—H bond decreases, thus it becomes weak and easily loses a proton and therefore it is more acidic.

(b) Due to $-I$ and $-R$ effect of $—NO_2$ group, delocalisation of – ve charge occurs and *p*-nitrobenzoate ion becomes more stable than benzoate ion. **(1)**

19. Refer to text on page 277. **(3)**

20.

(i) 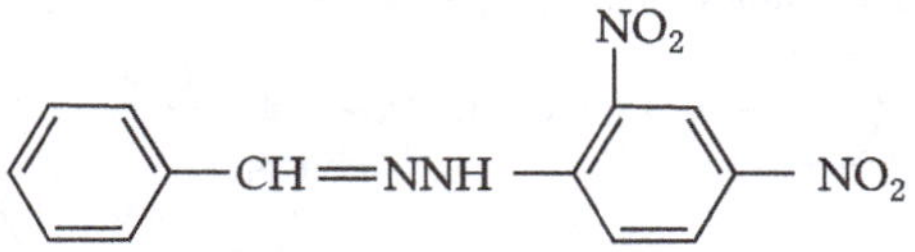 **(1/2)**

(ii) 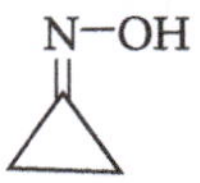 **(1/2)**

(iii) 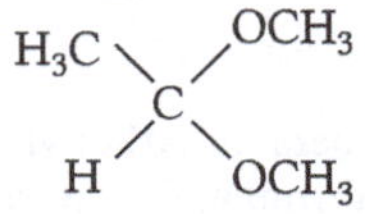 **(1/2)**

(iv) 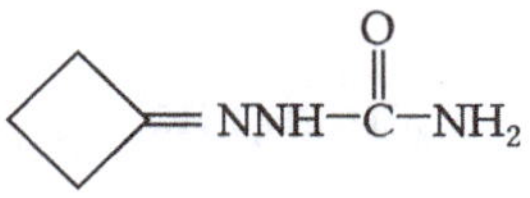 **(1/2)**

(v) 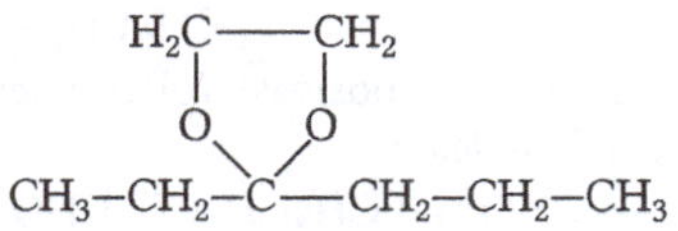 **(1/2)**

(vi) 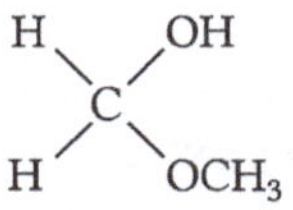 **(1/2)**

21. (i) $A = \underset{\text{Phenyl magnesium bromide}}{C_6H_5MgBr}$, $B = \underset{\text{Benzoic acid}}{C_6H_5COOH}$, $C = \underset{\text{Benzoyl chloride}}{C_6H_5COCl}$ **(1½)**

(ii) $A = \underset{\text{Acetaldehyde}}{CH_3CHO}$, $B = \underset{\text{3-hydroxy butanal}}{CH_3—\overset{OH}{\overset{|}{CH}}—CH_2—CHO}$,

$C = \underset{\text{But-2-enal}}{CH_3—CH{=}CH—CHO}$ **(1½)**

22. (i) **Etard Reaction**

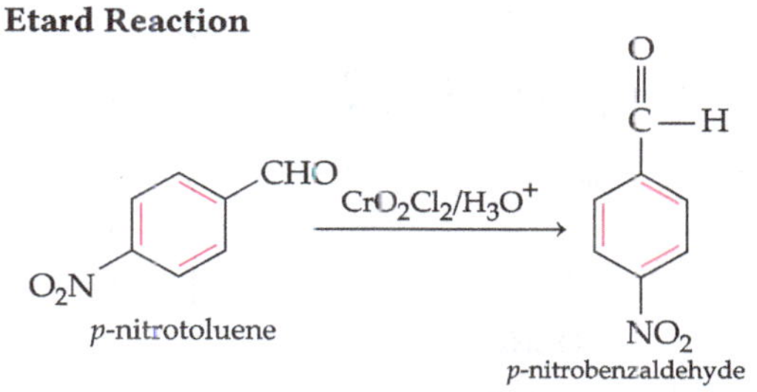 **(1)**

(ii) Benzoic acid undergoes extensive intermolecular hydrogen bonding, leading to the formation of dimer.

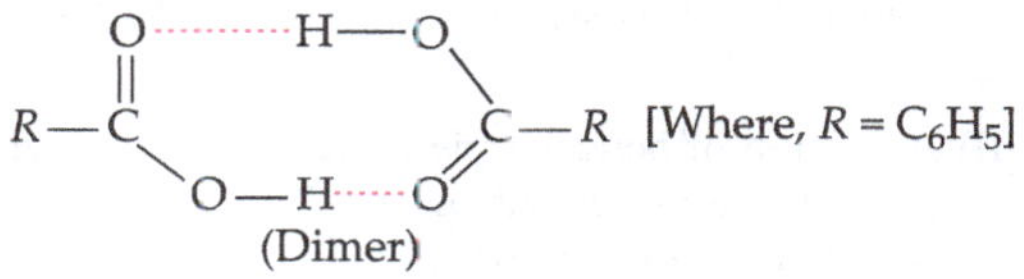 **(1)**

(iii) Benzoic acid does not undergo reaction with CH_3Cl i.e Friedel Craft reaction because the carboxyl group is deactivating and the catalyst aluminium chloride (Lewis acid) gets bonded to the carboxyl group. **(1)**

Or

(i) Compound '*X*' = Benzaldehyde,
Compound '*Y*' = Acetophenone **(1)**

(ii) 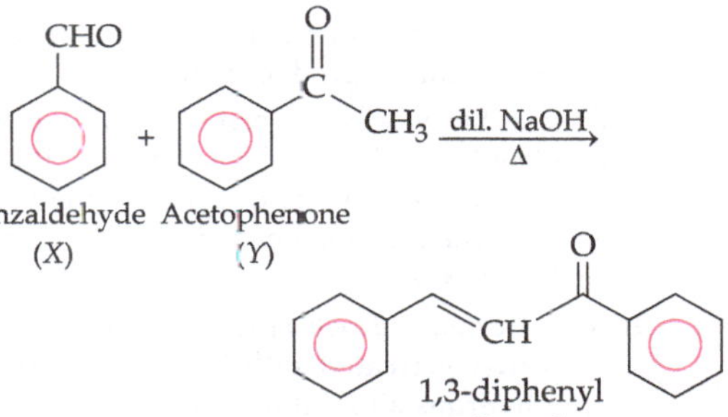

1,3-diphenyl prop-2-en-1-one (Major) Cross-Aldol product

(iii) Chemical test to distinguish between *X* and *Y* is the Tollen's Test .Benzaldehyde undergoes silver mirror test with Tollen's reagent and forms silver mirror . However, acetophenone does not react with Tollen's reagent.

$$\underset{\text{(Benzaldehyde)}}{Ph—CHO} + \underset{\text{Tollen's reagent}}{2[Ag(NH_3)_2]^+} + 3OH^- \longrightarrow$$

$$PhCOO^- + \underset{\text{Silver mirror}}{2Ag\downarrow} + 2H_2O + 4NH_3$$ **(1)**

23. $$\underset{\text{2-methyl propanal}}{(CH_3)_2CHCHO} + C_2H_5\overset{\delta-}{Mg}\overset{\delta+}{Br} \xrightarrow{\text{Dry ether}} (CH_3)_2CHCH(C_2H_5)(\overset{-}{O}\overset{+}{MgBr})$$

$$(CH_3)CHCH(C_2H_5)(\overset{-}{O}\overset{+}{MgBr}) \xrightarrow{H^+/H_2O} \underset{\text{(2- methylpentan -3-ol)}}{(CH_3)_2CHC(C_2H_5)(OH)}$$ **(3)**

24.

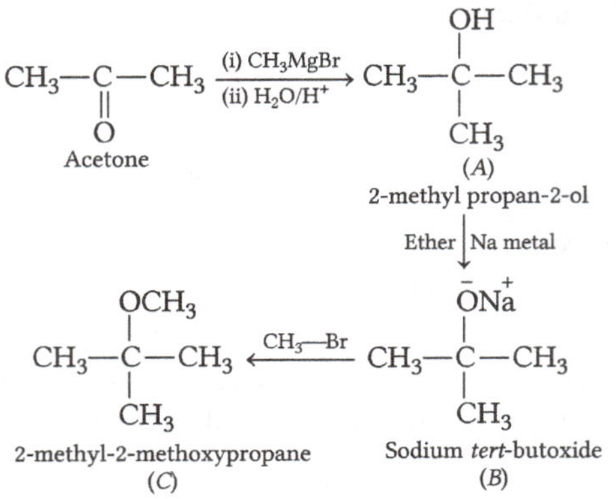

(3)

25. (i) Acylation of benzene yields acetophenone which on reduction gives ethylbenzene. The complete reactions can be shown as

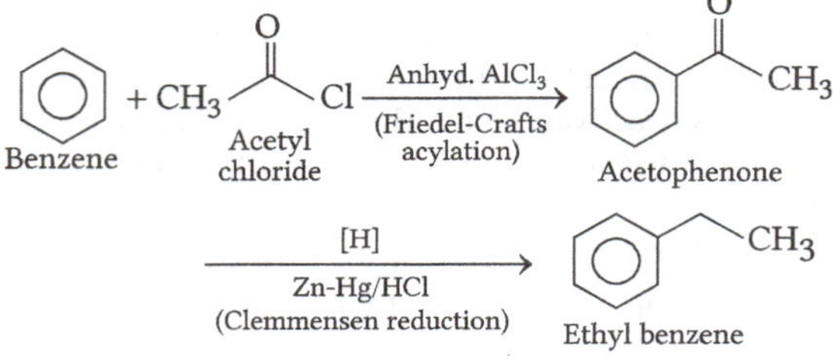

The direct alkylation cannot be performed because polysubstitution product is formed.

Or in other words, we can say that due to disadvantage of polysubstitution, the Friedel-Crafts alkylation reaction is not used for the preparation of alkylbenzene. Instead of that, Friedel-Crafts acylation is used. **(1½)**

(ii) In Gattermann-Koch reaction, benzene or its derivative is treated with CO and HCl in the presence of anhydrous aluminium chloride to produce benzaldehyde.

In this reaction, CO and HCl combine to form HCOCl, i.e., formyl chloride which gets substituted on benzene by the replacement of H-atom.

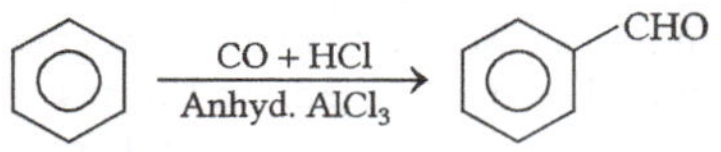

While in Friedel-Crafts acylation, acyl group is also transferred to carbon of benzene and acyl benzene is obtained as a result.This can be done by reaction of benzene with acyl chloride in the presence of anhydrous $AlCl_3$.

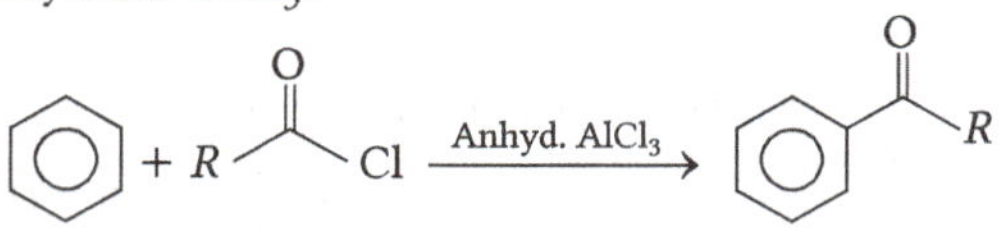

As, formyl chloride is unstable in nature. So, it can be prepared *in-situ* by treating CO and HCl in the presence of anhy. $AlCl_3$ by only Gattermann-Koch reaction, not by Friedel-Crafts reaction.

Since, in both the reactions, acylation takes place, hence, Gattermann-Koch reaction can be considered similar to Friedel-Crafts acylation. **(1/2)**

26.

(i)

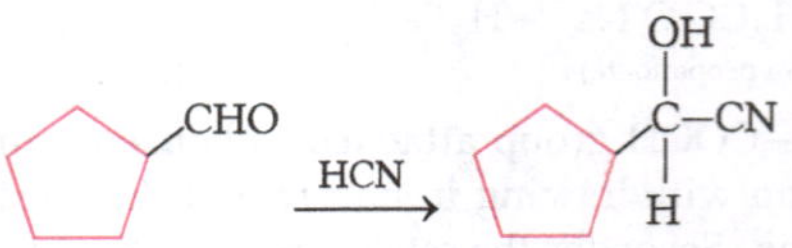

(1)

(ii)

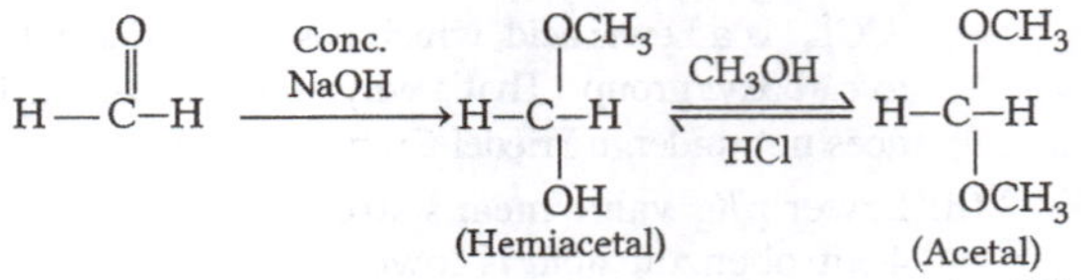

(1)

(iii) $2H-\overset{\overset{O}{\|}}{C}-H \xrightarrow[\Delta]{\text{Conc. NaOH}} CH_3-OH + HCO\overset{-}{O}\overset{+}{Na}$

(Cannizzaro reaction) **(1)**

27. Since, the given aldehyde does not undergo self aldol condensation, it will not contain α-hydrogen atom. Further it undergoes ozonolysis indicating the presence of unsaturation probably at two places as the products are benzaldehyde and two moles of (*B*). So, the structure of given aldehyde ($C_{11}H_8O$) is

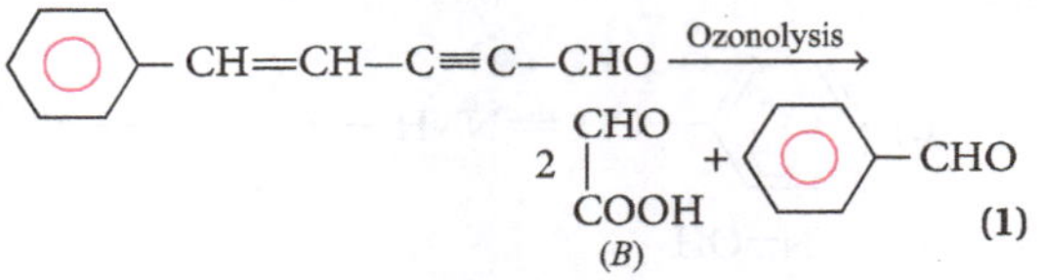

(1)

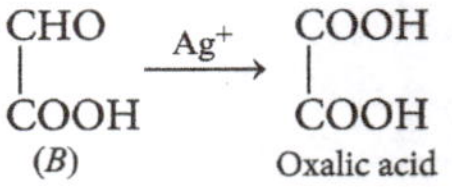

(1)

28. (i) The possible functional isomers of carbonyl compound with molecular formula, C_4H_8O are

$CH_3-\underset{}{\overset{CH_3}{\overset{|}{C}}}H-CHO$, $CH_3CH_2CH_2CHO$, $CH_3CH_2-\overset{\overset{O}{\|}}{C}-CH_3$

- Isomers (*A*) and (*C*) give positive Tollen's test, thus they must be aldehydes, i.e.

$CH_3-\underset{\underset{CH_3}{|}}{CH}-CHO$ and $CH_3CH_2CH_2CHO$

$$\underset{\text{Aldehyde}}{RCHO} + \underset{\text{Tollen's reagent}}{2[Ag(NH_3)_2]^+} \xrightarrow{\Delta} RCOO^- + \underset{\text{Silver mirror}}{2Ag\downarrow} + 2H_2O + 4NH_3\uparrow$$

- Isomer (*B*) does not give Tollen's test, but gives positive Iodoform test, thus it must be a ketone with $CH_3\overset{\overset{O}{\|}}{C}-$ group.

$$RCOCH_3 \xrightarrow{NaOX} RCO\overset{-}{O}\overset{+}{Na} + CHX_3 \quad [X = Cl, Br, I]$$

- Isomers (*A*) and (*B*) on reduction with Zn(Hg) / conc. HCl gives same product (*D*)

$$CH_3-\underset{}{\overset{CH_3}{\overset{|}{C}}}H-CHO + 4[H] \xrightarrow{\text{Zn-Hg/conc. HCl}} CH_3\overset{CH_3}{\overset{|}{C}}H-CH_3 + H_2O$$

$$CH_3-CH_2-CH_2-CHO + 4[H] \xrightarrow{\text{Zn-Hg/conc. HCl}} CH_3-CH_2-CH_2-CH_3 + H_2O$$

$$CH_3CH_2COCH_3 + 4[H] \xrightarrow{\text{Zn-Hg/conc. HCl}} CH_3CH_2CH_2CH_3 + H_2O$$

So, the structures of (*A*), (*B*), (*C*) and (*D*) are

$\underset{(A)}{CH_3CH_2CH_2CHO}$, $\underset{(B)}{CH_3CH_2COCH_3}$,

$\underset{(C)}{CH_3\overset{CH_3}{\overset{|}{C}}H-CHO}$, $\underset{(D)}{CH_3CH_2CH_2CH_3}$ **(1)**

(ii) The isomer (*B*) is least reactive towards addition of HCN. Since, ketones are less reactive towards nucleophilic addition reactions than aldehydes due to inductive and steric effects.

29. • According to the given information compound *A* (mol. formula C_5H_{10}) is an alkene.

- *A* on ozonolysis gives two carbonyl compound. (i.e. have $\rangle C=O$ group) *B* and *C*.
- *B* gives Fehling's test, so it is an aldehyde.
- *B* also gives positive idoform test, so it has $CH_3-\overset{O}{\overset{||}{C}}-$ group. That means, *B* is acetaldehyde.
- *C* does not give Fehling test, so it is a ketone. Also, it gives positive iodoform test and therefore, it contains $CH_3-\overset{O}{\overset{||}{C}}-$ group.
- Now, structure of alkene *A* can be obtained by writing the products of ozonolysis side by side with their $\rangle C=O$ groups facing each other. On removing the oxygen atoms and joining the remaining fragments by a double bond, the structure of alkene '*A*' can be obtained which is 2-methylbut-2-ene. **(1/2)**

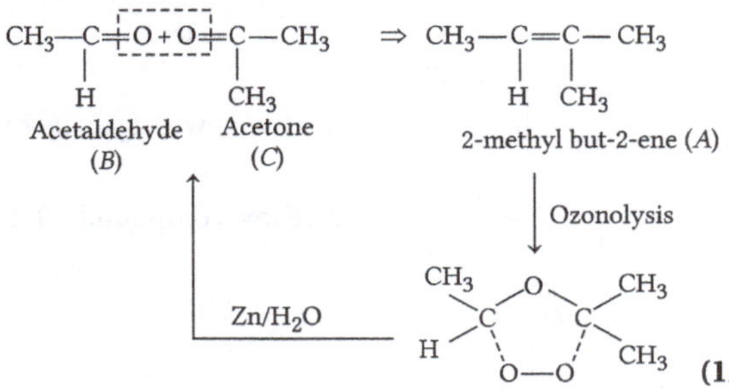

(1/2)

- **Fehling's test**

$$\underset{(B)}{CH_3CHO} + 2Cu^{2+} + 5\bar{O}H \longrightarrow CH_3COO^- + \underset{\text{(Red ppt.)}}{Cu_2O} + 3H_2O$$

$$CH_3COCH_3 + 2Cu^{2+} + 5\bar{O}H \longrightarrow \text{No reaction} \quad \textbf{(1/2)}$$

- **Iodoform reaction**

$$\underset{(B)}{CH_3CHO} + 3I_2 + NaOH \longrightarrow \underset{\text{Yellow ppt.}}{CHI_3\downarrow} + 3HI + HCO\bar{O}\overset{+}{Na}$$

$$\underset{(C)}{CH_3-\overset{O}{\overset{||}{C}}-CH_3} + 3I_2 + 4NaOH \longrightarrow \underset{\text{(Yellow ppt.)}}{CHI_3\downarrow} \quad \textbf{(1/2)}$$

$$+ CH_3CO\bar{O}\overset{+}{Na} + 3NaI + 3H_2O$$

$\therefore$ $A = CH_3CH=C(CH_3)_2$: 2-methylbut-2-ene
$B = CH_3CHO$: Acetaldehyde
$C = CH_3COCH_3$: Acetone **(1/2)**

30. (i) 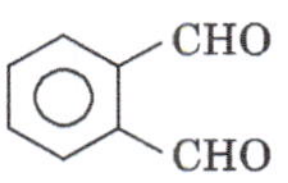 **(1)** (ii) 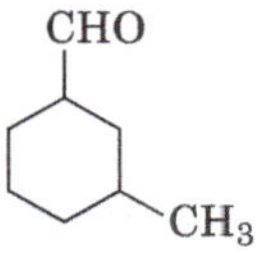 **(1)**

(iii) $CH_3-\overset{CH_3}{\overset{|}{C}}=CH-COOH$ **(1)**

31. Hint

(i) Carbon is more electronegative than silicon. **(1)**

(ii) sp^2-hybridised carbon is more electronegative than sp^3-hybridised carbon. **(1)**

(iii) *sp*-hybridised carbon of $C\equiv N$ is more electronegative than sp^2-hybridised carbon of $C=O$. **(1)**

32. Electron withdrawing group increases acidity carboxylic acids.

(i) CH_2FCOOH is a stronger acid. **(1)**

(ii) CH_2FCOOH is a stronger acid. **(1)**

(iii) CH_3CHFCH_2COOH is a stronger acid. **(1)**

(iv) F_3C— 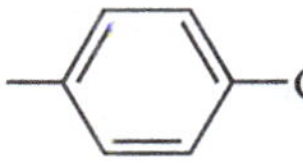 —COOH is a stronger acid. **(1)**

33. 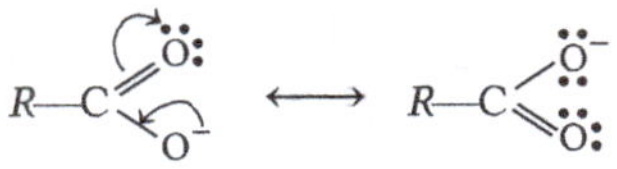 **(1/2)**

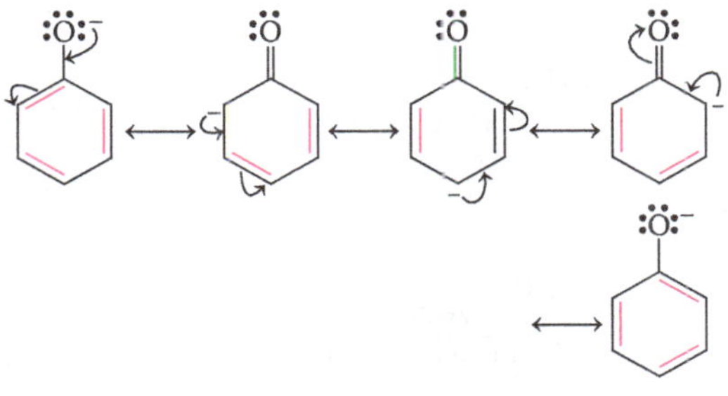 **(1/2)**

(i) Phenoxide ion has non-equivalent resonance structures in which the negative charge is at the lesser electronegative carbon atom, whereas in case of carboxylate ion both the resonating structures are equivalent. **(1)**

(ii) The negative charge is delocalised over two electronegative oxygen atoms in carboxylate ion, whereas in phenoxide ion, the negative charge less effectively delocalises over one oxygen atom and less electronegative carbon atoms. So, the carboxylate ion is more resonance stabilised than phenoxide ion. Thus, the release of proton from carboxylic acid is much easier than from phenol. Hence, carboxylic acid is a stronger acid than phenol. **(1)**

34. (i)

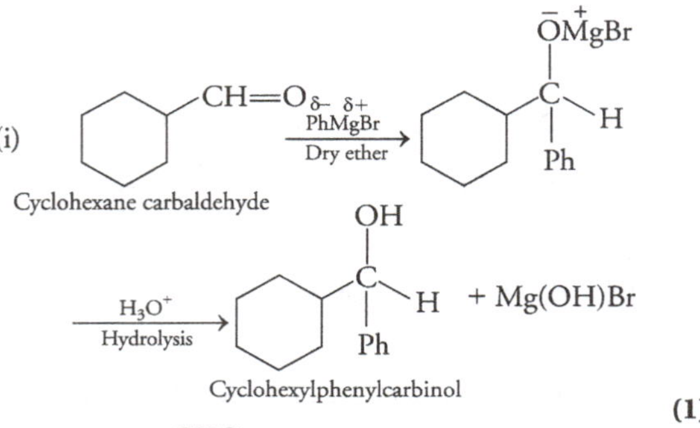

(1)

(ii)

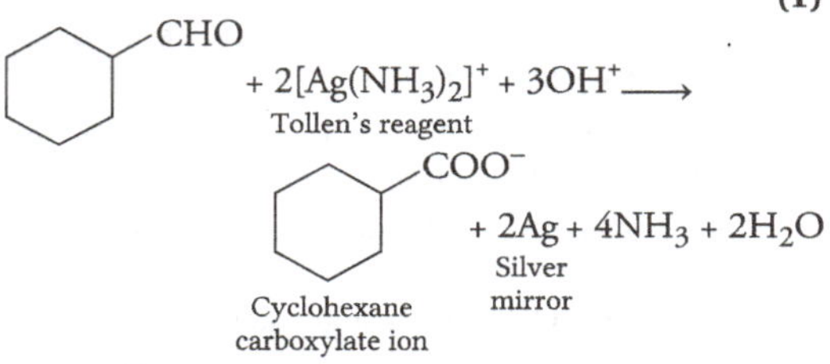

(iii)

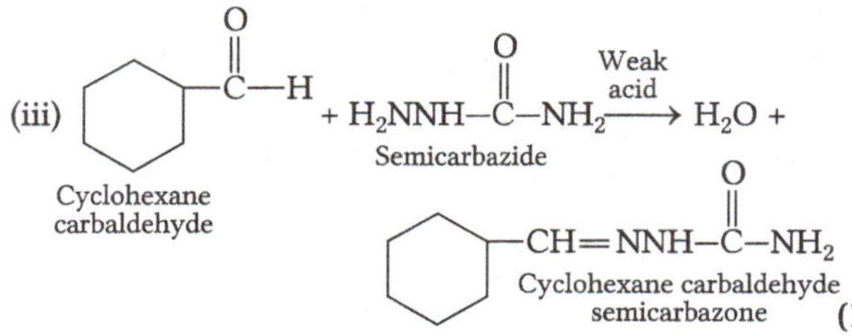

(1)

(iv)

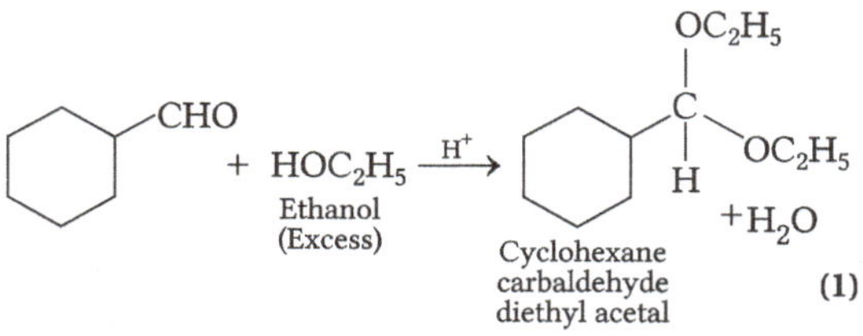

(1)

(v)

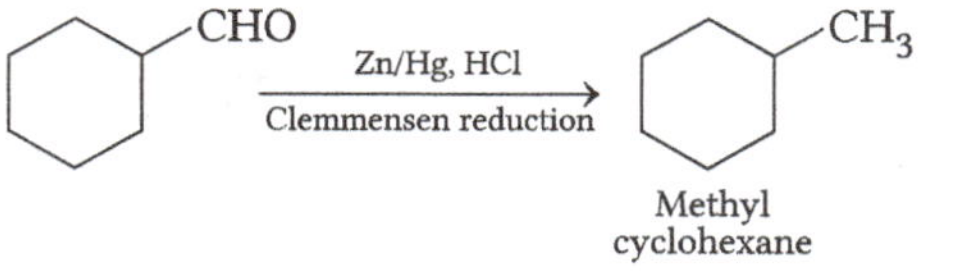

(1)

35. (i) (a) Reaction of acetone with sodium hypochlorite solution,

$$\underset{\text{(Acetone)}}{CH_3—CO—CH_3} + \underset{\text{(Sodium hypochlorite)}}{NaOCl} \longrightarrow \underset{\text{(Acetic acid)}}{CH_3COOH} + \underset{\text{(Chloroform)}}{CHCl_3}$$ **(1)**

(b) No, the carbonyl group in pentan-3-one is not linked to a methyl group which gets converted to chloroform in the reaction. Thus, it does not undergo haloform reaction. **(1)**

(c) Acetaldehyde/ethanal **(1)**

(ii) (a) (I) Aldehydes produce carboxylic acids having the same number of carbon atoms as the aldehyde.

(II) Ketones produce carboxylic acids having less carbon atoms than the ketone. **(1)**

- Aldehydes undergo oxidation without breaking of carbon-carbon bonds.

(b) Carbon-carbon bonds undergo cleavage on oxidation of ketones. **(1)**

36. *A, B, C* and *D* respectively are

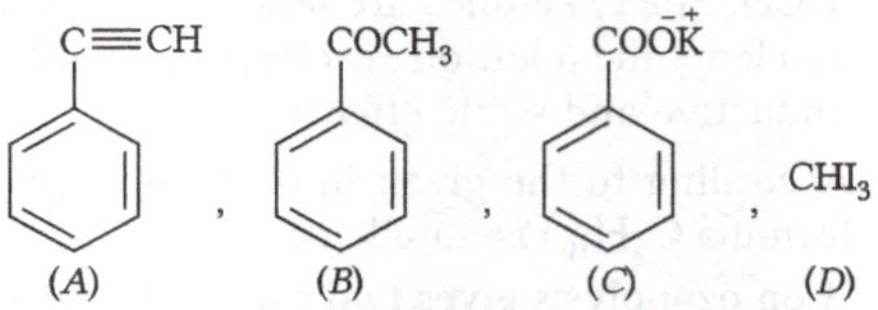

Complete reactions are as follows **(2)**

- C_8H_6 on reaction with dil. H_2SO_4, $HgSO_4$ gives

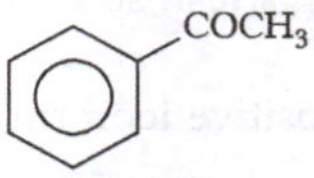

(*B*)

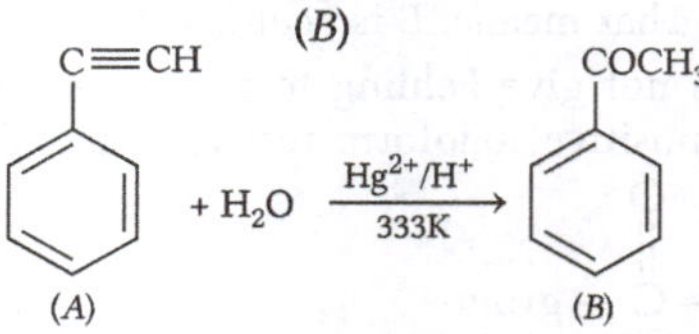

(1)

- $C_6H_5COCH_3$ (*B*) can also be obtained from benzene with acetyl chloride in presence of anhyd. $AlCl_3$.

This reaction is known as Friedel-Crafts acetylation reaction.

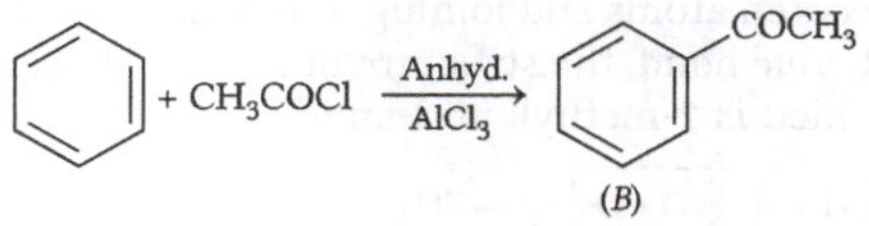

(1)

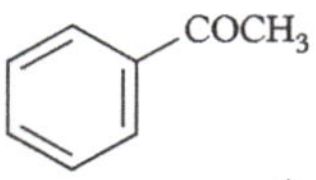

on treatment with I_2 in *aq.* KOH gives

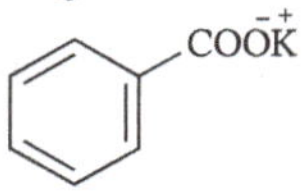

and yellow compound CHI_3

(*C*)

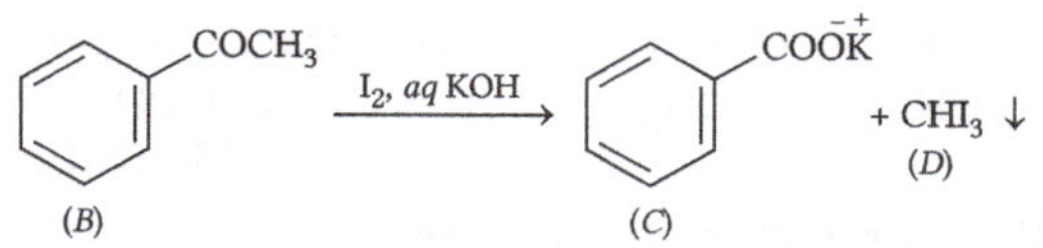

(1)

37. (i) $A \rightarrow$ An alkene, i.e., $(CH_3)CH{=}C(CH_3)_2$

$B \rightarrow$ An aldehyde with $—CH_3$ group, i.e., (CH_3CHO)

$C \rightarrow$ Methylketone (CH_3COCH_3) (1)

(ii) $\underset{\text{Acetaldehyde (B)}}{CH_3CHO} + \underset{\text{Tollen's reagent}}{2[Ag(NH_3)_2]^+} + 3\bar{O}H \longrightarrow$

$CH_3COO^- + 2Ag\downarrow + 4NH_3 + 2H_2O$ (1)

(iii) $\underset{\text{Acetone (C)}}{CH_3COCH_3} + NaOH + I_2 \longrightarrow \underset{\text{Iodoform}}{CHI_3\downarrow} + CH_3COONa$ (1)

(iv) $\underset{(B)}{CH_3COCH_3} + \underset{(C)}{CH_3CHO} \xrightarrow{Ba(OH)_2}$

$(CH_3)_2C(OH)CH_2COCH_3 +$
$CH_3CH(OH)CH_2COCH_3 +$
$CH_3CH(OH)CH_2CHO +$
$(CH_3)_2C(OH)CH_2CHO$

$\downarrow$ Heat

$(CH_3)_2C = CH—COCH_3 +$
$CH_3CH{=}CHCHO + (CH_3)_2C{=}CHCHO$
$+ CH_3CH{=}CHCOCH_3$ (2)

38. (i) Chemical equation of Cannizzaro reaction.

$$2H—\underset{\underset{H}{|}}{C}{=}O + \text{Conc. NaOH(50\%)} \xrightarrow{\Delta} \underset{\text{Methyl alcohol}}{CH_3—OH}$$

$$+ \underset{\text{Sodium formate}}{H—\underset{\underset{O}{\|}}{C}—O^-Na^+}$$ (1)

(ii) Carboxylic acids exhibit strong hydrogen bonding due to the presence of the hydroxyl (—OH) group. They often forms dimers in the liquid phase, which significantly increases their boiling points. (1)

(iii) $\underset{(A)}{CH_3—\overset{\overset{O}{\|}}{C}—CH_2—CH_2—\overset{\overset{O}{\|}}{C}H} \xrightarrow[\text{hydrazine}]{\text{NaOH, Glycol}} \underset{n\text{-pentane}}{CH_3CH_2CH_2CH_2CH_3}$

$$\underset{(A)}{C_5H_8O_2} \xrightarrow{NH_2OH} \underset{\text{Dioxime}}{CH_3—\overset{\overset{N—OH}{\|}}{C}—CH_2—CH_2—\overset{\overset{N—OH}{\|}}{C}—H}$$

Iodoform and Tollen's test reactions are as follows

$$CH_3\overset{\overset{O}{\|}}{C}—CH_2CH_2CHO \xrightarrow{I_2, NaOH} CHI_3 + \overset{+}{Na}\overset{-}{O}—\overset{\overset{O}{\|}}{C}—CH_2CH_2CHO$$

$$\xrightarrow[\text{Tollen's reagent}]{2[Ag(NH_3)_2]^+ + 3\bar{O}H} CH_3COOCH_2COO^- + 2Ag\downarrow + 4NH_3 + 2H_2O$$ (3)

39. **Compounds which will undergo aldol condensation (having α-hydrogen atom)** are follows

(ii) **2-methyl pentanal**

$$2CH_3CH_2CH_2—\overset{\alpha\text{-H}}{\underset{\underset{CH_3}{|}}{CH}}—CHO \xrightarrow[\text{Aldol condensation}]{\text{Dil. NaOH}}$$

2-methylpentanal

$$\overset{7\ \ 6}{CH_3CH_2}—\overset{5}{CH_2}—\overset{4}{\underset{\underset{CH_3}{|}}{CH}}—\overset{3}{\underset{\underset{OH}{|}}{CH}}—\overset{\overset{CH_3}{|2}}{\underset{\underset{CHO}{|1}}{C}}—CH_2—CH_2CH_3$$

3-hydroxy-2, 4-dimethyl 2-propylheptanal (1/2)

(v) **Cyclohexanone**

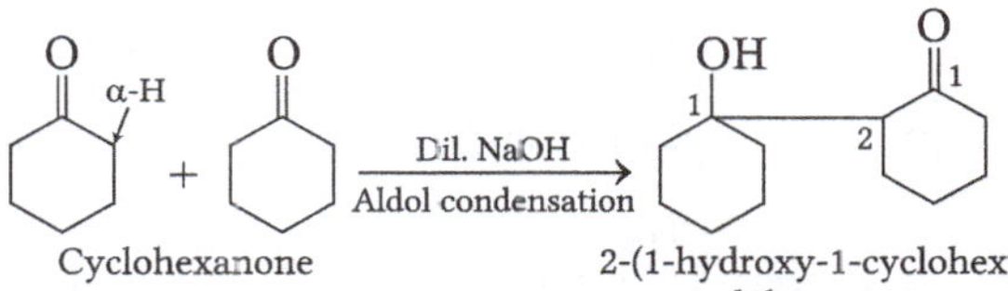

(1/2)

(vi) **1-phenyl propanone**

$$\underset{\text{1-phenyl propanone}}{C_6H_5—\overset{\overset{O}{\|}}{\underset{\underset{CH_2CH_3}{|}}{C}}} + \overset{\overset{C}{\|}}{\underset{\underset{\underset{CH_3}{|}}{CH_2 \leftarrow \alpha\text{-H}}}{|}}{C}}—C_6H_5 \xrightarrow[\text{Aldol condensation}]{\text{Dil. NaOH}}$$

$$C_6H_5—\overset{\overset{OH}{|}}{\underset{\underset{CH_2CH_3}{4|\ \ 5}}{\overset{3}{C}}}—\overset{2}{\underset{\underset{CH_3}{|}}{CH}}—\overset{\overset{O}{\|}}{\overset{1}{C}}—C_6H_5$$

3-hydroxy-2-methyl-1, 3-diphenylpentan-1-one (1/2)

(vii) **Phenyl acetaldehyde**

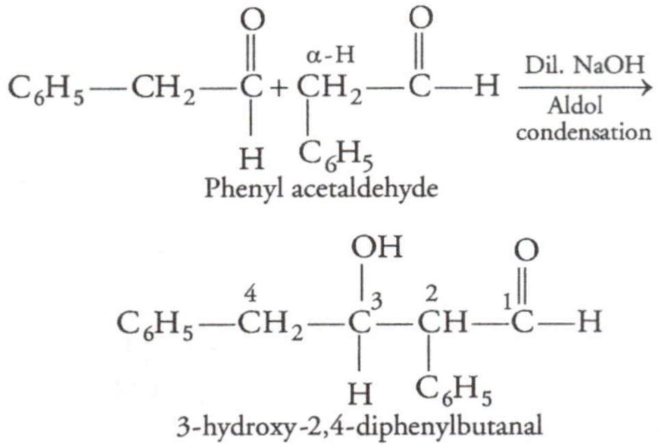

(1/2)

Compounds which undergo Cannizzaro reaction (only aldehydes without α-hydrogen atoms)

(i) **Methanal** Refer to text on page 288. (1/2)

(iii) **Benzaldehyde** Refer to text on page 288. (1/2)

(ix) **2,2-dimethyl butanal**

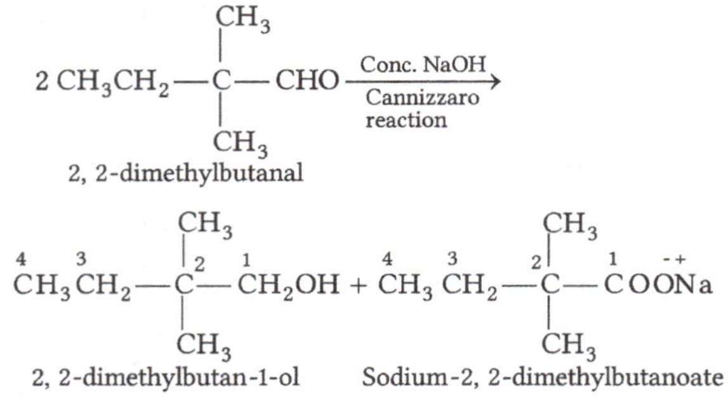

(1/2)

Compounds which undergo neither Cannizzaro nor Aldol reaction.

(iv) **Benzophenone** It is a ketone, so it does not undergo Cannizzaro reaction without α-hydrogen. It cannot participate in Aldol condensation.

(viii) **Butan-1-ol** It is an alcohol. So, it cannot participate in any of the above two reactions. (1½)

40. (i)

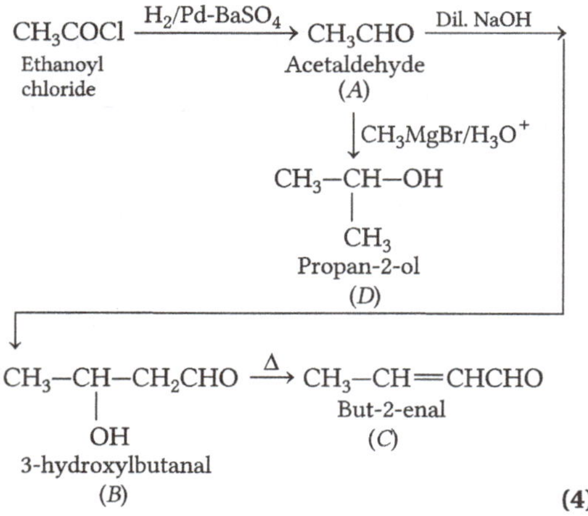

(4)

(ii) The correct increasing order of the boiling points is :

$$CH_3—O—CH_3 < CH_3CHO < CH_3CH_2OH < CH_3COOH$$ (1)

41 (i) (a) **Propanone to propene**

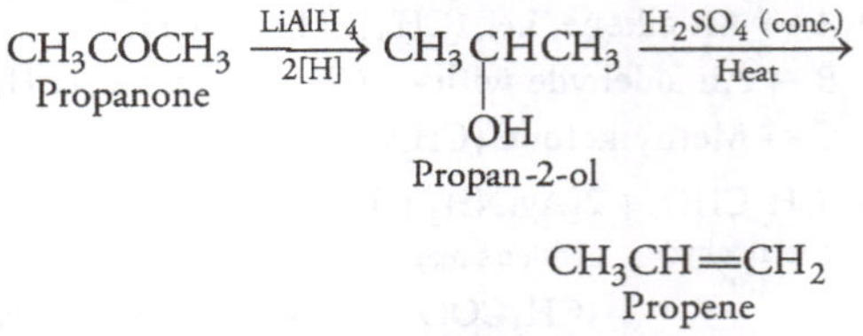

(1/2)

(b) **Ethanol to 3-hydroxybutanal**

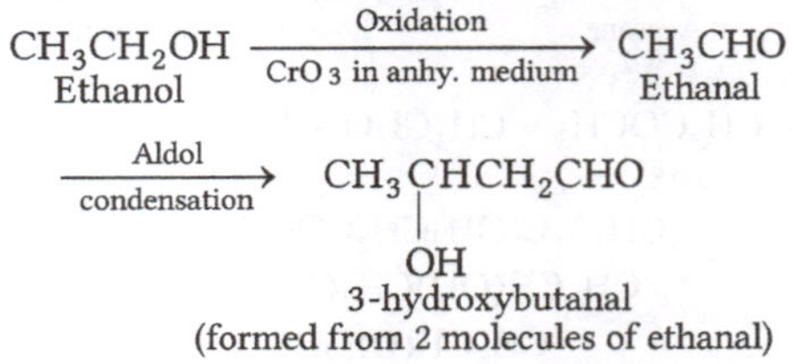

(1/2)

(c) **Benzene to *m*-nitroacetophenone**

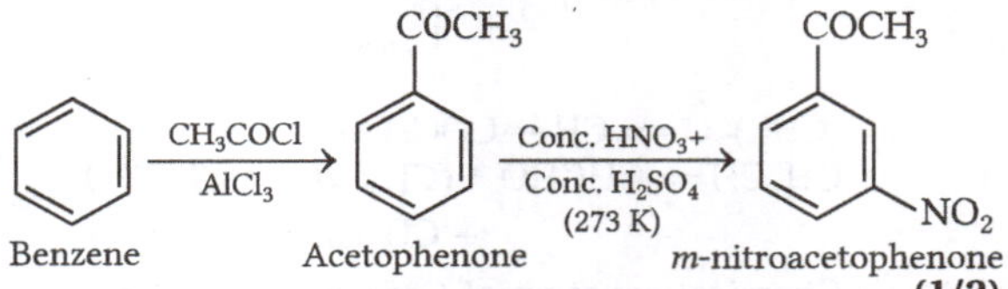

(1/2)

(d) **Bromobenzene to 1-phenylethanol**

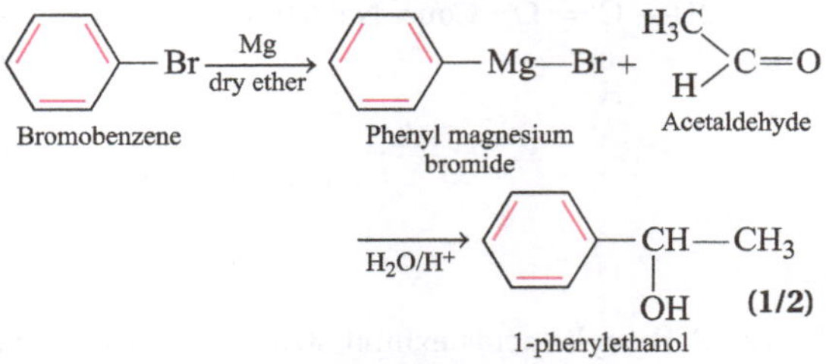

(1/2)

(e) **Benzaldehyde to benzophenone**

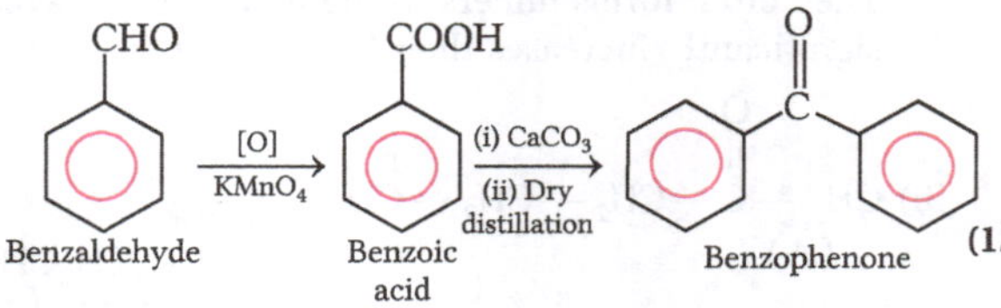

(1/2)

(f) **Benzaldehyde to α-hydroxyphenylacetic acid**

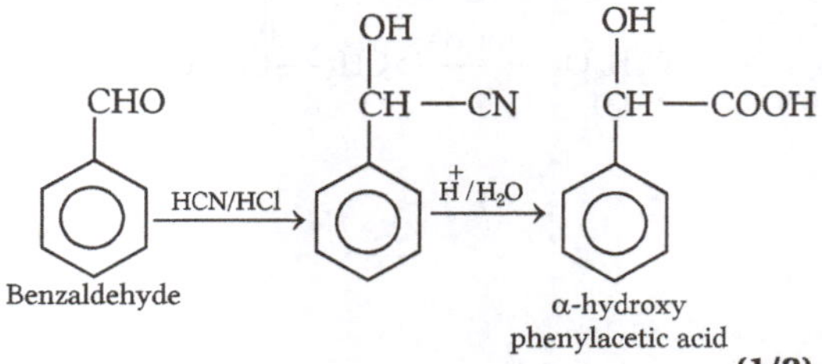

(1/2)

(ii) The reactivity of carbonyl compounds towards HCN addition decreases as the $+I$-effect of the alkyl group(s) increases or the presence of bulkier alkyl group increases, which causes steric hindrance to the nucleophilic attack by CN^- at the carbonyl carbon. Thus, the reactivity decreases in the order:

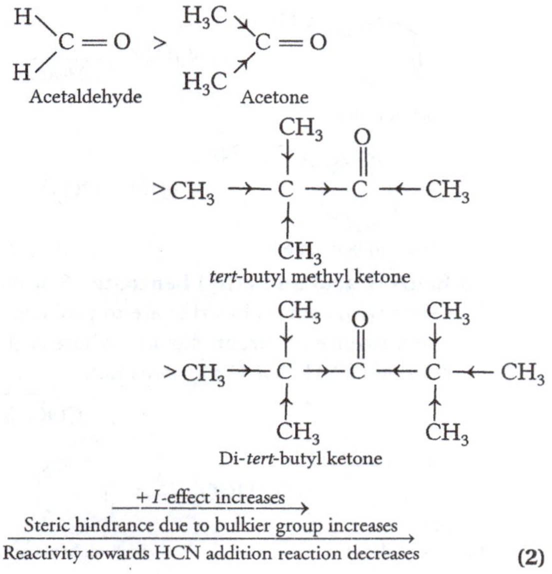

(2)

42. (i)

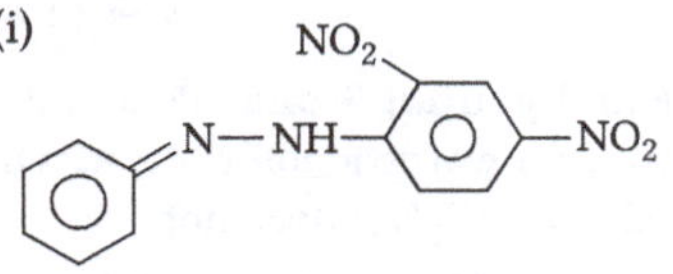

(1)

(ii) **Hint :**

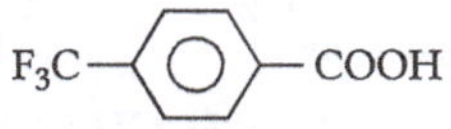

(1)

(iii) Refer to text on page 279. (1)

(iv) Refer to text on page 286. (1)

(v) Refer to Q. 45 (iii) (1)

43. (i) (a) When CH_3COCl is treated with $(CH_3)_2Cd$, then propanone is formed.

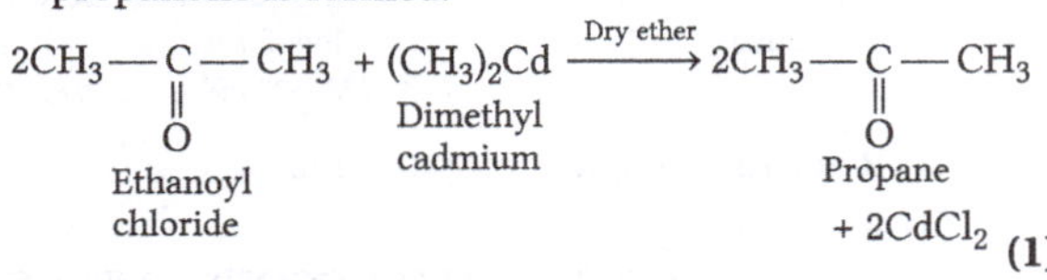

(1)

(b) When CH_3CHO is treated with HCN, then acetaldehyde cyanohydrin is formed.

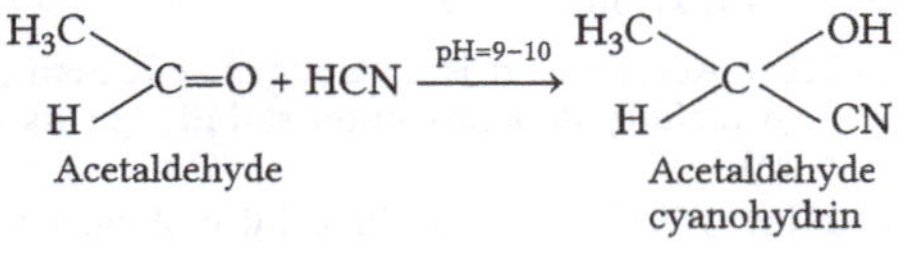

(1)

(c) When benzaldehyde is treated with conc. $(HNO_3 + H_2SO_4)$, *m*-nitrobenzaldehyde is formed.

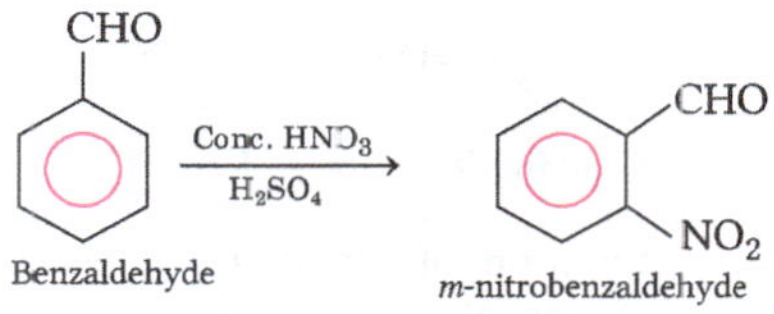

(1)

(ii) (a) Fluoroacetic acid, i.e., FCH_2COOH is a stronger acid than acetic acid, i.e., CH_3COOH. (1)

(b) *p*-nitrobenzoic acid i.e.,

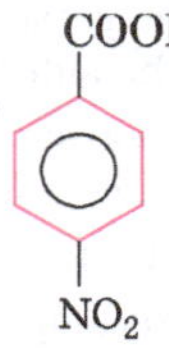

is a stronger acid than *p*-methylbenzoic acid, i.e.,

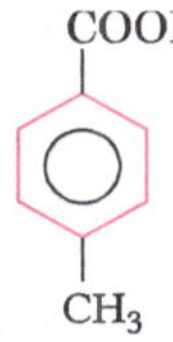

(1)

44. (i) Cross-aldol reaction is carried out between two different aldehydes or ketones (acetone and ethanal). It gives a mixture of two products.

$$CH_3COCH_3 + CH_3CHO \xrightarrow{\text{Dil. NaOH}}$$
$$(CH_3)_2C(OH)CH_2CHO + CH_3CH(OH)CH_2COCH_3$$
$$\xrightarrow{\text{Heat}} (CH_3)_2C{=}CHCHO + CH_3CH{=}CHCOCH_3$$

(2)

(ii) (a) **Benzyl alcohol to phenyl ethanoic acid**

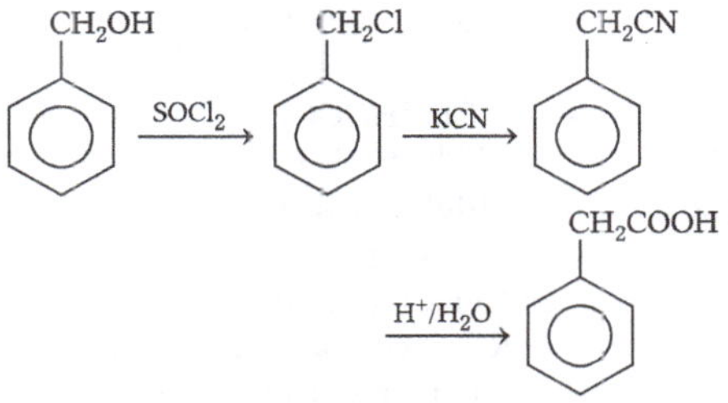

(b) **Propanone to propene**

$$CH_3COCH_3 \xrightarrow{H_2,\,Pd} CH_3CH(OH)CH_3 \xrightarrow{H_2SO_4} CH_3CH{=}CH_2$$

(c) **Benzene to *m*-nitro acetophenone**

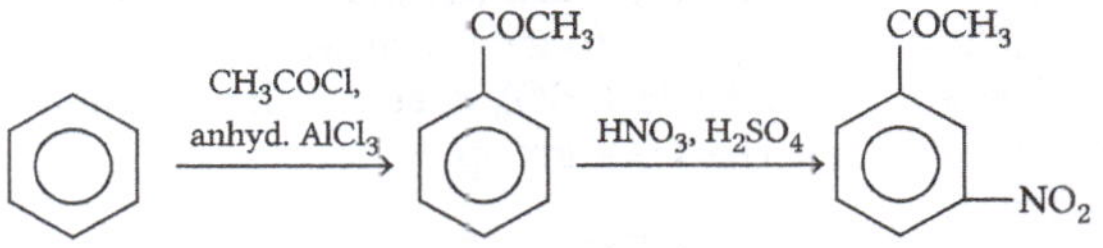

45. (i) (a) The α-hydrogens of aldehydes and ketones are acidic in nature. This is because of the strong electron withdrawing nature of the carbonyl groups and resonance stabilisation of the conjugate base in respective case.

Aldehyde Ketone **(1)**

(b) Oxidation of aldehydes is easier than ketones because of the presence of the hydrogen atom attached to the C=O double bond in the aldehyde, which is not present in ketone.

Thus, the presence of that hydrogen atom makes the aldehydes very easy to oxidise. **(1)**

(ii) (a) The decreasing order of reactivity towards nucleophilic addition reaction is

propanal > acetone > benzaldehyde. **(1)**

(b) The increasing order of boiling point is

propane < dimethyl ether < propanal < ethanol. **(1)**

(iii) **Test to distinguish between benzoic acid and benzaldehyde**

Benzoic acid being an acid reacts with $NaHCO_3$ solution to produce brisk effervescence due to the evolution of CO_2 while benzaldehyde does not give this test.

$$C_6H_5COOH + NaHCO_3 \longrightarrow C_6H_5COO^-Na^+ + CO_2\uparrow + H_2O$$

$$C_6H_5CHO \xrightarrow{NaHCO_3 \text{ solution}} \text{No effervescence}$$ **(1)**

46. (i) (a) Refer to text on page 284. **(1)**

(b) Refer to text on page 288. **(1)**

(c) $\underset{\text{Acetic acid}}{CH_3COOH} \xrightarrow{Cl_2/P} \underset{\text{Monochloroacetic acid}}{ClCH_2COOH} \xrightarrow{Cl_2/P} \underset{\text{Dichloroacetic acid}}{Cl_2CHCOOH} \xrightarrow{Cl_2/P} \underset{\text{Trichloroacetic acid}}{Cl_3CCOOH}$ **(1)**

(ii) (a) **Benzaldehyde and benzoic acid**

$NaHCO_3$ test Benzoic acid being an acid reacts with $NaHCO_3$ solution, to produce brisk effervescence due to evolution of CO_2, while benzaldehyde does not give this test.

$$C_6H_5COOH + NaHCO_3 \longrightarrow C_6H_5CO\overset{-}{O}\overset{+}{Na} + CO_2\uparrow + H_2O$$

$$C_6H_5CHO \xrightarrow{NaHCO_3 \text{ solution}} \text{No effervescence}$$ **(1)**

(b) **Propanal and propanone** Propanone responds to iodoform test, whereas propanal (CH_3CH_2CHO), does not due to the absence of CH_3CO— group.

$$\underset{\text{Propanone}}{CH_3COCH_3} + \underset{\text{Sodium hypoiodite}}{3NaOI} \xrightarrow[\text{Heat}]{NaOH, I_2} \underset{\substack{\text{(Yellow ppt.)} \\ \text{Iodoform}}}{CHI_3}\downarrow + \underset{\text{Sodium acetate}}{CH_3CO\overset{-}{O}\overset{+}{Na}} + 2NaOH$$ **(1)**

47. (i) **Acetophenone and benzophenone** Acetophenone ($C_6H_5COCH_3$) gives positive iodoform test, whereas benzophenone ($C_6H_5COC_6H_5$) does not. **(1)**

(ii) **Phenol and benzoic acid** Benzoic acid reacts with sodium bicarbonate to produce effervescence of carbon dioxide, whereas phenol (C_6H_5OH) does not.

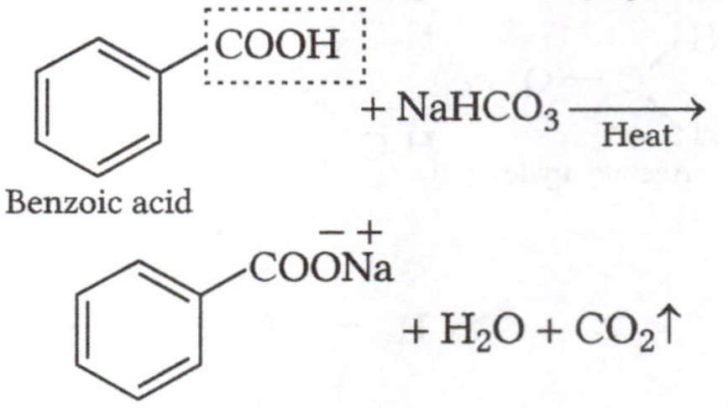

Benzoic acid → Sodium benzoate **(1)**

(iii) **Benzoic acid and ethyl benzoate** Benzoic acid reacts with sodium bicarbonate to produce effervescence of carbon dioxide, whereas ethyl benzoate ($C_6H_5COOC_2H_5$) does not.

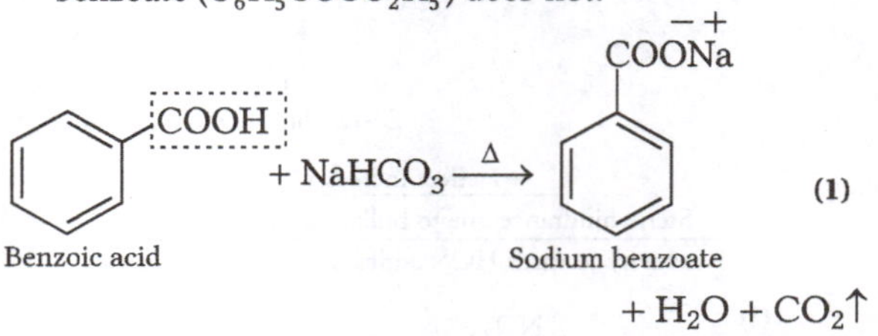

Benzoic acid → Sodium benzoate **(1)**

(iv) **Pentan-2-one and pentan-3-one** Pentan-2-one responds positively towards iodoform test, whereas pentan-3-one ($C_2H_5COC_2H_5$) does not.

$$\underset{\text{Pentan-2-one}}{CH_3-CO-CH_2-CH_2-CH_3} + 3NaOI \xrightarrow{\text{Heat}} \underset{\text{(Yellow ppt.)}}{CHI_3}\downarrow + CH_3CH_2CH_2CO\overset{-}{O}\overset{+}{Na} + 2NaOH$$ **(1)**

(v) **Ethanal and propanal** Ethanal responds positively towards iodoform test, whereas propanal (CH_3CH_2CHO) does not.

$$\underset{\text{Ethanal}}{CH_3CHO} + 3NaOI \xrightarrow{\text{Heat}} \underset{\substack{\text{Iodoform} \\ \text{(Yellow ppt.)}}}{CHI_3}\downarrow + HCO\overset{-}{O}\overset{+}{Na} + 2NaOH$$ **(1)**

48. (i) Refer to example 5 on page 292. **(3)**

(ii) Refer to page 295.

1. $O_2NCH_2COOH > CN(CH_2COOH) > FCH_2COOH$ **(1)**
2. Ethanal > Propanal > Propanone > Butanone **(1)**

Refer to text on page 282.

49. (i) (a) **Hint** Acrylic acid is a stronger acid than propanoic acid (acidity depends upon stability of its conjugate base). **(1)**

(b) **Hint** EWG increases the acidity of carboxylic acids. **(1)**

(c) **Hint** pK_a value of succinic acid is higher than pK_a value of malonic acid. **(1)**

(ii) (a) **Hint** (a) Br — CH_2COOH (b) Cl — CH_2COOH **(1)**

(b) **Hints**

I. Aliphatic aldehydes being more reactive reduce Fehling's solution to red ppt. of Cu_2O, while aromatic aldehydes do not.

II. Aromatic aldehydes on treatment with an alcoholic solution of KCN undergo benzoin condensation but aliphatic aldehydes do not. **(1)**

50. (*d*) Organic compound *A* is an ester, as on acid hydrolysis it gives a mixture of an acid and an alcohol. Oxidation of alcohol (*c*) gives carboxylic acid (*B*).

Hence, the number of carbon atoms in (*B*) and (*C*) are same.

Since, ester has eight carbon atoms, thus both (*B*) and (*C*) must contain four carbon atoms each.

Dehydration of (*C*) gives but-1-ene, therefore, (*C*) must be a straight chain alcohol (1°), i.e. butan-1-ol. Since, oxidation of (*C*) gives carboxylic acid (*B*), therefore (*B*) is butanoic acid.

Hence, ester (*A*) is butyl butanoate.

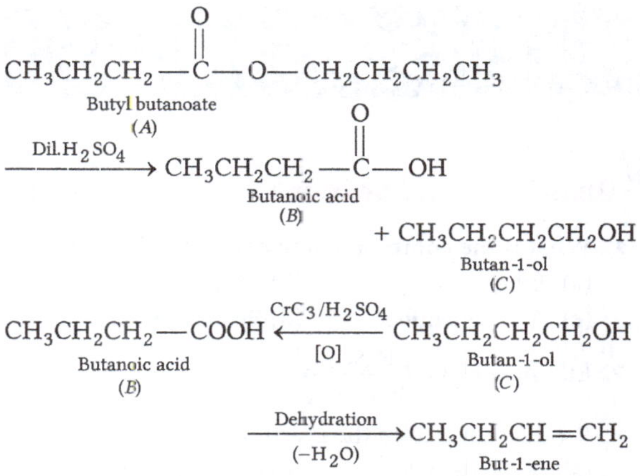

51. (i) Refer to text on page 286. **(1)**

(ii) Refer to text on page 287. **(1)**

(iii) Refer to text on page 279. **(1)**

(iv) Refer to text on page 288. **(1)**

(v) Refer to text on page 297. **(1)**

QR Code for Quick Test 1

QR Code for Quick Test 2

QR Code for Quick Test 3

QR Code for Quick Test 4

SELF ASSESSMENT TEST

Objective Type Questions [1 Mark]

1. What is the common name of dimethyl ketone?

(a) Ether (b) Acetone
(c) Acetophenone (d) Benzophenone

2. $\text{Ethyne} + H_2O \xrightarrow[\text{Dil. } H_2SO_4]{HgSO_4}$

Product formed in the given reaction is

(a) benzaldehyde (b) acetaldehyde
(c) ethanoic acid (d) ethanoyl chloride

3. In the reaction,

$$H_3C—CH{=}CH—CH_2—CH_2—CN \xrightarrow[\text{(ii) } H_2O]{\text{(i) AlH}(i\text{-Bu})_2}$$

Identify the product formed in the given reaction.

(a) $H_3C - CH_2CH_2CH_2CH_2CN$
(b) $H_3C - CH{=}CH - CH_2CH_2CHO$
(c) $H_3CCH_2CH_2CH_2CH_2CHO$
(d) None of the above

4. Match the reactions given in Column I with the suitable reagents given in Column II.

Column I (Reactions)	Column II (Reagents)
A. Benzophenone → Diphenylmethane	(i) $LiAlH_4$
B. Benzaldehyde → 1-phenylethanol	(ii) DIBAL-H
C. Cyclohexanone → Cyclohexanol	(iii) Zn(Hg)/Conc. HCl
D. Phenyl benzoate → Benzaldehyde	(iv) (a) CH_3MgBr (b) H_2O

(a) A-(iii), B-(ii), C-(i), D-(iv)
(b) A-(i), B-(iv), C-(ii), D-(iii)
(c) A-(i), B-(iii), C-(iv), D-(ii)
(d) A-(iii), B-(iv), C-(i), D-(ii)

5. $C_6H_5CHO + CH_3COCH_3 \xrightarrow[\Delta]{OH^-} C_6H_5CH{=}CH—COCH_3$

This reaction is known as

(a) Aldol condensation
(b) Cross-aldol condensation
(c) Cannizzaro's reaction
(d) Friedel-Crafts reaction

Assertion-Reason [1 Mark]

■ **Directions** (Q. Nos. 6-8) In the following questions, an Assertion (A) is followed by a corresponding Reason (R). Use the following keys to choose the appropriate answer.

(a) Both (A) and (R) are correct and (R) is the correct explanation of (A).
(b) Both (A) and (R) are correct but (R) is not the correct explanation of (A).
(c) (A) is correct but (R) is incorrect.
(d) (A) is incorrect but (R) is correct.

6. **Assertion** (A) IUPAC name of $HOOC\text{+}CH_2\text{+}_2\ COOH$ is butane-dioic acid.

Reason (R) In compounds containing more than one carboxyl group, '-e' of the alkane is retained, and prefix 'di' is added to the term-'oic'.

7. **Assertion** (A) Carboxylic acids have higher boiling liquids than aldehydes, ketones and even alcohols of comparable molecular masses.

Reason (R) More extensive association of carboxylic acid molecules through intermolecular hydrogen bonding is responsible for the high boiling point of carboxylic acid.

8. **Assertion** (A) Formaldehyde is a planar molecule.

Reason (R) It contains sp^2-hybridised carbon atom.

Short Answer Type I Questions [2 Marks]

9. (i) Explain why cyclohexanone forms cyanohydrin in good yield but 2,2,6-trimethyl cyclohexanone does not.

(ii) How will you obtain tertiary butyl alcohol from acetone?

10. (i) Give simple tests to distinguish between hexan-2-one and hexan-3-one.

(ii) Illustrate the Clemmensen reduction reaction giving suitable example.

Or

Give one chemical test for each to distinguish between the following pair of compounds.

(i) Acetaldehyde and benzaldehyde
(ii) Acetaldehyde and acetone

11. Answer the following questions.
   (i) Aromatic aldehydes do not give a reddish-brown precipitate on heating with Fehling's solution. Give reason.
   (ii) Why is benzaldehyde less reactive to electrophilic substitution reactions than benzene?

Short Answer Type II Questions [3 Marks]

12. (i) Give the chemical reaction involved when *p*-nitrotoluene undergoes Etard reaction.
   (ii) Why does benzoic acid exist as a dimer in an aprotic solvent?
   (iii) Benzene on reaction with methyl chloride in the presence of anhydrous $AlCl_3$ forms toluene. What is the expected outcome if benzene is replaced by benzoic acid? Give a reason for your answer.

13. An organic compound '*X*', does not undergo aldol condensation. However, '*X*' with compound '*Y*' in the presence of a strong base react to give the compound 1,3-diphenylprop-2-en-1-one.
   (i) Identify '*X*' and '*Y*'.
   (ii) Write the chemical reaction involved.
   (iii) Give one chemical test to distinguish between *X* and *Y*.

14. An organic compound (*A*) with the molecular formula $C_9H_{10}O$ forms 2,4-DNP derivative, reduces Fehling's solution and undergoes Cannizzaro reaction.
   On vigorous oxidation, it gives 1, 2-benzene dicarboxylic acid.
   (i) Identify the compound (*A*) and write its IUPAC name.
   (ii) Write the reaction of compound (*A*) with
      (a) 2, 4-dinitrophenyl hydrazine and
      (b) Fehling's solution
   (iii) Write the equation of compound (*A*) when it undergoes Cannizzaro reaction.

Case-Study [4 Marks]

15. Read the passage given below and answer the following questions.
   The characteristic chemical properties of carboxylic acids are the properties of the carboxylic group (—COOH). This group is made up of carbonyl group ($>C=O$) and a hydroxyl group.
   Thus, the properties of the carboxylic acids should be due to these groups. The properties of the —OH group get modified due to the presence of the carbonyl group. The carboxylic acids do not give the properties of the C—O group of the aldehydes and ketones due to resonance.
   Most of the reactions of the carboxylic acids can be divided into four principle type.
   - Reactions due to cleavage of O—H bond.
   - Reactions due to OH part of — COOH.
   - Reactions due to —COOH group.
   - Reactions due to alkyl group and benzene ring.

   (i) Give a balanced equation and name the products when acetic acid is treated with PCl_5.
   (ii) Arrange CCl_3COO^-, $CHCl_2COO^-$ and CH_2ClCOO^- in the increasing order of stability.
   Or What happens when benzoic acid reacts with hydrazoic acid in the presence of conc. H_2SO_4?
   (iii) Carbonyl group in carboxylic group does not give its usual nucleophilic addition reactions, why?

Long Answer Type Questions [5 Marks]

16. (i) Write the chemical equation for the following named organic reactions.
      (a) Wolff-Kishner reduction (b) Etard reaction
   (ii) How will the following be obtained? (Give chemical equations)
      (a) *m*-nitrobenzyl alcohol from benzoic acid
      (b) 3-phenylpropanal from benzaldehyde
   (iii) Arrange the following compounds in the decreasing order of their acidic strength.
      2, 2-dimethyl propanoic acid, acetic acid and *iso*-butyric acid.

Answers

1. (*b*)	2. (*b*)	3. (*b*)	4. (*d*)	5. (*b*)	6. (*a*)	7. (*a*)	8. (*a*)

09

CHAPTER

Amines constitute one of the most important class of organic compounds. They are present in a variety of naturally occurring and man-made organic compounds. In nature, they occur among vitamins, proteins, alkaloids and hormones. Synthetic examples include drugs, polymers and dyestuffs.

YOUR STUDY GOALS

9.1 Structure of Amines
9.2 Classification of Amines
9.3 Nomenclature of Amines
9.4 Preparation of Amines
9.5 Physical Properties of Amines
9.6 Chemical Reactions & Uses of Amines
9.7 Identification of 1°, 2°, 3° Amines
9.8 Diazonium Salts

YOUR PRACTICE GOAL

- Objective Type Questions (38 Qs ; 25 MCQs, 11 A-R, 2 Case Study)
- Subjective Type Questions (40 Qs; 14 SA-I, 22 SA-II, 4 LA)

Amines

Amines are the derivatives of ammonia, obtained by the replacement of one, two or three hydrogen atoms by alkyl/aryl groups. e.g.,

$$\underset{1^\circ \text{ amine}}{CH_3-NH_2},\quad \underset{2^\circ \text{ amine}}{CH_3-NH-CH_3},\quad \underset{3^\circ \text{ amine}}{CH_3-N\begin{matrix} CH_3 \\ CH_3 \end{matrix}}$$

9.1 Structure of Amines

- Like ammonia, nitrogen atom of amines is trivalent and carries an unshared pair of electrons. Therefore, the nitrogen orbitals in amines are sp^3-hybridised and the geometry of amines is pyramidal.
- Each of the three sp^3-hybridised orbitals of nitrogen overlap with orbitals of carbon or hydrogen depending upon the composition of the amines. The fourth orbital of N contains an unshared pair of electrons, in all amines.
- Due to the presence of unshared pair of electrons, the angle C—N—*E* (where, *E* is C or H) is less than 109.5°, e.g., In trimethylamine, angle is 108°.
- Due to the presence of lone pair of electrons on nitrogen which can be donated, amines act as a nucleophile.

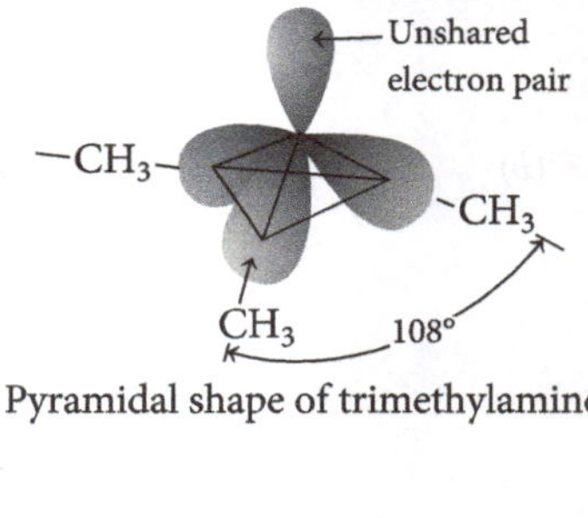

Pyramidal shape of trimethylamine

9.2 Classification of Amines

- **Depending upon the number of hydrogen atoms in ammonia** molecule replaced by alkyl (*R*) or aryl (Ar) groups, amines are classified as primary (1°), secondary (2°) and tertiary (3°). Thus, the sequence of classification of amine from ammonia can be shown as:

Types and Functional Group of Amines

S. No.	Amine	*n* (no. of H-atoms attached to N)	Types of amine	Functional group
1.	$R{-}NH{-}H$ (N bearing H)	2	1° (primary)	$-NH_2$
2.	R_2NH	1	2° (secondary)	$-NH-$
3.	R_3N	0	3° (tertiary)	$\gt N-$

- **Depending upon the number of alkyl or aryl groups** attached to the N-atom, amines are classified as simple and mixed amines. These are as follows:
  (i) **Simple amines** When all the alkyl/aryl groups are same, the amines are said to be simple amines.
  e.g. $(CH_3)_2NH$, $(CH_3CH_2)_3N$
  2° amine, 3° amine
  (ii) **Mixed amines** When all the alkyl/aryl groups are different, the amines are said to be mixed amines.
  e.g. $CH_3{-}NH{-}CH_2CH_3$,
  Ethylmethylamine (2°)
  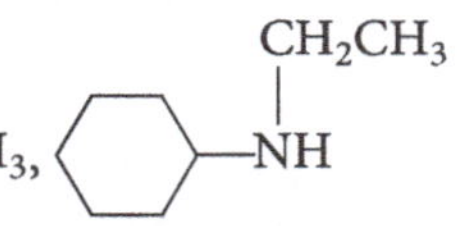
  Cyclohexylethylamine (2°)

Example 1 Classify the following amines as primary, secondary or tertiary. **NCERT Intext**

(i) 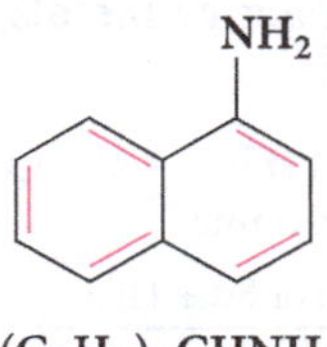 (ii) 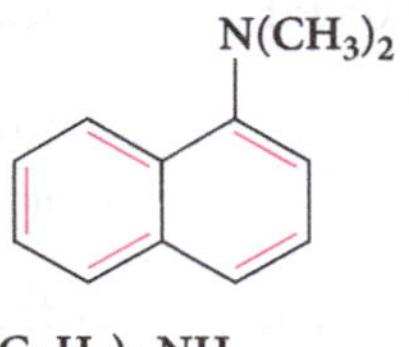

(iii) $(C_2H_5)_2CHNH_2$ (iv) $(C_2H_5)_2NH$

Sol. (i) Primary (ii) Tertiary
(iii) Primary (iv) Secondary

9.3 Nomenclature of Amines

Rules and steps to be followed while naming the amines are as follows:

- In **common system**, an aliphatic amine is named by adding suffix 'amine' to the name of the alkyl group attached to the nitrogen atom, e.g., methylamine.
- In 2° and 3° amines, when two or more groups are the same, the prefix di or tri is used before the name of the alkyl group.
  e.g. $CH_3{-}N(CH_3){-}CH_3$
  Trimethylamine
- In case of secondary and tertiary amines, locant N is used to designate substituent attached to a nitrogen atom, e.g., $CH_3NHCH_2CH_3$ is named as N-methylethanamine.
- In **IUPAC system**, amines are named as alkanamines, derived by the replacement of '*e*' of alkane by word 'amine'.
  e.g. CH_3NH_2, $CH_3{-}N(CH_3){-}CH_3$
  Methanamine, N, N-dimethylmethanamine
- If more than one amino group is present at different positions in the parent chain, then by assigning number, their positions are specified to the carbon atoms bearing $-NH_2$ groups and suitable prefix such as *di, tri* is attached to the amine.
  The terminal '*e*' of the name of the parent hydrocarbon is retained.
  e.g. $H_2N{-}CH_2{-}CH_2{-}NH_2$
  Ethane-1, 2-diamine
- The simplest **arylamine/aromatic amine** in which the $-NH_2$ group is directly attached to the benzene ring, i.e., $C_6H_5NH_2$ is called **aniline** and the substituted aromatic amines are named as derivatives of aniline.
  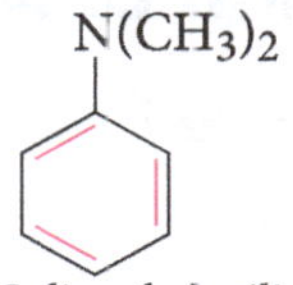
  N, N-dimethylaniline
- In IUPAC system, the terminal '*e*' of arene is replaced by 'amine'.
  e.g. $C_6H_5{-}NH_2$ (Benzenamine)

Nomenclature of some Important Alkanamines and Arylamines

Amine	Common name	IUPAC name
$CH_3-CH_2-NH_2$	Ethylamine	Ethanamine
$CH_3-CH_2-CH_2-NH_2$	*n*-propylamine	Propan-1-amine
$CH_3-CH(NH_2)-CH_3$	Isopropylamine	Propan-2-amine
$CH_3-N(H)-CH_2-CH_3$	Ethylmethylamine	N-methylethanamine
$CH_3-N(CH_3)-CH_3$	Trimethylamine	N,N-dimethylmethanamine
$C_2H_5-N(C_2H_5)-\overset{1}{C}H_2-\overset{2}{C}H_2-\overset{3}{C}H_2-\overset{4}{C}H_3$	N,N-diethylbutylamine	N,N-diethylbutan-1-amine
$NH_2-\overset{1}{C}H_2-\overset{2}{C}H=\overset{3}{C}H_2$	Allylamine	Prop-2-en-1-amine
$NH_2-(CH_2)_6-NH_2$	Hexamethylenediamine	Hexane-1, 6-diamine
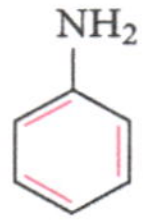	Aniline	Aniline or Benzenamine
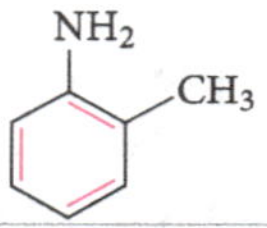	*o*-toluidine	2-aminotoluene or 2-methylaniline
	*p*-bromoaniline	4-bromobenzenamine or 4-bromoaniline
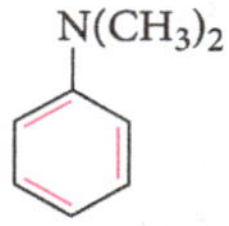	N,N-dimethylaniline	N,N-dimethylbenzenamine

9.4 Preparation of Amines

Amines are prepared by the following methods.

By Reduction of Nitro Compounds

Both aliphatic and aromatic primary amines can be prepared by the reduction of nitro compounds either catalytically with H_2 in the presence of finely divided Raney Ni, Pt or Pd or chemically with active metals in acidic medium.

e.g. $\underset{\text{Nitromethane}}{CH_3NO_2} + 3H_2 \xrightarrow[\text{Ethanol}]{\text{Raney Ni/Pt}} \underset{\text{Methylamine}}{CH_3NH_2} + 2H_2O$

$$\underset{\text{Nitrobenzene}}{C_6H_5NO_2} + 3H_2 \xrightarrow[\text{or Fe + HCl}]{H_2/\text{Pd in ethanol or Sn + HCl}} \underset{\text{Aniline}}{C_6H_5NH_2} + 2H_2O$$

Reduction with Fe scrap and HCl is preferred because $FeCl_2$ formed gets hydrolysed to release HCl during the reaction. Therefore, only a small amount of HCl is needed to initiate the reaction.

By Reduction of Nitriles

Reduction of nitriles with lithium aluminium hydride ($LiAlH_4$) or catalytic hydrogenation produces primary amines. This method is used to prepare amines containing one carbon atom more than the starting amine.

$$\underset{\text{Alkyl nitriles}}{R—C\equiv N} \xrightarrow[LiAlH_4 \text{ or } Na(Hg)/C_2H_5OH]{Ni/H_2} \underset{\text{Alkyl amines}}{R—CH_2—NH_2}$$

By Reduction of Amides

On reduction with $LiAlH_4$, amides yield amines.

e.g. $$\underset{\text{Alkyl amide}}{R—\overset{\overset{\large O}{\|}}{C}—NH_2} \xrightarrow[\text{(ii) } H_2O]{\text{(i) } LiAlH_4\text{, ether}} \underset{\text{Alkyl amines}}{R—CH_2—NH_2}$$

$$\underset{\text{Acetamide}}{CH_3CONH_2} \xrightarrow[\text{(ii) } H_2O]{\text{(i) } LiAlH_4\text{, ether}} \underset{\text{Ethylamine}}{CH_3CH_2NH_2}$$

By Hofmann Bromamide Degradation Reaction

This reaction is used for preparing amine containing one carbon less than the starting amide. This method was developed for the preparation of primary amines by reacting an amide with Br_2 / Cl_2 in an aqueous or ethanolic solution of NaOH/KOH.

In this reaction, migration of an alkyl or aryl group takes place from carbonyl carbon of the amide to the N-atom.

$$R—\overset{\overset{\large O}{\|}}{C}—NH_2 + Br_2 + 4NaOH \longrightarrow R—NH_2 + Na_2CO_3 + 2NaBr + 2H_2O$$

e.g. $$\underset{\text{Amide}}{CH_3CH_2CONH_2} + Br_2 + 4NaOH \longrightarrow \underset{\text{Amine}}{CH_3CH_2NH_2} + Na_2CO_3 + 2NaBr + 2H_2O$$

By Gabriel Phthalimide Synthesis

When a phthalimide is treated with ethanolic KOH, it forms potassium salt of phthalimide which on heating with alkyl halide followed by alkaline hydrolysis forms corresponding primary amines.

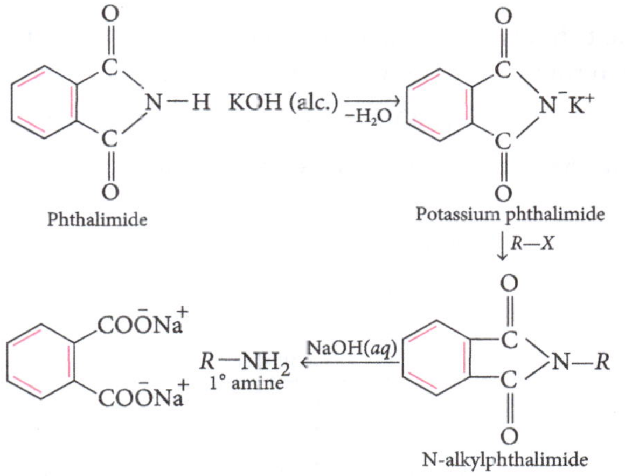

This method produces only primary amines without the traces of secondary or tertiary amines.

So, this method is preferred for the synthesis of primary amines.

> **TEACHER'S TIP**
> The above method is not useful for the preparation of aromatic primary amines because aryl halides do not undergo nucleophilic substitution with the anion formed by phthalimide.

By Ammonolysis of Alkyl Halides

This reaction is a nucleophilic substitution reaction carried out in a sealed tube at 373 K in which ammonia acting as a nucleophile, displaces the halogen atom. This process of cleavage of $C—X$ bond by ammonia is called **ammonolysis**.

$$\underset{\text{Ammonia}}{:NH_3} + \underset{\text{Alkyl halide}}{R—X} \xrightarrow[\text{Sealed tube}]{373\text{ K}} \underset{\text{Substituted ammonium salt}}{R—\overset{+}{N}H_3X^-} \underset{}{\overset{NH_3}{\rightleftharpoons}} \underset{1^\circ\text{amine}}{RNH_2}$$

The primary amine thus obtained behaves as a nucleophile and on subsequent reaction with alkyl halide forms 2°, 3° amines and finally forms quaternary ammonium salt.

$$\underset{(1^\circ)}{RNH_2} \xrightarrow{RX} \underset{(2^\circ)}{R_2NH} \xrightarrow{RX} \underset{(3^\circ)}{R_3N} \xrightarrow{RX} \underset{\text{Quaternary ammonium salt}}{R_4\overset{+}{N}\overset{-}{X}}$$

This method is not suitable for laboratory synthesis because the mixture obtained consists of different amine salts and the quaternary ammonium salt which is often difficult to separate.

On industrial scale, the mixture is separated by adding alkali to liberate free amines.

The primary and tertiary amines pass over, while the quaternary ammonium salt is left behind.

$$R—\overset{+}{N}H_3X^- + NaOH \longrightarrow R—NH_2 + H_2O + \overset{+}{Na}X^-$$

Note The order of reactivity of halides with amines is

$$RI > RBr > RCl.$$

Preparation of Amines (At a glance)

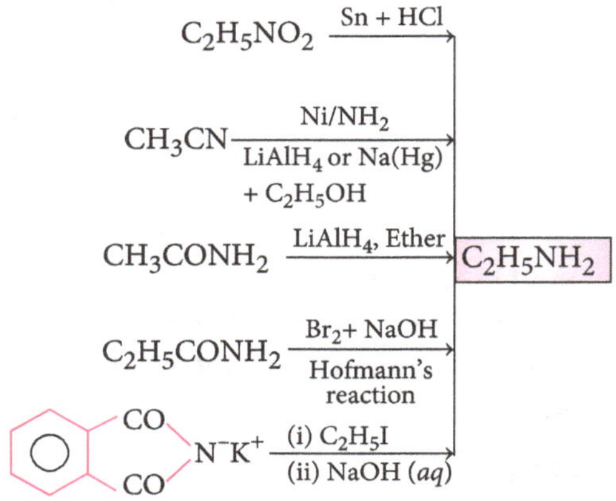

Example 2 **Write reactions of the final alkylation product of aniline with excess of methyl iodide in the presence of sodium carbonate solution.** NCERT Intext

Sol. **Hofmann's ammonolysis reaction** In the presence of excess of methyl iodide, aniline (primary amine) forms quaternary ammonium salt.

$$\underset{\text{Aniline}}{C_6H_5\ddot{N}H_2} + CH_3—I \longrightarrow \underset{\substack{\text{N-methylanilinium iodide}\\\text{(Intermediate)}}}{[C_6H_5\overset{+}{N}H_2CH_3]\,I^-}$$

$$2[C_6H_5\overset{+}{N}H_2CH_3]\,\overset{-}{I} + Na_2CO_3 \longrightarrow \underset{\text{N-methylaniline}}{2C_6H_5NHCH_3} + 2NaI + CO_2 + H_2O$$

$$C_6H_5\ddot{N}HCH_3 \xrightarrow[Na_2CO_3]{CH_3I} \underset{\text{N, N-dimethylaniline}}{C_6H_5N(CH_3)_2}$$

$$C_6H_5\ddot{N}(CH_3)_2 + CH_3—I \longrightarrow \underset{\text{N, N, N-trimethylanilinium iodide}}{[C_6H_5\overset{+}{N}(CH_3)_3]I^-}$$

$$2[C_6H_5\overset{+}{N}(CH_3)_3]\,\overset{-}{I} + Na_2CO_3 \longrightarrow \underset{\substack{\text{N, N, N-trimethyl}\\\text{anilinium carbonate}}}{[C_6H_5\overset{+}{N}(CH_3)_3]_2\,CO_3^{2-}} + 2NaI$$

Quick Test 1

1. Write the IUPAC names of the following compounds and classify them into primary, secondary and tertiary amines.
(i) $(CH_3)_2CHNH_2$ (ii) $CH_3(CH_2)_2NH_2$ NCERT
(iii) $CH_3NHCH(CH_3)_2$ (iv) $(CH_3)_3CNH_2$

2. Write down the IUPAC name of

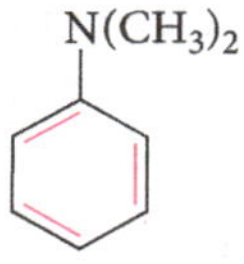

NCERT Exemplar

3. (i) Write the main product of the following reaction:

$$CH_3—\underset{\underset{O}{||}}{C}—NH_2 \xrightarrow{Br_2 + NaOH}$$

CBSE 2016 C

(ii) What is the best reagent to convert nitrile to primary amine? NCERT Exemplar

4. Give the structures of *A*, *B* and *C* in the following reaction.

$$CH_3CH_2I \xrightarrow{NaCN} A \xrightarrow[\text{Partial hydrolysis}]{OH^-} B \xrightarrow{NaOH + Br_2} C$$

NCERT

5. How will you convert the following? CBSE 2023
(i) Nitrobenzene into aniline
(ii) Ethanoic acid into methanamine

6. Identify *A* and *B* in the following reaction.

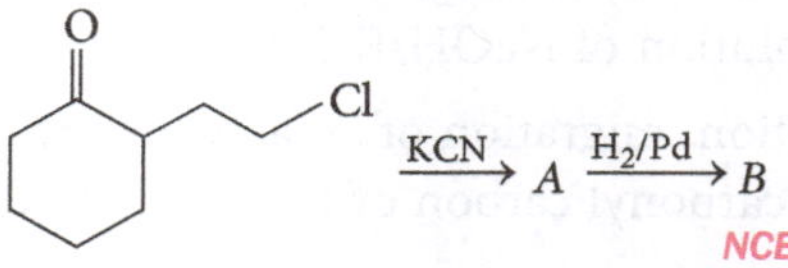

NCERT Exemplar

7. Ammonolysis of alkyl halides is not a good method to prepare pure primary amines. CBSE 2023

For Solutions, See QR Code on Pg. 356

9.5 Physical Properties of Amines

Physical properties of amines are as follows:

Physical State, Colour and Odour

- Pure amines are colourless but develop colour on keeping in air or on storage for long time, especially, the aromatic amines due to atmospheric oxidation.
- The lower aliphatic amines are gases whereas members of C_3 to C_{11} are volatile liquids and from C_{12} onwards are solids.
- Aromatic amines are toxic in nature.

Solubility

- Lower aliphatic amines can form hydrogen bonds with water molecules and hence are soluble in water.
- Solubility of amines decreases with increase in molar mass due to increase in the size of the hydrophobic alkyl part which retard the formation of H-bonds and hence, higher amines containing six or more carbon atoms are insoluble in water.
- Aromatic amines are insoluble in water but soluble in ether, alcohol and benzene.

Boiling Point

- Amines are polar and hence form intermolecular H-bonds between nitrogen of one and hydrogen of another molecule and therefore, they have higher boiling points. This intermolecular association depends upon the extent of H-bonding.
- 1° amines have two, 2° amines have one, while 3° amines have no hydrogen bonded to nitrogen.

  Therefore, the order of boiling point of amines is

  $$1^\circ \text{ amines} > 2^\circ \text{ amines} > 3^\circ \text{ amines.}$$

  The intermolecular hydrogen bonding in 1° amines is shown below:

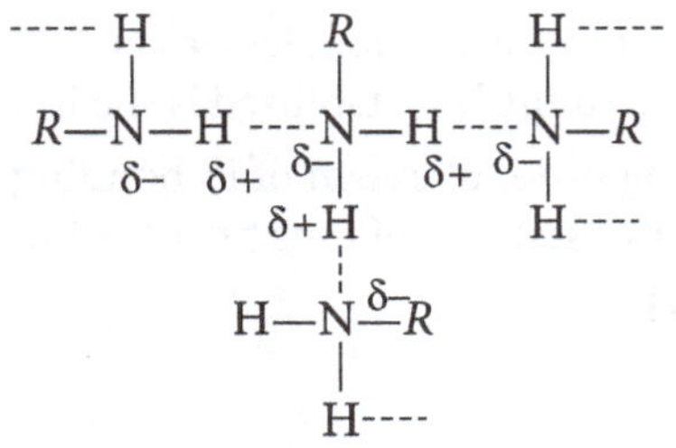

Intermolecular hydrogen bonding in primary amines

- Boiling points of amines, alcohols and alkanes of almost same molar mass are given in the following table.

Comparison of Boiling Points of Amines, Alcohols and Alkanes of Similar Molecular Masses

S.No.	Compound	Molar mass	Boiling point/K
1.	n-$C_4H_9NH_2$	73	350.8
2.	$(C_2H_5)_2NH$	73	329.3
3.	$C_2H_5N(CH_3)_2$	73	310.5
4.	$C_2H_5CH(CH_3)_2$	72	300.8
5.	n-C_4H_9OH	74	390.3

9.6 Chemical Reactions and Uses of Amines

Amines are very reactive due to the difference in electronegativity between nitrogen and hydrogen atoms and also, due to the presence of unshared pair of electrons over N-atom.

The number of hydrogen atoms attached to the N-atom decides the course of reactions of amine, that is why, amines differ in many reactions.

Some of the reactions of amines are described below

Basic Character of Amines

- Amines have an unshared pair of electrons over the nitrogen atom and hence, they behave as Lewis base. They readily react with mineral acids to form soluble salts.

$$\underset{\text{Amine}}{R—\ddot{N}H_2} + H—X \rightleftharpoons \underset{\text{(Salt)}}{R—\overset{+}{N}H_3X^-}$$

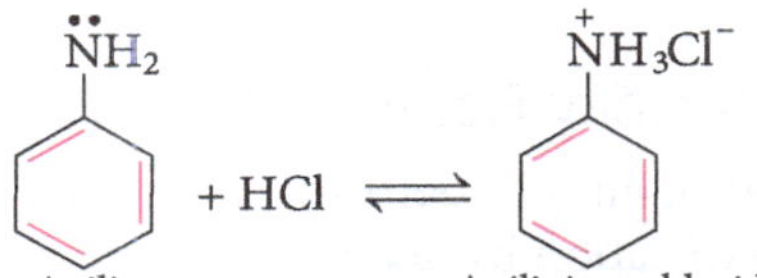

Aniline Anilinium chloride

- The amine salts on treatment with a base (NaOH), regenerate the parent amine.

$$R\overset{+}{N}H_3X^- + \bar{O}H \longrightarrow R\ddot{N}H_2 + H_2O + X^-$$

  Amine salts are soluble in water but insoluble in organic solvents like ether. That is why, this reaction is used for the separation of amines from the non-basic organic compounds which are insoluble in water.

- Basic character of amine can be better understood in terms of their K_b and pK_b values as explained below :

$$R—\ddot{N}H_2 + H_2O \rightleftharpoons R—\overset{+}{N}H_3 + \bar{O}H$$

$$K = \frac{[R—\overset{+}{N}H_3][\bar{O}H]}{[R—NH_2][H_2O]}$$

or $$K[H_2O] = \frac{[R—\overset{+}{N}H_3][OH]}{[R—NH_2]}$$

$$K_b = \frac{[R—\overset{+}{N}H_3][OH]}{[R—NH_2]}$$

$\Rightarrow$ $$pK_b = -\log K_b$$

Larger the value of K_b or smaller the value of pK_b, stronger is the base. e.g.

$$K_b \quad \underset{12.0\times 10^{-10}}{p\text{-toluidine}} > \underset{5\times 10^{-10}}{m\text{-toluidine}} > \underset{4.2\times 10^{-10}}{\text{aniline}} > \underset{2.6\times 10^{-10}}{o\text{-toluidine}}$$

$$pK_b \quad \underset{3.27}{(CH_3)_2NH} > \underset{3.38}{CH_3NH_2} > \underset{4.22}{(CH_3)_3N}$$

- Aliphatic amines are stronger bases than ammonia due to $+I$-effect (electron-donating power) of alkyl groups owing to which electron density on nitrogen atom increases and hence, they can easily donate their electrons.
- pK_b values of ammonia is 4.75 and pK_b values of aliphatic amine lies between the range 3 to 4.22.

Aliphatic amine

$CH_3 \rightarrow NH_2$
($+I$-effect)

Ammonia

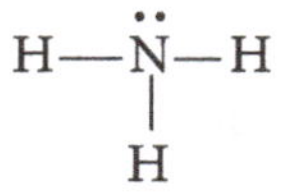

(no $+I$-effect)

On the other hand, aromatic amines are weaker bases than ammonia due to electron withdrawing nature of aryl group.

Structure-Basicity Relationship of Amines

Basic character of amines depends upon the ease for the formation of cation by accepting a proton from acid.

The more stable the cation is relative to the amine, more basic is the amine.

Alkanamines *versus* Ammonia

The basicity of alkanamine *versus* ammonia in gaseous and aqueous phase are discussed below.

I. Basicity in Gaseous Phase

The reaction of an alkanamine and ammonia with a proton is used to compare their basicity.

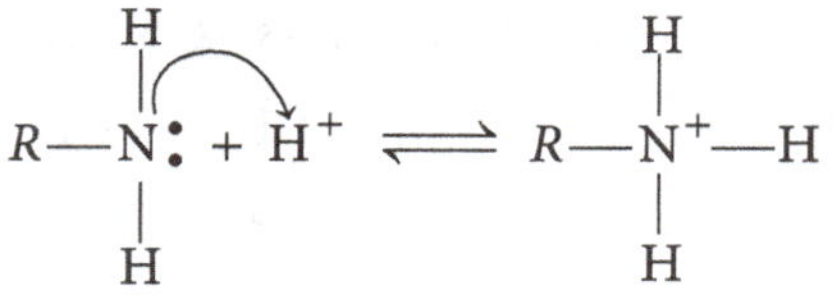

Alkanamine

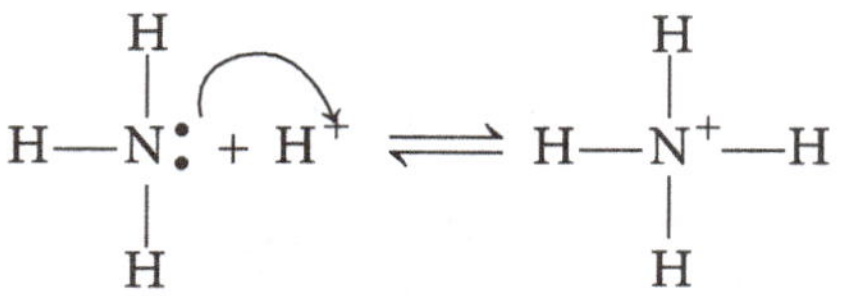

Ammonia

Due to electron releasing nature of alkyl group, it (R) pushes electrons towards nitrogen and makes the unshared electron pair more available for sharing with the proton of the acid.

The substituted ammonium ion formed from the amine gets stabilised due to dispersal of the positive charge by the $+I$-effect of alkyl group. Thus, basic nature of amine increases with increase in the number of alkyl groups.

Order of basicity of amines in gaseous phase is as follows:

Tertiary amine > Secondary amine > Primary amine > Ammonia

II. Basicity in Aqueous Phase

Basicity of an amine in aqueous solution depends upon the stability of ammonium cation formed by accepting proton from water. The stability of ammonium cation depends upon the following three factors

(a) **$+I$-effect** If we consider the first case, then as we increase the size of alkyl group, $+I$-effect increases and the positive charge of ammonium cation gets dispersed more easily. Therefore, the order of basicity is $3°$ amine $>$ $2°$ amine $>$ $1°$ amine.

(b) **Solvation effect** Substituted ammonium cation also gets stabilised by solvation with water molecules. The greater the size of ion, lesser will be the solvation and the less stabilised is the ion.

Decreasing order of extent of H-bonding in water and order of stability of ions by solvation is

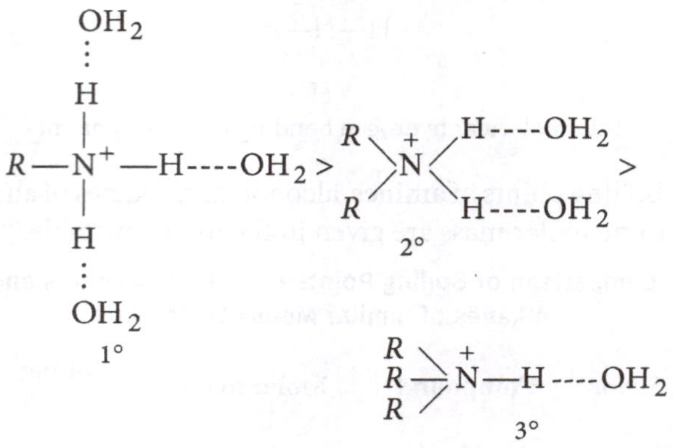

Greater the number of H-atoms on the N-atom, greater will be the H-bonding and, hence more stable is the ammonium cation.

So, order of stability is

$1°$ amine $>$ $2°$ amine $>$ $3°$ amine.

(c) **Steric effect** Steric factors refer to the crowding of alkyl groups around N-atom which causes hindrance to protonation of amine and also obstruction to H-bonding of protonated amine.

The steric effect increases with increase in size and in numbers of alkyl groups around N-atom, thus, the basic strength of amines decreases in the order 1° > 2° > 3° amine.

So, the two cases arise as:

Case I If we combine these 3 factors and if the alkyl group is small, i.e., $—CH_3$, then there is no steric hindrance to H-bonding and, hence H-bonding predominates over +*I*-effect. Since, all these effects are favourables for 2° amine. Therefore, 2° amine > 1° amine > 3° amine.

Case II If the alkyl group is bigger than $—CH_3$ group, i.e., $—C_2H_5$, then there is steric hindrance to H-bonding and hence, + *I*-effect predominates over H-bonding. Therefore,

2° amine > 3° amine > 1° amine.

There is a subtle interplay of the inductive effect, solvation effect and steric hindrance of alkyl group which decides the basic strength of alkyl amines in the aqueous state.

The order of basic strength in case of ethyl substituted amines and methyl substituted amines in aqueous solution is as follows:

$$(C_2H_5)_2NH > (C_2H_5)_3N > C_2H_5NH_2 > NH_3$$
$$(CH_3)_2NH > CH_3NH_2 > (CH_3)_3N > NH_3$$

Arylamines *versus* Ammonia

pK_b value of aniline is quite high due to the following reasons.

- As, $—NH_2$ group is directly attached to benzene ring, the lone pair of electrons on nitrogen atom gets delocalised over the benzene ring and thus, it is less available for protonation. Therefore, aromatic amines (aniline) are weaker bases than ammonia.
- If we consider the resonating structures, then we know that greater the number of resonating structures, greater is the stability.

  The five resonating structures of aniline are as follows:

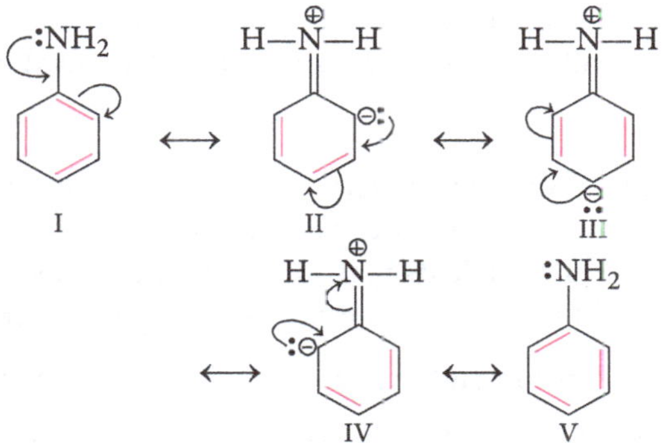

Resonating structures of aniline

In anilinium ion, there are two resonating structures, therefore, it is less stable than aniline.

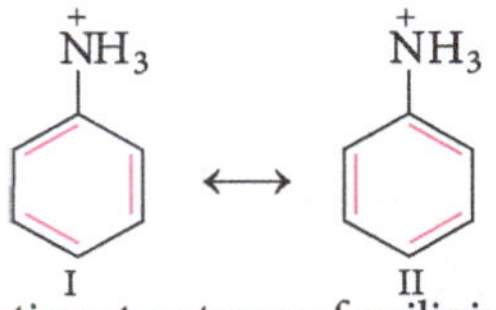

Resonating structures of anilinium ion

- In case of substituted aniline, electron releasing groups like $—CH_3$, $—OCH_3$, $—NH_2$ increases the basic strength, while electron withdrawing groups like $—NO_2$, $—X$, —COOH decreases the basic strength.

Alkylation

Amines undergo alkylation on reaction with alkyl halides.

$$\underset{\text{Ethylamine}}{CH_3CH_2NH_2} + \underset{\text{Ethyl bromide}}{CH_3CH_2Br} \longrightarrow \underset{\text{Diethylamine}}{(CH_3CH_2)_2NH} + HBr$$

$$\underset{\text{Diethylamine}}{(CH_3CH_2)_2NH} + \underset{\text{Ethyl bromide}}{CH_3CH_2Br} \longrightarrow \underset{\text{Triethylamine}}{(CH_3CH_2)_3N} + HBr$$

$$\xrightarrow{CH_3CH_2Br} \underset{\text{Tetraethylammonium bromide}}{(CH_3CH_2)_4\overset{+}{N}Br^-}$$

Similarly,

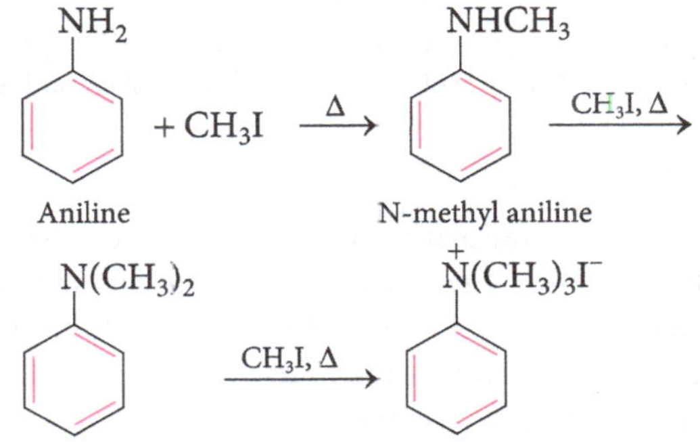

N,N-dimethylaniline Trimethylanilinium iodide

The process of conversion of a 1° amines into quaternary ammonium salt is called **Hofmann exhaustive alkylation.**

Acylation

Aliphatic and aromatic primary and secondary amines react with acid chlorides, anhydrides and esters by nucleophilic substitution reaction. This reaction is considered as replacement of hydrogen atom of $—NH_2$ or $>NH$ group by acyl group and the reaction is known as **acylation.** The reaction is carried out in the presence of a base stronger than amine like pyridine, which removes HCl so formed and shifts the equilibrium towards right hand side. The product obtained by acylation reactions are known as amides.

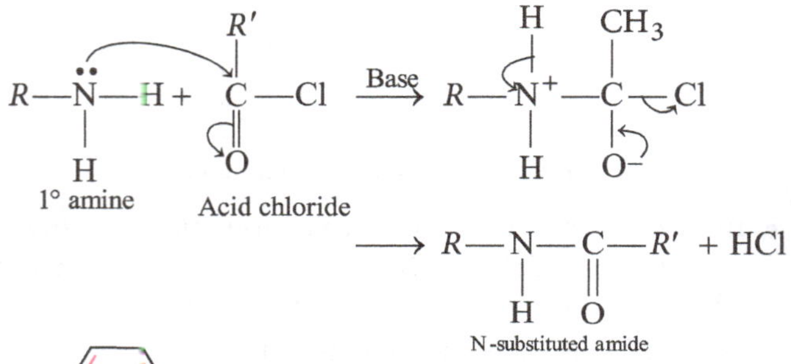

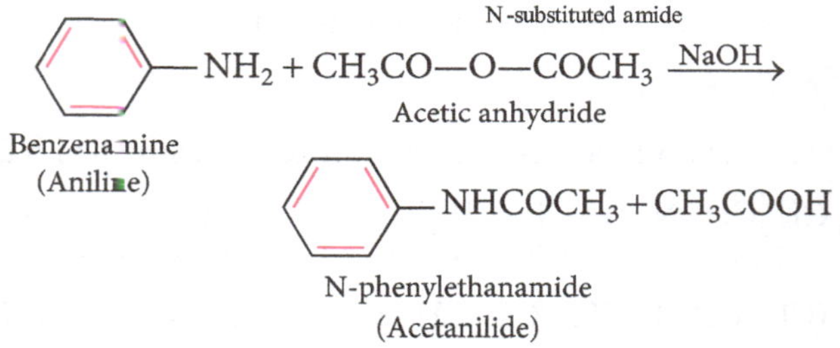

The process of introducing, $C_6H_5—\overset{O}{\overset{\|}{C}}—$ group in a molecule by treating amines with benzoyl chloride in the presence of a base is known as **benzoylation.**

$$\underset{\text{Methanamine}}{CH_3NH_2} + \underset{\text{Benzoyl chloride}}{C_6H_5COCl} \longrightarrow \underset{\text{N-methylbenzamide}}{CH_3NHCOC_6H_5} + HCl$$

Carbylamine Reaction

Primary amines (aliphatic and aromatic) on heating with chloroform and ethanolic potassium hydroxide form isocyanides or carbylamines which have a foul smell. This reaction is called **carbylamine reaction** or **isocyanide test** and is used to test primary amines.

In general,

$$\underset{\text{Amine}}{R—NH_2} + \underset{\text{Chloroform}}{CHCl_3} + alc.3KOH \xrightarrow{\Delta} \underset{\text{Alkyl or aryl isocyanide}}{R—NC} + 3KCl + 3H_2O$$

$$\underset{\text{Aniline}}{C_6H_5NH_2} + CHCl_3 + alc.3KOH \xrightarrow{\Delta} \underset{\text{Phenyl isocyanide}}{C_6H_5NC} + 3KCl + 3H_2O$$

Note **Secondary and tertiary amines** (both aliphatic and aromatic) do not give this test. Hence, this test is used to distinguish 1° amine from 2° and 3° amines.

9.7 Identification of 1°, 2° and 3° Amines

Following reactions can be used to distinguish between 1°, 2° and 3° amines.

I. Reaction with Nitrous Acid

Primary, secondary and tertiary amines react differently with nitrous acid (HNO_2) which is prepared *in situ* from a mineral acid and sodium nitrite.

Reactions with Nitrous Acid

Type of Amines	Method	Reactions Involved
Primary amines (1°)	Reacts with nitrous acid to form alcohol and nitrogen gas (as bubbles).	$R—NH_2 + HONO \longrightarrow ROH + N_2\uparrow + H_2O$
Secondary amines (2°)	Reacts with nitrous acid to form N-nitrosoamines which are water insoluble yellow oils. This reaction is also called **Libermann's nitrosoamine test.**	$R—\overset{R'}{\overset{\mid}{N}}—H + HONO \longrightarrow \underset{\text{N- nitrosoamine (yellow oil)}}{R—\overset{R'}{\overset{\mid}{N}}=O} + H_2O$
Tertiary amines (3°)	Reacts with nitrous acid to form trialkyl ammonium nitrite salts which are soluble in water.	$R_3N + HONO \longrightarrow \underset{\text{(Trialkyl ammonium nitrate)}}{R_3\overset{+}{N}HNO_2^-}$

Note Nitrogen gas liberated during reaction of primary aliphatic amines is used in estimation of amino acids and proteins.

II. Reaction with Arylsulphonyl Chloride

Benzenesulphonyl chloride $C_6H_5SO_2Cl$ (Hinsberg's reagent) reacts with primary and secondary amines to form sulphonamides. This can be shown in the table given below.

Reactions with Benzene Sulphonyl Chloride

Type of Amines	Method	Reactions Involved
Primary amines (1°)	Reacts with benzene sulphonyl chloride to yield monoalkyl sulphonamide which is soluble in alkali.	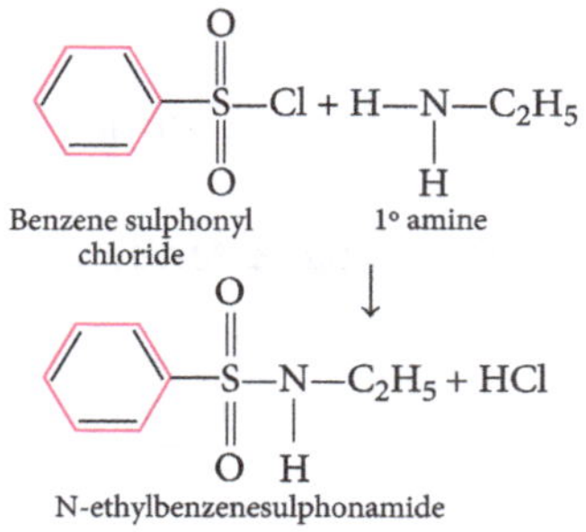
Secondary amines (2°)	Reacts with benzene sulphonyl chloride to yield N,N-diethylbenzene sulphonamide which is insoluble in alkali.	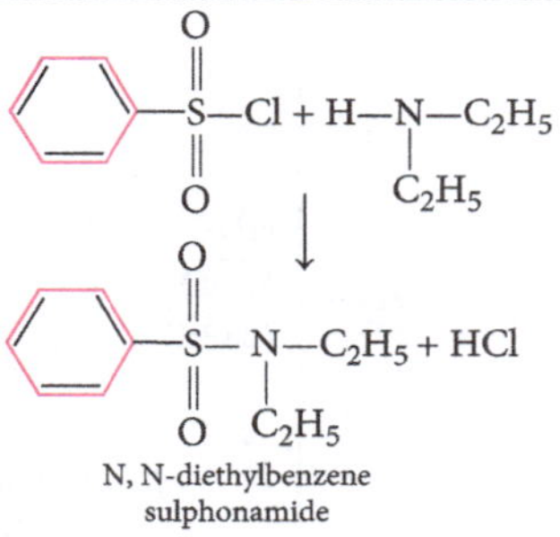
Tertiary amines (3°)	Do not react with benzenesulphonyl chloride.	

Note Now-a-days, benzenesulphonyl chloride is replaced by *p*-toluene sulphonyl chloride.

Electrophilic Substitution Reactions

In aniline, electron density at *ortho* and *para*-positions with respect to $—NH_2$ group is high. Therefore, $—NH_2$ group is *ortho* or *para*-directing and a powerful activating group.

(i) **Halogenation** (Bromination) In the absence of catalyst, aniline on treatment with bromine water at room temperature forms a white precipitate of 2, 4, 6-tribromoaniline.

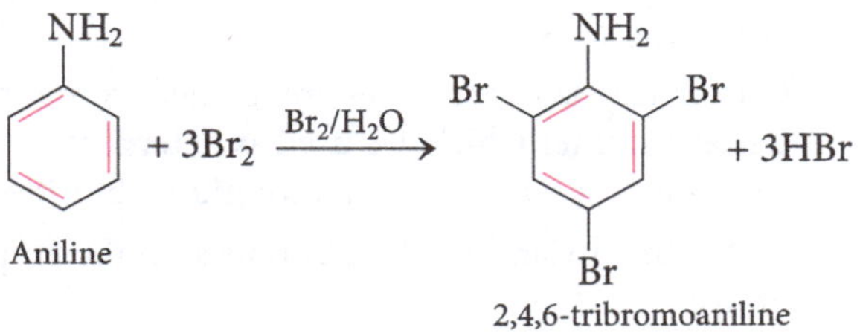

The main problem encountered during electrophilic substitution reaction of aromatic amine is that they have very high reactivity towards substitution at *ortho* and *para*-positions.

In order to get monohalogenated aniline derivative, the activating effect of $—NH_2$ group is controlled by protecting the $—NH_2$ group by acetylation with acetic anhydride and then halogenation is carried out. After halogenation, the acetyl group is removed by hydrolysis.

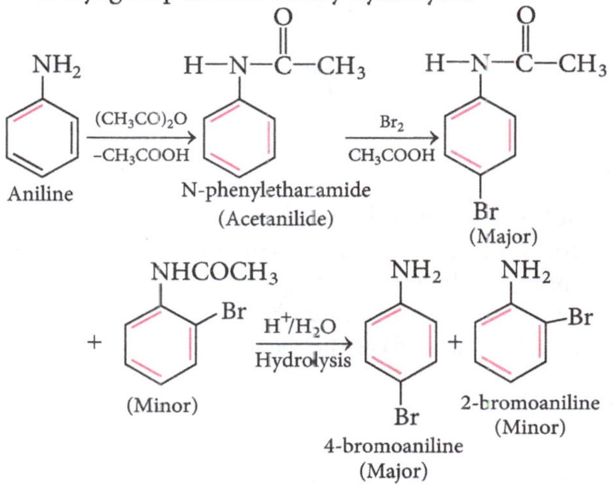

The lone pair of electrons on nitrogen of acetanilide interacts with oxygen atom due to resonance as shown below.

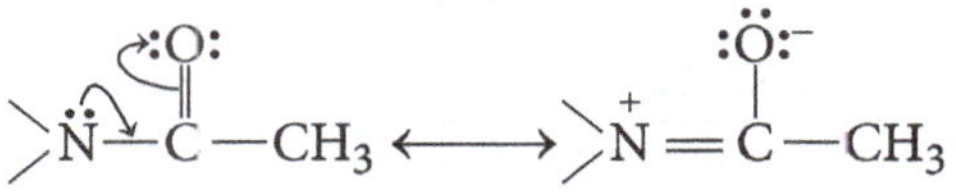

Hence, the lone pair of electrons on nitrogen is less available for donation to benzene ring by resonance. Therefore, activating effect of $—NHCOCH_3$ group is less than that of amino group.

(ii) **Nitration** In strongly acidic medium, aniline on nitration gives a mixture of *ortho*, *para* and significant amount of *meta*-nitroaniline. It is because aniline is protonated to form anilinium ion which is a *m*-directing group.

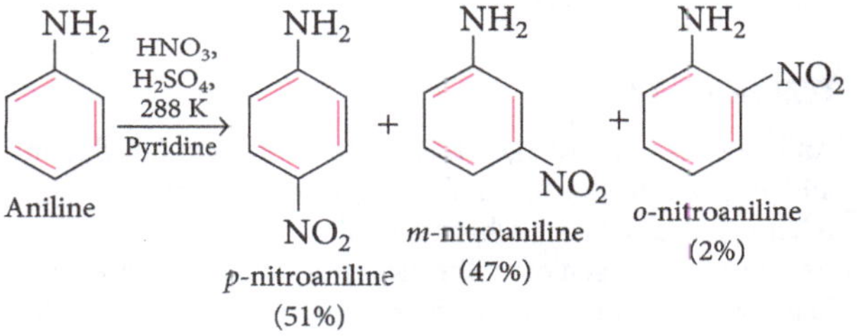

By protecting the $—NH_2$ group by acetylation with acetic anhydride, the reaction can be controlled and only *p*-nitro derivative as the major product is obtained.

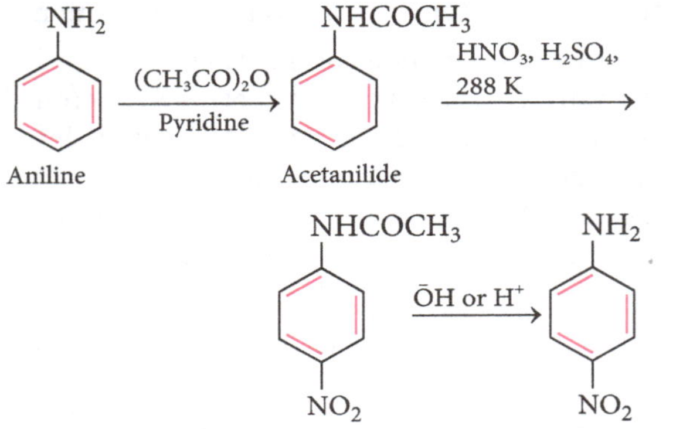

p-nitroacetanilide *p*-nitroaniline (Major)

(iii) **Sulphonation** Aniline when reacts with concentrated H_2SO_4, it forms anilinium hydrogen sulphate which on heating with H_2SO_4 at 455-475 K forms *p*-aminobenzene sulphonic acid (sulphanilic acid) as the major product.

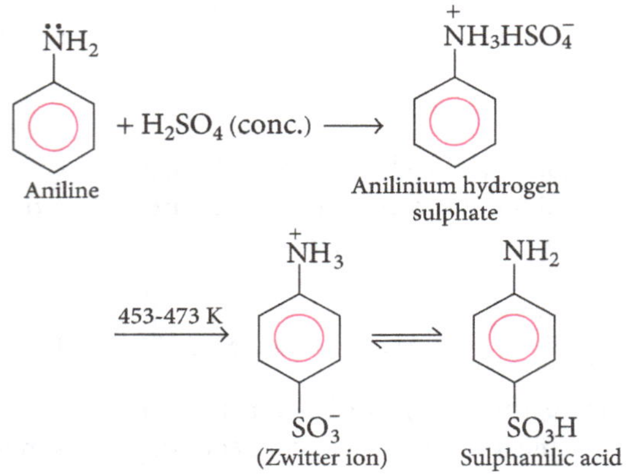

Zwitter ion

The ion which contains both positive and negative charges and also contains acidic and basic groups in the same molecule is known as Zwitter ion. e.g.

Structure of Zwitter ion

TEACHER'S TIP

Aniline does not undergo Friedel-Crafts reaction (alkylation and acetylation) due to salt formation with anhydrous $AlCl_3$, the Lewis acid, which is used as a catalyst.
As a result, nitrogen of aniline acquires positive charge and hence acts as a strong deactivating group for further reaction.

Chemical Reactions of Amines (At a glance)

(i) **Aliphatic/Aromatic Amines**

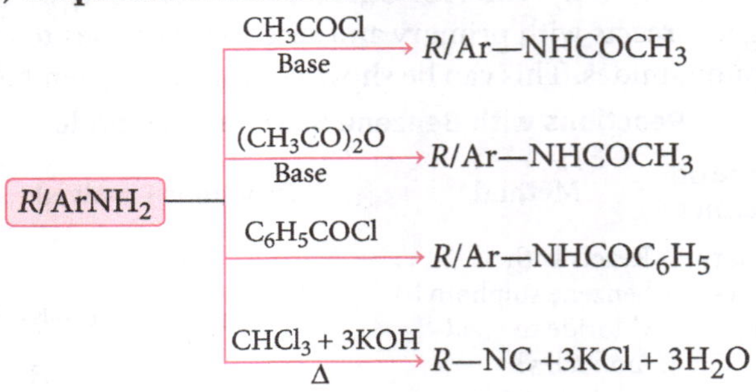

(ii) **Aromatic Amines**

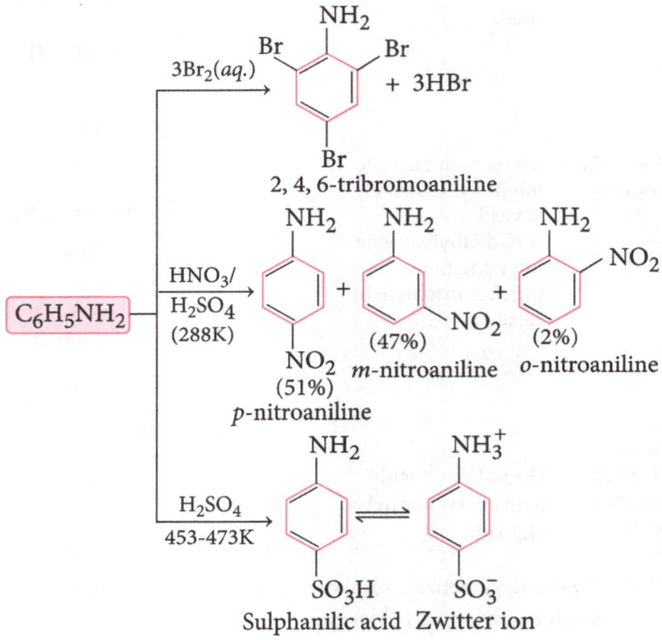

Uses of Amines

The uses of amines are as follows

- Aliphatic amines are used as solvents and intermediates in the manufacture of drugs namely adrenaline, ephedrine, novocain and benadryl.
- They are used as reagents in organic synthesis.
- Aromatic amines are used for the formation of polymers, dyes and drugs.
- Quaternary salts of amines are formed from long chain tertiary amines which are used as detergents, e.g. *n*-hexadecyl trimethylammonium chloride.
- N, N-dimethylaniline (DMA) is used in the preparation of dyes.

Quick Test 2

1. Give reasons for the following. *NCERT, CBSE 2024 C*

(i) pK_b of aniline is more than that of methylamine.

(ii) Ethylamine is soluble in water whereas aniline is not.

2. (i) Arrange the following in increasing order of their boiling points,

$C_2H_5OH, C_2H_5NH_2, (C_2H_5)_3N$ *CBSE 2023*

(ii) In the following reaction, which species behave as a Lewis base?

$$R—\ddot{N}H_2 + H—X \rightleftharpoons R—\overset{+}{N}H_3X^-$$

3. Complete the following acid-base reactions and name the products.

(i) $CH_3—CH_2—CH_2—NH_2 + HCl \longrightarrow$

(ii) $(C_2H_5)_3N + HCl \longrightarrow$ *NCERT Intext*

4. What is the role of pyridine in the acylation reaction of amines? *NCERT Exemplar*

5. Write the chemical reaction of aniline with benzoyl chloride and also write the name of the product obtained. *NCERT Intext*

6. Complete the following reactions.

(i) $C_6H_5NH_2 + CHCl_3 + \text{Alc. } 3KOH \longrightarrow$

(ii) $C_6H_5NO_2 \xrightarrow{Fe/HCl} A \xrightarrow[273\ K]{HNO_2} B$ *NCERT*

7. Complete the following reaction.

(i) $CH_3CH_2NH_2 + CHCl_3 + 3KOH\text{ (alc.)} \longrightarrow$

(ii) $C_6H_5NH_2 + H_2SO_4\text{ (conc.)} \longrightarrow$ *NCERT*

For Solutions, See QR Code on Pg. 356

9.8 Diazonium Salts

Diazonium salts are a group of organic compounds, having the general formula, $Ar\overset{+}{N}_2\bar{X}$, where Ar is abbreviated for the aryl group and $\bar{X}$ may be $Cl^-, Br^-, HSO_4^-, BF_4^-$, etc.

Nomenclature

The $\overset{+}{N}_2$, (i.e. $—\overset{+}{N}\equiv N$) is called **diazonium group (or diazo group)**. These are named by adding the suffix diazonium to the name of the parent hydrocarbon from which they are derived followed by the name of anion.

e. g. $C_6H_5\overset{+}{N}_2Cl^-$ is benzenediazonium chloride,
$C_6H_5N_2^+HSO_4^-$ is benzene diazonium hydrogensulphate.

Structure and Stability

The electronic structure of diazonium salts $(ArN_2^+X^-)$ is written as:

$$[Ar—\overset{+}{N}\equiv N: \longleftrightarrow Ar—\ddot{N}=\overset{+}{N}:]X^-$$

Primary aliphatic amines form highly unstable alkyl-diazonium salts.

Primary aromatic amines form arenediazonium salts, which are stable for a short time in solution at low temperature (0-5°C).

The stability of arenediazonium salt is due to the dispersal of the positive charge over the benzene ring.

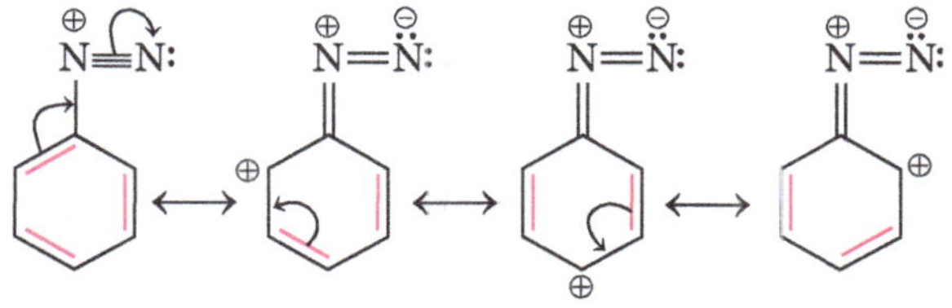

Note Resonance stabilisation is not possible in diazonium salts of aliphatic amines.

Methods of Preparation

Benzenediazonium chloride is prepared by the reaction of aniline with nitrous acid (which is produced by the reaction of $NaNO_2$ and HCl) at 273-278 K or 0-5°C.

$$C_6H_5NH_2 + NaNO_2 + 2HCl \xrightarrow{273\text{-}278\ K} C_6H_5\overset{+}{N}_2Cl^- + NaCl + 2H_2O$$

The conversion of primary aromatic amines into their diazonium salts is called **diazotisation**.

Due to its instability, the diazonium salt is not generally stored and is used immediately after its preparation.

Physical Properties

Physical properties of diazonium salts can be described as follows:

- Diazonium salts are generally colourless crystalline solids.
- These are readily soluble in water and stable in cold water. They react with water when warmed.
- These are unstable and decomposes in dry state, hence used in solution state.
- Their aqueous solutions are neutral to litmus and conduct electricity due to the presence of ions.
- Benzenediazonium fluoroborate is water insoluble and stable at room temperature.

Chemical Reactions

The chemical reactions of diazonium salts can be divided into two categories:

Reactions Involving Displacement of Nitrogen

Diazonium group being a very good leaving group, is substituted by other groups such as Cl^-, Br^-, I^-, CN^-, NO_2, H and OH^- which displace nitrogen from the aromatic ring. The nitrogen thus formed escapes from the reaction mixture as a gas.

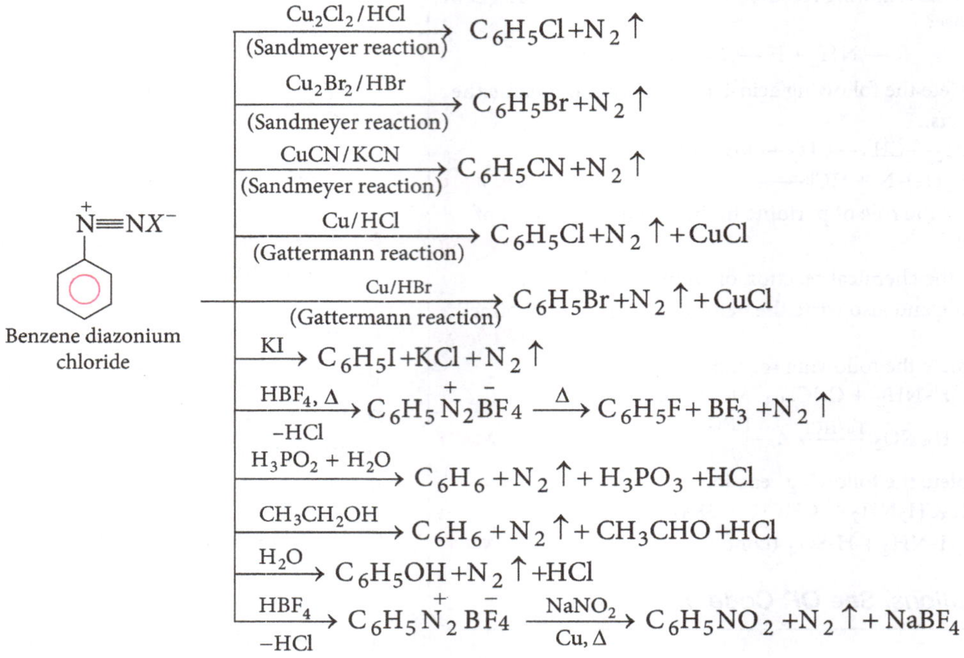

Note The yield in Sandmeyer reaction is better than Gattermann reaction.

Reactions Involving Retention of Diazo Group (Coupling Reactions)

Benzene diazonium chloride reacts with phenol in which phenol molecule at its *para*-position is coupled with diazonium salt to give the product *p*-hydroxyazobenzene, hence the reaction is known as **coupling reaction**. The azo products obtained having both the aromatic rings joined through the —N=N— bonds, are coloured and used as dyes.

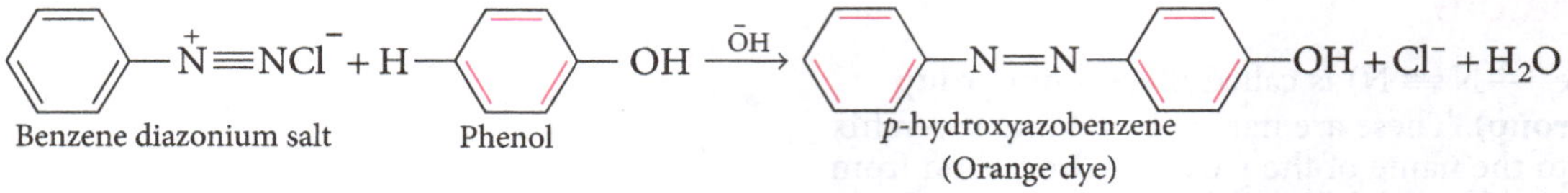

Similarly, the reaction of diazonium salt with aniline gives *p*-aminoazobenzene (yellow dye). This is an example of **electrophilic substitution reaction**.

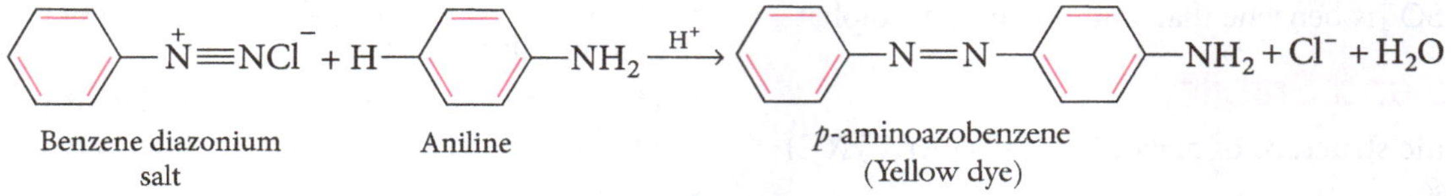

Note The reaction with phenols takes place in slightly alkaline medium ($pH = 9-10$), while with amines it occurs in slightly acidic medium ($pH = 4-5$).

Importance of Diazonium Salts in the Synthesis of Aromatic Compounds

These are important in the synthesis of aromatic compounds due to the following facts.

- These are very good intermediates for the introduction of —F, —Cl, —OH, —CN, —NO_2, etc., into the aromatic ring.
- Similarly, aryl fluorides and iodides cannot be prepared by the direct halogenation.
- Cyano group cannot be introduced by nucleophilic substitution of chlorine in chlorobenzene but cyanobenzene can be prepared from diazonium salts.
- Thus, replacement of diazo groups by the other groups is helpful in preparing those substituted aromatic compounds which cannot be prepared by the direct substitution in benzene or substituted benzene.

Quick Test 3

1. (i) Write a short note on diazotisation. *NCERT*

Or

The conversion of primary aromatic amines into diazonium salts is known as .... .

(ii) Complete the following reaction.

$$C_6H_5N_2Cl + C_2H_5OH \longrightarrow$$

NCERT, CBSE 2018, 2023

2. Complete the following reactions.

(i) $C_6H_5N_2Cl + H_3PO_2 + H_2O \longrightarrow$

(ii) $C_6H_5N_2Cl \xrightarrow[\text{(b) } NaNO_2/Cu]{\text{(a) } HBF_4}$ *NCERT*

3. Accomplish the following conversions.

(i) Aniline to 2, 4, 6-tribromofluorobenzene

(ii) Nitrobenzene to benzoic acid

(iii) Benzene to *m*-bromophenol *NCERT*

4. Give the structures of *A*, *B* and *C* in the following reactions.

(i) $C_6H_5\overset{+}{N_2}Cl^- \xrightarrow{CuCN} A \xrightarrow{H_2O/H^+} B \xrightarrow[\Delta]{NH_3} C$

(ii) $C_6H_5NO_2 \xrightarrow{Sn + HCl} A \xrightarrow[273\ K]{NaNO_2 + HCl} B \xrightarrow[\Delta]{H_2O/H^+} C$

NCERT, CBSE 2023

5. Convert :

(i) 3-methylaniline into 3-nitrotoluene.

(ii) Aniline into 1, 3, 5-tribromobenzene. *NCERT Intext*

6. Write the major product(s) in the following reactions.

(i) $C_6H_5N_2Cl \xrightarrow{KI} ?$

(ii) 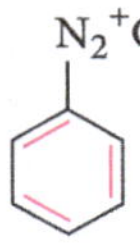 $\xrightarrow{Cu_2Cl_2/HCl}$? (iii) 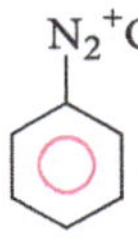 $\xrightarrow{CH_3CH_2OH}$

CBSE 2016, 2023

7. Give the structures of *A*, *B* and *C* in the following reactions.

(i) $C_6H_5NO_2 \xrightarrow{Fe/HCl} A \xrightarrow[273\ K]{NaNO_2 + HCl} B \xrightarrow[\Delta]{H_2O/H^+} C$

(ii) $C_6H_5NO_2 \xrightarrow{Fe/HCl} A \xrightarrow[273\ K]{HNO_2} B \xrightarrow{C_6H_5OH} C$ *NCERT*

(iii) 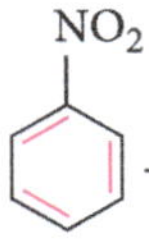 $\xrightarrow{Fe/HCl} A \xrightarrow[273\ K]{NaNO_2 + HCl} B \xrightarrow{C_2H_5OH} C$

CBSE 2023

8. Write a short note on coupling reaction.

Or Explain the coupling reaction. *NCERT*

For Solutions, See QR Code on Pg. 356

Mind Map

Amines

- Their solubility decreases but boiling point increases with increase in molecular mass.
- The order of bp is 1° > 2° > 3° amines.

Physical Properties

Diazonium Salts

They are colourless, unstable, soluble in water, neutral to litmus.

Methods of Preparation

(a) Reduction of —NO_2

$$R/Ar—NO_2 \xrightarrow[\text{metal + acid}]{H_2/Pd,\text{ethanol}} R/ArNH_2$$

(b) Reduction of —CN and —$CONH_2$

$$R—C \equiv N \xrightarrow[Na(Hg)/C_2H_5OH]{H_2/Ni} R—CH_2—NH_2$$

$$R—CONH_2 \xrightarrow[\text{(ii)} H_2O]{\text{(i)} LiAlH_4} R—CH_2NH_2$$

(c) Hofmann Bromamide Degradation Reaction

$$R—CONH_2 \xrightarrow[Br_2]{NaOH} R—NH_2$$

(d) Hofmann Ammonolysis

$$NH_3 \xrightarrow[-HX]{RX} RNH_2 \ (1°) \xrightarrow{RX} R_2NH \ (2°) \xrightarrow{RX} R_3N \ (3°) \xrightarrow{RX} R_4N^+X^-$$

(e) Gabriel-Phthalimide Reaction

Phthalimide $\xrightarrow{KOH}$ Potassium salt of phthalimide $\xrightarrow{R—X}$ N-alkyl phthalimide $\xrightarrow{NaOH}$ 1° amine (aliphatic)

Diazonium Salts ($C_6H_5\overset{+}{N}\equiv NCl^-$)

$$\underset{\text{1° amine (aromatic)}}{C_6H_5—NH_2} \xrightarrow[\text{or } NaNO_2 + HCl,\ 0\text{-}5°C]{HNO_2} \underset{\text{Diazonium salt}}{C_6H_5N_2^+Cl^-}$$

AMINES

Classification

Amines are classified as: 1° amine (RNH_2), 2° amine (R_2NH) and 3° amine (R_3N).

Nomenclature

Common Names

Aliphatic amine is named by suffix adding the amine to the alkyl group. In 2° and 3° amines prefix di or tri is put before the name of alkyl group.

IUPAC Names

Replacement of 'e' of alkane by the word amine. Suffix 'e' of arene is replaced by amine.

Chemical Properties

(a) Basicity

The order of basicity

(i) In gaseous state, 3° > 2° > 1° amine.

(ii) In aqueous solution, 2° > 3° > 1° > NH_3 if $R = C_2H_5$ and 2° > 1° > 3° > NH_3 if $R = CH_3$.

(b)

$R—NH_2$ (1°) $\xrightarrow[\text{Acylation}]{R'COCl,\ \text{base}}$ $R—N(H)—C(=O)—R'$ Substituted amide

$R—NH_2$ (1°) $\xrightarrow[\text{Carbylamine reaction}]{CHCl_3 + KOH,\ \Delta}$ $R—NC$

$R—NH_2$ (1°) $\xrightarrow[\text{Hinsberg's reagent}]{C_6H_5SO_2Cl}$ N-alkylbenzene sulphonamide (soluble in alkali)

R_2NH (2°) $\xrightarrow{\text{Hinsberg's reagent}}$ N,N-dialkylbenzene sulphonamide (insoluble in alkali)

R_3N (3°) $\xrightarrow{C_6H_5SO_2Cl}$ No reaction

RNH_2 — Electrophilic substitution (Here, $R = C_6H_5$)

- $\xrightarrow[H_2O]{Br_2}$ 2,4,6-Tribromoaniline
- (i) $(CH_3CO)_2O$/Pyridine (ii) Br_2/CH_3COOH (iii) OH^- or H^+ → 4-Bromoaniline
- $\xrightarrow[288\ K]{HNO_3,\ H_2SO_4}$ p-/m-/o-Nitroaniline (p-:51%, m-:47%, o-:2%)
- (i) $(CH_3CO)_2O$/Pyridine (ii) HNO_3, H_2SO_4, 288 K (iii) OH^- or H^+ → p-Nitroaniline
- (i) H_2SO_4 (ii) 453-473 K → Sulphanilic acid

Diazonium Salts

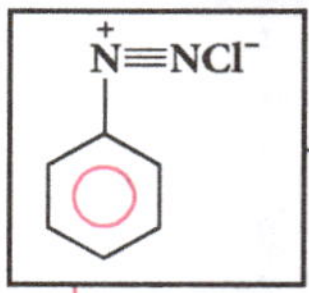

- $\xrightarrow[\text{(Sandmeyer's reaction)}]{Cu_2Cl_2/HCl}$ C_6H_5Cl
- $\xrightarrow[\text{Gattermann reaction}]{Cu/HX}$ C_6H_5X
- $\xrightarrow{KI}$ C_6H_5I
- $\xrightarrow[\Delta]{HBF_4}$ C_6H_5F
- $\xrightarrow{H_3PO_2 + H_2O}$ C_6H_6
- $\xrightarrow{H_2O}$ C_6H_5OH
- $\xrightarrow[\text{(Coupling reaction)}]{\text{Phenol},\ \bar{O}H}$ p-Hydroxy azobenzene (Orange dye)
- $\xrightarrow[\text{(Coupling reaction)}]{\text{Aniline},\ H^+}$ p-Amino azobenzene (Yellow dye)

Importance of Diazonium Salts in Synthesis of Aromatic Compounds

They are helpful in preparation of substituted compounds which cannot be prepared by the direct substitution in benzene or substituted benzene.

EXAM PATTERN QUESTIONS

Objective Type Questions

Multiple Choice Questions (MCQs)

[1 Mark]

1. **Which of the following is a 3° amine?** **NCERT Exemplar**
   (a) 1-methylcyclohexylamine
   (b) Triethylamine
   (c) *tert*-butylamine
   (d) N-methylaniline

2. **Which of the following reagents would not be a good choice for reducing an aryl nitro compound to an amine?** **NCERT Exemplar**
   (a) H_2(excess)/Pt (b) $LiAlH_4$ in ether
   (c) Fe and HCl (d) Sn and HCl

   Or

   Which of the following would not be a good choice for reducing nitrobenzene to aniline? **CBSE 2023**
   (a) H_2/Ni (b) $LiAlH_4$
   (c) Fe and HCl (d) Sn and HCl

3. **The best reagent for converting propanamide into propanamine is** **CBSE 2025**
   (a) excess H_2
   (b) Br_2 in aqueous NaOH
   (c) iodine in the presence of red phosphorus
   (d) $LiAlH_4$ in ether

4. **Ammonolysis of ethyl chloride followed by reaction of the amine so formed with 1 mole of methyl chloride gives an amine that** **CBSE SQP 2025**
   (a) reacts with Hinsberg reagent to form a product soluble in an alkali
   (b) on reaction with nitrous acid, produced nitrogen gas
   (c) reacts with benzene sulphonyl chloride to form a product that is insoluble in alkali
   (d) does not react with Hinsberg reagent

5. **In order to prepare a 1° amine from an alkyl halide with simultaneous addition of one —CH_2 group in the carbon chain, the reagent used as source of nitrogen is ....** **NCERT Exemplar**
   (a) Sodium amide, $NaNH_2$
   (b) Sodium azide, NaN_3
   (c) Potassium cyanide, KCN
   (d) Potassium phthalimide, $C_6H_4(CO)_2N^-K^+$

6. **The graphs below show the solubility of a primary, a secondary and a tertiary aliphatic amine *I*, *J* and *K* in water, at the same temperature. The number of carbon atoms in each of the compounds is three. Amine *I* is the tertiary amine, amine *J* is the primary amine and amine *K* is the secondary amine.**

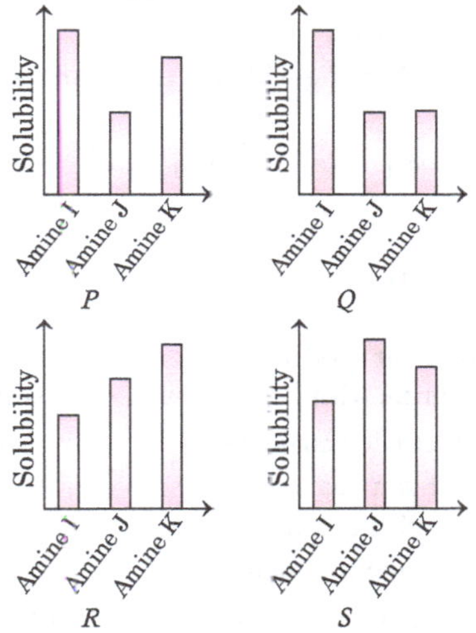

   Which of the following graphs identifies the three amines correctly? **Competency Based Que.**
   (a) *P* (b) *Q* (c) *R* (d) *S*

7. **The solubility in water of $C_6H_5NH_2$ (I), $(C_2H_5)_2NH$(II) and $C_2H_5NH_2$ (III) increase in the order of:** **Diksha**
   (a) II < III < I (b) I < II < III
   (c) III < II < I (d) II < I < III

8. **Two isomers, n-$C_4H_9NH_2$ and $(C_2H_5)_2NH$ have molar mass of 73 each.**
   Which of the following statement is correct about their boiling points? **Competency Based Que.**
   (a) The boiling point of n-$C_4H_9NH_2$ is higher than that of $(C_2H_5)_2NH$.
   (b) The boiling point of $(C_2H_5)_2NH$ is higher than that of n-$C_4H_9NH_2$.
   (c) Both the amines will have the same boiling point.
   (d) The boiling point of both the amines will be lower than that of water.

9. **Which statement is wrong about amine?** Diksha

(a) Aniline and other arylamines are usually colourless but get coloured on storage due to atmospheric oxidation.
(b) Amines are less polar than alcohol.
(c) The order of boiling point of isomeric amines is: Primary < secondary < tertiary.
(d) Higher amines are essentially insoluble in water.

10. **Amongst the following, the strongest base in aqueous medium is ....** CBSE 2020

(a) CH_3NH_2 (b) $(CH_3)_2NH$
(c) $(CH_3)_3N$ (d) $C_6H_5NH_2$

Or **Out of the following, the strongest base in aqueous solution is**

(a) methylamine (b) dimethylamine
(c) trimethylamine (d) aniline CBSE 2024 C

11. **Among the following which is the strongest base?** CBSE 2023

(a) 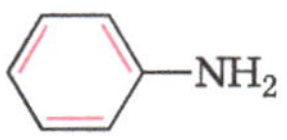
(b) 
(c) 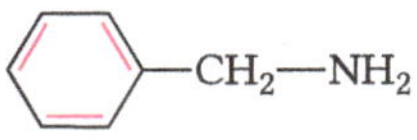
(d) 

12. **IUPAC name of product formed by reaction of methylamine with two moles of ethyl chloride is** CBSE SQP 2021

(a) N,N-dimethylethanamine
(b) N,N-diethylmethanamine
(c) N-methylethanamine
(d) N-ethyl-N-methylethanamine

13. **Match the reactions given in column I with the statements given in column II and choose the correct option from the codes given below.**

Column I	Column II
A. Carbylamine reaction	(i) Reaction of alkyl halides with NH_3
B. Hofmann bromamide reaction	(ii) Detection test for primary amines.
C. Ammonolysis	(iii) Amine with lesser no. of carbon atoms is obtained.

Codes

	A	B	C		A	B	C
(a)	(i)	(ii)	(iii)	(b)	(ii)	(iii)	(i)
(c)	(i)	(iii)	(ii)	(d)	(iii)	(i)	(ii)

14. **An organic compound (C_3H_9N) (*A*), when treated with nitrous acid, gave an alcohol and N_2 gas was evolved. (*A*) on warming with $CHCl_3$ and caustic soda gave (*C*), which on reduction gave isopropylmethylamine. Predict the compound (*A*).** Diksha

(a) $(CH_3)_2CH—NH_2$ (b) $CH_3—CH_2—NH—CH_3$
(c) $(CH_3)_2N—CH_3$ (d) $CH_3—CH_2—CH_2—NH_2$

15. **$—NH_2$ group in the aniline being an activating group proceeds reaction at**

(a) only *para*- position (b) only *ortho*- position
(c) *meta*- position (d) Both (a) and (b)

16. **The stability of arenediazonium ion is explained on the basis of resonance. Which of the following resonating structure is incorrect?**

(a) 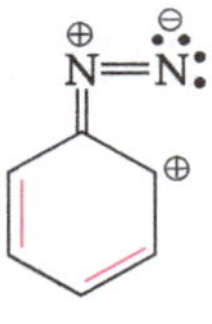
(b) 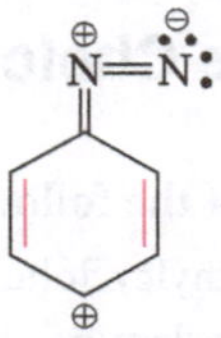
(c) 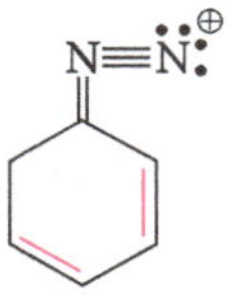
(d) 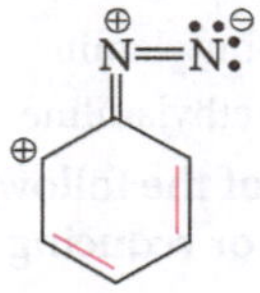

17. **The correct name of the given reaction is**

$$Ar—N_2^+X^- \xrightarrow[\text{Cu powder}]{\text{HBr}} Ar—Br + N_2$$ CBSE 2024

(a) Hofmann bromamide degradation reaction
(b) Gabriel phthalimide synthesis
(c) Carbylamine reaction
(d) Gattermann reaction

18. **The correct name of the given reaction is**

$$Ar—N_2^+X^- \xrightarrow{\text{CuCN/KCN}} Ar—CN + N_2$$ CBSE 2024

(a) Sandmeyer's reaction
(b) Gabriel phthalimide synthesis
(c) Carbylamine reaction
(d) Hofmann bromamide degradation reaction

19. **Benzene diazonium chloride on hydrolysis gives** CBSE 2023

(a) phenol (b) chlorobenzene
(c) benzene (d) aniline

20. **A student was preparing aniline in the lab. She took a compound "*X*" and reduced it in the presence of Ni as a catalyst. What could be the compound "*X*"?**

(a) Nitrobenzene (b) 1-nitrohexane
(c) Benzonitrile (d) 1-hexanenitrile

21. **The intermediate '*X*' in the following reaction is**

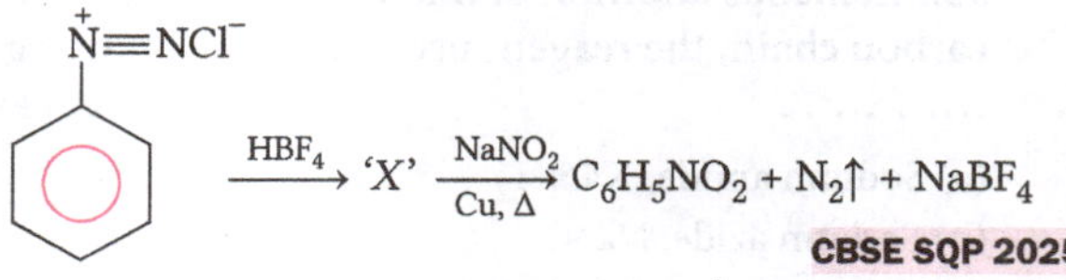

CBSE SQP 2025

(a) $C_6H_5N=BF_4$ (b) $C_6H_5\overset{+}{N}_2\overset{-}{B}F_4$
(c) $C_6H_5N_2^+BF_2^-$ (d) $C_6H_5N=NBF_4$

22. Consider the following table

Reactant	Reagent	Product
X	(i) $LiAlH_4$, ether (ii) H_2O	Ethylamine
Benzenediazonium chloride	Y	Benzene
Aniline	$CHCl_3 + alc.3KOH$	Z

X, Y and Z are

(a) X = Ethylnitrile, $Y = H_2O$, Z = Phenyl isocyanide
(b) X = Acetamide, $Y = HBF_4$, Z = Phenyl cyanide
(c) X = Acetamide, $Y = CH_3CH_2OH$, Z = Phenyl isocyanide
(d) X = Ethylnitrile, $Y = H_3PO_2 + H_2O$, Z = Phenyl cyanide

23. Which of the following reaction(s) is/are electrophilic substitution?

I. Bromination of acetanilide
II. Coupling reaction of aryl diazonium salts
III. Diazotisation of aniline
IV. Acylation of aniline

Choose the correct answer from the options given below.

(a) I and II (b) I, II and III
(c) III and IV (d) I and IV

24. Arjuna want to prepare an yellow dye. Which of the following species he should take for his experiment?

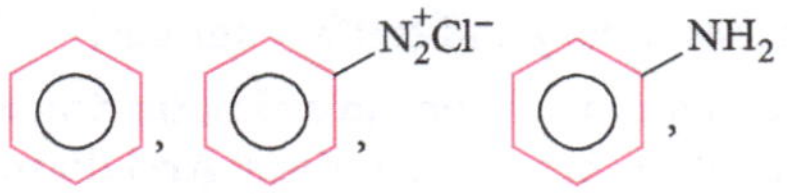

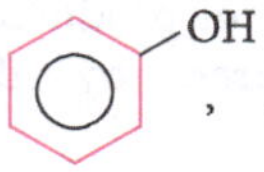

, HCl, $KMnO_4$, $K_2Cr_2O_7$

(a) 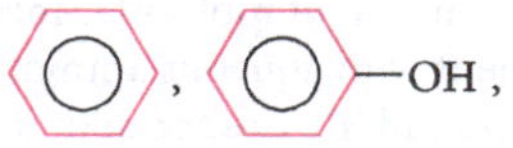

, HCl

(b) 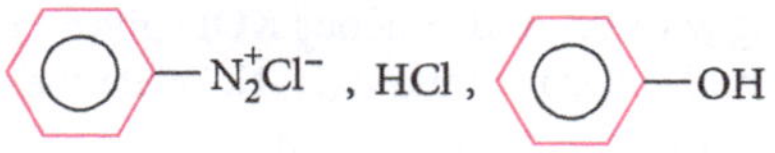

(c) 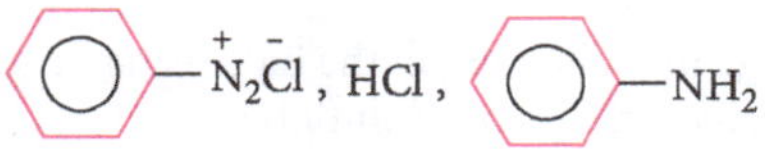

(d) 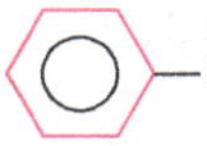 —NH_2, HCl, β-napthol

25. Which of the following compound will not undergo azo coupling reaction with benzene diazonium chloride? NCERT Exemplar

(a) Aniline
(b) Phenol
(c) Anisole
(d) Nitrobenzene

Assertion -Reason [1 Mark]

Directions (Q. Nos. 26-36) In the following questions. An Assertion (A) is followed by a corresponding Reason (R). Use the following keys to choose the appropriate answer.

(a) Both (A) and (R) are true and (R) is the correct explanation of (A).
(b) Both (A) and (R) are true, but (R) is not the correct explanation of (A).
(c) (A) is true, but (R) is false.
(d) (A) is false, but (R) is true.

26. Assertion (A) Only a small amount of HCl is required in the reduction of nitro compounds with iron scrap and HCl in the presence of steam.

Reason (R) $FeCl_2$ formed gets hydrolysed to release HCl during the reaction. NCERT Exemplar

27. Assertion (A) Hofmann's bromamide reaction is given by primary amides.

Reason (R) Primary amines are less basic than secondary amines. NCERT Exemplar

28. Assertion (A) Aniline cannot be prepared by Gabriel phthalimide synthesis.

Reason (R) Aryl halides do not undergo nucleophilic substitution. Competency Based Que.

29. Assertion (A) Tertiary butyl amine can be prepared by the action of —NH_3 on *tert*-butyl bromide.

Reason (R) Tertiary butyl bromide being 3° alkyl halide prefers to undergo elimination on the treatment with a base.

30. Assertion (A) Acylation of amines gives a monosubstituted product, whereas alkylation of amines gives polysubstituted product.

Reason (R) Acyl group sterically hinders the approach of further acyl groups. NCERT Exemplar

31. Assertion (A) In acylation reaction of amines, equilibrium shifts to the right hand side in the presence of pyridine.

Reason (R) In the presence of strong base, HCl is removed and reaction shifts toward the right hand side.

32. Assertion (A) N, N-diethylbenzene sulphonamide is insoluble in alkali.

Reason (R) Sulphonyl group attached to nitrogen atom is strong electron withdrawing group. NCERT Exemplar

33. Assertion (A) In strongly acidic solutions, aniline becomes more reactive towards electrophilic reagents.

Reason (R) The amino group being completely protonated in strongly acidic solution, the lone pair of electrons on the nitrogen is no longer available for resonance.

34. **Assertion** (A) Acetanilide is less basic than aniline.

Reason (R) Acetylation of aniline results in decrease of electron density on nitrogen. **NCERT Exemplar**

35. **Assertion** (A) Besides *ortho*-and *para*-nitroaniline, nitration of aniline in an acidic medium also gives the *meta* derivative.

Reason (R) In acidic medium aniline gets protonated forming anilinium ion. **Competency Based Que.**

36. **Assertion** (A) Benzene diazonium salts are soluble in water.

Reason (R) They are covalent in nature, so they are soluble in water.

Case-Study [4 Marks]

37. Read the given case and answer the questions that follow.

Organic compounds containing amine as functional group are present in wide variety of compounds namely amino acids, hormones, neurotransmitters, DNA, alkaloids, dyes etc. Drugs including nicotine, morphine, codein, heroin, etc., which have physiological effects on human also contain —NH group in one form or another. Amines are basic in nature due to presence of lone pair of electron on nitrogen. Adrenaline hormone and ephedrine drug, both containing secondary amino group are used for increasing blood pressure. Novacain, a synthetic compound contains both primary and tertiary amino group, is used as anaesthetic in dentistry. Benadryl, a widely used antihistamine drug contains tertiary amino group, quaternary ammonium salts of long chain, tertiary amines are used as cationic detergents. Diazonium salts are used for synthesis of azodyes and useful aromatic compounds.

(i) Convert aniline into *p*-nitroaniline.

(ii) Quaternary ammonium salts, derived from tertiary amines, particularly suitable as detergents. This is because of

(a) their ability to mimic hormones.
(b) their physiological effects on blood pressure.
(c) their high solubility in water and fats.
(d) their ability to react with DNA.

Or

Which of the following compounds contain secondary amino group?

(a) Adrenaline (b) Novocain
(c) Benadryl (d) Pyridine

(iii) The correct order of the basic strength of methyl substituted amines in aqueous solution is

(a) $(CH_3)_3N > CH_3NH_2 > (CH_3)_2NH$
(b) $(CH_3)_3N > (CH_3)_2NH > CH_3NH_2$
(c) $CH_3NH_2 > (CH_3)_2NH > (CH_3)_3N$
(d) $(CH_3)_2NH > CH_3NH_2 > (CH_3)_3N$

38. **Read the given case and answer the following questions.**

Amines are usually formed from nitro compounds, halides, amides, imides, etc. They exhibit hydrogen bonding which influences their physical properties. In alkyl amines, a combination of electron releasing, steric and hydrogen bonding factors influence the stability of the substituted ammonium cations in protic polar solvents and thus affect the basic nature of amines. In aromatic amines, electron releasing and withdrawing groups, respectively increase and decrease their basic character.

Influence of the number of hydrogen atoms at nitrogen atom on the type of reactions and nature of products is responsible for identification and distinction between primary, secondary and tertiary amines.

Presence of amino groups in aromatic ring enhances reactivity of the aromatic amines. Aryl diazonium salts provide advantageous methods for producing aryl halides, cyanides, phenols and arenes by reductive removal of the diazo group .

(i) An aromatic compound '*A*' of molecular formula $C_7H_6O_2$ on treatment with aqueous ammonia and heating forms compound '*B*'. Compound '*B*' on heating with Br_2 and aqueous KOH gives a compound '*C*' of molecular formula C_6H_7N. Write the structures of *A*, *B* and *C*.

(ii) Arrange the following in the increasing order of the pK_b values in aqueous solution :

$$C_2H_5NH_2\,,\,(C_2H_5)_2NH\,,\,(C_2H_5)_3N$$

Or

Aniline on nitration given a substantial amount of *m*-nitroaniline, though amino group is *o*/*p* directing. Why ?

(iii) Complete the following reaction giving main products.

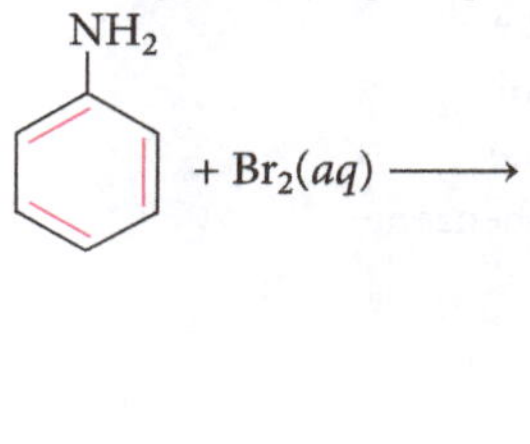

Subjective Type Questions

Short Answer Type I Questions [2 Marks]

1. How will you convert
(i) nitromethane into dimethylamine?
(ii) propanoic acid into ethanoic acid? **NCERT**

2. Suggest a route by which the following conversion can be accomplished.

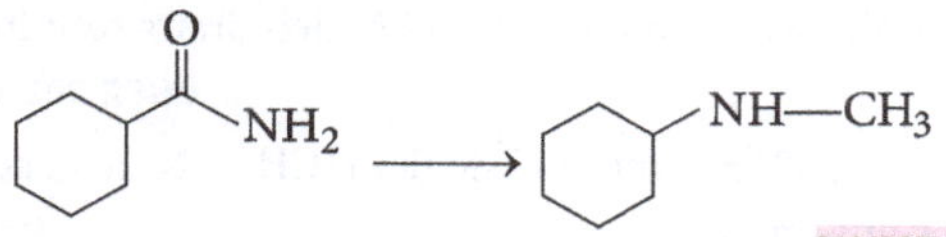

NCERT Exemplar

3. Write short notes on the following:
(i) Acylation (ii) Carbylamine reaction **NCERT**

Or

Write the reaction involved in carbylamine test. **CBSE 2023**

4. Of the two compounds *P* and *Q* given below, which one is more likely to be acidic in nature? Justify your answer. **Competency Based Que.**

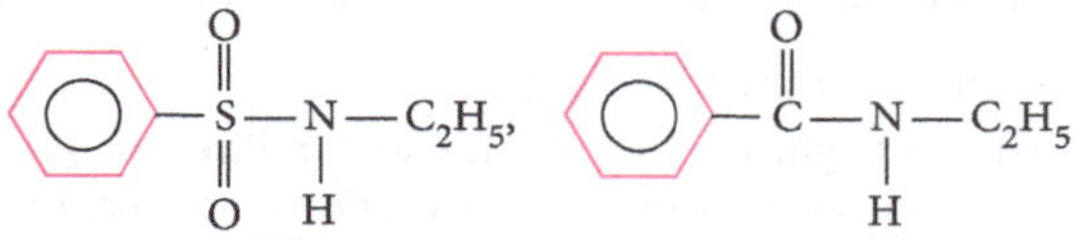

(*P*) (*Q*)

5. Give one chemical test to distinguish between the following pairs of compounds.
(i) Aniline and benzylamine
(ii) Aniline and N-methyl aniline **NCERT**

6. Account for the following:
(i) Aniline gets coloured on standing in air for a long time.
(ii) $MeNH_2$ is stronger base than MeOH. **NCERT Exemplar**

7. Why the hydrogen atoms of the methyl group in *o*-and *p*-nitrotoluenes are acidic in nature, while those of toluene are not?

8. Why does bromination of aniline, even under very mild conditions, gives 2, 4, 6- tribromoaniline instantaneously?

9. Identify *A* and *B* in each of the following reaction sequence
(i) $CH_3CH_2Cl \xrightarrow{NaCN} A \xrightarrow{H_2/Ni} B$
(ii) $C_6H_5NH_2 \xrightarrow[0\text{-}5°C]{NaNO_2/HCl} A \xrightarrow[H^+]{C_6H_5NH_2} B$ **CBSE 2025**

10. Give reasons for the following.
(i) Acetylation of aniline reduces its activation effect.

Or How can the activating effect of $—NH_2$ group in aniline be controlled? **CBSE 2023**
(ii) CH_3NH_2 is more basic than $C_6H_5NH_2$. **CBSE 2017**

11. (i) Identify the product of the following reaction:

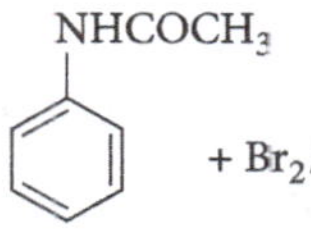

$+ Br_2/CH_3COOH \longrightarrow$

(ii) Convert bromoethane to propanamine. **CBSE 2023**

12. Give plausible explanation for each of the following
(i) Aromatic primary amines cannot be prepared by Gabriel phthalimide synthesis.
(ii) Amides are less basic than amines. **CBSE 2025**

13. Carry out the following conversions:
(i) Nitrobenzene to aniline
(ii) Aniline to phenol

Or **CBSE 2024**

(i) Write a chemical test to distinguish between dimethyl amine and ethanamine.
(ii) Write the product formed when benzene diazonium chloride is treated with KI.

14. Usually, benzene diazonium salts are unstable but benzene diazonium fluoroborate is stable. Why?

Short Answer Type II Questions [3 Marks]

15. Draw the structures of different isomers corresponding to the molecular formula, C_3H_9N. Write the IUPAC names of the isomers which will liberate nitrogen gas on treatment with nitrous acid. **NCERT Intext**

16. Account for the following. **CBSE SQP 2022 Term-II**
(i) Aniline cannot be prepared by the ammonolysis of chlorobenzene under normal conditions.
(ii) N-ethylethanamine boils at 329.3 K and butanamine boils at 350.8 K, although both are isomeric in nature.
(iii) Acylation of aniline is carried out in the presence of pyridine.

17. (i) Give the structures of *A*, *B* and *C* in the following reaction.

$$CH_3CN \xrightarrow{H_2O/H^+} A \xrightarrow[\Delta]{NH_3} B \xrightarrow{Br_2+KOH} C$$

(ii) Identify *A*, *B* and *C* in the following reactions.

$$CH_3CH_2Cl \xrightarrow{KCN} A \xrightarrow{H_2/Ni} B \xrightarrow{CH_3COCl/Base} C$$

CBSE 2017 C

18. Two beakers 'A' and 'B' contain aqueous solutions of methyl amine. It is observed that beaker A contains more OH^- than beaker 'B'

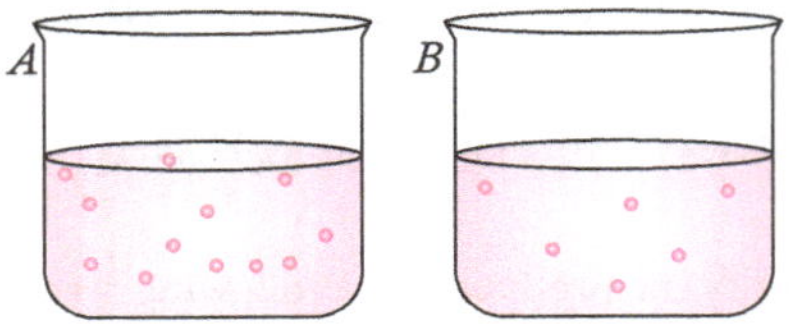

Prove which of the two solutions will have higher pK_b value and why? **Competency Based Que.**

19. $\underset{\substack{\text{(Optically active)} \\ (X)}}{C_5H_{13}N} \xrightarrow[\text{HCl}]{\text{Aq NaNO}_2} \underset{\substack{3^\circ \\ \text{alcohol}}}{Y} + \text{Other products}$

(i) Identify X and Y. (ii) Is Y optically active.

20. Write the main products of the following reactions.

(i) $CH_3CH_2NH_2 \xrightarrow[(0^\circ C)]{HNO_2}$

(ii)
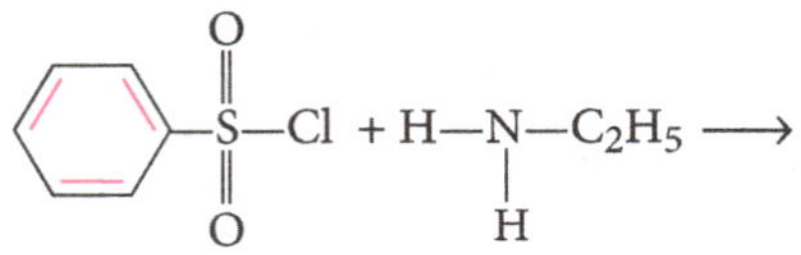

(iii)
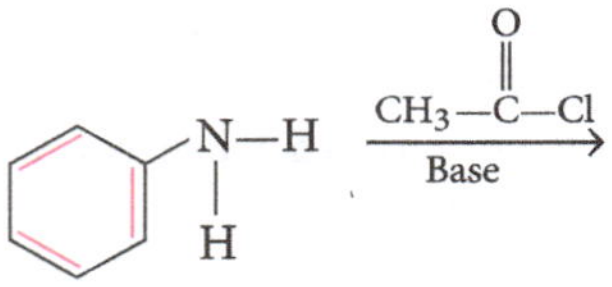

NCERT

21. What happens when **CBSE SQP 2022 Term-II**

(i) N-ethylethanamine reacts with benzene sulphonyl chloride ?

(ii) benzyl chloride is treated with ammonia followed by the reaction with chloromethane ?

(iii) aniline reacts with chloroform in the presence of alcoholic potassium hydroxide ?

22. How will you convert

(i) ethanamine into methanamine?

(ii) ethanoic acid into propanoic acid?

(iii) methanamine into ethanamine? **NCERT**

23. How will you convert

(i) ethanoic acid into methanamine?

(ii) hexane nitrile into 1-aminopentane?

(iii) methanol into ethanoic acid? **NCERT**

24. (i) Give a chemical test to distinguish between N-methylethanamine and N,N-dimethyl ethanamine. **CBSE SQP 2021**

(ii) Write the reaction for catalytic reduction of nitrobenzene followed by reaction of product so formed with bromine water.

(iii) Out of butan-1-ol and butan-1-amine, which will be more soluble in water and why?

25. An amine M reacts with sulphuric acid at 473 K to form compound N. Amine M cannot be prepared by the Gabriel phthalimide synthesis. It is the simplest amine of its type. **Competency Based Que.**

(i) Identify M and write its IUPAC name.

(ii) If electricity is passed through an aqueous solution of compound N and a bulb is connected to this circuit what will be your observation and why?

26. Give reasons for the following.

(i) Aniline does not undergo Friedel-Crafts reaction. **CBSE 2023, 2024 C**

(ii) $(CH_3)_2NH$ is more basic than $(CH_3)_3N$ in an aqueous solution. **CBSE 2023**

(iii) Primary amines have higher boiling point than tertiary amines. **CBSE 2016**

27. Give reason: **Diksha**

(i) Aniline does not undergo Friedel-Craft Reaction.

(ii) Although amino group is *ortho* and *para* directing in aromatic electrophilic substitution reactions, aniline on nitration gives a substantial amount of *m*-nitroaniline.

(iii) Aniline is a weaker base than cyclohexylamine. **Diksha**

28. Account for the following.

(i) Although, amino group is *o*-and *p*-directing in aromatic electrophilic substitution reactions, aniline on nitration gives a substantial amount of *m*-nitroaniline. **CBSE 2017, CBSE SQP 2019**

Or

Aniline on nitration gives good amount of *m*-nitroaniline, though —NH_2 group is *o/p* directing in electrophilic substitution reactions. **CBSE 2023**

(ii) Gabriel phthalimide synthesis is preferred for synthesising primary amines. **NCERT**

29. Accomplish the following conversions.

(i) Aniline to *p*-bromoaniline **CBSE 2023**

(ii) Benzamide to toluene

(iii) Aniline to benzyl alcohol **NCERT**

30. Give one chemical test to distinguish between the following pairs of compounds.

(i) Methylamine and dimethylamine

(ii) Secondary and tertiary amines

(iii) Ethylamine and aniline **NCERT**

31. Give the structures of A, B and C in the following reactions.

(i) $CH_3CH_2Br \xrightarrow{KCN} A \xrightarrow{LiAlH_4} B \xrightarrow[0^\circ C]{HNO_2} C$

(ii) $CH_3COOH \xrightarrow[\Delta]{NH_3} A \xrightarrow{NaOBr} B \xrightarrow{NaNO_2/HCl} C$

NCERT

(iii) 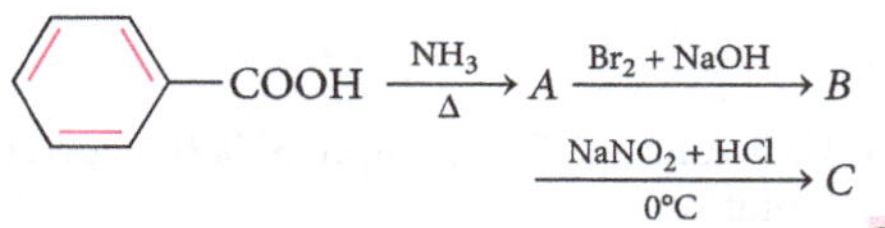

CBSE 2023

32. (i) Write the IUPAC name for the following organic compound. **CBSE SQP 2022 Term-II**

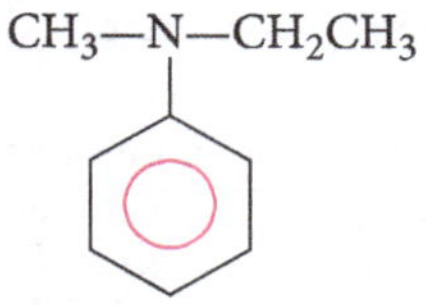

(ii) Complete the following.

$$C_6H_5NO_2 \xrightarrow{Sn/HCl} A \xrightarrow{Br_2/H_2O} B \xrightarrow[273\text{-}278\ K]{NaNO_2/HCl} C \xrightarrow[\Delta]{HBF_4} D$$

33. Write the structures of compounds A, B and C in the following reactions.

(i) $CH_3—COOH \xrightarrow{NH_3/\Delta} A \xrightarrow{Br_2/KOH(aq.)} B \xrightarrow{CHCl_3 + \text{Alc. KOH}} C$

(ii) $C_6H_5N_2^+BF_4^- \xrightarrow[\Delta]{NaNO_2/Cu} A \xrightarrow{Fe/HCl} B \xrightarrow{CH_3COCl/\text{pyridine}} C$ **CBSE 2017**

34. Write the products A and B in the following.

(i) 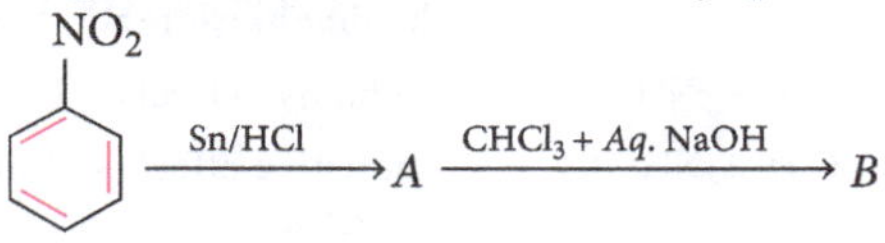

(ii) 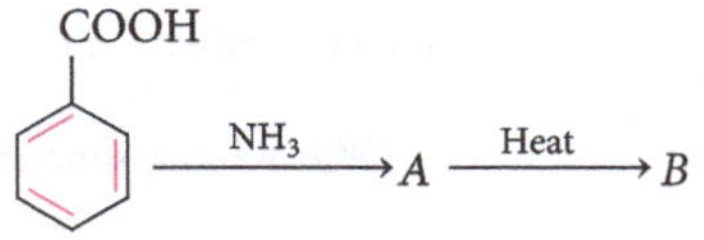

(iii) $C_6H_5\overset{+}{N}_2Cl^- \xrightarrow{Cu/HCl} A \xrightarrow{Cl_2/FeCl_3} B$

CBSE 2016 C

35. (i) Arrange the following in decreasing order of pK_b
Aniline, p-nitroaniline, p-methylaniline

(ii) Account for the following.

(a) Diazonium salts of aromatic amines are more stable than those of aliphatic amines.

(b) Methylamine in water reacts with $FeCl_3$ to precipitate hydrated ferric oxide. **CBSE 2025**

36. (i) What are coupling reactions? How does the electrophilic substitution reaction take place during this reaction?

(ii) List some important applications of diazonium salts.

Long Answer Type Questions [5 Marks]

37. An aromatic compound 'A' of molecular formula $C_7H_6O_2$, undergoes a series of reactions as shown below. Write the structures of A, B, C, D and E in the following reactions. **CBSE 2015**

$$\underset{A}{(C_7H_6O_2)} \xrightarrow{NH_3/\text{Heat}} C_6H_5CONH_2 \xrightarrow{LiAlH_4/\text{Ether}} D$$

$$C_6H_5CONH_2 \xrightarrow{Br_2 + NaOH} B \xrightarrow{(CH_3CO)_2O} C$$

$$B \xrightarrow{Br_2/(aq.)} E$$

38. (i) Write chemical equations involved when aniline is treated with the following reagents.

(a) $Br_2(aq)$

(b) HCl

(c) $NaNO_2$ + HCl at 0°C – 5°C

(ii) Write chemical reaction of aniline with benzoyl chloride and write the name of the product obtained.

(iii) Arrange the following in increasing order of boiling point: **CBSE 2025**

$C_2H_5OH, (CH_3)_2NH, C_2H_5NH_2$

39. An aromatic compound 'A' of molecular formula C_7H_7ON undergoes a series of reactions as shown below:

$$\underset{A}{(C_7H_7ON)} \xrightarrow{Br_2 + KOH} C_6H_5NH_2 \xrightarrow{CHCl_3 + NaOH} D$$

$$C_6H_5NH_2 \xrightarrow[273\ K]{NaNO_2 - HCl} B \xrightarrow{CH_3CH_2OH} C$$

$$B \xrightarrow{KI} E$$

Write the structures of A, B, C, D and E in the above reactions.

40. (i) Write the structures of main products when benzene diazonium chloride reacts with the following reagents:

(a) CuCN / KCN

(b) H_2O

(ii) Illustrate the following reactions giving suitable example in each case:

(a) Hofmann's Bromamide degradation reaction

(b) Carbylamine reaction

(c) Gabriel phthalimide synthesis **Diksha**

Hints & Solutions

Objective Type Questions

1. *(b)* Triethylamine is a 3° amine.

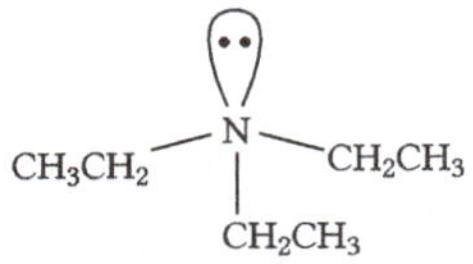

Triethylamine
(3° amine)

2. *(b)* $LiAlH_4$ is a strong reducing agent but is not suitable for reducing nitrobenzene to aniline. It reduces nitrobenzene to azobenzene or other partially reduced products instead of directly forming aniline.

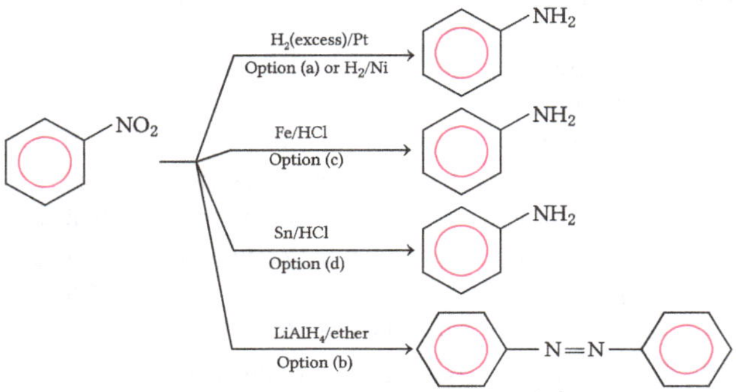

3. *(d)* The best reagent for converting propanamide into propanamine is $LiAlH_4$ in ether.

$$\underset{\text{(Propanamide)}}{CH_3-CH_2-\overset{\overset{\displaystyle O}{\|}}{C}-NH_2} \xrightarrow{LiAlH_4 \text{ in ether}} \underset{\text{Propanamine}}{CH_3-CH_2-CH_2-NH_2}$$

4. *(c)* Ethyl chloride (C_2H_5Cl) on reaction with ammonia (NH_3) undergoes ammonolysis to produce ethylamine ($C_2H_5NH_2$) and hydrochloric acid (HCl).

Ethylamine then reacts with one mole of methyl chloride (CH_3Cl) to form N-ethylmethylamine. N-ethylmethylamine is a secondary amine, thus on treating with Hinsberg's reagent (benzenesulphonyl chloride), it forms a product that is insoluble in alkali. This is because, the secondary amine formed does not contain α-hydrogen atom attached to nitrogen, which is acidic in nature.

5. *(c)* $RX + KCN \longrightarrow RCN + KX$

$$RCN \xrightarrow{\text{Raney Ni}/H_2} R-CH_2NH_2$$

6. *(d)* The degree of solubility of amines in water is primary amines > secondary amines > tertiary amines. Thus, amine *J* (Primary amine) will have highest solubility followed by *K* (Secondary amine) and *I* (Tertiary amine). Thus, graph '*S*' is the correct representation.

7. *(b)* $C_2H_5NH_2$ contains two H—atoms whereas $(C_2H_5)NH$ contains only one H—atom. Thus, $C_2H_5NH_2$ undergoes more extensive H-bonding than $(C_2H_5)_2NH$. Hence, the solubility in water of $C_2H_5NH_2$ is more than that of $(C_2H_5)_2NH$.

Further, the solubility of amines decreases with increase in the molecular mass. This is because the molecular mass of amines increases with an increase in the size of the hydrophobic part. The molecular mass of $C_6H_5NH_2$ is greater than that of $C_2H_5NH_2$ and $(C_2H_5)_2NH$.

Thus, the correct order is I < II < III.

8. *(a)* As primary amine has higher boiling point than secondary amine.

Thus, the boiling point of n-$C_4H_9NH_2$ is higher than that of $(C_2H_5)_2NH$.

9. *(c)* The correct order of boiling points for isomeric amines is primary > secondary > tertiary.

This is because tertiary amines lack free hydrogen atoms for bonding. So, there is no intermolecular association.

10. *(b)*

	Compound	Factors responsible for basic character
(a)	CH_3-NH_2	Inductive effect (+ *I*)
(b)	$(CH_3)_2NH$	Inductive effect (+*I*) and solvation
(c)	$(CH_3)_3N$	Inductive effect (+*I*)
(d)	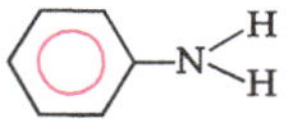	– *I* effect and resonance

Since, + *I*-effect and solvation increases basic character, while –*I*-effect and resonance decreases basic character. Hence, correct choice is (b).

11. *(c)* 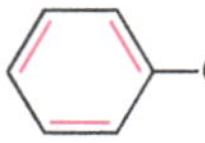 $-CH_2NH_2$ is the strongest base among the given bases. Due to the presence of methylene group between amino group and benzene ring, the resonance between the lone pair of electrons on N and the benzene ring is not possible.

Hence, the lone pair can be readily donated and therefore, benzylamine is the strongest base among the other given options.

12. *(d)* IUPAC name of product formed by reaction of methylamine with two moles of ethyl chloride is N - ethyl - N - methylethanamine.

Complete reaction is as follows:

$$CH_3NH_2 \xrightarrow{C_2H_5Cl} CH_3-\overset{H}{\overset{|}{N}}-C_2H_5 \xrightarrow{C_2H_5Cl} H_3C-\overset{C_2H_5}{\overset{|}{N}}-C_2H_5$$

Methyl amine — N-methyl ethanamine — N-ethyl-N-methyl ethanamine

13. (b) • Carbylamine reaction is used as a detection test for identification of primary amines.
- In Hoffmann Bromamide degradation reaction, amine containing one carbon less than the starting amide is produced.
- Ammonolysis is a reaction of alkyl halides with ammonia, i.e. NH_3. In this reaction, ammonia acts as a nucleophile and displaced the halogen atom.

Thus, the correct match is A-(ii), B-(iii), C-(i).

14. (a) The given amine gives alcohol when treated with nitrous acid, so it should be a primary amine.
As it also gives isopropylmethyl amine in carbylamine test, it should be an isopropyl amine and not *n*-propyl amine.

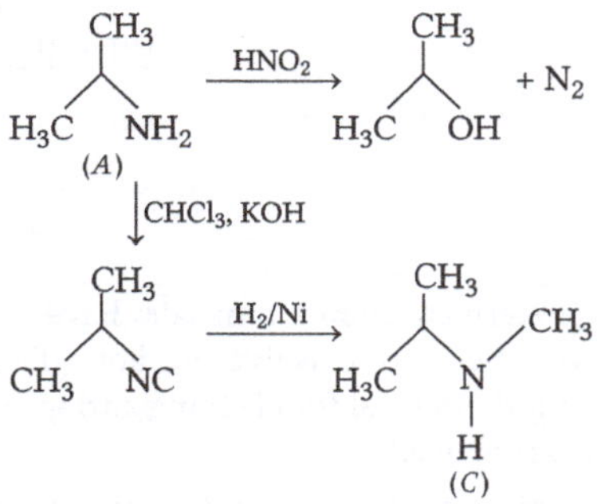

15. (d) *Ortho* and *para*-positions to the $-NH_2$ group have high electron density. Thus, $-NH_2$ group is *ortho* and *para*-directing and a powerful activating group.

16. (c) The stability of arenediazonium ion is explained on the basis of resonance as.

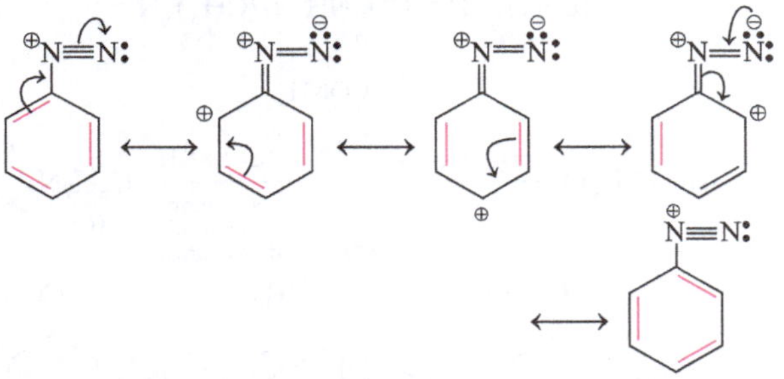

17. (d) The given reaction is Gattermann reaction.

18. (a) The correct name of the given reaction is Sandmeyer's reaction.

19. (a)

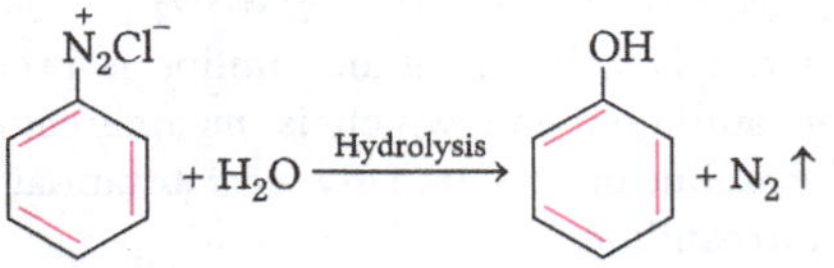

Benzene diazonium chloride — Phenol

20. (a) Nitrobenzene is the compound *X*
Nitrobenzene on reduction in the presence of nickel as a catalyst forms aniline.

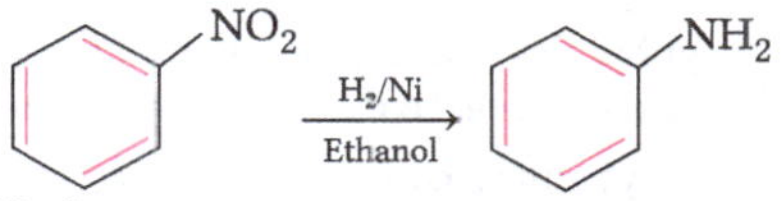

Nitrobenzene (*X*) — Aniline

21. (b) The intermediate '*X*' is $C_6H_5\overset{+}{N}_2\overset{-}{B}F_4$.

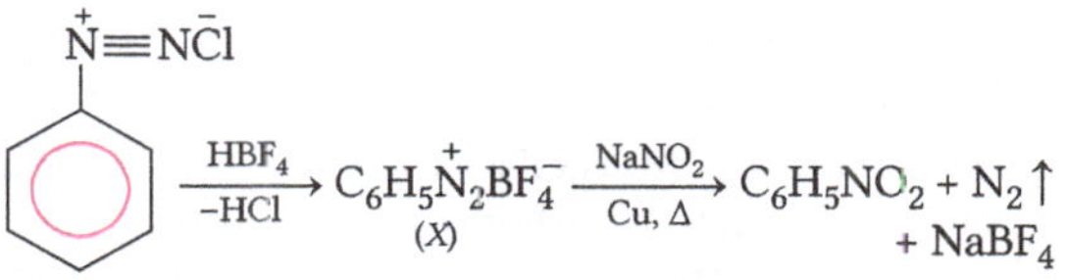

22. (c) The complete sequence of the given reactions are as follows :

- $CH_3CONH_2 \xrightarrow[\text{(ii) } H_2O]{\text{(i) } LiAlH_4\text{, Ether}} CH_3CH_2NH_2$
  Acetamide (*X*) — Ethylamine
- $C_6H_5N_2^+Cl^- \xrightarrow{CH_3CH_2OH\ (Y)} C_6H_6 + N_2\uparrow + CH_3CHO + HCl$
  Benzenediazonium chloride — Benzene
- $C_6H_5NH_2 + CHCl_3 + \text{Alc. } 3KOH \xrightarrow{\Delta} C_6H_5NC + 3KCl + 3H_2O$
  Aniline — Phenyl isocyanide (*Z*)

Hence, correct option is (c)

23. (a) Reactions (I) and (II) are electrophilic substitution reactions while reactions (III) and (IV) are nucleophilic substitution reactions.

24. (c) For preparation of an orange dye;
phenol, diazonium salt and HCl is required.

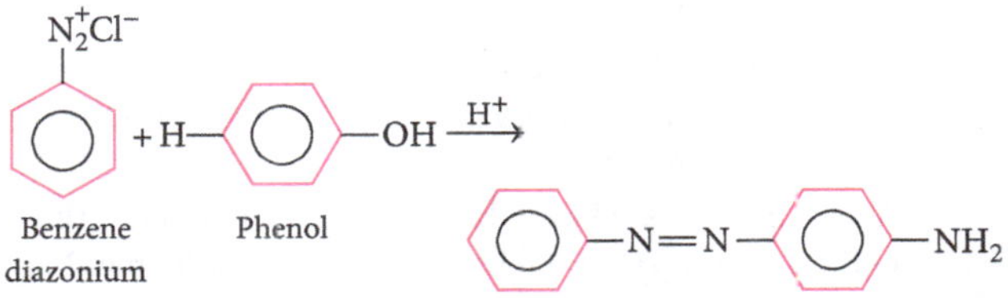

Benzene diazonium chloride — Phenol — *p*-aminoazobenzene (Yellow dye)

25. (d) Nitrobenzene will not undergo azo coupling reaction with benzene diazonium chloride, while other three undergo diazo coupling reaction very easily. Diazonium cation is a weak E^+ and hence reacts with electron rich compounds containing electron donating groups, i.e., $-OH$, $-NH_2$ and $-OCH_3$ groups and not with compounds containing electron withdrawing group, i.e., NO_2 etc.

26. (a) Only a small amount of HCl is required in the reduction of nitro compounds with iron scrap and HCl in the presence of steam, just to initiate the reaction as $FeCl_2$ formed gets hydrolysed to release HCl during the reaction.

27. (b) Hofmann's bromamide reaction is given by amides and resulting amines contain one C less than the parent amide. Moreover, primary amines are less basic than secondary and tertiary amines.

Thus, both (A) and (R) are true, but (R) is not the correct explanation of (A).

28. (c) Assertion is true, but Reason is false. The correct Reason is aryl halides undergo nucleophilic substitution reaction but are less reactive towards the same.

29. (d) Tertiary butyl amine cannot be prepared by the action of —NH_3 on *tert*-butyl bromide. This is because *tert*-butyl bromide prefer to undergo elimination rather than substitution on treatment with a base. The product is *iso*-butylene rather than *tert*-butylamine. Hence, (A) is false, but (R) is true.

30. (c) (A) is ture, but (R) is false. The correct (R) is the acyl group being electron withdrawing in nature reduces the nucleophilicity of the nitrogen atom and prevents further substitution.

31. (a) In acylation reaction of amines, equilibrium shifts to the right side in the presence of pyridine because it is a stronger base than amine which removes HCl so formed in the reaction. Thus, both (A) and (R) are true and (R) is the correct explanation of (A).

32. (b) N, N-diethylbenzene sulphonamide is insoluble in alkali because it has no acidic hydrogen. Moreover, sulphonyl group attached to nitrogen atom is an electron withdrawing group.

Thus, both (A) and (R) are true, but (R) is not the correct explanation of (A).

33. (d) The amino group being completely protonated in acidic solution, the lone pair of electrons on the nitrogen atom is no longer available for resonance. Hence, aniline becomes less reactive towards electrophilic reagents.

Thus, (A) is false, but (R) is true.

34. (a) Both (A) and (R) are true and (R) is the correct explanation of (A).

Acetanilide is less basic than aniline as in amides, the carbonyl group (C=O) has a stronger dipole than N—C dipole. Therefore, the ability of N—C group to act as H-bond acceptor (as a base) is restricted in the presence of a C=O dipole.

35. (a) Both (A) and (R) are true and (R) is the correct explanation of (A).

In strongly acidic medium, aniline is protonated to form the anilinium ion.

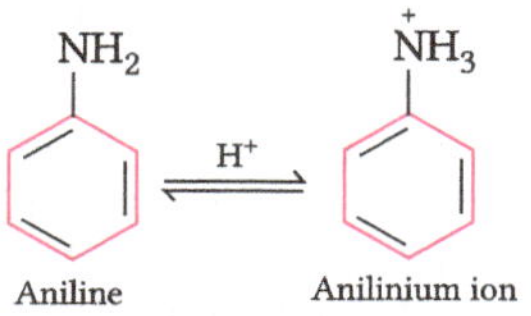

Since, anilinium ion so formed is *meta* -directing, thus besides *ortho* and *para* derivatives, significant amount of *meta* derivatives is also formed.

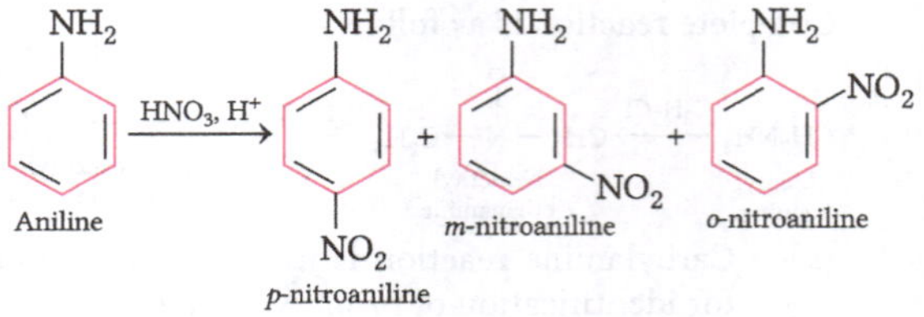

36. (c) Benzene diazonium salts are soluble in water because they are ionic in nature. Thus, (A) is true, but (R) is false.

37. (i)

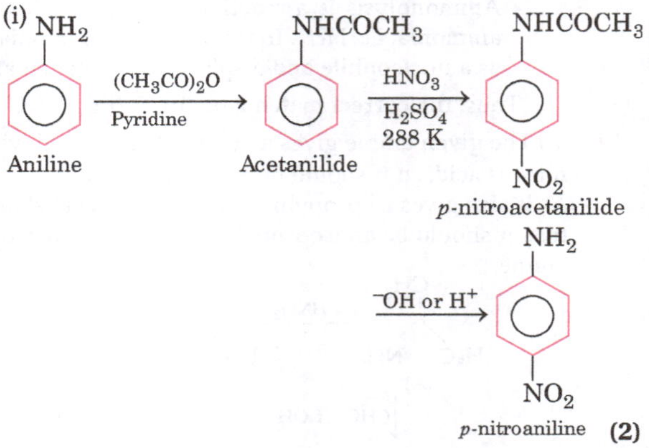

(2)

(ii) (c) Quaternary ammonium salts have a structure that allows them to dissolve in both fats and water, making them ideal for cleaning surfaces where grease removal is needed. **(1)**

Or (a) Adrenaline contains secondary amino group, whereas novocain, pyridine and benadryl contains tertiary amino group. **(1)**

(iii) (d) The correct order of basic strength of methyl substituted amines in aqueous medium will be

$$\underset{(2°)}{(CH_3)_2NH} > \underset{(1°)}{CH_3NH_2} > \underset{(3°)}{(CH_3)_3N}$$ **(1)**

38.

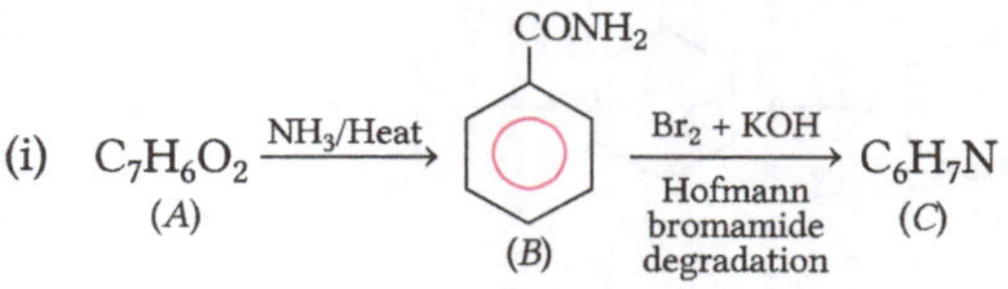

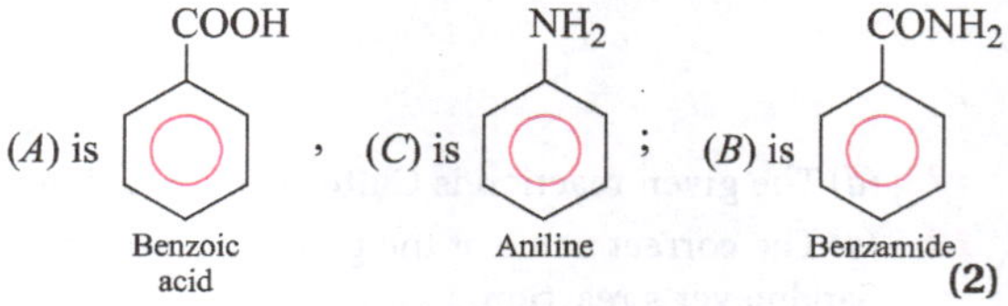

(2)

(ii) $(C_2H_5)_2NH > (C_2H_5)_3N > C_2H_5NH_2$ **(1)**

Or In strongly acidic medium, aniline is protonated to give anilinium ion which is *meta*-directing. That's why aniline on nitration gives a substantial amount of *m*-nitroaniline. **(1)**

(iii) 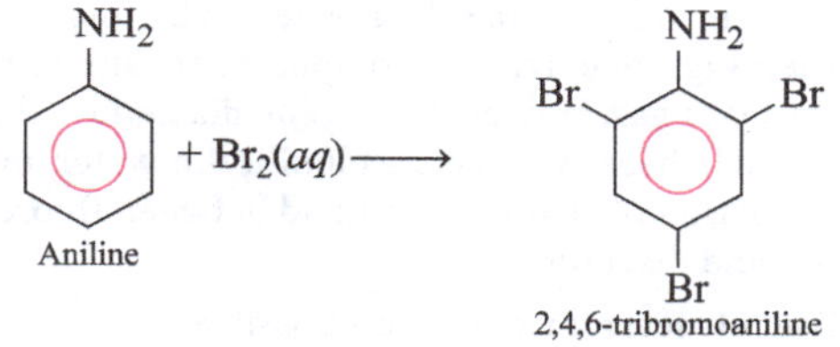

(1)

Subjective Type Questions

1. **Nitromethane into dimethylamine**

(i) CH_3NO_2 (Nitromethane) $\xrightarrow[\text{[H]}]{\text{Sn / HCl}}$ CH_3NH_2 (Aminomethane) $\xrightarrow{\text{CHCl}_3\text{ / KOH}}$ CH_3NC (Methyl isocyanide) $\xrightarrow[\text{[H]}]{\text{Na/C}_2\text{H}_5\text{OH}}$ CH_3NHCH_3 (Dimethylamine) **(1)**

(ii) **Propanoic acid into ethanoic acid**

CH_3CH_2COOH (Propanoic acid) $\xrightarrow{\text{NH}_3\text{/Heat}}$ $CH_3CH_2CONH_2$ (Propanamide) $\xrightarrow{\text{Br}_2\text{ / KOH}}$ $CH_3CH_2NH_2$ (Ethylamine) $\xrightarrow[-\text{N}_2,\ -\text{H}_2\text{O}]{\text{HONO}}$ CH_3CH_2OH (Ethanol) $\xrightarrow[\text{[O]}]{\text{K}_2\text{Cr}_2\text{O}_7/\ \text{H}_2\text{SO}_4}$ CH_3CHO (Ethanal) $\xrightarrow[\text{[O]}]{\text{K}_2\text{Cr}_2\text{O}_7\text{ / H}_2\text{SO}_4}$ CH_3COOH (Ethanoic acid) **(1)**

2. Complete conversion can be performed as

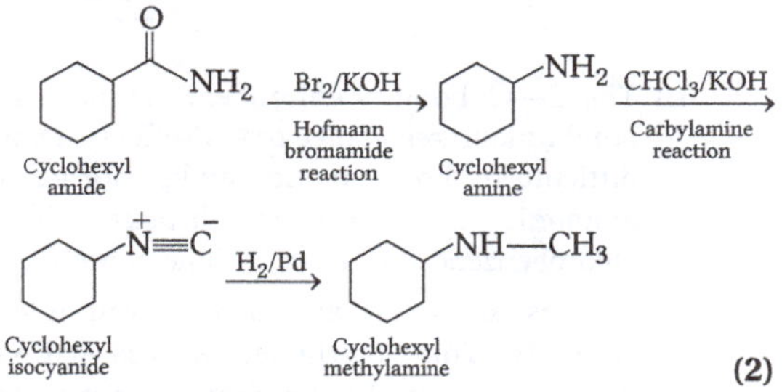

(2)

3. Refer to text on page 332. **(2)**

4. The sulphonyl group is a stronger electron-withdrawing group compared to the carbonyl group which makes the H atom attached to the N atom more acidic in nature. Hence, *P* is more likely to be acidic in nature than *Q*. **(2)**

5. (i) **Nitrous acid test** Aniline with HNO_2 (from $NaNO_2 + HCl$) gives benzene diazonium chloride which is stable at 273-278 K and hence, does not decompose to give N_2 gas.

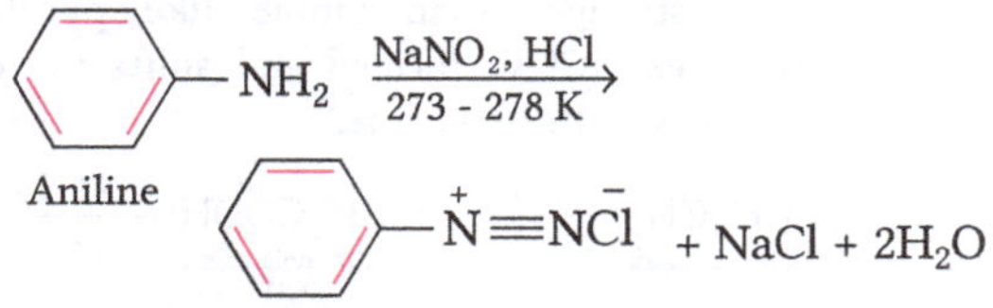

Benzene diazonium chloride

While benzylamine reacts with HNO_2 to give diazonium salt which being unstable at low temperature decomposes and gives N_2 gas.

$C_6H_5CH_2NH_2 \xrightarrow{\text{NaNO}_2\text{/ HCl}} [C_6H_5CH_2—\overset{+}{N}\equiv NCl^-]$ (Unstable)

$\xrightarrow{\text{H}_2\text{O}} C_6H_5CH_2OH + N_2\uparrow + HCl$
Benzyl alcohol **(1)**

(ii) Aniline is a primary aromatic amine while N-methyl aniline is a secondary aromatic amine. So, they can be distinguished by carbylamine test. **(1)**

For test, refer to text on page 332.

6. (i) Due to electron-donating effect (+*R*-effect) of $—NH_2$ group, the electron density on the benzene ring increases. As a result, aniline is easily oxidised on standing in air for a long time to form coloured products. **(1)**

(ii) Nitrogen is less electronegative than oxygen and therefore lone pair of electrons on nitrogen is readily available for donation. Hence, $MeNH_2$ is more basic than MeOH. **(1)**

7. **Hint** Due to the presence of electron withdrawing group in *o*-and *p*-nitrotoluene. **(2)**

8. Refer to text on page 333. **(2)**

9. (i) $CH_3CH_2Cl \xrightarrow{\text{NaCN}} CH_3CH_2CN$ (*A*) (Propane nitrile) $\xrightarrow{\text{H}_2\text{/Ni}}$ $CH_3CH_2CH_2NH_2$ (*B*) (Propanamine) **(1)**

(ii) 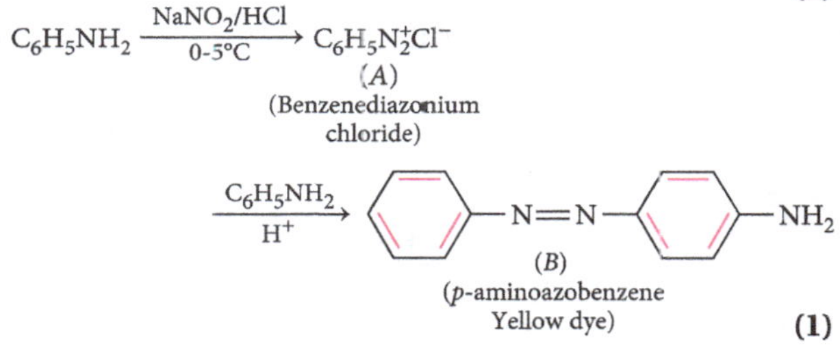

(1)

10. (i) Due to electron withdrawing effect of the acetyl group, the lone pair of electrons on N-atom is attracted by the group. As a result, lone pair of electrons on N-atom is not exclusively available for donation to the benzene ring and hence, activating effect of the — NH_2 group is reduced. **(1)**

(ii) In aniline ($C_6H_5NH_2$), the electron pair on nitrogen atom is involved in conjugation with ring and is less available for protonation than that in methylamine (CH_3NH_2). Therefore, aniline is less basic than methylamine.

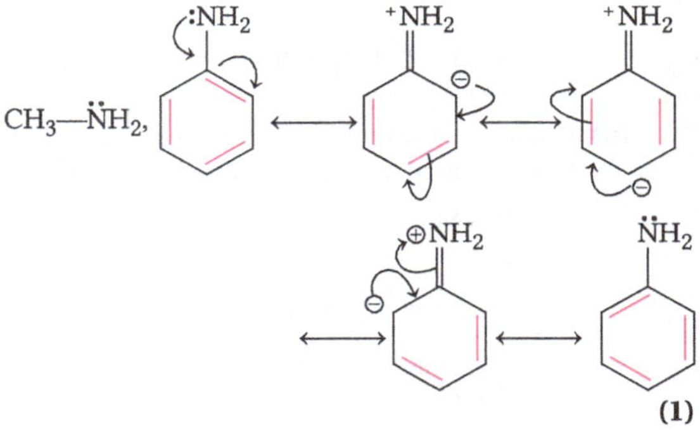

(1)

11. (i) Refer to text on page 333. **(1)**

(ii) $CH_3CH_2Br \xrightarrow{KCN} CH_3CH_2CN \xrightarrow{H_2/Ni} CH_3CH_2CH_2NH_2$ **(1)**

Bromoethane, Cyanoethane, Propanamine

12. (i) Refer to text on page - 327. **(1)**

(ii) Amides are less basic than amines because lone pair of electrons on nitrogen in amides is less available for donation due to the resonance with carbonyl

$(-\overset{O}{\overset{\|}{C}}-)$ group.

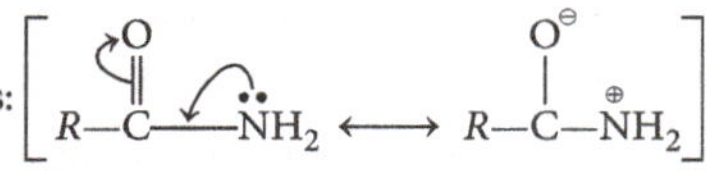

(1)

13. (i) **Nitrobenzene to aniline**

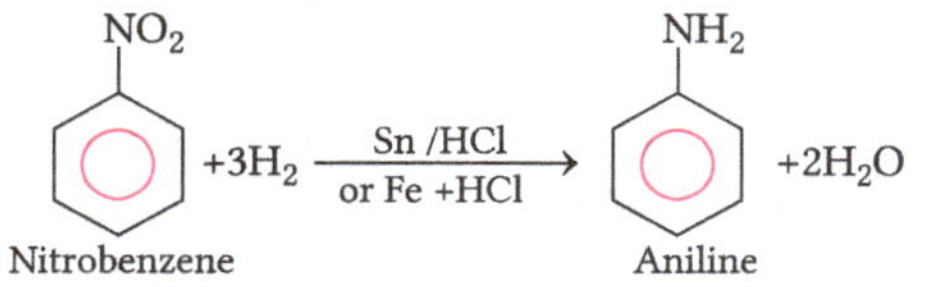

(1)

(ii) **Aniline to phenol**

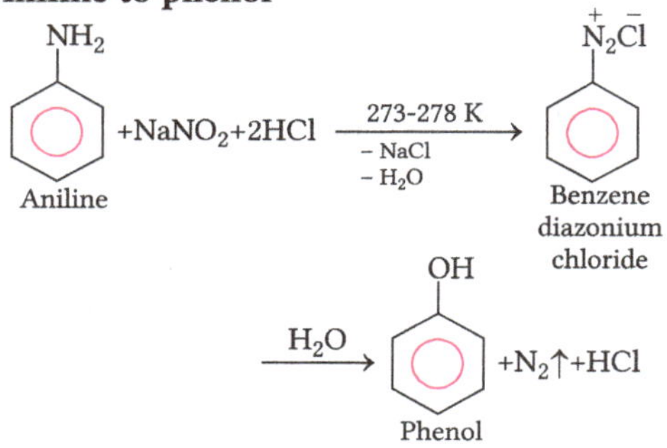

(1)

Or

(i) **Test for dimethyl amine and ethanamine**

Ethanamine, being primary amine, on heating with chloroform and ethanolic potassium hydroxide forms isocyanide which have foul smell whereas dimethyl does not give this kind of foul smell.

$$\underset{\text{Ethanamine}}{CH_3CH_2NH_2} + CHCl_3 + 3KOH \xrightarrow{\Delta} \underset{\text{Ethyl isocyanide}}{CH_3CH_2NC} + 3KCl + 3H_2O$$ **(1)**

$$\underset{\text{Dimethylamine}}{(CH_3)_2NH} + CHCl_3 + 3KOH \xrightarrow{\Delta} \text{No foul smell}$$

(ii) Benzene diazonium chloride when treated with KI form iodobenzene. The reaction involved is as follows

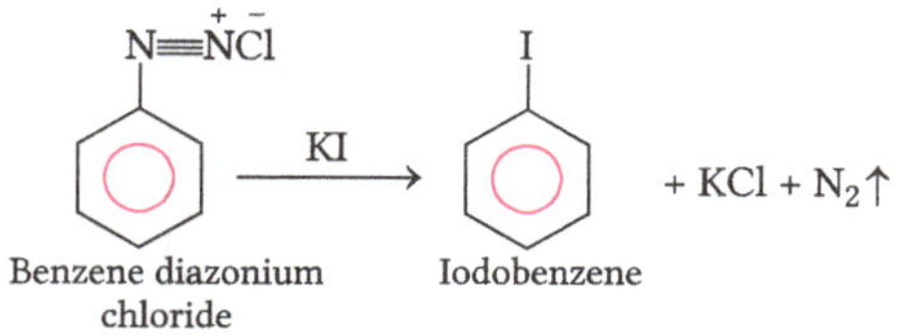

(1)

14. Benzene diazonium salts are generally unstable due to their high reactivity, decomposing readily to release nitrogen gas. However, benzene diazonium fluoroborate is stable because of its insolubility in water and it formation of strong ionic bond between fluoroborate ion and diazonium ion. **(2)**

15. Four structural isomers are possible.

$$\underset{\substack{\text{Propan-1-amine}\\(1^\circ \text{ amine})}}{CH_3-CH_2-CH_2-NH_2}, \underset{\substack{\text{N-methyl ethanamine}\\(2^\circ \text{ amine})}}{CH_3-NH-C_2H_5},$$

$$\underset{\substack{\text{Propan-2-amine}\\(1^\circ \text{ amine})}}{CH_3-\underset{NH_2}{\underset{|}{CH}}-CH_3} \qquad \underset{\substack{\text{N, N-dimethyl methanamine}\\(3^\circ \text{ amine})}}{CH_3-\underset{CH_3}{\underset{|}{N}}-CH_3}$$ **(1)**

Only 1° amines react with HNO_2 to give N_2 gas, i.e.,

$$\underset{\text{Propan-1-amine}}{CH_3-CH_2-CH_2-NH_2} + HONO \longrightarrow \underset{\text{Propan-1-ol (Major product)}}{CH_3-CH_2-CH_2OH} + N_2\uparrow + H_2O$$ **(1)**

$$\underset{\text{Propan-2-amine}}{(H_3C)_2CH-NH_2} + HONO \longrightarrow \underset{\text{Propan-2-ol (Major product)}}{(H_3C)_2CH-OH} + N_2\uparrow + H_2O$$ **(1)**

16. (i) The C—Cl bond of chlorobenzene has partial double bond (due to resonance or +*M*-effect). Thus, it is very difficult to break it. So, under normal conditions ammonia is unable to displace chlorine from chlorobenzene and hence, aniline is not formed. **(1)**

(ii) Amines are polar and hence form intermolecular H-bonds. This intermolecular association depends upon the extent of H-bonding. 1° amines have two, 2° amines have one, while 3° amines have no hydrogen bonded to nitrogen. Therefore, boiling point of butanamine is higher than N-ethylethanamine. **(1)**

$$\underset{\substack{\text{Butanamine}\\(1^\circ \text{ amine})}}{CH_3CH_2CH_2CH_2NH_2}; \underset{\substack{\text{N-ethylethanamine}\\(2^\circ \text{ amine})}}{CH_3CH_2-\underset{H}{\underset{|}{N}}-CH_2CH_3}$$

(iii) Acylation of aniline is carried out in the presence of a base stronger than amine like pyridine, which removes HCl so formed and shifts the equilibrium towards right hand side. **(1)**

17. (i) $$\underset{\text{Methyl cyanide}}{CH_3CN} \xrightarrow{H_2O/H^+} \underset{\substack{\text{Ethanoic acid}\\(A)}}{CH_3COOH} \xrightarrow[\Delta]{NH_3} \underset{\substack{\text{Ethanamide}\\(B)}}{CH_3CONH_2} \xrightarrow{Br_2 + 4KOH} \underset{\substack{\text{Ethanamine}\\(C)}}{CH_3NH_2}$$ **(1½)**

(ii) $\underset{\text{Chloroethane}}{CH_3CH_2Cl} \xrightarrow{KCN} \underset{\substack{\text{Ethylcyanide}\\(A)}}{CH_3CH_2CN} \xrightarrow{H_2/Ni}$

$\underset{\substack{\text{Ethanamine}\\(B)}}{CH_3CH_2NH_2} \xrightarrow{CH_3COCl/Base} \underset{\substack{\text{N-methylpronamide}\\(C)}}{CH_3CH_2NHCOCH_3}$ **(1½)**

18. Presence of more OH^- ions shows solution '*A*' is more basic. **(1)**

We know that, higher the concentration of OH^-, higher is the K_b, i.e., dissociation constant.

The reaction can be represented as;

$$CH_3—NH_2 + H_2O \longrightarrow CH_3NH_3^+ + OH^-$$

$$K_C = \frac{[CH_3NH_3^+][OH^-]}{[CH_3NH_2]}$$ **(1)**

(Here, $K_C = K_b$, i.e., dissociation constant of base in aqueous solution.)

But pK_b and K_b are related as

$$pK_b = -\log K_b$$

Thus, we can say pK_b value of solution '*B*' is higher because it has less concentration of OH^-. **(1)**

19. (i) Since, (*X*) gives alcohol and N_2 gas on treatment with $NaNO_2/HCl$, therefore, it must be a primary amine. Further, since *X* is optically active, therefore, it possess chiral structure.

Now, $—NH_2$ group cannot be directly attached to the chiral carbon because such amines readily undergoes racemisation due to inversion at N-atom..

Therefore, the probable structure of *X* is

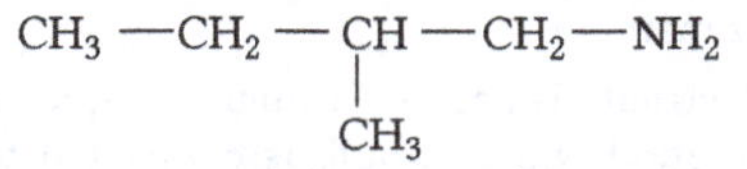

2-methylbutanamine (*X*)
(optically active) **(1)**

To determine the structure of 3° alcohol (*Y*)

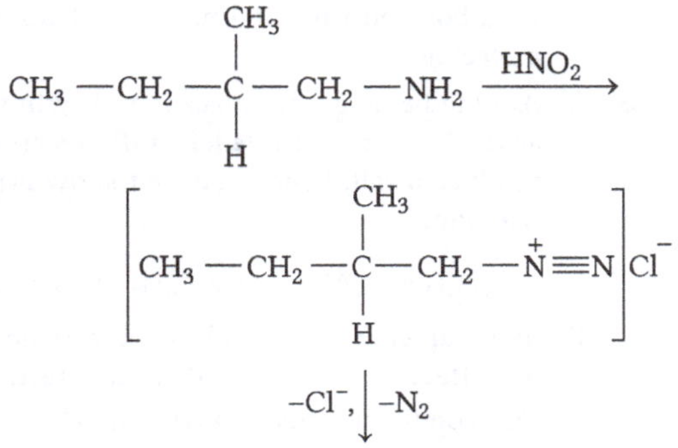

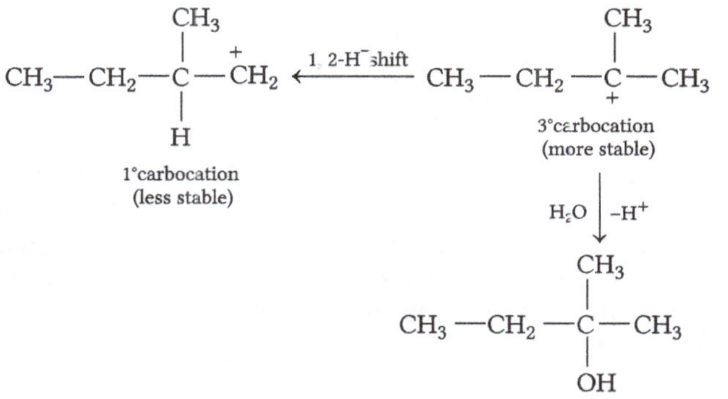

2-methylbutan-2-ol
(*Y*) (optically inactive) **(1)**

(ii) No, *Y* is optically inactive. **(1)**

20. (i) $\underset{\text{Ethylamine}}{CH_3CH_2NH_2} + HNO_2 \xrightarrow{0°C} \underset{\text{Ethyl alcohol}}{CH_3CH_2OH} + N_2\uparrow + H_2O$ **(1)**

(ii) Refer to text on page 333. **(1)**

(iii)

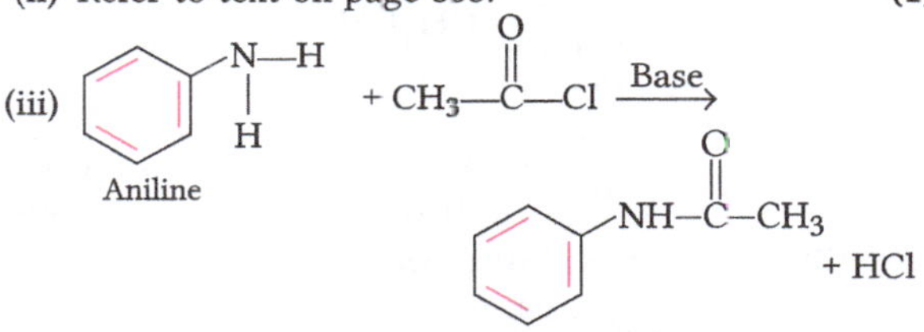

N-phenyl ethanamide
(Acetanilide) **(1)**

21. (i) When N-ethylethanamine (2°amine) reacts with benzenesulphonyl chloride then N, N-diethylbenzene sulphonamide is formed.

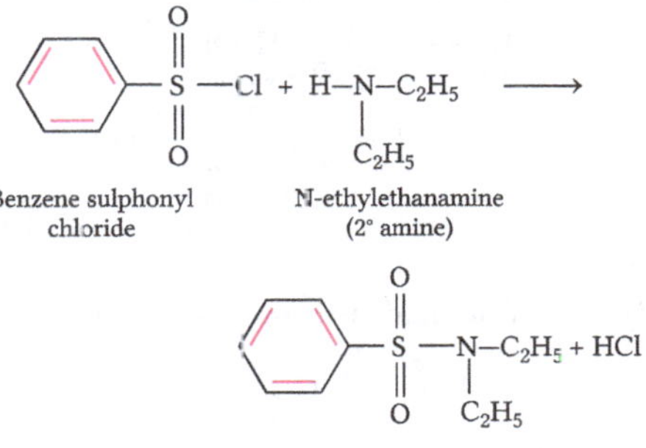

N, N-diethylbenzene sulphonamide
(Insoluble in alkali) **(1)**

(ii) When benzyl chloride is treated with ammonia, benzylamine is formed, which on further reaction with chloromethane yields a secondary amine, N, N-dimethylbenzylamine.

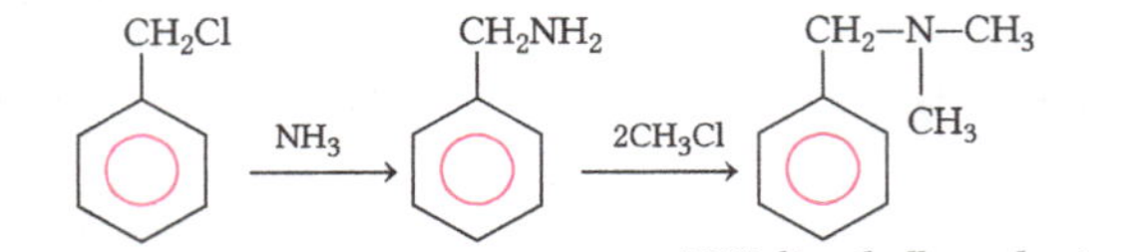

Benzyl chloride — Benzylamine — N-N-dimethylbenzylamine (2° amine) **(1)**

(iii) Aniline on reaction with chloroform in the presence of alcoholic potassium hydroxide gives phenyl isocyanides (or phenyl isonitrile).

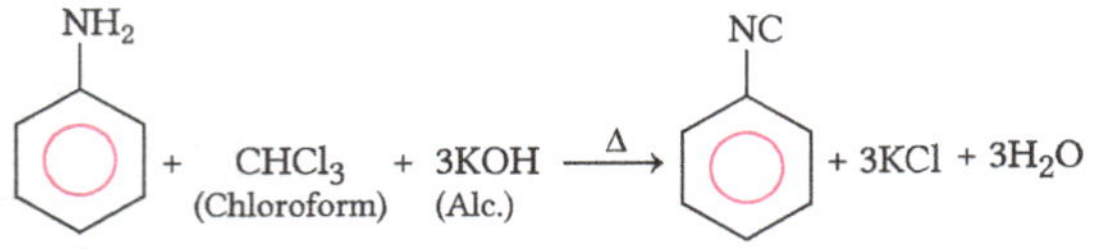

Aniline — Phenyl isocyanide **(1)**

This reaction is an example of carbylamine reaction.

22. (i) **Ethanamine into methanamine**

$$\underset{\text{Ethanamine}}{CH_3CH_2NH_2} \xrightarrow[-N_2-H_2O]{HONO} \underset{\text{Ethanol}}{CH_3CH_2OH} \xrightarrow[K_2Cr_2O_7/H_2SO_4]{[O]} \underset{\text{Ethanal}}{CH_3CHO} \xrightarrow[K_2Cr_2O_7/H_2SO_4]{[O]} \underset{\text{Ethanoic acid}}{CH_3COOH}$$

$$\xrightarrow[Heat]{NH_3} \underset{\text{Ethanamide}}{CH_3CONH_2} \xrightarrow{Br_2/KOH} \underset{\text{Methanamine}}{CH_3NH_2}$$ **(1)**

(ii) **Ethanoic acid into propanoic acid**

$$\underset{\text{Ethanoic acid}}{CH_3COOH} \xrightarrow{LiAlH_4} \underset{\text{Ethanol}}{CH_3CH_2OH} \xrightarrow{Red\ P/I_2}$$

$$\underset{\text{Iodoethane}}{CH_3CH_2I} \xrightarrow{KCN(alc.)} \underset{\text{Propane nitrile}}{CH_3CH_2CN} \xrightarrow{H_2O/H^+} \underset{\text{Propanoic acid}}{CH_3CH_2COOH}$$ **(1)**

(iii) **Methanamine into ethanamine**

$$\underset{\text{Methanamine}}{CH_3NH_2} \xrightarrow[-N_2,\ -H_2O]{HONO} \underset{\text{Methanol}}{CH_3OH} \xrightarrow{Red\ P/I_2}$$

$$\underset{\text{Methyl iodide}}{CH_3I} \xrightarrow{KCN\ (alc.)} \underset{\text{Ethane nitrile}}{CH_3CN} \xrightarrow[4[H]]{Na/C_2H_5OH/\ Reduction} \underset{\text{Ethanamine}}{CH_3CH_2NH_2}$$ **(1)**

23. (i) **Ethanoic acid into methanamine**

$$\underset{\text{Ethanoic acid}}{CH_3COOH} \xrightarrow{SOCl_2} \underset{\text{Ethanoyl chloride}}{CH_3COCl} \xrightarrow{NH_3(excess)}$$

$$\underset{\text{Ethanamide}}{CH_3CONH_2} \xrightarrow[\text{Hofmann bromamide reaction}]{Br_2/\ KOH} \underset{\text{Methanamine}}{CH_3NH_2}$$ **(1)**

(ii) **Hexane nitrile into 1-aminopentane**

$$\underset{\text{Hexane nitrile}}{CH_3(CH_2)_4CN} \xrightarrow[\text{Partial hydrolysis}]{H_3O^+} \underset{\text{Hexanamide}}{CH_3(CH_2)_4CONH_2}$$

$$\xrightarrow[\text{Hofmann bromamide reaction}]{Br_2/KOH} \underset{\text{1-aminopentane}}{CH_3(CH_2)_4NH_2}$$ **(1)**

(iii) **Methanol into ethanoic acid**

$$\underset{\text{Methanol}}{CH_3OH} \xrightarrow{PCl_5} \underset{\text{Chloromethane}}{CH_3Cl} \xrightarrow{KCN(alc.)}$$

$$\underset{\text{Ethane nitrile}}{CH_3CN} \xrightarrow{H_3O^+} \underset{\text{Ethanoic acid}}{CH_3COOH}$$ **(1)**

24. (i) N-methylethanamine is a secondary amine. When it reacts with benzene sulphonyl chloride it forms N-ethyl-N-methyl sulphonamide. On the other hand, N, N - dimethylethanamine is a tertiary amine. It does not react with benzene sulphonyl chloride. **(1)**

(ii)

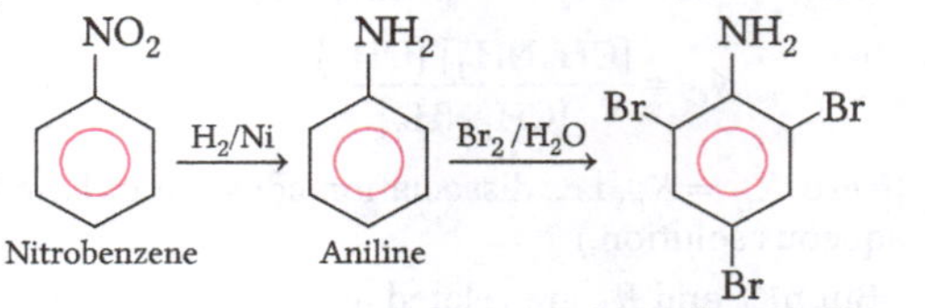

Nitrobenzene — Aniline — 2,4,6-tribromoaniline **(1)**

(iii) Butan-1-ol is more soluble in water. This is because alcohol forms stronger hydrogen bonds with water than formed by amine due to higher electronegativity of O in alcohol than N in amine.

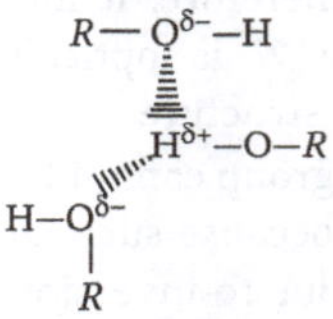

(1)

25. (i) Amine *M* is aniline and its IUPAC name is benzenamine. **(1)**

(ii) If electricity is passed through an aqueous solution of compound N and a bulb is connected to this circuit then the bulb will not glow. This is because compound N forms a zwitter ion in the reaction medium. Zwitter ions do not conduct electricity as it is a neutral ion with both positive and negative charges in the same molecule. **(2)**

26. (i) Aniline being a Lewis base, react with the Lewis acid $AlCl_3$ used in Friedel-Crafts reaction and produce a salt, hence does not show Friedel-Crafts reaction.

$$C_6H_5NH_2 + AlCl_3 \longrightarrow C_6H_5 \cdot \overset{+}{N}H_2 AlCl_3^- \text{ (Salt)}$$ **(1)**

(ii) In an aqueous solution, basic nature depends on + *I*-effect, H-bonding and steric-effect.

The combined effect shows that $(CH_3)_2NH$ is more basic than $(CH_3)_3N$ as H-bonding is more in case of $(CH_3)_2NH$ than in $(CH_3)_3N$, which predominates over the stability due to +*I*- effect of three —CH_3 groups. **(1)**

(iii) Primary amines (1°) show two hydrogen bonds, whereas tertiary amines (3°) show no hydrogen bonding. Thus, the net attractive force in case of primary amines is more than that of tertiary amines.

Hence, primary amines have higher boiling point than that of tertiary amines. **(1)**

27. (i) It is due to salt formation with aluminium chloride, the Lewis acid, which is used as catalyst. As a result of which, nitrogen of aniline acquires positive charge and hence acts as deactivating group. **(1)**

(ii) It is due to strong acidic medium, aniline gets protonated to form the anilinium ion which is *meta* directing in nature. **(1)**

(iii) In aniline, lone pair on nitrogen undergoes resonance in the ring, therefore, transfer of electron is not possible. Whereas, in cyclohexylamine, cyclohexyl group is electron donating group, so it increases the electron density at nitrogen and hence it become electron rich. Therefore, electrons are easily available for transfer. **(1)**

28. (i) Nitration is usually carried out with a mixture of conc. HNO_3 and conc. H_2SO_4. So, in the presence of these acids, aniline gets protonated to form anilinium ion.

Therefore, in the presence of these acids, the reaction mixture consists of aniline and anilinium ion. —NH_2 group in aniline is *o,p*-directing and activating, whereas the $\overset{+}{N}H_3$ group in anilinium ion is *m*-directing and deactivating.

Now, nitration of aniline mainly gives *p*-nitroaniline due to steric hindrance at *o*-position, the nitration of anilinium ion gives *m*-nitroaniline. In actual practice approx. 1 : 1 mixture of *p*-nitroaniline and *m*-nitroaniline is obtained.

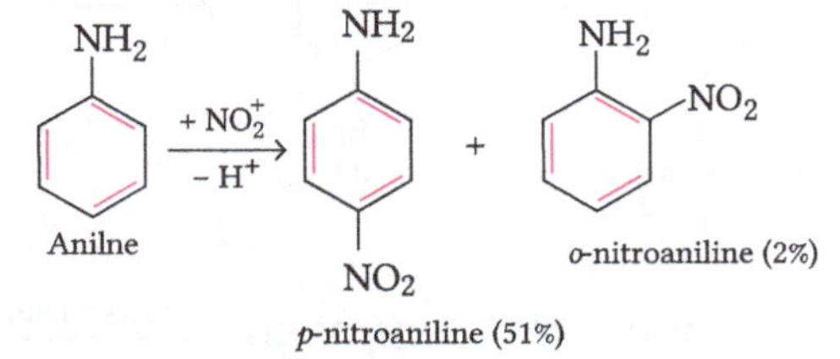

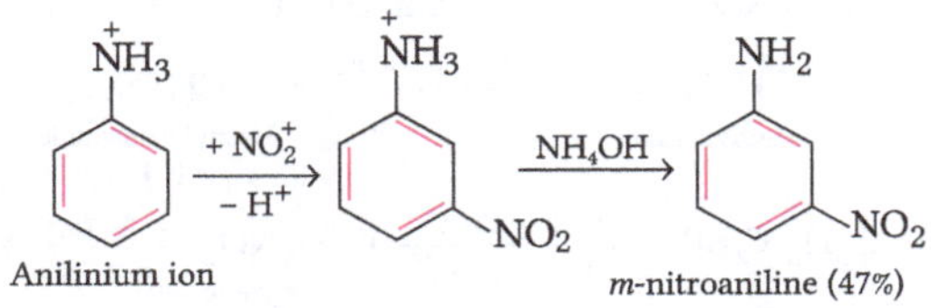

(1½)

(ii) Gabriel phthalimide synthesis produces primary amines only without the traces of secondary or tertiary amines. So, this method is preferred for the synthesis of primary amines. For reactions, refer to text on page 327. **(1½)**

29. (i)

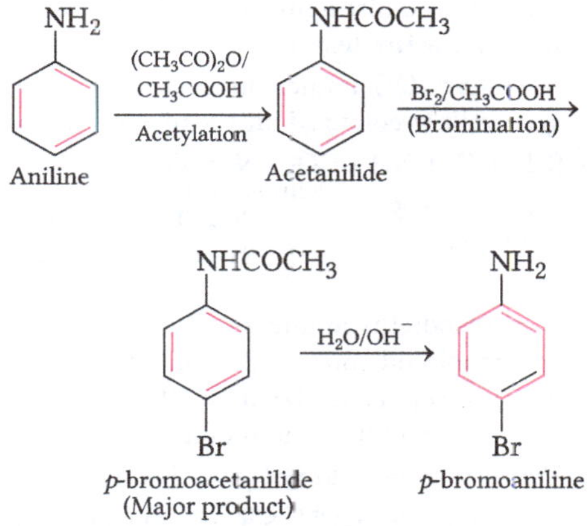

(1)

(ii)

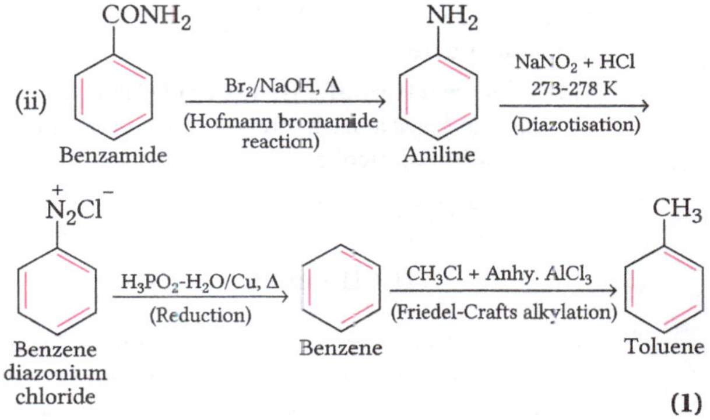

(1)

(iii)

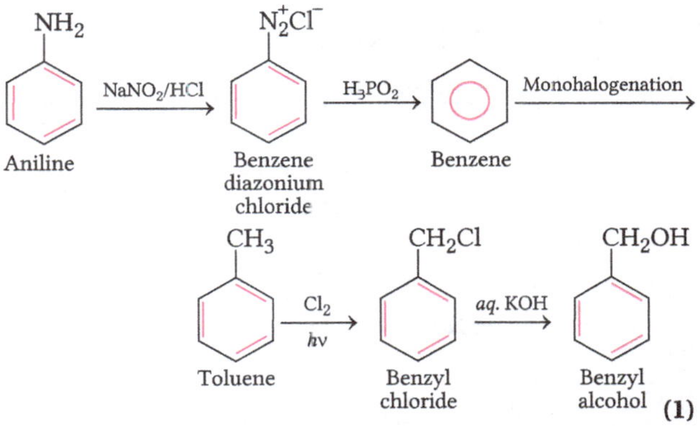

(1)

30. (i) **Carbylamine test** Methylamine is a primary amine, therefore it gives carbylamine test. When heated with an alcoholic solution of KOH and $CHCl_3$, it gives offensive smell of methyl isocyanide. Since, dimethylamine is a secondary amine, hence, it does not give this test.

For reaction, refer to text on page 332.

$$\underset{\substack{\text{Dimethylamine} \\ (2^\circ \text{ amine})}}{(CH_3)_2NH} \xrightarrow[\Delta]{CHCl_3/KOH(alc.)} \text{No reaction}$$

(1)

(ii) They can be distinguished by **Liebermann nitrosoamine** test.

Secondary (2°) amines on treatment with HNO_2, give yellow coloured oily N-nitrosoamines.

$$\underset{\text{Diethylamine (2° amine)}}{(CH_3CH_2)_2NH} + \underset{\text{Nitrous acid}}{HO—N{=}O} \longrightarrow \underset{\substack{\text{N-nitrosodiethylamine}\\ \text{(Yellow colour)}}}{(CH_3CH_2)_2N—N{=}O} + H_2O$$

N-nitrosodiethylamine, on warming with a crystal of phenol and conc. H_2SO_4, gives a green solution which when made alkaline with aqueous NaOH turns deep blue and then red on dilution.

Tertiary amines do not give this test. **(1)**

(iii) Ethylamine ($CH_3CH_2NH_2$) is a primary aliphatic amine, while aniline ($C_6H_5NH_2$) is a primary aromatic amine.

With the reaction of nitrous acid (HNO_2)

Ethylamine gives a brisk effervescence of N_2 gas with the formation of alcohol.

$$\underset{\text{Ethylamine}}{CH_3CH_2NH_2} + HONO \xrightarrow[\text{Dil. HCl(273-278 K)}]{NaNO_2} \underset{\text{Ethanol}}{CH_3CH_2OH} + N_2\uparrow + H_2O$$

Whereas, aniline gives benzene diazonium chloride which on treatment with alkaline solution of β-naphthol (2-naphthol) gives an orange dye (azo dye test).

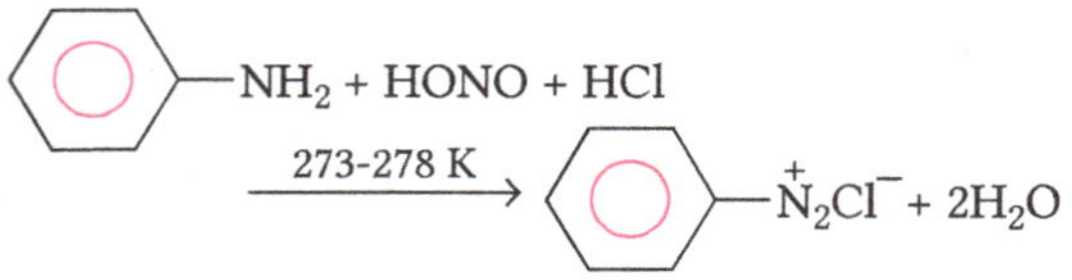

Benzene diazonium chloride

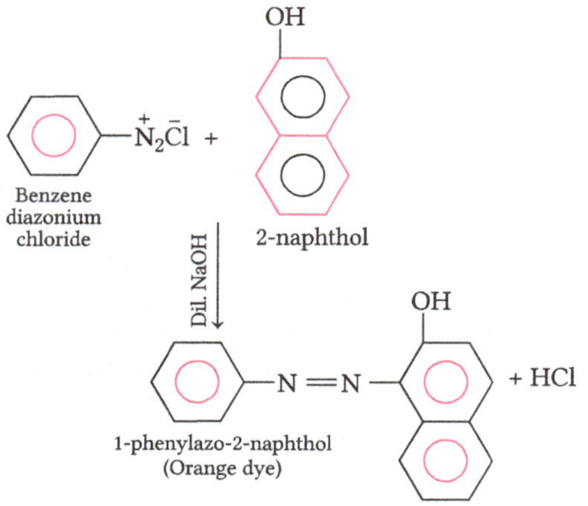

(1)

31. (i) $$\underset{\text{Ethyl bromide}}{CH_3CH_2Br} \xrightarrow{KCN} \underset{\text{Ethyl cyanide }(A)}{CH_3CH_2CN} \xrightarrow{LiAlH_4}$$

$$\underset{\substack{n\text{-propylamine}\\(B)}}{CH_3CH_2CH_2NH_2} \xrightarrow[0°C]{HNO_2} \underset{\substack{n\text{-propyl alcohol}\\(C)}}{CH_3CH_2CH_2OH}$$ **(1)**

(ii) $$\underset{\text{Acetic acid}}{CH_3COOH} \xrightarrow[\text{Heat}]{NH_3} \underset{\substack{\text{Acetamide}\\(A)}}{CH_3CONH_2} \xrightarrow{NaOBr}$$

$$\underset{\substack{\text{Methyl amine}\\(B)}}{CH_3NH_2} \xrightarrow{NaNO_2/HCl} \underset{\substack{\text{Methanol}\\(C)}}{CH_3OH}$$ **(1)**

(iii)

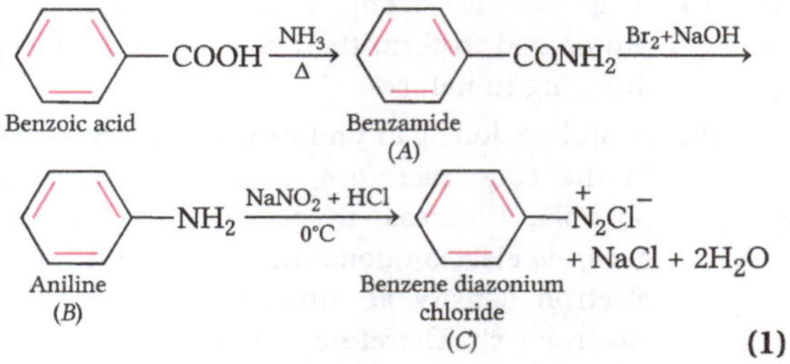

(1)

32. (i) IUPAC name of given compound is N-ethyl-N-methylaniline or N-ethyl-N-methylbenzenamine **(1)**

(ii) Complete reaction is as follows

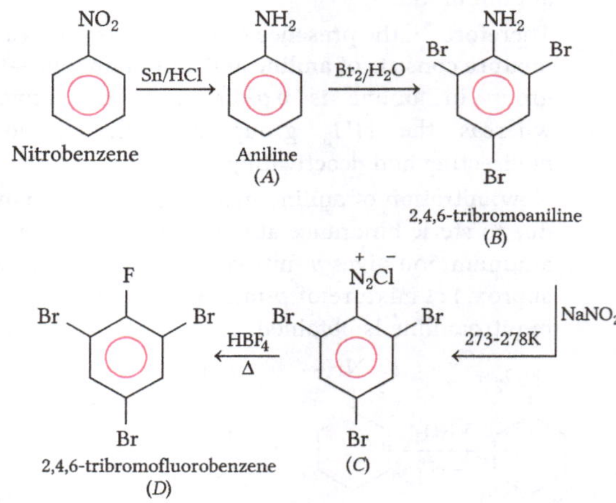

(2)

33. (i) $$\underset{\text{Acetic acid}}{CH_3COOH} \xrightarrow[-H_2O]{NH_3/\Delta} \underset{\text{Acetamide }(A)}{CH_3CONH_2} \xrightarrow{Br_2/KOH\,(aq)}$$

$$\underset{\substack{\text{Methylamine}\\(B)}}{CH_3NH_2} \xrightarrow{CHCl_3 + \text{alc. KOH}} \underset{\substack{\text{Methyl isocyanide}\\(C)}}{CH_3NC}$$ **(1½)**

(ii) $$C_6H_5N_2^+BF_4^- \xrightarrow[-N_2,\,-NaBF_4]{NaNO_2/Cu,\Delta} \underset{\substack{\text{Nitrobenzene}\\(A)}}{C_6H_5NO_2} \xrightarrow[\text{Reduction}]{Fe/HCl}$$

$$C_6H_5NH_2 \xrightarrow[-HCl]{CH_3COCl/pyridine} C_6H_5NHCOCH_3$$
Aniline (*B*) — Acetanilide (*C*) **(1½)**

34. (i)

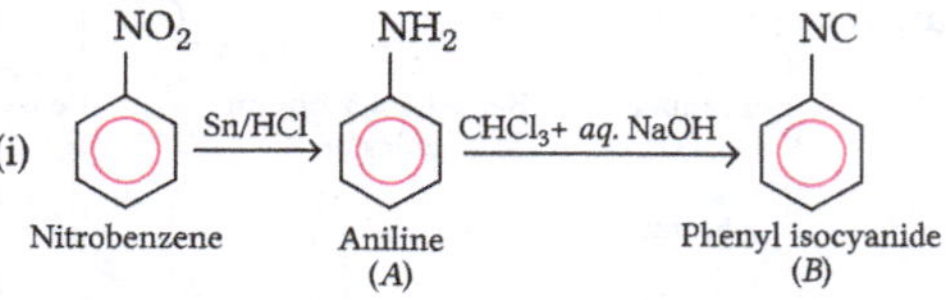

(1)

(ii)

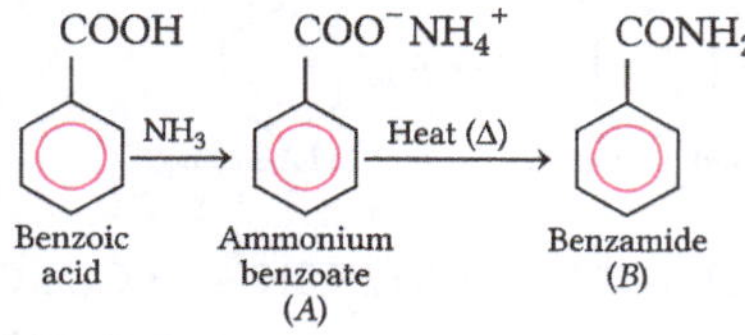

(1)

(iii)

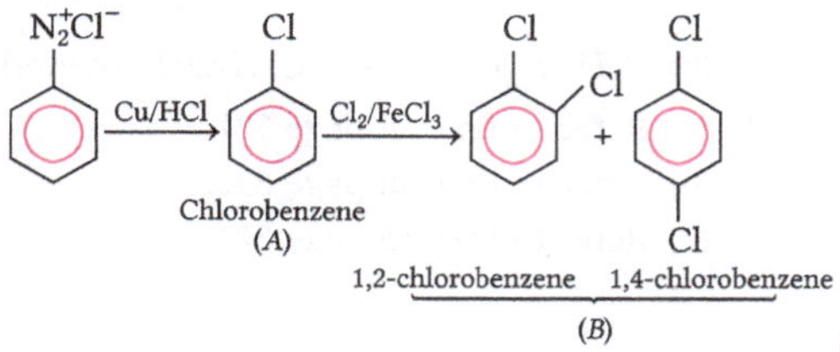

(1)

35. (i) Stronger base has a lower pK_b value. Electron releasing group, like —CH_3, increases the basic strength, whereas, electron withdrawing group like —NO_2, decreases the basic strength. Thus, the correct order of decreasing pK_b value is:

p-nitroaniline > Aniline > *p*-methylaniline **(1)**

(ii) (a) Refer to text on page 335. **(1)**

(b) Methylamine is a weak base that produces hydroxide ions in water. These hydroxide ions react with ferric ions in ferric chloride to form hydrated ferric oxide.

$$CH_3\ddot{N}H_2 + H\text{—}OH \longrightarrow CH_3\overset{\oplus}{N}H_3 + \overset{\ominus}{O}H$$
(Methylamine)

$$FeCl_3 \longrightarrow Fe^{3+} + 3Cl^-$$

$$2Fe^{3+} + 6OH^- \longrightarrow Fe_2O_3 \cdot 3H_2O \text{ or } 2Fe(OH)_3$$
Hydrated ferric oxide (Brown ppt.) **(1)**

36. (i) Refer to text on page 336. **(2)**

(ii) Refer to text on page 337. **(1)**

37.

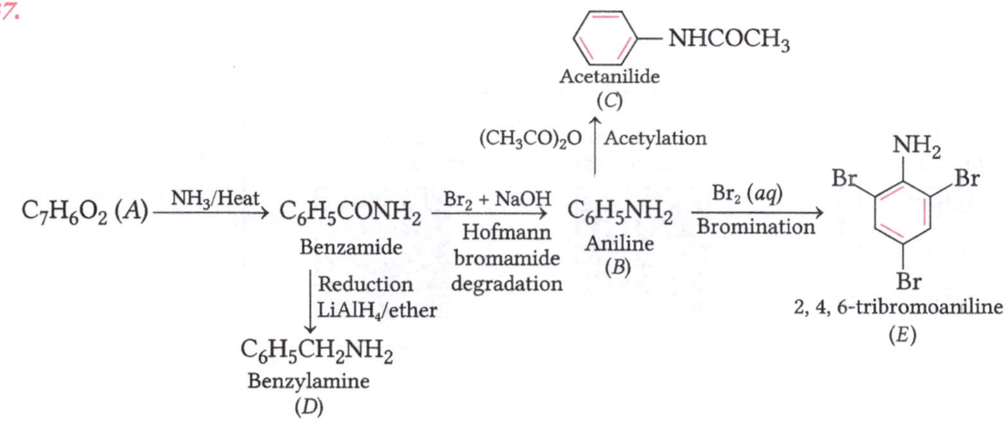

(3)

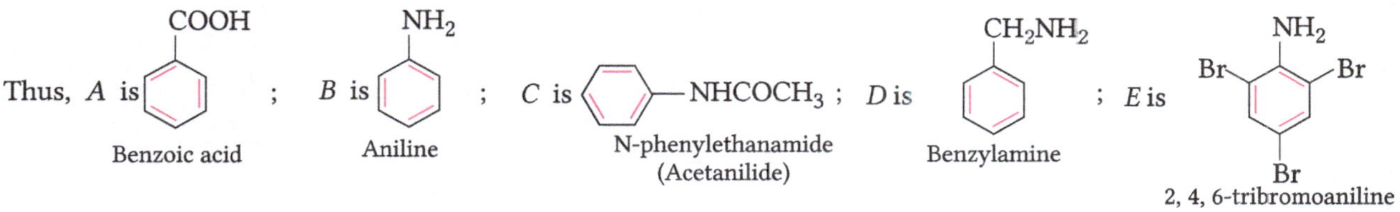

(2)

38. (i) (a) $C_6H_5NH_2 + Br_2(aq) \longrightarrow C_6H_5NH_2(Br)_3 + 3HBr$ **(1)**

(b) $C_6H_5NH_2 + HCl \longrightarrow C_6H_5NH_3^+Cl^-$ **(1)**

(c) $C_6H_5NH_2 + NaNO_2 + HCl \xrightarrow{0°-5°C} C_6H_5N_2^+Cl^- + NaCl + 2H_2O$ **(1)**

(ii) $C_6H_5NH_2 + C_6H_5COCl \longrightarrow C_6H_5NHCOC_6H_5 + HCl$

Name of compound is N-phenylbenzamide. **(1)**

(iii) $(CH_3)_2NH < C_2H_5NH_2 < C_2H_5OH$ **(1)**

39.

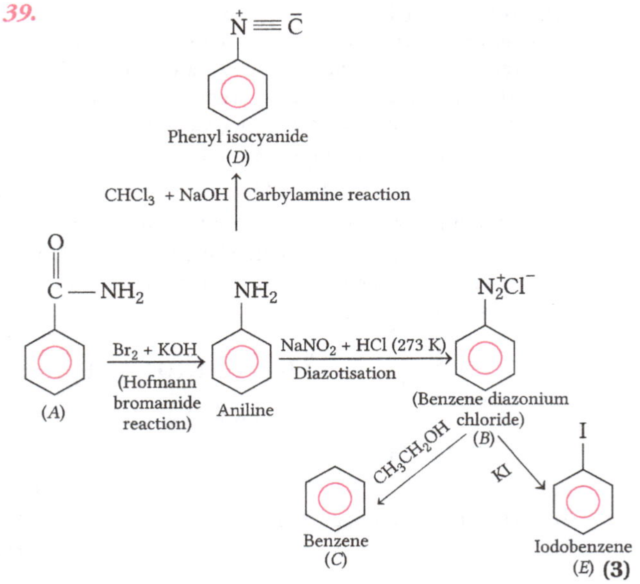

(3)

Thus, A is 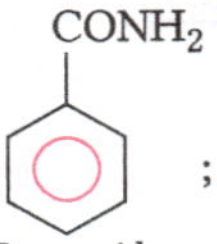 Benzamide ; B is 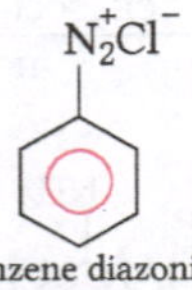 Benzene diazonium chloride ; C is  Benzene ;

D is 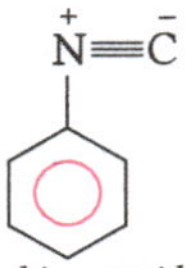 Phenyl isocyanide and E is 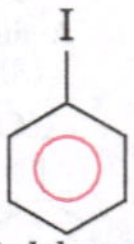 Iodobenzene **(2)**

40. (i) (a) $C_6H_5\overset{+}{N}_2\overset{-}{Cl} + CuCN/KCN \longrightarrow C_6H_5CN$ (Cyanobenzene) **(1)**

(b) $C_6H_5\overset{+}{N}_2\overset{-}{Cl} \xrightarrow{H_2O} C_6H_5OH$ (Phenol) **(1)**

(ii) (a) Refer to text on page 327. **(1)**

(b) Refer to text on page 332. **(1)**

(c) Refer to text on page 327. **(1)**

QR Code for Quick Test 1

QR Code for Quick Test 2

QR Code for Quick Test 3

SELF ASSESSMENT TEST

Objective Type Questions [1 Mark]

1. IUPAC name of $H_2N—CH_2—CH_2—NH_2$ is
   (a) ethane-1, 3-diamine (b) ethane-1, 2-diamine
   (c) ethyne-1, 2, diamine (d) ethene-1, 2, diamine
2. Propanamide on reaction with bromine in aqueous NaOH gives
   (a) propanamine (b) ethanamine
   (c) N-methylethanamine (d) propanenitrile
3. N-methylbenzamide is formed when methanamine reacts with benzoyl chloride. This reaction is known as
   (a) benzoylation (b) Hinsberg test
   (c) Schmidt reaction (d) Curtius reaction
4. Choose the correct order of the boiling point of isomeric amines.
   (a) Primary > secondary > tertiary
   (b) Secondary > tertiary > primary
   (c) Tertiary > primary > secondary
   (d) Tertiary > secondary > primary
5. Name the product(s) formed during the reaction of primary aliphatic amines with nitrous acid at room temperature?
   (a) $RN_2^+Cl^-$ (b) ROH
   (c) Both (a) and (b) (d) None of these

Assertion-Reason [1 Mark]

Directions (Q. Nos. 6-8) In the following questions. An Assertion (A) is followed by a corresponding Reason (R). Use the following keys to choose the appropriate answer.

(a) Both (A) and (R) are true and (R) is the correct explanation of (A).
(b) Both (A) and (R) are true, but (R) is not the correct explanation of (A).
(c) (A) is true, but (R) is false.
(d) (A) is false, but (R) is true.

6. **Assertion** (A) Ammonolysis of alkyl halides involves the reaction between alkyl halides and alcoholic ammonia.
   Reason (R) Ammonolysis of alkyl halides produces secondary amines only.
7. **Assertion** (A) Aniline does not undergo alkylation and acetylation.
   Reason (R) Nitrogen of aniline acquire positive charge in the presence of $AlCl_3$.
8. **Assertion** (A) Nitration of aniline can be conveniently done by protecting the amino group by acetylation.
   Reason (R) Acetylation increases the electron-density in the benzene ring.

Short Answer Type I Questions [2 Marks]

9. An organic compound [X] of molecular formula C_3H_5N, in one reaction produced a primary amine with $LiAlH_4$. In another case, the organic compound [Y] of same molecular formula C_3H_5N produced a secondary amine with $LiAlH_4$. Identify both the compounds [X] and [Y]. Why do these compounds form two different products?
10. Write chemical equation for the following conversions.
    (i) Nitrobenzene to benzoic acid
    (ii) Benzyl chloride to 2-phenylethanamine
11. Illustrate the following reactions by giving one suitable example in each case.
    (a) Coupling reaction
    (b) Acetylation of ethylamine

Short Answer Type II Questions [3 Marks]

12. Arrange the following in increasing order of property specified.
    (i) Aniline, ethanamine, 3-ethylethanamine (solubility in water).
    (ii) Ethanoic acid, ethanamine, ethanol (boiling point).
    (iii) Methanamine, N, N- dimethyl methanamine and N-methylmethanamine (basic strength in aqueous phase).
13. How will the following be converted? (Give chemical equations)
    (i) Benzene diazonium chloride to fluorobenzene.
    (ii) Nitrobenzene to phenol.
    (iii) Chloromethane to ethylamine.

14. Write chemical equations to illustrate the following name reactions,

(i) Benzoylation reaction

(ii) Gatterman reaction

(iii) Sandmeyer reaction

Case-Study [4 Marks]

15. Read the case given below and answer the questions that follow.

Amines are classified as primary. secondary and tertiary amines. Primary amines cannot be obtained by ammonolysis of alkyl halide because we will get mixture of 1°, 2° and 3° amines.

Cyanides, on reduction give primary amines where as isocyanides on reduction give secondary amines. Nitro compounds, on reduction also give primary amines.

Primary amines react with $CHCl_3$ and KOH to form foul smelling isocyanide. They react with HNO_2 and liberate N_2 gas. They react with Hinsberg's reagent to form salt soluble in KOH. Secondary amine form yellow oily compounds with HNO_2 and salt formed with $C_6H_5SO_2Cl$, is insoluble in KOH. 3° amines form salt soluble in water with HNO_2 but does not react with $C_6H_5SO_2Cl$.

Diazonium salts are prepared by reaction of aniline with $NaNO_2$ and conc. HCl at 0-5°C. Aromatic diazonium salts are more stable because phenyl diazonium ion is stabilised by resonance. Benzene diazonium chloride can be used to prepare halo benzene, phenol, nitro benzene. benzene, *p*-hydroxyazobenzene (azo dye) and large number of useful compounds.

(a) Complete the following reaction.

$$C_6H_5NO_2 \xrightarrow{Fe/HCl} A \xrightarrow[0\text{-}5°C]{NaNO_2\ +HCl} B.$$

Identify '*A*' and '*B*'.

(b) Distinguish between aniline and ethylamine.

Or Write the isomers of C_3H_9N which does not react with Hinsberg's reagent.

(c) 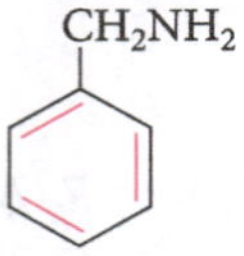

, on heating with $CHCl_3$ and KOH gives '*X*'. Identify '*X*'.

Long Answer Type Questions [5 Marks]

16. A hydrocarbon '*A*' (C_4H_8) on reaction with HCl gives a compound '*B*' (C_4H_9Cl), which on reaction with 1 mole of NH_3 gives compound '*C*' ($C_4H_{11}N$). On reacting with $NaNO_2$ and HCl followed by the treatment with water, compound '*C*' yields an optically active alcohol.

'*D*' Ozonolysis of '*A*' gives 2 moles of acetaldehyde. Identify compounds '*A*' to '*D*'. Explain the reactions involved.

17. (a) An aromatic compound '*A*' of molecular formula $C_7H_6O_2$ on treatment with aqueous ammonia and heating forms compound '*B*' which on heating with Br_2 and KOH forms a compound '*C*' of molecular formula C_6H_7N.

(i) Write the structures and IUPAC names of compound '*A*', '*B*' and '*C*'.

(ii) Give one method by which organic compound *C* can be prepared from *B*.

(iii) Write down the reaction in which *A* becomes its corresponding acid chloride.

Answers

1. (*b*) 2. (*b*) 3. (*a*) 4. (*a*) 5. (*b*) 6. (*c*)
7. (*a*) 8. (*c*)

10
CHAPTER

Biomolecules

All living systems are composed of various complex organic compounds namely carbohydrates, proteins, fats or lipids, nucleic acids, etc. These organic compounds are referred to as **biomolecules.** They interact with each other and constitute the molecular logic of life processes.
In addition to these, vitamins and mineral salts (simple molecules) also play an important role in the funciton of organisms. Therefore, structures and functions of some of these biomolecules are discussed in this chapter.

YOUR STUDY GOALS

YOUR PRACTICE GOAL

- Objective Type Questions (46 Qs ; 28 MCQs, 16 A-R, 2 Case-Study)
- Subjective Type Questions (29 Qs ; 14 SA-I, 13 SA-II, 2 LA)

10.1 Carbohydrates

- These are primarily produced by plants and form a very large group of naturally occurring organic compounds.
- Most of them have a general formula, $C_x(H_2O)_y$ and were considered as hydrates of carbon from where the name carbohydrate was derived.

e.g. The molecular formula of glucose ($C_6H_{12}O_6$) fits into the given general formula, $C_6(H_2O)_6$.

- All the compounds which fit into this formula may not be classified as carbohydrates, e.g. **Acetic acid** (CH_3COOH).
  Similarly, all the carbohydrates do not fit into this formula. e.g. **Rhamnose** ($C_6H_{12}O_5$) is a carbohydrate but does not fit in the formula.
- A large number of their chemical reactions have shown that they contain specific functional groups. Thus, chemically, the carbohydrates may be defined as *"optically active polyhydroxy aldehydes or ketones or the compounds which produce such units on hydrolysis"*.
- Carbohydrates are also known as **saccharides** (Greek : sakcharon means sugar).

Classification of Carbohydrates

On the basis of the behaviour towards hydrolysis, carbohydrates are broadly classified into the following three classes.

Monosaccharides

Simple carbohydrates which are composed of single unit of saccharide and cannot be hydrolysed further to give simpler unit of polyhydroxy aldehyde or ketone, are called **monosaccharides**.

It may consist upto six carbon atoms. About twenty monosaccharides are known to occur in nature, e.g., glucose, fructose, ribose, etc.

$$\underset{\text{Glucose or Fructose}}{C_6H_{12}O_6} + H_2O \xrightarrow{H^+} \text{No reaction}$$

Oligosaccharides

Carbohydrates which give 2-10 monosaccharide units on hydrolysis are called **oligosaccharides**.

They can be grouped further into di, tri, tetrasaccharides, etc., depending upon the actual number of monosaccharide units they give on hydrolysis. Amongst these, the most common are **disaccharides**.

e.g. Hydrolysis of sucrose,

$$\underset{\substack{\text{Sucrose}\\\text{(Disaccharide)}}}{C_{12}H_{22}O_{11}} + H_2O \xrightarrow{H^+} \underset{\text{Glucose}}{C_6H_{12}O_6} + \underset{\text{Fructose}}{C_6H_{12}O_6}$$

Note The two monosaccharide units obtained on hydrolysis of a disaccharide may be same or different. e.g. Sucrose (fructose + glucose) and maltose (glucose + glucose).

Polysaccharides

Carbohydrates which give a large number of monosaccharide units on hydrolysis are called **polysaccharides**, e.g. starch, cellulose, glycogen, etc.

$$\underset{\text{Starch}}{(C_6H_{10}O_5)_n} + nH_2O \xrightarrow{H^+} \underset{\text{Glucose}}{nC_6H_{12}O_6}$$

Note Carbohydrates which are sweet in taste are called **sugars**, while those which are not sweet are called **non-sugars**. Monosaccharides and disaccharides are sugars but polysaccharides are non-sugars.

- On the basis of reducing activity, carbohydrates can be classified as follows :

Reducing Sugars

Carbohydrates in which ketonic or aldehydic groups are free and are capable of reducing Fehling's solution or Tollen's reagent are known as **reducing sugars**, e.g. monosaccharides like glucose, fructose, ribose, etc.

Non-reducing Sugars

Carbohydrates in which aldehydic or ketonic group are bonded and are not capable of reducing Fehling's solution or Tollen's reagent are called **non-reducing sugars**, e.g. disaccharides like sucrose and polysaccharides like starch, cellulose, glycogen, dextrins, etc.

Monosaccharides

- As discussed earlier, monosaccharides are the simplest carbohydrates and also called **simple sugars**.
- These are classified on the basis of the functional group present in them, i.e., an **aldose** (monosaccharide containing an aldehyde group) and ketose (monosaccharide containing a keto group).
- Monosaccharides can be further classified into different categories depending upon the number of carbon atoms as shown in the table given below.

Different Types of Monosaccharides

Carbon atoms	General term	Aldehyde	Ketone
3	Triose	Aldotriose	Ketotriose
4	Tetrose	Aldotetrose	Ketotetrose
5	Pentose	Aldopentose	Ketopentose
6	Hexose	Aldohexose	Ketohexose
7	Heptose	Aldoheptose	Ketoheptose

I. Glucose

It is an aldohexose having molecular formula $C_6H_{12}O_6$ and occurs freely as well as in combined form in the nature. It is present in sweet fruits and honey. Ripe grapes contain glucose in large amounts, hence glucose is also known as **grape sugar**.

It can be prepared as follows

Preparation of Glucose

(i) **From sucrose (Cane sugar)** Glucose can be easily obtained in a laboratory by the hydrolysis of alcoholic solution of cane sugar, i.e., sucrose is boiled with dilute HCl or H_2SO_4 at 50°C to give glucose and fructose in equal amounts.

$$\underset{\text{Sucrose}}{C_{12}H_{22}O_{11}} + H_2O \xrightarrow{H^+} \underset{\text{Glucose}}{C_6H_{12}O_6} + \underset{\text{Fructose}}{C_6H_{12}O_6}$$

(ii) **From starch** On large scale (commercially), glucose is obtained by the hydrolysis of starch by boiling it with hot dilute H_2SO_4 at 393 K, under 2-3 standard atmospheric pressure.

$$\underset{\text{Starch or Cellulose}}{(C_6H_{10}O_5)_n} + nH_2O \xrightarrow[393\text{ K; 2-3 atm}]{H^+} \underset{\text{Glucose}}{nC_6H_{12}O_6}$$

Structure of Glucose

Two types of structures, the open chain structure and cyclic structure have been suggested for glucose which are discussed below.

Structural Evidences for Glucose

Glucose was assigned the open structure on the basis of the following evidences.

CHO ⟵ 1 Aldehydic group
$(CHOH)_4$ ⟵ Four CHOH (2° alcohol) groups
CH_2OH ⟵ 1 CH_2OH (1° alcohol) group
Glucose

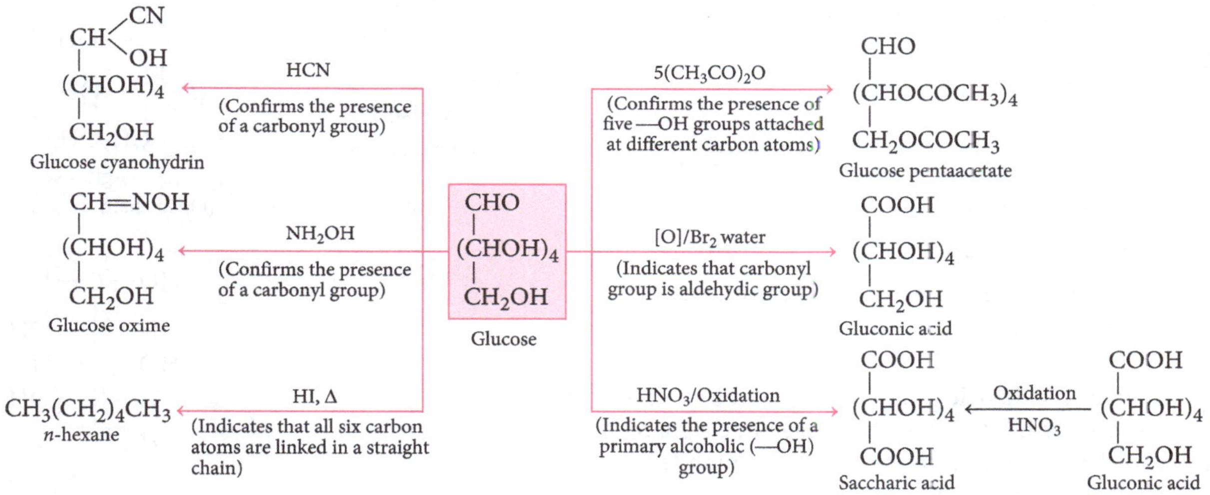

Glucose is named as D-(+)-glucose in which 'D' represents the configuration, whereas '(+)' represents the dextrorotatory nature of the molecule. Therefore, it is also known as **dextrose**.

Configuration of Glucose

Emil Fischer gave the exact spatial arrangement of different —OH groups in glucose after studying many other properties. Its configuration is correctly represented as I.

So, gluconic acid is represented as II and saccharic acid as III.

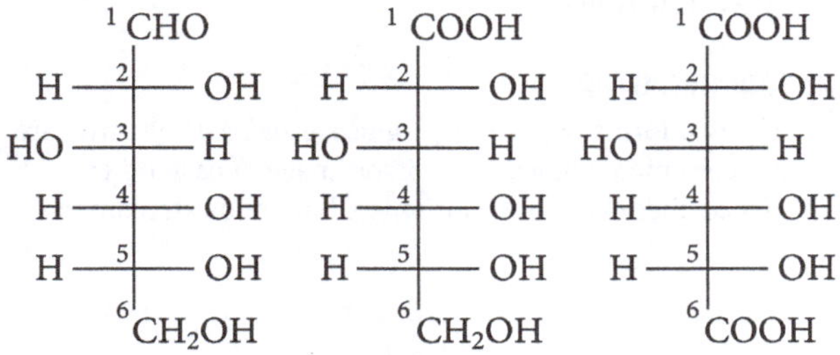

I D-(+)-glucose II Gluconic acid III Saccharic acid

D and L-Notations

- D and L before the name of any compound commonly indicate the relative configuration of a particular stereoisomer of a compound with respect to configuration of some other compound whose configuration is known.
- In the case of carbohydrates, this refers to their relation with a particular isomer of glyceraldehyde. Glyceraldehyde contains one asymmetric carbon atom and exists in two enantiomeric forms as given below:

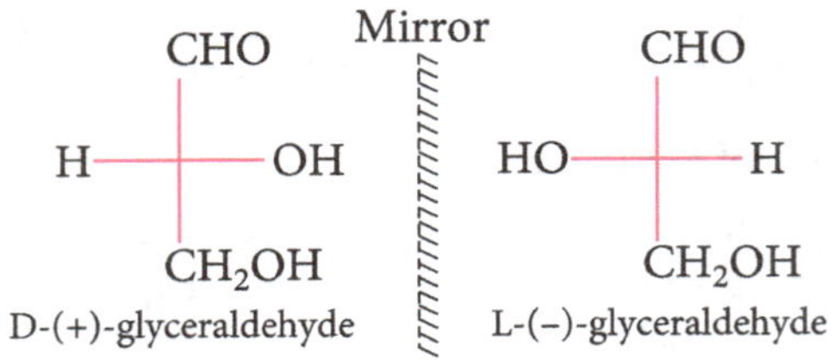

- Compounds which can be chemically correlated to D (+)-isomer of glyceraldehyde are said to have **D-configuration**, whereas those which can be correlated to L (–)-isomer of glyceraldehyde are said to have **L-configuration**.

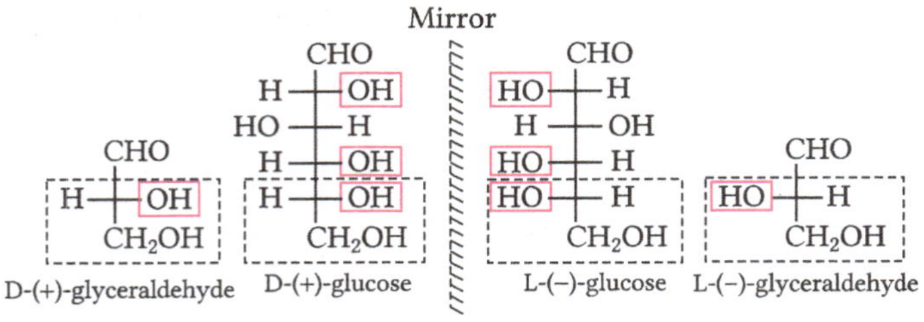

Note Moreover, for assigning the configuration of monosaccharides, it is the lowest assymetric carbon which is compared. D and L has no relation with the optical activity of the compound.

Cyclic Structure of Glucose

- The linear structure of glucose explained most of its properties but failed to explain the following facts and reactions.
  - (i) Even though an aldehyde group is present, the glucose does not react with NH_3, 2, 4-DNP reagent, Grignard reagent and it does not form the hydrogen sulphite addition product with $NaHSO_3$.
  - (ii) Glucose does not restore the pink colour of Schiff's reagent, despite having an aldehydic group.
  - (iii) The pentaacetate of glucose does not react with hydroxylamine which shows the absence of free —CHO group.
  - (iv) Glucose exists in two different crystalline forms which are named as α and β.
    - (a) The α-form of glucose (m.p. 419 K) is obtained by crystallisation from concentrated solution of glucose at 303 K.
    - (b) The β-form (m.p. 423 K) is obtained by crystallisation from hot and saturated aqueous solution at 371 K.
- All the given test or behaviour could not be explained by the open chain structure of glucose. Thus, it was suggested that one of the —OH groups may add to the —CHO group and form a cyclic hemiacetal structure.
- It was found that glucose forms a six membered ring in which —OH at C-5 is involved in the ring formation. This explains the absence of —CHO group and existence of glucose in two forms as shown below.

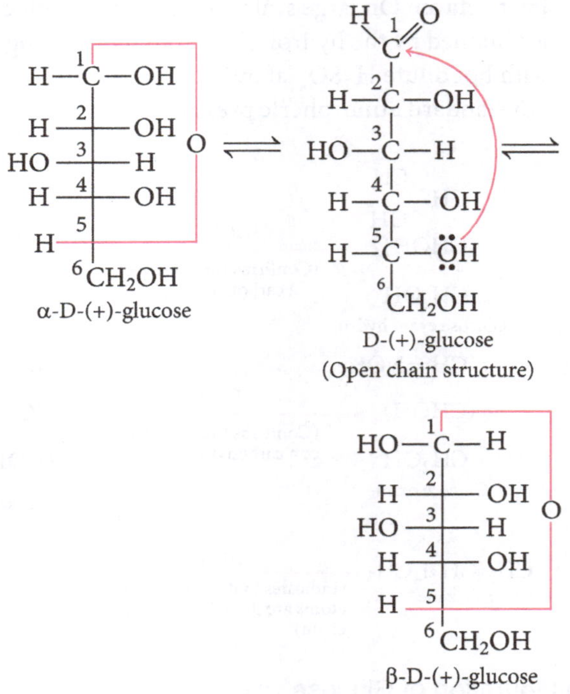

Fischer projection formulae

- The two cyclic forms (α - and β-forms) exist in equilibrium with open chain structure. These two cyclic hemiacetal forms of glucose differ only in the configuration of the hydroxyl group at C - 1 atom called **anomeric carbon** and such isomers, are called **anomers**.

TEACHER'S TIP

The two forms of glucose (α-glucose and β -D-glucose) are stereoisomers but are not mirror image of each other. Hence, these are not enantiomers but are diastereomers.

Mutarotation

- The specific rotation of α-D-glucose is +112.2°, while that of β-D-glucose is +18.7°, when either of α- and β- form of glucose is dissolved in water and allowed to stand for sometime, an equilibrium mixture is obtained. This mixture have specific rotation of +52.7°. This change in value of specific rotation implies that one form is converted into the other with a very small amount of the open chain form.

$$\alpha\text{-D-glucose} \rightleftharpoons \text{Equilibrium mixture} \rightleftharpoons \beta\text{-D-glucose}$$
$$[\alpha]_0 = +112.2^\circ \rightleftharpoons [\alpha]_0 = +52.7^\circ \rightleftharpoons [\alpha]_0 = +18.7^\circ$$

- This spontaneous change of specific rotation of an optically active compound with time towards an equilibrium value is called **mutarotation**.
- **Pyranose structure** (α- or β-) It is the six membered cyclic structure of glucose. It is analogous to pyran which is a cyclic organic compound with one oxygen atom and five carbon atoms in the ring.
- The cyclic structure of glucose is more correctly represented by **Haworth structures** as given below.

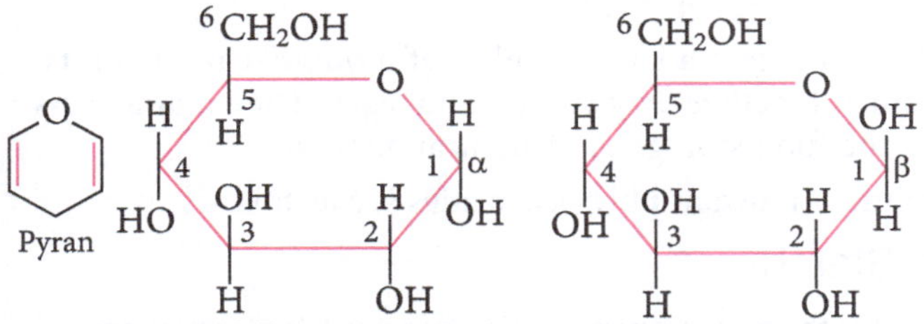

Pyran α-D-(+)-glucopyranose β-D-(+)-glucopyranose

Haworth structures of glucose

II. Fructose

It is an important ketohexose which is obtained along with glucose by the hydrolysis of disaccharide, sucrose. Its molecular formula is same as that of glucose, i.e. $C_6H_{12}O_6$.

Structure of Fructose

- Fructose have a ketonic functional group at C-2 and six carbon atoms in a straight chain as present in glucose.

  It is laevorotatory in nature hence, also known as **leavulose**. It is appropriately written as D-(−)-fructose.

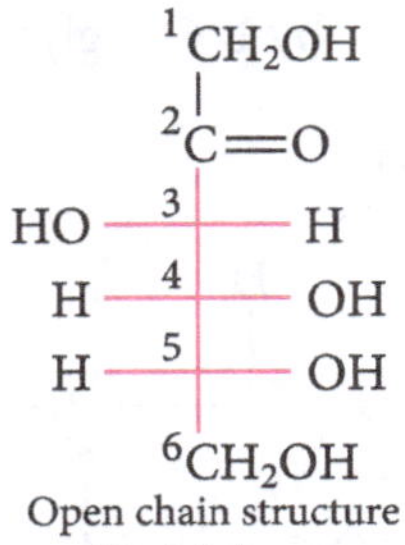

Open chain structure of D-(−)-fructose

- It also exists in two cyclic forms which are obtained by the addition of —OH at C-5 to the ($>C=O$) group.

  The ring, thus formed is a five membered ring named as furanose analogous to furan, which is a five membered cyclic compound with one oxygen and four carbon atoms.

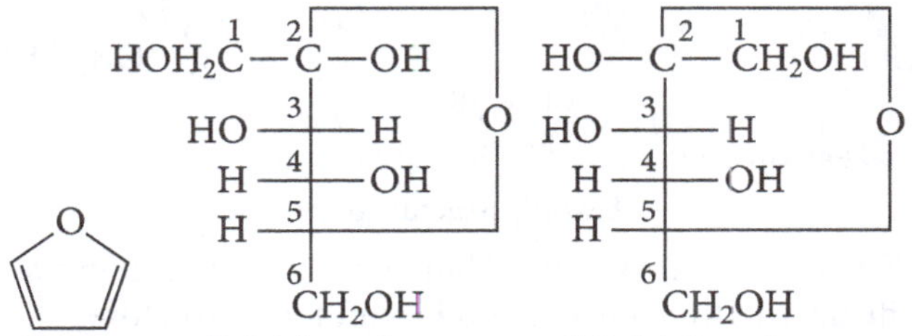

Furan α-D-(−)-fructofuranose β-D-(−)-fructofuranose

Fischer projection formulae

- The cyclic structures of two anomers of fructose are represented by **Haworth structures** as given below.

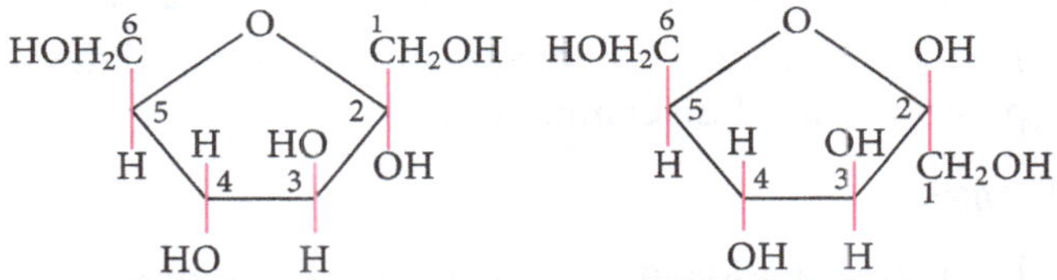

α-D-(−)-fructofuranose β-D-(−)-fructofuranose

Haworth structures of fructose

Disaccharides

Disaccharides on hydrolysis with dilute acids or enzymes give two molecules of monosaccharides. These molecules may be either same or different monosaccharides.

The two monosaccharide units are joined together through an oxide linkage, known as **glycosidic linkage**, which is formed by the loss of a water molecule.

Some important disaccharides are

I. Sucrose

- It is the most widely occurring disaccharides. It is commercially obtained from sugarcane or sugarbeets. On hydrolysis with acids or enzyme invertase, sucrose gives equimolar mixture of 1 mole of D-(+)-glucose and 1 mole of D-(−)-fructose.

$$\underset{\text{Sucrose}}{C_{12}H_{22}O_{11}} + H_2O \xrightarrow{HCl} \underset{\text{D-(+)- glucose}}{C_6H_{12}O_6} + \underset{\text{D-(−)-fructose}}{C_6H_{12}O_6}$$

These two monosaccharides are linked through a glycosidic linkage between C-1 of α-glucose and C-2 of β-fructose unit.

- Since, the reducing groups of glucose and fructose are involved in glycosidic bond formation, sucrose is a **non-reducing sugar**.

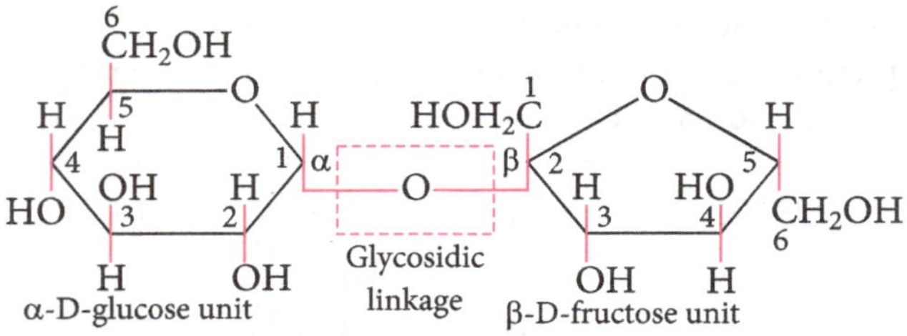

Haworth structure of sucrose

- Sucrose is dextrorotatory but after hydrolysis, it gives dextrorotatory glucose and laevorotatory fructose. The mixture is laevorotatory because specific rotation of fructose (–92.4°) is more than that of glucose (+52.5°).
- Therefore, hydrolysis of sucrose brings about a change in the sign of rotation, i.e., from *dextro* (+) to *laevo* (–). Hence, the product is known as **invert sugar** and the process is called **inversion of sugar**.

II. Maltose

- It is a disaccharide in which two D-glucose units are joined together by a glycosidic linkage between C_1 of one glucose (I) and C_4 of another glucose unit (II).
- It is a **reducing sugar** due to the presence of free aldehyde group which can be produced at C_1 of second glucose in solution.

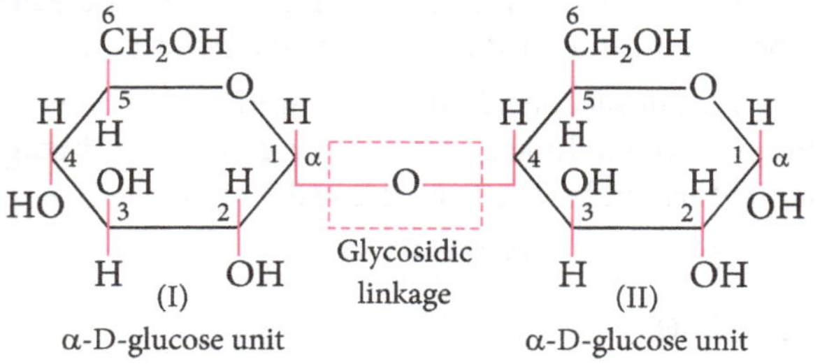

Haworth structure of maltose

III. Lactose

- It is commonly known as **milk sugar** because it is found in milk. On hydrolysis with dilute acid it gives one mole each of β-D-galactose and β-D-glucose.

$$C_{12}H_{22}O_{11} \xrightarrow[-H_2O]{H^+} \underset{\beta\text{-D-glucose}}{C_6H_{12}O_6} + \underset{\beta\text{-D-galactose}}{C_6H_{12}O_6}$$

- The linkage is between C-1 of galactose and C - 4 of glucose unit.

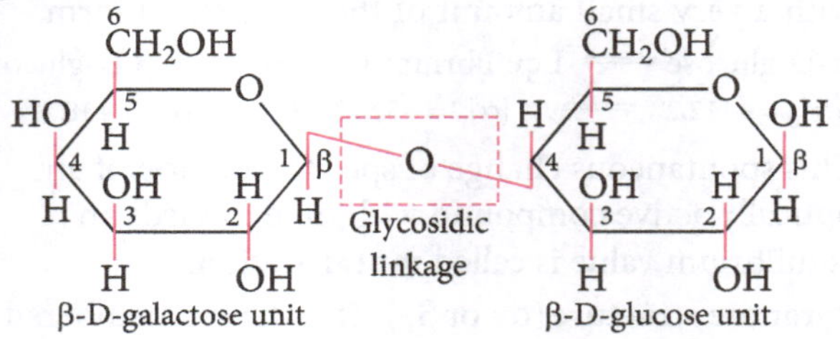

Haworth structure of lactose

- It reduces Tollen's or Fehling's solution hence, it is also called a **reducing sugar** in which glucose unit is in the reducing form.

Polysaccharides

These contain a large number of monosaccharide units joined together by glycosidic linkages. They mainly acts as the food storage or structural materials.

Some important polysaccharides are as follows

I. Starch

- It is the most important dietary source for human beings. It is found in cereals, roots, tubers and some vegetables.
- It is a polymer of α-glucose and consists of the following two components:
  (i) **Amylose** It is a long unbranched chain with 200-1000 α-D-(+)-glucose units held by 1, 4-α-glycosidic linkage. It is non-reducing in water.
  (ii) **Amylopectin** It is a branched chain polymer of α-D-glucose units. In this, chain is formed by 1, 4-α-glycosidic linkage, whereas branching occurs by 1, 6-α-glycosidic linkage.

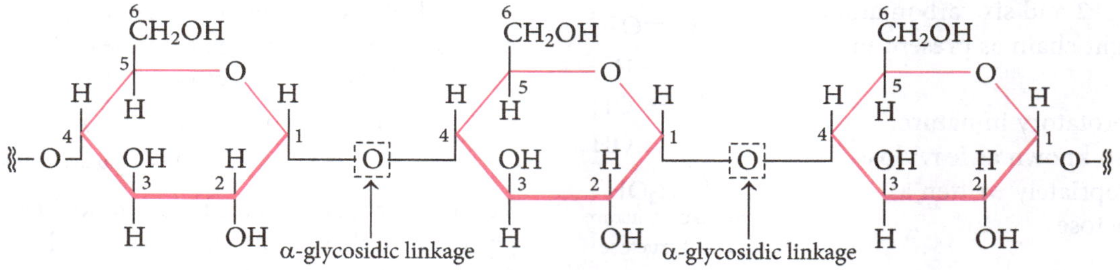

Structure of amylose

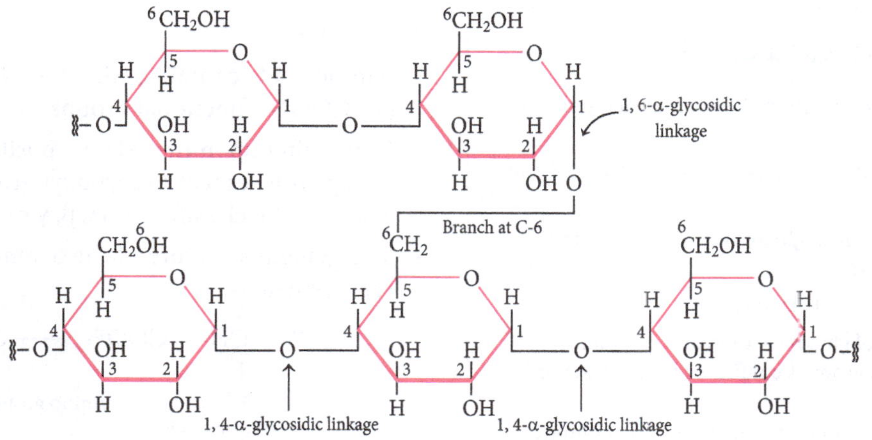

Structure of amylopectin

Differences between Amylose and Amylopectin

Amylose	Amylopectin
1. Amylose is soluble in water.	Amylopectin is insoluble in water.
2. It constitutes 15-20% of starch.	It constitutes about 80-85% of starch.
3. Chemically, amylose is a long unbranched chain with 200-1000 α-D-(+)-glucose units.	It is a highly branched chain polymer of α-D-glucose units.
4. α-D-(+)-glucose units are held together by C_1-C_4 glycosidic linkage.	Glycosidic linkage in glucose units is present between C_1-C_4 atoms, whereas the branching occurs through C_1-C_6 glycosidic linkage.

Note Starch on reacting with enzyme diastase yields maltose, while on boiling with dilute acid yields glucose.

II. Cellulose

- It is the most abundant organic substance in plant kingdom.
- It is a straight chain polysaccharide composed only of **β-D-glucose units**. These units are linked together by glycosidic linkage between C-1 of one glucose unit and C-4 of the next glucose unit. It is non-reducing in nature.

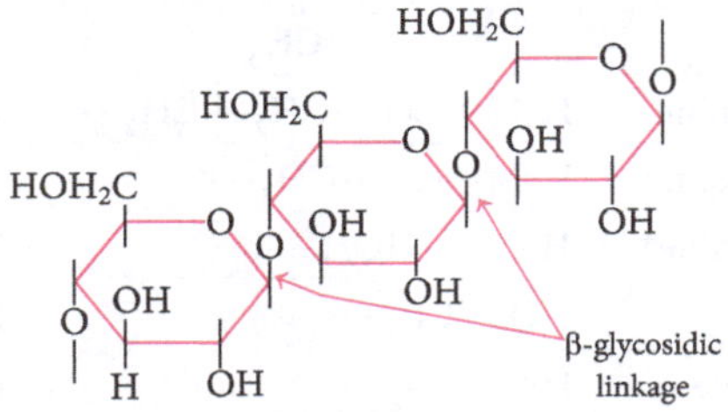

Structure of cellulose

III. Glycogen

- Its structure is similar to amylopectin and is highly branched that is why it is also known as **animal starch**.
- The main difference between glycogen and amylopectin is that average chain length in glycogen is 10-14, whereas in amylopectin it is 25-30 glucose units. It contains glycosidic linkage between C_1 and C_4 position of glucose.
- It is present in liver, muscles and brain. Glycogen is also found in yeast and fungi.

Importance of Carbohydrates

Carbohydrates are very important and essential for life in both plants and animals.

Few important roles of carbohydrates are listed below

- They form a major portion of our food. Honey has been used for a longtime as an instant source of energy by 'Vaids' in ayurvedic system of medicine.
- They are used as storage molecules like starch in plants and glycogen in animals.
- Cellulose in the form of wood is used to build furniture and clothes in the form of cotton fibres.
- They provide raw materials for many industries, like textiles, papers, breweries and lacquers.
- They act as a biofuel to provide energy for the functioning of living organisms.
- They (cellulose) act as constituents of cell membranes of plants and bacteria.
- Two aldopentoses (i.e. D-ribose and 2-deoxy-D-ribose) are present in nucleic acids.
- In living systems, carbohydrates are also found in combination with many proteins and lipids such as glycoproteins and glycolipids.

Quick Test 1

1. Classify the following into monosaccharides and disaccharides.
   Ribose, 2-deoxyribose, maltose, galactose, fructose and lactose. NCERT
2. What happens when D-glucose is treated with the following reagents? NCERT
   (i) HI (ii) HNO_3
3. Give the reaction of glucose with hydrogen cyanide. Presence of which group is confirmed by this reaction? CBSE 2023
4. How will you distinguish 1° and 2° hydroxyl groups present in glucose ?
5. What do you understand by the term glycosidic linkage? NCERT

Or What type of linkage is present in disaccharides? CBSE 2017 C

6. What are the products of hydrolysis of sucrose? NCERT, CBSE 2025
7. (i) How are carbohydrates stored in animal's body? Mention any one organ where they are present.
   (ii) What is the basic structural difference between starch and cellulose? CBSE 2023
8. What is glycogen? How is it different from starch? NCERT
9. Carbohydrates are essential for life in both plants and animals. Name the carbohydrates that are used as storage molecules in plants and animals.
   Also, name the carbohydrate which is present in wood or in the fibre of cotton cloth. NCERT Exemplar

For Solutions, See QR Code on Pg. 386

10.2 Proteins

- Another class of biomolecules which are essential for living systems, are **proteins**. These are the complex nitrogenous organic molecules and are also the most abundant biomolecules of the living system.
- The chief sources of proteins are milk, cheese, pulses, fish, meat, peanuts, etc.
- They are of different types and have many different biological functions. The word protein derived from Greek word "proteios" which means 'primary' or 'prime importance'.
- Chemically, proteins are the polymers in which the monomeric units are α-amino acids.

Amino Acids

- Amino acids contain amino (—NH_2) and carboxyl (—COOH) functional groups.
- Depending upon the relative position of amino group with respect to carboxyl group, the amino acids can be classified as α, β, γ or δ and so on.
- The general structure of the α-amino acids can be represented as,

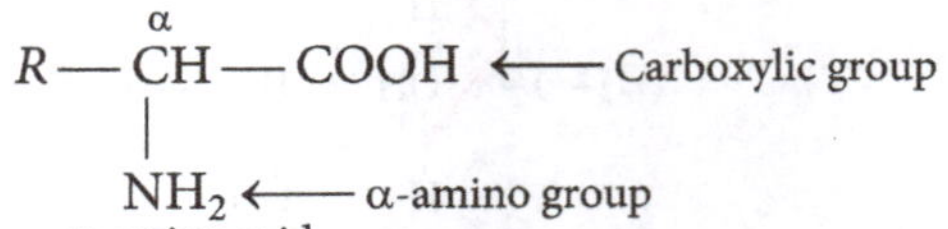

α-amino acid
(R = Alkyl or aryl side chain)

- On hydrolysis of proteins, only α-amino acids are obtained.

Proteins $\xrightarrow{\text{Hydrolysis}}$ Peptides $\xrightarrow{\text{Hydrolysis}}$ α-amino acids

Note The protein differ in the nature of R-group bonded to α-carbon atom.

Nomenclature of Amino Acids

Amino acids are generally represented by a three letter symbol, sometimes one letter symbol is also used.

The structures of some commonly occurring amino acids along with their symbols can be summarised as follows.

Natural Amino Acids

Name of the amino acids	Characteristic feature of side chain, R	Three letter symbol	One letter code
Neutral Amino Acids			
1. Glycine	H	Gly	G
2. Alanine	$—CH_3$	Ala	A
3. Valine*	$(H_3C)_2CH—$	Val	V
4. Leucine*	$(H_3C)_2CH—CH_2—$	Leu	L
5. Isoleucine*	$H_3C—CH_2—\underset{\underset{CH_3}{\vert}}{CH}—$	Ile	I
6. Glutamine	$H_2N—CO—CH_2—CH_2—$	Gln	Q
7. Asparagine	$H_2N—CO—CH_2—$	Asn	N
8. Threonine*	$H_3C—CHOH—$	Thr	T
9. Serine	$HO—CH_2—$	Ser	S
10. Cysteine	$HS—CH_2—$	Cys	C
11. Methionine*	$H_3C—S—CH_2—CH_2—$	Met	M

12. Phenylalanine*	$C_6H_5—CH_2—$	Phe	F
13. Tyrosine	(p) $HO—C_6H_4—CH_2—$	Tyr	Y
14. Tryptophan*	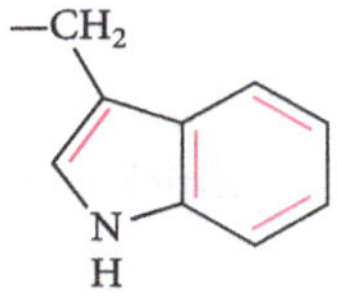	Trp	W
15. Proline	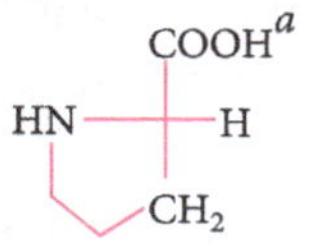	Pro	P
Acidic Amino Acids			
16. Glutamic acid	$HOOC—CH_2—CH_2—$	Glu	E
17. Aspartic acid	$HOOC—CH_2—$	Asp	D
Basic Amino Acids			
18. Arginine*	$HN{=}C(NH_2)—NH(CH_2)_3—$	Arg	R
19. Lysine*	$H_2N—(CH_2)_4—$	Lys	K
20. Histidine*	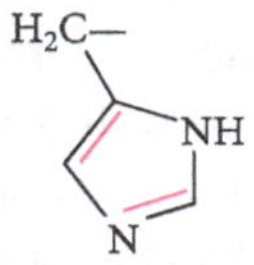	His	H

*Essential amino acids, a = Complete structure

Classification of Amino Acids

Classification of Amino Acids

- On the basis of relative number of amino ($—NH_2$) and carboxyl ($—COOH$) groups
  - **Acidic amino acids**
    No. of—COOH groups > No. of—NH_2 groups
    e.g. Aspartic acid, Glutamic acid
  - **Neutral amino acids**
    No. of—COOH groups = No. of—NH_2 groups. e.g. Glycine, Alanine, Valine
  - **Basic amino acids**
    No. of—NH_2 groups > No. of —COOH groups.
    e.g. Lysine, Histidine
- On the basis of their synthesis
  - **Essential amino acids**
    which can't be synthesised in the body and must be obtained through diet.
    e.g. Valine, Lysine, etc.
  - **Non-essential acids**
    which can be synthesised in the body.
    e.g. Glycine, Alanine, Glutamic acid

Properties of Amino Acids

Some of the important properties of amino acids are as follows

- Amino acids are usually colourless, crystalline solids. These are soluble in water and have high melting points.
- Amino acids contain both acidic (carboxyl group) and basic (amino group) groups in the same molecule due to which they behave like salts rather than simple amines or carboxylic acids.
- In aqueous solution, they neutralise each other involving transfer of a proton from the carboxyl group to the amino group, giving rise to a dipolar ion known as '**zwitter ion**'. It is neutral but contains both positive and negative charges.

$$R—\underset{\underset{:NH_2}{|}}{CH}—\overset{\overset{O}{\|}}{C}—O—H \rightleftharpoons R—\underset{\underset{\overset{+}{N}H_3}{|}}{CH}—\overset{\overset{O}{\|}}{C}—O^-$$

(Zwitter ion)

In Zwitter ionic form, amino acids show amphoteric behaviour as they can react with both acids and bases.

- Except glycine, all other α-amino acids are optically active as their α-carbon is asymmetric. These exist in both 'D' and 'L' forms.

Most of the amino acids have L-configuration in which $—NH_2$ group is on left hand side.

$$H_2N—\overset{\overset{COOH}{|\alpha}}{\underset{\underset{R}{|}}{C}}—H$$

L-amino acid

Peptide Linkage and their Classification

- Proteins are connected to each other by —CO—NH— bond which is called the **peptide bond** or the **peptide linkage**. Chemically, peptide linkage is an amide (—CO—NH—bond) formed between carboxyl group (—COOH) and amino group ($—NH_2$).
- Peptide linkages can be of various types, i.e., **dipeptide** (combination of amino group of one molecule with carboxyl group of other), **tripeptide** (three amino acids linked by two peptide linkages), **tetrapeptide, pentapeptide, hexapeptide** and so on.

e.g. Glycylalanine is formed when carboxyl group of glycine combines with the amino group of alanine.

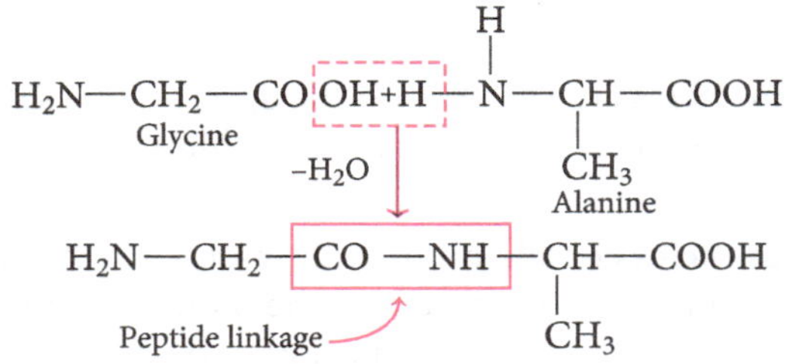

Glycylalanine (Gly-Ala)

- When the number of such amino acids is more than ten, then the products are called **polypeptides.**

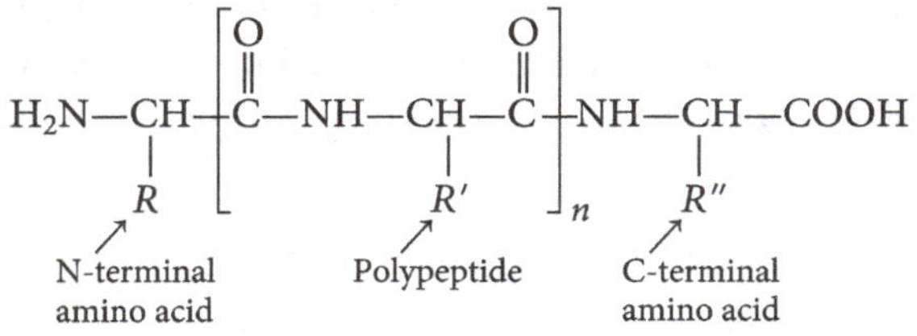

where, R, R', R'' may be same or different.

- A polypeptide with more than hundred amino acid residues, having molecular mass higher than 10,000u is called a **protein**.

Classification of Proteins

On the basis of their molecular shape, proteins are of two types

(i) **Fibrous proteins** They have thread or fibre like structures in which polypeptide chains run parallel and are held together by hydrogen and disulphide bonds. These proteins are insoluble in water.
e.g. Keratin (found in hair, wool, silk) and myosin (present in muscles).

(ii) **Globular proteins** They have spherical shape structure which results when the chains of polypeptides coil around. These are soluble in water.
e.g. Insulin and albumins.

Structure and Shape of Proteins

On the basis of structure and shape of proteins, four different levels are found.

(i) **Primary structure**

- The specific sequence in which various α-amino acids are linked with each other through peptide bonds to form a polypeptide, is called its **primary structure**.
- The change of just one amino acid in the sequence can alter its biological activity and can create a different protein.

(ii) **Secondary structure**

- It refers to the shape in which a long polypeptide chain can exist.
- The conformation in which the polypeptide chains assume as a result of hydrogen bonding between $-\overset{\overset{\displaystyle O}{\|}}{C}-$ and —NH— groups of the peptide bond is called secondary structure of proteins.
- It exist in two different structures which are as follows

(a) **α-helix structure** It is a spiral protein structure right handed helix structure stabilised by H-bonds between the $\rangle C{=}O$ group of one amino acid residue and the amino (—NH) group of the fourth amino acid residue ahead creating a compact, stable shape. Proteins such as keratin in hair, wool, nails and myosin in nucleus have α-helix structure.

Note All amino acids in the polypeptide chain have L-configuration. Thus, they can results in stable helix only if it is right handed.

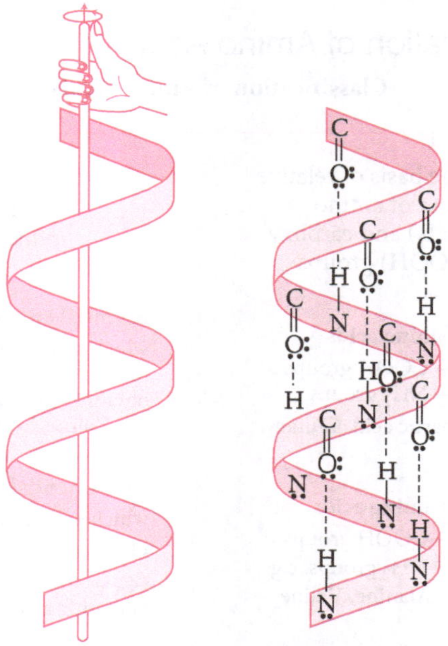

α-helix structure of proteins

(b) **β-pleated sheet structure** It is a protein structure where chains are aligned side-by-side and held together by H-bonds, creating a stable, *zig-zag* sheet-like form.

It can either be parallel or antiparallel. This structure is less compact and rigid as compared to α-helix structure. The structure so formed resembles the pleated folds of drapery and thus, it is known as **β-pleated sheet structure.**

Silk protein has β-pleated sheet structures.

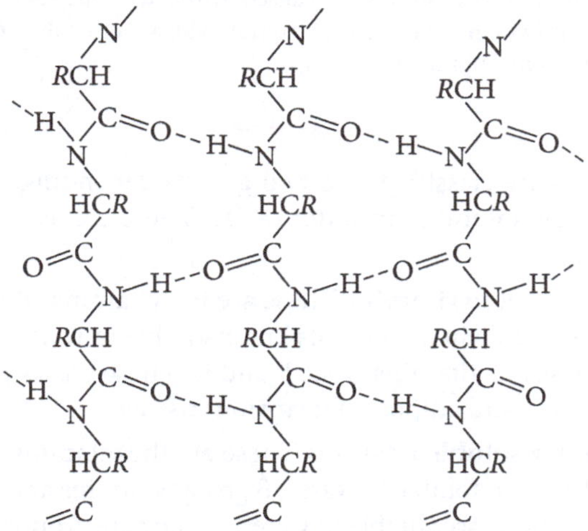

β-pleated sheet structure of proteins

(iii) **Tertiary structure** The further folding of the secondary structure of proteins is known as **tertiary structure.** It gives rise to two major molecular shapes, **fibrous and globular**. The main forces that stabilise 2° and 3° structures of proteins are hydrogen bonds, disulphide bonds, van der Waals' forces and electrostatic forces of attraction.

(iv) **Quaternary structure** Although many proteins exist as a single polypeptide chain, but some of the proteins are composed of two or more polypeptide chains called **sub-units.**

The spatial arrangement of these sub-units with respect to each other is known as quaternary structure. Like quaternary structure of haemoglobin involves four polypeptide chains.

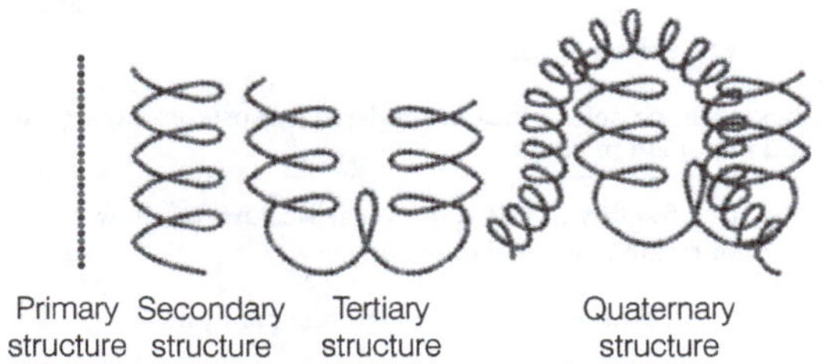

Diagrammatic representation of protein structure (two sub-units of two types in quaternary structure)

Denaturation of Proteins

- Protein found in a biological system with a unique three-dimensional structure and biological activity is called a **native protein.**
- When a native protein is subjected to physical change (like change in temperature) or chemical change (like change in pH), the hydrogen bonds are disturbed. As a result, globules unfold and helix get uncoiled and protein loses its biological activity. This is known as **denaturation of protein.**
- During denaturation, 2° and 3° structures are destroyed but 1° structure remains intact. e.g. Coagulation of an egg white on boiling and curdling of milk caused due to the formation of lactic acid by the bacteria present in milk.

10.3 Enzymes

- Enzymes are essential biological catalysts (or biocatalysts) which are needed to catalyse biochemical reactions. Almost all the enzymes are globular proteins.
- Enzymes are very specific for a particular reaction and for a particular substrate.
- They are generally named after the compound or class of compounds upon which they work. e.g. The enzyme that catalyses hydrolysis of maltose into glucose is named as **maltase.**

e.g. $$\underset{\text{Maltose}}{C_{12}H_{22}O_{11}} \xrightarrow[H_2O]{\text{Maltase}} \underset{\text{Glucose}}{2C_6H_{12}O_6}$$

- Sometimes enzymes are also named after the reaction, where they are used. The enzyme which catalyses the oxidation of one substrate with simultaneous reduction of another substrate are named as **oxidoreductase** enzymes. The ending of the name of an enzyme is '-ase'.

Mechanism of Enzyme Action

Enzymes are needed only in small quantities for the progress of a reaction. Like chemical catalysts, enzyme reduces the magnitude of activation energy.

e.g. Activation energy for acid hydrolysis of sucrose is 6.22 kJ mol^{-1}, while the activation energy is only 2.15 kJ mol^{-1}, when hydrolysed by the enzyme, sucrase.

Quick Test 2

1. Amino acids can be classified as α, β, γ, δ and so on depending upon the relative position of amino group with respect to carboxyl group. Which type of amino acids forms polypeptide chain in proteins? *NCERT Exemplar*
2. The melting points and solubility of amino acids in water are generally higher than that of the corresponding halo acids. Explain. *NCERT Intext*
3. What is the difference between fibrous protein and globular protein? *CBSE 2015, 2020, NCERT*
4. What type of bonding helps in stabilising the α-helix structure of proteins? *NCERT*
5. What are the common types of secondary structure of proteins? *NCERT*
6. Write the function of the following enzymes.
   (i) Invertase (ii) Urease (iii) Maltase *NCERT Exemplar*
7. Activation energy for the acid catalysed hydrolysis of sucrose is 6.22 kJ mol^{-1}, while the activation energy is only 2.15 kJ mol^{-1} when hydrolysis is catalysed by the enzyme sucrase. Explain. *NCERT Exemplar*

For Solutions, See QR Code on Pg. 386

10.4 Vitamins

- Vitamins are organic compounds required in the diet in small amounts to perform specific biological functions for normal maintenance of optimum growth and health of the organism.
- Most of the vitamins cannot be synthesised in our body but plants can synthesise almost all of them. Hence, vitamins are considered as essential food factors.

TEACHER'S TIP
In our body, **avitaminosis** is caused by the deficiency of more than one vitamin while **hypervitaminosils** is caused due to excess consumption of vitamins.

Classification of Vitamins

Vitamins are classified into two groups depending upon their solubility in water or fat. These are as follows :

(i) **Fat soluble vitamins** These are the vitamins which are soluble in fat and oils but insoluble in water. These are vitamins A, D, E and K. These are stored in liver and adipose (fat storing) tissues.

(ii) **Water soluble vitamins** These are the vitamins which are soluble in water. B group vitamins and vitamin C are soluble in water, so they are grouped together.

Water soluble vitamins must be supplied regularly in diet, because they are readily excreted in urine and cannot be stored (except vitamin B_{12}) in our body.

Some Important Vitamins, their Sources and Deficiency Diseases

Name of vitamins	Sources	Deficiency diseases
Vitamin A (Retinol)	Fish liver oil, carrots, butter and milk.	Xerophthalmia (hardening of cornea of eye) and night blindness.
Vitamin B_1 (Thiamine)	Yeast, milk, green vegetables and cereals.	Beri-beri (paralysis of legs, loss of appetite and retarded growth).
Vitamin B_2 (Riboflavin)	Milk, egg white, liver, kidney.	Cheilosis (fissuring at corners of mouth and lips), digestive disorders and burning sensation of the skin.
Vitamin B_6 (Pyridoxine)	Yeast, milk, egg yolk, cereals and grams.	Convulsions, anaemia, weakness.
Vitamin B_{12} (Cyanocobalamin)	Meat, fish, egg and curd.	Pernicious anaemia (RBC deficient in haemoglobin).
Vitamin C (Ascorbic acid)	Citrus fruits, amla and green leafy vegetables.	Scurvy (bleeding of gums).
Vitamin D (Egrocalciferol)	Exposure to sunlight, fish and egg yolk.	Rickets (bone deformities in children) and osteomalacia (soft bones and joint pain in adults).
Vitamin E (α-tocopherol)	Vegetable oils like wheat germ oil, sunflower oil, etc.	Increased fragility of RBCs, muscular weakness, yellow discolouration of enamel of teeth.
Vitamin H (Biotin)	Yeast, avocados, nuts and egg yolk.	Dermatitis, skin disease, loss of hair and paralysis.
Vitamin K (Phylloquinone)	Green leafy vegetables.	Increased blood clotting time.

10.5 Nucleic Acids

- Every generation of each and every species resembles its ancestors in many ways. Actually, the nucleus of a living cell is responsible for the transmission of inherent characters, also called **heredity**. The particles in the nucleus of the cell, responsible for heredity are called **chromosomes**. These are made up of proteins and another type of biomolecules called **nucleic acids.**
- Nucleic acids are long chain polymers of nucleotides, hence are also called **polynucleotides**. They are of two types, **deoxyribonucleic acid** (DNA) and **ribonucleic acid** (RNA).

Chemical Composition of Nucleic Acids

On complete hydrolysis of DNA (or RNA), nucleic acid gives three different compounds which are as follows:

(i) **Pentose sugar** DNA molecules contain, β-D-2-deoxyribose, a sugar moiety, whereas RNA contains β-D-ribose.

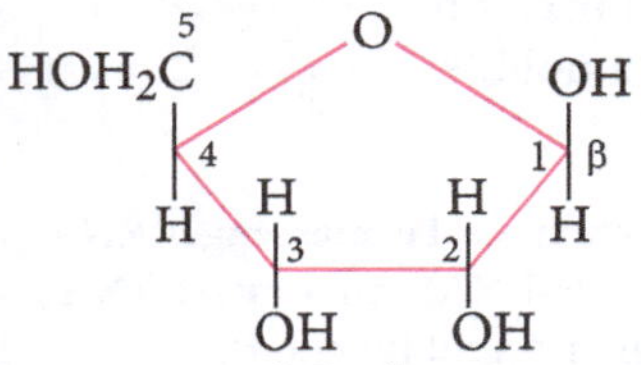
β-D-ribose

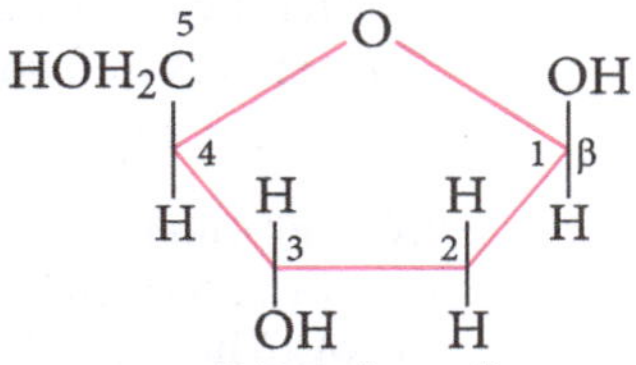
β-D-2-deoxyribose

(ii) **Phosphoric acid** It is the common product of hydrolysis of both DNA and RNA.

(iii) **Nitrogenous base** Nitrogen containing heterocyclic compounds are called **nitrogenous bases.**
Nitrogenous bases are of two types

(a) **Purines** - Adenine (A) and Guanine (G)

(b) **Pyrimidines** -Uracil (U), Thymine (T) and Cytosine (C)

DNA and RNA both contains three common bases; adenine (A), guanine (G) and cytosine (C). Thymine (T) is present in DNA but in place of thymine, RNA contains uracil (U).

i.e. DNA = A, G, C, **T** or RNA = A, G, C, **U**

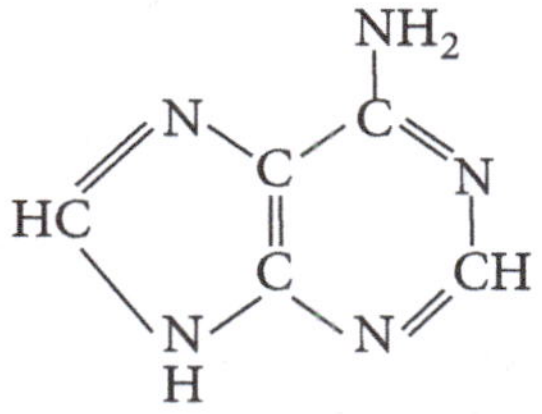
Adenine (A)

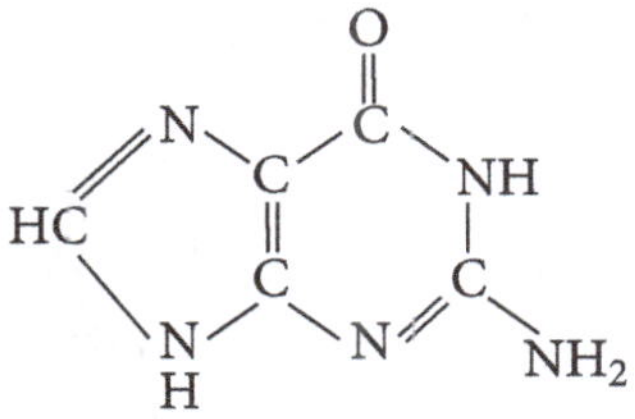
Guanine (G)

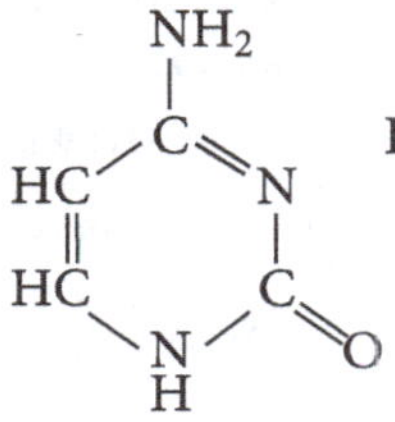
Cytosine (C)

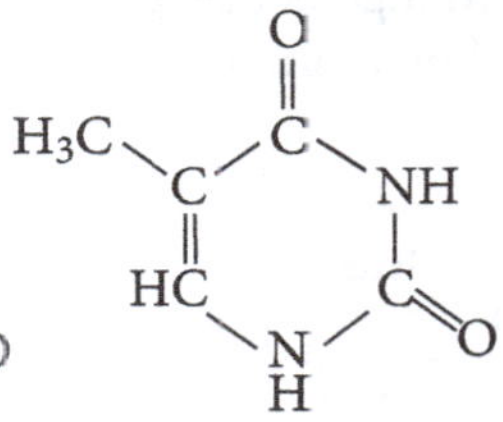
Thymine (T)

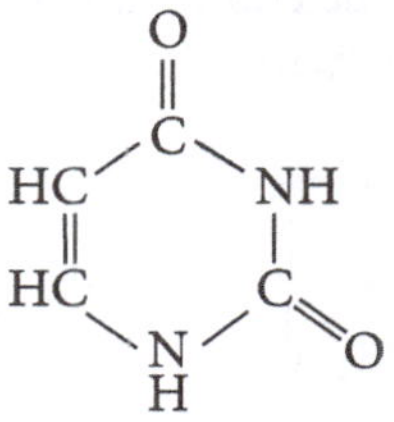
Uracil (U)

Structure of Nucleic Acids

The structure of nucleic acids is described as follows

(i) **Nucleoside** It consists of two basic components of nucleic acids, i.e. a pentose sugar and a nitrogenous base.

Actually, it is the unit in which the base is attached to 1′ position of sugar. In nucleosides, the sugar carbons are numbered as 1′, 2′, 3′, etc., in order to distinguish these from the bases.

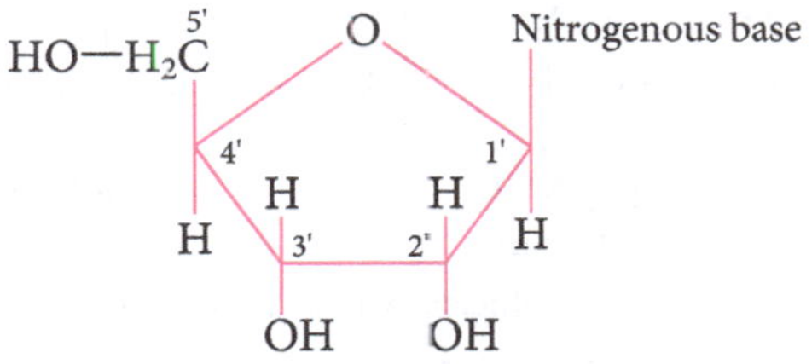

Structure of nucleoside

(ii) **Nucleotide** When nucleoside is linked to phosphoric acid at 5′ position of sugar moiety, a **nucleotide** is formed. Thus, a nucleotide contains three basic components of nucleic acids, i.e., a phosphoric acid, a nitrogenous base and a pentose sugar.

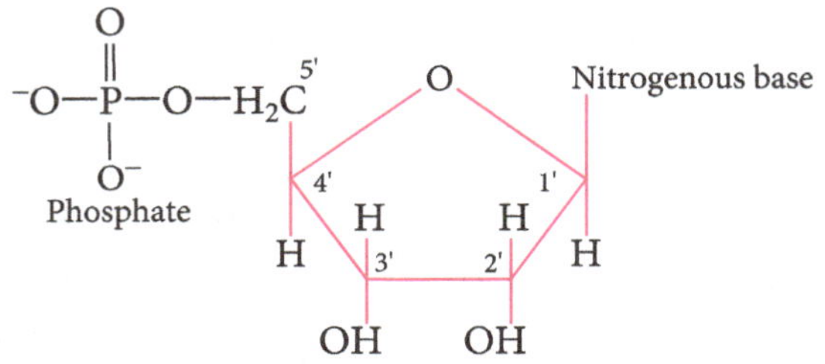

Structure of nucleotide

Nucleotides are joined together by phosphodiester linkage between 5′ and 3′ carbon atoms of the pentose sugar.

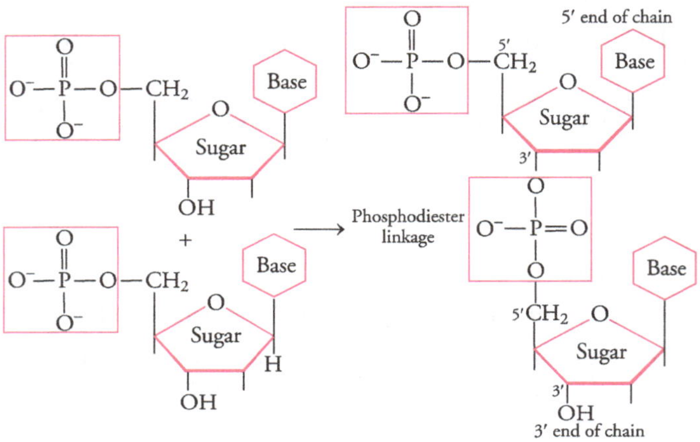

Formation of a dinucleotide

- When the large number of nucleotides are connected, they form **nucleic acid.**

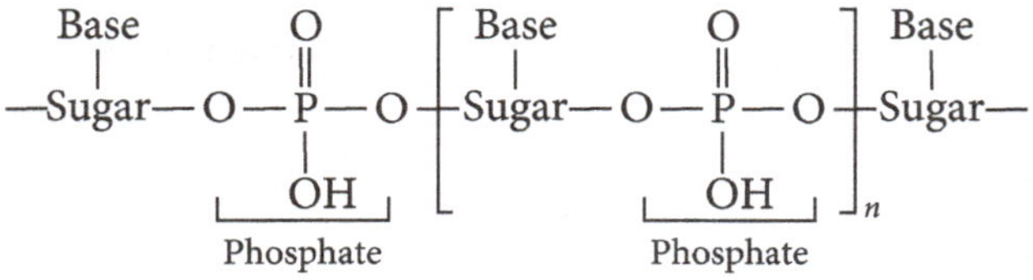

Nucleic acid or polynucleotide

- Structure of nucleic acid can be divided into two following categories (with special reference to DNA).
  - (i) **Primary Structure** The information regarding the sequence of nucleotides in the chain of nucleic acid is called its **primary structure**.
  - (ii) **Secondary Structure**
    - Two strands of polynucleotides coil around each other in the form of double helix. The backbone of each strand consists of sugar phosphate units and base units of each strand are pointed into the interior of helix and are linked through H-bonds. In this, 5′—3′ phosphodiester linkages run in opposite direction.
    - DNA has double stranded α-helix structure given by **James Watson** and **Francis Crick.** The two strands are complementary to each other becuase the hydrogen bonds are formed between specific pairs.
    - Adenine of one strand is hydrogen bonded to thymine of the other through two hydrogen bonds, whereas cytosine of one strand is hydrogen bonded with guanine of the other through three hydrogen bonds, i.e.

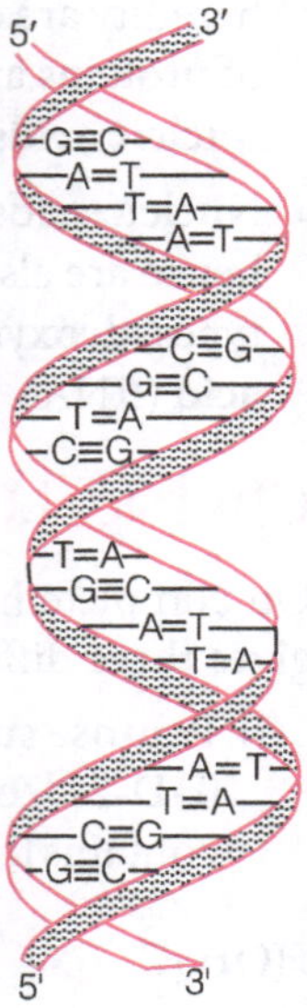

$A{=}T$ and $C{\equiv}G$
↑ 2 hydrogen bonds ↑ 3 hydrogen bonds

- In secondary structure of RNA, helics are present which are single-stranded but sometimes they fold back on themselves to form a double helix structure.

Note RNA molecules are of three types, i.e. **messenger RNA** (*m*-RNA), **ribosomal RNA** (*r*-RNA) and **transfer RNA** (*t*-RNA). They all perform different functions.

Differences between DNA and RNA

DNA (Deoxyribonucleic acid)	RNA (Ribonucleic acid)
• The pentose sugar present is deoxyribose.	The pentose sugar is ribose.
• The common organic bases are adenine (A), guanine (G), cytosine (C) and thymine (T).	The common organic bases are adenine (A), guanine (G), cytosine (C) and uracil (U).
• Adenine pairs with thymine and guanine with cytosine.	Adenine pairs with uracil and guanine with cytosine.
• Double-stranded α-helix structure.	Single-stranded α-helix structure.
• Undergoes replication.	Does not undergo replication.

Biological Functions of Nucleic Acids

The important biological functions of nucleic acids are given below

(i) **Heredity** It is considered as the reserve of genetic information and is also responsible for maintaining the identity of different species of organisms over millions of years.

(ii) **Replication** A DNA molecule is capable of self duplication (also called replication) during cell division and identical DNA strands are transferred to daughter cells.

(iii) **Protein synthesis** It is an important function of nucleic acids in the cell. Actually, the proteins are synthesised by various RNA molecules in the cell but the message for the synthesis of a particular protein is present in DNA. The synthesis of RNA by the DNA to conduct the message is called **transcription**, and synthesis of protein by these RNA is called **translation**.

The biological functions of nucleic acids can be concluded as **central dogma of the molecular biology** and can be represented as below.

$$\text{Replication} \circlearrowright \text{DNA} \xrightarrow{\text{Transcription}} \text{RNA} \xrightarrow{\text{Translation}} \text{Protein}$$

DNA Fingerprinting

A sequence of bases on DNA is unique for a person and information regarding this is called **DNA fingerprinting**.

The sequence on DNA is same for each and every cell of a body and these sequence cannot be altered by any known treatment.

Technique of DNA fingerprinting is used in the following ways.

- To determine the paternity of an individual.
- To identify the racial groups to understand biological evolution better.
- In forensic laboratories, for the identification of criminals.
- To identify dead bodies in case of an accident by comparing the DNA's of parents and children.

Note Dr. Har Gobind Khorana shared the Nobel Prize for medicine and physiology in 1968 with Marshall Nirenberg and Robert Holley for cracking the genetic code.

10.6 Hormones

- These are the chemical substances, produced by endocrine glands in the body and are released directly in blood stream. From here, these are transported to the site of their action.
- These act as intercellular messengers and control various body functions.

Various types of hormones are **steroids** (estrogens and androgens), **polypeptides** (insulin and endorphins), **amino acid derivatives** (epinephrine and norepinephrine). They help to maintain the balance of biological activities in the body.

Name, Sources and Functions of Some Hormones

	Name	Organ of secretion	Functions
Steroid Hormones			
1.	Sex hormones (a) Androgens (Androsterone and Testosterone)	Testes	Control the development and normal functioning of male sex organs during puberty; responsible for male characteristics (deep voice, facial hair, general physical constitution).
	(b) Estrogens (Estrone, Estradiol, Estriol)	Ovary	Control the development and normal functioning of female sex organs. Estradiol is the main female sex hormone. It is responsible for developement of secondary female characteristics and participitation in control of menstrual cycle.
	(c) Progesterone	Corpus luteum	Prepare uterus for implantation of the fertilised egg.
2.	Adrenal cortex hormones or corticoids (glucocorticoids, mineralocorticoides)	Adrenal cortex	Regulate the metabolism of fats, proteins and carbohydrates. Control the balance of water and mineral in the body.

Peptide Hormones		
(a) Insulin	Pancreas	Control the metabolism of glucose and decreases blood sugar level.
(b) Glucagon	Pancreas	Increases blood glucose.
(c) Endorphin	Pituitary gland	Response to relieve pain or stress.
Amine Hormones		
(a) Epinephrine and norepinephrine	Adrenal medulla, nervous system	Regulate the body's nervous system by raising the pulse rate, blood pressure, etc., during emergency.
(b) Thyroxine	Thyroid gland	Controls metabolism of carbohydrates, lipids and proteins.

Note

- Very low level of thyroxine leads to hypothyroidism, which is characterised by lethargyness and obesity.
- Increased level of thyroxine causes hyperthyroidism.
- Hypothyroidism is controlled by adding sodium iodide to commercial table salt ("Iodised" salt).
- If adrenal cortex does not function properly then one may suffer from Addison's disease characterised by hypoglycemia, weakness and increased susceptibility to stress.

Quick Test 3

1. Name the deficiency diseases resulting from lack of vitamins A and E in the diet.

2. Write one source and name of disease caused by the deficiency of vitamin B_{12}. *CBSE 2015, 2017*

3. (i) Deficiency of which vitamin causes scurvy?
(ii) Deficiency of which vitamin causes rickets?

Or

Write the name of vitamin whose deficiency causes bone deformities in children. *CBSE 2015*

4. How are vitamins classified? Name the vitamin responsible for the coagulation of blood. *NCERT*

5. What are nucleic acids? Mention their two important functions. *NCERT*

6. What products would be formed when a nucleotide from DNA containing thymine is hydrolysed? *NCERT Intext*

7. (i) Why nucleic acids are called polynucleotides?
(ii) Name the base that is found in the nucleotide of RNA only.

8. The two strands of DNA are not identical but are complementary. Explain. *NCERT*

9. What is the difference between hormones and vitamins?

For Solutions, See QR Code on Pg. 386

Mind Map

BIOMOLECULES

Nucleic Acids

- They are the polymers of nucleotides.
- They are of two types: Deoxyribonucleic acid (DNA) and ribonucleic acid (RNA) **Composition** In DNA, sugar is β-D-2-deoxyribose whereas in RNA, it is β-D-ribose. DNA contains A, G, C, T whereas RNA has A, G, C, U.

Structure

Nucleoside Formed by attachment of a nitrogenous base to 1′ carbon of the sugar.

Nucleotide Formed when a phosphate group is attached to the 5′ carbon of the sugar.

Enzymes

These are the proteins which catalyse reactions occurring in human body, so also called biocatalysts, e.g. maltase, zymase, etc.

Vitamins

These are essential but in very small amounts. Vitamins A, D, E and K are fat soluble while vitamin B and C are water soluble.

Proteins

- They are the polymers of α-amino acids.
- These contain amino as well as carboxyl functional group.

Classification

(i) On the basis of relative number of $—NH_2$ and —COOH groups.

(a) **Neutral** Equal number of $—NH_2$ than —COOH group.

(b) **Basic** More number of $—NH_2$ than —COOH group.

(c) **Acidic** More number of —COOH than $—NH_2$ group.

(ii) **On the basis of their synthesis**

(a) **Essential** cannot be synthesized in the body and must be obtained from the diet.

(b) **Non-essential** can be synthesized in the body.

(iii) On the basis of molecular shape

(a) **Fibrous** Fibre-like structure

(b) **Globular** Spherical shape

Structure

Peptide linkage

$$H_2N—CH_2—\boxed{CO—NH}—\underset{\displaystyle CH_3}{\underset{|}{CH}}—COOH$$

Structure of Proteins

- **1° structure** It shows the unique linear sequence of amino acids in a polypeptide chain.
- **2° structure** Exist in two different types α-helix and β-pleated sheet.
- **3° structure** Overall folding of polypeptide chains.
- **4° structure** Spatial arrangement of subunits (two or more polypeptide chain) with respect to each other.

Denaturation

- It is the process of destroying 2° or 3° structure of protein by heating and by changing pH.
- Due to this, protein loses its biological activity.
- e.g. Coagulation of egg white on boiling.

Carbohydrates

- These are polyhydroxy aldehydes or ketones or their derivatives, e.g. glucose, fructose, etc.
- Sugars are the carbohydrates having sweet taste. They may be reducing (e.g. glucose)or non-reducing (e.g. starch).

Classification

(i) Monosaccharides

Glucose ($C_6H_{12}O_6$)

- It is obtained by hydrolysing starch or cane sugar.
- Its reactions are as:

$$\underset{\text{(Glucose)}}{CHO—(CHOH)_4—CH_2OH} \xrightarrow[\Delta]{HI} n\text{-Hexane}$$

Glucose $\xrightarrow{NH_2OH}$ Glucose oxime

Glucose $\xrightarrow{3Br_2\text{ water}}$ Gluconic acid

Glucose $\xrightarrow{\text{Acetic anhydride}}$ Glucose pentacetate

Glucose $\xrightarrow{HNO_3}$ Saccharic acid

(ii) Disaccharides

Sucrose

- It contains D-(+)-glucose and D-(−)-fructose joined together by α-1,β-2-glycosidic linkage.
- It is also called invert sugar.

(iii) Polysaccharides

Starch

- It contains two components: amylose (water soluble, 20%) and amylopectin (80%, water insoluble).
- It is the reserve food of plants.

Cellulose

- Most abundant in plants. It contains β-D-glucose units, joined together by β-1,4-glycosidic linkage.

Importance

- Forms major portion of our food.
- Used as storage molecules.
- Act as a biofuel to provide energy for the function of living organisms.

Hormones

- These are the secretions of endocrine glands.
- These are of two types: Steroid hormones and non-steroid hormones.

EXAM PATTERN QUESTIONS

Objective Type Questions

Multiple Choice Questions (MCQs) [1 Mark]

1. Which of the following is a disaccharide? **CBSE 2020**

(a) Glucose (b) Starch
(c) Cellulose (d) Lactose

2. Disaccharides that are reducing in nature are **CBSE SQP 2021**

(a) sucrose and lactose
(b) sucrose and maltose
(c) lactose and maltose
(d) sucrose, lactose and maltose

3. In the following reaction, identify A and B

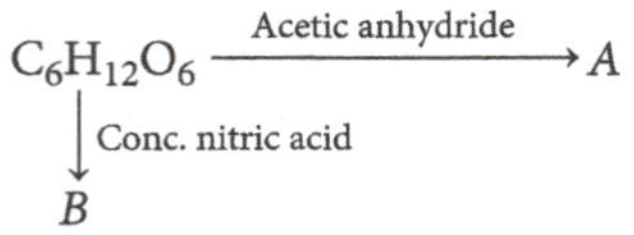

(a) $A = COOH—(CHOH)_4—COOH$,
$B = OHC—(CHOCOCH_3)_4—CH_2OCOCH_3$

(b) $A = COOH—(CHOH)_4—CHO$,
$B = OHC—(CHOCOCH_3)_4—CH_2OCOCH_3$

(c) $A = OHC—(CHOCOCH_3)_3—CH_2OCOCH_3$,
$B = COOH—(CHOH)_4—CHO$

(d) $A = OHC—(CHOCOCH_3)_4—CH_2OCOCH_3$,
$B = COOH—(CHOH)_4—COOH$

4. Which one of the following reactions is not explained by the open chain structure of glucose? **CBSE SQP 2021 (Term I)**

(a) Formation of penta-acetate of glucose with acetic anhydride.
(b) Formation of addition product with 2,4-DNP reagent.
(c) Silver mirror formation with Tollen's reagent.
(d) Existence of α- and β- forms of glucose.

5. Which of the following statements is not true about glucose? CBSE 2025

(a) It is an aldohexose.
(b) On heating with HI it forms n-hexane
(c) It exists in furanose form.
(d) It does not give Schiff's test.

6. Which of the following structures represents α-D-glucose? **CBSE 2023**

(a)
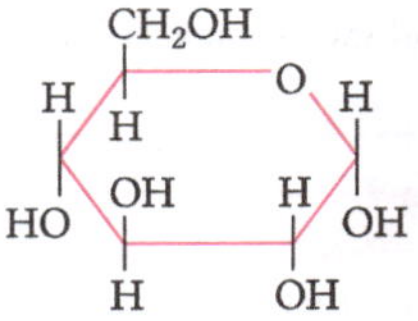

(b)
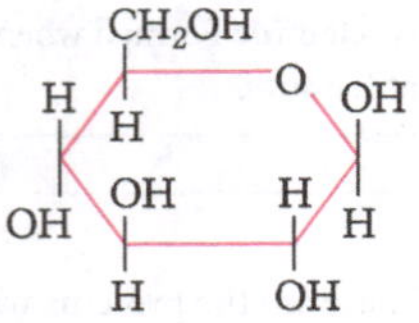

(c)
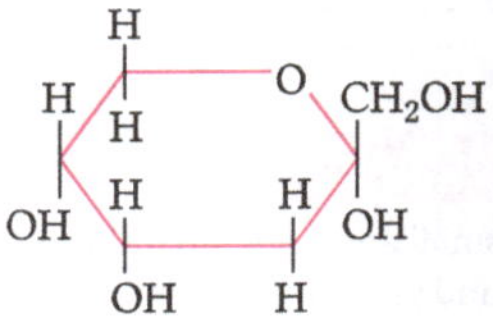

(d)
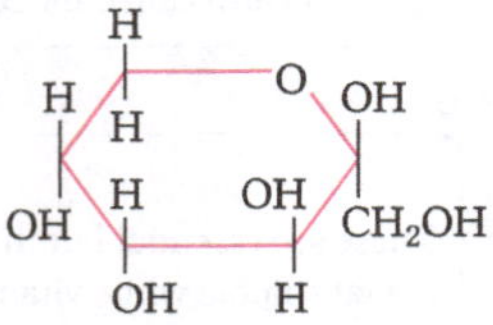

7. α-D-glucose and β-D-glucose differ from each other with respect to the **CBSE SQP 2021 (Term I)**

(a) number of —OH groups.
(b) configuration at the C-1 carbon.
(c) size of the hemiacetal ring.
(d) configuration at the C-5 carbon.

8. One molecule of sucrose on hydrolysis gives .... **NCERT Exemplar**

(a) 2 molecules of glucose
(b) 2 molecules of glucose + 1 molecule of fructose
(c) 1 molecule of glucose +1 molecule of fructose
(d) 2 molecules of fructose

9. Which one of the following statement is correct about sucrose? **CBSE SQP 2021 (Term I)**

(a) It can reduce Tollen's reagent however cannot reduce Fehling's reagent.
(b) It undergoes mutarotation like glucose and fructose.
(c) It undergoes inversion in the configuration on hydrolysis.
(d) It is laevorotatory in nature.

10. Hydrolysis of sucrose is called **CBSE 2023**

(a) inversion
(b) hydration
(c) esterification
(d) saponification

11. **On hydrolysis, which of the following carbohydrates gives only glucose?** **CBSE 2023**

(a) Maltose (b) Sucrose (c) Lactose (d) Galactose

12. **Which of the following is a polysaccharide?** **CBSE SQP 2021 (Term I)**

(a) Glucose (b) Maltose
(c) Glycogen (d) Lactose

13. **Shown below is the chain structure of an unknown compound *A*.**

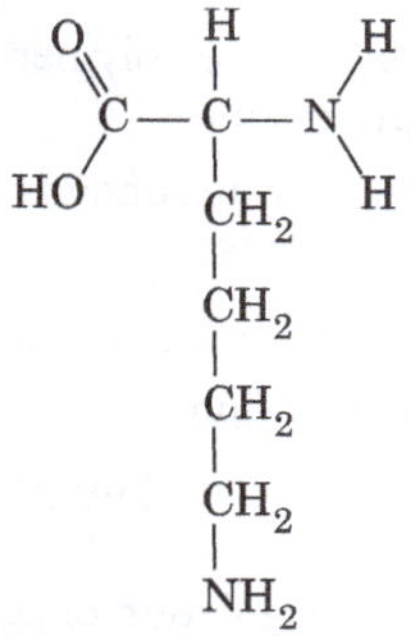

Which of the following statements is true for compound *A*? **Competency Based Que.**

(a) Compound *A* is neutral.
(b) Compound *A* is basic in nature.
(c) Compound *A* is acidic in nature.
(d) Compound *A* is ammonium salt.

14. **Which is the structure of a zwitter ion of an amino acid?** **Competency Based Que.**

(a) $H_3N^+ - CH - COO^-$
$\quad | $
$H_2C - CH_2 - CH_2 - CH_2 - \overset{+}{N}H_2$

(b) $H_3N^+ - CH - COO^-$
$\quad |$
$H_2C - COO^-$

(c) $H_2N - CH - COO^-$
$\quad |$
$H_2C - \overset{+}{O}H_2$

(d) $\overset{+}{H_3N} - CH - COO^-$
$\quad |$
$H_2C - SH$

15. **The specific sequence in which amino acids are arranged in a protein is called as** **CBSE 2024**

(a) primary structure (b) secondary structure
(c) tertiary structure (d) quaternary structure

16. **An α-helix is a structural feature of** **CBSE 2020, 2023**

(a) sucrose (b) polypeptides
(c) nucleotides (d) starch

17. **Tertiary structure of protein is stabilised by** **NCERT Exemplar**

(a) disulphide bonds (b) van der Waals' forces
(c) hydrogen bonds (d) All of the above

18. **Which of the following statements is/are correct?**

I. Amongst lysine, histidine and serine, lysine is the most basic in nature.
II. All non-essential amino acids are basic in nature.
III. Adding acids such as lemon juice into meat protein does not denature the primary structure yet tenderize meat. **Competency Based Que.**

(a) Only I (b) Only III
(c) I and III (d) I, II, and III

19. **Which of the following statements is/are correct for proteins or enzymes when they are subjected to physical changes as specified?**

I. The sequence of amino acids in the peptide changes in a protein when the pH of its environment is changed.
II. Most enzymes stop working above about 50°C.
III. Albumin, a globular protein found in egg whites, sets into an insoluble white solid when the egg white is heated. **Competency Based Que.**

(a) Only III (b) I and II
(c) II and III (d) I, II and III

20. **Deficiency of which of the following vitamins causes pernicious anaemia?** **CBSE 2023**

(a) Vitamin B_1 (b) Vitamin B_2
(c) Vitamin B_6 (d) Vitamin B_{12}

21. **Which of the following acid represents vitamin C?** **CBSE 2024**

(a) Saccharic acid (b) Gluconic acid
(c) Ascorbic acid (d) Benzoic acid

22. **Which of the following acids is a vitamin?** **NCERT Exemplar**

(a) Aspartic acid (b) Ascorbic acid
(c) Adipic acid (d) Saccharic acid

23. **Nucleotides are composed of a** **CBSE 2021 (Term I)**

(a) pentose sugar and phosphoric acid.
(b) nitrogenous base and phosphoric acid.
(c) nitrogenous base and a pentose sugar.
(d) nitrogenous base, a pentose sugar and phosphoric acid.

24. **Nucleic acids are the polymers of** **NCERT Exemplar**

(a) nucleosides (b) nucleotides
(c) bases (d) sugars

25. **Match the following columns.**

Column I	Column II
A. Amino acids	1. Protein
B. Thymine	2. Nucleic acid
C. Insulin	3. DNA
D. Phosphodiester linkage	4. Zwitter ion

Codes

	A	B	C	D
(a)	1	4	3	2
(b)	4	3	1	2
(c)	3	4	1	2
(d)	1	3	4	2

26. **The bases that are common in both DNA and RNA are** CBSE 2021(Term I)
(a) adenine, guanine and cytosine
(b) adenine, guanine and thymine
(c) adenine, uracil and cytosine
(d) guanine, uracil and thymine

27. **Helical structure of proteins is stabilised by**
(a) ionic bond (b) covalent bond CBSE 2023
(c) hydrogen bond (d) Van der Waals' forces

28. **The following image shows the structure of DNA, with the letters indicating the bases present.**

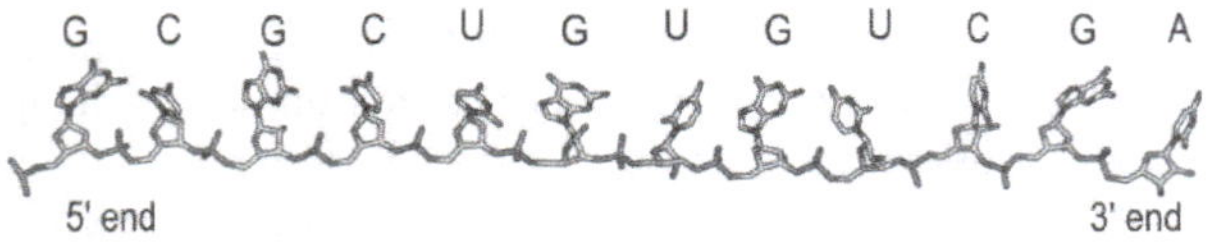

Which structure of DNA is represented above? Competency Based Que.
(a) Primary (b) Secondary (c) Tertiary (d) Quaternary

Assertion-Reason [1 Mark]

Directions (Q. Nos. 29-44) In the following questions an Assertion (A) is followed by a corresponding Reason (R). Use the following keys to choose the appropriate answer.
(a) Both (A) and (R) are true and (R) is the correct explanation of (A).
(b) Both (A) and (R) are true but (R) is not the correct explanation of (A).
(c) (A) is true but (R) is false.
(d) (A) is false but (R) is true.

29. **Assertion** Fructose is a reducing sugar.
Reason (R) Fructose does not reduce Fehling solution and Tollen's reagent. CBSE 2024

30. **Assertion** (A) Sucrose and fructose can not give positive Tollen's test.
Reason (R) Sucrose and fructose do not contain an aldehyde group. Competency Based Que.

31. **Assertion** (A) Glucose reacts with hydroxylamine to form an oxime and also adds a molecule of hydrogen cyanide to give cyanohydrin.
Reason (R) The carbonyl group is present in the open chain structure of glucose. CBSE SQP 2020

32. **Assertion** (A) D-(+)- Glucose is dextrorotatory in nature. NCERT Exemplar
Reason (R) 'D' represents its dextrorotatory nature.

33. **Assertion** (A) β-glycosidic linkage is present in maltose.
Reason (R) Maltose is composed of two glucose units in which C-1of one glucose unit is linked to C-4 of another glucose unit. NCERT Exemplar

34. **Assertion** (A) All naturally occurring α-amino acids except glycine are optically active.
Reason (R) Most naturally occurring amino acids have L-configuration. NCERT Exemplar, CBSE 2025

35. **Assertion** (A) All amino acids are solid at 20°C.
Reason (R) Amino acids can form zwitter ions. The ionic nature of the zwitter ions give amino acids with their relatively strong intermolecular forces of attraction. Competency Based Que.

36. **Assertion** (A) Proteins are polymers of α-amino acids connected by peptide bond.
Reason (R) A tetrapeptide contains 4 amino acids linked by 4 peptide bonds. CBSE 2023

37. **Assertion** (A) β-pleated sheet structure of proteins shows maximum extension.
Reason (R) Intermolecular hydrogen bonding is present in them.

38. **Assertion** (A) The coagulation of egg white occurs on boiling.
Reason (R) Denaturation of protein occurs when its native form is subjected to physical change or chemical change.

39. **Assertion** (A) In the presence of an enzyme, substrate molecule can be attacked by the reagent effectively.
Reason (R) Active sites of enzymes hold the substrate molecule in a suitable position.

40. **Assertion** (A) Vitamins A, D, E and K are stored in liver and adipose tissue.
Reason (R) Vitamins A, D, E and K are soluble in fats and oils.

41. **Assertion** (A) The two strands of DNA are complementary to each other. CBSE SQP 2021
Reason (R) The hydrogen bonds are formed between specific pairs of bases.

42. **Assertion** (A) In both DNA and RNA, heterocyclic base and phosphodiester linkages are at C-1′ and C-5′ respectively of the sugar molecule.
Reason (R) Nucleotides and nucleosides mainly differ from each other in presence of phosphate units.

43. **Assertion** (A) When RNA is hydrolysed, there is no relationship among the quantities of different bases obtained.
Reason (R) RNA molecules are of three types and they perform different functions.

44. **Assertion** (A) The backbone of DNA and RNA molecule is a chain consisting of heterocyclic base, pentose sugar and phosphate group. CBSE 2023
Reason (R) Nucleotides and nucleosides mainly differ from each other in presence of phosphate group.

Case-Study [4 Marks]

45. Read the given case and answer the following questions.

Organic compounds containing amine as functional group are present in a vivid variety of compounds, namely amino acids, hormones, neurotransmitters, DNA, dyes, etc. Amino acids are classified as acidic, basic or neutral depending upon the relative number of amino and carboxyl groups in their molecule. In aqueous solution, the carboxyl group can lose a proton and amino group can accept a proton giving rise to a dipolar ion known as zwitter ion. In zwitter ionic form, amino acids show amphoteric behaviour. CBSE 2024 C

(i) Give one point of difference between acidic and basic amino acid.

(ii) Name the linkage formed when carboxyl end of one amino acid condenses with amino end of other amino acid.

(iii) What are essential amino acids and non-essential amino acids?

Or What is meant by zwitter ionic form of amino acids? Why do amino acids show amphoteric behaviour?

46. Read the given case and answer the following questions.

Certain organic compounds are required in small amounts in our diet but their deficiency causes specific disease. These compounds are called vitamins. Most of the vitamins cannot be synthesised in our body but plants can synthesise almost all of them. So, they are considered as essential food factors. However, the bacteria of the gut can produce some of the vitamins required by us. All the vitamins are generally available in our diet. The term 'vitamin' was coined from the words vital + amine, since the earlier identified compounds had amino group.

Vitamins are classified into two groups depending upon their solubility in water or fat namely-fat soluble vitamins and water soluble vitamins.

Answer the following questions.

(i) Why can't vitamin C be stored in our body? Name the disease caused by the deficiency of this vitamin.

(ii) Which of the following vitamins helps in blood clotting?

(a) Vitamin A (b) Vitamin C
(c) Vitamin D (d) Vitamin K

Or

Which of the following is a fat-soluble vitamin?

(a) Vitamin B (b) Vitamin C
(c) Vitamin B_{12} (d) Vitamin K

(iii) Which vitamin is also known as cobalamin?

(a) Vitamin B_{11} (b) Vitamin B_2
(c) Vitamin B_{12} (d) Vitamin B_6

Subjective Type Questions

Short Answer Type I Questions [2 Marks]

1. Write the reactions involved when D-glucose is treated with the following reagents: CBSE 2024 C, 2025

(i) HCN

(ii) Br_2 water

2. Write the reaction when D-glucose reacts with the following: CBSE 2025

(i) NH_2OH (ii) Acetic anhydride

3. Monosaccharides contain carbonyl group hence are classified, as aldose or ketose. The number of carbon atoms present in the monosaccharide molecule are also considered for classification. In which class of monosaccharide will you place fructose? NCERT Exemplar

4. Sucrose is dextrorotatory but the mixture obtained after hydrolysis is laevorotatory. Explain. NCERT Exemplar

5. Label the glucose and fructose units in the following disaccharide and identify anomeric carbons atoms in these units. Is the sugar reducing in nature? Explain. NCERT Exemplar

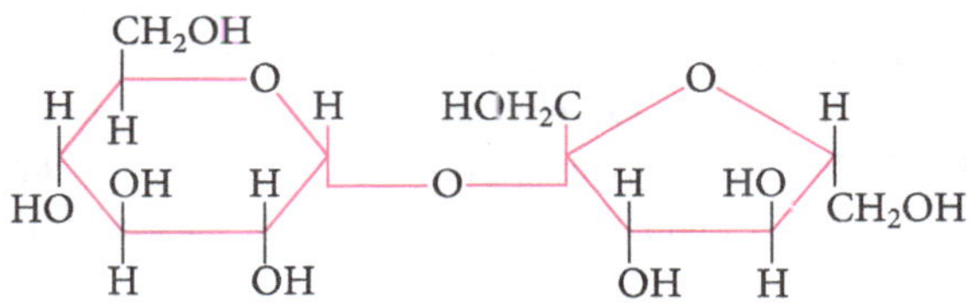

6. (i) Amylopectin and glycogen both have branched structures. How do they differ from one another?

(ii) Draw the structure of amylopectin.

7. Why do proteins form an indispensable part of our food?

8. (i) Name an amino acid which is optically inactive.

(ii) Draw the zwitter ion of an essential amino acid which contains phenyl ring.

9. Give reasons for the following: CBSE 2025

(i) The melting points of α-amino acids are generally higher than that of the corresponding carboxylic acids.

(ii) Amino acids show amphoteric behaviour.

10. Differentiate between CBSE 2023

(i) Peptide linkage and Glycosidic linkage

(ii) Nucleoside and Nucleotide

11. (i) What happens when glucose reacts with nitric acid? Write chemical equation.
(ii) Write one structural difference between DNA and RNA. **CBSE 2024**

12. (i) What happens when glucose reacts with bromine water? Write chemical equation.
(ii) Two bases are mentioned below, identify which is present in DNA and which one is present in RNA?
(a) Thymine (b) Uracil **CBSE 2024**

13. (i) What happens when glucose reacts with HI? Write chemical equation. **CBSE 2024**
(ii) Which type of bond holds a DNA double helix together?

14. Explain the role of nucleic acids in replication.

Short Answer Type II Questions [3 Marks]

15. Write the structure of product when D-Glucose reacts with the following. (Any three) **CBSE 2023**
(a) HI (b) Conc. HNO_3
(b) Br_2 water (d) HCN

16. Enumerate the reaction of D-glucose which cannot be explained by the open chain structure. **NCERT**

Or

Which type of reactions could not be explained by the open chain structure of glucose?
What alternative structure has been proposed for the glucose molecule? Draw the structure.

17. (i) Which of the following biomolecules is insoluble in water? Justify.
Insulin, Haemoglobin, Keratin
(ii) Draw the Haworth structure of α-D-glucopyranose.
(iii) Write chemical reaction to show that glucose contains aldehyde as carbonyl group. **CBSE SQP 2015**

18. Define the following terms : **CBSE 2024**
(i) Non-essential amino acids (ii) Monosaccharides
(iii) Anomers

19. (i) What is the difference between native protein and denatured protein?
(ii) Which one of the following is a disaccharide?
Glucose, Lactose, Amylose, Fructose
(iii) Which vitamin is a responsible for the coagulation of blood? **CBSE 2025**

20. Define the following terms. **CBSE 2025**
(i) Native proteins (ii) Nucleotide
(iii) Essential amino acid

21. Define the following as related to proteins. **NCERT CBSE 2015**
(i) Peptide linkage (ii) Primary structure
(iii) Denaturation

22. Write the four characteristic features of enzymes. Name an enzyme which catalyses hydrolysis of maltose into glucose.

23. Mr. Chatterjee was having pain in his joints. The shape of one his canines and some of his toes got deformed a bit. He visited the doctor. Along with the medications he was asked to take ample amounts of milk, and eggs. He was also asked to take cod liver oil capsules. The doctor asked Mr. Chatterjee to expose himself to sufficient sunlight every day. **Competency Based Que.**
(i) What is the most probable disease that Mr. Chatterjee is suffering from?
(ii) Mr. Chatterjee found one morning the milk had curdled. What could be a probable reason for his observation? Explain the observation.
(iii) How can exposure to sunlight help in improving the health condition of Mr. Chatterjee?

24. (i) Write the name of two monosaccharides obtained on hydrolysis of lactose sugar. **NCERT Intext, NCERT Exemplar, CBSE 2025**
(ii) Why vitamin C cannot be stored in our body? **NCERT Intext, NCERT Exemplar, CBSE 2025**
(iii) What is the difference between a nucleoside and nucleotide? **NCERT, CBSE 2016, 2020**

25. (i) What is the basic structural difference between starch and cellulose? **NCERT**
(ii) What type of linkage is present in nucleic acid?

26. What are the different types of RNA molecules which perform different functions?
Or What are the different types of RNA found in the cell? **NCERT**

27. What are hormones? Give an example for each of the following
(i) Steroid hormones (ii) Polypeptide hormones
(iii) Amino acid derivative

Long Answer Type Questions [5 Marks]

28. A compound *A* ($C_6H_{12}O_6$) is oxidised by bromine water into monobasic acid. It also reduces Tollen's reagent and reacts with HCN to give a compound *B* which on hydrolysis gives a compound *C*. On treating *C* with HI/red P, *n*-heptanoic acid is obtained. Compound *A* on treatment with excess phenyl hydrazine gave D-glucosazone. Name the compound *A* and draw its cyclic form.

29. On the basis of which evidences D-glucose was assigned the following structure? **NCERT Exemplar**

CHO
|
$(CHOH)_4$
|
CH_2OH

Hints & Solutions

Objective Type Questions

1. (*d*) Among the given carbohydrates, lactose is a disaccharide which is made up of β-D-glucose and β-D-galactose.
2. (*c*) Lactose and maltose are reducing in nature while sucrose is non-reducing in nature.
3. (*d*) Glucose ($C_6H_{12}O_6$) on reaction with acetic anhydride gives glucose pentaacetate, i.e.

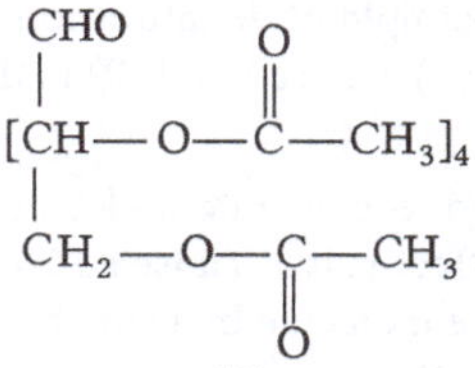

while on reaction with nitric

(*A*)

acid, it gives saccharic acid

$$(HOOC—(CHOH)_4—COOH)$$

(*B*)

4. (*d*) Existence of α- and β- forms of glucose is not explained by the open chain structure of glucose.
5. (*c*) Only statement (c) is incorrect. Its correct form is glucose exist in pyranose form.
6. (*a*) The correct structure of α-D-glucose is

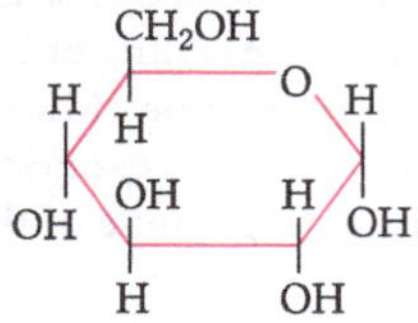

7. (*b*) α-D-glucose and β-D-glucose differ from each other with respect to the configuration at the C-1 carbon.
8. (*c*) Sucrose (cane sugar) is a disaccharide. One molecule of sucrose on hydrolysis gives one molecule of glucose and one molecule of fructose.

$$\underset{\text{Cane sugar}}{C_{12}H_{22}O_{11}} \xrightarrow[H^+]{H_2O} \underset{\text{D-(+)-glucose}}{C_6H_{12}O_6} + \underset{\text{D-(–)-fructose}}{C_6H_{12}O_6}$$

9. (*c*) Sucrose undergoes inversion in the configuration on hydrolysis.

   While the other statements correct form are as follows.
   - Sucrose being a non-reducing sugar is not capable of reducing Fehling's solution and Tollen's reagent.
   - Sucrose is dextrorotatory in nature.
   - Sucrose does not undergo mutarotation.
10. (*a*) Hydrolysis of sucrose to give glucose and fructose is called inversion of sugar. Hydrolysis of sucrose brings about a change in the sign of rotation, from dextro (+) to laevo (–) and the product is named as invert sugar.
11. (*a*) Hydrolysis of maltose yields two moles of α-D-glucose.
12. (*c*) Glycogen is a polysaccharide.
13. (*b*) Since, more no. of amino groups are present in the given amino acid, thus it is basic in nature.
14. (*d*) The zwitter ion of an amino acid has one basic group COO^- and one acidic group $—NH_3^+$.

    Thus, the structure (D) represents zwitter ion of an amino acid.
15. (*a*) The specific sequence in which various amino acids are linked with each other to form a polypeptide, is called its primary structure.
16. (*b*) α-helix is a secondary structure of proteins formed by twisting of polypeptide chain into right handed screw like structure.
17. (*d*) Tertiary structure of protein is mainly stabilised by hydrogen bonds, disulphide bonds, van der Waals' forces and electrostatic forces of attraction.
18. (*b*) Only Statement (III) is correct. The other given statements are incorrect. Their corrected form are as follows : Amongst lysine, histidine and serine, histidine is the most basic in nature. Further, all non-essential amino acids are not basic in nature.
19. (*c*) Statements (II) and (III) are correct while statement (I) is incorrect. Its correct form is

    The sequence of amino acids in a protein (also known as primary structure) remains intact when pH of environment is changed.
20. (*d*) Vitamin B_{12}
21. (*c*) Ascorbic acid represents vitamin C.
22. (*b*) Ascorbic acid is the chemical name of vitamin C, while others are not vitamins. Aspartic acid is an amino acid and adipic acid is a dicarboxylic acid having 6 carbon chain. Moreover, saccharic acid is a dicarboxylic acid obtained by oxidation of glucose using HNO_3.
23. (*d*) Nucleotides are composed of a nitrogenous base, a pentose sugar and phosphoric acid.
24. (*b*) Nucleic acids are polymers of nucleotides in which nucleic acids are linked together by phosphodiester linkage.
25. (*b*) In aqueous solution, amino acids exist in the form of dipolar ion, called **zwitter ion**.

    Thymine is a nitrogenous base present in DNA.

    Insulin is a protein hormone.

    Nucleotides are joined by phosphodiester linkage to form **nucleic acids.**
26. (*a*) Bases adenine (A), guanine (G) and cytosine (C) are common in both DNA and RNA.
27. (*c*) The helical structure of proteins is stabilised by hydrogen bond.
28. (*a*) The given structure shows the primary structure of DNA.

29. (*c*) Fructose is a reducing sugar because it has a free ketone or aldehyde group that can undergo oxidation thus reducing Tollen's and Fehling solution. The copper ions in fehling solution and silver ions in Tollen's reagent get reduced, resulting in the formation of a red precipitate of copper (I) oxide and a silver mirror respectively. Hence, (A) is true, but (R) is false.

30. (*d*) (A) is false, but (R) is true.

The correct form of Assertion is sucrose do not give Tollen's test but fructose gives positive Tollen's test.

31. (*a*) Both (A) and (R) are true and (R) is the correct explanation of (A). Glucose reacts with hydroxylamine to form an oxime and also adds a molecule of hydrogen cyanide to give cyanohydrin which confirms the presence of the carbonyl group in the open chain structure of glucose.

32. (*c*) (A) is true but (R) is false.
D-(+)-glucose is dextrorotatory because it rotates the plane polarised light to right.

Here, D represents relative configuration of glucose with respect to glyceraldehyde.

33. (*d*) (A) is false but (R) is true.
α-glycosidic linkage is present in maltose.

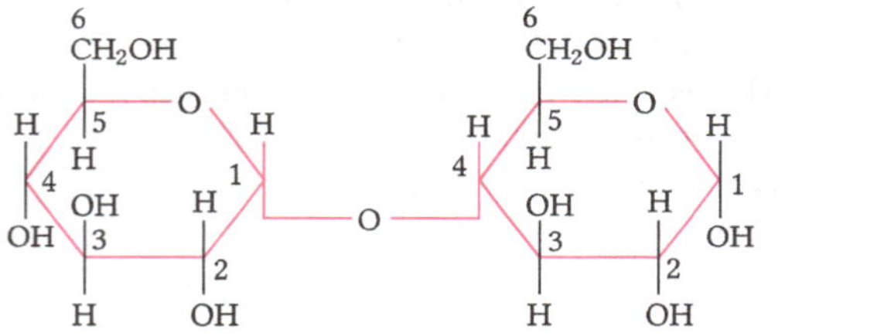

α-D-glucose α-D-glucose

Because maltose is composed of two glucose units in which C-1 of one glucose unit is linked to C-4 of another glucose unit.

34. (*b*) (A) and (R) both are true, but (R) is not the correct explanation of (A). All naturally occurring α-amino acids except glycine are optically active. Glycine is optically inactive because glycine does not have all four different substituents as shown below.

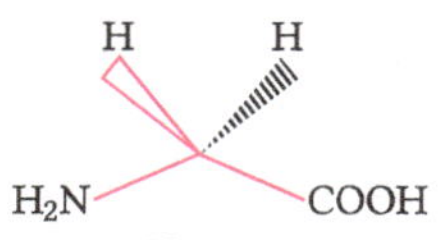

Glycine

35. (*a*) Both (A) and (R) are true and (R) is the correct explanation of (A).

36. (*c*) (A) is true, but (R) is false. The correct (R) statement is a tetrapeptide contains 4 amino acids linked by three peptide bonds.

37. (*b*) (A) and (R) both are true, but (R) is not the correct explanation of (A).

In β-pleated sheet structure, the polypeptide chains are held together by intermolecular H-bonds. Extension and contraction of β-pleated sheet structure of protein depends on the size of *R* group.

38. (*a*) When a protein in its native form is subjected to physical change like change in temperature or chemical change like change in pH, the hydrogen bonds are disturbed.

Due to this, globules unfold and helix get uncoiled and protein loses its biological activity. This is called denaturation of protein. The coagulation of egg white on boiling is the common example of denaturation of protein. Thus, both (A) and (R) are true and (R) is the correct explanation of (A).

39. (*a*) In the presence of an enzyme, substrate molecule can be attacked by the reagent effectively because active sites of enzymes hold the substrate molecule in a suitable position. Thus, both (A) and (R) are true and (R) is the correct explanation of (A).

40. (*b*) Some vitamins are soluble in fat and oils but insoluble in water. These are vitamins A, D, E and K. They are stored in liver and adipose (fat storing) tissues. Hence, both (A) and (R) are true, but (R) is not the correct explanation of (A).

41. (*a*) The two strands of DNA are complementary to each other because the hydrogen bonds are formed between specific pairs of bases. Adenine of one strand is hydrogen bonded to thymine of the other through two hydrogen bonds, whereas cytosine of one strand is hydrogen bonded with guanine of the other through 3 hydrogen bonds.

$A{=}T$ and $C{\equiv}G$
↓ ↓
2 hydrogen bonds 3 hydrogen bonds

Hence, both (A) and (R) are true and (R) is the correct explanation of (A).

42. (*b*)

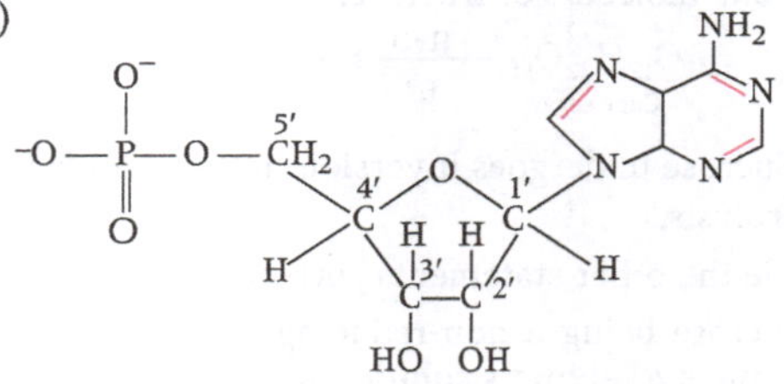

Nucleosides contain only sugar and a base, whereas nucleotides contain sugar, base and a phosphate group as well.

Thus, both (A) and (R) are true, but (R) is not the correct explanation of (A).

43. (*b*) When RNA is hydrolysed, there is no relationship among the quantities of four different bases obtained because in RNA, the bases don't occur in pairs as it is a single stranded structure.

RNA molecules are of three types and they perform different functions. They are named as messenger-RNA (*m*-RNA), ribosomal-RNA (*r*-RNA) and transfer-RNA (*t*-RNA). Thus, both (A) and (R) are true, but (R) is not the correct explanation of (A).

44. (*d*) (A) is false, but (R) is true. The correct Assertion is :
Backbone of DNA and RNA is composed of alternating pentose sugar and phosphate groups.

45. (i) Acidic amino acids contains more number of COOH groups as compared to amino groups. On the other hand, basic amino acids contains more number of amino groups as compared to carboxylic groups. **(1)**
(ii) Peptide linkage is formed when carboxyl end of one amino acid condenses with amino end of other amino acid. **(1)**
(iii) • Essential amino acids cannot be synthesised in the body and must be obtained through diet, e.g. valine, lysine, etc.
• Non-essential amino acids can be synthesised in the body, e.g. glycine, alanine, etc. **(2)**
Or Amino acids in aqueous solution neutralise each other involving transfer of a proton from the carboxyl group to the amino group, giving rise to a dipolar ion known as zwitter ion. **(1)**
In zwitter ionic form, amino acids show amphoteric behaviour because they can react with both acids and bases. **(1)**

46. (i) Vitamin C is a water soluble vitamin and is readily excreted in urine. Thus, it can't be stored in our body. Scurvy (bleeding gum) disease is caused by the deficiency of this vitamin. **(2)**
(ii) (*d*) Among the given, vitamin K helps in the blood clotting in the body. **(1)**
Or (*d*) The fat-soluble vitamins are vitamins A, D, E and K. These vitamins are absorbed more easily by the body in the presence of dietary fat. **(1)**
(iii) (*c*) Vitamin B_{12} is also known as cobalamin. **(1)**

Subjective Type Questions

1. Refer to text on page 361. (Structural evidence of glucose) **(2)**

2. (i)

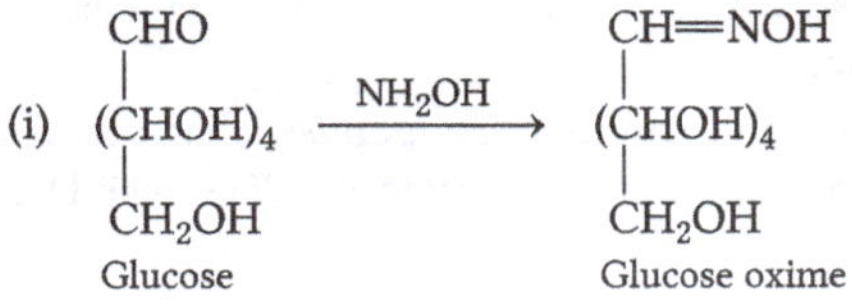

(1)

(ii)

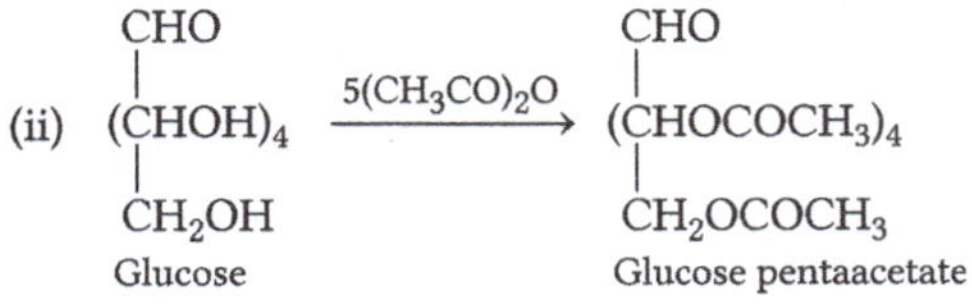

(1)

3. Monosaccharides contain carbonyl group. Hence, are classified as aldose or ketose. When aldehyde group is present, the monosaccharides are known as aldose.
When ketone group is present, the monosaccharides are known as ketose. **(1)**
Fructose has molecular formula $C_6H_{12}O_6$ containing **six carbon** and a **keto group**. It is classified as **ketohexose**.

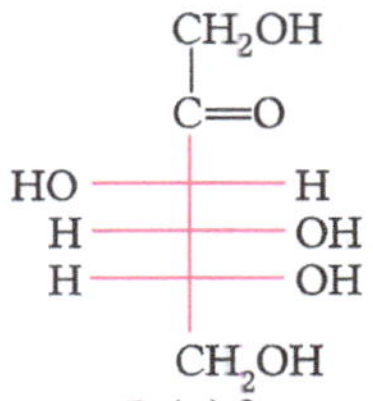

D-(−)-fructose **(1)**

4. Sucrose is dextrorotatory. On hydrolysis, it produces a mixture of glucose and fructose having specific rotation +52.5° and −92.4°. Thus, the net resultant mixture becomes laevorotatory.
Hence, the mixture is laevorotatory and product is known as invert sugar. **(2)**

5. C-1 of glucose unit and C-2 of fructose unit are anomeric carbon atoms in the given disaccharide.
The disaccharide is non-reducing sugar because —OH groups attached to anomeric carbon atoms are involved in the formation of glycosidic bond. **(1)**

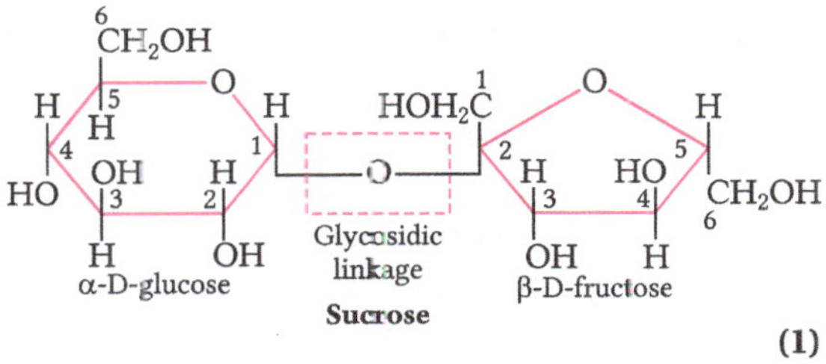

(1)

6. (i) Glycogen consists of 10-14 glucose units, while amylopectin consists of 25-30 glucose units. **(1)**
(ii) Refer to text on page 365. **(1)**

7. Proteins are the body building foods. They provide the chemical material for the growth and repair of body cells and tissues. At the time of emergency, proteins can also be oxidised in the body to release energy. Protein deficiency disease of young children is kwashiorkor. Which can lead to severe swelling, growth failure, etc. **(2)**

8. (i) Glycine **(1)**
(ii) Zwitter ionic structure of phenylalanine is as follow.

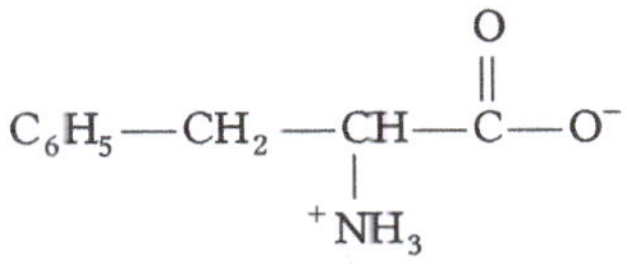

(1)

9. (i) α-amino acids exists as zwitter ions or dipolar ions. Due to this characteristic, they have strong interionic forces (dipole-dipole attractions) among them. Thus, their melting points are higher than the corresponding carboxylic acids. **(1)**

(ii) In aqueous solution, the carboxyl group of amino acid can lose a proton and the amino group can accept a proton to form zwitter ion. The zwitter ion can act as both an acid and a base, thus showing amphoteric behaviour. **(1)**

10. (i)

Peptide linkage	Glycosidic linkage
A peptide bond is formed when a carbonyl atom of one amino acid is linked to an amino of a different amino acid.	A glycosidic bond is formed when two carbon atoms of two different monosaccharides are linked together. **(1)**

(ii)

Nucleoside	Nucleotide
Nucleoside contains only sugar and a base.	Nucleotide contains sugar, base and a phosphate group as well. **(1)**

11. (i) When glucose reacts with nitric acid, it gets oxidised to saccharic acid.

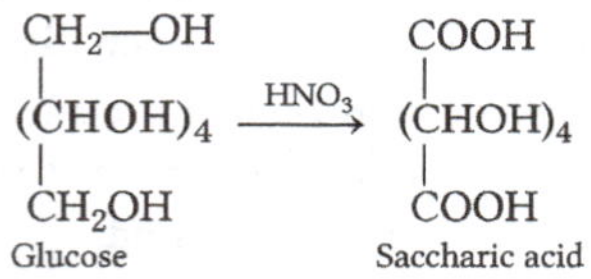

(1)

(ii) The structural difference between DNA and RNA are as follow.

	DNA	RNA
1.	The helical structure of DNA is double stranded.	The helical structure of RNA is single stranded.
2.	The sugar molecule is β-D-2-deoxyribose.	The sugar molecules is β-D-ribose. **(1)**

12. (i) Glucose gets oxidised in presence of bromine water to give gluconic acid. This reaction confirms the presence of aldehyde group.

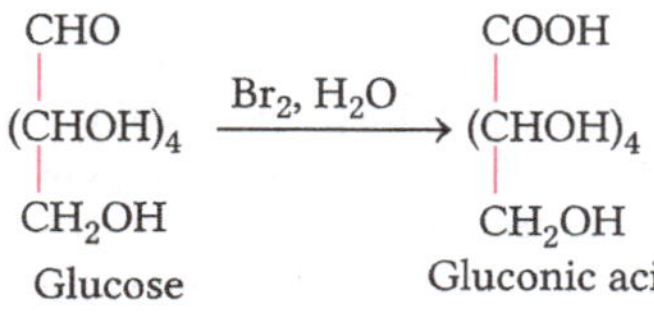

(1)

(ii) Uracil is present in RNA while thymine is present in DNA. **(1)**

13. (i) When glucose is heated with HI (reducing agent) it gets completely reduce to yield *n*-hexane.

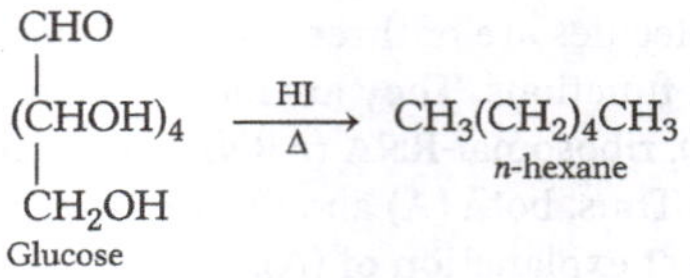

(1)

(ii) Hydrogen bond binds the nitrogen bases between the two strands of DNA. There are two H-bonds between A and T, three H-bonds between G and C. **(1)**

14. Refer to text on page 373. (Biological functions of nucleic acids). **(2)**

15. Refer to text on page 361. **(3)**

16. Refer to text on page 362. (Cyclic structure of glucose) **(3)**

17. (i) Keratin being a fibrous protein is insoluble in water. **(1)**

(ii)

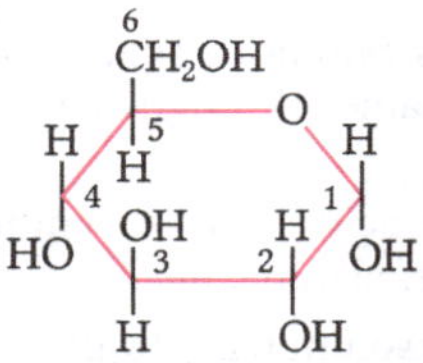

α-D-(+)-glucopyranose **(1)**

(iii) Glucose reduces Tollen's reagent to metallic silver.

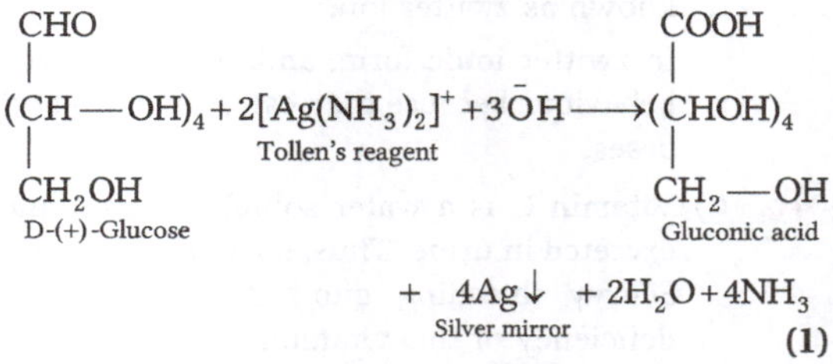

(1)

18. (i) Non-essential amino acids are those which can be synthesised in our body itself. Examples are glycine, alanine, etc. **(1)**

(ii) Monosaccharides are sugars that can't be broken down by hydrolysis into other simple sugars. e.g. Glucose, fructose, etc. **(1)**

(iii) A pair of stereoisomers which differ in configuration only around C-1 are called anomers. e.g. α-D-glucose and β-D-glucose are anomers. **(1)**

19. (i) Refer to text on page 369.

(ii) Lactose is a disaccharide, made up of D-galactose and D-glucose.

Glucose and fructose are monosaccharides. Amylose is a polysaccharide containing 200-1000 D-glucose units. **(1)**

(iii) Vitamin K is responsible for the coagulation of blood. **(1)**

20. (i) Refer to text on page 369. **(1)**
(ii) Refer to text on page 371 and 372. **(1)**
(iii) Refer to text on page 367. **(1)**

21. (i) **Peptide linkage** Refer to text on pages 367 and 368. **(1)**
(ii) **Primary structure** Refer to text on pages 368. **(1)**
(iii) **Denaturation** Refer to text on pages 369. **(1)**

22. Refer to text on page 367. **(2)**

23. (i) Mr. Chatterjee is decreased from osteomalacia. **(1)**
(ii) If the pH of milk is decreased, it curdles. The change in pH leads to breaking of the hydrogen bond in the protein molecules of milk. Thus, the proteins in milk get denatured and the milk curdles. **(1)**
(iii) Vitamin D helps in treating osteomalacia. It can be produced below the skin by irradiation of sterols with the UV rays present in sunlight. Thus, exposure to sunlight helps in improving the health condition. **(1)**

24. (i) D-glucose and D-galactose **(1)**
(ii) Since, vitamin C is a water soluble vitamin, it is excreted out through urine, hence cannot be stored. **(1)**
(iii) **Nucleoside** A unit formed by the attachment of a base to 1′ position of sugar is known as nucleoside.

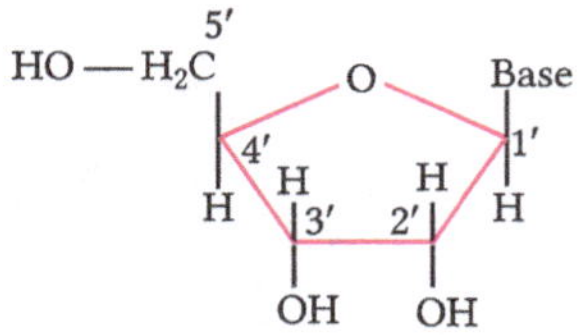

(Nucleoside)

Nucleotide When nucleoside is linked to phosphoric acid at 5′ position of sugar moiety, a nucleotide is obtained. They are joined together by phosphodiester linkage between 5′ and 3′ carbon atoms of the pentose sugar.

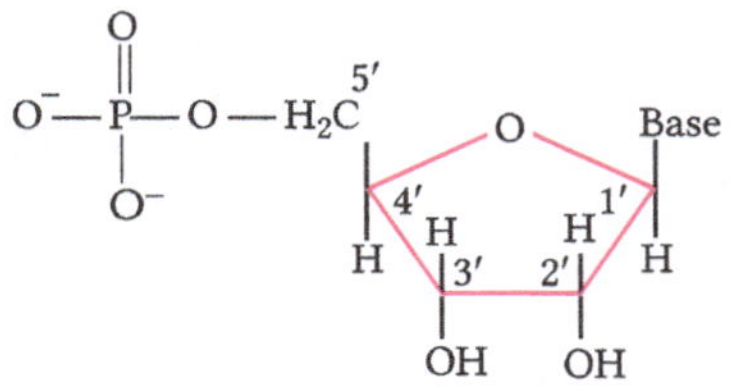

(Nucleotide) **(1)**

25. (i) Starch is a disaccharide of two components amylose and amylopectin, both are made up of D-glucose units linked through α-glycosidic linkages. Amylose is water soluble, while amylopectin is not. Cellulose, on the other hand, is straight chain polymer of β-D-glucose units linked together by β-glycosidic linkages. **(2)**
(ii) Phosphodiester linkage **(1)**

26. Three different types of RNA molecules are as follows
(i) Messenger-RNA (*m*-RNA)
(ii) Transfer-RNA (*t*-RNA)
(iii) Ribosomal-RNA (*r*-RNA) **(3)**

27. Refer to text on pages 373 and 374.
(i) Progesterone (ii) Insulin (iii) Thyroxine **(3)**

28. Compound *A* is glucose as it oxidised by bromine water into monobasic acid (gluconic acid). It also reduces Tollen's reagent and reacts with HCN to give a compound *B* (glucose cyanohydrin) which upon hydrolysis and reduction with HI acid, (in presence of red phosphorus) produces heptanoic acid. Further, compound *A* on treatment with excess phenyl hydrazine gave D-glucosazone. **(2)**

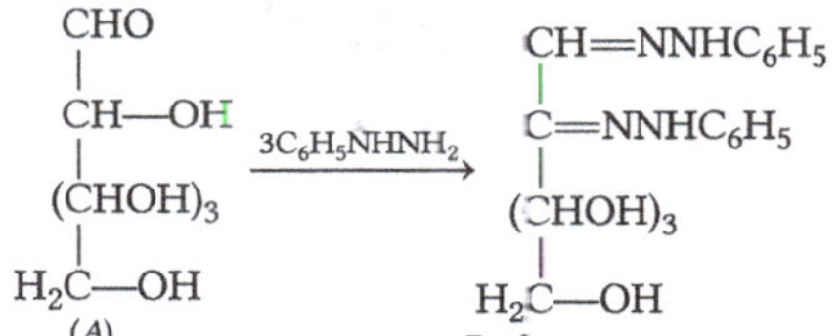

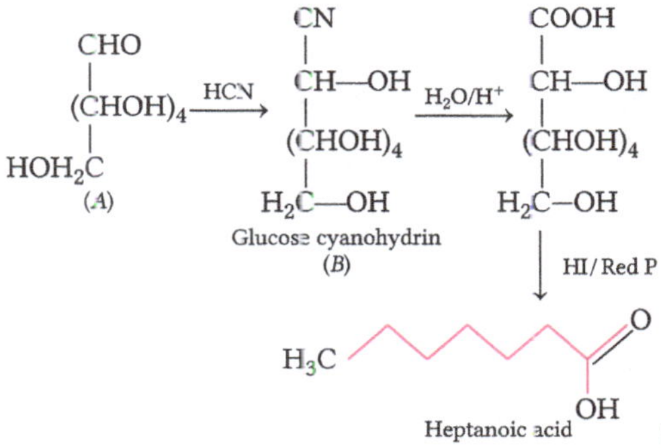

(2)

Cyclic form of glucose is

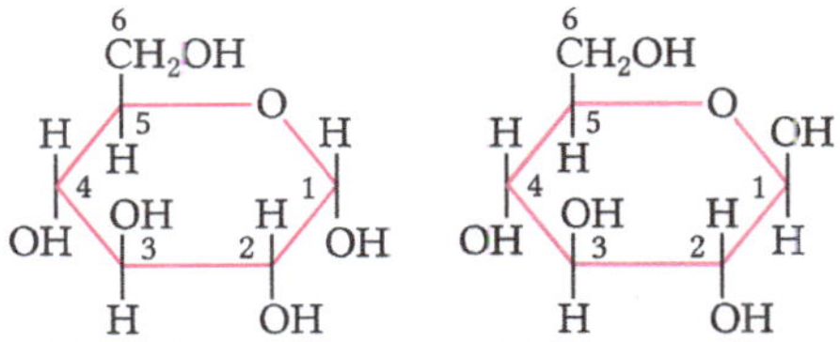

α-D-(+)-glucopyranose β-D-(+)-glucopyranose **(1)**

29. Evidences on the basis of which glucose was assigned the given structure are as follows

(i) Glucose on reaction with HI produces *n*-hexane which indicates that six carbon atoms linked in a straight chain.

$$C_6H_{12}O_6 \xrightarrow{HI} n\text{-hexane}$$ **(1)**

(ii) Glucose on reaction with acetic anhydride produces glucose pentaacetate which confirms the presence of five —OH groups.

$$C_6H_{12}O_6 \xrightarrow{Ac_2O} \text{Glucose pentaacetate}$$ **(1)**

(iii) Glucose on oxidation with bromine water produces gluconic acid which indicates the presence of —CHO group.

$$\text{Glucose} \xrightarrow{Br_2/H_2O} \text{Gluconic acid}$$ **(1)**

(iv) Glucose on reaction with HCN forms glucose cyanohydrin which confirms the presence of —CHO group. **(1)**

(v) Glucose on reaction with HNO_3 produces saccharic acid, which indicates the presence of one primary —OH group. **(1)**

QR Code for Quick Test 1

QR Code for Quick Test 2

QR Code for Quick Test 3

SELF ASSESSMENT TEST

Objective Type Questions [1 Mark]

1. Pair of compounds, which give positive test with Tollen's reagent is

(a) glucose and sucrose (b) fructose and sucrose
(c) glucose and fructose (d) All of these

2. Consider the following reaction,

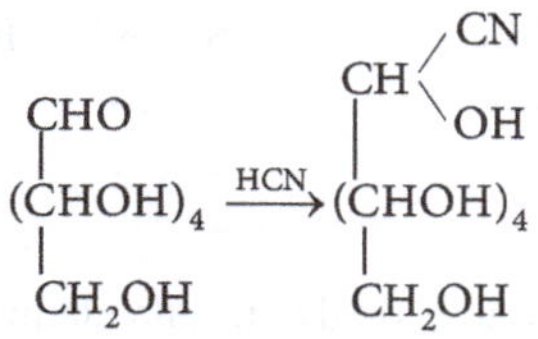

The given reaction confirms

(a) presence of primary alcoholic group.
(b) five — OH groups attached to different carbon atoms.
(c) all six carbon atoms are linked in a straight chain.
(d) the presence of a carbonyl group in glucose.

3. α-D-(+) glucose and β-D-(+) glucose are

(a) geometrical isomers (b) enantiomers
(c) anomers (d) optical isomers

4. Which of the following contains only β-D-glucose as its monosaccharide unit?

(a) Sucrose (b) Cellulose (c) Starch (d) Maltose

5. The manufacturing of alcohol commercially by fermentation method takes place in the following two steps.

Reaction steps	Enzyme Used
(i) X + Water ⟶ Glucose + Fructose	Invertase
(ii) Glucose ⟶ Ethanol + Carbon dioxide	Y

'X' and 'Y' in the above table are

(a) X = Sucrose, Y = Maltase
(b) X = Sucrose, Y = Zymase
(c) X = Lactose, Y = Zymase
(d) X = Maltose, Y = Maltase

Assertion - Reason [1 Mark]

Directions *(Q. 6 to Q. 8)* In the following questions, as Assertion (A) is followed by a corresponding Reason (R). Use the following keys to choose the appropriate answer. Select the most appropriate answer from the options given below.

(a) Both (A) and (R) are true and (R) is the correct explanation of (A).
(b) Both (A) and (R) are true, but (R) is not the correct explanation of (A).
(c) (A) is true but (R) is false.
(d) (A) is false but (R) is true.

6. Assertion (A) Tollen's reagent, Benedict's solution and Fehling's solution are reducing agents.

Reason (R) Mild oxidising agent like bromine water convert glucose into gluconic acid.

7. Assertion (A) Glucose does not form the hydrogen sulphite addition product with $NaHSO_3$.

Reason (R) Glucose exists in a six-membered cyclic structure called pyranose structure.

8. Assertion (A) In the presence of enzyme, substrate molecule can be attacked by the reagent effectively.

Reason (R) Active sites of enzymes hold the substrate molecule in a suitable position.

Short Answer Type I Questions [2 Marks]

9. Account for the following.

(i) Pentaacetate of glucose does not react with hydroxyl amine.
(ii) What happens when oxidation of gluconic acid takes place?

10. (i) The glycosidic linkage connects monosaccharide units in polysaccharides. Justify the statement.

(ii) Write the reaction to confirm the presence of carbonyl group in glucose molecule.

11. (i) Explain with the help of suitable reaction.

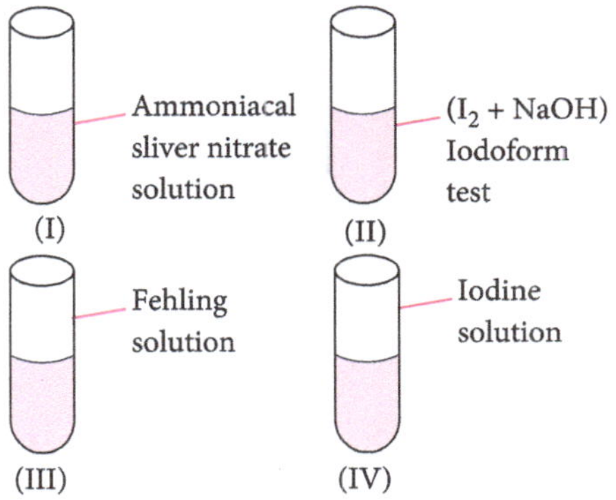

Out of given 4 solutions which will reduce glucose and why?

(ii) DNA and RNA contain four bases each. A base (say X) is present in DNA but not in RNA. Predict the name of base X.

Short Answer Type II Questions [3 Marks]

12. (i) Aradhana visits a physician as she is suffering from rickets and joint pain. Which fat-soluble vitamin should the physician prescribe to her?

(ii) Somesh put few drops of vinegar in milk. What change do you think he observed in the milk after some time? What is this phenomenon known as?

(iii) Name the product of hydrolysis of sucrose. Is it a reducing sugar or a non-reducing sugar?

13. (i) Rohan specifically used lemon juice while marinating meat. What can be the possible reason of doing that? Name the phenomena associated with it.

(ii) Name the base that is found in nucleotide of RNA only.

(iii) Glucose on reaction with acetic acid gives glucose pentaacetate. What does it suggest about the structure of glucose?

Case-Study [4 Marks]

14. **Read the given case and answer the following questions.**

Monosaccharides containing an aldehydic group are called aldoses while those containing a keto group are called ketoses. All monosaccharides containing five and six carbon atoms have cyclic structures, furanose (five membered) and pyranose (six membered).

During ring formation, C_1 in aldoses and C_2 in ketoses becomes chiral and hence all these monosaccharides exist in two forms called the α-anomer and β-anomer while C_1 and C_2 are called glycosidic or anomeric carbon atoms. In contrast, stereoisomers, which differ in configuration at any other chiral carbon other than the glycosidic carbon are called epimers.

Two molecules of the same or different monosaccharides combine together through glycosidic linkage to form disaccharides.

Based on the above information, answer the following questions.

(i) Explain essentially the difference between α-form of glucose and β-form of glucose.

(ii) Name the two monosaccharides obtained on hydrolysis of lactose sugar.

Or

What type of linkage is present in disaccharides?

(iii) Write one difference between peptide linkage and glycosidic linkage.

Long Answer Type Questions [5 Marks]

15. (i) (a) The structures of glycine and alanine are given below.

Show the peptide bond linkage in glycylalanine.

$$\underset{\text{Glycine}}{H_2N—CH_2—COOH}, \quad \underset{\text{Alanine}}{H_2N—\overset{\displaystyle CH_3}{\overset{|}{C}H}—COOH}$$

(b) What products would be formed when a nucleotide from RNA containing uracil is hydrolysed?

(c) What are reducing sugars? Give an example.

(ii) The presence of carbonyl group in glucose is confirmed by its reaction with hydroxylamine. Identify the type of carbonyl group present and its position. Give a chemical reaction in support of your answer.

Answers

1. (*c*) 2. (*d*) 3. (*c*) 4. (*b*) 5. (*b*) 6. (*d*)
7. (*b*) 8. (*a*)

CBSE
EXAMINATION PAPER 2025
CHEMISTRY

Time : 3 Hours | **Max. Marks : 70**

General Instructions

Read the following instructions carefully and follow them :

1. This question paper contains **33 questions**. All questions are **compulsory**.
2. This question paper is divided into **FIVE** sections - **Section A, B, C, D and E**.
3. **SECTION-A** questions number 1 to 16 are multiple choice type questions. Each question carries 1 mark.
4. **SECTION-B** questions number 17 to 21 are very short answer type questions. Each question carries 2 marks.
5. **SECTION-C** questions number 22 to 28 are short answer type questions. Each question carries 3 marks.
6. **SECTION-D** questions number 29 and 30 are case-based questions. Each question carries 4 marks.
7. **SECTION-E** questions number 31 to 33 are long answer type questions. Each question carries 5 marks.
8. There is no overall choice given in the question paper. However, an internal choice has been provided in few questions in all the sections except section A.
9. Kindly note that there is a separate question paper for visually impaired candidates.
10. Use of calculator is NOT allowed.

SET - I (Code 56/1/1)

Section-A

Questions No. 1 to 16 are Multiple Choice type Questions, carrying 1 mark each.

1. In case of association, abnormal molar mass of solute will

(a) increase
(b) decrease
(c) remain same
(d) first increase and then decrease

Sol. (c) Refer to Q.No. 21 on Pg. 22.

2. Standard electrode potential for Sn^{4+}/Sn^{2+} couple is +0.15 V and that for the Cr^{3+}/Cr couple is -0.74V. The two couples in their standard states are connected to make a cell. The cell potential will be

(a) +1.19 V (b) +0.89 V
(c) + 0.18V (d) +1.83 V

Sol. (c) Refer to Q.No. 3 on Pg. 60.

3. The magnetic moment is associated with its spin angular momentum and orbital angular momentum. Spin only magnetic moment value of Cr^{3+} ion (Atomic no : Cr = 24) is

(a) 2.87 B.M. (b) 3.87 B.M.
(c) 3.47 B.M. (d) 3.57 B.M.

Sol. (c) Refer to Q.No. 6 on Pg. 128.

4. Acidified $KMnO_4$ oxidises sulphite to

(a) $S_2O_3^{2-}$ (b) $S_2O_8^{2-}$ (c) $SO_2(g)$ (d) SO_4^{2-}

Sol. (c) Refer to Q.No. 18 on Pg. 129.

5. The correct IUPAC name of $[Pt(NH_3)_2Cl_2]^{2+}$ is

(a) diamminedichloridoplatinum (II)
(b) diamminedichloridoplatinum (IV)
(c) diamminedichloridoplatinum (0)
(d) diamminedichloridoplatinate (IV)

Sol. (c) Refer to Q.No. 9 on Pg. 166

6. Arrange the following compounds in increasing order of their boiling points:

(i) 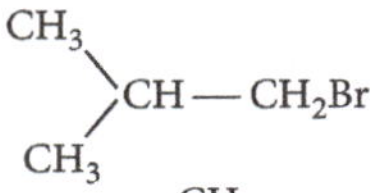 (ii) $CH_3CH_2CH_2CH_2Br$

(iii) 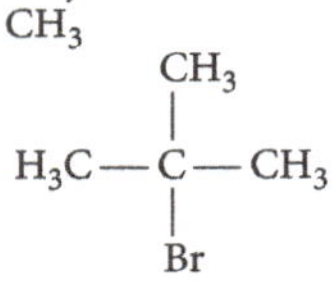

The correct order is

(a) (ii) < (i) < (iii)

(b) (i) < (ii) < (iii)

(c) (iii) < (i) < (ii)

(d) (iii) < (ii) < (i)

Sol. (c) Refer to Q.No. 10 on Pg. 212.

7. Alkyl halides undergoing nucleophilic bimolocular substitution reaction involve

(a) retention of configuration

(b) formation of racemic mixture

(c) inversion of configuration

(d) formation of carbocation

Sol. (c) Refer to Q.No. 15 on Pg. 213.

8. Which is the correct order of acid strength from the following?

(a) $C_6H_5OH > H_2O > ROH$

(b) $C_6H_5OH > ROH > H_2O$

(c) $ROH > C_6H_5OH > H_2O$

(d) $H_2O > C_6H_5OH > ROH$

Sol. (c) Refer to Q.No. 10 on Pg. 256.

9. The acid formed when propyl magnesium bromide is treated with CO_2 followed by acid hydrolysis is

(a) C_3H_7COOH

(b) C_2H_5COOH

(c) CH_3COOH

(d) C_3H_7OH

Sol. (c) Refer to Q.No. 17 on Pg. 301.

10. The best reagent for converting propanamide into propanamine is

(a) excess H_2

(b) Br_2 in aqueous NaOH

(c) iodine in the presence of red phosphorus

(d) $LiAlH_4$ in ether

Sol. (c) Refer to Q.No. 3 on Pg. 339.

11. Which of the following statements is not true about glucose?

(a) It is an aldohexose

(b) On heating with HI it forms *n*-hexane

(c) It exists in furanose form

(d) It does not give Schiff's test

Sol. (c) Refer to Q.No. 5 on Pg. 376.

12. An unripe mango placed in a concentrated salt solution to prepare pickle, shrivels because

(a) it gains water due to osmosis

(b) it loses water due to reverse osmosis

(c) it gains water due to reverse osmosis

(d) it loses water due to osmosis

Sol. (c) Refer to Q.No. 19 on Pg. 22.

Direction *For questions number 13 to 16, two statements are given – one labelled as Assertion (A) and the other labelled as Reason (R). Select the correct answer to these questions from the codes (a), (b), (c) and (d) as given below:*

(a) Both Assertion (A) and Reason (R) are true and Reason (R) is the correct explanation of the Assertion (A).

(b) Both Assertion (A) and Reason (R) are true, but Reason (R) is not the correct explanation of the Assertion (A).

(c) Assertion (A) is true, but Reason (R) is false.

(d) Assertion (A) is false, but Reason (R) is true.

13. **Assertion** (A) $[Cr(H_2O)_6]Cl_2$ and $[Fe(H_2O)_6]Cl_2$ are examples of homoleptic complexes.

Reason (R) All the ligands attached to the metal are the same.

Sol. (c) Refer to Q.No. 31 on Pg. 168.

14. **Assertion** (A) The boiling points of alkyl halides decrease in the order:

$$RI > RBr > RCl > RF.$$

Reason (R) The boiling points of alkyl chlorides, bromides and iodides are considerably higher than that of the hydrocarbon of comparable molecular mass.

Sol. (c) Refer to Q.No. 30 on Pg. 214.

15. **Assertion** (A) The boiling point of ethanol is higher than that of methoxymethane.

Reason (R) There is intramolecular hydrogen bonding in ethanol.

Sol. (c) Refer to Q.No. 30 on Pg. 258.

16. **Assertion** (A) All naturally occurring α-amino acids except glycine are optically active.

Reason (R) Most naturally occurring L-configuration

Sol. (c) Refer to Q.No. 34 on Pg. 378.

Section-B

17. Give reasons:

(a) Cooking is faster in pressure cooker than in an open pan.

(b) On mixing liquid X and liquid Y, volume of the resulting solution decreases. What type of deviation from Raoult's law is shown by the resulting solution? What change in temperature would you observe after mixing liquids X and Y?

Sol. Refer to Q.No. 7 on Pg. 25.

Or

(b) Define azeotrope. What type of azeotrope is formed by negative deviation from Raoult's law? Give an example.

Sol. Refer to Q.No. 8 on Pg. 25.

18. Complete and balance the following chemical equations:

(a) $2MnO_4^-(aq) + 10I^-(aq) + 16H^+(aq) \rightarrow$

Sol. Refer to Q.No. 48 (ii) (a) on Pg. 133.

(b) $Cr_2O_7^{2-}(aq) + 6Fe^{2+}(aq) + 14H^+(aq) \rightarrow$

Sol. Refer to Q.No. 16(i) on Pg. 131.

19. Would you expect benzaldehyde to be more reactive or less reactive in nucleophilic addition reactions than propanal? Justify your answer.

Sol. Refer to Q.No. 5 on Pg. 303.

20. Identify A and B in each of the following reaction sequence:

(a) $CH_3CH_2Cl \xrightarrow{NaCN} A \xrightarrow{H_2/Ni} B$

(b) $C_6H_5NH_2 \xrightarrow[0\text{-}5^\circ C]{NaNO_2/HCl} A \xrightarrow[H^+]{C_6H_5NH_2} B$

Sol. Refer to Q.No. 9 on Pg. 343.

21. Write the reactions involved when D-glucose is treated with the following reagents:

(a) HCN

(b) Br_2 water

Sol. Refer to Q.No. 1 on Pg. 379.

Section-C

22. A solution of glucose (molar mass =180 g mol^{-1}) in water has a boiling point of 100.20°C. Calculate the freezing point of the same solution. Molal constants for water K_f and K_b are 1.86K kg mol^{-1} and 0.512 Kkg mol^{-1} respectively.

Sol. Refer to Q.No. 20 on Pg. 26.

23. (a) State the following

(i) Kohlrausch law of independent migration of ions. Why does the conductivity of a solute decrease with dilution?

Sol. Refer to Q.No. 31 (ii) on Pg. 66.

(ii) Faraday's first law of electrolysis.

Sol. Refer to Q.No. 26(ii) on Pg. 66.

(b) Using E°_{values} of X and Y given below, predict which is better for coating the surface of iron to prevent corrosion and why?

Given : $E^\circ_{X^{2+}/X} = -2.36V$, $E^\circ_{Y^{2+}/Y} = -0.14V$

and $E^\circ_{Fe^{2+}/Fe} = -0.44V$

Sol. Refer to Q.No. 4 on Pg. 45.

24. A certain reaction is 50% complete in 20 min at 300 K and the same reaction is 50% complete in 5 min at 350 K. Calculate the activation energy if it is a first order reaction.

[$R = 8.314\ J\ K^{-1}mol^{-1}$; $\log 4 = 0.602$]

Sol. Refer to Q.No. 22 on Pg. 99.

25. The elements of $3d$ transition series are given as
Sc, Ti, V, Cr, Mn, Fe, Co, Ni, Cu, Zn

Answer the following:

(a) Copper has exceptionally positive $E^\circ_{M^{2+}/M}$ value, why?

Sol. Refer to Example 2 on Pg. 116.

(b) Which element is a strong reducing agent in +2 oxidation state and why?

(c) Zn^{2+} salts are colourless. Why?

Sol. Refer to Q.No. 9 on Pg. 131.

26. (i) Draw the structure of the major monohalo product for each of the following reaction:

(a) 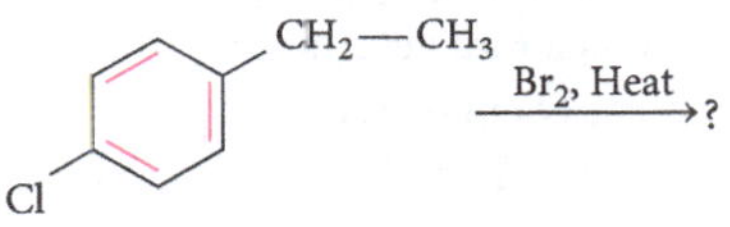

(b) 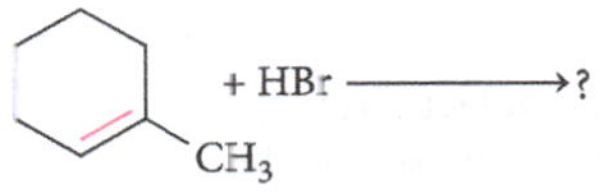

(c) 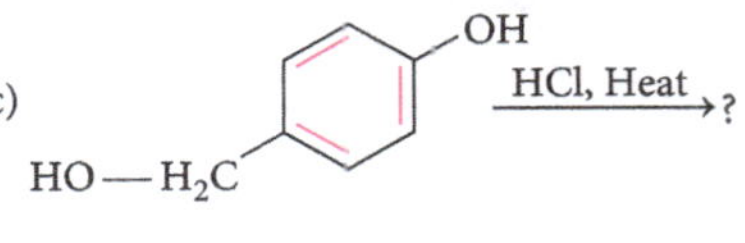

Sol. Refer to Q.No. 22 on Pg. 217.

(b) How do you convert:

(i) Chlorobenzene to biphenyl

(ii) Propene to 1-iodopropane

(iii) 2-bromobutane to but-2-ene.

Sol. Refer to Q.No. 23 on Pg. 217.

27. (a) Arrange the following compounds in increasing order of their boiling point:

$(CH_3)_2NH, CH_3CH_2NH_2, CH_3CH_2OH$

Sol. Refer to Q.No. 38 (iii) on Pg. 345.

(b) Give plausible explanation for each of the following:

(i) Aromatic primary amines cannot be prepared by Gabriel phthalimide synthesis.

(ii) Amides are less basic than amines.

Sol. Refer to Q.No. 12 on Pg. 343.

28. (a) What is the difference between native protein and denatured protein?

(b) Which one of the following is a disaccharide? Glucose, Lactose, Amylose, Fructose

(c) Which vitamin is responsible for the coagulation of blood?

Sol. Refer to Q.No. 19 on Pg. 380.

Section-D

The following questions are case based questions. Read the passage carefully and answer the questions that follow.

29. The rate of a chemical reaction is expressed either in terms of decrease in the concentration of reactants or increase in the concentration of a product per unit time. Rate of the reaction depends upon the nature of reactants, concentration of reactants, temperature, presence of catalyst, surface area of the reactants and presence of light. Rate of reaction is directly related to the concentration of reactant. Rate law states that the rate of reaction depends upon the concentration terms on which the rate of reaction actually depends, as observed experimentally. The sum of powers of the concentration of the reactants in the Rate law expression is called order of reaction while the number of reacting species taking part in an elementary reaction which must collide simultaneously in order to bring about a chemical reaction is called molecularity of the reaction.

Answer the following questions:

(a) (i) What is a rate determining step?

(ii) Define complex reaction.

(b) What is the effect of temperature on the rate constant of a reaction?

Or

(b) Why is molecularity applicable only for elementary reactions whereas order is applicable for elementary as well as complex reactions?

(c) The conversion of molecule X to Y follows second order kinetics. If concentration of X is increased 3 times, how will it affect the rate of formation of Y?

Sol. Refer to Q.No. 36 on Pg. 97.

30. Phenols undergo electrophilic substitution reactions readily due to the strong activating effect of OH group attached to the benzene ring. Since, the OH group increases the electron density more to *o*- and *p*- positions therefore OH group is *ortho*, *para*-directing. Reimer-Tiemann reaction is one of the examples of aldehyde group being introduced on the aromatic ring of phenol, *ortho* to the hydroxyl group. This is a general method used for the *ortho*-formylation of phenols.

Answer the following questions:

(a) What happens when phenol reacts with

(i) Br_2 / Cs_2

(ii) Conc. HNO_3

(b) Why phenol does not undergo protonation readily?

(c) Which is a stronger acid phenol or cresol? Give reason.

Or

(c) Write the IUPAC name of the product formed in the Reimer-Tiemann reaction.

Sol. Refer to Q.No. 38 on Pg. 259.

Section-E

31. (a) (i) Write the cell reaction and calculate the e.m.f. of the following cell at 298 K.

$Sn(s)|Sn^{2+}(0.004M)||H^+(0.02M)|H_2(g)(1Bar)|Pt(s)$

(Given, $E^\circ_{sn^{2+}/Sn} = -0.14$ V, $E^\circ_{H^+|H_2(g)}Pt = 0.00$ V

Sol. Refer to Quick Test 1, Q.No. 8 on Pg. 45.

(b) Account for the following:

(i) On the basis of E° values O_2 gas should be liberated at anode but it is Cl_2 gas which is liberated in the electrolysis of aqueous NaCl.

(ii) Conductivity of CH_3COOH decreases on dilution.

Sol. Refer to Q.No. 10 on Pg. 64.

Or

(a) Write the anode and cathode reactions and the overall cell reaction occurring in a lead storage battery during its use.

(b) Calculate the potential for half-cell containing 0.01 M $K_2Cr_2O_7(aq)$, 0.01M $Cr^{3+}(aq)$ and $10.\times10^{-4}$M $H^+(aq)$

The half-cell reaction is

$Cr_2O_7^{2-}(aq)+14H^{\oplus}(aq)+6e^- \rightarrow 2Cr^{3+}(aq)+7H_2O(l)$

and the standard electrode potential is given as $E^\circ = 1.38$V. [Given: log(10) = 1]

Sol. Refer to Q.No. 35 on Pg. 66.

32. Answer the following:

(a) Low spin tetrahedral complexes are not known.

Sol. Refer to Q.No. 38 (iii) on Pg. 171.

(b) Co^{2+} is easily oxidised to Co^{3+} in the presence of a strong ligand [At. No. of Co = 27]

Sol. Refer to Q.No. 36 (i) on Pg. 171.

(c) What type of isomerism is shown by the complex $[Co(NH_3)_6][Cr(CN)_6]$?

(d) Why a solution of $[Ni(H_2O)_6]^{2+}$ is green while a solution of $[Ni(CN)_4]^{2-}$ is colourless.
(At. No. of Ni = 28)

(e) Write the IUPAC name of the following complex: $[Co(NH_3)_5(CO_3)]Cl$

Sol. Refer to Q.No. 42 (i), (ii) and (iii) on Pg. 171.

Or

(a) What is meant by 'Chelate effect'? Give an example.

Sol. Refer to Q.No. 19 (ii) on Pg. 170.

(b) Write the hybridisation and magnetic behaviour of $[Fe(CN)_6]^{4-}$. (At. no. Fe = 26)

Sol. Refer to Q.No. 37 on Pg. 171.

(c) If $PtCl_2 \cdot 2NH_3$ does not react with $AgNO_3$ what will be its formula?

Sol. Refer to Q.No. 36 (iii) on Pg. 171.

33. (a) Carry out the following conversions:

(i) Ethanal to but-2-enal

(ii) Propanoic acid to ethane

Sol. Refer to Q.No. 17 on Pg. 304.

(b) An alkene *A* with molecular formula C_6H_{10} on ozonolysis gives a mixture of two compounds *B* and *C*. Compound *B* gives positive Fehling test and also reacts with iodine and NaOH solution. Compound *C* does not give Fehling solution test but forms iodoform. Identify the compounds *A*, *B* and *C*.

Sol. Refer to Q.No. 29 on Pg. 305.

Or

An organic compound (*A*) (molecular formula $C_8H_{16}O_2$ was hydrolysed with dilute sulphuric acid to get a carboxylic acid (*B*) and an alcohol (*C*). Oxidation of (*C*) with chromic acid produced (*B*). (*C*) on dehydration gives but-1-ene. Identify (*A*), (*B*) and (*C*) and write chemical equations for the reactions involved.

Sol. Refer to Q.No. 50 on Pg. 307

Set - II (Only Uncommon Questions from Set-I) (Code 56/1/2).

Section-B

18. When $FeCr_2O_4$, is fused with Na_2CO_3 in the presence of air it gives a yellow solution of compound (*A*). Compound (*A*) on acidification gives compound (*B*). Compound (*B*) on reaction with KCl forms an orange coloured (*C*). An acidified solution of compound (*C*) oxidises iodide to (*D*). Identify (*A*), (*B*), (*C*) and (*D*).

Sol. Refer to Q.No. 48(i) on Pg. 133

21. Give reasons for the following:

(a) The melting points of α-amino acids are generally higher than that of the corresponding carboxylic acids.

(b) Amino acids show amphoteric behaviour.

Sol. Refer to Q.No. 9 on Pg. 379

Section-C

22. A solution containing 15g urea (molar mass =60 g mol^{-1}) per litre of solution in water has the same osmotic pressure (isotonic) as a solution of glucose (molar mass =180 g mol^{-1}) in water. Calculate the mass of glucose present in one litre of its solution.

Sol. Refer to Q.No. 21 on Pg. 26

23. Calculate $\Delta_r G°$ and $\log K_C$ of the reaction:

$$Fe^{2+}(aq) + Ag^{+}(aq) \rightarrow Fe^{3+}(aq) + Ag(s)$$

Given $E^{\circ}_{Ag^{+}/Ag} = 0.80V$, $E^{\circ}_{Fe^{3+}/Fe^{2+}} = 0.77V$

$[R = 8.314 JK^{-1}mol^{-1},\ F = 96500 Cmol^{-1}]$

Sol. Refer to Q.No. 20 on Pg. 65.

24. (a) Arrange the following in decreasing order of pK_b

Aniline, *p*-nitroaniline, *p*-methylaniline

(b) Account for the following:

(i) Diazonium salts of aromatic amines are more stable than those of aliphatic amines.

(ii) Methylamine in water reacts with $FeCl_3$, to precipitate hydrated ferric oxide.

Sol. Refer to Q.No. 35 on Pg. 345

28. (a) Write the reaction when D-glucose reacts with the following:

(i) NH_2OH

(ii) Acetic anhydride

Sol. Refer to Q.No. 2 on Pg. 379

(b) Why vitamin C cannot be stored in our body?

Sol. Refer to Q.No. 24(ii) on Pg. 380

Section-E

32. For the complex $[Fe(en)_2Cl_2]Cl$, identify:

(a) the oxidation number of iron.

(b) the hybridization and the shape of the complex.

(c) the magnetic behaviour of the complex

(d) whether there is an optical isomer of the complex? If so draw its structure.

(e) IUPAC name of the complex.
(At. no. of Fe= 26)

Sol. Refer to Q.No. 54 on Pg. 172

Or

32. (a) Using IUPAC norms write the names of the following :

(i) $[Co(NH_3)_4Cl(NO_2)]Cl$

Sol. Refer to Q.No. 30(i), on Pg. 171

(ii) $K_3[Fe(CN)_6]$

Sol. Refer to Q.No. 29 (ii) on Pg. 171

(iii) $[Cr(C_2O_4)_3]^{3-}$

Sol. Refer to Q.No. 36 (ii) on Pg. 171

(b) What is crystal field splitting energy? Why low spin tetrahedral complexes are not formed?

Sol. Refer to Q.No. 19 (a) (i) on Pg. 170 and Q.No. 38 (iii) on Pg. 171.

Set - III (Only Uncommon Questions from Set-I & II) (Code 56/1/3)

Section-B

18. Complete and balanced the following chemical equation :

(a) $8MnO_4^- + 3S_2O_3^{2-} + H_2O \rightarrow$

Sol. Refer to Q.No. 39 (i) on Pg. 133

(b) $Cr_2O_7^{2-} + 3Sn^{2+} + 14H^+ \rightarrow$

Sol. Refer to Q.No. 48 (ii) (b) on Pg. 133

21. What are the hydrolysis products of

(a) sucrose ?

Sol. Refer to Quick Test 1, Q.No. 6 on Pg. 366

(b) lactose?

Sol. Refer to Q.No. 24 (i) on Pg. 380

Section-C

22. Henry's law constant for CO_2 in water is 1.67×10^8Pa at 298 K. Calculate the number of moles of CO_2 in 500 ml of soda water when packed under 2.53×10^5 Pa at the same temperature.

Sol. Refer to Quick Test 2, Q.No. 6 on Pg. 8

23. Calculate $\Delta_r G^\circ$ and $\log K_C$ of the reaction.

$2Cr(s) + 3Cd^{2+}(aq) \rightarrow 2Cr^{3+}(aq) + 3Cd(s)$

Given $E^\circ_{Cr^{3+}/Cr} = -0.74V$

$E^\circ_{Cd^{2+}/Cd} = -0.40V$

$[R = 8.314 JK^{-1} mol^{-1}, F = 96500 C\ mol^{-1}]$

Sol. Refer to Q.No. 21 on Pg. 65

24. The rate of a reaction quadruples when the temperature changes from 293 K to 313 K. Calculate the energy of activation of the reaction assuming that it does not change with temperature.

[Given:
$\log 4 = 0.602, \log 2 = 0.301, R = 8.314 JK^{-1} mol^{-1}$]

Sol. Refer to Q.No. 29 (ii) on Pg. 99

28. Define the following terms

(a) Native protein

(b) Nucleotide

(c) Essential amino acid

Sol. Refer to Q.No.20 (ii) on Pg. 380

Section-E

32. In the following complex ions, explain the type of hybridisation, shape and magnetic property.

(a) $[Fe(H_2O)_6]^{2+}$

(b) $[NiCl_4]^{2-}$

(At. Nos.: Fe = 26 and Ni = 28)

Sol. Refer to Q.No. 55 on Pg. 172

Or

(a) Write IUPAC names of the following:

(i) $[CO(H_2O)(CN)en)_2]^{2+}$

(ii) $[PtCl_4]^{2-}$

(iii) $Cr(NH_3)_4Cl(ONO)]^+$

(b) What is spectrochemical series? Write the difference between a strong field ligand and a weak field ligand.

Sol. Refer to Q.No. 51 (ii) on Pg. 172

SAMPLE QUESTION PAPER 1

A Highly Simulated Sample Question Paper for CBSE Class XII Examination

CHEMISTRY

Time : 3 Hours **Max. Marks : 70**

General Instructions

Read the following instructions carefully and follow them :

1. This question paper contains **33 questions**. All questions are **compulsory**.
2. This question paper is divided into **FIVE** sections - **Section A, B, C, D and E.**
3. **SECTION-A** questions number 1 to 16 are multiple choice type questions. Each question carries 1 mark.
4. **SECTION-B** questions number 17 to 21 are very short answer type questions. Each question carries 2 marks.
5. **SECTION-C** questions number 22 to 28 are short answer type questions. Each question carries 3 marks.
6. **SECTION-D** questions number 29 and 30 are case-based questions. Each question carries 4 marks.
7. **SECTION-E** questions number 31 to 33 are long answer type questions. Each question carries 5 marks.
8. There is no overall choice given in the question paper. However, an internal choice has been provided in few questions in all the sections except section A.
9. Kindly note that there is a separate question paper for visually impaired candidates.
10. Use of calculator is NOT allowed.

Section-A

The following questions are multiple choice questions with one correct answer. Each question carries 1 mark. There is no internal choice in this section.

1. In an alkaline medium, glycine predominantly exists as an
(a) cation
(b) anion
(c) Zwitter ion
(d) covalent form

2. Examine the following data for a reaction
$$A + B \longrightarrow P.$$
Concentrations of reactant A is varied, while the concentration of reactant B is kept constant.

Experiment	$[A]$ (M)	$[B]$ (M)	Rate (mol $L^{-1}s^{-1}$)
1	0.1	0.2	0.02
2	0.2	0.2	0.08
3	0.4	0.2	0.32

What will be the order of the reaction with respect to reactant A?
(a) 0 (b) 1
(c) 2 (d) 3

3. Identify the name of the reaction, bromoalkanes are prepared by refluxing the silver salts of acids with bromine in CCl_4.
(a) Borodine-Hunsdiecker reaction
(b) Finkelstein reaction
(c) Swarts reaction
(d) Balz-Schiemann reaction

4. The charge required to liberate 34.5g sodium from fused sodium chloride is
(a) 1 F (b) 1.5 F (c) 0.5 F (d) 2 F

5. Consider the table given below.

Coordination complex	Configuration of central metal ion	Hybridisation
$[Zn(NH_3)_4]^{2+}$	X	Y
$[Ti(H_2O)_6]^{3+}$	$[Ar]3d^1$	Z

Here, X,Y and Z are
(a) $X = [Ar]3d^{10}, Y = sp^3, Z = d^2sp^3$
(b) $X = [Ar]3d^9, Y = dsp^2, Z = sp^3d^2$
(b) $X = [Ar]3d^{10}4s^1, Y = sp^3, Z = d^2sp^3$
(b) $X = [Ar]3d^{10}, Y = dsp^2, Z = sp^3d^2$

6. Give IUPAC name of the compound given below.

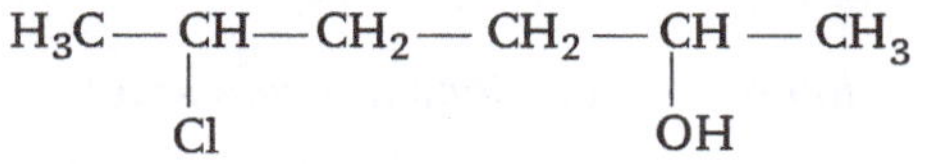

(a) 5-chlorohexan-2-ol
(b) 2-chlorohexan-5-ol
(c) 2-hydroxy-5-chlorohexane
(d) 2-chloro-5-hydroxyhexane

7. Identify the primary alcohol among the given options.

(a) 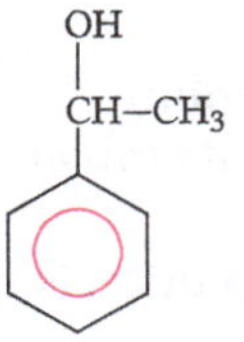
(b) 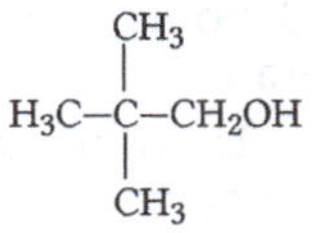
(c) 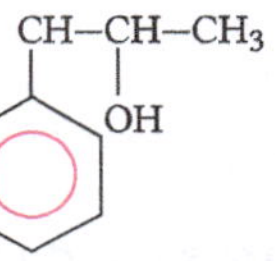
(d) 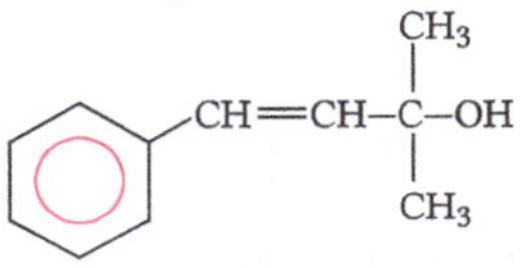

8. In the given reaction,

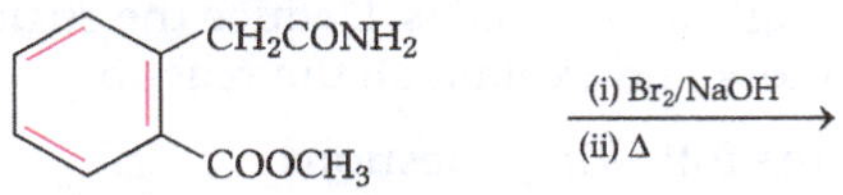

What would be the final product formed?

(a) 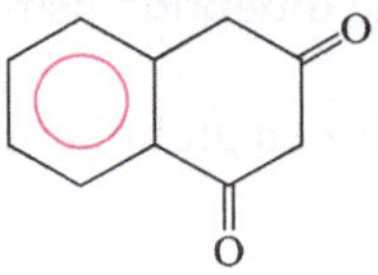
(b) 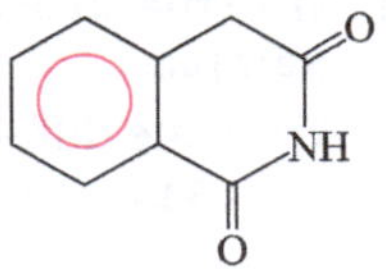
(c) 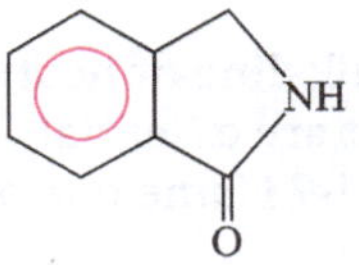
(d) 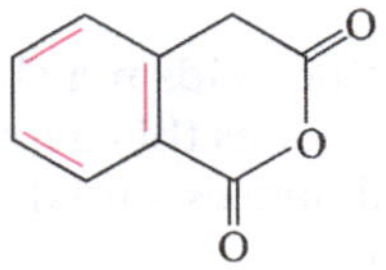

9. Match the magnetic moment with the ions of 3*d*-series.

(i) Cr^{3+}	(p) 5.92 BM
(ii) Mn^{2+}	(q) 3.87 BM
(iii) Fe^{2+}	(r) 4.90 BM
(iv) Sc^{3+}	(s) Zero

Select the correct option.
(a) (i)-(r), (ii)-(q), (iii)-(p), (iv)-(s)
(b) (i)-(r), (ii)-(s), (iii)-(p), (iv)-(q)
(c) (i)-(q), (ii)-(p), (iii)-(r), (iv)-(s)
(d) (i)-(s), (ii)-(r), (iii)-(p), (iv)-(q)

10. Which one undergoes S_N2 substitution reaction faster?

(a) 
(b) 
(c) 
(d) 

11. Alkenes react with water in the presence of acid as catalyst to form alcohols.

$$CH_3CH{=}CH_2 + H_2O \xrightleftharpoons{H^+} CH_3{-}\underset{\displaystyle OH}{\underset{|}{CH}}{-}CH_3$$

The reaction takes place in accordance with
(a) Hofmann elimination rule
(b) Saytzeff rule
(c) Markovnikov's rule
(d) anti-Markovnikov's addition

12. Identify the incorrect statement.
(a) Molecular formula of tetraamminediaquacobalt(III) chloride is $[Co(NH_3)_4(H_2O)_2Cl_3]$.
(b) $[PtCl_2(en)_2](NO_3)_2$ is the molecular formula of dichlorido*bis*-(ethane-1,2-diammine) platinum (IV) nitrate.
(c) Molecular formula of iron (III) hexacyanoferrate (II) is $Fe_4[Fe(CN)_6]_3$.
(d) If complex name starts with metal, it is an anionic complex.

Assertion-Reason

In the following questions (Q.No. 13-16), a statement of Assertion followed by a statement of Reason is given. Choose the correct answer out of the following choices.
(a) Both A and R are true and R is the correct explanation of A.
(b) Both A and R are true but R is not the correct explanation of A.
(c) A is true, but R is false.
(d) A is false, but R is true.

13. **Assertion** (A) If in a zero order reaction, the concentration of the reactant is doubled, the half-life period is also doubled.
Reason (R) For a zero order reaction, the rate of reaction is independent of initial concentration.

14. **Assertion** (A) The density of glycerol is higher than propanol.
Reason (R) Glycerol contain two —OH group due to which it shows extensive intermolecular H-bonding.

15. **Assertion** (A) Proteins are made up of α-amino acids.
Reason (R) During denaturation, secondary and tertiary structure of proteins are destroyed.

16. **Assertion** (A) *Neo*-pentyl chloride is formed when neopentyl alcohol reacts with HCl.
Reason (R) *Neo*-pentyl alcohol is a primary alcohol.

Section-B

This section contains 5 questions with internal choice in one question. The following questions are very short answer type and carry 2 marks each.

17. Explain, why the melting points and solubility of amino acids in water are generally higher than that of the corresponding haloacids?

18. What are interstitial compounds? Why are such compounds well known for transition metals?

19. (a) Write the effect of adding a non-volatile solute into solvent.
(b) What is the unit of molal depression constant?

20. How will you carry out the following conversion?
(a) Aniline to benzyl alcohol
(b) Benzene to *m*-bromophenol

Or

Account for the following:
(a) pK_b of aniline is more than that of methylamine.
(b) Ethylamine is soluble in water, whereas aniline is not.

21. (a) The conductivity of 0.2 M KCl solution is 3×10^{-2} ohm^{-1}cm^{-1}. Calculate its molar condutance.
(b) How molar conductance of a solution is related to the specific conductance?

Section-C

This section contains 7 questions with internal choice in one question. The following questions are short answer type and carry 3 marks each.

22. Complete the following reactions.
(a) $CH_3CH_2Cl \xrightarrow{KCN}$
(b) $CH_3CH_2CH_2Br \xrightarrow[\Delta]{\text{Alc. KOH}}$
(c) $C_6H_5O^-Na^+ + C_2H_5Cl \longrightarrow$

23. Write the balanced equations of the following reactions.
(a) Aniline and bromine water
(b) Ethylamine and nitrous acid
(c) Acetic anhydride and ammonia

24. (a) Give chemical tests to distinguish between the propanal and propanone.
(b) Arrange the following compounds in increasing order of reactivity towards HCN.
Acetaldehyde, acetone, di- *tert*- butylketone, methyl-*tert*-butylketone.
(c) Write a short note on Clemmensen reduction.

25. Compound *A* having molecular formula $C_4H_{10}O$ is found to be soluble in concentrated sulphuric acid. It does not react with sodium metal or potassium permanganate. On heating with excess of HI, it gives a single alkyl halides. Deduce the structure of compound *A* and explain all the reactions.

26. Answer the following questions.
(a) Give one example of an α-amino acid.
(b) Write the structure of the dipeptide using an example.
(c) Write one difference between globular and fibrous proteins.

Or

Amino acids may be acidic, alkaline or neutral. How does this happen? What are essential and non-essential amino acids? Name one of each type.

27. The rate constant for the decomposition of hydrocarbons is 2.418×10^{-5} s^{-1} at 546 K. If the energy of activation is 179.9 kJ s^{-1}, what will be the value of pre-exponential factor?

28. Calculate the $\Delta G°$ and log K_C for the following reaction at 298 K.
$2Cr(s) + 3Cd^{2+}(aq) \longrightarrow 2Cr^{3+}(aq) + 3Cd(s)$
[Given, $E°_{cell} = +0.34$ V, $F = 96500$ C mol^{-1}]

Section-D

The following questions are case -based questions. Each question has an internal choice and carries 4 (2+1+1) marks each. Read the passage carefully and answer the questions that follow.

29. The Crystal Field Theory (CFT) is an electrostatic model which considers the metal-ligand bond to be ionic arising purely from electrostatic interactions between the metal ion and the ligand.

In an octahedral coordination entity with six ligands surrounding the metal atom/ion, there will be repulsion between the electrons in metal *d*-orbitals and the electrons (or negative charges) of the ligands. Such a repulsion is more when the metal *d*-orbital is directed towards the ligand than when it is away from the ligand.

Thus, the $d_{x^2-y^2}$ and d_{z^2} orbitals which point towards the axes along the direction of the ligand will experience more repulsion and will be raised in energy and the d_{xy}, d_{zx} and d_{yz} orbitals which are directed between the axes will be lowered in energy relative to the average energy in the spherical crystal field.

Thus, the degeneracy of the *d*-orbitals has been removed due to ligand-metal electron repulsions in the octahedral complex to yield three orbitals of lower energy, t_{2g} set and two orbitals of higher energy, e_g set. This splitting of the degenerate levels due to the presence of ligands in a definite geometry is termed as crystal field splitting.

Answer the following questions.

(i) How many unpaired electrons are present in $[Co(CN)_6]^{3-}$ and whether it is a low spin or high spin complex.

(ii) Out of $[Mo(H_2O)_6]^{2+}$ and $[Cr(H_2O)_6]^{2+}$. Which has high Δ_o value and why?

Or

Write the correct order of increasing field strength of NH_3, en, CN^- and CO.

(iii) Why is Co^{2+} easily oxidised to Co^{3+} in presence of a strong ligand?

30. Electrochemistry is the study of production of electricity from energy released during spontaneous chemical reactions and the use of electrical energy to carry out non-spontaneous chemical transformations. A large number of metals, sodium hydroxide, chlorine, fluorine and many other chemicals are produced by electrochemical methods. An electrochemical cell is a device in which chemical energy of the redox reaction is converted into electrical energy, while electrolytic cell do the reverse.

Batteries and fuel cell convert chemical energy into electrical energy and are used in various instruments and devices. The reactions carried out electrochemically can be energy efficient and less polluting. Some of the examples of electrochemical cell batteries are Leclanche cell (dry cell), mercury cell, lead storage battery, etc.

Answer the following questions.

(i) Write the name of the cell which is generally used in hearing aids. Write the reactions taking place at the anode and the cathode of this cell.

(ii) Which of the following is not a type of electrochemical cell?

(a) Voltaic cell
(b) Photovoltaic cell
(c) Electrolytic cell
(d) Fuel cell

Or

Which of the following is not a secondary cell?

(a) Nickel cadmium cell
(b) Lead storage cell
(c) Lithium ion batteries
(d) Leclanche cell

(iii) Which of the following statement regarding primary cells is false?

(a) Primary cells cannot be recharged.
(b) They have low internal resistance.
(c) They have an irreversible chemical reaction.
(d) Their initial cost is cheap.

Section-E

The following questions are long answer type and carry 5 marks each. All questions have an internal choice.

31. (a) Complete the following reactions.

(i) $2H—\underset{\underset{O}{\|}}{C}—H \xrightarrow{\text{Conc. KOH}}$

(ii) 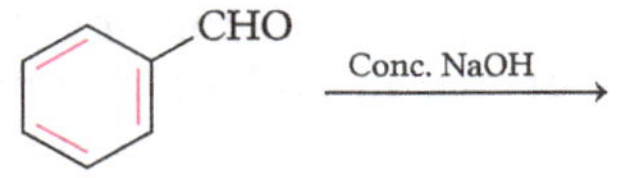

(iii) 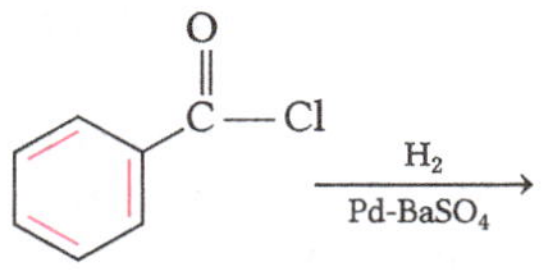

(b) Give one chemical test for each to distinguish between the following pair of compounds.

(i) Acetaldehyde and benzaldehyde

(ii) Acetaldehyde and acetone

Or

(a) How will you convert the following?

(i) Ethanal to 2-hydroxy propanoic acid

(ii) Toluene to benzoic acid

(b) Predict the products of the following reactions.

(i) $C_6H_5—CH_3 \xrightarrow[\text{(b) } H^+]{\text{(a) } KMnO_4/KOH} ?$

(ii) 

(c) Write the reagents required in the following reaction.

$$CH_3—COOH \xrightarrow{?} CH_3—CONH_2$$

32. A transition metal *A* has "spin only" magnetic moment value of 1.8 BM. When it is reacted with dil. H_2SO_4 in the presence of air, a compound *B* is formed. *B* reacts with compound *C* to give compound *D* with liberation of iodine. Determine metal *A*, *B*, *C* and *D*.

Or

(a) (i) For the first row transition metals, the $E°$ values are given below:

Elements	V	Cr	Mn	Fe	Co	Ni	Cu
$E°_{M^{2+}/M}$	−1.18	− 0.91	−1.18	−0.44	−0.28	− 0.25	+0.34

Explain the irregularity in the above values.

(ii) The halides of transition elements become more covalent with increasing oxidation state of the metal. Why?

(iii) Explain why Cu^+ ion is not stable in aqueous solution?

(b) Complete the following equations.

(i) $2CrO_4^{2-} + 2H^+ \longrightarrow$ (ii) $KMnO_4 \xrightarrow{\Delta}$

33. (a) (i) Will the molarity of a solution at 50°C be same at 25°C?

(ii) Out of 1 molal and 1 molar aqueous solution which is more concentrated?

(b) If the 40% (mass /mass) aqueous KI has density 1.202 gmL^{-1}. Calculate its

(i) molality

(ii) molarity

(c) What is the similarity between Henry's law and Raoult's law?

Or

(a) (i) Suggest the important type of intermolecular interaction for *n*-hexane and *n*-octane.

(ii) Acetonitrile (CH_3CN) and acetone (C_3H_6O).

(b) (i) Write any two limitations of (a) Henry's law

(ii) $\Delta_{sol}H$ of NH_4Cl is greater than 0. What is the effect of temperature on its solubility?

(c) State Raoult's law.

Solutions

1. (b) In alkaline medium, glycine predominantly exists as an anion. The reaction involved is shown as follows

$$H_3N^+—CH_2—COO^- + OH^- \longrightarrow \underset{\text{(Anion)}}{H_2\ddot{N}—CH_2—CO\bar{O}} + H_2O$$

2. (c) For the reaction, $A + B \longrightarrow P$

The differential rate law is

Rate $= k[A]^x[B]^y$

$\text{Rate}_1 = k(0.2)^x(0.2)^y$

$\text{Rate}_2 = k(0.2)^x(0.2)^y$

Thus, $\dfrac{\text{Rate}_2}{\text{Rate}_1} = \left(\dfrac{0.2}{0.1}\right)^x = \dfrac{0.08}{0.02}$

$\Rightarrow \quad 4 = 2^x$

Taking log on both sides

$\log 4 = \log(2)^x$

$\Rightarrow \quad \log(2)^2 = \log(2)^x$

$2\log 2 = x \log 2$

$\Rightarrow \quad x = 2$

Hence, order of the reaction with respect to reactant A is 2.

3. (a) Generally, bromoalkanes are prepared by refluxing the silver salts of acids with bromine in CCl_4.

This reaction is known as Borodine-Hunsdiecker reaction. The reaction can be depicted as

$$\underset{\text{Silver salt of acid}}{CH_3COO^-Ag^+} + Br_2 \xrightarrow{CCl_4} \underset{\text{Methyl bromide}}{CH_3Br} + \underset{\text{Carbon dioxide}}{CO_2\uparrow} + \underset{\text{Silver bromide}}{AgBr}$$

4. (b) For 23 g Na, charge required = 1F

For 34.5 g Na, charge required $= \dfrac{1}{23\text{g}} \times 34.5\text{g} = 1.5\,\text{F}$

5. (a) For the complex $[Zn(NH_3)_4]^{2+}$, the central metal ion is Zn^{2+} having electronic configuration (X) $[Ar]3d^{10}$.

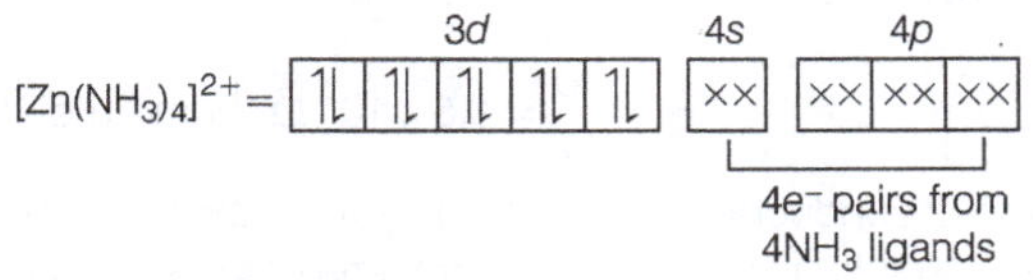

Thus, hybridisation (Y) is sp^3.

Similarily, for the complex $[Ti(H_2O)_6]^{3+}$, the central metal ion is Ti^{3+} having electronic configuartion $[Ar]3d^1$.

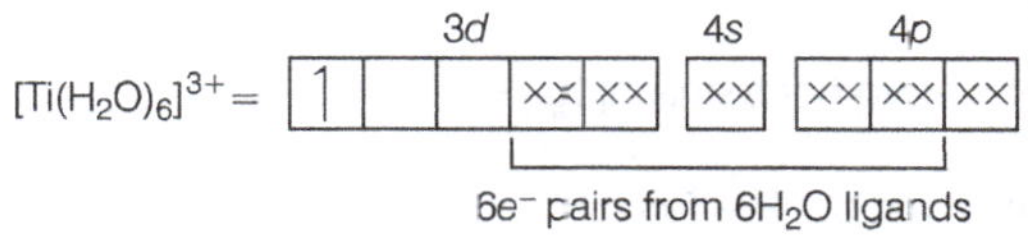

Thus, hybridisation (Z) is d^2sp^3.

6. (a) 5-chlorohexan-2-ol is the IUPAC name of given compound.

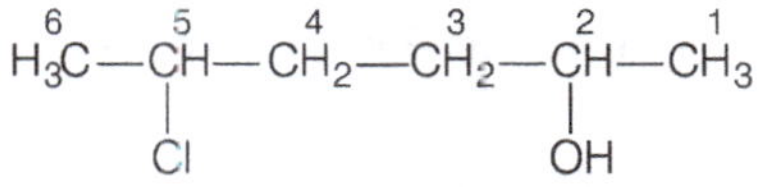

7. (b) Primary alcohols contain — CH_2OH group.

So, 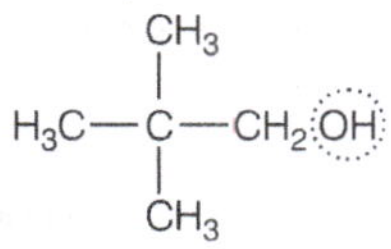 is a primary alcohol.

8. (c)

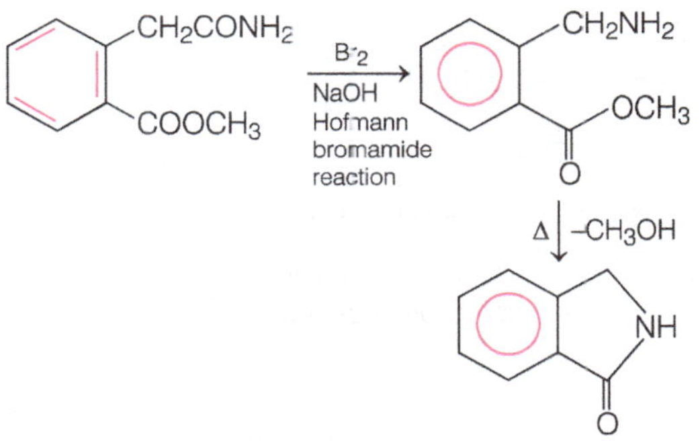

9. (c) The number of unpaired electrons in Cr^{3+}, Mn^{2+}, Fe^{2+} and Sc^{3+} are 3, 5, 4 and 0 respectively. By using formula for magnetic moment, i.e. $\mu = \sqrt{n(n+2)}$ where, n is number of unpaired electrons, the magnetic moment of Cr^{3+}, Mn^{2+}, Fe^{2+} and Sc^{3+} comes out to be 3.87 BM, 5.92 BM, 4.90 BM and 0 respectively.

Thus, the correct match is (i)-(q); (ii)-(p); (iii)-(r); (iv)-(s).

10. (a)  undergoes S_N2 reaction faster due to low C—I bond dissociation energy.

11. (c) Alkenes react with water in the presence of acid as catalyst to form alcohols. In case of unsymmetrical alkenes, the addition reaction takes place in accordance with Markovnikov's rule.

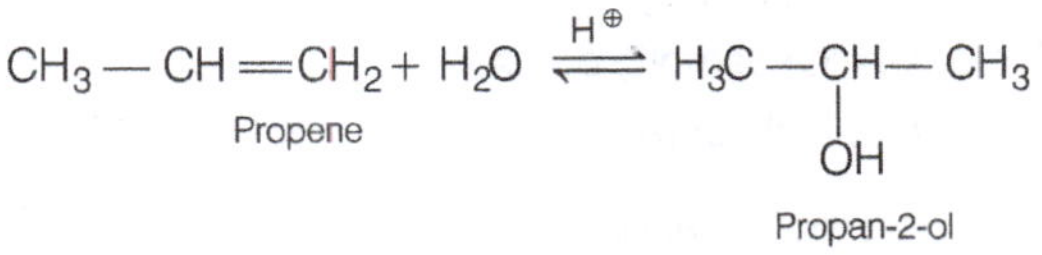

12. (a) The correct from (a) is the molecular formula tetrammine-diaquacobalt(III) chloride is $[Co(NH_3)_4(H_2O)_2]Cl_3$.

13. (b) Both A and R are true but R is not the correct explanation of A.

For a zero order reaction, $t_{1/2} = \frac{[A]_0}{2k}$.

14. (c) A is true but R is false.

The correct R is : The density of glycerol is higher than propanol, it is due to extensive intermolecular H-bonding. Glycerol contains three —OH groups, while propanol contains only one —OH group.

15. (b) Both A and R are true but R is not the correct explanation of A.

Chemically proteins are polymers in which the monomeric units are the α-amino acids.

16. (d) 2-chloro-2-methylbutane is formed when neopentyl alcohol reacts with HCl.

The initially formed primary carbocation undergoes rearrangement to form more stable tertiary carbocation.

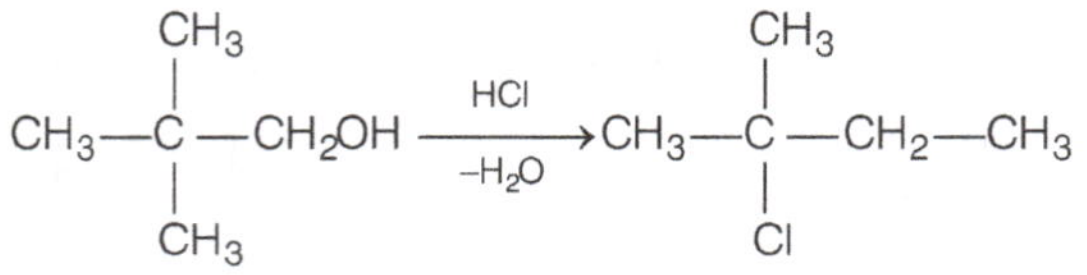

Therefore, A is false but R is true.

17. The amino acids exists as zwitter ions in aqueous solution. Due to this dipolar salt, they have strong dipole-dipole interactions.

Thus, their melting points are higher than corresponding haloacids is which do not have salt like character.

Secondly, they interact strongly with H_2O due to their salt like character. As a result, polar amino acids dissolve in polar solvents like H_2O. (2)

18. The compounds in which small atoms like H, C, N, etc., occupy interstitial sites in the crystal lattice are called interstitial compounds.

These compounds are well known for transition metals because small atoms can easily occupy the position in the voids present in the crystal lattices of transition metals. (2)

19. (a) The addition of a non-volatile solute into solvent

- lowers the vapour pressure
- lowers the freezing point
- increases the boiling point
- increases the osmotic pressure (1)

(b) The unit of molal depression constant is K kg mol^{-1}. (1)

20. (a) The conversion of aniline into benzyl alcohol can be carried out in the following manner.

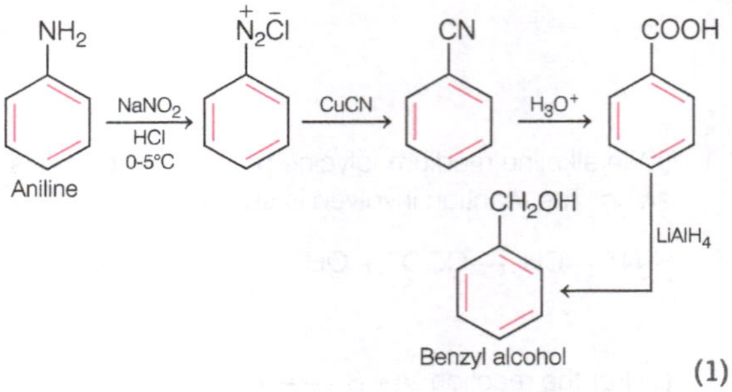

(1)

(b) The conversion of benzene to *m*-bromophenol can be carried out in the following manner.

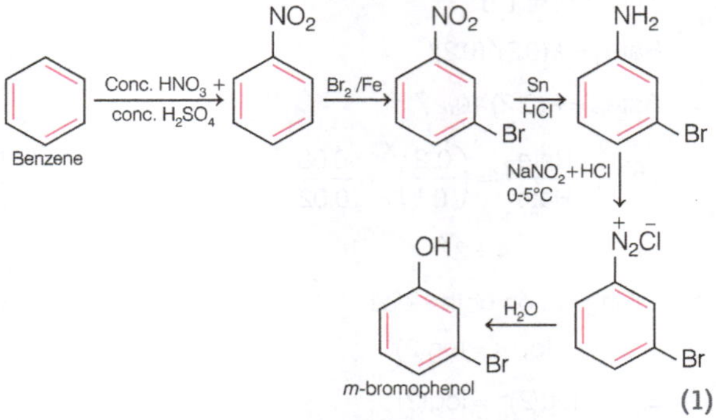

(1)

Or (a) In aniline, the electron pair on nitrogen atom is involved in conjugation with ring and is less available for protonation than that in methylamine.

Therefore, pK_b value of aniline is more than that of methylamine and aniline is less basic (as higher the pK_b value, weaker is the base). (1)

(b) Ethylamine is soluble in water due to hydrogen bonding.

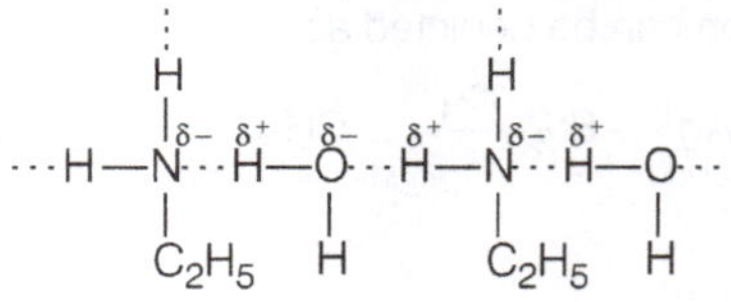

In aniline, due to bulky hydrocarbon part, the extent of hydrogen bonding is less and it is not soluble in water. (1)

21. (a) Given, $C = 0.2$ M, $\kappa = 3 \times 10^{-2}\ \Omega^{-1}\ cm^{-1}$

$$\because \quad \Lambda_m = \frac{\kappa \times 1000}{M}$$

Putting value, $\Lambda_m = \frac{1000}{0.2} \times 3 \times 10^{-2}$

$$= \frac{30}{0.2} = 1.5 \times 10^2\ \Omega^{-1}\ cm^2\ mol^{-1}$$ (1)

(b) Molar conductance is denoted by Λ_m. If the concentration of a solution is C mol/L, then volume of the solution containing 1 mole of the electrolyte will be 1/C L or 1000/C cc.

Hence, Λ_m and κ can be relates as $\Lambda_m = \frac{1000}{C} \times \kappa$, here, κ is specific conductance. (1)

22. (a) $CH_3CH_2Cl \xrightarrow{KCN} CH_3CH_2CN$ (1)
Ethyl chloride — Ethyl nitrile

(b) $CH_3CH_2CH_2Br \xrightarrow[\Delta]{Alc.KOH} CH_3CH{=}CH_2$ (1)
1- bromopropane — Prop-1-ene

(c) $C_6H_5\overset{-}{O}\overset{+}{Na} + C_2H_5Cl \longrightarrow C_6H_5{-}O{-}C_2H_5 + NaCl$
Sodium phenoxide — Chloroethane — Ethyl phenyl ether — Sodium chloride (1)

23. (a)

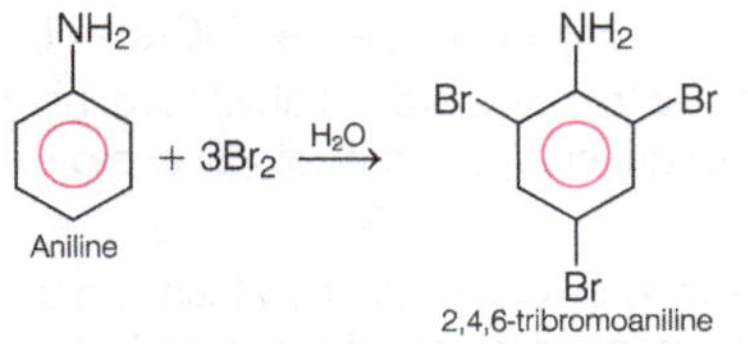

(1)

(b) $C_2H_5NH_2 + HNO_2 \longrightarrow C_2H_5OH + N_2\uparrow + H_2O$
Ethylamine — Ethanol (1)

(c) $(CH_3CO)_2O + NH_3 \longrightarrow CH_3COOH + CH_3CONH_2$
Acetic anhydride — Acetic acid — Acetamide (1)

24. (a) **Tollen's reagent test** Since, propanal is an aldehyde, it reduces Tollen's reagent to a shining silver mirror but propanone being a ketone, does not.

$$CH_3CH_2CHO + 2[Ag(NH_3)_2]^+ + 3OH^- \longrightarrow CH_3CH_2COO^- + 2Ag\downarrow + 4NH_3 + 2H_2O$$
Propanal — Silver mirror

$$CH_3COCH_3 \xrightarrow{\text{Tollen's reagent}} \text{No silver mirror}$$
Propanone (1)

(b) The reactivity towards HCN addition decreases as $+I$-effect of the alkyl group increases. Therefore, the correct order of reactivity is

Di-*tert*-butyl ketone < methyl-*tert*-butyl ketone < acetone < acetaldehyde. (1)

(c) **Clemmensen reduction** It involves the reduction of carbonyl group ($\rangle C{=}O$) to $\rangle CH_2$ group and it is carried out in the presence of Zn amalgam and conc. HCl.

$$\rangle C{=}O + 4[H] \xrightarrow{Zn\text{-}Hg/Conc.HCl} \rangle CH_2 + H_2O$$
Hydrocarbon (1)

25. (a) As compound *A* does not react with sodium metal or potassium permanganate, it cannot be an alcohol. (1/2)

(b) As compound *A* dissolves in conc. H_2SO_4, it may be an ether. (1/2)

(c) As compound *A* on heating with excess of HI, gives a single alkyl halide, therefore compound *A* must be a symmetrical ether. (1)

(d) The only symmetrical ether having molecular formula $C_4H_{10}O$ is diethyl ether.

Thus, compound *A* is diethyl ether,

$$CH_3{-}CH_2{-}O{-}CH_2{-}CH_3.$$

$$CH_3CH_2{-}O{-}CH_2CH_3 \xrightarrow{Conc.\ H_2SO_4} \left[CH_3{-}CH_2{-}\overset{+}{\underset{\displaystyle H}{O}}{-}CH_2{-}CH_3\right] HSO_4^-$$
Soluble oxonium salt

$$CH_3CH_2OCH_2CH_3 \xrightarrow[\Delta]{HI} 2CH_3CH_2{-}I$$
(*A*) Diethyl ether — Ethyl iodide (1)

26. (a) Alanine, $H_2N{-}\underset{\displaystyle CH_3}{CH}{-}COOH$ (1)

(b) When two α-amino acids combine, a dipeptide is formed with the loss of a water molecule.

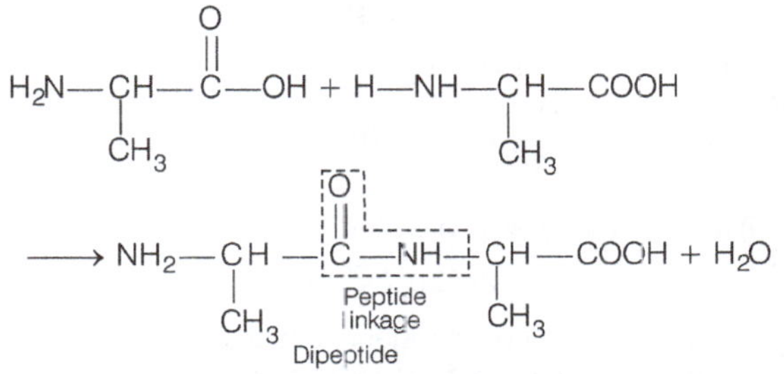

(1)

(c) (i) **Fibrous proteins** They have thread or fibre like structures in which polypeptide chains run parallel. These proteins are insoluble in water, e.g. keratin (found in hair, skin, nails, wool, silk) and myosin (present in muscles). (1/2)

(ii) **Globular proteins** They have spherical shape in which chains of polypeptides coil around. These are soluble in water, e.g. insulin and albumins. (1/2)

Or

Amino acids may be acidic, basic or neutral depending upon the relative number of amino and carboxyl groups present in the molecule.

Equal number of amino and carboxyl groups makes it neutral. More number of amino groups than carboxyl groups makes it basic and more carboxyl groups as compared to amino groups makes it acidic. (1)

(i) **Essential amino acids** are the α-amino acids which are needed for health and growth of human beings but are not synthesised by the human body, e.g. valine, leucine. (1)

(ii) **Non-essential amino acids** are the α-amino acids which are needed for health and growth of human beings and are synthesised by the human body, e.g. glycine, aspartic acid. (1)

27. According to Arrhenius equation,

$$\log k = \log A - \frac{E_a}{2.303RT}$$

We have, $k = 2.418 \times 10^{-5} s^{-1}$;

$E_a = 179.9$ kJ mol^{-1}

or $\quad 179900 \text{ J mol}^{-1}$;

$R = 8.314 \text{ J K}^{-1}\text{mol}^{-1}$; $T = 546\text{K}$

$$\Rightarrow \quad \log A = \log k + \frac{E_a}{2.303RT}$$

$$= \log(2.418 \times 10^{-5} \text{s}^{-1}) + \frac{179900 \text{ J mol}^{-1}}{2.303 \times (8.314 \text{ JK}^{-1}\text{mol}^{-1}) \times 546 \text{ K}}$$

$$\log A = -4.6165 + 17.21 = 12.5935$$

$$A = \text{antilog } 12.5935 = 3.9 \times 10^{12}\text{s}^{-1}$$ (3)

28. $\Delta G° = -nFE°_{cell}$; $n = 6$

$$= -6 \times 96500 \text{ C/mol} \times 0.34 \text{ V}$$

$$= -196860 \text{ J/mol} = -196.860 \text{ kJ/mol}$$

$$\therefore E°_{cell} = 0.059\, V/n \times \log K_C$$

$$\log K_C = \frac{0.34V \times 6}{0.059V} = 34.5762$$ (3)

29. (i) For the complex, $[Co(CN)_6]^{3-}$,

$$Co^{3+} = 1s^2 2s^2 2p^6 3s^2 3p^6 3d^6$$

CN^- is a strong field ligand and as it approaches the metal ion, the electrons must pair up.

The splitting of the d-orbitals into two sets of orbitals in an octahedral complex $[Co(CN)_6]^{3-}$ may be represented as $t_{2g}^6 e_g^0$.

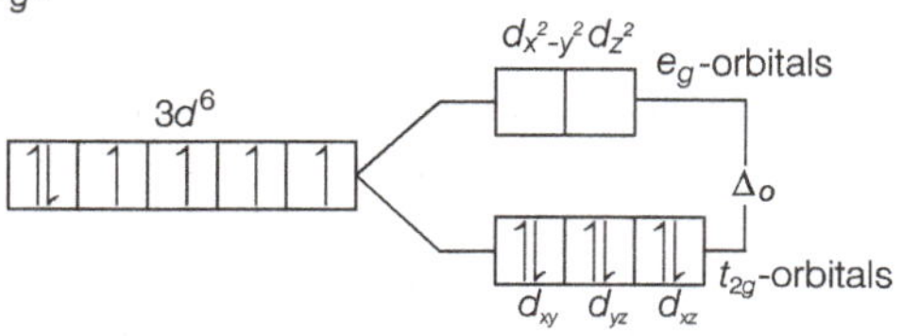

Here, for d^6 ions electrons pair up in t_{2g} orbital giving rise to low spin complex (strong ligand) field.

$\therefore$ $[Co(CN)_6]^{3-}$ has no unpaired electron and will be in low spin configuration. (2)

(ii) CFSE increases with increasing principal quantum number, i.e. $3d < 4d < 5d$, when the ligand, oxidation state and d-electrons are the same.

So, Δ_o of $[Mo(H_2O)_6]^{2+} > [Cr(H_2O)_6]^{2+}$ (1)

Or

Based on spectrochemical series, ligands arranged in increasing order of crystal field strength are as (1)

$$NH_3 < en < CN^- < CO$$

(iii) In the presence of a strong ligand, $Co^{2+}(3d^7)$ has an electronic configuration of $t_{2g}^6 e_g^1$, whereas, $Co^{3+}(3d^6)$ has a stable electronic configuration of t_{2g}^6 as electron is lost from e_g level. Thus, Co^{2+} is easily oxidised to Co^{3+} in presence of a strong ligand. (1)

30. (i) Mercury cell is suitable for low current devices like hearing aids, watches, etc.

The electrode reactions of a mercury cell can be written as

At anode,

$$ZnHg + 2OH^- \longrightarrow ZnO(s) + H_2O + 2e^-$$

At cathode,

$$HgO + H_2O + 2e^- \longrightarrow Hg(l) + 2OH^-$$

Overall reaction,

$$ZnHg + HgO(s) \longrightarrow ZnO(s) + Hg(l)$$ (2)

(ii) (b) Photovoltaic cells are not an electrochemical cell as it converts light energy into electrical energy.

Or

(d) A secondary battery is one which can be charged, discharged into a load and recharged many times. Nickel-cadmium cell, lead storage cell and mercury cell are examples of secondary cells whereas Leclanche cell is an example of a primary cell.

(iii) (b) Primary cells cannot be used again and again. Since there is no fluid inside, these cells are also known as dry cells. The internal resitance is high and the chemical reaction is irreversible. Their initial cost is cheap.

31. (a) (i)

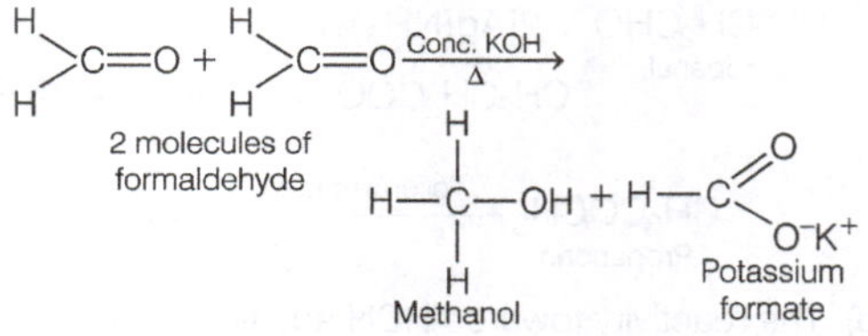

(1)

(ii)

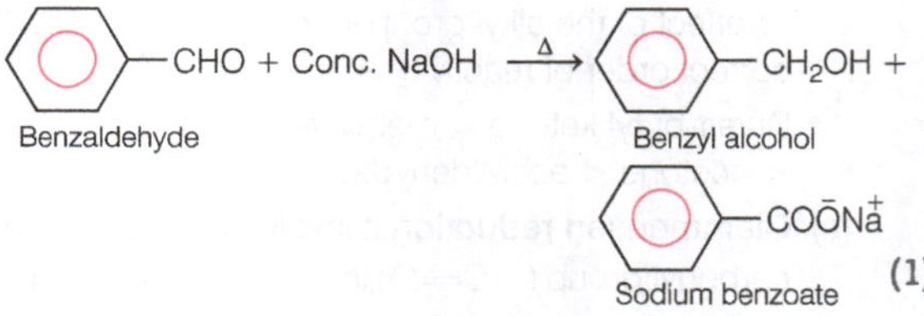

(1)

(iii)

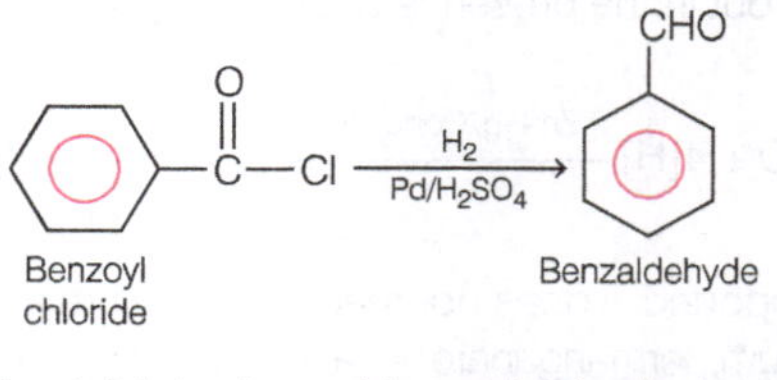

(1)

(b) (i) **Acetaldehyde and benzaldehyde** Acetaldehyde acts as reducing agent which reduces Fehling's solution. It gets oxidised to carboxylate ion and reduces Cu^{2+} to cuprous oxide.

$$\underset{\text{Acetaldehyde}}{CH_3-\overset{\overset{}{}}{\underset{\underset{O}{\|}}{C}}-H} + 2Cu^{2+} + 5OH^- \longrightarrow \underset{\text{Carboxylate ion}}{CH_3-\overset{\overset{O}{\|}}{C}-O^-} + \underset{\text{(red ppt.)}}{Cu_2O\downarrow} + 3H_2O$$

Benzaldehyde is not oxidised by Fehling solution. (1)

(ii) **Acetaldehyde and acetone** Acetaldehyde gives a silver mirror test when heated with Tollen's reagent.

$$\underset{\text{Acetaldehyde}}{CH_3CHO} + \underset{\text{Tollen's reagent}}{2[Ag(NH_3)_2]^+} + 3OH^- \longrightarrow CH_3COOH + \underset{\text{Silver mirror}}{2Ag\downarrow} + 4NH_3 + 2H_2O$$

Acetone does not give this test because it does not have α-hydroxy ketone group. (1)

Or

(a) (i) **Ethanal to 2-hydroxy propanoic acid**

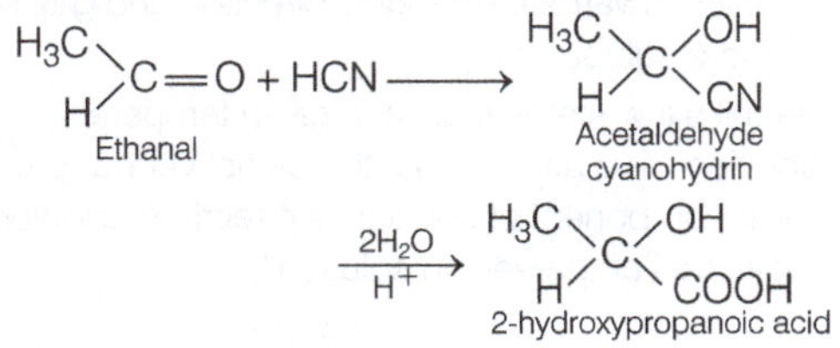

(1)

(ii) **Toluene to benzoic acid**

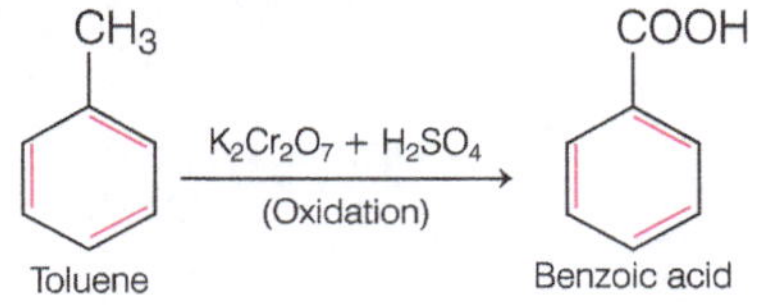

(1)

(b)

(i)

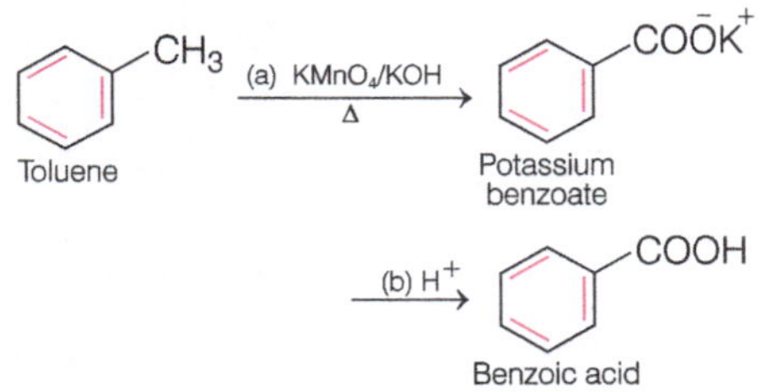

(1)

(ii)

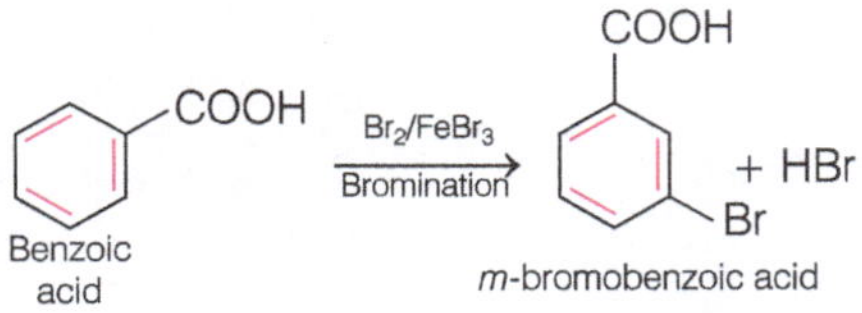

(1)

(c) $CH_3—COOH \xrightarrow[-H_2O]{NH_3/Heat} CH_3—CONH_2$ (1)

32. The spin only magnetic moment is given by

$$\mu = \sqrt{n(n+2)}$$

Thus, $\sqrt{n(n+2)} = 1.8$

Squaring both sides,

$$n(n+2) = 3.24$$
$$n^2 + 2n = 3$$
$$n^2 + 2n - 3 = 0$$
$$n^2 + 3n - n - 3 = 0$$
$$(n-1)(n+3) = 0$$

$\Rightarrow n = 1$, but $n \neq -3$ is not possible,

Thus, $n = 1$

It means that one unpaired electron is present, i.e. it is copper.

Thus, $\underset{(A)}{2Cu} + 2H_2SO_4 + O_2 \longrightarrow \underset{(B)}{2CuSO_4} + 2H_2O$

$$\underset{(B)}{2CuSO_4} + \underset{(C)}{4KI} \longrightarrow 2K_2SO_4 + 2CuI_2$$

$$2CuI_2 \longrightarrow \underset{(D)}{Cu_2I_2} + I_2$$ (5)

Or

(a) (i) It is due to irregular variation of sublimation enthalpies and ionisation enthalpies for elements of 3*d*-transition series. (1)

(ii) This problem is based on the concept of Fajans' rule. As the oxidation state increases, size of the ion of transition element decreases. As per Fajans' rule, when the size of metal ion decreases, covalent character of the bond formed increases.

Therefore, the halide of transition elements become more covalent with increasing oxidation state of the metal. (1)

(iii) In aqueous solution, copper (I) undergoes disproportionation reaction.

$$2Cu^+(aq) \longrightarrow Cu^{2+} + Cu(s)$$

The highest stability of Cu^{2+} ion in aqueous solution is due to negative enthalpy of hydration.

Hence, Cu^+ is not known (or unstable) in aqueous solution. (1)

(b) (i) $2CrO_4^{2-} + 2H^+ \longrightarrow Cr_2O_7^{2-} + H_2O$ (1)

(ii) $2KMnO_4 \xrightarrow{\Delta} K_2MnO_4 + MnO_2 + O_2$ (1)

33. (a) (i) No, molarity at 50°C will be less than at 25°C as it decreases with rise in temperature. (1)

(ii) 1 molar aqueous solution is more concentrated than 1 molal aqueous solution. Because in 1 m solution, 1 mole of solute is present in 1000 g of solvent while in 1 M solution, 1 mole of solute is present in 1 litre of solution which include both solute and solvent. (1)

(b) (i) Weight of KI in 100 g of solution = 40 g

Weight of water in the solution

$= (100 - 40)\,g = 60\,g = 0.06\,kg$

Molar mass of KI $= 39 + 127 = 166\,g\,mol^{-1}$

Molality of the solutions $(m) = \dfrac{\text{Number of moles of KI}}{\text{Mass of water (in kg)}}$

$$= \frac{(40g)\,/\,(166\,g\,mol^{-1})}{(0.06\,kg)}$$

$$= 4.02\,mol\,kg^{-1} \approx 4\,m.$$ (1)

(ii) Weight of the solution = 100 g

Density of the solution $= 1.202\,g\,mL^{-1}$

Volume of the solution $= \dfrac{\text{Weight of solution}}{\text{Density}}$

$$= \frac{(100\ g)}{(1.202 g\ mL^{-1})}$$

$= 83.19\ mL = 0.083\ L$

Molarity of the solution (M)

$$= \frac{\text{Number of moles of KI}}{\text{Volume of solution in litres}}$$

$$= \frac{(40\ g)/(166\ g\ mol^{-1})}{(0.083 L)}$$

$= 2.9\ mol\ L^{-1} = 2.9\ M$ (1)

(c) Both the laws are applied to volatile component in solutions. (1)

Or

(a) (i) Since both are non-polar. Hence intermolecular interactions between them are london dispersion forces. (1)

(ii) As both are polar molecules. Hence, intermolecular interactions between them will be dipole-dipole interactions. (1)

(b) (i) Two limitations of Henry's law are :

Henry law is applicable when,

1. temperature is not too low.
2. the gas should not undergo any chemical change. (1)

(ii) As dissolution of gas in liquid is an endothermic process. So, on increasing the temperature, equilibrium shifts towards the forward direction and gas tends to be more soluble in liquid. (1)

(c) Raoult's law states that "at a given temperature, for a solution of volatile liquids, the partial vapour pressure of each component of solution is directly proportional to its mole fraction present in solution".

$$p_A \propto \chi_A$$ (1)

SAMPLE QUESTION PAPER 2

A Highly Simulated Sample Question Paper for CBSE Class XII Examination

CHEMISTRY

Time : 3 Hours **Max. Marks : 70**

General Instructions

Read the following instructions carefully and follow them :

1. This question paper contains **33 questions**. All questions are **compulsory**.
2. This question paper is divided into **FIVE** sections - **Section A, B, C, D and E.**
3. **SECTION-A** questions number 1 to 16 are multiple choice type questions. Each question carries 1 mark.
4. **SECTION-B** questions number 17 to 21 are very short answer type questions. Each question carries 2 marks.
5. **SECTION-C** questions number 22 to 28 are short answer type questions. Each question carries 3 marks.
6. **SECTION-D** questions number 29 and 30 are case-based questions. Each question carries 4 marks.
7. **SECTION-E** questions number 31 to 33 are long answer type questions. Each question carries 5 marks.
8. There is no overall choice given in the question paper. However, an internal choice has been provided in few questions in all the sections except section A.
9. Kindly note that there is a separate question paper for visually impaired candidates.
10. Use of calculator is NOT allowed.

Section-A

The following questions are multiple choice questions with one correct answer. Each question carries 1 mark. There is no internal choice in this section.

1. The rate of the reaction,

$CCl_3CHO + NO \longrightarrow CHCl_3 + NO + CO$

is equal to rate $= k[CCl_3CHO][NO]$. If concentration is expressed in mol/L, the unit of k is

(a) $L\ mol^{-1}s^{-1}$

(b) $mol\ L^{-1}s^{-1}$

(c) $L^2mol^{-2}s^{-1}$

(d) s^{-1}

2. A glycerine solution at 393 K has a molality of 4.53 molal and molarity of 7.42 M.

Which of the given relation would be correct for molarity and molality of the same glycerine solution at 640 K?

(a) Molarity = 7.42 M, Molality = 4.53 molal

(b) Molarity > 7.42 M, Molality = 4.53 molal

(c) Molarity < 7.42 M, Molality < 4.53 molal

(d) Molarity < 7.42 M, Molality = 4.53 molal

3. Give the name of

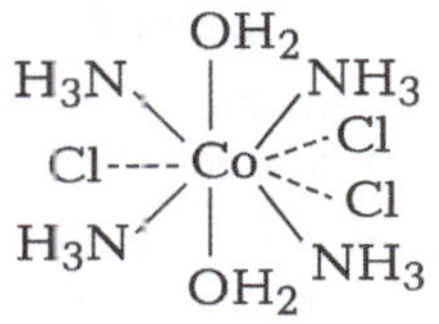

(a) tetraammineaquacobalt chloride

(b) tetraamminediaquacobalt(III) chloride

(c) tetraamminediaquacobalt(IV) chloride

(d) None of the above

4. Reaction of chloroform with chlorine is an example of fraction order reaction.

Its rate law expression is rate $= k[CHCl_3][Cl_2]^{1/2}$. If both are assumed in gaseous state and pressure is measured in bar, then units of rate and rate constant respectively are

(a) bar min^{-1}, bar^2 min^{-1} (b) bar min^{-1}, $bar^{-1/2}$, min^{-1}

(c) $bar^{-1/2}$, min^{-1}, bar^2min^{-1} (d) bar min^{-1}, $bar^{-1/2}$ min^{-1}

5. Iodoform test is not given by
(a) pentan-2-one (b) pentan-3-one
(c) ethanal (d) ethanol

6. The manufacturing of alcohol commercially by fermentation method takes place in the following two steps.

	Reaction steps	Enzyme Used
(i)	X + Water $\longrightarrow$ Glucose + Fructose	Invertase
(ii)	Glucose $\longrightarrow$ Ethanol + Carbon dioxide	Y

'X' and 'Y' in the above table are
(a) X = Sucrose, Y = Maltase
(b) X = Sucrose, Y = Zymase
(c) X = Lactose, Y = Zymase
(d) X = Maltose, Y = Maltase

7. The electrophile used in Reimer-Tiemann reaction is
(a) $CCl_3^{\oplus}$ (b) $:CCl_2$ (c) $Cl^{\oplus}$ (d) H_2O

8. Salicylic acid and phenol can be distinguished by the use of
(a) bromine water (b) neutral $FeCl_3$
(c) 5% NaOH solution (d) $NaHCO_3$ solution

9. Which of the following element show catalytic property?
(a) Ca (b) Fe (c) Na (d) None of these

10. Match the properties given in Column I with the metals given in Column II.

	Column I		Column II
(i)	An element which has highest second ionisation enthalpy.	(p)	Mn
(ii)	3*d*-block element that show only +3 oxidation state.	(q)	Zn
(iii)	3*d*-block element with lowest melting point.	(r)	Sc
(iv)	An element which can show +7 oxidation state.	(s)	Cu

Select the correct option.
(a) (i)→(p), (ii)→(s), (iii)→(r), (iv)→(q)
(b) (i)→(s), (ii)→(q), (iii)→(r), (iv)→(p)
(c) (i)→(s), (ii)→(r), (iii)→(q), (iv)→(p)
(d) (i)→(r), (ii)→(s), (iii)→(p), (iv)→(q)

11. Which of the following molecule is achiral?
(a) 2-chlorobutane (b) 2,2-dichlorobutane
(c) Bromochloridoiodomethane (d) 2-bromobutane

12. Which of the following is not correct?
(a) $PhCH_2Br > PhCHBrCH_3 > PhCBr(CH_3)_2$ (S_N1)
(b) R—I > R—Br > R—Cl (S_N2)
(c) $CH_2{=}CH{-}Cl < CH_2{=}CH{-}CH_2{-}Cl < PhCH_2{-}Cl$ (S_N1)
(d) R—Cl < R—Br < R—I (S_N1)

Assertion-Reason

In the following questions (Q.No. 13-16), a statement of Assertion (A) followed by a statement of Reason (R) is given. Choose the correct answer out of the following choices.
(a) Both A and R are true and R is the correct explanation of A.
(b) Both A and R are true but R is not the correct explanation of A.
(c) A is true but R is false.
(d) A is false but R is true.

13. **Assertion** (A) Phenol is less acidic than *p*-nitrophenol.
Reason (R) Phenolate ion is more stable than *p*-nitrophenolate ion.

14. **Assertion** (A) Order of the following reaction, $2NO(g) + 2H_2(g) \longrightarrow 2H_2O(g) + N_2(g)$ is 3 and its rate equation is rate = $k[NO]^2[H_2]$
Reason (R) Order of the reaction with respect to given reactant is the power of the reactant's concentration in the rate equation.

15. **Assertion** (A) Glucose does not gives 2, 4-DNP test.
Reason (R) Glucose exists in cyclic hemiacetal form.

16. **Assertion** (A) Aldehydes and ketones both react with Tollen's reagent to form silver mirror.
Reason (R) Both aldehydes and ketones contain a carbonyl group.

Section-B

This section contains 5 questions with internal choice in one question. The following questions are very short answer type and carry 2 marks each.

17. List any four factors on which the colligative properties of a solution depend.

18. What is the difference between hormones and vitamins?

19. Write the structure of the major organic products in each of the following reactions.
(a) $CH_3CH_2CH_2OH + SOCl_2 \longrightarrow$
(b) $CH_3CH_2CH{=}CH_2 + HBr \xrightarrow{\text{Peroxide}}$

20. Consider the following, ln [*R*] *vs* time (min) plot.

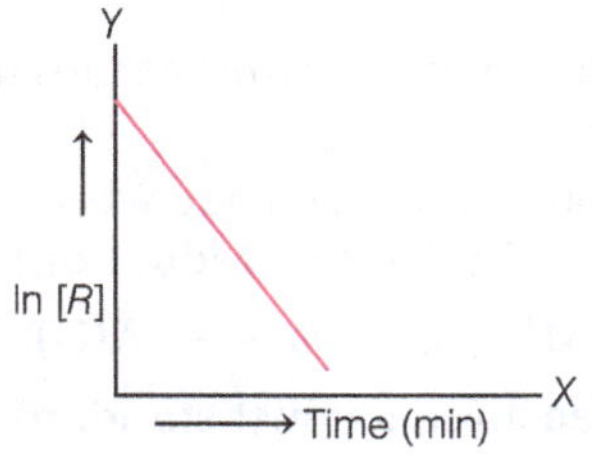

(a) What is the order of the reaction?

(b) What are the units of rate constant, (*k*) for the reaction?

21. Consider the following reactions.

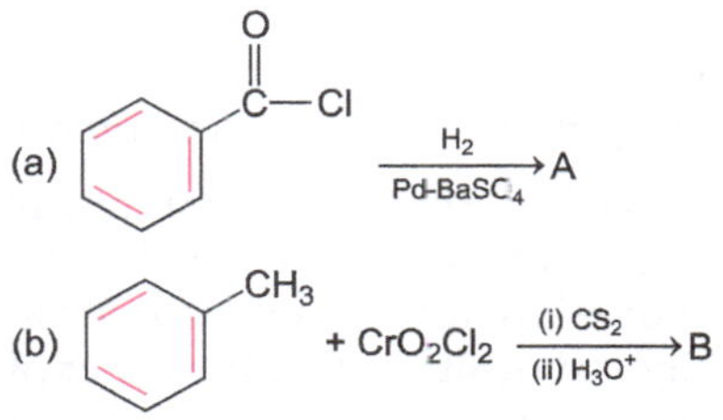

Write the product and name of the reaction.

Or Convert

(a) Acetaldehyde to formaldehyde

(b) Propanal to butanone

Section-C

This section contains 7 questions with internal choice in one question. The following questions are short answer type and carry 3 marks each.

22. Give the half-cell reactions in the following batteries.

(a) Mercury cell

(b) Lead storage battery

(c) Nickel-cadmium battery

23. $[CoF_6]^{3-}$ is a coordination complex ion.

(a) What is the oxidation number of cobalt in the complex?

(b) State the magnetic behaviour of the complex.

(c) Give the IUPAC name of the complex.

24. How will you convert

(a) benzene to acetophenone?

(b) propanone to 2-methylpropan-2-ol?

(c) ethanal to butane-1,3-diol?

Or

Swati was experimenting in the lab to study the properties of esters. She has an organic compound '*A*' with molecular formula $C_4H_8O_2$ undergoes acid hydrolysis to form two compounds '*B*' and '*C*'. oxidation of '*C*' with acidified $KMnO_4$ also produces '*B*'.

(a) Identify '*A*', '*B*' and '*C*'.

(b) Out of '*B*' and '*C*' which will have higher boiling point?

25. How may be the following transformation carried out (in not more than six steps)? Ethyl alcohol to vinyl acetate.

26. (a) Write a chemical reaction in which iodide ion displaces diazonium group from diazonium salt.

(b) A solution of KOH hydrolyses $CH_3CHClCH_2CH_3$ and $CH_3CH_2CH_2CH_2Cl$. Which one of these is more easily hydrolysed?

(c) Why iodoform has appreciable antiseptic property?

27. Activation energy for the acid catalysed hydrolysis of sucrose is 6.22 kJ mol^{-1}, while the activation energy is only 2.15 kJ mol^{-1}, when hydrolysis is catalysed by the enzyme sucrase. Explain.

28. For the reaction, $2NO(g) + Cl_2(g) \xrightarrow{\text{Slow}} 2NOCl(g)$

The following data were collected. All the measurements were taken at 263 K.

Exp. No.	Initial [NO] (M)	Initial $[Cl_2]$ (M)	Initial rate of disappearance of Cl_2 (M/min)
1.	0.15	0.15	0.60
2.	0.15	0.30	1.20
3.	0.30	0.15	2.40
4	0.25	0.25	?

(a) Write the expression for rate law.

(b) Calculate the value of rate constant and specify its units.

(c) What is the initial rate of disappearance of Cl_2 experiment 4?

Section-D

The following questions are case-based questions. Each question has an internal choice and carries 4 (2+1+1) marks each. Read the passage carefully and answer the questions that follow.

29. Valence bond theory describes the bonding in complexes in terms of coordinate covalent bonds resulting from overlap filled ligand orbitals with vacant metal hybrid orbitals. This theory explains magnetic behaviour and geometrical shape of coordination compounds.

Magnetic moment of a complex, compound can be determined experimentally and theoretically by using spin only formula.

Magnetic moment $\sqrt{n(n+2)}$ BM

(where, n = no. of unpaired electrons)

Answer the following questions

(i) Write the state of hybridisation, shape and the magnetic behaviour of the $[Cr(H_2O)_2(C_2O_4)_2]^-$.

(ii) Why s-orbital does not show preference to any direction?

(iii) Describe the type of hybridisation, shape and magnetic properites of $[Co(NH_3)_4Cl_2]Cl$. {Given : At. no. of Co = 27}

Or

(iv) Explain the geometry and magnetic character of complex $[Cr(NH_3)_6]^{3+}$.

30. The standard potentials are always measured under standard conditions, i.e. when the pressure of a gas is 1 atm, concentration of ions is 1 mol dm^{-3} and the temperature is 298 K.

However, practically standard conditions are hardly achieved or used.

The potential of the electrode whose reaction can be written (in the form or reduction) as

$$M^{n+}(aq) + ne^- \longrightarrow M(s)$$

Which is measured against standard hydrogen electrode, is written as

$$E_{(M^{n+}/M)} = E^\circ_{(M^{n+}/M)} - \frac{RT}{nF} \ln \frac{[M]}{[M^{n+}]}$$

This is known as the **Nernst equation.**

(i) What does the standard electrode potential of a metal being negative ($E^\circ_{Zn^{2+}/Zn} = -0.7632$) indicate?

(ii) What is the number of electrons transferred in an equation if the Nernst equation is $E_{(cell)} = E^\circ_{cell} - 9.83 \times 10^{-3} \times \log_{10}$ (Anode/cathode)?

(a) 2 (b) 6

(c) 4 (d) 1

Or

Calculate the electrode potential of the given electrode.

Pt, $Cl_{2(2\ bar)} | 2Cl^-_{(0.02\ M)}$; $E^\circ_{(Cl_2/2Cl^-)} = 3.4V$

(a) 3.51 V (b) 3.55 V

(c) 1.26 V (d) 2.95 V

(iii) The equilibrium constant for a cell reaction, $Cu(s) + 2Ag^+(aq) \longrightarrow 2Ag(s) + Cu^{2+}(aq)$ is 4×10^{16}. Find the E_{cell} for the reaction.

(a) 0.63 V (b) 0.49 V

(c) 1.23 V (d) 3.24 V

Section-E

The following questions are long answer type and carry 5 marks each. All questions have an internal choice.

31. Answer the following questions

(a) Which of the following are amphoteric oxides?

Mn_2O_7, CrO_3, Cr_2O_3, CrO, V_2O_5, V_2O_4

(b) Calculate the 'spin only' magnetic moment of $M^{2+}(aq)$ ion. ($Z = 27$)

(c) Why are the E° values of Mn, Zn more negative than expected?

(d) Draw the structures of manganate ion and permanganate ion.

(e) Why there is striking similarities (horizontal and vertical) among successive members of the transition series?

Or

(a) The table of the third ionisation enthalpy of a few transition elements is given below :

Element	Sc	Ti	V	Cr	Mn	Fe	Co
Ionisation enthalpy (kJ mol^{-1})	2393	2657	2833	2990	3260	2962	3243

What is the reason for the break in the trend of steady increase in third ionisation enthalpy as shown in the table.

Based on this, what can be said about the second ionisation energy of Cr as compared to that of Mn?

(b) Write the ionic equations for the oxidising action of MnO_4^- in acidic medium with (i) I^- ion (ii) Fe^{2+} ion.

32. (i) At 25°C the vapour pressures of benzene (C_6H_6) and toluene (C_7H_8) are 93.4 torr and 26.9 torr, respectively. A solution is made by mixing 35.0 g of benzene and 65.0 g of toluene. At what applied pressure, in torr, will this solution boil at 25°C ?

(ii) The freezing point of benzene decreases by 0.45°C when 0.2 g of acetic acid is added to 20 g of benzene. If acetic acid associates to form a dimer in benzene, percentage association of acetic acid in benzene will be (K_f for benzene = 5.12 K kg mol^{-1})

Or

At some temperature, the vapour pressure of pure C_6H_6 is 0.256 bar and that of pure $C_6H_5CH_3$ (toluene) is 0.0925 bar. If the mole fraction of toluene in solution is 0.6.

Then,

(i) what will be the total pressure of the solution?

(ii) what will be the mole fraction of each component in vapour phase?

33. (i) Give reasons for the following.

1. Aniline does not undergo Friedel-Crafts reaction.
2. Acetylation of aniline reduces its activation effect.

(ii) Arrange the following.

1. In the decreasing order of pK_b values $C_2H_5NH_2, C_6H_5NHCH_3, (C_2H_5)_2NH$ and $C_6H_5NH_2$.
2. In the increasing order of basic strength CH_3NH_2, $C_6H_5NH_2$, $C_6H_5CH_2NH_2$ and $(CH_3)_3N$.

(iii) Which among the given is weakest base aniline, *p*-nitroaniline, *p*-toluidine ?

Or

(i) Complete the following acid-base reactions,

1. $CH_3—CH_2—CH_2—NH_2 + HCl \longrightarrow$
2. $(C_2H_5)_3N + HCl \longrightarrow$

(ii) 1. What are coupling reactions?
2. List some important applications of diazonium salts.

(iii) Define Gattermann reaction.

Solutions

1. (a) Rate $= \frac{dx}{dt} = k[CCl_3CHO][NO]$

$$k = \frac{dx}{dt \times [CCl_3CHO][NO]}$$

$$= \frac{mol/L}{s \times mol/L \times mol/L} = L\,mol^{-1}s^{-1}$$

2. (d) Since, with increase in temperature, molarity decreases due to increase in volume.

Thus, molarity < 7.42 M. On the other hand, temperature has no effect on molality as molality does not depend on volume.

Thus, the correct relation will be

molarity < 7.42 M, molality $= 4.53$ molal.

3. (b) The IUPAC name of the given compound is tetraamminediaquacobalt(III) chloride.

4. (d) Given, rate $= k\ [CHCl_3]\ [Cl_2]^{1/2}$

$\because$ Order $= 1 + \frac{1}{2} = \frac{3}{2}$

$\therefore$ Units of rate constant

$$= \frac{\text{Units of rate}}{[CHCl_3]\ [Cl_2]^{1/2}} = \frac{\text{bar min}^{-1}}{\text{bar}^{3/2}} = \text{bar}^{-1/2}\text{min}^{-1}$$

and units of rate is bar min^{-1}.

5. (b) Since, 3-pentanone does not contain $\left(CH_3-\overset{\overset{\large O}{\|}}{C}-\right)$ group, it does not give iodoform test.

6. (b) Following reactions takes place in the manufacturing of ethyl alcohol commercially by fermentation method.

$$\underset{\text{Sucrose}}{C_{12}H_{22}O_{11}} + H_2O \xrightarrow{\text{Invertase}} \underset{\text{Glucose}}{C_6H_{12}O_6} + \underset{\text{Fructose}}{C_6H_{12}O_6}$$

$$\underset{\text{Glucose}}{C_6H_{12}O_6} \xrightarrow{\text{Zymase}} \underset{\text{Ethanol}}{2C_2H_5OH} + 2CO_2 \uparrow$$

7. (b) The electrophile used in Reimer-Tiemann reaction is $:CCl_2$. It is formed by the reaction of $CHCl_3$ with NaOH.

8. (d) $NaHCO_3$ is used as specific test for acids.

9. (b) Transition metals and their compounds show catalytic property.

10. (c) (i) The second ionisation enthalpy is highest for copper (Cu) having electronic configuration $[Ar]3d^{10}4s^1$.

(ii) Scandium (Sc) show only +3 oxidation state.

(iii) Zinc (Zn) has the lowest melting and boiling point because it does not contain any unpaired d-electrons.

(iv) Manganese (Mn) in Mn_2O_7 shows +7 oxidation state.

Thus, the correct match is (i) → (s), (ii) → (r), (iii) → (q), (iv) → (p).

11. (b) The molecules containing symmetrical carbon i.e. carbon bearing two or more similar groups are called achiral molecules. Thus, 2, 2-dichlorobutane is achiral.

12. (a) Trend given in option (a) is incorrect.

In case of halides, 3° halides undergoes S_N1 reaction very fast because of the high stability of 3° carbocation followed by 2° and 1° carbocation.

Hence, the correct order is

$$Ph\underset{3°}{\overset{+}{C}}(CH_3)_2 > Ph\underset{2°}{\overset{+}{C}}HCH_3 > Ph\underset{1°}{\overset{+}{C}}H_2$$

Rest of the other trends are correct.

13. (c) Phenol is less acidic than p-nitrophenol because $-NO_2$ is strongly electron withdrawing group and further, p-nitrophenolate ion is more stable than phenolate ion. Hence, A is correct but R is incorrect.

14. (a) Order of the following reaction, $2NO(g) + 2H_2(g) \longrightarrow 2H_2O(g) + N_2(g)$ is 3. As we know that, order of the reaction with respect to given reactant is the power of the reactants concentration in the rate equation. Thus, both A and R are true and R is the correct explanation of A.

15. (a) Both A and R are true and R is the correct explanation of A.

16. (d) Ketones do not react with Tollen's reagent to give silver mirror test, because ketone cannot reduce silver ions of Tollen's reagent to give silver metal.

Aldehydes react with Tollen's reagent to form silver mirror. Hence, A is false but R is true.

17. Following are the factors.

- Number of particles of solute.
- Association or dissociation of solute.
- Concentration of solution.
- Temperature. (2)

18. The main points of differences are listed below.

	Hormones	Vitamins
(a)	They are produced in the ductless (endocrine) glands, e.g. testes of males and ovaries of females.	They are are not produced in the body, have to be supplied in food (except vitamin D which may be supplied in the food or produced in skin by irradiation of sterols present in oils and fats, with UV light). (1)
(b)	They are not stored in the body but are continuously produced.	They may remain stored (except vitamin C and some vitamins of group B) to fight against the diseases. (1)

19. (a) $\underset{\text{Propan-1-ol}}{CH_3CH_2CH_2OH} + SOCl_2 \xrightarrow{\text{Pyridine}} \underset{\text{1-chloropropane}}{CH_3CH_2CH_2Cl} + SO_2\uparrow + HCl$ (1)

(b) $CH_3CH_2CH = CH_2 + HBr \xrightarrow{\text{Peroxide}} CH_3CH_2CH_2CH_2Br$ (1)

20. (a) The given plot shows the first order reaction. (1)

(b) Unit of $k = (\text{mol L}^{-1})^{1-n}\,\text{s}^{-1}$

$= (\text{mol L}^{-1})^{1-1}\,\text{s}^{-1} = \text{s}^{-1}$ (1)

21. (a)

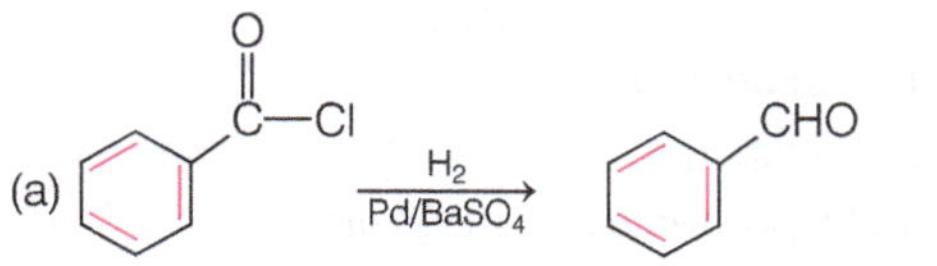

Benzaldehyde

(Rosenmund reduction) (1)

(b)

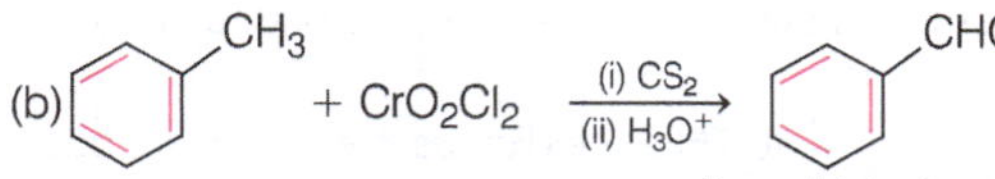

Benzaldehyde

(Etard reaction) (1)

Or

(a) $\underset{\text{Acetaldehyde}}{CH_3CHO} \xrightarrow{K_2Cr_2O_7} CH_3COOH \xrightarrow{\text{NaOH}} CH_3CO\bar{O}\overset{+}{Na}$

$\xrightarrow{\text{Soda lime}} \underset{\text{Methane}}{CH_4} \xrightarrow{Cl_2} CH_3Cl \xrightarrow{\text{Aq. KOH}} CH_3OH \xrightarrow{\text{Cu}} \underset{\text{Formaldehyde}}{HCHO}$ (1)

(b) $\underset{\text{Propanal}}{CH_3CH_2CHO} + CH_3MgBr \xrightarrow{H_2O} CH_3CH_2CH(OH)CH_3$

$\xrightarrow{CrO_3} \underset{\text{Butanone}}{CH_3CH_2-\overset{O}{\overset{\|}{C}}-CH_3}$ (1)

22. (a) For mercury cell,

Half-cell reaction,

At cathode, $HgO + H_2O + 2e^- \longrightarrow Hg(l) + 2OH^-$

At anode, $Zn(Hg) + 2OH^- \longrightarrow ZnO(s) + H_2O + 2e^-$ (1)

(b) For lead storage battery,

Half-cell reaction,

At cathode :

$PbO_2(s) + SO_4^{2-}(aq) + 4H^+(aq) + 2e^- \longrightarrow PbSO_4(s) + 2H_2O(l)$

At anode : $Pb(s) + SO_4^{2-}(aq) \longrightarrow PbSO_4(s) + 2e^-$ (1)

(c) For nickel-cadmium battery,

At cathode,

$2NiO(OH)(s) + 2H_2O(l) + 2e^- \longrightarrow 2Ni(OH)_2(s) + 2OH^-(aq)$

At anode, $Cd(s) + 2OH^-(aq) \longrightarrow Cd(OH)_2(s) + 2e^-$

(1)

23. (a) Let the oxication number of Co in the complex ion $[CoF_6]^{3-}$ is x, then $x + 6(-1) = -3 \Rightarrow x = +3$ (1)

(b) Electronic configuration of Co = $[Ar]\,3d^7 4s^2$

Co atom = $3d^7$: ⥮ ⥮ 1 1 1 ; $4s^2$: ⥮

For $Co^{3+} = [Ar]3d^6 4s^0$

Co^{3+} ion = $3d^6$: ⥮ 1 1 1 1 ; $4s^0$: (empty)

4 unpaired electrons

Therefore, there are 4 unpaired electrons. (1½)

Thus, it is paramagnetic.

(c) Hexafluoridocobaltate (III) ion. (1/2)

24. (a) **Benzene to acetophenone**

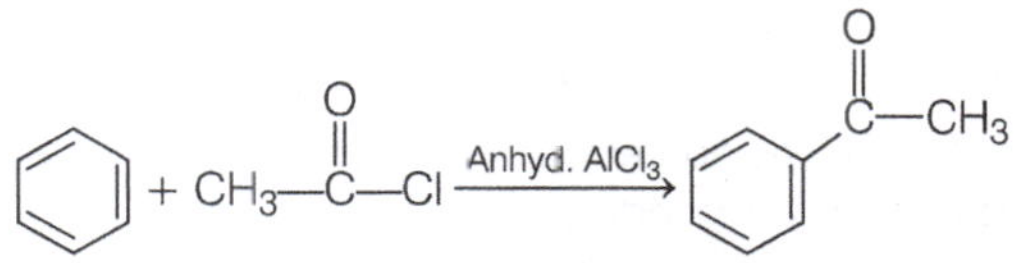

(1)

(b) **Propanone to 2-methylpropan-2-ol**

$CH_3-\overset{O}{\overset{\|}{C}}-CH_3 + \overset{\delta+}{CH_3}\overset{\delta-}{MgX} \longrightarrow CH_3-\underset{CH_3}{\overset{CH_3}{C}}-\bar{O}\overset{+}{Mg}X$

$\xrightarrow{H_2O} CH_3-\underset{CH_3}{\overset{CH_3}{C}}-OH$ (1)

(c) **Ethanal to butane-1, 3-diol**

$\underset{\text{Ethanal}}{2CH_3CHO} \xrightarrow[\text{(Aldol condensation)}]{\text{Dil. NaOH}} \underset{\text{3-hydroxybutanal}}{CH_3CHOH-CH_2-CHO}$

$\xrightarrow{NaBH_4\text{ (Reduction)}} \underset{\text{Butane-1,3-diol}}{CH_3-CHOH-CH_2-CH_2OH}$ (1)

Or

The organic compound 'A' ($C_4H_8O_2$) is $CH_3COOC_2H_5$.

$\underset{(A)}{CH_3COOC_2H_5} \xrightarrow{\text{Hydrolysis}} \underset{\text{Ethanoic acid }(B)}{CH_3COOH} + \underset{\text{Ethanol }(C)}{C_2H_5OH}$

$\underset{(C)}{C_2H_5OH} \xrightarrow{\text{Acidified }KMnO_4} \underset{\text{Ethanoic acid }(B)}{CH_3COOH}$ (1)

(a) (A) : Ethyl acetate ($CH_3COOC_2H_5$)

(B) : Ethanoic acid (CH_3COOH)

(C) : Ethanol (C_2H_5OH) (1)

(b) Among ethanoic acid and ethanol, ethanoic acid will have higher boiling point because it has high extent of H-bonding with water due to which they exist as associated molecules. (1)

25. $CH_3CH_2OH \xrightarrow[\Delta]{\text{Conc. } H_2SO_4} CH_2{=}CH_2 \xrightarrow{Br_2} \underset{Br}{CH_2}{-}\underset{Br}{CH_2} \xrightarrow{NaNH_2}$

$H{-}C{\equiv}C{-}H \xrightarrow[Hg(CH_3COO)_2]{CH_3COOH} \underset{\text{Vinyl acetate}}{CH_2{=}CH{-}OCOCH_3}$ (3)

26. (a) Replacement of the diazonium group by iodine is done simply by shaking the diazonium salt with potassium iodide.

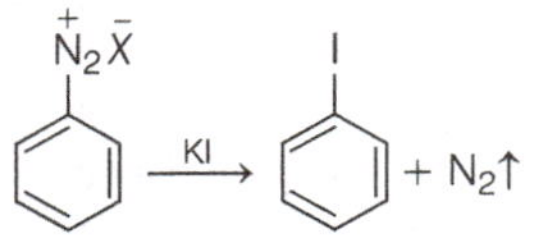

(1)

(b) $CH_3CHClCH_2CH_3$ upon ionisation gives more stable 2° carbocation, while $CH_3CH_2CH_2CH_2Cl$ gives less stable 1° carbocation.

Thus, $CH_3CHClCH_2CH_3$ is more easily hydrolysed. (1)

(c) Iodoform has appreciable antiseptic property due to the liberation of free iodine.

$$4CHI_3 + 5O_2 \xrightarrow[\text{Heat}]{SO_2} 6I_2 + 4CO_2 + 2H_2O$$ (1)

27. Enzymes are the essential biological catalysts which are needed to catalyse biochemical reactions. Enzymes are needed only in small quantities for the progress of a reaction like chemical catalysts.

Enzymes reduces the magnitude of activation energy by providing alternative pathway.

e.g. Hydrolysis of sucrose, the enzyme sucrase reduces the activation energy from 6.22 kJ mol^{-1} to 2.15 kJ mol^{-1}.

Thus, enzyme catalysed reaction occurs at a much faster rate. (3)

28. (a) The rate law for the reaction,

$$\text{Rate} = k[NO]^2[Cl_2]$$ (1)

(b) Rate constant can be calculated by substituting the value of rate, [NO] and $[Cl_2]$ for any of the experiments.

$$k = \frac{\text{Rate}}{[NO]^2[Cl_2]} = \frac{0.60}{(0.15)^2(0.15)}$$

$$= 177.78 \text{ mol}^{-2} \text{ L}^2 \text{ min}^{-1}$$ (1)

(c) Let initial rate of disappearance of Cl_2 in experiment 4 is r_4.

$$\therefore \quad r_4 = k[NO]^2[Cl_2]$$

$$= 177.78 \times (0.25)^2(0.25) = 2.78 \text{ M/min}$$ (1)

29. (i) $[Cr(H_2O)_2(C_2O_4)_2]^-$

In this complex, Cr is present as Cr^{3+}

$Cr^{3+} = [Ar]3d^3 4s^0$

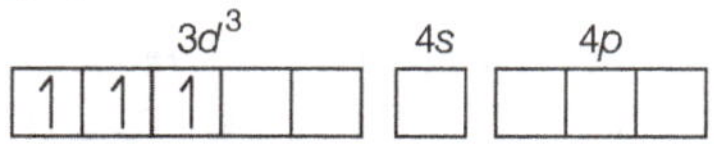

$[Cr(H_2O)_2(C_2O_4)_2]^- =$

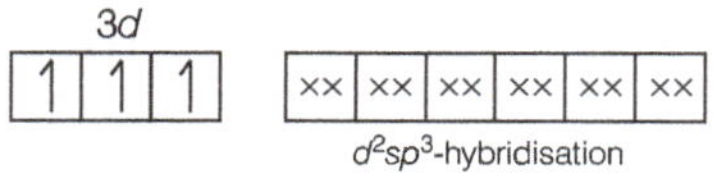

[∵ Oxalate is a bidentate ligand, one oxalate occupies two orbitals].

Hybridisation d^2sp^3

Shape Octahedral

Magnetic behaviour Paramagnetic (as 3 unpaired electrons present).

Hybridisation d^2sp^3 octahedral shape magnetic behaviour Paramagnetic (as 3 unpaired electrons present). (2)

(ii) The s-orbtial is spherically symmetrical in shape, so it does not show preference to any direction.

It is same from all the directions. (1)

(iii) **Hybridisation** d^2sp^3

Shape Octahedral

Magnetic properties Diamagnetic. (1)

Or

Octahedral complex including d^2sp^3-hybridisation. It is paramagnetic due to the presence of three unpaired electrons. (1)

30. (i) $E^\circ_{Zn^{2+}/Zn} = -0.7632$ V indicates that zinc electrode acts as anode when coupled to NHE.

Since, oxidation takes place at anode, therefore oxidation potential is positive but reduction potential is negative. (2)

(ii) (b) Nernst equation is given as,

$$E_{cell} = E^\circ_{cell} - \frac{0.059}{n}\log_{10} \text{(Anode/cathode)}$$

On comparing both the formula, $\frac{0.059}{n} = 9.83 \times 10^{-3}$

$$n = 6$$

Or

(a) The electrode potential is $Cl_2(g) + 2e^- \longrightarrow 2Cl^-$

$$E = E^\circ - \frac{0.059}{n}\log([Cl^-]^2 / P_{(Cl)})$$

$$E = 3.4 - \frac{0.059}{2}\log(0.02^2/2) = 3.51 \text{ V}$$

(iii) (b) Given : equilibrium constant $K_C = 4 \times 10^{16}$

$$E^\circ_{cell} = \frac{0.059}{2}\log_{10} K_C$$

$$= \frac{0.059}{2}\log_{10}(4 \times 10^{16}) = 0.49 \text{ V}$$

31. (a) V_2O_5 and Cr_2O_3 are amphoteric oxides because both react with alkalies as well as acids. (1)

(b) Magnetic moment $\mu = \sqrt{n(n+2)}$ BM

Electronic configuration of $M = [Ar]3d^7 4s^2$

$$M^{2+} = [Ar]3d^7 4s^0$$

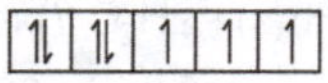

So, $\mu = \sqrt{n(n+2)}$

$= \sqrt{3(3+2)} = \sqrt{15} = 3.89$ BM. (1)

(c) Negative E° values of Mn^{2+} and Zn^{2+} are related to stabilities of half-filled and completely filled configuration respectively. (1)

(d)

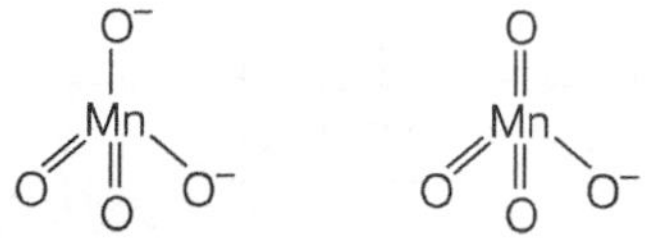

Manganate ion Permanganate ion (1)

(e) This is because of the fact that along a horizontal row, electrons enters an incomplete inner shell while outer shell remains unchanged. In vertical columns, similarities are due to similar electronic configurations. (1)

Or

(a) Mn^{2+} has $3d^5$ configuration, which is more stable than $3d^6$ configuration of Fe^{2+}. This makes removing an electron from Mn^{2+} more difficult than from Fe^{2+}. Since, Cr^+ has $3d^5$ configuration, it is more stable than Mn^+ and so Cr will have higher second ionisation enthalpy as compared to Mn. (3)

(b) (i) $2MnO_4^- + 16H^+ + 10I^- \longrightarrow 2Mn^{2+} + 8H_2O + 5I_2$

(ii) $MnO_4^- + 8H^+ + 5Fe^{2+} \longrightarrow Mn^{2+} + 4H_2O + 5Fe^{3+}$ (2)

32. (i) This solution of benzene and toluene will boil at 25°C when the pressure above the solution is equal to the sum of the vapour pressures of benzene and toluene in the solution.

Partial vapour pressure of benzene, $p^\circ_{C_6H_6} = 93.4$ torr

Partial vapour pressure of toluene,

$p^\circ_{C_6H_5CH_3} = 26.9$ torr

Mass of $C_6H_6 = 35$ g and mass of $C_6H_5CH_3 = 65$ g

Molar mass of $C_6H_6 = 12 \times 6 + 1 \times 6$
$= 72 + 6 = 78 \text{ g mol}^{-1}$

Therefore, the number of moles of C_6H_6,

$$n_{C_6H_6} = \frac{35\text{g}}{78\text{g/mol}} = 0.449 \text{ mol}$$ (1/2)

Molar mass of $C_6H_5CH_3 = 12 \times 6 + 1 \times 5 + 12 + 1 \times 3$
$= 92 \text{ g mol}^{-1}$

Therefore, the number of moles of $C_6H_5CH_3$,

$$n_{C_6H_5CH_3} = \frac{65\text{g}}{92\text{ g/mol}} = 0.707 \text{ mol}$$ (1/2)

Now, the mole fractions of C_6H_6 and $C_6H_5CH_3$ are

$$\chi_{C_6H_6} = \frac{n_{C_6H_6}}{n_{C_6H_6} + n_{C_6H_5CH_3}}$$

$$= \frac{0.449 \text{ mol}}{0.449 \text{ mol} + 0.707 \text{ mol}}$$

$$= \frac{0.449 \text{ mol}}{1.156 \text{ mol}} = 0.388$$ (1/2)

$$\chi_{C_6H_5CH_3} = \frac{n_{C_6H_5CH_3}}{n_{C_6H_5CH_3} + n_{C_6H_6}}$$

$$= \frac{0.707 \text{ mol}}{0.707 \text{ mol} + 0.449 \text{ mol}}$$

$$= \frac{0.707 \text{ mol}}{1.156 \text{ mol}} = 0.612$$ (1/2)

Therefore, vapour pressure of C_6H_6 and $C_6H_5CH_3$ are

$$p_{C_6H_6} = p^\circ_{C_6H_6} \times \chi_{C_6H_6}$$
$$= 93.4 \text{ torr} \times 0.388 = 36.24 \text{ torr}$$
$$p_{C_6H_5CH_3} = p^\circ_{C_6H_5CH_3} \times \chi_{C_6H_5CH_3}$$
$$= 26.9 \text{ torr} \times 0.612 = 16.46 \text{ torr}$$ (1/2)

Total vapour pressure of the so ution,

$$p_{\text{total}} = p_{C_6H_6} + p_{C_6H_5CH_3}$$
$$= 36.24 \text{ torr} + 16.46 \text{ torr}$$
$$= 52.7 \text{ torr}$$ (1/2)

(ii) Let the degree of associaon of acetic acid (CH_3COOH) in benzene is α, then

$$2CH_3COOH \rightleftharpoons (CH_3COOH)_2$$

	$2CH_3COOH$	$(CH_3COOH)_2$
Initial moles	1	0
Moles at equilibrium	$1-\alpha$	$\frac{\alpha}{2}$

$\therefore$ Total moles $= 1 - \alpha + \frac{\alpha}{2} = 1 - \frac{\alpha}{2}$

or $i = 1 - \frac{\alpha}{2}$ (1/2)

Now, depression in freezing point (ΔT_f) is given as

$$\Delta T_f = i K_f m \quad \ldots \text{(i)}$$

where, K_f = molal depression constant or cryoscopic constant and m = molality

$$\text{Molality} = \frac{\text{number of moles of solute}}{\text{weight of solvent (in kg)}}$$

$$= \frac{0.2\text{g}}{60\text{g/mol}} \times \frac{1000\text{g}}{20\text{g}}$$ (1/2)

Putting the values in Eq. (i),

$$\therefore \quad 0.45 = \left[1 - \frac{\alpha}{2}\right](5.12)\left[\frac{0.2}{60} \times \frac{1000}{20}\right]$$

$$1 - \frac{\alpha}{2} = \frac{0.45 \times 60 \times 20}{5.12 \times 0.2 \times 1000}$$

$$\Rightarrow \quad 1 - \frac{\alpha}{2} = 0.527 \Rightarrow \frac{\alpha}{2} = 1 - 0.527$$

$$\therefore \quad \alpha = 0.946$$

Thus, percentage of association = 94.6% (1)

Or

(i) According to Raoult's law,

For toluene, $p_1 = p_1^\circ \times \chi_1$

$p_1^\circ = 0.0925$ bar and $\chi_1 = 0.6$

Then, $p_1 = 0.0925 \times 0.6 = 0.0555$ bar (1)

For benzene, $p_2 = p_2^\circ \times \chi_2$

Mole fraction of benzene,

$$\chi_2 = 1 - \chi_1 = 1 - 0.6 = 0.4$$

and $p_2^\circ = 0.256$ bar

Then, $p_2 = 0.256 \times 0.4 = 0.1024$ bar (1)

Total vapour pressure of solution

$$p_{total} = p_1 + p_2$$
$$= 0.0555 + 0.1024 = 0.158 \text{ bar}$$ (1)

(ii) Mole fraction of toluene in vapour phase

$$y_1 = \frac{p_1}{p_{total}} = \frac{0.0555 \text{ bar}}{0.158 \text{ bar}} = 0.351$$ (1)

Mole fraction of benzene in vapour phase

$$y_2 = \frac{p_2}{p_{total}} = \frac{0.1024 \text{bar}}{0.158 \text{ bar}} = 0.648$$ (1)

33. (i) 1. Aniline being a Lewis base, reacts with the Lewis acid $AlCl_3$ used in Friedel-Crafts reaction and produces a salt, hence it does not show Friedel-Crafts reaction.

$$C_6H_5NH_2 + AlCl_3 \longrightarrow C_6H_5 \cdot \overset{+}{N}H_2AlCl_3^- \text{ (Salt)}$$ (1)

2. Due to electron withdrawing effect of the acetyl group, the lone pair of electrons on N-atom is attracted by group.As a result, lone pair of electrons on N-atom is not exclusively available for donation to the benzene ring and hence, activating effect of the $—NH_2$ group is reduced. (1)

(ii) 1. $C_6H_5NH_2 > C_6H_5NHCH_3 > C_2H_5NH_2 > (C_2H_5)_2NH$ (1)

2. $C_6H_5NH_2 < C_6H_5CH_2NH_2 < (CH_3)_3N < CH_3NH_2 < (CH_3)_2NH$ (1)

(iii) Among the given compounds *p*-nitroaniline is weakest base due to the delocalization of the nitrogen non-bonding electron pair into the aromatic ring. (nitro group is also showing electron withdrawing effect). (1)

Or

(i) 1. $CH_3—CH_2—CH_2—\ddot{N}H_2 + H—Cl \longrightarrow CH_3—CH_2—CH_2—\overset{+}{N}H_3Cl^-$ (1)

($CH_3CH_2CH_2NH_2$: *n*-propylamine; product: *n*-propyl ammonium chloride)

2. $(C_2H_5)_3\ddot{N} + H—Cl \longrightarrow (C_2H_5)_3\overset{+}{N}HCl^-$ (1)

(Triethylamine → Triethylammonium chloride)

(ii) 1. The reactions that involves the joining of two hydrocarbon fragments which are coupled with the help of a metal catalyst.

e.g. When benzene diazonium chloride reacts with phenol in which the phenol molecule at its para position couples with diazonium salt to form *p*-hydroxyazobenzene.

2. The important applications of diazonium salt are :

- These are important in the synthesis of aromatic compounds.
- They are used as intermediates for introducing —F, —Br, —Cl, —I, NO_2, —OH and —CN groups into the aromatic rings. (2)

(iii) Chlorine or bromine can be introduced in the benzene ring by treating the diazonium salt solution with corresponding halogen acid in the presence of copper powder. This is known as Gattermann reaction. (1)

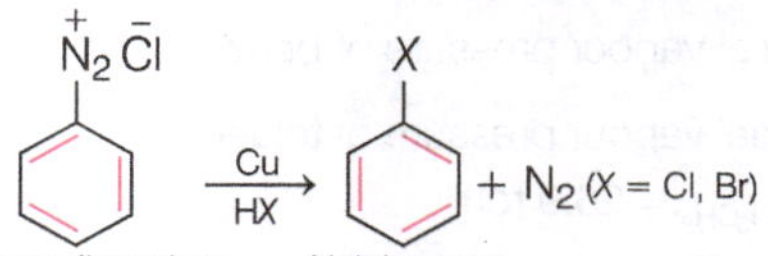

Benzene diazonium chloride Halobenzene

SAMPLE QUESTION PAPER 3

A Highly Simulated Sample Question Paper for CBSE Class XII Examination

CHEMISTRY

Time : 3 Hours **Max. Marks : 70**

General Instructions

Read the following instructions carefully and follow them :

1. This question paper contains **33 questions**. All questions are **compulsory**.
2. This question paper is divided into **FIVE** sections - **Section A, B, C, D and E**.
3. **SECTION-A** questions number 1 to 16 are multiple choice type questions. Each question carries 1 mark.
4. **SECTION-B** questions number 17 to 21 are very short answer type questions. Each question carries 2 marks.
5. **SECTION-C** questions number 22 to 28 are short answer type questions. Each question carries 3 marks.
6. **SECTION-D** questions number 29 and 30 are case-based questions. Each question carries 4 marks.
7. **SECTION-E** questions number 31 to 33 are long answer type questions. Each question carries 5 marks.
8. There is no overall choice given in the question paper. However, an internal choice has been provided in few questions in all the sections except section A.
9. Kindly note that there is a separate question paper for visually impaired candidates.
10. Use of calculator is NOT allowed.

Section-A

The following questions are multiple choice questions with one correct answer. Each question carries 1 mark. There is no internal choice in this section.

1. According to IUPAC nomenclature, sodium nitroprusside is named as

(a) sodiumpentacyanonitrosylferrate (II)
(b) sodiumpentacyanonitrosylferrate (III)
(c) sodiumnitroferricyanide
(d) sodiumnitroferrocyanide

2. The cell constant of a conductivity cell

(a) changes with change of electrolyte.
(b) changes with change of concentration of electrolyte.
(c) changes with temperature of electrolyte.
(d) remains constant for a cell.

3. When a solution of formaldehyde and KOH is heated, it will give

(a) acetylene and methane
(b) methanol and potassium formate
(c) methanol and methane
(d) methanol and acetylene

4. Which amino acid has phenolic —OH group as it backbone?

(a) Glycine (b) Leucine (c) Serine (d) Tyrosine

5. Match the complexes with their hybridisation.

I.	$Ni(CO)_4$	p.	sp^3
II.	$[Co(NH_3)_6]^{3+}$	q.	dsp^2
III.	$[MnF_6]^{4-}$	r.	sp^3d^2
IV.	$[Ni(CN)_4]^{2-}$	s.	d^2sp^3

(a) I-p, II-s, III-r, IV-q (b) I-q, II-p, III-s, IV-r
(c) I-s, II-r, III-p, IV-q (d) I-s, II-p, III-q, IV-r

6. The method used to separate primary, secondary and tertiary amines is

(a) Hoffmann method (b) Lucas method
(c) Victor Meyer method (d) Kolbe's method

7. Which one of the following gases has the lowest value of Henry's law constant?

(a) N_2 (b) He (c) CO_2 (d) O_2

8. Replacement of Cl from chlorobenzene to give phenol requires drastic conditions but chlorine of 2, 4-dinitrochlorobenzene is readily replaced because
   (a) NO_2 makes ring electron rich at *ortho* and *para* position.
   (b) NO_2 withdraws electrons from *meta* position.
   (c) NO_2 donates electron to *meta* position.
   (d) NO_2 withdraws electrons from *ortho* and *para* positions.

9. Basicity order of amines in aqueous solution.
   (a) $3° > 1° > 2° > NH_3$ (b) $3° > 2° > 1° > NH_3$
   (c) $2° > 1° > 3° > NH_3$ (d) $2 < 1° < 3° < NH_3$

10. Chlorobenzene is
   (a) less reactive than benzyl chloride.
   (b) more reactive than ethyl bromide.
   (c) nearly same reactive as that of methyl chloride.
   (d) more reactive than isopropyl chloride.

11. How many alcohols with molecular formula $C_4H_{10}O$ are chiral in nature?
   (a) 1 (b) 2 (c) 3 (d) 4

12. What will be the order of reaction for a chemical change having $\log t_{50\%}$ *versus* log concentration of (a) curves as

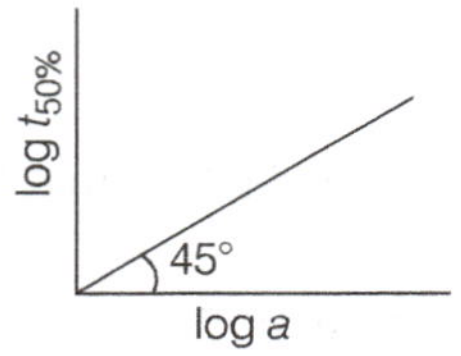

   (a) 0 (b) 1 (c) 2 (d) 3

Assertion-Reason

In the following questions (Q.No. 13-16), a statement of Assertion (A) followed by a statement of Reason (R) is given. Choose the correct answer out of the following choices.
   (a) Both A and R are true and R is the correct explanation of A.
   (b) Both A and R are true but R is not the correct explanation of A.
   (c) A is true but R is false.
   (d) A is false but R is true.

13. **Assertion** Glucose and fructose are reducing sugars.
   Reason Glucose and fructose contain a free aldehydic and ketonic group adjacent to a >CHOH group respectively.

14. **Assertion** Addition of HCN to carbonyl compounds gives cyanohydrins.
   Reason Pure HCN reacts with aldehydes and ketones.

15. **Assertion** 2-chloro-3-methylbutane on treatment with alcoholic potash gives 2-methylbut-2-ene as major product.
   Reason Above reaction occurs according to Saytzeff's rule.

16. **Assertion** The reaction, $H_2 + Br_2 \longrightarrow 2HBr$ has molecularity of two.
   Reason Order of the given reaction is 2.

Answers

1. (a) **2.** (d) **3.** (b) **4.** (d) **5.** (a) **6.** (a)
7. (c) **8.** (d) **9.** (c) **10.** (a) **11.** (a) **12.** (a)
13. (a) **14.** (c) **15.** (a) **16.** (c)

Section-B

This section contains 5 questions with internal choice in one question. The following questions are very short answer type and carry 2 marks each.

17. Arrange the following compounds in the increasing order of dipole moment. Give reason.
   $CH_3CH_2CH_3$, $CH_3CH_2NH_2$, CH_3CH_2OH

18. Give one test to distinguish :
   (a) Glucose and fructose
   (b) Lactose and sucrose

19. Aqueous copper sulphate solution (blue in colour) gives
   (a) a green precipitate with aqueous potassium fluoride.
   (b) a bright green solution with aqueous potassium chloride.
   Explain these experimental results.

20. (a) The value of $\Lambda°$ for HCl, KCl and CH_3COOK are 425.1, 121.3 and 94.15 respectively. Calculate $\Lambda°$ for acetic acid (CH_3COOH).
   [**Ans.** $\Lambda° = 397.85\ Scm^2mol^{-1}$]
   (b) How many coulombs of charge are required for the reduction of 1 mole of Cu^{2+} to Cu?
   [**Ans.** 193000 C]

21. (a) What will be the value of van't Hoff factor for a dilute K_2SO_4 in water?
(b) It is advised to add ethylene glycol to water in car radiator while driving in hill station. Why?

Or

(a) Will the depression in freezing point be same or different, if 0.1 mole of sugar or 0.1 mole of glucose is dissolved in 12 g of water?
(b) What role does the molecular interaction play in solution of alcohol and water?

Section-C

This section contains 7 questions with internal choice in one question. The following questions are short answer type and carry 3 marks each.

22. (a) Write the IUPAC names of $[Co(NH_3)_6]Cl_3$ and $[Pt(NH_3)_2Cl\ (NH_2CH_3)]Cl$
(b) Draw all the isomers (geometrical and optical) of $[CoCl_2(en)_2]^+$.
(c) Calculate the oxidation state of Cu in $[Cu(NH_3)_4]SO_4$.

23. (a) It is very difficult to separate Zr and Hf. Give reason.
(b) Why the Fe^{3+} is more stable than Fe^{2+}?
(c) Why are the different oxidation states exhibited by the lanthanoids?

24. (a) What is glycogen ? How is it different from starch?
(b) Which one of the following is a disaccharide?
Starch, Maltose, Fructose, Glucose.
(c) Name the deficiency diseases resulting from lack of vitamin A and E in the diet.

25. Give the structure of various amines with molecular formula C_3H_9N. State whether they are primary, secondary or tertiary amines.

26. Define the following terms
(a) Activation energy
(b) Rate constant
(c) Molecularity of reaction

27. Sucrose decomposes in acid solution into glucose and fructose according to the first order rate law, with $t_{1/2} = 3$ h. What fraction of sample of sucrose remains after 8 h?

28. Primary alkyl halide $C_4H_9Br(A)$ reacts with alcoholic KOH to give compound *B*. Compound *B* is reacted with HBr to give *C*, which is an isomer of *A*. When *A* is reacted with sodium metal, it gives compound *D*, C_8H_{18} which is different from the compound formed when *n*-butyl bromide is reacted with sodium.

Give the structural formula of *A* and write the equations for all the reactions.

Or

State reasons for the following.
(a) *n*-butyl bromide has higher boiling point than *t*-butyl bromide.
(b) Racemic mixture is optically inactive.
(c) *Neo*-pentyl chloride does not follow S_N2 mechanism.

Section-D

The following questions are case -based questions. Each question has an internal choice and carries 4 (2+1+1) marks each. Read the passage carefully and answer the questions that follow.

29. The magnitude of conduction depends upon the nature of the material. It also depends upon the temperature and pressure at which the measurements are made. Materials are classified into conductors, insulators and semiconductors. It depends on the magnitude of their conductivity.

Electrical conductance through metal is due to the movement of electrons and termed as electronic or metallic conductance. It depends upon the nature and structure of metal, number of valence electrons per atom and temperature (it decreases with increase of temperature).

Pure water has very low conductivity but when electrolytes are dissolved in water, they furnish their own ions in the solution, hence its conductivity increases. The conductance of electricity by ions which are present in the solutions is called electrolytic or ionic conductance.

The conductivity of electrolytic solutions depends on the nature of the electrolyte, size of the ions produced and their solution, nature of the solvent and its viscosity, concentration of the electrolyte and temperature.

Answer the following questions.

(i) The specific conductance of 0.1 N KCl solution at 23°C is 0.012 $ohm^{-1}cm^{-1}$. The resistance of cell containing the solution at the same temperature was found to be 55 ohm. Calculate the cell constant. **[Ans.** 0.66 cm^{-1}]

(ii) The variation of molar conductivity with concentration of an electrolyte (X) in aqueous solution is shown in given figure.

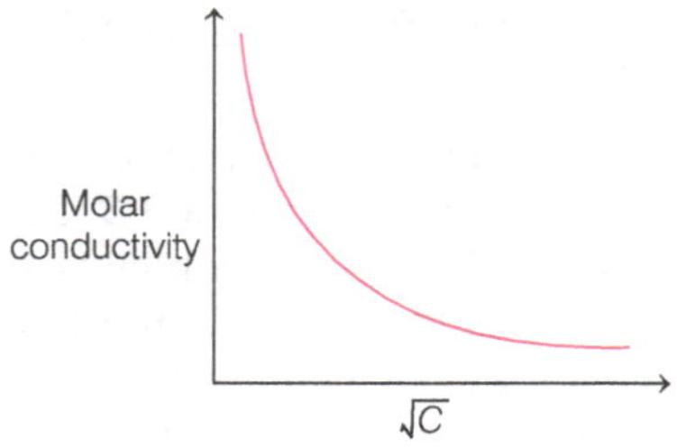

Identify the electrolyte X.

Or

What is the SI unit of molar conductivity?

(iii) The conductivity of 0.01 N solution is found to be 0.005 $ohm^{-1}cm^{-1}$. What is the equivalent conductivity of the solution?

[Ans. 500 $ohm^{-1}cm^2 eq^{-1}$]

30. The spontaneous flow of solvent molecules from solvent side to solution side or from a region of lower concentration to a region of higher concentration through a semipermeable membrane is called osmosis. It is different from that of diffusion, where the movement is in reverse direction.

The minimum pressure that has to be exerted/applied on the solution to prevent the entry of solvent into solution through semipermeable membrane is called osmotic pressure.

This concept is used in desalination of sea water. The growth of plants depends mainly on the phenomenon of osmosis. Two solutions having same osmotic pressure are called **isotonic**.

Osmotic pressure is a colligative property. Molecular mass of a solute can be determined from the osmotic pressure measurements. Osmotic pressure is represented by π.

The osmotic pressure can be experimentally measured by using Berkeley Heartley method.

Answer the following questions

(i) 6.8 g of a compound is dissolved in 100 g water. Calculate the osmotic pressure of this solution at 298 K, when boiling point of solution is 100.11°C, K_b for water is 0.52 K kg mol^{-1} and $R = 0.082$ L atm K^{-1} mol^{-1}. **[Ans.** $\pi = 5.17$ atm]

(ii) Osmotic pressure of a solution is 0.0821 atm at a temperature of 300K. The concentration in moles/litre will be **[Ans.** c]

(a) 0.33 (b) 0.666
(c) 0.3×10^{-2} (d) 3

Or

0.05 M glucose solution is iso-osmotic with which of the following solution? **[Ans.** c]

(a) 0.10 M NaCl (b) 0.05 M NaCl
(c) 0.025 M NaCl (d) 1 M NaCl

(iii) The relationship between osmotic pressure at 273 K, when 10 g glucose (P_1), 10 g urea (P_2) and 10 g sucrose (P_3) are dissolved in 250 mL of water to form separate solution is **[Ans.** c]

(a) $P_1 > P_2 > P_3$ (b) $P_3 > P_1 > P_2$
(c) $P_2 > P_1 > P_3$ (d) $P_2 > P_3 > P_1$

Section-E

The following questions are long answer type and carry 5 marks each. All questions have an internal choice.

31. Answer the following questions.

(a) Yb^{2+} act as a reductant while Tb^{4+} act as an oxidant. Why?

(b) Which transition element in 3d-series has positive $E^\circ_{M^{2+}/M}$ value and why?

(c) Name a member of lanthanoid series which is well known to exhibit (+4) oxidation state and why?

(d) Why paramagnetism is shown by lanthanoid ions?

(e) What is lanthanoid contraction? What causes lanthanoid contraction?

Or

(a) Why the lowest oxide of a transition metal is basic, the highest is amphoteric or acidic ?

(b) Account for the following.

(i) In the 3*d*-transition series, zinc has the lowest enthalpy of atomisation.

(ii) Cu^+ ion is unstable in aqueous solution.

(iii) Actinoids show more number of oxidation states than lanthanoids.

32. (a) Suppose a reaction between *A* and *B*, the initial rate of reaction (r_0) was measured for different initial concentrations of *A* and *B* as given below.

A/ mol L^{-1}	0.20	0.20	0.40
B/mol L^{-1}	0.30	0.10	0.05
r_0/ mol $L^{-1}s^{-1}$	4.08×10^{-5}	4.08×10^{-5}	2.34×10^{-4}

Answer the following questions.

(i) Find the order of reaction with respect to *A* and *B*. [**Ans.** 2.5, 0]

(ii) Determine the rate law expression for the reaction.

(iii) Calculate the rate constant. [**Ans.** 2.28×10^{-3} $mol^{-1.5}L^{1.5}s^{-1}$]

(b) Two reactions of the same order have equal exponential factors but their activation energies differ by 24.9 kJ/mol.

Calculate the ratio between the rate constants of their reactions at 27°C.
($R = 8.314 JK^{-1}mol^{-1}$) [**Ans.** 2.157×10^4]

Or

(a) For the given graph

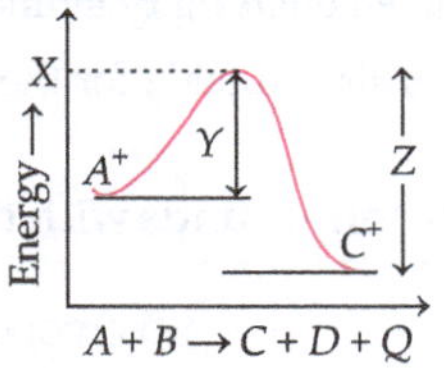

(i) Identify *X*, *Y*, *Z* and *Q*.

(ii) If the rate constant, the activation energy and Arrhenius parameter of a reaction at 25°C are $3\times10^{-4}s^{-1}$, 104.4 kJmol^{-1}, and $6.0\times10^{14}s^{-1}$ respectively. What is the value of rate constant at $T \longrightarrow \infty$? [**Ans.** $6.0\times10^{14}s^{-1}$]

(b) Two reactions,

(i) $A \longrightarrow$ Products,

(ii) $B \longrightarrow$ Products, follow first order kinetics.

The rate of reaction (a) is doubled when the temperature is raised from 300 K to 310 K. The half-life for this reaction at 310 K is 10 min. At the same temperature, *B* decomposes twice as fast as *A*. If the energy of activation for the reaction (ii) is half that of reaction (i), calculate the rate constant of the reaction (II), at 300 K. [**Ans.** $1.57\times10^{-9}s^{-1}$]

33. (a) How will you convert the following ?

(i) Acetophenone to benzoic acid.

(ii) Ethyl cyanide to ethanoic acid.

(iii) Benzoic acid to benzaldehyde.

(b) Write the structures of *A* and *B* are the following.

(i) $CH_3-\underset{\underset{O}{\|}}{C}-CH_3 \xrightarrow[\text{(ii) } H_2O]{\text{(i) } CH_3MgBr} A \xrightarrow[\text{Ether}]{\text{Na- metal}} B$

(ii) $CH_3CH_2Br \xrightarrow{NaOH\,(aq)} A \xrightarrow{PCC} B$

Or A ketone *A* (CH_2H_8O) which undergoes a haloform reaction gives compound *B* on reduction, heating with sulphuric acid gives a compound *C* which forms mono-ozonide *D*. *D* on hydrolysis with zinc dust gives only *E*. Identify *A, B, C, D* and *E*. Write the reactions involved.

How does compound *A* gives iodoform reaction?

SAMPLE QUESTION PAPER 4

A Highly Simulated Sample Question Paper for CBSE Class XII Examination

CHEMISTRY

Time : 3 Hours **Max. Marks : 70**

General Instructions

Read the following instructions carefully and follow them :

1. This question paper contains **33 questions**. All questions are **compulsory**.
2. This question paper is divided into **FIVE** sections - **Section A, B, C, D and E**.
3. **SECTION-A** questions number 1 to 16 are multiple choice type questions. Each question carries 1 mark.
4. **SECTION-B** questions number 17 to 21 are very short answer type questions. Each question carries 2 marks.
5. **SECTION-C** questions number 22 to 28 are short answer type questions. Each question carries 3 marks.
6. **SECTION-D** questions number 29 and 30 are case-based questions. Each question carries 4 marks.
7. **SECTION-E** questions number 31 to 33 are long answer type questions. Each question carries 5 marks.
8. There is no overall choice given in the question paper. However, an internal choice has been provided in few questions in all the sections except section A.
9. Kindly note that there is a separate question paper for visually impaired candidates.
10. Use of calculator is NOT allowed.

Section-A

The following questions are multiple choice questions with one correct answer. Each question carries 1 mark. There is no internal choice in this section.

1. The electrolytic purification of copper can be carried out in an apparatus similar to the one shown below.

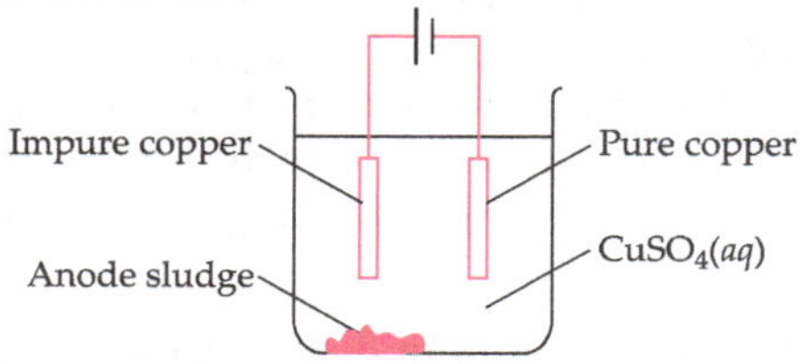

The half equation for the reaction at the anode is

(a) $Cu(s) + 2e^- \longrightarrow Cu^{2+}(aq)$

(b) $Cu(s) \longrightarrow Cu^{2+}(aq) + 2e^-$

(c) $Cu^{2+}(aq) + 2e^- \longrightarrow Cu(s)$

(d) $Cu^{2+}(aq) \longrightarrow Cu(s) + 2e^-$

2. In the given reaction,

$$\underset{}{NH_3} + RX \longrightarrow \underset{(1°)}{RNH_2} \xrightarrow{RX} \underset{(2°)}{R_2NH} \xrightarrow{RX} \underset{(3°)}{R_3N} \xrightarrow{RX} R_4N^{\oplus}X^-$$

Select an appropriate statement(s) about the reaction.

(a) In this reaction, NH_3 act as an electrophile nucleophile.

(b) In this reaction, RX is the nucleophile.

(c) $R_4N^{\oplus}X^-$ is called quaternary ammonium salt.

(d) This method is also suitable for the preparation of aryl amines.

3. Match the given compounds with their IUPAC names.

I.	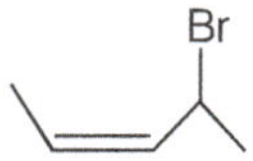	p.	4-bromopent-2-ene
II.	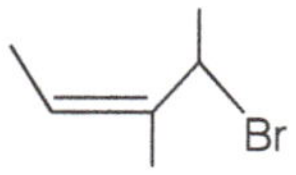	q.	4-bromo-3-methylpent-2-ene
III.	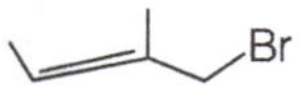	r.	1-bromo-2-methylbut-2-ene
IV.	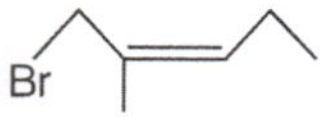	s.	1-bromo-2-methypent-2-ene

(a) I-p, II-q, III-s, IV-r (b) I-p, II-q, III-r, IV-s
(c) I-q, II-p, III-s, IV-r (d) I-q, II-s, III-r, IV-p

4. For d^4 ions, the fourth electron enters one of the e_g orbitals giving the configuration $t_{2g}^3 e_g^1$, when

(a) $\Delta_o > P$ (b) $\Delta_o < P$
(c) $\Delta_o = P$ (d) $\Delta_o \geq P$

5. Identify *A*, *B* and *C* in the given sequence of reactions,

$$H_2C = CH_2 + \underset{(B)}{Br_2} \xrightarrow{A} \underset{(C)}{BrCH_2CH_2Br}$$

	(*A*)	(*B*)	(*C*)
(a)	CCl_4	Colourless	Reddish brown
(b)	CCl_4	Reddish brown	Colourless
(c)	CBr_4	Colourless	Reddish brown
(d)	CBr_4	Reddish brown	Colourless

6. In a first order reaction, reactant concentration '*C*' varies with time '*t*' as

(a) *C* decreases with $\frac{1}{t}$
(b) log *C* decreases with $\frac{1}{t}$
(c) $\frac{1}{C}$ increases linearly with *t*
(d) log *C* decreases linearly with *t*

7. Atomic number of Mn, Fe and Co are 25, 26 and 27 respectively. Which of the following inner orbital octahedral complex ions are diamagnetic?

(a) $[Co(NH_3)_6]^{3+}$ (b) $[Mn(CN)_6]^{3-}$
(c) $[Fe(CN)_6]^{4-}$ (d) $[Fe(CN)_6]^{3-}$

8. Which of the following graph is the correct representation of λ_m *vs* $\sqrt{C}$ for $AgNO_3$?

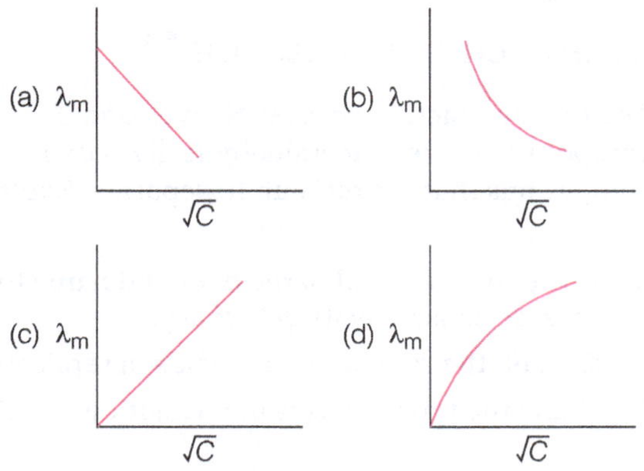

9. The most suitable reagent for the conversion of $RCH_2OH \longrightarrow RCHO$ is

(a) $KMnO_4$ (b) $K_2Cr_2O_7$ (c) PCC (d) CrO_3

10. In Tollen's test, aldehydes

(a) are oxidised
(b) are reduced to alcohol
(c) neither reduced to alcohol nor oxidised
(d) precipitate Ag as AgCl

11. The reaction by which benzaldehyde is converted into benzyl alcohol is

(a) Fitting reaction (b) Cannizzaro reaction
(c) Wurtz reaction (d) Aldol condensation

12. Thymine is held by two H-bonds to the nitrogenes base

(a) guanine (b) cytosine
(c) thymine (d) adenine

Assertion-Reason

In the following questions (Q.No. 13-16), a statement of Assertion followed by a statement of Reason is given. Choose the correct answer ouf of the following choices.

(a) Both A and R are true and R is the correct explanation of A.
(b) Both A and R are true but R is not the correct explanation of A.
(c) A is true but R is false.
(d) A is false but R is true.

13. **Assertion** (A) Sucrose is a non-reducing sugar.

Reason (R) It has glycosidic linkage.

14. **Assertion** (A) Conductivity always increases with decrease in concentration for strong and weak electrolytes.

Reason (R) Number of ions per unit volume decreases on dilution.

15. **Assertion** (A) Phenol is more stronger acid than ethanol.

Reason (R) Phenoxide ion is more resonance stabilised than ethoxide ion.

16. **Assertion** (A) $Cl—CH_2COOH$ is a stronger acid than CH_3COOH.

Reason (R) —Cl group exhibits $+I$ effect.

Answers

1. (d) 2. (c) 3. (b) 4. (b) 5. (b) 6. (d)
7. (c) 8. (a) 9. (c) 10. (a) 11. (b) 12. (d)
13. (b) 14. (d) 15. (a) 16. (c)

Section-B

This section contains 5 questions with internal choice in one question. The following questions are very short answer type and carry 2 marks each.

17. The rate of a first order reaction is $0.04 \text{ mol L}^{-1}\text{s}^{-1}$ at 10 min and $0.03 \text{ mol L}^{-1}\text{s}^{-1}$ at 20 min after initiation. Find the half-life of reaction. **[Ans.** 24.06 min]

18. Equal weights of two substances X and Y are dissolved in equal volumes of water. The osmotic pressure of the solution containing Y is five times the osmotic pressure of the solution containing X. What is the molecular weight of X if that of Y is 60 g/mol? **[Ans.** $X = 300 \text{ g mol}^{-1}$]

19. (a) How will you distinguish between glucose and sucrose?

(b) Write relevant equation to convert fructose to osazone.

Or

(a) How will you convert glucose to osazone?

(b) Which one of the following is a disaccharide? Fructose, Glucose, Sucrose, Maltose.

20. Write the hybridisation and magnetic character of the following complexes.

(a) $[Fe(H_2O)_6]^{2+}$ (b) $[Ni(CN)_4]^{2-}$

Atomic no : Fe = 26, Ni = 28

21. Draw the structure of the following compounds.

(a) 2,2-dimethyl-1-bromobutane

(b) 2,2,4,4-tetramethyl hexane

Section-C

This section contains 7 questions with internal choice in one question. The following questions are short answer type and carry 3 marks each.

22. (a) Write the structure of 2-(2-bromophenyl) butane.

(b) Among the given compounds, 2-bromopentane, 2-bromo-2-methylbutane, 1-bromopentane.

(i) Which is optically active?

(ii) Which is most reactive towards β-elimination reaction?

23. 0.05 M NaOH solution offered a resistance of 31.6 Ω in a conductivity cell at 298 K. If the cell constant of the cell is 0.367 cm^{-1}, calculate the molar conductivity of the NaOH solution. **[Ans.** $232.3 \text{ S cm}^2/\text{mol}$]

24. The chemical reaction, $2O_3 \longrightarrow 3O_2$ proceeds as follows

$$O_3 \rightleftharpoons O_2 + O \quad \text{(Fast)}$$

$$O + O_3 \longrightarrow 2O_2 \quad \text{(Slow)}$$

What should be the rate law expression?

25. Using valence bond theory, explain the following in relation to the complexes, given below. $[Mn(CN)_6]^{-3}, [Cr(H_2O)_6]^{3+}$

(a) Type of hybridisation

(b) Magnetic behaviour

(c) Inner or outer orbital complex.

26. Write the products in the following reaction.

(a) 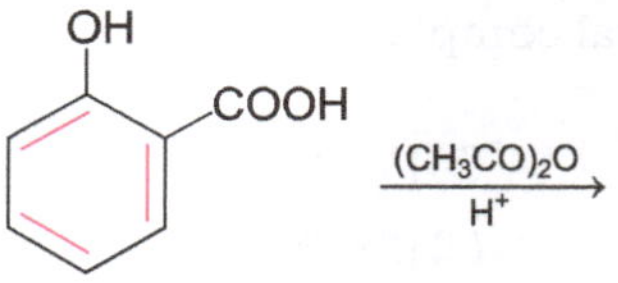

(b) $CH_3-\underset{\substack{|\\CH_3}}{CH}-O-CH_2-CH_3 \xrightarrow{HI}$

(c) $CH_3-CH=CH-CH_2-OH \xrightarrow{PCC}$

27. Acetone on reaction with HCN gives one compound whereas acetaldehyde gives two compounds that are difficult to separate. Explain why?

28. (a) Write the chemical name of B_1 and name the disease caused by its deficiency.

(b) Explain the role of nucleic acids in replication.

(c) Name the type of bases in nucleotides of RNA.

Or Two nucleotides are shown below:

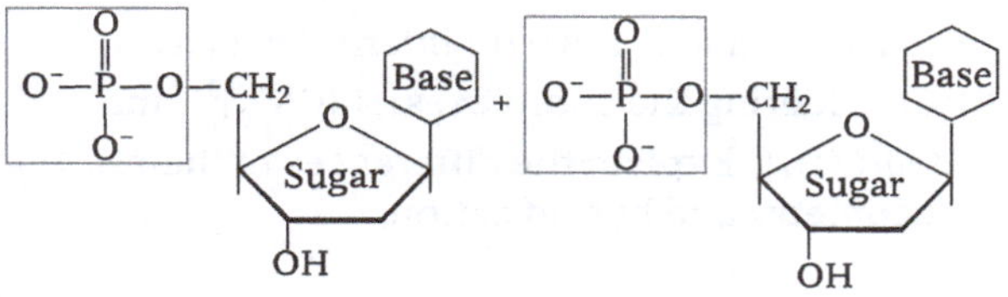

(a) Draw the structure of the dinucleotide formed.

(b) How are the nucleotides joined together?

(c) What is the primary structure of a nucleic acid?

Section-D

The following questions are case -based questions. Each question has an internal choice and carries 4 (2+1+1) marks each. Read the passage carefully and answer the questions that follow.

29. Transition metals combine with oxygen at high temperature to give metallic oxides. Except Sc, all the metals upto Mn form monoxide (*MO*), which are ionic in nature.

As oxidation number increases, covalent nature and acidic character increases.

In general, the oxides in lower oxidation states of metal are basic and in their higher oxidation states, they are acidic whereas in the intermediate oxidation state, the oxides are amphoteric.

Behaviour of oxides of manganese

$\overset{+2}{MnO}$ $\overset{+8/3}{Mn_3O_4}$ $\overset{+3}{Mn_2O_3}$ $\overset{+4}{MnO_2}$ $\overset{+7}{Mn_2O_7}$

MnO: Basic; Mn_3O_4, Mn_2O_3, MnO_2: Amphoteric; Mn_2O_7: Acidic (Covalent green oil)

Basic oxides Sc_2O_3, TiO, Ti_2O_3, VO, V_2O_3, MnO FeO, CuO, CoO, NiO, Cu_2O, CrO

Acidic oxides Mn_2O_7, CrO_3, OsO_4

Amphoteric oxides
CuO, TiO_2, ZnO, CrO_3, Cr_2O_3, Mn_2O_3, MnO_2, V_2O_5, Mn_3O_4, Fe_3O_4

Answer the following questions.

(i) Complete the following chemical equations.

(a) $MnO_4^-(aq) + C_2O_4^{2-}(aq) + H^+(aq) \longrightarrow$

(b) $Cr_2O_7^{2-}(aq) + Fe^{2+}(aq) + H^+(aq) \longrightarrow$

(ii) Which one of the following characteristics of the transition metals is associtated with higher catalytic activity? **[Ans.** (d)**]**

(a) High enthalpy of atomisation

(b) Paramagnetic behaviour

(c) Colour of hydrate ions

(d) Variable oxidation states

Or

The property which is not characteristics of transition metals is **[Ans.** (d)**]**

(a) Variable oxidation states

(b) Tendency to form complexes

(c) Formation of coloured compounds

(d) Natural radioactivity

(iii) Total number of unpaired electrons and the most stable species in Mn^{3+}, Cr^{3+} and V^{3+} gaseous species is **[Ans.** (c)**]**

(a) 4, 3 and 2 ; V^{3+} (b) 3, 3, and 2 ; Cr^{3+}

(c) 4, 3 and 2 ; Cr^{3+} (d) 3, 3 and 3 ; Mn^{3+}

30. The chemical reactivity of amines is mainly due to the presence of a lone pair of electrons on N atom due to which amines act as nucleophiles or bases. A nucleophile is a species that attacks an electron deficient carbon and a base is a species that attacks an electron deficient hydrogen, i.e., proton.

In aromatic amines, the lone pair of electrons on nitrogen atom activates the aromatic ring towards electrophilic substitution.

The number of hydrogen atoms on the amine nitrogen also affect the course of some reactions.

Answer the following questions.

(i) What happens when phenyl cyanide is treated with dilute mineral acid?

(ii) Write the chemical reaction to obtain methylamine from acetamide.

Or How is *m*-nitroaniline obtained from nitrobenzene?

(iii) Write a balanced chemical equation for the reaction of methyl amine and silver chloride.

Section-E

The following questions are long answer type and carry 5 marks each. All questions have an internal choice.

31. Answer the following questions.

(a) 1.5 A current is following through a metallic wire. If it flows for 3 hrs, how many electrons would flow through the wire?

[**Ans.** 1.0×10^{23} electrons]

(b) What will be the weight of silver deposited, if 96.5 A of current is passed into aqueous solution of $AgNO_3$ for 100 s? [**Ans.** 10.8 g]

(c) Why does a dry cell become dead after a long time even if it has not been used?

(d) Rusting of iron is quicker in saline water than in ordinary water. Give reason

(e) Write the chemistry of discharging the Leclanche cell, highlighting all the materials that are involved during cell reactions. State its use.

Or

(a) The resistance of a conductivity cell, when filled with 0.05 M solution of an electrolyte *x*, is 100 Ω at 40°C. The same conductivity cell filled with 0.01 M solution of electrolyte *y*, has a resistance of 50 Ω.

The conductivity of 0.05 M solution of electrolyte *x* is 1.0×10^{-4} S cm^{-1}. Calculate

(i) cell constant. [**Ans.** 10^{-2} cm^{-1}]

(ii) conductivity of 0.01 M *y* solution. [**Ans.** 2×10^{-4} S cm^{-1}]

(iii) molar conductivity of 0.01 M *y* solution. [**Ans.** 20 S cm^2 mol^{-1}]

(b) Using the $E°$ values of *X* and *Y*, predict which is better for coating the surface of iron to prevent rust and why?

Given : $E^\circ_{Fe^{2+}/Fe} = -0.44$ V,

$E^\circ_{X^{2+}/X} = -2.36$ V, $E^\circ_{Y^{2+}/Y} = -0.14$ V

[**Ans.** Metal *X*]

32. (a) Explain linkage isomerism. Give an example of complexes which exhibit this type of isomerism.

Also, find out the type of isomerism in the given pair of coordination compounds $[Cr(H_2O)_5Cl]Cl_2 \cdot H_2O$ and $[Cr(H_2O)_6]Cl_3$.

(b) Considering the complexes $[Ni(CN)_4]^{2-}$ and $[Ni(CO)_4]$. Explain the differences in their geometry and hybridisation.

Or

(a) Name the type of isomerism shown by the following pairs of coordination compounds.

(i) $[Co(NH_3)_5Cl]SO_4$ and $[Co(NH_3)_5SO_4]Cl$

(ii) $[Co(NH_3)_2(NO_2)_2(py)_2]NO_3$ and $[Co(NH_3)_2(ONO)_2(py)_2]NO_3$

(ii) $[Co(NH_3)_4Cl_2]^+$ and $[Co(NH_3)_4Cl_2]^+$

(b) Using VBT, predict the hybridisation of the complex, $[Cr(NH_3)_6]^{3+}$. State whether it is a high spin or low spin complex. (Atomic number of Cr = 24)

33. An organic compound *A* (molecular formula = $C_8H_{16}O_2$) was hydrolysed with dilute sulphuric acid to give a carboxylic acid *B* and an alcohol *C*. Oxidation of *C* with chromic acid also produce *B*. '*B*' on treatment with chlorine in the presence of small amount of red phosphorus and H_2O gave '*D*' and in presence of PCl_5, it gives '*E*'.

On dehydration, *C* gave but-1-ene. Identify *A*, *B*, *C*, *D* and '*E*'.

Or

(a) How will you convert

(i) formaldehyde to methanol?

(ii) benzaldehyde to *m*-nitrobenzaldehyde ?

(b) Write the structures of *A*, *B* and *C* in the following :

(i) $CH_3CH = CHCHO + NH_2\overset{O}{\overset{\|}{C}}NHNH_2 \xrightarrow{H+} A$

(ii) 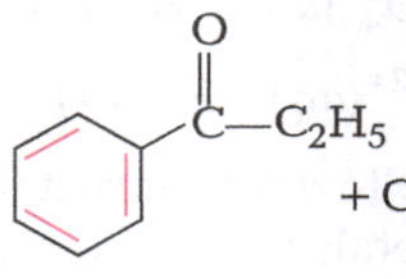 $+ CH_3NH_2 \xrightarrow{H^+} B$

(iii) $CH_3COCH_3 \xrightarrow[KOH/glycol, \Delta]{H_2NNH_2} C$

SAMPLE QUESTION PAPER 5

A Highly Simulated Sample Question Paper for CBSE Class XII Examination

CHEMISTRY

Time : 3 Hours **Max. Marks : 70**

General Instructions

Read the following instructions carefully and follow them :

1. This question paper contains **33 questions**. All questions are **compulsory**.
2. This question paper is divided into **FIVE** sections - **Section A, B, C, D and E**.
3. **SECTION-A** questions number 1 to 16 are multiple choice type questions. Each question carries 1 mark.
4. **SECTION-B** questions number 17 to 21 are very short answer type questions. Each question carries 2 marks.
5. **SECTION-C** questions number 22 to 28 are short answer type questions. Each question carries 3 marks.
6. **SECTION-D** questions number 29 and 30 are case-based questions. Each question carries 4 marks.
7. **SECTION-E** questions number 31 to 33 are long answer type questions. Each question carries 5 marks.
8. There is no overall choice given in the question paper. However, an internal choice has been provided in few questions in all the sections except section A.
9. Kindly note that there is a separate question paper for visually impaired candidates.
10. Use of calculator is NOT allowed.

Section-A

The following questions are multiple choice questions with one correct answer. Each question carries 1 mark. There is no internal choice in this section.

1. In which case Raoult's law is not applicable?

(a) 1 M NaCl (b) 1 M Urea
(c) 1 M Glucose (d) 1 M Sucrose

2. On increasing the pressure three fold, the rate of reaction of $2H_2S + O_2 \longrightarrow$ products, would increase

(a) 3 times (b) 9 times
(c) 12 times (d) 27 times

3. How many ions are produced from $[Co(NH_3)_6]Cl_3$ in solution?

(a) 6 (b) 4
(c) 3 (d) 2

4. The correct order of dehydration of alcohol is

(a) 1° > 2° > 3°
(b) 3° > 2° > 1°
(c) 2° > 1° > 3°
(d) 1° > 3° > 2°

5. On the basis of the following observations made with aqueous solutions.

	Formula	Moles of AgCl precipitated per mole of the compounds with excess $AgNO_3$
I.	$PdCl_2 \cdot 4NH_3$	2
II.	$NiCl_2 \cdot 6H_2O$	2
III.	$PtCl_4 \cdot 2HCl$	0
IV.	$CoCl_3 \cdot 4NH_3$	1
V.	$PtCl_2 \cdot 2NH_3$	0

The secondary valencies of I and III is

(a) 4 and 5 respectively
(b) 4 and 6 respectively
(c) 6 and 4 respectively
(d) 2 and 4 respectively

6. The potential energy diagram for the reaction $R \rightarrow P$ is given below

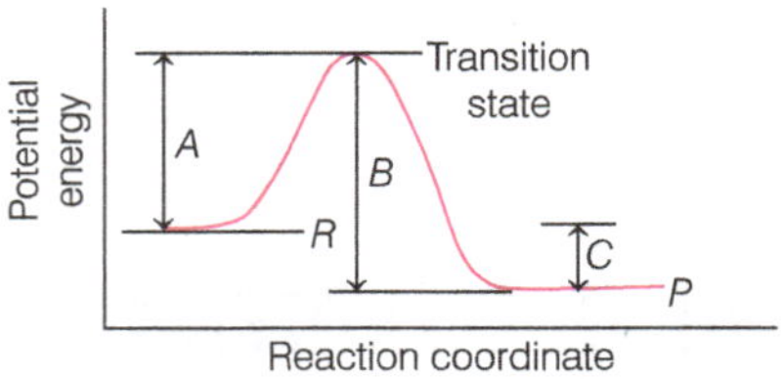

$\Delta H°$ of the reaction corresponds to the energy

(a) A (b) B
(c) C (d) $A + B$

7. Arrange the following compounds in the increasing order of their densities.

(i)  (ii) 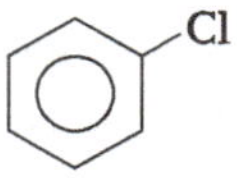

(iii) 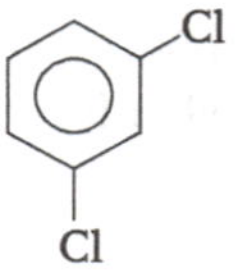

(iv) 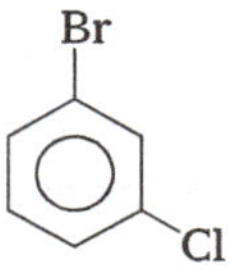

(a) (i) < (ii) < (iii) < (iv) (b) (i) < (iii) < (iv) < (ii)
(c) (iv) < (iii) < (ii) < (i) (d) (ii) < (iv) < (iii) < (i)

8. The IUPAC name of the compound is

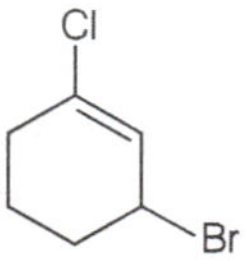

(a) 2-bromo-6-chlorocyclohex-1-ene
(b) 6-bromo-2-chlorocyclohexane
(c) 3-bromo-1-chlorocyclohexene
(d) 1-bromo-3-chlorocyclohexene

9. Ground state configuration of element having atomic number = 24 is $[Ar]3d^5 4s^1$. This is because,

(a) the energy of $3d$ and $4s$-orbitals is very low
(b) $3d$ and $4s$-orbitals are of comparable energy
(c) energy of $3d$-orbital is lower than the energy of $4s$-orbital
(d) energy gap between third and fourth shell is very large

10. Formic acid and acetic acid are distinguished by

(a) $NaHCO_3$ (b) $FeCl_3$
(c) Victor Meyer test (d) Tollen's reagent

11. Match Column I with Column II.

	Column I		Column II
A.	Lechlanche cell	1.	Converts energy of combustion into electrical energy.
B.	Ni-Cd cell	2.	Does not involve any ion in solution and is used in hearing aids.
C.	Fuel cell	3.	Rechargeable
D.	Mercury cell	4.	Reaction at anode, $Zn \longrightarrow Zn^{2+} + 2e^-$

Codes

	A	B	C	D		A	B	C	D
(a)	4	3	1	2	(b)	1	4	3	2
(c)	3	4	2	1	(d)	4	3	2	1

12. Krishna went to a chemistry lab. There he get following beaker in which 1°/2°/3° amines were placed. He needs methylamine for his experiment/work. Now by which test he can distinguish methylamine easily from other solutions? (Note Beakers are not labelled with name)

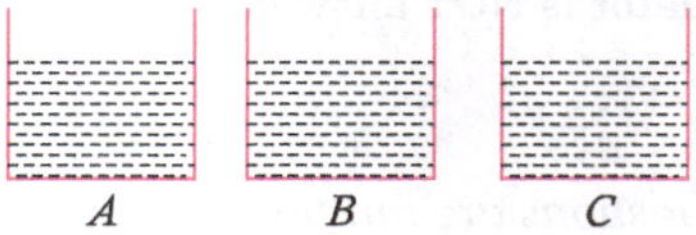

(a) Hinsberg's test
(b) Iodoform test
(c) Tollen's test
(d) Diazotisation test

Assertion-Reason

In the following questions (Q.No. 13-16) a statement of Assertion followed by a statement of Reason is given. Choose the correct answer out of the following choices.

(a) Both A and R are true and R is the correct explanation of A.
(b) Both A and R are true but R is not the correct explanation of A.
(c) A is true but R is false.
(d) A is false but R is true.

13. **Assertion** (A) It is difficult to replace chlorine by —OH in chlorobenzene in comparison to that in chloroethane.

Reason (R) Chlorine carbon (C—Cl) bond in chlorobenzene has a partial double bond character due to resonance.

14. **Assertion** (A) Phenols give *o*- and *p*-nitrophenol on nitration with conc. HNO_3 and H_2SO_4 mixture.

Reason (R) —OH group in phenol is *o*-,*p*-directing.

15. **Assertion** (A) Chromium is a typical hard metal, while mercury is a liquid.

Reason (R) In Cr, there are six unpaired electrons, whereas in Hg, there is no unpaired electron.

16. **Assertion** (A) α-hydrogen atoms of carbonyl compounds are acidic.

Reason (R) The strong electron releasing effect of carbonyl group make the stabilisation of the conjugate base by the resonance.

Answers

1. (a)	**2.** (d)	**3.** (b)	**4.** (b)	**5.** (b)	**6.** (c)
7. (a)	**8.** (c)	**9.** (b)	**10.** (d)	**11.** (a)	**12.** (a)
13. (a)	**14.** (d)	**15.** (b)	**16.** (c)		

Section-B

This section contains 5 questions with internal choice in one question. The following questions are very short answer type and carry 2 marks each.

17. Complete the following reactions.

(a) $C_6H_5NH_2 + CH_3COCl \longrightarrow$

(b) 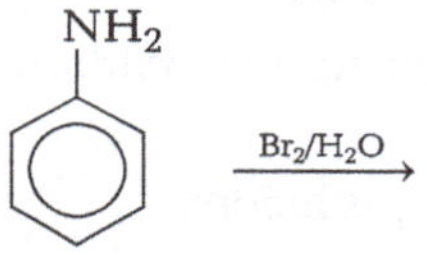

18. The standard oxidation potential of Ni/Ni^{2+} electrode is 0.236 V. If this is combined with a hydrogen electrode in an acidic solution, at what pH of the solution will measured emf be zero at 25°C? (Assuming $[Ni^{2+}] = 1$ M) [**Ans.** ≈ 4]

19. Answer the following.

(a) $[Ni(en)_3]Cl_2$ is more stable complex than $[Ni(NH_3)_6]Cl_2$.

(b) Arrange the following complex ions in increasing order of crystal field splitting energy (Δ_o).

$[CrCl_6]^{3-}$, $[Cr(CN)_6]^{3-}$, $[Cr(NH_3)_6]^{3+}$

Or (a) Write the IUPAC nomenclature of $[Cr(NH_3)_4Cl_2]^+$ and $[Co(en)_3]^{3+}$ complex.

(b) Magnetic moment of $[MnCl_4]^{2-}$ is 5.92 BM. Give reason.

20. 0.5 M aqueous solution of sodium chloride show higher value of osmotic pressure than 0.5 M glucose solution at the same temperature. Why?

21. How will you bring about the following conversions?

(a) $CH_2{=}CH_2 \longrightarrow \begin{array}{l} COOH \\ | \\ COOH \end{array}$

(b) 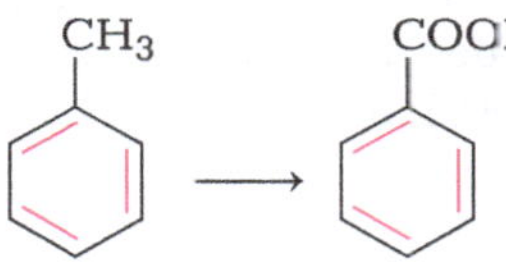

Section-C

This section contains 7 questions with internal choice in one question. The following questions are short answer type and carry 3 marks each.

22. (a) Complete the following reactions.

$$CH_3CH_2\underset{\underset{Cl}{|}}{C}HCH_3 \xrightarrow{\text{Alc. KOH}}$$

(b) Write the structure of an isomer of compound C_4H_9Br which is most reactive towards S_N1 reaction.

(c) $C_2H_5OH + SOCl_2 \longrightarrow$

23. An aromatic compound *A* on treatment with aqueous ammonia on heating forms a compound *B*, which on heating with Br_2 and KOH forms a compound *C* of molecular formula C_6H_7N. Write the structures and IUPAC names of compounds *A*, *B* and *C*.

24. (a) Express the relation between conductivity of a solution and cell constant.

(b) Determine the values of equilibrium constant (K_C) and $\Delta G°$ for the following reactions as 25°C.

$$Ni(s) + 2Ag^+(aq) \longrightarrow Ni^{2+}(aq) + 2Ag(s),$$

$E° = 1.05\ V$ $\quad [F = 96500\ C\ mol^{-1}]$

[**Ans.** $\Delta G° = -202.65$ kJ, $K_C = 3.16 \times 10^{39}$]

25. Answer the following questions.

(a) Aldopentoses named as ribose and 2-deoxyribose are found in nucleic acids. What is their relative configuration?

(b) In nucleoside, a base is attached at '1′' position of sugar moiety. Nucleotide is formed by linking of phosphoric acid unit to the sugar unit of nucleoside. At which position of sugar unit is the phosphoric acid linked in a nucleoside to give a nucleotide?

(c) Predict whether the following compound has 'D' or 'L' configuration.

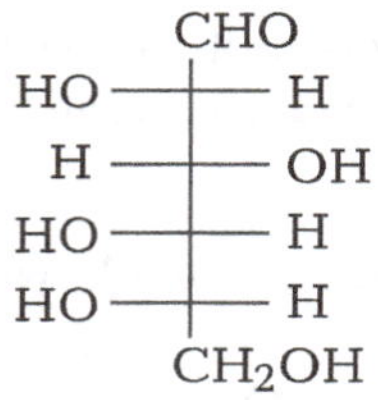

Or

DNA is relatively rigid, a puzzling finding in view of the large number of single bonds (5 per nucleotide) in the phosphate-sugar back.

D.N.A.

BASE—SUGAR
>PHOSPHATE
BASE—SUGAR
>PHOSPHATE
BASE—SUGAR
>PHOSPHATE
BASE—SUGAR
>PHOSPHATE
BASE—SUGAR

Answer the following questions.

(a) Draw the structure of purines present in DNA.

(b) Of the two bases (thymine and uracil), which one is present in RNA and which one is present in DNA?

(c) Among DNA and RNA, which has double stranded α-helix structure?

26. Give examples and suggest reasons for the following features of the transition metal chemistry.

(a) The lowest oxide of transition metal is basic while the highest is amphoteric/ acidic.

(b) A transition metal exhibits highest oxidation state in oxides and fluorides.

(c) MnO is basic while Mn_2O_7 is acidic.

27. Calculate $E°_{cell}$ for the following reaction at 298 K.

$$2Al(s) + 3Cu^{2+}(0.01M) \longrightarrow 2Al^{3+}(0.01M) + 3Cu(s)$$

Given, $E°_{cell} = 1.98\ V$ [**Ans.** 2 V]

28. Degree of dissociation of pure water is 1.9×10^{-9}. Molar ionic conductances of H^+ ions and OH^- ions at infinite dilution are 200 S $cm^2\ mol^{-1}$ and 350 S $cm^2 mol^{-1}$ respectively. What is the molar conductance of water? [**Ans.** 1.045×10^{-6} S $cm^2 mol^{-1}$]

Section-D

The following questions are case -based questions. Each question has an internal choice and carries 4 (2+1+1) marks each. Read the passage carefully and answer the questions that follow.

29. One of the most important classes of biomolecules is carbohydrates. These include sugars, starch, glycogen, cellulose, etc. These are formed by plants under a process called photosynthesis and make up about 70% of plant material. Carbohydrates provide us food, clothing and shelter in the form of starch, cotton and wood respectively.

Earlier carbohydrates were called as hydrates of carbon $C_x(H_2O)_y$. But this definition is not applicable in all cases. Carbohydrates are also called saccharides. These can be monosaccharides, oligosaccharides and polysaccharides. Carbohyderates can also be classified as sugar and non-sugar. All the monosaccharides and oligosaccharides are sugar.

The polysaccharides are non-sugar. All those carbohydrates which reduce Tollen's reagent or Fehling solution are called reducing carbohydrates, while others which do not reduce these reagents are called non-reducing carbohydrates. All monosaccharides are reducing. All polysaccharides are non-reducing.

Answer the following questions.

(i) Why does the mixture obtained after hydrolysis of cane sugar is laevorotatory through sugar itself is dextrorotatory?

(ii) Which of the two components of starch are water soluble?

Or

Why are carbohydrate generally optically active?

(iii) Write the reactions involved when D-glucose is treated with the HCN.

30. Transition elements are elements that have partially filled d-orbitals. IUPAC defines transition elements as an element having a d-subshell that is partially filled with electrons, or an element that has the ability to form stable cations with an incompletely filled d-orbital.

In general, any element which corresponds to the d-block of the modern periodic table (which consists of groups 3-12) is considered to be a transition element. Even the f-block elements comprising the lanthanides and the actinides can be considered as transition metals. However, since the f-block elements have incompletely filled f-orbitals, they are often referred to as inner transition elements or inner-transition metals.

Transition metals show a great variety of oxidation state (or variable valency). However, due to large gap in energy of $4f$ and $5d$-subshells, the number of oxidation state is limited in case of lanthanoids. On the other hand, actinoids show a variety lanthanoids. On the other hand, actinoids show a variety oxidation states due to comparable energies of $5f$, $6d$ and $7s$ energy levels.

Answer the following questions.

(i) Silver atom has completely filled d-orbital ($4d^{10}$) in its ground state. How can you say that it is a transition element?

(ii) The configuration which exhibits highest oxidation state in transition metals is

(a) $(n-1)d^8 ns^2$ (b) $(n-1)d^5 ns^2$

(c) $(n-1)d^3 ns^2$ (d) $(n-1)d^5 ns^2$

Or

(ii) Terbium belongs to $4f$-series. it's atomic number is 65. Which of the following is the correct electronic configuration of terbium?

(a) $[Xe]4f^9 6s^2$ (b) $[Xe]4f^9 5s^1$

(c) $[Xe]4f^7 5d^2 6s^2$ (d) $[Xe]4f^6 5d^3 6s^2$

(iii) The actinoids resemble the lanthanoids in having more compounds in

(a) state (b) +4 state

(c) +5 state (d) −2 state

Section-E

The following questions are long answer type and carry 5 marks each. All questions have an internal choice.

31. Answer the following questions.

(a) For a reaction $A + B \longrightarrow P$, the rate is given by

$$\text{Rate} = k[A][B]^2$$

How is the rate of reaction affected, if the concentration of B is quadrupled?

[**Ans.** 16 times]

(b) What is the overall order of the above reaction if A is present in large excess ?

(c) A first order reaction takes 23.1 min for 50% completion. Calculate the time required for 75% completion of the reaction.

[**Ans.** 46.2 min]

(d) For which type of reactions, order and molecularity have the same value?

(e) In a reaction, if the concentration of the reactant R is quadrupled, the rate of reaction becomes sixty four times.

What is the order of reaction? [**Ans.** 3]

Or

(a) Calculate the value of E°_{cell} cell and ΔG° that can be obtained from the following cell under the standard conditions at 25°C.

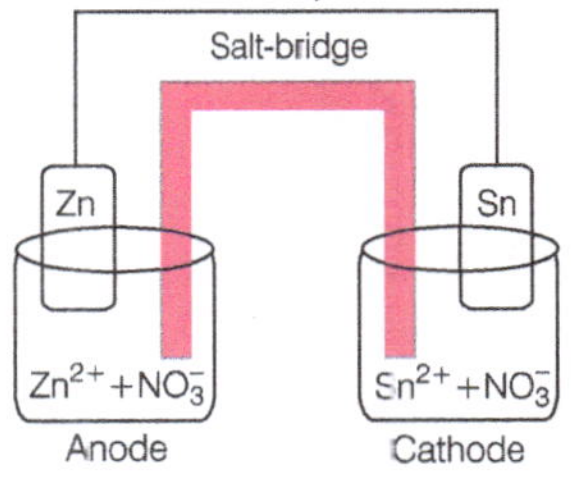

Given : $E^\circ_{Zn^{2+}/Zn} = -0.76$ V ;

$E^\circ_{Sn^{2+}/Sn} = -0.14$ V

1 Faraday = 96500 C mol^{-1}

[**Ans.** $E^\circ_{cell} = 0.62$V, $\Delta G^\circ = -119.66$ kJ]

(b) How much electricity in Faraday is required for the complete reduction of MnO_4^- ions present in 500 mL of 0.5 M solution to Mn^{2+}? [**Ans.** 1.25 F]

32. (a) The molecular weights of sodium chloride and glucose are determined by the depression of freezing point method. Compared to their theoretical molecular weight, what will be their observed molecular weights when determined by the above method? Justify your answer.

(b) What will be the vapour pressure of a solution containing 5 moles of sucrose ($C_{12}H_{22}O_{11}$) in 1 kg of water, if the vapour pressure of pure water is 4.57 mm of Hg? (C = 12, H = 1, O = 16) [**Ans.** 4.192 mm of Hg]

(c) Calculate the mass of compound (molar mass = 256 g mol^{-1}) to be dissolved in 75 g of benzene to lower its freezing point by 0.48 K ($K_f = 5.12$ K kg mol^{-1} [**Ans.** $W_2 = 1.8$ g]

Or

(a) What is a colligative property? Give two examples.

(b) A solution of lactose containing 8.45 g of lactose in 100 g of water has a vapour pressure of 4.559 mm Hg at 0°C. If the vapour pressure of pure water is 4.579 mm Hg, calculate the molecular weight of lactose. [**Ans.** = 348 g/mol]

(c) What volume of 95% sulphuric acid (density = 1.85 g/cm^3) and what mass of water must be taken to prepare 100 cm^3 of 15% solution of sulphuric acid? (Density = 1.1 g / cm^3)

[**Ans.** Volume of H_2SO_4 = 9.4 mL, mass of water = 90.6 g]

33. An organic compound '*A*' with molecular formula C_6H_6O reacts with zinc dust to give a hydrocarbon '*B*', which upon reaction with CH_3Cl in the presence of anhydrous $AlCl_3$ gives '*C*'. Compound *C* on oxidation with alkaline $KMnO_4$ gives compound *D*. Compound *A* on further reaction with NH_3 in the presence of anhydrous $ZnCl_2$ gives '*E*'.

Identify the compound *A*,*B*,*C*,*D* and *E*, also justify your answer by giving relevant chemical equations.

Or

(a) How will you convert

(i) phenol into picric acid ?

(ii) cumene into phenol ?

(b) Write the structures of *A* and *B* in the following reactions :

(i) 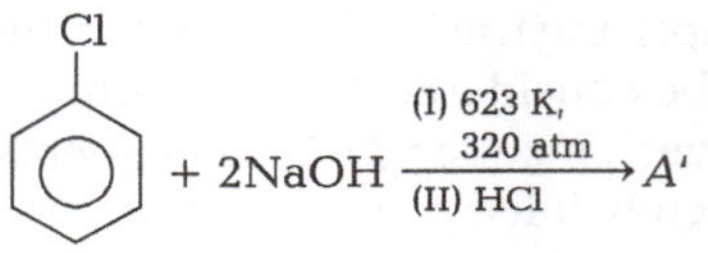

(ii) $CH_3OCH_2Cl + CH_3MgI \xrightarrow{\text{Dry ether}} A + B$

(iii) 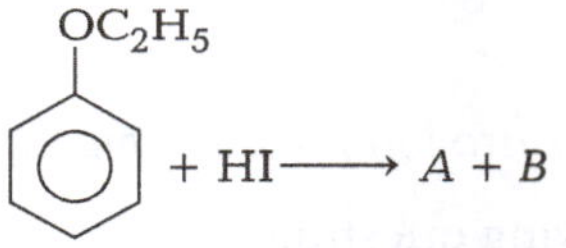